Contemporary
Literary Criticism

Guide to Gale Literary Criticism Series

When you need to review criticism of literary works, these are the Gale series to use:

If the author's death date is: **You should turn to:**

After Dec. 31, 1959
(or author is still living)

CONTEMPORARY LITERARY CRITICISM

for example: Jorge Luis Borges, Anthony Burgess,
William Faulkner, Mary Gordon,
Ernest Hemingway, Iris Murdoch

1900 through 1959

TWENTIETH-CENTURY LITERARY CRITICISM

for example: Willa Cather, F. Scott Fitzgerald,
Henry James, Mark Twain, Virginia Woolf

1800 through 1899

NINETEENTH-CENTURY LITERATURE CRITICISM

for example: Fedor Dostoevski, Nathaniel Hawthorne,
George Sand, William Wordsworth

1400 through 1799

LITERATURE CRITICISM FROM 1400 TO 1800
(excluding Shakespeare)

for example: Anne Bradstreet, Daniel Defoe,
Alexander Pope, Francois Rabelais,
Jonathan Swift, Phillis Wheatley

SHAKESPEAREAN CRITICISM

Shakespeare's plays and poetry

Antiquity through 1399

CLASSICAL AND MEDIEVAL LITERATURE CRITICISM

for example: Dante, Homer, Plato, Sophocles, Vergil,
the Beowulf poet

(Volume 1 forthcoming)

Gale also publishes related criticism series:

CHILDREN'S LITERATURE REVIEW

This ongoing series covers authors of all eras.
Presents criticism on authors and author/illustrators
who write for the preschool to junior-high audience.

CONTEMPORARY ISSUES CRITICISM

This two-volume set presents criticism on
contemporary authors writing on current issues.
Topics covered include the social sciences,
philosophy, economics, natural science, law, and
related areas.

ISSN 0091-3421

Volume 43

Contemporary Literary Criticism

Excerpts from Criticism of the
Works of Today's Novelists, Poets,
Playwrights, Short Story Writers, Scriptwriters,
and Other Creative Writers

Daniel G. Marowski
Roger Matuz
EDITORS

Robyn V. Young
ASSOCIATE EDITORS

Gale Research Company
Book Tower
Detroit, Michigan 48226

STAFF

Daniel G. Marowski, Roger Matuz, *Editors*

Robyn V. Young, *Associate Editor*

Sean R. Pollock, Jane C. Thacker, Thomas J. Votteler,
Bruce Walker, Debra A. Wells, *Senior Assistant Editors*

Kent Graham, Michele R. O'Connell, David Segal, *Assistant Editors*

Jean C. Stine, *Contributing Editor*

Melissa Reiff Hug, *Contributing Assistant Editor*

Jeanne A. Gough, *Production & Permissions Manager*
Lizbeth A. Purdy, *Production Supervisor*
Denise Michlewicz Broderick, *Production Coordinator*
Kathleen M. Cook, *Assistant Production Coordinator*
Suzanne Powers, Jani Prescott, *Editorial Assistants*
Linda M. Pugliese, *Manuscript Coordinator*
Donna Craft, *Assistant Manuscript Coordinator*
Jennifer E. Gale, Maureen A. Puhl, Rosetta Irene Simms, *Manuscript Assistants*

Victoria B. Cariappa, *Research Supervisor*
Maureen R. Richards, *Assistant Research Coordinator*
Filomena Sgambati, Laura B. Standley, Mary D. Wise, *Research Assistants*

Janice M. Mach, *Permissions Supervisor, Text*
Susan D. Battista, Sandra C. Davis, Kathy Grell, *Assistant Permissions Coordinators*
Mabel E. Gurney, Josephine M. Keene, Mary M. Matuz, *Senior Permissions Assistants*
H. Diane Cooper, *Permissions Assistant*
Eileen H. Baehr, Anita Ransom, Kimberly Smilay, *Permissions Clerks*

Patricia A. Seefelt, *Picture Permissions Supervisor*
Margaret A. Chamberlain, *Assistant Permissions Coordinator*
Colleen M. Crane, *Permissions Assistant*
Lillian Tyus, *Permissions Clerk*

Special thanks to Carolyn Bancroft and Sharon Hall
for their assistance on the Title Index.

Frederick G. Ruffner, *Chairman*
J. Kevin Reger, *President*
Dedria Bryfonski, *Publisher*
Ellen T. Crowley, *Associate Editorial Director*
Laurie Lanzen Harris, *Director, Literary Criticism Division*
Dennis Poupard, *Senior Editor, Literary Criticism Series*

Library of Congress Catalog Card Number 76-38938
ISBN 0-8103-4417-3
ISSN 0091-3421

Computerized photocomposition by
Typographics, Incorporated
Kansas City, Missouri

Printed in the United States

Contents

Preface

Literary criticism is, by definition, "the art of evaluating or analyzing with knowledge and propriety works of literature." The complexity and variety of the themes and forms of contemporary literature make the function of the critic especially important to today's reader. It is the critic who assists the reader in identifying significant new writers, recognizing trends in critical methods, mastering new terminology, and monitoring scholarly and popular sources of critical opinion.

Until the publication of the first volume of *Contemporary Literary Criticism (CLC)* in 1973, there existed no ongoing digest of current literary opinion. *CLC,* therefore, has fulfilled an essential need.

Scope of the Work

CLC presents significant passages from published criticism of works by today's creative writers. Each volume of *CLC* includes excerpted criticism on about 45 authors who are now living or who died after December 31, 1959. More than 1,800 authors have been included since the series began publication. The majority of authors covered by *CLC* are living writers who continue to publish; therefore, an author frequently appears in more than one volume. There is, of course, no duplication of reprinted criticism.

Authors are selected for inclusion for a variety of reasons, among them the publication of a critically acclaimed new work, the reception of a major literary award, or the dramatization of a literary work as a film or television screenplay. For example, the present volume includes Reynolds Price, who won the National Book Critics Circle Award in fiction for his novel *Kate Vaiden;* Joe Orton, whose brief, controversial career as a dramatist is portrayed in the recent film *Prick Up Your Ears;* and Tama Janowitz, whose short story collection *Slaves of New York* received much critical and popular attention. Perhaps most importantly, authors who appear frequently on the syllabuses of high school and college literature classes are heavily represented in *CLC;* W. H. Auden and Jean Cocteau are examples of writers of this stature in the present volume. Attention is also given to several other groups of writers—authors of considerable public interest—about whose work criticism is often difficult to locate. These are the contributors to the well-loved but nonscholarly genres of mystery and science fiction, as well as literary and social critics whose insights are considered valuable and informative. Foreign writers and authors who represent particular ethnic groups in the United States are also featured in each volume.

Format of the Book

Altogether there are about 700 individual excerpts in each volume—with an average of about 14 excerpts per author—taken from hundreds of literary reviews, general magazines, scholarly journals, and monographs. Contemporary criticism is loosely defined as that which is relevant to the evaluation of the author under discussion; this includes criticism written at the beginning of an author's career as well as current commentary. Emphasis has been placed on expanding the sources for criticism by including an increasing number of scholarly and specialized periodicals. Students, teachers, librarians, and researchers frequently find that the generous excerpts and supplementary material provided by the editors supply them with vital information needed to write a term paper, analyze a poem, or lead a book discussion group. However, complete bibliographical citations facilitate the location of the original source and provide all of the information necessary for a term paper footnote or bibliography.

A *CLC* author entry consists of the following elements:

- The **author heading** cites the author's full name, followed by birth date, and death date when applicable. The portion of the name outside parentheses denotes the form under which the author has most commonly published. If an author has written consistently under a pseudonym, the pseudonym will be listed in the author heading and the real name given on the first line of the biographical and critical introduction. Also located at the beginning of the introduction to the author entry are any important name variations under which an author has written. Uncertainty as to a birth or death date is indicated by question marks.

- A **portrait** of the author is included when available.

- A brief **biographical and critical introduction** to the author and his or her work precedes the excerpted criticism. However, *CLC* is not intended to be a definitive biographical source. Therefore, *cross-references* have been included to direct the reader to these useful sources published by the Gale Research Company: *Contemporary Authors,* which includes detailed biographical and bibliographical sketches on more than 87,000 authors; *Children's Literature Review,* which presents excerpted criticism on the works of authors of children's books; *Something about the Author,* which contains heavily illustrated biographical sketches on writers and illustrators who create books for children and young adults; *Contemporary Issues Criticism,* which presents excerpted commentary on the nonfiction works of authors who influence contemporary thought; *Dictionary of Literary Biography,* which provides original evaluations and detailed biographies of authors important to literary history; *Contemporary Authors Autobiography Series,* which offers autobiographical essays by prominent writers; and *Something about the Author Autobiography Series,* which presents autobiographical essays by authors of interest to young readers. Previous volumes of *CLC* in which the author has been featured are also listed in the introduction.

- The **excerpted criticism** represents various kinds of critical writing—a particular essay may be normative, descriptive, interpretive, textual, appreciative, comparative, or generic. It may range in form from the brief review to the scholarly monograph. Essays are selected by the editors to reflect the spectrum of opinion about a specific work or about an author's literary career in general. The excerpts are presented chronologically, adding a useful perspective to the entry. All titles by the author featured in the entry are printed in boldface type, which enables the reader to easily identify the works being discussed.

- A complete **bibliographical citation** designed to help the user find the original essay or book follows each excerpt.

Other Features

- A list of **Authors Forthcoming in *CLC*** previews the authors to be researched for future volumes.

- An **Appendix** lists the sources from which material in the volume has been reprinted. It does not, however, list every book or periodical consulted during the preparation of the volume.

- A **Cumulative Author Index** lists all the authors who have appeared in *CLC, Twentieth-Century Literary Criticism, Nineteenth-Century Literature Criticism,* and *Literature Criticism from 1400 to 1800,* along with cross-references to other Gale series: *Children's Literature Review, Authors in the News, Contemporary Authors, Contemporary Authors Autobiography Series, Dictionary of Literary Biography, Something about the Author, Something about the Author Autobiography Series,* and *Yesterday's Authors of Books for Children.* Users will welcome this cumulated author index as a useful tool for locating an author within the various series. The index, which lists birth and death dates when available, will be particularly valuable for those authors who are identified with a certain period but whose death date causes them to be placed in another, or for those authors whose careers span two periods. For example, Ernest Hemingway is found in *CLC,* yet a writer often associated with him, F. Scott Fitzgerald, is found in *Twentieth-Century Literary Criticism.*

- A **Cumulative Nationality Index** lists the authors included in *CLC* alphabetically by nationality, followed by the volume numbers in which they appear.

- Beginning with Volume 40, in response to suggestions from many users and librarians, a **Cumulative Title Index** has replaced the Cumulative Index to Critics. The Cumulative Title Index lists titles reviewed in *CLC* from Volume 1 through the current volume in alphabetical order. Titles are followed by the corresponding volume and page numbers where they may be located. In cases where the same title is used by different authors, the author's surname is given in parentheses after the title, e.g., *Collected Poems* (Berryman), *Collected Poems* (Eliot). For foreign titles, a cross-reference is given to the translated English title. Titles of novels, novellas, dramas, films, record albums, and poetry, short story, and essay collections are printed in italics, while all individual poems, short stories, essays, and songs are printed in roman type within quotation marks; when published separately (e.g., T.S. Eliot's poem *The Waste Land*), the title will also be printed in italics.

Acknowledgments

No work of this scope can be accomplished without the cooperation of many people. The editors especially wish to thank the copyright holders of the excerpted essays included in this volume, the permissions managers of many book and magazine publishing companies for assisting us in securing reprint rights, and the photographers and other individuals who provided portraits of the authors. We are grateful to the staffs of the Detroit Public Library, the Library of Congress, the University of Detroit Library, the University of Michigan Library, and the Wayne State University Library for making their resources available to us. We also wish to thank Anthony Bogucki for his assistance with copyright research.

Suggestions Are Welcome

The editors welcome the comments and suggestions of readers to expand the coverage and enhance the usefulness of the series.

Authors Forthcoming in *CLC*

Contemporary Literary Criticism, Volume 44, will be a yearbook devoted to an examination of the outstanding achievements and trends in literature during 1986. Volumes 45 and 46 will contain criticism on several authors not previously listed and will also feature criticism on newer works by authors included in earlier volumes.

To Be Included in Volume 45

Kathy Acker (American novelist and scriptwriter)—Acker has attracted critical attention for her experimental novels *Great Expectations* and *Don Quixote,* in which she uses pornography, plagiarism, autobiography, and dream fragments to subvert literary conventions and to attack traditional social values.

Eric Bogosian (American performance artist)—In *Drinking in America,* a series of satirical monologues, Bogosian examines the psyches of several obsessed male characters. This work shared the 1986 Obie Award for best off-Broadway play.

Guillermo Cabrera Infante (Cuban-born novelist, short story writer, journalist, and critic)—In his recent novel, *Infante's Inferno,* Cabrera Infante continues the use of humorous wordplay and narrative experimentation which won him international recognition with his earlier novel, *Three Trapped Tigers.*

J. P. Donleavy (American-born Irish novelist, dramatist, short story writer, and nonfiction writer)—Donleavy is best known for his first novel, *The Ginger Man,* in which his protagonist searches for love and stability amid a hostile society and a chaotic personal life. Among the recent novels to be covered in his entry are *Schultz, Leila,* and *De Alfonce Tennis.*

William Humphrey (American novelist, short story writer, and essayist)—Humphrey's fiction is usually set in the American Southwest and depicts families and individuals struggling to survive in an often hostile environment. His recent publications include *The Collected Stories of William Humphrey* and *Open Season: Sporting Adventures,* a volume of essays.

Joseph Kesselring (American dramatist and scriptwriter)—An author of popular Broadway comedies during the 1940s and 1950s, Kesselring is best remembered for his domestic farce *Arsenic and Old Lace.*

Ursula K. Le Guin (American novelist, short story writer, poet, and essayist)—A respected award-winning author of fantasy and science fiction, Le Guin is best known for her *Earthsea Trilogy.* Her recent works include *Always Coming Home* and *The Eye of the Heron.*

Thomas McGuane (American novelist, short story writer, scriptwriter, and essayist)—A leading contemporary American satirist, McGuane writes irreverent fiction that focuses on what he terms America's "declining snivelization." Works to be covered in his entry include the novels *Nobody's Angel* and *Something To Be Desired* and the short story collection *To Skin a Cat.*

Alice Munro (Canadian short story writer and novelist)—Munro writes humorous, well-crafted stories about the disturbing undercurrents that affect the ordinary lives of her characters, who inhabit a rural area in southwestern Ontario. Her recent collection, *The Progress of Love,* has attracted significant critical attention.

Lewis Nkosi (South African novelist, critic, and dramatist)—Nkosi, who has lived in exile in England, the United States, and Zambia for over twenty-five years, is well known for his essays on contemporary African literature. His first novel, *Mating Birds,* centers on a young Zulu man who is sentenced to die by the South African government for allegedly raping a white woman.

Charles Tomlinson (English poet, translator, and critic)—Considered one of England's most distinguished post-World War II poets, Tomlinson writes verse which displays his precise attention to detail and his concern with metaphysical themes. Tomlinson's recent collections include *The Flood* and *Notes from New York and Other Poems.*

Rex Warner (English novelist, nonfiction writer, poet, and translator)—Warner was a scholar of classical literature and history whose novels evidence his early interest in Kafkaesque techniques, his concern with contemporary political and social issues during the World War II era, and his later use of historical narratives to focus on universal themes.

Alice Adams (American novelist and short story writer)—In her fiction, Adams often explores the emotional lives of upper middle-class professional women. Her recent works include a novel, *Superior Women,* and a short story collection, *Return Trips.*

Louise Bogan (American poet, critic, editor, translator, and autobiographer)—A distinguished figure in twentieth-century American literature, Bogan wrote classically structured poetry that passionately explores the extremes of experience. Her collections of verse have been complemented by the publication of *Journey around My Room: The Autobiography of Louise Bogan.*

Len Deighton (English novelist, short story writer, nonfiction writer, and scriptwriter)—Deighton is a highly popular author of spy thrillers who delighted critics and readers with the parodic elements in his first novel, *The Ipcress File.* Recent works to be covered in his entry include *Mexico Set* and *London Match.*

Jean Genet (French dramatist, novelist, and poet)—Described by Jean Cocteau as France's "Black Prince of letters," Genet was a controversial author who sought to replace Western values with his own system of antimorality. Among his most respected writings are the plays *The Maids* and *The Balcony* and the prose works *The Thief's Journal* and *Our Lady of the Flowers.*

Ken Kesey (American novelist, essayist, and short story writer)—Best known for his experimental novel *One Flew Over the Cuckoo's Nest,* Kesey has ended a long publishing hiatus with *Demon Box,* a collection of essays and short stories.

John Montague (American-born Irish poet, short story writer, and editor)—Montague's recent volumes of verse, *Selected Poems* and *The Dead Kingdom,* have secured his reputation as one of contemporary Ireland's leading poets.

Alberto Moravia (Italian novelist, short story writer, essayist, critic, dramatist, and script-writer)—Regarded as one of the foremost twentieth-century Italian literary figures, Moravia often presents a world of decadence and corruption in which his characters are guided primarily by their senses and by sexual obsession. Recent works to be covered in his entry include *Erotic Tales* and *The Voyeur.*

Vladimir Nabokov (Russian-born American novelist, poet, short story writer, essayist, dramatist, and critic)—Considered one of the greatest stylists of twentieth-century literature and renowned for his experimentation with language, Nabokov has gained renewed attention with the posthumous publication of his novel *The Enchanter.*

John Cowper Powys (English novelist, poet, autobiographer, essayist, and critic)—A prolific author in several genres, Powys is admired for the depth of imagination, ornate prose style, and philosophical beliefs displayed in such novels as *Wolf Solent, A Glastonbury Romance,* and *Weymouth Sands.*

Bernard Slade (Canadian-born dramatist and scriptwriter)—A popular Broadway dramatist best known for *Same Time, Next Year, Tribute,* and *Romantic Comedy,* Slade combines humor with emotionally affecting situations in plays about marital and familial love.

Tristan Tzara (Rumanian-born French poet, dramatist, and essayist)—Tzara was the founder of Dadaism, an intellectual movement of the World War I era that espoused intentional irrationality and repudiated traditional values of art, history, and religion. Tzara's nihilistic precepts continue to influence contemporary artists of all genres.

Anzia Yezierska (Russian-born novelist and short story writer)—Yezierska is best known for her fiction detailing the experiences of female Jewish immigrants in the United States at the beginning of the twentieth century. Since her death in 1970, several of Yezierska's works have been reissued, prompting renewed critical interest in her writings.

W(ystan) H(ugh) Auden

1907-1973

English-born American poet, critic, essayist, dramatist, editor, translator, and librettist.

Auden is considered to be one of the preeminent poets of the twentieth century. His poetry centers on moral issues and evidences his strong political, social, and psychological orientations. In his work, Auden applied conceptual and scientific knowledge to traditional verse forms and metrical patterns while assimilating the industrial countryside of his youth to create an allegorical landscape rife with machinery, abandoned mines, and technological references. His canon represents a quest for a systematic ideology in an increasingly complex world. This search is illuminated in its early stages by the teachings of Sigmund Freud and Karl Marx and later by the influences of philosopher Sören Kierkegaard and theologian Reinhold Niebuhr. Auden's poetry is versatile and inventive; ranging from terse, epigrammatic pieces to book-length verse, it incorporates his vast knowledge and displays his efforts to discipline his prodigious talent. Affirming his tremendous influence on twentieth-century poetry, Seamus Heaney commented: "Auden was an epoch-making poet on public themes, the register of a new sensibility, a great sonneteer, a writer of perfect light verse, a prospector of literature at its most illiterate roots and a dandy of lexicography at its most extravagant reaches."

Auden was born and raised in the heavily industrialized region of northern England. Both his father, a prominent physician whose knowledge extended into the mythology and folklore of his Icelandic ancestry, and his mother, a strict Anglican, exerted strong influences on Auden's poetry. Auden's early interest in science and engineering earned him a scholarship to Oxford University, where his fascination with poetry caused him to change his field of study to English. His attraction to science never waned, however, and scientific references are frequently found in his poetry. While at Oxford, Auden became familiar with modernist poetry, particularly that of T. S. Eliot, which was to heavily influence his early writing. It was also at Oxford that Auden became the pivotal member of a group of writers that included Stephen Spender, C. Day Lewis, and Louis MacNeice, a collective variously labeled the "Oxford Group" or the "Auden Generation." These writers adhered to various communist and anti-fascist doctrines and expressed social, political, and economic concerns, all of which are evident in Auden's work of the 1930s.

In 1928, Auden's first book, *Poems,* was privately printed by Stephen Spender. That same year, T. S. Eliot accepted Auden's verse play *Paid on Both Sides* for publication in his magazine *Criterion*. This play, along with many poems from the 1928 collection, appeared in Auden's *Poems* (1930), which was published upon Eliot's urging. Critics noted that these early poems display the influences of Thomas Hardy, Laura Riding, Wilfred Owen, and Edward Thomas and have commended the collection for its ability, in M. D. Zabel's words, to "evoke a music wholly beyond reason, extraordinarily penetrating and creative in its search for significance behind fact." Stylistically, these poems are fragmentary and terse, relying on concrete images and colloquial language to convey Auden's political and psychological concerns. In his next volume, *The Orators: An En-*

glish Study (1932), Auden implements modernist and surrealist techniques to detail and satirize fascism and British stagnation, although much of the work consists of private allusions, jokes, and references to Auden's friends. Despite its abstruseness, *The Orators* was praised for its adventurous experimentation with literary styles and its lively and original use of English verse and prose. During the next few years, the pieces Auden sporadically published in periodicals and anthologies marked a gradual change in his verse style. Many of these poems are collected in *Look, Stranger!* (1936; published in the United States as *On This Island*), in which Auden's development of a more disciplined style is expressed in the volume's dedication to Erika Mann: "Since the external disorder, and extravagant lies, / . . . What can truth treasure, or heart bless, / But a narrow strictness?" These poems are written in a more intensely formal style that implicitly eschews Romantic idealism and modernism and is seemingly intended to offset contemporary chaos. The change in Auden's approach prompted Gavin Ewart to comment: "Mr. Auden's verse has undergone a considerable simplification and a more severe formal discipline, emerging both concise and emotive, in the political poems of very great powers and in the love poems . . . of very great sympathy and tenderness."

Auden's poems from the second half of the 1930s evidence his many travels during this period of world trouble. "Spain"

(1937), one of his most famous and widely anthologized pieces, was written upon his return to England from the Spanish Civil War. *Letters from Iceland* (1937), a travel book written in collaboration with Louis MacNeice, contains Auden's poem "Letter to Lord Byron." This long epistolary poem to the author of *Don Juan* derives from that work the metaphor of the journey for artistic growth and displays Auden's mastery of *ottava rima*. *Journey to War* (1937), a travel book on China written with Christopher Isherwood, features Auden's sonnet sequence and verse commentary "In Time of War." The first half of the sequence recounts the history of humanity's move away from rational thought, while the second half addresses the moral problems faced by humankind on the verge of another world war.

In 1939, Auden left England and became a citizen of the United States. His first book as an emigrant, *Another Time* (1940), contains some of Auden's most memorable poems, among them "September 1, 1939," "Musée des Beaux Arts," and "Lay Your Sleeping Head, My Love." *Another Time* also contains Auden's elegies to such poets as A. E. Housman, Matthew Arnold, and W. B. Yeats, from whose careers and aesthetic concerns Auden was beginning to develop his own artistic credo. The famous line from "In Memory of W. B. Yeats"—"Poetry makes nothing happen"—presents Auden's complete rejection of romantic tenets. Auden's increasing concentration on ethical concerns in *Another Time* points to his reconversion to Christianity, a decision influenced by his disillusionment with secular political solutions, his reading of the works of Sören Kierkegaard, and his personal friendships with Charles Williams and Reinhold Niebuhr. These concerns are central to *The Double Man* (1941) and *For the Time Being* (1944). *The Double Man* contains "New Year Letter," a long epistolary poem outlining Auden's readings of Christian literature, while *For the Time Being* features two allegorical pieces that present in prose and verse his views on art and life. The title poem of *For the Time Being* is a rendering of the Nativity that utilizes technical language derived from modern science and psychology in order to intellectually rationalize Christian faith. Even more ambitious is "The Sea and the Mirror: A Commentary on Shakespeare's *Tempest*," considered by many critics to be Auden's best extended poem. Taking characters from *The Tempest*, "The Sea and the Mirror" represents, according to Herbert Greenberg, "Auden's conception of the true function of art; both mimetic and paradigmatic, its purpose is not only to show us as we truly are but also, by its example of order, to suggest that we might be different and better."

Auden's next volume, *The Collected Poetry* (1945), in which he revised, retitled, or excluded many of his earlier poems, solidified his reputation as an esteemed poet. *The Age of Anxiety: A Baroque Eclogue* (1947), winner of the Pulitzer Prize in poetry, features four characters of disparate backgrounds who meet in a New York City bar during World War II. Written in the heavily alliterative Anglo-Saxon style, this poem explores the attempts of the protagonists to comprehend themselves and the world in which they live. These individuals eventually fail to attain self-realization and succumb to their immediate desires rather than adhering to a spiritual faith. Auden's next major work, *Nones* (1951), includes another widely anthologized piece, "In Praise of Limestone," and the first poems of the "Horae Canonicae" sequence. This sequence, and another entitled "Bucolics," are contained in *The Shield of Achilles* (1955), for which Auden received the National Book Award. These works, although less overtly Christian in content

than his early verse, are serene meditations on human existence informed by the philosophy of Martin Heidegger, historical events of the Christian church, and elements of nature. *Homage to Clio* (1960), in similar fashion, begins the sequence "Thanksgiving for a Habitat," which is published in its entirety in *About the House* (1965). In these poems, Auden expresses the conflict between the private and public spheres of an artist's life.

In his later years, Auden wrote three more volumes—*City without Walls and Other Poems* (1969), *Epistle to a Godson and Other Poems* (1972), and the posthumously published *Thank You, Fog: Last Poems* (1974)—which are noted for their lexical range and humanitarian content. Auden's penchant for altering and discarding poems has prompted the publication of several anthologies since his death. *Collected Poems* (1976) is faithful to Auden's last revisions, while *The English Auden: Poems, Essays, and Dramatic Writings, 1927-1939* (1977) includes the original versions of Auden's early writings as well as portions of his dramatic and critical pieces. Included in *The English Auden* is an uncompleted work, *The Prolific and the Devourer,* an epigrammatic piece written in the manner of Blaise Pascal and William Blake.

Auden's dramatic work consists of *Paid on Both Sides,* a complex blending of the theories of D. H. Lawrence and American psychologist Homer Lane with Norse mythology, and *The Dance of Death* (1933), a ballet with acting and singing that was commissioned by Rupert Doone's Group Theatre. With Christopher Isherwood, Auden coauthored *The Dog Beneath the Skin; or, Where Is Francis?* (1935), *The Ascent of F6* (1936), and *On the Frontier* (1938). Auden also collaborated with Chester Kallman on libretti for works by Benjamin Britten, Igor Stravinsky, Wolfgang Mozart, and others. As a critic, Auden is best represented by *The Enchafèd Flood; or, The Romantic Iconography of the Sea* (1950), which informs much of his poetry of the 1950s, *The Dyer's Hand and Other Essays* (1962), and *Forewords and Afterwords* (1973). These last two volumes are noted for reflecting the soundness of Auden's critical judgment.

Auden's distinguished career as a man of letters has been the subject of much reevaluation in recent years. While some critics contend that he wrote his finest work when his political feelings were less obscured by religion and philosophy, others defend the later material as the work of a highly original and mature intellect. Many critics echo the assessment of Auden's career by the National Book Committee, which awarded him the National Medal for Literature in 1967: "[Auden's poetry] has illuminated our lives and times with grace, wit and vitality. His work, branded by the moral and ideological fires of our age, breathes with eloquence, perception and intellectual power."

(See also *CLC*, Vols. 1, 2, 3, 4, 6, 9, 11, 14; *Contemporary Authors*, Vols. 9-12, rev. ed., Vols. 45-48 [obituary]; *Contemporary Authors New Revision Series*, Vol. 5; and *Dictionary of Literary Biography*, Vols. 10, 20.)

PETER PORTER

[*The English Auden: Poems, Essays and Dramatic Writings, 1927-1939*] prints an unpublished and unfinished work entitled *The Prolific and the Devourer* which is touching in its rawness. Here are the main ideas which dominated Auden's life right up to his death, but there seems to be no control of their presentation. Had he been able to work them into a properly planned book, the world might well have lost much of the mature poetry he wrote thereafter. These fragments remain like thematic sketches in a composer's notebook: we see the dominating shapes of his imagination, but as yet there is no proper indication of how richly he is going to expand them and counterpoint them in his work. At first sight, these perceptions seem confined to political issues, but the working-out of their consequences can be found in *For the Time Being,* **"The Sea and the Mirror"**, *The Age of Anxiety* and well into the poems of the Fifties and Sixties. Auden always saw politics as an expression of the health of the imagination, and there is a sense in which the later Horatian poetry is quite as politically directed (or as unpolitical if you want to put it that way) as the work of the Thirties. The last quoted entry from *The Prolific and the Devourer* reads: "Tolstoy, who, knowing that art makes nothing happen, scrapped it, is more to be respected than the Marxist critic who finds ingenious reasons for admitting the great artists of the past to the State Pantheon." The date is 1939, but the sentiment is perfectly in keeping with the ideas of the "Mid-Atlantic Goethe" of the Sixties. It makes general sense to state that Auden not only wrote well and ill at all stages of his career, but that his abiding interests and characteristics did not change very much over forty years' devotion to poetry. He is an artist who resists the famous three periods of production: his work is like a well-cut gem, it reveals different facets of itself at certain times. It does not get more mature or develop particularly, except in the one sense of literary professionalism. After settling in America, Auden's concern for the technical finish of his poems became more fastidious. In **"Profile,"** written in 1965-6, he paints a picture of himself as a descendant of the craftsmen-artists of the past—"Vain? Not very, except / about his knowledge of metre, / and his friends." And in a contribution to an anthology entitled *Let the Poet Choose,* he introduced **"In Due Season"** as the only English poem since Campion written in accentual asclepiads.

But *The English Auden* leaves the strong impression that this growth of professionalism was not all gain. Mixed up with the rough and ready finish of much of his poetry of the Thirties, there is also a marvellous authority and originality which the later poetry does not possess. After all, the conviction that a new genius of English poetry had arrived, which was felt so powerfully by so many people in the Thirties (not just Auden's immediate contemporaries), did not come about accidentally. *Poems 1930* must be one of the most unexpected books ever to have made its author's reputation. Where, except perhaps in Laura Riding's verbal defoliation and Wilfred Owen's pararhymes, are there any precedents for the first poems of this twenty-three-year-old genius? The material of the poems is not without ancestry—chiefly the sagas, the public school fantasies of himself, Isherwood and friends, and the gnomic marginalia of Blake—but the tone is completely new. And like Byron's tone, which enabled him to wake one morning and find himself famous, Auden's won instant recognition. It is only when we scrutinise these early poems closely that we perceive how far they depart from the canons of poetical propriety which the later Auden set up for himself. For a start, they are *sui generis,* and not fashioned by imitation of some admired model, some apt and brilliant recognition of the mileage a modern poet could get out of the sonnet, or terza rima, or even blank verse. There are shadows of past structures in them (I cannot imagine how anybody could write convincingly poetry which was entirely *ab ovo*), but they come very close to being unclassifiable formally—uncomfortably so, for the taste of the mature Auden,

perhaps, though he always remained fond of the bulk of them and included them, under however many changes of title, in his various collections from the Forties onwards. By 1931 . . . Auden was ready to employ the sestina—there is one in *The Orators*—and two years later was experimenting with the sonnet as a vehicle for his examination of the psychology of love. *The Orators* (finished 1932) has several poems in rhyming doggerel, as well as an uneven but highly stimulating series of odes in its Bruckner-length coda. *The Dance of Death* (1933) is packed with songs, jingles and doggerel choruses as well.

After 1930, rhymes, metrical devices, stanza structures, in fact all the traditional armoury of poetry, are applied in full knowledge of their effectiveness and the formal demands they make upon the poet's skill and imagination. But the early poetry is different. It is packed with close rhymes, pararhymes, and cadences out of the nursery, but these are held dissolved in verse of a sleepwalking authority. This is just the way an oracle would speak, we think, as we read such poems as **"From the very first coming down"**, **"Taller today"**, **"Love by ambition"**, **"Watch any day his nonchalant pauses"**, **"Will you turn a deaf ear"**, and **"Consider this and in our time."** Those first readers in the Thirties who thought they were hearkening to the voice of a new leader, and who interpreted Auden's poems as messages from the battlefront, soon identified with Communism, were not wrong in their impulses, though wholly mistaken in their interpretations. As Edward Mendelson points out, the early poems speak of defeat, of separation, of stories which are not simply incomplete but of which there were probably never any definitive versions. We may wonder how anybody could take *Poems 1930* or even *The Orators* as a call to the collective life, though G. S. Fraser has discerned a Fascist tinge in *The Orators*—unconvincingly, to my mind. But Auden himself must have been persuaded to think that his talent was amenable to the cause of Communism: for all his brilliance of mind, he was not gifted with total self knowledge.

His was a most unusual case—a very young poet whose first work was recognised by his contemporaries as new and authoritative. Combined with his didactic bent, this discovery of his authority pushed him towards an explicitness which was sometimes at variance with his talent during the Thirties. After 1930, it seems to me, Auden's work is a sort of development section reworking themes to which the first book of poems gave the exposition. Ideas out of the hauntingly complete early poetry are now subjected to overt elaboration. Except for his remarkable lyrics and songs, many of which were gathered into *Look, Stranger,* the rest of the Thirties poetry is not as fine as his first published work. Only after he went to America and realigned himself with Christianity did he experience another surge of power of the kind with which he began. But he could never be so innocently assertive again—hence his courses of reading, his insistence on a Goethean apparatus during the American years.

Now that we have most of Auden's output of the Thirties in one volume . . . , we can see more clearly than we could by consulting the original individual volumes or looking through his much-revised and reorganised *Collected Poems* that the revolutionary art seemingly promised by his earliest work was something he was either unaware of or something he had no intention of providing. The anti-modernist counter-reformation which he led in later years is prefigured as early as *The Orators*. And if in the Thirties he was content to take up forms and influences with an almost games-playing enthusiasm, he quickly turned himself into a virtuoso, whose maturity was accelerated by the more professional air of the United States. James Fenton has pointed to a common misunderstanding of Auden's turning his back on Modernism. Fenton sees him not as a lost leader but as a liberator, showing the next generation of poets the opportunities still open to them in traditional forms. For Fenton, it is really the strenuousness of Modernism which is the self-denying ordinance. The United States is, of course, the home of the academic avant-garde but Auden did not interest himself in this. It was American professionalism which concerned him, and he was more likely to discern it on Broadway than on Black Mountain.

It is hard to read *The English Auden* without wondering equally at the memorable language and the wilful extravagance. The two occur together most frequently in *The Orators* and *The Dog Beneath the Skin*. . . . (pp. 64-6)

But having praised the exuberance, I can't say I am surprised that Auden quickly outgrew and came to regret the crudity of many of the ideas in the poems of his time of poetical loosening-up. . . . [An] ode addressed to the newly-born John Warner contains the following lines:

> The few shall be taught who want to understand,
> Most of the rest shall live upon the land;
> Living in one place with a satisfied face
> All of the women and most of the men
> Shall work with their hands and not think again.

Had he meant that, and many similar passages in *The Orators, The Dance of Death* and the other plays, there would be some truth in the claim that his direction was as Fascist as it was Communist. It was, I believe, neither, and we should look at all the other kinds of writing produced in Auden's Thirties for a truer picture of his concerns. Auden's personality being so strongly didactic, his creative gift had to stand in for the Old Adam in him. He was drawn to the wilder shores of the healers (Homer Lane, Lawrence and "loony Layard"), but also to Freudian orthodoxy and to his mother's Anglicanism. Without the urge to portray the sickness of our species in poetry as exuberant and memorable as anything he wrote in praise of health, he would have been an insufferable prig as an artist. Time and again in the Thirties, the resolution of the conflict between his anarchy and his dirigism is made in lyrics of healing beauty. It is as though he were anticipating his later doxological statement, "praise what there is for being."

Not the least of the attractions of *The English Auden* is its reminder that this knowing artist once exhibited character faults like ours, and didn't merely anatomise them. He had not yet put his guard right up. *Poems 1930* is all Old Adam—a wonderful assortment of warnings and battle scenes, not just from ruined industrial landscapes and the haunted pastures of old feuds, but as much concerned with the High Streets and mass culture of an England bleeding to death in the Depression. The one really severe loss suffered by Auden in America was his sense of place. He recaptured it in a touristy sort of way in his poems about the Mezzogiorno and lower Austria, but the real (as distinct from the mythic) America seems never to have entered his imagination at all forcefully. Not even New York is fleshed out in his late poetry. From **"New Year Letter"** onwards, the landscape of his poems comes from books, and emblematic ones at that. And when he does record more concretely, the scene is usually England again. In dozens of poems and prose passages in *The English Auden* (as well as in **"The Last Will and Testament"** in *Letters from Iceland*) and in the plays with Isherwood, he sets these islands before us like a

map. It is much more than a geographical poetry; the vision is of the field of folk itself, whether the view is from Birmingham to Wolverhampton or down in Surrey among "the old-world cottages . . . [where] . . . nervous people who will never marry live upon dividends with an animal for friend or a volume of memoirs." The Flying Scot heads south, the Bristol Fighter flies, the Night Mail crosses the border: the British Isles come alive in Auden's imagination. . . . "Get there if you can and see the land you once were proud to own" begins one of the poems in Auden's first book. So much of what Auden saw at that time is undated and disturbingly true today. In America Auden moved on to other concerns, but the country he left behind remains very much as he diagnosed it.

The English Auden should enable all those commentators who have been saying for years that he left his gift behind him when he went to America to check on their memories of his work in the Thirties. It is not just the convenience of having the contents of many books in one volume, including several which are out of print, which pleases, but the texts themselves have been restored to their original state. I do not intend to go into the question of Auden's multiple revisions or de-fusings of his poems. It seems to me a poet has a perfect right to trim and prepare his canon for posterity, provided the public can choose his earlier versions if it prefers them. Edward Mendelson's editing has now removed any cause we had to complain of the mayhem Auden perpetrated on much-loved poems when preparing his progressively decimated *Collected Poems*. Anyone with *The English Auden* on his shelves can skip the texts of **"In Memory of W. B. Yeats"**, **"Dover"**, **"Oxford"** and **"The Witnesses"** in *Collected Poems* and go straight to their vastly preferable originals. Old favourites completely banished from court also return—**"August for the People"**, **"Spain"** and **"September 1st 1939."** (pp. 67-8)

[*The English Auden* includes several poems which appear] for the first time in book form. *Collected Poems* (the 1966 version) raided a notebook in the British Museum for Auden's early Blakcan jottings, but now we get a few more. . . . **"Happy New Year"** is a great joy for anyone who has had to borrow a friend's copy of *New Country* (1933). This is one of Auden's happiest pieces of relaxed writing, and the Langland-like vision is not to be deprecated because of the Boy Scout tone of some of the verse. It appears in one of the appendices, and is much more worthwhile than the similar dream poem, **"The month was April"**, which comes from a notebook and was first published last year. . . . (pp. 69-70)

There is a good deal more which I have not mentioned, some of it very slight, but all of it engaging to read. *The English Auden* will be most useful to those readers who have all Auden's early volumes. It will be a valuable concordance and source of textual information. This, however, is not the right note on which to end a review. There are dozens of masterpieces in its pages, some of them the most familiar and loved poems of our century. Has there been a writer of lyrics in English since Rochester who was Auden's equal? That claim can be substantiated on his first decade's production alone— the greater part of it present in this cornucopia of a book. (p. 70)

Peter Porter, "Auden's Cornucopia: The 1930s Texts," in Encounter, Vol. L, No. 2, February, 1978, *pp. 64-70.*

FRANK KERMODE

[*The English Auden*], though it in no way matches the idea people of my age must have as to how an Auden collection should look, is nothing like as hideous as *Collected Poems,* which seems to have been designed as part of a plot to stop people reading Auden. I myself am not quite old enough to have been part of the orginal audience of *Poems,* but I read *Look, Stranger!* soon after it appeared (and, having heard the word from Cambridge that it demonstrated the collapse of Auden's talent, rushed off to get the early book, wondering what marvels it contained). And it really is a great pleasure to see the poetry of this period decently available once more, unexpurgated, uncorrected, unamended in accordance with a later creed of taste, morals, politics, and religion. (p. 610)

There is a genuine and sad perversity in [the] failure of Auden to understand himself. It is as if he came to find himself boring, or became unable to connect with himself, as in life he grew less and less able to connect with others. All those schemes and formulas he invented to systematize his views on everything from history to ethics—it was a habit early formed, as we see from some of the prose selections in [*The English Auden*]—served to fence him in, to prevent any real conversation with others, or with his former self. His earlier rhetoric failed later ethical tests, and in acquiring a poetic personality that could live with these faintly schoolboyish standards of truth-telling he lost all sense of the valuable strangeness of the personality it supplanted. He says of Edward Lear that he "became a land"; he himself had been a land, with many settlers. But he wished to impose on them institutions invented by his own internal bureaucracy—they are represented by all those words and phrases with capital letters, like the Just City and the Truly Weak Man. The poet of the Prologue to *Look, Stranger!* was one of the first to leave.

It should be said that many of the changes are of a kind that any poet might make, for example the deft, simple improvements in the poem **"Legend."** But it still seems to me that much of the early work is travestied. Even the titles, when they are ironical or dismissive (**"Venus Will Now Say a Few Words"**), tend to put the poems down. The very early work suffers least, perhaps because it is usually gnomic and opaque, not speaking aloud what the later, moralizing poet did not want heard. *Paid on Both Sides,* certainly a work of genius, is spared. The poems which are not are probably lesser works, but they speak out, and in unacceptable tones. Auden's reason for disliking them is hinted at in a casual piece of prose, here reprinted, and dated 1936: "the commonest cause of badness in the arts is being really interested in one subject while pretending to be interested in another. The secret of good art is the same as the secret of a good life: to find out what you are interested in, however strange, or trivial, or ambitious, or shocking, or uplifting, and deal with that, for it is all you can deal with well. 'To each according to his means; from each according to his powers,' in fact." This last quotation would presumably have disappeared had Auden revised the piece for publication later; but one sees what is in process. He decided that some of his poems were only pretending to be interested in what they were saying. And out goes the Prologue to *Look, Stranger!,* "O Love, the interest itself in thoughtless heaven," with its tremendous concluding thirteen-line sentence and its exalted conceits. This poem has an intellectual and technical range quite different from that of *Paid on Both Sides,* but the poet had ceased to be interested in that "possible dream, long coiled in the ammonite's slumber," and now supposed that he never really had been. There is something wrong with a set of rules that excludes so fine a poem from the canon; and there is something wrong with an editorial policy that excludes it from

the *Collected Poems* and prints it in a supplementary volume which, however sumptuous, is still only an appendix.

One is glad to have the specimens of early prose. Like other young reviewers, Auden was educating himself in public, and there are passages here that he would certainly have found blush-making in his later years—for example, the 1934 review of Liddell Hart's *T. E. Lawrence,* which compares Lawrence's enlistment in the R.A.F. with Lenin's requirement ("to go hungry, work illegally, and be anonymous"), adding that Lenin and Lawrence were the two "whose lives exemplify most completely what is best and significant in our time, our nearest approach to a synthesis of feeling and reason, act and thought, the most potent agents of freedom and to us, egotistical underlings, the most relevant accusation and hope." Is this "pretending"? He never rejected **"Our Hunting Fathers,"** written presumably at the same moment as the review; perhaps it was sufficiently obscure, perhaps the Lenin quotation was sufficiently susceptible of ironical reading.

The best of the prose has to do with psychoanalysis, for the young Auden had thought seriously about it, and what he had to say is still worth reading for its own sake. The excursions on light verse, though repetitive, are also worth attention, for Auden's doctrine of light verse was soon to become his doctrine of poetry in general. And of course he was always remarkably good at it. [Editor Edward] Mendelson kindly prints, for the first time in full, a charming, innocently obscene song called **"Alice Is Gone,"** and some others as well. (pp. 612-14)

Now for some praise. The editor's Introduction is valuable, making a modest use of material only he has access to. [*The English Auden*] probably establishes the outline of Auden's career most likely to be used in future, from the first authentic poem **"Who stands, the crux left of the watershed"** through the abandonment of quasi-utopian politics signaled by the newly-printed dream-allegory **"The month was April,"** to a crucial spiritual experience associated with the poem called **"A Summer Night."** I hope this poem, which may be about a Vision of Agape, will not in consequence assume importance disproportionate to its merit; it is already overvalued, partly because of Britten's setting. And we old men who still think of the poems of the 'thirties as part of an almost incomparably good time for modern poetry—when you picked up the literary journals and read a late poem of Yeats, or *East Coker,* or a new Auden—are not going to sit idly by and allow it to be said that he was really in a bad patch of pretending, but eventually got it right; and that people will come to see that he did, abandoning their allegiance to the older texts and the banned poems. At least *The English Auden* will do nothing to strengthen that kind of propaganda. (p. 614)

Frank Kermode, "Another Auden," in The Yale Review, *Vol. LXVII, No. 4, Summer, 1978, pp. 609-14.*

ANTHONY THWAITE

F. R. Leavis has argued for many years that 'the Auden who conquered the literary world with such ease was the undergraduate intellectual', with all the disabilities of the type—precocious sophistication, lack of real seriousness, 'a surprising radical adolescence that should have been already well outgrown'. What seems particularly to have galled Leavis is what he took to be the smell of conspiracy in the reception that greeted Auden's poetry from the beginning, and that went on greeting it. By 1937—when Auden was still only thirty—the acclaim was such that the periodical *New Verse* devoted the whole of a special issue to the man, his work, and estimates (mainly congratulatory, though Ezra Pound was indignantly contemptuous) of both. No other English poet of the century has commanded such early and continuous praise. Put in such terms, one can see how Leavis shuddered . . . at what seemed to be the machinations of a clique, a publicity campaign.

I think Leavis was wrong, and that dislike of a 'system' prevailed over his literary judgement. The Auden that emerged in 1929 and 1930 was indeed more than a prodigy, a university phenomenon, writing work which (in Leavis's opinion) 'might have represented the very green immaturity of a notable creative talent'. Auden's contemporaries did well to be impressed by him, and to take him as their representative voice. The occasional silliness, arrogant obscurity and intellectual pretentiousness of some of the early work are plain for all to see; but these faults are not paramount. (pp. 54-5)

[Auden's wide appeal from the early days derived from the fact] that he was not impenetrably 'difficult', much of the time, for all his assured modernity, so that he was not the preserve simply of clever undergraduates and metropolitan intellectuals, but spoke equally—and eloquently—to provincial schoolboys. . . . He was 'modern', he spoke of the time in which he lived, but he did not seem to presuppose (for example) an apparatus of polyglot scholarship such as *The Waste Land* appeared to present.

Much has been written about Auden as a political poet—even *the* political poet—of the 1930s; but in fact the direct political content of *Poems* (1930) and *Look, Stranger* (1936) is small. Even the strange 'English Study', *The Orators,* that appeared between these two books, for all the Marxist notions that have been read into it, is much more a work that has its roots in Jung, Groddeck and Layard—psychologists, prophets of the psyche rather than political analysts. It is a fantasy, a journal of personal obsessions too, which has a relationship with the grotesque and almost surrealist invented world of 'Mortmere'—that private country, or private joke, of Isherwood and Edward Upward, described by Isherwood in *Lions and Shadows*. It was not really until the late 1930s—in *Spain* (1937) and *Journey to a War* (1939)—that Auden dealt in other than generalized terms with the political world; and by that time he had shed whatever didactic partisan views he may once have held. (I should perhaps mention *The Dance of Death,* an early dramatic satire in light charade form: it is his most consistently Marxist piece, in which Marx himself appears and is seen at the end as a logically inevitable but also rather comic figure.) No totally committed political animal could have written, as Auden did in *Spain,* of 'the flat ephemeral pamphlet and the boring meeting'; as for 'the necessary murder'—that notorious phrase which enlisted the scorn of George Orwell, and which Auden later somewhat neutralized to 'The conscious acceptance of guilt in the fact of murder', before eventually abandoning the whole poem—it has always seemed to me as much a piece of role-playing as anything in *The Orators:* a rhetorical, schoolboy-gang phrase. In this sense, Leavis is right about Auden's posture as an arrested adolescent. But the **"In Time of War"** sequence (from *Journey to a War*) strikes no such attitudes: it has a distinct detachment, even from events in that year when

> Austria died and China was forsaken,
> Shanghai in flames and Teruel retaken.

What the sequence looks for—and it is summed up in the **"Commentary"** with which it ends—is that 'change of heart'

forecast in a poem several years before. In this **"Commentary"**, he concludes:

> Ruffle the perfect manners of the frozen heart,
> And once again compel it to be awkward and alive,
> To all it suffered once a weeping witness.
>
> Clear from the head the masses of impressive rubbish;
> Rally the lost and trembling forces of the will,
> Gather them up and let them loose upon the earth,
>
> Till they construct at last a human justice,
> The contribution of our star, within the shadow
> Of which uplifting, loving and constraining power
> All other reasons may rejoice and operate.

Such an injunction leads naturally towards the acceptance of Christian teaching and Christian discipline which Auden found in the early 1940s, and which some of his admirers found so disconcerting (as happened, too, with those who were appalled or contemptuous at Eliot's 'conversion' in 1927). The progression can be seen as one that leads on without strain from Auden's mind-healing preoccupations in the 1930s. (pp. 57-9)

[A] frequent objection is that Auden's adoption of the United States as his new home at the beginning of 1939 marked not only a rejection of his native country but the start of a rapid decline in his poetry. Some critics would like to see the episode as a dramatic break, a sloughing-off of Europe, and a consequent lapsing into a cosy and languidly didactic style. Those who had 'placed' Auden in the 1930s, and who had certain fixed ideas about him, were disconcerted; some of their objections had as much to do with an outraged sense of patriotism as anything else. In fact, Auden (together with his friend Christopher Isherwood) left for America in January 1939, a time when, it has been pointed out, the British government was asserting that the prospects for peace had never been brighter. So it was nothing to do with 'deserting the sinking ship' or escaping from danger: Auden had voluntarily faced danger in Spain in 1937 and in China in 1938.

But, quite apart from his motives, was there indeed a decline in his subsequent poetry? I think not. Almost to the end—and certainly up to *Epistle to a Godson* (1972)—there are poems in his successive books which can properly stand alongside his best earlier work. . . . In *City Without Walls* (1969), **"Prologue at Sixty"** is a self-elegy which combines, in the authentic Auden manner, high seriousness about important things with that lightness of tone which distinguished him from the beginning—that sardonic wit, sometimes even clownish, which so often combined with a note of urgent warning or impending doom; one can see it in such poems of the 1930s as **"Law Like Love"**, in many of the sonnets in his sequence **"The Quest,"** in what he grouped together as 'Songs and other musical pieces', and at its briskest and most amusing in **"Letter to Lord Byron"**, the long discursive poem which runs through the book he worked on with MacNeice, *Letters from Iceland* (1937). Finally, to mention one more late poem, **"An Encounter"** (in *Epistle to a Godson*) shows Auden's concise and reverberant historical sense at work as perfectly as his *Spain* almost thirty-five years earlier; the poem observes a meeting between 'Attila and his Hun Horde' and Pope Leo by the River Po in the year 452, and makes a telling point about the mysteries of civilization and barbarism.

It could be said that Auden gradually became a sage and not a prophet; but whichever function he took upon himself, he was supremely an entertainer, a brilliant teacher and preacher, a virtuoso who believed that poetry can display many voices, many skills, and that it has something to do with the disinterested intelligence. . . . He was a prolific poet and (as one should expect of a prolific poet—think of Wordsworth, Byron, Tennyson) some of his work is careless, coy, laborious, occasionally boring. But the general level and impact of over forty years of constant writing is exhilaratingly high. Along with Eliot, he has been the most influential Anglo-American poet of the century. . . . (pp. 59-61)

Anthony Thwaite, "W. H. Auden," in his Twentieth-Century English Poetry: An Introduction, *Barnes & Noble, 1978, pp. 54-61.*

AUSTIN WARREN

The sheer bulk of Auden's writing—two substantial volumes of critical prose and a hugely unwieldy **Collected Poems** in small print—makes the effort to say anything comprehensive about him seem unmanageable. One could address oneself to the task by dividing it into three essays—one on the man, one on the poetry, and one on the criticism, chiefly, but by no means exclusively, literary. But with Auden that seems unsatisfactory, for in him the three parts coexisted: he never segregated his personal life from his work (as Eliot so rigidly attempted to do), nor his critical mind from his poetic work: after his early poetry his critical mind, his acute intelligence, more and more takes the upper hand over his unconscious. He was never really the romantic poet, the Rimbaud, he used to seem, nor the "pure poet" of images and rhythms either. Perhaps in a sense one should read Auden's poetry backward—the latest written, first.

After 1939 he had renounced one of the persistent grandiose conceptions poets have entertained of themselves, the conception entertained by Shelley of the immense power poets wield over human lives: that they are prophets and shapers of destiny and changers of history. Instead he assigned poetry, his own included, to the humbler position which earlier ages than the romantic had given to literature, including poetry: that of a craft with words, which described, characterized—perhaps even, in one of Auden's favorite words and concepts, "diagnosed"—human life in its more permanent, as well as its more transient, more agebound, features. Poetry can never take the place of religion: here Auden distinguishes his position from that modified romantic Arnold or, with less rigidity, allies himself with Eliot. Poetry cannot change history or even morally reform or spiritually regenerate a single man. It can soften or refine, but cannot alter, character. It can harmlessly entertain our idle hours or, at a higher level, educate and subtilize our sensibility; it can interpret. Further the orginality of the poet is not in his philosophic thought (as Eliot said long ago of Dante) but in the adequacy with which he translates a world view into appropriate aesthetic expression.

Auden was a highly intelligent man with a wide range of interests; he was not, except incidentally, a confessional poet. When he writes about himself directly, as he does delightfully in his **"Letter to Lord Byron,"** it is as simple delivery of a case history, not as a revelation of supposed importance to mankind. A lifelong practitioner of what his friends call his "clinical" method, he treats himself with (almost) the same objectivity with which he treats others. (pp. 229-30)

[To approach Auden] is to approach a poet through his self, his character, his knowledge and his wisdom, not through his poetry. In Auden's case this is not a bizarre procedure, for

though he is finally to be considered as all he ever claimed to be, a poet, he is much more than the diminished thing the contemporary poet often seems to be: he is a poet on the older, larger lines of Milton and Dryden and Goethe, one whose perceptions, intuitions, and purely literary felicities do not rule out the humane dimensions of the universal man. Like the three I cite, Auden is a master of prose as well as poetry, ambidextrous. Not an original speculative mind like, say, Kierkegaard or Nietzsche, he is far better balanced and more synoptic than either existentialist (unlike these two, ever aware of the community as well as the gifted individual); he takes within his conceptual grasp and sweep Freud, Marx, and Christian thinkers; and though he finally takes his stand with the Christian thinkers, it is in no manner a sectarian way. His prose mind, trained on science and philosophical criticism, is what gives ballast and substance to his poetry. (pp. 247-48)

Austin Warren, "The Quest for Auden," in The Sewanee Review, *Vol. LXXXVII, No. 2, Spring, 1979, pp. 229-48.*

ARNOLD KETTLE

What Auden did supremely well in his early poetry was to explore and speculate on the condition of Britain in the period between the wars. One of the characteristics of this poetry is that it has at the same time a very individual, idiosyncratic, sometimes private flavour (which at its least successful depends on a certain cliquishness and on 'in' jokes) and is yet preoccupied with general, public, impersonal yet central factors and ideas. His lyrics are as intellectually subtle and sometimes as intellectually challenging as his more obviously argumentative poetry. It has been well pointed out that what allows him to be 'unselfconsciously personal' is 'his awareness of being the spokesman for, or representative of, many people'. His almost constant use of a 'persona' is a device which allows him to dramatize situations without depersonalizing them or adopting the rather heavy, hectoring tone which poetry concerned with public issues can easily fall into.

He has an extremely sharp instinct for significant trends and for contemporary atmosphere and he was interested in everything. If psychology was his major preoccupation, to emphasize this can easily give a false impression, partly because it wasn't just Freud but a wider selection of 'healers' (Lawrence, Blake, and Homer Lane) whom he drew on, partly because there was so much else that interested him: many aspects of science and scientific theory, history and anthropology, music, religion and philosophy and of course—supremely—literature. What he had to say was not always true but it was always intelligent and stimulating and very seldom sentimental. So that his poetry at its best had the effect of opening up the modern world rather than leading the reader inwards into his personal obsessions and limitations. Although clearly a very unusual and quirky man, he managed on the whole, as a poet, to see himself objectively and humorously.

Auden's involvement in political struggle during the thirties, though it never brought him to a theoretical position which Marxists would be likely to consider very satisfactory, seems to me to have been an altogether positive factor in his development as a poet for several reasons. In the first place, it led him to explore continuously the connections between his private or purely personal experience and the public, historical developments of the time. In the second, it encouraged him to find out what he had in common with other people and to see himself as a part of a social situation, not merely as one lonely man, uncertain and afraid. In the third place it helped him, at least for a time, towards a view of language and indeed of poetry itself which was fruitful precisely because it was outward-turning and socially orientated.

Now it is true that by the end of the thirties Auden was denying the active, social role of poetry:

> Art is not life and cannot be
> A midwife of society. . . .

But a few years earlier he had written

> No artist, however 'pure', is disinterested

and

> You cannot tell people what to do, you can only tell them parables; and that is what art really is, particular stories of particular people and experience, from which each according to his own immediate and peculiar needs may draw his own conclusions.

This last statement is a rejection of poetry as propaganda; but it is an acceptance of the political role of the poet and of the fact that poetry can and does make something happen. And it was during the period in which he held this view that his strongest and most political poetry was written.

For a poet to think of himself as a 'mouth' or 'voice' is fair enough. Saying things is what he is good at. It is when the voice becomes abstracted from changing reality that the trouble starts. It is then that it is likely to begin talking, as Auden in his later years did more and more, about the poet's duty or responsibility being to 'the language', rather than to something impure like human need. This is what purism involves: the treatment of 'language' or 'poetry' or 'art' as though they had some unchanging purity of their own, some autonomy like that of the celestial voice which crops up at critical moments in Italian opera, though always in practice in a specific human context. Celestial voices are all right as long as everyone agrees (even if they don't quite say so) that they are just another convention to help get past difficult moments. But when the poet *really* thinks his duty is to the Language or to Poetry, what actually happens is that he capitulates to conceptions of language and poetry that the ideologists of those with power have found suitable to their deeper purposes. (pp. 93-5)

Political poetry, I would suggest, is poetry in which the question of power gets recognition and expression. Experience is presented not in a cocoon (the poem's form tending all the time to separate it from everything outside itself), not in some sort of purity and isolation as an autonomous whole, but in a way that gives a sense of the power-forces present in the situation evoked. Too strong an emphasis on the autonomy of any human experience or activity always tends to remove it from the pressures, the power-forces, which go towards making it what it is. Poetry that makes us conscious of power opens up the world rather than attempting to enclose a part of it in some sort of mystic purity. One of the virtues of the best poetry of the thirties was that it arose out of and helped define the power struggles of the time.

The impact of Auden's poetry on young intellectuals in the thirties was so great, I think, not because he was offering them the theoretical truth or the confirmation of their existing prejudices but, rather, because with great intellectual and verbal energy his poetry probed and explored many areas of con-

sciousness—scientific, psychological, sociological, political, aesthetic—and came up with striking and stimulating connections embodied in phrases and images of vivid contemporary resonance. (p. 100)

> Arnold Kettle, "W. H. Auden: Poetry and Politics in the Thirties," in Culture and Crisis in Britain in the Thirties, *edited by Jon Clark and others, Lawrence and Wishart, 1979, pp. 83-101.*

JOHN BAYLEY

"All I have is a voice", [Auden] wrote, in his early work, and its potency depended on its impersonal authority. Charles Madge's reaction—"There waited for me in the summer morning, / Auden, fiercely, I read, shuddered and knew"—was common among those at the time who understood the nature of new utterance in poetry and were unconsciously awaiting it. That it was not the voice of an individual was, in terms of the Zeitgeist, so much the better: a bleak impersonal severity was in fashion, as was the idea of communal enterprise, in poetry as in society. But Auden never did develop his individuality. The cosy mannerisms of his later period are no more personal than the youthful tones, but are just as much something in the air, the sound of the leader of a group or fashion, though no longer one that was minatory and exhilarating.

Not infrequently it happens that the tone was not altered at all between the early and the late periods. As soon as the undergraduate of 1926 was introduced by his friend Tom Driberg to *The Waste Land* he took to writing stanzas like

> In Spring we waited. Princes felt
> Through darkness for unwoken queens;
> The itching lover weighed himself
> At stations on august machines

which has not only ceased to be Eliot and become Auden but is the same Auden—although not as accomplished—as the one who around 1950 was to write for Cyril Connolly that most plummy of camp poems, **"The Fall of Rome."**

> Fantastic grow the evening gowns;
> Agents of the Fisc pursue
> Absconding tax-defaulters through
> The sewers of provincial towns.

The always questionable relation between self and group is characteristic of this poetry, the sign of a duality both accepted and exploited by the poet. [In *Early Auden*, Edward] Mendelson observes that as he began his career Auden wanted "both absolute isolation and absolute community, one for the mind, the other for the flesh", and "in his poems he had no need for a dramatic mask; he was invisible without one" [see excerpt below]. This may be a way of saying that the poems do not necessarily believe in their own air of complete confidence, of assertiveness over and rapport with the reader. They seem to be in personal charge but disappear into the isolation of art. Barbara Everett comments that "it is the sound of a man who knows that he sounds like this, assents to sounding like this, but is not like this". Then what is he like? Nothing else. The art is all, as it is in Mozart or Shakespeare; it is the art (as Auden put it in *The Age of Anxiety*) of "the sane who know they are acting", rather than "the mad who do not". Sanity for this poet is keeping the show on the road.

The poet is what the poetry seems; part of the art of the contraption is to make up an impression—a disconcerting or alluring one—of the man inside it. The uniqueness of Auden's poetry lies in its being the result of an act of will. A similar act of will might have made him a doctor, a geologist, a brilliant teacher. That he turned out to be a brilliant poet does not alter the essential arbitrariness of his decision to become one. And his attitude to his art ("we *may* write, we *must* live") remained permanently affected by that decision. The paradox is that other poets who have, as it were, found themselves in their poetry, take their dedication to it for granted: their art is for them the most important *human* activity, proclaiming poet as man and man as poet, paired in harmony. Gabriel Josipovici blames Auden for his attitude to art, rightly seeing in it a rejection of the slow, painful exploratory process which results in the organic creation of a Mallarmé, a Joyce, an Eliot, a Wallace Stevens or a Montale. Auden's act was that of scald or court poet, lead man in a team, the analogy again being with modern activities like physics or filmmaking. For such an act, art must be highly decorated but untrustworthy, halcyon but bogus, beautifully made to be true to nothing else. Auden is the "half-witted Swedish deckhand" whom Basil Wright and Harry Watt, the directors of [the film] *Night Mail,* saw scribbling "the most beautiful verse" for them on an old GPO table and telling them to "just roll it up and throw it away" when its profuseness had to be checked. *Night Mail* is the strongest magic ever brewed by Auden, a magic that completely enchants and dispossesses what it celebrates.

The brilliant creature who looks like a Swedish deckhand is also an image of the Mozart who so affronted the serious Salieri, a legend dramatized with elegant intensity by Pushkin and vulgarized in the play *Amadeus.* Artists dedicated as and for themselves recognize such genius but secretly, almost unconsciously, hate and envy it, for it discredits their labours to bring their own special gifts to fruition. "Negative capability" takes on a special meaning in Auden's case. He comes as close as any poet in the post-romantic age to what Coleridge said of Shakespeare—"a very Proteus of the fire and flood"—naming and inhabiting people and things, entering into being while having no being of his own. In our time this primary activity of the naïve poet is no longer possible. Auden could not get into things and people, but he got instead into the spirits and sense of the age, into its moods and dreams, its fears and neuroses, its fashions and crazes, from Homer Lane to Sheldon, from the yo-yo to the carbon date. He turned into hard magic everything in the consciousness of the time that was questioning and uncertain, muddled and apprehensive, everything that was reaching out, as the poetry itself seemed to be doing, for new devices and solutions, new images of wholeness and salvation.

Poetry eternalizes these things, but also embodies in the process the very weakness it transforms, its "flat ephemeral" nature. Poetry only survives "in the valley of its making". That marvellous poem **"Spain",** which chastened liberals disapprove of today, gets its power from its accurate conjuration of the illusions of a special moment, its fidelity to that moment's sense of "Today, the struggle", and tomorrow (which never comes in poem or history) the idyllic social utopia. Auden, as he told Isherwood, knew they could only live among lunatics, and the same is true of his poems. Unlike most great poetry they do not beckon to another world but make one out of the absurdities of the present. (p. 1431)

The success of an Auden poem, especially an early one, depends on its simplicity. When he pursues a complex argument as in **"Meiosis"** . . . , the poem sustains the complexity by making a special thing of it, like an ingenious pump or gear,

but calls in magic too as an insurance (the Dantesque last line) and ends up with all its bits and pieces seeming strewn on the page around it. . . . The poem is an impressive, even satisfying contraption, but there is no life in it. In his maturity Auden would have been more genial, more cunning and more clear, but it is doubtful if he would have been more inspiring. The poem lacks sex and its excitement of the group, the excitement that is so extraordinary and has such controlled success in **"Consider":**

> Then, ready, start your rumour, soft
> But horrifying in its capacity to disgust
> Which, spreading magnified, shall come to be
> A polar peril, a prodigious alarm,
> Scattering the people, as torn-up paper
> Rags and utensils in a sudden gust,
> Seized with immeasurable neurotic dread.
>
> (pp. 1431-32)

The ideal Auden poem of this date always moves outwards into a public scene imagined in its significant details and observed as if from the air or by radio ("Supplied elsewhere to farmers and their dogs / Sitting in kitchens in the stormy fens"). The torn-up paper is reminiscent of the famous shot in *Things to Come,* where the camera focuses on a ragged scrap of newsprint caught on wire, giving news of ultimate war-horrors. The image of the helmeted airman, with his lordly perspective, is superb but farcical, too, just as his exhortation is also a spell of comfort against the horrors that a demoralized society imagines are awaiting it. Auden's poetry is deeply aware that the group want both to be thrilled by their bard and to joke with him, and that the ideal shaman is both a power and a figure of fun. . . .

Together with the charade *Paid on Both Sides, The Orators* developed the Auden technique later adopted in the plays he wrote with Isherwood: exotic and mythical matter from the past and present and transposed into the group life of English schools and homes. Such a transposition was standard practice among the modernists—Eliot had used it in *The Waste Land*— but Auden gave it not only the special emphasis of a game among initiates but a corresponding and disarming frivolity (though *Paid on Both Sides* is significantly more serious, and more moving, than *The Orators*). As usual there is a discrepancy, particularly grotesque in the latter case, between the impact of the work of art and what the artist and his critics have said about it. Auden wrote to Naomi Mitchison that "the theme was the failure of the romantic conception of personality"; and expressing dissatisfaction to another correspondent he said the result was "far too obscure and equivocal"—what was intended as a critique of the Fascist outlook "might be interpreted as a favourable exposition". That, indeed, is one reason why *The Orators* comes off as well as it does, for Mendelson emphasizes that however much the early Auden wanted to respond "positively" to the challenge of the time and become the young poet spokesman for enlightenment and left-wing ideals, his art would not oblige. The group was essential to it, the cause was not. And neither was the Message. However much he tinkered with *The Ascent of F6,* the end remained a muddle, though the individual speeches and poems are so effective; and compared with its group liveliness the satire of *The Dog Beneath the Skin* operates on the most elementary level. . . .

The reader's feeling of intimacy with most poets takes two forms. First, that the poet is revealing to him, quite naturally and by the act of composition, something he could not reveal to anyone else; second, and conversely, that the poet "in touching our hearts by revealing his own", as Hardy puts it, also reveals that he has a self to keep back. The second does not apply to later confessional poetry, like Lowell's and Berryman's, whose convention is a complete avowal to the reader; and neither applies to Auden. His early intimacy of threats and promises is like the disclosures of an older and dazzling schoolboy prodigy to the reader as younger child; and this changes to the reader being accepted as one of a group of comrades and initiates, the poet forthcoming and unbuttoned but retaining his powers of fascination and omniscience. The poems written in Brussels in 1938-39, **"Musée des Beaux Arts"**, **"Gare du Midi"**, **"The Capital"** and **"Epitaph on a Tyrant"**—are good examples of this, and the success of such a style of communication reveals the hollowness, embarrassment even, when the group seems to have disappeared, and the poet of **"Lay your sleeping head"** and **"I sit in one of the dives / On Fifty-Second street"** is talking to us on our own. The residue of discomfort and unreality in such poems is produced by a suggestion of contrived aloneness, a person-to-person relation does not come naturally. . . .

Everything that the young Auden wrote has a bottom of good sense. His poetry's hospitality towards crazes of every kind, crackpot or otherwise, carries into its art one of the most universal of human tendencies, and corrects it with a faith and a scepticism that, again as with most human beings, are almost identical. "You cannot have poetry unless you have a certain amount of faith in something, but faith is never unalloyed with doubts." A true magic is its own antidote. For Auden as for Nabokov, "art is a game of intricate enchantment and deception", but Auden also wrote that "in so far as poetry, or any of the arts, can be said to have an ulterior purpose, it is, by telling the truth, to disenchant and disintoxicate". It was by his genius for resolving this paradox that Auden became, as Mendelson justly claims, "the most inclusive poet of the twentieth century, its most technically skilled, and its most truthful". (p. 1432)

John Bayley, *"The Flight of the Disenchanter,"* in The Times Literary Supplement, *No. 4106, December 11, 1981, pp. 1431-32.*

EDWARD MENDELSON

In childhood, before he wrote a line of poetry, Auden imagined himself an architect and engineer, the maker of a fictional landscape. Between the ages of six and twelve he devoted much of his waking thought to what he later called "the construction and elaboration of a private sacred world, the basic elements of which were a landscape, northern and limestone, and an industry, lead mining." This world was a fantasy, its fabrication a game, but the principles that gave it order were among those that governed the material world. "I decided," he recalled, "or rather, without conscious decision, I instinctively felt that I must impose two restrictions upon my freedom of fantasy." In choosing the objects that might go into his private world he must choose among objects that really exist; and "In deciding how my world was to function, I could choose between two practical possibilities a mine can be drained either by an adit or a pump—but physical impossibilities and magic means were forbidden." He felt, "in some obscure way, that they were morally forbidden," that the rules of his game must represent both the laws of nature and the laws of ethics. Eventually, still during childhood, "there came a day when the moral issue became quite conscious." Among the equipment

he needed for his imaginary mines was a device, used for washing the ore, which was available in two different designs. "One type I found more sacred or 'beautiful,' but the other type was, as I knew from my reading, the more efficient. At this point I realized that it was my moral duty to sacrifice my aesthetic preference to reality or truth."

Auden recounted these childhood decisions in later years as a way of characterizing his work as a poet. Mines were places of symbolic depths and hidden meaning, passages to a dark source of mystery and power. But even as a child he knew them also to be functioning artifacts, made for practical mundane reasons, and causing real and possibly dangerous effects. As an adult he wrote poems that found richness of meaning in the moral complexities of fact. He had no wish to achieve an imaginative triumph over common reality; he used his poetry to comprehend the world he shared with his audience, and he wrote his poems as public acts of homage to the truths he perceived. His truthtelling never led him to prefer in literature what he called "Plain cooking made still plainer by plain cooks." As in childhood he delighted in the elaborate machinery of mines, in his adult years he indulged his love of poetic artifice: "Riddles and all other ways of not calling a spade a spade," "Complicated verse forms of great technical difficulty," "Conscious theatrical exaggeration." Yet he put his dazzlingly irresponsible virtuosity to responsible use. Through it, he insisted that his poems were connected to the ordinary world by their craftsmanship, just as they were connected to it by their dedication to fact. His poems were not visionary autonomous objects, exempt from the practical and ethical standards appropriate to all other human works. They were made to be judged both for their art and for their truth.

These elements from Auden's childhood fantasy, its commitment to fact and its deliberate artifice, were present in his poetry almost from the start of his career. But in his earliest poems they were subordinate to a different element of his fantasy. "It is no doubt psychologically significant," he wrote, "that my sacred world was autistic, that is to say, I had no wish to share it with others nor could I have done so." In the same way, his first adult poetry, the work of a young man of twenty, was overwhelmingly concerned with his own emotional isolation, rather than with truths he could share with his audience. In contrast to the complex stanzaic contraptions of his later years, he wrote many of his first poems in irregular free verse. During the first twelve years of his career, . . . Auden made the difficult passage from a private poetry to a public one, from apparent formal disorder to manifest artifice, and from lonely severity to a community of meaning. When he began writing he found in his personal psychology the condition of the age. As he grew older, he sought in science and history a range and variety of knowledge that he knew no individual could hope to organize on personal or aesthetic principles alone. He began as the deliberate inventor of the new poetic language he felt his isolation required. Then he refused the imprisonment of a reflexive personal voice and chose to write in stanzaic forms that, as he said later, "forbid automatic responses, / force us to have second thoughts, free from the fetters of Self."

Two kinds of poetry, two ideas of the poet's task, two poetic traditions contend against each other in Auden's early years. Because his work, from the start, was large in its sympathies and powers, and densely linked to the traditions of poetry, the issues dividing it were those that perennially divide literature and show no signs of ever being resolved. (pp. xiii-xv)

The first critic who judged between these two kinds of poet, the civil and the vatic, was the god Dionysus. In Aristophanes' *The Frogs* Dionysus is the god of wine, but he is also a god of Athens, and he seeks a poet who can save his city from disaster. Descending into the underworld, he presides over a contest between the shades of Aeschylus and Euripides, and weighs in his scales the art of civil responsibility against the art of inner vision. Aeschylus prays to the traditional gods, invokes the ancient tradition of the poet as moral teacher, and condemns the self-centeredness encouraged by his rival. Euripides prays to a private pantheon of the sky and his own tongue and senses, claims that when he writes his extravagant modern fictions he does no harm to society, and praises the doubt and questioning his work provokes in Athens. Dionysus finds he loves both poets equally, but at last he must select one of them for his city. He chooses Aeschylus. So, in effect, did Auden. (p. xvi)

[In] 1927-28 Auden wrote the first of the intensely modernist verse he gathered in his 1930 *Poems*. For a young poet whose early ambition was to write the great poems of his generation, there seemed no turning back.

And Auden did not turn back. He was the first English writer who absorbed all the lessons of modernism, but also understood its limits, and chose to turn elsewhere. He successfully challenged the vatic dynasty after more than a century of uncontested rule. When he renounced the goals of his immediate predecessors he made no effort to revive the native lyric tradition of Hardy—now often proposed as the alternative to international modernism, but in fact another branch of the same vatic line, equally lonely and nostalgic, equally in exile from the shared life of the city. Instead he retained from Hardy the vast historical perspectives of *The Dynasts,* its conjunction of great aeons and distances with minute local detail, and put it to different use. Where Hardy stood ironically aloof from a brute mechanistic history, Auden saw an obligation to bring knowledge to the service of responsibility. He placed Hardy's perspectives in the context of a civil tradition of poetry that extended from Chaucer through Shakespeare, Dryden, and Pope. In the modernist era the chief representative of this tradition was Kipling, whose attitudes seemed to many readers to be adequate proof that his mode of writing had grown moribund or outdated. But its potential was as large as it had ever been. George Orwell did not realize when he dismissed Auden as "a sort of gutless Kipling" (a phrase he soon retracted) that he was in fact honoring him; it was precisely Kipling's "guts" that were most damaging to Kipling's genius. In 1929 Auden wrote of doomed violent heroes, "Fighters for no one's sake / Who died beyond the border." Ten years later he chose a different tone, celebrating those like Freud "who were doing us some good, / And knew it was never enough but / Hoped to improve a little by living."

In the same year, 1939, Eliot looked sadly back at the triumphs of modernism, and saw in them "rather the last efforts of an old world, than the first struggles of a new." In the midst of these triumphs, before modernism began its manifest decline, Auden was exuberantly at work, writing in ways that modernism insisted were impossible. Eliot had written of the "great labour" and "continual self-sacrifice" a writer must endure to find a tradition. Auden made tradition his ordinary experience, his daily means of perception. The poets of modernism felt they could bring tradition into the present only as battered ironic fragments, or by heroic efforts to make it new. For Auden it had never grown old.

Had Auden been alone in the course he pursued in his poetry, his career might now seem an historical dead end, offering few prospects for later writers to explore. But he was following in the same direction taken by the greatest of his near-contemporaries in Europe, Bertolt Brecht. Auden and Brecht both began as romantic anarchists, violently amoral, but matured into a chastened public orthodoxy, Christian in Auden's case, Communist in Brecht's. Renouncing the brash menacing styles of their early work, both chose didactic manners suitable for irony and celebration. Both taught through parables. Where modernism had used innovative forms to speak of historical necessity, Auden and Brecht adopted traditional forms to speak of freedom and choice. They both enlarged the genres they adopted by restoring to literary language the content and manner of historical analysis, public oratory, moral philosophy, social and literary criticism, even gossip, and they restored to poetry an encyclopedic fullness of subject matter and style; yet they never pretended that what they wrote was sufficient unto itself or that it gave order to the world. Rejecting the romantic premise that individual vision was the true source of poetry, each willingly submerged his personality in collaborations with other writers. (When their paths crossed in the 1940s they collaborated on an adaptation of *The Duchess of Malfi*.) Both kept themselves open to the full range of literature and diction, taking influences where they found them. Unlike the modernists, they used popular forms without the disclaimer of an ironic tone. Each preferred mixed styles to lyric intensity, imperfect truth to pure resonance. Neither would entrust serious issues to the inflation of the grand manner, and neither was afraid to be vulgar. Each dreamed for a time of a perfect society; each woke to the recognition that an ideal order imposed on a recalcitrant citizenry, which included themselves, would be an arid despotism. (pp. xx-xxi)

One of the last modernists, Vladimir Nabokov, wrote that art is "a game of intricate enchantment and deception." Auden wrote that "In so far as poetry, or any of the arts, can be said to have an ulterior purpose, it is, by telling the truth, to disenchant and disintoxicate." He knew that poetry, for all its formal excitement and elaboration, could never be independent, and could never adequately be understood in terms of its internal or linguistic order. The emotional power of poetry leads readers to sympathize, however subtly or unknowingly, with the attitudes it embodies. Attitudes such as nostalgia or hero-worship eventually translate into action, with results less beautiful than any poem. Knowing this, Auden found himself in the curious position of taking poetry far more seriously than his critics did who regretted his apparent lack of High Seriousness—critics who accepted the vatic principle that art was its own reason for being and who, therefore, lacked any standard of judgement that could distinguish seriousness of tone from seriousness of meaning.

When Auden wrote in opposition to the canons of modernism, he did so in the understanding that came of accepting them earlier. He explored all the fields of poetry familiar to his age, and discovered rich fields his age had neglected or abandoned. Isolated, intense, and severe in his earliest writings, he came to write poetry that, more than any other, contributed to the understanding of his time. He became the most inclusive poet of the twentieth century, its most technically skilled, and its most truthful. (p. xxiii)

As the problem Auden faced in his first poems is abstract and difficult to define, so, notoriously, are the poems. Readers who try to resolve the difficulties by finding allegories of Freud and Marx, or who devise a unified narrative myth as a context for individual incidents, or who hunt out clues in the mythical landscapes of the writings of Auden's friends, largely miss the point of the early work, although they are responding to a quality that pervades it. The poems suggest that they are fragments of a larger whole but do not provide enough data to identify that whole. The reader is made to feel that some vital clue is lacking which, if one had it, could make sense of everything. But Auden hid nothing. The absence of a clue is the clue itself. The poems' central subject is their own failure to be part of any larger interpretive frame. Their metaphors refer to their own state of division and estrangement. As soon as one stops looking for the key to a set of symbols, and recognizes that the poems focus on the self-enclosing patterns that bar their way to a subject in the world outside, their notorious obscurity begins to vanish. (p. 10)

Yeats, Pound, and Eliot had all felt the loss of an earlier, nobler state of poetic language, and continually stressed how difficult was their self-imposed task of restoring it. But they never said the task was impossible, which is precisely what Auden said. He absorbed the modernist notion of a catastrophic break in literary tradition; he accepted that break as irreparable; and he set out to find a new poetic language, nonsymbolic and noncommunicative, that would give voice to the new conditions. (p. 11)

Separated like all the modernists from both audience and tradition, Auden could not, in his ruined world, enjoy a stable relation with any subject matter he might share with his readers. He could not be didactic, because the conditions in which questions had memorable answers were lost in the past. And he could not enjoy a sense that his own work built on a coherent tradition of which it could now become a part. A poet would now recollect older literary forms only to recognize how inappropriate they are in the present, how distant is the world where they enjoyed their proper functions. He could remember the *forms* of tradition, not its meaning—"Only . . . the method of remembering"—and could remember them only in a different, modern way. His historical evidence for such ideas would have been the Eliot of "Gerontion" or *The Waste Land,* who echoed ancient forms for only a few lines at a time, before the pressure of modern desolation twisted the forms to the breaking point.

Yet while Auden's predominant tone was one of warning and crisis, the tone suited to an apocalyptic age, he added overtones of deliberate fustian and buffoonery. There was no turning back from the disaster; best to accept it, even enjoy it as an occasion for poetry. (pp. 11-12)

The elusiveness of his first poems brought consequences he never intended, effects that eventually helped persuade him to revise his modernist projects. Where the poems presented themselves as discrete parts of an unspecified whole, the poems' readers, then as to a large extent now, concluded that the poems really did imply the nature of that greater whole. The poems were taken as fragments of an activist allegory whose key, although hidden, really did exist. Auden's readers, while agreeing on this view, divided into two hostile camps: those who complained that the key was a private myth or private joke reserved for a coterie of cronies and insiders, and those who felt *they* were the insiders, by virtue of membership in Auden's generation, and proceeded to fill the gaps in his broken pattern with their own political and psychological enthusiasms. . . . Auden implied connections and relations only to announce their absence or failure. Readers hailed or denounced him as a

spokesman; he never wrote as one. There were one or two moments in the 1930s when he hoped he might learn to speak on behalf of inarticulate masses, but he saw the vanity of this wish, and its half-heartedness, as soon as he tried to achieve it. When he did write with conviction of civil relations and responsibilities, in the 1940s and after, readers protested that he was distorting or betraying causes that, in fact, he had not hoped to serve. In recent years critics have often prefaced their discussion of Auden's earliest work with a faintly puzzled comment that we can no longer feel the revolutionary excitement it generated in the 1930s, but these critics have been misled by the poems' early reception. The thrill of their contemporary imagery has faded, but the poems still speak as urgently as they ever did of their own conditions. What we can no longer feel is the excitement produced by the first misreadings.

To say this is not to blame Auden's original audience. He scarcely made matters easy for them. His work first reached the eye of a small but influential readership when the dauntingly obscure charade *Paid on Both Sides* appeared in Eliot's quarterly *The Criterion* in January 1930. Later that year the charade and thirty short poems, none of them illuminated by a title or epigraph, appeared in a small blue-wrappered volume of *Poems* published by Faber & Faber. It is still striking to see how anonymous the poems seem, how difficult they make any speculation on the character of the poet behind them, how easy they make it to project on them meanings that might be in the air. Auden had learned the virtues of an anonymous style from Eliot, but Eliot had at least identified his special social milieus and had implicitly defined his sensibility through the personal events his consciousness chose to record. Auden refused to do even that. His poems displayed only intermittent and fragmentary correspondences with the young man visible to his friends—that improbable figure, autocrat of what he called "the dreadful literary conversations when I always talk such pompous nonsense," half genius, half poseur, who made imperial pronouncements on the cure of neurosis at one moment, at another donned a false beard and extravagant hat. In his personal life these were animated masks hiding a silent isolation. In his poems he had no need for a dramatic mask; he was invisible without one. (pp. 13-15)

The Auden of later years—the avuncular, domestic, conservative, Horatian, High Anglican poet of civilization, who sees language not as a sublimation of violence but as a safeguard against it, and whose "sounded note is the restored relation"— would seem to show few traces of the anarchic stringencies of his younger self. Yet although Auden transformed or inverted his early theories, civilized them with public contexts, and made them responsible to a moral order, he never entirely gave them up. The ethically sober late Auden retains the form and outline of the amorally fervid early one. . . . In Auden's later writings the young anarchist neither retreats nor recants, but he has learned the necessary cost of his independence and is willing to pay it.

The great social theme of Auden's later work is the mutual implication of violence and civil order, the penalty in human life that every peaceful well-lit city must pay to survive. As he wrote in the 1950s: "without a cement of blood (it must be human, it must be innocent) no secular wall will safely stand." This is hardly a new discovery in Western literature—it is the burden of the *Aeneid* and of Shakespeare's histories—but in English poetry since the eighteenth century it has been virtually forgotten. Both romantics and modernists focused their attention on one side or the other of this double recognition: either regarding all societies as irredeemably brutal and imagining instead a realm of universal harmony; or celebrating, with Yeats, Lawrence, and Pound, the grand isolated violence of a lofty hero. The first of these alternatives denies the real hatred in the human will, the second denies the unique humanity of its victims. Auden was able to reject both these partial visions because he reached their extreme forms early enough in his own work to sense their limits and inadequacies.

The intensely isolated and reflexive character of Auden's earliest poems has been obscured by the more public character of his later work. It was obscured also because the critical climate was not yet receptive to it. In the atmosphere that later developed around existentialism and around structural theories of language and culture—the atmosphere propitious for the later Beckett—Auden's earliest work would have seemed comfortably at home. Late in life Auden was fascinated with the concept of prematurity in scientific and philosophical thought, the prematurity of ideas, like Vico's, that emerged before there was an audience, whether conventional or avant-garde, that was capable of absorbing them. (pp. 19-21)

Like the later critical theorists who confuse the local conventions of modernism with universal truth, Auden in his early poems treats the separation of language from the world as the ultimate subject to which all writing refers. In his later poems he treats the gulf between language and world in a very different way—as a condition that must be accepted but that does not prevent language from being shared, or prevent it from illuminating and affecting a physical and ethical world whose order and events are not only verbal ones. In other words, Auden moves from a world *without* choice to a world *with* choice: from a world of limits where differences are absolute and the proper literary mode is the tragedy of helplessness and isolation, to a world of possibility where differences are overcome by mutual forgiveness and responsibility and the proper literary mode is the comedy of reconciliation. Auden's early poems are for intense love affairs that end quickly; the later poems are for marriage.

Auden's early work may be seen as the culmination of the romantic heritage in English poetry, in the same way that recent theories of poetic language are the culmination of romantic literary theory. Attempts to continue in the same course, efforts to extend the modernist revolution either in poetry or in criticism, lead to arid parodies of what came before. In each instance the next step cannot be one that moves *beyond* the last—as the idiom of progress would suggest—but one that moves in a different direction. Late romanticism, in the earliest Auden, focuses on the frontier of perception between the self and a dead inaccessible world outside—a world of discrete objects that may be put to use only by the poetic imagination. In the later Auden there is no need for a romantic imagination, because there are no objects. Instead there are *creatures,* created beings with rights of their own, and Auden is concerned more with their peculiarities and relations than with any difficulty he might have in perceiving them. (pp. 21-2)

> *Edward Mendelson, in his* Early Auden, The Viking
> *Press, 1981, 407 p.*

HAYDEN CARRUTH

No other poet, not even Frost, has given me as much trouble in my own mind as Auden; none has simultaneously attracted and repelled me so forcibly. (I mean in his writing, of course.

I never met him.) I think I have reviewed all his books of poetry since 1945 and a good many of his other books as well. Yet I doubt that any two of my reviews come close to saying the same thing. What attracted me first, nearly forty years ago, was Auden's astonishing verbal facility, which was something I was brought up to recognize.... Auden could write badly; but then he wrote so *much* and so much of it was *brilliant.* He could, for instance, take the tritest forms from all periods of English literature and, without display, turn them to new account.... (p. 336)

In the long run, however, what attracted me more than his technique was his honesty. Auden did what we all told ourselves, when we were young, that we should do but that we seldom did, namely, to fight *against,* not for or with, one's talent. Auden is the only poet I know who consistently improved his old poems by revising them long after they were written. He did it again and again with each succeeding collection of his work. And always his revisions were in the direction of simplicity and clarity, suppressing whatever was in the least inflated or mushy or unearned. For honesty he threw away the products of his rhetorical genius without a qualm, and many of us complained about the loss of favorite passages and phrasings. Yet I believe his alterations were almost invariably improvements. (p. 337)

Finally what attracted me throughout, and still attracts me, is Auden's intellectuality, which he often called, without the least complacency, his necessary way of being in the world. Sometimes it seems as if he was sensorily defective; one can find implications of this even in his sexuality, both in his poems and in [Humphrey] Carpenter's biography; and certainly the imagery of his poems is seldom sensually evocative. His poems, like Donne's, function intellectually as they move in their sentences and figures.... Yet is Auden less the poet for this? I insist, in spite of all the palaver during my lifetime about the necessity of the "concrete," the "objective" image, that he was not. "As you know," he once wrote in a letter, "my dominant faculties are intellect and intuition, my weak ones feeling and sensation. This means I have to approach life via the former; I must have knowledge and a great deal of it before I can feel anything." But isn't this true of all of us who take the trouble to be honest? Are the feelings raised in us by immediate perceptions of things as powerful and constructive as the feelings that come after study and thought? In his best work, which I think is limited to the shorter poems, Auden was a profoundly emotional writer, and I fail to see how any reader can miss that quality in his writing, that force, that humility, even when the knowledge is specialized—Auden was fond of scientific writing and by no means unschooled in it—and the thought is complex or quirky. For me, the poet who shows me his mind as well as his heart (Blake) is always more interesting than the one who shows me his heart alone (Smart).

What repels me in Auden is his cutesy-campy manner, which doubtless derives in part from his homosexuality, or rather from the ways of expressing his homosexuality that were forced on him by the society of his time and place, but which derives, I think, even more from the whole cultural conspectus of English middle-class, public-school life before World War II. Auden called *The Orators* a charade; that means a game; and gamesmanship became a more and more important analogue for art in his theoretical writings throughout his life, until in the book called *Secondary Worlds* (1969) he asserted outright that the world of the imagination is separate, totally disjunct, from the "primary world" of life, society, politics, and morality. It is true that a charade is not only a game, but a puzzle implying a solution, and I think this is what prevented Auden from drifting off completely and always into the secondary world of, for instance, Lewis Carroll and J.R.R. Tolkien, two of his favorite authors. Nevertheless the game-theory of life in a boarding school, life in a Christ Church quad, life in a homosexual café in Berlin was controlling in much of Auden's writing after the late 1930s, when he gave up a social view and resolutely turned to religion and privacy.

I could not disagree more with such a view of art and experience. To me it is not only dangerous and irresponsible, it is intellectually disgusting. For years I could never understand how a man of Auden's mind and sensibility, who had so marvelously mingled his social with his erotic and cultural concerns when he was doing the poems of the mid-1930s, could end by rejecting the responsibility of the artist to his real and human environment. Now I have read *The Prolific and the Devourer,* and I can see more clearly how his mind was working, though this does not take away an iota of my disagreement. The arguments are clearly stated in his book of *pensées,* however, which he began in imitation of Pascal, and some of them are abstruse, too complex to reproduce here. But they amount to nothing, while the commonest argument, both in this book and elsewhere, is the simple, not to say simple-minded, iteration of the ''fact'' that neither his own poems nor those of other ''proletarian'' poets in the 1930s had forestalled one death, one injustice, or one even infinitesimal wavelet in the advancing tide of fascism. Well, in the first place, how did he know, how could he tell? And in the second, did anyone ever expect poetry to produce a demonstrable and immediate political result? That is not the way it works. Quite aside from the immanent obligation of the member to the group, an obligation altogether compatible with the state of freedom, we know that a kind of cultural tensility or tone determines the quality of any civilization, and we know that it comes about through the combining, sometimes conflicting, efforts of artists, scientists, moralists, and politicians, i.e., the imaginative, cognitive, practical, and active components of human intelligence. Artists must do their part, no matter how difficult it is.

I am reminded of a time when I was in correspondence with Ezra Pound. I don't think I was influenced by Auden, I'm quite sure I was thinking only of the Cantos, but in one letter I asked Pound what was the point of putting social and political materials into poetry when the world was so obviously going to hell in a handbarrow anyway and the whole notion of social change was at odds with our experience of human feasibility. Pound fired back his answer: ''Pheezability aint got nawthin to do with it. Besides, nobody said it was easy.''

Auden had a glimpse of this, and some of his best early poetry came from that glimpse. Even in fond retrospect, it is good to know that he met and briefly worked with Bertolt Brecht; that moment of hope, or more strictly of possibility, existed. [Edward Mendelson (see excerpt above)] has a sentence describing Brecht's position that I cannot improve on. ''Instead of composing his unique experience into idiosyncratic structures, transmitting the forms of his vision to an audience of the aesthetically initiated, an artist must convey knowledge that is not exclusively his own, and that he and others can put to use.'' To rebel, in other words, against what we now call modernism. Brecht did it, he did fifty years ago, and Auden almost did it. Then Auden, despondent and never able to reach a settled intellectual position, permitted himself to be co-opted again by modernism, and who can tell what might have been the

course of Anglo-American writing, or what might be the condition of poetry today, i.e., instead of the ever more attenuated running-down of modernism we actually have, if that had not happened?

Auden at his best was a first-rate, hard-working writer. He did his best work alone. His collaborations with homosexual friends and lovers, Isherwood, Britten, Kallman, and others, were too tricky and dilettantish; the best of them is probably the libretto for Stravinsky's *The Rake's Progress.* Beyond this, his best collaborations were in translations of poetry where he used the literal cribs furnished by someone else. Such a work was his translation of poems by Pär Lagerkvist done with Leif Sjöberg, *Evening Land,* published in 1976 after Auden's death, poems so lovely and showing so effectively a *writer's* sanative genius that I wonder why no one but I has ever noticed them; the title is not even included in the bibliography at the end of Carpenter's book.

Beyond this I will risk saying, after all, that I think Auden's two finest works were written just before and not long after his coming to the United States. The first is the sequence of sonnets done as a consequence of the journey he and Isherwood made to China in 1938 at the height of the war with Japan. Originally it was called ''In Time of War,'' but I prefer the retitled and considerably rewritten version in the *Collected Poems* (1976) called simply ''**Sonnets from China.**'' The second is ''**Horae Canonicae,**'' a sequence of poems based on the Offices of the Church and the events of Good Friday, published in its complete form in *The Shield of Achilles* (1955) but begun some years earlier. Significantly, Auden did not rewrite ''**Horae Canonicae,**'' once it was published, and in the last edition of his poems which he himself supervised, *The Collected Shorter Poems* (1967), he placed ''**Horae Canonicae**'' out of chronological order at the end of the volume. Then, of course, there are some dozens of separate short poems that are superb, though more from the 1930s and 1940s than from his later decades, and brilliant passages in some of the long poems like ''**New Year Letter**'' and *The Age of Anxiety,* even if, taken in their wholenesses, not a single one of his long poems is satisfactory.

Often I get down my copy of *The Collected Shorter Poems,* flipping the pages at random as one does, being disappointed and elated by turn. I think I always will.

Some day, I suppose, a biographer . . . will try to discover why a writer as gifted as clearly Auden was could produce, out of the enormous mass of his work, so little that endures. Such a biographer will need prodigious finesse, as critic, historian, sociologist, psychologist, and even metaphysician. Could it be done? I think probably not. Sartre failed miserably—and grandiosely and selfishly—when he tried to do it for Jean Genêt. But wouldn't it be a wonderful book if it could be done? It would tell us more about art and life than any number of biographies and critical studies devoted to the other great literary figures of the half century from 1910 to 1960, those who fared better than Auden in this matter of the proportion of satisfactory to unsatisfactory work. (pp. 337-40)

Hayden Carruth, ''Wystan Hugh Auden,'' *in* The Hudson Review, *Vol. XXXV, No. 2, Summer, 1982, pp. 334-40.*

EDWARD CALLAN

In the forty-four years between his first volume, *Poems,* 1930, and his final collection, *Thank You, Fog!,* published some months after his sudden death in September 1973, W. H. Auden produced a body of poems, plays, opera libretti, and criticism unmatched in the twentieth century. He wrote rapidly, and sometimes he was slipshod; but his best and most characteristic work achieved what good arists are commonly remembered for: the highlighting of some facet of truth that was always there, but outside the circle of our recognition until brought into focus by their art.

At one time or another Auden sought to reach a variety of audiences and tastes, from popular to highbrow. He could range widely in tone from shrill name-calling in a political broadside—"Beethameer, Beethameer, bully of Britain,/With your face as fat as a farmer's bum" . . .—to erudite bookish allusion that assumed everyone who read Auden had also read Freud (and as time went on, Goethe and Kierkegaard, too). As his choices for *The Oxford Book of Light Verse* (1937) attest, he liked all sorts of light verse, and in his own includes ballads, blues, limericks, clerihews, and cabaret songs—forms attuned in some degree to the tinselled social atmosphere of the twenties in which he grew up. But the things that most excited his imagination had an intellectual reach; and if the term *intellectual* implies an aptitude for thought coupled with a well-stocked, witty, and logical mind, Auden was an intellectual. He particularly respected books by "thinkers"—R. G. Collingwood and A. N. Whitehead as well as Freud, Jung, and Groddeck in his earlier years in England where his reputation as a poet was first established in the 1930s; and Paul Tillich, Reinhold Neibuhr, Simone Weil, and Hannah Arendt, as well as Kierkegaard and other existentialists in his later years in America.

He valued books for their language as well as for their ideas, and he had a special passion that increased with age for dictionaries, crossword puzzles, and linguistic oddities of all sorts. He was pleased when his usage was cited in dictionaries—a pleasure given him by several entries in the unabridged *Webster's Third* (1961) where, for example, the instance cited for *egoist* in the sense of *egocentric* is his, and the instance given of *abrupt* as a verb is "let brazen bands abrupt their din" from *The Age of Anxiety* (1947). His playful late poem **"A Bad Night: A Lexical Exercise"** exhumes gnarled dialect words like *hirple, glunch,* and *sloomy;* but even his earliest verse employed unusual words—typically with the clinical air of a detached observer. At nineteen, for example, he wrote a poem on lovers' partings ("Consider if you will how lovers stand") that brought surprise to this genre with words like *suction, heartburn, clinically-minded,* and *ligatured*—this last in a laconic phrase of the kind that became his early hallmark: "Have ligatured the ends of a farewell." (pp. 3-4)

Although it may have become so in old age, Auden's youthful fascination with words was not a sterile one. The first quality in his work that proclaims him an artist—the marked ability to give to "airy nothing/A local habitation and a name"—is manifest in his effective figurative use of clinical terms like "ligatured"; and in the comic extravagance of a metaphorical line like: "Or hum of printing presses turning forests into lies," to depict the partisan slant of mass-circulation English dailies in the thirties. But his gift for imaginative "naming" went beyond verbal marksmanship. It enabled him to discover a poetic mythology for the times. (p. 4)

The range of Auden's poetic imagery, and the scope of the several technical vocabularies he from time to time employed show him remarkably aware of twentieth-century intellectual trends, and more attuned to discoveries in the natural sciences than either Eliot or Yeats. One may encounter in his poetry,

on the one hand, technical terms from the specialized vocabularies of existentialist thinkers like Jaspers, Heidegger, Kierkegaard, and Buber; and on the other, precise images from various natural sciences—from the chemistry of cellular division, for example, in **"Meiosis"**; from paleontology in **"Winds"**; and from microbiology in **"A New Year Greeting"** (a humorous *tour de force* first published in *Scientific American*). Given the wide range of his interests, there is little to be gained from approaching Auden's art—as was once commonly done—by comparing it with the work of his Oxford contemporaries in "The Auden Group": Louis MacNiece, Cecil Day Lewis, and Stephen Spender, none of whom grew and changed to the extent that he did, or continued to deploy new technical equipment to meet the challenge of new themes. Auden is more aptly classed in the company of Pope and Wren whose names recall an age. (pp. 7-8)

Whatever their deeper differences, both Pope and Auden were committed to their craft; and both were primarily occasional poets. Pope wrote *The Rape of the Lock* in the hope of mending a family quarrel, and his other more memorable works are in such traditional occasional forms as the verse essay and the epistle. Auden also wrote many letters in verse, including the two long works **Letter to Lord Byron** and **New Year Letter,** a number of shorter verse letters in **Letters from Iceland,** and the title poem in **Epistle to a Godson.** Pope wrote few elegies and a great number of epitaphs. Auden wrote few epitaphs: one of them for a favorite cat, Lucinda, that he and Chester Kallman owned in Ischia, but none of them for specific people. However, he often turned to the elegy as an occasional form. A remarkable proportion of the poetry of his later years is elegiac including memorial poems for his housekeeper at Kirchstetten, Frau Emma Eiermann, and for his New York doctor, David Protetch, M.D. Several of his elegies, including **"In Memory of W. B. Yeats," "At the Grave of Henry James,"** and **"In Memory of Sigmund Freud,"** are among his better known occasional poems.

Auden represented himself not in the high Romantic manner as a lover of the Muse—an *amateur*—but as a professional who could produce verse for a play, a libretto, an epistle, or an elegy as the occasion demanded. In the English cricketing terms of his day he was a "Player," as professionals were then called, not one of the amateur "Gentlemen." At a time when some literary theorists found traditional forms suspect, he preferred to believe that a poet's first duty was to master the technical elements of his craft. For more than forty years he commanded a greater variety of poetic forms than any poet writing in English. Readers who have sampled his poetry from time to time may well recall a cluster of ballads; various sonnets and sonnet sequences; instances of the villanelle, ballade, and canzone; a number of sestinas—four of them in "Kairos and Logos"; and sustained passages of terza rima and of alliterative verse. Some of the more complex stanza forms in the poems of his middle years—those employed in **"Streams"** and **"In Transit,"** for example—are derived from elaborate courtly metrical forms whose names he brought back into the general vocabularly: the Welsh englyn, and the Skaldic drott-kvaett; and in his sixties he perfected other syllabic forms, derived ultimately from Greek prosody, but more immediately based on Goethe's hexameters and Horace's Sapphics and Alcaics. He imposed on himself even stricter limitations than those inherent in the traditional forms he adopted. (pp. 9-11)

[There] was a strong utopian strain in Auden's work of the early 1930s welcomed by a generation struggling out from the quagmire of war and depression. Many among his contemporaries nursing a sense of betrayal by their elders whose policies had led to the mass slaughter of the 1914-18 war were delighted by the irreverent vision he set before them of England's ruling caste beguiled by its native forms of oratory: the lies of press lords; the dubious rhetoric of pulpit and political platform; and the vapid talk above the old school tie. The poetry of Wilfred Owen had linked the patrician rhetoric of these elders—*Dulce et decorum est pro patria mori* [Horace: "It is sweet and fitting to die for one's country"]—to the slaughter in the trenches, and it was to Owen's banner that Auden rallied with lines like the one about "printing presses turning forests into lies." Many among Auden's contemporaries also welcomed the fresh combination of qualities in his verse that gave rise to the term *Audenesque:* a clinical air, clipped phrase, sharp ironical eye, and deft control of line and rhythm. Such verse seemed designed to probe the infected spots on the body politic like a surgical scapel. Auden was soon a newspaper celebrity in England at a time when the growing Fascist power in Germany, Italy, and Spain seemed to outweigh all other dangers, so much so that from 1931 onward it brought socialists and liberals into an alliance with the Communist Party in a Popular Front against Fascism.

The Popular Front rallied to the Republican cause during the Spanish Civil War—a war that presented intellectuals in the West with a crisis of conscience comparable to that faced by Americans during the Vietnam War thirty years later—and Auden's widely heralded intention to serve in an ambulance unit that resulted in a short visit to the Spanish war zone in 1937, together with his subsequent journey, in 1938, to the Sino-Japanese war front, seemed to set him on the high road to a poetry grafted to political Romanticism. In retrospect, Auden saw in his politicallly oriented poetry of the mid-thirties a departure from the true line of his poetic development. He also felt on looking back that the public acclaim given him and his fellow poets in the thirties was undeserved. In the second half of life he turned the search light of his art on the Romantic obsession with oracular truth within, not only in the realm of politics but in the realm of poetry, where so many of the Romantic poets, including some older contemporaries he had admired, like W. B. Yeats and D. H. Lawrence, had fancied that they had discovered truth anew within themselves.

Auden's misgivings about the Romantic imagination were not apparent in his writings until 1937-38, when he was thirty years old and already fairly widely acclaimed as the leader of a new and politically oriented poetic movement, consisting mainly of his friends, C. Day Lewis, Stephen Spender, and Louis MacNeice. Then, partly through a re-examination of his own personal values and of his public role as a poet, he began to question the conventional Romantic assumption that the artist-genius was more than commonly privy to the truth and that his creative imagination was geared exclusively to the service of freedom. This questioning first becomes evident in his sonnet sequence from China in *Journey to a War* (1938). His later American work expresses a conviction that Romanticism's deification of the imaginative original genius spawned the modern totalitarian dictator, whether of the Left or of the Right.

By 1940 he had come to recognize, perhaps with the aid of Kierkegaard's categories, that an analogous urge for the creation of perfect order marked both artist and tyrant—the one in the aesthetic sphere, the other in the political. He felt that the artist, habituated to shaping or discarding his materials at will, was by cast of mind inclined to seek tyrannical solutions

in civil affairs—a weakness he had begun to diagnose in himself. Conversely, he felt that tyrants like Hitler or Stalin who sought to mould human societies to utopian ideals were artists out of their spheres. For, in pursuit of civil order, tyrants display the quality of ruthlessness with which the poet, for aesthetic reasons, liquidates unsound rhymes or removes whole stanzas to some other part of his design. (pp. 14-16)

Now that Auden's work is complete it can be seen that his long identification with the *avant garde* of the thirties is not the whole measure of his art. His perspective changed with time, but he continued to illuminate in his poetry obscure areas of individual human freedom necessarily circumscribed in each life by ties to nature and to history; and he scorned W. B. Yeats for reviving outmoded cyclic theories in which, as in Greek religion, nature and history were confused. He regarded formal restrictions in art and natural limitations in life as both circumscribing and nurturing liberty by contributing to creative ingenuity. As he put it in an essay on Valéry where he also says it is more becoming in poets to talk of versification than of mysterious voices: "The formal restrictions of poetry teach us that the thoughts which arise from our needs, feelings, and experiences are only a small part of the thoughts of which we are capable.". . . This is the theme of his **"Ode to Terminus"** honoring the Roman god of limits and boundaries whom he thanks "for giving us games and grammar and metres.". . . The couplet from his **"In Memory of W. B. Yeats,"** now inscribed on Auden's memorial in the Poets' Corner of Westminster Abbey,

> In the prison of his days
> Teach the free man how to praise, . . .

is but one instance of the type of analogy he liked to draw between vitality arising from imposed restraint in the making of a poem and from natural limitations in the life of a free man. (pp. 16-17)

Auden's conception of man's responsibility for Nature's freedom—less common perhaps among poets than among physicists—sets him apart from those poets among his contemporaries more immediately concerned with social and political ideologies, and . . . it certainly set him apart from W. B. Yeats. The difference is fundamental. Therefore simplistic charts of his changes of attitude toward questions of politics or religion help little toward the enjoyment of his later, more philosophical, poems that are so frequently concerned with the nature of man and the origins of creativity. Having thought as a schoolboy that his future lay in mining engineering, in time he came to regard his choice of a poetic vocation as providential—given his life circumstances. (p. 20)

As there is no way back to lost innocence in science, so there is no way back in art; not even in the particular case of Auden's art. He was not simply a poet of the thirties. The significance of his work, early and late, transcends local loyalties. His perennial themes were consciousness and the human condition; and no other writer has so consistently chosen for theme the gap between the world of consciousness where the responsibilities of freedom begin and the unconscious natural world where necessity rules. His works in prose explore this theme also; and a measure of the qualities of mind he brought to criticism was his capacity for turning such occasional pieces as reviews and introductions into essays of permanent value. But his reputation as an artist rests, ultimately, on the poetry; and—apart from a Romantic emphasis on the spirit where Auden would include the flesh—what Sir Herbert Grierson said of seventeenth-century metaphysical poetry—that it was a poetry inspired by a philosophical conception of "the role assigned to the human spirit in the great drama of existence"—applies to Auden's poetry three centuries on. (pp. 266-67)

Edward Callan, in his Auden: A Carnival of Intellect, *Oxford University Press, 1983, 299 p.*

HUGH HAUGHTON

You don't have to be a devotee of *Rezeptionstheorie* to realize that Auden's poetry depended on a peculiarly close, even conspiratorial relationship with his audience and his time. "Consider this and in our time", his poetry said, and they did—reading its cryptic reports and lyrics from strange but strangely familiar frontiers and battlefields as "the very age and body of the time its form and pressure". At least in the 1930s. From the start Auden's unnerving use of the first person plural (as in "*our* time") and the constant appeal to his contemporaries, in a situation of shared emergency ("The situation of our *time*"), proved subtly seductive and created a profound sense of identification in his audience. "This poetry was ours", said Bernard Knox recently, speaking for his generation. At the outset the late William Empson thought **Paid on Both Sides,** the macabre family charade first published in Eliot's *Criterion*, a work that defined "the attitude of a generation". By 1939 Philip Henderson (in "The Poet and Society") could look back on "The Age of Auden".

That identification between poet, generation and decade was to haunt Auden and his readership for the rest of his restlessly mobile career.... Perhaps the first major poet to share the twentieth-century obsession with generations, epochs and decades, with social and cultural obsolescence, Auden may also have been the first to fall a victim to it. In 1937 Louis MacNeice thought it "a blessing to our generation" that Auden's verse was full of interesting subject-matter, "including the subject-matters of psycho-analysis, politics and economics", and praised it "for always taking sides". Ten years later this might have come to seem a mixed blessing for the generation (and poet), when Auden was observed to have *changed* sides—of the Atlantic in the first place, but also on many of the crucial, ideological issues which figured in his early verse....

There is still no general agreement about Auden's Progress (or Regress); his "development" and successive revisions of the canon remain thoroughly problematical. 1940 is widely accepted as a watershed..., but thereafter opinions are divided. Did Auden rise on stepping-stones of his dead selves to higher things, as both Edward Mendelson's and Edward Callan's recent studies imply [see excerpts above]? Or is it a story of decline and fall, with the poet trampling on his dead selves on the way down—as the Auden-influenced poets Randall Jarrell, Delmore Schwartz and Philip Larkin maintain? (p. 457)

There is an ironic connection between the themes of his early work, and subsequent readings of his career (his diagnoses were always infectious). The novel evolutionary sense he introduced into poetry—whether of geological epochs, Marxist class analyses, Freudian stages of infantile development, or technological obsolescence—was turned against him. His opponents attacked him for failing to evolve properly, failing to grow up, failing to wean himself from his bourgeois class-background, becoming part of the Old Gang he had guyed in his young days, filling his late Horatian verse with what Terry Eagleton saw as "obsolete historical postures". There are two sides to this—the political and the psychological....

Donald Davie, in a telling review in 1955, wondered whether "this poet has made his peace with society too wholeheartedly and too soon". This argument seems to me right in the main, but overlooks the continuity between the subversive tyro of **Poems** (1930) and the cosmopolitan homemaker of **"Thanksgiving for a Habitat"**: age heightens his sense of historical obsolescence while it diminishes his relish for it and—even though theology replaces Marxism—Auden remains the most thoroughly anthropological poet of the modern world....

Auden called Tennyson the poet of the nursery, and Auden is the poet of the school-room. The relations between low seriousness and high levity, light verse and social commentary, high style and high jinks, were always uneasy in Auden's work—from **Dance of Death** to **Thank You, Fog.** At its best, this constitutes a buoyant and provocative critique of seriousness—and "maturity". Freud's startling rewriting of childhood provided Auden with a way of jazzing up the Wordsworthian version, establishing a new set of shared references with his audience and an effective handle for a kind of psychoanalytic satire—a device for revealing the "low" desires behind the "high" seriousness of his class, as well as the bizarre "convolutions of the simple wish". (p. 458)

Hugh Haughton, "Auden's Progress," in The Times Literary Supplement, *No. 4230, April 27, 1984, pp. 457-58.*

MARTIN LEBOWITZ

Auden was a brilliant, all-inclusive mirror of modern culture—Freud, Jung, Marx and the contemporary mythopoetic function not only of Shakespeare but also of science, all of which he understood very well—yet he writes with the didactic hand of an emancipated cleric . . . whose liberation consists in a highly ambiguous enjoyment of worldly folly and corruption. He was an ironic sensualist very much in the modern spirit, viewing the English ruling class as the "living dead" because they lack the *joie de vivre* to survive.

In the last analysis however, Auden was a religious humorist. Tertullian's remark—"I believe because it is absurd"—is profoundly relevant to an age of science in which the act of religious belief reflects an antinomy; the conflict inherent in consciousness itself which assigns a deterministic order to experience while expressing will power and freedom of choice.

Auden's famous description of the ascent of man—"He faulted into consciousness"—became his spiritual preoccupation; his view of the spirit is that it is a transcendental attribute struggling to cope with the causal order upon which freedom is contingent, the paradox being that freedom and determinism are reciprocal concepts. Hence the serenity of nature implies the tragic character of man caught in the struggle between the unconscious will—determinism—and conscious freedom at once ostensible and real.

Thus Auden was a dualist; the appearance of emergent evolution in his thinking is superficial because, very much like Yeats, he regards human nature as the incarnation of spirit. Beauty in this view is emblematic, paradoxically, of both the Fall (man's natural incarnation including his temptations) plus the possibility of his redemption. Auden's view of the flesh is that—in expressing the potential for both good and evil—it reveals the dialectical inconsistency of the moral life, thereby implying the final necessity of complete self-transcendence. It is for this reason that time and anxiety are synonymous; one cannot exist without the other not because nature is unreal but because, in its beauty, animism, and unconscious serenity, it is a mirror image reflecting a higher order—supernatural in its eternal preexistence, the Reality preceding the false dualities of moral action and intellectual discourse. (pp. 119-20)

Of course, no reading of Auden can fail to suggest that the worst feature of modern life—high up in its catalog of sins—is greed. It is just possible that Auden's austerity on the one hand and his sensualism on the other both express contempt for this cardinal abomination. (p. 121)

> *Martin Lebowitz, "Faulted into Consciousness: Recent Writing on Auden and Eliot," in* The Kenyon Review, *n.s. Vol. VII, No. 3, Summer, 1985, pp. 118-22.*

(Sir) John Betjeman

1906-1984

English poet, nonfiction writer, critic, and editor.

The Poet Laureate of England from 1972 to 1984, Betjeman had been known primarily as an authority on English architecture until the unprecedented popular success of his *Collected Poems* (1958), which sold over 100,000 copies in its original edition. Although some critics attributed the volume's success to Betjeman's fame as an authority in several nonliterary fields and to his deliberate disregard of stylistic complexity, most concurred that the appeal of his poetry resulted from his blend of light, sentimental humor and nostalgia for England's vanishing past. A traditionalist in style and form who borrowed his rhyme schemes and meters from eighteenth- and nineteenth-century poets, Betjeman distanced himself from the modernist concepts of T. S. Eliot and Ezra Pound and never identified himself with any particular movement or school of poetry. Betjeman is often referred to as a topographical poet concerned with describing actions and events as they relate to human themes in specific geographic locations. Philip Larkin maintained that Betjeman's lifelong fascination with buildings and landscapes was inseparable from his lack of interest in innovation or experimentation and his search for ''a poetry which embraces architecture and an architecture which embraces poetry.'' Betjeman regarded buildings as manifestations of the society which constructed them—a society he alternately celebrated for its love of tradition and condemned for its progressive, materialistic values which threatened remnants of the past.

Betjeman was educated at Marlborough and Magdalen Colleges at Oxford University but left without a degree. While there he edited a literary magazine, *Cherwell,* and developed an interest in architecture and poetry. Betjeman's first book of verse, *Mount Zion: or, In Touch with the Infinite* (1931), established his recurring topics: topography, particularly that of English suburbia; nineteenth-century architecture, especially churches, railways, and old towns; religious faith and doubt; the fear of death; and the transitoriness of existence. Society and Victorian propriety are the topics of such collections as *Continual Dew: A Little Book of Bourgeois Verse* (1937), *Old Lights for New Chancels* (1940), and *New Bats in Old Belfries* (1945). The poems in these collections helped establish Betjeman's reputation as a light versifier with little serious intent. Such early, frequently anthologized poems as ''Slough,'' ''The Varsity Students' Rag,'' and ''How To Get On in Society'' were so popular that they overshadowed such serious efforts as ''The Town Clerk's Views'' and ''The Planster's Vision,'' antiprogressivist poems which, according to Derek Stanford, attacked ''bad taste, folly, presumption.''

Critics began to note the serious intent of Betjeman's verse with the publication of *Slick But Not Streamlined: Poems and Short Pieces* (1947), a volume of early works selected by W. H. Auden and intended to introduce Betjeman to American readers. Louise Bogan praised Betjeman's ''serious and emotional contribution to the modern lyric'' and defended his seemingly trivial preoccupation with places as ''visible and concrete symbols of middle-class pretensions and yearnings.'' *A Few Late Chrysanthemums* (1954) focuses upon Betjeman's fear of mor-

Photograph by Mark Gerson

tality and his ambivalence toward religion. *Poems in the Porch* (1954) similarly confirms his religious doubts yet also evidences his growing faith in the Church of England. The tremendous popularity of *Collected Poems* prompted critical reappraisal of Betjeman's work. While some critics regarded Betjeman's style and approach as a popular substitute for the deeper themes of contemporary poetry, faulting his satire for lack of depth, most praised the sincerity and emotion conveyed in his work. Critics particularly noted such poems as ''In Willesden Churchyard'' and ''The Metropolitan Railway.'' ''In Willesden Churchyard'' is set in a graveyard in which a poet and his lover reflect on the possibility that a deceased author and an unknown woman laid to rest beside him may have had a love affair. In ''The Metropolitan Railway,'' a young couple travel to London for work and pleasure, unaware of the possibility of death.

Betjeman's verse autobiography, *Summoned by Bells* (1960), covers his life from early childhood to his departure from Oxford in 1928. The book reflects Betjeman's increasing preoccupation with death and mortality, as he recalls the various church and school bells he heard during his youth and the emotions these evoke. The tentative response to modernity in Betjeman's early poems gradually develops into a well-defined critique of postwar Britain in such works as *High and Low* (1966) and *A Nip in the Air* (1974). Betjeman's last book,

Uncollected Poems (1983), was noted for his refinement of style and his attempt to universalize topics in the context of the self and its immediate environment.

Betjeman's prose works, including *First and Last Loves* (1950) and *A Pictorial History of English Architecture* (1972), have earned him a reputation as a defender of antique buildings and other historical bastions. He is generally credited with having revived public appreciation for Victorian and other early architectural styles. In addition to editing several anthologies, Betjeman served briefly as a weekly columnist for *The Spectator* and as book critic for *The Daily Telegraph*.

(See also *CLC*, Vols. 2, 6, 10, 34; *Contemporary Authors*, Vols. 9-12, rev. ed., Vol. 112 [obituary]; *Dictionary of Literary Biography*, Vol. 20; and *Dictionary of Literary Biography Yearbook: 1984*.)

LOUISE BOGAN

[*The essay from which this excerpt is taken was originally published in* The New Yorker, *September 13, 1947.*]

John Betjeman's *Slick But Not Streamlined* brings the reader up against some unexpectedly weighty considerations. Modern poetry, although filled with nostalgia of various kinds and degrees, is notably lacking in pathos. Pathos, it might be said, is an emotion derived from contemporary objects or contemporary experiences; it is not a yearning for the past. Modern poets have so firmly eliminated pathos from their work that the suspicion sometimes arises that they are incapable of experiencing it, that the modern sensibility has become so hardened and abstract that entire areas of emotional response are outside its range. We would not wish, certainly, for a return to the sentimental repining of early and middle Romanticism. Yet this lack of true pathos deprives modern verse of a whole set of emotional effects and reverberations. Betjeman has nevertheless made a serious and emotional contribution to the modern lyric. . . . Satirist and wit Betjeman surely is, but a special kind of gravity underlies a good deal of his work. Nothing is further from pathos than parody, which is Betjeman's manner of projection, and it is an unexpected experience to find him now and again pushing parody over into the region of pure feeling. . . . Betjeman brings off his effects with the greatest deftness. He is capable of writing in the most glittering way about British middle-class mores; he is capable, too, of abruptly stepping into another dimension, where sensibility is all. Suddenly, we are in the midst of pathos before we realize what response is being demanded of us. Because Betjeman's interests are basically topographical and architectural, he goes directly toward visible and concrete symbols of middle-class pretensions and yearning: churches and chapels, parsonages, suburbs, provincial gaslit towns and seaside lodgings, railways, viaducts, factories, tearooms, and hotels. He involves these various locales and structures in perfect replicas of nineteenth-century verse forms, not forgetting the hymn. But he matches form to feeling, rather than the other way around. So, instead of getting a stream of sly jokes and satirical cuts, we get poems whose high spirits and sharp observation are continually breaking off to admit the spirit of place and of character, the sadness of human beings and of things. The dangers in Betjeman's method are obvious. Some of his poems hang in a hair's-breadth balance between the success of sincerity and the failure of smartness. The tone of "**The Arrest of Oscar Wilde at the Cadogan Hotel**" is not quite a success. On the other hand, "**Parliament Hill Fields**" (a note of nostalgia, it must be admitted), "**Death in Leamington**," "**Sudden Illness at the Bus-Stop**," and the exquisitely satirical "**Bristol and Clifton**" are perfect examples of how emotion may be smuggled into the modern lyric without restricting its freedom or dulling its finish and point. (pp. 55-6)

Louise Bogan, *"John Betjeman," in her* A Poet's Alphabet: Reflections on the Literary Art and Vocation, *edited by Robert Phelps and Ruth Limmer*, McGraw-Hill Book Company, 1970, pp. 55-8.

IRWIN EDMAN

[John Betjeman's] talent is not easy to define. In verse it is allied to that of Auden's who has selected the writings in [*Slick But Not Streamlined*] and has written for them an introduction, at once witty and enlightening. In prose [Betjeman] might be described a sharper latter-day Max Beerbohm. In verse he writes the sort of light verse that has genuine poetic feeling at its heart and technically he has a gift for expressing the most modernistic sentiments or railleries in a fashion so subtly traditional that at moments one feels this is Housman one is reading or some seventeenth century ballad or Tennyson. But when the meaning as well as the metre is noted, it becomes quite clear that this is something else again. . . .

Mr. Betjeman deftly satirizes what he clearly loves: the ordinary furniture of very English life, the ritual of the English church, teashops, and particularly vestiges of a vanishing England, suburbs, provincial towns and garden cities.

He feels and focuses the contrast between these and a time "when England is all council houses and trunk roads and steel and glass factory blocks in the New Europe of after the war."

Mr. Betjeman pokes fun at Oxford dons in "**A Don Looks at His Fellows**" but he obviously loves them, even the stuffiest and most foolish of them. He embroiders, sometimes ironically on church ritualism, but he is plainly enchanted by it. He is affectionately erudite on the rise and fall of English architecture and gives both an entertaining and fact-packed account of the history of the grand English countryside in "**An Apostrophe to One of the Landed Gentry**." Mr. Betjeman is well known as a student of English architecture and he makes a brilliant defense of easily libelled Victorian taste.

The net quality of this book is that of highly civilized entertainment, and of something more; of tenderness and understanding of things English, and of wry insight into the mixture of the new and the traditional, the traditional and the sceptical in modern English intelligence.

There are some to whom the humor of this book and its attachments will be too, too, frightfully English and altogether too local. One would perhaps have had, like Mr. Auden, to have gone to school with Mr. Betjeman to enjoy everything in these pages. But Mr. Betjeman is an accomplished man of letters and turns local affections into universal art. And the more serious prose pieces wonderfully focus the history of taste, of art, of politics and religion in England.

Mr. Auden's introduction and his selections offer a good introduction to Mr. Betjeman's quality. These hors d'oeuvres make one eager for a whole meal of Betjeman. He would not be the first very English writer to be admired in America. For he is not only English; he is first rate.

Irwin Edman, *"Tender Satire on English Ways,"* in
New York Herald Tribune Weekly Book Review,
September 14, 1947, p. 6.

THE TIMES, LONDON

The success of Mr. Betjeman' poems, as one small volume follows another, provides a fascinating example of the vagaries of taste. For in an age which positively enjoys wrestling with words, and far more readily spends its time upon the sibylline than on the enjoyable, he has built up a steady following . . . by employing for the most part the easy grace which in the past has been associated with names like Tom Moore, Thomas Haines Bayly, and Jean Ingelow.

This grace, however, he uses with a difference. While keeping closely in touch with the main themes of English lyric poetry, Mr. Betjeman twists each theme into a demurely eccentric shape. He is often in love—but with the gym tunic quite as much as with its wearer. He loves the country, but above all the country seen from the District Railway. He suffers agonizing twinges of guilt, but bravely incurs the reproaches of a delicate conscience by going on exactly as before. And all this is set down in strains of deceptive innocence (marred occasionally by an unnecessary metrical jolt) while the reader, ever prepared to be amused, suddenly finds his heart touched as well by an entirely original skill.

[Whether the poems in *A Few Late Chrysanthemums*] are to be accounted among Mr. Betjeman's best it is too early to say. His field of vision is deliberately limited, and so the particular pleasure to be gained from each new volume is that of watching much the same experiences set out with increasing precision. His jokes remain pointed and fresh, however—there is a wicked example of scholarly procedure, for instance, called **"A Literary Discovery"**—and the voice of conscience, which is more insistent than usual, nags with properly chilling authority. October is breaking on Mr. Betjeman's garden, maybe, but the chrysanthemums are still undamaged by frost.

"Mr. Betjeman's Verse: Mount Zion Revisited," in
The Times, *London, July 14, 1954, p. 10.*

JOHN BETJEMAN

[*In the essay from which this excerpt is taken, Betjeman addresses the critical reception to his poetry collection,* A Few Late Chrysanthemums.]

As early as I can remember I have read and written verse. I have always preferred it to prose, known that its composition was my vocation and anything else I have written in my life has been primarily a means of earning money in order to buy the free time in which to write poetry.

My verses are my children, sometimes too private to be shown in public. They are part of me and attacks on them I take as personal and feel inclined to answer in terms of personal abuse. When they are published my verses have generally grown up into comparative strangers. But they are still mine. Some I would gladly disown, notably three which seem to have stuck to me, try to get rid of them as I may: **"In Westminster Abbey," "Come friendly bombs and fall on Slough,"** and, in [*A Few Late Chrysanthemums*], **"Phone for the fishknives, Norman."** These now seem to me merely comic verse and competent magazine writing, topical and tiresome.

Verse-writers will know the lengthy and painful business of giving birth to a poem. First there is the thrilling or terrifying recollection of a place, a person or a mood which hammers inside the head saying, 'Go on! Go on! It is your duty to make a poem out of it.' Then a line or a phrase suggests itself. Next comes the selection of a metre. I am a traditionalist in metres and have made few experiments. The rhythms of Tennyson, Crabbe, Hawker, Dowson, Hardy, James Elroy Flecker, Moore and Hymns A & M are generally buzzing about in my brain and I choose one from these which seems to me to suit the theme. On the backs of cigarette packets and old letters, I write down my lines, crossing out and changing. When I reach home I transfer the whole to foolscap and cross out and change again. Then I start reciting the lines aloud, either driving a car or on solitary walks, until the sound of the words satisfies me. Then I try reading the poem out to a patient friend whose criticisms I gladly accept, provided they are of detail only. After that I may have the courage to send it all to a magazine.

This may explain why verses are the children of their creator and so deeply personal. Reactions of readers to a man's verses are personal reactions to him. (p. 443)

Poems are personal and that means that they must be sincere. What I was when I published my first volume of verse in about 1930, I am not today. Nor, I hope, are you. In those days my purest pleasure was the exploration of suburbs and provincial towns and my impurest pleasure the pursuit of the brawny athletic girl. When most of the poems in [*A Few Late Chrysanthemums*] were written, I was the self-pitying victim of remorse, guilt and terror of death. Much as I dislike trying to conform to Christian morality (which makes Peter Quennell detect a note of Martin Tupper in my verse), the only practical way to face the dreaded lonely journey into Eternity seems to me the Christian one. I therefore try to believe that Christ was God, made Man and gives Eternal Life, and that I may be confirmed in this belief by clinging to the sacraments and by prayer. This is sometimes implicit in my latest poems. An anonymous friendly critic in *The Times* [see excerpt above] certainly knows a thing or two when he says: 'He suffers agonising twinges of guilt, but bravely incurs the reproaches of a delicate conscience by going on exactly as before.' That means he recognises my verses at least as sincere. For there is no doubt that fear of death (a manifestation of the lack of the faith I deeply desire), remorse and a sense of man's short time on earth and an impatience with so-called 'progress,' did inform many of the poems in my latest volume. Since then I have grown a little more cheerful and thankful and hope to produce some poems expressing the joys of being alive.

It has pleased me to find long and understanding notices in Christian papers . . . , and to find avowed Christians like Tom Driberg, Evelyn Waugh and Frank Singleton and G. B. Stern and John Arlott appreciating the reasons for the gloom of some of my verse. It is doubly pleasing when this change of mood is recognised and accepted by critics who may not subscribe to my religious beliefs. That fine poet and critic Geoffrey Taylor expresses his reaction neatly when he says . . . , 'It is rather as though something friendly, familiar and furry and easily frightened had turned at bay and bitten one in the bathroom.' . . . Indeed to summarise the helpful criticism I have received from so many papers and journals, . . . I would say they advise me to keep off satire and anger. This is sound advice.

The criticism of poetry can only be really useful if it is written by poets, even if they be not popular poets. They know the meaning of words like 'technique' and 'rhythm' as applied to poetry. And criticism of poetry is useless and stultifying if the critic does not recognise the change of mind and outlook in an author he is criticising. A bad critic is like the sort of schoolmaster who sets himself up as perfection, remains static in that ridiculous position, and regards any deviation from his own norm as a step in the wrong direction. Inevitably there were a few people like this who wrote or spoke about my verses. They blamed them for not containing qualities they were never intended to have. I can only reply that I was not addressing myself to the *vieux jeu avant garde*—if I may string four French words together—which still lingers on. . . . (pp. 443-44)

John Betjeman, *"John Betjeman Replies," in* The Spectator, *Vol. 193, No. 6589, October 8, 1954, pp. 443-44.*

THE TIMES LITERARY SUPPLEMENT

Mr. Betjeman really is unique among modern poets, and there can be no question about the popularity of his poems. But is that popularity "a fitting tribute" to his genius? Lord Birkenhead, who has contributed an excellent preface to [*Collected Poems*], is perhaps nearer the mark when he hints that it may represent "a calculated risk." . . .

Waking to find himself not only famous but a public humorist, in the preface to [*A Few Late Chrysanthemums*] Mr. Betjeman had to explain to his readers that they had misunderstood him: he was not, he protested, a funny poet. He loved certain places— country, suburb, town—for what they meant to him. To him they were like people: one is fond of them because they have been kind to one; one is attached to them because they belong to one's background, because they form part of one's life. . . . [Those subjects not derived from his immediate background were chosen by Betjeman] because for him they had an intrinsic charm and exercised upon him an attraction that was almost perverse.

It is upon the perverse element in his poetry that, in spite of his protests, his readers—and more recently his "listeners" and "viewers"—have fastened, and fastened with such enthusiasm that he must have been tempted to accept the role that they have thrust upon him. . . . [However, such] fame might well cramp poetic growth. Mr. Betjeman has not wholly resisted temptation; Lord Birkenhead has wisely omitted a few pieces . . . in which Mr. Betjeman seems to be merely imitating, or parodying, himself; and a severer critic might have weeded out as many more. But, taken as a whole, this collection—which contains, besides selections from the *juvenilia,* almost the whole contents of *Old Lights for New Chancels* (1940), *New Bats in Old Belfries* (1945), and *A Few Late Chrysanthemums* (1954), and a score or so of more recent poems— demonstrates the multiplicity of its author's talents. If he is indeed a "funny poet" the first part of that composite characterization does not negative the second, and the description leaves out of account by far the most successful and important elements in his work. For Mr. Betjeman shows himself between the covers of his *Collected Poems* to be a serious poet in two senses of the word: in his own strange way he is often deeply moving, and by virtue of his solid and varied achievement he must be "taken seriously" by any critic who seeks to give an adequate account of English poetry in the twentieth century.

The multiplicity of Mr. Betjeman's talents reflects the complexity of his personality, and the oddity and the "literariness" of some of his poems result from an eccentricity which is quite unaffected and a sophistication which is entirely natural. It is when he looks at life from his own odd angles that his poetry is most successful. He really sees a poem in such situations as **"Sudden Illness at the Bus Stop," "Invasion Exercise on the Poultry Farm," "The Irish Unionist's Farewell to Greta Hellstrom in 1922."** And who but he would find poetry—mingled with reminiscences of Yeats and Francis Thompson—in the licorice fields of the West Riding? . . . Nothing could well be stranger or more sophisticated than that. To call it "amusing" would be an inadequate, if not an inaccurate, description: it is at once a successful picture and a successful poem. When he chooses a more conventionally emotional situation, Mr. Betjeman seems to make a poem out of it, rather than to see a poem in it, and the result is not so happy. Witness the brave little wife on the specialist's doorstep in **"Devonshire Street, W.1":**

> No hope. And the X-ray photographs under his arm
> Confirm the message. His wife stands timidly by . . .

The touch has faltered, the thing does not come off.

Equally—and this perhaps is more surprising—the touch falters, the materials do not fuse, in those poems which seem to be direct expressions of personal emotion, such as **"Remorse," "Portrait of a Deaf Man," "Pershore Station,"** and **"A Child Ill."** . . . One does not doubt the sincerity or the depth of the feeling, any more than one doubts the depth and sincerity of the feeling that inspires [Betjeman's] diatribes on the Hygienic Public House, Welfare Cities in a Welfare State, and the inanities of "Progressive" talks on Sex in the Civic Centre; but somehow neither in elegy nor in satire does the feeling fuse into poetry. It seems that Mr. Betjeman's subject must reach him from a distance, along the paths of imagination or of memory, if it is to "inspire" him. Then he can give us poems of fantasy and description which lift him far above the ranks of "minor" poets. For fantasy, take **"Sir John Piers"** or **"The Heart of Thomas Hardy,"** a Stanley Spencer vision of resurrection in a country churchyard; for imaginative description, take the closing lines of **"Beside the Seaside."** . . .

As for [Betjeman's] "amatory" poems, if they never become love-poems in the full sense, that is because he never, as a poet (except to indulge, or repress, **"Late-flowering Lust"**), outgrows the calf-love of a schoolboy. He is the landscape poet, not the nature poet, of love: he neither analyses, nor reflects; he sees. Even his fear of death—and Mr. Betjeman, who is much obsessed with death, spares us none of its horrors . . .—is still the fear that he caught from the "cheap nursery maid" he tells us of in one of his newest poems, and for more than one of his most poignant lyrics he might have borrowed Mrs. Meynell's title, "Intimations of Mortality, from Recollections of Early Childhood."

His "religious" poetry falls into the same pattern. Almost all of it, like **"Sunday Afternoon Service in St. Enodoc Church, Cornwall,"** draws upon the recollection of going to church as a child. "Almost all," for in one or two pieces—and here his touch is as uncertain as it is in elegy and in satire—he seeks to convey the mystical adoration with which he reveres the sacrament of the Mass; the rest of his "religious" poetry is not religious poetry but Church poetry—Church of England poetry. . . .

[Only one poem from *Poems in the Porch*] has been preserved by Lord Birkenhead. Introducing those delightful verses, their author modestly said that "they do not pretend to be poetry." But whether or not all Mr. Betjeman's verse is poetry, all his poetry is verse, and in this it is a pleasant change from the shapeless and unarticulated matter, the "fluid puddings," offered us by so many of his contemporaries. For Mr. Betjeman is a born versifier, ingenious and endlessly original; his echoes of Tennyson and Crabbe, Praed and Father Prout, are never mere *pastiche;* and he is always attentive to the sound of his words, the run of his lines, the shape of his stanzas. . . . "Where are the words?" Mr. Betjeman [asks in **"Wantage Bells,"** but he] has found them; they solicit the ear with an artistry as sure and as subtle as Tennyson's. Alone among his contemporaries, he is a master of that most difficult of mediums, blank verse. And it is not caprice, nor merely the desire for euphony, that dictates the highly original conformation of many of his stanzas, but an instinctive sense of tune, of the way in which the shape of a stanza can help in the expression of what the poet has to say; and it is this sense, quite as much as his idiosyncrasy of vision and of feeling, that makes Mr. Betjeman indeed "a unique figure among modern poets."

"A Serious Poet," in The Times Literary Supplement, *No. 2963, December 12, 1958, p. 720.*

BERNARD BERGONZI

[In *Collected Poems,* Mr. Betjeman] appears as a thoroughly up to date figure. Mr Eliot or Mr Pound seem, in comparison, somewhat archaic. Mr Betjeman, too, has turned his back on free verse and symbolist allusiveness, and writes in verse forms that might have been used by a number of Victorian poets (and most of them were). His subject is, quite simply, Culture; not in the highbrow or aristocratic sense, but rather in the homely democratic sense implied by Mr Raymond Williams when he claims that 'Culture is Ordinary', the whole way of life of a community, or the common elements in our experience. So Mr Betjeman's seaside golf links, Kia-ora bottles, Metropolitan line trains, restored parish churches, tennis clubs, and children's parties, are all cultural objects, all partial reflectors of our English way of life. Contemplating them, we contemplate essential elements in our own experience; the delight inherent in Mr Betjeman's poetry is the delight of recognition. Here, at least, is the myth, and it is quite sufficient to account for his present immense popularity. (p. 130)

[Yet despite his acclaim, the] image of Mr Betjeman as a good-hearted celebrant of the English Way, a kind of poetic Orwell, minus the politics and the rancour seems, if anything, too simple. For reading through the *Collected Poems* has reinforced my existing impression that Mr Betjeman is a complex and ambiguous figure. There is no doubt, of course, that he *is* a poet, and at his best a very good one. The moving and admirable poem on the death of King George V, for instance, takes an assemblage of 'cultural' bric-a-brac and makes a unity out of them which does somehow focus the concern of a whole society. Again, **"Love in a Valley",** with its combined richness and precision of imagery, its delicate blend of sadness and irony, succeeds very well. . . . And some of [Betjeman's] best poetry comes when the verse is ostensibly at its lightest. As in **"Sun and Fun",** where the accuracy of observation, the horror of what is observed, and the lighthearted manner, combine in a significance which is ultimately moral. . . . Here the feeling for social fact and the verbal finesse are deplorably coarsened or even, perhaps, caricatured. (pp. 130-32)

Betjeman's sense of social fact is his principal strength, but it leads directly to his major weakness, which is best described as a lack of intellectual grasp or conviction. This is by no means essential equipment for a poet, but the lack of it in Betjeman means that his satirical impulses are directed only by a sense of social—or cultural—habit. In a way his imagination is *too* concrete, for he is apt to be guided in his valuations only by what he already knows very well. This leads to his rule-of-thumb snobbery and a curious uncertainty of attitude when faced with an unfamiliar situation. And since by the nature of the world we inhabit such unfamiliar situations are apt to occur increasingly often, the poet's stance becomes more and more shifty and ambiguous. It is, of course, true that Betjeman is a believing and practising Anglican. Yet the Erastianism of the English Church, its intimate identification with and even submersion in existing social and cultural patterns, is reflected microcosmically in Betjeman's religious poems. Though he believes in the Real Presence, the Eucharist seems to engage his poetic attention and affections on much the same level as do the ecclesiastical architecture and church furnishings to which he is so addicted. . . . (p. 132)

[In the] final stanzas from **"St Saviour's, Aberdeen Park",** one sees that Betjeman's devotion to 'that Bread so white and small' is part of a larger complex of attitudes which includes filial piety and his affection for the 'great red church of my parents'. This is in no way to impugn the sincerity of Betjeman's religious convictions, but it does, I think, suggest that they don't assert any very clear intellectual dominance over his other attitudes. Mr Betjeman's God is not transcendent, but culturally immanent; an integral part of the Anglican—and English—tradition. In poetic terms, his religion works as a kind of totemism, with a variety of non-religious accretions. The reference, too, to the 'chain-smoking millions and me', coming where it does in the poem, suggests that even in the presence of his God the poet is unable to feel secure without consciously assuring himself of his separation from the mass of infidels outside.

This kind of uneasiness has, I think, had an increasingly unhappy influence on his poetry. In his earliest work he was a satirist of considerable powers, as in **"The Wykehamist"** or **"The Varsity Students' Rag".** But in the later satire, admittedly directed at bigger targets, Betjeman seems to lose his sense of social realities and the attack becomes correspondingly unfocused, as is apparent in [**"Huxley Hall"**]. . . . [The poem] is unsatisfactory, not because it manifests doubts about progress and a distaste for the workers (as good a poetic attitude as any other), but because the poem suggests no very good reason for the attitudes it adopts. Its most precise feeling is a kind of generalized disgust, though nothing so respectable as a metaphysical anguish, and, so far as one can see, without any specific object, for it is impossible to be sure what precise aspect of our society **"Huxley Hall"** is supposed to represent. The targets it offers are too many and various for much point to be made. . . . It is neither good satire, good light verse, nor good poetry. Lord Birkenhead, in his inept and unnecessary introduction to this volume, admits that Betjeman's satire is defective, but claims this is 'because he is lacking in the cruelty and spite that are inseparable from that art'. It seems to me, rather, that Betjeman fails as a satirist because he has no very clear convictions from which to direct his attacks. Sometimes, though not as often as one would like, he is able to project ironically his own uncertainties on to his characters; he does this in **"The Old Liberals",** one of the best of his later poems, which contents itself with delicately posing a question, and does not attempt an answer.

Betjeman's basic weakness lies, in fact, in his arbitrary attempt to criticize the values of Subtopia by those of Suburbia, giving these terms the widest possible meaning; in Betjeman's own work they stand for, respectively, aspects of society with which he is not familiar and those with which he is. What he forgets is that the differences between these two worlds, considered in a wider historical and cultural context than he allows himself, are much smaller than he imagines. To-day's Subtopians may easily be to-morrow's Suburbans. It is one thing to complain that

> Mere anarchy is loosed upon the world,
> The blood-dimmed tide is loosed, and everywhere
> The ceremony of innocence is drowned,

if one is writing with the aristocratic standards of a Yeats, and quite another to make a similar complaint if one's own cultural heroes are vulgarians like the Pooters (see, for instance, **"Thoughts on *The Diary of a Nobody*"**). Hence, I think, the failure of such poems as **"Huxley Hall"**. Indeed, I am convinced that Mr Betjeman, as well as being a skilful parodist of other people's verse, is also, on a deeper and perhaps less conscious level, a parodist of the attitudes of other and greater poets. Eliot and Pound and Yeats have all in their different ways sought a cultural continuity with past civilizations and their major monuments. The approach of these poets . . . is now unfashionable, and seems to smack of an unhealthy cosmopolitanism. So, true to our times, Mr Betjeman celebrates a native—and largely suburban—tradition in much the same tone; instead of Yeats's Byzantium or Pound's Provence, he writes of Margate and Middlesex. . . . Mr Betjeman has been about this parodic business, both in prose and verse, for a good many years now, and one does, in a way, admire him for keeping it up so well. But sooner or later one has to ask: is it all an enormous joke or not? If it is, then it is liable to degenerate into a fixed and unfunny pose, and if, by some chance, it is not, then one can only regret the association of so much cleverness with so little real intelligence.

But fortunately there is more to Betjeman's poetry than this elaborate and doubtful traditionalism. By many readers he is most admired for his love-poems, where an individual eroticism mingles with acute social observation. Here the moral concern which is apparent in **"Sun and Fun"** and is dissipated into irrelevant feelings in **"Huxley Hall"** operates successfully. The dominant emotion is not romantic love, nor passion, but, quite simply, lust, in an archaic and almost medieval sense, where an intense physical desire and an equally intense guilt are combined in the same emotion. . . . The reader's embarrassment and even repugnance are an integral part of the poetic intention, for he thereby participates in the poet's own sense of torment. It is in these poems, where the range is restricted and a personal emotion is wholly appropriate, that Betjeman most often succeeds, I feel. Perhaps the finest, and most unambiguously beautiful, is **"Youth and Age on Beaulieu River, Hants"**, where potentially erotic feelings about a young girl sailing her boat are sublimated into the admiration and regret and loneliness of an older woman watching her from the shore. (pp. 133-36)

Equally successful, for the most part, are those even more personal poems that look back to the poet's childhood or forward to his death. One of the best, and most recent, is **"N.W.5 & N.6"**, where a memory of childhood is recaptured with almost Proustian exactness, with memory sifting 'Lillies from lily-like electric lights and Irish stew smells from the smell of prams'; the poet tells how a nursery-maid—'sadist and puritan as now I see'—first instilled into him a fear of eternity: 'I caught her terror. I have it still'. It is a powerful poem. Betjeman, in fact, writes better poetry when he is expressing the negative aspects of his religious beliefs, the doubt or near-despair, than when he is attempting to be positive. In this context, one may mention **"Before the Anaesthetic"** and **"The Cottage Hospital"**. In another recent and very personal poem, **"Pershore Station"**, Betjeman expresses a mood of unusually intense remorse and guilt; the lush and heavy movement of the verse effectively contrasts with the inner disturbance. . . . (pp. 136-37)

Betjeman is a challenging and difficult poet, even though much of what he writes can be classed as light verse; and his admirers do him no great service by presenting him merely as a simple and straightforward singer of the good things of English life. It is often hard to decide how a poem of his should be read, which of the several possible dominant tones is the correct one. And to this extent he can be very puzzling. The ambiguity, as I have implied, is a result of the somewhat erratic operations of his social perceptions; proceeding by a series of 'hunches', he tends to know what he likes and what he doesn't like, rather than why in either case. So he can be alternately shrewd and silly and false, sometimes all in the same poem. Where something in the nature of an informed and positive judgement is required—as when facing the kind of world that has grown up in the last twenty years—he tends to fall down rather badly. He is a poseur without being insincere, a nostalgic suburban elaborately mimicking an aristocratic regret for a vanished past. And where his idiosyncratic feelings and moral concerns can operate without him getting out of his social depth, he can write good poetry. (p. 137)

Bernard Bergonzi, "Culture and Mr Betjeman," in The Twentieth Century, Vol. 165, No. 984, February, 1959, pp. 130-37.

DEREK STANFORD

Those who believe in progress as distinct from social improvement may be forgiven for believing Mr. Betjeman to be a poetic die-hard. Such poems as **"Huxley Hall"**, **"Group Life, Letchworth"** and **"The Planster's Vision"** are farcical skits upon the Radical faith in science, franchise and moral emancipation. So thoroughly saturated is our culture in the presuppositions of the creed of progress that it is difficult for most people to stand outside them and view them with detachment. Even such a keen and able critic as Mr. Bernard Bergonzi obviously sides instinctively with those attitudes which the poet attacks, just as automatically he feels put off by most of the poet's own convictions. In his essay **"Culture and Mr. Betjeman"** [see excerpt above] he quotes [**"Huxley Hall"**] and comments upon it. . . . (p. 286)

Mr. Bergonzi is right, I think, in speaking of the poem's "generalized disgust" and by the same argument wrong in seeing it as chiefly directed at the working- or manual-class. . . . What Mr. Betjeman dislikes is not a matter of upper- or lower-class thought and conduct, but an over-all attitude to life shared by many of whatever rank or status. What annoys the poet is the indiscriminate scrapping of traditional social props. One does not have to be a bigot or reactionary to believe that the nursemaids of progress have thrown both baby and bath-water away. (p. 287)

Both Lord Birkenhead and Mr. Bergonzi are agreed that the poet's satire is defective, though they offer different explanations. Lord Birkenhead holds that if "Betjeman has not on the whole succeeded as a satirist, it is only because he is lacking in the cruelty and spite that are inseparable from that art." Mr. Bergonzi, on the other hand, maintains that "Betjeman fails as a satirist because he has no very clear conviction from which to direct his attack." The kindness and compassion of the poet are clearly to be recognized. Yet this imaginative charity does not prevent him at times from being devastatingly angry. In 1937, before the first bombs fell, he wrote the superb commination **"Slough"**—a poem so vitriolic in feeling that only the awful excrescence of the place could excuse the destructiveness of its tone:

> Come, friendly bombs, and fall on Slough,
> It isn't fit for humans now,
> There isn't grass to graze a cow
> Swarm over, Death. . . .

This is the *saeva indignatie* of Swift—the outright invocation of a curse. But it is followed by a qualification—a prayer to save not Sodom but the helpless ones within it. . . . (pp. 287-88)

In the gross ignominious capitalism of pre-war England this was a poem as anti-capitalistic in sentiment as any by the "Pylon Poets". But whereas these poets tended to opt for Communism, Mr. Betjeman was not himself jumping out of the frying-pan into the fire. In fact, he preferred the frying-pan—but only the more humane aspects of it. His detestation of the vulgar exploiter and his feeling for the pawns and victims of the game sprang from no party-line propaganda concerning the oppressor and the oppressed. Mr. Betjeman did not need to read Marx in order to learn sympathy with those inhumanly done by or neglected.

The more closely one looks at the satirical poems, the clearer it becomes that it is not class but error or presumption which provide the subject matter. There is no question of the poet staging a contest of Workers *versus* Gentlemen. He is not, in this sense, an exclusive poet in the manner of Praed or Locker-Lampson. Members of varying income-groups and classes come in for nasty knocks. In **"The Old Liberals"** representative figures of the ancient leisure-class are under satirical fire. In **"Winthrop Mackworth *Redivivus*"** the victims are the members of a Higher Civil Servant's family. **"The Dear Old Village"** castigates the modern farmer and farm-worker (with a dig at the Women's Institute as a gossiping, backbiting guardian of morals). **"The Village Inn"** deals with roughly the same group. . . . **"The Town Clerk's Views"** and **"The Planster's Vision"** are both anti-progressivist pieces. "A man with bye-laws busy in his head," the town clerk is socialist middle-class; the Planster, who says "chum", one social rung lower. In **"Group Life, Letchworth"**, the characters are lower-middle-class culture fads, all eagerly engaged in the arts of self-expression ("line-cut", "leather-work", folk-tunes and free-love). In **"Huxley Hall"** the cast is mixed.

It is obvious that class *per se* is not the target of Mr. Betjeman's satire. It is, rather, bad taste, folly, presumption (particularly in terms of pseudo-ideas), which the poet pillories. (pp. 288-89)

Between the reality of a social class and some ideological image of it, there is all the difference in the world. The sacrosanct notion of the working-class (seldom entertained by its own members) is one of those shibboleths of the Party-mind as stupid and dishonest as the opposite notion of some hypothetical bowler-hatted *élite*. It is the militant T.U. myth of working-class aggressiveness which the poet satirises in **"The Dear Old Village"** rather than normal working-class behaviour. . . . It could, doubtless, be argued that however just the architectural strictures passed on "progressive planning" in **"The Town Clerk's Views"**, the satire tells only one side of the story. The thatched cottages and "lumpy churches"—which make way for civic centres, concrete lamp-standards, light industry and pylons—may offer a legitimate cause for regret. But to switch from country to town is sometimes to see "progressive planning" in a more positive light. Here the sky-scaling blocks of workers' flats, with pastel-painted balconies—for all their often flimsy air—are at least visually an improvement on the bombed benighted terraces of grimy and grim artisans' dwellings. This is not a side to "progressive planning" noticed by Mr. Betjeman in his poems. Socially the change is all to the good, but his architectural eye is not yet satisfied with what has been done, and there is no good reason why it should be. (p. 289)

> *Derek Stanford, "Mr. Betjeman's Satire," in* Contemporary Review, *Vol. 197, May, 1960, pp. 286-89.*

WALTER ALLEN

Autobiographies in verse are rare, and John Betjeman's **Summoned by Bells** could well be subtitled, like [William Wordsworth's] *The Prelude,* "Growth of a Poet's Mind." Yet, though written mainly in blank verse, its nearest analogue is not so much Wordsworth as Auden's *Letter to Byron.* Like Auden, Betjeman . . . has never made a distinction between poetry *au serieux* and what is usually called light verse. A serious poet, he has always kept his poetry light, something that baffled many of his readers for years. . . .

Judged simply as autobiography, **Summoned by Bells** is an almost exact equivalent in verse of the traditional English first novel: lonely, sensitive son of solid bourgeois parents is bullied and unhappy at school, finds solace in books and nature (in Betjeman's case, in church architecture and High Church religion as well), wants to be a writer, thereby quarreling with his father, who wishes him to go into the family business, and discovers freedom and himself at Oxford.

Summoned by Bells, however, can't be judged simply as the equivalent of an autobiographical novel. Whatever the final verdict on it may be, it is an extraordinarily accomplished, sustained exercise in narrative verse. At its core, as at the core of all Betjeman's best work, is a curious nostalgia for what in England are usually the objects of satire—suburbia, calf love, middle-class tennis clubs, nineteenth-century churches, street-cars, and the like, the whole normal environment of middle-class childhood, in fact. (p. 5)

[Although based upon conversation], Betjeman's blank verse can become the vehicle of exquisitely Tennysonian renderings of landscape . . . and rise to the utterance of deeply felt emotion, as when he writes of his religious faith and doubts.

Within the limits he is careful never to stray beyond, Betjeman is a virtuoso both in verse and in feeling. In **Summoned by Bells** he brings to life a Georgian boyhood in London and Cornwall, which culminates in a dazzlingly brilliant account of Oxford in the Twenties. . . . (p. 30)

> *Walter Allen, "A Georgian Boyhood," in* The New York Times Book Review, *November 27, 1960, pp. 5, 30.*

PHILIP LARKIN

One of the most striking passages in this first instalment of Mr. Betjeman's verse autobiography [*Summoned by Bells*] describes how, as a schoolboy in Highgate, he fancied that his poems were 'as good as Campbell now':

> And so I bound my verse into a book
> *The Best of Betjeman*, and handed it
> To one who, I was told, liked poetry—
> The American master, Mr. Eliot.

The scene is worthy of a nineteenth-century narrative painter: 'The Infant Betjeman Offers His Verses To The Young Eliot.' For, leaving aside their respective poetic statures, it was Eliot who gave the modernist poetic movement its charter in the sentence, 'Poets in our civilisation, as it exists at present, must be *difficult*.' And it was Betjeman who, forty years later, was to bypass the whole light industry of exegesis that had grown up round this fatal phrase, and prove, like Kipling and Housman before him, that a direct relation with the reading public could be established by anyone prepared to be moving and memorable.

It is ironic that, up to a point, the poetry of Betjeman (and also that of his contemporary W. H. Auden) is precisely the kind Mr. Eliot foresaw. 'Our civilisation,' the passage continues, 'comprehends great variety and complexity, and this variety and complexity, playing upon a refined sensibility, must produce various and complex results.' So it has. Betjeman does more than genuflect before Victorian lamp-brackets and shudder at words like 'serviette': despite the flailing introduction to *First and Last Loves* . . . , he is an accepter, not a rejecter, of our time, registering 'dear old, bloody old England' with robustness, precision and a vivacious affection that shimmers continually between laughter and rage, his sense of the past casting long perspectives behind every observation. . . .

Summoned by Bells comprises nine chapters of the kind of reminiscential verse Mr. Betjeman has already given us (**"Original Sin On The Sussex Coast"**), demurely pedestrian, Leica-sharp in detail, recounting by selective episodic narrative his life from boyhood to involuntary departure from Oxford, done not in the spirit of farcical or shocking revelation (much of his material is as familiar as his manner), but with an eager pleasure in re-creating incidents and circumstances that still have power to move him. The personality is in abeyance. And indeed what first emerges from a reading of this poem is that Betjeman, though an original, is not an egoist: rather, he is that rare thing, an extrovert sensitive, not interested in himself but in the experiences being himself enables him to savour, including that of being himself. . . . [Time] and again in scenes where interest might be expected to focus on the author's feelings we find it instead shifting to the details. . . .

None the less, the connecting theme of the narrative is highly personal. . . . Only son of a forceful father and semi-invalid mother, Mr. Betjeman was expected to carry on the family business. . . . He refused—implicitly, when young, by incompetence; explicitly, when older, with defiance. This was a grave defection for an only son, and Mr. Betjeman does not minimise his father's anger ('Bone idle, like my eldest brother Jack, A rotten, low, deceitful little snob') nor his own feelings of remorse ('A sense of guilt increasing with the years') that spread like a discoloration across his whole life. The excuse he gives is single and unvarying:

> I was a poet. That was why I failed.

The lame self-importance of this attitude must be interpreted by what we know of Betjeman today. Destined to be one of those rare persons who can say, 'Simply the thing I am shall make me live,' he was holding off with an instinctive obstinate wisdom anything that might hinder contact with the factors that were to form his particular nature. And one by one we see them enter—Cornwall and the sea, Oxford and church architecture, London and railway stations; then religion, announced by the strangest of all the bells that summon him throughout the narrative—it hangs on an elm bough, beaten by a bearded book-reading priest outside a ruined church; then, lastly, Magdalen, where for the first time his sullenly smouldering character bursts into violent flame, and the extraordinary blend of interests that we label Betjemania becomes recognisable. Thus although the book ends in ostensible failure ('Failed in Divinity!'), it is really a triumph. Betjeman has made it. He has become Betjeman.

The value of . . . [*Summoned by Bells*] will no doubt be hotly disputed. . . . For the moment it is enough to name two of its virtues. First, Betjeman has an astonishing command of detail, both visual and circumstantial. It makes the surface of his flat, *Task*-like blank verse . . . [glitter] in accumulations of flotsam from its author's remarkable memory. . . . This imaginative and precise evocation is part of the poem's purpose, and is accomplished with splendid competence.

Secondly, although it remains a mystery how Mr. Betjeman can avoid the traps of self-importance, exhibitionism, silliness, sentimentality and boredom, he continues to do so. . . . How, without alienating us, can he confess his social climbing into 'the leisured set in Canterbury Quad,' or admit his infatuation with the Firbanky world of Harold Acton . . . without attracting to himself some of the impatience that today it rouses in us? No doubt sincerity is the answer, a sincerity as unselfconscious as it is absolute, but it is helped by his own attitude to himself, scrupulously free of what they no doubt called 'side' at Marlborough and disinfected by his palpably greater interest in things other than himself. It may irritate us that it should be so marketable. But one finishes the book with a considerable respect for this almost moral tactfulness. It will be interesting to see if it can be maintained as Mr. Betjeman's memory, like Poe's pendulum, sweeps closer and closer to the present.

> Philip Larkin, "The Blending of Betjeman," in The Spectator, *Vol. 205, No. 6910, December 2, 1960, p. 913.*

V. S. PRITCHETT

[Readers of Mr Betjeman's *Summoned by Bells*], a poem that glances from incident to incident in the first 20 years of his life, must observe that Mr Betjeman's real subject is not nostalgia, but the sense of insecurity, the terror of time and pain. The laughs come at the point of agony. . . .

Mr Betjeman's originality starts from the unbearable twinges of shame and remorse; and in this he is in the familiar tradition of all English light verse from Hood, Thackeray, Carroll to Newbolt and Auden—poets given to parody, pathos, sing-song or the thumping emotions of our hymns, when the eyes wander sinfully as we swell out for the last verse. The genre is very English; it is perpetuated only by very clever, frightened, defensive people who are given sedulously to ritual: ritual prevents feeling from having its head and confines one rigorously to sentiment. . . . [Mr. Betjeman's] peculiar contribution is to have substituted religious feeling for the usual Play-up-Play-up-and-Play-the-Game kind of patriotism. . . .

Mr Betjeman's device for concealing violence, passion, wilfulness and brilliance, is first of all 'a love of the dim'. He studiously collects the faded photographs, gives silly expression to their feelings, all the more to dodge the terrible implication that wild feeling once lived in these people, and that the feelings were sat on—just as aces are 'sat on' in bridge—so that the effort is desperate and choking. He laughs to increase the pain of it.

In terror of time, he avidly collects what is dated: the point is that these lives were novelties, manifestations of the lust of the eye and the pride of life. . . . The nostalgia and affection for the past are there; 'a slight sense of something unfulfilled.' The laughter, the mockery of . . . suburban memories is sharpened by remorse and by a sense of being alone in a wilderness of guilt. 'Summoned by bells' is a phrase that quite literally refers to Mr Betjeman's lasting passion for architecture; but equally it refers to things more disturbing—how the bells are 'hollowing out the sky', and to the apprehension of the appalling summons that a laugh will not avert. For living in the past is a game just as Carroll's brainy fantasies were games: the game of snubbing fear.

Light verse depends for its effect on the catchiness, the spirit of its tunes and rhythms and the power of wit to turn the feeling as the poem whizzes to its dangerous corner. The two or three lyrics in *Summoned by Bells* are shapely and exhilarating. The main body of the poem is in blank verse that is 'as near prose as [I] dare'; it is sometimes poor prose rather than flat verse. . . . At a first reading one is restfully passing from the commonplace to the 'amusing' . . . and Mr Betjeman moves on with such suicidal quickness that nothing builds up until the episodes at Marlborough and Oxford. The former is moving, for Mr Betjeman is the poet of love in glum places; the latter is boldly ludicrous and very well done.

But, at a second and third reading, this novel in verse discloses its more important quality: he is a true excavator of drama. In the evocation of suburban youth and family troubles; the visit to father's works; the conflict between father and son, the miseries of prep school and public school, the romantic holidays in Cornwall, we recognise the fidelity of observation, the painful anxiety for truth in the determination to amuse and touch. But these would be fatally lulling but for the short thrilled power of dramatising a scene in a line or two. Nervous of prolonging these scenes, Mr Betjeman makes often too quick a getaway; but they whizz back like a cane and are sharp enough to raise a weal. The sadness or the pathos of Mr Betjeman are the rector's old gumboots which a fierce, wilful and even violent man is pretending to slop along in. Indeed, pretending to be a rector. In these brief flashes of drama the dullness wears off and we see Mr Betjeman hard and accomplished. The slackness which is his weakness as a poet vanishes.

> *V.S. Pritchett, "Betjeman in Pooterland," in* New Statesman, *Vol. LX, No. 1551, December 3, 1960, p. 894.*

JOHN WAIN

[*The essay from which this excerpt is taken was originally published in* The Observer *in 1960.*]

[Mr. Betjeman's *Summoned by Bells*] is autobiographical. So, of course, is all his poetry; even where it is not directly about himself, it is an expression of his particular viewpoint, emanating from a personality at once vivid and immediately recognisable. (p. 168)

Since the new poem goes over the same ground that all Mr. Betjeman's readers have trodden before, this seems a good moment to try to sum up his work as a poet and try to account for its vast popularity. In some quarters the high sales of Betjeman's volumes are taken to indicate a 'revival of poetry'. I cannot be so optimistic, and the best way of explaining my attitude is to give some account of what I take to be the reasons for his appeal to such a wide audience.

To begin with, his poetry is warmly sympathetic. It bears the stamp of his character, and that character is honest, likeable and generous. Secondly, it is nostalgic. The English middle class, and particularly its upper layer, has lived for fifty years in a world less and less organised for its comfort, appreciative of its virtues, indulgent to its failings. As a result, nostalgia is widespread among such people even when they personally are too young to remember the good times. And Mr. Betjeman's nostalgia is not the ordinary kind that springs from mere selfishness. The virtues whose disappearance he mourns were real virtues; the things he hates in modern life are for the most part genuinely hateful. Thus he appeals to an easily aroused response and at the same time makes it respectable.

Thirdly, he is completely free of any wish to be smart. If he finds something moving, he writes about it and confesses his feelings, even when the subject is one that many writers would avoid for fear of sounding sentimental. . . . And yet his honesty never leads him to be searing or shocking. About sexual emotions, for instance, he writes a good deal, but never in a way that could challenge or disturb. He is at his best when describing passion before puberty. . . . [Adult sexual relationships] are seen mainly as a disruptive and ugly calamity.

Fourthly and finally, the all-important reason, the heart of the matter. English middle-class people, if they are at all intelligent, nearly always find themselves trapped in an ambivalent attitude towards their own *lares et penates*. All this rich clutter in which they live their formative years, . . . is, in their eyes, both lovable and ridiculous. In a word, they can't decide whether it is what they love most or what they hate most. And this is where Betjeman steps in. His account of the clutter, the terms in which he describes it, the comments he makes on it, all mirror that same ambivalence. He, too, cannot decide whether the way of life he describes is damnable or admirable. It stirs his emotions, but what emotions? From minute to minute he is never quite sure. Hence the decision to write in verse rather than prose. Because the thumping metre, the comic rhymes, the refrains so redolent of parody . . . all convey the idea that the whole thing is a joke. Having conveyed that, he has no need actually to make the joke. The verse-form does that for him.

Summoned by Bells, like *Paradise Lost,* has a prefatory 'note on the verse'. 'The author has gone as near prose as he dare. He chose blank verse, for all but the more hilarious moments, because he found it best suited to brevity,' etc. The word 'hilarious' is the give-away here, with its invitation to the reader to take the whole performance as a joke. Especially since (as we find when we look into the poem) the passages in various rhymed metres are not by any means all hilarious, or even mildly comic; they include most of the poem's more intense moments. . . . (pp. 168-70)

The pathetic inadequacy of such verse to deal with important matters is readily forgiven by the reader who has accepted the suggestion contained in the word 'hilarious'. It is this same suggestion that acts as a lightning-conductor to protect the verse from critical censure. Once agree that we are all going to play a nice cosy game together, and it becomes bad form to introduce serious standards. And yet timid reviewers, who feel unsafe when serious issues are raised, feel perfectly free to break this rule in the poet's favour. To insinuate that high standards can be invoked when it is a question of praising rather than blaming. Hence the squeals of adulation. 'He brings back to poetry a sense of dramatic urgency it had all but lost.' 'It would be difficult to point to a contemporary poet of greater originality or more genuine depths of feeling.' It's pure relief. At last, a poet who doesn't order us to tidy away our toys and come out of the nursery!

The reviewers who write like that are, of course, making fools of themselves. But it does not follow from this that Betjeman's work is foolish. It is merely that the strength and appeal of what he writes lie elsewhere, away from the kind of discriminations that must be used when 'real' poetry is in question. That is why it is not harmed by the writer's almost complete lack of the skills of the true poet, his wooden technique, his water-colours slapped at the canvas, his incuriosity about literary art.

Most of his poems are written either in hymn-metres or in metres usually associated with 'light' and comic verse. These forms, themselves loaded with the kind of suggestion he means to convey, are the literary counterpart of Betjemanian *bric-à-brac* in the world of objects. . . . To manipulate them needs no more skill than is shown by the men who write the jingles on Christmas cards. And that so many people find Mr. Betjeman the most (or only) attractive contemporary poet is merely one more sign that the mass middle-brow public distrusts and fears poetry.

Mr. Eliot once remarked that people speak as if thought were precise and emotion vague, whereas in fact there is vague emotion and precise emotion. The vogue for Betjeman shows how unready the English still are, and perhaps will always be, for precise emotion. And the kind of poetry that could benefit from a 'revival' starting from this point is not likely to be either durable or satisfying. (pp. 170-71)

> John Wain, "Four Observer Pieces: John Betjeman," in his Essays on Literature and Ideas, Macmillan and Co. Ltd., 1963, pp. 168-71.

R. E. WIEHE

In the midst of atom bombs, industrial uncertainty, and general social upheaval, the generation in its fifties and sixties can take Betjeman's recollections with the reassuring knowledge that this is real poetry, not too hard to understand, and culturally rewarding. A goodly number of local references, conveying the sense of British solidarity, helps to keep up the illusion. Yet when one has admitted this, and one has granted the differences from our usual unrhymed metaphysical, abstract free verse, Betjeman still remains a poet capable of receiving serious attention.

It is true that he plays with a familiar English subject—class and manners. He has been accused of an unlovely snobbery in at least one review, but **"How to Get On in Society"** with its rollicking briskness . . . undercuts that attitude. The poem al-

ludes to the bits of refinement required for a proper tea party. These become the medium of an ironic commentary masked under a garrulous apology. The speaker is keeping up the amenities of her position but without conviction. Betjeman's detachment from gentility is apparent in the tones of another speaker in **"Camberley,"** where the gossipy parentheses of idle conversation . . . underscore the vacuous insincerity of good society. Though his conversational rhythm in these pieces functions well in expressing that discrepancy between motives and manners, his longest exercise in class analysis is in blank verse. **"Beside the Seaside"** details the seasonal peregrination of various classes to the beach and the struggles of children in their peer groups. Jennifer, facing a humiliating demotion from being last year's queen of the young, found "That life-long tragedy . . . / Which ate into her soul and made her take / To secretarial work in later life." The trivial tone here underscores a whole class attitude. As Jennifer laments over her status— and Betjeman is an analyst of childhood frustration and demoralizing fear—so her family amid endless rounds of winkle-eating, golf, and bicycling worry over [their social status]. . . . This parodied ritualism detaches [Betjeman] from commitment to class respectability. Like Robert Frost he is concerned with the problem of keeping self-respect and maintaining communication with others in our loneliness.

The simple diction of "She died in the upstairs bedroom / By the light of the evening star" occurring in **"Death in Leamington"** reminds us of Frost, but other lines in the poem have less of his calm restraint and more of Auden's mordant voice (**"As I Walked Out One Evening"**). An invalid lies dead as her nurse, bustling in "chintzy cheeriness," evades the fact. While the finality of death is unfelt, the poet himself obliquely insists on the fact of life's decay: "Do you know that the stucco is peeling?" (pp. 37-8)

If town organizing becomes anathema to Betjeman, perhaps his care for old churches provides the reason. The number of poems about them bulks heavily in his work, and he is a life-long student of ecclesiastical architecture. This subject matter may endear him to those readers in Britain for whom preservation and description of church monuments is a major hobby. He uses his churches on occasion for more than merely sentimental picture-making. One can find poems like **"A Lincolnshire Church"** where his religious experience becomes moving and poetically impressive. (p. 39)

If the Church keeps a sense of ritual continuity alive, the city with its endless improvements represents an alien disruption. "For us of the steam and the gas-light, the lost generation / The new white cliffs of the city are built in vain," he says in **"Monody on the Death of Aldersgate Street Station."** There may be a trifle of irony in finding a poet educated during World War I, coming into manhood during the twenties, and now celebrating the Victorian world, who calls himself a member of "the lost generation." For many of his readers the truth is more than a literary phrase. The sense of organic community has gone, and his indictment of the new-model metropolis in **"The Town Clerk's Views"** and **"The Planster's Vision"** is their scientific planning uninformed by beauty, proportion, or spiritual dedication. By contrast the individuals whom he depicts in a period poem recalling the dignity which the late nineteenth century could have, are a Victorian father and daughter, indulging in a purely personal activity, a duet. Though the poem is called **"The Old Liberals,"** the reference is less to politics than to a middle-class, progressive household. . . . Betjeman's own Edwardian home is distilled in **"N.W. 5 and**

N. 6" where he recalls the "red stone cliffs" of Lissenden Mansions where stew smells mingled with "lily-like electric lights" and caterpillars on the privet hedge. The caterpillars introduce an ambivalent note, one of fear, which colors much of Betjeman's retrospect.... The poem ends with his confession of the continuing strength of his terror even in later years.... The sense of childhood pain is found too in **"Original Sin on the Sussex Coast"** in which a young boy, presumably Betjeman himself, experiences the harassment of other youngsters, not too severe, but inflicting a casual sadism which affected him deeply. He refers in *Summoned by Bells* to a schoolboy contemporary who suffered as an outcast after being found "guilty" by his upper-division elders. And the same work describes his panicky refuge in a lie about a sick parent to escape a dishonorable retreat from a fight with a gentlemanly swaggerer. A historical scene is recaptured in **"An Incident in the Early Life of Ebenezer Jones, Poet, 1828,"** a poem describing a school-usher, who finding his charges with a stray dog, drags the beast upstairs to fling it down amid cries of "You shall not! shall not!" The usher, adds Betjeman, shakes Heaven's walls by breaking a boy's heart. Betjeman is driven to search out cruelty practiced by elders or youths. In this respect he reminds us of Dickens and the traumatic experience of the blacking-factory. Betjeman emphasizes his dislike of the Calvinism which was his religious heritage and that his own sense of uneasy fear led him into Anglicanism.

Betjeman's father is often presented as estranged from him.... In this context it is interesting to note one of his best poems, **"A Child Ill."** Written as an elegiac lyric, it has an idealism reflecting the poet's desire, perhaps, for a real identity with his father. The child, lying on its bed, scrutinizes the father, and the expression recalls *his* own father's as he had looked into his father's eyes one past occasion. The father's refrain, "Oh little body, do not die / The soul looks out through wide blue eyes" invokes a Stoic classicism. The communion of child and father is in spirit, not words.... The vision which the father has of the child's soul, "wordless as the windy sky," suggests the neo-Platonic concept of divine breath. And the father's reference to the son's soul as "This other light alight" might suggest the Biblical "light unto all generations," tacitly identifying the child with the divine message, or the Plotinian spark of divinity alight in each man. These bare allusions and lyrical phrasing make this one of the best poems.

The real difficulty in meeting the world, which Betjeman found in his relations with father and his own contemporaries is reflected humorously in poems about overpowering females.... The partner of the opposite sex whom he ordinarily celebrates is vital, aggressive, Junoesque, one for whom he can play the weak fool. Pam in **"Pot Pourri from a Surrey Garden"** overcomes him forcefully in a tennis match and her "bountiful body" is paralleled by the more-than-life stature of the heroine of **"The Olympic Girl."** Though overpowering women may reflect Betjeman's own lack of real contacts as a schoolboy and collegian, his humor may spring out of an odd inversion of Romanticism. Instead of the burning will and strength overcoming obstacles, as in the Byronic hero, there is submission, escape, fear, weakness offered with a certain romantic egotism. His mockery of the passive lover appears again in some lines with a turn of T. S. Eliot, **"Pershore Station, Or a Liverish Journey First Class."** A Prufrockian traveler recalls his abandonment of love, leaving his lady wrapped only in "her self-protection," without giving "one word" which "would have made her turn." He adds: "But the word I never murmured and now I am left to burn." The colloquialism underscores a

senseless reticence about love which the direct young Junos have at least overcome. Betjeman elsewhere croons in waltz time a little lyric about love, **"In the Public Gardens,"** in which he proclaims: "You so white and frail and pale / And me so deeply me." Jennifer, whom we have already mentioned in **"Beside the Seaside,"** pokes in solitude among seaside rocks and sands, lonely but "always ME." And like Betjeman, she finds consolation in Nature. This lonely personality is reflected in a minor descriptive poem about a typist named Eunice. She frets in her spinsterly emptiness until she returns to her native garden in Kent. In the poem **"Business Girls,"** the daily bath ritual symbolizes the empty hedonism of meaningless lives. Steam clouds rise from the bath, foreshadowing the heedless rush of morning trains; dahlia gardens below the bathroom are metamorphosed into steamy nothingness.... Using bits of abstract experience, Betjeman skillfully montages a trivial busyness without purpose. The external image of despair for him is a woman lost without love or sense of place.

Since the *Collected Poems* do embody poetic talent and a certain depth of psychological insight, it is well to consider the autobiography, *Summoned by Bells,* in the light of Betjeman's development. This work displays qualities of earlier poems— local color in particular.... [Poems] again provide nostalgic precision of detail which can conjure up for many readers a particular period of prosperity and progressive assurance. Names appeal to Betjeman as to many poets.... Names, like bells, have a sonorous satisfaction of their own. What diminishes the achievement is an overwrought accuracy, which sometimes produces lines that the early Wordsworth might have envied: "An old gas engine smelling strong of oil / Its mighty wheel revolved a leather belt." ... Then too a smug Victorian hortatory tone mars "Let those who have such memories recollect / Their sinking dread of going back to school." Certain scenes take on a picture-postcard quality.... The pictorial approach to experience is asserted in lines about Pusey House, Oxford, where Betjeman went to find faith. For him the truth was found in stained glass, vestments, stoups, incense, and crossings. Here is the same paraphernalia which is used to establish the religious intensity of **"Holy Trinity."** Oxford itself for Betjeman was a wallowing in "All that was crumbling, picturesque and quaint." Granting his own honesty in showing his youthful inexperience, we might question his motivation as a poet: "I wanted to encase in rhythm and rhyme / The things I saw and felt (I could not think)." After all, the poet's business *is* to think. And poetry-making is not merely jelling bits of experience in a casing of metrics. Wordsworth showed that trivial fact can enter into blank verse for the sake of fidelity to experience. But his effort pointed up the need for significance in the experience. In this connection Betjeman's description of a meeting with the bearded rector of ruined St. Ervan's at Evensong, encountering a sympathetic friendship in the charms of an evening's reading about the Grail quest, remains unconvincing. Since the scene is paired against the one involving his revolt against his father, by implication the comradeship meant much to Betjeman, growing toward college age in a somewhat uncongenial school atmosphere. However, the details of the evening bell, the sycamore, the bearded priest, and the Grail story—all fragments of Arthurian legend—do not really show his emotional response nor any particular depth of feeling for it. It is a set piece of local color.

What remains more memorable is the reaction against his restricted childhood, not a new subject after Butler, Huxley, and the World War I generation. The evident delight in escaping his "pokey, dark and cramped" home in Chelsea by exploring the Underground, or escaping his adolescence in bicycle tours keep the chronicle alive. There is his account of the liberation of books, which he purchased with all available pocket money, making their old plates come alive in his imagination, and his later undergraduate delight in poetry, which he explored under Maurice Bowra's direction at Wadham College. . . . In general his time at Oxford was lacking in intellectual distinction, and he himself dismisses his achievement in a quip: "While we ate Virginia hams / Contemporaries passed exams." The record of his failure in divinity includes his account of the embarrassing foolery of a coterie of precious Oxfordians gathered at "Colonel" Kolkhorst's. . . . At best he faces this absurd flight from reality with honesty, although one might question the suitability of the events for inclusion in a serious poem. There is in Betjeman's lines in *Summoned by Bells* the continuing problem of style vs. subject—we are not prepared to see a man take himself seriously when he so often lapses into a naïve total recall. The tone of the poem does not help the reader to attain the proper perspective and attitude.

Considering Betjeman's poetry in terms of vocabulary and meter, we observe that his fluency is in some cases a source of difficulty rather than strength. In **"Our Padre"** he refers to the preacher's voice: "His voice would reach to Heaven, and make / The Rock of Ages Roll." He continues: "Our padre is an old sky pilot / He's tied a reef knot round my heart. . . ." The desire to indulge in punning, word play, and humorous metaphor tends to make language its own master. The poem may be a devastating criticism of cliché, but the tone of jolly awe, if indeed that is what he is striving for, reveals a less sardonic awareness. What does one feel about the dissonant suggestiveness of "sky pilot" and "reef knot" (in what way are pilots tied in reef knots or the makers of them?) in these lines? His use of sprung rhythm provides a necessary touch of wonderment which he associates with his subject, but the phrasing . . . leaves the poem breathlessly obscure. Alliteration is a favorite device, sometimes successful and sometimes not. . . . That the effect to be successful need not be comic is made clear in the pathos of "Oh little body, do not die" and "this other light alight" which are supported by subtle alliteration and assonance elsewhere in **"A Child Ill."** The gossipy comment of "A drawing room in mauve, I think" or ironic aside, "I knew we were a lower, lesser world / Than that remote one of the carriage folk," . . . show his skillfulness in ironic or comic effects. Against the lush vocabulary of **"Holy Trinity"** there is the metaphysical concision of "I cling to you inflamed with fear" in a love poem. His language can display Victorian diction—"wold," "gentle eminence," "a-maying" and descend shortly to "bloody old England" or create coinages like "tractor-drowned." . . . The verse in *Summoned by Bells* displays an ease of handling that is significant. "I heard the church bells hollowing out the sky, / Deep beyond deep, like neverending stars." These two lines have four major stresses, these major ones reinforced by alliteration in part, and the feet show variant iambic-trochaic rhythm as well as longer feet made possible through weaker stressing. By contrast the poem, **"The Town Clerk's Views"** uses rather stiff couplets, partly to emphasize the unreality of his visions. Thus Betjeman's work is characterized by technical variety. If he has imitated Eliot, Auden, and Spender, sometimes unhappily, he still has an originality which redeems his more naïve, erratic moments of verse-making. Like a number of British poets, he is best when conveying the melancholy of nature. As it instills in us the sense of youth passing (the Kennet River passage in *Summoned by Bells*), the urgency of personal meeting with God (**"A Lincolnshire Church"**) or the timelessness of life (**"Beside the Seashore"**), we find Betjeman in his strongest mood, most able to communicate with his readers. . . . Betjeman refers in his autobiography to the freckled cowrie as a "core of peace" for him. Nature then provides the background for his expression of pain, need for companionship, and sympathetic human values in his best poems. When he succeeds in creating metaphors which can embrace his themes, extending them with overtones of meaning, and using his technical command of verse to bear the weight of the meaning, Betjeman becomes a strong poet. It is not possible to dismiss him as merely distilling a fashionable middle-brow nostalgia. (pp. 41-9)

R. E. Wiehe, "Summoned by Nostalgia: John Betjeman's Poetry," in Arizona Quarterly, Vol. 19, No. 1, Spring, 1963, pp. 37-49.

MARIUS BEWLEY

In comparison with some of his earlier work John Betjeman's latest volume of poems, *High and Low,* is disappointing. It may be that one is less prepared to accept the repetitive and the slightly fatigued from a writer of light verse than one is from, say, the writer of *Ecclesiastical Sonnets*. However that may be, there is nothing here that can in any way compare with an early piece like **"The Arrest of Oscar Wilde at the Cadogan Hotel."** . . . (pp. 32-3)

[Although Wilde briefly reappears in a poem in *High and Low,* it] is unpleasantly coy rather than funny or witty, and it is a world away from the earlier poem. Betjeman returns to a favorite theme in these poems, the destruction of England's landscape. In earlier verses—the monologue of 1948 called **"The Town Clerk's Views,"** for example—Betjeman made his point with a good deal of humor and crispness. There seems little purpose in coming back to it repeatedly in inferior verse such as this:

> Encase your legs in nylons,
> Bestride your hills with pylons
>   O age without a soul;
> A way with gentle willows
> And all the elmy billows
>   That through your valleys roll.

Betjeman's verse at its best displays a mildly ironic, critically humorous vision of contemporary society, heavily salted with nostalgia for Edwardian or late Victorian England. Superimposed on the conventional metrics and rhythms of his early admirations in poetry, the result has often been highly successful. But the irony has grown a little tired, the humor thinner, and those early admirations begin to show through too plainly. (p. 33)

Marius Bewley, "Good Manners," in The New York Review of Books, Vol. VIII, No. 9, May 18, 1967, pp. 31-4.

DAVID McCORD

[Despite Mr. Betjeman's popularity in England, in the United States] the author of *High and Low* remains for us a special taste. There are several good reasons for this.

In spite of his name, Mr. Betjeman is deeply, urbanely, organically English, with a sidearm embrace of Ireland; in rhyme and in unexperimental meter and love of toponymy, he looks on the page like a held-over Georgian. But if his woodshed is Georgian, his tools are not. For one thing, he is an antiquary of great distinction and taste; a master of a new kind of anti-quarian prose—see **"First and Last Loves"** (1952) rather than **"Ghastly Good Taste"** (1933). For another, he is an unrelenting champion of the middle class and of middle-class life . . . , yet a loather of cheap vulgarity, obsidian false front, throughways, massive messes in concrete, despiser of whatever little "ranchos" may be called in England; a true and compassionate voice against cruelty, vandalism, desecration, . . . [and a] defender of things and people ignored or overlooked. . . .

[Mr. Betjeman's] headlong enthusiasm for "mineral railways, provincial towns, and garden cities" is reflected in dozens of poems. And if none of those about rolling stock has the exquisite lyric quality of Stephen Spender's "The Express," one hears "the elate meter of her wheels." Often he is swayed between wit and the macabre, between bucolic tragedy or comedy and the deepest personal drama: a merchant in the little things of large portent. . . .

In no sense a "funny" poet, Mr. Betjeman has a devastating wit. Who does not know his inspirational Miss Joan Hunter Dunn? Or his passion for the Amazonic? One of these ladies turns up in the current volume in **"Agricultural Caress":**

> God shrive me from this morning lust
> For supple farm girls: if you must,
> Send the cold daughter of an earl—
> But spare me Thelma's sister Pearl!

The Georgian technique, but far from vapid. At times Mr. Betjeman is the surrealist in the gazebo. If *High and Low* is not the best of the poet, it is still a good introduction. . . . The longish poem, **"Cricket Master,"** shows the non-sporting Betjeman at his best. A man of deep friendships, the death of a friend "strikes him with a terrible impact," as the Earl of Birkenhead has observed. **"The Hon. Sec.,"** possibly fictional, is a threnody worthy of a place with that earlier one which ends: "I am deaf to your notes and dead / by a soldier's body in Burma."

If a book feeds me, as Edward Thomas once said, that is all I ask. Did Mr. Betjeman derive solely from one English nursery rhyme, it would be enough: "I went to Noke, / But nobody spoke; / I went to Thame, / It was just the same; / Burford and Brill / Were silent and still, / But I went to Beckley / And they spoke directly."

> *David McCord, "A Special Taste," in* The New York Times Book Review, *September 24, 1967, p. 57.*

PHILIP LARKIN

[Betjeman's poetry as exemplified in *Collected Poems* makes] up the most extraordinary poetic output of our time. By extraordinary I don't necessarily mean good: good poems are surprising rather than extraordinary, keeping the power to inflict their tiny pristine shock long after they have become familiar; but good poems can seem extraordinary too at first . . . , and it is only when this extraordinariness wears off that we can see whether the surprise remains. (p. xvii)

"Betjeman has a mind of extraordinary originality; there is no one else remotely like him." The speaker is Sir Maurice Bowra, as reported by The Earl of Birkenhead, when both Birkenhead and Betjeman were Oxford undergraduates. The words have the ring of careful consideration, and came from a clever man: what can we infer from them? . . . What Bowra meant was that

the sort of thing he heard this ex-Marlborough undergraduate say when he invited him to dinner in Wadham College was completely unlike the common talk of the day. (p. xx)

[Betjeman's themes] were resolutely opposed to the spirit of the century in two major ways: they were insular, and they were regressive. To compare Betjeman with a real figure of the Twenties, a Harold Acton, is to see immediately what a poor figure he would have cut in the Paris of Stein and Cocteau: he was not, and never has been, a cosmopolitan. To understand this we have to realise that at Betjeman's heart lies not poetry but architecture—or, if the concepts are allowed, a poetry that embraces architecture and an architecture that embraces poetry. . . . (pp. xxi-xxii)

[Betjeman's writings on architecture imply] that his fundamental interest is human life, or human life in society, and that architecture is important in human life because a good society is one dwelling in well-proportioned surroundings. This would seem to place him with writers such as Ruskin and Morris, people for whom the appearance of things approached a morality, and in a way this is true, for with Betjeman the eye leads the spirit: he tells us that he came to the Christian religion by means of church architecture and formal ritual. But Betjeman has always mocked Morris . . . , and we shall see that it is not so much the architecture of a building that appeals to him as its relation to human use, to human scale and size, and the degree to which it reflects human life and emotions.

The quality of regressiveness I mentioned earlier might indeed be taken as no more than a latter-day version of the anti-industrialism Morris and Ruskin and their followers so vehemently professed. If the spirit of our century is onwards, outwards, and upwards, the spirit of Betjeman's work is backwards, inwards, and downwards. . . . If the age is agnostic and believes everyone is a socialist nowadays, Betjeman embraces the Christianity of the Church of England and proclaims a benevolent class system the best of all possible worlds. In a time of global concepts, Betjeman insists on the little, the forgotten, the unprofitable, the obscure. . . . (pp. xxiii-xxiv)

All this is a necessary prelude to an understanding of Betjeman's poems, partly because a great deal of what he writes is, overtly or covertly, propaganda for what he believes, partly because his poetic aesthetic is only another version of his social aesthetic. The first thing to realise about Betjeman as a writer of verse is that he is a poet for whom the modern poetic revolution has simply not taken place. Insularity and regression rule here as there. For him there has been no symbolism, no objective correlative, no T. S. Eliot or Ezra Pound, no reinvestment in myth or casting of language as gesture. . . . He addresses himself to his art in the belief that poetry is an emotional business and that rhyme and metre are means of enhancing that emotion, just as in the days when poetry was deemed a kind of supernatural possession . . . ; the result is that Betjeman's poems, however trivial or lighthearted their subjects, always carry a kind of primitive vivacity that sets them apart from the verses of his contemporaries and captures the reader's attention in advance of his intellectual consent:

> Miss J. Hunter Dunn, Miss J. Hunter Dunn,
> Furnish'd and burnish'd by Aldershot sun,
> What strenuous singles we played after tea,
> We in the tournament—you against me!

> (pp. xxv-xxvi)

[Betjeman is] someone to whom every poem seems to *matter* in a rare refreshing way. For Betjeman's poems, forthright, comprehensible, and couched in the marked button-holing rhythms of Praed or Tennyson, are nothing if they are not personal: they are exclusively about things that impress, amuse, excite, anger or attract him, and—and this is most important— once a subject has established its claim on his attention he never questions the legitimacy of his interest. Energy most contemporary poets put into screening their impulses for security Betjeman puts into the poem.

The result is, at first sight, a poetic corpus of extreme oddity: Betjeman, we remember, has a mind of extraordinary originality; there is no one else remotely like him. And yet his actual subjects, insofar as they are classifiable, are familiar enough: topography, religion, satire, death, love and sex, people and childhood take care of four fifths of the pieces, and really only an occasional poem is totally eccentric (for instance, **"The Heart of Thomas Hardy"**). The uniqueness lies in his approach, a blend of the direct and the round-about. The verse just quoted is the opening of a love poem, yet what could be simultaneously more personal and ironic than the first line? The passionate reiteration of the beloved's name in a form in which it would appear, say, on her visiting card conveys that she is clearly seen by the poet in the context of the middle classes, and that this increases her attraction for him. Betjeman has told us that the poem was the expression of his feelings for a superintendent in the canteen of the Ministry of Information during the war, but even in such a traditionally direct exercise he has to invent the *persona* of a subaltern (or junior army officer), stage an imaginary (and somewhat masochistic) tennis match in Aldershot, and follow it with the most suburban of club dances. All this apparatus is necessary before he can say what he wishes to say: . . . the poem's feeling is genuine, even if the properties are fiction—yet even the properties have, perhaps, a kind of truth. (pp. xxvi-xxviii)

[The subject of **"The Metropolitan Railway"** is] a young Edwardian married couple (''your parents''—or his?) who come to London to work and shop respectively, and meet at Baker Street Station in the evening to go back together to ''autumn-scented Middlesex again.'' In this case Betjeman first fixes our attention on a light-fitting of the period that remains in the station buffet the pair would have used: slowly he ''tracks'' (the cinematic metaphor is almost inevitable) to the couple's arrival and day in Edwardian (''safe hydraulic lift'') London; sharply the poem ''cuts'' to the poignantly brutal:

> Cancer has killed him. Heart is killing her.
>   The trees are down. An Odeon flashes fire
> Where stood their villa . . .

and its last line takes us back to the station buffet again with its hanging electrolier, the *art nouveau* of an age when ''Youth and Progress were in partnership,'' but now we see it with a new understanding of its place in the poem. (pp. xxviii-xxix)

[This kind of poetry] has its parallel with Betjeman's kind of architecture: just as that meant ''our whole over-populated island,'' so the poetry means the furniture of our lives: **"The Metropolitan Railway"** is about the lives of an Edwardian married couple, and by implication all married couples, but take away the early electric suburban railway, the period light-fitting, the ''sepia views of leafy lanes in Pinner,'' and the poem collapses. Betjeman is a true heir of Thomas Hardy, who found clouds, mists and mountains ''unimportant beside the wear on a threshold, or the print of a hand'': his poems are about the threshold, but it and they would be nothing without the wear. (pp. xxix-xxx)

Betjeman is consistent: he has said what he believes in, whether in architecture or poetry, and it is the backbone of his verse, at once its strength and its appeal. Of course it is not always imbued with compassion; sometimes it is tinged with fun—it would be a poor account of Betjeman that didn't say he is a master of the comic and the absurd—sometimes with amorousness, sometimes with satire: for someone often accused of tenderness towards the establishment, Betjeman spends an unusual amount of time attacking things, sometimes with quite remarkable ferocity (**"Slough," "In Westminster Abbey"**). (pp. xxxi-xxxii)

It is customary to say that Betjeman fails as a satirist: he is certainly too kind a writer to be really savage. . . . But in fact Betjeman is an accepter, not a rejecter, of his time and the people he shares it with. The notion that he is a precious aesthete whose sensibilities are perpetually either quivering before Victoriana or shuddering at locutions such as ''toilet'' is totally misguided. On the contrary, he is a robust and responsive writer, registering ''Dear old, bloody old England'' with vivacious precision and affectionate alliteration quite beyond most avowed social realists. His gusto embraces it all— the mouldy remnants of the nineteenth century, the appalling monoliths of the twentieth . . .—all the sadness and silliness and snobbery is potential Betjeman material. I have sometimes thought that [*Collected Poems*] would be something I should want to take with me if I were a soldier leaving England: I can't think of any other poet who has preserved so much of what I should want to remember, nor one who, to use his own words, would so easily suggest ''It is those we are fighting for, foremost of all.'' This may not be an orthodox critical judgment, but I don't see why it shouldn't be taken into account.

I have every sympathy with the American reader faced with the task of arbitrating on the value of these poems. To start with, Betjeman constitutes a kind of distorting mirror in which all our critical catch-phrases appear in gross unacceptable parody. He is *committed, ambiguous,* and *ironic;* he is *conscious of literary tradition* (but quotes the wrong authors); he is a *satirist* (but on the wrong side); he has his own *White Goddess* (in blazer and shorts). And he has done all those things such as *forging a personal utterance, creating a private myth, bringing a new language and new properties to poetry,* and even . . . *giving back poetry to the general reader,* all equally undeniably, yet none of them in quite the way we meant. No wonder our keen critical tools twitch fretfully at his approach.

From this point of view alone he represents a worthwhile challenge to readers of any country: I can well imagine the American demurring, however, on the grounds that Betjeman is like cricket, something absolutely peculiar to these islands and in consequence absolutely unexportable. . . . Such an attitude would be understandable, but there are several points to be made in reply. First, and perhaps rather unexpectedly, an English reader would go some of the way with it. I know Brent, Wembley, Northolt, and so on are in Middlesex, because Betjeman tells me so, but I've never been there and what I feel about them depends entirely on what he tells me about them: they might as well be in New York State. In **"The Metropolitan Railway"** the same applies to all the place names; I don't know what the Bromsgrove Guild was (though I can guess), and I don't know where the quotation comes from in the last stanza. Some of Betjeman's poems are completely incomprehensible to me (e.g., **"The Irish Unionist's Farewell to Greta Hellstrom in 1922"**) while remaining emotionally potent. In sum, the English reader is going to need an annotated Betjeman almost as soon as the American.

Secondly, it isn't outrageously novel to expect a little topographical and period background to a work of literature on the part of its reader: think of James Joyce's Dublin. The crucial point is whether the reader gets enough out of the work initially to make it worth his while solving the references to deepen his enjoyment. In the case of Betjeman there are enough universal situations . . . to make this so; at a lighter level, there is enough fun to be had from the rhymes and metres. (pp. xxxii-xxxvi)

Betjeman is serious: his subjects are serious, and the fact that his tone can be light or ambivalent should not deceive us into thinking he does not treat them seriously. His texture is subtle, a constant flickering between solemn and comic, self-mockery and self-expression. . . . To compare him with Housman or Hopkins tempts one to talk in terms of poetic ballistics: they penetrate deeper, but he makes a bigger hole, by which I mean only that while I doubt if any of Betjeman's pieces can be advanced against "Tell me not here," or "I wake, and feel the fell of dark" (still less "The Wreck of the Deutschland"), he can claim a much greater range of theme and manner and metre. He offers us, indeed, something we cannot find in any other writer—a gaiety, a sense of the ridiculous, an affection for human beings and how and where they live, a vivid and vivacious portrait of mid-twentieth-century English social life. (p. xxxvii)

> *Philip Larkin, in an introduction to* Collected Poems
> *by John Betjeman, Houghton Mifflin Company, 1971,*
> *pp. xvii-xli.*

PETER THOMAS

In an extremely interesting and perceptive essay "On English and American Poetry" . . . , Stephen Spender pointed out how "the English poet still instinctively trusts to his own taste and to habits of composition handed down to him." Philip Larkin's own poetry he praised for its "peculiarly intimate English quality of personal, private witness" and found the most English characteristic of Robert Graves' work to be "an honesty; . . . the sense he gives of proving his statements by the test of his experienced feelings in actual living" so that "the literal event seems to coincide with the poetic one." All this could be said with equal truth of John Betjeman's closely wedded art and insight. Exercising his craft within the habits of rhyme and meter he has contentedly inherited from the past, his honesty of private witness not only evokes a very strong sense of atmosphere and place but also communicates a precise metaphysical awareness that irradiates the often trivial, often shady, actuality of his scenes with an intuition of the larger context of his Christian faith.

Nowhere is this better done than in the poem **"Christmas."** . . . The atmosphere evoked is comprehensively English in its juxtaposition of banal detail and generous intention. We are carried from city to country churches, from "provincial public houses" to "London shops on Christmas Eve," while "The bells of waiting Advent" ring over all. . . . Then comes a questioning of the image and its meaning that has set all this absurdly inadequate activity in motion, contrasting the "Baby in an ox's stall" seen in a stained-glass window with

> Bath salts and inexpensive scent
> And hideous ties so kindly meant,

until they are all caught up in the single, central astonishing Truth

> That God was Man in Palestine
> And lives to-day in Bread and Wine.

The "props" are those of *A Christmas Carol* (bells, stoves, oil-lamps, holly and bunting and clerks from the City), the mood is not unlike that of *A Child's Christmas In Wales,* but the vision is distinctively Betjeman's own, transforming all these "sweet and silly Christmas things" by referring them back to the Child who is also "The Maker of the stars and sea."

Looking at the versification, one is struck not merely by its polish but by its happy acceptance of well-tried prosodic forms. Betjeman writes, in fact, as if Eliot and Pound had never invented "Modern Poetry" or William Empson discovered "Seven Types of Ambiguity"—or poetry itself been smothered in the Halls of Academe with their proliferating light industry of literary criticism. He is not above weeping at Victorian ballads, says Larkin, or roaring out Edwardian comic songs. He is rash enough to believe that he can still address himself to the intelligent (and general) reader who knows what he likes and likes what he knows. This does not mean, however, that the work is trite or shoddy. On the contrary, while the tone varies from the serious to the very funny, the style itself shows consistently able craftsmanship and that sort of intelligence in the deployment of language which C. S. Lewis defined as *"wit-ingenium."* Betjeman may not stand with Shakespeare or Milton among the giants of English poetry, but he is certainly among the very gifted and accomplished. Larkin places him with Thomas Hardy, Tennyson, Crabbe and Cowper in a dynasty not to be despised.

Like Hardy, with whom his poems conduct a skirmish or two . . . , Betjeman cherishes a passion for architecture, especially English church architecture. Many of his titles are simply the name of a town, a village, a county or a building and many more of his poems are filled with place names euphoniously or ironically used. He has an eye for the significant, characteristic detail and dwells, lovingly or disgustedly, on the object or environment of his choice. An Oxford bus-stop, a London railway station, even a dated electrolier in the Baker Street Metropolitan Railway Station Buffet: none is beneath his notice. (pp. 290-92)

[An] acute and comprehensive awareness of the aspirations inherent in a faded past and the indignities embodied in a strident present give strength and body and edge to poem after poem. Essentially a polite and charitable man, Betjeman is nonetheless capable of a just and terrible anger (as in **"Slough,"** where he prays for "friendly bombs" to blow its ugliness to smithereens) or a controlled and deadly indignation (as in **"Harvest Hymn,"** where another fine hymn is parodied to show us what the countryside has now become at the hands of slick exploiters). He achieves a more poignant, though no less telling, apposition of what once we were and what are now in the strange ambivalence of the love poem **"In Willesden Churchyard."** In the tradition of Marlowe and of English folk song, the poet-swain invites his beloved to walk with him "to Neasden lane." They visit the grave of Laura Seymour where the coffin of Charles Reade, author of *The Cloister And The Hearth,* "lies with hers" and the poet speculates whether Laura was Reade's mistress and gave him her tender inspiration when the monkish Oxford don came down by coach.

This may suggest that the poem lies somewhere between Marvell's "Coy Mistress" and Gray's "Elegy"; and so, to a point, it is a conjuration of both these. What gives it a grimly modern edge is what has happened in the churchyard:

> The chemicals from various factories
> Have bitten deep into the Portland stone
> And streaked the white Carrara of the graves
> Of many a Pooter and his Caroline,
> Long laid to rest among these dripping trees. . . .

There is none of Gray's gentle, romantic melancholy here; nor the wryness of Marvell's "fine and private place." Nor will the swain allow either his girl or us to remain in addled surmise over the possibly clandestine relationship between Laura and her friend. . . . (p. 292)

[The poem moves from] old mortality to fear of death to God's present immanence in the neighboring tabernacle: what a movement to grow out of a visit to a grave! Within its brief compass, this poem follows a pattern not unlike some of the meditations in Sir Thomas Browne's *Religio Medici*. (p. 293)

Looking again at **"In Willesden Churchyard,"** one is compelled to admire the ease with which so many complex elements have been woven into its structure. There is a sense of history and of immediate setting, an easy familiarity with fellow poets who have handled similar themes in similar forms, and a dramatic awareness of those (both dead and dying) who are in the churchyard now. But these are qualities common to all Betjeman's work—and taken together they may help to explain what "architecture" really means in this context and why Larkin feels that architecture takes priority over poetry in Betjeman's heart. Better still, one might say that he cultivates a vision in which the two are inseparably mated. "For architecture," he has written in a passage Larkin quotes with obvious approval, "means not a house, or a single building or a church . . . but your surroundings; not a town or a street, but our whole over-populated island."

Inevitably, that vision has darkened through the years as the poet has watched the age of progress bring increasing damage to the people and their environment. In his **"Harvest Hymn"** he sees them "spray the fields and scatter / The poison on the ground." . . . Country towns grow equally ugly and increasingly congested, seaside resorts charge ever-higher prices for ever-shoddier service and London itself becomes ever more impersonal and undistinguished as historic buildings of humane size and proportion are replaced by gigantic blocks of concrete, steel and glass.

People often ask me here what Britain is really like. Now I can offer them a guidebook far more revealing, because far more honest and perceptive, than anything put out by the sellers of the tourist trade. It is all there in John Betjeman's *Collected Poems*. . . . (pp. 293-94)

Peter Thomas, "John Bull Speaks: Reflections on the Collected Poems of John Betjeman," in Western Humanities Review, *Vol. XXVII, No. 3, Summer, 1973, pp. 289-94.*

G. M. HARVEY

In this essay I wish to discuss briefly what seem to me to be the central features of Betjeman's commitment to life, to suggest a few of the reasons for the growing sense of urgency in his writing, and by considering his poetry of almost the last decade, collected in his latest volume, *A Nip in the Air* (1974), I want also to indicate something of the complexity of his technique. I also hope to answer his critics' main objection to his work, which is still made occasionally against Larkin, that his poetry ignores important issues. (p. 112)

[Although] he writes from within the essentially middle-class tradition of English liberal humanism, Betjeman has been a consistently subversive force in modern English poetry, and it is clear from his latest poems that his criticism of English society has taken on an angrier tone. A second element in his writing is the increasingly powerful note of spiritual anguish, a deepening of the religious doubt and despair which was evident in an earlier poem, **"Tregardock,"** in his volume, *High and Low* (1966). . . . In his later poems it is the urgency of Betjeman's social anger and spiritual anguish which seem to me to characterise his response to life as it really is, but the depth of his personal commitment does not hinder the poetry from exploring some of the fundamental issues of twentieth-century life and expanding into an accurate general statement of the human condition.

In an important sense, his subversive attack on the values of contemporary society is a corollary of his profound reverence for places. Betjeman insistently questions the validity of the notion of progress, in the headlong pursuit of which the modern world heedlessly destroys both the community and the natural environment. In **"Dilton Marsh Halt"**, for instance, his defence of a small country railway station threatened with closure is not mere sentimental preservationism or debased romanticism. The station is worth preserving, not for economic reasons or even to gratify nostalgia, but because it retains for us in a vital way a close contact with the realities of the natural world, imaged by the red sky and the cedar tree, insistent reminders of our human scale, which we ignore at our peril. The poem mocks our allegiance to the illusory idea of progress, for our linear view of time is merely the creation of human reason, expressing the human ego on a cosmic scale. Time, Betjeman reminds us, is not linear but cyclical, like the life which envelops the little station. . . . (pp. 112-13)

The interdependence of time and space and the crucial importance of our retaining a fundamentally human perspective of their relation in our lives is the subject of **"Back from Australia."** The irony of the natural image in the first stanza of the travelers "Cocooned in Time, at this inhuman height" stresses the unnaturalness of the claustrophobic environment [of an airplane]. . . . Betjeman's savage mockery of this technological miracle and "all the chic accoutrements of flight" is rooted in his profound awareness of how it distorts the human scale and the second, counterpointed stanza makes a full and complete contrast as he stands with relief at home in Cornwall looking up at the night sky. Surrounded by the permanent realities of land, sea and sky in their natural frame, he experiences a sense of space and time expanding again to their proper dimension and real significance. Seen from the human point of view, the "hurrying autumn skies" form a dramatic and vital relation with the land, . . . while the cosmic interrelation of time and space is emphatically present in the rhythm of the seasons. Betjeman's technique of contrapuntal points of view serves to stress once more the paradoxically dehumanising effect of human progress. In the totally human world of the airplane our attention is dominated by the paraphernalia employed to obliterate time, while in the second stanza the isolated figure standing amidst the huge grandeur of the natural world focusses our vision on the human perspective . . . and the poet experiences the liberating sanity of true human scale.

Betjeman's concern for the preservation not merely of fine buildings but the human frame of things which they represent is not reactionary but, ironically, in modern society with its commitment to size, growth and change for their own sakes, economically and politically subversive. As its whimsical title suggests, **"The Newest Bath Guide"** satirises "progressive" development. Old Bath, with its chapels, assembly rooms, springs, terraces and sordid backstreets asserted the sheer variety of human life. Modern Bath, however, is symbolised for Betjeman by the stark monolithic structure of its new technical college. Life is now governed, not by a humanistic ethic but by the technological, commercial ethic, and taste now finds expression in "working out methods of cutting down cost". Because purely human and aesthetic needs are no longer considered significant, proportion and texture are lost in a "uniform nothingness". There is, Betjeman suggests, a fundamentally and powerfully reciprocal relation between people and their environment. The vital humanity and frank sexuality of eighteenth-century Bath have been destroyed by the Puritan work ethic, by the consequent emasculation of its architecture, and the climax of the poem makes a satirical statement of the concomitant, profound loss of human stature.... (pp. 114-15)

Betjeman's criticism of bureaucracy for its blind acquiescence in the debasement of human values is amplified in **"Executive"**, which ... castigates the corruptibility of public officials by private interests. Fundamentally the poem, which records a chance meeting between a young developer and the aging preservationist, makes a savagely accurate attack on a modern idol who is really a modern monster.... At first the young man's brash assurance and obsession with status symbols seem harmless and amusing, but this mask is abruptly dropped when his style and the brutal reality it habitually conceals are juxtaposed in the couplet: "A luncheon and a drink or two, a little *savoir faire*—/I fix the Planning Officer, the Town Clerk and the Mayor". This sudden emergence of his covert thuggery reveals him as a profound threat to social order.... [His] habitual debasement of the language of human intercourse both masks and symbolises his endless destruction of the traditional, civilised values of order, integrity and humanity, while his childlike love of dangerous toys and his boast of slaughtering pedestrians with his sports car display his fundamentally anarchic and nihilistic impulses. (pp. 115-16)

For Betjeman, this young man is the modern hero, embodying the values of his society. And while the new, rootless, uncommitted elements in Enigsh society attack its physical and moral fabric, Betjeman feels that one can no longer rely on the traditional, conservative influence of the landed class to assert its civilising power and prop up the tottering structure. In the savagely satirical poem, **"County"**, he turns his anger on the county set, the "Porkers" as he calls them symbolically. Devoid even of political principles, they have lost their historical sense of social obligation and surrendered to the modern acquisitive culture. Their world now revolves around the domestic trivia of tax-evasion, servants' wages and interminable shopping. Bereft of their social function, they employ traditional rituals to mask the hollowness of their useless lives. But the men's shooting is also a potent symbol of the anarchic, destructive instincts which threaten to pierce the well-bred vacuum, just as the social competition of the dominant women reveals neuroticism and moral fatigue.... As the covert parallel in their loud talk of "meets and marriages" implies, neurotic, self-indulgent, bored, this is a predatory society which has turned inwards upon itself. Fundamentally, Betjeman portrays a claustrophobic, nihilistic world, bound by meaningless

tradition and not strong enough to resist the insidious corruption of materialism. This stratum of society, affectionately dealt with in Betjeman's early poetry, is now seen as morally as well as physically flabby.... At the end of the poem Betjeman's residual sympathy for the county set comes as something of a surprise; but this is part of its covert rhetoric of irony.... [His] sympathy implies nothing less than a damning indictment of the moribund class structure of English society, in which habitual attitudes and moral and social realities no longer reflect each other.

Betjeman's consistent, remorseless probing of the weaknesses of English social institutions includes the church. **"Lenten Thoughts of a High Anglican"** is a quietly whimsical poem, which on closer reading turns out to be subtly and powerfully subversive. Fundamentally it challenges not only the church's doctrines but the whole relevance of institutionalised religion. The poem describes his religious response to a beautiful woman worshipping at his church.... However, the poem is a carefully conceived structural irony, and his celebration of the human in a religious setting leads directly to the poem's central statement in the pivotal fourth stanza:

> How elegantly she swings along
> In the vapoury incense veil;
> The angel choir must pause in song
> When she kneels at the altar rail

This paradox, that the divine must also worship the human, which involves a daring reversal of perspective, counterpoints the parson's pious warning that staring around in church hinders our search for the "Unknown God". Like Blake, in "The Divine Image", Betjeman recognises that every man and woman is a perfectly unique centre of religious experience, and this stands in contrast to the church's traditional teaching of Pauline theology. Betjeman suggests that we learn the world's spiritual frame by knowing its Creator in another and in oneself, and he does so with a wry yet emphatically satirical apology to institutionalised religion.... Like Blake's child in "A Little Boy Lost", the poet's wise innocence and imagination quietly confound bureaucratically guarded knowledge, with its emphasis on mystery, the arduous search for God, the centrality of church ritual and the discipline of the instincts symbolised by Lent. For Betjeman the church provides quite inadvertently the context for worship of an instinctive and spontaneous kind. His God frankly embraces femininity, sexuality and emancipated modernity, and there is a subdued zest in his kicking over theological and ecclesiastical traces in order to illuminate a spiritual truth.

Most of his later poems which deal with religious themes are governed by his deepening horror at the facts of life and death, by a sense of doubt and loss. **"Aldershot Crematorium"** is a truthful and compelling response to the modern way of death. Sandwiched between the swimming-pool and the cricket-ground, the crematorium creates a dominant image of the casual interpenetration of life and death, but this is only fully experienced in the shock of seeing the smoke from the furnace chimney.... [The] brutal juxtaposition of the vital solidity of the flesh with the air into which it dissolves enforces our true reverence for the human body, particularly because our sense of another's identity depends so much on purely physical attributes. More importantly, perhaps, the hideous incongruity of the transformation, like a grotesque conjuring trick, denies death its proper human dimension and baffles our natural responses.

The crematorium, tastefully hidden in the suburbs, hygenic and efficient, also represents modern society's peculiar treatment of death. It is an obscenity. But although death can be ignored, it will not go away. . . . This paradox is humanised as the mourners talk anxiously about the weather and living (" 'Well, anyhow, it's not so cold today' ") but the undercurrent of macabre irony lurking in this mundane phrase only pierces their thin facade and reinforces by grim contrast their underlying thoughts of the furnace. Betjeman thus makes the whole situation of the poem focus our attention on its central paradox. Cremation emphasises so insistently the incontrovertible reality of a merely material universe that simple but profoundly human questions about the nature of resurrection and the possible form of a new spiritual identity become, for the modern sceptical age, irrelevant. Modern man seeks to escape his fear in the temporary oblivion which materialism affords, but for a believer, like Betjeman, death presents a constant challenge to his own sense of spiritual identity. . . . (pp. 116-19)

Betjeman's anguish at being trapped in the vacuum between faith and doubt proceeds from an often appalling sense of cosmic isolation. In **"Loneliness"** he explores the personal paradox of his simultaneous belief and unbelief. In tone and feeling he frequently recalls Matthew Arnold, in "Dover Beach" for instance, but his confrontation with his personal hell of doubt and despair is more dramatic and urgent. The poem proceeds on two levels in a vain attempt to relate the natural and metaphysical worlds, symbolised by nature and the Easter bells; but the poem's organising symbol is an infinitely expanding and contracting universe, which bewilders and terrifies the poet and which gives the poem its emotional tautness. The Easter bells, with their message of assurance, open for him huge vistas of spiritual joy, . . . but this is at once qualified by the poet's scepticism ("O ordered metal clatter-clang!/Is yours the song the angels sang?"), and the universe immediately shrinks to the compass of his own timid, shivering ego. . . . (p. 119)

In the second, contrapuntal stanza [of **"Loneliness,"**] Betjeman seeks refuge in nature, but finds there only further cruel paradoxes. He extends the bitter image of himself as the last year's leaves on the beech waiting to be pushed aside by new growth, for the springtime regeneration of the natural world reminds him of the certainty of his own decay and death. Ironically, the only new growth possible for him will itself hasten dissolution: "For, sure as blackthorn bursts to snow,/Cancer in some of us will grow". This cruel image underlines the paradox that, although part of the natural world, the poet is cut off from its cycles of death and rebirth. Like the bells, nature is impassive to this suffering, nor can a materialistic society offer any consolation. . . . For the total sceptic the "tasteful crematorium door" can shut out temporarily the roar of the furnace, but for Betjeman the bells repeatedly speak of his death, yet also hold the painful echo of an irretrievably lost faith. In the last stanza the sound of the Easter bells infinitely extends a universe which is now appallingly deserted and which strikes answering hollow depths in his own being. . . . The bells represent for Betjeman what the Dover sea did for Arnold, but unlike Arnold he can find no consolation either in human love or in the natural universe.

These later poems of Betjeman are important because they deal with large issues, although they are often located in the local and familiar, and like Arnold's, Betjeman's personal crises expand into a poignant general statement of the human condition. The poem **"On Leaving Wantage 1972"** explicitly records such a crisis, which is employed to explore the complex relations between place, time, faith and identity. Betjeman's

leaving Wantage with his wife after twenty years raises the issue of the nature of human identity in an acute form. The poem opens with a lyrical evocation, rich in colour and movement, of the centrality of place in human life. . . . But essentially it is an imagistic poem, developing its metaphysic from the conjunction of disparate and concretely realised images, which force the reader to adopt an altered point of view. . . . [While] the poem is apparently about a particular place and the poet's clinging to the things he loved there for reassurance of his identity, . . . its true subject is time, for time is contained in place and humanised by it. Betjeman examines the ways, trivial and magnificent, in which time is manifested in place. There is the tedious succession of days, of which he is reminded by the faint reek of last night's fish and chips, the weekly newspapers emphasising our linear view of time, the rhythms of the seasons and of the Christian calendar, and beyond that stretches the whole history of Christianity and the timelessness of its faith. . . . The central paradox of the poem is that place contains all time, while here time also contains and unites place.

Betjeman's clinging to a particular place where time has been contained and ordered, where this peculiar synthesis has in a real sense created and sustained human identity, is an attempt to find a temporary refuge from time manifested outside place which, for the sceptic, becomes an impersonal abstraction and a force of dissolution. The poet feels that time in this form is the enemy of human significance and therefore that leaving Wantage is a symbolic act forshadowing death as they are whirled away "Till, borne along like twigs and bits of straw,/ We sink below the sliding stream of time." A further irony is concealed in the time frame of the poem, which is given as the third Sunday after Easter. Equidistant between the Resurrection and Pentecost, it reminds him of his own suspension between hope and faith, of his inability to achieve the bells' promised transcendence of place and time, and the poem ends with an honest, painful statement of confusion and loss.

Behind the covert horror of so much of Betjeman's later writing there also lies a hard-won equilibrium of temper. It is this Augustan sense of balance between private and public, imagination and reason, commitment and detachment, sympathy and irony, which marks the fundamental sanity of his poetry. This balance controls the tone and form of **"Hearts Together"**, which describes an occasion in Betjeman's youth, the solitary encounter of two adolescent lovers on a Dorset beach. Its situation, its theme—the human capacity for self-deception and the power of time to correct this distortion of values—and the colour and rhythm of the opening lines ("How emerald the chalky depths/Below the Dancing Ledge!") are Hardyesque, but the development of the poem is quintessentially Betjeman.

The lovers' sexual encounter occurs after a swim during which they pull up jelly-fishes and thoughtlessly leave them to die on a hedge in the hot sun, thus creating by an act of gratuitous cruelty, their own appropriate sexual symbol. . . . As Betjeman's heavy irony stresses, they create the universe in the reflex of their own egos and the ensuing meeting of their intellects is also incongruously and comically out of touch with reality. . . . [The] familiar Betjeman counterpoint is apparent in the two distinct tones of voice which he employs, the youthful voice of innocence, carrying the rhetoric of sympathy, and the mature voice of experience, enforcing the perspective of irony. (pp. 119-22)

[The lovers'] self-consciously modern equation of rationality and happiness is simply ironic because it conceals from them the supremacy of the purely physical in their relationship, while their youthful arrogance in explaining the universe is made ludicrously ironic by the worlds of beauty and mystery by which they are surrounded and which they ignore or casually destroy. Thus the poem's most significant irony lies in the parallel which Betjeman makes between the jelly-fish's ''self-effacing'' physical death in the sun and their own moral oblivion as they lie scorched on the beach imprisoned in narrow egoism. For Betjeman a moral universe which embraces the arts but cannot include nature reveals a profound ignorance of the importance of true human scale and, from the point of view of the poet's maturity, an ignorance of the power of time to alter moments which seem eternally significant. So by the end of the poem the full irony of its title emerges. What he has recollected is not, as he once thought, a union of emancipated hearts, but a casual conjunction of youthful bodies and minds bound together by self-indulgence, naivete, cruelty and egoism. True emancipation, the poem suggests, lies in the lovers' mature ability in the present to place the illusions of the past in their proper temporal frame. However, the severity of this judgment is tempered by the affectionate, mocking tone which conveys the poet's sympathy for his youthful self and his realisation that his past is only part of a universal experience.

In Betjeman's poetry his commitment to life as it really is is balanced by his insistence on the need to maintain a comic stance towards it, and in this he is, I think, closer to the Augustans than to the Victorians or the moderns. In his early poetry comedy was a form of social celebration, but in his later writing it has also become both an instrument for satire and for personal defence against the horrors of age and death. In **''The Last Laugh''**, which has a splendidly Yeatsian economy and objectivity, Betjeman's final pleas is not for joy, or assurance, or even consolation, but for laughter:

> I made hay while the sun shone.
>   My work sold.
> Now, if the harvest is over
>   And the world cold,
> Give me the bonus of laughter
>   As I lose hold.

The humanising quality of comedy allows Betjeman to transcend the anger and anguish of life, and his choice of laughter to help him towards death testifies to his profound belief in the importance of human scale and human values. It is this fundamental commitment to life as it really is that makes Betjeman a truly significant poet. (pp. 123-24)

> G. M. Harvey, *"Poetry of Commitment: John Betjeman's Later Writing,"* in The Dalhousie Review, *Vol. 56, No. 1, Spring, 1976, pp. 112-24.*

STEPHEN MEDCALF

A few months ago there were published some characteristically acerbic and urgent letters from Evelyn Waugh accusing John Betjeman of regarding religion ''as a source of pleasurable emotions and sensations'' and calling on him to come out of the Church of England, round which, in that spirit, he had built his ''life and learning and art''. *Church Poems* and the new edition of *Parish Churches* might be regarded as Sir John's equally characteristic response, oblique, gentle and triumphant. *Church Poems* contains thirty poems of which two are new, the rest from *Poems in the Porch* and other earlier collections. . . .

Like any notable poet, Betjeman may be taken in two ways: as the maker of a handful or two of absolute poems which rest for technique on a mass of craftsmanlike verse: or as the utterer of a unique voice which varies in power but which always, in some degree, for those who have been caught by it, enchants. . . . No doubt *Church Poems* (although it contains half a dozen that should be counted absolute poems) was compiled primarily for those to whom the voice is irresistible. But it is in the end fatal to good reading to separate the two kinds of appreciation.

If Waugh were right, then the voice would only be concerned with chatting on about churches and the humours of those that use them. In fact, it is not accidental nor dispensable that many of Betjeman's poems end by talking about the *function* of a church as a place to pray in.

For in Betjeman's world, churches are not isolated as a source of aesthetic sensation. They are inseparable from the general life of the community. . . . And they are inseparable from their function . . . ; the introduction to *Parish Churches* [states], ''the purpose of the church remains . . . to be a place where the Faith is taught and the Sacraments are administered''. . . .

Betjeman's articulation of love may not seem to be everybody's. ''Odi et amo'', he says in the introduction to *Parish Churches,* sums up the general opinion of the Church of England among the few who are not apathetic, and although he substitutes for this the motto ''To God's Glory and the honour of the Church of England'', still ''I hate and I live'' may seem no bad description of ''Betjemanic irony''.

But then there are objects for which intelligent love could only take that form: a good many of the environments, for example, of which the Church of England forms the heart and identity:

> Church of England bells of Westgate . . .
> You have one more message yet
> ''Plimsolls, plimsolls in the summer
> Oh goloshes in the wet!''

Comic: yes, and when the same bells recall the children . . . , even a little sickening; but true. Humanity finds it very difficult to accept an attitude which is neither passionately adoring nor passionately disillusioned nor weary of both: and Betjeman's poems are often called ironic or eccentric when they are merely (as Charles Williams said of a not altogether dissimilar poet, Swift) ''actuality circumfused by poetry''.

But the tradition to which Betjeman belongs is too kindly to be Swift's. It is certainly, nevertheless, Church of England: and where it goes back to is a matter that might concern Evelyn Waugh, since it touches on the question of continuity—whether the Church of England or the Church of Rome better represents the English Church of the Middle Ages. Gentle, satirical, odd, lustful, pious, sceptical, humorous, aware of being the style of little man, yet self-confident, deeply attached to that aspect of the Church of England . . . where sacrament and folk-custom overlap, the line seems to me to go back through Herrick and Corbet to Skelton and Hawes. . . . [Above] all it is by their self-confident insecurity, which causes their tone to be continually escaping the reader, that those poets are linked [to Betjeman].

The whole tone is one of many products of a church which tries to adjust itself to, and yet to consecrate actual human society. But Betjeman has further qualities which put him above Corbet and Hawes, perhaps above Skelton or Herrick. His own personal voice, plaintive, confiding, full of doubt but self-possessed, learned, seeming to dare its readers not to be interested in everything that interests him, has an amazing power to change our apprehension of the world. The power to make up love, a little, such environments as Westgate is obvious. . . . But the conquest of new areas of language is as remarkable. . . .

> The chandeliers would twinkle gold:
> As pre-Tractarian sermons roll'd
> Doctrinal, sound and dry.

I suppose it is the placing of the one obviously praising word of three, ''sound'', between the normally deadly ''doctrinal'' and ''dry'' that enables the whole line to take its place in a context of passionate nostalgia and even devotion, and itself to express those feelings. . . .

Such delicacy with words makes it not unreasonable to compare Betjeman with one of the greatest of poets, of whose balance and eye for detail the first word used is again ''irony'': Chaucer, to whom after all most traditions in English poetry do go back. To believe in the Christian God; to be nevertheless obsessed with time and death, yet to love life in its complexity; to have a sharp eye for detail, especially topical, and a gift for creating characters at once eccentric and universal; to be a deft maker of poetry of all kinds, and yet to be most naturally associated with humorous verse; to cultivate a poet's persona, but with the implication that such a persona is only important if it amuses; to make no absolute boundary of decorum between humorous and solemn: these are all qualities at once Betjemanic and medieval (the ecclesiastical nature of so many of Betjeman's satiric objects of course helps here). . . . but they are most particularly Chaucerian. It is possible to come closer to the tone of the lines:

> Nas never pyk walwed in galauntine
> As I in love am walwed and ywounde

which have puzzled commentators, than to imagine a topical simile from a Betjemanic love poem? To such similes the question—serious or not serious?—is almost inapplicable: they are just the products of men who see things with a singular realism, from a series of odd angles.

Betjeman implies that understanding of the Middle Ages comes to him rarely and dimly ''on a hot summer Sunday morning in the country when I have been reading Chaucer to the sound of bells pouring through the trees''. But then has a day passed when Betjeman has not been listening to the sound of bells, which, like Froude, he thinks the last echo of the Middle Ages? They echo through his poetry. I suppose he likes them because they are at once ephemeral and permanent, something to be compared to what he loves similarly, the waves of the sea or a river. . . . They ring thanks for him, and doom, birth and marriage and death. They embody his feeling for the Church. . . .

So often Betjeman seems to become the humorous self-deprecating English Proust, whether in social observation, the oddity of his sexual persona. . . . or that quasimystical sense of time and something beyond time. It is the bells above all that create this sense, sounding differently at different times and angles, but always the same. Betjeman's latest verse, scarcely a poem, rather an ''improvement'' like one of Beerbohm's on some lines from the Reverend James Hurdis's ''Village Curate'', tells us the same thing of Magdalen bells: ''When I was twelve, as deep they were to me/As now they sound when I am seventy-three''—just the same ''loud exhilarating peal,/Now dying all away, now faintly heard'' by Hurdis in the 1780s. For this effect, Betjeman transforms Hurdis's lines, which are full of

boyish exuberance in the original . . . into a Nunc Dimittis. That underlines the desired effect: which is further enlarged by the setting of the lines in *Church Poems* as a pendant to **''Church of England Thoughts occasioned by hearing the bells of Magdalen Tower from the Botanic Garden, Oxford on St. Mary Magdalen's Day.''** There the bells, as in **''House of Rest''**, summon to Eucharist, and the end of it all is

> I thank the bells of Magdalen Tower.

The ''heart and identity'' of Betjeman's poems, as of the Christian religion which he professes, is thanksgiving.

> *Stephen Medcalf, ''To the Sound of Bells,'' in* The Times Literary Supplement, *No. 4069, March 27, 1981, p. 335.*

JOHN CAREY

In England, Hilaire Belloc once noted, the mention of poetry will disperse a crowd faster than a fire hose. English poets, if they want an audience, have to find ways of neutralizing this native distaste, and Sir John Betjeman's solution has been to masquerade as a sad clown—a loveable, woebegone Peter Pan, keening over the nursery teas and teddy bears of his lost Elysium. It has proved wildly successful. . . .

And quite right too. For beneath the clown's mask can be descried traits that have, in the past, signalled major poets: the howling gulfs of implacable emotion, the rigorous technical mastery, the lonely, uncompromising vision. With Betjeman, appearances are always deceptive. The affable bumbler seethes with hate inside: it escapes, now and then, in acrid spurts—**''Come, friendly bombs, and fall on Slough''**, for example, or the joyous paean at the scene of a car crash where ''the first-class brains of a senior civil servant'' lie scattered on the road.

Deceptive, too, is the air of misty nostalgia the poems give off. No poet is in fact more precise, as Philip Larkin, an eager disciple, has insisted. Betjeman's poetic realm brims with exact locations like a street directory, its actuality certified by swarms of brand names and architectural data. Alone among the poets of his generation, Betjeman has catalogued our real suburban world in which housewives queue at MacFisheries and Elaine, in well-cut Windsmoor, daintily alights at Ruislip Gardens. Nor (it's another of his enriching complications) does his rapture over such mundane epiphanies prevent him from looking forward with satisfaction to the day when humankind will wipe itself out, and leave the globe to the starfish and the hawthorn. . . .

[*Uncollected Poems* includes], among some duds, poems no sensible reader will miss. The best of them touch on dying, that undying Betjeman bug-bear. Whatever his relations with contemporary life, he is unchallengeably the laureate of contemporary death, and has traced, in poem after poem, its horribly normal advance from the preliminary twinge . . . to the fatal X-ray photographs and the hospital bed, conveniently placed for you to hear your relatives, in the car park below, making off cheerily to tea and telly.

Unlike most poets, Betjeman has added terrors to death, presenting moments so real that they become part of your own premonitions. This is true, for instance, of **''Devonshire St., W. I''**, arguably his best poem, where the doomed patient steps aghast from the consulting room into a newly alien world:

> No hope. And the iron nob of this palisade
> So cold to the touch, is luckier now than he.

Uncollected Poems contains nothing as haunting as that, but there is a plaintive monologue spoken by a retired postal clerk . . . which catches the triteness of grief with cruel accuracy, and there are two poems about hell. . . .

Betjeman and hell have always been a problem. What, you wonder, has he done to make him so sure he'll go there? True, there are several rather enigmatic poems about betraying a girl and leading a double life (a new one, **"Guilt"**, appears here); but even supposing these were autobiographical, such a lapse could hardly merit eternal combustion. Or could it? . . . Betjeman's hellfire God has puzzlingly little in common with the gracious diety portrayed in other poems (**"Christmas"**, say), and the intellectual difficulties of a belief in hell are never faced. . . .

Of course, no Christian's terror of hell will be diminished by rational argument, least of all Betjeman's. His brain is poised on an extremely sensitive ejector seat, and at the merest mention of religion it vanishes with a melodious whizz. Its loss doesn't matter much in the long run, because his poetry always draws on emotion rather than reason for its strength. His basic conviction that the world ought ideally to be organized for the preservation of thatched cottages and old railway lines is not conspicuously reasonable, though it appeals to something stubbornly regressive in many thinking people.

His social views, in the satirical poems, depend likewise on irrational loathing—of businessmen, oilmen, admen, and planners of every sort. Only a simpleton could subscribe to the blanket vilification of such callings that Betjeman urges on us, or could believe, as he seems to, that there are bureaucrats at large eager to cover England with workers' flats and fields of soya beans. Betjeman substitutes these wild fantasies for rational thought because rational thought has demonstrably done nothing to stop the erosion of the England he loves, and because only the extravagance of unreason can match his disgust at the atrocities we surround ourselves with. . . .

[Betjeman's] belief in hell, and the shuddering anticipation of being tortured there himself, can be seen as facets of Betjeman's masochism. He gets delicious shivers, as the poems abundantly testify, from the idea of prostrating himself before muscular, sporty girls who whack things. . . . Betjeman's punitive God is, in one respect, an apotheosis of these beefy lovelies—a deity in drag, as it were, equipped with the divine equivalents of jodhpurs and riding whip. We should not laugh: or rather we should admire Betjeman for letting us laugh. Part of his stature comes (to quote Larkin again) from his being prepared to release feelings that we are ashamed of and so ridicule.

Besides, the wish to feel hurt is ultimately what prompts Betjeman's most poignant and beautiful lyrics. When he mourns for the enormous hayfields of Perivale, or the lovertrod lanes that once rambled round Tooting Bec, he is deliberately stimulating grief, as any poet must who aims to touch the buried springs of tenderness in us.

> *John Carey, "Love and the Laureate of Death," in*
> The Sunday Times, *London, January 9, 1983, p. 43.*

GAVIN EWART

Any book of verse by John Betjeman is likely to be understandable and enjoyable. [*Uncollected Poems*] is no exception, although it consists of work rejected from the previous books and 'occasional' poems (such as a very good book review in

verse). Some poems are low-grade by Betjeman standards. Often it is the ending of a poem that is weak (**"Interior Decorator"**). **"The Retired Postal Clerk"** is sheer Victorian sentimentality. **"The Lift Man"** is a performance piece—comic monologue. There are near-misses like **"Cheshire"**, the kind of topographical description that Betjeman has done better elsewhere. But there are some fine poems—**"Guilt"** in particular. **"The Old Land Dog"** is a very funny parody of Newbolt, while **"The Shires"** encapsulates a way of life. There are also some beautiful and effective lines, trees 'billowing like heaps of cushions on the sofa of the land'. Tennyson's power of matching a mood and a landscape is also Betjeman's. A liking for the diction and metres of *Hymns Ancient and Modern* has never left him, though it is not too obtrusive here. A line like 'Tis evening in the village school' looks eccentric in a living poet, but Betjeman has his own unmistakable voice, his own attitudes and his own honesty.

> *Gavin Ewart, in a review of "Uncollected Poems,"*
> in British Book News, *February, 1983, p. 116.*

THE LISTENER

[*The excerpt below is taken from a program originally broadcast on English radio. In this discussion, Anthony Thwaite and a group of poets and critics assess Betjeman's influence following his death.*]

'When Sir John Betjeman died in May 1984,' said Anthony Thwaite, . . . 'he'd been for many years, and had increasingly become, a national figure: not simply Poet Laureate, or television personality, or lovable eccentric, but a sort of mascot or emblem incorporating all of these and much more.' . . .

But what did other poets and critics really think of him? 'He is infernally difficult to get any sort of critical callipers on,' said Donald Davie. But Philip Larkin and Kingsley Amis both spoke out categorically in praise of him, and made their points in some detail.

Larkin said that he remembered the first poems very well, 'because I was at Oxford at the time, and they hit me like a bomb. . . . We'd never had this kind of primitive rhythm and sort of mad celebration. [Betjeman's poetry] wasn't a fine-drawn thing at all: it was just sheer, ludicrous, farcical excitement. What effect did [the poems] have on me?—well, they had no effect at all except to make me, I suppose, see that poetry could be something other than what it had been up till then, which was Auden and Eliot and Yeats and Dylan Thomas and all the people that we'd been reading.

'He seemed to me to bring a new kind of poetry into being. I know he wrote several sorts of poetry, but there was a kind of poems about places in terms of people, and poems about people in terms of places. . . . You can't really say this [poem] is about a place, or that's about a person; they're kind of mingled, you know, and that I don't think has been done by anybody else. You remember the advice his father gave him: "Let what you write be funny, John, and be original"—and that advice he carried out to the letter.

'I think he will survive as a poet of great energy. Once you begin reading a poem by Betjeman you immediately feel you're in good hands; he's not going to let you down. I love that feeling; it's a feeling I get from very few poets. But he seems to me more a dark poet than a light poet—a great obsession with death. The first poem in the first book he published—

"**Death in Leamington**"—it epitomises Betjeman: death on the one hand, the precise place on the other.'

Kingsley Amis also recalled his first impressions: 'I remember distinctly the first poem that sank in, which was "**Croydon**" in his first collection. I had naturally taken him to be what so many people already thought him to be and so many people still think of him as—a light, entertaining, extremely funny versifier. But then, you see, I paid especial attention to "**Croydon**", because I grew up near there. . . . [Reading the first few lines], I thought "This is sly fun going on." It's like an affectionate little postcard—a suburban scene. But then we see that it isn't just that and it ends with saying . . .

> Pear and apple in Croydon gardens
>   Bud and blossom and fall,
> But your Uncle Dick has left his Croydon
>   Once for all.

And I remember thinking "My God, I hadn't bargained for that." It's a very characteristic Betjeman thing, of course: it's that horrible dig in the ribs. Very often the message is, it seems, in the midst of life we're in death. It's not always that way but in the midst of ordinary, boring, amusing, vaguely entertaining life there's something unexpected done with incredible speed and incredible concentration.'

Tom Paulin, the Northern Irish poet, was impatient with all this admiration. 'He represents that anti-intellectual antiquarian streak that there is in English culture. For me he goes with a children's book I once read about a character called Molesworth, who tends to find things like old ear-trumpets in Hull. It's that kind of whimsy which, after a while, becomes terrible and frightening and surreal and bizarre, because of its enormous, trivialising stupidity.

'I don't think the work develops. I frankly find him a very absurd figure. . . . I think that when one looks at Betjeman from a European perspective he does seem to be an utterly ridiculous figure. Because he's so much on the surface, there's no complexity there: really he would interest somebody with a sociological approach to literature, and I think one could construct an interesting argument based on that. But in purely literary terms I don't think there's any interest at all, though one might like to compare him with Marvell. There's something similar there, . . . that fascination with long, hot afternoons and big girls. . . . It's there in Lewis Carroll. Perhaps it's the tradition they belong to, phantasmagoric Anglicanism.

'What he did was to take up Auden's interest in High Anglicanism in the Victorian Gothic and in minor Victorian poets, and in ancient industrial machinery. All these are things that one associates with Auden—in fact Auden said, late in life, that he thought that he had invented Betjeman while he was at Oxford. Betjeman processed them for a general public. But really everything was invented by Auden, I think, and Betjeman just took it over.' (p. 20)

Is part of the problem that Betjeman needs immediate recognition of all his allusions? There were two very different views on this. Larkin acknowledged that 'Betjeman doesn't export. In a way I can understand this, but again, having just witnessed the surprising but quite incontrovertible exportability of Barbara Pym, I am surprised by it. Why Barbara Pym should go down in America and Betjeman not, I don't know. They seem to me to be very much of a background. As for his needing glosses, well, he needs glosses in England. I mean, there's quite a lot in Betjeman I don't understand. . . . There are some poems of Betjeman I find completely incomprehensible. "**The Irish Unionist's Farewell to Greta Hellstrom in 1922**", for instance.' . . .

But Peter Porter didn't agree: 'Englishness is not a barrier to people that are not English understanding something, the reason being quite simply that the English have exported their Englishness, as it were, in such effective terms that people all round the world who have never set foot in the Home Counties can read Betjeman and understand him instantly. I think this is because Betjeman's Englishness, although wonderfully detailed in its surface with the Windsmoor scarves and the bottles of hair shampoo, and all his thousand-and-one brand-name details which people rejoice so much in getting from his poems— every bit of that is completely followable and will be found to be moving by people who have never set foot in modern England. You don't have to have travelled on the Metropolitan Railway out of Marylebone Station to understand Betjeman's world, because it is a world which has been so well sold by the English to the rest of the world that everyone knows it.'

Let Donald Davie have the last word: 'I think he might very well revert to being an élite reputation, which he was to begin with, because, after all, it seems to me that really to esteem these curious poems, so unlike anybody else's, you need to be very sophisticated. In their curious way, they're making extraordinarily sophisticated, intricate play with convention. But if we say that, that only means that he reverts, you see, to the élite that I would say that the true poet always does inhabit.' (p. 21)

"The Teddy Bear and the Critics," in The Listener, *Vol. 113, No. 2910, May 23, 1985, pp. 20-1.*

Rachel Billington

1942-

English novelist, scriptwriter, and author of children's books.

Billington's novels usually center on affluent but unhappy English men and women who search for fulfillment in their lives. Many of Billington's protagonists are shallow and vain individuals whose exaggerated sense of self-importance contributes to their discontent. Although Billington is sometimes faulted for her unsympathetic treatment of her protagonists, she is commended for depicting their vanities with perceptiveness and wit.

Billington's first novel, *All Things Nice* (1969), focuses on a rich, self-centered young English woman living in New York City whose interest in the problems of people she befriends is revealed to be superficial. *The Big Dipper* (1970) concerns the mental collapse of a middle-aged executive after his wife leaves him. Billington treats the breakdown in a humorous manner, detailing the man's subsequent indulgences in women and food with what one critic called "a giggling venom." *Lilacs out of the Dead Land* (1971) details an adulterous affair between an insecure young schoolteacher and a middle-aged businessman. In *Cock Robin* (1972), a clever Oxford scholar takes revenge against three female students who had taken advantage of him. *Beautiful* (1974) is the story of a narcissistic woman who uses her beauty to gain social status. *A Painted Devil* (1975) concerns a selfish artist who is eventually murdered by one of his models.

A Woman's Age (1979) deviates from Billington's previous novels and is considered her most ambitious work. This book chronicles the colorful life of Violet Hesketh from her birth in 1905 to her death in 1975. By depicting Violet's life and the lives of her unusual female friends, Billington examines the changing roles of women in the twentieth century. Although critics found the work somewhat overburdened with facts, they praised Billington's extensive research and her vivid sense of history. In *Occasion of Sin* (1982), Billington returns to the themes of her previous novels, centering on a woman who abandons her husband and son to live with her lover. This work recalls Leo Tolstoy's novel *Anna Karenina,* as Billington's heroine attempts to reconcile her scandalous conduct with her previous moral standards. *The Garish Day* (1985) focuses on a disillusioned young British diplomat whose failure to find fulfillment nearly results in his suicide. Clancy Sigal described this book as "a funny, playful novel about deeply serious matters."

(See also *Contemporary Authors,* Vols. 33-36, rev. ed.)

© *Jerry Bauer*

The New York which entertains Rachel Billington's graceless English dolly of a heroine [in *All Things Nice*] is that documentary cliché, the city of extremes, the place where even the most desultory searcher will encounter anglophile millionaires, junkies and evidence of a colour problem. Kate is escaping her background, which is upper-class. . . . She is suitably introduced and quickly makes the grade in a world of chattering, politically aware girls and the rich men who manage, and occasionally sleep with, them. . . . Predictably, she has a go at commitment . . . , and is briefly caught up in the problems of a junkie married to a Negro girl. She undertakes to get the couple cured in a Kentucky hospital and to write an article about it all. She's out of her depth here, though, and relieved though apologetic when the man dies of cancer and his wife returns to her genteel whoring. She's relieved and apologetic too to discover she loves the dogged Englishman she's been avoiding.

The novel is squalid and unfeeling not for what it reveals about New York but for what New York reveals about its heroine: an empty, glumly swinging chick, who blames her dabbling on a world which accepts her bleakness as fashionable and English and rewards her appropriately.

A review of "All Things Nice," in The Times Literary Supplement, *No. 3,509, May 29, 1969, p. 589.*

THE TIMES LITERARY SUPPLEMENT

In *The Big Dipper,* Ian, a handsome, greying man, late of the Foreign Office now in television, is left by a tiresome wife.

He reacts with apparent indifference, even pleasure, indulging a mild interest in girls and a more serious passion for food. The paraphernalia of greed, the lengths to which a compulsive eater might go to find a box of chocolates in his boss's filing-cabinet are amusingly described. It is difficult to maintain such detachment through Ian's toppling into mental breakdown and premature senility. A giggling venom runs through the book, which is acceptable so long as the hero is seen as just another vain, middle-aged man, dining out on his distinguished appearance and a rich young wife, whose hysterical need for love he ignores. There *is* something disgusting about the way he treats the mindless young girls he sleeps with and his obsessional craving for food. But since it is not clear why the departure of a wife to whom he was indifferent should have caused his collapse, the reader is bound to be more wary than the author has been of condemning the poor chap as a sybarite with nasty habits who is getting his deserts. *The Big Dipper* is more controlled and accomplished than *All Things Nice,* Mrs. Billington's first novel, but a little affection for her characters would give another dimension to her need to be witty at all costs.

"*I Like Older Men,*" *in* The Times Literary Supplement, *No. 3,561, May 28, 1970, p. 578.*

MARK HOLLEBONE

Gourmets do not willingly regress from syllabub to candyfloss, but it can happen, as Rachel Billington's unhappy hero, Ian Harrad (ex-Foreign Office, now TV executive) weirdly demonstrates in this macabre piece of character slaughter [*The Big Dipper*]. The collapse of his marriage leads him—why, we are not told—with lightning speed to total breakdown, physically and mentally to the viscous mess of candyfloss, via the failed escape of a travel, a girl or two, and a palate that deteriorates as fast as his appetite grows. Rachel Billington is quite funny and is a good observer and certainly should be able to make her wit and perceptiveness work for her more successfully. But in this novel, her second, she shows no interest in her central figure, presenting him to us merely as a whipping boy for various nastinesses. (pp. 668, 670)

Mark Hollebone, "A Trio of Novels," in The Tablet, *Vol. 224, No. 6,789, July 11, 1970, pp. 668, 670.*

THE OBSERVER

[*Lilacs out of the Dead Land* is a] set-piece 'affaire' based on mutual self-esteem and the need for an emotional prop. A young schoolteacher missing a father and a past-40 publisher cherishing his physique grope at each other through a hot London summer and a holiday in Sicily. The situation is abandoned with more animosity than compassion leaving the reader without a markedly clearer picture of the two than at the outset. Though tinged with bitterness, and less amusing than [Billington's] two previous novels, this one succeeds in capturing the imagination and is written with assurance.

A review of "Lilacs out of the Dead Land," in The Observer, *June 6, 1971, p. 29.*

THE TIMES LITERARY SUPPLEMENT

[In *Lilacs out of the Dead Land*], her third novel, Rachel Billington has abandoned the comic and grotesque strain she introduced into her second, *The Big Dipper,* and has returned, a little defeatedly, to the elegiac tone of her first [*All Things Nice*], which had a well-brought-up young lady blunder, blinkered and narcissistic, through other people's tragedies. In *Lilacs out of the Dead Land,* April is ashamed of her dirty underclothes when she stays with her nice parents in Dorset, ashamed of her nice accent when she is drinking tea in the staffroom of the primary school where she teaches, and ashamed to have to admit that she is the prettiest girl on the staff. . . .

The process engages April less as daughter and teacher than as juvenile temptress to a middle-aged and married publisher who knows his way around. Together they travel to Sicily, sampling its decadence and marvelling at temples. Elaborate flashbacks chart the course of their affair in London, and these in turn divide into passages of third-person narrative and direct reflections from April herself. Her sulky silences and bursts of unaccountable temper are duly traced back to this London self, with its search for identity and a unifying principle to life; but beyond this they simply record the couple's beddings, their embraces and endearments, and some scurrying episodes when his wife telephones to announce her arrival.

Inexplicably moved to kick her lover down a cliff, April dashes off in their rented car to the hotel to find him waiting for her there, quite well-disposed towards her would-be murderer and ready to set her free. Free for what? It is to be hoped that the myopic wanderings of this particular girl go unrecorded, that she will learn to wash her underwear, forget her accent and accept, like her nice mother, that it is time she relinquished her claim to the novelist's attention.

"*Overprivileged,*" *in* The Times Literary Supplement, *No. 3,619, July 9, 1971, p. 815.*

JOHN SPURLING

Rachel Billington is one of the writing Pakenhams. Her novels, which at first give the impression of treating a rather odious world of the smart, the rich, the beautiful and the well-educated in altogether too uncritical, even romantic a spirit, are slyer than they seem. Her latest, *Cock Robin,* is slyer than ever; it describes the triumph of a metaphorical eunuch over three girls from Oxford, princesses as it were (in both the Tennysonian and the Arabian Nights senses), who have used him as a factotum without giving him sexual satisfaction in return. But we are left at the end wondering whether the revenging Robin is not after all the greatest villain of the piece. Lady Rachel has a mild manner and the makings of a cruel satirist, but the combination is uneasy: there is a slight lack of focus, as if she were talking to you and looking at someone else, or vice versa.

John Spurling, "Four Encounters," in New Statesman, *Vol. 85, No. 2,196, April 20, 1973, p. 591.*

THE TIMES LITERARY SUPPLEMENT

Rachel Billington's *Cock Robin* (sub-titled *A Fight For Male Survival*) is—in intention at least—the sort of book we should be getting more of. If "the end of all scribblement is to amuse", as Byron wrote, then the less gloomily it is all done, the better.

Robin himself, a tall, thin Old Etonian, diffidence personified, tells the story in language both simple and direct as well as conventionally novelistic. It begins at Oxford in 1966, where he is friendly, in his negative way, with three undergraduettes: Sophy (a Lady), Jemima (working-class beneficiary of the football pools), and Gail (an American). . . . The interest throughout centres on the three girls. Robin remains a bit of a cipher. He also does rather a lot of gasping at not very shocking statements (eg, "Sexually, of course, she's voracious").

Gervaise, the bisexual ex-monk, is the most successful character, though unfortunately only a minor one. The high-pitched sexy girls are sufficiently physically and psychologically differentiated. For social comedy, for situation comedy, for sexual comedy, this is all that is necessary. But this kind of novel, since it never sets out to be profound, must be entertaining. The entertainment here is intermittent. There are stretches where the author seems to be trying too hard. "How Lady Rachel can write!" cried the *Sunday Express*, reviewing an earlier book. One can see how, and guess why. At this level of sophistication, however, greater talent is required. Anybody can write from the heart; writing from the head is a good deal harder.

"The Group," in The Times Literary Supplement, *No. 3,711, April 20, 1973, p. 437.*

PETER PRINCE

Beautiful is an enormously silly book about a society lady called Lucy whose features are so intensely fascinating that after one glance practically all men, and quite a few women, are enslaved forever. I guess you had to be there: on the printed page Lucy's charms seem highly resistible. I just can't take seriously a heroine who remarks of her latest flame that though it was his looks that got to her first, it was 'an added bonus to discover that he was a creative director in a high-powered advertising agency'. Not that this is the dimmest moment, by any means. Author Rachel Billington spends most of the novel teetering on the brink of disaster. And at the end, in a finale of unparalleled corn, she bellyflops over.

Peter Prince, "Euthanasia," in New Statesman, *Vol. 87, No. 2,254, May 3, 1974, p. 776.*

THE TIMES LITERARY SUPPLEMENT

Rachel Billington has had problems with her narrators before. Either they have been used confessionally, to give ingratiating or apologetic accounts of themselves, or they have dangled outside the story equipped with telescopic eyesight, some surprising information and a settled mood of incredulity. This presents special problems in Mrs Billington's latest novel, *Beautiful,* which might have stood a fairer chance of success if its heroine had told her own story. As it is, the characters of Lucy Trevelyan and her supporting cast depend upon assertions and a shared and almost supernatural gullibility.

Lucy is thirty-six, beautiful and admired and loved by her husband, children, friends and a patient queue of lovers. Her life is full, ordered and elegant. Lucy's lovers are welcomed by her family and gloriously and meltingly by her. She is thought clever and ravishing by everyone, it seems, but her creator. Lucy made herself a beauty at twenty-three, though the intriguing possibility that she may have started life as a genuinely ugly duckling is not explored. Her golden curls are dyed. She is famous for her conversational gifts, yet the author grudgingly allows her only some elliptical asides in dinner-party French. Her success as an interior decorator is reduced to an eye for the main chance and a way with house plants. Her sexiness is compared to an addiction and seems not wholly unlike nymphomania. As she lies rosily in her bath, the author points to physical blemishes which are missed by Lucy and

ignored by her admirers. Steely rather than good will is made to account for the harmony of her life, which is achieved at the expense of her husband and her children. Mrs Billington dislikes her heroine very much, and the malice which inspires those quotations from *Romeo and Juliet* at the beginning of chapters is two-edged, for one is reminded by them that Shakespeare, after all, delights in Juliet because Romeo does.

Mrs Billington has a beady eye, but she has not yet found a character she cares enough for to understand. She seems to regard novel-writing as an exercise in punitive candour about people she must, after all, take responsibility for. Until she lets them speak and act for themselves she will find it hard to enlist the reader's support for her strictures.

"Self-Made Beauty," in The Times Literary Supplement, *No. 3769, May 31, 1974, p. 591.*

ANNE BARNES

Edward Aubrey is a young, beautiful and ruthless painter with the skills of an adult and the emotions of a five-year-old. Around him flutter his various lovers, a friend of long standing who, when rejected, takes to drugs and proceeds to prison; a rather strainedly romantic girl whom he marries, neglects and drives to dramatic suicide; and others of more or less plausibility and usefulness. Towering over these is Austin, a window-cleaner, not exactly the noble savage but here to counteract Edward's aesthetic preoccupations by his unpretentious practicality and warmth. Edward makes use of him as a model but cannot subjugate him by turning him into a picture, and is finally murdered by him in his own studio.

There is a lot of emphasis in Rachel Billington's [*A Painted Devil*] on blood, wrinkled flesh, sweat and sick, but each traumatic scene is presented largely in terms of its pictorial composition. . . . This aspect of the novel is carefully worked out and the fact that the characters are so flimsily set up might not matter so much if their life styles—the food they eat, the wittiness of their clothes and so on—were thought to be of less interest. . . . Every event is judiciously hinted at beforehand and the climactic scenes are powerful enough, but in spite of the decorative people, the scenery, and the careful structure, it is a rather empty unattractive novel.

Anne Barnes, "Thinner than Water," in The Times Literary Supplement, *No. 3836, September 19, 1975, p. 1041.*

KATHA POLLITT

[*A Painted Devil*], Rachel Billington's fifth novel, is the sort of elegant English piffle it's hard not to like. Somehow what is absurdly theatrical in her people is sheer fun in her decor, from chic London restaurants and grand country houses to ibis-feather bookmarks and white silk tuxedos. Next time she should give her scenery to characters who are able to relax and enjoy it.

Katha Pollitt, in a review of "A Painted Devil," in The New York Times Book Review, *December 28, 1975, p. 18.*

ANNE TYLER

A Woman's Age has a serious purpose. It attempts to show, through examination of one woman's life, what forces might have shaped any woman's life during the first three-quarters of this century. Violet Hesketh, the heroine, is an Englishwoman born in 1905, when the lawns were still full of croquet and no lady went without a hat. She dies in 1975, while touring India in ankle socks and sandals to investigate the problem of population control.

You can't call her life typical, however typical the social pressures upon her may have been. Abandoned by her flighty, self-centered mother at an early age and later reclaimed, Violet grows up in seclusion in a fairytale island castle. She has a succession of unlikely lovers and husbands, and surrounds herself with people who are extreme in one way or another—a baby-machine, a secret agent, an Egyptian "princess" and so on. For her first 35 years—exactly half her life—she tries to content herself with what she imagines to be a woman's lot. The second half of her life is spent escaping that lot, first in volunteer work and then in political activity.

Strangely enough, Rachel Billington chooses to show us the second half—from Violet's political debut on—through the eyes of Violet's daughter, also named Violet. This is jarring at first, coming as it does after 300-odd pages of events seen solely through the older Violet's eyes. It must have jarred even Rachel Billington: for some time, the daughter tends to slip into an impossibly knowledgeable tone of voice. She tells us her mother's innermost thoughts, and occasionally, like an omniscient narrator, reveals the thoughts of distant acquaintances as well. . . . But gradually the daughter settles in, and her own story begins to engage our interest—even to obscure her mother's story, as she herself copes with marriage, career and child-rearing. Could it be that the author switched narrators simply because the life of a socialist politician, whether male or female, is not really all that interesting? It's ironic to find that the liveliest parts of this book are those that swarm with nannies and fat babies.

In its best moments, *A Woman's Age* resembles one of those enormous, overpopulated battle paintings where so much is going on at once, so many people waving flags and galloping past and dying, that you find something new wherever you look. And the mere progression of time, after all, is affecting in itself: the aging of someone we knew as a child, the reappearance of a character we thought long gone, the sight of a once purposeless woman gathering strength and coming into her own. But there is something unfiltered about this book. Events are simply catalogued and arranged in the proper sequence. Historical events, in particular, are set down in stiff clumps, as if fresh off the researcher's legal pad. And not once is a moment in history allowed to pass unnoticed. The novel is so firmly, determinedly anchored in world affairs that at times it reads like a textbook. . . . (p. 15)

[*A Woman's Age*] has an absorbing plot and interesting characters, but there's no special slant of view to make us stop and think. When we've finished, we've merely been well entertained by a multitude of lives. Nothing in those lives has in any way altered our own. (p. 37)

> Anne Tyler, "Woman Coping," in The New York Times Book Review, *February 10, 1980, pp. 15, 37.*

JEAN STROUSE

Reading Rachel Billington's new novel [*A Woman's Age*] is like being invited to a weekend house party and finding yourself

suddenly passing through a time warp with a thoroughly delightful (and often quite batty) set of traveling companions. "Sometimes it seemed to me," says one of the story's narrators, "that people spent most energy either tangling themselves into knots with each other or trying to get the knots untangled." An infinite variety of human knots fastens down this large family saga that spans four generations of upper-class Englishwomen, and Billington handles it all with assurance, ease, warmth and wit. . . .

Billington is up to more than telling charming stories. In her well-researched but never heavy-handed scan of the twentieth century, she traces the vast changes that have taken place at the intersections of history and private life—specifically, female private life. As a child, Vi follows the Great War on maps "as closely as any general." Her Oxford friends discuss Synge, D. H. Lawrence, Huxley and Virginia Woolf, and help out in the General Strike of 1926. Molly, a red-haired rebel with brains, becomes by turns a scholar, vegetarian, feminist, lesbian, Catholic and Spanish Civil War fighter. Earth-mother Araminta has eight babies, cries a lot and champions self-sacrifice.

Vi herself passes from lonely Edwardian waifdom, through the rituals of adolescence and early marriage, to a strange resolution of her own. After her divorce she falls in love with Nettles . . . , they marry, move to Kettleside, have two children, and Vi takes "cover in my reproductive organs" from news of Hitler and Mussolini. But not for long. The drumbeats of history have so far been heard mainly offstage; now, having found a sense of herself at 35, Vi feels the twin pulls of motherhood and a larger world. She leaves her family for a stint of London war work—and never really returns. She becomes a Labor M.P. and a life peeress.

To every one of these women, questions about motherhood loom large. Looking at [her mother] Eleanor's "lunatic, meaningless isolation," Vi wonders "how far we are programmed by our mothers." Eleanor deserted her for pleasure; she deserts her own daughter, Violet (who takes over the narration on page 308) for work. Daughter Violet aims to be the perfect mom—and *her* daughter, Ethne, runs away to live . . . with Eleanor and have an illegitimate child (at last, a boy). In 70 years, the contours of these questions have changed a great deal: new social attitudes, economics and contraception have made it easier for women to work *and* raise children. But the questions haven't really changed, and Billington wisely offers no simple answers, because there aren't any. Instead, she provides a searching, entertaining look at the tangling and untangling knots in a woman's age.

> Jean Strouse, "Mothers and Daughters," in Newsweek, *Vol. XCV, No. 8, February 25, 1980, p. 84.*

HELEN MARIE HRICKO

[*A Woman's Age*] is centered around the life of Violet Hesketh and her search for fulfillment. . . . She spends the first part of her life in the traditional female roles. Although she is raised on the secluded island "paradise" of Eureka with her mother and her mother's lover, she "comes out," attends college and occupies herself with several lovers and an unsuccessful marriage. She eventually settles down, marries her mother's lover and spends several years satisfied with her role as mother and wife. At the beginning of World War II, the course of her life changes once again as she abandons this world for a place in politics, where she ultimately finds personal satisfaction.

The strength of *A Woman's Age* lies in the sharp contrasts Ms. Billington creates within and between her characters, especially her women. Aside from the radical differences in Violet's personality, there is a sharp contrast between her and Araminta, who is completely satisfied with her role as mother, to the point of giving up her potential career as an artist. Violet's close friend, Molly, who is caught up with a strong religious fervor, dedicates herself to social work. Even Violet's own daughter is pleased with her own marriage and family life. All serve as strong examples of the evolution of the female role in this century.

Reading *A Woman's Age* was enjoyable, but unfortunately, not challenging. Ms. Billington fails to take advantage of the situation she has created to make direct personal observations or to challenge her readers' opinions. To be sure, the characters who populate these pages are flamboyant, radical, and unique, but the novel tends to be a mere chronicle of events and people's actions with very few insights into the characters' personalities that will leave a lasting impression with the reader. (p. 3)

> *Helen Marie Hricko, in a review of "A Woman's Age," in* Best Sellers, *Vol. 40, No. 1, April, 1980, pp. 2-3.*

LINDSAY DUGUID

In Roman Catholic doctrine an "occasion of sin" is a set of circumstances which would lead someone to sin; if you place yourself knowingly in such circumstances, then you are already committing a sin. Rachel Billington's [*Occasion of Sin*] deals with just such a set of circumstances, describing in some detail how her vaguely Catholic heroine Laura progresses from being a "good" to a "fallen" woman. Laura falls in love with a young computer expert, Martin, and having tried to resist temptation for a few chapters, abandons her QC husband, their son, her lovely home and the au-pair to live with him and bear his child.

As with other novels concerned almost solely with adultery, the success or failure of *Occasion of Sin* depends on the attractiveness of its heroine. Rachel Billington has tried to make all this talk of sin seem worthwhile by endowing Laura with the correct attributes.... Laura is clearly intended to embody an ideal of beautiful yet vulnerable womanhood and accepts that other people take her to be a paragon of virtue. What comes over most strongly, however, is the speciousness of these attractions, the superficial nature of Laura's feelings and the callousness of her behaviour towards her husband and son. It is unfortunate too that the author's decision to note in detail each one of Laura's confusions and vaccillations ensures that her "mysterious remoteness", remarked upon by other characters, is denied to us.

There is superficiality, too, in the way in which her affair with Martin is charted as a series of treats—compliments in hoarse whispers, wine, picnics, lunches, trips to New York, Ireland and Italy—all equally glossy....

The introduction of serious themes—the religious dimension—and the way the narrative keeps breaking into the present tense to convey intensity show that the book is meant to be taken seriously, but like the many echoes of *Anna Karenina*, only serve to emphasize its emptiness.

> *Lindsay Duguid, "Falling for the Gloss," in* The Times Literary Supplement, *No. 4,152, October 29, 1982, p. 1,203.*

ABIGAIL McCARTHY

Rachel Billington takes the title of this story of a woman and her midlife experience of love and passion [*Occasion of Sin*] from an old Roman Catholic teaching....

But although Laura sometimes attends mass, seeks out the confessional at intervals and talks about St. Anthony, her story is not really the story of the struggle of a soul. In fact, her battle with temptation is scarcely a battle at all, let alone a spiritual one. The touches of Catholicism seem to serve only to give a fillip and something of a frame to an ordinary story of an ordinary woman in an ordinary middle-class marriage in London who falls suddenly and unreasonably in love with a younger man and leaves her husband, home and child. Nevertheless, because sin perceived as sin is always interesting, because the author is a mistress of her craft and because she has an uncanny ability to pin down the moment-to-moment shifts of feeling of a woman in love, this is a memorable novel.

Structured like *Anna Karenina*, from which it takes its epigraph, it begins on a train as Laura goes to save the marriage of her brother, whose wife threatens to leave him because of his most recent infidelity. Laura herself has been married 10 years to a successful barrister and is the mother of a 7-year-old son, the very thought of whom makes her smile lovingly. She is generally admired by her husband, her family and her friends. "It was strange that a brother and sister should have such different attitudes," she thinks. "She didn't find it difficult to be faithful. On the contrary, she enjoyed the feeling of security it gave her. Perhaps, too, a sense of virtue." Then she catches a glimpse of Martin Keane on a station platform, and her whole life begins to change.

It is Rachel Billington's accomplishment that in an era of easy liaisons, she has written a convincing novel of passion. She details Laura's slide from grace—for it is a slide and not the result of conscious decision—with nuanced precision.... Laura seized by passion is completely believable. We understand that this pretty, complacent woman who liked the thought of her own virtue is so swept away that she can fly off with her lover without stopping to pack a bag, that she can be separated from her adored son and feel only intermittent flickers of pain. (p. 11)

Like Anna Karenina's, her whole world changed. "By leaving Miles she had broken herself apart. Was there anything left now to put together?" Passion has ebbed, and, as [her lover] Martin says, the world has come in. She now sees people as they really are and no longer through the prism of her own feelings. But she does not understand herself. She has traded a life in which she dealt with certainties for one in which she does not know whom she loves or hates or what she wants to do.

In the last scene, Laura is on a train again, traveling toward her brother's house, where her son waits. At a stop she jumps off. "Her sensation of freedom was so great that she wanted to run, laugh, cry. It seemed to her that this touching down in the middle of nowhere was the first free decision she'd ever made in her whole life." But her baby by Martin is on the train. The train starts again. What she does then suggests that this is perhaps a novel of the spirit after all. (p. 17)

> *Abigail McCarthy, "A Virtuous Woman's Slide from Grace," in* The New York Times Book Review, *May 1, 1983, pp. 11, 17.*

T. J. GRANAHAN

Rachel Billington's elaborately detailed novel [*Occasion of Sin*] focuses on a woman's struggle between the constraints of stiffling responsibility and the attraction and uncertainty of unbridled desire. It is a journey of developing disintegration. (p. 80)

Cast upon wholly unfamiliar emotional ground, Laura attempts to gain a perspective. She is a Catholic with a catechism notion of sin. The book's title is derived from the idea that willfully placing oneself in temptation's path is a sin. The actual surrender to temptation is an additional sinful act. It is a kind of spiritual double jeopardy. Laura uses this notion as a rationale for adultery. Having sought out the apple, she feels obliged to have a bite.

The view of the Catholic Church found in *Occasion of Sin* is recognizably British. But it is not the active presence found in the writing of Evelyn Waugh nor is it the spiritual albatross vexing the characters of Graham Greene. The Church is viewed from the narthex, as a relic institution, a repository of rules governing behavior and responsibility. Laura is not capable of reconciling her position with her belief in Church and Marriage; she comes, instead, to an uneasy self-awareness. By the story's end, she is a fallen woman not only in the conventional sense of the term, but also in the sense that she has taken on bitter knowledge (original sin?).

The process of Laura's struggle for order is represented by her confused state, and at times it is shared with the reader in greater detail than seems necessary. As a result, an otherwise well-crafted narrative becomes overburdened with emotional minutiae, and wanders into weary melodrama. The reader, consequently, shares a greater degree of Laura's frustration than the author may have intended. (pp. 80-1)

T. J. Granahan, in a review of "Occasion of Sin," in Best Sellers, Vol. 43, No. 3, June, 1983, pp. 80-1.

MIRANDA SEYMOUR

Harry Hayes-Middleton's story, as related by Rachel Billington in *The Garish Day,* is a modern *Bildungsroman,* a long, slow haul over the coals from pride to humility. Pride comes easily enough to Harry as the bright and only son of Lionel, a shrewd and lecherous diplomat, and Beatrice, his tolerant, plucky wife. Cooed over by the English ladies of India and Ceylon, educated at English prep and public school, Harry has no greater desire than to follow his father into the Foreign Office; which, after a cheerfully unsuitable affair with an Irish farm-girl and an ill-fated marriage to a fellow undergraduate at Oxford, he does.

The trouble with Harry is that conventionality has always been a mask rather than a conviction. Disoriented by a life of constant travel . . . and by a lack of moral standards—his best friend, Belinda, is the daughter of one of the many women he knows as his father's "sisters"—Harry is dangerously inclined to ask questions of the "What is the meaning of life?" variety: not a virtue in an ambitious young diplomat.

Flavia, his wife, takes off with an Argentinian. His wild friends of the 1960s are settling into well-orchestrated lives as financiers, diplomats, entrepreneurs. His old friend Belinda turns up again as a feminist pacifist, while Harry struggles, vainly, to find the kindly light amid the encircling gloom of New York. (The book's title comes from Newman's hymn.) Neither the loyalty of his anxious friends nor the invitingly open arms of

Donna, Roxy, Belinda and others can provide an answer. Religion proves as fruitless an endeavour as his attempt to jump off the Trade Centre. . . . It takes his mother's funeral to bring Harry to a somewhat puzzling nirvana. . . .

The Garish Day is ambitious in its time-span and social scope, and tersely written in short and snappy sentences which make for slow reading. Rachel Billington is at her most assured when she is dealing with Harry's family—the mother, Beatrice, is a splendid portrait of an honourable woman making the best of a bad marriage—but she lessens their impact by swamping them in socio-historical detail. Everything is liberally chronicled, from the rise of the mini-skirt to the Israeli invasion of Jordan in 1967. . . . It is hard to see Billington's secondary characters as more than specimens, useful social types whose unlikely progressions are incorporated to help define the period rather than to give the reader any larger understanding of their natures. I would like to see Rachel Billington's next novel concentrating less on the setting and shifting of the scenes and more upon—horrible term—character motivation.

Miranda Seymour, "Encircling Gloom," in The Times Literary Supplement, No. 4,301, September 6, 1985, p. 972.

GEOFFREY TREASE

As a novelist and a radio and television playwright, Rachel Billington is practised in storytelling and the depiction of character through dialogue and situation. She is less successful in the persuasive elucidation of an internal conflict demanding our sympathetic entry into the thought processes of a tormented individual. This is vital in [*The Garish Day*], a tale of father and son, both career diplomats. Sir Lionel belongs to an earlier tradition, ossified in his unquestioned prejudices and assumptions. He rises to the top of the tree as successively High Commissioner in New Delhi and ambassador in Washington. . . . His son Harry follows him in the foreign service but, like many of the post-war generation faced with the problems of a radically altered world, loses faith in the wisdom of his seniors. Secretly baptized a Roman Catholic in infancy, by a mother always in silent rebellion against his father, he is now as an adult vaguely drawn to the Church but finds little comfort therein. He behaves oddly in public, develops suicidal impulses, and resigns from the service. We are left in doubt as to the nature of his mental disturbance. . . . The author is clearly trying to say something in this book, but it is not clear what she is trying to say.

Geoffrey Trease, in a review of "The Garish Day," in British Book News, November, 1985, p. 682.

CLANCY SIGAL

Readers of Graham Greene and other Catholic novelists will be familiar with Rachel Billington's steadily unradiant gaze [in *The Garish Day*]. She helps us see through Harry's eyes the total absurdity and futility of a rhetorically seeking heart. Among the novel's funnier scenes are Harry's encounters, drunken and sober, with poor Father Bernard, a simple Irish-born priest in London who quails at the larger questions put by desperate souls several social cuts above him. Curiously, it is Father Bernard who may be the author's real hero—a tough, sensible man all too aware of his deficiencies but who comes through magnificently at the end when he is most needed.

It's a serious plot lightly told. Mrs. Billington takes us from Harry's birth through his school years, Oxford, and, later, a failed marriage, a globe-encircling mental breakdown (or spiritual reorganization, depending on your theological bias), culminating in a grandly comic funeral scene—Father Bernard nervously, then triumphantly, presiding—when Harry's mother dies. Her death releases in her son an almost-joy, a semiacceptance. I cannot vouch for the religious authenticity of Harry's experience. And Mrs. Billington, a subtle and vivacious novelist, sometimes makes her shadow-man Harry a little too shadowy to grasp in a full, human sense. But psychologically he makes all too much sense. As his school friend Julian, a hippie turned movie producer, says with some justice, "Extreme conventionality, such as Harry displayed . . . is almost certainly a cover for total insanity." This is a funny, playful novel about deeply serious matters.

Clancy Sigal, "Spiritually Reorganizing Harry," in The New York Times Book Review, *June 15, 1986, p. 22.*

Paul Blackburn

1926-1971

American poet and translator.

In his poetry, Blackburn combined structural experimentation with colloquial speech and rhythms to create a visual, aural, and psychological reading experience. Although he was affiliated with such Black Mountain poets as Robert Creeley and Charles Olson and shared many of their compositional techniques, including projectivist verse, Blackburn was not an active participant in the Black Mountain College experiment. Major influences on his work included Ezra Pound, with whom Blackburn corresponded for several years, and William Carlos Williams, whose dictum "No ideas but in things!" Blackburn applied to his own verse. These influences notwithstanding, most critics agree that Blackburn produced an original body of work characterized by a relaxed, conversational tone that masks the innate rhythm of his poems. Blackburn's verse addresses such personal concerns as love, friendship, and the places where he had traveled. Gilbert Sorrentino noted that "the poems, over his entire career, return again and again to these things and each time extend their possibilities in terms of Blackburn's deepening understanding of them."

Several of Blackburn's early poetry collections—including *The Dissolving Fabric* (1955), *Brooklyn-Manhattan Transit: A Bouquet for Flatbush* (1960), *The Nets* (1961), and *The Reardon Poems* (1967)—were printed in limited editions, and much of his other work was not published until after his death. These four volumes and several uncollected poems are included in *Early Selected y mas: Poems, 1949-1966* (1972). Blackburn's two major volumes published during his lifetime are *The Cities* (1967) and *In, On, or About the Premises: Being a Small Book of Poems* (1968). The poems collected in *The Cities*, which are set in New York and various foreign locales, were written in the 1950s and early 1960s and earned Blackburn a reputation as an urban poet. In his note to this volume, Blackburn wrote that the poems are linked by his "recognitions of those constructs not my own that I can live in." The importance of place and its relationship to self are also key elements in the poems of *In, On, or About the Premises*. These pieces depict some of Blackburn's favorite Manhattan neighborhoods, where he observed people and listened to their conversations in order to gather material for his verse. The poems in the posthumously published volume *Halfway Down the Coast* (1975) detail Blackburn's experiences while traveling in Europe.

Blackburn's most widely acclaimed work is *The Journals* (1975), a collection of poetry and prose pieces which, according to Paul Christensen, evokes "a superb sense of visual-placement of language on the page." These poems were written after Blackburn was diagnosed as having terminal cancer. *The Journals,* wrote Michael Stephens, "is remarkable for many reasons, among which are the maturity of Blackburn's poetry and poetics, the energy and intelligence of the writing, and the human courage informing every utterance." The poems in *Against the Silence* (1980) chronicle Blackburn's troubled second marriage and subsequent divorce. Reviewers noted that in both books Blackburn confronted those painful periods in his life with frankness and humor. Since the publication of *The Collected Poems of Paul Blackburn* (1985), Blackburn's verse

© 1987 Thomas Victor

has begun to attract a wider audience and has undergone substantial critical reevaluation.

Blackburn was also a noted translator and scholar. His translations of medieval Provençal verse, collected in *Proensa: An Anthology of Troubadour Poetry* (1978), are considered among the finest in the genre. Blackburn freely translated the works of Arnault de Marueill and other European artists to make them more accessible to English audiences. Blackburn is remembered as well for organizing and recording poetry readings by the Black Mountain poets and the Beat poets during the late 1950s and early 1960s.

(See also *CLC*, Vol. 9; *Contemporary Authors*, Vols. 81-84, Vols. 33-36, rev. ed. [obituary]; *Dictionary of Literary Biography*, Vol. 16; and *Dictionary of Literary Biography Yearbook: 1981*.)

M. L. ROSENTHAL

The Renascents (Allen Ginsberg, Gregory Corso, and others) have struck a false note from the start of their phosphorescent little history. Theirs was a cry, not of the heart, but of the groin—a revulsion from official repression that expressed itself in belches, obscenities, incoherent manifestoes, and great shrieks of *"Libertad!"* . . . Yet there was, and there remains, something valid in it. It appealed to an instinct in the young everywhere to lash out with blind energy against almost everything, good or bad, that "authority" has constructed. Empty as much of this poetry has been, it has cleared a little place for itself that may be permanent.

But also emerging now is a little-known, ultimately more serious and mature body of non-traditional verse. It is represented by the work of Charles Olson, Denise Levertov, Paul Blackburn, Robert Duncan and Robert Creeley. Their poetry shows the same intensified intransigence as does that of Ginsberg and Co., the same fundamental assumption that the crack-up of values prophesied by an older generation has completed itself. Indeed, these qualities are at the heart of almost all the more impressive new work, traditional or not. . . . In the Olson group, a renewed emphasis on the feel of specific moments of awareness—as if they were totally detachable from the rest of life—is indispensable to the reordering of sensibility.

Denise Levertov and Paul Blackburn are the most "open" and sensuous writers in this group. Neither is content with sharp physical awareness alone, but both have a freshness that engages you even when what they present seems abstract. . . . [Several of Miss Levertov's poems] seem to regard the civilization against which they react as a sort of cobweb brushing the face, something alien and strangely cold, yet almost unreal.

Blackburn, too, gives this impression, but more humorously and evasively than Miss Levertov. His poem **"The Assistance"** riddles out a ridiculous but real big-city predicament almost casually. The subject is trivial and embarrassing, but Blackburn conjures up a personal universe through his treatment of it. You would think, for the moment (as in actual life you might), that this was the whole of things:

> On the farm it never mattered;
> behind the barn, in any grass, against
> any convenient tree,
>   the woodshed in winter, in a corner
> if it came to that.
>
> But in a city of eight million, one
> stands on the defensive. . . .

Sunken into Existential reality, without pride, definitive, Blackburn's poems seem at times to reduce themselves to an uncritical savoring of consciousness. Whatever is, is; and what you give a damn about is not what it means but what it feels like. The poet's spirit floats and absorbs whatever is there; in **"The Term,"** he speaks of sitting in the Spanish sunlight and

>   watching
>   weeds grow out of the drainpipes
>   or burros and the shadows of burros
>   come up the street bringing sand
>   the first one of the line with a
>   bell
>   always. . . .

There is another, darker brooding beneath this surface acceptance; but it too is fatalistic rather than critical in its presentation:

Another bell sounds the hours of your sun
> limits
>   sounding below human voices,
> counts the hours of weeks, rain, darkness, all with a
> bell.

I do not say that what these two poets do is in the key of the future—and yet this is the way that intellectual universes *are* shattered. Not through head-on assault, but through indifference, or the refusal to take the present seriously on its own terms. No bang, no whimper, just a new way of looking at things. (pp. 324-26)

> *M. L. Rosenthal, "In Exquisite Chaos," in* The Nation, *Vol. 187, No. 14, November 1, 1958, pp. 324-27.*

ALLEN PLANZ

[*The Cities*], the first full-sized presentation of Paul Blackburn's poems, reminded me of the things said of his work in the years it was widely published but never adequately collected. Of contemporary American poets, he has been reputed to have the best "ear," to be in the firmest control of the line break, to be the most persistently experimental younger poet in the innovative tradition advanced in our times by Pound and Williams. This book abundantly demonstrates those virtues, and more: it presents the work of a master poet. Unfortunately, many of the poems for which he is justly famed are not here. . . . Blackburn literally needs lots of space, and while he has the wit and grace to snap out incisive short poems, he also has the power to sustain marvelously long constructions. The rich, multifarious music of *The Cities* is at once fulfillment and prelude.

Most contemporary poets, attempting to bring their craft into greater consciousness, heightened self-awareness, settle for a style which if not ruthlessly evolved can lose freshness and become mannerist. But Blackburn's forms remain open, fluid, expansive; his awareness of language—his love of it—carries a dedication that identifies it at the heart of the creative act. Each poem has its own measure, discovered by the poet's voice (which can whisper, sing, harangue, yell, talk quietly or loudly—and all in one poem). **"Sirventes"** is an extravagant example.

And he succeeds in making you hear. Blackburn redirects one's attention to the act of reading creatively, so that one hears more, even while reading silently. His repertoire of technical devices—which another poet would invoke to combat rhetoric—are used to convey the precise reading of the poem, to orchestrate the silences within it and without, to reveal nuances and depths previously unsuspected in the most casual word. (p. 247)

Blackburn is really concerned with, and immersed in, the vitality of language, the American language, as it is spoken, felt, and heard. Robert Frost claimed that his own greatest gift was in getting the sound of his voice in his lines. It is also Blackburn's gift. Other voices, sounds, noises, events, and even things get in too, as the organic unity of the poem directs—though, to be sure, they sometimes get in the way, when, as relief, they lower the textural intensity of the poem. The risks Blackburn runs are enormous, but worth it.

There are many masterly pieces in the book. . . . Plus a lot of fun, hilarity, joking and clowning, that give this book an unusual character, the work of an original man.

In a prefatory note Blackburn tells us the book "is the construct out of my own isolations, eyes, ears, nose, and breath, my recognitions of those constructs not my own that I can live in. The Cities." The poems in this book, then, reveal an unyielding, existential engagement with the metropolis—using all the resources of language to explore what concerns the poet. Yet these recognitions do not resolve into rites of passage, or abscond to myth: rather, they expand to a vision that, for all its gentleness, its celebration of passion and youth and craft, is essentially tragic. Hence the resonance of the remarkable technical proficiency becomes finally song, eloquence, out of which the paradigm of the book becomes clear. Our cities. On this score, Blackburn is our most engaged poet. (p. 248)

> *Allen Planz, "A Line to the City," in* The Nation, *Vol. 207, No. 8, September 16, 1968, pp. 247-48.*

THE TIMES LITERARY SUPPLEMENT

Sunk in egocentricity, [Paul Blackburn, in his collection *In, On, or About the Premises*], is obsessed with the jobs of ingestion, elimination and coition. But he knows how to shake the kaleidoscope of his fragmentary perceptions and find delicate, evocative patterns in them. Like W. C. Williams he enlarges the estate of poetry by domesticating words and experiences normally excluded from polite speech. Judged by the standard of his masters, he falls short. Cummings on the death of Harding is more dramatic and witty than Blackburn on McKinley. Pound's subtlety of intellectual association gives the best *Cantos* an elegance of sound and structure which a poem like "**The Watchers**" lacks. Mr. Blackburn's ear for American talk is not the same as Pound's instinct for poetic rhythms. But it remains a pleasure to watch the ends of Mr. Blackburn's poems flower suddenly out of their start and middles, or to hear his bright changes rung on repeated words or images. . . .

Mr. Blackburn avoids the impression of diffuseness that is the commonest peril of free verse.

> *"Enlarging the Estate," in* The Times Literary Supplement, *No. 3478, October 24, 1968, p. 1202.*

CHARLES STEIN

Two small groups, "**The Ale House Poems**" and "**The Bakery Poems**," are included in this handsome collection of Blackburn's [*In, On, or About the Premises*]. These are fast-paced, open-form poems, whose witty surfaces belie a darker, almost desperate content: Bowery derelicts, barroom situations of various descriptions, urban characters in urban poses. Blackburn assumes a number of voices in his poems which realize a compassion that is at once generous and alarming. The poems' matter-of-fact diction and the poet's suggested identification with his characters save him from self-congratulation and make his material potent and immediate. Disparate aspects of a given moment are presented: in one poem, the assassinated President McKinley is lowered in his tomb as a shop-keeper finishes making love to his typist. The connection between these events is that they are observed (really by the poetry, not the poet) at the same time, as part of the same occasion. Time is felt as the *subject* of the poetry. Simultaneity does not merely unite disjunct happenings, but taken together, happenings reveal a meaning of the moment in which they occur.

> *Charles Stein, in a review of "In, On, or About the Premises," in* The Nation, *Vol. 208, No. 7, February 17, 1969, p. 217.*

ROBERT D. SPECTOR

Paul Blackburn sustains a lyrical assault on the way we live now. Blackburn must be tired of being labeled a Black Mountain poet, a disciple of William Carlos Williams, and, in fact, he is quite unlike any other modern poet. In "**The Ale House Poems**" of *In, On, or About the Premises* . . . , he recalls the Goliardic poetry of the Middle Ages, an odd combination of irreverence, earthiness, and erudition. Blackburn masks his learning in a seeming casualness and his difficult craftsmanship in his unaffectedness. Affairs of pomp and ceremony become more pretentious when juxtaposed with vignettes of sex. With quiet humor, precise rendering of American speech, and sharp detail, his voice cuts to the marrow. (p. 34)

> *Robert D. Spector, "Lyrics, Heroic and Otherwise," in* Saturday Review, *Vol. LII, No. 11, March 15, 1969, pp. 33-5.*

M. L. ROSENTHAL

[Paul Blackburn's] emphasis is always on the quality of movement of something when one is in the middle of it. The dominant motif in *The Cities*, the speaker going through the motions of living, thinking, and sensing the passing moments in the wake of a broken marriage, sets the pitch and direction for a number of the poems. Mr. Blackburn's love of the American lingo and capacity to be absorbed in any moment of existential awareness as though he were married to it lead the poems out in various directions—humorous, sensuously recreative of the concrete outside world, speculative (especially about sex and love and their contemporary meaning or, rather, the way we are changing in our experience of them), and collagist. But the harsh central situation keeps reasserting itself in a number of poems that present its different emotional phases through a precisely weighted rhythmic ordering. . . . (p. 129)

As the poet says in his "Author's Note", this poetry "is a construct out of my own isolations, eyes, ears, nose, and breath, my recognitions of those constructs not my own that I can live in. . . . Let me use Lorca's term: *duende* is that faculty of making / into which you subsume yourself. . . ." Mr. Blackburn, like some others among our contemporaries, has but focused on the essential process engaging the poet as the poem gets under way, making the process itself a disciplining *subject* of the poem as well as its range of action. (pp. 129-30)

> *M. L. Rosenthal, in a review of "The Cities," in* Poetry, *Vol. CXIV, No. 2, May, 1969, pp. 129-30.*

CLAYTON ESHLEMAN

Early Selected Y Mas spans the years 1945 to 1966—however the bulk of the writing takes place from 1953 through 1961; very definitely a "selected" and not a "collected." To grasp the fulness of these years, when Blackburn lived in Europe— mainly southern France and Spain—from 1954 through 1957, then returning to New York City, the reader should also consider about 17 poems in *The Cities* . . . and a poem called "**The Letter**" which is collected in *A Controversy of Poets.* . . . The body of poetry that Blackburn achieved relative to his four years in Europe is, for me, the high point of all his poetry, and places him among the very best poets of his generation. It is a period in which he found a splendid continuum of attention and feeling, a period in which all of his virtues and hardly any of his weaknesses are present. In back of this writing is his translation-work on the Provençal troubadours; one feels, during this period, a nearly perfect balance between translatory source and original work. When Blackburn returned to New York City in 1958 he lost this balance and never found it again. True, he wrote terrific poems after 1958 and well into the 60s, and he did some very fine translations too, mainly of Paz, Lorca and Nicolas Guillen—however a complex of factors, among which was certainly New York City itself, slowly undermined his work. I realize that by putting it this way I may only be expressing a like for one aspect of Blackburn and a disinterest in another aspect; be that as it may, I feel no other American poet of our times so vividly and pathetically records the difference between living on foreign soil, in a town ambience against that of living in the large American city, namely New York City. Blackburn's prime nourishment came from sky, sea and natural landscape, stone and wine, the moon, watching and feeling people, recording a kind of spare narrative. I am aware that I may be talking about the maturation process in the poet, or his failure to imaginatively mature, as well as New York City; Blackburn lived in Europe when he was a young man and he was forced, or I should say *chose* to confront his own development in New York, a place which is a potential death to the frail lyrical bearing, a place where the stark nobility of the Spanish peasant is converted to the street bum etc.,—in short the heart of New York City is critical prose, and Blackburn's gift, which is nearly as delicate and soft as his pregnant cat [in **"The Café Filtre"**], was crushed there. He lived there for a decade, probably as cleanly as a poet could—his decency to others, his refusal to play poetry politics, his steady though weakening persistence with his art in the face of an almost surly neglect by virtually all of the poets of his own generation—these qualities, to carry them off especially in New York City, strike me as almost saint-like. Yet I do not mean to invoke pity for him. The sadness of the matter is that the cold, the impersonal, the bitter and the odd have come to be taken for granted as essential ingredients of an art, or pseudo-art, made in New York City in our time.

It is appropriate to mull over these things here because the curve of *Early Selected* begins in New York City, bends to Europe and in the end returns to Manhattan. Blackburn's first book, *The Dissolving Fabric,* with which *Early Selected* begins, is a tight unit of 14 poems, which in a kind of ambiguous way explores identity, and seeks out the poet's own presence in the world. The opening and ending poems focus on the death of a woman, and provide an ominous controlling image that the other poems seem to be in the service of. The best poem in this book is **"The Search"** which anticipates a lot of later work and to a certain extent fixes Blackburn's identity. Yet the fabric continues to dissolve—a curious image of sea and cloth, as if to suggest that there is something essentially "off" in coherence. Most of the poems in this first book were written between 1951 and 1954.

The next two sections in *Early Selected* consist of previously uncollected poems, 21 in all. In these poems Blackburn seems to feel a rootlessness even more, acutely at points, but the Spanish landscape soothes, and the best poems find their form on its terms. One thing that is interesting to note in this section is the way he brings in his life-long preoccupation with "the line." I mean, one of the first things that strikes any reader of Paul Blackburn is the poet's ability to sculpt and "tone" a line. Given this gift, it is natural to find the poet first experiencing it as sensation, as a line, a kind of limit, evoking death, that enters him when he sleeps as well as moving around in his room in vague relation to a woman. This section ends with a poem called **"Spring Thing"** which as a narrative is an

advance on **"The Search."** In its precise yet relaxed tone it is similar to **"The Café Filtre"** and is a good example of a typical Blackburn poem, in which a scene is constructed with the poet himself moving through it.

The second book in *Early Selected* is *The Nets,* 20 poems, most of which were written from 1957 through 1959. There are at least four very fine poems in *The Nets,* and along with the poems in *The Cities* it contains Blackburn's strongest poetry relevant to Europe. This book is constructed somewhat in the same way that *The Dissolving Fabric* was; like the former book, it has a beginning and ending poem that set a tone for the rest of the book—in the case of *The Nets* the ambiguous death of a woman becomes more actual, piercing, a realization of the inability to live love. With the final poem of *The Nets,* **"The Purse-Seine"** one is confronted with what will be the central ache of Blackburn's poetry from here on. This poem has a compelling fugal structure in which while on one hand the woman becomes openly identified as a killer, on the other hand, the poet keeps returning with her to the bed. It is as if within release there is no real release—**"The Purse-Seine"** is a very strange poem—it feels like a masterpiece yet it also keeps its action at one remove so that at the end of it one has the feeling of not knowing what really happened; the experience remains veiled, in contrast to the openness that Blackburn has when he is with landscape or things (or food, or animals, say, as in **"The Café Filtre"**). This veiledness, which granted is intriguing as well as frustrating, is most imaginatively worked in two poems that draw upon the Boibel-Loth tree alphabet worked out by Robert Graves in his book *The White Goddess.* Graves claims to be deciphering a secret alphabet that ancient European poets used to camouflage their real meanings, and Blackburn in a kind of serious parody of this method works certain images out of Graves that when related back to the tree alphabet reveal two sets of letters. . . . While the first poem [**"Venus. The Lark. . ."**] turns on destruction, the second turns on rebirth, and the two together become a motor, the internal driving power for the entire book. Both of these poems were written in 1958 after Blackburn had returned to New York City. Both, especially the second—**"The Vine. The Willow . . ."**—stand in stark contrast to the next book in *Early Selected, Brooklyn-Manhattan Transit,* five poems published in 1960. . . . (pp. 642-45)

The feel of the [*Brooklyn-Manhattan Transit*] booklet is light-verse, which Blackburn could handle let us say very entertainingly at times, set against utter despair: **"Meditation On the BMT."** In contrast to the inspiring Spanish landscape we have Brooklyn backyards seen from a subway train. It is a terribly sleepy and sentimental poem—yet it works. For in contrast to the feeling the line remains taut.

The next section of 12 poems, all of which were written in New York City, brings in Manhattan in several poems, but Blackburn's memory of Spain is still strong enough to feel and find a sensuousness there (the kind of poem, say, that he will go ahead to write several years later in **"The Bakery"** series). The majority of the poems in this section look back at Europe and, as one might expect, they are alternatingly poignant and elegiac. . . . Perhaps the most memorable poem in this section, and one of Blackburn's greatest, is **"The Mint Quality"** written in 1961 and never published until now. . . . It is an elegy for a young woman named Christiane who was killed, or who killed herself—this is left intentionally unclear—wrecking her Jaguar in southern France. The center of the poem is a long monologue by the dead woman, extremely rich in emotional dimension—it is as if her being entered Blackburn and contacted a lot of feelings about himself that he did not want to confront but would utter in the frame of his friend's death. Which is to say, the piece has an archetypal feel to it, a hauntedness beyond explication. (p. 645)

The final section of *Early Selected* is another small book, **"The Reardon Poems."** . . . **"The Reardon Poems,"** written on the occasion of a writer friend's death in 1966, bring an *Early Selected* to its complete title, *Early Selected Y Mas*. . . . Compared to his poetry of the late fifties, **"The Reardon Poems"** are meaninglessly talkative, they ramble, occasionally connect—they are accurate in the sense that they evoke the world of McSorley's Ale House on 7th Street which both Blackburn and Reardon frequented.

I have mentioned . . . Blackburn's ability to handle the poetic line. . . . The stanza from **"The Birds"** contains the seeds of many things to follow:

> And I was young
> and neck began to wobble clear, but feet
>   were rooted in his beach, for I
> feared the dark march to the sun again; and each
> stiff inner motion moved me into song
>   instead of into living:
> but now I know what thing is worth the having
> and fear the imperfection in my singing; but now
> can lie here and swim my mind in it
>   and still know when to leave
>   touch bottom to darkness where
> I no longer fear to ask much of the gods.
>   It has taken me a long time to realise
> I want them to come here
> I want to see them here.

This is the first appearance of the gull which will over the years become Blackburn's totemic creature, as well as the first poem in which the presence of the provençal is felt—or let us say the tone of voice Blackburn chose to use in the provençal translations. . . . In the 7th line of the stanza quoted above this other voice comes in, holds for two lines, then leaves. It feels a little archaic, the diction not really forced but of another era—in fact those two lines may be from the provençal. We do not hear them again in Blackburn's own poetry and one reason I quote that stanza here is to suggest the poet's point of departure. Blackburn brought a prosody to the provençal material, fashioning his translations with a lightness and openness similar to that which he discovered in his own poetry— the pull the provençal seemed to have on him, and it was certainly a powerful one, for he reworked his translation for years, never completely sure that he had it right, was thus more psychic than linguistic—the attitude toward the "lady" was in many ways compatible with Blackburn's own sense of "the white goddess" and one of the most problematic things about his own poetry is that he never seemed to have entered into a relationship in which he could find a basis to fully exercise, or uphold, his mythology. (pp. 646-47)

"El Camino Verde" opens positing two roads which are and are not the same: "The green road lies this way. / I take the road of sand." As the poem winds through its images, the road of sand becomes identified with "Days when / the serpent of wind plucks and twists the harp of sun." and the green road, the traditional road of life becomes that which is "filtered thru / leaves that cast obscene / beautiful patterns / on roads and walls." where "under the burning wind" there is "the wet

heat of an armpit,"—for a moment this demanding concentration of contraries is relieved by the appearance of a gull, brought to birth through the dove-tailing of opposites (the potential distinction between contraries and opposites is never calculated by Blackburn)—the poet prays to "hold the mind clear in the dark honey of evening light," but he is beyond any easy clarity, and caught up in a great creative flow—

> the serpent
> hidden among sweet-smelling herbs, down there
> a small palm offers its leaves to the wind.
>   On the mountain, olive,
> o, live wood,
> its flawless curve hangs from the slope.
>
> Hot . sirocco . covers everything
> and everyone, all day, it blows all day as if
> this were choice, as if
> the earth were anything else but
> what is is, a hell. But
> blind, bland, blend the flesh.
> Mix the naked foot with the sand that caresses it, mix
> with the rock that tears it, enter
>   the hot world.
>
>   Cave of the winds
> What cave?   the
>   reaches of Africa
>   where an actual
>   measure
>   exists.

Blackburn's use of the floating period, which he first began to experiment with in 1955, here achieves a functional identity with content. His own character which I have described before as being passive and watchful, here meshes with the timelessness of the road, and the floating period not only pauses as we read, but integrates itself into the syntax of the vision itself— it is the slow eternality of the universe that most fascinated Paul Blackburn when he was in Spain, that slow slow process that is movement as season and cloud yet as movement is enchased in a greater motionlessness—yet not really motionless either, more a feeling of the passing-through, warm wind through blossoms, hunger in the walls of the stomach, people slowly gathering and leaving a stone bench—the time we most naturally associate with childhood, real time in contrast to clock time. Yet the reaches of Africa represent something political as well as time/spatial—

> a hope—it MUST be there, my
> desire realized in what the word Africa calls up—
>   yet if we have
> accepted the "naked foot" mixed with "sand"
>   we have gone with Blackburn
>   into death—
>   the foot cannot be mixed with sand unless the
>   primal
> boundary is destroyed—

(pp. 647-48)

Clayton Eshleman, "A Mint Quality," in boundary 2, *Vol. II, No. 3, Spring, 1974, pp. 640-48.*

MICHAEL STEPHENS

Halfway Down the Coast is a good place to begin reading the poetry of the late Paul Blackburn. It is also a good book to reacquaint oneself with this writer. If jacket copy is the place for good news, then it certainly is welcome to read that "Paul Blackburn had published some fourteen books of poems and translation. Yet those books represented perhaps not even half of his existing work." This verdant coast, then, is a poetic terrain, like Apollinaire's coast between Mobile and Galveston. It is coastal also in the sense that the reader can get "next to" the poems quite easily. Once there, the vistas are magnificent, not dwarfing, not overly refined, not rarefied though certainly heady like mountain air. They are also healthy, in the manner of Henry Miller, full of life, and, as Blackburn used to call it, *duende,* though if he were alive today, still living downtown on the East Side, he might just call it—*salsa!* These are poems of life without apology, without posturing (the uninitiated might find Blackburn's stance too hip, though), and from the opening poem, **"The Surrogate,"** driven by an intelligent whimsy:

> She stole ma hat
> ma hat . was in the lounge
> with ma jacket
> The jacket she dint take it, but
> ma hat, she tukkit,
> clean
> out a the place

to the more philosophical ending of the last poem, **"Backsweep/ Black":**

> Time
> gone now
> and again
> recurs

Blackburn's snapshots go nicely with his shorter, imagistic poems—the singular observations *in place.* The Matisse drawings on the covers are appropriate since both artists were capable of a sustained lyricism throughout their respective careers. The poet also shares this gift of stamina and pacing with one of his poetic influences, William Carlos Williams. It is his own best tribute that Blackburn was able to maintain a high emotional shape throughout his career, giving an overall form from earliest volumes to the present. Quite probably the forthcoming posthumous volumes will continue this energized, overall shape.

This shape is certainly one of the most deceptive in modern poetry, because Blackburn was able to appear effortless while working in complex forms.... Many unaware writers and critics failed to discern the complex forms, the sly intelligence, and reserved elegance of that lyrical gift. Put another way, Blackburn was as socially and literarily accessible as lesser poets, and yet he was cut from the fabric of genius.

One facet of Blackburn's poetic gift had to do with his ability to listen to the overheard cadences of common speech.... [He] seemed to love people, and in some lapsed Roman Catholic way, he enjoyed giving of himself. In turn, he received stories, spoken images, vignettes, exaggerations, blarney and, like James Joyce after a night of drinking with the proles, Blackburn got out his notebook, wrote it down, typed it up, immortalized obscure men and women, and gave dignity to common man's articulations.

When his poetry is rolling it has the gentle flow of natural speech:

> what softness we run toward
> and the rock of wool pulled short the
> mountains stand
> under the forks of rivers

> The bowman lays it out and keeps us
> down
> no names
> that give us not our death,
> O swift current, O buffalo.

The poem was written for the ear to ejoy, and yet it holds in its simple lyrical form a manifold content. In the preceding quote from **"Baggs,"** there is enough allusion to satisfy a Chinese and Pound scholar ("Song of the Bowmen of Shu"); a Jesuit scholar ("give us not our death"); and an American Indian scholar ("O buffalo").

The dying Blackburn is no different than the vital one, which is to say that he is always able to outflank lesser poets. He comes rushing out with rage and humor in the manner of W. B. Yeats in old age.

> Listen, Death
> Beth, see, it's
> not so bad . . . .

But the possibility of death in *Halfway Down the Coast* becomes the reality of dying in *The Journals.* This latter book is a poetry and prose chronicle from 1967, when the poet was lively, to 1971, when he died of cancer.... As the book progresses, the idea of death is superseded by the daily elements of physical decline and the actuality of dying. This book is remarkable for many reasons, among which are the maturity of Blackburn's poetry and poetics, the energy and intelligence of the writing, and the human courage informing every utterance. *The Journals* presents consummate Blackburn. The book culls deep intelligence, vast energy which refuses to wane with cancer, experience, and boldface originality. As the book presents new hope for poetry, it simultaneously breaks new ground for prose. Novelists of the future should read the work. (pp. 189-90)

And yet the most startling aspect of this book is not its poetic applications but rather the human emotion, the steady lyrical progression from full life to carcinoma....

Blackburn was always a poet of cities, thus the title of his only commercial volume, *The Cities,* but the slow wasting must have been costly on his energies, and the last years of his life were spent teaching in Cortland, a central New York farm town with a state university. Instead of indulging cancer dreams, Blackburn deals with his growing pain as though it were a toothache or what he calls a pain in the shoulder. Whereas the earlier sections of this book were unique in form, the latter sections are *sui generis* for form wedded to passionate content....

The June entries contain references to his lack of strength and loss of weight. In mid-month his physical energies collapse, and he is unable to build a fence in his back yard. Nevertheless, a superhuman mental vigor accompanies the physical deterioration; the energetic intelligence is still groping for forms, the overhead sense of beauty in spoken language is not lost. The self-effacing hip posture, the love of drink and poetry, do not leave the poet. The last entry is dated July 28, 1971, about six weeks before his death. This remarkably creative man dies, without once being maudlin or lugubrious. Never a man to pass up a humorous, deadpan, tragicomic line, Blackburn ends the journal: "Bigod, I must have been full of shit." (p. 190)

Michael Stephens, "Common Speech & Complex Forms," in The Nation, *Vol. 223, No. 6, September 4, 1976, pp. 189-90.*

JOEL OPPENHEIMER

Paul Blackburn, poet, began his studies in Provencal poetry 30 years ago. Turned on by Ezra Pound's introduction to the work, and fueled by his own taste for Mediterranean and Latin culture, Blackburn pursued this body of verse until he died, too early, in 1971. *Proensa* was essentially ready for publication in 1958 but has had to wait until now to show itself to us.

That these poems constitute a very real beginning for post-Roman literature throughout Europe and then America is without question. What is more readily apparent in this version is the close connection over nine centuries between those poets and their work, and today's poets and theirs—and Paul Blackburn was ideally suited to delineate it. . . . [He] saw the poems as living things, to be recreated as poetry in *American*.

He succeeded admirably, so that this is not a scholar's book but a reader's. . . .

Let those who will learn from this work, as well as enjoy it. It is a major contribution and should do much to pull down the elitist obfuscating veil that the litterateurs have thrown over the art of poetry.

Which is to say, again, that these poems were written as living things, and Blackburn has translated them as such. They are fresh and meaningful today, too; they are our beginnings and yet they breathe now. . . .

> *Joel Oppenheimer, in a review of "Proensa: An Anthology of Troubadour Poetry," in* The Village Voice, *Vol. XXIV, No. 7, February 12, 1979, p. 90.*

PAUL CHRISTENSEN

Blackburn was a modern pastoral poet whose sensibilities experience easily bruised. He wrote often of his loneliness, of watching others, of his shy sexual longings, of fantasies arising out of the banality of daily life, always attempting to protect his vulnerability by affecting a certain toughness or indifference. His first poems are somewhat callow in their emotional simplicity. . . . In his later poetry he wrote as a man who ventured into the world with too much tenderness. Tone is the delicate nuance of his best verse, and innocence of mind that is forever dissolving and reemerging from a tough antilyric vocabulary. He is the pastoral poet set loose in the drab, impersonal streets of New York. In the poems of *Brooklyn-Manhattan Transit* (1960), he describes the slight possibilities of romance in the dreary compartments of the subway train:

> The tanned blond
>   in the green print sack
> in the center of the subway car
>   standing
> tho there are seats
>   has had it from
> 1 teen-age hood
> 1 lesbian
> 1 envious housewife
> 4 men over fifty
> (& myself), in short
>   the contents of this half of the car.
>   (pp. 195-96)

Blackburn died leaving a canon of work, including his last-written poems, *The Journals,* which Robert Kelly edited in 1975. In his editorial note, Kelly claims that *The Journals,* are

"Blackburn's quintessential work." As early as 1968 Blackburn had a premonition of his impending death by cancer, to which he succumbed in 1971, and from that date, Kelly says, "his work, especially *The Journals,* reads like a *carnivale,* a joyous farewell to the flesh of the world." Perhaps "joyous farewell" is more than the text of the poems would bear out; many of the individual entries in the poet's journal are touching and poignant, sometimes starkly lyrical.

In these last poems, too, there is a superb sense of visual placement of language on the page: Blackburn communicates half of the content of his words merely by their location. The objective, mundane content is lined up against the left margin, the moodier passages and subjective embellishments against the right, and the play of the mind ranges down the center in steep terraces. There is an exact sense of spacing in the lines, a keen ear-sense as well in the way he dangles the terminal word of a line or halts a line and then introduces the key word in full capitals. These typographical techniques, so bold and controversial fifteen years before, appear under Blackburn's hand as the new conventions of modern poetic speech; they do not shout or violate the reader's expectations, they simply occur with precise, satisfying effect.

The Journals are also Blackburn's successful effort at a long poem, in which he recorded his late travels through Europe and the final months of his life in Cortland, New York, where he was teaching. As the title implies, these poems constitute his daybook, the form many poets of the short lyric have imposed on themselves to achieve a work of length and continuity. But whereas other poets have used the daybook as a rhythmic device, Blackburn seizes upon the form with a richer intent: the days themselves are increasingly more valuable as he senses his approaching death.

He avoids making a deliberate plot of his death; rather, the thought of it erupts intermittently in the flow of his brief lyrics. The last poems are not final in any thematic sense; they continue to make records of daily life as though the process were to go on forever. For the contemporary poet, death is an intractable subject. Its final meaning is unclear, and the fuller the treatment of it, the more the poet feels required to address himself to its religious and philosophical implications. Blackburn succeeds in treating the theme by approaching it with naive inquisitiveness. . . . As it was for Emily Dickinson before him, death is a shock into greater consciousness which the poet explores precisely, openly, using every resource of language and technique to map and understand it. (pp. 196-98)

> *Paul Christensen, "Olson and the Black Mountain Poets," in his* Charles Olson: Call Him Ishmael, *University of Texas Press, 1979, pp. 161-212.*

PIERRE JORIS

Paul Blackburn, sadly, died nine years ago . . . , and in his death we mourn the loss of a major voice of American poetry. Besides 'sharing the same hopes for poetry, the same angers at what we considered its slack misuses', as [Robert] Creeley says in his thoughtful introduction to *Against the Silences,* he and Paul Blackburn shared common roots in New England. Creeley's thought and work, down to its tight, bare and rock hard structures, has always retained an essentially New England quality. Blackburn, on the other hand, rejecting the harsh puritanism that seems to go hand in hand with those bleak Vermont winters, turned his imagination to the South 'and the generous permission of unabashed sensuality'. The present book is a selection culled from a larger manuscript which the poet kept in a loose-leaf binder and to which he periodically added poems during the decade preceding his death. All the poems concern his relationship with his second wife. They are, in a sense, very private occasions, charting the breakdown of the marriage and the eventual separation and divorce. For a lesser poet this could mean sentimentality. But Blackburn, even in those moments of extreme personal anguish, never falls prey to this danger. His earthiness, his delight in life, his sensuality guard him as does his exquisite craftsmanship. The poems are deceptively simple on the surface, due to his use of colloquial American language and its speech rhythms. But that easy-going surface hides an extremely accomplished craftsman. One of the major problems of 'free verse', from its inception on, is the question of where to break the line. If a poem's form is to emerge from 'the poem understand' in the very process of writing, and if that form is to be the only accurate form for that poem, then line-breaks have to show a near-total internal necessity. Blackburn brilliantly solved this problem by using his breath as the basic measure (one needs to read these poems *aloud* to savour their rhythmic intricacies and complex texture. . . . Even though the poems are a record of failure and loss, of sexual frustration—as made clear by that haunting image of the 'Six men of some desert tribe, their women / for that time unclean', who 'stand about the camp's / fire / jacking off' which the poet sees as an offering to Moloch—there is humour here too, in no way ironic or sarcastic, a humour springing from a deep love for the world and whatever, good or bad, that world contains. . . .

[What] is most engaging in the work is the way a single poem of, say two pages, will let so much, so many different perceptions in, following the Creeley saying: Form is never more than an extension of content. No one who wants to know what can be done in a lyric poetry that is not simply 'confessional poetry' can afford to miss Blackburn's work. (p. 20)

> *Pierre Joris, "Reinventing Love," in* New Statesman, *Vol. 100, No. 2592, November 21, 1980, pp. 20-1.*

THOMAS MEYER

Paul Blackburn's Lorca translations [in *Lorca/Blackburn: Poems of Federico Garcia Lorca*] lack something, the contrast between ingenious elegance and folk simplicity never quite comes across, and so the stark surprise of the originals is often lost. . . . I miss a definite metallic edge in Blackburn's Lorca, that snappiness Spicer got hold of in *After Lorca.* But I'm ready to admit my judgment, if at all informed, may be off target. Looking back over *Lorca/Blackburn,* the rendering of "Agosto," to pick just a single short lyric, is plain testament to Blackburn's skill as poet and translator. About that I have no quibble. The economies he exercises in English upon a poem whose original Spanish is already tight as a drum are dazzling. . . .

Still I'm uneasy, perhaps with the frequent cognates, or with Blackburn's attempts to make Lorca's repetitions asymmetrical, often destroying the effect of a haunting refrain. Perhaps some of the work is simply overwrought, or the selection itself too scant, I don't know. But this is not to deny that *Lorca/Blackburn* is a book well worth anyone's reading and re-reading. As poet-translator and translated-poet they are ultimately mismatched. Blackburn while he obtains a polish, doesn't have Garcia Lorca's *sangre fria,* nor that bitterness born of mistrusting then dishonoring emotion by distorting it.

Which is why Blackburn's Provencal translations, imitations and gleanings are brilliant and his Lorca strikes me as a bit lackluster. Federico Garcia Lorca is much too heartless a poet for the author of *Against the Silences* and no matter how sophisticated one's technique, the heart once admitted can't be ignored. . . .

Against the Silences describes the breaking up of a marriage, an ordinary, nevertheless painful event riddled with personal inconclusiveness and legal uncertainty. . . . As always, how can we recover the fleeting details of our lives and redeem them?

How Blackburn does it so well and so openly is a delicate yet deliberate exercise of great skill. To describe the loss of his wife's affection, the severing of their intimacy, the vicissitudes of their sex life he quietly reports the turnings away abed, unshared meals, absences, toilet habits and sleeplessness so that the growing losses of a man "who wishes for a subdued life of leisurely gestures" reach their extreme when the poet finally has no details to make his poems from but the most painful: a song about his wife's taking a lover, a sort of two-step about the quickie divorce, a meditation on his attempt to relieve the new sexual frustration of being left alone. The complexities of such an everyday but marked crisis oddly enough are always handled in these poems with lyric rather than psychological adherence to detail. Thus they remain poetry rather than becoming *Madame Bovary* or even *The Golden Bowl.* Blackburn refuses to render his emotions in any other form than their direct statement, that is, as they are perceived. The result is a laconic dissociation of verbal meaning which provides the poet with metrical grounding in common speech but never draws him headlong into full satire or cynicism. Its effect is the discreet presentation of a startling, honest emotional reality whose rare accomplishment preserves the feeling nothing has been tampered with. (p. 2)

These two books, back to back, make odd bedfellows. Yet each is precious as probably one of the last Blackburn books we'll have. From hereon in it'll be a matter of the Collected, the Selected, the Annotated etc., while it is as single volumes appearing in their own time that a man's work touches us with those vital pressures he himself labored under. By that freshness Paul Blackburn's work makes clear, I think, how important it is that we take our lives as actual, and by honoring such actualities as these, come to regard their occasional nature as tender. Such is their ultimate, and only value. (pp. 2-3)

> *Thomas Meyer, in a review of "Lorca/Blackburn Poems of Frederico Garcia Lorca" and "Against the Silences," in* The American Book Review, *Vol. 3, No. 3, March-April, 1981, pp. 2-3.*

TOBY OLSON

In not too long a time we will have the late Paul Blackburn's collected poems in hand. It will be a large gathering, and one trusts that justice will follow that appearance, placing this poet, his special and various talents where they belong, beside those few others of major importance in recent years. Until then, the poems come to us piecemeal, in small groupings. But Blackburn's care was thorough, and *Against the Silences* is of his own choosing and ordering. So we have here yet another carefully arranged aspect of his concern, thrust, as it always is, into celebration. And that celebratory quality of his work is all the more startling in his case; these are the painful pieces, ones that he did not choose to publish in book form while he was alive, that deal both with the knowledge of his death and the other death of his broken marriage. The book is a kind of companion piece to *The Journals*. . . . In general, these are the darker poems, the riskier and more painful ones. There is more anger here. With . . . a mix of searing, disjunctive poems and lovely lyrical pieces, *Against The Silences* is a fine pearl for the string of any Blackburn collection.

> *Toby Olson, in a review of "Against the Silences,"*
> *in New Letters, Vol. 48, No. 2, Winter, 1981-82, p.*
> *108.*

PETER SCHJELDAHL

The Collected Poems of Paul Blackburn. . . . rescues Blackburn from a near oblivion that is itself "very 60's." That was a time of Balkanization in poetry, when poets turned hermetic not only in their work but in their sense of audience. On the Lower East Side, where Blackburn figured as a coffeehouse impresario . . . , the ruling idea was that you wrote for your circle of friends and let fame take care of itself. Fortunately for Blackburn and us, fame is at last being given a hand. . . .

[A frequent] translator of troubadour poetry, Blackburn was a latter-day troubadour, squeezing sweetness from bitter life. The life was his own, that of a person who seems not to have interested him very much. He had an obvious distaste for introspection and any other experience that could not be turned directly into song.

Blackburn's fierce commitment to songfulness—a formalism aimed not so much to express feelings as to invent them—makes him troubling in a way that is resonant with the glory and misery of an epoch when people really did try to edit themselves as if they were poems. The cocky, slangy, profane persona of Blackburn's work is a kind of translucent fiction in which one sees the dim shadows of suppressed emotions. At his worst, he flaunts the fiction, a barroom boor. More often he is a selfless hero of art, laying down his very life for a good line.

Blackburn was a city poet, one of the best at lyricizing the crowded, scuffling existence in which "nature" reduces to greenery in an air shaft and pigeons wheeling overhead. He also wrote wonderful dialect poems, pitch-perfect vignettes from the New York streets. But his main themes are erotic. Lust, incautiously obeyed, is his master metaphor.

> Love is a weakness, a
> sickness, a fear & a terror, and—
>
>   I love I can do that
>   and risk
>   that evil thing
> wherein our own heart go forth from us

The "sickness" has some unlovely symptoms. History has not been sympathetic to Blackburn's brand of chivalry, typical of a time when sexual freedom seemed a man's privilege and a woman's fate. Of course, bad attitudes have never been inconsistent with good poetry, a perverse truth that Blackburn proves.

Blackburn's work holds an extreme variety of pleasures. I particularly enjoy him as a serious comedian, a springer of laconic traps that make velleities extravagant. . . .

Another of Blackburn's modes was the pop-style poem that merely arranges, rather than trying to penetrate, the mediating surfaces of urban culture. **"Obit Page"** is an amazingly moving tour de force:

> O god.
> First the greatest right-handed batter in history
> Rogers Hornsby
>   (hit .424 in   1924)
>   with a lifetime average of .358
> and now   William Carlos Williams

Williams's name tolls slowly and vastly, summoning worlds of significance. . . .

Blackburn's poems keep a running commentary on world events of the 60's, though in terms that jealousy guard, and reinforce, poetry's autonomous value. His antiwar poems are essentially antipolitical, or else they reflect the notion, current in the 60's, that the personal is political. Blackburn was anguished by the way public rhetoric, however virtuous, distorts private truth, including even the inconvenient and vile truth of war's esthetic appeal. . . .

In his last years, when he was dying and knew it, Blackburn wrote poetry that was a loose-knit journal full of the doings and musings of "a doomed man planting tomatoes." Relentless in-jokes and an air of distraction mar these poems, but the voice in them is never less than appealing. Blackburn was chipper to the end. Surveying himself in the bath, he remarks, "I haven't had a body like this since I was 15," and the last line in this book is an exultant profanity. The muttering sprawl of his late work was historically apt, as always. It figured forth the deltalike spread, the entropy, of a decade's torrential energies. "Make it new," Pound had ordered. Blackburn couldn't seem to make it any other way.

> *Peter Schjeldahl, "Fever Charts of the 1960's," in*
> The New York Times Book Review, *November 10,*
> *1985, p. 30.*

PAUL CHRISTENSEN

[A] shared conviction gathers together much of [twentieth-century American poetry] as the collective voice of protest against life in the modern city. . . . Early in the century, Ezra Pound struck the note of discord in poetry when he began dissecting the city as a vortex of mechanistic ideals, in which usury and commerce were bulwarks against an alternative order Pound discerned in pagan myths, the Greek world-view, in the lust gods of nature, Dionysus and Aphrodite. "Learn from the green world," he exhorted. . . .

Blackburn's "green world" lay somewhere in the unconscious, in what is primal of human nature. His eye was always searching for some tidbit of human resistance to city monotony, "but such accidents of fate or inner nature/are certainly occasional," he reports in a wry goat song, **"Cabras."** His notational style here and throughout [*The Collected Poems of Paul Blackburn*] springs from Pound's poetry, which Blackburn began reading in his early twenties. Like William Carlos Williams, Blackburn believed in "no ideas but in things," hence these *trompe l'oeil* lyrics catching sight of minute particulars of nature in the mechanical city. The machine age, Blackburn thought, was merely puritanism with a new face, a grinding work ethic poised against pleasure and surprise. His poems . . . are the art of detecting the life force as it seeps out of the cracks of the street, from the manhole covers clamped down on it. Even Blackburn's pitiful last days battling cancer, recorded in his journals, thrust up the opposition between primordial vitality and modern entropy; he is witty and sensuous to the end of his life, a steady apostle of Pound's vision of the old *élan*.

Paul Christensen, "Notes from the Green World," in Book World—The Washington Post, *January 5, 1986, p. 6.*

TOM CLARK

Some of the best of our poetry comes out of the late 1950s and early 1960s, a time when the discoveries of William Carlos Williams and Ezra Pound were approaching full realization in the work of a group of younger writers intent on keeping the language equally true, fresh and alive. One of the talented young progressives of that period was New York poet Paul Blackburn, whose early allegiance to Williams and Pound . . . had brought him into contact with writers of his own generation like Charles Olson and Robert Creeley. Along with Olson, Creeley and other writers of the Black Mountain group, Blackburn devoted himself to exploring and extending the Pound/ Williams breakthrough—in so doing, creating a whole new terrain for American poetry.

That's one area of the culture where the maps keep changing constantly, however. By the 1970s, Blackburn's innovative work was already hard to find, scattered through ephemeral, often out-of-print volumes that hadn't been easy to turn up even when new. Reading Blackburn became impossible for anyone lacking the hours (or the dollars) of a serious collector. All that changes now, with the 523 poems lovingly and laboriously assembled by Edith Jarolim into [*The Collected Poems of Paul Blackburn*]—a book that gives us the first organized body of work by which to assess this prolific writer.

Blackburn died in 1971, at age 44, of a cancer that came almost as an objectification of the longing for unconsciousness, the deathward swoon, expressed in much of his later poetry. . . . For this poet committed to the ideal of Eros, Death was the ultimate lover, a final tunnel of extinction "at spur's end" beyond the "nets of lust" and the last BMT stop—releasing one into "the jaw of what softness we rut toward . . . To roll into it / and stay there warm" (**"Baggs"**).

The vision in many of Blackburn's poems may be as dark as a subway tunnel, but the voice is always clear. His early immersion in the regular-guy, man-on-the-street discourse of William Carlos Williams . . . had a permanently salutary effect, keeping Blackburn's poems as honestly expressive and dem-ocratically engaging as the pluralistic urban society whose surfaces they reflect. Confidential, wry, knowing, but somehow modest—the Blackburn voice is always there, as easy to trust as a loyal friend.

Blackburn kept the man-on-the-street modesty as his standard. "To write poems, say, / is not a personal achievement," he suggests in one poem, thereby dismissing his own years of careful practice with a single calculated shrug, as if to say, "anyone can do it." (But of course, anyone can't, as Blackburn well knew.) Or again: "Poems will not do. / It is a kind of minuteness of application of whatever blessed / things the goddess has put in our hands" (**"Winter Solstice"**).

Blackburn found that his own dalliance with "the goddess," both in her divine and too-human manifestations, brought its special costs. "Wounded so many times by love" in his poems, in real life he went through three wives and numerous temporary attachments, repeatedly bouncing back up, only to be pulled down into the whirlpool-vertigo of love (or "lust," as he called it in an unconscious echo of his Catholic upbringing) all over again.

It was as if not only in poetry but in reality Blackburn had to live out the Provencal troubadour poet-lover's fate of heart-loss and perpetual victimization at the feet of the remote, cruel, Unkind Lady. Adopting this troubadour persona as a distancing device for a mock-plaintive lyricism, he used poetry to give him courage in love, and vice versa. . . .

In his last years, Blackburn abandoned the strict form of his poems in favor of a looser-structured kind of verse "journal," which gradually became a diaristic catch-all for his daily doings, domestic life, travels and creative process. This increasingly painful poetic home movie keeps rolling almost to the bitter end, as we see the dying poet surveying his wasted body in the bath, "waiting for the ache . . . to go away."

"Let / each man's words be his own," he writes a few months before death, echoing the close of one of his finest early poems, **"The Dissolving Fabric,"** about a suicide: "she possessed her own life, and took it." The self-possession always to be found at the center of Blackburn's poetry, holding it all together with a steady, controlled presence, was the last thing to leave him. In the poems, it remains.

Tom Clark, in a review of "The Collected Poems of Paul Blackburn," in Los Angeles Times Book Review, *January 19, 1986, p. 6.*

Jimmy Breslin

1930-

American novelist, journalist, and nonfiction writer.

Breslin's intimate knowledge and understanding of New York City street life informs his novels as well as his nationally syndicated newspaper columns and contributed to his being awarded the 1985 Pulitzer Prize for commentary. His vision of the pervasive corruption of life, reflected in his focus upon such characters as Mafia leaders, drug dealers, teenage hoodlums, and cynical alcoholics, is tempered with compassion and hope. Breslin's aggressive, visceral prose is often compared to that of Damon Runyon: both writers create colorfully authentic portraits of city life replete with urban colloqialisms, violence, and fast-paced, tragicomic narratives.

Breslin's first novel, *The Gang That Couldn't Shoot Straight* (1969), is a comic tale concerning an incompetent South Brooklyn Mafia underling who wants a bigger role in his organization's dealings. However, he squanders his opportunity and resorts to violence against the mob. While some critics faulted Breslin for awkwardly handling several subplots, most considered the book informed, realistic, and humorous. In his next novel, *World without End, Amen* (1973), Breslin relates the story of Dermot Davey, a twenty-nine-year-old alcoholic policeman. Faced with career failures, a faltering marriage, and an alcoholic mother, Davey travels to Northern Ireland to reconcile with his father. He and his father remain distant, however, and Davey is left alone to encounter Northern Ireland's social troubles. While some critics faulted Breslin for attempting to incorporate too many themes into the novel, others praised his delineation of Davey's spiritual poverty.

Breslin's next book, *.44* (1978), written in collaboration with Dick Schaap, is a thinly-veiled account of the "Son of Sam" murders that terrorized New York City residents during 1976 and 1977. Alan A. Ryan, Jr. described the book as an "amalgam" of fiction and nonfiction which "succeeds only on its least ambitious level: it is a passably good story of cops and a killer, the killer's victims and the fear he brought to a city." Breslin's fourth novel, *Forsaking All Others* (1982), concerns an ambitious young Hispanic who attempts to make his mark in the narcotics business, and his friend, a lawyer who becomes adulterously involved with the daughter of a powerful mobster. Filled with detailed descriptions of the drug trade, irreverence toward religion and authority, and explicit portrayals of sex and violence, the novel offers a painfully authentic picture of the criminal world and its effects on individuals.

In his recent novel, *Table Money* (1986), Breslin explores the complexities of marriage. Set in Queens in the early 1970s, the novel centers on Owney Morrison, an alcoholic laborer who is preoccupied with his aggressive masculine image, and his wife Dolores, who begins to assert her independence and revives her ambition to become a doctor. Often praised as Breslin's strongest work of fiction, *Table Money* is, according to James Carroll, "an important novel about what it is to be men and women trying to build and rebuild lives and meanings in America today." Breslin has also written several nonfiction books, including *How the Good Guys Finally Won: Notes from an Impeachment Summer* (1975), which details the demise of

© 1987 Thomas Victor

Richard Nixon's presidency, and *The World According to Breslin* (1984), a collection of his newspaper columns.

(See also *CLC*, Vol. 4 and *Contemporary Authors*, Vols. 73-76.)

THOMAS MEEHAN

Jimmy Breslin, the tough-guy chronicler of New York low life, . . . has turned out a comic tale about a South Brooklyn gang of Mafia small fry who botch a series of attempts to gun down a Cosa Nostra overlord.

Written in the neo-Runyonesque style familiar to readers of Breslin's magazine and newspaper pieces, *The Gang That Couldn't Shoot Straight* is more cinematic in its origins than literary. . . . [It] seems to have been influenced strongly by movies like *Big Deal on Madonna Street*, in which a grab-bag of incompetent but lovable crooks ludicrously fail at some major robbery. In this instance, however, the incompetents are professional killers, and the crime they're out to commit is nothing less than cold-blooded murder. Nor are they all that lovable, though Breslin desperately tries to make them so.

Anyway, he has assembled a cast that is virtually a circus sideshow of freaks. It includes, for instance, a dwarf and a 425-pound fat man, and most of its members have comic names— Kid Sally, Big Jelly, Tony the Indian. (The gang even has a pet lion that Breslin drags into the action from time to time.) The comedy in this novel, however, is mostly that of mayhem—funny, perhaps, to those capable of getting a laugh out of someone being blown up, garroted, or pitched head first off a bridge.

Breslin's plot deals with the rivalry between the South Brooklyn gang, led by Kid Sally Palumbo, a semimoron of 29 who has made a minor reputation for himself by helping to run over a gangster named Georgie Paradise, and the Mafia Establishment, as represented by a 68-year-old overlord called Baccala. Aware of dissident rumblings, Baccala at first tries to placate Kid Sally by permitting him to arrange and run a six-day bicycle race, on which the Mafia plans to make book. When the race fails to come off, however, (mainly because of blunders by Kid Sally and his lieutenants) open warfare breaks out between the two factions, and most of the rest of the book is simply the detailing of murders, attempted murders, and gangland funerals.

Getting all the worst of it, several members of Kid Sally's gang are brutally eliminated by Baccala's men, and each of these killings is treated as though it were slapstick comedy. Breslin, too, includes a love affair, a pallid romance between Kid Sally's younger sister and one of the six-day bicycle racers. Sex raises its head scarcely at all in the novel, however. If there is pornography in *The Gang That Couldn't Shoot Straight,* it is the pornography of violence.

Here and there, Breslin gets in some satirical knocks at the New York Police Department, at TV, radio, and newspaper reporters, and at City Hall. At times, too, as in the best of his journalistic pieces, there are sharply observed bits of New York detail. . . . At the Museum of Modern Art were "men in the uniform of Wall Street retirement: black Chesterfield coat, rimless glasses, and the Times folded to the obituary page." Indeed, the best parts of the novel (and Breslin addicts should agree) are such throwaway details as these—again, the sort of thing this author does so well in his magazine and newspaper pieces.

All of this isn't to suggest, however, that Breslin doesn't evidence some talent as a novelist. He may just need another race over the track, and could surprise when not having to be funny about the Mafia—a subject that, along with nerve gas, must certainly rank among the least comic of our time. (pp. 5, 52)

Instead of *The Gang That Couldn't Shoot Straight,* one somehow wishes he had written a novel of Irish-American family life in lower-middle-class Queens—about which maybe nobody could write better than he. A serious novel, too, rather than a comic one.

Breslin, with his broad and curiously cruel sense of humor, isn't half as funny as he thinks he is. Or, to put it another way, he is perhaps a more serious man than he realizes. (p. 52)

> Thomas Meehan, "*Kid Sally Palumbo Took on the Mafia,*" in The New York Times Book Review, *November 30, 1969, pp. 5, 52.*

L. J. DAVIS

[*The Gang That Couldn't Shoot Straight*] is about the time in Brooklyn, not so very long ago, when the Gallo boys declared war on the Profaci mob and a lot of people got killed. It is a journalistic book in the best sense of the word: crisp, informed, funny, cruel, and at times very real. Breslin's gangsters are vicious but not very smart, and they are endowed with all the compassion and moral fiber of men who would set fire to cats for the fun of it. In short, they are like real South Brooklyn gangsters.

Breslin's knowledge of the Mafia and its workings is extensive and accurate, but it is not the sort you are likely to find in the newspapers or most books. It is street knowledge. It may have its facts a little twisted and its body counts may be inflated, but it has other qualities. For example, it is true. (p. 4)

A book of this sort is heavily dependent on—and limited by— its tone of voice. It is the voice of the precinct house, the city room, the Irish bar, the political club: cynical, fluent, romantic and humane, and very much the product of an oral and not a literate tradition. It is a beautifully effective tool for describing a police captain, a gangster's funeral, a bumbled murder, a stupid crook, the way South Brooklyn looks in the morning, and the process by which the Mayor of New York receives vital crime news from outlying boroughs (he reads about it in *The New York Times,* just like the rest of us). Breslin is most at home with his subject in these moments, his touch is absolutely sure, and his sense of the tragic absurdity of human affairs is most apparent and effective; and he does not yield an inch to the implicit temptation in writing of this sort to be merely funny or merely clever. (pp. 4-5)

What a narrative voice like this cannot do is take us to the Palm Court at the Plaza Hotel. It tries to and it fails, and this brings us to the novel's principal weakness: a subplot involving art forgery, an Italian bicycle racer, and the insurgent gangster's kid sister. It is not a very interesting subplot and it keeps getting in the way of the rest of the novel. One gets the impression that Breslin is not very interested in it either, but that he nonetheless plugged doggedly away at it from a mistaken notion that the book needed more "human interest" and "contrast." It is a journalist's mistake. The narrative thrust of the novel is weakened, the tone of voice falters and goes flat, and not much of importance is accomplished. Angela, the sister, grows more and more to resemble a sentimental cliché and the bike rider is so fitfully relevant to the main action that it would have been better if he'd been dispensed with entirely. . . .

At its best, this is a very fine, very strong and often remarkable book. It will undoubtedly be a success, and it deserves to be. (p. 5)

> L. J. Davis, "*Inside Gangland,*" in Book World— The Washington Post, *December 21, 1969, pp. 4-5.*

JEFF GREENFIELD

The Gang That Couldn't Shoot Straight is a very funny novel, and if you don't think that's significant, try to think of the last book since *Catch-22* that made you put it down and laugh.

Breslin's plot concerns a rivalry within the Brooklyn Mafia family under the direction of Anthony Pastrumo, Sr.—Baccala to his friends (he doesn't have any) and hierlings (lots). An incompetent lieutenant, Kid Sally Palumbo, wants a bigger piece of the pie, and Baccala lets him try his hand at organizing a six-day bicycle race which the mob will use for gambling purposes. The race turns into total catastrophe, and when Baccala announces that Palumbo is to be humiliated, Kid Sally revolts and the war is on . . . sort of. . . .

What makes it all work is not so much this rickety plot as the characters from Breslin's world who people the book. There is Big Jelly Catalano, professional degenerate (as a schoolboy, he used to lean over and whisper into girls' ears "sodomy," "period," and "come"). There is Big Mama, offering pithy advice to grandson Kid Sally ("you watch you ass"). There is the Mayor, a tall, good-looking, harrassed Protestant (obviously a figment of Breslin's fertile mind). There is a large and hungry lion.

There are also the little gems that flavor the book. Breslin has a two-page history of the FBI and the Mafia that's worth a dozen National editorials, and a one-paragraph explanation of Italian-Puerto Rican hostility that would take the Times a 40-man task force to find. One caveat—he can't write about sex at all. At one point, describing a liaison between his heroine and a bemused Italian visitor who gets trapped in the gang warfare, you aren't sure whether the girl is making love to the guy or throwing up all over him.

Small pickings. The fact is this is a funny book and a good one. . . .

> *Jeff Greenfield, in a review of "The Gang That Couldn't Shoot Straight," in* The Village Voice, *Vol. XV, No. 1, January 1, 1970, p. 7.*

RICHARD BROWN

In [*World Without End, Amen*] it doesn't matter whether [Breslin's characters] are the comparatively affluent members of the New York area working class, or Northern Irish proletariat, it is their spiritual poverty . . . that concerns him, and it applies equally to the small, mean lives led on the streets of the Borough of Queens across the East River from Manhattan and in the Catholic ghettos of Derry and Belfast.

The protagonist is Dermot Davey, a 29-year-old cop whose life is going to pieces. A black-out drinker who cannot be trusted anymore with a gun, he has been reduced to serving on the police department's "bow and arrow" squad, a combination disciplinary-therapeutic program for troubled cops. Dermot Davey was once a decent and naively dedicated enforcer of the law, but the facts of police life have brutalized and corrupted him. Not yet 30, and with $20,000 of pay-off money tucked away, he is comfortably slogging out his time to an early retirement, a pension and a job as a bank guard. He is contemplating suicide as well.

Davey's mother is alcoholic, and they don't talk anymore. He has a wife, a mother-in-law and a sister about whom he cares little and children to whom he is largely indifferent. His off-duty hours are spent boozing in bars and talking sports. The women of his family are defined by children, supermarkets, bingo parlors and neighborhood hairdressers. An evening at home with them would be spent in front of the television from 7:30 to bedtime.

Bedtime has brought its own traumas to them all, and Davey is one of the men who stand smoking in front of the stoops at night to give their wives a chance to at least feign sleep so that they will be spared the embarrassment of acknowledging, or ignoring, their waking presence in a bed.

That is Irish Catholic Queens, a bleak picture of repressed sexuality, anger, narrow prejudices and petty enthusiasms. Because Davey's life is coming apart, the reader might well expect that his visit to the land of his forbears will open up new vistas,

not only of social conscience but of meaning, and that the ruined cop will somehow find himself quixotically in the cause of the Irish Republic. The expectation is encouraged by the fact that the trip to Ireland has been prompted by news that Davey's long-lost father is living off an insurance settlement somewhere in the North. This is not the author's intent, however, and except for a moving encounter between father and son in a bar in Derry, during which they awkwardly discuss the pitching prowess of one-time Yankee great Whitey Ford, the found father is of little significance, and the idea of Ireland as homeland is of even less.

Essentially, this is a socio-ethnic novel, and what Breslin is up to is, I think, more motivated by his sense of the shortcomings of his own kind here in America than by any desire to dramatize the latest chapter of Ireland's eight centuries of resistance to the Anglo-Saxon tyrant. (pp. 2-3)

Breslin doesn't really care about the stolen kingdom of Ulster, and though he may care personally about the civil rights question in the North, here it is the irony of the situation that interests him most. The general Irish-American inclination to conservatism is, in areas like Queens, sometimes almost redneck in its intensity, and Dermot Davey, with a cop's angers and frustrations, is even more given to a bigot response than are his neighbors. He hates blacks, Italians, homosexuals, hippies and the Jewish lawyers who plead their cases in the courts. Given the chance (and he takes it whenever he can), he'd beat up on them all.

It is something of a shock, then, for him to go to Northern Ireland and find that the shiftless, unreliable, foul-smelling, breed-like-rabbits element of the population are his own kind— all Murphys, Coogans and O'Briens. . . .

Gone to Ireland in search of a father, Davey finds a mother, too, at least a mother-figure of sorts, in the person of a strong, young socialist lieutenant to Bernadette Devlin. An attractive woman his own age, with sensibilities and intelligence, she challenges all that he believes in. What happens in their relationship constitutes the novel's romantic plot line, and Breslin's handling of it, both for the purposes of his story, and in what it reveals of an old-time Irish-Catholic sensibility, is at the core of the work.

Having said all this is not to have said enough. This is a surprisingly serious novel. It is not without flaws, but they are small ones. The achievement is large and rich and rewarding. *World Without End* is the kind of thing Breslin should have been applying his considerable talent to a long time ago. (p. 3)

> *Richard Brown, "The Tearing of the Green," in* Book World—The Washington Post, *August 12, 1973, pp. 2-3.*

RALPH McINERNY

Breslin's *World Without End, Amen* is a book which, like its hero, has a tendency to fall between stools. The choice of the concluding words of the Lesser Doxology for a title suggests the ambiguities of the book. Why should a paean to the Trinity be chosen to name this story? One suspects that the words are lodged in Breslin's deepest memories but that he has forgotten their context and just plucks them forth, perhaps because they suggest just one damned thing after another, the apparent nihilism of the book, its unconvincing suggestion that nothing makes any sense. Unconvincing because here and there the likable pre-literary Breslin you thought you knew comes irrepressibly through. . . .

His protagonist, Dermot Davey, is a brutal boozy sadistic cop, a character who invites at first the disgust and then the disinterest of the reader. Why in the name of God did Breslin think him important enough to occupy the center of a novel? Apparently he had the idea that, if you took a cop who oppresses, beats, even shoots, the citizens he is employed to protect, and put him in the reversal of his situation, make him one of the oppressed, say as a Catholic in Northern Ireland, well . . . Well, what? If we hold Breslin to this theme, the answer to our unfinished question is: nothing. Zero. Dermot Davey will end as he began. Does Breslin want his novel to say that there is nothing to choose between the oppressor and the oppressed? I would have settled for a clear affirmative answer to that. The clarity is not vouchsafed.

Then there is Theme Two. Davey is a father and of course he had one of his own. His father deserted his mother and went back to Ireland. So the trip to Ireland is a search for his father, for reconciliation. He will meet his father and he will come to understand why the man left and as a result love or hate him for it. Davey meets his father, in a bar, of course, and the one is as inarticulate as the other. . . . On his second visit to the bar, Dermot is told this by his father: "You know, once you let one day go, it's a very easy thing to let a hundred days go." And Dermot replies, "I know." That kind of recognition of failure is possible only in a moral universe. Infrequently, in scenes like these, a real novel seems to underlie what we have been given.

Theme Three, I fear, is the one Breslin may think he developed, one I choose to think was foisted on him by some dum-dum unaware of his real powers as a writer. Why not think of the Catholics in Bogside as the niggers of Northern Ireland? Then poor dumb Dermot Davey can be lectured by every bellicose tosspot, Bernadette Devlin and Marxist Mother Machree for the dreadful things he has done to Angela Davis. Now anyone who can seriously entertain the comparison between the Catholics of the Six Counties and the blacks in America is thinking on the level of a television documentary. That such an analogy is facile sometimes troubles even Davey in the sodden recesses of his brain but he is incapable, and Breslin is unwilling, to explore the phoniness of it. Indeed one of the major missed opportunities of the novel is Breslin's failure to develop what is candidly admitted by his guide, namely that the current troubles are in large part television drama. (pp. 440-41)

As has been mentioned, Breslin's strengths as a writer come upon the reader unexpectedly, rising out of a dead prose which seems printed in capital letters. The basic weakness is structural; these seventeen chapters simply do not form a coherent whole. They *say* a lot, but they do not *tell* us anything. . . .

From time to time an effort is made to rise above the wire service level of the prose, but too often—I think because Breslin has lost his voice or is practicing ventriloquism—this leads to such infelicities as the description of Derry "sitting at the foot of a finger of water." And there is the incessant lighting of cigarettes and the endless boozing. . . .

So what are the strengths? The scenes with the father. An episode, recounted with authoritative economy, in which a Catholic garbageman who has spent years hanging on to the back of the truck brings his wife and kids along on the morning when he is to be promoted to driver. They stand on the pavement, waiting for the truck to emerge from the garage, with the proud man at the wheel. But he is passed over in favor of a Protestant much his junior and, when the truck emerges, a shamefaced husband and father clings to the back of it, his face averted. There, without wooly rhetoric and cheapening parallels with the plight of the children of slaves, is tragedy enough for any writer and any reader. Given his instinct for the viscerally significant, Breslin could have made this a novel of a brute's awakening to his humanity and if Davey should later lapse from this awareness, revert to his former self, well, we might weep but we would not be surprised. This is the story Breslin lost by transposing it onto a political level his hero is too dumb to understand and which Breslin as author must therefore handle on a tabloid level. The attempt to write a novel of ideas with a central character whose scarcely evolved brain is anyway numb with booze invited a shambles. (p. 441)

> *Ralph McInerny, "Hamill, Breslin & Flaherty, Ltd.," in* Commonweal, *Vol. XCIX, No. 17, February 1, 1974, pp. 439-41.*

ALLAN A. RYAN, JR.

[*.44*] is Jimmy Breslin's and Dick Schaap's transparently disguised account of the "Son of Sam" murders which terrorized New York. . . . They say it is "based on historical realities" but is "not itself historically accurate," presumably because "we have invented people, places and dates." Thus it is intended not to be "factual," only "truthful." Here, as in reality, the killer wields a .44 caliber Charter Arms Bulldog and signs his notes "Son of Sam." But David Berkowitz becomes "Bernard Rosenfeld." Jimmy Breslin of the *Daily News,* himself a dramatis persona because the killer wrote him a letter (which appears here verbatim), becomes "Danny Cahill" of the "Dispatch." Stacy Moskowitz, the killer's last victim, becomes "Mitzi Levinson," and so forth. This is neither fiction nor nonfiction, but an amalgam of both, labelled a novel.

This book succeeds only on its least ambitious level: it is a passably good story of cops and a killer, the killer's victims, and the fear he brought to a city. It fails on its most important level, for it tells us almost nothing about Berkowitz/Rosenfeld. It is, in both respects, a sort of urban *Jaws,* with Berkowitz as the shark: primitive, driven and unchanging, random in his choice of victims and ultimately beyond understanding. That one-dimensional portrait will do in *Jaws,* for there the killer was only an animal. But Berkowitz is a human being. Breslin and Schaap simply tell us that Berkowitz is possessed by visions of slavering dogs and have us assume that he is therefore crazy. But these visions should be the beginning of the inquiry, not the end. (p. E1)

There is no attempt to explain the basic riddle of Berkowitz's mind: why the dogs laid peacefully in his psyche for months on end and then cried havoc. Here, Rosenfeld sees a pretty young girl; the dogs howl in his head, and he kills. Next month, he hunts again, but the dogs don't howl and so he goes home. Two months later, they howl again, and he kills again.

One cannot overlook or excuse this frustrating neglect of analysis, for Breslin and Schaap had the best of both worlds: the compelling fact that there is a real Berkowitz who murdered, and the novelist's freedom—indeed, duty—to explore, speculate and create. . . . The reason they pass up such exploration, one senses, is that in the end they are less interested in Berkowitz than in those he affected—the police, the reporters, the men and women who ride the subways and read the *Daily News* in New York. Breslin has always been very good at capturing the strengths and weaknesses and foibles of such people. There is a compassionate and no doubt accurate portrayal of the dedication of the New York police in tracking down the Son of Sam. And there are also some genuinely funny ripostes at Rupert Murdoch and the *New York Post,* glamorpuss TV reporters, and PR advisors to the Mayor.

But Berkowitz was not, after all, a member of the gang that couldn't shoot straight. He was, as the authors constantly remind us, both a cunning killer and a frighteningly tormented madman. One cannot write him off by telling us that fiery-eyed dogs roamed his skull. What possessed him to bring a city to its knees is a story that remains to be told. (p. E6)

> Allan A. Ryan, Jr., "Son of Son of Sam," in Book World—The Washington Post, *May 21, 1978, pp. E1, E6.*

EVAN HUNTER

In *The Gang That Couldn't Shoot Straight,* Jimmy Breslin tried to combine a Runyonesque sort of humor with a serious love story, which is difficult for the best of writers; ultimately that novel was a hybrid failure. The beginning of *World Without End, Amen* was a brilliant portrait of an alcoholic New York City cop; it fell apart when Mr. Breslin took the story to Ireland and the warfare there. [In *.44*], collaborating with Dick Schaap, the sports director of WNBC-TV, Mr. Breslin has written a book that similarly cannot make up its mind.

The introductory disclaimer is fair-enough warning of the book's ambivalence: "This is a novel. It is based on historical realities—the Son of Sam killings in New York City in 1976 and 1977—but it is not itself historically accurate. It is not supposed to be. . . ." [We] have invented people, places, and dates, everything except the terror. The terror was real. This is a novel. It is not factual. We hope it is truthful."

I can only speculate on the legal advice that prompted the authors to tell this familiar story as fiction. Someone should have advised them simultaneously that a novel doesn't *have* to be either factual *or* truthful; a novel, for that matter, can perhaps best be defined as inspired lying. I confess that I did not follow the real-life Son of Sam case day by day, hour by hour, but nowhere in this "novel" could I find any discernible difference between what the authors *pretend* to pretend and what anyone living in or around New York City remembers as actually having happened. Nowhere, in short, is there the spark of invention that might have propelled the basic material into that rarefied realm of fiction—the inspired lying one would have wished from Mr. Breslin, who was so intimately involved in the real hunt for the killer.

The book is a *non*-novel, *non*-nonfiction mutant without any characters who are more than pasteboard figures slavishly linked to an actual event that—because of its worldwide coverage—unfolds here with neither mystery nor suspense. It is a book that would have been more "truthful" and might perhaps have dared to illuminate (as any true novel should) had it been written straight. But, even then, I would have asked the only pertinent question: *Why?* (p. 6)

> Evan Hunter, "Murderous Fact and Fiction," in The New York Times Book Review, *July 2, 1978, pp. 6, 14.*

EVAN HUNTER

Jimmy Breslin's new novel [*Forsaking All Others*] is so good that I feel an intense personal obligation to persuade you to read it. You may have been put off by the derivative Runyonesque humor of his first novel, *The Gang That Couldn't Shoot Straight.* You may have felt excluded by the strong Irish-American slant of his next novel, *World Without End, Amen.* You may have been entirely alienated, as was I [see excerpt above], by what seemed to be a commercial exploitation of the notorious Son of Sam murders in *.44,* the novel he wrote with sports reporter Dick Schaap. But none of these previous works will prepare you for the power of *Forsaking All Others.*

Somewhere, somehow, Mr. Breslin seems to have searched deep within himself, exorcised himself of whatever it was in the past that had kept him at arm's length from his subject matter and then immersed himself completely in a setting that would seem entirely foreign to him. He has chosen to write about hope, corruption, disillusionment and despair; to illustrate these important themes, he has selected as his protagonists two young Hispanic men and a young Italian-American woman.

Ramon Solivan, whose street name is "Teenager," comes to New York from a Puerto Rican "town of shacks" in 1966, when he is 17. He brings with him $37, a note to his uncle on West 93rd Street, his 14-year-old wife and the wild hope that he can use his strength to become rich in America. Ten years later, he is being paroled from the Albion Correctional Facility, where he's already been credited with 681 days of jail time, after a criminal career that has included arrests for possession with intent to sell, robbery first, grand larceny first, assault first, assault second and homicide; as a member of the parole board puts it, "These were just a few of the things you did out there." At 27, he is back on the teeming streets of the South Bronx.

Maximo Escobar is four years younger than Teenager. He was born in a shack in La Playa de Ponce, two doors down from the one in which Teenager was born. He is a graduate of De Witt Clinton High School, Lehman College and, most recently, Harvard Law School. Maximo despises drug peddlers. At the same time, he loves Teenager, who—immediately upon his release from prison—begins building the ambitious narcotics empire that will serve as the catalyst for the novel's action. Maximo wants to help his people; when he passes his bar exam, he wants to "place his standard atop the rubble and the breeze would cause the colors to dance and the people would be attracted."

Nicki Mariani is the 26-year-old daughter of the boss of the Mafia family running the Bronx. She has been married for 42 months to a man who has been in prison for 36 of those months, serving four to life on a narcotics conviction. . . . While waiting faithfully for her husband's eventual parole, dutifully taking home-cooked lasagna and sausage and peppers to him on her periodic conjugal visits to the prison ("For two days all you do is drink wine and get raped," she tells a girlfriend), Nicki works as a well-paid skip-tracing supervisor for a New York bank. When Teenager comes to visit her father in New Jersey on drug "business" one weekend, he brings along with him his friend Maximo. Nicki takes one look—and the seeds of tragedy are sown.

Their illicit Romeo and Juliet romance unfolds against the gritty backdrop of a realistically viewed South Bronx. . . . We are presented with the criminal element in these streets. But we are also given valuable insights into the lives of these honest, hard-working citizens struggling to reconcile the deeply rooted traditions and superstitions of the old world with the demands of a system seemingly designed to render them as burned-out as the tenements surrounding them. The police figure largely in Mr. Breslin's story—they could not fail to in a plot that revolves around a full-scale narcotics war—but they are not the "good guys" as opposed to the "bad guys." They too are merely human. (pp. 10-11)

Forsaking All Others is a novel about people who refuse to allow their lives to fall about them like pleats. The tragedy is that their heroic stand, their struggle to avoid a fate that seems preordained, ends in failure. Mr. Breslin's achievement is to make this failure appear a triumphant cry of the human spirit. (p. 33)

> Evan Hunter, "Street Scene," in The New York Times Book Review, *June 20, 1982, pp. 10-11, 33.*

SEYMOUR KRIM

How about a doomed love affair between the daughter of a Mafia boss and a sweet Puerto Rican kid just out of Harvard Law School? If it sounds a little like an updated *West Side Story,* and you can feel the heart-strings already tugging, that's the general idea [of *Forsaking All Others*]. Jimmy Breslin is the proverbial tough guy with a quiver full of Cupid's arrows jammed under his bullet-proof vest. He is also a shrewd, funny, sardonic observer of big-city ways.

The result is a romantic novel with very sharp teeth. Dreamers and weepers will probably buy the somewhat improbable love affair, while buffs of the urban absurd and grotesque will applaud such prime Breslin touches as: New York's Finest throwing up all over the insides of a search helicopter and three Doberman pinschers who have undergone delicate throat operations that prevent them from making a sound before they kill.

Also credit Breslin with being one of the very few white/Anglo writers to plunge into the teeming underside of Manhattan Hispanic life. Italicized Spanish peppers his pages like buckshot—a little too conspicuously?—and middle-class readers get a scary education in the packaging and selling of huge amounts of heroin. It is all rough stuff. But Jimmy Breslin is a hard-hat troubadour who works heroically to find sunshine in the sleaze until the final eclipse, when his Puerto Rican hero is killed for the wrong reasons and nasty business as usual goes on in its cheerful way.

Breslin's authenticity as a writer is in his small details. He knows the cigarette-smoking anxiety of a cheating wife. He can show us lazy detectives bullying the helpless as if he once wore a shield himself. . . . He is as observant as a cat. But this veteran newspaperman also has a booming romantic streak, in the tradition of vintage Manhattan tale-tellers from O. Henry to Damon Runyon, and he hangs all this encyclopedic knowledge on a plot that could serve for a hard-boiled operetta.

The prime mover in his fable is a lusty young bull from the Caribbean side of Puerto Rico who storms the East Bronx to take over the drug trade and be king for a day. His name is Teenager and his goal is to do for heroin what John D. Rockefeller did for oil. Under his wing is his pride and joy: the clean-cut, straight, upright Maximo Escobar, who through dint of hard work has put himself through Harvard Law and is about to embark on a beautiful career helping his people.

But all of this is changed forever when Maximo accompanies Teenager to a Mafioso's home across the Hudson River. Here, while the two bad guys split up the Bronx drug-turf, Maximo meets Nicki, the daughter of Boss Mariani. It's blind passion at first sight, folks, even though Nicki and all the Marianis normally despise blacks and Puerto Ricans as unthinkingly as they do odors from an open sewer. . . .

Anyway, Maximo and Nicki begin a perilous affair while she waits for her mob-guy husband to be released from jail. If her father ever finds out about it Maximo's head will decorate a caesar's salad down on Mulberry Street. In the meantime Teenager and Boss Mariani have fallen out over the spoils and had the other team's pushers murdered several times over. A contract goes out on Teenager and his henchmen. (p. 4)

The bare bones above certainly don't indicate the thick swath of life Breslin gets into his prose, although the story-line clearly shows that this book is aiming for a wide, popular, bittersweet appeal. . . .

Serious readers and connoisseurs of metropolitan black humor will savor much of the accurate, unflattering and sometimes savage observation in these pages; they will also sense something manufactured in the dutiful boy-girl scenes. Escapist readers, on the other hand, may very well be dismayed by the street-level rawness of the normal Breslin vision every time he gets away from the silk and satin Band-Aids of romance. Of course it's possible that a fresh generation raised without any illusions except the most famous—the salvation of romantic love—can take it all in without splitting their emotions. We'll have to wait and see.

Until then just let it be said that this reviewer, who sides with those who will value this novel for its iconoclastic truths of observation rather than its torchy centerpiece, wishes Breslin had tucked in more loose ends before releasing this book. A case in point is an 11-year-old boy who is raped in the Bronx children's jail. The boy tells Maximo that his rapist has threatened to kill him if his identity is revealed. The boy reveals it. But by then Breslin has gotten involved in his bread-and-butter love story once again, and we never know if the death-threat is attempted. It haunts us to the last page, because in these areas Jimmy Breslin knows things that we will never know and it's frustrating when he just flips them away like half-smoked cigarettes. (p. 8)

> Seymour Krim, "At the Hard Core of the Big Apple," in Book World—The Washington Post, *July 4, 1982, pp. 4, 8.*

ANNE TYLER

Forsaking All Others is less than a love story. The man and woman involved seem propelled by sex alone, lacking any real understanding of each other. But it's also more than a love story. It's a long, rich, gritty poem about the seamy side of life in the Bronx.

The so-called lovers are Maximo and Nicki. Maximo is a young Puerto Rican poverty lawyer, a childhood friend of the drug lord known as Teenager. Nicki is the pampered daughter of Teenager's Italian competitor. She's married, but her husband is in prison at the moment. . . .

Maximo and Nicki meet, with predictable results. Nicki thinks Maximo looks just like a movie star. Nicki herself has a "long cheerful body," as we're told three times, and "legs beginning at the hips.'' (It's not clear where else they would begin.) This discussion of looks is important, for the couple connects only on the surface. Nicki thinks of Maximo as a ''Spic,'' lowest of the low, and continues to make exaggeratedly bigoted remarks about Puerto Ricans during the entire course of their affair. Maximo unaccountably misses almost every insult, and fails to notice that she keeps arranging to have them seated in the rear of restaurants.

As you might imagine, their conversations are laughably wide of the mark. While Maximo embarks on what he considers a compelling discussion of Section 235 housing rehabilitation, Nicki is constructing her fantasy of him as a lithe, dangerous panther from a Puerto Rican jungle. She is mildly impressed that he went to Harvard, because Harvard is a ''sleepaway school.'' He is baffled by her plan to spend all of one Saturday shopping for a ''collar shirt with ombre stripes.'' We're supposed to hope for their happiness, obviously, but we can't care that much. Their affair is as static and unrealistic as those in the old romantic movies where a couple fought bitterly through every reel but was somehow expected to fall into a perfect marriage once the credits rolled up on the screen.

Notice, though, the absolute rightness of those details—that collar shirt with ombre stripes. Notice Nicki's prim, fussy routine when she comes home from work every night: the shoes put away in one of the boxes neatly aligned in her closet, the silk shirt hung to air, the ritual of special soap, toner, and moisturizer for complexion care. Or the etiquette for prison wives: the tinfoil-wrapped trays of lasagna and chicken *scarpariello* prepared before every visit; the $130 kelly-green Adidas jogging suit purchased to appease a whining convict husband. . . . (p. 42)

In short, the couple's failure to enlist us in their courtship is not a failure of characterization; it's that they have been characterized so well. We know them too intimately—Maximo with his seriousness and dedication, Nicki with her shallowness—to see any prospects for their union. Breslin is a master at observing and cataloguing the clues that inform us of all this. He sets up an atmosphere that is palpable: the constant threat of violence contrives to produce, of all things, a feeling of stifling confinement, and this result is so surprising that it's instantly convincing. (pp. 42-3)

The complicated ins and outs of the drug trade are described offhandedly, with none of the compulsive didactic zeal that characterizes an obviously ''researched'' novel. People speak of ''half los'' and ''white'' that ''you can step on seven times.'' Rubbery black ovals of poppy gum, brought up from Mexico, are transformed into heroin by a man in surgical mask and undershorts, working from a recipe written on the wall of his garage. You begin to worry about how Jimmy Breslin knows so much—the ultimate compliment to any writer of fiction.

The book goes on far too long; and with its huge cast of characters and complicated wheelings and dealings, it's occasionally difficult to keep track of. There are enough gruesome acts—torture and chain-saw murders, among other things—to make certain sections downright unpleasant. And always, we are being asked to sympathize with an oddly unsympathetic love affair. Even so, *Forsaking All Others* is well worth reading. It's crisply paced and authoritative, and it possesses an abundance of vitality. (p. 43)

Anne Tyler, ''South Bronx Story,'' in The New Republic, *Vol. 187, No. 3, July 19 & July 26, 1982, pp. 42-3.*

JOSEPH BROWNE

In Jimmy Breslin's excellent novel, *Forsaking All Others,* every decibel of [the cry of the ghetto] is accurately recorded and every graffiti-pocked brick of the wall which entombs tens of thousands within the South Bronx ghetto is graphically visualized. Each objective and subjective dimension of ghetto existence, from disease and obscene housing to hopelessness and hostility, is delineated in its every debilitating and repulsive detail.

The incipient talents manifested in Breslin's earlier novels, *The Gang that Couldn't Shoot Straight* and *World Without End, Amen,* are fully developed in *Forsaking All Others.* Having done Italian-Americans and Irish-Americans in the first novels, Breslin now turns to a brilliant ethnological dramatization of Puerto Rican-Americans which surpasses the combined worth of its predecessors. Perhaps through a lack of confidence in his powers of characterization with Puerto Ricans, Breslin has included an Irish-American cop and an Italian-American femme fatale to strengthen what he apparently considered a less-than-convincing dramatis personae without their presence. Although both characters are totally credible in themselves, their involvement in the plot is, at times, awkwardly contrived and tenuous. This relatively minor weakness, however, is further diminished by the book's considerable strengths. (p. 78)

Teenager and Maximo have survived their wretched slum backgrounds to achieve relative prominence in their respective, albeit antithetical, careers. They are also equally but unknowingly doomed by an inexorable law of consequences over which they have no control, but which is predicated upon the realities of who they are and where and when they came into being. Whether it is Teenager murdering a rival drug dealer with a chain-saw to maintain his power within the ghetto, or Maximo cultivating a relationship with Nicki Mariani, the Mafia Boss's daughter, to transcend the racist rules of the ghetto, both have tragically deluded themselves into thinking they can control their own destinies because they have some control over the destinies of others.

In *Forsaking All Others* Jimmy Breslin has forsaken no one. In this fact lies the novel's major accomplishment. Beyond the forsaken exterior of the South Bronx which he has so convincingly and comprehensively shown, Breslin also shows the inner vitality and spirit that allow these human beings to endure dehumanization today in hope of more fulfilling tomorrows, regardless of how distant and how many generations away those tomorrows may be. (pp. 78-9)

Joseph Browne, in a review of ''Forsaking All Others,'' in America, *Vol. 147, No. 4, August 7-August 14, 1982, pp. 78-9.*

R. Z. SHEPPARD

Booze is the thematic undercurrent of Jimmy Breslin's fifth novel [*Table Money*], a brutal slab of working-class life set among the Irish in the New York City borough of Queens. This is where Breslin learned his own trade as a newspaperman, reporting on the ways and means of the Archie Bunker set. His headlong bowling-ball prose can currently be found in the New York *Daily News,* where he is a Pulitzer-prizewinning columnist. There, as here, Breslin's lack of subtlety is his greatest strength. His characters are undereducated, abusive and conflicted by feelings of pride and shame. *Table Money* is burdened by stereotypes, although this is not necessarily a bad thing. Breslin knows what few members of the gentility are willing to acknowledge: that there would be no stereotypes if groups and classes did not demonstrate distinguishing characteristics.

Owney Morrison is descended from a long line of drinkers. He likes beer for breakfast and whiskey and beer chasers at lunch. ''Just one'' after work frequently turns into one too many. Sometimes Owney sleeps it off overnight in the hog house, the dressing room at the construction site [where he works]. This does not please his wife Dolores, who wants to study medicine but is stuck at home with a baby. Dolores is a latter-day stereotype and one that Breslin is less sure of than he is of the guys and dolls along Queens Boulevard. Still, she is vital and feisty enough to make his point about the gulf between blue-collar men and their women.

There are two kinds of courage in *Table Money.* Owney's is physical, as he displayed in Viet Nam by winning a Congressional Medal of Honor. Dolores proves her valor by overcoming generations of inertia and fatalism. She does it by demonstrating that behind the male swagger there is usually an unsteady little boy in need of a firm maternal hand. When a neighborhood Rambo threatens to shoot at police from his window, Dolores arms herself with a basket of wet wash and gets him to help her hang it. . . .

Hanging laundry is not a bad analogy for the way Breslin works. His book relies less on plot than on the cumulative effect of colorful anecdotes flapping on a slack story line. There are tales of the old sod, immigration and Boss Tweed's New York. The first male Morrison in the U.S. walks off the boat in 1870 and is put right to work sandhogging for 75¢ a day plus three hots and a cot. He soon discovers that he is restricted to the construction camp because the nearby Hudson River town of Beacon, N.Y., does not want muddy foreigners on its streets. (p. 73)

Breslin sets most of his action in the early '70s, after Owney returns from Viet Nam. His war experiences are locked inside him, and he has thrown away the key. He is literally and figuratively an underground man, emotionally detached from his family but bound by code and tradition to his brother sandhogs.

Table Money has its affectionate touches, like the etiquette for throwing out the trash: ''The proper Glendale housewife keeps such a small garbage can in the kitchen that it must be emptied four and five times a day. The sweater tossed over the shoulders goes with the chore.'' There is a salute to the Delahanty Institute, which prepared generations of young men for the police- and fire-department exams, and a bitterly funny scene in which two sandhogs find themselves in a midtown Manhattan bar filled with three-piece suits and attaché cases.

But the comedy of class consciousness is only a distraction. Breslin is interested not in sociology but in evil. His Queens has more than its share of ethnic Snopeses, gangsters, murderers and thieves. These are the people who truly stimulate the author's descriptive instincts for the deadly sins. . . . Breslin puts a lot of life on the page. Like a good barroom storyteller, he can make you miss your bus with one more for the road. (pp. 73, FB4)

R. Z. Sheppard, ''Just One More for the Road,'' in
Time, *Vol. 127, No. 18, May 5, 1986, pp. 73, FB4.*

JAMES CARROLL

What we never expected from Jimmy Breslin is what we have here—a serious literary novel, a superior work of fiction. *Table Money* is set in Queens in the early 70's, and it concerns Owney Morrison and his wife Dolores, two of the most compassionately drawn characters I have encountered in a novel this year. The story is about their love for each other and how it promises to redeem their circumscribed, dreary lives. But their love is crippled early by Owney's weakness and by Dolores's strength.

At one level *Table Money* is about what it has come to mean to be an American male. Owney Morrison is one of those good-looking guys we see in the beer commercials, a denim-shirted beau ideal. He was a hero in Vietnam. He is a faithful son, a good buddy, a natural leader revered by his co-workers on a grueling, dangerous job—digging tunnels in the earth hundreds of feet beneath the streets of New York. He is at his best when a physical calamity occurs. Mr. Breslin's descriptions of men like Owney risking their lives in war or in work or in defiance of hoodlums are gripping examples of action writing at its best. And because we, as readers, have been moved by the sight of ordinary men behaving heroically, we too think they deserve it when they hit the tavern after work in their meager ritual of daily celebration. . . .

If Morrison's work takes him below the surface of things so does Mr. Breslin's. . . . This hero's story, like that of many all-too-American males, becomes the painful story of an alcoholic. Mr. Breslin tells it with an unsparing, almost cruel detachment—sheer truthfulness—that leaves the reader wincing each time Morrison veers into yet another friendly neighborhood bar. But at the same time, in one of this novel's achievements, the author relates the experience of alcoholism as if from inside it, and the reader is left in the grip of an infinite sorrow. . . .

What may be lost to Owney is the love of his wife Dolores. *Table Money* brings together a man increasingly at the mercy of his self-doubt and a woman who with great courage lays claim at last to her own self-esteem. Suddenly the survival of the marriage to which she was supposed to dedicate her life becomes far less important than her own survival. Dolores loves Owney, but she is not going to destroy herself for him. That becomes the given of their marriage, the fact, the basic truth between them, and it is as hard as the bedrock through which Owney and his fellow sandhogs tunnel. And as reliable. On New York's bedrock the greatest city in the world has been built; and on Dolores's, perhaps a new life for both of them can be.

Thus *Table Money* is not the usual story in which a woman's self-discovery comes at the expense of her prior commitment. In an act of profound fidelity, Dolores invites Owney, in effect, to rebuild himself on the foundation of her fierce will. Whether he can or not provides *Table Money* with its excruciating tension. Oh, how we want these lovers to triumph over what would keep them apart.

But what keeps them apart is not war or work or danger, not class oppression or absurdities of the age or the arms race. It is something buried deep in the psyche of Owney Morrison, for he has his idea of what it is to be a man. And that idea is what threatens to keep him, finally and ironically, from being one.

You don't have to be on a bar stool in Queens to have Morrison's problem and you don't have to be in a failing marriage to dread his kind of loneliness. Mr. Breslin has set this story in a world he knows better than most, and he has told it with both eyes on its details, on the crackling talk and the gritty feel of these streets and these rooms, which are unlike streets and rooms elsewhere in New York or anywhere. But this particularity explodes to include everyone of our generation and of our culture. Jimmy Breslin has written an important novel about what it is to be men and women trying to build and rebuild lives and meanings in America today.

James Carroll, "Dolores Won't Take It Anymore," in The New York Times Book Review, *May 18, 1986, p. 9.*

PETER S. PRESCOTT

Two elements account for [*Table Money*'s] particular success. One is its energy, its muscularity; the other, its thickly textured portrait of a world and a way of life that most people who read books know little of. Breslin's world is Queens, and his people are working-class stiffs: sandhogs who risk their lives drilling tunnels through subterranean rock and then knock back small beers and shots of Fleischmann's in a bar while their wives wait at home with the children. (The title refers to the money a man puts on the kitchen table for his wife to use—after he has left a lot in the bar.)

Owney Morrison, scion of a hard-drinking line of Irishmen who built the tunnels that bring water to New York City, returns from Vietnam with a Congressional Medal of Honor. He marries a woman who, though raised in the convention of subservient Roman Catholic housewives, develops an independence that surprises even her. So it is that when Owney begins to drink, failing to come home nights and missing days at work, seizing that first icy can of beer that gets the morning going, Dolores does not behave as Queens wives do. First she warns him to stop, then she and their infant daughter move out. Dolores is still in her early 20s and, whatever happens to Owney, she has a life of her own to make. . . .

Breslin resolves his characters' dilemmas as you would expect: the good guys sort things out, the bad guys get what they deserve and justice serves character, not law. Which is to say that Breslin's populist vision of the human condition, like Henry Fielding's, has little to do with irony or tragedy, with stoicism or ambiguity; it honors the difficulties of living and moves on to become pointedly comic. It's also digressive: the columnist who has a couple of points to make on any subject enlarges his story with a number of marvelous scenes and satirical observations.

Yet for all its expansiveness, there's very little fat in *Table Money.* Reading it is like walking with an athlete who keeps the pace fast, who has something to say about each landmark on the route. Breslin explains exactly why the ethnic hard hat respects the blacks on his job and ridicules them as he walks away from the pit. He shows us railroad conductors buying drinks with the ticket money they collect on trains. He gives us more tunnel technology than we may be willing to absorb, then shows us Dolores telling her teacher that on the basis of what he wrote, Hemingway couldn't have liked women. This book works in part because of its contrasts. It's tough to make a drunk sympathetic, but Breslin does. Owney's helplessness becomes poignant because it's set against the unrestrained outrageousness of the way his father and friends behave.

Peter S. Prescott, "A Muscular Hard-Hat Saga," in Newsweek, *Vol. CVII, No. 21, May 26, 1986, p. 70.*

BRUCE COOK

Breslin has, with varying degrees of success, written about Brooklyn Mafia Italians (in *The Gang That Couldn't Shoot Straight*), the Puerto Rican drug trade in the Bronx (*Forsaking All Others*), and the IRA's struggle against the Prots and the Brits in the Six Counties of Northern Ireland (*World Without End, Amen*), he had yet to write a full book about the Irish-Americans with whom he grew up in Queens. (The first third of *World Without End, Amen* put his Irish cop at home in Queens, and it is pure gold; the remainder, alas, is not.) And so, for a long time, people who followed Jimmy Breslin, who really believed in the guy, have sensed that he had a really terrific novel in him, one about his "own kind," just struggling to be let out. *Table Money* is it.

It tells the story of Owney Morrison, a Vietnam Medal of Honor winner and a sandhog from a family of sandhogs. Breslin starts his narrative far back with Florence Morrison, who emigrated from Ireland to New York in 1869, and he traces the history of the family in its efforts to escape the poverty that dogs succeeding generations in their moves from Manhattan to the Bronx to Queens. But this is Owney's story, and that of his wife Dolores, and the genealogical first chapter that precedes it seems there to give it all a kind of epic quality. This may seem a bit bombastic for what at least in outline is a domestic drama, but it's also Breslin's intention to present the panorama of Queens, to give a sense of the whole place and the people who live there. And that would seem to justify the use of this device. Once you finish *Table Money,* you will never again be able to think of the borough in quite the same way. (pp. 1, 6)

Owney Morrison meets Dolores Kaufhold, half-German and half-Irish (though not quite that either, for she was informally adopted as an infant by her childless parents), at a soda fountain the day before he is to ship off for Vietnam. She, a freshman at Queens College with ambitions for medical school, is attracted to the big, good-looking Irish guy and falls in love with him by mail. His agonized, graphic letters from the war affect her so deeply that when he returns a hero she marries him after the briefest of courtships. When she becomes pregnant almost immediately and is forced to leave college, it looks as though the two will be trapped into living the lives their parents lived. And while this may not seem so bad to Owney, Dolores resists. She wants something more for him—and for herself. . . .

What Jimmy Breslin has put before us in *Table Money,* though he does not belabor it, is fundamentally a tragedy of class. Owney Morrison is a pure product of the working class. No matter that he makes more money than most white-collar types, and no matter that he may eventually wind up in the union leadership—he's working class all the way.

Dolores, on the other hand, is middle-class—not just in her aspirations, which are pure bourgeois (a doctor, after all), but also in her grasp of life's difficulties. Confronted with problems, she sees proximate and obvious solutions, nothing heroic—which is, of course, the middle-class way of dealing with things. She really has no idea what Owney is all about. . . .

More than a class tragedy, this is also a tragedy of the sexes, a commentary on marriage (or a lot of marriages) today. Owney has the potential for greatness in him; Dolores has the potential for a nice, tax-sheltered income.

But I promised you the panorama of Queens laid before you and believe me, Jimmy Breslin delivers. It's there in bits of dialogue: A mother complains of her son driven nutty by the war, "I'll tell you, it's an accident living with him." When a black woman calls her man a dog, he responds, "Then you nothin' but a . . . leash!" And the wild characters—Philip McNiff, an off-the-wall lawyer who rescues Owney and Dolores separately from trouble; Sharon, the little bar waitress who gets even in a big way; and old man Kramer who swallowed his Medicare card just to teach his wife a lesson. (Breslin can't mention a name without telling you a story.) It's there, too, in the little essays he delivers on the mores and folkways of Queens—the Mungo Park of Flushing Avenue.

And it works! It's glorious, just the sort of riotous, discursive writing that makes a novel wonderful reading in the woolly old Dickens tradition. I haven't read a better American novel this year, and I certainly don't expect to read one as good in what's left of it. (p. 6)

Bruce Cook, "Jimmy Breslin: King of Queens," in Book World—The Washington Post, *June 1, 1986, pp. 1, 6.*

Rita Mae Brown

1944-

American novelist, poet, essayist, and scriptwriter.

Best known for her novels *Rubyfruit Jungle* (1973) and *Southern Discomfort* (1982), Brown writes seriocomic fiction revolving around strong, often homosexual characters who are distinguished by their beauty, humor, and ambition. By focusing upon what Annie Gottlieb termed "the misfit between human passions and societal conventions," Brown strives, through humor and sensitivity, to undermine society's attempts to limit the expression of human desire. Although some critics fault Brown for being excessively didactic, others praise her energetic, irreverent prose and applaud the determination and resiliency of her characters.

In her first novel, the semiautobiographical *Rubyfruit Jungle*, Brown relates the experiences of Molly Bolt, a fiery young lesbian. This work begins in her early childhood and extends, in picaresque fashion, through her graduation from college and into her professional career as a writer. Marked by Molly's refusal to conform to social standards, *Rubyfruit Jungle* celebrates individualism and advances Brown's attempts to dispel the stereotyped image of homosexual women as unattractive and self-destructive. While some critics admonished Brown for exhorting her personal views in the novel, others praised her authentic evocation of Molly's childhood and her strong characterizations.

Brown's next novel, *In Her Day* (1976), is the story of two lesbians of disparate ages who attempt to reconcile the choices they have made regarding their homosexual lifestyles. Some critics found the book unfocused and lacking the inventive prose that enlivened *Rubyfruit Jungle*. In *Six of One* (1978), Brown chronicles three generations of an American family by alternating between 1909 and 1980 and by using a mock-epic narrative style that combines fantasy and slapstick humor. While she continues to focus on female characters, Brown broadens her fictional scope in *Six of One* by exploring the psychological disposition of a small American town through the sensibilities of many of its residents. Brown's next novel, *Southern Discomfort*, is set in Montgomery, Alabama, during the 1920s and involves a beautiful white socialite whose passionless marriage has driven her to an affair with a fifteen-year-old black boy. Despite Brown's attempts to explore some of the situation's complexities, Charlotte M. Meyer stated that *Southern Discomfort*, as well as Brown's earlier novels, "are fairy tales wherein the heroines are larger than life—although very lovable—and suffer none of the inner doubt or the frustration and anger of normal, mortal women who are redefining their femininity." Meyer concluded, however, by stating that *Southern Discomfort* is "nevertheless a funny, vigorous, irreverent novel."

Brown considers her next novel, *Sudden Death* (1983), to be a diversion from her creative progression. A revealing glimpse into the world of women's professional tennis, the book resulted from Brown's promise to her friend, Judy Lacy, a sportswriter dying from a brain tumor who had wanted to write a novel about the sport. *Sudden Death* is regarded by many, however, as a *roman à clef* of Brown's relationship with tennis star Martina Navratilova. In *High Hearts* (1986), an extensively

Courtesy of Rita Mae Brown

researched and panoramic novel about the Civil War that recalls Margaret Mitchell's *Gone with the Wind*, Brown details the story of a young southern woman who disguises herself as a man and joins the cavalry in order to be near her husband. The novel provides a vivid account of the varying roles women assumed during the war. Brown has also published two volumes of poetry, *The Hand That Cradles the Rock* (1971) and *Songs to a Handsome Woman* (1973), and a collection of essays, *A Plain Brown Rapper* (1976).

(See also *CLC*, Vol. 18; *Contemporary Authors*, Vols. 45-48; and *Contemporary Authors New Revision Series*, Vols. 2, 11.)

ANNIE GOTTLIEB

Ever since *Rubyfruit Jungle*, her tough-talking, tenderhearted story of a girl who loves girls, Rita Mae Brown's subject has been the misfit between human passions and societal conventions. Imagine a Rubens nude trying to squeeze into a size 6 corset, and you've got the comic futility and wasteful pain that Miss Brown sees in the effort to confine desire within one standard form: respectable heterosexual marriage. In her view,

80

sexuality is a first cousin of imagination, involving an irrepressible urge to honor and rival the crazy abundance of life.

Unexamined heterosexuality, in *Rubyfruit Jungle,* is a pressure cooker of far-out fantasies. The most dogged champion of decency in the small town of her boisterous novel *Six of One* is discovered, at age 80, to keep pornography under her mattress. And in Miss Brown's latest novel, *Southern Discomfort,* nearly all the good husbands of 1918 Montgomery, Ala.—including the judge and the chief of police—relieve the pressures of propriety *chez* Banana Mae Parker and Blue Rhonda Latrec, prostitutes of Water Street.

For Miss Brown, such duplicity is the stuff of human comedy. But her last two novels boasted women characters who dared to tell the naked truth and to love whom they pleased. . . . There is no such character in *Southern Discomfort*—no embodiment of passion triumphant, of fearless love and guiltless pleasure—and the novel is stronger for it.

Rita Mae Brown still believes in the fundamental innocence of passion, but for the first time she gives the old adversaries—rules, roles, prohibitions, limitations—a grudging respect, a kind of equal time. (p. 10)

At the beginning of *Southern Discomfort,* icy, blonde Hortensia Reedmuller Banastre, a Montgomery aristocrat, is 27 and still untouched by life. Her marriage to wealthy Carwyn Banastre is "a brilliant social match" but loveless and sexless. (Carwyn has long since turned to Banana Mae.) Hortensia feels dimly fond of her older son and utterly distant from her younger, Paris. She is elegant and cynical. And then she and a 15-year-old black aspiring boxer named Hercules Jinks fall totally in love.

This love affair does not happen *because* it is forbidden. It is a pure and absolute event, like a star falling in perilous innocence of its surroundings. Hortensia and Hercules have to hide their love carefully, but both lovers are made ecstatically happy, and Hortensia is transfigured. Of course, given the social context, their relationship can't last. Rather than submit her characters to the Southern novel's cliché of disclosure of a forbidden love and lynching fever, Miss Brown disposes of Hercules in an accident—though her *deus ex machina* device does involve a casual and, consequently, even more chilling instance of racism. Hortensia is devastated, not least because she has hesitated to run away to the North with Hercules. (Much later she can admit that she would never have had the courage to leave; her social *place* is too much a part of what she is.) She is also pregnant.

Ten years later, in 1928, a sullen summer of heat and cicadas, their child, Catherine—raised by a black servant in Hortensia's house—wonders about her parentage, her curly red hair and green eyes, *her* lack of place in a world that is either black or white. And everyone around her—from the grandmother, Ada Jinks, who tutors her in Latin, to her jealous half-brother Paris—wonders too, until at last the secret has to burst out. As Catherine comes into her singular heritage, Blue Rhonda, dying of leukemia, reveals a secret of her own. She, too, exists right on the boundary line between categories people believe to be absolute: black and white, female and male, good and bad, gay and straight. Not out of splendid defiance, but simply by accepting what she is, both of these women bring into their milieu an eerie breath of freedom.

It's rare to say that a book would be better if it were longer, but I suspect that in a less impatient era *Southern Discomfort* would have been a 700-page epic that slowly revealed the roots of character and the intertangling of disparate lives. As it is, the book often seems abrupt and arbitrary, jump-cut as if it were a two-hour movie. Lacking space to let us discover her major characters at their living, Miss Brown flatly tells us who they are: "Hortensia wanted control over everybody and everything." It's a while before these authorial puppets come to life. Meanwhile, minor characters, like Hercules's boxing manager, Sneaky Pie, are so vivid that they cry out for more space. The plot moves in fits and starts. A fistfight between mother and son is perfectly rendered, but a later, even more crucial scene of violence is rushed and anticlimactic. The reader is left feeling charmed, moved—and a little bit cheated. (pp. 10, 29)

Annie Gottlieb, "Passion and Punishment," in The New York Times Book Review, *March 21, 1982, pp. 10, 29.*

CHARLOTTE M. MEYER

Rubyfruit Jungle and *Six of One* present sexual aberrations of all sorts in a very positive light: the Gospel according to Brown supersedes the old Victorian dispensation and preaches instead an exuberant and guilt-free eroticism. The messiah in this gospel is a tall, beautiful, athletic, sexually uninhibited, self-possessed genius of a lesbian who fears not the Pharisees.

The central character of *Southern Discomfort* departs from that job description in one detail only: she is heterosexual. Hortensia Banastre is a young matron who dominates the high-society of Montgomery, Alabama, in the 1920s. She is a beautiful, cold, bored mother of two young sons, but she comes to life when she falls madly in love with a sixteen-year-old black boy. And there are other provocative lines of action in the book. One subplot is set on Water Street where Montgomery's prostitutes flourish. The reader becomes involved with two that are particularly engaging, Blue Rhonda and Banana Mae. In partnership these two service many of the town's notables, including Hortensia's husband Carwyn. A third plot follows the careers of another Montgomery belle, Grace Deltaven, who goes off to Hollywood, then a brand new industry, and returns home triumphant, a great star, to stage her spectacular but ill-fated Hollywood-style wedding.

Braided into these plot lines with all the now-familiar Rita Mae Brown twists are incest, transvestism, adultery, homosexuality, miscegeny, filicide, suicide, alcoholism et al. It isn't the presence of all these so-called aberrations that make me uncomfortable, however; it's the way they are worked out, or rather, *aren't* worked out. Although her setting is the South between the two world wars, she's really writing about the issues that women struggle with today. There are some anachronisms in the psychology of the characters as a result, but it is the pedagogy of the novel that is the real problem.

The narrator's tone is close and familiar and it urges its readers between the lines to shun their hang-ups and sexual hesitations. What Brown presents, however, are idealizations of liberated female consciousness, not the process for arriving at them. Nor does she work out the psychological implications of enacting such liberated attitudes in a hostile, male-dominated, racist society. *Southern Discomfort* and the earlier two novels are fairy tales wherein the heroines are larger than life—although very lovable—and suffer none of the inner doubt or the frustration and anger of normal, mortal women who are redefining their femininity.

For example, when Hortensia is in her late thirties, stunningly beautiful and at the very pinnacle of the social heap, she begins to roll in the hayloft with Hercules Jinks, the black teenager who delivers wood to her back door. Like the super heroines of Brown's novels, Herules is larger than life—sweeter, stronger, cleaner, kindlier, more handsome and intelligent, and better educated than any southern black boy that ever was. Richard Wright's *Black Boy* presents an autobiographical picture of how young black men were taught to react to white women in the South, especially expensive ones like Hortensia, with self-abnegating courtesy and downcast eyes. And Faulkner devotes hundreds of pages to the subtleties of the insurmountable color barriers between aristocracy and their black servants. But Brown's Hortensia and Hercules have sex after two or three meetings, roll around in the stable for awhile and then rent a love nest down on Water Street where Hortensia thinks to "pass" by swapping coats with her maid. At one point they are even walked in on by a white client of Blue Rhonda. The repercussions for an older white wife-and-mother conducting a secret affair with a black teenager would be monumental even today, but we see none of the fear or overwhelming confusion in Hortensia we might legitimately expect. . . .

The private and social costs involved in committing oneself long term to such an affair are not worked out either because Hercules is accidentally—and conveniently—killed in the act of saving his father's life. Shortly afterwards, Hortensia, who has not slept with her own husband in years, discovers that she is pregnant. Next comes a pregnancy implausibly concealed by a long trip to Chicago, then the return of Hortensia and the simultaneous sudden arrival of an infant girl, half-black with Hortensia's unusual green eyes, passed off as the daughter of her black maid who was never pregnant, in a town where everyone knows everyone else's business: the plot turns on creaky hinges.

Not only do these flaws in plotting weaken the credibility of the novel, but worse, they cheat the reader out of real resolutions to the problems the novel boldly poses. . . .

There is another important example. Her second son, Paris, is love-starved and over-sexed because, he figures, Hortensia was cold to him throughout his childhood. He is jealous of the little pampered mulatto girl who has the run of the house and who is the apple of Hortensia's eye. He has guessed that little Catherine is his half-sister (*mirabile dictu*, her husband hasn't). Paris threatens to reveal Catherine's true identity to her unless Hortensia sleeps with him. She is persuaded in no time at all, such is her love for Catherine and her ignorance of blackmail, and she even responds to his skill in bed. When he comes back for more and is rebuffed, he begins to beat up little Catherine. Unable to pull him off of her, Hortensia grabs her handy old pistol and shoots off the back of his head. When the Chief of Police arrives and asks a few questions, he says, "Let's forget it. He shot himself cleaning his pistol." Reason? Once long ago the courteous Hercules had done him a small favor. "I owe Catherine's father one," he explains. Why would a southern police chief, charged with the responsibility of keeping blacks in their place, still consider himself in Hercules' debt once he discovered that Hercules had impregnated a white woman? These acrobatics in the plotting of the novel sidestep once again the resolution of the problem at hand, this time, incest. What kind of relationship do a mother and son have after they've slept with one another? Paris, like Hercules, gets bumped off and so does the whole interesting provocative problem. Miscegeny, adultery, incest, murder—Hortensia walks

away without a scratch. Why write a character who never has to pay consequences?

This is nevertheless a funny, vigorous, irreverent novel, as the earlier ones have been, but it needed more careful craftsmanship. Rita Mae Brown's devoted following of readers deserve it.

Charlotte M. Meyer, in a review of "Southern Discomfort," in The American Book Review, *Vol. 5, No. 2, January-February, 1983, p. 22.*

ELISABETH JAKAB

For a short book, there's a great deal of plot rattling around in Rita Mae Brown's *Sudden Death,* an energetic account of a lesbian scandal that erupts on the women's pro tennis circuit. As might be expected, the battles on the court pale by comparison with the struggles going on behind the scenes.

In one corner is Carmen Semana, a young Argentine émigré who is a top ranked player. Carmen is in love with Harriet, a college professor who has put her own career on hold to travel the circuit with Carmen while she attempts to win the Grand Slam: the French Open, Wimbledon, the U.S. Open and the Australian Open. Although basically a good-hearted sort, Carmen is seldom capable of handling anything beyond her encounters on the tennis court.

In the other corner is Carmen's arch enemy, Susan, a player who vows that if she can't win the Grand Slam herself, she will prevent anyone else from doing so. Susan had been Carmen's first lover and treated her very shabbily. Susan treats all her women lovers badly, forcing them to sneak around in the shadows while she herself poses for photographs with her husband and young daughter. Unable to halt Carmen's progress on the court, Susan confides Carmen's romantic situation to a friendly reporter. A scandal might not only cause Carmen's "green card" to be revoked and thus get her deported, it could also result in her losing hundreds of thousands of dollars in endorsement money. Susan believes in getting at people where it really hurts.

Milling about in the middle of all this is such an extensive supporting cast that it's difficult to sort out the players without a program. The most important characters seem to be the tournament organizers and Carmen's brother Miguel, a lawyer who is hard at work forging Carmen's signature to several shady deals he feels she is better off not knowing about. The tour directors are panicked that their sponsor—a cosmetics manufacturer—will withdraw financial support if a scandal surfaces.

Miss Brown, the engaging and exuberant storyteller of *Southern Discomfort* and *Rubyfruit Jungle,* is not at her best here. The world of tennis does not seem to be congenial terrain for her, and her usually natural and easy style seems cramped. The novel tends to read like the casebook of an anthropologist stranded in the midst of a disappointingly boring tribe. She does what she can, but there's just not that much to work with. In *Sudden Death* we can almost hear the pieces of the plot clanking into their proper slots, and there's an overly familiar air to the satirical dissections of several tennis stereotypes.

The result is a rather cluttered book in which the reader is never quite sure where the focus is supposed to be since the author, while she doesn't give everyone equal time, does incline to give them equal weight. The main story actually turns out to concern the disintegrating relationship between Carmen and the stalwart, loyal Harriet, who eventually emerges as the book's true heroine. (pp. 12, 21)

Elisabeth Jakab, "Tennis and Diplomacy," in The New York Times Book Review, *June 19, 1983, pp. 12, 21.*

GARY DAVENPORT

In *Southern Discomfort* Rita Mae Brown is interested in the repressiveness of southern Protestant morality. . . . One of the two main characters, Hortensia Banastre, scandalizes Montgomery, Alabama, by her adulterous relationship with a black teenager. The other principal is a first-class whore (complete with a heart of gold) named Blue Rhonda Latrec. Blue Rhonda engages in theological combat of a very adolescent sort with a Bible-thumping crusader named Linton Ray and is thus the "philosophical" focus of the book, although any character is inclined to wax sententious. The basic point seems to be that we are all hypocrites about sex and the like—and that we should just be honest about it and live full and beautiful lives. (Bigotry, war, and a few other evils are also dealt heavy blows.) What better way to attack sexual hypocrisy than to display the children of Adam in flagrante delicto as often and as variously as possible? (The only known or imaginable variation that is unrepresented, to the best of my knowledge, is zooerasty.)

The novel is ostensibly historical, set in 1918 and then 1928, but the language (even the clichés) and the whole ambience are vintage 1982 ("Everyone acted like a total twit"). Ultimately it is on their control of language and narrative voice that most works of fiction stand or fall, and such control is in *Southern Discomfort* at best erratic. The reader doesn't believe in this novel because the author—or a presence that appears to the reader as the author—is constantly visible in the wings, injecting sex, injecting philosophy, injecting southernness ("Southerners always had the wisdom to realize that form is as important as content"), winking at us chummily, holding up Applause and Laughter signs, and generally hellbent on producing a rollicking good story. (pp. 441-42)

Gary Davenport, "The Fugitive Hero In New Southern Fiction," in The Sewanee Review, *Vol. XCI, No. 3, Summer, 1983, pp. 439-45.*

MARCELLE THIÉBAUX

[Since *Rubyfruit Jungle*] achieved popularity, Brown's fiction has largely identified her as an outspoken champion of gay women. Certainly the baiting and persecution of homosexuals and their exclusion from professional opportunities are to be deplored. *Sudden Death* will probably not accomplish much, however, for the cause of humanizing the homosexual in the public eye. Most of the gays are shown to be as cruel and perfidious as the straights. Brown's characters, whatever their age and sex, all have a way of sounding like gleefully naughty little girls. Why they love, suffer, and betray, is dealt with only superficially. Structurally, breaking the 13 chapters into breathless mini-scenes that go pinging by like tennis balls stifles the development of motivations and relationships.

Brown likes to treat explosive topics with edgy, giggly hilarity. Representative jokes are about douche powder, diaphragms, kick-starting your vibrator, and decorating your uterine walls. Similarly, in *Southern Discomfort* . . . incest, murder, madness, interracial strife and love, prostitution, and drag are handled with goofy humor in a big shambling plot. It's her way

of getting readers to confront the issues. The risk, however, is of trivializing issues all too comfortably.

Marcelle Thiébaux, in a review of "Sudden Death," in Best Sellers, *Vol. 43, No. 4, July, 1983, p. 120.*

AMY WILENTZ

I sometimes wish there were no libel laws. Not because everything I have to say about Rita Mae Brown's new book, *Sudden Death,* is unprintable, but because it would spare readers of romans à clef so much time and worry if the authors who insisted on writing them could call a spade a spade, or, in this case, a Martina a Martina.

Decoding who's who becomes even more annoying when the changes from fact to fiction seem designed solely to disguise the identities of potential plaintiffs. It's one thing for a writer like Gore Vidal to say that in his early years, he was "often pleased to be identified with the protagonist of *The City & the Pillar*—a male prostitute." It is another for a lesbian tennis aficionada like Brown to be, in her not so early years, eager for identification with her protagonist, a lesbian tennis aficionada in her not so early years. The one implies an imaginative interest in notoriety, the other a desire to exploit an unearned—and uninteresting—celebrity. . . .

Sudden Death begins with the usual disclaimer: "None of these events actually occurred and any resemblance to individuals of the [women's tennis] circuit is purely coincidental." Well, if Page Bartlett Campbell of *Sudden Death* isn't the spitting image of Chris Evert Lloyd of the circuit, why did Brown give her those rattling three names? It's only the strong arm of the libel law that stops me from telling you the names of the other figures Brown so barely disguises—the stars as well as the fringe elements.

Now I do remember that when *Rubyfruit Jungle* and *Southern Discomfort* were published, Rita Mae Brown was hailed as a talented new writer. She has also been on the right side of many battles, including the one in which she was purged from NOW. And even if the plot of [*Rubyfruit Jungle*] was a tiny bit cribbed from Vidal's [*The City & the Pillar*], there was some strong writing there, some verve, some guts. Here—nada.

"When they came, they were as two moths caught in brightness. Finding the flame, they burned their wings and quickly fell to earth." Remember, this is not Petrarch and Laura, not Gertrude and Alice, not Verlaine and Rimbaud, not even . . . [Vidal's] Jim and Bob, but Harriet Rawls, an intellectual (like Brown) who teaches God knows what at Cazenovia (yes Cazenovia) College, and Carmen Semana, an Argentine tennis star who bears a distinct resemblance to Navratilova, and whose name, Carmen Semana, in nearly literal translation means "Red Week," if you catch my drift. Moths? Flame?

But don't imagine that the moth/flame bit is typical of the style of the book. There is no style to this book: "Jeffrey Campbell was a handsome, virile quarterback for the San Francisco Forty-Niners." "Susan's body went rigid." "If a fart were a scab, that man would pick it off his asshole." (This last, an instance of Brown's celebrated "outrageousness," as *People* magazine calls it.)

For drama, Brown reverts to the Billie Jean King lesbian palimony event of several years ago. . . .

Brown's fictionalization, though, is hardly as wittily played out as the true story. A scandal breaks, Harriet and Carmen are forced apart by heavies in the tennis business, and Harriet loses her job back at Cazenovia (again, we wait, breath bated, to discover what it was she taught so devotedly—but no). As backdrop to all this action, a friend of Harriet's dies (remarkably, a friend of Brown's actually *did* die, we learn from the introduction, which is called "Genesis"), and Harriet takes to reading the bible in her time of trouble.

"'If there is life after death,'" Harriet says at the end of the book, "'I'd like to think we'll all find each other again . . . I'd like to think that God will strengthen the love between us. Is that such a foolish dream? Is there never a time when people are bound by more than scar tissue?'" As someone once said, "There are more things in heaven and earth, Rita Mae, than are dreamt of in your philosophy." Reading the religio-soap operatic finale, one is tempted to conclude that Brown has had just one too many Martinas.

Amy Wilentz, in a review of "Sudden Death," in The Village Voice, Vol. XXVIII, No. 29, July 19, 1983, p. 35.

LESLIE FISHBEIN

Rubyfruit Jungle is a celebration of the joys of lesbian life, in contrast to the tragic emphasis of much of the earlier literature. . . . *Rubyfruit Jungle* clearly reflects and exalts a woman's experience taken from the perspective of a spunky, outrageously funny, poor white lesbian growing up in the rural South and finding new-found freedom in the urban North. For Molly Bolt, lesbian love is always joyous; she finds in it no guilt and only pleasure.

The novel also seeks to debunk traditional stereotypes used to dismiss lesbianism. Despite its comic nature, the novel is essentially didactic and polemical. Her high school friend Connie reveals that, despite her veneer of sophistication, she is nervous and apprehensive that Molly will rape her. Molly makes it clear that lesbians are not violent sexually and do not seek to coerce or seduce the innocent: "Now it was my turn to be shocked. 'That's crazy. What do you think I do, run around panting at every female I see? I'm not going to leap on you like some hyperthryoid ape. Goddammit!'" She completely repudiates the butch-femme distinctions of the traditional lesbian world. When her friend Calvin takes her to a gay bar, she is upset by the butch-femme divisions, having had no prior notion of them. Molly tells him: "That's the craziest dumbass thing I ever heard tell of. What's the point of being a lesbian if a woman is going to look and act like an imitation man? Hell, if I want a man, I'll get the real thing not one of these chippies. I mean, Calvin, the whole point of being gay is because you love women." Brown's heroine breaks the stereotype of lesbianism being a parody of straight life. When her first lover, Leota, now broken by marriage and motherhood, tells her some day she will meet the right man and settle down, Molly replies indignantly: "Let's stop this shit. I love women. I'll never marry a man and I'll never marry a woman either. That's not my way. I'm a devil-may-care lesbian."

Nevertheless, there are a number of fundamental problems with this novel that unfit it as the celebration of lesbian feminism that many of its reviewers claimed it to be. The critic in *Ms.*, Marilyn Webb, portrayed the book as "an inspiring, bravado adventure story of a female Huck Finn," but while this novel purports to be a *Bildungsroman*, or novel of education, in the Huck Finn tradition, in fact, it is not. Molly is like Huck Finn in bridling at the restraints of civilization. However, she is unlike him because she neither grows nor changes. She never learns anything new about the world; she is always uninhibited personally and sexually. She develops no new insights as a result of her experiences, whereas Huck comes to understand that his comrade Jim is a human being and is willing to risk his own soul to free Jim from slavery.

Rita Mae Brown makes lesbianism too exclusively sexual. She emphasizes the homosexual and not the homoerotic. In contrast, many modern lesbians object to reducing lesbianism to sexual activity alone. If many lesbians and feminists object to Freud's notion of penis envy as a result of its anatomical reductionism, Rita Mae Brown's novel simply does the obverse in celebrating the vagina. The book clearly establishes the anatomical inferiority of males in a virtual parody of Freudian theory. . . . She claims to Polina that lesbian sex is more intense than the heterosexual variety and definitely superior to it: ". . . it's the difference between a pair of roller skates and a Ferrari."

The book is no feminist tract because there is no genuine affection for women; Molly never truly loves the women with whom she sleeps. Women make good lovers, but they are not portrayed as friends. For example, Molly respects Connie for her values and intellect but sleeps with Carolyn Simpson, the head cheerleader, who is physically more attractive but who also is completely hypocritical about her lesbiansim and essentially a superficial person. . . . Molly continues sleeping with Polina for quite a while despite the woman's repulsive sexual fantasies about being in a men's urinal.

Molly's closest relations are with men rather than women. Her cousin Leroy tells her repeatedly that she always has been the only girl he can talk to, and the two of them do share personal and sexual intimacy. He makes himself vulnerable to her, confessing his fears about being a homosexual, and she is genuinely caring in allowing him to prove his heterosexuality by sleeping with her. She develops a trusting relationship with Calvin, the black gay with street smarts who initiates her into New York life. Her most loving relationship is with her stepfather Carl, a man who is proud of her academic accomplishments and her fighting spirit. He actually encourages her independence and is the only family member to accept and endorse her decision never to wed: "You wouldn't look too hot on the other side of an apron and between us, it'd kill me to see you buckle under to anyone, especially a husband." Carl also enunciates what is to be her philosophy regarding sex and life, possibly because we later learn of his own sexual vagaries, loving two women at the same time: "'Listen to me,' his voice got stronger, 'you go on and do whatever you want to do and the hell with the rest of the world.'"

Molly's reconciliation with her stepmother, Carrie, at the end of the novel is not adequately foreshadowed in the first half of the book. It seems arbitrary and forced, a concession to the feminist formula that women must come to accept their mothers as sisters if they are to affirm their own identity. For the first half of the book Carrie is portrayed as hateful, jealous, vindictive. She wants to keep Molly from fulfilling her potential so that Molly will be trapped in the same culture of poverty that confined her. When Molly returns to film Carrie as part of her cinema education, the woman is transformed. Instead of spurning her stepdaughter, Carrie says, "Course you didn't turn out like I expected but you're still mine. All I got in this world." And Molly for the first time is able to express her gratitude and love for Carrie.

Rubyfruit Jungle is fundamentally amoral without being self-reflective about the consequences of its amorality. Molly's sexual life is organized around essentially hedonistic rather than ethical principles. . . . The novel never deals with the emotional or moral consequences of life in a world in which all sexual taboos have been dissolved, in which everyone is a potential sexual partner. (pp. 156-58)

Brown's novel celebrates lesbianism as an alternative life style, but, in fact, it is as compulsive about homosexuality as heterosexuals have been about heterosexuality. Clearly, homosexuality is portrayed as the only viable sexual choice. Everyone in a heterosexual marriage—Leota, Leroy, Carl, Carrie—is miserable; and heterosexual intercourse is comparatively dull. Motherhood is portrayed almost as if it were a disease. Twenty-four-year-old Leota is depicted as looking forty-five, "and she had two brats hanging on her like possums." Seeing Leota makes Molly eager to return to New York City, where she "can be more than a breeder of the next generation."

The novel is completely narcissistic and selfish. It is an utterly individualistic tale that has no social consciousness or sense of commitment to a lesbian community. When lesbians are portrayed in groups, they are viewed as butches and femmes, as sexual predators as in the bar and party scenes. The novel never evokes lesbian support networks or genuine gay friendships. Nor does it have any social consciousness. The only oppression it seeks to correct is Molly's own. In that sense, *Rubyfruit Jungle* becomes the perfect document of the ME generation: it takes the new selfishness and makes it both gay and good. (pp. 158-59)

> Leslie Fishbein, "'Rubyfruit Jungle': Lesbianism, Feminism, and Narcissism," in International Journal of Women's Studies, *Vol. 7, No. 2, March-April, 1984, pp. 155-59.*

PUBLISHERS WEEKLY

If *Gone with the Wind* had been written from the point of view of soldiers in the midst of battle, it might have read something like [*High Hearts,* an] appealing novel that deals with the stupidity of the Civil War and its effect on women. . . . Brown (*Rubyfruit Jungle, Sudden Death*) extensively researched this novel; her bibliography includes weather reports and family chronicles from the 1860s. As a result, an obsession with military tactics interferes with her storytelling. Although the chain of events is formulaic and the outcome less than surprising, Brown's style is energetic, her message humane, and her characters unconventional and lively.

> A review of "High Hearts," in Publishers Weekly, *Vol. 229, No. 13, March 28, 1986, p. 52.*

MARK CHILDRESS

[*High Hearts,* an] expansive novel of the Civil War, contains what must surely be the first in-saddle marital squabble between two members of a Virginia cavalry regiment. Geneva Chatfield, tall for her 18 years and an excellent horsewoman, can't stand the idea of her new husband, Nash Hart, running off to the cavalry and leaving her back on the plantation. So she cuts off her hair, convinces her mother and her best slave friend, Di-Peachy, to stay quiet about it, and sneaks off to join up. . . . Rita Mae Brown's childhood fascination with Virginia battlefields—and her extensive research for this book—serve her well. She knows her horses, and the movements of a cavalry

unit in the battles of First Manassas and the Seven Days are excitingly painted. Women did indeed dress as men and fight in the war, and this idea comes alive. While the story rides breathlessly in Geneva's saddle, all is well. But the author's intention is to render the larger story of women's roles in the war, to create, she says, a "monument" to them. After all the careful interweaving of feuding slaves, sainted mothers, gossiping Richmond hostesses and the inevitable gold-hearted madam, the sound of guns comes to seem a relief. Luckily, the author keeps things light with some fine comic scenes and smart-talking characters. A deft touch is required to pull off a gender-switch à la *Yentl, the Yeshiva Boy* and blend it with *The Red Badge of Courage.* Rita Mae Brown takes an admirable turn at it.

> Mark Childress, in a review of "High Hearts," in The New York Times Book Review, *April 20, 1986, p. 22.*

FLORENCE KING

With the 50th anniversary of the publication of *Gone With the Wind* upon us, southern novelist Rita Mae Brown, author of the underground best seller *Rubyfruit Jungle* and other outré contemporary works, has turned her considerable if uneven talents to [*High Hearts*], a Civil War novel set in and around Charlottesville, Virginia, where she now lives.

The story opens on the eve of Fort Sumter at the Chatfield plantation. Mother Lutie, driven half-mad by her husband's infidelities, sees ghosts, talks to a familiar named Emil, and dreams of a bat who wears ruby earrings and sings Mozart. Below stairs, a slave named Auntie Sin-Sin provides a restrained Virginia version of the voodoo element, while a younger maid, Di-Peachy, has light skin, hazel eyes, and breasts that "stuck straight out like hard melons." The men of the household are the silver-haired master, Henley, who breeds horses and may have fathered Di-Peachy; and son Sumner, a Tarleton-twin type well on the way to useless but endearing cavalier-hood.

What the Chatfields do not have is a resident belle. Daughter Geneva is six feet tall and so skinny she could wash in a gun barrel. Horse-crazed, she is seldom out of the saddle and, although 18, hardly ever menstruates. The last is of some concern, for the eve of Fort Sumter is also her wedding day.

She marries Nash Hart, who is slim, blond, sensitive, and intellectual—and if that isn't Ashley enough for you, consider what happens to him on his wedding night: "She grabbed him. She was strong and squeezed the breath out of him." Despite the role-reversal, Nash performs his husbandly duties so well that Geneva cannot bear to be parted from him when he goes off to war, so she cuts her hair, dons men's clothes, and follows him to Harper's Ferry, where she joins the First Virginia Cavalry and fights by his side at the battle of Manassas. . . . (p. 3)

Besides coping with the spectacle of Rhett Butler in a menstruation-free tomboy heaven, we must also cope with Brown's literary style. Whether from a tin chronological ear or carelessness or both, she puts jarringly modern phrases into the mouths of her 19th-century characters and into her own exposition: "don't waffle," "didn't know beans about," "what's the big idea?," "a pain in the ass," "she chewed her out," and "navy" blue—surely not a color term at this time. Even more unsettling than any of the foregoing is "Jesus H. Christ," an oath that, to the best of my recollection, first saw the light of print in a John O'Hara novel.

She uses pretentious words like "noctilucent" and "hellacious" and strains for metaphors. . . . Worse, she doesn't strain for metaphors, as in the sex scene when she has Nash reflect: "He thought he died and went to heaven." Her grammar is shaky: "bid" for "bade" and "snuck" for "sneaked.". . . [And] her research sticks out, as when Henley checks into "the Spotswood Hotel at the southeast corner of Eighth and Main Streets in Richmond."

This is one of those books that start getting good just when the reader is about to throw them across the room. Once Brown leaves Geneva to her adolescent sex-change fantasies and turns to other characters and events, she finds her stride and gives us a vivid and soul-searing picture of the psychological effects of war on decent and intelligent human beings.

Her finest moment comes in a train depot scene when a mother who has volunteered for nursing work opens a coffin and finds the body of her son. (pp. 3, 8)

She does a splendid job on behind-the-scenes power struggles in the Confederate bureaucracy, and proves that she can weave her research into her story when she makes, effortlessly, the interesting and heretofore ignored point that, as a brand-new nation, the Confederacy had no party out of power to force the government into a more balanced stand.

She also proves that she can turn a phrase. Brushing the flies away from the corpses of the soldiers, the grieving mother "noticed as she squashed one that it smelled like the rotting flesh it had been eating." while an expert rider mounting a horse "sprang on the animal like a cricket."

As with Dickens, Brown's minor characters are better than her major ones. . . . She de-canonizes General J.E.B. Stuart and turns him into an interestingly flawed human being instead of the unrelievedly gallant *beau sabreur* other writers have made him. She captures with underwritten subtlety the dumb misery of unrequited love in the slave Big Muler, and she paints an accurate psychological portrait of the interior struggles of a woman who is far too intelligent to be a southern belle, but who tries to be one anyway. . . .

Stick with this novel, it will grow on you. Brown's stylistic faults are the kind that can be easily corrected in future works; meanwhile, she has proved that she can make the jump to a new genre. That in itself is rare and commendable. (p. 8)

Florence King, "Rita Mae Brown's Tomboy Scarlett O'Hara," in Book World—The Washington Post, May 4, 1986, pp. 3, 8.

DIANE COLE

A novel that should keep readers turning pages is Rita Mae Brown's *High Hearts*. . ., an entertaining historical tale that presents the war between men and women as a subplot to the War Between the States. (p. 32)

Unfortunately, the writing can be clumsy and the dialogue awkward. Anachronisms can also be troubling. Brown's depiction of slavery on the enlightened Chatfield estate seems less akin to Virginia in the 1860s than to the gentle paternalism the Edwardians displayed toward their servants in "Upstairs, Downstairs." All these difficulties arise, I think, from Brown's strained attempts to reconcile the Confederacy and what it stood for with her own liberal and antiwar convictions. Even so, who can help but be enchanted by the hardfighting Geneva and her dashing suitor, Major Mars Vickers? At its best, *High Hearts* is a kind of feminist *Gone with the Wind*. (pp. 32,34)

Diane Cole, in a review of "High Hearts," in Ms., Vol. XIV, No. 12, June, 1986, pp. 32,34.

Dennis Brutus

1924-

(Has also written under pseudonym of John Bruin) Rhodesian-born South African poet and essayist.

Brutus is regarded as one of the most distinguished contemporary South African poets. Influenced by John Donne and William Butler Yeats, Brutus employs traditional forms and rich language in his poetry to detail without self-pity or bitterness the physical and mental anguish he has suffered as a political prisoner and an exile. Brutus is also well known for his involvement in the anti-apartheid movement. His activism has led some critics to accuse Brutus of using his poetry for propagandistic purposes and others to fault him for being too restrained in condemning the South African government. However, most critics find Brutus's poems to be powerful in their subtlety and compassion.

Several poems in Brutus's first collection, *Sirens, Knuckles, Boots* (1963), denounce South Africa's racial policies. These poems, like many of Brutus's later pieces, are highly personal and meditative, interweaving personal references while developing such themes as love, pain, and anger. Brutus combines tenderness in the poems with a firm commitment to the liberation of his nation's citizens. The political nature of this volume contributed to Brutus's arrest and imprisonment in 1963. Following his release in 1965, Brutus was banned by the South African government from publishing any form of creative writing. Consequently, in his next collection, *Letters to Martha and Other Poems from a South African Prison* (1968), published after he left South Africa for England in 1966, Brutus recounts his prison experiences through letters to his sister-in-law. These poems, which describe the deprivation and fear of prison life, were praised for their objectivity and lucidity. Courage and humility are intermixed in the poems which condemn apartheid, as Brutus combines a polished, low-key approach with descriptions of the system's brutal acts. Critics also noted that the poems in this volume are different in style from those in Brutus's first collection; Brutus acknowledged that he altered his technique in favor of simpler idioms which make his verse more accessible to the average reader.

Brutus resided in London until 1970, when he moved to the United States and became a member of the English faculty at Northwestern University. Brutus's first volume of poetry published after leaving England, *A Simple Lust* (1973), includes his earlier work related to prison and exile in addition to new poems. Tanure Ojaide described Brutus's characteristic persona, which becomes most prominent in *A Simple Lust,* as "a troubadour who fights for a loved one against injustice and infidelity in his society." In the new poems in this collection, Brutus writes with passion of the homeland for which he yearns and of his compatriots who remain behind. His anxiety over their suffering is intensified by the contrast between his life as a free individual and their restricted lives. In *Stubborn Hope: New Poems and Selections from China Poems and Strains* (1978), Brutus again writes about his prison experiences and the inhumanity of apartheid. Endurance and hope are dominant themes in this volume, as Brutus extends his concern with the oppressive conditions of his homeland to a universal scale and assumes the role of spokesperson for all suffering people.

Photograph by Layle Silbert

(See also *Contemporary Authors,* Vols. 49-52 and *Contemporary Authors New Revision Series,* Vol. 2.)

MYRNA BLUMBERG

Dennis Brutus is a writer whose work can resuscitate a limp reader knocked out by power knockabouts. At his best, in the deft simplicity of the first part of [*Letters to Martha, and Other Poems from a South African Prison*] he has grace and penetration unmatched even by Alexander Solzhenitsyn—or perhaps Brutus is just less shockable and less verbose about the levels of degradation and joy, the nature of human nature, he has seen and felt. This is his first book published here although his earlier poems and some prose have been widely published in Africa.

Born in Rhodesia but schooled in South Africa, he served 18 months, mostly breaking stones, in the devilish Robben Island Prison off the Cape Coast; the poems he wrote there were confiscated, but he tried to re-create them when he was later under house arrest and still banned from writing for publication. . . .

Some of his earlier lyrics seem less successful, but this finely produced collection also includes moving recent poems, taut with religious doubts, challenging with personal and communal resilience. Buy it.

Myrna Blumberg, "Of Degradation and Joy," in The Guardian Weekly, Vol. 100, No. 10, March 6, 1969, p. 14.

PAUL KAMEEN

A Simple Lust is a collection of all Brutus' poetry relating to his experience of jail and exile. He is a serious-minded man, capable of subtle thought and large passion, who writes his best when these qualities are integrated and well-disciplined— i.e., in sustained meditation. His earliest work, written before he was jailed, is shot through with a strident tone of protest. Yet it is strained beyond its capacity by excess. Real feeling is either desiccated by ostentatious diction . . . or lost in a maze of self-indulgent prose. . . . Like Brutus, "suddenly one is tangled in a mesh of possibilities"—too many possibilities to allow a poem to come to life.

For Letters to Martha, the prison poems, Brutus eschewed much of this excess in favor of a more direct, authentic voice. . . . Such lines as "Or logic obfuse with semantic ambiguities" are more the exception here than the rule. The poems, as a result, are more convincing, and often poignant.

In his most recent work, "After Exile," the voice of meditation dominates. When Brutus follows its will to "state the bare fact and let it sing" he produces some fine lyric passages. But when his "mesh of ideas webs the entranced mind" the problem of excess returns to dismember the poetry.

Paul Kameen, in a review of "A Simple Lust," in Best Sellers, Vol. 33, No. 13, October 1, 1973, p. 298.

C. J. DRIVER

I find it difficult to write about Dennis Brutus's poems. I have known him a long time, in good times and bad; I admire him a great deal; I am much in debt to him; and there is nothing as hurtful as the criticism of friends. Yet I often find myself unable to like Dennis Brutus's poems; I find them unnecessarily polysyllabic, formless—their main form is the occasional jotting, the diary entry rather than the shaped artifact—and too generalized and generalizing. Yet the Letters to Martha, actually written while he was in gaol, strike me as very fine indeed.

Partly this is because for once the form of occasional reflections seems justified. The poems were apparently included in letters to his sister from prison, and 'decoded' afterwards; small wonder, in other words, that they are jottings, and great wonder that he was capable of writing them at all. Certainly they have a directness and simplicity only occasionally marred by the polysyllabic or abstract generalizing of some of the earlier or later poems. For instance:

> Particularly in a single cell
> but even in the sections
> the religious sense asserts itself;
>
> perhaps a childhood habit of nightly prayers
> the accessibility of Bibles,
> or awareness of the proximity of death:

> and, of course, it is a currency—
> pietistic expressions can purchase favours
> and it is a way of suggesting reformation
> (which can procure promotion);
>
> and the resort of the weak
> is to invoke divine revenge
> against a rampaging injustice;
>
> but in the grey silence of the empty afternoons
> it is not uncommon
> to find oneself talking to God.

It is not, I think, a faultless poem ('grey' silence, 'empty' afternoon), though as always it is intelligent and sensitive (I never doubt Brutus's considerable intelligence or his sensitivity) but it comes close to the true voice of feeling. . . . [The] groundswell of tragic feeling is there, even when obscured by clumsy writing and stale images. What is happening is too terrible for the empty gestures of absurdists; this is the destruction of real people, not of theatrical shadows, but—heroically—they refuse to accept their own destruction. They go out shouting or singing or silently, not whimpering. In a strange way, one does not feel pity for them, because they have made their choices and are suffering out of will, not passivity. When Dennis Brutus forgets the large gestures and the striving for the large image, and relies on his own natural, sombre, dark voice, he writes poems of considerable power. (pp. 113-14)

C. J. Driver, "The View from Makana Island: Some Recent Prison Books from Africa," in Journal of Southern African Studies, Vol. 2, No. 1, October, 1975, pp. 109-19.

EZEKIEL MPHAHLELE

The poems in Strains date back to September 1962 and come as far as 1973. "Jagged streets in Vrededorp / under the papery pre-dawn moon," "hoarse tubercular rooms," "thunderheads . . . in the night," "fractured metals," "shattering releasing tide,"—these are all images that are anchored in a familiar, specific place and time. Vrededorp is a slum suburb in Johannesburg. The "fractured metals" echo sabotage when power plants and trains were being blown up following upon the Sharpeville massacre. It is also the phase of loaded rows of epithets in Brutus's career, some of which epithets are mere thick plaster. The epithets become sparser as we move to the 1970's. He broods over his own stagnation, when he is "pooled in desperation," standing like a heron on one leg. When the verbs do more work when the epithetical plaster is knocked off, there is energy in the poem. "It is the human form / that you see mutilated" . . . is an example of this energy. He warns the spectator that "the instrument of terror" will yet reach him where he stands. "Because the ship sinks while you dance / I must command your choice for you: / It is prison you must choose." And so much for freedom of the will!

The single idea visualized, the single emotion or set of emotions felt about it and the ripples of feeling and thought pushing out from the center—these provide muscle in Brutus's poems structured on this premise: instruments of terror, prison, the spiritual feud with himself, etc.—the specific experiences that give so much of his previous A Simple Lust . . . a sustained focus. There are several trivia in Strains, which don't tell us much and sound like snatches of a tune or a dream begun and abandoned because the rest of it could not take shape. They also give one the uneasy feeling that they are a running commentary on the changing moods in a man traversing oceans and continents, filing through airport gates. The single object or mental experience, the single emotion or set of emotions as the starting point lend force also in **"No matter for history"**—about the late Latin American poet Pablo Neruda, and in **"Returning to the continent."**

Brutus's language maintains the lucidity of *A Simple Lust* and rings as clear as a bell, except when his epithets rush on you as if jostling for prominence. Brutus the champion of justice and beauty is still here with us. But there is lacking in the book the strong link between the various items that makes *A Simple Lust* readable and much more meaningful. If *Strains,* as the blurb tells us, has all the major strains in Brutus's poetry, it has, unfortunately, spread itself too thin. (pp. 118-19)

> *Ezekiel Mphahlele, in a review of "Strains," in* Okike,
> *No. 9, December, 1975, pp. 118-19.*

JANE GRANT

Dennis Brutus's last major collection of poems, *A Simple Lust,* appeared in Britain in 1973. . . . Since then smaller collections have been published in the United States (where Brutus teaches at Northwestern University), notably *Strains* . . . and *China Poems* . . . but these were not readily available here. For that reason alone *Stubborn Hope* would be welcome, making available to us poems from the two earlier collections, as well as Brutus's contribution to another American publication of poems by himself and several fellow countrymen, *South African Voices.* . . . (p. 75)

A Simple Lust was sub-titled 'Collected Poems of South African Jail and Exile', and this new collection, described as 'Selected Poems of South Africa and a Wider World', is largely parallel in subject-matter. . . . [A] major portion of *Stubborn Hope* consists, like *A Simple Lust,* of poems written in South Africa or soon after his departure into exile in 1966, following his imprisonment on Robben Island.

But even in those poems in *Stubborn Hope* which one imagines must have been written later, significant images recur from the earlier collection. Of central importance in both collections is the image of the troubadour and other vocabulary of chivalry which Brutus seems to have retained from his childhood admiration of Tennyson and Wordsworth. *A Simple Lust* opens with a famous poem of this type:

> A troubadour, I traverse all my land
> exploring all her wide-flung parts with zest . . .

The use of the image has changed in more recent poems.

> I will be the world's troubadour
> if not my country's
> Knight-erranting
> jousting up and down
> with justice for my theme. . . .

The earlier example could be read as a love poem to Brutus's beautiful doomed homeland. Although in the present collection we once again find many poems which express, often in images of great tenderness and sensuality, his passionate involvement with the land of South Africa, we are never allowed to forget the ugliness beneath the surface beauty. For example **"In this country"** celebrates the beauty of the land, but ends ominously. . . . The image of Robben Island remains one of the most potent in Dennis Brutus's poetry, and *Stubborn Hope* contains several poems which deal directly with the traumatic

period of his life when he was imprisoned on the island, after having been shot while trying to escape arrest. While the earlier prison poems, *Letters to Martha* (addressed as letters to his sister-in-law because it was illegal for a banned person to write poetry, but it was legal to write letters) had shown a remarkable cool control and lack of bitterness, in this new collection the bitterness breaks through. . . . But even here the tendency remains to under-rather than over-state and to refuse the hero's role:

> On torn ragged feet
> trailing grimy bandages
> with bare thin legs
> I puttered around the prison yard awhile
> while politicos learning of me gaped
> wondering how they had managed to make of
> me a thing
> of bruises, rags, contempt and mockery.
>
> In time things grew better. . . .

The use of 'puttered', like the throw-away last line, seems an almost perverse attempt by Brutus to play down his own suffering and courage.

The self-effacing mood recurs in the poems of exile which describe his travels around the world in the course of his many anti-*apartheid* activities. . . . This brings us to the theme of endurance, of hope almost against the odds, which is the most constant feature of the recent poems in the volume, and which gives us its title. The contrast between the present poems—for example [**"Stubborn Hope"**] to the collection ('Endurance is a passive quality, transforms nothing, contests nothing')—and the confident prediction of 1966 when he entered exile is marked:

> Peace will come
> We have the power
> the hope
> the resolution.
> Men will go home. . . .

From early on there seems to have been an inner conflict between Brutus, the activist against *apartheid,* and Brutus, the highly literate writer of difficult, complex and lyrical poetry. The months in solitary confinement on Robben Island seem to have led him to a radical reassessment of his role as a poet. . . . (pp. 75-6)

What came out of these decisions was the less complex, more straightforward statement of *Letters to Martha,* and the trend culminates in the extreme brevity and economy of the *China Poems* (the title refers both to where they were written and to the delicate nature of the poems), which are included in *Stubborn Hope.* They are seldom more than a few lines long, and are influenced by the Japanese *haiku* and its Chinese ancestor, the *chueh chu.* The trick, as Brutus puts it in the original edition, is 'to say little (the nearer to nothing, the better) and to suggest much—as much as possible'. While I am glad that not all his recent poetry follows this trend, some of the 'China poems' succeed very well. . . . Yet Brutus is still capable of returning to Blake's powerful tone of anger to express his bitterness about the realities of Britain today (in earlier years he was more struck by 'England's seducing charms'). . . . *Stubborn Hope,* as a collection, is undoubtedly uneven in quality, but certain poems stand out in their agony and power, and we can only hope that this talented and courageous man will continue to write. (p. 77)

Jane Grant, "Exile's Progress," in Index on Censorship, *Vol. 8, No. 4, July-August, 1979, pp. 75-7.*

DAVID SWEETMAN

The evidence of an exile's pilgrimage is scattered throughout [Brutus's] latest collection, **Stubborn Hope**—Teheran, Kabul, Lagos, even a trip to the Lake District, and everything speaks of keeping going, of continuing the fight. . . .

The problem is that these quiet, stubborn insights are too often drowned in a rush of words, by the massive overkill that we have seen in his previous books. Many of the 97 poems, old and new, in this collection should never have got past the poet let alone his editor. Take this *complete* work:

> Perhaps
> all
> poems
> are simply
> drafts
>
> (p. 592)

Fortunately Brutus does frequently abandon these attempts at minimalism and return to what he is best at, the straight presentation of experience; as here in a recollection of Robben Island where . . .

> some mornings we lined up for hospital
> —it meant mostly getting castor oil—
> but what a varied bunch we were!
> for all had injuries—but in such variety
> split heads; smashed ankles, arms;
> cut feet in bandages, or torn and bloodied legs:
> some under uniform wore their mass of bruises
> but what a bruised and motley lot we were!

That same light, self-mocking touch is at work in one of the best poems in this collection, **"From Shannon"**, where the poet describes the smoke-greys and slate-blues of the Lake District while recalling his love of Wordsworth and Coleridge only to realise, bitterly, that words will not work . . . The transfer of the colours as a symbol of the transfer of language and poetry from England to Africa along with the awareness of the limits of the poet's role in the face of tyranny add a modest power to the poem that the more self-regarding pieces lack. The non-African reader will probably appreciate most these quieter poems, concerned as they are with love and landscape, yet Brutus's popularity with exile groups and young activists here and in the States comes not from the more thoughtful pieces, set as they are in the European tradition, but rather from those works of his that are meant to be shouted in protest or chanted in prison. (p. 593)

David Sweetman, "Children of the Lion," in New Statesman, *Vol. 99, No. 2561, April 18, 1980, pp. 592-93.*

GESSLER MOSES NKONDO

Those who know South Africa, particularly certain places like the coastal city of Port Elizabeth, overwhelmed by the sky which is so dominant a feature of the landscape, will have been struck by the Mediterranean quality of the light. I am reminded of this when I think of the work of one of the most distinguished of contemporary South African poets, Dennis Brutus. Brutus is learned, passionate, skeptical—and in his work there is an insistent, almost fierce sense of a Western Latin tradition.

Perhaps one is misled by the analogy of the Latin light. It may be that the creative impulse is discrepancy, an aching consciousness of the dissimilarity between the decorative density of Europe and the native splendor of the country. More probably both impulses work together in the South African English sensibility, work together and work on one another, sharpening into positive existence the Latin elements—not just the linguistic ones—latent in the English language. Certainly Brutus [in his **Stubborn Hope**] is concerned in a most unusual way, for those currently writing in English, with order and coherence of feeling and with lucidity and precision in presentation. This preoccupation is a constant presence in the poetry—not always successfully realized, of course—and we have no need to go outside the verse to find a sanction for the claim I have made. (p. 32)

"The rosy aureole of your affection" is a remarkably contained poem, each verbal edge firmly finished off and each syntactical contour exactly defined. Two bold images, "our focussed shaped projection" and the "ancient foetus-hungry incubus" are separately drawn out and then drawn together. The tranquil, mellowed richness of the love scene, "the rosy aureole of your affection," is put into opposition and balance with the awe-inspiring aura of "older mouths from oozy shores." Together the images, locked at once in antagonism and passion, produce the strength and scent of sexual encounter. The actual tension and embrace of love are poised above and sustained by the profound processes of organic life: "The rosy aureole of your affection / extends beyond our urban bounded knowledge / to tangled undergrowths of earlier time."

The poem, keeping its varied complexities in place and in connection along a lucid descriptive line, grasps first at the physical basis of life and experience, at the flesh and the earth and the calm sagacity it generates, and then touches the quick of human experience at its exquisite crisis in the mysterious meeting of love. The mystery is an essential part of the experience which the poem offers. It includes not only the joyful, physical energy of sexual love, . . . but also a tissue of social memories and images. These are both serene ("bright labyrinths of the mind") and terrifying ("older mouths from oozy shores"). In the poem the act of love appears as a model of all human experience which has its ancient sources buried in the earth, but which is also immediate and adapted to the light and further transformed by the imagination, itself always a carrier of a more than merely personal cargo, a conductor of both compulsion and aspiration, honor and grace.

Sexual love is a recurrent theme in Brutus's work. Occasionally he celebrates it as the beneficent completion of life and personality. More frequently he is concerned with its Lawrentian vigor and aboriginal vitality. . . . [In **"Nightsong: country"**] love is seen restoring the warmth and purity of the ancient earth and in which Brutus's energy of articulation is given a singing, aspiring quality. . . . The sense of unalloyed delight in love, spiritual as well as physical, is almost always present in Brutus's poetry. It is true that whenever he writes of love he conveys in a masterly way the pleasure of the senses and the richness and beauty of the body. But there is almost always something breaking in, something sinister or ugly or mean. Monstrous and cogent fears about the police, who supply many of the fictions in Brutus's verse, intrude on the enclosed world of lovers—sirens, knuckles, boots: "over our heads the monolithic decalogue / of fascist prohibition glowers / and teeters for a catastrophic fall; / / boots club the peeling door." This stanza from **"Somehow we survive"** . . . , contrasting sharply and yet following naturally on the informal and casual opening (the brilliant twist of mood is completely logical), is an example of Brutus's supple virtuosity in modulation from the casual and throwaway to the stately and measured. It calls up the great name of Yeats, for whom Brutus has made no secret of his admiration.

But while Yeats is clearly a vital (and absorbed) influence in Brutus, his idiom is his own, being at once less gorgeous and Byzantine when full out and more flatly contemporary in the lower register. . . . [An] example of this calculatedly flat manner, and one . . . thoroughly charged with the macabre—the attraction of which for Brutus suggests a certain nauseated disgust with ordinary life as part of his response to experience—is the last stanza of **"When last I ranged and revelled"**:

> When last I ranged and revelled all your length
> I vowed to savour your most beauteous curves
> with such devout and lingering delight
> that they would etch themselves into my brain
> to comfort me throughout the prisoned night.
>
> But waking early in the frowsty dawn
> and finding you dishevelled and unkempt
> my heart arose as though you showed your best
> —and then I wryly knew myself to be
> the slave of an habituated love. . . .

Having said this—that the appeal of the macabre for Brutus testifies to some perverse disrelish for common experience—I am immediately conscious of the need to correct or qualify it. There is something nasty, an occasional gratuitous reveling in the garbage bin and perhaps the puritan self-hatred to which this is often the clue, in a few of Brutus's poems. . . . But more often some quality in the tone, a quaver of amusement, a glint of wit, a touch of self-mockery, even a cry of innocent astonishment, shows that the macabre is being put to a more complicated and controlled use. It becomes an instrument instead of a dead end, another gateway through which the poet's imagination can enter an odd, disturbed but somehow valid world. (pp. 32-4)

I have referred . . . to Brutus's writing in the formal Yeatsian mode, to his flatter, more contemporary manner and to work of the kind I call "macabre-grotesque," although I recognize the infelicity of the term, which misleadingly suggests some Gothic thrill-inducing intention on the part of the poet, when the most notable thing about these poems is the control and application with which the genre is put to serious, indeed somber, purposes. Use, management, the employment of a style for purposes beyond what it seems capable of is even more strikingly evident in another set of poems which look immediately to be more than deliberate imitations. Two members of this series are **"At a funeral"** and **"Gaily teetering on the bath's edge."** These poems are strongly reminiscent of certain religious poems of the English seventeenth century.

What in the seventeenth century Brutus fastens on is a composite sensibility made up of the passionate subtleties and the intellectual sensuousness of the metaphysical poets and the masculine, ironic force of Donne. *Why* the seventeenth century should be looked to as the source has to do with the congruence between Brutus's own poetic nature and the adult, ardent, almost mathematical reasoning habit of the metaphysicals: a balance further modified by another, the symmetry between Brutus and his admired Donne's gift of sensitive manliness, his way of being at once independent and level with his experience, however intricate; and modified yet again by Brutus's sym-

pathetic understanding of Donne's skill in calling upon a range of poetic resonance within a strictly defining, disciplining pattern. Nor should we overlook that Brutus had to make his choice of exemplar at a particular time and from within a certain literary tradition, not only the wider one grounded in the English language and the English literary tradition, but within the local African one based on the altered language of his own country. It could not be a purely personal choice, although it had to be primarily a personal one, answering to the need felt in the poet's own nerves. The poet as poet is not engaged in any explicit mission to renovate a literary tradition. But of course he is involved in such an undertaking, and the more significant a poet he is, the more profound is his involvement. Brutus's "conservatism" in fact is truly radical. His poetry has to be freed from the influence of home, from a tradition still too much domesticated within the nineteenth century in which British gentility and blandness were curiously reinforced in their parochialism by an unambitious—and suspicious—South African philistinism. The seventeenth century, so different from the nineteenth in its inclusiveness and in the very assurance of its skepticism to which poets in Britain earlier directed their attention, could be the same cleansing, tonic influence for South Africa, above all if the connection were made by a South African poet. (pp. 34-5)

"So, for the moment, Sweet, is peace" [is] a sardonic extrapolation from **"The Canonization,"** and **"The sounds begin again,"** a grim evocation of inner turmoil which is Roman in the strength of its despair. Both these poems are written in vigorous conceits which have something of Donne's wit and force: Donne's because the medium, handled by Brutus with remarkable naturalness, is used as the instrument of strength rather than delicacy. Indeed the conceit, employed in an easy, open way, is splendidly adapted to communicate the peculiar quality of Brutus's poetry which one is aware of even in his earliest, lightest pieces. This is its powerfully, almost physically energetic character. It is muscular, quick and solid, with the relaxed poise of the gifted athlete who brings all his force to bear rhythmically and without strain. Brutus is the least neurotic of poets, and even when he is scrutinizing his own romantic love, as in one of his best poems, **"Nightsong: City,"** his regard is gravely objective without the least touch of narcissistic droop or any suspicion of anxious self-interest. Right from the start of Brutus's poetic career, the reader is aware of the formed personality beneath the finished literary character. It is positive, independent and radical in an un-South African manner; the accepted South African literary convention lacks precisely this very virtue. It is free of the frog of middle-class pretension and gentility: sharp where that was bland and harsh where that was cozy. At the same time Brutus's poetry asserts a profound commitment to the great constitutive works of the Western—not just the British—tradition, and not only in poetry but also in thought and morality. It accepts and asserts, namely, the principles of intellectual integrity, and in doing so avoids, or ignores, the clogging dangers of South African parochialism. The result is a powerful and unfashionable maturity which joins a naked freshness of original response to a richly realized conception of an ideal order.

This is a conjunction which appears in . . . **"Kneeling before you in a gesture,"** the fable of which seems to be taken from *Antony and Cleopatra* or some of Donne's crabbed, more passionate outbursts. The despair which is implicit in the situation and the grimness of a passionate love call to powers deep in Brutus's nature and are transformed in his treatment to become the implacable conditions of tragic human life itself. It is written in language which very much obeys the prescription Brutus lays down: that the language of poetry should be concrete, lucid, coherent, logically connected, syntactically exact and firmly based in current idiom and usage. It begins with sharp, plaintive, clearly effective phrases, in a rhythm and in a voice which has nothing in it but tenderness. . . . The poem, mingling sadness and sensuousness in a strange, dry way, manages unfalteringly to convey at once the coldness of present misery and the radiance of remembered passion. Not that the effect is at all romantically intimate or soft. The logical structure, the carefully worked-out syntax, both of grammar and feeling, generalize the experience into something highly organized and impersonal, so that the love passages, luminous and distant in the memory, have the refinement and the deadliness of expert swordplay, abrasive and bleakly affecting. Here is the conclusion, in which we see the particular aspiring through the lucidity of form toward a larger, general order:

> and answering, you pressed my face against your womb
> and drew me to a safe and still oblivion,
> shut out the knives and teeth; boots, bayonets and
> knuckles:
> so, for the instant posed, we froze to an eternal image
> became unpersoned and unageing symbols
> of humbled vulnerable wonder
> enfolded by a bayed and resolute maternalness.

"Kneeling before you in a gesture" is a statement—but more than a mere "statement"—about the ideal order which is implicit in, and which by means of poetry can be extracted from, the grubby detritus of life. But of course the poet could be, and is, as concerned with the other side of the duality, with the disordered elements in their chaos. In another poem, **"Erosion: Transkei,"** he speaks of that preoccupation. . . . The "ravaged land" describes very well the form under which society and the modern world appear to this tough-minded, independent poet. "My possessing" describes the general, bracing aim which keeps his observations tart, the fervent steps, the self-confidence of the approach. The tone of these social poems, which include some of Brutus's most effective and personal work, is better seen in **"Let not this plunder be misconstrued."** . . . The tone here, untensed and self-mocking, is a recognition that we are all, not excluding the poet himself, "poor wordless bodies" gnawed by "lonely desire," in the same cage, and an almost amused confession of innocence, in that whatever is wrong—and so much is, both in the lover and the beloved—derives from a common impersonal fault. It is the classical Western awareness—but light, wry and quite without guilt—that everything issues from a single, tainted source, an original flaw or sin.

Yet at other times the poet collects himself into a more feline and separate contempt. **"Off The Campus: Wits"** spits at the mass-communicating world, **"The Mob"** at the malevolently stupid mob, **"Our aims our dreams our destinations"** at the formal cruelties of religion, and **"Longing"** straight into "Science's logistics." Sometimes the tone is harsh and disgusted. The poet squarely rejects those with all the answers. . . . [**"Mirror Sermon"**] mocks at "sensual intellection."

> This cold reflection
> of our interlocking nudity
> moralizes ascetically
> on sensual intellection
> or mortality. . . .

The poem makes solemn, wicked fun of the reductive habit of the contemporary mind, of its technique at getting beneath the delusive surface in the interests of uttering some pure abstract truth. Brutus combines a gravely ironic parody of psychiatric investigation with a medievally gruesome pondering on the horrors of the body, including "twitching strings of lust." Clothes, skin, flesh are peeled off until the sage lays bare the "body's aberrations." . . . The Swift-like gravity of procedure, simultaneously recommending and undermining the modest monstrous proposal, and the hideous exposure of the skinned body are devices used in the service of a serious intention but one which can express itself in a less ferocious, more bantering species of ridicule than the master of devastation would ever allow himself. The touch of tolerant lightheartedness is confirmed by the crisply humorous conclusion. It holds out a small hope that a sense of reality is perhaps recoverable, but only as the issue of total absurdity. (pp. 36-7)

"Blood River Day" is a powerfully meditative poem on the theme of man's sacredness and of our kinship with nature. It makes the characteristically solid impact of Brutus's best poems, seeming to have behind it the weight of personal experience which has been grasped and deeply pondered. (p. 37)

"Blood River Day" is a strongly objective poem, written in a mood of dry, almost grim composure, in which the settled author, unfrayed by his own situation and its pathos, stares at what is the case: namely, the twin realities of bloodthirsty Afrikaner patriots and the perfume of the earth. Much of the intensity of the poem's effect comes from the simultaneous and equal treatment of the two themes, not in a way which uses the political figure as a simple analogy or parable but as an exercise in positive ambiguity. South Africans are sometimes thought to be fustily conformist—it is a criticism the South Africans often make of themselves—but there is also in the South African psychology a quality of lissome independence corresponding, perhaps, to the marvelous bodily suppleness generated by a regimen of sun, protein and sport. Only a South African, and one with Brutus's gifts—only Brutus himself, I suppose—could use the antiquarian vocabulary in the last lines of **"In the greyness of isolated time"** (from the **"Letters to Martha"** sequence) with such unembarrassed lack of self-consciousness. There the words are, his attitude seems to imply, still with a quirky flair of life not yet quite snuffed out, as well as with a degree of dubious charm. Let me use them therefore, taking advantage of their antique attractiveness and consciously manipulating them in a new direction, like a batsman who makes not simply an unorthodox but an astonishingly original stroke, staying all the time strictly within the rules.

> Coprophilism; necrophilism; fellatio;
> penis-amputation;
> and in this gibbering society
> hooting for recognition as one's other selves
> suicide, self-damnation, walks
> if not a companionable ghost
> then a familiar familiar,
> a doppelgänger
> not to be shaken off. . . .

There is a checked or controlled comic impulse at work here which enables Brutus to use a set of superannuated terms as though they were colloquialisms, and to employ what could easily be units of rhetoric as terms of slang. Two modes of discourse, rhetorical and familiar, run together through the poem. At one point, as in the first few lines, the rhetorical is more strongly present; at another, as in the closing five lines, the casually colloquial is emphasized. The half-amused, shoulder-shrugging tolerance keeps the rhetorical from becoming fustian while it gives a sardonic edge to the slang. (p. 38)

In **"Under House Arrest"** the stony, stoical quality and the almost regular edge of the verse match the author's notation of the "screaming tensions" between artistic form and the raw material of experience. In **"Our aims our dreams"** a milder but equally critical regard is turned upon the myth of Gethsemane. In cool, almost strict verse the poet questions the grandeur of splendid Gethsemane. He registers the humanity of the myth and the irony by which evil is supposed to be brought out of good. Some critics may find metaphysical complexities in this poem, a view of the world and a sense of sin; but to me the poem seems most remarkable for its directness and simplicity. A tranquil, pagan eye, not by any means without humor, is turned upon the Judeo-Christian story. This itself makes for freshness. And it is the naturalness of the event in the fable which the poet suggests, and the human incongruity of the story; the theological implications are somewhat suppressed.

If one wanted a Mediterranean but more intimately personal and self-involved poem, one would go to **"Landscape of my young world."** . . . Brutus brings to bear upon his enigmatically impalpable subject, the vaguely glimmering beginnings of his existence, not external measuring instruments but the most refined and disciplined of faculties, the matured poetic consciousness. The glimpse of, the hint about, the beginning of his life has a poetic definition and actuality of being, and the whole poem itself has the solidity of an event. He registers first his point of entry, the memory which is triggered as much by his immediate as by his total situation. . . . The Browningesque reminiscence reminds us not to forget Brutus's characteristic and wholly unaffected daring. But such nerve is justified by the naturalness with which the poem starts, and the propriety and evenness with which the body of it flows from the opening. He next hints at the location, Port Elizabeth, where the "soft" hills and the aloes together with the dreaming firs and the green slopes combine the genius of South Africa and Britain, that particular blend of sensibility which is the poet's genius too. This place, the product of two national sources, is not just an enclosing context but an inward condition of the child's psychology. Implicit in that is a powerful sense of distance, of distance as a positive and creative dimension of imagination. (p. 39)

Brutus is a remarkable poet, one of the most distinguished South Africa has produced. His very positive literary character is both grainily individual and strongly in the main Western literary tradition to which he adheres: for accretions, whether modish or cliquish, he has no use, and indeed considerable scorn. The lucidity and precision which he is at pains to develop in his work are qualities he admires from artistic conviction, as a humanist opposed both to romantic haze and conventional trends. But they also testify to a profound cultivation of spirit, a certain wholeness and harmony of nature, as they do too to a fine independence of literary fashion. (pp. 39-40)

       Gessler Moses Nkondo, "Dennis Brutus: The Domestication of a Tradition," in World Literature Today, *Vol. 55, No. 1, Winter, 1981, pp. 32-40.*

CHIKWENYE OKONJO OGUNYEMI

In his collection, **Letters to Martha,** Dennis Brutus gives a hint of his attitude towards his prison material: "I cut away the public trappings to assert / certain private essentialities." It is

the private angle of prison life with its humanistic emphasis which the public figure, Brutus, examines urbanely and objectively and with a remarkable ironical distancing. This apparently calm exterior, a recognizable black South African pose in racial politics, covers up an inner turmoil and seething. In one dramatic vignette, he presents himself as unprotected, but we perceive an inner resilience that only the spiritually strong can possess when opposing a contemptible but powerful enemy. . . . His courage in the unequal struggle is the mark of his victory and heroism. He can therefore afford to be matter of fact in reporting the deplorable conditions under which he and the other prisoners find themselves on Robben Island:

> Cold
> the clammy cement
> sucks our naked feet
>
> . . .
> we sit on the concrete,
> stuff with our fingers
> the sugarless pap
> into our mouths. . . .

Brutus' choice of aspects of prison life to emphasize demonstrates his acute awareness of the humiliating experience that is prison life, its emasculation of the black South African in a hideous system that remains apparently unchanging.

Brutus touches on the perennial conflict between the warder and the gaoled, a relationship that the reader readily extends to the apartheid rulers and the black populace. . . . It is with such disarming simplicity and a hint of innocence that the poet manages adroitly to put his enemy in the wrong. The factual reporting allows the reader to make even extreme associations, between the situation reported and the brutality of the Nazis towards the Jews, for example. It is intended to arouse the moral awareness of the international community, to get us to view seriously the individual scenarios that take place in South African prisons, and by extension, in South Africa itself. Brutus' strategy is to engage in a quiet, unobtrusive, and insistent attack on his enemies, in an approach that is compatible with Martin Luther King's philosophy of political non-violence. Part of his attitude is a modesty and humility that will not jubilate over victory in any form. Instead, Brutus feels a certain selflessness in his

> vague heroism
> mixed with self-pity
> and tempered by the knowledge of those
> who endure much more
> and endure. . . .

Yet he too has endured, and has the poetic ability to let us share his experience.

Brutus maintains a detached mood and achieves self-effacement with the use of imprecise pronouns like "one," "you," "your" instead of "I." His objectivity lends an air of truth and sincerity to his account as he explores the degeneration of the human mind in prison through observing various prisoners and their ways of coping with their terrible status. Deprived of basic necessities of life like sex and music and prevented from watching objects of nature like stars and the carefree bird, some prisoners take recourse in psychosomatic illnesses or fantasizing. Others move towards "Coprophilism; necrophilism; fellatio; / penis amputation." . . . Sodomy is rampant. Many find peace from their cares in the very private world of the insane. Yet through it all, with patience and without self-praise, Brutus not only survives the numerous hardships, the lot of the prisoner, but, like Malcolm X, matures through contact with so much hideousness and suffering. Here he differs markedly from Soyinka, . . . who delights in engaging in battle with the enemy. Rather, Brutus acknowledges the status of the political prisoner and from that premise continues to fight the opposition. . . . (pp. 67-9)

With such a limited day-to-day experience, "clichés about the freedom of the birds . . . become meaningful" . . . and a subtle metamorphosis takes place in the prisoner. Brutus suggests the poignancy of his plight in an incident when he switches off the light in an attempt to catch a glimpse of the stars but receives a "warning bark" in reply that arouses fear and destroys the meditative, romantic mood that the poet found himself in. Brutus knows the psychology of fear, as shown in **"A Letter to Basil,"** and his knowledge gives him spiritual strength amidst the vicissitudes of his life:

> To understand the unmanning powers of fear
> and its corrosive action
> makes it easier to forgive. . . .

These lines express the length and the roughness of the road that Brutus had patiently trod. He has learnt to forgive and even pity the offensive prisoner who cannot help being perfidious to his kind out of fear of the authorities. Also, Brutus' South African whites, referred to as "O my people" in a poem, **"The Mob,"** brutal from fear and so unmanly, become, in a sense, Brutus' fellow prisoners. In an ironic but humanistic mood, he pities them and forgives them for their wrongdoings in a surprising spirit of maturity and brotherhood reminiscent of Christ's indomitable reaction to Peter's denial of him. When Brutus arrives at the tragic conclusion that the whole of South Africa is a prison, he has to work out a *modus vivendi* for himself. . . . His feeling of pity is similar to Baldwin's in the American situation as expressed in his letter to his nephew in *The Fire Next Time*. Brutus triumphs over the sadism of the South African government through his humanism, which pleads for imitation by the authorities. His rebellion against the dehumanization is the act of writing; the power of his cosmopolitan truth and urbane tones all the more condemns the apartheid regime, which emerges by contrast as primitive.

It is therefore surprising that "an African writer thinks that the poet's social involvement in Dennis Brutus's poems is a check on the artistic effect," although, as D. S. Izevbaye is quick to add, "most critics do not endorse this view, nor do they agree that as a rule poets should be less vociferous about social problems." This raises a perennial issue about aesthetics and the social involvement of the writer, and here the issue must be resolved in the writer's favour. It is obvious from the *Letters* that the occasion and experience of prison life that political imprisonment affords have given poetic inspiration to Brutus, as it has to other writers in other parts of the world. His turning his experience into a work of art is certainly as valid as a poet who turns to nature for inspiration. Brutus deals with the nature of man in power, the artist as prisoner, and these are powerful modes of knowing man and his ways. Brutus' writing is artistic rather than overtly propagandistic. He writes to connect his inner life with the outside world and those who love him so that his mind and theirs can be, relatively, at rest. . . . That need to connect with posterity, a reason for the enduring, is a genuine artistic feeling. By handling the subject of prison life, mulling over it, seeing its corrosive effect on both the gaoler and the gaoled, Brutus grapples through it with the existential human predicament that man finds himself in. His message,

even if ultimately didactic, as most good literature is, is humanistically convincing and artistically enunciated. (pp. 69-71)

> *Chikwenye Okonjo Ogunyemi, "The Song of the Caged Bird: Contemporary African Prison Poetry," in Ariel, Vol. 13, No. 4, October, 1982, pp. 65-84.*

COLIN GARDNER

The problem with Dennis Brutus . . . is that his writings are banned in the Republic of South Africa. Brutus as a writer exists, as far as the Pretoria government is concerned, as a vacuum, an absence; in the firmament of South African literature, such as it is, Brutus could be described as a black hole. But it is necessary to find him and read him, to talk and write about him, to pick up the light which in fact he does emit, because he is at his best as important as any other South African who has written poetry in English. (p. 354)

Brutus began to write in the 1950s; and his first volume of poems, *Sirens, Knuckles, Boots,* was published in Nigeria in 1963 while he was on Robben Island. He is therefore in one sense a poet of twenty years ago, though he has continued to write, often very successfully, while he has been in exile. I am conscious that, in directing an appreciative spotlight on Brutus's poetry and its methods and implications, I might be accused in some quarters of wearing a cloak of mild boldness in order to mask a critical intention which is in fact profoundly conservative, if not positively retrogressive. The truth is that while I recognize that Brutus's writing, especially that of the early 1960s, belongs to a particular moment in South African sensibility and South African history, I do not believe that his finest poems are confined to their period, although they express it so well: achieved art never dates in any simple sense. This does not mean that I deny or call into question the striking developments that have taken place in the direction and practice of verse in South Africa, particulary among black writers, in the last twelve or fifteen years. It is nevertheless often dangerous to insist that one stream of literary development, no matter how creative and dominant it may be, is the only valid and valuable current. It may be even more important for us to remember that Dennis Brutus, even though he is in exile, is still alive and writing and still a figure in contemporary South African literature. (p. 355)

Reading [the poems collected in *Sirens, Knuckles, Boots*] today, one is struck by the degree to which they are different from recent black verse: one thinks of the tangy and sometimes epigrammatic irony of the early Mtshali, who lets the carefully handled "facts" appear to speak for themselves; of the vigorous, impassioned, but subtle and sensitive, almost communal voice of Serote; of the sophisticated, seemingly relaxed but half-despairing deadpan joking of Sepamla; and of the various modes and moods of sharp indignation, analysis, and resoluteness in the more memorable of the *Staffrider* and *Wietie* poems.

The world evoked by Brutus—both the internal and the external world—is quite other. The poems are quiet, peculiarly personal, meditative. We are introduced to, or rather into, a persona, which is capacious, generous, observant, anxiously dedicated, morally and intellectually scrupulous. Everything that the poems touch on is translated or transformed to become a part of the landscape or the furniture of this inner world—not that there is anything egocentric or solipsistic about the effect that the poems achieve. [For example] "The sounds begin again," has become, by the end of the poem, "*My* sounds begin again." What is happening here is of course not merely a process of internalization, of compassionate appropriation: the poet indicates, by a subtle shift, that he himself physically participates in the suffering of which he writes.

This production of a meditating persona, a richly presented working mind and sensibility into which we are drawn by the strong, spiderlike threads of the poetic structure, is a phenomenon which has been very common in Western and perhaps particularly in English poetry, from Eliot back through Wordsworth and Shakespeare to Wyatt and Surrey. And of course Brutus is a traditional poet, nourished in the classic English tradition, in a way that is largely foreign to the poets of Soweto. ("Traditional" may seem a dangerous word to apply to anyone, in the present climate of innovation, but let me draw attention to Eliot's view that a certain kind of traditionality may be highly original.) It is at this point that I introduce my reference to Shakespeare. [Brutus's line] "It is the constant image of your face" might almost have been the opening line of a Shakespearean sonnet; so might "A common hate enriched our love and us," except that the circumstances are rather special. It is significant that Brutus has described himself as a lyrical poet and has added that "'protest elements' are only incidental, as features of the South African scene obtrude." He has said that his favorite poets are Donne, Hopkins, and Browning. In some of his work one can sense the influence of those three writers and of others, but the quietly dramatic unfolding of a delicate pattern of feeling and thought seems to me to owe most—if "owe" is quite the right word—to the Shakespeare of the sonnets. But of course those sonnets are themselves related to the soliloquies in the plays, and there are perhaps a few minor links with Brutus there too. It may not be wholly fanciful, indeed, to invoke the other Brutus, the central character in *Julius Caesar*—troubled, self-analytical, caught between the love of his wife, Portia, and his allegiance to what he feels to be essential justice and values in Rome.

This brings me back to the poet's subject matter. I think Brutus was right to see himself as primarily a lyrical poet, but he seems to me to have misinterpreted his work when he described "protest elements" as "incidental." The phrase "protest elements" is inadequate and was probably designed merely to suggest a contrast with some of the more strident forms of black American verse. But the distinctive qualities of the four poems [that were first published as the sequence **"Nightsong: City"** in 1963] depend entirely on the poet's particular response to a specific sociopolitical situation. In the first poem he addresses his love, inviting her to enjoy what momentary peace she can have in a situation of violent emotions and antagonisms, and he then reveals, in the last line, that his love is the land itself—the land and its peoples, clearly. In the third of these poems, the poet's love for the woman he addresses is defined in terms of, has indeed been given its identity and richness by, the surrounding political tension and horror. The interaction between personal and political, between the inward and the outward, is complete, even though it involves a paradox: "hate gouged out deeper levels for our passion." What is suggested is that the hate and the love meet at a newly discovered depth, in an impulse which is both violent and generous. In the fourth poem the structure of the love relationship is differently depicted: the loved woman and the loved land are in a state of rivalry, and the poet tries, urgently but with affection and good humor, to reconcile his two allegiances.

The sensibility that Brutus displays in these poems is clearly his own, but at the same time it offers us something of the feeling of the early 1960s, what Raymond Williams would call that period's "structure of feeling." The poet is aware that he has comrades in his political campaigns and struggles, but under intense government pressure, there is no real sense of a mass movement. The fight for liberation will be a long one, and a sensitive participant cannot but feel rather isolated. This isolation is an important aspect of the poet's mode and mood. (By the late 1960s and early 1970s, on the other hand, blacks, particularly those in the larger urban townships, were beginning to develop a corporate confidence of a wholly new kind.)

Some critics have disapproved of the methods and attitudes which prevail in Brutus's poems. Bahadur Tejani, for example, has expressed grave reservations about Brutus's inwardness and compassion, his hopefulness and "a sense of underlying religiousness in his poetry which makes him suspect"; Tejani would prefer more of the "protest elements," something distinctly more militant. But such critics as Abasiekong and Egudu have recognized the richness and complexity of Brutus's apprehension and of his language and have suggested that his sympathetic understanding of what he feels to be the universality of human frailty represents a position not of weakness but of strength.

Brutus's sense that he was largely alone in his efforts can be seen in retrospect to have prepared him for his tragically long exile. New situations, new movements of thought and feeling, have produced new types of verse in South Africa. But the struggle for radical social change is of course far from over. Some of the euphoria of the mid-1970s has died away or been transmuted into newer directions, and it would be difficult to argue that the voice of isolated resolve and of exile has lost its relevance. . . . Brutus's best poetry has a resonance which both articulates and generalizes his specific themes; he has found forms and formulations which dramatize an important part of the agony of South Africa and of contemporary humanity. (pp. 357-60)

> *Colin Gardner, "Brutus and Shakespeare," in* Research in African Literatures, *Vol. 15, No. 3, Fall, 1984, pp. 354-64.*

TANURE OJAIDE

The poet is consistently represented as a troubadour and this persona unites all of Brutus's poems. Brutus acknowledges in an interview:

> . . .there recur in my poetry certain images from the language of chivalry—the troubadour, in particular. The notion of a stubborn, even foolish knight-errantry on a quest, in the service of someone loved; this is an image I use in my work, because it seems to me a true kind of shorthand for something which is part of my life and my pursuit of justice in a menacing South Africa.

The troubadour was a medieval knight "who was also a poet and who dedicated his life to the service of a lady (usually called a mistress) and whose unattainable love he praised in poetry. Often his service entailed fighting in order to rescue the mistress from monsters and other unfaithful knights." This mask of a troubadour who loves and fights for his mistress is transplanted from medieval European times to the modern world to represent the non-white poet in the apartheid society of South Africa.

The troubadour mask is extended and complicated after *Sirens Knuckles Boots, Letters to Martha,* and early exile poems. The later poems present an alienated exile, still a troubadour in his being a poet of the open road. There is a close correlation between the poetic personality and the man in Brutus's poetry. The poet is familiar with his country and the world and speaks of human suffering because of socio-political injustice from the wealth of his individual experience as a sage and philosopher in his struggle to free the oppressed. Brutus uses this mask of a troubadour with ambivalence, but his position remains a valid poetic standpoint.

The opening poem of *A Simple Lust* establishes the poet as a troubadour.... In the poem the troubadour is represented in diverse ways. The upturned thumb, drawn from the salute of the African National Congress, is also an image of the troubadour who is hiking, hitching. According to Brutus, Don Quixote also in the poem is a variation of the troubadour, "the man who travelled across Europe, fighting and loving and singing. It's the combination of conflict and music in the troubadour which interests me—the man who can be both fighter and poet, and this is a kind of contradiction which is also present in Don Quixote." The poet wears the mask of this romantic knight on the road fighting in defence of his mistress.

The poet is a troubadour who fights for a loved one against injustice and infidelity in his society. He is the spokesman for his oppressed people and exposes the brutality of the oppressors, South Africa's white minority. The poet takes the side of the majority but oppressed non-whites against the perpetrators of apartheid, the monsters the knight has to fight for the security of his mistress. It is a case of "we" against "them." The poet establishes his spokesmanship for the oppressed by varying his use of pronouns to show himself as both individual and representative. The "I" and "me" of the poems show the poet as one of the many oppressed. In **"Nightsong: City,"** when the poet exhorts "my land, my love, sleep well," he is talking about the country at large. It is in the same light that "my sounds begin again" ... should be seen. In **"The sounds begin again"** the poet speaks not only for himself but for all "the unfree" against "their woe." The representative voice is clear in the poet's use of the first person plural. His "we" and "us" identify the poet's group—the oppressed non-white people of South Africa—and create the tone of a spokesman. (pp. 55-7)

In addition, Brutus often uses "one" to express both personal and representative experiences.... Also the poet uses "one" mainly in the prison and exile poems to avoid self-centredness by distancing himself from the experience to avoid sentimentality. In any case, "one" succeeds in portraying the poet's experiences as representative of the black inmates'. This representative voice creates a sense of solidarity among the oppressed and establishes the poet as a prime mover in his society.

Conversely, the whites are referred to as "they," as in **"Blood River Day"**:

> Each year on this day
> *they* drum the earth with their boots
> and growl incantations
> to evoke the smell of blood
> for which *they* hungrily sniff the air:
>
> guilt
> drives *them* to the lair
> of primitiveness
> and ferocity....

And in **"Their Behaviour,"** the contrast is clear as "Their guilt / is not so very different from ours.".... The contrast of the two socio-political groups which causes tension in real life also brings tension to the verse. Besides, the poet stands out as taking the side of justice, for he is satirical and critical of the apartheid oppressors.

As spokesman, the poet speaks about South Africa to South Africans and all of humankind. He speaks of the brutality of the apartheid system.... As spokesman the poet explains the state of the oppressed and imprisoned to the outside world. Because he has been a victim himself, the poet understands the oppressive situation and tells others the true state of things. This helps to make outsiders view the oppressed sympathetically.... The poet thus explains things to outsiders so that they will be able to understand the predicament of the non-whites.

The role of the poet as a fighter is manifested in diverse ways. To discredit and embarrass the establishment on the one hand and inspire the oppressed non-whites on the other, the poet acts as a reporter and chronicles the atrocities of the "monsters" so that history will confirm the guilt of the oppressors. **"For a Dead African"** is about "John Nangoza Jebe: shot by the police in a Good Friday procession in Port Elizabeth 1956.".... He thus gives the correct but unofficial account of things in South Africa. The fight is not physical but mainly psychological—making "them" feel guilty and embarrassed so as to stop the inhuman policies of apartheid. (pp. 58-60)

As part of the struggle for justice, the poet encourages his people. He believes that despite their current plight the oppressed will be free. As a singing troubadour, he instils hope in his people, thus contributing positively to the psychological upliftment necessary for a successful struggle.... By fighting for and encouraging his people, the poet is his brother's keeper as he continues the fight even after his release from jail. He believes that as long as others are in jail or suffering, he is himself not free.

The troubadour has his mistress whom he loves. Brutus subtly symbolizes South Africa—his land and his country—as the mistress; hence his personification of the land:

> exploring all her wide-flung parts with zest
> probing in motion sweeter far than rest
> her secret thickets with an amorous hand....

Besides, "my land takes precedence of all my loves.".... It is in pursuing the motif of the troubadour in defence of his mistress that the poet laments that "—no mistress-favour has adorned my breast / only the shadow of an arrow-brand.".... In other words, unlike the troubadour who is rewarded for his service by his mistress, the poet receives wounds from the South African regime. Therein lie the irony and ambivalence of the poet in the apartheid state—that this "Dear my land" should evoke "love and pain.".... The poet loves the country but hates the inhumanity practised in it. This tension runs through the poetry of Brutus. The poet fights for his mistress to achieve justice which in the social context of the poems involves condemning apartheid and embarrassing its perpetrators. The poet thus fulfills his troubadour roles of lover and fighter in the poems. (p. 61)

The troubadour motif also dominates the poems after exile. Exile itself is a journey, a quest which corresponds to the wanderings of the troubadour. However, different facets of the poet's personality emerge.... The poet gives the impression of lack of confidence, of fighting a losing battle in this post-exile stage. Despair is immanent in the ineffectual role the poet sees himself playing. He can only

> remouth some banal platitudes
> and launch-lodge some arrows
> from a transient unambitious hand,
> a nerveless unassertive gripe. . . .
>
> (p. 63)

Perhaps the poem that best expresses the wandering nature of the poet in the post-exile stage is **"And I am driftwood."** The repetition of "I am driftwood" emphasizes the wandering nature of the poet who drifts from place to place not of his own volition, but as an act of destiny. . . . Here the purpose of the wandering is spelt out: a quest for meaning to human existence. The meaning the poet looks for is socio-political justice that will free the victimized non-whites of the apartheid system. All "the restlessness, the journeyings, the quest, / the queryings, the hungers and the lusts" . . . are towards social justice.

In the quest two things stand out about the poet. He is both an alienated being and a spokesman for his people. He is an "alien in Africa and everywhere" . . . a state exacerbated by Brutus's mixed blood. He is dogged by the burden of responsibility and imagination so that even in exile, he thinks of those suffering in Robben Island, "the men who are still there crouching now / in the grey cells, on the grey floors, stubborn and bowed." . . . As in earlier poems, the poet's plight is representative of the suffering group in South Africa. It is for this that he is spokesman telling the world of the plight of the victims of apartheid:

> only I speak the others' woe:
> those congealed in concrete
> or rotting in rusted ghetto-shacks;
> only I speak their wordless woe,
> their unarticulated simple lust. . . .

So far the poet is still a troubadour, a poet of the open road in his exile and a fighter in his protest. The troubadour image is reinforced by quester-related metaphors. In *Stubborn Hope* different quest metaphors describe the poet in his exile. Most of *Stubborn Hope* are travel poems, since the poet is in flight, "one more wide range on a troubadour's earth." The poet is still on the road and this time the whole world is the setting of his poems and the experiences are universalized. . . . And he is a pilgrim who shuffles "through the waiting rooms / and the air-terminals of the world." . . . The pilgrim as a metaphor for the poet has the same role as the troubadour; the pilgrim quests for an ideal. The poet is thus a Christian knight and the shrine is symbolic of the romantic mistress he seeks and defends. To the knight the mistress meant adoration, and the implication that the mistress could be a Christian saint is significant. (pp. 63-5)

The pain and suffering the poet witnesses are not restricted to South Africa as in the early poems but are a world-wide phenomenon. . . . [Wherever] the poet finds himself, he lives with the burden of the suffering people. . . . (pp. 65-6)

As a result of general suffering the poet praises endurance and stoicism. The title poem, **"Stubborn Hope,"** is an ode on endurance:

> Yet somewhere lingers the stubborn hope
> thus to endure can be a kind of fight,
> preserve some value, assert some faith
> and even have a kind of worth. . . .

This is the undaunted will of the troubadour in his relentless struggle. To him, "Endurance is the ultimate virtue" . . . a shield against despair. Other poems. . . . emphasize the poet's extolling the resolve to endure oppression with hope. By doing this, the poet does not give the oppressors the opportunity to rejoice in defeating the oppressed. (pp. 66-7)

A Simple Lust and *Stubborn Hope* clearly present the poet who is a fighter for justice at home and abroad, struggling to realize his poetic aims. The troubadour image is consistent in all of the poetry of Brutus. (pp. 67-8)

His choosing the persona of the troubadour to express himself is particularly significant as the moving and fighting roles of the medieval errant, though romantic, tally with his struggle for justice in South Africa, a land he loves dearly as the knight his mistress. The movement contrasts with the stasis of despair and enacts the stubborn hope that despite the suffering, there shall be freedom and justice for those *now* unfree. (p. 68)

> *Tanure Ojaide, "The Troubadour: The Poet's Persona in the Poetry of Dennis Brutus," in* Ariel, *Vol. 17, No. 1, January, 1986, pp. 55-69.*

Jean (Maurice Eugene Clement) Cocteau

1889-1963

French dramatist, filmmaker, scriptwriter, poet, novelist, critic, essayist, librettist, and autobiographer.

Among the most versatile, innovative, and prolific literary figures of the twentieth century, Cocteau is best remembered for his dramas and films in which he utilized myth and tragedy in modern contexts to shock and surprise his audiences. Identifying himself as a poet and referring to virtually all of his works as poetry, Cocteau rejected naturalism in favor of lyrical fantasy, through which he sought to create a "poetry of the theatre" consisting not of words but of such stage devices as ballet, music, and pantomime. The fantastic, or "le merveilleux," is made manifest in Cocteau's plays through inanimate objects and symbolic characters, which embellish our understanding of "reality" by making the impossible possible. Like Charles Baudelaire and Arthur Rimbaud, Cocteau made use of the romantic myth of the *poète maudit*—the poet blessed with artistic powers of creation yet cursed to remain a misunderstood social outcast. Alienation is an important theme in Cocteau's work; his related subjects include the origin of artistic creation and inspiration, the limitations of free will, and the relationships between such opposing forces as adolescence and adulthood, illusion and reality, and order and disorder.

Cocteau was born into a wealthy Parisian family from whom he gained an appreciation for the performing arts. Although he briefly attended the Lycée Condorcet in Paris, Cocteau detested school and left to pursue a writing career. His first, traditional volume of poetry, *Le lampe d'Aladin* (1909), anticipated few of his later concerns. Cocteau's surrealist poetry written during and after World War I, included in *Le cap de Bonne-Espérance* (1919), *Escales* (1920), *Vocabulaire* (1922), and *Plain-chant* (1923), is classical in meter and rhyme and metaphysical in subject, containing images of and allusions to angels, sailors, statues, dreams, and heaven. *Le discours du grand sommeil* (1920), a long piece about pain and friendship set during World War I, is considered among Cocteau's most ambitious poetic works. In *Opera: Oeuvres poetiques, 1925-1927* (1927), Cocteau blends elements of paganism and Christianity, stating his famed maxim, "I am the lie that always tells the truth." The later poetry in *Leone* (1945; *Leoun*) also reflects Cocteau's interest in myth, recalling Dante's *Paradiso* in its description of an angelic figure who accompanies the poet toward a transcendent realm.

During World War I, Cocteau wrote his first novel, *Le potomak* (1919), a seemingly random collection of writings and drawings that is unified by a sense of spiritual quest as it relates to the poet, the nature of poetry, and the poet's place in the world. *Le grand écart* (1923; *The Grand Ecart*), one of Cocteau's most accomplished novels, is a semiautobiographical chronicle of youthful disillusionment. Cocteau's experiences with a civilian ambulance unit at the German front inform *Thomas l'imposteur* (1923; *Thomas the Imposter*), about a lyric poet's detached journey in a world where war is revealed to be a treacherous joke of fate. *Les enfants terribles* (1929; *The Children of the Game;* later published as *The Holy Terrors*), a classic allegory of human destiny, describes the intermingled

fates of two siblings whose private world is threatened when two peers compete for their individual attentions.

Toward the end of World War I, Cocteau became associated with the avant-garde movement at Montparnasse, which included such poets as Guillaume Apollinaire and Blaise Cendrars. Cocteau's early ballets, *Parade* (1917) and *Le dieu bleu* (1921), were inspired by Serge de Diaghilev and his Ballet Russes and featured music by Eric Satie and set designs and costumes by Pablo Picasso. *Parade* depicts a festival and its bizarre promoters, who attempt to entice an onstage audience to enter a mysterious tent; however, the ballet ends without the spectators having entered the tent, implying that Cocteau's interest is not in the event itself but in the visual occurrences which surround it. Although a complete failure at its first production, *Parade* is generally regarded as one of the twentieth century's most innovative ballets. *Les mariés de la tour Eiffel* (1921; *The Wedding on the Eiffel Tower*), an irreverent satire of bourgeois values, centers on a banal wedding party at the base of the Eiffel Tower. This work features two actors dressed as phonographs who comment on the action and a huge camera prop from which animals and characters emerge and retreat. Cocteau's later ballets include *Le train bleu* (1924), *Le jeune homme et la mort* (1946), and *La dame à la licorne* (1953).

Despite his involvement with central artistic figures of post-World War I France, Cocteau never allied himself with any school or movement. In *Antigone* (1922), Cocteau adapted Sophocles's tragedy to what he called "the rhythm of our times," thus initiating a lifelong preoccupation with contemporizing Greek mythologies. *Orphée* (1927; *Orpheus*) is among Cocteau's most innovative adaptations, focusing on the poet as interpreter of the supernatural and the poet's relationship to the source of inspiration. In this drama, objects, animals, and characters become symbols of ritual and acquire startling new associations. Cocteau also attempted several adaptations of the Oedipal myth during his career. The first, *Oedipus-rex* (1927), is an opera-oratorio on which he collaborated with composer Igor Stravinsky. *Oedipe Roi* (1928), a free adaptation which Cocteau revised in 1962 as an attempt at "total theatre," combines virtually all the performing arts to evoke lyric tragedy. Cocteau's best-regarded reworking of the Oedipal myth is *La machine infernale* (1934; *The Infernal Machine*), a drama exploring the relationship between free will and determinism which makes use of modern vernacular and musical forms. Unlike Sophocles, Cocteau opens his drama when Oedipus first enters Thebes—a free man about to realize his own mortality and unalterable fate. Henri Peyre called *The Infernal Machine* "the best modernization of the Oedipus story in our generation."

Of his original dramas, *La voix humaine* (1929; *The Human Voice*) is probably Cocteau's most often-performed work. Written as a "monodrama," a one-act play for a single character, the drama consists entirely of a woman's one-sided conversation with a boyfriend who has abandoned her. The dualistic conflict between good and evil is the subject of *Les chevaliers de la table ronde* (1937; *The Knights of the Round Table*), an adaptation of the Arthurian legend in which King Arthur and the sorcerer Merlin are pitted against one another. *Les parents terribles* (1938; *Intimate Relations*), a drama about family conflict, jealousy, and manipulation, reveals the influence of Greek tragedy but derives its form from Parisian boulevard theater. Cocteau's plays of the 1940s are generally considered less successful than his earlier works. *L'aigle à deux têtes* (1946; *The Eagle Has Two Heads)*, his best-known work of this period, is a melodrama in which a young poet, allegorically representing the angel of death, falls in love with a puppet empress and tragically attempts to help her regain her power.

Cocteau's films of the 1940s are regarded as his most accessible and engaging works. He intended many of his films to be vehicles for his acting protégé, Jean Marais. Cocteau found in the cinema a means superior to all other media in depicting his poetic view of death and the fantastic. His first film, *Le sang d'un poète* (1930; *The Blood of the Poet*), is a surreal interpretation of the relationship between the poet and the world of dreams. *La belle et la bête* (1945; *Beauty and the Beast*) allowed Cocteau to explore his fantasies of integrating other visual arts within the two-dimensional frame of the film and is considered among his most enduring cinema creations. Many of Cocteau's films, including *Les parents terribles* (1948) and *Les enfants terribles* (1948), are cinematic adaptations of his novels and plays. In such original works as *Orphée* (1950) and *Le testament d'Orphée* (1959), Cocteau employs classical legend and such visual effects as vanishing mirrors, vertical frames, and double images. Although some critics consider Cocteau's films difficult and obscure, he is generally regarded as a filmmaker of original talent and vision striving to realize his conception of film as "not a dream that is told but one we all dream together."

Throughout his career, Cocteau engaged in a variety of artistic ventures, ranging from decoration of public buildings to ce-

ramics and the composition of music. *Le rappel à l'ordre* (1926; *A Call to Order*) is a collection of working notes on theater in which Cocteau mixes observations on the nature of art with personal reminiscence. Among his most important collections of essays are *Essai de critique indirecte: Le mystère laïc—Des beaux arts consideres comme un assassinat* (1932) and *La difficulté d'être* (1947; *The Difficulty of Being*).

(See also *CLC*, Vols. 1, 8, 15, 16; *Contemporary Authors*, Vols. 25-28; and *Contemporary Authors Permanent Series*, Vol. 2.)

FRANCIS FERGUSSON

[*The essay from which this excerpt is taken was originally delivered as a lecture at the English Institute at Princeton University in 1949, and first published in* Institute Essays *in 1950.*]

The question of poetic drama—its possibility in our time—is perhaps *the* question of the contemporary theatre. There is no better way to see into the nature and the limitations of the theatre as we know it, than to ask the perennial question, Why don't we have a living poetic drama?

But this question has occupied some of the best minds of our time and has received a vast variety of answers. It would take a book, at the very least, to handle the matter at all adequately. In a brief paper one can do no more than suggest one approach. . . . I have chosen Cocteau's **Infernal Machine** for this purpose. (p. 590)

It is probable that the theatrical dexterity of [many post-World War I] poetic theatre works is largely due to the influence of the Paris Theatre, and . . . especially to Cocteau. In other words it is certain that Cocteau is one of the chief sources of contemporary theatre poetry, or poetry in the theatre, even in English. (p. 591)

When Cocteau started to write in Paris just after World War I, he found artists from all over Europe gathered there; and he found a theatrical life nourished from Russia, Italy, Germany, Sweden, as well as a fairly lively native theatre. Copeau's Théâtre du Vieux Colombier for instance, had been in existence since 1912. Paris in the twenties still looks fabulous to us: Bergson and Valéry, Joyce and Picasso and Stravinski; Pirandello and the Moscow Art Theatre, Milhaud and Gide and Maritain and Ezra Pound—if we think over some of the names associated with that time and place, we can see very clearly what an impressive effort was being made, in the center of Europe, to focus and revive the culture which had been so shaken by the war. If there was to be a favorable opportunity in our time to build a poetic drama, it should have been there and then, where the most enlightened audience and greatest talent were concentrated. (pp. 591-92)

The collection of [Cocteau's] early critical writings, **The Call to Order**, throws a great deal of light upon his labors in this period. He was trying to sort out the extremely rich influences which bore upon him; and to select the elements of a contemporary, and *French*, theatre poetry.

In very general terms, I think one may say that he was trying to fuse two different traditions, one ancient, the other modern. What I call the ancient tradition was that of myth, of ritual, and of primitive or folk art. What I call the modern tradition was French—that classical spirit of intelligence, wit, measure and proportion, which the French are supposed to have at their best—especially the French since Racine and Molière. The formula which Cocteau invented to describe the fusion of these two strands was *une poésie de tous les jours*—an everyday poetry. He was looking for a dramatic or theatrical art which should be poetic as myth, ritual, and the inspired clowning of the Fratellinis is poetic—and yet at the same time acceptable to the shrewd and skeptical Parisians in their most alert moments and as part of their daily lives. . . . He wanted to acclimatize mythopoeia in the most up-to-date, rational, and disillusioned of modern commercial cities.

You will I am sure remember that during this period many other artists were trying to nourish themselves upon myth, upon ritual, and upon primitive and popular forms of art. . . . Eliot was writing *The Waste Land;* Joyce was between *Ulysses* and *Finnegan's Wake*. When Cocteau and his friends began, most of this work was still to come; Cocteau himself was one of the pioneers in the movement. When he looked around for clues to the ancient and perennial theatre art he was seeking, forms which he might imitate or adapt, he found, not the works I have just mentioned, but Wagner and the all-pervasive Wagnerian influence.

Wagner was in a sense a forerunner of this whole movement. He had made use of myth in his operas, elaborated a whole theory of mythic drama, and worked out a singularly potent poetic theatrical form in the very heydey of bourgeois positivism. Cocteau remembered that Baudelaire had greeted Wagner as an ally against the Parisian Philistines of his day. Baudelaire's studies of Wagner remain one of the fundamental documents for any modern theory of poetic drama. Nevertheless Cocteau and his friends found Wagner extremely unsympathetic. . . . [For] Cocteau and his friends, the Wagnerian taste or habit of mind became the great enemy, in spite of their respect for Wagner's achievement. They saw Wagnerianism as an alien mode of awareness which was impeding the development of native French forms of art. The Wagnerian tradition, Cocteau says in *The Call to Order*, is like "a long funeral procession which prevents me from crossing the street to get home." Probably he felt in Wagner's magic the potent elements which the Nazis were so soon to use for their own purposes—drowning not only the French spirit but the physical life of France also.

However that may be, Cocteau developed his own conception of poetic drama, as it were, in answer to Wagner's. He too wanted to tap the ancient sources of myth and ritual, but without resorting to religiosity, hypnosis, or morose daydreaming. He wanted to bring mythopoeia and some of the ancient myths themselves into the center of the faithless, nimble, modern city—but he sought to establish them there by the clarity and integrity of art.

The Call to Order is a collection of working notes and critical *obiter dicta* from the very beginning of Cocteau's career, between 1918 and 1926. *The Infernal Machine* was published in 1934; and yet that play seems to be exactly the poetic drama which he had planned and foreseen fifteen years earlier. It presents a very ancient myth, the myth of Oedipus, not as a joke, but as a perennial source of insight into human destiny. Yet at the same time the play is addressed to the most advanced, cynical, and even *fashionable* mind of contemporary Paris. It is at one and the same time chic and timeless—rather like the paintings of Picasso's classic period, or his illustrations for Ovid. If one were to try to describe it briefly, one might say

it shows the myth behind the modern city: both the mysterious fate of Oedipus and the bright metropolitan intrigues for pleasure and power which go on forever. To have achieved such a fusion of contradictory elements is, of course, an extraordinary feat of virtuosity. And therefore this play illustrates, from one point of view at least, *the* problem of modern poetic drama: that of presentation on the public stage, at a time when poetry has lost almost all public status. (pp. 592-94)

The story of *The Infernal Machine* is the same as that of Sophocles's tragedy, *Oedipus the King*. Before the curtain goes up, a voice reminds us of the main facts.

Jocasta, Queen of Thebes, was told by the oracle of Apollo that her infant son Oedipus would grow up to murder his father and marry his mother. To avoid this terrible fatality she has the infant exposed on Mt. Kitharon with his feet pierced. But a shepherd finds him on the mountain and saves him, and eventually the young Oedipus makes his way to Corinth, where the childless king and queen adopt him as their son. He is brought up to think he is really their son; but in due time he hears the oracle, and to escape his fate he leaves Corinth. At a place where three roads cross, he meets an old man with an escort; gets into a dispute, and kills him. The old man is, of course, his own father Laius. Oedipus continues his journey, and reaches Thebes, where he finds the Sphinx preying on the city. He solves the riddle of the Sphinx and like other young men who make good, marries the boss's daughter, the widowed Queen Jocasta, his own mother. They rule prosperously for years and raise a family; but at last, when Thebes is suffering under the plague, the fate of Oedipus overtakes him. The oracle reports that the plague is sent by the gods, who are angry because Laius's slayer was never found and punished. Oedipus discovers his own identity and his own guilt—but thereby becomes once more, and in a new way, the savior of the city.

Such are the facts, in Cocteau as in Sophocles. But the question is how Cocteau presents them. What attitudes, what dramatic and theatrical forms does he find to bring the ancient tale alive in our time? His dramaturgy is utterly unlike Sophocles's; he presents *both* the mythic tale, and, as it were, the feel, or texture, of contemporary life, in which no myth is supposed to have any meaning.

When the curtain goes up we see the stage hung with nocturnal drapes, as Cocteau calls them; in the center of the stage there is a lighted platform, set to represent the city wall of Thebes. The play is in four acts, and each act is set upon that lighted platform. Everything that occurs in the set on the lighted platform is in the easy, agile style of the best sophisticated modern comedy—Giraudoux's *Amphitryon*, or the acting of Guitry. In other words Cocteau tells the story in the foreground in a way that his blasé boulevard audience will accept. Thus he achieves the "everyday" part of his formula for "everyday poetry." But the tinkling modern intrigue is itself placed in a wider and darker setting represented by the nocturnal curtains—and in this vaster surrounding area the cruel machine of the gods, Oedipus's fate, is slowly unrolled. . . . Thus the "poetry" part of the formula is ironically hidden; it is to be found in the background, and in the mysterious relation between the hidden shape of the myth and the visible shape of Oedipus's ambitious career.

The first scene on the lighted platform represents the city wall of Thebes. It is the night when Oedipus is approaching the city. Two young soldiers are on guard. They have seen Laius's ghost, who is trying to warn Jocasta not to receive Oedipus when he comes. Queen Jocasta herself has heard rumors of this ghost, and arrives with the high priest Tiresias to investigate. But the ghost cannot appear to Jocasta; he can appear only to the naive, "the innocent, the pure in heart," such as the young soldiers; and Jocasta departs none the wiser.

The second scene shows the suburbs of Thebes, where the Sphinx lies in wait for her prey. Occurring at the same time as the first act, it discloses Oedipus's interview with the Sphinx. The Sphinx is not only a goddess but a very mortal woman, who falls in love with Oedipus and lets him guess her riddle in the hope that he will fall in love with her. But he is more interested in his career than in love; he takes her mortal remains to town as a proof of his victory, while she departs to the realm of the gods, thoroughly disgusted with mortals. She is willing to let him get away with his heroic pretenses because she sees the terrible fate in store for him.

In both of these scenes the most important characters—Jocasta in the first and Oedipus in the second—are unaware of their fate. It is separated from them as by a very thin curtain; they *almost* see what they are doing, but not quite. Moreover, in both scenes the characters and the dialogue are felt as modern, like the scandals in the morning paper. (pp. 594-96)

[When Jocasta arrives in the first act, responding to reports of the ghost, she] is sharply modern: she speaks, Cocteau tells us, with the insolent accent of international royalty. . . . Jocasta is full of forebodings; she is nervous and overwrought; she complains about everything—but she does not have the naïveté or the "purity of heart" to grasp her real situation, or to see the ghost which appeared to the soldiers.

In the second act the young Oedipus is also a modern portrait, almost a candid-camera picture in the style of Guitry or Noel Coward. He is an ambitious and worldly young Latin—he might be the winner of a bicycle marathon or a politician who managed to stabilize the franc for a day. It is inevitable that he and Jocasta should get together—two shallow careerists, seekers after pleasure and power. The third scene shows their wedding night. It is set in the royal bedroom, and beside the royal bed is the crib which Jocasta kept as a memento of her lost son. In this scene the tenuous curtain of blindness which keeps them from seeing what they are doing is at its thinnest. But they are tired after the ceremonies of the coronation and the marriage; and they proceed sleepwalking toward the fated consummation.

In these first three acts of his play, Cocteau keeps completely separate the mythic fate of Oedipus and the literal story of his undoing, in so far as Oedipus and Jocasta themselves are concerned. The audience is aware of the fact that the terrible machine of the gods is slowly unwinding in the surrounding darkness; but the audience also sees that the victims are winning their victories and building their careers in total ignorance of it. In this respect the plan of *The Infernal Machine* resembles that of Joyce's *Ulysses*. Joyce also shows the lives of the people of a modern city in the form of an ancient legend which they are quite unaware of. Bloom wanders through his Dublin life according to an abstract scheme like that of the Odyssey; the reader sees this, but Bloom does not. The audience of *The Infernal Machine* sees Oedipus both as a contemporary politician and as the character in the myth. But at this point the resemblance between Cocteau's play and Joyce's novel ends. For Cocteau proposes to bring the two levels sharply together—to confront the city with the myth, and the myth with the city. This he proceeds to do in the fourth and last act.

We have been prepared all along for the sudden shift in point of view—for the peripety and epiphany of the last act. . . . [At] the beginning of the play, and at the beginning of each of the first three acts, a Voice bids us relish the perfection of the machine which the gods have devised to destroy a mortal. The emphasis is on mortal stupidity and upon the cruelty of the gods. But before the last act, the Voice reminds us of a different meaning in these events; the Voice makes the following proclamation: "After false happiness, the king will learn real unhappiness: the true ritual, which will make out of this playing-card king in the hands of the cruel gods, at long last, a man."

The fourth act, unlike the other three, follows fairly closely the order of events in Sophocles's tragedy. Oedipus feels, like an unsuccessful bluffer in poker, that the jig is up; he receives the evidence of the messenger and the old shepherd which unmistakeably reveals him as his mother's husband and his father's killer. Tiresias, who had half-guessed the truth all along, watches this terrible dénouement and explains it to Creon and for the audience. When Oedipus gets the final piece of evidence which convicts him, he runs off to find Jocasta. . . . As in the Sophoclean tragedy, Jocasta kills herself and Oedipus puts out his eyes, while their bewildered child Antigone tries to understand. Cocteau, like Sophocles, imagines these horrors with great intimacy, sparing nothing. But Cocteau brings the play to an end on a different note. In Sophocles the final pathos and enlightenment of Oedipus is presented in a series of steps, and by the time we finally see him blind in the end, the chorus has pretty well digested, or at least accepted, the tragic and purgatorial meaning of it all. But Cocteau ends the play with a *coup de théâtre*, a spectacular effect, a piece of theatrical sleight-of-hand, which visibly presents the tragic paradox on which the whole play is based.

The dead Jocasta appears to Oedipus, who is blind and can therefore see—but she appears not as the corrupt queen and dishonored wife of the sordid tale, but as a sort of timeless mother. "Yes, my child," she says to Oedipus, "my little son. . . . Things which seem abominable to human beings—if you only knew how unimportant they are in the realm where I am dwelling." The blind Oedipus, the child Antigone, and the ghostly Jocasta depart on their endless journey. Creon can see Oedipus and Antigone, if not Jocasta, and he asks Tiresias, "To whom do they belong now?" to which Tiresias replies, "To the people, to the poets, to the pure in heart." "But who," asks Creon, "will take care of them?" To which Tiresias replies, "La Gloire"—glory, or renown.

The effect is to remind us, all of a sudden, that Oedipus, Jocasta, Antigone, are not only literal people as we know people, but legends, figures in a timeless myth. We had in a sense known this all along; but during the first three acts we forgot it—we laughed at Oedipus's youthful vanity, grinned with cynical understanding when we saw his shallow ambition, his bounder-like opportunism. Now he and Jocasta are safe from our irony—as poetry and myth are safe—both more human and less human than the intriguing puppets which we found so familiar in the first three acts. (pp. 596-98)

The whole play of *The Infernal Machine,* if properly understood, may be read as a discussion of the most general problem of dramatic poetry in our time: how are we to place upon the public stage . . . a poetic image of human life? The play, as we have seen, answers this question in its own wonderful way . . . ; but the general question is the same as Wagner answered according to his taste, and Yeats and Eliot according to theirs. *The Infernal Machine* thus takes an important place in the long line of attempts which have been made, for over a hundred years, to build a modern poetic drama. (pp. 599-600)

[*The Infernal Machine* is not written] in verse; and though the language is beautifully formed, the poetry is not to be found in the first instance in the language at all. The play is *theatre-poetry*, as Cocteau defines it in his preface to *Les Mariés de la Tour Eiffel*:

> The action of my play is in images, while the text is not. I attempt to substitute a poetry *of* the theatre for poetry *in* the theatre. Poetry *in* the theatre is a piece of lace which it is impossible to see at a distance. Poetry *of* the theatre would be coarse lace; a lace of ropes, a ship at sea. . . . The *scenes* are integrated like the *words* of a poem.

Though the language in *The Infernal Machine* is of course more important than it is in *Les Mariés* (essentially a dance pantomime), Cocteau's description of the underlying structure applies also very accurately to *The Infernal Machine*. The poetry is to be found in the relationships of all the main elements: the relationship between the lighted platform in the center of the stage with the darker and vaster area around it; between Oedipus's conscious career with the unseen fatality that governs it; between the first scene and the second, which ironically occurs at the same time; and between the first three acts, when we see Oedipus as a contemporary snapshot, and the last act, when we see him as a legend. In other words, the basic structure, or plot—the primary form of the play as a whole—embodies a poetic idea; and once that is established the language need only realize the poetic vision in detail.

If Cocteau, more than any other contemporary playwright, is thus a master of poetic-dramatic form, it is partly because he has learned from the neighboring arts of music, painting and ballet, and partly because he found his way back to a root notion of drama itself, that which Aristotle expressed when he said the dramatic poet should be a maker of plots rather than of verses. If Auden and MacNeice do not succeed in making poetic drama, it is because they do not understand the poetry of the theatre—they take an unpoetic well-made plot from the commercial theatre and add, here and there, a pastiche of verses. (pp. 600-01)

[Poetic] drama, real poetic drama, comparable to the landmarks of the tradition, when the ancient art has really flourished—cannot be invented by an individual or even a small group. If it is to perform its true function it must spring from the whole culture and be nourished by sources which we may perhaps recognize, but can hardly understand. Will such a drama ever reappear? We do not know. In the meantime, all we can do is pick together the pieces, save and cultivate such lesser successes as have been achieved. *The Infernal Machine* is one of these successes—one of the clues, so to say—to the nature and the possibility of poetic drama in our time. (p. 601)

> Francis Fergusson, "Excursus: Poetry in the Theatre and Poetry of the Theatre, Cocteau's 'Infernal Machine'," in Literary Criticism—Idea and Act: The English Institute, Selected Essays, 1939-1972, edited by W. K. Wimsatt, University of California Press, 1974, pp. 590-601.

GERMAINE BRÉE AND MARGARET GUITON

[*The essay from which this excerpt is taken was originally published in* An Age of Fiction: The French Novel from Gide to Camus *in 1957*.]

The novel, as used by Cocteau, is somewhat experimental, halfway between the traditional nineteenth century novel and a totally new conception of the novel form. It is only with his last major novel, *Les Enfants terribles* (*The Children of the Game*), 1929, that Cocteau is altogether successful. And even here his theme is more restricted than in the case of his two best plays, *Orphée*, 1926, and *La Machine infernale* (*The Infernal Machine*), 1934. But from the point of view of the novel itself, the Cocteau novel is an interesting experiment.

The everyday world of recognizable people and places naturally plays a greater role in Cocteau's novels than in his poetry and theater. But Cocteau, by his choice of scene and atmosphere, sees to it that this world is fragmentized, disrupted, torn apart. (p. 141)

Disorder, for Cocteau, especially for Cocteau the novelist, is merely the "rejection of the conventional equilibrium" that precedes the poet's ascent to a higher and more intimate equilibrium of his own, an equilibrium found only in death, the symbolic death of the poet to the world. The theme of poetic "ascesis," which Cocteau apparently attempted to act out himself in his experiments with dadaism, opium and Catholicism, recurs in all his works. Even if the theme is not explicit, it is felt in the icy, mineral quality of Cocteau's imagery: his statues and snowballs, his demonic mechanical contrivances, his constant transposition of reality into artifice.

This latter device no doubt explains Cocteau's popular reputation as a literary charlatan. But for Cocteau, artifice is a serious matter. He sees in it that depersonalization, that dehumanization of reality, which to him is an essential attribute of poetry. (p. 142)

Jacques Forestier, the hero of *Le Grand Ecart* and the most directly autobiographical of Cocteau's fictional characters, represents the case of a potential drug addict who never finds his drug, a diver in his heavy diver's costume forgotten on the surface of the earth: "To rise again, to take off the helmet and the costume; that is the passage from life to death. But there comes to him through the tube an unreal breath that allows him to live and fills him with nostalgia."

This opening passage suggests interesting possibilities; but Cocteau never succeeds in deriving the substance of a novel out of Jacques's fatal unadaptability to life. What he has done is to graft this introductory theme onto the conventional story of an adolescent in the throes of disenchantment. And Cocteau, who specifically relates his hero to the typical Balzac adolescent arriving in Paris from the provinces, seems to have taken a good part of the story out of Balzac's *Le Père Goriot* (*Old Goriot*). Jacques Forestier, adrift in Paris, bears a fleeting resemblance to Eugène de Rastignac; the squalid pension where he lives, to the Pension Vauquer; his heartless mistress, Germaine, to the Baronne de Nucingen. Indeed, a principal cause of Jacques's final disillusionment is directly transcribed from Balzac's famous novel. Just as Balzac's baroness stubbornly refuses to believe that her father is dying, because she wishes to attend a fashionable ball, Germaine conceals a telegram informing her of her father's death, because she wants to go to the theater.

Cocteau's undisguised debt to Balzac is not in itself a weakness—Proust also has borrowed from Balzac—and Cocteau's treatment of the Balzacian theme of "lost illusions" is skillful. He knows how to turn the knife in the wound. Unfortunately, however, this theme is not really connected with Cocteau's original and more important subject: the poet's death to the world. The original subject recurs, somewhat abruptly, in the final pages of the novel when Jacques poisons himself and experiences a momentary illumination: "Jacques rises. He loses footing. He sees the other side of the cards. He is not aware of the system that he is disrupting, but he has the presentiment of a responsibility." But Jacques's attempted suicide is unsuccessful, and he returns to life, less as an exiled poet than as a disillusioned lover.

The unsuccessful suicide provides a more pathetic ending to this novel than death—the conclusion of Cocteau's two later novels—would have provided. Still, this element of human pathos, which no doubt stems from Cocteau's personal involvement in the story, is incompatible with his conception of the poet. Who *is* Jacques? the reader is left to wonder. A poet astray on the surface of the earth, or a nice, if somewhat spineless, young man who has fallen into bad company? And what *is* disorder? The eternal dissonance of poetry and life or the misplaced sentiments of an untidy heart? The universal and the particular in this novel are badly jointed. Instead of reinforcing one another, they rub and jar; and at these points of friction the fine edge of poetry is worn down to mere sentimentality, none the better for its superficial disguise of modernism, paradox and bravura. Cocteau's concluding sentence is worthy of de Musset at his very worst: "To live in this world one must follow its fashions, and the heart is no longer worn."

Thomas the Impostor, the hero of [*Thomas l'Imposteur*], is another displaced adolescent, but one who has found an artificial equilibrium in a fictional existence. Guillaume Thomas, taking advantage of the confusion during the early months of the war, has lied about his age (sixteen), borrowed the uniform of a friend, and finally posed as the nephew of a famous general, Fontenoy. Cocteau hastens to inform us, however, that this is not an ordinary imposture, a vulgar means of "getting ahead." Guillaume, floating on the edges of a dream, is more at home, more himself, in a fictional than in a real existence. Aided by a Polish princess and her daughter, Henriette, Guillaume soon finds a place for himself in a hastily improvised ambulance service and is eventually expedited to his predestined environment, the fantastically camouflaged confusion of the northern front.

At the end of the novel the two conflicting personalities, Guillaume Thomas and Thomas de Fontenoy, are finally reconciled: Guillaume, who has volunteered to carry a message to another post under extremely dangerous conditions, is spotted by an enemy patrol and shot down.

"'—A bullet, he said to himself. I am lost if I don't pretend to be dead.' But fiction and reality, in him, were one. Guillaume Thomas was dead."

Thomas l'Imposteur, in contrast with *Le Grand Ecart*, is written with considerable detachment. Its hero is modeled not on Cocteau himself but on a young impostor that Cocteau encountered during the war. Self-pity thus gives way to sparkling irony. At first glance we seem to be confronted with a pure satirical fantasy in the early manner of Evelyn Waugh. We soon realize, however, that Thomas is actually another incarnation of the poet, a poet who succeeds in divesting himself of his human identity and whose "imposture" is ultimately authenticated by death.

The symbol is no doubt valid as a symbol, but is it anything more than an abstract symbol? We are quite willing to believe that artifice, under certain circumstances, can become real; lies, true; disorder, art. But has Cocteau really shown that this has

happened? That Guillaume should die at the very moment he is pretending to be dead provides a neat conclusion to the novel. Does this, as Cocteau would apparently have us believe, really give retrospective reality to Guillaume's whole imposture? And the elegant detachment of Guillaume and his Polish patroness, their attempts to exploit the wartime situation in such a way as to enjoy the best possible view of the fireworks, the ambiguous emotional relationship that binds the two of them together—does this whole moral climate of exquisite snobbery really attain the "higher equilibrium" of poetry? It seems rather to be the Cocteau version of an atmosphere that Stendhal used for an entirely different purpose.

Here again Cocteau has taken an existing novel theme, that of Stendhal's *La Chartreuse de Parme* (*The Charterhouse of Parma*) as the vehicle for a totally unconventional novel subject. And here again the experiment, however interesting as such, is not entirely successful. Like one of those pioneering ventures in aviation, *Thomas l'Imposteur* never quite gets off the ground.

Cocteau's latest try, *Les Enfants terribles,* is, within its given limitations, a conspicuous success. His formula is simple: to push to their extreme consequences the fierce passions, strange tribal conventions and innocent perversions of a group of children living in a universe completely insulated from adult interference.

Childhood, Cocteau tells us, is a kingdom unto itself like the animal and vegetable kingdoms. In this novel the kingdom is constituted by the relationship of a young girl, Elizabeth, and her younger brother, Paul. Situated in their wildly disordered bedroom, "the room" as it is called, this private universe has its own language, fetishes and rituals . . . ; it offers a dangerous enchantment, of which Paul is the passive conductor and Elizabeth, the jealous guardian.

As Elizabeth is aware, this enchantment is constantly threatened by shifting relationships and loyalties—or the normal process of growing up. For this, however, she is prepared. Two possible threats, Paul's schoolmate, Gérard, and her own friend, Agathe, are neutralized by adoption and come to live in "the room." When Elizabeth realizes that Gérard has fallen in love with her and Agathe with Paul, she again neutralizes the two intruders by persuading them that each is morally bound to marry the other. (pp. 142-46)

The real danger to "the room" lies not in adult reality but in a counterenchantment; not in Agathe and Gérard but in Dargelos, a heartless, older schoolboy hopelessly adored by Paul. It is this external factor that originally sets the plot in motion and finally brings it to its catastrophic conclusion.

In a prologue to the novel, set in the enchanted light of a winter's afternoon, Paul wanders through an abandoned courtyard searching for his idol, Dargelos. Suddenly he is struck full in the chest and seriously hurt by a snowball that Dargelos has thrown. Unable to return to school, he lives from then on under Elizabeth's watch in "the room." At the close of the novel Dargelos happens to meet Gérard in the street, ironically asks after Paul, and, as a test of his own powers, sends Paul a package of poison—a "black pellet" counterbalancing the snowball of the prologue. Paul takes the poison, and a last-minute struggle sets in between Agathe, Elizabeth and the absent Dargelos for the final possession of Paul's soul.

At first it seems that Agathe will win out, for she arrives upon the scene before Paul dies, and Elizabeth stands by in impotent fury while the two lovers unravel the subterfuges that have hitherto kept them apart. In an excess of rage Elizabeth seizes a revolver, then suddenly controls herself, and with a feverish lucidity, a supreme effort of the will, rediscovers the magic words, associations and memories that will restore the charmed atmosphere of "the room." Paul's expression of hatred gives way to curiosity, curiosity to complicity, as Elizabeth, her finger on the trigger of the revolver, waits for her brother's death spasm. Paul's head falls back. Elizabeth presses the revolver against her forehead and pulls the trigger. But she has struck too soon. Paul is not yet dead, and Elizabeth, falling, brings down a screen hiding the window.

As the corrupt Danish court, in the last act of *Hamlet,* disintegrates at the sound of Fortinbras's martial trumpets, the perverse enchantment of "the room" is dissipated, for evermore, by the pale light of the frosty windowpane, by the ghostly spectators that lurk outside. Paul recognizes these spectators—the noses, the cheeks, the red hands, the capes, the scarves of the memorable snow fight of several years before—and resumes, in his last moments of consciousness, his original quest for Dargelos.

Les Enfants terribles, in striking contrast to Cocteau's earlier and more impressionistic novels, has the rigorous economy of means, the geometrical construction, the almost claustrophobic *unité de lieu* of a classical tragedy. As Cocteau himself reminds us in a number of incidental references, the theme is somewhat similar to that of Racine's *Athalie*—a pattern better adapted to Cocteau's purposes than that provided by a nineteenth century novelist's treatment of the theme of adolescence. That necessity of a "rigorous equilibrium" for those who reject the conventional equilibrium, seems to apply not only to the poetic sensibility but also to the technique of novel-writing. This most ordered of Cocteau's novels also has the strongest poetic impact.

The basic ingredients are as down to earth, as credible, as one could wish. But they are also capable of unlimited expansion. . . . Elizabeth is entirely understandable as a passionate young girl who refuses to relinquish her childhood; but she is also the savage priestess-queen of *Athalie.* Dargelos is a thoroughly recognizable classroom criminal; but he is also the angel that preys on poets—the "Ange Heurtebise" of Cocteau's poem and of his *Orphée.* In contrast again with Cocteau's earlier novels, the universal and the particular, the poetic and the novelistic, are here indissolubly fused.

Les Enfants terribles was written in three weeks during a "cure." And the experiences that Cocteau describes, "the game," "the room" and the breath-taking poetic ascension that precedes the double suicide, are very similar to his descriptions of the effects produced by opium. It would thus seem possible that Cocteau, in his struggle to abandon opium, momentarily recovered the childhood reality for which opium had acted as an artificial substitute. "All children," Cocteau writes, "have a fairy-like power to change themselves into whatever they want. Poets, in whom childhood is prolonged, suffer greatly from losing this power. Indeed this is one of the emotions that drives them to use opium." This momentary return to childhood may provide the key to Cocteau's best novel; but it also shows the limitations of this novel, of the novel form itself as used by Cocteau: an incapacity to carry the poetic vision into the enlarged and more complex realm of adult consciousness. (pp. 146-48)

Germaine Brée and Margaret Guiton, "Escapes and Escapades," in their The French Novel from Gide

to Camus, *1957. Reprint by Harcourt, Brace & World, 1962, pp. 132-79.*

JACQUES GUICHARNAUD with JUNE BECKELMAN

[*The essay from which this excerpt is taken was originally published in* Yale Romantic Studies, Second Series, *in April, 1961.*]

Cocteau began to write for the theatre in 1916, when the battle for reform was at its most acute. He started as a revolutionary and continued as a revolutionary. And we know that in general, any immobility, any rigidity was distasteful to him. If his works often give more the impression of a great to-do and confusion than of revolution, it is because his desire for complete change was opposed to an unquestionable narcissism.

To the conflicts and struggles of Cocteau's subjects and themes are added the unexpected contrasts of the works as a whole. His theatre would seem to have covered all possible genres, from the avant-garde spectacle to commercial cinema, everything that could be represented or played by actors of every category. . . . Such diversity of means gives Cocteau's works a disparate appearance, a sort of Jack-of-all-trades or amateur aspect that makes him seem rather like [his character] Georges in *les Parents terribles.* Cocteau has tried to perfect already existing genres and make them more effective just as Georges, having tried other experiments, wants to perfect the spear gun and make it shoot bullets.

With each work, Cocteau plays the game he has chosen to play. In theatre he plays at being a playwright. . . . His prefaces often give the impression that . . . [each] work is an exercise in style, imposed by external circumstances. The "idea" of theatre comes first and varies according to the period, the year, the month. Every play is an example, a model, an illustration. Cocteau's works are presented as a group of occasional plays—to enhance actors or actresses, to satisfy a request from the Vicomte de Noailles, to scandalize a certain public.

Once he has decided to go along with such or such circumstance, Cocteau starts to work as if the genre of the play he is writing were the only one possible. In fact he is more actor than playwright. . . . He is an understudy of genius. When there is a comedy lacking on the French stage, Cocteau is ready to plug up the hole. He provides an avant-garde spectacle when needed. . . . [Cocteau] was the first of his generation, even before Giraudoux, to reinterpret Greek tragedy because the new era needed a Racine. *Bacchus* shows a certain fatigue in that respect, for there he was a follower. The general impression is that Cocteau has always something to do, if not always something to say. The problems he would seem to pose are of an aesthetic and even technical order, for he is more interested in the secrets of workmanship than in the actual material of the product.

If there is an evolution in Cocteau's works, it is based on a twofold movement: he wanted both to create fashions and revive them. In most of his prefaces he affirms the necessity of saying no to whatever is established, as soon as it is established. One must never become immobilized in a game. Once the rules are fixed, "the rules must be changed." His is indeed the psychology of a great dress designer. And in his perpetual invention of new rules, Cocteau constantly refers back to a certain past—now a lost naïveté, that of primitive theatre or childhood; now the bygone age of the theatre of actors, the sacred monsters. The ancient tunic is made old-fashioned by knight's armor; the suit, by Second Empire uniforms. Just as

Antoine was right to have imposed "real quarters of meat and a fountain" on a public used to painted objects, Cocteau was to consider it his duty as an artist to impose painted canvas on a public accustomed to real quarters of meat, or to reinvent the Boulevard for a public that had come to demand modernist theatre. . . . The objective of such an operation is to keep the public's esthetic consciousness in a state of alert. However, a multiplicity of changes ends by resembling constancy. And in spite of the unexpected and the novelty, every one of Cocteau's plays can be recognized by a group of permanent features which might be called the writer's signature.

For Cocteau has more of a signature than a style. The handwriting is always the same, while the style changes. To whatever genre it may belong, a Cocteau play can be recognized by certain words, certain formulas, certain images. . . . (pp. 48-51)

On another level, we find that the milieu of nearly all Cocteau's plays is "the family." Doubtless it includes an idea of the couple in the manner of Giraudoux, but it also includes the idea of a household: the households of Orpheus, King Arthur, Jocasta, Yvonne, and Esther, all characterized by a feeling of bedroom slippers and slammed doors never found in those of Giraudoux's Alcmene, Clytemnestra, Lia, or Lucile. The novel *les Enfants terribles* and the play *les Parents terribles* have fixed the theme of family promiscuity at the center of Cocteau's works—a promiscuity of people (mother-son, sister-brother) and also of intimate objects. But even in the deliberately anti-naturalistic plays, Cocteau introduces a realism of intimacy through the mention of pieces of clothing, physical contact, and childish quarrels. (p. 52)

Intimacy and witchcraft often have a meeting point in the object—more or less ordinary—that lies about, goes astray, or behaves in unexpected ways. "Even the familiar objects have something suspicious about them," wrote Cocteau in his description of the stage set for *Orphée.* The objects that furnish his stage are therefore intimate or ordinary, but also magical. Whereas in *les Mariés de la Tour Eiffel* the phonograph and camera are magical (the camera produces an ostrich and a lion that eats generals), the rest of his works are strewn with object-witnesses, chosen amongst the most ordinary and suddenly gifted with supernatural powers. . . . Sometimes the language and sometimes its physical aspect accentuate the object's mystery or secret in a kind of expressionism rare on the French stage until Adamov and Ionesco.

The objects often acquire their powers through disorder. Out of their usual places, they seem stripped of their usual functions, diverted from their roles in this world, and free therefore to assume new functions. The incongruity of the object not in its proper place creates an uneasiness in the spectator which comes from the consciousness of pure unjustified being. The transcendency of being that appears when being is stripped of the habitual relationships established with it becomes magic in the hands of a poet, the sign of, or a door opening onto, the supernatural. Through not belonging, the being of things becomes strange. The point at which consciousness bumps up against an impenetrable transcendency—a fact or an exceptional or monstrous relationship—is the point at which the poet, by an act of faith, affirms that *there* the world of poetry begins and that the imagination, the poet's "deep night," is called upon to give perceptible content to the ensuing uneasiness. (pp. 53-4)

An object which is not in its place can be poetic: a lion on the Eiffel Tower, theatrical costumes in a bourgeois house, even

a stray shoe under an armchair. The same holds true for the characters. Cocteau tries to poetize them by isolating them, displacing them, making them somewhat foreign. On the simplest level, he does it by a disparity of class: Stanislas in the Queen's room (*l'Aigle à deux têtes*); Hans, the poor mad peasant, chosen as king for a week (*Bacchus*). . . . In a more visual way, he disguises or masks the character in a decisive scene: Margo, in *la Machine à écrire,* is dressed up like Lucrezia Borgia during most of the first act; Esther, in *les Monstres sacrés,* completely covers her face with cold cream when Liane confronts her with cruel facts. The displacement is complete in *la Machine infernale,* in which Jocasta speaks and gesticulates like a foreigner. . . . [Cocteau uses this device], as in the other cases, to isolate the character by an accidental peculiarity, or at least seemingly accidental.

In the same way, Cocteau hoped for revelations from certain coincidences, certain unexpected encounters. . . . [The] music of Bach as background to the film *les Enfants terribles* was to furnish "accidental synchronisms" out of which the most original beauty would spring. At the beginning of every Cocteau play, a certain amount of chance, coincidence, and accident must be accepted in addition to the usual dramatic conventions: Orpheus' poetry dictated by a horse and his guardian angel in the form of a glazier . . . ; Stanislas as the image of the dead King. The process is similar to a combination of fairy tale illusion and surrealist experiment. Cocteau's world is made up of disparate beings and elements, each one generally familiar but isolated from its context, whirling about in a vacuum, fastening on to one another as if by chance, and thus perhaps creating poetry. Cocteau has said that the great writer is he whose "aim is straight." He himself gives the impression of hoping to aim straight while closing his eyes, like the characters of certain comic films who haphazardly shoot in the air and out of the sky falls a duck or a balloon. In that way, Cocteau hopes to shoot down the blue bird.

More than a vision of the world, it is a device, and a device that can lead to every extravagance—legitimate to the extent that the incongruity of the combined elements is a protestation against the superficial coherence of psychological theatre or the theatre of ideas, and also against the traditions surrounding myth and certain great subjects. The poetry of *les Mariés de la Tour Eiffel* consists in replacing traditional coherence by an inner chance that is quite contrary to the logic of everyday reality. "The scenes fit together like the words of a poem," says Cocteau in his preface. Here the poem would be a surrealist *divertissement* or, to be more explicit, a collage. Its interest lies both in its amusing absurdity and its challenge to accepted forms of poetry or painting. Cocteau counts on "the part that belongs to God" to make the symbol emerge, just as a chemist's apprentice might haphazardly choose two substances, mix them together in a test tube, and hope for an explosion. Of course there is the danger of obtaining no more than a bit of smoke and a change in color. (pp. 54-6)

Cocteau's experiment in *les Mariés* in 1921 might seem old-fashioned today, for it is essentially a document, a polemic argument that took place during a quarrel, now established in history. It does not have the weight of either Jarry's *Ubu Roi* or Apollinaire's *les Mamelles de Tirésias,* in which the revolution in form was accompanied by a true theme. Yet *les Mariés,* in the intransigency of its conception, is still a call to order every time a resurgence of naturalism in the theatre begins to exercise its charms. It remains a warning against psychologism, earnestness, and want of imagination.

The plays that follow, from *Orphée* to *Bacchus,* and whatever the genre, reaffirm the poet's right to search for a synchronism of chance between elements drawn from the familiar world and the most exalted forms of myth or art. The Parisian vulgarity and banter of the demon Jinnifer in *les Chevaliers,* the duality of Jocasta and the Sphinx in *la Machine infernale,* the great themes of incest and death embodied in Boulevard characters in *les Parents terribles* are most striking examples of it. But do the shocks thus provoked have real dramatic value? There is no doubt that they create a tension between the play and the audience (surprise, indignation, irritation). However the determining factor is largely "the part that belongs to God," with the result that the juxtaposition of disparate elements may be rich in living tensions or turn out to be sterile, the spectator's interest being caught up in the play's ingeniousness or absurdity rather than in the drama itself.

A theatre of exorcism, Cocteau's works drive the demon out so effectively that there is hardly time to see him. The spectator is usually too busy watching the exorciser's pirouettes and incantations to think about the person possessed. Whence the clear division of public and critics into raving admirers and rabid disparagers, into those who see Cocteau's works as the reflection of a deep and intense drama and those who see Cocteau as the entertainer of a certain high society with a taste for anarchy.

> Three managers organize the publicity. In their terrifying language, they tell each other that the crowd takes the parade for the inner spectacle, and they grossly try to make the crowd understand it.
>
> No one enters. . . .

Such, in general, is the scenario of the ballet *Parade,* produced in collaboration with Picasso, Erik Satie, Diaghilev, and Leonide Massine. Besides its value as a manifesto, it has a theme that might serve as a symbol for the whole of Cocteau's works: Cocteau keeps his public outside. The true spectacle of the inner circus remains forbidden, despite the poet's innumerable invitations to enter. And perhaps that inner circus is no more than an absolute vacuum, as Eric Bentley has suggested.

Yet beyond the parade, beyond the enormous differences of style and tone that are so many theatrical variations of an outer ceremony, there is the suggestion of a real drama, if not its total realization. Almost all Cocteau's plays lead toward the same resolution. They are often directed toward a violent death and the hero generally appears more like a victim of the drama than the tragic master of his fate. Victims of either magic spells or very special circumstances, Cocteau's heroes submit to action more than they direct it. (pp. 56-8)

Cocteau is eminently representative of modern drama, which draws as near to tragedy as possible, yet most often remains on this side of it. Tragic heroism for the Greeks consisted in going all the way through an ordeal, to the point of giving any final acceptance the value of a challenge, and finding true grandeur in the catastrophe itself. Today this conception is replaced by a taste for victimization, still colored by Romanticism.

Cocteau uses the basic elements of tragedy in his dramas: the misunderstanding, a source of tragic irony, and the play of supernatural forces or obscure powers. Yvonne is mistaken about the meaning of her love for Mik just as Oedipus [in *la Machine infernale*] is mistaken about the oracle and the en-

counters in his life, and the interiorization of fate and its expression in psychological terms detract nothing from its transcendency. But either the characters, following in the path of fate, stop just on the edge of the revelation that might have elevated them (Yvonne dies without having really got to know herself, in *les Parents terribles*); or the development of the action remains outside the character, who is victimized and then liberated without having had any determining effect on the drama (King Arthur, in *les Chevaliers,* does no more than talk about the forces that "intoxicate" and then "disintoxicate" him); or, as is most frequently the case, the characters accelerate the final movement and precipitate their own deaths in gestures that are more evasive than fulfilling (Solange's suicide in *la Machine à écrire,* the anticipation of Hans who kills himself, in *Bacchus*).

Although the precipitated denouements are far removed from classical tragedy, they have two great merits. One, their theatricalism is effective. The foreshortening, the elements of spectacle, the effects of surprise and shock do create an unquestionable climate of finality. The spectacle is carried away by an increasingly rapid whirlpool of scenic movements and at the end death is imposed, so to speak, on the spectator's nerves. Two, they reveal a conception of freedom which is Cocteau's own. In the preface to *les Mariés de la Tour Eiffel,* Cocteau wrote:

> One of the photographer's lines could be used on the title page: *Since these mysteries are beyond us, let's pretend to be their organizer.* It is our line par excellence. The conceited man always finds refuge in responsibility. Thus, for example, he prolongs a war after the phenomenon that had been its deciding factor is over.

Freedom would then be shown in the acceleration or slowing down of the necessary developments, in their foreshortening or extension. Freedom is Cocteau's "pretense" and the others' "conceit." And Cocteau has no illusions about his own characters. When at the end of *Bacchus* Hans cries out "Free . . .," his way of dying should be seen not as "tragic death par excellence, both fated and chosen" but as a pretense, a voluntary illusion. Hans' final freedom is in fact abstract. It consists only in anticipating an already determined event. (pp. 58-60)

Therefore what Cocteau's plays reveal is not a traditional tragic vision, but a particular conception of destiny very near to fatalism, wherein the best man can do is to live "as if" he were capable of controlling his fate. That "as if" can be found in all the eloquent affirmations, costumes, grand gestures, and at the extreme limit, in art itself. In *la Machine à écrire* many inhabitants of the city claim, at one point or another, to have written the anonymous letters. The play explains that in making the claim they hope to get out of the mediocrity in which they are imprisoned. They want to be recognized even in crime and their desire is so powerful that they end by believing their own lies. Actually their mythomania picks up the "pretense" and "conceit" of the preface of *les Mariés.* Caught in a development of events that is beyond them and for which they are not responsible, they want to have themselves put in prison so that everything will happen *as if* the scandal was their own work. In short, the only escape from fate is in the lie. And the game of lying must be played to the very end, that is, all the way to total illusion, until the mask of freedom is seen as the very flesh of man. Man's only recourse is to deceive himself and others.

Death by suicide, in Cocteau's works, is the highest form of human pretense. By precipitating death, it often appears as an escape. The character disappears before the last illuminations of his ordeal. He wants to testify before it is too late and makes himself the martyr of certain values (poetry, love, grandeur, humanity) at the very moment that those values may be shown as impossible. As soon as the character realizes that the world has tricked him, he answers with the definitive trickery of suicide. He neither triumphs nor makes his peace. He retires. The deep and despairing cry of Cocteau's works is in the agitation of man who is caught and either ignores the fact or succeeds only in reconstructing a higher ignorance in the form of illusion. But although gilded by language and adorned with all the devices of mind and imagination, the trap remains merciless. By means of theatrical devices, Cocteau has invented a masked ball and he is the first to proclaim its vanity.

Cocteau's heroes—pure, still not disillusioned, preys to circumstance—are victims of chance, victims of a *fatalitas* often similar to that of melodrama. They believe that they benefit from it until, having gone too far in the game, they are seized with an unbearable mistrust which leads to a voluntary illusion. Cocteau's universe is not one of tragedy but of danger. The cosmos surrounding the characters is not that of a great moral order in the Greek manner, in conflict with man's affirmation of himself. It is a Coney Island contraption, a lay-out of pitfalls. . . . Those who fall into the traps—who are marked out for them—are the naïve and the pure in heart: poets, idealized adolescents, dewy-eyed revolutionaries. . . . Characterized by adolescence—a state of both grace and malediction, and a combination of impulsive acts, ignorance, purity, disorder, and youth—Cocteau's heroes are to a certain extent "going forces" in the Romantic manner, and "going" in a treacherous universe filled with every danger. Actually the adjective "Romantic" does somehow describe Cocteau's works. The variety of forms, the esthetic debates surrounding the plays, the justifying abstractions of the subject matter (poetry, youth, impure order, pure disorder) only partially disguise the underlying theme of isolation, an isolation of the individual destined for better and for worse. In *Scandal and Parade* Neal Oxenhandler emphasizes the theme of the *poète maudit*, the cursed poet, found throughout all of Cocteau's works. The ambiguity of benediction-malediction, generally identified with adolescence, is also, directly or indirectly, identified with the situation of the poet. (pp. 60-2)

The problem of the cursed protagonist is complicated by the fact that the young hero in each of his plays . . . cannot be considered individually. . . . The female role (mother, sister, queen) is just as important in Cocteau's plays as the leading male role, except perhaps for Eurydice in *Orphée*, who is a bit pale and simple-minded. Because of a kind of allegorical redistribution of qualities that somehow evoke Tennessee Williams and, in certain cases, Jean Genêt, Cocteau's hero can only be truly understood as part of the couple, young man-older woman. The poet-martyr's identification with his persecuted or rebel hero is obvious, but so is his identification with the feminine mask. "*I am Yvonne,*" Cocteau might have said, paraphrasing Flaubert's "*I am Madame Bovary.*" All more or less Jocastas, Cocteau's women are at once incarnations of the poet's feelings with regard to the young hero, and women-obstacles, now an outer obstacle (mother, wife, lover), now an inner one ("le fantôme de Marseille" in *Théâtre de Poche*).

The comparison with Tennessee Williams seems even more evident when we consider that Cocteau chose to adapt *A Streetcar Named Desire* for the French stage. . . . Obviously the heavy sexual atmosphere of Williams' works is foreign to Cocteau's, or at least considerably relieved in the major plays. Yet the general pattern—the duos, even the trios—are analogous. The unity of the couples reveals that they are but two faces of one basic individual—an eagle with two heads or with two sexes, as it were. In minor works such as *le Fantôme de Marseille,* the hero remains undivided by also playing the part of a female impersonator. In fact the hero in Cocteau's dramas and certain of Tennessee Williams' plays is not one character but a couple, a divided hermaphrodite who tries to possess himself—an often impossible desire, and always tormenting.

The idea of the hermaphrodite can be seen in the complicity of intimacy so characteristic of Cocteau's atmosphere: the complicity of Yvonne and Mik, of Jocasta and Oedipus, of Maxime and Margot, of Maxime and Solange, of the Queen and Stanislas, of Hans and Christine, of Guinevere and Lancelot, parallel to that of King Arthur and the false Gawain. In Cocteau's theatre there are always at least two who are marked out—marked out for poetry, grandeur, disorder, or love. (pp. 63-4)

[Fate] serves as an archetype for the metaphors of danger and universal fatality which constitute the unchanging hidden drama in Cocteau's works. Each story consists in the search for union, realization, equilibrium, right up until the last scene, when an unexpected meaning breaks through in the form of catastrophe, a price to pay, a fatal incompatibility. The rest is surface effect. By means of a kind of baroque or rococo disproportion, the surface effects conceal the drama's underlying structure and are in fact taken for it—an obtrusive "parade," intentionally created by Cocteau who, through the diversity and exuberance of his talents, wanted both to disclose *and* to mask the danger in order to give the true equivalent of man's condition. (p. 65)

Mistrust is characteristic of Cocteau's sensibility and creates a primitive and somehow pre-tragic terror in his works. He never intellectualizes his fear but preserves it in its integrity, in its extreme discomfort. Theatre is one of man's maneuvers to appease a threatening Nature or super-Nature—an illusory maneuver, since despite all the embellishments and digressions, the universe can only be portrayed as implacable. Whereas Giraudoux resolved the problem of tragedy through intelligence, Cocteau, completely involved in a world for which the time of brilliant solutions is past or yet to come, does the dance of a man who is condemned to death, with no appeal possible. His masquerade is a staggering metaphor of the hesitation of a consciousness before its condemnation. Man can be seen innocently claiming freedom or the realization of values, desperately clinging to those desires, plunged in a defeat which is masked by a voluntary illusion. In a parallel way, the playwright himself plays an analogous double game. He puts all his effort into raising the exalting or blinding illusion to the rank of reality while preserving enough illusionism to keep the reality from ever being reached.

Success—a synthesis of the hermaphrodite, the triumph of poets or lovers, the realization of a total and happy equilibrium, excluding all hazards or perils—is not of this world. It is in a beyond where Orpheus and Eurydice, Guinevere and Lancelot, Patrice and Nathalie (the Tristan and Isolde of the film *l'Eternel retour*) are reunited. The price for union is death. . . . In this world everything must be paid for and the deal is transacted above man and without his consent. (pp. 66-7)

A grim and anguished theatre, full of surface glitter that is no more than an illusion of esthetic satisfaction, Cocteau's plays are outwardly like entertainments of the twenties and thirties. He has used all the devices of the entertainment, from avant-garde forms to the Boulevard, in order to express the meeting between the illusionism of that time and the personal and sincere perception of a basic dimension of man's condition. Cocteau searched the present and a recent past for all the masks imaginable. Clowns, Music Hall stars, the favorite actors of the bourgeoisie and other classes are all buffoons in a masquerade addressed as much to the Prince de Beaumont as to the masses who attended vaudeville theatres during the time of the Popular Front. What gives Cocteau's theatre its value is its cry of warning addressed, whatever may be said, to all men.

Added to that is his fidelity to an uncompromising idea of theatre. He is a modernist not only when he concretizes psychological or metaphysical phenomena on stage, with the freedom of today's poets, but also in his "Boulevard" plays. Even *la Machine à écrire,* generally considered his worst play and one that he himself repudiated, is infinitely superior to plays of the same genre in that, while continuing to play the Boulevard game to the very end, Cocteau goes beyond the document on life in the provinces and succeeds, through dialogue and action, to actualize a theme of pure theatre: that of illusion, as both mask and instrument of the inexorable destructibility of man.

Cocteau has a love of the theatre which is evident from his general declarations, but which can also be found in the conception of his plays themselves. A metaphor of illusion, theatre should be presented with all the signs of illusion. At certain moments, the reality of what unfolds on stage must be forgotten so that the spectator may once again become conscious of the actor's number. . . . In *les Parents terribles* the characters constantly remind us that they are acting out a play—vaudeville, drama, or tragedy, depending on the moment and situation. Allusions to dreams and magic, now represented by living beings or objects, now evoked by metaphors of language, should also be interpreted in the sense of a diversion from the real. What happens on stage is never absolutely true, despite appearances. Each play is presented as a trance or comedy, throwing man into a story that is fictional or dreamed up by some god.

A Protean theatre, it is the faithful image of a Protean universe. The number of forms that the traps of the universe can take is infinite; so are the forms taken by man's illusory defenses. The meaning of reality is finally lost in the game of lies and counter lies. Through an intransigence recalling the Baudelairian dandy, Cocteau, as the only possible affirmation of his identity, succeeded in immobilizing two elements of the confusion: theatre and the emotion of fear. His double game is tragic even though individually, his plays are not. It is a recognition, a voluntary act. For Cocteau, writing a play is taking man's part—but he takes it all in lucidity, for by resorting to devices and descriptive illusion, he affirms that he defends a lost cause. (pp. 67-8)

> *Jacques Guicharnaud with June Beckelman, "The Double Game: Jean Cocteau," in their* Modern French Theatre from Giraudoux to Beckett, *Yale University Press, 1961, pp. 48-68.*

J. L. STYAN

[Cocteau] was not only versatile in trying his hand at every artistic medium, but he also experimented endlessly in the media he chose; it is understandable if the criticism that he

was a showman has clung. His gift of creating striking and unique visual images can be seen in play and film alike. 'Astonish me!', demanded Diaghilev, and Cocteau responded with *Parade,* the first of many attempts to astonish his audiences. When it was performed at the Théâtre du Châtelet, he ironically called it a 'ballet réaliste'. . . . [Music and dance] tended to suppress any dialogue Cocteau had supplied in his libretto. The music was by Eric Satie and the ballet had a mobile Cubist set by Picasso. This collaboration by a trio of highly temperamental avant-garde artists made it a miracle that a performance of *Parade* ever took place. The idea was to set illusion against reality, and the 'parade' of the title referred to the bizarre display outside a circus tent before the show, designed to lure spectators inside to see the 'reality'. The side-show consisted of three Managers encased in scenery, with a cast of two acrobats, a Chinese prestidigitator and 'a little American girl', who looked like Mary Pickford in a sailor suit about to face *The Perils of Pauline.* The dancing was accompanied by outrageous sound-effects produced by sirens, whistles and typewriters, and the dancers were made to seem like unreal, Craig-like pieces of moving machinery inside the frame of the stage. The audience was denied a view of what was really inside the tent, and was scandalously made to feel it was part of the grotesque show it was watching. The production was received with the customary mixture of cheers and catcalls, and was also followed by public insults and lawsuits. But this was Cocteau's début, and *Parade* ensured that his reputation was truly launched.

Like any playwright, Cocteau was searching for a style to match his content, and in his surrealistic plays the two are certainly inseparable. He believed that the action in his next play was pictorial, and he explained that he was trying to substitute what he called 'poésie de théâtre', 'theatre poetry', for the usual poetry *in* the theatre, the poetry being in the structure of the play rather than in its language. Hence, he emphasized visual and theatrical effects at the expense of words. *Les Mariés de la Tour Eiffel* (*The Wedding on the Eiffel Tower*) [was also designed as a ballet]. . . . This play, however, reclaims the text, which asserts much more control over the performance: while the performers mime the action in masks, two music-hall compères, dressed as gramophones with horns for mouths, recite the lines and narrate what is happening. This arrangement produces the singular effect of dissociation between actor and character, an effect which Brecht would pursue on a later occasion for other reasons. . . . (pp. 56-7)

With a foretaste of Ionesco, the dialogue is a series of clichés ('cliché' in French signifies both a commonplace and a snapshot), spoken by the gramophones quickly and loudly. It is accompanied sarcastically by a variety of contrapuntal funeral marches, waltzes and other musical forms. . . . The whole play had the effect of a preposterous dream, madly irreverent and wildly comic. In his preface of 1922, Cocteau declared that instead of trying to lessen the absurdity of life, he had emphasized it: 'I try to paint *more truly than the truth*' (Cocteau's italics). He wanted to 'rejuvenate the commonplace', and present it in such a light that it 'recaptures its youth'. If his play seems elementary, he asks, 'Aren't we still in school? Aren't we still deciphering what is elementary?' Accused of buffoonery, he cites Molière in his own defence: 'The attitude of the buffoon is the only one that allows certain audacities.'

This remarkable preface comes near to advancing Cocteau's theory of symbolism. 'The true symbol is never planned', he says; 'it emerges by itself'. . . . He reported that it was the candour of *Les Mariés* that caused it initially to be mistaken for a piece of esoteric writing—apparently what is mysterious inspires a kind of fear in the public. But in this play, he insists,

> I renounce mystery, I illuminate everything, I underline everything. Sunday vacuity, human livestock, ready-made expressions, dissociation of ideas into flesh and bone, the fierce cruelty of childhood, the miraculous poetry of daily life: these are my play. . . .

And Cocteau suggests that a line by the photographer might do well for his epigraph: 'Since these mysteries are beyond me, let's pretend that I arranged them all the time.' (pp. 57-9)

While Cocteau continued to mix music and mime, ballet dancing and circus acrobatics, his dramatic work grew more substantial. Yet it is a nice irony that some of his best writing for the stage, like *Les Parents terribles* (1938), was in the vein of psychological realism. For while he declared his opposition to realism, he also considered that Jarry's *Ubu* and Apollinaire's *Les Mamelles de Tirésias* consisted at the same time of symbolism and a species of drama *à thèse*, that they had successfully merged symbolism and realism. It could well be true that a play which manages to draw upon both symbolism and realism is likely to be the more universal and durable. (p. 60)

> *J. L. Styan, "Dada and Surrealism in France: Tzara to Cocteau, 'The Wedding on the Eiffel Tower'," in his* Modern Drama in Theory and Practice: Symbolism, Surrealism and the Absurd, Vol. 2, *Cambridge University Press, 1981, pp. 51-60.*

NEAL OXENHANDLER

Cocteau's work for the theater falls into three periods. First there were the works of "minor beauty"—ballets and adaptations created during and after World War I. Then came the works of the late 1920s and 1930s which (even though sometimes based on the classics) achieved a powerful originality and brought him fame. Finally, the success of these plays allowed him to finance his major films during the 1940s. The plays written during the 1940s, however, tended to be derivative and unconvincing.

Cocteau's first works for the stage were ballets. . . . Not only did Cocteau write the plots for these ballets, he intrigued to bring all the artists involved—Picasso, Satie, Auric, Poulenc, Honegger, Milhaud—together in wartime under conditions of extreme duress. Throughout his career, he was to manifest a genius for reconciling difficult personalities. This gives to his work a quality of improvisation and spontaneity. Each work becomes a minor miracle pulled off by bravado and skill.

The ballets represent what Cocteau called "minor beauty," which is full of tricks and surprises. It's found in costume or sleight-of-hand, in puns and plays on words. It's the beauty of the street singer, the nightclub *chansonnier,* the carnival mime. Cocteau associated himself with these self-taught artists as he studied to learn how he might enter the world of traditional French theater. (p. 126)

In his early works Cocteau displayed an amazing ability to use the *truc,* or trick, whether of language or spectacle. "The *truc,*" he once said, "is art itself. Poetry is a vast pun." Clearly, a long moral and artistic development had to be undergone before he could enter the house of Molière.

After the ballets, Cocteau wrote a number of adaptations: *Antigone, Romeo and Juliet, Oedipus the King.* These were streamlined versions of the originals. ***Romeo and Juliet*** was described by Cocteau as a "pretext for a choreographic production." He directed the play and also played the role of Mercutio. It seemed impertinent of him, to those who dismissed Cocteau as a frivolous jack-of-all-trades, to meddle with Shakespeare's text. But Cocteau had the instinct of a born dramatist who knows that the great works of the past must be reinvented. While stripping Shakespeare's play of much of its verbal lyricism, he added to it a poetry of motion. . . . The behavior of the play's protagonists anticipated the unpredictability of those adolescents who would appear in most of Cocteau's later works. Romeo throws a tantrum and Juliet lies on her stomach to talk to Romeo over the edge of the balcony. Cocteau was always a child at heart; it is not surprising that teenagers were to become his favorite heroes and heroines.

Cocteau's work up to this point is characterized by the title of his first ballet, ***Parade.*** In that ballet gesticulating Managers with immense cardboard heads try to persuade the crowd to come inside their street fair. "The real show is on the inside." But nobody buys a ticket and gets to see. (p. 130)

French theater in the 1920s divided into two streams. One of these, which tempted Cocteau later in his career, was Naturalism, the theater that attempted to "imitate" life. Sometimes this involved putting a butcher shop, complete with raw meat, on the stage. More often, as in the plays of Ibsen, it meant revealing human motives that were shocking to bourgeois society. The other current, with which Cocteau was more clearly attuned, had come down from Symbolism. It was a theater of atmosphere, of fantasy and invention. (p. 132)

In 1928 Cocteau wrote to Jacques Maritain that "mystery" was his obsession, his "*idée fixe.*" Clearly the path to the exploration of mystery lay not in imitating life but in going behind appearances—even through death itself, as he claimed to do in his first important play, *Orpheus.* Mystery meant many different things to Cocteau in the various stages of his career. In *Orpheus* it meant primarily the supernatural, the realm of the dead, entered through a mirror. "Look in a mirror and you will see death working like bees in a hive." On the other side of the mirror, the dead continue their lives amid monsters and marvels, but the only emotion they display is hostility toward the living.

Orpheus, produced in 1926 . . . , can be seen now in the 1980s as a brilliantly conceived homage to the supernatural. One aspect of Cocteau's genius was his ability to synthesize, to bring together fragments of the past and present, to create momentary unity out of the debris of 2,500 years of Western culture. So the play takes the ancient story of Orpheus, prince of poets. He and his wife, Eurydice, live like some upwardly mobile middle-class couple in a cozy *nouveau* Greek house. . . . He writes poetry and is involved in literary one-upmanship with other Thracian literati, who are for the most part mediocre. When his work takes him away from Eurydice, she runs with a gang of wild girls, the Bacchantes. (pp. 132-34)

The scene is the couple's home at Thrace. There is a mirror on the left wall and at stage rear a white horse, protruding from a niche. As the play begins, Orpheus is trying to interpret a message that the horse is tapping out with his hoof. Eurydice expresses her jealousy of this supernatural nag who takes so much of her husband's time. (p. 134)

The horse may be interpreted as the devil, the unconscious, or simply the marvelous. At any rate, the poem he taps out for Orpheus turns out to be a trick. It consists of one line: *MADAME EURYDICE REVIENDRA DES ENFERS* (MADAM EURYDICE WILL COME BACK FROM HELL). Orpheus enters the poem in a contest, but the judges are infuriated because the initial letters of the words when placed together spell *MERDE*.

While Orpheus is at the contest, Eurydice is murdered by her ex-friends, the Bacchantes. Returning, Orpheus decides to rescue her from death. Instructed by the angel, he passes through the mirror. He returns with Eurydice, but life together is impossible, since he is not allowed to look at her. To make matters worse, the Thracian public, led by the Bacchantes, comes to harass Orpheus, claiming that he has submitted an obscene poem.

One scenic trick follows another. Orpheus is decapitated by the Bacchantes. Eurydice leads him back through the mirror. The angel places Orpheus's head on a pedestal, where, in answer to questions from the police, it announces that it is Jean Cocteau and gives Cocteau's address, 10 rue d'Anjou. This apparent intrusion of ''reality'' into the play does not break the illusion. It mingles daily life with the play's fictions and enhances that sense of complicity between the author and the supernatural that had so possessed Cocteau during the writing of this play. . . . As the play ends, Orpheus, Eurydice, and their angel return to live together in harmony as the set mounts on wires into the loft.

Because of the flatness of the characters, this first major work of Cocteau's was called ''superficial.'' But as always, Cocteau was ahead of his time. He knew that the psychologism of the boulevard plays of Sardou, Bernstein, and Lenormand was phony. He knew that a sense of character in the theater is not created by the typology that defines one man by his having an inferiority complex, or another as a womanizer. The well-made plays that had dominated French theater since the end of the nineteenth century belonged to an exhausted genre. Cocteau's theater is poetic in exactly the same way as that of his great contemporaries, Giraudoux and Anouilh. All of them show human complexity and open out onto life's mystery. Cocteau's plays also resemble those of Giraudoux and Anouilh in the balance among the parts. Cocteau claimed that he learned this neo-classic sense of form from his young friend Radiguet. Radiguet taught him to walk the tightrope above the pitfalls of eclecticism.

The various impulses of *Orpheus* fuse around its major theme: the genealogy of the poet. (pp. 135-37)

Cocteau identified himself as a poet, which meant running the risk of provoking public outrage and even martyrdom, as in the case of *Orpheus*. True, Cocteau bore his share of insults and humiliations, which were magnified by the extreme sensitivity of a fragile ego. But persecution and martyrdom are more than a theme, more than a neurosis in Cocteau's work; they constitute one level of its deep mythic structure. Even after he was elected a member of the French Academy and was honored by Oxford, he always felt that he was working in a kind of psychic no-man's-land and that he belonged to that tribe of *poètes maudits* who are in a deep sense outcasts from the society of their time.

Cocteau's first work to be accepted by the Comédie-Française was *The Human Voice*. . . . [This] monologue for the female voice is more than a curtain-raiser. It shows that Cocteau could create a character wounded in her deepest emotions, not a poet this time but an ordinary woman, speaking in anguish over the phone to her lover. (p. 137)

The Human Voice was one of the first of several swings that Cocteau was to make in the direction of naturalism. Although fantasy was his homeland, he was able to work successfully in the much more constricting Naturalist form in which a room is only a room, a voice only a voice. But his success in this genre was limited to the monologues and *Les Parents terribles (Intimate Relations)*, a play which successfully transposes his adolescent hero into the Naturalist mode. Other works in this genre, such as the heavy-handed mystery story *The Typewriter*, were dismal failures.

The Infernal Machine has always been considered Cocteau's greatest work for the theater. . . . [The] play appeared within the context of other myth-modernizations, by Giraudoux and Anouilh as well as by Cocteau. This fascination with myth can be attributed in part to the neoclassical revival, initiated a number of years earlier by André Gide and Jacques Rivière, editor of the *Nouvelle Revue Française*. French schoolchildren in the 1930s still read Latin and Greek. Ever since the seventeenth century, Greece had been the mirror image of France; Racine and Corneille had used classical models.

Jean Cocteau saw more in Greece than Giraudoux's famous description, ''some goats browsing on marble.'' Besides a concept of style and the acceptance of homosexual love, Cocteau saw in Greece the ultimate model of ''purity.'' ''Purity,'' like ''mystery,'' has a variety of meanings, but its root meaning in Cocteau's lexicon is similar to what we now call authenticity—being true to one's deepest self. (pp. 137-39)

The story of Oedipus, which has been described as the first detective story, exactly conveyed Cocteau's own search for identity. Oedipus was a man who fled from a horrible prediction—that he would kill his father and marry his mother—only to find that his flight made the oracle come true. At the age of fifteen Cocteau too had run away. He ran away to Marseilles, perhaps to join the navy, perhaps only to try opium and engage in some torrid sexual experimentation. It was the first of his many flights in search of himself. The truth that Cocteau finally learned about himself, while in no way as horrible as that which Oedipus found, was equally unexpected.

The play begins with a prologue spoken by Cocteau's resonant voice. (As Molière before him, and Hitchcock and Godard after him, Cocteau made cameo appearances in his own works.)

Lights up, dim. We are on the ramparts of Thebes. Two guards discuss the disasters that have befallen the city; it might be the opening of *Hamlet*. We learn that the ghost of Laïus, their dead king, has appeared to them. Moments later the queen, Jocasta, climbs the stairs to their post. . . . She is followed by her blind adviser, the soothsayer Tiresias. The ghost fails to appear to Jocasta and Tiresias. They leave the ramparts unaware that not far away a young man is racing across the desert toward Thebes.

Already in this collage of borrowings, erudition, and private jokes we hear Cocteau's highly personal style. Everything seems improvised—from the high seriousness of Sophocles to the high camp of incest jokes. It is the voice that holds it all together. Once again the actors are choreographed. Once again Cocteau's voice endows each fragment with the genetic imprint of style. (pp. 139-41)

[In the desert Oedipus meets the Sphinx, who has assumed the form of a young woman who casts a spell on him.] The Sphinx is disarmed by Oedipus, and tells him the answer to her riddle. Triumphant, he seizes as his trophy the mask of Anubis, the jackal, and rushes off toward Thebes.

The Sphinx and Anubis are an invention; there is no such fairy-tale fantasy in the Sophoclean model. Yet Cocteau is reaching toward a deep truth. In the fairy-tale the hero slays the monster and marries the princess. The princess, of course, is always mother because the fairy-tale hero is a child. No one before Cocteau had realized that *Oedipus* is a story for children.

In Act III we find ourselves in Jocasta's bedroom, "red like a little butcher shop amid the architecture of the city." Throughout the play, Cocteau tried to achieve a miniaturization of the myth, reducing everything in scale. Later productions of the play have moved it in other directions—toward an exaggeration of its implicit violence and obscenity, or toward a representation of those vengeful gods who have set the "infernal machine" of the plot in motion. I have seen several productions of the play, including one that used projections of monstrous leering faces on a screen above the nuptial bed. In another, the bed was a marbleized altar tilted toward the audience, to which Oedipus and Jocasta were offered like sacrificial victims. (p. 142)

The conflict between free will and fatality (the gods) had by this time become the central theme of Cocteau's theater. It was again the question of identity. How can I choose to be myself when events and other people conspire against me?

Cocteau's heroes are all threatened by the world or by events they cannot control. These events force them to make choices. Oedipus chooses to run away from the oracle, he chooses to kill Laïus at a crossroads, he chooses to marry Jocasta. He has found the identity for which he unknowingly searched, but the price is high. Jocasta strangles herself, Oedipus punctures his eyes. As the play ends, the sacred scapegoat is led out by his small daughter, Antigone, to wander the world.

This play, which began as a pastiche of *Hamlet,* then seemed at times to be turning into a boulevard comedy, ends as a mystery play. Like all great religious works, it warns us that there are limits. These limits are ambiguous; we know only when it is too late that we have transgressed them. In the age of nuclear threat, mass murder, and terrorism, Cocteau's *Infernal Machine* remains wholly contemporary. It is a play for all time. (pp. 142-44)

Three other works were produced in the late 1930s, marking this decade as the height of Cocteau's dramatic career. There was his *Oedipus the King,* a streamlined version of Sophocles in the manner of his 1922 adaptation of *Antigone.* . . .

Oedipus the King was Cocteau's third Oedipean work and was based on his first reworking of the myth, the oratorio *Oedipus Rex* that he wrote for Igor Stravinsky. Produced in 1927 in honor of Serge Diaghilev, the somber Latin text was a notable failure at its first performance. (p. 144)

[*The Knights of the Round Table*], in which Cocteau sought to elude his "Grecian mania," pits two old men against each other—the evil magician, Merlin, and King Arthur, who is seeking to restore peace and prosperity to his troubled land. But the King is bewitched by Ginifer, Merlin's valet. Like a valet in Molière, Ginifer continually gets his master into and out of trouble. Ginifer supplies much of the magic in this delightful work of fantasy. He is never seen in his own Puckish form, but appears now as Gawain, now as Queen Guinevere, now as Galahad himself. Galahad's mission is to restore peace to the land, crushed under plague, poverty, and famine. Merlin's machinations account for some of the trouble. Lancelot's adulterous relationship with the queen is a dangerous transgression that must be paid for by all the people of the realm.

Galahad arrives at the Round Table, and is dubbed the "All Pure." His purity, we are told, is the equivalent of poetry. What this means becomes clear as the play ends. Galahad exposes the sinister Merlin and makes the Grail appear. He alone cannot see it. "I will never see it. I am he who makes it appear to others."

The poet is scapegoat and sacrificial victim. His role is to give insight to the community by purifying its language and reconciling its antagonisms. But to accomplish this, he himself must give up any possibility of happiness. Through Galahad, Cocteau once again signals his own membership in the race of *poètes maudits*. Cocteau's poetry and his theatricality fuse in the interchangeable characters of Galahad and Ginifer.

The last play of the 1930s is Cocteau's finest work in the Naturalist vein, *Les Parents terribles.* (p. 145)

The characters: Yvonne and Georges, parents of Michel; Léonie (Léo), Yvonne's sister, secretly in love with Georges; and a young woman named Madeleine. Act I shows us Yvonne's room, lit by a small bedside lamp and by sinister light from the building next door. Bathrobes and nightgowns lie on the floor. The room, like that of the children in Cocteau's novel *Les Enfants terribles (The Holy Terrors)*, reveals a family in disorder. The opening *coup de théâtre* is the discovery by Léonie and Georges that Yvonne, a diabetic, has nearly killed herself with an overdose of insulin. She is frantic with worry over Michel, who has spent the night away from home. The plot builds rapidly, with that repressed intensity so typical of what Freud called "the family romance."

Michel returns home, radiantly happy. He is in love with a young woman, has spent the night with her. His mother claws him in jealousy. The act ends with the awful discovery that Madeleine, Michel's fiancée, is also the mistress of his father.

The play's effectiveness does not lie merely in the demonstration of Sartre's famous line, "Hell is other people" (especially if they happen to be related). Merely tightening the screws on a group of characters is a common theatrical device. The difference is that Cocteau does it in a bravura style. Even within the Naturalist formula, the dialogue is built around metaphors:

> LÉO (next to Yvonne, holding her still): Another thing, Yvonne. Our worst suffering comes from being unable to imagine the place where those we love avoid us. Aren't you curious about that woman whom Mik used to hurt you, even though you can't give a precise name to that hurt? If an object is stolen from you, don't you try to imagine where it's hiding?

No doubt the concept of jealousy here comes from Proust, with the incestuous feature added by Cocteau. But the dramatization of that jealousy, the way Yvonne is manipulated by her sister to accept the visit to Madeleine—this moves past psychology into metaphor.

In Act II the family, or "gypsy caravan," as they call themselves, goes to visit Madeleine. Michel, innocent and unknowing, assumes the visit to be friendly. But his mother and father, each for his/her own reason, intend to destroy the relationship. Georges threatens Madeleine. He will reveal the truth to Michel. She has no alternative but to tell Michel that she is in love with somebody else. He leaves in despair, a mood swing that signals the play's second peripety.

In Act III the peripeties succeed each other like explosions. Michel is out of his mind with despair. His mother commits suicide. The young couple may find happiness after all—they have passed through the country of disorder. (pp. 146-47)

The plays of the 1940s included *Les Monstres sacrés (Sacred Monsters)*.... Although it has had several revivals, it was never a notable success. In 1941 *The Typewriter* was little more than an unfortunate echo of Henry Becque's great play, *The Crows*. Both deal with anonymous letters and provincial life, but Cocteau was too much of an urbanite to convey the underside of rural life.

At fifty-one, Cocteau was beginning to discover the limits to his versatility. This did not, however, prevent him from writing a tragedy in verse on a theme from the Italian poet, Tasso. The play, *Renaud et Armide,* [was] written entirely in alexandrine verse.... The action of the play, which takes place in an enchanted garden, recounts the love of the soldier-hero, Renaud, for the siren, Armide.

Cocteau had written verse since childhood, and the poetry of this play was no mere pastiche of French neo-classicism. The plot was traditional—the torments of love in an enchanted garden. But within these constraints, Cocteau evoked a view of love that was thoroughly modern. The enchanted garden became the symbol of all those obstacles to love that Cocteau himself had experienced. The danger of mere infatuation, the inability to find privacy, and the fear, familiar to all celebrities, of being used by parasites. But the chief threat to love lies in oneself. How can love achieve stability when the self is constantly changing? (pp. 147-48)

As the decade of the 1940s drew to an end, Cocteau made two final attempts to win back his place in the theater. His two historical plays, *L'Aigle à deux têtes (The Eagle with Two Heads)* (1946) and *Bacchus* (1951), were attempts to deal with political reality. Although both plays were set in Germanic countries split by unrest and rebellion, the reference to postwar France was unmistakable.

L'Aigle portrays a fanciful queen who has lost all interest in life until she falls in love with a poet, Stanislas. He is pursued into her room by the queen's own guards (once again, a hunted poet). The poet and the queen, the two-headed eagle, struggle to ward off the evil designs of the queen's enemies. The play is political in a negative sense. Cocteau seems to be saying, people such as these, who live in the realm of imagination,

should not be called upon to take responsibility. They do not deal with reality—they invent it. He is defending not only poets but mythomaniacs, beings whose theatricality is a kind of detour to the truth.

From the very beginning of his career, Cocteau had been accused of lacking seriousness. Now, in the early 1950s, Jean-Paul Sartre was making his plea for political *engagement*. Cocteau had no interest in building a classless society or bringing about a revolution; such programs in fact made him uncomfortable.

Bacchus was his answer to these ideas. It tells of a young man, the village idiot, who is crowned Bacchus for one day and given the privilege of ruling the city. In fact no idiot at all, he takes over and tries to bring about essential reform. Despite his idealism and heroic strength, he is killed as the result of political intrigue. The hero and heroine of *L'Aigle* had also shown that poets' gifts lift them above the world of politics. When out of generosity they traffic with this world, it turns on them and kills them.

Cocteau's play seemed hackneyed when compared to the complex moral issues presented in Sartre's *Le Diable et le bon Dieu (The Devil and the Good Lord),* which was produced at the same time. Cocteau defended himself with his usual paradoxes: "... my engagement was in myself and not exterior to me." Or as Hans, his hero, puts it: "To engage oneself in a party is a comfort, since that party supports us and spares us the anguish of nuances to the advantages of a single color." (pp. 148-49)

[Cocteau's last work for the theater], called *L'Impromptu du Palais-Royal,* brings Molière and Louis XIV themselves out of the gloom of history. There, on the stage of Molière's own theater, they gossip and argue with a variety of dukes, marquises, and other hangers-on, including that notorious gossip, Saint-Simon.

Here, in a brief soliloquy, Cocteau evokes "the great century" as the time when theatricality was at its peak. Dancing and playacting were the very mode of courtly life. Everything, from the king's first waking to the after-dinner violins, was part of the great play of existence: "Dance, gentlemen.... Dance between heaven and earth.... Dance on the strings our invisible author manipulates overhead."

Cocteau has passed through the mirror, but the marionettes he left behind still dance his dramas and his endlessly inventive dreams. (p. 151)

*Neal Oxenhandler, "The Theatre of Jean Cocteau,"
in* Jean Cocteau and the French Scene, *edited by
Alexandra Anderson and Carol Saltus, Abbeville Press
Publishers, 1984, pp. 125-51.*

Paul Durcan

1944-

Irish poet.

Durcan writes intense, emotionally-charged verse featuring an exuberant and playful use of language. Infused with surrealistic imagery and humor, Durcan's poetry satirizes various social and religious values and celebrates love and nature. Maurice Harmon stated that Durcan "is a poet of fierce rejections and of passionate loves: rejection of repression and conformity, of violence and mediocrity of poeticism; love for fertility and sensuality, individuality, natural beauty, words." While some critics regard his output as uneven, Durcan is praised for his command of tone and his experimentation with form, which contribute to the lyrical and visionary qualities of his verse.

The Selected Paul Durcan (1983), which contains poems drawn from his four previous volumes, *O Westport in the Light of Asia Minor* (1975), *Teresa's Bar* (1976), *Sam's Cross* (1978), and *Jesus, Break His Fall* (1980), was Durcan's first book to draw substantial critical attention. Gerald Dawe commented: "Durcan's poems are about people, a montage of the banal and exotic that, by their seemingly random juxtaposition, expose the hypocrises, loves and bitter enmities of Irish life." The poems in *Jumping the Train Tracks with Angela* (1984) evidence Durcan's characteristic scorn of repressive social and religious practices and his repulsion of the violence in Northern Ireland. In other poems, Durcan writes with whimsical humor on such universal topics as love and social relationships. Critics were divided in their assessment of this volume; some argued that Durcan's conversational approach helps make his work accessible, while others contended that his unstructured style detracts from his observations. *The Berlin Wall Café* (1986) was more roundly praised. The poems in this volume focus upon modern urban life and include colorful characters and insightful social criticism.

EDNA LONGLEY

The titles of Paul Durcan's four full collections—*O Westport in the Light of Asia Minor, Teresa's Bar, Sam's Cross* and *Jesus, Break His Fall*—cover both the visionary and the Irish aspects of his poetry. They also imply a likely friction between the two; since Sam's Cross was the birthplace of the murdered Michael Collins, while **"Teresa's Bar"** represents an antidote to all the hurts and constraints of society:

> But Teresa deep down had no time for time
> Or for those whose business has to do with time.

Durcan is visionary, first of all, in his faith. This faith extends to literature itself, as when he salutes a significant Trinity of writers:

> I have not 'met' God, I have not 'read'
> David Gascoyne, James Joyce, or Patrick Kavanagh:
> I believe in them.

Durcan's own work achieves extra-literary qualities too, if occasionally at the expense of certain literary ones. His 'mystical entrances' affirm lost Edens, like Ireland **"Before the Celtic Yoke"**, or an ideal peaceable kingdom: 'Even the grey pools by the bridge cannot help / But be motherfathers to wild-flowers' (**"Letter to Ben, 1972"**). But such visions, including more personal oases of love, are often hard-won from time, space, and the potential destructiveness of all relationships within the human family. (p. xi)

Even when celebratory, Durcan's perceptions have a bizarre aura which shades into disturbing possibilities. In [a] love poem (**"Hymn to Nessa"**) the two watchers convey peril as well as intensity:

> I looked back and saw her wave towards me
> She burned through her eyes
> I looked back and saw her wave towards me
> Her face burning in coals

Although surrealistic or fantastic effects may underline the oneness of phenomena—all the hats of humanity in **"The Hat Factory"**—they chiefly strike discords: the refrain uttered by a dying man ('Rider Haggard, Rider Haggard: / Storm Jameson, Storm Jameson'), the scenario of **"The Head Transplant"**, the cosmic strangeness of **"La Terre des Hommes"**. . . . Surrealism is also Durcan's most powerful satirical weapon, crystallising incongruities between the ideal and the actual. **"Two History Professors"** take a questioning West Indian at his word when he complains 'They are using a bacon-slicer on my mind'. . . . Satire is perhaps too cool and intellectual a term for such poems. It might be truer to say that Durcan's negatives fiercely invert his positives: that his vision encompasses dreams and nightmares.

As regards specific attacks on Irish society, Durcan continues where Patrick Kavanagh rather feebly left off. *The Great Hunger* apart, Kavanagh lampooned Dublin's "Bohemian Jungle" and the 'evil Mediocrity', from a subjective and narrowly literary point of view. Durcan's broadly-based outrage, which sometimes breaks through his verbal control, indicts the concrete jungle, the Church, the repression of sex and women, the bourgeoisie, the murder of bodies and minds. Fiction, if not poetry, may have thoroughly savaged these targets already. However, Durcan is not only peculiarly sensitive to Ireland's changing line-up of anti-life forces, but able to embody them in vivid symbols, portraits and fables. Materialism and the social consequences of expansion provide an area of richly urgent concern. **"Please Stay in the Family Clovis"** and **"The Day of the Starter"**, for instance, illustrate how maternal and marital affection can become confused with curtains, cutlery and cars. . . . Durcan's naturally religious cast of mind recoils from the Catholic Church's ingenious hostility to life and love. Many poems subvert puritanism, while **"Bishop of Cork Murders his Wife"** hammers the accepted superiority of violence to sex, and maleness to femaleness. A subtler skit, **"Irish Hierarchy Bans Colour Photography"**, exploits an appropriate analogy for black-and-white attitudes and stunted awareness. On the other hand, **"Teresa"**, **"Polycarp"** and **"Fat Molly"** personify fertile sexuality and sensuality. The latter, a carnal incarnation of Cathleen ní Houlihan and thus another version of primal Ireland, lives 'On the other side of the forest from the monkfort at Kells'.

Durcan's critique of the South is sharpened by his sense of the North. No other Southern Irish poet has so painfully and continuously responded to the Ulster Troubles. . . . Some of Durcan's whispers take the form of irony—**"National Day of Mourning for 12 Protestants"**. Others emphasise that bigotry is not confined to one sect or province (**"What is a Protestant, Daddy?"**), or function as reminders of the Protestant tradition in the South (**"Protestant Old Folks' Coach Tour"**, **"The Weeping Headstones of the Isaac Becketts"**). Perhaps his quietest and most effective comment is **"The Night They Murdered Boyle Somerville"**. An old man, during a train journey that traverses up much history and geography, simply remarks:

> I found out what was in it, and was not in it,
> The night they murdered Boyle Somerville;
> I knew then that it was only the sky had a roof.
>
> (pp. xii-xiv)

Durcan's alternative Ireland not only includes 'Desire under the steeples and spires', and excludes the IRA, but must be fit for his heroes and heroines. The diverse integrity of his real-life idols is matched by the idiosyncrasies of his invented models: Teresa, Polycarp, Fat Molly, **"The Kilfenora Teaboy"**, Constance Purfield who 'prefers the trees', **"Nora and Hilda"**, **"The County Engineer"** and his wife. In this truly human family, makers of love not war, there is compassionate room for marginal and ambiguous figures like **"The Butterfly Collector of Corofin"**. Durcan can characterise with names alone: **"Gogo's Late Wife Tranquilla"**. And the fictional names of his heterogeneous dramatis personae interact oddly with actual

placenames: this contributes to the shifting projection of the country's real features against a Platonic conception. Durcan has named more places than most Irish poets. He sometimes just states and hates middle Ireland—**"I've Got the Drimoleague Blues"**—but generally placenames become 'magic passwords into eternity' (**"Going Home to Mayo, Winter, 1949"**). In **"Birth of a Coachman"** implicit resonance creates the 'magic' of a more hopeful symbolic journey than that of **"The Night They Murdered Boyle Somerville"**:

> Praising the breasts of the hills round Port Laoise;
> Sailing full furrow through the Curragh of Kildare,
> Through the thousand sea-daisies of a thousand white
> sheep . . .

These richly textured lines evince an open Romanticism rare in contemporary poetry. Their obvious assonance raises the ghost of Gaelic metre, but the Irishness of Durcan's language depends more on conversational idiom—for example, the pervasive 'used [to]'—and its various rhetorical extensions, such as the amplified sentence . . . , or a stately elaboration:

> . . . while the cradle is but a grave
> The grave is not a cradle but is for ever . . .
> And I see that all church-architecture is but coiffure
> And all mystical entrances are through women's faces.
>
> (**"Phoenix Park Vespers"**)

No loader of every rift with ore, though capable of startling concentration, Durcan resembles D. H. Lawrence in his tendency to write 'the poetry of the present moment', or adopt a biblical style of prophecy. But while some poems over-saturate their subjects—some titles nearly exhaust them!—he can also renew the simplest ballad-forms. **"Backside to the Wind"**, which wistfully imagines 'a French Ireland', combines an old air with a down-to-earth refrain:

> Yet I have no choice but to leave, to leave,
> And yet there is nowhere I more yearn to live
> Than in my own wild countryside,
> Backside to the wind.

That quatrain might exemplify the way in which Paul Durcan's poetry seems in touch with the deepest wells of native Irish sensibility, yet radically challenges their pollution. In addition to his other achievements, he has developed the conscience of the race. (pp. xiv-xv)

> *Edna Longley, in an introduction to* The Selected Paul Durcan *by Paul Durcan, edited by Edna Longley, The Blackstaff Press, 1982, pp. xi-xv.*

GERALD DAWE

[The essay excerpted below was first presented at the fifth triennial conference of IASAIL (The International Association for the Study of Anglo-Irish Literature) in July, 1982.]

I think [Durcan] is a poet whose work represents a liberating force in contemporary Irish poetry, all the more significant because that force is richly endorsed by the style and content of his poems. For if it is fair to say that two constants are generally to be found in Irish poetry, given also that such a monolith exists, they are non-experimentalism and . . . a dependence on the imaginative resourcefulness of natural imagery. Durcan's poetry in its wild exuberance offers formally and in the choice of material, an opposing countenance.

Durcan's poems are about people, a montage of the banal and exotic that, by their seemingly random juxtaposition, expose the hypocrisies, loves and bitter enmities of Irish life. It would be wrong, however, to suggest that Durcan merely documents, with a provocative laugh, Irish life. His poetry exists on a more profound level than this: the laugh bears a chastening image, fixed in the actual intransigence of language to mean what he wants it to say. . . . Yet, Durcan's poetry absorbs the traditional Irish legacy of an inherited 'poetic language' as a stock of images that are able to passively render meaning. Durcan transforms this legacy and explores its moral bankruptcy with a narrative and dramatic range of subtle intonations closely attuned to the reading voice rather than for the consequential eye. (pp. 182-83)

In a poem like **"Going Home to Mayo, Winter 1949"**, he points to the Dublin of the day and contrasts it with the 'magic passwords' of the towns he passes through *en route* to home but this is not a simple pastoral; rather it is a reluctant, even angry acceptance and redefinition of himself in urban terms:

> And in the evenings
> I walked with my father in the high grass down by the
>   river
> Talking with him—an unheard-of thing in the city.
> But home was not home and the moon could be no
>   more
> outflanked
> Than the daylight nightmare of Dublin city:
> Back down along the canal we chugged into the city
> And each lock-gate tolled our mutual doom;
> And railings and palings and asphalt and traffic-lights,
> And blocks after blocks of so-called 'new' tenements—
> Thousands of crosses of loneliness planted
> In the narrowing grace of the life of the father;
> In the wide-wide cemetery of the boy's childhood.

The childhood passes into a sombre, chaotic world where **"Margaret Thatcher Joins the IRA"**, **"Irish Hierarchy Bans Colour Photography"**, **"Bishop of Cork Murders his Wife"**, **"Minister Opens New Home For Battered Husbands"**, **"Communist Cardinal Visits Dublin"** and **"A Connacht Doctor Dreams of an African Woman"**. These poem-titles suggest that Durcan is more than willing to enjoy himself by stretching or overthrowing our customary expectations about what an 'Irish Poem' is about. His poems deal with the nervous system of Irish Catholic life, with the duplicities of contemporary Irish politics and with the obscure, lost and repressed souls like **"The County Engineer"**, or they celebrate figures with whom Durcan identifies, such as the sculptor Seamus Murphy, Michael MacLiammoir, or Cearbhall O' Dalaigh. . . . The confidence with which Durcan writes these laments, his sense of voicing genuine public feelings at historic events, like the death of a President, takes on an expansive, hectic force of disruption that bursts through the traditional decorum of modern Irish poetry, tapping on ancient resource perhaps, but rooted also, one feels, in the bitterness of Kavanagh. . . . (pp. 183-84)

> *Gerald Dawe, "The Permanent City: The Younger Irish Poets," in* The Irish Writer and the City, *edited by Maurice Harmon, Barnes and Noble Books, 1983, pp. 180-96.*

MAURICE HARMON

Paul Durcan is a poet of fierce rejections and of passionate loves: rejection of repression and conformity, of violence and mediocrity, of poeticism; love for fertility and sensuality, individuality, natural beauty, words. The dissonance at the heart of his perception yields oblique, fleeting lines of lyricism which are all the more appealing for being housed with such jarring company. There are compelling juxtapositions of the bad and the beautiful; the poetry creates bizarre situations and releases the eccentric and the idiosyncratic, the magic of make-believe, and metamorphosis. Durcan's irreverent and iconoclastic vision is a liberating force in contemporary Ireland. [*The Selected Paul Durcan*] should bring him wide recognition. (pp. 116-17)

> *Maurice Harmon, in a review of "The Selected Paul Durcan," in* Irish University Review: A Journal of Irish Studies, *Vol. 13, No. 1, Spring, 1983, pp. 116-17.*

JOHN WAIN

Durcan writes about Irish life, in its sadness and its comicality and its deep, narrow resentments and longings, in its immense vistas backward and its short vistas forward. Not all these qualities are specifically Irish, but like most good writers Durcan reaches to the universal through the particular; he writes about universal human experience as if it only happened in Ireland, and after all James Joyce did the same.

[In *The Selected Paul Durcan* he] writes about enmity and scorn and disapproval, but he also writes about love. . . . [A] poem about married love, **"Anna Swanton"**, tells how the young man met the girl as he hurried along a country road to the railway station; they walked together, found the train did not run any more, and in due course finished up living together in the stationmaster's cottage, with their children 'playing real trains':

> And yet although I live in terror of the tracks
> For fear that they should prove our children's grave
> I live in greater terror of the thought
> Of life without Anna Swanton on this earth:
>
> Or of how I might be rich in far-off Nottingham
> And married to another kind of girl;
> I'd rather rain for ever in the fields with Anna Swanton
> Than a car or a goddess in the sun.

Not only the loved woman, but the loved country, can make it worth staying in one's own place instead of being 'rich in far-off Nottingham' or wherever. (pp. 74-5)

There is, of course, the other side of the coin also—the bitterness and harshness of Irish life and of the judgements that Irish people pass on one another. Behind Durcan's satiric or elegiac poems one senses the figure of Yeats murmuring,

> Out of Ireland have I come;
> —Great hatred, little room.

Mention of Yeats reminds one that Durcan would be an even better poet if he had the good fortune to live in an age with a decent literary tradition. Modern slovenly habits of writing, the absence of anyone to encourage pleasure in craftsmanship, have done their melancholy work in his poems. He is a natural lyric poet with a good ear for language and an open, musical idiom, and his inborn impulse is to make language dance and sing; but what usually happens is that he gets going in fine style with a good verse-pattern and then, presumably at the first hint of difficulty, drops it and lapses into the ordinary standard chopped-up prose that is the modern convention in 'poetry'. Examples are too numerous to bother with; just look at any of the poems that start out as if they were going to sing and dance, and follow them through. It would be unfair to blame Durcan for this; he is writing in a culture that wouldn't notice if he carried his music, and his dance, and his vigorous rhythm, all through the poem. People don't read poems for those qualities any more; they read them for Statements, or for ingenious games with metaphor. (p. 75)

> *John Wain, "Celts," in* London Magazine, *n.s. Vol. 23, No. 4, July, 1983, pp. 74-8.*

DAVID PROFUMO

Paul Durcan is a genuinely inventive poet whose work [as evidenced in *The Selected Paul Durcan*] ranges from the gnomic distich to the long improvisatory monologue, and he is by turns outlandish, sentimental and depressing. His poems are distinguished by their idiosyncratic titles, which often tell a little story in themselves, like newspaper headlines—**"Three Hundred Men Made Redundant"**, **"Minister Opens New Home for Battered Husbands"**—and by an exotic cast of characters. Although a few of his poems are designed primarily as entertainments, Durcan's work represents an extraordinary amalgam of the Romantic and the blackly humorous. His chief targets, witheringly portrayed, are institutional figures who stultify the life of the nation—these can include judges, architects, teachers and the religiously dogmatic. Hypocrites of the Church, especially, stalk through his poems: one bishop murders his wife, another dreams of a harlot, a Reverend Mother gets pregnant, and all are socially tolerated in a world reminiscent of Skelton's or Chaucer's. But this humorous dimension is darkly shaded, as in **"Two History Professors Found Guilty of Murder"** where the academics (both named Cantwell) are excused the butchering of a black colleague who "had consistently encouraged his students to ascertain the true facts / of the history of Ulster".

This vision is brought to bear on any force—and there are seen to be many—that counteracts the life-affirming qualities of Irish culture. Some poems chart the bourgeois confusion of love with material possessions (**"Please Stay in the Family Clovis"**) while others lambast the advocates of genteel sexual mores (**"Polycarp"**), but the most rigorous denunciation is reserved for the agents of physical violence. Durcan's recent verse has moved increasingly towards elegy and the condemnation of murder, but he is resolutely non-partisan: all sects and parties, the British included, are implicitly and collectively guilty; they have created by fear "a country where words also have died an unnatural death" (**"Tribute to a Reporter in Belfast, 1974"**) and what is at stake is the survival of an Ireland where true heroism, one of the spirit, can flourish once more. One of Durcan's achievements is to balance his fractured vision of modern Ireland with a precise sense of the relationship between its spiritual ancestry and the much-invaded history of more recent centuries. For against the contemporary follies that he treats, Durcan sets up a dream world of legend where heroes and "speakers of truth" have influence; his own Catholic upbringing he satirizes (**"What is a Protestant Daddy?"**), but a humanistic passion has taken its place.

> *David Profumo, "Recording with Honesty," in* The Times Literary Supplement, *No. 4194, August 19, 1983, p. 886.*

DEREK MAHON

[Durcan is] an established name in Ireland, where he is thought of in the two-fold guise of satirist and surrealist: a title like **"Irish Hierarchy Bans Colour Photography"** will give you some idea. Edna Longley, in her introduction to *The Selected Paul Durcan* [see excerpt above], reads this one as an attack on 'black-and-white attitudes'. Durcan, she rightly says, is 'peculiarly sensitive to Ireland's changing line-up of anti-life forces'. He is peculiarly sensitive to much else besides. The synoptic two-line epigram **"Ireland 1972"**—

> Next to the fresh grave of my beloved grandmother
> The grave of my firstlove murdered by my brother—

is intensely painful and resonant; but no less typical is another epigram, **"La Terre des Hommes**—

> Fancy meeting *you* out here in the desert:
> Hallo Clockface—

which takes us into a different sphere altogether. Durcan's is a radical humanist sensibility at work on contemporary Ireland; but it is also a metaphysical sensibility at work on the nature of reality itself. His poems can be strange, bitter, tender, hilarious and very moving. (pp. 27-8)

> *Derek Mahon, "Quaat?" in* New Statesman, *Vol. 106, No. 2747, November 11, 1983, pp. 27-8.*

JOHN LUCAS

Jumping the Train Tracks With Angela is, as the title suggests, on the manic side, but it's a good read. Durcan goes in for ballads which forget to be ballads and he also has a line of monologue which gives the impression sometimes of Stevie Smith imitating Damon Runyan, sometimes of one of Beckett's clowns in a more than usually desperate search for a listener. There are a great many jokes, of which the good ones are good and the bad ones are even better. In other words, Durcan has a professional rogue-ishness about him. He keeps an eye on his audience to make sure it isn't getting restless, and this inevitably limits his satiric thrusts at contemporary Irish matters. Still, **"The Problem of Fornication in the Blarney Chronicle"** is a rough beast with a bite, and the same is true of a handful of others from the same pack. (p. 24)

> *John Lucas, "Truth, Dare, Slush or Promise?" in* New Statesman, *Vol. 107, No. 2763, March 2, 1984, pp. 23-4.*

PETER PORTER

Paul Durcan is not the sort of poet you expect to find coming from Ireland. There they are still lining up to try on Yeats's robes, with Seamus Heaney at the head of the queue. Anyone who thinks this is a cliché hasn't read the new Irish poetry. Even when it is sardonic, or committed to a cause, it insists on formal decorum and on looking Prince Posterity full in the face. Style and illumination will always be given precedence over any other shaping force, except in the work of James Simmons and Michael Foley, and now Paul Durcan as well.

Durcan is a poet whose manner and whose means we know from our own practitioners. [In *Jumping the Train Tracks with Angela*, he] is whimsical, satirical, jokey—a Playboy of Western Surrealism. But his verse has an oddity and plangency which the work of the English circuit entertainers often lacks. It also has fierce faults: it is too often wordy, wasteful and rhythmically becalmed. Durcan will begin a ballad as though he thought that the straitjacket of metre and rhyme were the point of the thing, and then forget his chosen restraints and let the poem ramble to its end.

The Catholic Church very properly comes in for a large share of his distaste, but the whole Republic is included—a typical Durcan title is **"The Perfect Nazi Family is alive and well and prospering in modern Ireland."** He is usually good when he pushes his fantasy further than satire would require, and he can be lyrical and relaxed.

> Peter Porter, *"The Playful Muse," in* The Observer, *March 11, 1984, p. 25.*

MARTIN BOOTH

Paul Durcan is an astonishing and remarkable poet.... His poetry is what poetry should be—and Irish verse usually is, by tradition—in that it speaks to people at large, not just to the smart-mouthed literati, and seeks to expand their worlds into a greater consciousness. It is about everyday life, trouble, love, politics and general being. What is more, it is about people and is inhabited by people. It contains the core of the human condition and, Ireland being what it is, this means a very mobile state of flux.

In some ways, Durcan is the reviewer's plague—one has to be critically observant when reading work, detached and distant in order to gain the perspective to assess and discuss. With this man's work, it's impossible. To read five lines is to be captured by the mood, tone and vitality of his muse, drawn hard and fast into a world of love and life, Irishness, pathos and considerable beauty. There is not a mediocre poem in [*Jumping the Train Tracks with Angela*]. What is not movingly beautiful is ironic, witty, touching, direct and—what sums all Durcan's poetry up—full of real life. Durcan is a poet of the first rank, a writer of his times with more than a fair share of the genius one so often yearns for but seldom discovers in modern verse. (pp. 308-09)

> Martin Booth, *in a review of "Jumping the Train Tracks with Angela," in* British Book News, *May, 1984, pp. 308-09.*

DAVID PROFUMO

[Durcan's] off-beat, convulsive imagination is capable of producing writing that is sublime and banal by turns. The occasions of his verse [in *Jumping the Train Tracks with Angela*] continue to be as eccentric as ever, his inventiveness equally unpredictable, and certainly he is often funny; but he is exceedingly uneven. At its best, his comedy is reductive rather than merely entertaining, the jokiness underpinned by a dark humour that portrays in strange perspectives the violent indifference of humans to each other's sufferings, or their sexual hypocrisies. Here, poems such as **"The Night They Put John Lennon Down"** or **"The Perfect Nazi Family"** anatomize self-interest but elsewhere there is a warmer vitality at work in the extravagant variety mimic, and his characters often show confused, even crazed, patterns of thought. Their monologues can be both amusing and frightening—a bisexual priest, a lascivious interviewer—but there is also a body of gentler characters. In the second section of the book there are more poems that deal feelingly with loneliness, the frustrations and excitements of love, and this more sentimental, celebratory vein shows Durcan at his best, including the two good poems **"Dave Loves Macker 14.2.83."** and **"The Athlone Years"**.

A large proportion of this collection is none the less disappointing. The odd surreal simile (''She laughed like a prehistoric rabbit, unperturbed by the firing squad'') is not enough to energize a whole poem, nor is it satisfactory for the verse to lapse so often into a kind of corrugated vernacular prose. Such stuff reads poorly on the page; puns and catchlines begin to look like resorting to literary fast-food rather than the real thing. The variety of tone is often clearly geared for reading aloud, but this sort of versatility lacks the quality of anything lasting, whatever immediate appeal it makes....

> David Profumo, *"In the Family Way," in* The Times Literary Supplement, *No. 4252, September 28, 1984, p. 1105.*

PETER PORTER

To adapt Pound's saying, poetry should be at least as readable as prose. A book like Paul Durcan's [*The Berlin Wall Café*], where each poem urges you on to the next, with some of the page-turning impetus you expect in novels, must surely be a happy arrival on the scene. Yet the killjoy critical spirit insists on asking: will I want to read these poems again? isn't the surrealism too easy? don't the verbal jokes and one-liners exude a suspicious charm?

Disquiet centres on the relentless contemporaneity of Durcan's verse. *The Berlin Wall Café* is to poetry (especially the poetry of Ireland) what ''The Comic Strip'' and ''The Young Ones'' are to older TV comedy. You can see the words fading on the page. Yet Durcan is a serious writer, charting with wit and lightness some of the grimmer reaches of life, especially the failure of marriages and the pointlessness of the poet in the modern world. The book is a great advance on his last one, *Jumping the Train Tracks with Angela.* It has a much sharper focus, and its buttonholing style is imbued with real warmth.

Its *mise-en-scène* is attractive to anyone who wants poetry to turn back to the city from its rural obsessions. With Durcan, you are firmly in the built-over purlieus of post-war Europe. When he is not applying the surrealist detail with too broad an impasto, his poems resemble stories by William Trevor. Durcan's Ireland has thrown off the seemingly inescapable literary clobber of the past, even the Joycean past. Students of modern Ireland could use his poem **"The Vasectomy Bureau in Lisdoonvarna"** to illustrate the changes which have taken place in both the country and its literature. The old terrors are the same—the Catholic clergy, sexual inhibition, the scourge of booze—but the new response is jagged and combative.

Durcan's monologues are not artless, but he sacrifices too many of poetry's traditional skills to gain his urgency. Nothing could be further from the crafting of Seamus Heaney's verse. Everything depends on the tone of voice and on echoes and distortions of familiar turns of speech.... Whether you find the facetiousness or the pain uppermost here will probably dictate your reaction to Durcan.

> Peter Porter, *"The Grimmer Reaches," in* The Observer, *January 26, 1986, p. 50.*

MEDBH McGUCKIAN

[In her Introduction to *The Selected Paul Durcan* (see excerpt above), Edna Longley states:] 'No other Southern Irish poet has so painfully and continuously responded to the Ulster Troubles'.... Ms Longley might have omitted the 'Southern' appellation; as an 'outsider' he can afford to be more direct, more vitriolic, than any Northern poet has dared, to extend or even discard metaphor without appearing partisan. His castigation equally of the I.R.A. and the reactionary Catholicism of the Republic exorcises the worst of Unionist fears, although he is careful to place what he condemns in the context of general political decadence. As a result, he gets away with a certain amount of myopia himself. . . .

Selected Poems (1982) is still eminently relevant and enjoyable for its sardonic humour, its innocence. To hear Durcan intoning his own verse on a good night is a revelation. He has been compared as 'poet-in-the world' and 'visionary' with Yeats. He is certainly as prolific if not as disciplined or serious, though in his evangelism he more resembles Whitman. The naming of real personalities and the dating of real events coincides with absurd characters of his own making, from **"The Kilfenora Teaboy"** to **"The Most Beautiful Protestant Girl in Muggalnagrow"**, to people a landscape meaner and more hypocritical than Yeats created. His versatile forms range from the epigram to the epistle, he is a master of repetition, strong endings, refrain, the periodic sentence. By taking his fantasies to literal extremes, he transcends the personal and the observed.

The Berlin Wall Café, admittedly traumatic and self-pitying, furthers his themes while covering old ground, (as in **"High Speed Car Wash"**). It falls too tritely into its opposed halves, is too monotonously bound by Cold War clichés. As **"Checkpoint Charlie"** he tries too hard to make Ireland's divisions a symbol of marital breakdown and vice versa. Only in England, in fact, were he and his wife ever happy (**"Around the Corner from Francis Bacon"**). He continues to lash the Church with Chaucerian satire, as being in league with the lowest kinds of media entertainment. But an advance in control is shown in the initial narrative with its parody of "The Song of Songs" and its blasphemous shades of *Jesus Christ, Superstar*. It is ironically when he overcomes his absorption with Nessa by becoming her, or expressing the woman's viewpoint, that Durcan is most authentic, as in **"The Haulier's Wife"**, as previously in **"The Daughter Finds her Father Dead"**, as in **"Raymond of the Rooftops"** which made me laugh more than I have since Paul Muldoon was last under *my* rooftop. In the Swiftian **"Man Smoking a Cigarette in the Barcelona Métro"** he achieves a universality which Ted Hughes, if not Yeats, would appreciate. (p. 23)

Medbh McGuckian, "Bawling across the Hearthrug," in Books and Bookmen, *No. 365, March, 1986, pp. 23-4.*

SEAMUS HEANEY

[What] holds true for the Czechoslovakian [Milan Kundera] applies equally to the case of Paul Durcan whose . . . volume, *The Berlin Wall Café*, deepens his claim to be one of the most original and undaunted imaginations at work in our favor anywhere today.

Poetry, Kundera declared,

> means not just a literary genre; rather it's above all a conception of the world, an attitude towards the world . . . The lyric poet always identifies himself with his feelings. The anti-lyrical attitude consists of the conviction that an infinite distance exists between what one thinks about oneself and what one really is, an infinite distance between feelings and existence, between what things want to be, or believe they are, and what they are.

It is precisely this tension between the lyrical and the anti-lyrical, between intensity and irony, between innocence and fear, that we experience in Paul Durcan's work. . . . There shimmers at the heart of these poems a something which we might call "The Morning Offering Vision," the belief that nothing is trivial and everything is holy and wholly important when offered up and taken in in the spirit of love. The poetry resides in this "attitude to the world." Yet this vision or attitude is constantly threatened by the anti-lyricism of a realist's laughter; the cold blast of self-mockery blows menacingly close to the marshlight of tenderness.

It has been the fate of Durcan's imagination to inhabit this world of hiatus, to tremble on the fulcrum between comedy and self-pity, to be doomed to compensate for need or loss with a hyperactive inventiveness. The longer he writes, the more he closes the gap between a style and a destiny, the more purely he transforms the intimate into the universal. . . .

[While] his poems are enormously popular and highly regarded in Ireland, they have had less notice than they deserve in Britain and the U.S. In fact, it's time some American publisher did a volume of this poet, who, with Paul Muldoon and a number of women, are among the ones who are "changing the game" (to use Lowell's downbeat phrase) in Ireland.

To keep to Kundera terms, we might call *The Berlin Wall Café* a book of laughter and remembering, a book which demonstrates the bearable heaviness of being. There are plenty of the old merry routines here about the crudity of the Irish male and the bully-boys of the Irish hierarchy. There are the hit-and-miss fantasias we have come to look forward to, the great zany odysseys of an Irish everyman into a dream Russia or an actual Acapulco. But behind his chanter music, there is the great drone of a central theme. A marriage breaks, distances intervene, the heart breaks and must heal itself and its distances again, must contain in itself a Jesophat of memories and desires. To say that Durcan's poetry is equal to the task is only to begin to give the book its due praise. What was once necessary writing has become necessary reading.

Seamus Heaney, "Three Irish Poets to Watch," in Irish Literary Supplement, *Vol. 5, No. 1, Spring, 1986, pp. 1, 27.*

Friedrich Dürrenmatt

1921-

Swiss dramatist, novelist, short story writer, scriptwriter, essayist, and critic.

Best known for his play *Der Besuch der alten Dame: Eine Tragische Komödie* (1956; *The Visit: A Tragi-Comedy*), which is considered a classic of contemporary drama, Dürrenmatt is among the most celebrated German-language dramatists to emerge after World War II. Unlike such contemporary playwrights as Albert Camus and Samuel Beckett, Dürrenmatt considers the world neither absurd nor incomprehensible but rather an alternately cruel, grotesque, or paradoxical human stage where existence may assume limited significance. In his seminal dramaturgical manifesto, *Theaterprobleme* (1955; *Problems of the Theatre*), Dürrenmatt illustrates the inappropriateness of tragedy to the modern age, stating that only comedy can adequately depict a planet "about to fold like ours." Although Dürrenmatt rejects Bertolt Brecht's notion that the world may be changed through art, he generally tempers his pessimism with exuberant humor and a nondefeatist attitude. For Dürrenmatt, "the world . . . stands as something monstrous, an enigma of calamity that must be accepted but to which there must be no surrender."

Dürrenmatt grew up in a prestigious intellectual family which included several artists and writers. After studying theology, philosophy, literature, and science at the University of Bern, Dürrenmatt enrolled at the University of Zurich but abandoned his studies to pursue a writing career. In his first, unproduced satirical drama, *Komödie* (1943), Dürrenmatt establishes his characteristic tragicomic approach to theater. In his morality plays *Es steht geschrieben* (1947; *It Is Written*) and *Der Blinde* (1948; *The Blind Man*), he purposely animates historical and religious events with two-dimensional characters who function as vehicles for his rhetorical concerns. Although both plays are overtly polemical and regarded as imperfect in form, they serve to reveal Dürrenmatt's debt to such influences as the Viennese folk theater of Johann Nestroy, the expressionist drama of Brecht, and the representational works of Frank Wedekind and Thornton Wilder. Dürrenmatt achieved his own style and tone with his first important play, *Romulus der Grosse: Eine Ungeschichtliche historische Komödie in vier Akten* (1949; *Romulus the Great*), a satire based on the Teutonic attack on Rome in 476 A.D. Described by Dürrenmatt as an "un-historical historical comedy," the play depicts the last Roman emperor as a chicken enthusiast who, despairing of the force necessary for retaining rule, deliberately allows his empire to fall. According to H. F. Garten, Romulus is among the first of Dürrenmatt's many heroes who "refute the absurdity of the world by accepting it."

Dürrenmatt established his international reputation with *Die Ehe des Herrn Mississippi* (1952; *The Marriage of Mr. Mississippi*), a surrealistic play in which an upper-class couple who have killed their respective spouses unite to inflict "absolute justice" on the rest of humanity. Such a system of rigorous ideals is revealed to be futile as the protagonists discover that "everything can be changed, except man." *Ein Engel kommt nach Babylon: Eine Fragmentarische Komödie in drei Akten* (1954; *An Angel Comes to Babylon*) is a morality

play about the impossibility of selfless love in a material world. In this religious parable, an angel sends a righteous young girl on a mission to love the world's most abased beggar, but love turns to chaos when a selfish king takes the beggar's place and discovers that he must choose between the girl and his kingdom. The drama received praise for Dürrenmatt's use of complex theatrical devices and secured his popularity in Europe.

Dürrenmatt received the New York Drama Critics Circle Award in 1959 for *The Visit*, which Max Frisch deemed "the greatest play in the German language since Brecht." The drama revolves around Claire Zachanassian, a rich old woman who returns to her impoverished native village and offers one million dollars to the villagers in return for the death of Alfred Ill, who years earlier had falsely denied responsibility for Claire's pregnancy. Although the villagers profess righteous indignation, they eventually defend their murder of Ill by claiming to "serve justice." *The Visit* prompted diverse critical interpretations; most disagreement centered on the question of whether Ill atones for his crime against Claire and attains heroic stature by accepting his sentence of death, or whether he becomes an absurd figure, since his death fails to significantly alter the inhumanity of the villagers. Dürrenmatt again received international praise for *Die Physiker* (1962; *The Physicists*). Set in a mental asylum, the drama centers on a scientist who feigns insanity to conceal his "discovery of universal value," which he believes humanity incapable of managing. Because of his exclusivism and his distrust of mankind, however, his discovery is usurped by an insane psychiatrist who plots world domination.

Dürrenmatt largely ceased writing dramas in the late 1950s, choosing to devote himself instead to adaptations of existing plays. Most of these works are considered less accomplished than his earlier plays. *Frank der Fünfte, Oper einer Privatbank* (1958), in which an industrious son murders his father, a corrupt banker, in the interest of restoring his bank's reputation, is a musical parody recalling Brecht's *Threepenny Opera. Die Wiedertäufer* (1967), an epic which was also compared to Brecht's work, is essentially a revised version of *It Is Written. Play Strindberg* (1969; *Play Strindberg: The Dance of Death Choreographed*) is an oppositional adaptation of August Strindberg's *Dance of Death* and Dürrenmatt's best-received adaptation. The new version functions, according to Dürrenmatt, as an "attempt to clarify Strindberg's theatrical vision to a modern audience" by transposing the subtle conflicts of Strindberg's bourgeois marriage tragedy into a twelve-round boxing match. *König Johann* (1969; *King John*) and *Titus Andronicus: Eine Komödie nach Shakespeare* (1969; *Titus Andronicus*) are among Dürrenmatt's other adaptations. Dürrenmatt's later plays include *Porträt eines Planeten* (1971; *Portrait of a Planet*), *Der Mitmacher* (1973), and *Die Frist* (1977). Most critics concur that these works do not attain the stature of Dürrenmatt's best dramas.

Early in his career, Dürrenmatt wrote short stories and brief prose sketches in the tradition of Franz Kafka, many of which were collected in *Die Stadt: Prosa I-IV* (1952). Dürrenmatt soon gained a reputation as the first German-speaking detective novelist to achieve international recognition. Gary Giddins described Dürrenmatt's novels as "dreams, hallucinations in which the demarcation between good and evil is constantly threatened by chance and obsession." *Der Richter und Sein Henker* (1952; *The Judge and His Hangman*) features the ambiguous Komissär Bärlach, who attempts in his experiments with evil to catch a murderer. In the book's sequel, *Der Verdacht* (1953; *The Quarry*), Dürrenmatt reverses the conventional mystery formula, making use of predictable conclusions, intellectual discourse, and other antinarrative elements. Although the novel disappointed mystery readers, critics maintained that its relative value depends upon whether it is considered a mystery novel or a scholarly tract. A similar dualism characterizes *Das Versprechen Requiem auf den Kriminalroman* (1957; *The Pledge*), an allegorical novel which parodies nineteenth-century detective stories by focusing on a brilliant detective who fails to solve a murder and goes insane. Chance and accident are determinants of human fate in *Grieche sucht Griechen* (1958; *Once A Greek . . .*), a light satirical novel based on the myth of Cinderella. In this book, a naive clerk rises to inexplicable success through marriage to a beautiful woman who, unbeknownst to him, has bestowed her sexual favors on his country's major political figures.

Dürrenmatt has also served as theater critic for the weekly Zurich newspaper *Die Weltwoche*. He has written many scripts for radio, including *Herkules und der Stall des Augias* (1954; *Hercules and the Augean Stables*), *Das Unternehmen der Wega: Ein Hörspiel* (1955; *Operation Wega*), and *Abenstunde im Spätherbst: Ein Hörspiel* (1959; *An Evening in Late Fall*). Among Dürrenmatt's best-known nonfiction works is *Theater, Schriften, und Reden* (1966), a collection of essays and speeches on theater craft.

(See also *CLC*, Vols. 1, 4, 8, 11, 15 and *Contemporary Authors*, Vols. 17-20, rev. ed.)

ARTHUR DARACK

[Duerrenmatt] has produced a series of comic plays and detective stories where the crime is major (murder), the criminal minor (all of us), the solution either absurd or, what is worse, rational. Chance or accident, he implies, is one of the chief initiating factors in human affairs—this with the authority of Aristotle and other comic metaphysicians who . . . attempt a logical exposition of what they have just defined as illogical.

Tragedy, Duerrenmatt has said, is impossible in the atomic age, and the writer must use comedy to reveal the tragic condition of man. This apparently paradoxical esthetic is no more mystifying than Sartre's *No Exit*, which in fact exemplifies it. Does this make Duerrenmatt an Existentialist? No. He is a kind of moral logician writing plays and novels. The novels, of which *Once a Greek. . .* is the latest, are not so well known as the play *The Visit*, in which revenge for an ancient wrong is a sardonic sonata played savagely. . . .

In *Traps* Duerrenmatt turned an intellectual game, in which justice is examined, into a grisly conclusion; and in *The Pledge* he began to see the limitations of moral argument presented as mystery. To be sure, the mystery thriller with its format of clue and implication seems close to moral argument with its logical parade of data, development, and conclusion. It may be rejoined that sexual promiscuity, in part the theme of *Once a Greek. . .*, is close in biological programming to sacred matrimony; but it cannot on that count alone receive holy sanction. That is because bizarre details, however realistically they may be urged upon us, do not determine the form of an act, but only its outward trappings. The detective thriller, like the promiscuous adventure, trades on what is exotic, unexpected—in a word, accidental. . . .

Duerrenmatt tried nobly in *The Pledge* to rescue the thriller as moral agent; he failed, and produced another engaging murder story with heady overtones. He then switched to satiric farce for *Once a Greek. . .*, thus suggesting that his comic-play technique . . . is equally applicable to the novel.

Once a Greek. . . is a novel from which every serious consideration has been removed except the point, which is, as in the past, the assertion that chance plays sardonic tricks on us. The best will in the world, though informed by morality, justice, economy, and industry, all geared to what is predictable, cannot triumph over what is not. The importance of this message, in an age of totalitarian dedication, cannot be over-estimated.

The book tells a story of a clerk, raised to exalted status because he blundered into a projected marriage to the most famous courtesan in the country. Chloé has dispensed her favors to the chief of state, the leading industrialist, bishop, etc., all of which gentlemen are now anxious to be rid of her for reasons that are never made clear.

Chloé possesses every allure and every vice; Archilochos, the clerk, has every common virtue—thrift, continence, sobriety, industry. Duerrenmatt, like every male writer worth his salt, will reverse the historic injustice that considers great feminine allure and its enjoyment a vice, and masculine stuffiness a virtue. Every male reader will cheer Duerrenmatt on; every female will be puzzled at his failure. If a woman is so desirable, a man ought to find reasons and a morality to justify access to her; if he cannot, he is the worst of failures—the moralist whose principles stand in the way of natural law.

The comic situations made inevitable by this familiar juxtaposition are varied, spasmodic, and unpredictable. They are exactly the reverse of the prim logic of Duerrenmatt's detective novels. They are also more entertaining.

Chloé, the classic Greek temptress, having exposed the hypocritical structure of modern society—Communist or capitalist—by means of her great physical beauty and powerful seductions, decides to chuck it all for the simple, good life. She will marry a true son of Greece and live happily ever after.

The monumental scorn implicit in this situation is treated whimsically; the humor also entails incidents in which slapstick, as well as high and low comedy, is conspicuous. Archilochos is slightly reminiscent of Dorcon in the Daphnis and Chloé legend; in other words, he is oafish. Duerrenmatt does not worry very much about the niceties of character development. He shifts his man from servile clerk to personage of power in the manner of Molière and the old Italian playwrights.

Satiric farce offers the widest latitude: it can be poetic, as with Molière; scathing, as in the case of Sheridan; highly polished and glittering, as with Wilde. Duerrenmatt steers a safe, effective middle course. The result is a play disguised as a novel, amusing and easy to read.

> *Arthur Darack, "An Accident of Life," in* Saturday
> Review, *Vol. XLVIII, No. 29, July 17, 1965, p. 36.*

SANDRA SCHMIDT

For Friedrich Dürrenmatt the pins that hold the universe together are hidden behind the commonest folds of life, within the least affirmation or denial of action, and the smallest trace of innocence or too much knowledge is sufficient to dislodge them. Dürrenmatt is a poet of horror. Catastrophe, super-reality encroach upon and swallow the ordinary with no more warning than the hand-sized shadow of a cloud on a far snowfield. Everything moves at nightmare pace, by jerks, slowly and painfully or with runaway speed. Everything happens with a hard, sharp clarity that makes horror seem matter-of-fact and inevitable. . . .

[*Once a Greek* centers upon] innocent, middle-aged Archilochos. When he meets the beautiful Greek girl who answers his ad for a wife, it seems natural that the sun should immediately shine, that the mayor, the banker, even the president should suddenly say hello to him in the street, that he should be promoted from Assistant Bookkeeper to Director in charge of Obstetrical Forceps and Atomic Cannon, that he should mysteriously own a small castle and a small fortune.

It is only at his wedding that the final pin of his innocence gives way—but then, . . . Archilochos must make the decision that is the culmination of the experience of all Dürrenmatt's characters. Can he accept the flawed love, the mixed motives, the cracked nature of his universe—because it is all the universe he has? Has he the strength to compromise, to give love, to live? And can he survive the national events that his actions have set in motion? . . .

Dürrenmatt has, in [*Once a Greek*], written a movie script. In his plays, peripheral events reflect the emotional quality of the main action. Distant revolutions intensify immediate inner rebellions. Tigers move through the streets as the beast in human beings struggles with its bonds. Here, impossible on the stage, Dürrenmatt has bent the weather to his will. As the sun shines, or icicles form, or fog drifts, you can follow the emotions of the principal characters and the state of Dürrenmatt's peculiar universe in a cinematically sophisticated, highly artistic manner. . . .

Ads for the book have featured exclamation-starred quotes hailing *Once a Greek* as a brilliant satire of something or other. Satire is beside the point. The publishing and entertainment worlds are awash with satires, and highly salable they are, too. But *Once a Greek* is a much more important contribution, an addition to a body of work—that achievement belonging only to artists who have something of import and significance to say.

> *Sandra Schmidt, "Dürrenmatt's Hidden Pins," in*
> The Christian Science Monitor, *July 22, 1965, p. 11.*

THE TIMES LITERARY SUPPLEMENT

[*Once a Greek . . .*, a "prose comedy", as Dürrenmatt] called it, is more closely related to his dramatic works than his other novels. Like his play *The Visit . . .* , *Once a Greek . . .* is a semi-realistic fable about the contemporary world; like it also, it is drily funny, grotesque in parts, and grimly satirical throughout. Yet it is neither wholly "absurd" nor nihilistic. The alternative endings of the original version, of which the more conventionally "happy" one has been adopted here, suggest an admirable reluctance on the author's part to drive home a single moral; and this reluctance points to one of Herr Dürrenmatt's outstanding virtues. One of the limitations inherent in the moral fable is that it is apt to become schematic, allowing little scope either for invention or for fantasy. Another is that it tends to reduce characters to types, sacrificing complexity and ambiguity.

Herr Dürrenmatt has avoided the first danger, and the openness of his plot does much to compensate for the lack of psychological depth. True, we are presented with an English couple, the archaeologists Mr. and Mrs. Weeman, who between them say nothing more than "Well" and "Yes"; but the farcical convention that breeds such caricature would have seemed less acceptable in so serious a work if the author had subordinated his imagination to a preconceived moral thesis. As it is, Herr Dürrenmatt's comic zest is beautifully integrated with his grimness as a moralist. Because it is rooted in charity, his sense of fun permits the possibility of a happy ending that has to do with love.

The Greek of the title, Arnolph Archilochos, is the Assistant Bookkeeper of an Assistant Bookkeeper in a large industrial concern. A celibate, teetotaller, non-smoker and vegetarian, he lives in squalid obscurity, sustained by the heroes of his "ethical cosmos". These include the President of the country in which he lives—a country most reminiscent of France, but not necessarily identical with France—[and] the almost mythical owner of the concern that employs him. . . . Together, the eight heroes of [Arnolph's] moral cosmos represent the powers that be, though Number Eight, Arnolph's brother Bibi, with his terrible delinquent family, represent the seamy side of the social order, redeemed in Arnolph's eyes only by his own belief in his sponging brother's fundamental goodness. A complete reversal in the hero's status and values occurs when he advertises for a marriage partner, another Greek. It is only after the marriage ceremony that he discovers why all the heroes of his moral cosmos step down from their pedestals to accept him as their equal or superior; all of them had been lovers of his wife, the beautiful courtesan Chloé, whom he had believed to be a housemaid. For a time the meek hero turns into a furious avenger. He is almost persuaded to assassinate the President and so lend himself to the designs of the revolutionary Fahrcks. . . . As in other works by Herr Dürrenmatt, the arts are not excluded from his devastating satire. Petit-Paysan, the tycoon, reads Hölderlin, and the great painter Passap, one of Arnolph's heroes, provides some of the most hilarious episodes in the book.

Arnolph's disillusionment makes him wiser, but not more cynical. Whether he returns to his former status and way of life, in a garret adjoining the w.c.s in Mme. Bieler's establishment, or goes off with Chloé to Greece to unearth a statue of Aphrodite, we can be sure that his modesty and kindness are unimpaired. The tale stops short of nihilism because Friedrich Dürrenmatt believes in the virtues of ordinariness. All the values by which ordinary people live may be so much cant, but in his creator's eyes Arnolph is a true hero. Herr Dürrenmatt's choice of a medium that permits only rudimentary characterization is no accident; like other Swiss writers before him, he is profoundly suspicious of the pretensions that go with highly developed individuality and with individualism. . . . Herr Dürrenmatt's modernity—his drastic and sometimes savage exposure of false values, or his readiness to let satire proceed well beyond the limits of the real or plausible—owes very little to the fashionable cult of absurdity, much more to the traditional moral preoccupations of Swiss writers. This is more apparent in the demotic quality of Herr Dürrenmatt's German than in translation.

"At the Housemaid's Knee," in The Times Literary Supplement, *No. 3358, July 14, 1966, p. 609.*

SAAD ELKHADEM

[Dürrenmatt's] first mystery novel *Der Richter und sein Henker (The Judge and his Hangman,* written in 1950) is undoubtedly one of the most exciting and entertaining novels in German literature. Its popularity is based mainly on its gripping incidents and breath-taking plot. From a narrative point of view, this pure event-novel testifies to the remarkable talent of Dürrenmatt as an imaginative fabulist and beguiling storyteller. Throughout this novel, Dürrenmatt never loosens his grip on the narrative strings or permits real moral questions and serious philosophical issues to slink into the story and obstruct the unfolding of the plot.

Dürrenmatt's by now well-known anti-illusionistic devices (such as the presentation of extremely grotesque situations, the inclusion of absurd and implausible events, the portrayal of bizarre characters, and the ample use of ironic, satirical, and sarcastic elements), which play an important role within his dramatic works, are kept here at a minimum. By avoiding the use of his favorite "estrangement effects" as much as possible, and by employing a plain and straightforward style, Dürrenmatt has considerably reduced the literary and artistic merit of his first novel, but has, in return, created a very suspenseful story.

Dürrenmatt's third novel, *Das Versprechen (The Pledge,* written in 1957) which has the subtitle *Requiem auf den Kriminalroman (Requiem for the Mystery Novel),* is also a very exciting one in spite of the author's intention to ridicule the traditional pattern of the nineteenth-century detective story. That his "ge-

nius" protagonist, inspector Matthäi, fails to apprehend the murderer (contrary to what the reader of conventional mystery stories expects) . . . , does not change the fact that Dürrenmatt has succeeded in narrating a very enthralling incident. This success is also due to the absence of serious issues and philosophical questions . . . , and to the terse and lucid style the author employs in relating the events.

Aside from the few ironic and witty remarks made by the author and the narrator from time to time (which deal with the difference between serious poetry and trivial literature, or the discrepancy between the investigation of a crime in fiction and in real life), and except for the grotesque and highly theatrical scene featuring the dying and confessing wife of the murderer, Dürrenmatt has succeeded in controlling his intellectual whims and dramatic impulses and in dedicating all his efforts to the narration of the story. (p. 178)

[Dürrenmatt's second novel, *Der Verdacht*], which also deals with the detection of a crime, differs greatly—intrinsically as well as extrinsically—from his other two works. Because the author reveals the identity of the murderer and unveils the mystery surrounding Dr. Emmenberger and his hospital very early in the game, this novel has been regarded by a few critics as a defective work which ignores the very nature of the mystery novel. While in the *Richter* the identity of the murderer of police lieutenant Ulrich Schmied is kept in the dark till the very last pages, and in *Das Versprechen* the fate of the criminal is disclosed at the end of the book, in *Der Verdacht* the reader is told in the middle of the story that Dr. Emmenberger is the *SS-Folterknecht* (Nazi torturer), exactly as inspector Bärlach—and the reader—has suspected. And this, of course, causes great disappointment for the typical reader of mystery novels. A much more important reason for the reader's dissatisfaction with the *Verdacht* is caused by the novel's relatively high intellectual content as well as by its many anti-illusionistic, and thus anti-narrative, elements.

More than in his other two mystery novels, or, for that matter, more than in any other work by Dürrenmatt, *Der Verdacht* is—especially in its second part—full of sermonizing passages and lengthy ponderous speeches which deal with serious philosophical issues. . . . Dürrenmatt incorporates many satirical remarks on Switzerland, its people, its cities, and its institutions . . . , as well as earnest comments on humanity and the state of the world. For no apparent stylistic or narrative reason does he insert these meditative remarks which—although sharp-witted and penetrating—could not be artistically justified. Also by referring to famous authors, thinkers, and artists, and by alluding to mythological figures and dramatic characters, Dürrenmatt has increased the intellectual substance of his book; but the question now is whether these elements have supported or damaged the intrinsic structure of this "mystery" novel.

If compared with Dürrenmatt's other two mystery novels, *Der Richter und sein Henker* or *Das Versprechen,* the style used in the *Verdacht* is much more sophisticated. The peculiar diction and phraseology of *Der Verdacht,* the rhetorical nature of many passages, and the affluence of controversial issues make this work . . . something that could be read, reread, and always enjoyed. (pp. 178-79)

Of course, for the reader who is interested solely in the unfolding of the plot, these stylistic and philosophical elements would be regarded as "estrangement effects," as obstacles which hinder—or at least slow—the vigorous and continuous narrative flow which he expects to experience when he sees the tag *"Kriminalroman."* This kind of reader not only appreciates suspense and entertainment more than enlightenment and information, but he is also accustomed to certain stereotyped characters rather than to the unpredictable and highly dramatic ones he encounters in *Der Verdacht* (such as the terminally sick but extremely bold protagonist).... These overdimensional characters who would enliven the dullest play, would also blunt the most exciting mystery novel, for they continuously divert the reader's attention from the action.

Mystery stories are usually noted for their adventurous but plausible events; in *Der Richter* as well as in *Das Versprechen,* the plot is very gripping without being unbelievable. In *Der Verdacht,* however, the reader, even by stretching his imagination to the extreme, will not be able to believe that a criminal surgeon like Dr. Emmenberger "who kills out of love"..., could run his hellish sanatorium in the center of a big city undisturbed by the relatives of the murdered rich people and unsuspected by the authorities....

The portrayal of Dr. Emmenberger (a mixture of Raskolnikov and Dr. Faustus), and the many unbelievably gruesome crimes he commits and philosophically justifies, make him the personification of evil rather than a real and convincing character. Also the way the other figures talk, act, and react, shifts this story towards the allegorical, the grotesque, and even the absurd.... [The] reader is not only encouraged, but strongly urged to look for deeper meanings and profounder significance. (p. 180)

All of these elements combine to make *Der Verdacht* less of a mystery story and more of a literary novel. By increasing the intellectual substance and the poetic merit of this book, Dürrenmatt has created a highly sophisticated work of literature instead of a pure adventure story as he had originally intended. *Der Verdacht* is undoubtedly Dürrenmatt's only "mystery" novel which invites serious literary examination and tolerates different philosophical interpretations. But at the same time, and because of this, it is his most labored and tedious story. (p. 181)

> *Saad Elkhadem, "Dürrenmatt's 'Der Verdacht': A Defective Mystery Story or a Sophisticated Novel?"* in The International Fiction Review, *Vol. 4, No. 2, July, 1977, pp. 178-82.*

KENNETH S. WHITTON

Interpretations of [*The Visit of the Old Lady*] range from the conventional: Bänziger's "Probably *the* tragicomedy of our age" or Weber's "A sort of second national drama for the Swiss", through the political: a play about the "secrets of Fascism" (Tolschenova) or Kühne's "judgement on the philistine bourgeoisie", to the Biblical: "A modern presentation of the Passion Play" (Hortenbach) or an illustration of the "victory of grace" (Buri) or of the "principle of moral steadfastness" (Profitlich) to the psychological, economic and political interpretations of Askew, the cheerfully admitted bafflement of a younger critic, Hugo Dittberner, and Murray Peppard's summing-up: "There is no single, simple message or moral in *The Visit,* but rather a powerful action with a wide range of suggestibility". Max Frisch saw it, *tout court,* as "the greatest play in the German language since Brecht", while one of the latest pronouncements is Gerhard Knapp's: "So we can see that the way to over-interpretation leads over rough places, because of an exaggerated love of pre-pigeon-holing". (p. 101)

[In 1957, a group of critics at Basle, Switzerland] decided that the play had been overtreated "from the theological, philosophical and psychological point of view" and that people had forgotten "that the author is writing for the stage": And this must be my point of view, too, since I have been striving to show that Dürrenmatt's concern *at all times* is with the *living,* critical theatre.

The *point de départ* is the sub-title: "A tragic *Komödie*". For the first time, the adjective "tragic" appeared in the title of a Dürrenmatt play, and it is surely no coincidence that his *Problems of the Theatre* was published in 1955, shortly before the première of this play in 1956. (pp. 101-02)

[In *Problems of the Theatre*], Dürrenmatt had compared the tragic and comic modes of writing and had concluded that "pure tragedy" was not compatible with our age.... In this chaotic, disintegrating world, a fate is decided by "bad luck" rather than by "guilt". "Guilt nowadays is a personal achievement only, a religious deed". Tragedy is no longer possible, and "only the *Komödie* can reach us now". (p. 102)

In their discussion of [*The Visit of the Old Lady*], Soergel and Hohoff say that, apart from the conclusion, it is a classical comedy, a statement which begs, of course, a rather large question. Although this view of the work accords more with mine than, say,... the many performances that I have seen of Maurice Valency's [American] "adaptation", I feel that it goes too far. Where producers of the latter sort have failed to note the author's admonition in the *Note:* "Nothing will damage this *Komödie* (which ends tragically) more than deadly seriousness" and have played the work as a pure tragedy, producers of the former brand have treated the play as a too-typical Dürrenmatt *Komödie*. (p. 103)

[Most of Dürrenmatt's earlier plays] were meant to be played as *Komödien,* where the sense of the tragic is nullified by the overriding significance of the elements of the comic in structure, language and characterization. But *The Visit of the Old Lady* is clearly different; where, in the other plays, one was dealing with a *potentially* tragic character in an *actual* comic situation, here we are dealing with an *actual* tragic character in an *actual* comic situation. The examinations of these plays revealed that the main characters were "spiritual clowns" whose laughable fates might evoke sympathy, but certainly not Aristotelian "pity" or "terror". The elements of the comic in the concept of the character and in the situation had removed any sense of the tragic. For this reason, I called the plays *Komödien* rather than "tragicomedies", where there must be a true sense of the tragic present.

H. M. Waidson rightly asserts that "humour in this play... is for the most part demonstrated in the minor characters". There are four such groups: the Teacher and the Parson; the Mayor and the Policeman; Ill's family, and fourthly, the popular (*das Volk*) of Güllen. Although it would appear, at first sight, that these groups could all be classed as "buffoons", whose rôle was simply the creation of a "mood of festivity" and little else..., this is not the case. They are, in fact, an important and essential ingredient of the plot.

These characters are, however, all "impostors"; they possess many of the characteristics of the classical alazon-type; pedantry, pretentiousness, hypocrisy, mendacity, static obtuseness and obsessiveness. The comic here is "reductive", in the Hobbesian sense; it aims at "bringing down", at stripping them of their illusions. But, when we laugh at them, we have here the uneasy feeling that we are laughing at ourselves. (pp. 103-04)

[The] main sources of laughter in the play *are* to be found in these four groups, but they cannot be regarded *simply* as mindless buffoons, as could some of the characters in the earlier plays. Here, I would suggest, they form in fact *one* main antagonist to Ill, a permanent record of Man's inhumanity to Man. This is no *Komödie*. Nevertheless, as these figures lose their humanity and become unthinking stereotypes, they do become clowns whose automatic gestures and responses evoke comic laughter. Jacob Scherer has rightly noted how Dürrenmatt's "attack on our age for its loss of humanity becomes more urgent with each play", and it has seemed to me that this strongly political element in his work can best be illustrated by studying the use he makes of the traditional comic techniques which mercilessly reveal the in- and non-humanity of his chosen characters. (p. 110)

It might be of some use here to interpolate a few of the more provocative interpretations of the play. East German critics have taken the comic in the [minor] characters . . . as a satire on western capitalism. Erich Kühne praises Dürrenmatt for his attack, but suggests that he has missed his target, or, rather, that he has chosen the wrong one: "The weapon of his comedy-based satire does not strike at the major class of imperialistic society but at an intermediate class, the petit bourgeois fellow-travellers and the hangers-on of the monopolistic bourgeoisie . . .". Jürgen Kuczynski, defending Dürrenmatt against another East German, Rainer Kerndl, who had called the play "social criticism, but anti-human", since it was not truly "realistic" in the "socialist" sense, finds the play "a parable of a people who succumbed to fascism until it 'honestly believed in it', of a people who are succumbing today to the psychological warmongering of the imperialists".

Hans-Georg Werner, seeing Dürrenmatt as a "moralist" praises the "accuracy of his attacks on the capitalist social system" and sees the theme of the play as "the corrupting force of money". Maurice Valency, the author of the American "version" agrees. He writes: "The propulsive force of the action is neither external fate . . . nor guilt; it is the power of money—not even money itself only the smell of it, its influence".

Now, all of these are fairly predictable, but they do show, firstly, the reason for Dürrenmatt's popularity in the Eastern bloc countries, and, secondly, the reasons for the suspicions of some of his critics in the west. Here, the play, a masterpiece of the twentieth century by common consent, has been interpreted from an all too narrow "religious" standpoint. The approach is, of course, a valid one, but the vast theses built up on a purely religious argument seem, to me anyway, often wide of the mark. Jenny Hortenbach's attempt, for example, to find Biblical parallels everywhere is [overstated]. . . . The same could be said of M. Askew's psychologically-orientated study which energetically seeks to prove that Ill was a sufferer from the classical castration-complex, that he was a modern Oedipus. A recent study by Ulrich Profitlich perhaps concentrates too much on the "minor" works and he sees Ill as one of that group which is "exempted . . . from comic and ludicrous characteristics" which, as will shortly be seen, is not quite accurate.

Some of these writers seem to me to have overstrained theses (which are useful in themselves), and omitted to relate the work closely enough to the stage—its only and proper medium. Not that the work need lack a "message"—but its meaning lies in the performance on the stage and not in the professional study. It is a dramatic work—not a theological, political or psychological tract—not 'theatre as dissertation', as Dürren-

matt once remarked. This is what Dürrenmatt always has in mind when he speaks on the critics' love of "profundity". "Stick to my flashes of inspiration" he wrote in the *Notes* to **The Visit of the Old Lady**, "and forget about profundity". . . . It seems to me that a performance which emphasized more the elements of the comic . . . and which would ensure the "atmosphere of mad hilarity" which H. P. Guth claimed should appear in a performance . . . , would not only please the author, but would also deepen the play's significance by creating that "new sublime incongruity" of which Wilson Knight wrote . . . , and which is the peculiar merit of this "tragic comedy". (pp. 110-12)

It would seem at first sight that Alfred Ill was to be one of our "spiritual clowns"; when Claire arrives, he seems ready to deceive himself into thinking that she will be as susceptible to his charms as she was 45 years before. . . . As has been seen, one of the attributes of the comic character is his proneness to be perpetually deceived. It is clear, however, that Ill has a feeling of guilt from the outset, for the opening scene shows a petty bourgeois with a conscience; the bribe of the next Mayorship hangs heavy over Ill's head, making him a party to the hypocrisy of his fellow-citizens. (p. 112)

Jacob Steiner has written that "the tragic hero need become laughable only once—and he is finished as a tragic hero". There would seem to be no "heroic" in this self-pitying little man. Part of the comic here lies in the grim incongruity of Claire's teleological comments on Alfred's statements of despair. He claims that he married Mathilde for Claire's sake: "She had money", Claire answers. The future belonged to Claire, so Alfred renounced his future for her: "And now the future is here", says Claire. Alfred has lived in a hell since Claire left him: "And I've become Hell itself," is Claire's frightening answer. . . . (pp. 112-13)

When Claire says that she will not abandon him, Alfred is "fooled" and the deception is comically symbolized by the "false" bird-calls of the "unnatural" people of Güllen and by his discovery of her artificial limbs!

But—do we laugh here? Perhaps. . . . Claire's external appearance, her grotesque false limbs, are all grotesquely comic; her incongruous, often illogical ("absurd") answers are comic—but the two characters, the one ridiculous in his hypocritical self-pity, the other mysteriously paradoxical, are diffused with an emotion which is patently *un*-comic and which "freezes" our laughter.

Alfred is a comic character up to the banquet scene: ". . . Klara has a golden sense of laughter! These jokes'll kill me!", he says innocently. . . . [Claire soon announces]: "A milliard for Güllen if someone will kill Alfred Ill". . . . From that point on, Alfred Ill ceases to be a comic character. Some, the Mayor, the Policeman, Ill's family, the people of Güllen, become more ridiculous, others, the Teacher, the Parson, the Doctor, less so, but they all still serve as sources of comic laughter. Alfred detaches himself from them; by going his own way, he ceases to be the generalized "typed" character of the comedy and becomes an individual, a "human being". (p. 113)

Calvinistically conscious of his own guilt, [Ill] must now wrestle with his conscience like the tragic hero of old. The whole point of Act II is to make Ill aware of his guilt and the comic situation throws Ill's agony into high relief. (pp. 113-14)

In Act III, the people become more inhuman and likewise more comical; on the other hand, Ill attains a true humanity by accepting the burden of his guilt: "I've made Klara what she is and me what I am, a dirty, big-headed shopkeeper".... Later, to the Mayor, who has tried to make him commit suicide, Ill says: "But now I have made my decision, conquered my fear . . . I shall submit to your verdict, whatever it may be. For me it is justice—what it is for you, I do not know" . . . , for, to commit suicide, would be to avoid the consequences of his guilt and (incidentally) would remove the guilt for his death from Güllen.

This is what makes the village meeting comically ironical for the audience. It knows that all that is being said and done is ambiguous—the people of Güllen swear to stamp out injustice because they cannot tolerate a crime in their midst and so on— but we know that this very vow implies a crime. Only Ill's dramatic and parodistic cry: "My God!"—his horror at the hypocritical inhumanity of the proceedings—is genuine. . . . (p. 114)

Does Ill die a tragic death? Hans Mayer thinks not: "The vast nexus of relationships between the Old Lady and the town of Güllen did not allow the normal play between guilt and repentance. . . ." Jan Knopf, on the other hand, has no doubt that the *end* is tragic: "And in the analysis of what has gone before, Ill's guilt is gradually revealed. He atones by his death, by the tragic conclusion".

The importance of this death for my study is whether it nullifies the effect of the various comic elements which have been examined. Where is the weight to be laid? On Ill's "tragic" death—or on the comic situation? Is the play a *Komödie*, is it a tragedy in the guise of a tragicomedy, or is it an actual tragicomedy as, say, Karl Guthke has defined the genre? Is a "tragic *Komödie*" in Dürrenmatt's terminology something quite different? Are the comic elements to be treated simply as "comic relief", or do they in fact help to create Wilson Knight's "new sublime incongruity"? . . .

Dürrenmatt's portrayal of the character of Claire Zachanassian will help us to answer these questions. . . .

I am unhappy with those attempts to table all of Dürrenmatt's comic elements under the heading of "grotesque", however defined. I do not deny the presence of the grotesque in his work, of course, but I believe that much of what has been termed grotesque is, in fact, only a dramatization, a sensationalization, an exaggeration of the comic. The grotesque is indeed in danger of becoming what Dürrenmatt said the absurd was: a superficial catch-phrase.

My own view is that the grotesque should show three major traits:

    a) an ugly "deformation",
    b) a dark and ludicrous comic,
    c) the demonic or fearsome.

(p. 115)

In the figures of Claire and her retinue, and in the nature of her impediments, one must acknowledge the presence of the true grotesque. Our laughter is not only uneasy, it is often "frozen" when we have had time to consider the retinue in its entirety. The butler Boby "about 80, with dark glasses"— are these not perhaps *the* grotesque symbol of twentieth-century stage, screen and TV?; Boby, after whom, we learn, all Claire's (seven and eventually nine) husbands have been named. Claire possesses him for life since he was the judge at Alfred's successful paternity-suit trial. The duos, the two "Herculean, gum-chewing monsters" who carry her sedan-chair and who are

acquitted murderers, and "two little fat old men with gentle voices", the castrated witnesses bribed by Ill to swear that they were "the father" of Claire's child. The underlying demonic makes the normally merely "comic" multiplication (of husbands) and "automatism" (of the eunuchs) grotesque. (pp. 115-16)

From her first action, the unheard-of stopping of a train in Güllen, it is made clear to us that Claire is not of this world. She is the stranger "from outside", certainly, but she is no *alazon*, although she is, like most of these characters that we have studied, "inhuman" and, like them too, she sets the action in motion. Their "inhumanity", however, is figurative and usually makes them ridiculous. Claire's is literal and it makes her fearsome and awe-inspiring. (p. 116)

To return then to our question: Was Ill's death tragic? Is the play a tragedy rather than a "tragic comedy"? Claire's words to the Teacher may answer the first question: If he had really wanted to better Güllen with Claire's money, then his true humanity would not have permitted him to take part in the execution. Since he did take part in it, the money was a bribe and his humanity (the humanity of traditional culture, of "Goethe and Brahms", be it remembered), a sham. Claire shows him that her money meant nothing to her—she wants *revenge* only. By "stringing along with her", Güllen executes Alfred Ill for the money alone. His death is therefore no Grecian tragedy; it becomes death by executioner (he is clearly strangled by the gymnast) in surroundings of hypocritical rôle-playing. The Doctor diagnoses "heart failure", the Mayor says "Death from joy" and the whole event takes place—on a stage. But it is no "comic death" either, unlike the death of the characters in, say [*The Marriage of Mr. Mississippi*]. Alfred does not come back to life.

Further, the parodistic Sophoclean ode to a dehumanized economic boom which closes the work shows clearly that Alfred's life has been what George Steiner might have called "an allegory of pure waste", rather than a tragedy. The two choruses, in evening-dress in the middle of their rebuilt town, a universal "Happy Ending", sing finally the joys of prosperity. There is no remorse, no sense of guilt. They (like Frisch's *Biedermann* chorus) have learned nothing. . . .

Yet Alfred Ill *has* risen once to the greatness of the tragic hero, this was his "personal achievement"; his fate was brought about, not by Chance, but by *hamartia,* that "great error on his part", as Aristotle put it in *The Poetics,* an error which he sought to correct. The "lost world order", lost, as was noted, when Claire's arrival suspended the natural laws, is restored to him when he refuses the Mayor's suggestion to commit suicide and decides to face the judgement of Güllen. It is however restored to *him*, the "individual", the only citizen willing to accept the responsibility for his actions as a human being—to stand up and say: NO! Nothing has been changed with his death and nothing will change or can change until, as the drunken "half-human" Teacher tells the people of Güllen, an "Old Lady" comes to *them*. As has been noted, *The Visit* is one of Dürrenmatt's answers to Brecht's maxim about the changeability of the world.

Such fates are warnings; they do not necessarily depict what has happened, but what might happen if mankind continues to deny Freedom to Man. (p. 118)

"The actual tragic character in the actual comic situation", of which I wrote earlier, seems to me to be a workable working definition for modern tragicomedy. Dürrenmatt's earlier plays postulated a potentially tragic character who was finally prevented from taking the step which would have made his fate a tragic one. The comic situation is common to both types. That type of play can therefore be called a *Komödie* since the tragic is not "realised". The comic remains comic, the "darkness" is only a shadow and is never truly threatening as it is in *The Visit of the Old Lady*. (pp. 119-20)

Out of all the characters created by Dürrenmatt, [Ill] is still the one who most nearly makes a tragedy out of the comedy. (p. 120)

Kenneth S. Whitton, "The Masterpiece," in his The Theatre of Friedrich Dürrenmatt: A Study in the Possibility of Freedom, *Oswald Wolff, 1980, pp. 101-23.*

ENOCH BRATER

Play Strindberg is in many ways a unique work of contemporary theater, but it is that much more in terms of design than of execution. For in this play Dürrenmatt has succeeded in elevating a production concept into a literary genre of its own. "I directed it as I wrote it," he observed recently. "Theater is a composition; it takes place in time. Theater is a practical affair; you can't do it without others. You can't do it by yourself." An act of interpretation becomes in Dürrenmatt's hands an act of sheer invention. [August Strindberg's] *The Dance of Death* is the raw material for the new creative process or, to use the playwright's own words, "The dramaturgy of existing materials is replaced by the dramaturgy of invented materials." Let us review for a moment the special circumstances which led to the writing of this play. Dürrenmatt turned his attention to Strindberg in 1968, when he . . . planned a revival of *The Dance of Death*. But the plan misfired. "We played it," said Dürrenmatt, "and the actors protested and were all very depressed. So I said, "'I'll do it for you' and wrote it straightaway. . . . It was as with [*King John*]," referring to his earlier adaptation of Shakespeare's *King John*, "practical theatre." In production, moreover, the practical elements became even more basic than Dürrenmatt's comments imply, for the cast took an active part in revising the script. Incorporating improvisational techniques, a major portion of the work was done during rehearsals. *Play Strindberg* is, then, an elaborate exercise in collaboration, not only with Dürrenmatt's source material, but perhaps even more significantly with his actors. Here is a piece of theater written *with* actors, not *for* them, offering us a "tight total structure with an improvising, cabaret-like tone." Dürrenmatt was himself aware of his own literary starting-point, for he stated at the time, "I do not write my plays for the actors any more, I compose my plays with them." (pp. 13-14)

In bringing the classics to modern audiences the Germanic dramaturge-director is the real star of the show. It is not enough to "recreate" the basic structure of the original text; one must enter a dramatic world created by someone else, give it a new twist, and make a statement of one's own. If production, when judged from the point of view of theater in the English-speaking world, runs perilously close to appropriation, so much the better. It allows for spontaneity and vitality. Sometimes it even allows for creativity. This is a director's, not a playwright's theater. In this respect Dürrenmatt has brought off a *coup* in more than mere mechanistic terms: the making of *Play Strindberg* takes production out of the director's hands and gives it back where it more properly belongs, to the playwright. Or in any case it brings that much neglected playwright back into

the arena—no pun intended. Seen in this light, Dürrenmatt's accomplishment in *Play Strindberg* is not nearly so radical as it initially appears to be. Combining the dual roles of director and dramaturge and then superseding them, Dürrenmatt in *Play Strindberg* returns to his primary vocation as a writer for the stage. The road he travels critically determines the turn his drama now takes. And in his "anti-Strindberg" play the turn Dürrenmatt takes is the "worst possible one"—towards comedy.

To accomplish this goal it becomes necessary for Dürrenmatt to ride roughshod over his fellow playwright August Strindberg. The results are hilarious. Yet comedy in *Play Strindberg* is the direct result of staging. Concept is made concrete; period characters in period costumes collide with comic precision in a decidedly un-period setting, a boxing-ring. Married life is hell, but on stage the end-game can be made bearable by dividing it into twelve rounds announced in advance by the characters and beginning and ending with a gong. Tonight we improvise: this is Dürrenmatt playing with Strindberg, Pirandello, Brecht, and Beckett all at once. Dürrenmatt's non-naturalistic set is a flamboyant flight of fancy, a sustained doodle which makes the façade of *The Dance of Death* fall down like Alice's house of cards. (pp. 14-15)

For this exercise in theatrical decomposition Dürrenmatt has constructed an ingenious simultaneous set. Before the actors enter the ring at the sound of a gong, they wait for their cues on the benches in full sight of the audience. Once they have been blocked on Dürrenmatt's simultaneous set, moreover, these players are fated to have no exit. As the three characters in search of an author combine and recombine into a series of combative duets, the third member of the triangle, a momentary odd-man-out, is visibly waiting in the wings regaining his composure or silently recalling his next lines. . . . Dürrenmatt enforces a strict minimalism to displace Strindberg's fourth-wall illusionism. Only the most necessary props are employed, and when they are used, the actors carry them onto the "set" themselves. No extras are allowed to get in the way of these three principals; this is, after all, a play for actors. The effectiveness of this set, however, creates its impact only because the audience has come to the theater expecting to see something else. . . . [Strindberg's original stage] elements are gone, but they are certainly not forgotten. The sensationalism of Dürrenmatt's set relies on their absence. Everything we do not see is simultaneously there in our mind's eye. For Dürrenmatt has been counting on us to fill in the missing gaps. And when we do so, the frank theatricalism of his own minimalist staging becomes even more striking.

Set design is then the principal means through which Dürrenmatt establishes a dramatic tension between Strindberg's original and the radical features of his new hybrid form. This conflict will be heightened even further when actors are blocked on these boards. In the boxing arena each player's moves are precisely charted on a narrowly circumscribed space. This is not a room, but a small circle full of sharp light. The possibilities for movement, compared to the style of naturalistic interpretation, are therefore limited. When an actor fades out of the arena, he does so only to enter the lesser light of the make-believe "offstage" bleachers. Here his muscles relax and he is free to breathe more naturally—or we should say more naturalistically. (pp. 15-16)

Once back in the arena his body movement as well as his pacing are again subject to severe restriction. He must play Strindberg. And as he does so he is literally trapped in a closeted drama from which there is no escape until the gong releases him once more. In this way Dürrenmatt's tightly constructed one-act play orchestrates a pattern of tension alternating with brief periods of relaxation. But in this play no one relaxes for long—least of all, the audience. For Dürrenmatt's strategy of twelve rounds has implicated us in its action and involved us in a conflict of our own. Against the panorama of Dürrenmatt's spectacle we are staging in our own minds a separate but certainly more traditional production of *The Dance of Death*. . . . Frustrated in our activity, we are before long taking the arena-like action we see in the spotlights for the "real" *Dance of Death*. But duration is never permitted to evoke the luxury of familiarity. . . . We too find ourselves trapped; the joke has suddenly turned on us. Just when we thought we were watching an eccentric but nonetheless stimulating interpretation of *The Dance of Death*, we are jolted into recognition that before our eyes something quite different has been taking its course.

Language, too, pinpoints the same conflict. Each "round" in *Play Strindberg* develops the rhythm of those same "little canters" we normally associate with *Waiting for Godot*. . . . Beckett's "little canters" are here, but these characters have long ago given up on waiting for Godot—or anything else for that matter. Every "little canter" will end not in uncertainty, but in negation. Before almost every pause a negative statement will undermine the integrity of what has been said before. This language, we suspect, will end in a draw.

In *Play Strindberg* characters use language in the same way it has been designed to function in Pinter's plays: to put one another in checkmate. From one verbal fencing match to the next, each can claim some modest success. . . . At the end of each round, however, every runner stumbles. No referee calls out the name of a winner. Language as used by this threesome has been a highly inefficient weapon. Its structures take them nowhere. Reducing the scope of emotions it encompassed in *The Dance of Death*, the range of language in *Play Strindberg* is as circular as the limited space of a boxing ring. . . . "What is there to keep me here," asks Beckett's Clov [in *Waiting for Godot*]. "The dialogue," quips Hamm. But in Dürrenmatt's boxing arena the dialogue is, as [Hugo Leber] called it, a "word ping-pong" which takes the characters back to where they began. Repetitions make a line, at first uttered in earnest, a joke. "We'll say no more about it," Edgar will say to Kurt. . . . But he soon proceeds to do the reverse of what he says. "We'll say no more about it" therefore becomes a litany which cues the audience in to his intention of saying everything he says he is not going to say. (pp. 16-19)

What makes Dürrenmatt's language work so well in *Play Strindberg* is everything that has been left out of it. For dialogue in this play has been subjected to the same process of cancellation and omission we have already discussed as a particular virtue of the set. Restricted language on a minimalist set makes us yearn all the more for Strindberg's selective expressionist mode, where syncopated variations of pace and rhythm reveal in performance a method of distributing event and reaction within the fabric of the dialogue itself. In *Play Strindberg* what you hear is what you get. But what you don't get in this truncated language makes you remember all the more the tragicomic eloquence of Strindberg's haunting lines.

Losses, however, are not necessarily without accompanying gains. This is especially true of Dürrenmatt's distortion of Strindberg's diction, for it is precisely this shift in accent which establishes in its cumulative effects what amounts to an entirely new play. What is at stake here is something more than a

relaxed view of *The Dance of Death*: it is, in fact, the whole methodology of theatrical adaptation. Dürrenmatt's playing with Strindberg makes out of a middle-class tragedy a comedy about middle-class tragedies. But it is successful at doing so only because Dürrenmatt has shifted our attention from content to form. This shift in focus is therefore far more impressive than any of the changes critics might notice as Dürrenmatt's special stamp on the original's scenic details. To be sure, the uncanny stage effects of this rewriting of Strindberg with tragedy as well as tragicomedy in bit parts have been largely responsible for our initial fascination with this piece. (pp. 19-20)

This performance, we realize, is neither straight tragedy nor melodrama, neither comedy nor tragicomedy, but something in between. Our difficulty in identifying the species is precisely the element responsible for the dynamic tempo that unfolds in *Play Strindberg*. As the twelve rounds progress we move back and forth from one possibility to the next, while the drama as a whole moves so fast that it elides any neat system of synchronization. Abandoning any modernist notions of heroes and anti-heroes, the conflict on this stage is no longer restricted to a duel of protagonists and antagonists, but is instead situated dead in the center of the competing levels of theater experience. Is this travesty or parody, adaptation or invention? We never know for sure.

Play Strindberg therefore expands the bag of tricks a clever dramatist might use to generate new conflicts in his theater. An accumulation of styles in a realm prior to resolution yields interesting results in the metaphorical boxing-ring sometimes known as life. But let us bring all of this back to the continuing possibility of theater. For in this arena Dürrenmatt is important in still another sense: after *Play Strindberg*, *The Dance of Death* will never be quite the same again. And although it is usual to think of the impact of *The Dance of Death* on the writing of *Play Strindberg*, we must now consider the effects the new rhythms in *Play Strindberg* will have on subsequent productions of *The Dance of Death*. (p. 23)

The production concept that led Dürrenmatt on the road to invention has, curiously enough, made us rediscover a classic through inversion. This is the oldest rule of the theater game, for the remodeling of Strindberg serves to remind us that every production of every play is in some very basic sense an adaptation. Every play will tell us something more about itself each time it is successfully brought to its real life on the stage. (p. 24)

Enoch Brater, "'Play Strindberg' and the Theater of Adaptation," in Comparative Drama, *Vol. 16, No. 1, Spring, 1982, pp. 12-25.*

GARY GIDDINS

Duerrenmatt's novels are dreams, fairy-tales, hallucinations in which the demarcation between good and evil is constantly threatened by chance and obsession. They are filled with magical numbers and reversals, with details that shimmer. The world is out of whack and nothing is what it seems—not even epiphany, not even metaphor. At the sight of a child's raped and dismembered body, townspeople stand silently while "from the lashing trees great raindrops continued to fall, glittering like diamonds." Good men attempt to stem the tide of villainy, ruminating ponderously on the human condition, but much of the talk is blather; guilt lurks everywhere and honor is up for grabs. What better modus operandi for Duerrenmatt's purposes than the detective novel, a spreadsheet of facts and assumptions? All of his novels except *Once a Greek*. . . are thrillers, and even that satire on morals and cultural identity moves at a thriller's pace. They are set in European cities and villages cornered by postwar temptations: the absolute evil of the Nazi past, the blandishments of American consumer goods, and the assurances of revolution. Like his plays, Duerrenmatt's fiction asks the big questions but idles uneasily over the answers.

[*The Judge and His Hangman*] introduced Duerrenmatt's Police Commissioner Barlach, the first of those monsters whose attitude toward good and evil is based entirely on caprice. To snare the devil, Barlach will be the devil. He is a patient in the more fantastically conceived *The Quarry* . . . , submitting himself to torture in his determination to track down a Dr. Mengele-type war criminal who he believes is running a chic sanatorium. His aides are a giant Jew named Gulliver and a killer dwarf. In *Once a Greek*. . . , Duerrenmatt's most flippantly satirical and least known book, Cinderella is the source of a fable about a dim middle-aged patriot and virgin who advertises for a bride. He is promptly engaged to a fabulously wealthy and beautiful courtesan—a prototype of Claire in *The Visit*—and dispatched from one mythical land (bureaucratic Europe) to another (the Greece of Aphrodite and Chloe). *Traps* . . . is really a longish short story about a modern Macbeth, a ruthless and superstitious businessman undone by three witches in the garb of ancient, gluttonous ex-members of the bar. The last novel is perhaps his best—*The Pledge* . . . , told in the second-person narrative style Camus used in *The Fall*. A Little Red Riding Hood is brutally murdered on her way to grandmother's house and a tragically scrupulous detective swears by his "soul's salvation" to find the fiend.

Duerrenmatt's obsessions wax with cumulative power in these five novels. Scenes and settings are painted in the broad strokes of folk literature; changes in the weather are like musical accompaniment to the action. He doesn't waste words, though some characters are given to windy preachments; his occasional literary flourishes gleam like silver in these dark woods. Duerrenmatt's precise, conversational prose has been translated with calculating clarity . . . so that his cold irony never fails to balance his infrequent sentimentality. His plots don't make much sense, but then they're not of this world. They are as logical as dreams, and not much longer. . . .

> Gary Giddins, "Save These Books: The Novels of Friedrich Duerrenmatt," in VLS, No. 23, February, 1984, p. 18.

ROBERT P. RENO

[In *The Physicists*, Dürrenmatt addresses the] paradoxical relationship between science and religion to show that these two most distinctive of human endeavors are finally inseparable. Fresh, original, and highly provocative, Dürrenmatt's exploration of the intersection of science and religion is based partly on epistemology and partly on imagination. Epistemologically, *The Physicists* encourages its spectators to remember that science and religion both are ways of knowing; imaginatively, it centers on the role of the Knower, of the one to whom knowledge has been revealed. The play reminds us that, from an epistemological point of view, knowledge is knowledge. It therefore makes little difference whether the Knower calls himself a physicist or a prophet; the important consideration is rather that each holds a special insight that has profound implications for all mankind. From an imaginative perspective, the play challenges us to contemplate the beginning and the end of man's search for knowledge. From whence does knowledge come, and to what does it lead? Dürrenmatt suggests in *The Physicists* that true wisdom begins and ends with the Creator, that all that man knows must be attributed to a God who knows all.

In addition to his particular juxtaposition of science and religion, of physicist and prophet, Dürrenmatt's play also collapses the universal into the particular by insisting that one is invariably implicit in the other. One prophet waking in the night is given a vision for all mankind; one physicist working alone in his cell formulates what Dürrenmatt calls the "Principle of Universal Discovery." . . . Dürrenmatt often treats religious themes, but *The Physicists* is unique in its use of a story about a scientist to examine the concerns of the spirit. Throughout the play, this conflation of science and religion, reinforced by the identification of the universal with the particular, forms the basis of an attack on the exclusivity of knowledge, whether scientific or religious. This attack is launched to advance the thesis that man's only hope for surviving the scientific and technological developments of the twentieth century rests ironically in the ancient biblical plea for openness, sharing, and trust among the people of all nations.

When he was a young student finishing his doctoral dissertation, the protagonist of *The Physicists,* Johann Wilhelm Möbius, suspected he was on the verge of discoveries which could bring about the destruction of humanity. In an attempt to avert this possibility, Möbius pretended to be insane and was soon "clapped into a madhouse," as he puts it. . . . At the opening of the play, he has been a patient at Les Cerisiers for fifteen years, insisting all the while that he is visited by King Solomon. Recently, Möbius has been joined by two other physicists, one of whom claims to be Sir Isaac Newton, and the other Albert Einstein. By the end of the first act, each scientist has "proven" his insanity by committing a murder, the investigations of which introduce the idea of justice and the law.

In the second act, Newton and Einstein reveal that they are really Kilton and Eisler, physicists turned agents who work for competing superpowers, presumably the United States and the Soviet Union. Quite by chance, each had stumbled upon Möbius' dissertation and had been led thereby to suspect his true genius. Each spy has come to Les Cerisiers at the same time with the intention of returning Möbius to the service of his respective government. But Möbius is so convincing in his argument that "today it's the duty of a genius to remain unrecognized" that Kilton and Eisler finally agree to live out their lives in the asylum, "mad but wise . . . prisoners but free . . . physicists but innocent." . . . However, just as their feeling of generous self-sacrifice reaches a crescendo, Mathilde von Zahnd, head psychiatrist and proprietor of Les Cerisiers, announces that she, too, has seen visions of the Golden King. Hit with this reversal, Möbius retreats rapidly to rationalism and [explains his true motives]. . . . But unlike Kilton and Eisler, the Fräulein Doktor is beyond convincing, for she has already begun to exploit Möbius' discoveries in the most Machiavellian manner.

The Physicists thus ends on a somber note. The events that Möbius most feared have come to pass—his knowledge has fallen into the wrong hands, and as Eisler observes, the world has succumbed to the domination of an apparently insane female psychiatrist. . . . To close the play, each physicist reverts to his initial role and intones a brief biography of his assumed character. . . . Möbius no longer claims simply to see King Solomon, but now assumes an absolute identity with this biblical figure. . . . In this somewhat ambiguous conclusion, one point is clear—Möbius realizes at long last that he shares essential characteristics with the ancient king to whom he has so often referred; in a moment of deep insight, he comes to understand that what is true of Solomon is true also of himself.

As a familiar symbol of knowledge and wisdom, King Solomon is essential to *The Physicists* as a constant source of motivation and allusion. . . . Anointed as the third king of Israel, Solomon is so afflicted by a sense of inadequacy that he beseeches the Lord to give him the knowledge he needs to rule his people. . . . God rewards this humble attitude by giving Solomon not only knowledge and wisdom, but riches and power as well. (pp. 70-2)

Scripture makes points about Solomon: first, God is the source of his knowledge, and second, this knowledge is granted with the intention that it be used. These points suggest a covenantal relationship between God and Solomon. . . . When Solomon and Israel later fall on evil times, it is not because knowledge is destructive, but because Solomon no longer requires his people to walk in the way of the Lord. Forgetting his early dependence on God and allowing pride and arrogance to replace his humility, he begins to assume that his knowledge is his own, that he is wise in his own right. His faith destroyed by pride, Solomon is cut off from the source of true knowledge and is forced to rely increasingly on human knowledge.

As the archetype of the Knower, of the one to whom knowledge has been revealed, Solomon has special relevance to Möbius. Through most of *The Physicists,* however, Möbius does not realize that Solomon has any actual significance at all. Instead, he sees him as a device, as merely a convenient method of gaining credibility as a madman. . . . Until his closing speech, Möbius seems to accept all he knows, even the Principle of Universal Discovery, as a matter of course, as the expected consequence of scientific inquiry. . . . Though Möbius may be acting with the best of intentions, his attitude toward knowledge is nevertheless reductive and deadening, for it treats the extraordinary as familiar and the miraculous as mundane. (pp. 72-3)

Möbius' complacent and self-assured attitude is a primary aspect of his identification with Solomon. Though one is a modern scientist and the other an ancient king, Dürrenmatt shows that both believe knowledge to reside in the individual; each believes that he is solely responsible for his knowledge, and each is determined to limit and control what he knows in any way he wishes. But Solomon's story establishes that God is the source of all understanding, and the books of the Old Testament suggest again and again that what God reveals to one person or group, He intends to be shared by all people everywhere. Like Solomon, Möbius has been granted knowledge far beyond that of any other person, but he decides that his great discoveries must never be shared or even suspected. With this decision to keep his knowledge to himself at all costs, Möbius leaves Solomon behind and becomes a type of Jonah, a modern example of the reluctant prophet who will go to any extremes to keep from revealing his knowledge. (pp. 73-4)

[In the Bible], Jonah chooses to board ship and flee the presence of God rather than carry his message to the hated Ninevites. In like manner, Möbius chooses to abandon his family and flee to a madhouse rather than share his knowledge with the rest of humanity. Cast into the sea, Jonah is swallowed by a great fish, therein to endure a harrowing confinement lasting three days and three nights. Similarly, for fifteen years, Möbius "lives for himself," as Dürrenmatt says, "wrapped in the cocoon of his own little world." (p. 74)

[The] Book of Jonah can be taken as a model argument against exclusivism and restrictiveness. . . . The Hebrew Bible shows clearly that Israel was chosen for a task, and that task was nothing less than to carry the knowledge of Yahweh to all mankind. In the familiar words of Isaiah, Israel was to be a light unto all nations. The temptation to shirk this duty . . . was ever present. . . . But every attempt to do so, every decision to restrict the spread of this special and wonderful knowledge, resulted in suffering to Jew and Gentile alike.

With this background, it is easy to see *The Physicists* as a similar protest against exclusivism, in this case intellectual or scientific exclusivism. . . . Whether one's knowledge is labelled as an example of divine inspiration or of scientific genius makes no difference; the force of revelation cannot be bottled up, either in the belly of a fish or in the cell of an insane asylum. . . . Expressed in its simplest form this argument is based on the principle that no man can bear the burden of decision for all mankind. . . . Whether we like it or not, we must have faith in one another, for the conditions of life in this world demand a mutual trust and dependence. (p. 75)

But of course, until the final moments of the play, Möbius understands none of this. . . . He has comprehended to the last, lingering detail the secrets of the physical universe, but he has no understanding at all of the spiritual mysteries of faith, hope, and charity. Because of this spiritual blindness, Möbius is poorly qualified to make this inevitably moral decision that will profoundly affect the lives of all people everywhere. Paradoxically, the same blindness leads him to assume that no one is more highly qualified than he to make such a decision. (p. 76)

No matter how reasonable it may seem for nations to attempt to out-smart their enemies through the careful control of scientific knowledge, *The Physicists* argues that such a policy leads only to disaster. . . . All efforts to keep knowledge hidden invariably require a separation. As time passes, this initial separation hardens into alienation as the Knower is increasingly cut off from his fellowmen, his God, and finally himself. Like Solomon, he is brought low when he is severed from the source of his wisdom; like Jonah, he is washed over by the flood of isolation and despair; like Israel, he is crushed under the burden of the knowledge he refuses to share. (p. 77)

Because twentieth-century science has so often been associated with the weapons of destruction and the economics of oppression, Dürrenmatt's call for the sharing of knowledge may at first seem new, offbeat, and even radical. To the contrary, his plea is completely in accord with the great tradition of the ideal scientific community in which money, politics, and competition have no bearing, but in which cheerful cooperation and universal publication are rendered without exception, and in which the fact of mutual dependence is readily acceded. (pp. 77-8)

While *The Physicists* is about science, it is also about religion, and although it concerns all people everywhere, it also concerns each person in his own particular existence. This concern with the individual is emphasized in the final scene of the play, by the very specific and personal image of Möbius alone on stage repeating over and over ["I am Solomon"]. . . . So focused and intense is this closing scene that some commentators have suggested that Möbius is now mad in good earnest. But a more consistent interpretation argues that he has never seen things more clearly, that he is experiencing not a moment of madness, but a moment of remarkable insight and wisdom. . . . In identifying with King Solomon, Möbius is confessing that he, too, has been blinded by pride and misled by expediency. He is admitting that he, too, is limited and helpless without God's love and support. Having made his confession, Möbius returns to his room filled with the grace and glory of God.

Even given the recognition that Möbius has received a special grace, we must beware of one last temptation. Because Möbius' epiphany is delayed until the final moment of the play, we are likely to dismiss it as too little, too late. . . . But to accept this prediction as an accomplished fact is to reveal that we still do not fully comprehend Dürrenmatt's message, for in assuming that the world will surely be destroyed, we display the same failure of faith and hope that Möbius has nurtured for fifteen years. . . . The role of the prophet, whether in religion, science, or drama, is to sound the alarm, to spread the warning. In *The Physicists,* Dürrenmatt cries out loudly and well against the pride and presumption of intellectual exclusivism. (pp. 78-9)

Robert P. Reno, "Science and Prophets in Dürren-matt's 'The Physicists'," in Renascence, *Vol. XXXVII, No. 2, Winter, 1985, pp. 70-9.*

Andrea Dworkin

1946-

American nonfiction writer, essayist, novelist, and short story writer.

A self-avowed radical feminist and a leading voice in the women's movement, Dworkin is best known for her controversial nonfiction works in which she examines sexual politics and the status of women in modern society. Believing that women have been subjected to sexism and violence by men as a means of control and possession, Dworkin advocates a revolution through which conventional sexual roles are abolished. She also urges reform of the cultural institutions that nurture misogynic behavior. While Dworkin's extremist position has led to condemnation of her work, her strong commitment to feminist issues and her passionate prose style are widely admired.

Dworkin's first two books, *Woman Hating: A Radical Look at Sexuality* (1974) and *Our Blood: Prophecies and Discourses on Sexual Politics* (1976), introduce her views of women as victims of male hostility. In both works, Dworkin contends that traditional myths and fairy tales are antifemale in content, and she cites footbinding practices in the Orient and witchburning in Europe and the United States as historical evidence of what she considers "gynocide" against women. In perhaps her most controversial book, *Pornography: Men Possessing Women* (1981), Dworkin argues that pornography is less a creative expression of eroticism than an instrument of power used by males to humiliate and subjugate females. *Right-Wing Women* (1983) focuses on women whose fear of male violence, according to Dworkin, has forced them to forfeit their individuality and to accept the traditional female role of subservience in exchange for security.

Dworkin has also published a novel, *Ice and Fire* (1986). This story of a young, college-educated prostitute was faulted for its graphic depictions of sex and violence. While most critics questioned Dworkin's reliance on the themes and subject matter that she has condemned in her nonfiction, Jean Hanff Konelitz stated that Dworkin's intent in the novel was to "make the reader feel what pornography does to women."

(See also *Contemporary Authors*, Vols. 77-80 and *Contemporary Authors New Revision Series*, Vol. 16.)

© *Jerry Bauer*

it, its art, its churches, its laws." Dworkin's language [in *Woman Hating*] is crude, often obscene by most local standards; her philosophy, a vicious and strident extension of many important and valid points made by the women's movement today. . . . It's harsh, it's argumentative (the author's note details her struggle with her publishers), and it's not for the uninitiated.

Ellen Gay Detlefsen, in a review of "Woman Hating," in Library Journal, *Vol. 99, No. 11, June 1, 1974, p. 1531.*

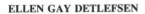

ELLEN GAY DETLEFSEN

What can you say about a book that says this of Cinderella's stepmother. "She loved her daughters the way Nixon loves the freedom of the Indochinese, and with much the same result." What can you say about a book with chapters on Chinese footbinding as a form of genocide ("gynocide")? Or say about a book with the avowed purpose "to destroy patriarchal power at its source, the family [and] in its most hideous form, the nation-state . . . to destroy the structure of culture as we know

JEANNE KINNEY

The subtitle of [*Woman Hating: A Radical Look at Sexuality*] hints at the revolutionary nature of the approach the author takes in exploring the male-female relationship. And radical she is—in ideas, language and emotion. She attacks the foundations of our culture and would destroy all the institutions and begin again. She represents the most radical Woman's Liberation philosophy, one that attributes all the evils of the world to the master-slave roles inculcated into society most basically by the male-dominant, female-submissive level of cultural experience. She has searched through history and our present culture for the extremes and graphically describes them without a blush. While much of the material repulsed me, it also awakened me to Woman as Victim in ways I never knew existed. (p. 165)

Yet despite [the book's] weaknesses, it contains the germ of truth often buried a layer or two beneath the surface of the Woman's Movement—that the role polarity of sex in our culture, which stresses the differences of man and woman, creates problems of power and violence that a culture which stresses the similarities between the sexes can peacefully avoid. The solution according to Andrea Dworkin is in creating a new consciousness of androgyny. She focuses on anthropology for her proofs and conclusions. The discovery for her is that "man" and "woman" are fictions, cultural constructs, and that the earliest myths described androgynist persons, which were both male and female. Our rigid role definitions are a corruption of earlier thinking which had male and female all together. Our polar definitions lead to oppression since otherness is always a threat, while the androgynist coming together leads to co-operation since the familiar is comfortable. . . .

The author embodies the sincerity of purpose and idealism of youth, as well as the frank outspokenness and impatience of the late 60's which produced the student rebels. At twenty-seven this is her first book. The bibliographic entry catalogues it under these titles: 1. Woman's Liberation Movement 2. Sex role. 3. Woman—Psychology. 4. Literature, Immoral. Any mature individual interested in these categories and indeed in human liberation will find a certain amount of graphic sexual abuses described here but more significantly an energetic effort to find out the truth about woman's sexuality. (p. 166)

> *Jeanne Kinney, in a review of "Woman Hating," in Best Sellers, Vol. 37, No. 7, July 1, 1974, pp. 165-66.*

CAROLE ROSENTHAL

Back in the mid-1960s, I first encountered Andrea Dworkin in the New York newspapers. . . . Eighteen years old and arrested for protesting at an antiwar demonstration, she was dragged off to the Women's House of Detention and subjected to the usual inmate routine: brutal internal examination, bullying, authoritarian contempt. She left prison after four days, hemorrhaged vaginally for two weeks, and then went public: demanding to know, in newspapers, on TV, why a woman—*any woman*—should be humiliated in so sexual a way. (p. 45)

Dworkin's public inquiry, her outrage, shocked me. It called attention to something secret and squeamish, but something we all knew about, of course: our female sex organs, and the constant verbal and physical abuse we received as women. It was so obvious I wondered why I'd never thought of it before.

Not surprisingly, Andrea Dworkin has since emerged as one of the most compelling voices in the Women's Movement. And her gift to readers of *Our Blood,* a collection of nine essays, is to make radical ideas seem clear and obvious again, much in the same way she did for me 12 years ago with the questions she raised in the media. She scrutinizes historical and psychological issues, including female masochism, rape, the slavery of women in "Amerika," and the burning of nine million witches during the Middle Ages. Then she calls for—insists upon, really—a complete cultural transformation, the rooting out of sex roles from our society.

Equal pay and sexual equality beneath the bed sheets are not enough, she states. Women must make a deeper and a different

commitment than merely to mimic men. In fact, the notion of equality is rejected altogether. (pp. 45-6)

Instead, she calls for revolutionary action at the most personal levels of our lives, asking us to reexamine the "male" and "female" personality structures we have come to think of as our own. Women must stop saying "I can't," "I don't want to," or "I don't know how." Casting out female masochism—that deeply entrenched "nonidentity" that women have learned—is the first priority. The second is to destroy the overaggressive "phallic identity" in men, and to overturn the male sexual model.

"All forms of dominance and submission, whether it be man over woman, white over black, boss over worker, rich over poor, are tied *irrevocably* to the sexual identities of men and are derived from the male sexual model," Dworkin argues. Pointing to thousands of years of poverty and racism, of "gynocide," of violence and wars, she paints an agonizing picture of Humankind lined up on two sides, against itself, and blames the male sexual model for this division. . . . Only when what Dworkin calls the "revolutionary kernel" of the feminist vision becomes a reality—that is, only when sex roles have been so completely given up that they become dim memories or museum relics for our descendants—does she believe that the world will be free.

This analysis is interesting to mull over, but many don't agree with Dworkin when she moves to the question of countermeasures. On the subject of men's responsibility in creating this new culture, she is at her most controversial. She tracks ideas down to the farthest reaches a conclusion can go. In the essay called **"Renouncing Sexual 'Equality',"** first delivered as a speech at the National Organization for Women's Conference on Sexuality, she writes: "For men I suspect that this transformation [of the male sexual model] begins in the place they most dread—that is, in a limp penis. I think that men will have to give up their precious erections and begin to make love as women do together. . . . They will have to excise everything in them that they now value as distinctly 'male'." This speech . . . takes us over some logical pathways that lead to a plain dead end, it seems to me. It asks for the defiance of male anatomy. Nevertheless, I admire the relentless courage of Dworkin's revolutionary demands.

It is difficult to remain neutral or unmoved by such passionate language and conviction. But however strongly a reader agrees or takes issue with the essays in this book, Dworkin will never be found dull or dishonest or glib. She is a genuine visionary—bold, thoughtful, willing to take risks. *Our Blood* poses questions that enlighten us in exploring our lives; it constantly tugs and stretches at the imagination's boundaries. These are trailblazing essays. They can alter your mental map of the world. (p. 46)

> *Carole Rosenthal, "Rejecting Equality," in Ms., Vol. V, No. 8, February, 1977, pp. 45-6.*

SALLY O'DRISCOLL

Pornography is a disappointing book: taking off from a section of her earlier, more interesting, *Woman Hating,* it promises a deeper exploration that it doesn't produce. Dworkin cops out on a difficult discussion of the subtle ways pornography affects both men and women, and settles for a narrow, vehement exposition of her single thesis—what the existence of pornography means about men.

Dworkin's ideas aren't new—that men's sexuality, and indeed their whole nature, depends for pleasure on the victimization of others, which leaves women as the constant victims of the image that's forced upon them. Dworkin has a high stake in maintaining this patronizing view of women's passivity. Women as victims have no complicity in pornography, so they don't clutter her thesis that pornography is not simply an expression of male nature but a massive conspiracy to rationalize it. She believes that men make pornography to justify their treatment of women in real life, but at the same time men treat real women that way because pornography proves that's how they are. It's a vicious cycle—women are whores because they are depicted as whores. Dworkin shows men as neurotically incapable of confronting women unless they bolster themselves with a whole array of images, their fantasies of the "secret truth about women" which become real in pornography and thus take on the power to prove that women are really like that.

Dworkin's book is in fact a long elaboration of Women Against Pornography's slogan, "Pornography is the theory, rape is the practice." It's disturbing that the best-publicized feminist critiques of such an important subject are based on such simple-minded rhetoric. And it is an important subject: women *are* in the process of redefining their sexuality, and pornography is just about the rawest way possible for women to confront what does or doesn't turn them on—away from the intimacy of domestic sex and out there in public, on the line sexually in a way that women haven't been used to. Women are also not accustomed to freely expressing their sexual desires, and rabid anti-pornographers like Dworkin are exploiting women's sexual guilt—not for the purpose of liberating them but to proselytize for their own idea of the "right" view of female sexuality. (Remember, Dworkin was the one who wrote a few years ago that sex with men was okay as long as the man's penis wasn't erect.)

I'm ambivalent about pornography, but I have enjoyed some of it and I resent being pushed into a moral corner. No woman reading **Pornography: Men Possessing Women** could fail to be upset by some of Dworkin's descriptions of books and films in which women are raped, beaten, tortured and then fucked (and often shown as *liking* all of it), or by the rape and wife-beating statistics, or by the sexiest quotes from Kinsey. But Dworkin's obsessive one-atrocity-after-another style is fundamentally manipulative, and the result is a picture of men as monsters, a view so extreme that the questions Dworkin obscures in her anger emerge to undermine her thesis. . . .

Having described men as such monsters, Dworkin predictably implies that male and female sexuality are almost diametrically opposed. She sees objectification and fetishism as completely alien to women, for example, and, in passing, she offers this comparison: "Generally, boys and girls who have active sexual longings do not imagine the hit-and-run sexuality of the adult male. They are still tied, to differing extents, to the nonphallic, more diffuse eroticism they experienced with their mothers. They have longings and desires that are not reducible to genital sexual contact."

That quote reveals Dworkin's ideological obsession with how women *should* be. What makes this book so frustrating is that the real women are missing, along with their real experiences. The only reaction that Dworkin allows women to have is horror at how they are being used. **Pornography** is a diatribe, not a

discussion, and there's no room for dissent because dissent in the context that Dworkin has set up implies a betrayal of all women.

> *Sally O'Driscoll, "Andrea Dworkin: Guilt without Sex," in* The Village Voice, *Vol. XXVI, No. 29, July 15-21, 1981, p. 34.*

STANLEY REYNOLDS

Ms Dworkin writes like a Leon Trotsky of the sex war. Short, sharp sentences, full of repetitions but never boring. She is full of power and energy. She writes—dare I say it?—with an aggressive manner, like a man. Except that no men write with such utter conviction these days. Most of **Pornography: Men Possessing Women** is unquotable because what she is doing here is analysing pornographic stories, showing how they all—even those dealing with homosexuals—demonstrate the male lust for violence and power. If she overstates her case it is because she is a true revolutionary. (pp. 244-45)

> *Stanley Reynolds, "Valentine Massacred," in* Punch, *Vol. 282, February 10, 1982, pp. 244-45.*

CAROL RUMENS

It is hardly surprising that many of Andrea Dworkin's ideas, extremist though they are, seem familiar; most of the speeches collected together in **Our Blood** were first delivered in the mid-70s, and they reverberate with the increasingly separatist theories being developed at that time. They are, however, well worth reading. Controlled anger does wonders for the prose-style, as many a great speech or sermon can testify.

Many are also important reminders of what has still to be achieved in terms of justice for women. There is a strikingly well-argued and impassioned essay on rape which one feels should be on every school reading list, particularly in 'Amerika' (as Ms Dworkin insists on spelling it). In New York, according to a recent survey, one in four young girls can expect to be sexually assaulted. More generalised tirades against the phallus are, however, weakened by the writer's failure to face biological fact—if you abolish the male erection, you abolish the human race, at least until an alternative means of reproduction is perfected.

There is, of course, a dangerous side to polemical talent. Andrea Dworkin advocates censorship, not just of pornography, but of all 'masculinist' art. An appalling historical naivety seems to blind her to the obvious parallel with fascism. But there are moments when a more humanitarian spirit breaks through the ideology. (p. 31)

> *Carol Rumens, "Bondage to the Brute," in* The Observer, *May 16, 1982, p. 31.*

ANNE TYLER

Why are so many women on the right side of the political fence? Why are so many men, for that matter?—but Andrea Dworkin, author of several other books on feminist topics, prefers to treat women as a separate issue [in **Right-Wing Women**].

The usual explanation offered for women's conservatism, she says, is that their childbearing, child-nurturing role encourages them to stick to the safe, to the status quo. . . .

True, she says, women do tend to be traditionalists, but that's out of fear of male violence; and the right makes use of that fear. It promises to protect women by offering "form, shelter, safety, rules, and love." In addition, it posits an outside enemy, whether black or foreign or Jewish or homosexual, to direct women's anger and frustration away from the men in their immediate lives.

In a chapter called "The Coming Gynocide," the grim future predicted for the aging in America is redefined, logically enough, as the future for aging women, since it's mostly women who live to be old. For the same reason, the patients in those nursing homes that everyone deplores are also women—ditched because they no longer serve a reproductive function, Andrea Dworkin says; though that seems a roundabout reason in a country where loss of economic function is a much greater sin. And finally, even younger women face a subtle form of annihilation—if not through poverty and an appallingly discriminatory welfare system, then through the widespread, casual prescription of mood-altering drugs for everything that troubles women, from menstrual cramps to abusive husbands.

When she sticks to the particular, Andrea Dworkin makes her points well. She's good on specific issues, particularly abortion. (Why is it, she wonders, that men so often infer their own deaths from the death of a fetus—as in, "If abortion had been available to my mother, I might not be standing here today"?) She offers a crisp, amusing summary of the careers of Marabel Morgan, Anita Bryant, Ruth Carter Stapleton, and Phyllis Schlafly. (Marabel Morgan teaches "how to cater to male pornographic fantasies in the name of Jesus Christ." Phyllis Schlafly "might be viewed as that rare woman of any ideological persuasion who really does see herself as one of the boys, even as she claims to be one of the girls.") And her own personal recollection of arguing with anti-E.R.A. delegates is a combination of scary and funny. (pp. 34-5)

The problem is that for the most part, *Right-Wing Women* avoids the particular and makes generalizations so sweeping that the reader blinks and draws back. "All housewives are economically exploited; all working women are," we're told. And "Girls are taught in order to make them compliant: intellectual adventurousness is drained, punished, ridiculed out of girls." (Notice she doesn't say "some girls," or "many girls," or even "most girls." Just "girls," period.) And, "Neither men nor women believe in the existence of women as significant beings." . . .

That these statements are true in some situations, some of the time, anyone with eyes must admit; but it would be foolish to claim they were universally true. Yet *Right-Wing Women* acknowledges no exceptions; it makes broadside pronouncements. Its language is florid—often beautiful, as a matter of fact, very like a sort of martial poetry, but it's far too emotionally charged for a political analysis.

And there's a strangely limited view of men. "Only women die one by one," Andrea Dworkin says, implying that men die . . . how? In grinning comradely gangs, perhaps. She tells us that women feel, "Without the children, I am not worth much," and many women do feel that; but then, of course, many men feel the same way: if not for their children, who require a breadwinner, they're afraid they wouldn't be valued by their wives.

When Ruth Carter Stapleton is accused of being a witch, "in typical female fashion Stapleton disclaims responsibility for her own inventiveness and credits the Holy Spirit, clearly male," we're told, as if generations of male religious leaders had not

done the same thing, surely not "in typical female fashion." If a man had written that line, wouldn't we call it prejudice? . . .

There is plenty to think about in this book. Much of it is intelligent, original, deeply felt. In order to accept it part and parcel, though, you would have to accept its pervasive sense of a world where the sexes exist in an unremitting tooth-and-nail relationship; where men and women have absolutely no hope of any genuine connection with each other; where they have never once experienced a disinterested, kindly affection for each other. And that is simply not true. (p. 35)

Anne Tyler, "The Ladies and the Tiger," in The New Republic, Vol. 188, No. 7, February 21, 1983, pp. 34-5.

MARION GLASTONBURY

As its title implies, this incisive study [*Right-Wing Women*] encompasses a wide range of unsisterly postures, from the clenched fist of the religious zealot to the cowed shrug of the captive housewife. Some tamed shrews have gained fame and fortune by telling the story of their conversion and advocating the sort of conjugal devotion that substitutes Jesus for the husband in the mind's eye. But, although anti-feminist ideology may occasionally furnish a career, it offers, according to Dworkin, none but self-defeating solutions: a bid for survival that is tantamount to suicide.

Coming to terms with patriarchy, conforming to male requirements and propitiating male power, women subordinate their human potential and personal integrity to one of two ideals: 'the brothel or the farm', in the belief that beauty and breeding, the proper functions of their sex, will be socially valued, win approval, disarm hostility and ensure protection. That these are equally vain hopes can be seen, first, from the fate of such bright stars as Marilyn Monroe, and, second, from the present state of modern warfare and the labour market neither of which now requires mass recruitment from each generation. So what price the fecundity of Mrs Average? More than ever before, women are becoming expendable. The progress of reproductive technology may soon render child-bearers as redundant as their pauperised elders, 'displaced homemakers' who now languish in Medicaid institutions, having outlived their usefulness. (p. 26)

The intuitive analysis that Dworkin applies to her compatriots, their history and recent political experience works well on Sixties radicalism, the economics of prostitution and the effects of American chauvinism. . . . Only as she moves further afield do her prophecies begin to seem farfetched, her imputation of motives dubious, her passion ever so slightly misplaced. In the interpretation of Judaic law and Christian dogma she tends to rely on guess-work; in her approach to literature on hyperbole. A good case need not be overstated. Why call George Eliot, Jane Austen and Virginia Woolf 'the greatest writers in the English language'? It may well be true that all cultures at all times manifest the underlying logic of male supremacy if you look hard enough. But lay sermons to this effect should include some acknowledgment that lust is not always violent, coition not always painful, pregnancy not always unwanted and children not an unmitigated curse. (pp. 26-7)

Marion Glastonbury, "Unsisterly," in New Statesman, Vol. 106, No. 2732, July 29, 1983, pp. 26-7.

JOHN WALSH

Andrea Dworkin is an eloquent American polemicist, author of four tough feminist tracts of which the best known in this country is *Pornography: Men Possessing Women.* Her first novel, *Ice and Fire* . . . , is as outspoken and uncompromising as you'd expect such a radical theorist to be when freed from the demands of non-fictional forms of debate.

Ms Dworkin begins like a pussycat with memories of childhood games, piggyback rides and ghost stories, the sense-data of a time when the sexes laughed together at the pretension of romance, and wondered at the mysteriousness of nuns as though they were alien beings.

But her early innocence abruptly shatters as the novel moves to the present day and the boiling sidewalks of the Lower East Side of Manhattan. . . . The narrating voice tells of her life as a writer-cum-film-maker-cum-prostitute in an apartment whose other inhabitants and their gentlemen callers are known by their initials alone. They go to clubs, and jazz venues endlessly chasing the luxury of 'a safe fuck'; they shoot up, pop pills and so on in the now established (indeed clichéd) fashion of modern Americana, while trying to fund a movie together. The girls make love with young blades, sharp musicians, cool sadists and casual Puerto Ricans, with each other, with love-demanding women, with absolutely everyone. In between these activities, the New Yorkers are stricken time and again by the beauty of light, air, colour and all the debris of excess. They embrace the sleaze, lose themselves in the sweat and ragged music, immerse themselves in the ragged underworld of violence. This contradiction is never resolved. . . .

Comparisons with Burroughs, Miller, Hubert Selby and Kathy Acker spring to mind, inevitably, with this brand of overwrought literary hate-mail. Ms Dworkin, however, brings her own, genuinely affecting sensibility to bear on the relentless catalogue of squalor. By the end, after a trip to Europe (what would Henry James make of it?), she achieves a kind of *faux de mieux* happiness as a writer, for which we must be grateful. This is a book of calculated nastiness, earnest pretentiousness and pyrotechnic prose: undeniably impressive, but almost wholly unlikeable.

> *John Walsh, in a review of "Ice and Fire," in* Books and Bookmen, *No. 366, April, 1986, p. 37.*

BARNEY BARDSLEY

[*Ice and Fire*] is an extraordinary book. It reads like a religious litany, but with words of almost pornographic passion and sacrilegious lust. In her first novel, Andrea Dworkin, fierce feminist polemicist on pornography and violence against women, has come close to the edge of hell—and takes us with her. She bites on the truth of daily existence and spits it in our faces. This novel is dangerous.

It starts off harmlessly enough, with an account of an American East Coast childhood—the games, the fears, the small triumphs and desolations. But as the protagonist grows into adulthood, the raw edges begin to bleed through. New York as a young woman. Post-hippy haze of drugs and sex. And oh, the endless fucking: of men, of women, of herself. The waking dream of excess, turning rapidly to nightmare as the acid eats her brain and the angry pimps claim her body. . . .

If you're a woman and you've ever felt used in your body—and ever felt the burning need to write about it, read this book.

If you're a man and you've ever wondered how it feels to be fucked, mind and body, till you're numb down to your very soul, please read this book.

Andrea Dworkin is a poet and a prophet. She uses words as weapons. Her art is a volatile emotion. In her book she quotes Henry James: "The great thing is to be saturated with something—that is, in one way or another, with life; and I chose the form of my saturation". Andrea Dworkin is soaking wet with life. She is ice and fire. Read her. Be dangerous.

> *Barney Bardsley, "Close to the Edge of Hell," in* Tribune, *Vol. 50, No. 16, April 18, 1986, p. 8.*

MAUREEN FREELY

Andrea Dworkin has made a career out of being America's most militant feminist. Whether or not one agrees with her, one cannot to fail to notice when she throws herself into a crusade, or to marvel (quietly, and at a safe distance) over the extent to which her prose style echoes the rapist drug-addicts she portrays in *Ice and Fire.* By wearing farmer's dungarees, talking dirty to reporters and defending her own right to free expression whilst suing magazines that lampoon her efforts to curtail theirs, she has revealed a large talent for public relations.

Her first novel displays considerably less talent for fiction and imitates the pattern of her own life. . . .

It is a trite story riddled with interesting contradictions. What she is trying to do is write a prose poem about all the ugliest things she has ever seen in her life and all the people who have ever let her down—in other words, to elevate the temper tantrum to an art form. If she falls short of the mark, it is partly because the English language contains too few synonyms for blood and urine. . . .

Dworkin's attempts at 'shocking' realism are as dated as flower power or bra-burning. A better way to unsettle a reader these days is to masquerade as the soul of convention and then remove your costume a piece at a time.

> *Maureen Freely, "Ordure of the Day," in* The Observer, *April 27, 1986, p. 26.*

JEAN HANFF KORELITZ

Dworkin, perhaps best known here and in America for books such as *Pornography: Men Possessing Women,* has said that the purpose of *Ice and Fire* is to make the reader feel what pornography does to women. This won't be a pleasant read, her publisher warns us; we may be stunned, perhaps even revolted. No such luck: Dworkin completely fails to flesh out any of the points made in her non-fiction works; her heroine is middle class, college educated and a prostitute by choice. . . . She is nonchalant about selling herself, and unoppressed by an exploiting pimp; it seems to beat a job. As a result, and despite the plentiful scenes of gratuitous violence, gang-rape and sadism to which they are subjected, one can't seem to drum up any interest in or sympathy for the narrator and her chums.

Apparently, Dworkin had some trouble finding an American publisher for *Ice and Fire,* and the resulting grudge has its place among her novel's mess of over-articulated discontents.

The fate of the narrator's own novel, unsurprisingly, "strangely resembles" that of Dworkin's:

> The book has been finished now. Many publishers have refused to publish it. There is virtually no one left to despise it, insult it, malign it, refuse it: and yet I have been refining it, each and every night, writing until dawn. Now I am tired and the book is perfect and I am done, a giant slug, a glob of goo.

Dworkin is mistaken in her belief that by anticipating her critics she has repudiated them.

Jean Hanff Korelitz, "Tough Little Number," in The Times Literary Supplement, *No. 4340, June 6, 1986, p. 622.*

Gus Edwards

1939-

West Indian-born American dramatist.

Edwards writes naturalistic dramas characterized by their vivid recreation of the squalid slums of New York City, where most of his plays take place. Although his characters often ignore conventional moral standards, Edwards focuses on their redeeming qualities. Edith Oliver described Edwards's characters as "the sort of people who are often made the subject of worthy documentaries on public television, yet Mr. Edwards, writing with irony, humor, and understanding, insists upon their complexity and their humanity and, above all, their spirit." Some critics have faulted portions of Edwards's dramas for being melodramatic and predictable, while others praise his authentic dialogue and the stark realism of his settings.

Edwards's first major play, *The Offering* (1977), depicts the power struggle between a retired professional killer and his ex-protégé. His subsequent dramas concentrate on domestic conflicts. *Black Body Blues* (1978) is an ironic play about a gentle black man who is exploited by everyone except his white employer. The play ends when the protagonist is shot and killed by his oppressive brother. Edwards's next play, *Old Phantoms* (1979), examines the bittersweet relationship between a domineering widower and his children by alternating between the past and the present. *Weep Not for Me* (1981) centers on a South Bronx family whose decadent lifestyle is metaphorically related to the deteriorating neighborhood in which they live.

Edwards's later plays are lighter in subject matter and tone. *Manhattan Made Me* (1983) is a satire involving an affluent white couple, their sophisticated black companion, and a wise derelict, who all take turns using each other. *Louie and Ophelia* (1986) depicts one year in a stormy relationship between two lovers who are not suited for each other.

(See also *Contemporary Authors,* Vol. 108.)

Photograph by A. Vincent Scarano

EDITH OLIVER

Most of the action in Gus Edwards' *The Offering* . . . takes place between (and behind) the lines. The lines—very good ones—are just surface manifestations of what is actually happening onstage and off, and of what happened many years before. The setting is the living room of the West Side apartment of Bob Tyrone, a man in his late sixties, and his wife, Princess, who is thirty years younger. We see him first dozing in front of a television set in the middle of the night, so listless that when Princess gives him a drink he lets it slip from his hand. A doorbell rings downstairs, and they ignore it, but the next day, when the doorbell rings again and Princess answers it, admitting a youngish man named Martin and Ginny, his white girlfriend, things change. Martin, a former colleague and apprentice of Bob's, is now living in Las Vegas, where Ginny works as a chorus girl. He is obviously very prosperous, and the reason he has come is to give Bob some money—three thousand dollars, in bills, which he tosses on a table. Princess, not surprisingly, questions Martin about where he got the money, and at last finds out that he is a professional killer. When, in some terror, she reports this to Bob, he replies, "I know. I taught him." Money is not the offering that Bob has in mind; it is Martin's Ginny he wants, and gets. Without giving away any more of the plot, I can say that the play is about a number of struggles for sexual dominance, that the mounting pressure of sexual urgency and threat is what gives it its frightening tension and momentum, and that its humor and small moment-to-moment detail are what keep it buoyant. Bob's bawdy, callous reminiscences of old Harlem days are very funny indeed.

Mr. Edwards has written *The Offering* with classic construction and spare, classic simplicity, as episode follows episode. A few of these episodes seem somewhat arbitrary—we are aware of the playwright at work—but most of them are acceptable without question.

Edith Oliver, "Three Grand," in The New Yorker, Vol. LIII, No. 43, December 12, 1977, p. 92.

DEAN VALENTINE

Ntozake Shange would be appalled by . . . *The Offering,* a work marking the debut of a young black playwright, Gus Edwards. His thesis is that black men have just one thing in mind; so do all women, who are drawn to the meanest fellow (Edwards identifies nastiness with élan) with the amplest supply of bedroom tricks.

A synopsis will give you the idea. Bob Tyrone, an aged, once no-good black, now retired, leads a boring life; he watches TV, drinks brandy and ignores his wife, Princess. Martin, a toothy, amiable black sharpie, and his white dumb chorine girlfriend, come to visit Bob, who it turns out taught Martin everything about surviving in the world. Of course the older man still has some life in him, and he spirits Ginny into the bedroom; but not before Martin has revealed to Princess that what he does for a living is, gasp, kill people. Happily, he is not violent ("I kill only for money") and he settles for Princess (she has no say in the matter). In the last act, Bob suffers a heart attack and dies, and Edwards thus disposes of whatever dramatic tension existed in the situation. Martin leaves for Las Vegas with Princess, she presumably having understood that the young triumphs over the old. Ginny remains in New York to attend dance classes.

[*The Offering*] is sheer Grand Guignol, not "the brutal urban world suffused with menace, sexuality and the ever-present threat of violence" that a flyer accompanying my program claimed.

Dean Valentine, in a review of "The Offering," in The New Leader, *Vol. LXI, No. 1, January 2, 1978, p. 29.*

WALTER KERR

"I put a bullet in your master and I freed you," says a black man to his brother in Gus Edwards's **Black Body Blues**. . . . Ten years ago that line would have been taken at face value. The master would have been white, he'd have been directly or indirectly oppressing the play's leading black, and the shot that finally dropped him would have been a shot meant to be heard around the world. If black liberation had to be violent, so be it. The time had come. Whites *knew* it had come and nodded assent, in the theater at least.

Now—suddenly, subtly—the line is riddled with irony. In **Black Body Blues,** the "master" is still a white man, but he is a white man much admired by the servant he employs. That servant, a likable and intelligent do-gooder named Arthur, is still something of a menial: he does every sort of chore around the white man's house, genially puts on a tuxedo nights to officiate at parties. "You look good in your monkey suit—for a monkey," his visiting brother sneers. But Arthur, in or out of his tuxedo, is no Uncle Tom. He is grateful to his employer for a clear, strongly affirmed reason: he's the only one who treats him as a person, the only one who's ever taught him anything useful.

His first loyalties, however, remain firmly rooted in the black world he inhabits. He shares a shabby-neat apartment in the Times Square area with a girl who was once a dancer and a model . . . but is now a drug addict. He's picked her up, helpless, on the street and given her house-room, though the gesture hasn't earned him any love. She cheats on him regularly, with a pusher, with almost anyone at hand.

When his younger brother appears, on the run from the police after a long string of bank robberies, Arthur makes him instantly and completely welcome. He is loyal to his kinfolk, particularly loyal to the onetime lad he grew up with. His tolerance is infinite and extends to the ravings of a mentally

and physically shattered victim of World War II, now scarred and blinded and beating the floor with his cane in a flat just above. Easygoing, amiable, quietly ambitious. Arthur spends his time listening to Beethoven whenever the others cease haranguing him, which isn't often.

His generosity never falters, and he is happy to get his brother and the pusher jobs serving a dinner party with him at the "master's" house. Brother and pusher repay him by returning to the house, late that night, to burglarize it. Caught, there is a shootout: employer kills the fleeing pusher, brother kills the employer. At which point the line we began with—"I put a bullet through your master and freed you"—is spoken.

And our heads reel as all the old values seem to turn inside-out. Arthur has been "freed" from his immediate means of bettering himself. He has been "freed" by the man who has actually oppressed him most, betrayed him at every turn: by the brother who will, in a moment, gun Arthur down, too. Watching the play, we see Arthur as victimized indeed, but victimized by a random sampling of his own people. The oppressors here aren't white, but black.

Mr. Edwards isn't writing a didactic play. He is certainly not saying, in any schematic sense, that it is blacks who keep blacks from rising. Neither is he saying that a black man's only hope of economic or intellectual advancement lies in a direct attendance on whites. Rhetorically speaking, the play isn't *saying* anything. It is showing us something, showing us a series of vignettes (each beginning as a still-life, then gliding into an exploration of freshly rearranged relationships) that ultimately explode into a violent event. The event may have happened just this one time, in this one particular place, and we generalize from it at our own risk. (In the end, by the way, too much happens; the author's brushwork is too light, his language too spare, to absorb the multiple catastrophes that crowd his final sequence.)

Still, there is no question where our sympathies lie. They are lodged with Arthur, the endlessly gentle and generous Arthur who was once a boxer but had to give it up because he lacked "the killer instinct," the Arthur who likes the white man he works for. . . . And there is an extension of sympathy. Because Arthur likes his employer, we suppose that we should like and/ or trust him, too, though he does not appear in the play and is never described in any detail. (pp. 1, 7)

We leave the theater pondering one last question: have we come to the end of the "get whitey" play, have black playwrights—once so justifiably inflamed—now surrendered the single note of rage in exchange for a much more complex view of things? Mr. Edwards doesn't commit himself to a tendentious position either way. Instead he seems to probe, explore and re-explore, the sadly crossed wires of a black-white society, searching for an objectivity that may advance no one's ideology but that does—in its relative detachment—constitute an artistic game. He even permits the blinded intruder an odd, possibly a comic, burst of enthusiasm for the Beethoven that Arthur is playing. "I recognize it," he cries, "because the white man's heart and soul is in it!" . . .

Ten years later a tide may have turned. I don't know that. But the play, as performed, *feels* it. (p. 7)

Walter Kerr, "Is the 'Get Whitey' Play Obsolete?" in The New York Times, *Section II, February 12, 1978, pp. B1, B7.*

JOHN SIMON

Black Body Blues is the second play by Gus Edwards, now presented by the Negro Ensemble Company in repertory with his first, *The Offering*. Though more daring in concept, both ideologically and technically, it is much the less successful of the two. It is the story of Arthur, a former boxer who proved too gentle to be a great fighter, and who has now opted for a placid existence as the butler of a white man who treats him squarely. The employer gives Arthur not only food to take home but also food for thought, such as a recording of Beethoven's Ninth, and incentive to educate himself. As Arthur observes, his white boss is the only person who takes him seriously. Joyce, the black hooker and drug addict whom Arthur took in as a live-in girl friend, does not really care for him: She still turns tricks to pay off Andy, her pusher and former pimp, whenever she needs a fix. Andy, of course, only pretends to be Arthur's friend. Fletcher, the fanatical blind man who lives upstairs, also professes appreciation for Arthur's kindness, but is more than willing to have sex with Joyce in Arthur's bed.

The worst exploitation, however, comes from Louis, Arthur's older and cleverer brother. Louis is on the run from the police, who want him for several bank robberies and a killing. Arthur decently puts him up in his dingy apartment off Times Square, and even gets him a job with his employer. This kindness proves fatal: Arthur ends up losing everything, probably even his life. Now, it is a temerarious thing for a black playwright to suggest that a white man may be a black man's sole benefactor. Unfortunately, however, Edwards has made his hero too simple—both mentally and as a dramatic character. The latter impoverishment he shares, moreover, with the other dramatis personae, all of whom are too one-sidedly eager to use him. True, Joyce blames his sedentary reclusiveness for the stagnation of their relationship, but she does this precisely when he has brought home champagne to celebrate her birthday, which detracts from the merit of her claim. The conflicts, then, lack plasticity and complexity; *Black Body Blues* is hardly more than an outline for a play. This, I take it, is largely deliberate, and constitutes the author's technical audacity: Edwards has tried to strip the plot, characters, and dialogue down to the bone—an apter title might have been "Black Bone Blues." Such reduction, however, requires people and situations less obvious and predictable than these: mystery that is bone-deep.

John Simon, "Black and White in Monochrome," in New York *Magazine, Vol. 11, No. 7, February 13, 1978, pp. 74-5.*

MEL GUSSOW

In the opening scene of Gus Edwards's new play, *Old Phantoms,* . . . one young man stares blankly out of a window, another man sits down and casually sprawls one leg over an arm of the chair, and a woman dressed in black stands as still as a sentinel. The images and the performances are so precise that even before the dialogue is spoken, we know the time, place and character. These are brothers and a sister, separated in a lonely house. There has been a death in the family, a death that has a different impact on each of the survivors.

For the duration of the play, we are enveloped in the atmosphere and by the confidence and certainty of the author's writing. Effortlessly, and with a kind of homely poetry, Mr. Edwards moves back and forth from present to past to a third spectral level, until we have an indelible collage of a family at war with itself.

In his first two plays, *The Offering* and *Black Body Blues,* . . . Mr. Edwards was revealed as a playwright with a terse Pinteresque feeling for omen and menace. Without abandoning his gift for understatement, he moves in his new play to a situation that might have been recognized by O'Neill or Ibsen. That's *Old Phantoms,* as in "ghosts."

The father of the family . . . , deceased in the first scene and encountered in a flashback, is hard and demanding—a proud black landowner in a small Southern town. With his wife dead, he becomes father and mother, teacher and tyrant.

He expects his children to live up to his impossibly high standards, and when they disappoint him—the older son . . . is slow, the younger and brighter son . . . easily falls into a life of crime—he takes it as a personal affront. With his daughter . . . , he has the most ambiguous relationship. She is his abject admirer, but because she is a woman, he subjugates and depersonalizes her, dismissing her suitor with an almost Jamesian sense of position.

Although the image of the father hovers over the household, the play is actually more concerned with the thwarted lives of the children. Each is compartmentalized in an emotional void. As much as anything, the play is about the absence of love, the corrosion of blood ties.

In outline, the story may sound cold and bleak, but Mr. Edwards writes with enormous sympathy and humor. We are moved by these people, even by the autocratic father, and especially by the older son as he spurns the father, his memory and his property.

As was demonstrated in his earlier plays, Mr. Edwards's theater begins naturalistically, but moves on to a plane that is both lyrical and imaginative. The [characters] are called upon to change from adults to children and back again without accompanying changes of makeup, costume or scenery. . . . [A] slight lifting of the voice, a youthful stance and walk—all three siblings convincingly remove years from their shoulders. . . .

Up to a point, the playwright's spare method—the brief, almost cinematic vignettes—is an exact match for the subject. We learn about this family through an accretion of incidents and observations. However, the style is occasionally inconsistent (some but not all properties are mimed) and several encounters seem like shorthand sketches for scenes still to be written. The evening ends precipitously instead of climactically. At this early stage of what we assume will be a long and rewarding career, Mr. Edwards seems unprepared to make that final, piercing journey into his characters and their psyches. . . .

Mel Gussow, " 'Old Phantoms,' a New Gus Edwards," in The New York Times, *February 9, 1979, p. C3.*

FRANK RICH

[*Weep Not for Me*] is a view of the South Bronx from the inside: its characters are middle-class black people who have lived there for 15 years and have nowhere else to go. To be sure, Mr. Edwards doesn't present the neighborhood as a Shangri-La: his South Bronx, like the one in *Fort Apache,* is a hell of crime, drugs and bombed-out buildings. But the playwright unearths both the dignity and the wit of people who do their best to keep going in desperate circumstances.

As a play, *Weep Not for Me* eventually fails—it collapses totally in Act II—but it is clearly the work of a born writer. In Act I, Mr. Edwards introduces us to a household full of intriguing, idiosyncratic characters. The proverbial family matriarch, Lillian . . . , is not the mournful sufferer one expects, but a strong-willed woman who has sublimated her misery into a giddy affair with a much younger man. Her husband, Jake . . . , is a retired Army sergeant who insists on showering his unfaithful wife with love, not revenge. The family's adult children—all Lillian's by a previous marriage—include a deranged rape victim . . . , a neurotic divorced woman . . . , a sex-crazed aspiring model . . . and a drug-addict brother . . . , who lusts after his sisters. Mr. Edwards doesn't settle for making these sad people sympathetic; he makes them all likable as well.

The playwright accomplishes this feat by viewing the family with clear-eyed, far from uncritical, affection, rather than hand-wringing pity. The tone is set by Jake. The father knows that his stepchildren, like his wife, are selfish and spiritually sick, and yet he refuses to abandon either his sense of humor or his compassion. Lounging about the living room in his underwear, he steadily drinks beer and picks up after the others without much complaint. Though his family insists on running away from responsibility, Jake takes stubborn pride in doing the reverse.

[Jake]—at once bemused, morose and self-mocking—ushers us into Mr. Edwards's flinty, unsentimental point of view. There are laughs where one least expects them. . . . Mr. Edwards sees pungent gallows humor in people who survive against all hope. . . .

Act II, unfortunately, is quite another matter. Mr. Edwards abruptly abandons his initial approach and turns *Weep Not for Me* into a conventionally apocalyptic ghetto melodrama—complete with random, multiple murders that wipe out almost half the cast. The fierce screams of pain at the final curtain are undoubtedly genuine, but they belong to another, far easier play. Instead of delving further into his complex people—of working out their lives in dialogue—the playwright turns them into symbolic martyrs and ends their lives with bullets. Once he does, *Weep Not for Me* becomes Weep for Me—just another predictable funeral epitaph for the South Bronx. One weeps not for Mr. Edwards's dead characters, however, but for the life-filled play that he unaccountably let slide away.

> *Frank Rich, "'Weep Not for Me', Inside the South Bronx," in* The New York Times, *February 9, 1981, p. C15.*

EDITH OLIVER

Weep Not for Me, by Gus Edwards, . . . is a portrait of a black family in the South Bronx whose lives are deteriorating as inexorably as the neighborhood they live in. Several stories are told to the accompaniment of ambulance and police sirens and the constant sound of a drill outside the family's apartment, where all the action takes place, yet the strength of the play is in its mood and its depiction of a kind of life in which people become so used to horrors—to drugs, rape, incest, and even murder—that they are almost casual about them. These are the sort of people who are often made the subject of worthy documentaries on public television, yet Mr. Edwards, writing with irony, humor, and understanding, insists upon their complexity and their humanity and, above all, their spirit. . . . The play, for all its sad and harrowing and even frightening moments, is never grim; there are tender scenes and funny scenes.

Nor is it short on plot and action . . . but its principal interest (for me, at any rate) is in its characters.

Although *Weep Not for Me* lacks the power and artistry of Ed Bullins' plays about slum life, and although there are a few lumps of undigested exposition, it has merit, and, . . . every moment is believable and alive. (pp. 59-60)

> *Edith Oliver, "No Tears in the Bronx," in* The New Yorker, *Vol. LVI, No. 52, February 16, 1981, pp. 59-60.*

STEPHEN HARVEY

Long before shotgun-blasted bodies start littering the doorways of the tenement living room in which . . . *Weep Not for Me* takes place, you can't help figuring that the Hendricks clan will come to a woeful end—and not just because they're secreted in New York's most notorious slum neighborhood, either. This family may be intended to represent the hapless victims of a brutal urban milieu, but as author Gus Edwards has depicted them, they are so myopically obtuse as to all but invite every bit of mayhem the playwright can hurl in their direction. . . .

[Much] of *Weep Not for Me* has the audience in stitches. [Jake's] irate bluster and mystified double takes are in the best sitcom tradition of dimwitted, put-upon dads, transposed downward from the bourgeoisie.

In a more original vein, Edwards displays a rare gift for the comedy of human self-centeredness raised into the realm of pure chutzpah. There's a delicious digression from the juggernaut plot in the form of a cozy gossip-fest between Lillian and a neighbor lady. . . . There's more genuine insight and lively writing in these brief passages than in all the Hendricks's plunges into the apocalypse, and I hope Edwards's next play further explores the caustic side of his talent, stripped of all that spurious redeeming social value.

This time around, however, the author teeters queasily between farce, *Grand Guignol* with a sociological tinge and the clanging symbolism and turgid phrasemaking of that previous chronicler of the Bronx's lower-middle depths, Clifford Odets. It's regrettable that many of *Weep Not for Me*'s laughs are earned at its own expense, when the play is temporarily in dead earnest. Edwards's characters have a way of dropping terse clinkers of exposition to cue the spectator in on their respective past traumas, and these don't begin to explain the genesis of the lurid conflicts taking place before our eyes. Edwards underscores the psychological distress of these figures with some intrusive off-stage sound effects to convey the inescapable force of the environment that is crushing them. Principal among these is the leitmotif of a demolition crew's incessant pneumatic drilling; in one of Willie's rare lucid moments, he confides his fear that the ever-encroaching workmen are likely to smash their very own walls at any minute. This is one metaphor that literally works overtime since, the din persists even while these people plot and fornicate in the middle of the night. (pp. 283-84)

Weep Not for Me isn't nearly as reprehensible a piece of exploitation as the current movie *Fort Apache, the Bronx,* but it likewise reduces real-life tragedy to the pulp of facile melodrama, dehumanizing the victims into disposable pawns. Gus Edwards's ill-fated family unit isn't trapped by the menace of life in a slum without a future—it's snuffed out by the theatrical machinations of the author's own devising. (p. 284)

Stephen Harvey, in a review of "Weep Not for Me,"
in The Nation, *Vol. 232, No. 9, March 7, 1981, pp.*
283-84.

EDITH OLIVER

Gus Edwards' *Manhattan Made Me,* . . . is a cynical, satiric, and sporadically funny play about blacks and whites in this city, and it should have come off with much more style than it did. . . . [It] is an endless succession of small scenes linked by interminable bridges of popular music and moving sluggishly along without any springs or tension. Its hero, so to speak (heroism seems to be the last thing on Mr. Edwards' mind), is a young, urbane black named Barry Anderson, who is the close friend and companion of a white couple, Alan and Claire McKenzie. Claire appears to be very rich, and the pair have moved to New York from somewhere or other because Alan wants to try his hand at acting. He is a drunk and spends much time, he reports, picking up and bedding down an assortment of women. The fourth character in the play is one Duncan, who, standing in the shadows outside the set that represents the McKenzies' lavish apartment, functions through most of the action as a kind of mocking chorus. He is a black derelict, a sardonic old buddy of Barry's, given to disreputable reminiscence and bits of down-home philosophy, which he delivers in low, pungent street language. Alan leaves to make a television pilot in California, Barry moves in with Claire, and Alan, when he returns, is expelled in tears and rage. . . . Alan comes back again, drunk and maudlin and declaring his eternal love for Barry, and he is again turned out, ending up as yet another street-corner derelict, in some terrible weather (made manifest by some terrible sound effects). Claire, a Sunday painter, decides to ask Duncan to pose for a portrait, despite heavy objections from Barry. Soon, Duncan, quitting his effective post as Chorus, moves into bed with Claire, and furious Barry, shouting in a number of foreign tongues, becomes a raving animal before our eyes. At the end, Duncan, having progressed from rags to brocade smoking jacket, is in residence, and the action has petered out into predictability.

The pity of it is that *Manhattan Made Me* could have been a strong and original piece of work, given one more pass through the typewriter by Mr. Edwards—a good writer, whose *Weep Not for Me,* of a couple of seasons ago, was one of the best plays ever done by the N.E.C. . . .

Edith Oliver, in a review of "Manhattan Made Me,"
in The New Yorker, *Vol. LIX, No. 15, May 30, 1983,*
p. 86.

JOHN SIMON

In *The Offering,* Edwards was imitating Pinter, quite successfully, until the play fell apart in the second act. In *Manhattan Made Me* (a feeble pun, by the way), Edwards imitates Murray Schisgal quite successfully, though in this endeavor success is hardly better than failure.

Barry Anderson—young, gifted, and black—is an unemployed art director sponging off a white couple: Claire and Alan McKenzie, a rich amateur painter from Virginia and her boozing, wenching, tough-talking husband, who has come to New York to make it as an actor. Barry spends all his time in the McKenzies' fashionable high-rise apartment—drinking, eating, gabbing with Alan, and trying to conquer Claire. She, however, is a model wife, loving Alan and blind to his esca-

pades. Barry keeps running into Duncan, a former friend turned derelict, who hangs out near the McKenzie place and gives Barry teasing streetwise jive about his enviable position as a successful parasite.

These four are interestingly conceived and could be the spokes and spokesmen in the sophisticated, satirical whirligig Edwards had in mind. But there is immediate trouble: Claire not only seems but also is thoroughly decent and devoted at first; when Alan goes to Hollywood for a TV pilot and forgets even about her birthday, she reluctantly accepts physical consolation from Barry while still affirming her love for her husband and suffering pangs of guilt. It makes no sense then, even in a non-realistic parable, for her to be suddenly revealed as a former, present, and future man-eating bitch. Similarly, all three men undergo schematic reversals, too pat even for an ostensible allegory.

In a speech of Duncan's—by far the best writing in the play—Edwards conveys that he is not considering women here (itself a damaging admission), only men, each of them a "m————r" of one of three kinds. An M1 is born into that condition and unable to help it; an M2 has it thrust upon him and won't shake it off; an M3 is the worst sort—he is and remains an M without even knowing it, and wreaks the most havoc. I assume that Alan is M1, Barry M2, and Duncan M3. Nice, if only Edwards knew how to dramatize it.

What he *can* do very well is the black street talk with which Duncan alienates the *embourgeoisé* Barry, and the black-and-white cat-and-mouse banter of the interracial threesome, in which one never knows who is cat and who mouse. What he can't do is work out the overarching schema (whatever, exactly, it is) in non-comic-strip terms, or write long, serious speeches, of which there are many, all bad. Here Edwards, apparently taking it for fine writing, embarrassingly apes the worst slick-magazine fiction.

Yet an author who can manage Duncan's aforementioned speech, ending with the racy metaphor about New York, which "will bust you apart and leave you a cripple, and then offer you tap-dancing lessons for free," cannot be discounted. Scarcely less good are Alan's sardonic comments about actors' auditions complete with homosexual stage managers on the make, and other flashes of social and sexual insight that ignite intermittently. But Edwards does not seem aware—or sufficiently so—of the latent implications of the Barry-Alan and Barry-Duncan relationships; on the other hand, he sometimes creates swiftly effective scenes without words. (p. 87)

John Simon, "Unreal, Surreal, Hyper-Real," in New
York *Magazine, Vol. 16, No. 23, June 6, 1983, pp.*
87-9.

MEL GUSSOW

In dozens of scenes that take place over a period of about one year but seem to last an eternity, Gus Edwards tells the pathetic story of *Louie and Ophelia,* a mismatched couple that never realize how different one is from the other. Perhaps if the author had removed every other scene, one might have had more patience with the characters.

The two meet in a Bronx bar and, despite Ophelia's apparent moral austerity, they are soon living together. At least in the beginning, she keeps the romantic relationship a secret from her young children. Later, when she tells them of Louie's presence, she repeatedly warns them that if they don't study, they will end up with a job like his.

Louie, the hero of Mr. Edwards's new two-character play . . . , is a cook—and not a bad fellow. . . . One demonstration of his generosity is his devotion to the daughter of one of his ex-lovers, a devotion that repeatedly enrages Ophelia. She regards it as the equivalent of an act of infidelity. . . .

[Ophelia] is a nag and, at times, a termagant, more concerned with her own comfort than with the needs of her supposed loved ones. But when Louie bristles at her insults, she briskly retreats. As we know, within minutes she will be back on the attack.

The story is as shallow as a sitcom and almost entirely without atmosphere. We find out little about Louie except for the fact that he learned to cook while in the Army, and even less about Ophelia except that her husband abandoned her and their children. That unseen character is a man to envy.

Watching and waiting for something, anything, to happen, we look for relief from the domestic doldrums. Perhaps one of the children, not listed in the program, may make a surprise appearance, or Louie might bring a friend home from the restaurant where he works. Variety, such as it is, is provided by the use of film. Several of the scenes are projected on a small overhead screen while the actors mime the events on stage. . . .

Despite the chasm between the two characters, one suspects that there will be a happy ending, foreshadowed when a title is projected indicating that the next—and final—scene takes place ''a month later in the depths of winter.''

The disappointment is increased by the fact that Mr. Edwards is such an accomplished playwright. Two of his early plays . . . **The Offering** and **Old Phantoms,** were intense and deeply atmospheric dramas about people facing severe crises. In contrast

to the henpecked Louie and the officious Ophelia, the earlier characters earned every minute of their stage time.

Mel Gussow, ''Negro Ensemble's 'Louie and Ophelia','' in The New York Times, *May 25, 1986, p. 58.*

EDITH OLIVER

Gus Edwards' play [**Louie and Ophelia**] tells the story, in one brief episode after another, of . . . [a] love affair—and it's love, all right, although many of the episodes are stormy, and most of them are humorous. Ophelia is a bossy woman, stubborn and assertive, very edgy about the position of blacks in every situation, and insistent that her children never stop studying, as she herself studies, so that they can rise in the world. . . . Louie, just as intelligent and strong as she is, though barely literate, is easygoing. Her behavior toward him seems impossible—she constantly puts him down and challenges everything he says—yet on the occasions when he asserts himself her remorse is complete, and one is always aware that her self-discipline is as fierce as any discipline she imposes on anyone else. Both are lonely and long for a kind of family stability. In time, Louie realizes that he and this exasperating woman are mismatched, and he walks out—but temporarily, because he also comes to realize, in a wry, bittersweet ending, that love is love, and there is nothing they can do about it.

Mr. Edwards' great strength as a dramatist is his ability to examine with depth and humor and understanding characters we meet most frequently in case histories or documentaries or cheap television shows. Ophelia and Louie are as free of cliché and full of surprises and humanity as any of the characters in Mr. Edwards' **Weep Not for Me.**

Edith Oliver, in a review of ''Louie and Ophelia,'' in The New Yorker, *Vol. LXII, No. 14, May 26, 1986, p. 87.*

Hans Magnus Enzensberger
1929-

German poet, essayist, critic, editor, translator, and dramatist.

A controversial figure in contemporary West German literature, Enzensberger is known for the polemical social, political, and cultural criticism he presents in his poetry and essays. He first drew attention in Germany for his unconventional and often vituperative poetry. With the publication of essays during the early 1960s on such topics as popular culture, German society, and international politics, Enzensberger became an important literary figure. Although Enzensberger's criticism is often motivated by his socialist beliefs, critics note that the range of his opinions makes him difficult to categorize. Neil McInnes stated: "[Enzensberger] is a learned Marxist, a radical critic of industrialism, of parliamentary democracy and of what he curiously calls 'bourgeois science,' but at the same time he scornfully rejects Soviet communism, fellow-travellers, ecological politics and the romantic revolutionism of Fidel Castro and Che Guevara." Enzensberger was awarded the Georg Büchner Prize in 1963 and became a member of *Gruppe 47,* the prestigious association of post-World War II German writers.

Many of the poems in Enzensberger's first two volumes, *Verteidigung der Wölfe* (1957) and *Landessprache* (1960), voice contempt for the complacency and materialism in German society. *Blindenschrift* (1964), Enzensberger's third collection, is viewed as his most accomplished early volume of poetry. Critics noted that in this work Enzensberger achieves a more controlled and effective tone, and his poems of social criticism were compared to those of Bertolt Brecht. Other poems in Enzensberger's first three collections are lyrical meditations on such topics as love and nature. Selected poems from these early works were published in both German and English in *Poems for People Who Don't Read Poems* (1968).

Enzensberger's position as a significant literary figure was solidified with several early volumes of essays. *Einzelheiten* (1962), his first collection, won popular and critical acclaim in Germany and was reissued in a two-volume paperback edition comprising *Bewusstseins-Industrie* (*The Consciousness Industry: On Literature, Politics and the Media*), which concerns popular culture and the various media which influence public opinion, and *Poesie und Politik* (*Poetry and Politics*), which includes essays of literary and social criticism. *Politik und Verbrechen* (1964; *Politics and Crime*) contains essays on such topics as treason, capitalism, communism, and the interaction of various revolutionary movements in Russia during the nineteenth and early twentieth centuries. Selections from these volumes and from *Deutschland, Deutschland unter anderm* (1967) appear in English translation in *Raids and Reconstructions* (1977) and *Hans Magnus Enzensberger: Critical Essays* (1982). Many of these essays propound radical ideas which some critics found contentious and disconcerting. For example, in "A Critique of Political Ecology," Enzensberger blames pollution on the excesses of capitalism and claims that the ecology movement is promoted in part by large corporations that manufacture high-priced antipollution technology. However, most critics praised Enzensberger as a stimulating commentator on a variety of topics, and several included him in the tradition of German essayists that includes Friedrich von Schlegel and Gotthold

Ephraim Lessing. John Simon, in his foreword to *Critical Essays,* refers to Enzensberger as a "Renaissance man," claiming that the essays give "a generous inkling of his diversity, and attest to the benefits of a complex literary sensibility's latching on to political matters, and, conversely, of a historically and politically astute mind's addressing itself to our arts and culture."

After having concentrated on prose since the mid-1960s, Enzensberger published *Mausoleum: 37 Balladen aus der Geschichte des Fortschritts* (1975; *Mausoleum: Thirty-Seven Ballads from the History of Progress*). This work contains prose and verse biographies of people whom Enzensberger believes profoundly influenced the course of Western civilization. Enzensberger's next volume of poetry, *Der untergang der Titanic* (1979; *The Sinking of the Titanic*), contains thirty-three cantos centered on the ill-fated journey of the *Titanic.* Enzensberger uses the ocean liner as a metaphor for society; he comments on differences between the conditions and fates of poor and rich passengers, describes events from several perspectives, and invokes a number of historical and personal references to extend the implications of his themes. Some critics found the poem's symbolism heavy-handed, citing a series of allusions that link Enzensberger's work with Dante's *Divine Comedy.* However, others viewed the cantos as an ambitious sequence in which Enzensberger displays a command of various tones and ideas. In *Die Furie des Verschwindens* (1980), Enzensberger returns to the shorter lyrical forms of his early poems. Of this work Michael Hamburger commented: "The social criticism is more incisive, more knowing, more searching than ever before; but it is so because Enzensberger has learnt to dispense with the utopian reformer's vantage point, as well as with the rhetorical bravura of his early verse."

While Enzensberger has won recognition primarily for his poetry and essays, he is also respected for his many other literary endeavors. Enzensberger has edited politically-oriented journals and poetry anthologies and has translated into German the works of such poets as William Carlos Williams and Pablo Neruda. *Das Verhör von Habana* (1970; *The Havana Inquiry*), which was well received in several European countries, is a documentary play based on the televised interrogation of prisoners of war captured by Cuba during the Bay of Pigs invasion. Enzensberger has lived and taught in a number of countries outside of Germany, including the United States, Cuba, and Norway.

(See also *Contemporary Authors*, Vols. 116, 119.)

D. J. ENRIGHT

It is scarcely the case that we live in a time when literary conventions are so narrow and stifling that "poetry" must become, for the poet, a dirty word. Far from it. Poetically, anything goes, and the louder the faster, though perhaps not very far. So the more one considers the title of Hans Magnus Enzensberger's volume of selected poems [*Poems for People Who Don't Read Poems*] . . . the more sadly irrelevant or even senseless it comes to seem. People who don't read poems don't read poems.

In the longest piece here, "**summer poem**," the phrase *"das ist keine kunst"* keeps recurring—"that's not art." In a note the author describes the phrase as "the traditional objection of a bourgeois aesthetic against every innovation." True, such was the situation, once upon a time. But far more often today we hear the complaint "but that's *art*," the false artist's by now traditional objection to the suggestion that art should be something more than a howl, a slash of paint, or a tangle of old iron. The genuine artist—and there is clear evidence here of Enzensberger's genuineness—oughtn't to be wasting his time and energy on this sort of shadow-boxing.

Enzensberger has set his face against Rilke, Bach, Hölderlin ("what can we do / with everyone / who says hölderlin and means himmler"), seemingly because their work failed to prevent the Nazi extermination camps, because indeed some camp commandants were actually connoisseurs of music and poetry. Are Rilke, Bach, and Hölderlin to blame for this? Should they have written only for good men to read? Maybe in a few score years the work of Enzensberger will be judiciously appreciated by the monsters of some new regime, whose withers are left unwrung, or are probably unwringable anyway? . . .

A good deal of what Enzensberger cries out against in Germany is in fact universal. Some of it is trivial. Since the artist *must* select, anyway, it is best that he *does* select. And selection appears to be this poet's weak point. Embroidered napkins, whipped creams, wage negotiators, plastic bags, chambers of commerce, murderers' dens, bonus vouchers, chamois beard

hats, Coca Cola and arsenals, Rilke and Dior, branflakes and bombs—they all feature as expletives in a lengthy curse, all of equal weight apparently or, in the end, of equal weightlessness. To be angry about everything is to be angry about nothing. Enzensberger's rage declines into rant, his fierce indignation into smashing-up-the-furniture. One thinks of Brecht's poems, and of his gift for selecting the one detail, the one image, the one reference which will tell all, or as much as he set out to tell.

The last poem in this book is called "**joy**," and it begins,

> she does not want me to speak of her
> she won't be put down on paper
> she can't stand prophets. . .

It is a more hopeful poem than most of Enzensberger's, for it ends by speaking of Joy's *"siegreiche flucht"* ("her long flight to victory") but it is a little too abstract, too willed, and deficient in the urgency and the implied compassionateness of similar poems by Brecht. . . . (p. 21)

Yet for me Enzensberger is at his best when at his nearest to Brecht, and when he eschews length, as in "**bill of fare**," "**poem about the future**," the grimly comic "**midwives**," and (a very fine poem) "**the end of the owls**." . . . These are Enzensberger's most moving, most impressive poems—and I don't mean (if indeed it means anything at all) "aesthetically." These, by implication, contain the horror and disgust of the longer pieces, but go beyond horror and disgust, not by annulling them, by selling out to "art," but by assuring us that the poet is not himself merely a destroyer with a grievance against bigger and better destroyers. Here he is not making war but speaking, soberly and lucidly, of the pity of war. In his longer poems, Enzensberger's weapon is the blunderbuss, where it should rather be the rapier. Or is that too much like "art"? In an age of nuclear weapons the rapier cannot be said to be noticeably less effective than the blunderbuss or the bludgeon, and it is certainly more discriminating. The poet, unlike the atom bomb, ought to discriminate still. (p. 22)

> D. J. Enright, "Between Hölderlin and Himmler," in The New York Review of Books, Vol. X, No. 7, April 11, 1968, pp. 21-2.

MICHAEL WOOD

Enzensberger's remarks in prose tend to be stiff and fussy, too much concerned with saying where he stands. There are traces of this in his verse—a simplified anger, a rather crude declarative tone—and there is a huge hint in the title of [*Poems for People Who Don't Read Poems*] with its swipe at people who *do* read poems. We know what happens to people who read poems. They become commandants of Auschwitz and Dachau: very cultured people. They say Hölderlin and mean Himmler, as Enzensberger puts it. Perhaps. But what about the uncultured camp commandants, the ones who didn't read poems? Is Enzensberger writing for them, for their philistine children, their heirs?

Enzensberger, like Günter Grass with his practical politics, like Peter Weiss with his emotional Marxism, wants to atone for German literature, for its quietist past, its echoing imagery of accepted autumns and afternoons, its defection in the face of Hitler. His atonement takes the form of a wide invective against the new Germany, the land of the miracle, a 'fallow, silenced and hostile land,' where 'the dead are outvoted,' where 'the future grits its false teeth,' and where 'the rich poor /

smash their cinema seats for sheer joy.' 'Here the rule is: be ruthlessly nice to each other.' The phrase is marvellous, and reminds us that when Enzensberger turns to verse much of his falseness, much of his simplicity, vanishes.

He still has a heavy hand at times . . . , but more often there is an acute wit controlling and refining Enzensberger's unfocused anger, converting diatribe into irony, converting a posture into a complex personal statement. The practical, committed poet, for example, admits to being tempted by flight, by isolation. He writes from a remote house in a northern landscape. Yet he feels guilty there, he is hounded by the noises of the world he has left. . . . Enzensberger, like Camus, like Sartre, like Norman Mailer, feels a form of shame at writing so much and doing so little. Yet Enzensberger also knows that action can become an alibi, that poets need time to think—that, as Proust said, not even the Dreyfus case is a sufficient excuse for refusing to face yourself.

At his best, in poems like **"joy," "a panting," "a field of carnations," "the end of the owls,"** Enzensberger is very good indeed, a lyric poet of the first order.

> Michael Wood, "Deutschland unter alles," in The Observer, *August 11, 1968, p. 23.*

MICHAEL ROLOFF

Asked, after a visit, how he liked Germany Andrei Voznesensky, the Russian poet, replied: "Enzensberger makes up for everything." After a visit to the same country Irving Kristol, editor of *The Public Interest,* commented that he would be perfectly happy as long as the Germans aimed at nothing higher than a Mercedes. The reader who agrees with the more cynical of these two travelers' views, who prefers a Germany content in the squalor of its affluence, will not like poetry that makes up for this squalor and that disrupts the contentment. . . .

[**"man spricht deutsch"** and] poems like **"lachesis lapponica," "to all telephone subscribers," "summer poem,"** and **"foam,"** which makes A. Ginsburg's "Howl" sound like the mopings of a puppy, are some of the best poems by Germany's best postwar poet. His work [contained in *Poems for People Who Don't Read Poems*] is not for people who read poems only in the sense that they are not pretty, but lucid, technically brilliant, contemporary, as critical of the poet himself as of his society and the world.

The key sentence to Enzensberger's poetry and his related activities is: "absently i am here." At age 38 he is Germany's most important literary catalyst, a brilliant essayist, a discoverer and rediscoverer of literary talent, a translator from numerous languages (he has reworked some of his own poems into English), and editor of the politically and internationally oriented *Kursbuch,* compared with which similar American quarterlies seem safely settled in their indigenous version of cozy parochialism.

The theme of being and yet not being part of something which is characterized by spiritual destitution is the poet's central conflict and subject. Voznesensky, perhaps meaning to be flippant, could not have given a more accurate appraisal of what Enzensberger seeks to accomplish with everything he does. Admittedly, that is an unhappy task, and so it is not surprising that the dominant tone underlying his poetry should be one of unmistakably pure concealed melancholy.

> Michael Roloff, "Two Germans," in The New York Times Book Review, *August 18, 1968, p. 4.*

G. H. A. BECKMANN

The most public-minded if not the best of contemporary German poets, Hans Magnus Enzensberger feels too strongly about the way the world goes to be a steady and self-critical craftsman. It is important that this excellent bilingual collection [*Poems for people who don't read poems*] should include an unsuccessful poem like **"man spricht deutsch."** Its outspoken, often crudely argued disgust with a smug, sticky society, an almost ritual despair of identity and the sheer physical need to lash out indicate a frustration that bars the dimension of art. When Enzensberger attempts, as he does again in the long ambitious **"foam,"** a general satire, he loses control of his material. There is no clear perspective. Wild statements slip in for descriptions. The use of metaphor and symbol is unqualified, and the tone frequently lapses into mere aggressiveness or sentimentality. . . . Both poems mentioned, documents if you like of the late fifties and the radical mood of a younger generation, point out limitations that in some measure remain characteristic of nearly all Enzensberger's poetry. He is not a highly imaginative writer, and in many cases his poems are elaborations of obvious or even cliché ideas. (p. 129)

These warnings are not meant to deny Enzensberger his very considerable merits. He may at times lack originality, yet he makes effective use of his materials and is remarkably free from poetic inhibitions. His social realism, combined with a stringently reasoned appeal to his readers as political animals has reclaimed a basic social responsibility for the poet and his work. The importance of this should be particularly clear [in England], for social realism as such may easily lead to irrelevancies of observation and triviality of style and subject matter. Enzensberger's poetry shows an intellectual grasp that transcends the situation he touches, and where his ironic ruthlessness is substantially set and focused his verse of social involvement carries conviction. A notable example is the **"wolves defended against the lambs,"** upbraiding the discontent meek

> and tell me who sews the ribbons
> all over the general's chest? who
> carves the capon up for the usurer?
> who proudly dangles an iron cross
> over his rumbling navel? who
> rakes in the tip, the thirty pieces
> of silver, the hush money? listen: there
> are plenty of victims, very few thieves. . . .

The social realism is established in an argument with the readers who are drawn into a relentless process of social self-criticism that tightens owing to the brilliantly handled pattern of imagery and allusion. The entire structure of the poem, with its symmetry of questionnaire and verdict, mounts an inquisition on public behaviour. Poems like these channel a strictly political response and impart a sense of the urgency of social action and revolution, or, alternatively, of despicable self-contempt if not imminent annihilation. In his radical incitement, the poet assumes the function of the political moralist.

Enzensberger likes to address or, at least, involve the reader directly and he does so, irony always playing part and provoking thought, in a variety of moods that range from the highly inflammatory to the elegiac sadness in one of his greatest poems, **"the end of the owls,"** on thermo-nuclear war. He can be a master of understatement (. . . **"his middle-class blues"**) and also raise his questions in the form of expressionist nightmare as in **"the midwives,"** or in a masterpiece of symbolical description and assessment like **"historical process."** To avoid the wide-spread Anglo-Saxon impression that Enzensberger is a peculiar German writer who tackles the problems of his country in a rather unpatriotic way, one should begin with these poems instead of **"foam"** or **"man spricht deutsch."** Enzensberger's scope and significance has a wider than national truth and he should not be read as a kind of literary information on a new Germany.

Critics who have little taste for Enzensberger's political verse, or for politics, have singled out the love-poetry of his first volume [*Verteidigung der Wölfe* (1957)] for praise, and claim that while politics got in the way of poetry in the second volume [*Landessprache* (1960)] Enzensberger has re-discovered a personal style in the third [*Blindenschrift* (1964)]. . . . *Poems for people who don't read poems*, rightly I think, emphasizes the public side of Enzensberger's works. Contrary to the opinion quoted above there is evidence of a growing political awareness and a correspondent capacity for poetic articulation. **"Lachesis lapponica"** is likely to be one of the outstanding and lasting poems of the sixties. It may be interpreted as a self-portrait of the poet in nature, desperately trying to be absorbed by the scenery but finding his active social conscience taking his concentration. The interplay of imagination and dry irony, of various tones and voices in this poem shows Enzensberger at the height of his powers. It would indeed be a pity if he were to give up poetry for politics now he has reached a maturity of expression that vindicates poetry as an urgent and honourable means of self-understanding that keeps in touch with human needs at all levels. (pp. 130-31)

G. H. A. Beckmann, "Poetry of Public Concern," in Agenda, Vol. 6, Nos. 3 & 4, Autumn & Winter, 1968, pp. 129-32.

THE TIMES LITERARY SUPPLEMENT

The televised interrogation by pro-Castro journalists of forty-one prisoners-of-war in Havana, at the end of the Bay of Pigs fiasco, is Enzensberger's starting-point [in *Das Verhör von Habana*]. From a transcript of the proceedings (more than 1,000 pages of it) he has selected, arranged, translated, and—as distinct from "translated"—interpreted the ten texts which supposedly best suit his purpose; the purpose, that is, of exposing the evils of counter-revolution reflected in the actions and attitudes of Castro's bourgeois capitalist enemies. The interpretation takes the form of a forty-four-page introductory essay, without which the undiscerning reader might not fully grasp the damnable message inherent in the prisoners' testimony. The apparatus at the end of the book includes excerpts from a very long conversation between Castro and some of his prisoners (April 26, 1961), from a prisoner's statement about C.I.A. machinations and the plight of Cuban exiles in Miami (April 28, 1961), and from the court's verdict after the trial which followed the interrogations (April 7, 1962—there were 1,113 accused altogether). The final pages are devoted to photographs of Dr. Enzensberger's selected few, of their interrogators, and of the conversing Castro.

Although the interrogations in *Das Verhör von Habana* are said to constitute neither a play nor a film script, it is also said that they *can* be performed, on stage or television screen, and it is implied that they should be, as a sort of visual aid to learning. What is envisaged is a lesson not in the history of Cuba but in the ways far larger parts of the world work and will continue to work until the C.I.A. and those it serves . . . have perished. The mentality of those who in turn, whether they know it or not, serve the C.I.A. (e.g., the thwarted invaders) is one with which readers or viewers may initially identify but which, having watched or read on, they are expected finally to reject. It is the mentality, for example, of the rich man who admits that, had the invasion succeeded, he would have tried to get back the property he lost when Castro took over. . . . Not that all Enzensberger's specimens come from the same socio-economic strata. An unemployed waiter and disenchanted mechanic represent the dupes and underdogs of "the system", a Spanish priest stands for some of its willing accomplices, and a professional thug (subsequently executed) for its stooges. The eight senior journalists conducting the hearing are allegedly representative too: "they directly represent the Cuban people". Reference to biographical data at the back of the book reveals, however, that officially most of them do so no longer—only one, it seems, has any real say in the Cuba of 1970.

Enzensberger has in fact, in *Das Verhör von Habana,* a tendency at times to manipulate his material with an artlessness which is little short of baffling. To those who either read him quickly or need no persuading, such tendencies may not matter. But Enzensberger himself clearly calls for careful readers. How else than by taking a long hard look can the uncommitted, to whom the book is surely addressed, see through the apparent virtues of the villains on display? To regard the expression of progressive views by top people in capitalist societies as suspect is perhaps to be realistic; but the proposition that what such people say is nothing better than self-deception calls for more in the way of proof than *Das Verhör von Habana* provides. And to dismiss with contempt the fortitude, the dignity, and the awkward ability to argue evinced by some of the prisoners is to cheapen rather than to sell.

"Shrill Anti-American Voices," in The Times Literary Supplement, No. 3561, May 28, 1970, p. 588.

JAMES NELSON GOODSELL

The Bay of Pigs invasion of Cuba in April, 1961, was a total fiasco, a perfect failure. It was, as one commentator wrote, "a failure of mind, of imagination, of common sense."

If anything, it did the opposite of what it sought to do. Instead of eliminating or weakening the government of Cuban Prime Minister Fidel Castro, it strengthened his hold on the Cuban people—and inflated his prestige in the world.

The Havana Inquiry is a clear case in point. A documentary play on the CIA-supported invasion, it has been performed with wide acclaim before audiences in Germany and France.

Using the public testimony of 10 participants, Hans Magnus Enzensberger has woven together a fascinating—albeit one-sided—dialogue showing that those who took part in the landing were primarily from the ruling classes that Castro had deposed.

In truth, not all participants in the Bay of Pigs fiasco were from the ruling class; there were hundreds who came from very humble families. Enzensberger's play is essentially a political treatise, a sharp Marxist-oriented attack on the United States and its role in the Western Hemisphere, particularly in Cuba.

His attitude is so doctrinaire that it falls far short of objective analysis. . . .

However, the play remains valuable for its depiction of basic conflicts which were inherent in Cuba when Fidel Castro took power in 1959, and which still exist today. *The Havana Inquiry* is not the whole story, nor is it a balanced story, but it will give new insight into modern-day Cuba.

> *James Nelson Goodsell, in a review of "The Havana Inquiry," in* The Christian Science Monitor, *July 17, 1974, p. 11.*

ROGER SHATZKIN

Applying a nondoctrinaire dialectical method [in the essays collected in *The Consciousness Industry: On Literature, Politics and the Media,* Enzensberger] takes on the notions of both bourgeois and traditional leftist aesthetic criticism. Although some of the essays are overly abstract in spots, occasionally fragmented (he likes lists), and at times esoteric to the reader unfamiliar with European political and critical traditions, Enzensberger's methodology and insights ultimately command respect. He argues persuasively that the production of culture cannot be understood by ignoring or idealizing history, but rather by measuring culture within the context of the immediate historical and political moment. Difficult but important essays.

> *Roger Shatzkin, in a review of "The Consciousness Industry: On Literature, Politics and the Media," in* Library Journal, *Vol. 99, No. 14, August, 1974, p. 1953.*

PUBLISHERS WEEKLY

[*Politics and Crime* is] a powerful grouping of [Enzensberger's] political essays covering the past decade or so, felicitous and often brilliant in the writing and meaningful to serious American readers even when the author ponders German guilt (during Eichmann's trial) or examines Castro's Cuba (1969). Among more abstract subjects Enzensberger offers some horizon-widening essays on treason, official government secrets, political "ecology" and a magnificent piece on 19th century Russian revolutionary movements. Scarcely a paragraph lacks an indelibly aphoristic line or two.

> *A review of "Politics and Crime," in* Publishers Weekly, *Vol. 206, No. 19, November 4, 1974, p. 66.*

GEORGE WOODCOCK

We have all observed, not without a touch of *Schadenfreude,* how the strength of the great nuclear powers has proved to be somewhat illusory, since the very danger of atomic war gives a disproportionate nuisance value to small countries in turbulent regions like the Middle East. . . .

Much the same kind of situation has arisen in what Hans Magnus Enzensberger chooses to call "the consciousness industry." By this he means something more than what we generally call "communications" and the "media." [In the essays collected in *The Consciousness Industry,* he] includes education, the arts to the degree they have a popular appeal, everything that directly or indirectly influences public opinion.

One of the basic paradoxes of this multifarious industry, he observes, is that it "presupposes independent minds, even when it is out to deprive them of their independence." Moreover, the accuracy of that presupposition is ultimately fatal to those

who seek to manipulate the human mind through the media: Too many hands are involved for control to be easily centralized, and the new technologies of communication are becoming increasingly available to those who wish to subvert the officially sponsored world view.

So far, well and good. Just as we have seen how the nuclear powers fear the ability of smaller powers to use apparent irresponsibility as a form of blackmail, we can appreciate how modern technology has made states more vulnerable from within than they ever were in the past. Indeed, as Enzensberger suggests at one point, it can be argued that the French establishment was saved in 1968 mainly because the student rebels did not understand their own strength and romantically seized the Odeon Theatre instead of realistically invading the radio and television stations.

The great powers, he further contends, have been similarly spared by the failure of revolutionaries—lost in outdated Marxist dreams—to perceive the potentialities for popular participation in the dissemination of news and opinion that new communications advances have placed in their hands. In other words, Enzensberger is presenting a post-Orwellian view that denies the feasibility of monolithic control over the media as envisaged in the novel *1984*.

Even this is largely true. But the conclusions he draws from the situation I find both false and disturbing. Despite his attacks on Marshall McLuhan, he is really no less destructive of genuine cultural values and no less dominated by an uncritical acceptance of mechanical processes. Often he reads like nothing other than McLuhan paraphrased to suit the particular brand of radical chic that obtains in Germany.

Thus Enzensberger, too, regards the age of the book as brief and doomed—this notwithstanding the vast increase in book sales and library circulation in recent years. But when he speaks with stale absurdity of the "exclusive class character" of the book, equating it with the easel painting as a bourgeois luxury, he is not merely reaching for effect; he is derogating the intellectual capacities of the masses whose interest he would promote.

He goes on to propose that through the camera, the tape recorder and other products of technology (which, incidentally, cost much more than paperback books and would therefore seem nearer to the world of bourgeois luxury) every man can now become his own artist. In Enzensberger's view, the role of the writer today is to hasten that goal. . . . (p. 19)

Enzensberger merely perpetuates the Proudhonian, and Tolstoyan, myth that there is an art of the people as opposed to "bourgeois" art. Perhaps one need say no more than that in Tolstoy's case such an attitude resulted in the evaluation of *Uncle Tom's Cabin* as a better book than Count Leo's own novels *War and Peace* or *Anna Karenina*!

Enzensberger protects himself from this kind of absurdity by carefully avoiding discussion of specific works of literature, so that we never know who his electronic-age Harriet Beecher Stowe may be. He writes almost entirely in oracular statements, in barbed and sometimes stinging aphorisms. There is a great deal of talk in the abstract about the goal of poetry and the duties of poets, but he never quotes a line to show what he considers good verse, and very few to show what he thinks is bad. Consequently, as a critic promoting our understanding of literature he is entirely nugatory. (pp. 19-20)

Like other radical critics whose creativity is dubious or frustrated, Enzensberger is at his best as a reporter on the aberrations of the Left. The book's most successful essay—the one that is truly vivid because for once he is effectively concrete in his statements—is his **"Tourists of the Revolution."** This brilliant analysis of that audacious and economical instrument of corruption used by the Communist countries—the *delegacija* system, the subsidized tour for the fellow traveler—deserves a place beside the essays of Orwell, whom Enzensberger in his shallow arrogance dismisses, and of Dwight Macdonald, whom he would doubtless despise with equal injustice.

Yet **"Tourists of the Revolution"** is the exception that makes one all the more conscious that most of *The Consciousness Industry,* like most aphoristic writing, consists of gratuitous and pontifical pronouncements. In the end, one is led to suspect that the mask of the iconoclast merely conceals the mandarin manqué. (p. 20)

> George Woodcock, *"The Mask of a Mandarin Manqué," in* The New Leader, *Vol. LVIII, No. 2, January 20, 1975, pp. 19-20.*

DAVID CAUTE

I have noticed—have painfully wrestled with the same disease in myself—that modern writers of the European Left whose talents, interests, and energies are both "artistic" and intellectual, who oscillate between fiction, poetry, or drama on the one hand, and the political-ideological essay on the other, do tend to banish all artistry, all humor, indeed all humility from the harsh, flat, remorselessly rationalist prose by which they expose the scandalous disparity between the real and the ideal. Sartre, it is true, brought an artist's insights and recognizable human smells to the pages of *Saint Genet* and *Being and Nothingness,* but Brecht, the modern German writer with the most profound impact on Enzensberger, hurried from the quick, physical, colloquial atmosphere of the Theater am Schiffbauerdamm to his study, where he indulged in the relaxation of confiding to his notebook dry and categorical dogmas that no actress could possibly absorb and yet remain sane. (As he knew.)

This is Enzensberger's problem, too [in *Politics and Crime* and *The Consciousness Industry*]: a prose in search of a truly human future, but without a truly human phrase. The theoretician keeps the poet at arm's length. . . . (p. 476)

Despite his immense intelligence and—my prejudices announce—generally impeccable political judgment, this challengingly gifted poet seems to share the general Left Continental horror of acknowledging that a question of taste, in poetry as well as food, is quite liable to be just a question of taste. In his essay **"Poetry and Politics,"** for example, he cites several examples of sickeningly sycophantic poetry from the time of Plato to Johannes Becher's eulogy to Stalin, then hurries to insist: "The root of the scandal does not lie where it is usually sought: it lies neither in the person of him who is praised nor him who praises." Evidently a third person is also ruled out of account—the reader—for Enzensberger goes on to insist, in a manner so characteristic of intellectuals influenced by the Hegelian-Marxist tradition, that the true explanation for our dislike of Becher's eulogy resides in the fact that "the language of poetry refuses its services to anyone who uses it to immortalize the names of those exercising power. The reason for this refusal lies in poetry itself, not outside it."

Facets of this approach, of course, are admirable, most notably the rejection of the crude and hitherto prevalent Marxist search for the political value of a work of art in its "objective" portrait of society (Lukács), its overt celebration of the Party, etc. (Zhdanov), or its author's attitude toward the Berlin Wall or the Great Wall of Mao. Like Mayakovsky, Tretyakov, Breton, and Brecht before him, Enzensberger is both Marxist and modernist. Unfortunately, so great is the pressure within the Continental Left never to let one's pants drop and be caught floundering, bare-buttocked and erect, in the bourgeois whorehouse of personal taste, that Enzensberger feels constrained to counter Lukács, etc. with an "objectivity" no less rigorous than their own.

Now I admire Enzensberger's talents (he is also a gifted linguist), and I salute that part of him, a most considerable part, that penetrates the rhetoric and postures of his fellow-rebels, laying bare the democratic sham of the Cuban Communist Party as clear-sightedly as he earlier exposed the democratic sham of Germany's great coalition. He is a writer who is not afraid to be found alone, even at the cost of being ostracized by all the clans and cliques who support their identities with the flying buttresses of the hour. I have nevertheless found his essays, which span a wide variety of subjects, from the meaning of treason to the "media industry," the avant-garde, and political ecology, difficult to enjoy. They lack warmth, vitality, and contact with everyday life, even though such qualities are recognized by Enzensberger in passages he quotes by other authors such as Jan Myrdal and Susan Sontag.

Part of the trouble, I suspect, lies in his periodic capitulation to the very habits of mind he rightly distrusts. The monster manipulating the machine keeps reappearing even when Enzensberger is at pains to stress that the monster *is* the machine; and while valuably pointing out that the Left would do well to scrutinize the manipulation of the media manifest in every actual social system, Cuba no less than the United States, he is irresistibly drawn by the soft chocolates of anticapitalist reductionism: "the ruling class," "the revolution," and, of course, "the system." How seriously should one take a commentator who declares the problem of violence and illegality to be, simply, superfluous for those "who make the revolution," even though as he points out himself, all known revolutionaries have carried the poisons they wish to eject from the social bloodstream? Why superfluous? Because, says Enzensberger, opponents of the system must "operate at the limits of legality and constantly transgress the limits in both directions." Sounds very dialectical but what does it mean? (pp. 476-78)

I know how easily one can begin an essay, as he does, by knocking Orwell's pessimism as "undialectical," how stylishly one can conclude it with a flourish, as he does, about deepening contradictions. I know, too, how impossibly difficult it is to write an essay half as true to life as any one of Orwell's. (p. 478)

> David Caute, *"Systems Analysis," in* Partisan Review, *Vol. XLIII, No. 3, 1976, pp. 475-78.*

EDWIN MORGAN

[It] is hard not to admire the energy and range of a postwar German poet like Hans Magnus Enzensberger . . . who can turn out a series of acute essays on many aspects of contemporary society without letting his poetry go by default.

It may be that, given the times he has lived through, particularly in Germany, he has an abnormally keen awareness of the dangers of passivity, a theme that recurs through his verse and prose, and that, therefore, he wants the impossible task of 'an eye on everything'; an eye trained to see a long way off the wads of wool waiting to be pulled over it. However that may be, his essays are sharp, knowledgeable and thought-provoking.

Raids and Reconstructions has the subtitle "Essays in Politics, Crime and Culture", and its contents date from 1962 to 1973. It is an uneven collection, where, perhaps, most readers will single out subjects that interest them, rather than attempt to digest the whole.

Two essays have a brittle, deliberately provocative, rather Shavian (the author would say Brechtian) approach to emotive issues in the area of crime. **"Towards a Theory of Treason"** argues that treason is now not much more than a taboo, and that far from being a crime, it is 'nothing but the juristic name for revolution'. Consequently, the continued and almost religious interdiction of treason serves only 'as the one-sided instrument of the rulers'. **"Reflections Before a Glass Cage"** makes the point that since the days of the 'final solution', Hiroshima and Eichmann, it is almost impossible to use, and certainly impossible to define, the words 'crime' and 'criminal'; the ordinary 'criminal', like the 'traitor', has become merely mythological, and far from terrifying society, the criminal today really keeps it happy and complacent: 'For he only does what everyone would like to do, and he does it on his own without a concession from the state.' The answer to these two essays, of course, is 'Yes, but—'.

Possibly a clearer 'yes' would be given to his probing political analysis of the current ecology-and-conservation movement, in **"A Critique of Political Ecology"**. . . . Also of much interest is **"Constituents of a Theory of the Media"**, where he deplores the somewhat stagnant concept of media 'manipulation', admits, nevertheless, that 'there is no Marxist theory of the media', attacks the apolitical avantgarde of Warhol and Cage, but, equally, holds out a capacious dustbin for Lukács and Adorno as backward lookers, and ends with a strong plea for the artist or author not to stand aside from the mass media, for all their contradictions, but to show how capable he is of 'using the liberating factors in the media and bringing them to fruition'. And it is the very transience of the media, their refusal to provide tangible objects for the 'heritage', that is liberating. Three cheers for that!

Mausoleum, subtitled "Thirty-seven Portraits of the History of Progress", is a dazzlingly ironic, wry, indignant, scathing biographical collage of famous figures from the 14th to the 20th century—a poetry packed with reference and statement and quotation, a little after the manner of Marianne Moore, and equally incisive, but much more angry and concerned. Here is praise of Machiavelli and Chopin, hatred of Campanella and Leibniz and Sir Henry Stanley; wonder at Malthus ('merriest of men'), Darwin the hypochondriac, and Charles Messier . . . ; great insight into Piranesi, great horror at the animal and human experiments of Spallanzani and Ugo Cerletti; and most fascinating of all, a lyrically dialectic conversation with the revolutionary anarchist, Bakunin. The language is vivid . . . , the juxtapositions are startling, the assault on the reader's ease of mind is relentless; the overall effect is destructive, yet exhilarating. This is a collection not to be missed.

Edwin Morgan, "An Eye on Everything," in The Listener, *Vol. 97, No. 2506, April 28, 1977, p. 546.*

NEIL McINNES

In the somewhat conformist, *bien pensant* climate of the Federal Republic of Germany, Hans Magnus Enzensberger has long seemed an unclassifiable oddity. He is a learned Marxist, a radical critic of industrialism, of parliamentary democracy and of what he curiously calls "bourgeois science", but at the same time he scornfully rejects Soviet communism, fellow-travellers, ecological politics and the romantic revolutionism of Fidel Castro and Che Guevara. He frankly admires terrorists. There is nothing in [*Mausoleum* or *Raids and Reconstructions*] to show what he thinks of the Baader-Meinhof gang but there is plenty to suggest that he sees himself as doing with words what they did with bullets, that is, making cruel, desperate, hopeless attacks on random targets chosen in a system they all feel is hateful but invincible.

Enzensberger is lucid enough to see that there is a sort of complicity between the bomb-throwing terrorists and the more authoritarian forces in our societies. The terrorists fight the secret police, and the secret police justifies its existence (and its big, unaudited budget) by reference to the terrorists. The spies and traitors steal and sell secrets that never needed to be kept secret, and the counter-espionage agencies justify their even bigger and less audited budgets by reference to the "unseen enemy". This complicity can become outright collusion, in the person of the double agent and *agent provocateur*. In his essay on pre-Revolutionary Russian terrorists, Enzensberger says it is hard to say whose side a man like Asev was on: he was paid by the Ochrana to perpetrate genuinely revolutionary acts.

Now, although Enzensberger sees that ambiguous relation (any other Marxist would call it a dialectical relation, but Enzensberger does not talk jargon) at the level of physical terrorists, he does not notice that he himself is caught in it, at the intellectual level.

He wants to terrify the complacent educated class but he insists that this must be done from within existing institutions by opponents who are educated, fair, critical and immensely learned. He writes "political poetry" and mocks the coarseness and ignorance of communists and ecological freaks. He no doubt shocks many solid German burghers but, to the communists and ecologists, he must look like Asev. "Whose side is he on?", they will ask. He is entitled not to abide their question, since a radical critic is not obliged to choose political sides. But he is obliged to state his own position, and that Enzensberger never does. In these books, at least, there is no more than a hint that he launches his attacks from a vague proto-Marxism, of which the one dogma would be: exploitation and mystification will continue as long as men produce commodities. Since there is no imaginable way from our society to one where men would not produce commodities (ie, to one where they would do as they wished and live their hobbies), the only thing to do is stay with the well-paid, learned, refined and beautiful people and throw the odd bombshell.

The duplicity of this position is plain in the notion of "political poetry". By that, Enzensberger does not mean agitprop doggerel or proletarian art, but polished, learned and beautiful poems that cultivate an anti-industrial sensibility, not by talking about flowers and moonbeams but by talking about machines, engines and electroshock therapy. The "37 ballads from the history of progress" that make up *Mausoleum* are about inventors, technicians, scientists, scholars and politicians who made important contributions to industrial society. Many of them I had never heard of. Since Enzensberger entitles each poem only with initials and dates, one has to consult indexes, and dictionaries of biography, to see who it is he is writing about. . . .

To suggest an attitude is enough for a poet, but a political analyst must do more. I doubt if Enzensberger does more in *Raids and Reconstructions*. . . .

Take the theory of treason. Enzensberger says there is no such objective crime, just a taboo. It is eighty years since scholars took up the question of whether there was any information Dreyfus could possibly have given the German General Staff that would have hurt the French people, and decided there was none. Enzensberger thinks there still is none. "Information deficits" are filled by spy-satellites and careful analysis of the press. Traitors and counter-espionage agents just play cops and robbers in a primeval dream-world. Yet he does not examine any contemporary treason case, as other authors have done with great care. He thereby evades the fact that senior diplomats insist there do exist secrets of state that are in some sense precious to a community. And he dodges the obvious fact that industrial espionage certainly exists, and thus, since today's rivals are "military-industrial complexes", there must be information about weapons-systems and the like that it would be advantageous to obtain, damaging to divulge. That our thinking about treason is riddled with irrational respect for tribal taboos is plain, but that does not dispense the analyst from asking if there is not something more. . . .

The visible pleasure with which Enzensberger tells the story of the Russian terrorists (this is the longest thing in the book) is accounted for in the last lines: terrorists are good because they frighten the tyrants. "One such dreamer, an anonymous one in the crowd, suffices to instill dread into all those who hold power on this earth." Yet the worst tyrannies have come after the nihilists and have consisted in anti-terrorist dictatorships. If Stalin, Hitler, Franco and the rest were scared of terrorists, everyone suffered for it, and the dictators were never brought down by terror. That is so obvious for physical terrorists that I only mention it in order to ask what good intellectual raiders like Enzensberger do. I suspect they consolidate the system they pretend to oppose so radically. Effective social criticism is based on a coherent position, a rational morality that can be translated into real social institutions such as a political party or a reform movement. In contrast, hit-and-run raiders who can only shock without stating a case simply encourage the complacent educated class in its belief that its only opponents are crazy "dreamers of the absolute".

> Neil McInnes, "The Intellectual Terrorist," in The Times Literary Supplement, *No. 3925, June 3, 1977, p. 667.*

DENNIS D. DORIN

Politics and Crime is a collection of seven Hans Enzensberger essays on such topics as the theory of treason, genocide in the name of the nation-state, regicide as a last resort against tyranny, the potential for revolution in the Western industrialized states, the role of the Communist Party of Cuba, and the political implications of the ecology movement. (p. 636)

"Dreamers of the Absolute (Part I)—Pamphlets and Bombs" (1964) and **"(Part II)—The Beautiful Souls of the Terror"** (1964) provide an insightful account of the small bands of Russian terrorists of the late nineteenth and early twentieth centuries who sought personal and national salvation through the assassination of high-ranking officials of the czarist government. Such zealots, Enzensberger asserts with obvious satisfaction, constitute a threat to every regime founded upon its subjects' suffering. One of them, anonymous in the crowd, is enough to instill dread into "all those who hold power on the earth.". . . (p. 637)

"A Critique of Political Ecology" (1973) paints an apocalyptic picture of a world approaching ecological breakdown as a result of the excesses of capitalism. While Enzensberger believes that industrialization is far advanced in its destruction of the earth's sources of fuel, food, water, and air, he regards the "ecology movement" as nothing more than a propaganda campaign of the bourgeois and capitalist classes. The rescue of the environment, he argues, will not be attained through taxing the masses to pay for antipollution technology. Nor will it be achieved through exhortations to Third World peoples to restrict their birth rates. The abolition of the automobile, the desalinization of sea water, wars for raw materials, will prove only to be stop-gap measures. As long as capitalism survives, the quality of life can be expected to deteriorate. The world's hope, Enzensberger concludes, has to be socialist revolution. Only socialism can bring about the reconciliation of humanity with nature essential to survival.

This collection has its problems. Enzensberger's style is frequently ponderous and cryptic. His attempts to employ symbolism occasionally detract from the clarity of his arguments. Enzensberger demonstrates more intellectual force in assaults upon the ideological positions of others than in the development of his own. The title, *Politics and Crime,* implies that the anthology has more of a central theme than it does. But, each essay is stimulating. Enzensberger plays a valuable role in challenging major assumptions of Western and Communist political theory. (pp. 637-38)

> Dennis D. Dorin, in a review of "Politics and Crime," in The American Political Science Review, *Vol. 72, No. 2, June, 1978, pp. 636-38.*

DIETHER H. HAENICKE

For more than fifty years now, critics and historians of literature alike have assured us that the epic poem became an extinct genre in German literature at the turn of the century. But [in *Der Untergang der Titanic*] we have an epic poem again— transformed into a vastly modernized structure and independent of many of its traditional characteristics, but an epic poem nevertheless. And it turns out that the genre is by no means obsolete and inadequate but that, on the contrary, it provides a highly effective and versatile medium for the subject matter at hand. . . .

In thirty-three cantos Enzensberger "narrates" the famous story of the *Titanic,* which sank in the Atlantic Ocean in 1912. (p. 499)

The poet constantly changes his narrative position and perspective. He gives seemingly detached, objective reports in one canto; in another one he creates visionary scenes of the catastrophe; he offers wrathful comments on the inhuman treatment of the poor immigrant passengers; he mingles with the crew who are driven back to the flooded engine room, and he shares their fear of death; he sits with the dead who look back at the disaster with detestation for the survivors. Changes of meter and structural variations occur from canto to canto, corresponding with the continuous changes in the narrator's view-point.

The poem furthermore transcends the historical dimension of the time of the catastrophe. Not only does Enzensberger alternate his physical perspective, he also views the event from different perspectives in time: as an imaginary eyewitness on the boat, as a contemporary poet writing about the *Titanic* in the seventies, and from the timeless viewpoint of the deceased victims of the marine disaster. The multiformity of the individual cantos and the constant change of historical and narrative perspective make for a highly complex and almost bewildering poetic structure. Nevertheless, this epic poem may well be one of Enzensberger's strongest contributions to modern German literature. (p. 500)

> *Diether H. Haenicke, in a review of "Der Untergang der Titanic," in* World Literature Today, *Vol. 53, No. 3, Summer, 1979, pp. 499-500.*

MICHAEL HAMBURGER

Like most long or longer poems written in this century, *The Sinking of the Titanic* is not an epic but a clustering of diverse, almost disparate, fragments around a thematic core. The main event of the poem, the shipwreck of the *Titanic* in 1912, becomes a symbol and a microcosm, with extensions, parallels, repercussions on many different levels. The *Titanic* is also Cuba, East Berlin, West Berlin . . . , an updated version of Dante's Hell and many other places besides, including any place where any reader of the poem is likely to be. Not content with that much telescoping, Enzensberger also includes historical flashbacks to the fifteenth, sixteenth and nineteenth centuries, all to do with doubts, self-doubts, about art and the relation of art to reality. Other digressions are even more explicit in their questioning of the truthfulness and usefulness of poets and poetry. These also introduce Dante by name, though he is present in the whole poem as a prototype of what poetry can and cannot achieve.

I shall not attempt to list all the many theses and subtheses ironically advanced in the poem, usually to be challenged or contradicted by others, because it is the business of poems to do that as succinctly as possible; yet one brief quotation does seem to subsume the main message:

> We are in the same boat, all
> of us.
> But he who is poor is the first
> to drown.

Characteristically for Enzensberger, that assertion is supported by statistics of the passengers—first-class, second-class, steerage and crew—drowned and saved in the *Titanic* disaster. Much other material of that kind, including a menu, has been drawn upon. The most lyrical, i.e., songlike, canto of the thirty-three in the book—not counting the unnumbered interpolations—is the twentieth, adapted from *Deep Down in the Jungle: Negro Narrative and Folklore from the Streets of Philadelphia*. Documentary collages have been one of Enzensberger's specialties in verse and prose, and they are prominent as ever here, as in the Thirteenth Canto, made up of snatches of miscellaneous hymns and popular songs. Another is the permutation of simple colloquial phrases into puzzles or tautologies, not simple at all, but devastating, as in the interpolated section **"Notice of Loss."**

Yet the most impressive and reassuring parts of the sequence, poetically, are those in which Enzensberger lets himself go again a little at last, relying less on his bag of tricks—a formidable one—than on the imaginative penetration of specific experience, other people's and his own. A high-spirited, often comically cynical desperation is his peculiar contribution to the range of poetry; it becomes affirmative, if not joyful, in the concluding canto of this poem, a celebration of bare survival.

As for the other side of his gifts, his sheer accomplishment, cleverness and adroitness, one instance of it is his success in translating so intricate and ambitious a sequence into a language not his own. In earlier English versions of his own poems, he allowed himself the freedom of "imitation." This one is a close rendering, with no loss of fluency or exuberance, and very little of the idiomatic rightness of his German original. (pp. 529-30)

> *Michael Hamburger, "The Usefulness of Poets," in* The Nation, *Vol. 230, No. 17, May 3, 1980, pp. 528-30.*

MICHAEL HAMBURGER

Sixteen years have passed since Hans Magnus Enzensberger last published a collection of new short poems. Although "silence" seems quite the wrong word to use of a poet who has been active and conspicuous enough in other capacities, not least as an anti-poetic, anti-literary polemicist, but also as the author of two long sequences [*Mausoleum* and *The Sinking of the Titanic*] in which the quarrel between the poet and the anti-poet was fought out, the new collection [*Die Furie des Verschwindens*] does bridge a gap of sixteen years.

Die Furie des Verschwindens links up with the volume of 1964, *Blindenschrift*, by finally lifting the ban publicly imposed by Enzensberger on the kind of poetry that springs from moments of intense experience—experience inevitably subjective up to a point, however objective the correlatives; and it completes the breakthrough begun in [*The Sinking of the Titanic*] into a new phase that is also a continuation of his first. Brilliant though his early poems were, and masterly as his workmanship remained even in the least lyrical of his longer sequences, *Mausoleum*, the short poems in this new book are as consistently excellent as any he has written.

Many of the poems are character studies which allow him to achieve an unprecedented balance between the social criticisms he had always regarded as his main function and the spontaneity with which that function tended to conflict. By getting under the skin of, for example, a thirty-three-year-old woman, an uneasy male business executive, an equally uneasy employee on holiday in Spain—each a "short history of the bourgeoisie", as another poem is called—Enzensberger is now able to present a whole complex of delicate interactions from the inside; and it no longer matters whether the social criticism is subjective or objective, whether the inside is the poet's own or another person's. The fusion is so complete, the execution so impeccable, that there is no relevant distinction to be made between poems of immediate personal experience and successful projections into fictitious characters and their situations; nor, for that matter, between "confessional" poetry and satire.

The social criticism is more incisive, more knowing, more searching than ever before; but it is so because Enzensberger has learnt to dispense with the utopian reformer's vantage point, as well as with the rhetorical bravura of his early verse. One reason for that may be that he has come to include himself among those—bourgeois or otherwise—whose prospects are summed up in the poem **"Unregierbarkeit"** (ungovernability): "on legs getting shorter and shorter/power is waddling into the future."

Michael Hamburger, *"Causes for Pessimism,"* in The Times Literary Supplement, *No. 4045, October 10, 1980, p. 1153.*

R. J. HOLLINGDALE

The Sinking of the Titanic is in thirty-three "cantos", with sixteen intercalated poems; the cantos, by and large, tell the story, the intercalated poems refer to it obliquely, some of them very obliquely. When he allows himself to do so, Enzensberger can write very powerful and convincing narrative verse: the fifth Canto is forty-six excellent lines on the failure of the steerage passengers of the Titanic to take their rescue into their own hands; the twelfth Canto is twenty-eight excellent lines on the evacuation of the ship; the fourteenth Canto is thirty-two excellent lines on the ship slowly filling with water; the seventeenth Canto is twenty-two excellent lines on the ship going down; the eighteenth Canto is twenty-five excellent lines on the survivors in the boats listening to the cries of the survivors in the sea—strong narrative quite capable of engaging those "people who don't read poems" for whom Enzensberger produced his first volume of verse in English. . . .

And there is more fine verse: four of the inserted poems, for instance, are descriptions of painters and their paintings. They may be imitations of Browning, perhaps as communicated by Pound; they are certainly Browningesque, whether by design or not, and they would easily establish their author's reputation if he were unknown.

But—and it's a big but—everything about *The Sinking of the Titanic* is not as happily achieved as this. There is the matter of its wilful complexity. The *Purgatorio* of Dante, you will recall, is also in thirty-three cantos, and the otherwise unmotivated appearance of Dante in several places here (the poem **"Identity Check"**, inserted after the twenty-third Canto, is wholly devoted to him), and as a passenger aboard the doomed liner, must be intended to draw attention to this fact. We are being invited, it seems, to regard *The Sinking of the Titanic* as Enzensberger's *Purgatorio*. The invitation is pressed home through the employment of a simple *leitmotif* technique. In the fourth Canto, the author tells us that he has written a poem called "The Sinking of the Titanic"—"It was a good poem", he adds, rightly shunning false modesty—and that it was "pencilled / into a notebook, wrapped up / in black oilcloth"; in the last canto, in a list of seafarers who are heading for destruction, we are told that "the gentleman clad in white, / holding a manuscript wrapped in black oilcloth, is undoubtedly Dante." Let us not dwell on the awful risk of annihilation Enzensberger is running by inflicting this comparison upon himself: we should, however, not fail to notice the pretentiousness of his scheme, nor to question whether anything except complexity is really gained by the imposition of Dante upon the sinking of the Titanic.

But this is not nearly all. The story told by *The Sinking of the Titanic* is not, as you might think, the story of the sinking of the Titanic. It is the story of Enzensberger's life from the late 1960s, when he was in Havana, to the late 1970s, when he was in Berlin. The "Sinking of the Titanic" is a poem he wrote which was lost in the post; the shipwreck scenes we are given here are as much of it as he can remember. That at least appears to be the case. I am not saying that this is a fiction invented so as to make use of pieces of an epic poem on the Titanic which he was in fact unable satisfactorily to complete or, possibly, to make lengthy enough for the kind of publication he had in mind; but I do say that the further complexity of the text thus resulting constantly imperils whatever dramatic pressure the narrative—whether of Enzensberger's life or of the sinking of the Titanic—may have. It makes this a very "literary" work—in the pejorative sense.

From the technical point of view, Enzensberger has attempted something which has defeated him and which would probably have defeated even Joyce. Question: what do the North Atlantic in April 1912, Havana in the 1960s and Berlin in the 1970s have in common? Answer: they all had people in them. Apart from that they have nothing in common, and that is why the task he has undertaken of combining them into a single idea has proved insuperably difficult except at the level of extreme generalization—"It's all Purgatory, mate!" Havana and Berlin appear in this poem presumably only because Enzensberger happens to have lived in them—which was bad luck for him, since neither city lends itself very easily to being likened to the floundering Titanic. Technically, the nearest he gets to a successful fusion of at any rate two of his disparate locations is in the ninth Canto, in which he describes a visit to a Havana cinema, where he sees "Barbara Stanwyck . . . hopping about with Clifton Webb" in a film set on a ship: even here, though, he withholds the information that the film is called *Titanic* and features the never-to-be-forgotten night to remember as its climax and conclusion. That, however, is the best he can do: the worst, perhaps, occurs at the end of the third Canto, when he

> looked out with an absent mind
> over the quay at the Caribbean Sea,
> and there I saw it . . .
> I saw the iceberg, looming high
> and cold . . .

An—or rather "the"—iceberg off Havana? Of course, it is an illusion—"I was the only one to see it"—but is it not, artistically speaking, very forced? A failure, in fact?

Enzensberger has, it seems to me, been unable to elude the younger of the twin ancestral curses of the house of German letters: inferior imitation of foreign models. The third Canto, for example, begins:

> I remember Havana, the plaster coming down /
> from the walls, a foul insistent smell / choking
> the harbor, the past voluptuously fading, / and
> scarcity gnawing away, day and night, / at the
> Ten Year Plan . . .

Whom does that remind you of? There is a touch of Hemingway in it: "You know how it is there early in the morning in Havana with the bums still asleep against the walls of the buildings; before even the ice wagons come by with ice for the bars?" (*To Have and Have Not*). But the chief resemblance is to another writer of Cantos [Ezra Pound]. . . . **"News Wires of April 15, 1912"**, inserted after the nineteenth Canto, is John Dos Passos, even to the American "wires". The thirteenth Canto is put together from bits of hymns, like a travesty of *The Waste Land*.

There are other obscurities in the text, of a kind that reflection—mine, at least—cannot pierce. . . .

Taking **The Sinking of the Titanic** as a whole, I find it hard to believe that that fine poet and much honoured man, Hans Magnus Enzensberger, now in his fifty-second year, can be truly satisfied with this far-too-diversified production, in which a potentially excellent poem about a shipwreck—which tells its own story and whose further implications the reader may draw for himself if he cares to and can—is all but swamped by waves of over-ambition. Might a rescue not be attempted at some future time? It would be a pity if what is worth saving went down with what isn't.

R. J. Hollingdale, "Wails from the Icy Water," in The Times Literary Supplement, No. 4075, May 8, 1981, p. 509.

LAURENCE LERNER

[**The Sinking of the Titanic** is] all relaxed and colloquial in style, vast and symbolic in subject. The fact that in the fifteenth Canto the poet appears, telling his sceptical readers ("Rather passé, we should have thought, all these hidden meanings") that there *are* no hidden meanings, that "metaphors do not exist", will of course deceive nobody. The poem *is* an allegory, and yes, of course, we are all passengers on the *Titanic,* heading for disaster, but we mustn't give up: in the very last line of all, the poet is still swimming.

It all sounds horribly obvious, yet in the event the poem is a good read, always entertaining, sometimes brilliant, written with a Brechtian impudence that saves it almost completely from pretentiousness. It is hard to see that the sections on paintings have much to do with the rest, except in the obvious sense that they are about the relation between art and life, but they are well done, especially **"Apocalypse: Umbrian Master, about 1490."** . . . As for the narrative itself, the most brilliant sections seem to be Canto 5 in which an unnamed agitator fails to persuade the steerage passengers to take their rescue into their own hands, to "throw the bastards overboard", because, though "they understood what he said, they did not understand him": Canto 14, which describes the ship steadily filling with salt water: and Canto 18, which describes the lifeboats not picking up those in the water, in a long sentence of intricate and terrible flatness. . . .

[Enzensberger] is a reminder that one can after all be modern without being obscure. He is one who puts things in rather than leaves them out. (p. 69)

Laurence Lerner, "Wrestling with the Difficult," in Encounter, Vol. LVII, No. 3, September, 1981, pp. 62-9.

JOHN SIMON

Renaissance men (or women) are in short supply these days. Rare indeed is the writer who can hold his own as poet, translator, critic, playwright, polemist, anthologist, and editor of two remarkable—and very different—periodicals. But Hans Magnus Enzensberger is all of those things (and probably a few others I forgot to mention), and manages them with a wit and polish that belie their profundity. Yet what makes him so extraordinary is that even within each individual field he is a bit of a Renaissance man.

Thus there is no end to the themes and forms that Enzensberger's poetry, for example, has espoused; yet from volume to volume, and even from poem to poem, it is able to be as various as verse can get, without losing, however, the feel and scent of its author's unmistakable identity. There seem to be, as when a ball of mercury is rolled across a smooth surface, a great number of glittering little Enzensbergers that in the end coalesce all the same into one dazzling mind and sensibility.

We are presented [in **Critical Essays**] with a selection of Enzensberger's essays that, of necessity, cannot encompass the full range of the man. Even so, they do give a generous inkling of his diversity, and attest to the benefits of a complex literary sensibility's latching on to political matters, and, conversely, of a historically and politically astute mind's addressing itself to our arts and culture. (p. vii)

Enzensberger knows how to deal with complicated ideas and fine discriminations in a style that, though anything but inelegant, is nevertheless stunningly straightforward and plain. . . . He may have begun as an adherent of Marxism, but by now even that -ism—at least in its doctrinaire form—has been left behind. With the more modish and obscurantist ones he never had any truck. The only -ism that persists in his work is humanism. There are no hobby horses; only horse sense. (p. viii)

I should like to quote a poem of his; partly in order to remind you of a very important other aspect of his talent, but even more so as to give you a sense of the essential Enzensberger expressed most tersely, yet with those persistently, understatedly reverberating ironies that I urge you to notice in the prose as well. The poem is called **"Remembrance."**

> Well now, as concerns the seventies
> I can express myself with brevity.
> Directory assistance was always busy.
> The miraculous multiplication of loaves
> was restricted to Düsseldorf and vicinity.
> The dread news came over the ticker tape,
> was taken cognizance of and duly filed.
>
> Unresisting, by and large,
> they swallowed themselves,
> the seventies,
> without guarantee for latecomers,
> Turkish guest workers and the unemployed.
> That anyone should think of them with leniency
> would be asking too much.

The tone, *mutatis mutandis,* is very much the one of Enzensberger's best essays: the chiseled mockery of a civilized man who has not given up the fight, but who chooses his weapons fastidiously: the implication-drenched detail, hearty irony, incitement to thought.

This is in the best tradition of the German essay. . . . And here it behooves us to recognize how few of our English and American essayists had this kind of sardonic acumen to apply equally to culture and politics: George Orwell, of course, and Edmund Wilson, and doubtless a few others. But they are precious few, and Hans Magnus Enzensberger, in good English translations, readily assumes a place beside them as their equal. For what gives him the finishing touch of the Renaissance man is his internationalism. However much we might wish, defensively, to relegate him to otherness—to being German, European, Continental, or whatever—it won't wash. He stands right beside us, whoever we are. He is one of us. (pp. viii-ix)

John Simon, in a foreword to Critical Essays by Hans Magnus Enzensberger, edited by Reinhold Grimm and Bruce Armstrong, The Continuum Publishing Company, 1982, pp. vii-ix.

REINHOLD GRIMM

It happened nearly two decades ago, yet I can recall it as vividly as if it had occurred yesterday. The scene: Frankfurt University; the year: 1964. A slender, fair-haired, almost boyish-looking man of thirty-five was mounting the rostrum. He was greeted with a veritable uproar of applause. His first public address as the newly appointed poet-in-residence had been the talk of the town; in fact, town and gown—both students and scholars, critics and fellow writers, the representatives of the big publishing firms and of the mighty media, as well as the city's dignitaries—all were in attendance. Not even the largest lecture hall could hold this crowd: the event had to be broadcast by short-circuit to an adjacent hall. The late Theodor W. Adorno, editor of Walter Benjamin and West Germany's leading philosopher, sociologist, and aesthetician, had volunteered to present the speaker. Adorno declared, to cheers: "All we have in German literary criticism, nay, in criticism as such, is Hans Magnus Enzensberger . . . and a few scattered attempts" (*Wir haben ihn und Ansätze*). This is precisely what the great scholar Ernst Robert Curtius had once stated in regard to the seminal critic and essayist Friedrich Schlegel, and what Schlegel himself had said of Gotthold Ephraim Lessing, founder of a comparable literary criticism.

When Enzensberger was hailed in the mid-sixties as a latter-day Lessing or Schlegel by his friend and mentor, only two volumes (albeit weighty and sizable ones) of his critical and essayistic output had appeared, but he had already brought out three volumes of poetry, containing some of the finest postwar verse written in German. His lyrical breakthrough in 1957 had been likened to the meteoric rise and lasting fame of Heinrich Heine, and in 1963 he had been awarded the prestigious Büchner Prize which commemorates Heine's contemporary, Georg Büchner. More achievements were to follow: a documentary play and a documentary novel, a pair of libretti, an epic, another three volumes of poetry, and two more volumes of essays and criticism. Enzensberger was also active as a prolific and conscientious editor who enjoyed that rarest of editorial gifts: serendipity. With his two journals alone, *Kursbuch* (timetable or railroad guide—a title abounding in ambiguities and allusions) and *Transatlantik*, founded in 1965 and 1980 respectively, he might safely boast of having ensconced himself as the most innovative and stimulating literary promoter and critical mediator of his generation. (pp. xi-xii)

Enzensberger's very concept of art and literature and their function is reflected in [his] pattern of steady development and restless change. Since his first publications in the mid-fifties, he has expanded his horizons, but he also became absorbed in nearly insoluble problems—he has proceeded from local and national to global and international and therefore ever graver concerns. His earliest collection of essays, *Einzelheiten (Odds and Ends; Details)*, first published in 1962, was soon after brought out as a two-volume paperback comprising *Bewusstseins-Industrie (The Consciousness Industry)* and *Poesie und Politik (Poetry and Politics)*. The collection featured an acid polemic against the *Frankfurter Allgemeine Zeitung*, the foremost West German newspaper, and an unmasking of *Der Spiegel*, West Germany's equivalent of *Time* Magazine, and its jargon. On the other hand, his last such collection to date, *Palaver: Politische Überlegungen (Palaver: Political Consider-*

ations), which appeared in 1974, contained a broad and strongly self-critical satire on the leftist intelligentsia of all countries and their cherished "tourism of the revolution." It analyzes their traveling and fellow-traveling to socialist paradises and tellingly culminates with the penetrating **"Critique of Political Ecology,"** which is scarcely Marxist in any orthodox sense, but is certainly Marxian. The two earlier collections of 1964 and 1967 reveal in their choice of titles, *Politik und Verbrechen* (*Politics and Crime*) and *Deutschland, Deutschland unter anderm (Germany, Germany Among Other Things),* that duality of centrifugal expansion and centripetal absorption, entanglement though never total engulfment, which distinguishes Enzensberger's manifold and seismographic oeuvre. As controversies are unavoidable, so are contradictions. Enzensberger's widening gyre reveals itself as a deepening vortex as well.

Yet precisely this complexity makes him exemplary for our present age; it elevates his writings—with their unceasing dialectic of past and future, closeness and distance, commitment and resignation, hope and despair, even utopia and apocalypse—to an outstanding contribution to world literature and modern life. His essays can perhaps be best summed up by drawing on their author's own binary formula: they treat, basically, either "poetic" or "political" issues, just as his creative work at large consists, for the most part, of either poetry or critical prose. The texts assembled [in *Critical Essays*] represent the scope and topicality of Enzensberger's approach to questions of art, literature, culture, to history, sociology, ecology. (pp. xiv-xv)

[A] reference book I consulted does not list even one German title or author under the heading "Essay." Do not Lessing and Schlegel deserve mention, not to speak of Goethe, Schiller, Heine, Nietzsche? And what about such widely divergent modern classics as Thomas Mann, Gottfried Benn, and Bertolt Brecht? What about Brecht's friend Walter Benjamin and, in his train, Adorno? The German tradition offers a wealth, not only of genuine essays worth reading, but also of pertinent insights well worth pondering. For example, Schlegel's aphorism has it that it is as detrimental to a writer to have a solid system as to have no system at all; he must sustain a dialectical unity, if not balance, of contradictions. This definition illuminates both the content and structure of Enzensberger's work in the genre as well as that of many other writers.

It is to be hoped that the essays of Hans Magnus Enzensberger will succeed in redressing the general state of neglect and ignorance of German achievements in the essay form from the time of Lessing and Schlegel. These essays preserve and enliven a rich tradition. In form and essence, and for all the tentativeness and subjectivity peculiar to their kind, they partake of much of Lessing's humanistic verve and straightforwardness, much of Schlegel's literary urbanity and wit—to mention again two of Enzensberger's earliest ancestors. Steadfastly, Enzensberger continues to take up and face, more than any other essayist I know of, the burning issues of our time. (pp. xv-xvi)

Reinhold Grimm, in an introduction to Critical Essays *by Hans Magnus Enzensberger, edited by Reinhold Grimm and Bruce Armstrong, The Continuum Publishing Company, 1982, pp. xi-xvi.*

William Gaddis

1922-

American novelist.

Gaddis's three novels, *The Recognitions* (1955), *JR* (1975), and *Carpenter's Gothic* (1985), have established him as an important, if somewhat obscure, contemporary novelist. *The Recognitions,* generally regarded as his most accomplished work, is considered an influential precursor to postmodernism, an experimental literary movement which included John Barth and Thomas Pynchon among its seminal contributors. Like other postmodern novelists, Gaddis employs self-reflexive narrative techniques, fragmented structures, and extensive use of parody and satire while examining social, artistic, and cultural themes. He relies largely on disjointed and fragmented dialogue to convey the labyrinthine plots and rapidly shifting settings that characterize his work. According to Bruce Allen, Gaddis displays an overriding concern with "the omnipresence and dominance of mendacity and greed in human dealings, and the likelihood . . . that this folly is suicidal, and may lead to extinction."

The Recognitions is an immense work replete with literary, historical, mythological, and religious allusions. The story centers on Wyatt Gwyon, a clergyman's son who abandons his aspirations for the ministry to become an artist and, ultimately, a forger of classical Flemish paintings. *The Recognitions* contains an array of bizarre characters and intricate subplots, each amplifying Gaddis's central themes of falsehood, fragmentation, sterility, and decline, which he sees as characteristic of modern civilization. Carol Iannone observed: "The novel suggests that copying, in the sense of reverential 'recognition' of the vision of the masters, is more genuinely creative than the spurious originality sponsored by sentimental romantic values." Gaddis also suggests the absurdity of prolonging religious and social rituals that have been rendered meaningless by the chaos of modern life. In this work, Gaddis parodies a variety of literary works, including the Bible, Sir James Frazer's *The Golden Bough,* and James Joyce's *Ulysses,* and includes passages written in several different languages. Although considered by many to be abstruse and pretentious, *The Recognitions* is lauded by Gaddis's supporters as a landmark in American fiction.

Gaddis won the National Book Award for his second novel, *JR.* In this work, he retreats from the cosmopolitan breadth of *The Recognitions* to revile what he perceives as the decadent influence of American capitalism. This novel is an account of the corporate adventures of an eleven-year-old boy who amasses, through cunning and deceit, an enormous financial empire. Among Gaddis's thematic concerns in *JR* is entropy, a theory of thermodynamics which suggests that systems tend to move from energy and order toward chaos and inertia. Gaddis employs this theory as a metaphor for American capitalism. According to Carol Iannone, "The entropic decline in *JR* is seen by Gaddis as the result of the subordination of all values in capitalist America to greed and profit." In *JR,* Gaddis relies almost exclusively on dialogue to show how modern uses of language reflect social decline. While some critics found this technique convoluted and distracting, others praised it as an exemplary instance of an artist uniting form and content.

© 1987 Thomas Victor

Carpenter's Gothic is an attempt to capture the disorder of contemporary life that Gaddis believes is contributing to the decline of American society. Set in a ramshackle Victorian house along the banks of the Hudson River, *Carpenter's Gothic* focuses on a few days in the life of Elizabeth Booth, an heiress to her father's mining fortune, and Paul, her ruthless husband. Overwhelmed with information from electronic and print media, Liz and numerous minor characters engage in garrulous and often unintelligible dialogue that illustrates the banality and redundancy of contemporary life. *Carpenter's Gothic* has been viewed as a metaphorical novel, with the tawdry American Gothic houses built in imitation of the architecturally sound European prototypes serving to represent American art and society. "The real story of *Carpenter's Gothic,*" observed Terrence Rafferty, "isn't the end of the world, [but] the end of the imagination, the world gone dark in the writer's head."

(See also *CLC*, Vols. 1, 3, 6, 8, 10, 19; *Contemporary Authors,* Vols. 17-20, rev. ed.; *Contemporary Authors New Revision Series,* Vol. 21; and *Dictionary of Literary Biography,* Vol. 2.)

CHRISTOPHER LEHMANN-HAUPT

One comic scene in William Gaddis's remarkable new novel [*Carpenter's Gothic*]—his first in nearly a decade and his third in 30 years—reveals Paul Booth, a Vietnam veteran turned media consultant, frantically drawing a diagram for his harried wife, Elizabeth. In it, he tries to show her certain outlandish schemes he is currently working on. . . .

> He had a blunt pencil,—here's Teakell . . . and a smudged circle appeared and shot forth an arrow.—Got his own constituency here . . . a blob took roughly kidney shape,—Senate committees and the big voice for Administration policy up here . . . something vaguely phallic,—and his whole big third world Food for Africa program over here . . . and an arrow shot to distant coastlines shaped up abruptly in a deformed footprint.

About 20 pages later, another character, a man named McCandless who owns the house overlooking the Hudson River that the Booths are renting, pays a call on her and remarks, "I didn't know you had children?" She sees that he is looking at her husband's "blobs and crosses, lightning strokes, hails of arrows" and says, "Oh, oh that that's just, nothing."

This little joke illustrates any number of things about Mr. Gaddis's compressed, complex novel, not least of them Paul Booth's nutty patronization of his deceptively compliant wife. But, more significant, the incident is typical of the way that the discovery of innocent-seeming objects is the instrument by which the plot of *Carpenter's Gothic* unfolds. Indeed the novel could be described as a mosaic of curious objects, which seem to have lives of their own and must be viewed just so if the pattern they form is to be seen.

And, most important of all, the joke of the diagram evokes one of the novel's major themes, which has been sounded only a moment earlier when McCandless echoes Liz Booth's lament of the Halloween mess that the neighborhood kids have made. "Like the whole damned world isn't it," he says, "kids with nothing to do."

In this respect, Mr. Gaddis's new novel reverses the situation of his earlier work of fiction, *JR* . . . . For if *JR* focused its plot on an 11-year-old boy who parlays a school assignment into a vast financial empire, then *Carpenter's Gothic* is about a scheming grownup who makes a child's mess of everything.

Or does he really? Another character, a C.I.A. agent, looks at Paul Booth's diagram and says, "it's Cressy. I just figured it out. It's the battle of Cressy," meaning of course the village of Crécy-en-Ponthieu, where in 1396 the English fought the French in one of the most significant battles in history. Paul's doodling may not be so childish after all. Just as the objects in Mr. Gaddis's plot have multiple ways of presenting themselves, so do the actions of his characters. It may just be that Paul succeeds in his plan to start a war in Africa by promoting the interests of a fundamentalist preacher named Reverend Elton Ude. On the other hand, Paul may amount to nothing but words and empty gestures.

It depends to some degree on which of the several meanings of the novel's title one chooses to emphasize. Most literally, *Carpenter's Gothic* refers to the style of the house that the Booths are renting. . . .

But the title may also refer to the rude and barbarous Christianity that Reverend Ude has made of what history's most

famous carpenter began. Or to McCandless's embittered view of American civilization. . . .

Or one might apply the title to the form of the novel itself. This seems appropriate in several ways. Out of the simple situation of a married couple renting a house, Mr. Gaddis has "carpentered" "grotesque and violent events, and an atmosphere of degeneration and decay," to cite one dictionary's definition of literary gothic. More satisfying still is to compare the present book with Mr. Gaddis's previous two novels, both of which seemed to this reader at least virtually unreadable because of their length, their repetitiousness and their complexity. Not least among the things for which one can be grateful is that if *The Recognitions* and *JR* were grandiose, then Mr. Gaddis has taken their visions and in *Carpenter's Gothic* has brought them down to "human scale."

Some of Mr. Gaddis's more passionate admirers may regard this act of becoming comparatively accessible as one of stepping down in esthetic class and compromising the best things he has stood for. But I disagree. In *Carpenter's Gothic* Mr. Gaddis hasn't so much reduced the complexity of his fiction as compressed it. By doing so he has transformed a tiresome task into an inviting challenge—in short, something very like an entertainment.

> *Christopher Lehmann-Haupt, in a review of "Carpenter's Gothic," in* The New York Times, *July 3, 1985, p. C22.*

MALCOLM BRADBURY

It's exactly 30 years ago that William Gaddis published his vast and remarkable novel about fiction and forgery, *The Recognitions*. It showed a world of dark and complex plots where the faked and the forged seemed the basic conditions of human existence. To a number of critics, including myself, it was the starting place for a whole new direction in contemporary American fictional experiment, opening the path for Thomas Pynchon and the modern labyrinthine novel. We waited for Gaddis' second novel; but over 20 years were to pass before he came out with *JR,* another extraordinary book, about a sixth-grader who masters and manipulates the plots and systems of conglomerate capitalism.

The critics tried to find the right words for Gaddis' special qualities. This was the "cybernetic" novel, committed to the styles and techniques that could capture the noise and the redundancy of a technetronic age. His style, like Pynchon's, was the "paranoid" style, a way of writing of a world so made of plots and conspiracies that the individual is swamped by external systems and discourses. The terms are useful in catching at Gaddis' complex and baroque method, though they hardly suggest one of his strongest qualities: his enormous satiric vitality. What is clear is that Gaddis is one of the great talents of the recent American novel, though his books remain still something of a cult item. (p. 1)

At a mere 262 pages, Gaddis' new book [*Carpenter's Gothic*] is, in his terms, hardly more than a novella, lacking the overwhelming mass of the two earlier novels. But it shows no lack of his striking and baroque technique, or his talent for constructing labyrinthine plots and vast conspiracies. The direct action of the story is held over a few days in and around one single rented house up on the Hudson. Here lives Liz, the book's passive "heroine" and still center, the heiress to a corporation fortune which is still in litigation. Here comes and goes her husband Paul, an opportunist media consultant who is wheeling and dealing in the world of international corporations, law, Washington politics and fundamentalist religion. Here too, in a locked room, are the papers of the owner of the house, the geologist McCandless. Liz, damaged after a plane crash, consoles herself with Gothic fantasies, especially images from Orson Welles' film of the finest of Gothic novels, *Jane Eyre*. But meanwhile the world enters, endlessly, through the telephone's ceaseless ringing, the mailbox, the newspaper headlines (TEARFUL MOM), TV and the unstoppable, incomprehensible penetration of the corrupt political, commercial and religious practices of hyped-up, born-again America.

The house, appropriately, is built in carpenter's Gothic, the American domestic style based on the European Gothic forms, but using the skills and materials locally to hand. . . . These houses were built from the outside and the inside rooms filled in later—an unmistakable parallel for those who live there now, trying to sustain their own "conceits, borrowings, deceptions" against the pressure of the world. Like Pynchon's Oedipa Maas (in *The Crying of Lot 49*), Liz can only struggle to find some way of making sense of random interruption and disorder in a world of vast systems, picking up loose connections from the words in dictionaries, the images in books and films, and a brief love-affair with the decent but defeated McCandless, lost amid the disorder of his own papers. (pp. 1, 11)

The world outside and beyond Liz is a world of dark imperialism, shrouded in the ignorance of an age of raging fundamentalist faiths. Paul promotes the cause of the media evangelist the Reverend Ude, who attacks evolution and science, abortion and Marxism, in a mission that is a cover for the exploitation of mineral resources in Africa. The old Heart of Darkness is as dark as ever, a continent where fanatics from every faith conduct their jihads in a new era of mindless revealed religion, as if hungry for apocalypse.

As in Gaddis' earlier novels, the characters are ritual talkers, makers of tales and interpretations which compete to structure the accumulating plots and conspiracies of life. All stories conceal some falsehood. Liz herself seeks "some hope of order restored, even that of a past itself in tatters, revised, amended, fabricated in fact from its very past to reorder its unlikelihoods, what it all might have been. . . ." Both Liz and McCandless write fictions, but they are powerless before the fictions of life, the conspiracies that do have power, and in their ever-unravelling complexity take us to the book's bleak ending.

But, like Gaddis' other novels, *Carpenter's Gothic* has a marvelous stylistic precision and a sharp satirical bite. Gothic fiction has always been about reason's struggle with extremity. It has also shown the power of as well as the defeat of the inventive process of fiction. Gaddis' own fine patchwork of "conceits, borrowings, deceptions" has rebuilt the form to write a novel of our own irrational fundamentalist and apocalyptic age. This fine and tightly-made book shows again that Gaddis is among the first rank of contemporary American writers. (p. 11)

> *Malcolm Bradbury, "The House That Gaddis Built,"* in Book World—The Washington Post, *July 7, 1985, pp. 1, 11.*

FRANCES TALIAFERRO

Carpenter's Gothic is not a restful novel. It is, however, agreeably free of authorial judgments, preachings, pronouncements or ego-spillages. Neither are there authorial incursions into any character's psyche. We know only what is expressed or implied in rapid conversation.

The central characters, Liz and Paul Booth, have recently rented a Victorian house somewhere on the Hudson River. Liz, a beautiful redhead, is an heiress whom Paul married for her money. Paul, a Vietnam veteran, has grandiose plans for his future as a media consultant.

Paul's big client is the Rev. Elton Ude, an evangelistic preacher who leads a movement called Christian Recovery for America's People (note the acronym it forms). Ude, a slick operator, runs a mission in Africa whose fortunate location will enrich him when he sells the mineral rights to a large mining combine; Liz's late father was once that organization's chief executive, but he died in ambiguous circumstances in which Paul was implicated. McCandless, the owner of the house Liz and Paul have rented, is involved in further ambiguities: A geologist and a writer, he has information that the combine wants and will probably do violence to get.

This small summary only begins to suggest the elusive complexity of a plot that also entertains a dozen or more minor characters and seems to sprout in just as many directions. . . .

As a satirical novel, *Carpenter's Gothic* is about American disorder: political paranoia, religious corruption, sexual laxity, even domestic mess. The Booths' kitchen is just as squalid as their lovemaking, a multimedia event that includes a movie of *Jane Eyre* on the bedroom TV and Paul's simultaneous running commentary on a couple of lawsuits he and Liz have filed.

Mr. Gaddis also takes a crack at some literary subgenres: spy thrillers and novels of intricate betrayal; "dark continent" novels resonant of both Conrad and Waugh; even drawing-room comedies complete with telephone and maid (the phone functions here as a separate character).

And, of course, he also works in the Gothic romance suggested by the title. The house the Booths live in is "a classic piece of Hudson River carpenter gothic," built by country architects and carpenters with the aid of "style books." As McCandless, the owner, explains it, "it was built to be seen from outside . . . it was all derivative wasn't it, those grand Victorian mansions with their rooms and rooms and towering heights and cupolas and the marvelous intricate ironwork." It seems reasonable to suppose that here Mr. Gaddis has provided an ironic message about the construction of his novel: built to be seen from outside, "a patchwork of conceits, borrowings, deceptions," expertly derivative.

Carpenter's Gothic is a clever, well-made book, full of ironies and provocations. Like many other novels of the past few years, it is also about the making of fiction and the nature of art, but let that not intimidate any reader who is hoping for mere entertainment. You need not feel daunted; you may even want to turn now to *The Recognitions* and *JR*.

> *Frances Taliaferro, "From the Outside In,"* in The Wall Street Journal, *August 26, 1985, p. 14.*

ROBERT TOWERS

For 30 years William Gaddis's 900-page first novel, *The Recognitions,* has been whispered about as though it were buried treasure—or a sacred shrine to which only a few highly qualified devotees were permitted entry. If you hadn't read it, you were probably unworthy of reading it in the first place. The fact that Gaddis did not produce another novel for 20 years has lent a special note of purity to his reputation: obviously such a man doesn't have to write for a living, or lower his standards to broaden his appeal.

While I am not aware that a comparable cult has formed around his second novel, *JR* has nonetheless been held out as a sort of challenge or endurance test. . . . It will be interesting to see whether the relatively brief *Carpenter's Gothic,* whose publication is accompanied by the reissue of its weighty predecessors, will nourish the cult—or perhaps drive a stake through its collective heart. It is in any case unlikely to profane the shrine by becoming a popular success.

The Recognitions is indeed a prodigious book. Erudite and intricate, both polyglot and polymath, its scope embraces Flemish painting, demonology, alchemy, patristic theology, the science of perspective, aesthetics, and a whole galaxy of philosophical conundrums. Its settings range from Spain to New England, from Paris to Greenwich Village, and they are all delineated with a wealth of social and historical and physical detail. If Wyatt Gwyon, the novel's pivotal figure who produces "original" Flemish masterpieces, his wife, Esther, and a host of subsidiary figures do not emerge as exactly memorable characters, they are nonetheless somewhat more accessible to the reader's sympathies than the grotesques who populate Gaddis's later books. The tone of Olympian detachment with which the characters and other multitudinous concerns of the novel are presented precludes any really close involvement. It is very much an intellectual's book.

If the tone of *The Recognitions* is godlike in its aloofness, that of *JR* is simultaneously as angry and as icy as if the book had been engendered by the devil's semen. With consummate mimicry, Gaddis reproduces the dialogue—telephonic as well as face-to-face—of a batch of scheming knaves and bustling fools: school teachers and school administrators who speak the language of Board-of-Education directives; vapid and garrulous spinsters; a misfit composer; frantic stockbrokers and their rapacious clients; secretaries, company directors, and PR men; generals, senators, and drunks; nurses and hospital attendants—and, above all, a pushy, obnoxious sixth-grader, JR himself, who, mastering the jargon of business manipulation and paper-capitalism, manages to build a financial empire that is also a house of cards. Gaddis's own mastery of the jargon of wheeling-and-dealing is spectacular, and exhausting.

JR has been acclaimed as a comic masterpiece. There is indeed a good deal of comedy of a raucous and saturnine sort, derived mostly from the interruption or tripping-up of characters in their headlong verbal pursuit of their current obsessions. While the incongruities are sometimes harshly funny, they offer little relief—no leavening of wit, no trace of tender or forgiving humor—and should be regarded, I think, as implements of Gaddis's relentless indictment of our crass and acquisitive society. As a satirist, Gaddis makes the most of his uncannily accurate ear for banality, greed, hypocrisy, and stupidity as they reveal themselves in nonstop dialogue. His knowledge of the technicalities of commercial transaction is formidable and he uses it to create an elaborate metaphor of self-perpetuating folly.

But the impact of *JR* as satire is seriously weakened by the paltriness of its human targets and their petty concerns. The book cries out for a monster of Tartuffian proportions. Alexander Pope also slapped bugs, but he did so with an exuberance of fantasy and invention that is largely precluded by the tape-recorder technique that Gaddis employs. For a work of such length, *JR* produces an oddly airless and claustrophobic effect; 20 pages into it, I felt as if I had been trapped inside a telephone booth with a maniac constantly screaming into the phone—and there were still 700 pages to go.

Carpenter's Gothic might well have been subtitled "JR Junior." It, too, is written mostly in dialogue with a minimum of punctuation. The maniac is still screaming into the telephone. Mercifully, the new book is only about a third of the size of its parent.

Carpenter's Gothic spans a brief period in the lives of a blustering Vietnam veteran named Paul Booth, his much-abused wife, Liz, her brother Billy, a belated hippie who talks about Karma, and McCandless, a burned-out, despairing geologist from whom Paul and Liz have rented a ramshackle Victorian house—the "carpenter's gothic" of title. These are the principal onstage characters. (pp. 30-1)

Gaddis establishes Paul as a thoroughly repellent character whose strident voice dominates the novel to the point where the reader wants to clasp his hands to his ears. McCandless is more complex and intelligent, and serves as a kind of *raisoneur* or spokesman for the raging despair and disgust that is the novel's ultimate message—a message that Liz at one point tries to rebut but so feebly as to have little effect. Some attempt is made to work up a degree of sympathy for poor Liz, to allow her a moment of hope and spirit when she goes to bed with McCandless, but she is too pathetic a creature to arouse much interest, let alone sympathy.

In both *JR* and *Carpenter's Gothic,* Gaddis is working in that very contemporary mode of abrasive paranoia that Pynchon and Don DeLillo have also exploited. His emotional scope is narrower than theirs—and his tone is more bleakly misanthropic. Misanthropy in the hands of a master—Swift and Céline come to mind—can be invigorating; it can purge the reader's bile through the discharge of the author's. But the masters of misanthropy have known the importance of range, of variety, of extravagance, and even of playfulness. They do not set out to bore the reader—as Gaddis seems deliberately to do. Reading *JR* and then *Carpenter's Gothic,* one senses a melancholy contraction, or withering, of the spirit of the intellectually avid young man who three decades ago produced *The Recognitions.* (p. 32)

Robert Towers, "Talk Show," in The New Republic, *Vol. 193, No. 10, September 2, 1985, pp. 30-2.*

BRUCE ALLEN

Author of just three novels in 30 years, William Gaddis has attained the status of a contemporary James Joyce. His books are complicated and difficult constructions. They eschew straightforward communication with the reader because their manifest intent is the expression of a single controlling theme: the omnipresence and dominance of mendacity and greed in human dealings, and the likelihood—stronger than ever in [*Carpenter's Gothic*]—that this folly is suicidal, and may lead to extinction.

Gaddis's great first novel, *The Recognitions* (1955), a labyrinthine analysis of art forgery and "fakery" in general across the international scene, is a vast, ramshackle edifice so filled with comic subplots and bizarre personalities that it's an invigorating joy to plow through. *J. R.* (1975), which won a National Book Award that was probably belated "recognition" for its predecessor, struck me when new as a brilliant and imaginative satire on American commerce and commercial appetite. It's the story, told almost entirely through dialogue, of a preadolescent boy who becomes a powerful business tycoon; rereading it recently, I found it turgid and exhausting. . . .

[*Carpenter's Gothic*] is shorter and shapelier than either of them. But it falls far short of the comic brio and synthesizing power of *The Recognitions,* and even deeper into the trap of obsessive mannerism that snared *J. R.*

It contains the usual Gaddis mixture of energetic monomaniacs and the ineffectual people who try, and fail, to oppose them. The book is mostly dialogue: Its characters shout and rant and insist on their visions of things—and they do not communicate. Telephones keep ringing: the calls are cryptic or meaningless, or are placed to persons who aren't there to answer. Conversations—when they are that, and not just self-enclosed monologues—are carried out in run-on sentences continually interrupted by distractions and second thoughts. Nothing that's begun gets completed, and nobody tunes in to what anybody else is saying. (p. 25)

There is indeed promising material for satire [in *Carpenter's Gothic*], and some parts of the novel are monstrously funny. Images of failure and breakdown, both domestic and global, are artfully scattered about, and there are several wonderful set-pieces (such as Paul's long, fawning phone conversation with the minister's teen-age son Bobbie Joe).

But it's all too schematically pessimistic. Gaddis's Jeremiah-like emphasis on the lust for money and power becomes unrelenting and monotonous. Worse, the characters aren't strong enough to leap forth from the frame and command our attention. Paul is a cacophonous bore. McCandless (he's candleless, without light) is a cardboard diabolist. His "vision of disorder" and "sense of wrongness" aren't rooted in anything credibly personal; they're simply there, haranguing us. Even Liz, potentially sympathetic because she's their victim, is annoyingly passive.

It's also excruciatingly hard to get through. Relax your attention for a single paragraph, and you've missed something crucial, and must reread. If the vision the novel offers were sufficiently striking or original, I'd say: work at it; it's worth it. Alas, it isn't. *Carpenter's Gothic* can be recommended only to William Gaddis's most devoted admirers. The rest of us may be grateful for the reemergence of *The Recognitions,* in the hope it will find the new generation of readers it unquestionably deserves. (p. 26)

> Bruce Allen, *"Gaddis's Dense Satire of Greed Is Often Amusing, Mostly Confusing," in* The Christian Science Monitor, *September 17, 1985, pp. 25-6.*

TERRENCE RAFFERTY

No good modernist would dream of writing a novel that didn't include a critique of itself. In *Carpenter's Gothic,* his third novel, William Gaddis provides the following exchange between a sinister character named Lester and the mysterious McCandless, a geologist/adventurer/novelist who owns the house where all the action takes place:

> —It doesn't end it just falls to pieces, it's mean and empty like everybody in it is that why you wrote it?—I told you why I wrote it, it's just

an afterthought why are you so damned put out by it. This novel's just a footnote, a postscript.

As auto-critiques go, that's unusually harsh—and accurate. *Carpenter's Gothic* is full of elaborate schemes and hinted-at conspiracies, huge autonomous chunks of plot looming behind a screen of fragmented diction and teasing us with the possibility of coherence, only to fly apart in the end. And the people *are* pretty sickening. McCandless has a little dignity (he's the closest thing to a stand-in for the author), but the main characters are his tenants, a loutish P.R. hustler named Paul and his dishrag wife, Liz, whose only response to Paul's daily bullying is meek, hopeless withdrawal. What the slimy Lester says about McCandless's novel (his only one) is a perfect description of Gaddis's too. Does the author know? Is he, like his fictional novelist, simply too exhausted to care? Or is he playing a con man's game, poking us with his finger and daring us to understand him?

Carpenter's Gothic is, in any event, no ordinary game: it begins as Monopoly and ends as Russian roulette. The novel has a single setting, the musty Victorian house on the Hudson that Liz and Paul have rented from McCandless, and each of its long scenes consists almost entirely of run-on, Mametlike dialogue about Paul's various scams, which are at first local (an insurance case, a publicity campaign for a fundamentalist preacher) and then widen to a global conspiracy involving a multinational corporation, a senator and a South African mine. For a while, we may even imagine we know how we're meant to read this book—the game, we think, is to piece together the absurd international-thriller plot from fragments of conversation, and the prize will be the revelation of the dark connections between things, the resolution into a single plot of all the information received secondhand from visitors to the house, from radio and newspaper reports, from the constantly ringing phone. But that's not what Gaddis is up to at all. Carefully constructed as *Carpenter's Gothic* is, it doesn't reward the detective reader's diligent analysis. The plots don't add up, the architectural/geological/political/economic/theological/esthetic metaphors cancel one another out and the jangling, disconnected style turns out to be only mimetic—a mirror of chaos. It seems inconceivable, but this novel—Gaddis's first in ten years—is *designed* to be skimmed like a newspaper, half heard like a call-in show on the kitchen radio.

It's as if Gaddis had conceived a mammoth, complex work of fiction—on the scale of his earlier novels, *The Recognitions* and *JR*—and then lost heart and written this slender shadow play instead. *Carpenter's Gothic* is the ghost of a novel, not the living, breathing thing, and all that keeps us reading is the possibility of touching the narrative body it may have once inhabited. What kept Gaddis writing for ten years is harder to figure: maybe it was the impulse to justify a loss of faith in fiction, to produce an apologia for his sense of futility. There's a strange, uncalculated urgency to this novel, a rage that has nothing to do with the chilly formalism of its style. Gaddis seems to loathe his characters and their culture with a hatred too universal and too indiscriminate for satire. He's like an angry god appalled at something he's created in his own image.

Halfway through the book, the burnt-out McCandless delivers this soliloquy on the house he owns:

> It was built that way yes, it was built to be seen from outside . . . yes, they had style books, these country architects and the carpenters it was all derivative wasn't it, those grand Victorian man-

sions with their rooms and rooms and towering heights and cupolas and the marvelous intricate ironwork. That whole inspiration of medieval Gothic but these poor fellows didn't have it, the stonework and the wrought iron. All they had were the simple dependable old materials, the wood and their hammers and saws and their own clumsy ingenuity bringing those grandiose visions the masters had left behind down to a human scale with their own little inventions . . . a patchwork of conceits, borrowings, deceptions, the inside's a hodgepodge of good intentions like one last ridiculous effort at something worth doing even on this small a scale, because it's stood here, hasn't it, foolish inventions and all it's stood here for ninety years.

So the American novel isn't a cathedral. So the style is borrowed from European "masters," our culture provides material too humble and debased to be the vehicle of great visions, and all the artist can do is disguise his poverty with imitation and pathetic "little inventions." So *Carpenter's Gothic* is thin and deliberately superficial because it can only be "seen from outside"—because the inside doesn't bear (or deserve) scrutiny. And that's why, Gaddis tells us, there will only be afterthoughts from here on, no more grand edifices like *The Recognitions* or *JR*. He's seen the light at last, made the bitter discovery that his world just isn't good enough for his art.

This is an astonishing message, but it's the only possible reason for the book's existence, the only explanation for its sour, contemptuous tone and its formal bad faith. The real story of *Carpenter's Gothic* isn't the end of the world, it's the end of the imagination, the world gone dark in the writer's head. And the real art of this novel is the art of the suicide note, the nasty, labored-over kind that pins the blame on everything and everyone that dares to remain alive. (p. 496)

Terrence Rafferty, "*Postmodern Maladies,*" *in* The Nation, *Vol. 241, No. 16, November 16, 1985, pp. 496, 498.*

CAROL IANNONE

To millions it may have seemed the promised land, but to certain of its native sons, post-World War II America had gained the whole world only to lose its soul. Such, at any rate, was the view that impelled the evolution of "metafiction" in the postwar years—a fiction whose form and content were meant to mirror, in an ironic way, the extravaganza of hype, fraud, and mounting materialism that the United States, its critics said, had finally been revealed to be. The writers of "metafiction" now include such near-venerable men of letters as John Barth, Thomas Pynchon, and, perhaps less well known, William Gaddis, who in hindsight can be seen as a pioneer of the form.

Gaddis's *The Recognitions* (1955), a thousand-page "meta-novel" about forgery, religion, art, and the quest for meaning in the contemporary wasteland, brought the principles of late literary modernism to bear upon the American novel. Lacking an authoritative narrative voice and the usual signs of fictional organization, full of complex mythological, literary, religious, historical, and occult allusions, *The Recognitions* uses and parodies many sources, among them T. S. Eliot (especially "The Waste Land"), Sir James Frazer's *The Golden Bough,* Goethe's

Faust, and a 3rd-century Christian work, *Recognitions of Clement.*

The Recognitions was widely reviewed—and widely damned. In what a Gaddis supporter has since called "one of American criticism's weakest hours," all but a few of *The Recognitions*' first reviews—there were fifty-five of them—ranged from cool dismissal to sputtering outrage that focused especially on the novel's bulk and complicated technique. But the book gradually began to gain a reputation as an underground classic. . . . Favorable revaluations by John W. Aldridge, Tony Tanner, and David Madden appeared, and Anthony West predicted that *The Recognitions* would "one day take a place in classic American literature." Academic critics, who soon enough rallied to the Gaddis banner, have indeed maintained that *The Recognitions* is an American masterpiece on a par with *Moby-Dick.* . . .

By 1975, the year of Gaddis's second novel, *JR,* a corrosive diatribe against capitalist corruption told in 700 pages of near-hysterical running dialogue, Gaddis's voice fell on eagerly receptive ears. *JR* was awarded the coveted National Book Award—in part, as has been suggested even by Gaddis's admirers, because a lot of critics felt obligated to undo past damages. . . .

Gaddis's most recent novel, *Carpenter's Gothic,* another and even more corrosive diatribe against capitalist and sundry other corruptions, again told in near-hysterical running dialogue, but this time only 262 pages of it, has been greeted with enormous enthusiasm and respect. . . . [Gaddis] has, in fact, become something of a cult figure among the young, and his most loyal academic followers have worked energetically to establish his reputation as an American master. (p. 62)

The Recognitions has a multitude of intersecting plot lines. The main one concerns Wyatt Gwyon, son of a minister. Left motherless at the age of four, Wyatt comes into the care of his dour, punitive, Calvinist Aunt May. . . .

Wyatt declines to study for the ministry and some years later, after the failure of his own sterile marriage, he begins to forge works of art in the style of the masters of the Flemish Guild. Others cash in on his forgeries, but Wyatt is an innocent. He actually thinks of himself as a "master painter in the Guild, in Flanders," using "pure materials" and working "in the sight of God." The novel suggests that copying, in the sense of reverential "recognition" of the vision of the masters, is more genuinely creative than the spurious originality sponsored by sentimental romantic values.

Nevertheless, Wyatt sickens of the dishonesty involved in forgery. Declining into mental breakdown, he begins a search for his true self. . . . Wyatt, who has now changed his name to Stephen, eventually comes to spend time at the monastery to which his father had retreated years before. . . .

Eventually, Stephen seems to leave the monastery, having arrived at a sort of salvation by means of "recognitions." . . . (p. 63)

[The] texture of *The Recognitions* is fabulistic, parodistic, and self-parodistic, layering fiction upon fiction. The book builds upon linguistic games and literary devices and allusions to a variety of languages. Even the annotated *Reader's Guide to William Gaddis's "The Recognitions"* admits that it is often hard to get hold of what is actually happening or to judge if some event is meant to be real or hallucinatory. Bizarre comic events continually intrude into an already surrealistic narrative, mingling the ridiculous and the serious, the ordinary and the mythic. Characters have names like Rectall Brown, Agnes Deigh, and Frank Sinisterra. Several large sections of the book are devoted to recording at great length and in intricate detail—and to no effective purpose—the vapid, superficial, deceitful conversation at artistic gatherings among the various hangers-on in the "creative" world.

There is heavy emphasis in *The Recognitions* on sterility—in the general sense that characters can bring nothing original to pass, and in the particular sense that couples cannot or will not conceive, or even carry out plans to adopt, a child. Another emphasis is on sexual confusion. *The Recognitions* features several homosexuals, an apparent hermaphrodite, and one character who is taken to be a homosexual, apparently without reason. And of course, forgery, plagiarism, fakery, impersonation, counterfeiting, and many other kinds of dishonesty abound, all metaphors for Gaddis's chief point—that the world is a fraud.

As Gaddis sees it, religion, art, medicine, all the supposedly salvific structures of modern life are false and empty rituals—counterfeits of ancient ones—that have been superimposed upon a reality too fragmentary and remote for recovery except perhaps through momentary "recognitions," when "all of a sudden everything [is] freed into one recognition, really freed into reality that we never see" (as Wyatt puts it). Yet unfortunately *The Recognitions* is itself but another symptom of the disease it seeks to diagnose. Nothing in the novel is alive; everything is self-conscious, sterile, entirely an affair of the head. The characters have neither texture nor vitality, but are instead just limply executed mouthpieces for points of view which remain contradictory and unresolved.

Gaddis is a writer who goes about saying a writer must not go about saying what he means but leave that task to the critics. Reading *The Recognitions* one begins to suspect that this is because he does not know what he means. Even the concept of "recognition" is fuzzy; sometimes compared to Joyce's "epiphany," it lacks Joyce's luminous conviction of the concreteness of reality. Disintegration, dissolution, decline, fragmentation are not just the themes but the overriding experiences of this book and Gaddis lacks the aesthetic (or moral) energy to counter them. (pp. 63-4)

The fact that Gaddis engages issues of great seriousness and importance—faith, salvation, the function of art—only makes the more exasperating his refusal to see his work through to resolution, his yielding instead to an impulse of aimless accumulation. As he himself remarks in a recent interview: "Once one gets a theme in one's mind it becomes obsessive. If it happens to be forgery, then everywhere you look all you see is forgery, falsification—of religious values, of art—plagiarism, stealing." Of course, if everything is a forgery, then there is little point in working to make distinctions of any kind and nothing then can be worth much effort. As Wyatt remarks, never have there been so many things not worth doing. To this principle, Gaddis's work bears eloquent testimony.

Given Gaddis's abrogation of his own role as an artist, which precisely involves the making of necessary distinctions, *The Recognitions* becomes itself a bit of a fraud, one of those elaborate manipulations of reality—like the tricks performed by the magicians of Pharaoh's court—which impress mightily at first but collapse finally of their own emptiness. Some critics have placed *The Recognitions* within the modernist tradition, or on the cusp that hinges modernism with post-modernism; others have suggested that it stands in a line of savage and

uniquely American comedies that include certain works of Mark Twain and Herman Melville's *The Confidence Man*. But once divested of its show of erudition, its literary parodies, its complex array of ultimately pointless mythological allusions, *The Recognitions* is actually closer to the type of 1950's melodrama exemplified by Arthur Miller's *Death of a Salesman* (approvingly cited by Gaddis in his essay on failure in American life) and such sub-middlebrow efforts as *Marty* and *Requiem for a Heavyweight:* vaguely adolescent tales about sensitive souls adrift in a harsh modern world saturated with fraud, commercialism, cruelty, and vulgarity. Stripped of its surface complexity, *The Recognitions* is reminiscent of nothing so much as an especially ambitious episode of the old TV series, Playhouse 90, though without the resolution demanded of the popular form and consequently without even its modest yield of satisfaction.

Gaddis's two subsequent novels do not employ the elaborate structure of mythological and literary allusion characteristic of *The Recognitions*. They are, to be sure, difficult books to read, but more because of their quotient of counterculture faddism than because they are experiments in the avant-garde. For whatever reason, with the passing of the 50's, Gaddis seems to have found his voice. Now his protest is not muffled but open and focused, his nihilism untroubled by lukewarm gestures in the direction of "salvation."

If fraud is the leitmotif of *The Recognitions,* in *JR* it is entropy, i.e., the tendency of systems toward disorder and inertness. As a character remarks in *JR,* "Order is simply a thin, perilous condition we try to impose on the basic reality of chaos."

The entropic decline in *JR* is seen by Gaddis as the result of the subordination of all values in capitalist America to greed and profit. Language must of course reflect such a decline, and in *JR,* the language—almost entirely dialogue—is frantic, fast-paced, fragmentary, full of jargon, cliché, evasion, hesitation, deceit, apology, interruption, irrelevancy, manipulation. Characters seem to possess no identities that have not been corrupted or devastated by the "system." (Perhaps for that reason their names are seldom given; they often have to be identified through their speech habits, as in the favorite epithet of the main character, the eleven-year-old JR, "holy shit.") Settings switch during the brief, blink-and-you'll-miss-them narrative sections, and the whole book proceeds at breakneck speed.

JR is a sixth-grade entrepreneur who parlays his social-studies lessons in free enterprise into a corporate empire. His conglomerate comes to be known as the JR Family of Companies, an irony since the actual families portrayed in the book, including his own, are all fragmented or deteriorating in one way or another. The JR Corporation markets all kinds of improbable and fairly useless goods like wooden picnic forks, pork bellies, and green aspirin, and runs a series of deficient services, like an interlocking chain of nursing homes and funeral parlors. JR operates out of phone booths, chiefly the one in his school, using a handkerchief over the mouthpiece to disguise his boyish voice.

Very little, "educationwise," goes on in school. The principal, Mr. Whiteback, is also a banker, who strives for such goals as "the full utilization potential of in-school television." One of the school's teachers tells his class, "You're not here to learn anything, but to be taught so you can pass these tests." JR enlists the help of two of the school's teachers, a writer and a composer, in operating his companies out of a catastrophically disordered apartment. A large cast of supporting characters—bankers, brokers, politicians, public-relations men, businessmen, writers, artists, and a number of wives and girlfriends—are either driven ragged by or are perpetrators of the chaos caused by ringing telephones, blaring radios, intrusive advertising, bureaucratic scheming, snoopy reporters, and assorted other disorders deriving from the junky, kitschy culture they inhabit.

Corporate values have destroyed everything, Gaddis thunders in *JR:* family, education, morality, love, all social structures, relationships between men and women, sex, and even art. Nor can there be any doubt that the corruption is not an aberration but intrinsic to the system. (pp. 64-5)

Gaddis does evince a certain skill in *JR* at capturing the speech patterns of different contemporary types, and at building an intricate, ingenious plot. But the book's monomania, with its Cyclopean vision of the horrors of capitalism as the cause of every evil, pretty thoroughly discredits this achievement. *JR* displays the same helplessness as *The Recognitions* in the face of its material.

This kind of one-note thinking also characterizes Gaddis's latest novel, *Carpenter's Gothic,* although it is shorter and takes place in a single setting. . . .

"*Carpenter's Gothic* . . . is about getting it wrong and stupidity," the author vouchsafed in one of his rare explications of himself. "It's about stupidity and ignorance, stupidity and greed. . . . Stupidity is, as someone says in the book, a hard habit to break." It is also about the Third World—Africa in the novel but, according to Gaddis, Central America as well. "Stupidity and sentimental values are guiding us in Central America right now." "Can't we stop wandering off in other people's wars and pushing people around?" he wonders. "The Nicaragua picture—it is beyond belief what we are doing, and stupid, stupid."

In *Carpenter's Gothic,* Gaddis means to show us the consequences of stupidity. His wrath is unleashed on all kinds of "true believers," not only fundamentalists and creationists but anti-Communists and diehard capitalists who persist in holding blindly to their creeds and in inflicting them on others. ("Revealed truth is the one weapon stupidity's got against intelligence," quoth McCandless.) The true believers, aided by blandly corrupt government lackeys, and prodded by what Gaddis calls the "unswerving punctuality of chance," move toward a denouement in which several characters die violently, a nuclear device is exploded by the U.S. off the African coast while the President rages in headlines against the Evil Empire, and everything apparently returns to business as usual in this black Disneyland.

In a way that even *The Recognitions* and *JR* do not, *Carpenter's Gothic* shows that Gaddis is not so much an artist as an anti-artist, working with cartoon characters and disembodied ideas. Instead of shaping, he flattens; instead of synthesizing, he fragments; instead of ordering, he disorders; instead of sifting the chaff from the wheat, he collects the chaff and blows it in our faces.

Gaddis enthusiasts have of course insisted that the form of his work is appropriate to its content. And, at different points in his novels, Gaddis himself shows his awareness of the kind of criticism he inspires by denouncing the simpleminded mentality that demands ready-made solutions from art. But what is this if not a by-now hackneyed justification for an impotent imag-

ination? In undercutting the creative act, Gaddis does more to break down the human spirit than any system he opposes. It is true that our current funhouse state of literary criticism in one way or another encourages novels like *JR* and *Carpenter's Gothic*—tons of bloodless verbiage and sweaty contrivances to make incomparable banality sound like truth. But in this corruption, from which he (unlike the various struggling artists of his fiction) has handsomely profited, William Gaddis himself has had a prominent hand. (p. 65)

Carol Iannone, "Gaddis Recognized," in Commentary, *Vol. 80, No. 6, December, 1985, pp. 62-5.*

PETER KEMP

Bedlam is William Gaddis's fictional speciality: the uproarious recording of near-terminal derangement. It's hard to imagine noisier novels than *The Recognitions* or *JR* . . . or *Carpenter's Gothic,* the latest of his sonic chronicles. Capturing with sizzling precision the tones and idioms of hundreds of voluble characters, they emit a kind of high-fidelity pandemonium: the farcical, fearsome hubbub of an America that is stridently disintegrating.

At the centre of the tumult of talk in *The Recognitions*—Gaddis's first novel, published in 1955—is an art racket. A painter with a taste for emulating pictures of the Flemish school of the 15th and 16th centuries is battened upon by a crooked dealer who passes off his canvases—after they've been through a process of cosmetic dilapidation—as long-lost masterpieces by the Van Eyck brothers and the like. Around this chicanery throng numerous variations on the motif of forgery. (p. 28)

Falsity is exhibited everywhere: two characters sport wigs; another totes an uninjured arm round in a sling. Conversationally, the accent falls on phoniness—from a gold-digger's squeal, 'Are they real di-mins?', to the bogus music-enthusiast's solemn claim that Handel's *Judas Maccabaeus* sounds better in 'the original German'. Pretence and pretentiousness—especially among 'the bumped buttocks and wasted words' of dilettante parties in Greenwich Village and expatriate Montmartre—are picked up with sharp jabs of irony. Sexual sham and charades come in for repeated observation: transvestites flit round the story's margins; there's a climactic sequence at a Harlem drag ball where a brassière is inched with pseudo-titillation off a male chest.

Flashy top-dressings frequently attract Gaddis's satiric scrutiny, especially among the 'sincere theatricals' of religion. Presenting Christianity as itself an accretion—its theology merely an overlay on older myths—he revels, like a more robust Ronald Firbank, in the baroque excrescences that have embellished it: tales of wrestlers with demons, mittened stigmatics, flagellants, charismatic insomniacs and visionary recipients of census figures from hell. (pp. 28-9)

Straying from the contemporary American scene down these recherché by-ways gives *The Recognitions* a high-spirited colour absent from Gaddis's later work. When he returned to fiction—two decades later—with *JR,* he focused on a creed closer to home and one whose ecstasies and excesses he finds less beguiling. After the cosmopolitan expansiveness of *The Recognitions* (a novel that echoes with snatches of French, Spanish, German, Hungarian dialect and Latin, and whose teasing conclusion demands a knowledge of Italian), *JR* moves in—amid a welter of financial jargon, advertising sloganeering and Business Studios sub-talk—on what Gaddis sees as America's real religion: capitalism and its zealots.

Early in the novel, its eponymous hero—an 11-year-old fascinated by finance—is heard rehearsing for a school performance of *Das Rheingold* in which he is to play Alberich, Wagner's stunted, stunting devotee of lucre. From this point on, though JR only re-appears fleetingly, his influence—like that of Alberich in *The Ring*—pervades everything that occurs: capitalist zest, personified as juvenile, underlies and undermines all aspects of American life.

Conveying this, Gaddis takes his technique of satire by damning dialogue to tasking lengths. With scenes spliced together into a kind of montage that seems all soundtrack and no visuals, the novel is composed almost entirely of speech, and speech presented so obliquely that it's often hard to establish who is talking or when and where. *The Recognitions* deplored authors writing for 'people who read with the surface of their minds, people with reading habits that make the smallest demands on them'. Linking this literary slovenliness with a malignant laxness sapping society, Gaddis's books swing to the opposite extreme. Under their demotic din, they are intricate, subtle, thought-demanding—exemplars of those qualities he feels are being hounded out of America by screaming headlines and rampant stupidity.

Carpenter's Gothic, his latest and grimmest book, dramatises this situation, showing the last flickers of enlightenment guttering as bigotry and benightedness howl through a country becoming another 'Dark Continent'. Shorter than Gaddis's earlier books . . . *Carpenter's Gothic* is a mere 262 pages, and far more compressed in structure. . . .

As in all Gaddis's work, fraud is particularly prominent. Carpenter's Gothic, we're reminded, is a style of architecture that is fake. All façade, it's designed to look impressive, dignified and venerable from the exterior. Behind this, though, with rooms packed in anyhow, everything is murkier, more paltry and crooked. For Gaddis, this stands as an image of his nation now: striving to hold up an imposing front but, in actuality, a warren of darkness and disorientation.

A particularly rackety contemporary instance of this, the book suggests, is another kind of Carpenter's Gothic: the grotesque twists given by fundamentalists to Christianity, the creed preached by 'the carpenter's son'. . . .

The book's hottest mockery is trained on Creationism, singled out by Gaddis's spokesman in the book as the culminating instance of stupidity's assault on intelligence. Sardonically demonstrating the brute ignorance of those who oppose evolutionary ideas, Gaddis gives a further harsh twist to things by depicting an evangelical mission to Africa being used as a cover for political infiltration. In the novel's final pages, as a result of this, a global war liable to exterminate the species is breaking out over an African rift valley from which man's ancestors emerged.

This apocalyptic ending is merely the most intense instance of the novel's acridity. The action occurs in autumn, amid withered leaves and rotting vegetation. Inside the cobwebbed and chaotic house, trash and breakages accumulate. From outside comes a ceaseless clamour of callousness, exploitation and violence. The Bible Belt quackery—air-wave appeals for 'prayerful tax deductible gifts', regressive re-writings of science textbooks—blurs into political graft, aggression and homicidal treachery. At the conclusion of the book, Liz—betrayed by the two people she has trusted—is dead; corpses heap the narrative's periphery; overseas, war wreaks havoc. A scathing, exacerbated *tour de force*, *Carpenter's Gothic* seems the last word on a society whose doomed babble it so vehemently transmits. (p. 29)

Peter Kemp, "Fearsome Hubbub," in The Listener, *Vol. 115, No. 2951, March 13, 1986, pp. 28-9.*

Jane Gardam

1928-

English novelist, short story writer, and author of children's books.

Gardam is praised for her sharply humorous observations about English society. Although several of her early works have been categorized as young adult literature, critics acknowledge that Gardam's wit and polished prose style make these books of interest to a wider audience. Gardam weaves allusions to well-known literary works and figures into her narratives, enriching her tales of social misfits who seek acceptance. One reviewer noted that Gardam's characters are "observed with unwavering directness, their emotional hang-ups and outlets quietly understated."

Gardam's early novels and stories explore various problems of adolescence. Her young heroines must often cope with chaotic home lives as well as with the uncertainties of growing up. The stories in *A Few Fair Days* (1971) revolve around a young girl and her happy, carefree childhood in a small seaside town before World War II. *God on the Rocks* (1978), which takes place in the same setting and time period as *A Few Fair Days*, features a protagonist who is faced with the breakup of her parents' marriage and, later, her father's death. In *A Long Way from Verona* (1971), a thirteen-year-old girl must cope with the usual problems of adolescence amidst the horrors of World War II and a family life disrupted by her father's sudden career change. Teenaged girls struggling with self-doubts and questions about their impending womanhood are central characters in both *The Summer after the Funeral* (1973) and *Bilgewater* (1976). Patricia Craig noted that Gardam handles these familiar situations "with a splendid original recklessness."

Black Faces, White Faces (1975) was Gardam's first work of adult fiction. Considered a novel by some critics and a short story collection by others, the book comprises a series of vignettes linked by several recurring characters and the common setting of a resort hotel in Jamaica. *Black Faces, White Faces* was widely praised for Gardam's accomplished style; Peter Ackroyd commented that she "has taken the form of the short story as close to art as it is ever likely to reach." The title story of Gardam's next collection, *The Sidmouth Letters* (1980), concerns the discovery of several letters written by Jane Austen to the man she loved and the discoverer's decision to destroy them. Several of the stories depict unusual characters and situations and focus on small details which affect larger events. The stories in *The Hollow Land* (1981) also evidence Gardam's use of episodic narrative structure as they depict the ongoing relationship between a lower-class family in England's Lake District and an upper-class family that vacations there every year. Many of the pieces in *The Pangs of Love and Other Stories* (1983) feature English characters in foreign settings; the most successful of the stories, contends Anthony Thwaite, are those that depict "faintly disturbing happenings among people who don't fit in."

Crusoe's Daughter (1985) helped confirm Gardam's reputation as an important and skillful chronicler of English life. This novel follows more than eighty years in the life of its protagonist, Polly Flint. Orphaned at a young age and brought up in

Photograph by Mark Gerson

an isolated house on the British moors, Polly reads Daniel Defoe's *Robinson Crusoe* and adopts the adventurous Crusoe as her guiding spirit. During her lifetime, Polly witnesses industrial progress, war, and the changing social strata in England. Critics generally praised Gardam's balance of comic action and serious social and literary observations.

(See also *Contemporary Authors*, Vols. 49-52; *Contemporary Authors New Revision Series*, Vols. 2, 18; *Something about the Author*, Vols. 28, 39; and *Dictionary of Literary Biography*, Vol. 14.)

THE TIMES LITERARY SUPPLEMENT

Jane Gardam's first novel must be greeted not with the superficial "beam, beam and BEAM" which the headmistress in *A Long Way from Verona* is observed by the heroine Jessica Vye to accord to a visiting lecturer, but with genuine delight. For Jane Gardam is a writer of such humorous intensity—glorious dialogue, hilarious set-pieces—that when one reads her for the first time one laughs aloud and when re-reading her, the acid test for funny books, one's admiration increases a hundredfold.

Set in Yorkshire during the Second World War, *A Long Way from Verona* is a first-person novel "written" by Jessica who is thirteen and suffering accordingly. Through Jessica Mrs Gardam recreates the fun of being thirteen, the naivety, the self-absorption, the definite opinions, the lack of respect for establishment views—coupled with the awareness that there are such things as great novels, poems and paintings even if for the moment *The Cloister and the Hearth* appears to be "an awful long book and dead boring", Rupert Brooke's "Grantchester" makes you feel slightly sick (though he's so handsome you keep his portrait by your bedside) and you can't quite get over the shock of seeing Gauguin's picture of naked green ladies up on the wall of the Senior English teacher's sitting room.

In Jessica Vye, who was told when she was very young that she was "a writer beyond all possible doubt" and who spent the rest of her school life developing her literary talents (forty-eight-page essays scornfully dismissed by the English mistress), Jane Gardam has created a heroine whom most girls a little older than the acutely observant Jessica will find outrageously funny, breathtakingly outspoken and enviably off-beat; anyone of that age who is also a burgeoning writer will immediately recognize Jessica's agonies and compulsions as their own.

Mrs Gardam, not content with pinpointing the awfulness of the Searle-type school in which Jessica operates in her own wildly maverick fashion, matches this with a relentlessly focused picture of Jessica's erratic and sometimes rather alarming home. Father had been a housemaster but decided late in life to become a curate—very left-wing, rebellious, jolly, talkative and insensitive: a man who sings hymns to the cat on the stairs, makes his spinster parishioners blush and invariably has to dash off to Eucharist if a family upheaval is brewing. Mother, who had managed admirably as a housemaster's wife—polite tea-parties and a maid—is now plunged into an almost penniless existence and is pulled this way and that by the conflicting demands of parish and household. . . .

The flavour of this brilliantly witty and agonizingly true-to-life first novel is impossible to convey.

> *"A Writer's Childhood," in* The Times Literary Supplement, *No. 3640, December 3, 1971, p. 1512.*

BARBARA BADER

One inclines naturally to identify Jessica [the protagonist of *A Long Way From Verona*] with Jane Gardam: the book has the nubbiness of memoir and, in the conventional sense, no plot. But no plot does not mean no progression. Equally critical—what sustains *A Long Way From Verona* as the novel it would be—is the fact that Jessica's narrative is less confession than revelation. We don't need steady Florence Bone's "Calm down . . . We like you all right" to know that she is not the outcast she presents us with. . . . And long before her father's remark that Cissie Comberbach looks "utterly wretched" catches Jessica up, making her wonder if she really does know what's in people's minds, it is apparent that what she attributes to others, the disgust and dismay, are her own dark thoughts.

That is to say, Jessica's telling, her first-person (help!) narrative, is not a device or a dodge, it is itself the story. Just as the subject isn't for once alienation or angst or antithis-Establishmentarianism. . . . The book is Jane Gardam's, and this, her first novel, makes her immediately an author to watch

for, but the story is Jessica's in all its glorious passage from self-intoxication to tentative self-searching. Read her.

> *Barbara Bader, "The Nubbiness of Memoir and No Plot," in* The New York Times Book Review, *May 7, 1972, p. 28.*

ELIZABETH MINOT GRAVES

[*A Long Way From Verona*] is the story of Jessica Vye, a teenage girl with a passion for writing, whose strong and original character and whose compulsion to tell the truth often get her in trouble with the Establishment, including three demerits one terrible day at school. A wry description of awakening interest in the opposite sex, it describes Jessica's first beau who takes her to the slums on a date, as he is in love with reforming, and of her disillusionment with him during an air raid. The minor characters are all unusually well realized, including Jessica's friends and teachers at school, her father, a minister with Socialistic ideals, and her mother, who looks back nostalgically at the days when she had more fashionable friends. This is a story of family life as well as adolescence, of England during World War II, and most important of all of what it means to be a writer and to feel you have created something really good.

The author's own writing is strong, terse, witty and full of exuberance for life. The subthemes are extremely well integrated into the whole; there are many hilarious sad-happy incidents, with much to say on many levels.

A Few Fair Days, laid in a town on the Yorkshire coast just before World War II, is more loosely knit than *A Long Way From Verona* and a little slower and quieter in pace, but then it is about a younger child. Lucy, however, is very much like Jessica Vye for she too is imaginative, vulnerable, often wild, and "probably a little bit mad because in her heart she felt she was not Lucy at all but really the Princess of Cleves." This is a series of vignettes of her escapades and happy days growing up in a town filled with relatives, filled with nostalgia that will appeal to adults. As Lucy loves to read poetry and her parents strongly resemble the Vyes, one is left with the feeling that both Jessica and Lucy are probably Jane Gardam at different stages of her childhood. Why, one wonders, has Mrs. Gardam waited all these years to be published? One can only give thanks that she is writing in earnest at last, and hope for many more books with the same humor, insight and wonderfully natural conversation as these.

> *Elizabeth Minot Graves, "Children's Novels: Alive and Well," in* Commonweal, *Vol. XCVII, No. 7, November 17, 1972, pp. 156-58.*

THE TIMES LITERARY SUPPLEMENT

[*The Summer after the Funeral*] is riotously funny, alive with visual imagery ("her stockings lay in two sad pinkish heaps at her feet, like dead roses") and shot through with social comment of devastating accuracy. Its pattern, like that of an Iris Murdoch satire, is as intricate and delicate as that of a mazurka.

The central character of *The Summer after the Funeral* is Athene Price who was sixteen when her father, a very old and somewhat eccentric vicar, died. Athene was a beauty; but "all sunshine she was not, and her summery face was the very highest achievement, the head behind it holding dismal and complex troubles''. . . .

In a needlework lesson at school, staring at a frontispiece portrait of the Brontë family in a copy of *Jane Eyre,* Athene discovered her extraordinary resemblance to Emily and became instantly convinced that she had lived before, was indeed the reincarnation of that gifted but ill-fated lady. And as if this were not enough to turn a girl's mind, Athene found herself having to cope with its awful implications in isolation; for during that August and September the Price children were sent away from the Rectory (Athene to stay with one after another of her parents' friends) while the widowed Mrs Price, selflessly selfish, was making arrangements for her ''*much diminished* [as she wrote in one of her rambling letters] life''.

Neither rich old Posie who lived in a hotel and never stopped eating nor timid Sybil . . . was likely to understand, any more than Athene's chemistry mistress had . . . that Emily Brontë, in the shape of Athene Price, had come among them. But wandering in Posie's hotel garden who should Athene see, for a split second during a thunderstorm on the summer-house steps, but Heathcliff. . . .

All very disturbing, and not less so when she managed to escape from feminine company, first into the arms, almost literally, of a fat and balding artist, and then to Sebastian's empty boarding school where middle-aged and susceptible Mr Bell befriends her and takes her to Haworth (of all places) to celebrate her seventeenth birthday. Athene is already half in love with Mr Bell . . . and the day at Haworth surrounded by ghastly tourists gawping at Emily-Athene's sofa is the step over the precipice.

But fate plays a hand in Athene's life, and all ends happily in a dramatic family reunion; even the Heathcliff of the summer-house materializes, by a most well thought-out coincidence. Not an accident, a coincidence. Nothing in Jane Gardam's brilliantly compact, mocking and witty novel is unplanned. The characters, young and old, are observed with unwavering directness, their emotional hang-ups and outlets quietly understated. . . . The lightness of touch, the resistance to overplaying the comedy in the farcical set-pieces, is truly admirable: to enjoy the full impact of this marvellously entertaining book one cannot afford to skip a single word.

> *''Who Is Athene?'' in* The Times Literary Supplement, *No. 3742, November 23, 1973, p. 1429.*

PENELOPE FARMER

The English writer Jane Gardam arrived on the literary scene recently with two books published almost simultaneously: *A Few Fair Days* . . . and *A Long Way From Verona,* set during World War II. Both were eminently readable, witty, perceptive, vivid and consequently highly praised—justifiably I think.

Well, Mrs. Gardam marches on. Her new book [*The Summer after the Funeral*], if more polished, lacks *Verona*'s fierceness and rather interesting edginess. But it is beguilingly well-written and quite as funny; about beautiful Athene, a kind of juvenile Zuleika Dobson, lucky girl, but who, appearances notwithstanding, has problems. And who breaks out of her amenable exterior at last while being shunted round a succession of unsuitable adults after her aged parson father dies.

Mrs. Gardam once again is very good on young grief, desperation, elation, first love—American teen-agers should iden-

tify also; very good on settings . . . , very good on subsidiary characters, mostly English spinsters, auntlike if not actually aunts. There are some darker Freudian undertones such as Athene and her brother's disquiet at being fathered by so old a man—hints, too, at adult wretchedness. But generally the tone is discreet, contained.

It seems to me that both books, but this one especially, move towards a very particular genre of English adult fiction in which female writers describe the vicissitudes of strong-charactered, sensitive, middle-class heroines amid a gallery of middle-class eccentricity; a genre ranging from writers as distinguished as Elizabeth Taylor at one end to lightweight novels like *I Capture the Castle* at the other. Jane Gardam can write as well as the best of them, but generally I'd put her at the lighter end. A definite if muted element of wish-fulfillment is one reason her books are so readable. This is not to belittle them; nor to accuse her of sentimentality. . . .

But turning the convention upside down, superlatively well, and being exact and strong and truthful within it, makes it no less a convention and so, ultimately, safe. The families in her books may be poor, may live in or visit houses which smell of cabbage or even poverty with unspeakable mould growing in their larders, but fundamentally they are safe too—the bell may toll very close, but we know it will never, actually, toll for them.

> *Penelope Farmer, in a review of ''The Summer after the Funeral,'' in* The New York Times Book Review, *February 17, 1974, p. 8.*

VICTORIA GLENDINNING

Jane Gardam's *Black Faces, White Faces* is very good indeed, not on account of originality of plot or even of character, but because she writes so well. Her very personal style is light and clean, with an effective economy of punctuation:

> For years in her quiet way and particularly in Harrods Lady Fletcher (wife of the judge) had looked forward to the title. She received it and was disappointed.

Put commas in that first sentence, and its style is destroyed. It is a small point, but characteristic of Mrs Gardam's cool directness. She has until now written novels for children, which may account for a deceptive naivety that goes straight to the heart of the matter in every episode of her novel.

For the novel is so episodic as to be hardly a novel at all; it is written to the formula that has made dozens of successful books and films, that of a group of ill-assorted people fortuitously brought together, each with a story, a past, and the remains of a future. The place is Jamaica, and the people are there on holiday; they may watch each other, dine together, even help each other . . . but their lives remain separate. . . . There are middle-aged ladies in the wrong clothes, flares of sexuality towards the wrong partners, and everywhere the friendly smiling faces of the black people who suddenly, shockingly, produce guns or hurl stones or insults at the ignorant well-meaning tourists. Terror and farce in equal parts lurk beside the hotel pool, but neither is allowed above the surface in this short, elegant book.

> *Victoria Glendinning, ''Fellow Travellers,'' in* The Times Literary Supplement, *No. 3836, September 19, 1975, p. 1041.*

PETER ACKROYD

Black Faces, White Faces strikes me as a very accomplished book. [Jane Gardam] has a simple and easy prose which artfully masks some cunning observations and a nice line in wit. All of the stories are set in Jamaica, and they all have a combination of brilliant surface colour and interior tension which is characteristic of that island.... Jane Gardam has that highly sophisticated gift of writing simply; and you can sometimes see a universe in a grain of sand, especially in Jamaica. In "**Saul Alone**", a rich old man, paralysed down one side of his body, eavesdrops on his wife's shrill talk. Simplicity, it seems, can be the most revealing tone of all. *Black Faces, White Faces* is actually called a collection of 'incidents', since the same characters appear and reappear within different frames, but in fact Jane Gardam has taken the form of the short story as close to art as it is ever likely to reach and in doing so has joined the company of such writers as William Trevor and Ian McEwan.

> *Peter Ackroyd, "Shorts," in* The Spectator, *Vol. 235, No. 7692, November 29, 1975, p. 704.*

RAYMOND SOKOLOV

[Jamaica continues] to attract rich tourists from London, despite the ugly post-colonial hostilities so well reported in the press and sung in reggae anthems. The Jamaicans grudgingly accept the foreign exchange they need to survive and the white vacationers manage to pretend that the palmy isolation of their resort hotels exempts them from the anger all round them. This lush, oasis life is the world of Jane Gardam's novella [*The Pineapple Bay Hotel* (published in Great Britain as *Black Faces, White Faces*), a work] ... of deceptive simplicity that looks wryly at an odd assortment of English visitors and how they pass their expensive time away from home.

Gardam does not, for the most part, burden us with dramatic confrontations between tourists and islanders. There is one hilarious collision: two old-maid schoolmarms spook some local thugs and show that British eccentricity can still be a force in the Third World. But mainly this is a very skillfully assembled series of vignettes of people cut loose from their regular lives and set down in a tropical bower. Travel is not necessarily broadening, but it almost always provides the opportunity for going to bed with strangers.

That, at least, is the theory adopted by Anne Shaw, normally complacent wife of a conventional lawyer whom she has innocently allowed to junket off to Jamaica without her for an extended combination of business and pleasure. His letters—bland and clogged with travelogue—arouse her doubts, and the casual mention of a new-found friend, female and Bolivian, accelerates the quiverings of Anne's anxieties. As luck and the laws of plot would have it, Anne has guessed exactly right.... Anne gathers up her inner resources and flies to the Caribbean, where she apparently has no trouble saving her marriage.

I say "apparently" because the extirpation of La Boliviana takes place off camera, as it were, as does so much of the "action" of this book. What we see, or, rather, what we read, is a series of cinematic cuts that comment on, or frame, action we don't see. Letters that try to conceal the love affair are, for example, the main source of information about the affair itself. Indeed, the Shaws do not at first seem to be the central actors in the tale. There are so many other people packed into the landscape. Only when you look closely do you see that there

is a good deal more to this gaily unfolding hotel pastoral than mere holiday enjoyment by the sea.

Gardam makes you do the work. Her manifold traps are hidden away under glass and satin. The voice you hear is an odd combination of girl and grande dame, a voice that trills out the most sinister truths as if they were part of the court circular. If the writing sometimes gets out of hand and means less than it sounds ... such lapses do not much mar the exuberant flow of the well-wrought story. Then, too, there are so many cameo performances to admire, like the honeymoon interlude of Catriona ("Pussy") Fox-Coutts Fielding or Lady Fletcher's finding that she has fallen for a man who likes men. And you will also admire, when you stop to think about it, the wonderfully graceful shifts of tone both in dialogue, from British to American to Jamaican patois, and in narrative voice. Short and surprising, this is a mature book for mature people, and by that I don't mean that it is especially erotic. In point of fact, it is as discreet about sex as it is about everything else. Also, it will save you the discomfort and expense of going to Jamaica yourself.

> *Raymond Sokolov, "Let Them Drink Rum," in* Book World—The Washington Post, *May 2, 1976, p. L6.*

MARTIN LEVIN

[*The Pineapple Bay Hotel* has] a fine cast of characters who introduce themselves in 10 separate interludes. But they touch only tangentially, leaving unplumbed possibilities for catalytic action. The two episodes with the most direct connection deal with the anxieties of a lawyer's wife whose husband has gone to Jamaica for a convention. In "**The First Declension**," Anne Shaw finds disturbing messages between the lines of her husband's suspiciously effusive letters. In "**Monique**," it turns out that Mrs. Shaw's worst fears were justified.

There is a pleasant infusion of wit in these stories, as in "**Something to Tell the Girls**," in which two elderly but energetic schoolmistresses explore the upcountry by car, protected by the god who looks after such innocents. Two other stories of Englishwomen getting light-headed in the tropics suggest that the world hasn't changed all that much since Maugham left it.

An engaging collection of vignettes that would have had many times the candlepower had they been fused.

> *Martin Levin, in a review of "The Pineapple Bay Hotel," in* The New York Times Book Review, *May 2, 1976, p. 60.*

SALLY EMERSON

[In *Bilgewater*, a] girl nicknamed Bilgewater tells of her former trials from the lofty age of eighteen. The tone and style of her writing is lively but riddled with rather more jocularity and naïvety than I would expect from a girl of that age. Bilgewater lives with her widowed housemaster father in a boys' boarding school. The eccentric schoolteachers are wittily described, the affection of the brisk matron for her and her father carefully suggested, but Bilgewater's sense of her ugliness and stupidity is stated too cheerfully to be credible. Before this ugly duckling swans into a place at Cambridge and wins the heart of a good man she falls under the dangerous spell of the beautiful but bad Grace, has a crush on the handsome headboy who turns out to be worthless, and falls for the strange boy Terrapin she'd previously detested who breaks her heart by running off with

Grace. It's an easy read but far above the standard of pappy adult romantic fiction; the passages describing her nightmare visit to the bridge-playing house of Jack Rose and the turret filled with marionettes made by Terrapin are especially powerful.

Sally Emerson, in a review of "Bilgewater," in Books and Bookmen, *Vol. 22, No. 3, December, 1976, p. 82.*

PATRICIA CRAIG

The first epigraph [in *Bilgewater*] fixes the mood: "Youth is a blunder" (Disraeli). The theme is familiar, but Jane Gardam handles it with a splendid original recklessness. Bilgewater is far more memorable than the usual dotty or awkward adolescent. The rueful, chatty, engaging tone of the archetypal first-person teenage narrative is compressed here into something altogether fiercer and wittier. On the brink of social disaster, Bilgewater flees or does something unpredictable; but her behaviour has an inverted kind of style. Even when she indulges in self-pity, against the advice of forthright Paula Rigg, the young school matron, she guys the emotion ("I wetted the exercise book with tears").

The diverting events in the second half of the novel are linked by the figure of Mrs Deering, a grotesque and slightly malevolent old body who sticks in kiosks, chews meat sandwiches on the bus and appears at crucial moments in Bilgewater's life. Technically, her function is to dissolve tension and to relieve the author of the necessity to deal seriously with emotion; but her presence helps also to raise contrivance to the level of literary accomplishment.

Bilgewater is a comedy of false trails and misalliances. The structure is flexible, the quotations apt and sparing, and the narrative fluent. Only the omission of many commas confuses the syntax; only the epilogue is less scintillating than slick. Jane Gardam took something of a risk with her title, with its slang meaning of nonsense or rubbish: but it has to be stated that the content of this novel is a long way from bilge.

Patricia Craig, "Blundering Youth," in The Times Literary Supplement, *No. 3900, December 10, 1976, p. 1549.*

JEREMY TREGLOWN

[*God on the Rocks*] is a completely unponderous, elegantly constructed story about the daughter of a Fundamentalist couple between the wars—the puritanical father falling for the nanny, and the wife reverting, in revenge, to a childhood lover. The coastal setting establishes a strong layer of reference to non-conformist images of salvation and damnation—shipwrecks and lifeboats, and the rocks of the title—and a deftly extended time-scheme enables the events to reflect big changes of attitude brought about partly by the first world war. At the end, soldiers roll up the barbed wire on the beach. The painful and unnecessary tangles of religious superstition and sexual taboo, we are made to feel, have been similarly swept away. There are some successful passages of near-lyrical writing, and an unexpectedly hilarious episode of high bedroom farce. (p. 480)

Jeremy Treglown, "On the Side," in New Statesman, *Vol. 96, No. 2482, October 13, 1978, pp. 479-80.*

JANE MILLER

It is through the eyes of Margaret [in *God on the Rocks*] . . . that we scrutinize, at first, the world in which she grows up between the wars. She lives in a brown house in a north-eastern seaside town with her parents, a new baby brother she abhors, and a maid called Lydia, whom Margaret's father plans to seduce from her rumbustious ways to the gloomy crankiness his religion and his nature assure him would be to her advantage. He is the leading member of the town's small band of "Saints", lugubrious Brethren, who preach and forswear a lot. His wife is a convert to all this, and, it turns out, a convert by nature, who abides by the certainties of a series of other people. Observed by their daughter they seem irrational, even stupid, but unchangeably what they are and must always have been.

It is on recently introduced weekly treats, expeditions to a neighbouring town with Lydia, that Margaret gets glimpses of a life outside her home for the first time. What she sees extends and mimics what she already knows, and is interpreted in the light of the bizarre secrecies she associates with the grown-up world. . . . Just at the moment when the people she knows begin to unfurl for her, to acquire histories and proclivities, Margaret is ejected as the viewer of it all, and the author takes over.

The author's treatment of Margaret exactly parallels the way the adults in the novel shut the child out, disregard her need to know, while appearing to want her to flourish. Later she will take her revenge on them for expecting her to listen quietly to cryptic adult talk, which hints at her mother's having a past, and at adults generally behaving erratically and in response to private promptings they do not divulge to children. So that behind her back, so to speak, and for the reader, Margaret's mother is allowed to be more than she has seemed to her daughter. Her resumed friendship with a "clever" brother and sister who live together is explained. She had been going to marry the brother before his patrician mother intervened to prevent a liaison with a working-class girl. Retribution, something Margaret has been brought up to believe in, has been visited on that mother and on both her children, and Margaret's mother is seen to have undergone several conversions by the time she married. . . .

The last chapter leaps, disconcertingly, twelve years. Margaret is at university, and has survived and not drowned as we were left to expect. Her swimming out to sea, "showing off", killed her father, who was trying to save her. Her mother is now married to the vicar. There are things Margaret still wants to know. "But it's my business. At least it's other people's, not mine. Their business to tell me", she says to her mother's old friend, who replies: "No. It's other people's business, but not to tell you. I can't be the one to talk to you about your mother." An important reason for telling stories is that children need to know things which are hard to tell them in other ways. It is as if Jane Gardam had written her novel in order to tell its heroine those sorts of things: that her father's plans to seduce Lydia were more conventional than they seemed, for instance, and that her mother was in bed with her old lover at the moment when Margaret hoped to get her parents' attention by swimming out to sea.

Jane Gardam has a spectacular gift for detail, of the local and period kind, and for details which make characters so subtly unpredictable that they ring true, and her humour is tough as well as delicate. It can be no serious criticism to say that the compression and explosiveness of this tightly controlled novel are disappointing only for suggesting that the author has used up material which would serve for several novels.

Jane Miller, "Other People's Business," in The Times Literary Supplement, *No. 3993, October 13, 1978, p. 1141.*

JOHN NAUGHTON

Jane Gardam's *God on the Rocks* is a most peculiar novel, a free-floating account of some family doings in a small seaside town in the north-east of England. The time is sometime in the interwar years, yet the feel of the narrative and the dialogue is more reminiscent of the 1950s. The central character is a young girl, Margaret Marsh, and the book is really about her breakthrough into the crazy reality of adulthood. Into her path, however, stray the most desolate crowd of cast-off personalities: a religious maniac of a father; a petit-bourgeois wistful snob of a mother; various drunks, alcoholics and sundry degenerates; and the only real character in the book—a vulgar, sensuous, impertinent maid named Lydia, whose lines would be awfully funny if only they had been written in English rather than phonetic Geordie. In producing such a strange world, and staffing it with such a cast, Jane Gardam has left more than God on the rocks. (p. 519)

John Naughton, "Kids' Week," in The Listener, *Vol. 100, No. 2582, October 19, 1978, pp. 518-19.*

SIMON BLOW

As a short story writer [Jane Gardam] has two essential assets: style and a quick eye for the extraordinary. She can pick on the small incident and find that behind it lies the bizarre, or the chilling, uncomfortable edge.

Why, in **"The Dickies"** [from her collection *The Sidmouth Letters*], does Jo-Jo Dickie, Pauline's nice, ex-military husband make a play for a woman's hand at the dinner table? Why should a patently honourable man be keeping his wife in neurotic fits for years by his philandering? Her women friends agree that he may be a charmer, but he's an utter cad. It is the dinner-table details that leads on to the clue to the mystery. It is through such carefully chosen minutiae that Jane Gardam finds her truths.

But Jane Gardam is on less sure ground when she moves into areas with which she can only be familiar by hearsay. Placing herself in the character of a tramp in **"The Great, Grand, Soap-Water Kick"** she produces a monologue that is unconvincing as either realism or parody. . . .

Yet, on other accounts, she can deal superbly with the single situation. . . .

The title-story of this volume [**"The Sidmouth Letters"**] is the moral of the *Aspern Papers* updated. It centres round the discovery of some letters from Jane Austen to the man she was abortively attached to at Sidmouth in 1801. The story has some excellent comic moments but it does not rate alongside the four or five stories in this book that display Jane Gardam's intuitiveness for noting the elusive disturbance, funny or sad. In a society where it has become increasingly hard to grasp the whole, her brief, spare writing very much has its place.

Simon Blow, "Quick Eye," in New Statesman, *Vol. 99, No. 2560, April 11, 1980, p. 558.*

VICTORIA GLENDINNING

Jane Gardam has received literary prizes and laudatory reviews, which are all very well, but for some reason the high quality of her fiction for adults has not got through to readers as emphatically as it might. *The Sidmouth Letters,* her new collection of short stories, may help to put this right. She is a very English writer, in that her observation is at its sharpest on matters of class and status, and her most poisonous darts are reserved for the upper middle classes, or rather for the female residue who no longer have servants to exploit and are ending their days in seedy stinginess. . . .

Women come in for more scrutiny and more punishment from Mrs Gardam than do men. In **"The Dickies"** there are two shrewd portraits. Pam is a denizen of "Rhododendria"—i.e., Surrey—a middle-aged "Betjeman girl", relentlessly philistine but redeemed by courage and kindness; whereas her hysterical friend Mrs Dickie is accorded no virtue. . . .

The actual plot of the story is over-contrived, turning on the menopause Ophelia's neurotic need to have a faceless husband to complain about, thus forcing him into the role of unwilling philanderer. Also contrived is the plot of **"Lychees for Tone"**, which depends for its point on an unintended pun. Mrs Gardam is better at people than at plots. But in the latter story she removes herself from the cocktail belt and gives the interior monologue of a working man's mother, with a totally distinct set of foibles and prejudices, and brings this off as well. She goes very much further in **"The Great Grand Soap-Water Kick"** and enters, in every sense experimentally, the mind of a verminous tramp who has lost the power of speech but knows how to have a good time. This is a bravura performance, the most original piece in the book and the funniest. In another, her narrator is a homosexual, losing his one glimpse of the possibility of heterosexual love. The tone is right for the man in question, overwrought and prissily didactic. . . .

The versatility shown in this collection is impressive. **"Hetty Sleeping"**, a "brief encounter" story set in Connemara, is women's magazine fiction of a superior sort. **"Transit Passengers"** is about teenagers: the boy and the girl, bedraggled and in love, have spent a summer together in Crete. He dreads the airport parting, she is supercool. But, after, it is he who recovers almost instantly, and she who sends desperate telegrams. This has the ring of truth. There is also a ghost story, which has the ring of neither confidence nor truth, self-consciously entitled **"A Touch of Gothic"**.

The title story [**"The Sidmouth Letters"**] however, is firmly back in the prevailing middle-class, grown-up world. . . . The story hinges on the discovery—and the destruction—of letters from Jane Austen to the man she loved. It is notable for the portrait of a terrible American academic who writes scholarly books that "read like railway timetables" and spices his reputation with suggestive articles for the *TLS* about "how far Keats got with Fanny Brawne". Foiled in his attempts to reveal all about the immortal Jane, he is at last heard of in Dublin, "lecturing on something unpleasant he had discovered about Yeats".

Victoria Glendinning, "Denizens of Rhododendria," in The Times Literary Supplement, *No. 4021, April 18, 1980, p. 430.*

MARY CADOGAN

There is warmth as well as wit in Jane Gardam's *The Sidmouth Letters* and each story in this collection proceeds at a galloping pace with an outrageous and satisfying twist to its tail. The author skilfully conveys a strange assortment of events—from a working-class mother's worried preparations for the visit of her son's Chinese girl-friend to Gothic goings-on beneath a full-moon in Wensleydale: from the reunion at Harrods of a haggle of desiccated diplomatic wives to the rare ablution rituals of a ghastly old tramp.

Several of the stories are told in first person narratives which have to sustain dialects or unusual modes of speech. This technique could make for tedious reading but on the whole it is well manipulated by Jane Gardam to add colour and vitality. Flexibility of style is best reflected in the episode concerning the hobo who feels in sudden need of his bi-annual clean-up. This unappetising individual comes alive as his thought process unfolds in atmospheric half-sentences and disconnected words. Though he is inwardly articulate, his conversations are gibberish to the other characters in the story but clear to the reader. . . .

The academic background of ["**The Sidmouth Letters**"] is in marked contrast with the mood of self-protective anarchy in the tramp's soliloquising. Its theme is the presumed discovery of some letters sent by Jane Austen to her lover in Sidmouth. All the stories are absorbing, and whether Jane Gardam's leading participants are hippy drop-outs or personifications of affluent decay she never resorts to type-casting. There are streaks of the bizarre in her most ordinary characters and of solid, human warmth in those that are flamboyant or calculating.

> *Mary Cadogan, in a review of "The Sidmouth Letters," in* Books and Bookmen, *Vol. 25, No. 9, June, 1980, p. 43.*

SUSAN JEFFREYS AND MARY ANNE BONNEY

The Batemans, Londoners on holiday, soon find [in *The Hollow Land*] that there is more to country life than fresh air and new-laid eggs when the Teesdale family sets about hay-making in the Home Field that surrounds the house the "incomers" rent. Jane Gardam's descriptions of natives and strangers, of adults and children, from the metal whiskered egg witch to the household name's daughter Poppet are sharp and lively, but it is the place, and not the people that is the star of *The Hollow Land*. . . . The Cumbrian fells, riddled with underground streams, set the pace for, and link together the chapters/stories, and provide a time scale which extends effortlessly into the future, and towards eternity. Jane Gardam's writing may be gentle but it is not soft.

> *Susan Jeffreys and Mary Anne Bonney, in a review of "The Hollow Land," in* Punch, *Vol. 281, August 5, 1981, p. 235.*

PATRICIA CRAIG

> Christ keep the Hollow Land
> Through the sweet spring-tide
> When the apple blossoms bless
> The lowly bent hill side.

Jane Gardam's epigraph [to *The Hollow Land*] is taken from William Morris, and her setting is the Cumbrian fells: "hollow" not in the sense of being opposed to hilly, as in the Yeats poem, but because of the disused mine workings which lie beneath the ground. It is a place of distinct character, with becks, tarns and quarries at every turn. In the opening episode

the narrator (eight-year-old Bell Teesdale) remembers the derelict farmhouses scattered all along the dales. . . . Abandoned to weather and birds and sheep—until holidaymakers, tired of the Lake District, think of buying or leasing the little stone dwellings.

Light Trees is the farmhouse the Bateman family rents. Batemans and Teesdales nearly fail to get along at first, before Bell and young Harry Bateman take a hand (these two meet and quickly become friends for life). Friction—the result of a misunderstanding—is smoothed over and an alliance established between the two families. Summer after summer the London Batemans come; and often in the winter as well. The place is rich in anecdotes and alarms; something is always going on, and everything is relished to the utmost. . . .

With this book, Jane Gardam has reverted to the "linked stories" framework of her earlier *Black Faces, White Faces*. . . . In each episode a satisfactory advance in neighbourliness is achieved or a disaster averted. . . . In the long concluding story, "**Tomorrow's Arrangements**" (set in the year 1999), the Bateman family (or at least grown-up Harry) is threatened with the worst misfortune of all: the loss of Light Trees. Against a spectacular background, however—an eclipse of the sun—their would-be supplanter is sent about his business.

The children's story traditionally ends on a bright note, as these stories do; nothing else in Jane Gardam's approach is conventional. She makes the most, as always, of the subtle and the untoward. Her work has always created problems of classification: when she writes about children, it is in a way that does not exclude an adult readership. *The Hollow Land* is typical in this respect: there is not a limited, trite or chatty observation in it. It creates an overwhelming impression of vigour and freshness. The aids to picturesque living it enumerates—the lovely red-and-white patchwork quilts, the old oak settles and grandfather clocks—all contribute to the sense of order and continuity which is part of the countryside's charm. . . .

Jane Gardam's writing is as exact, as condensed and striking as ever. Underlying the engaging plots of these stories—plenty of frolics and fun—is a single theme: attachment to a special locality.

> *Patricia Craig, "A Country of Customs," in* The Times Literary Supplement, *No. 4094, September 18, 1981, p. 1065.*

ANNE DUCHÊNE

"And there you were with bright, ridiculous, marvellous, mocking eyes and long hard hands", thinks the narrator about her newly-deceased husband in one of the stories [in *The Pangs of Love and Other Stories*], and while one is still pondering the attraction—indeed, even the appearance—of "ridiculous eyes", she continues:

> It was not right or dignified to love so much. To let a man rule so much. It is obsession and not love, a mental illness not a life. And of course, with marriage came the quarrelling and pain because I knew there were so many others, and you not coming home, and teasing when you did and saying that there was only me but of course I knew it was not so because of—cheap and trite things like—the smell of scent. It was worst just before the Robertsons went away. . . .

One needs to ask the reader's pardon for opening with such quotations. Also the writer's: it is presumably not for this kind of writing that Jane Gardam's seven books have variously attracted the Whitbread Award, the David Higham Award, and the Winifred Holtby Award, as well as runner-upship in the 1978 Booker hurdles. No one unfamiliar with her work can lightly ignore such a consensus; the reason has the more carefully to be sought why this present collection seems strained and unsatisfying, and the tone of the prose so often what has to be called pert. . . .

[The blurb] helpfully notes that the author is "married to a Q.C. with an international practice, and has travelled with him extensively, particularly in the Far East". And truly, without frivolity, the reader may come to the conclusion that she has been travelling too much. Too many time-zones and time-tables, too many dazzling, exhausting, exotic *locales* outside too many air-conditioned hotels, have begun to parch her roots.

Not surprisingly, several stories concern Englishwomen who are visiting far-flung places. . . .

The Englishwomen are all very nice, and intelligent, and respond strongly to the dreadful poverty they encounter before they have to move on. And the author herself, with her note-books in her hand-luggage, seems to have become so experienced a visitor that she is not much at home in England either. A noticeably high proportion of these stories have recourse to eccentrics or to old bundles of geriatric mischief, black or benign: a fairly frequent resort these days for writers *en mal de matière,* but even the eccentrics here lack persuasiveness.

The common property of all these stories, however, is efficiency; not a quality that promises much resonance or delicacy. One can see, for instance, that **"Stone Trees"**, which supplied the opening quotations here, began with the observation that the fossilized trees in shallow water on the Isle of Wight are restored to movement by the incoming tide, and that this suggested an image of the restoration of feeling to a numbed heart. Whose numbed heart? A childless widow's heart?—and hey presto! a story taking in Cambridge and Sacramento (for fashionable academic early married life), and the new widow's visit to their old friends the Robertsons, and her seeing, in one of Mrs Robertson's small sons, the exact replica of her husband (even to the "long hard hands"). In eight pages, this communicates itself as a pretty rushed job.

In assembly-line terms, these stories would probably be called a hiccup. Which does not stop one hoping that their designer will tear up some at least of her air-line tickets, and go back to the drawing-board to work in increased tranquility.

> *Anne Duchêne, "Highly Arched," in* The Times Literary Supplement, *No. 4167, February 11, 1983, p. 131.*

ANTHONY THWAITE

The blurb to Jane Gardam's book of stories, *The Pangs of Love,* seems at pains to hammer them into a unity, as variations on the love theme; but it seems to me that Mrs Gardam's strengths are both more various and more limited than this. She is a chronicler, an observer, rather than a fabulist or a moralist, and it's when she tries to extend her range of manner and tone that she goes wrong—as in the title story ["**The Pangs of Love**"], which is an embarrassing bit of whimsy aiming to play feminist tricks with Hans Andersen's mermaid, or in **"Stone Trees,"** the style of which too fretfully draws attention to itself.

What she is best at is faintly disturbing happenings among people who don't fit in: a rigidly disciplined English family in an Italian pensione in **"An Unknown Child,"** an English-woman lost in Hong Kong in **"The Pig Boy,"** and in other stories a succession of spinsters, church workers, odd school-girls and eccentric shoppers. In all these Jane Gardam unerringly goes for the precise detail, the accurately astringent phrase.

In several stories (such as **"The Kiss of Life"** and **"A Seaside Garden"**) she finishes with a twist or surprise which cleverly undercuts one's expectations. Most originally, in **"The First Adam"** she catches marvellously a moment of temptation—averted temptation—in the life of an old Eastern hand, miles away from Welwyn and wife, sweating over the work he loves in one of those desert Intercontinental Hotels.

> *Anthony Thwaite, "Small Pockets of Disturbance," in* The Observer, *February 13, 1983, p. 32.*

JOHN SUTHERLAND

The short story would seem to be Jane Gardam's criticism of life. Her view of things is sharp, yielding nothing more expressive than tolerant amusement at some of life's more elegant little ironies. In what I take to be the best piece in *The Pangs of Love,* a story called **"The Easter Lilies"**, a dotty old lady resents buying Easter flowers when the things grow wild in Malta. Sacrificing custom regulations to common sense, she has a bunch sent over. The rich ungrateful bitch acting as courier drops her pearls in the bouquet. The old lady tries them on, expires at the bedecked altar and, leaving everything to the church, saves it from demolition. It's mechanical, but in its way an almost perfectly satisfying story.

Gardam's people are, typically, comfortably off but hopelessly uprooted. She has a very good line, for instance, in travelling executives and their camp-following womenfolk. . . . [Accidental encounters] dictate Gardam's world. In **"The Kiss of Life"**, a lonely man and woman are brought together after he resuscitates the supermarket kleptomaniac who has been persecuting her. Unmediated mouth-to-mouth contact between the principals is unthinkable. Like Shakespeare's mechanicals, they can only kiss through walls.

Gardam's sharpness stops this side of cruelty. If her work has a fault, it is one inherent in the short story form, I think; namely, a propensity to being too clever. Doing things in short compass . . . seems to encourage showing-off. In this respect, the title piece, **"The Pangs of Love"** (the mermaid and her prince, updated and given a feminist slant), is the weakest offering in an otherwise consistently good collection.

> *John Sutherland, "Short Is Sharp," in* London Review of Books, *Vol. 5, No. 2, February 3 to February 16, 1983, p. 15.*

CARROLL KLEIN

Jane Gardam's book of short stories, *The Sidmouth Letters,* came with an assurance from no less august an authority than the *Guardian* that it was "deliciously barbed, perceptive, entertaining." Having just read a tedious, arch, and ever-so-clever novel with approximately the same claim on the cover, I was skeptical. The friend who sent me the book had included a written proviso that Gardam was "not really our cup of tea, rather romantic and certainly not a feminist." So it was with some curiosity but with limited expectation that I approached the eleven stories in this collection; the reward of discovering yet another woman who writes with sense and sensibility was therefore even greater than it might have been.

With irony, and some affection, Gardam peoples her stories with ineffectual, occasionally absurd, characters, with the walking wounded, the intellectually incompetent, and with those hovering on the edge of social approbation. Her perspective is complex and varied, often romantic but as often anti-romantic. (p. 89)

The scope of her characterization is remarkable. She is as much at home with adolescents living on the beaches of a Greek island as she is with a zany tramp housebreaking in order to have his biannual bath. Devoted parents and their impossible adult children are at once touching and infuriating; retired diplomatic wives hold conversations that are like fingernails on chalkboards. She is familiar with the genteel and not-so-genteel poor, with the middle-class inhabitants of Guildford, and with those whose lives are circumscribed by a vague and worrying sense of never having quite come up to the mark. (pp. 89-90)

Gardam could not be considered in the vanguard, or even the rearguard of feminist writing though her stories are peopled by women professionals, painters who have uneasily abandoned their art for motherhood, working mothers and reprehensibly useless women who are a burden to their men and to society. The subtlety of her writing salvages and often enhances her reticence in making direct statements. She sets up a situation, creates brilliantly realistic dialogue, and lets the reader conclude what she will. After the instructive (and powerful) writing of many feminist writers, Gardam may appear initially to be slight, a denizen of a polite garden-party world who strays from time to time, hatted and gloved, into seedier environs in order to observe the behaviour of the lower classes. This is an understandable but ultimately unfair judgement. She observes class structure and male-female relationships with deadly precision and the lack of a feminist polemic detracts not a moment from her art. She is certainly worth a read though she may not, in fact, be to the taste of all women. A story-teller first and foremost, she does her work well. (p. 90)

> *Carroll Klein, in a review of "The Sidmouth Letters," in* Room of One's Own, *Vol. 8, No. 3, 1983, pp. 89-90.*

ALANNAH HOPKIN

Polly Flint is dumped at the yellow house on a pair of maiden aunts in 1904 at the age of six. Her sea-faring father goes down with his ship shortly after. Her mother is already dead. Polly stays at the yellow house on the salt-marsh, a house so close to the sea and so battered by the wind that at times it "seemed to toss like a ship", until her death in 1985. In *Crusoe's Daughter* she recalls the events of her long, strange life.

If *Crusoe's Daughter* were only the story of Polly Flint most readers would be well satisfied. She is a grand character: sensible, strong, intelligent but fallible, and endowed with a wry sense of humour. However, *Crusoe's Daughter* is much more than the story of Polly Flint; it is also a sustained meditation on the nature of the novel from its 18th century beginnings to its "quite canonically boring" present day manifestations—"all about politics or marital discord." Because of Polly's lifelong obsession with *Robinson Crusoe,* her interest in the nature and purpose of the novel as a literary form is an integral

part of her character, and the intellectual activity never mars the story-telling.

"Every serious novel must in some degree and *unnoticeably* carry the form further" says Polly. Jane Gardam has put her cards on the table, and one can only congratulate her for managing to live up to the demands of her heroine. This is a remarkable achievement, and must surely establish Jane Gardam as one of the most interesting and accomplished novelists in England today.

> *Alannah Hopkin, "An Isolated Life," in* Books and Bookmen, *No. 355, May, 1985, p. 31.*

BARBARA HARDY

Jane Gardam's new novel [*Crusoe's Daughter*] is fresh and vivid, but in it something old and something new are at odds. At the centre is an old-fashioned, fully-blown character, Polly Flint. She is comic, touching, eccentric and English. Her story takes us on a historical crash course from 1898 to her death in 1985. It includes industrial growth, wars, class mobility, concentration camps and nuclear waste. In private and public, comedy and pathos join hands. Images of place, time, and people are sharp and surprising. It is a bit like an early Joyce Cary, in bounce, brightness and observation, though it does not plumb his depths.

Cary wrote in his essay *Art and Reality* that a symbol wholly known was a symbol drained of life. One of the problems in *Crusoe's Daughter*—as in much modern fiction—is the thoroughly explicit and explicated nature of its literary symbols. Reference is preferred to resonance. The heroine's adventures, rambling but stay-at-home, are blended with the story of another story, *Robinson Crusoe*. A cleverly articulate but conventional novel of character and manners is promoted to a work of literary reflection and reflexiveness. Though Defoe's great novel is the object of meditation and love, it is hard not to see its pesence here as determined by fashion. In the critics' forum which is becoming as obligatory as the death-bed and sex-scene were in their day, Polly complains to the benign shade of Crusoe that modern fiction has become "canonically boring", all about "politics and marital discord. Minutiae." There seems to be a touch of self-approval here, since this novel conspicuously skirts both subjects, but the word "canonically" prompts the thought that its own subjects of fiction and feminism are now as popular as those the heroine frowns on (and, like all subjects, boring or not according to their authors' imaginative powers). . . .

It is amusing to use the routinely lit-critical novel for throwing out ideas without needing to develop them, but it is a rash and sometimes superficial game. Polly is an amateur of Defoe. Jane Gardam's use of Crusoe as a kind of role-model involves the neglect of his materialism, his sentimental attack on materialism, his colonialism and his cruelty. There is talk of Defoe's metaphysical landscape, but the word seems scarcely applicable to this novel. The woman's life is isolated and islanded, though Polly's is also crowded and companionable. This image of Crusoe's daughter is much less worked-out than Virginia Woolf's character of Shakespeare's sister. The Woolfs make a brief appearance at a house-party, but Defoe's feminism, in journalism and novels, doesn't get a mention. Crusoe says that we don't hear about his daughter, but I'm not so sure; Polly's name is a variant of Moll Flanders. Defoe's stories of marooned daughters are violent, complex, frightening and comic. Moll and Roxana put Polly Flint in the shade. Polly tells Crusoe that she has been in love for years, ''like a dumpling in broth'', and he approves: ''My creator liked a homely image''. One thinks of the grim folk-wisdom of Moll's image, ''by the steps and the string'', or her comparison of a desolate woman to ''a bag of money or a jewel dropt on the highway''.

Despite the caves threatened by nuclear waste, there is an emotional softness about this novel which is shown up, not modified, by the invocation of Defoe. I dare say this is to take the analogue too humourlessly. There is one delicious scene where Polly is on her way to take a class and plans a lecture on Defoe and the history of fiction which would have kept her going, if it hadn't caused a riot, for a year at least. The book is at its best when it is light-hearted and does not tease us into thinking too hard about great novels.

> Barbara Hardy, *''Islanded, Companionable,'' in* The Times Literary Supplement, *No. 4287, May 31, 1985, p. 599.*

PATRICIA CRAIG

There is at present something of a fashion for novels reflecting other novels, ironically and obliquely. . . . With Jane Gardam's latest novel [*Crusoe's Daughter*] the background book, and enriching ingredient, is *Robinson Crusoe*. Mrs Gardam is not new to the practice. **The Summer after the Funeral** (1973) has a heroine . . . who feels an affinity between herself and Emily Brontë, to the point of thinking deeply about reincarnation. *Wuthering Heights* has left its mark indirectly on this novel. *Crusoe's Daughter,* with its heroine Polly Flint metaphorically cast away, and not cast down by it, is rather more open about its literary appropriations.

Polly Flint, though, is a good deal more than Crusoe's parrot. Crusoe, for her, is both a solace and an exemplar, stuck there on his island—as she says late in the novel—'like women have to be almost always . . . Imprisoned.' Stranded, imprisoned, but calmly getting on with things. . . . Among the children eventually fathered by Robinson Crusoe, after his 28 years of sexual abstinence, Defoe mentions a daughter: but this daughter promptly disappears from the history of the central character. . . . It's a masterstroke of Jane Gardam's to bag the role for a 20th-century woman, daughter of a sea-captain drowned in 1904 on the coal run to Belfast. This is the year when the novel opens. Motherless Polly, soon to be fatherless at six years old, is landed at a tall yellow house on a saltmarsh, somewhere on the Northumbrian coast. . . .

At the yellow house live Polly's Aunt Mary and Aunt Frances, both too religious for their own good—a temperamental defect well understood by Jane Gardam: one is overtaken in the end by vagueness, the other by unaccountable flightiness, after a late marriage, on a voyage to India. . . .

During the greater part of the novel, Polly's age is less than 20; and so Jane Gardam is able to re-do certain set-pieces like the one in which a nervous but determined young girl confronts someone's grand, unlikeable and disconcerting mother. Adolescence offers plenty of scope for the kind of high comedy,

elliptically presented, at which this author excels. But *Crusoe's Daughter* isn't a novel of adolescence, or a social comedy, or commentary, or a piece of pure historical evocation . . . , though it conforms to the rules of each of these categories in turn. It's not exactly an allegory either, more a sustained salting of one set of fictitious memoirs with another—a subtle undertaking. Jane Gardam, following her usual practice, creates dazzling effects out of bits and pieces: an Edwardian pony-and-trap coming joyously along a beach, a train drawing away from the platform at Darlington station, a telescope on a roof. Nothing is out of place in the details of setting or mood; as with other novels which assimilate some crucial text . . . , and thereby gain the freedom to shift away from straightforward narration, certain kinds of verisimilitude seem not greatly to the point. Jane Gardam, for instance, makes no bones about endowing her under-age heroine with an unnatural cogency; and truly, it wouldn't have done to make Polly's literary judgments correspond with those we might expect to hear from an unschooled 16-year-old brought up long ago in a house full of women. 'Form,' she declares—at this formless age, and in a bygone age, not that it matters in the least—'is determined by hard secret work—in a notebook and in the subconscious and in the head.' And *Crusoe's Daughter,* no less than *Crusoe,* could be said to bear out the effectiveness of the process. (p. 20)

> Patricia Craig, *''Crusoe and Daughter,'' in* London Review of Books, *Vol. 7, No. 11, June 20, 1985, pp. 20-1.*

BOB COLEMAN

[*Crusoe's Daughter*] has many virtues: a Dickensian sense of character, some fine comic touches, an abundance of beautiful description. More impressive, however, is Mrs. Gardam's adaptation of venerable novelistic techniques to address present-day political and social concerns. The fluid narratives of those older novels, their clarity and readability, argued the existence of a human community that transcended differences of class, gender and experience, and placed unalterable obligations upon its members.

For Mrs. Gardam, that community and those obligations remain unchanged by the horrors of two world wars, the Holocaust, and numerous other crimes and injustices of the modern age. Polly's view of woman's powerlessness and isolation might have produced a much harsher feminism; instead, when at last she finds her way, it is not by radical means but by modest choices. Her life becomes both tolerable to herself and essential to others.

It is not a quibble to call *Crusoe's Daughter* an unlucky title. Readers expecting a robust story of exotic adventure will be disappointed. More to the point, those who would savor an act of literary faith, a skillfully and affectionately told story of a young woman's survival in 20th-century England, may never discover *Crusoe's Daughter.* That would be a pity.

> Bob Coleman, *''Polly Came Through,'' in* The New York Times Book Review, *April 27, 1986, p. 39.*

Tony Harrison

1937-

(Has also written as T. W. Harrison) English poet, translator, dramatist, and librettist.

Harrison writes traditionally structured poetry in which he combines vernacular with classical language to explore the conflict between his working-class upbringing and his formal education and literary career. A central theme in Harrison's poetry is his alienation from his family, community, and social class, a consequence of his education and his abandonment of the less eloquent language of his ancestors. Yet Harrison is also concerned with the social, economic, and political implications of the suppression of working-class language by the educated classes. By filtering his observations through travels to Africa, Eastern Europe, and the Americas, Harrison has, according to Jeffrey Wainwright, widened his sense of silenced language and "the cultural disinheritance that came to him with the contradictory gift of his education" to include "the wider spread of imperialism that has obliterated languages and cultures across the globe."

Harrison attended England's prestigious Leeds grammar school on a scholarship. He later studied at Leeds University, where he received his bachelor's degree in classics and a postgraduate diploma in linguistics. Harrison's first book, *Earthworks* (1964), is a collection of conventional poems which anticipate few of his later thematic and structural concerns. His first full-length volume, *The Loiners* (1970), is a five-section poem describing the sexual exploits of Harrison and his fellow "loiners," the residents of the city of Leeds. Written in octosyllabic couplets, the book also celebrates expatriate loiners in Africa and other countries and conveys Harrison's characteristic blend of sophistication and commonality in its witty treatment of masturbation, homosexuality, and other sexual practices. Also included in *The Loiners* is Harrison's previously published autobiographical poem, "Newcastle Is Peru," which focuses on the importance of homecoming in establishing one's sense of place. While some critics contended that the explicit nature of Harrison's language overshadowed the book's virtues, Alan Brownjohn deemed *The Loiners* "a rough, oddly touching mixture of crudity and intellectual sophistication, shoddy effects and formal accomplishment."

From "The School of Eloquence" and Other Poems (1978) is a sequence consisting of sixteen-line sonnets whose form derives from George Meredith's *Modern Love*. These poems revolve around Harrison's recurring themes of family, society, class, and language and also encompass art, history, and culture. "The School of Eloquence" describes Harrison's childhood in Leeds during the 1940s and 1950s, his years as a student, the death of his mother, and his return home as a successful poet. *Continuous: Fifty Sonnets from "The School of Eloquence"* (1981) adds thirty-three poems to the sequence and centers on Harrison's life with his aging father, his father's death, and the role of language in determining working-class oppression. Although some critics considered Harrison's portrayal of himself as a dislocated scholarship boy to be artificial and melodramatic, others praised the work for its sensitively delineated ironies, its subtle comedy, and its successful blend of incongruous elements. *Selected Poems* (1984) contains rep-

Photograph by Layle Silbert

resentative works from Harrison's previous volumes and includes his previously published poem, "A Kumquat for John Keats."

Harrison is also highly respected as a dramatist and a translator. His translations cover a wide range of material, including *Aikin Mada* (1965), an Africanized version of Aristophanes's *Lysistrata; The Misanthrope* (1973), from Moliere's drama *Le Misanthrope; Phaedra Britannica* (1975), from Racine's drama *Phèdre;* and *The Oresteia* (1981), from Aeschylus's play of the same title. *Pallades: Poems* (1975) contains selected translations of the verse of Palladas of Alexandria, while *U.S. Martial* (1981) is a collection of first-century Latin poems by Marcus Valerius Martialis. Harrison has also collaborated with actors and musicians on such original theater pieces as *The Passion* (1977) and *Bow Down* (1977).

(See also *Contemporary Authors*, Vols. 65-68 and *Dictionary of Literary Biography*, Vol. 40.)

ALAN BROWNJOHN

The Loiners are the inhabitants of Leeds, and Tony Harrison is drawn to them in their sexual role in his boisterous sketches of city characters and lecherous expatriates in Africa. The clash of old and new cultures, of the civilised and the raw, of education with environment, provide the subjects for poems which mirror the conflict: crude, earthy, modern life in Leeds and abroad comes out in slangy, vigorous but highly formal couplets:

> Stroked nylon crackled over groin and bum
> Like granny's wireless stuck on Hilversum.

Harrison's poetic personality is bitter, ironic and noisy, his themes full of unresolved dilemmas. *The Loiners* is a rough, oddly touching mixture of crudity and intellectual sophistication, shoddy effects and formal accomplishment: uncomfortable bedmates, but it would seem idle to wish these qualities separate. (p. 94)

> *Alan Brownjohn, "Masquerades," in* New States-
> man, *Vol. 80, No. 2053, July 24, 1970, pp. 93-4.*

THE TIMES LITERARY SUPPLEMENT

Tony Harrison's [*The Loiners*] is a trenchant, pugnacious, hard-bitten book, a single five-part poem which moves from tales of sexual adventures in Leeds to the jottings of a lecherous colonial expatriate, and then back home to Leeds for some reflections on what seems to Mr. Harrison the pointlessly circulating vortex of birth, copulation and death. Mostly, however, copulation: "Loiners" means citizens of Leeds, but the anatomical pun is clearly more to the point in a poem which rattles and blisters its way through accounts of masturbation, sodomy and straight sex in Leeds, West Africa, Newcastle, Prague and various other locations.

Most of this has, at the very least, an above-average novelistic interest. Mr. Harrison has the rare knack of manipulating his ironically regular iambics to sustain a story-line or sketch a quick character, and at this level the poem succeeds much of the time as a kind of verse-parody of a goodish late 1950s naturalistic novel, given to tidy chunks of straight-faced throw-away humour:

> We knew those adult rumours just weren't true.
> We did it often but our minds stayed strong.
> Our palms weren't cold and tacky and they never grew
> Those tell-tale matted tangles like King Kong.

The rhythmic clumsiness of that third line is, in fact, fairly unusual in the poem; for it's a capacity to shackle within formal restraints what continually threatens to become a sprawling, turbulent naturalism which accounts for much of the book's limited success. At work beneath the cluttered, abrasive anecdotes is an acute feeling for economy and ellipsis, owing a good deal (one would guess) to Lowell; so that, at the best, the heavy-handed monotony of the sexually obsessive subject-matter can be just sufficiently invigorated by a craft self-effacingly attentive to movement and sound. . . .

In the end, though, the monotony wins out. Despite a lack of pretentiousness remarkable for such a no-holds-barred technique (achieved in part by the use of dramatic personae), the poem has little finally to offer beyond its ocean of immediate sensations. If it avoids a cultic toughness, it does so only because it sticks to a grimly empiricist level hostile to most kinds of meditation, indifferent to attitudes and attitudinizing alike. Its lack of swagger and self-consciousness depends not just on its undoubted wit but on an inability to feel and reflect above the level of the action: to analyse the "finer feelings"

which one of Mr. Harrison's lechers claims wistfully to possess. Sex is real, even if the rest is dizzying vortex: and though that sense of metaphysical dizziness does finally emerge for explicit treatment in the last part, it's appropriate that the poem invites us to put it down to the effect of too much Newcastle Brown as much as to an excess of angst.

> *"Iambic Attitudes," in* The Times Literary Supple-
> ment, *No. 3576, September 11, 1970, p. 994.*

DOUGLAS DUNN

Tony Harrison's first book is *The Loiners* (named for the inhabitants of Leeds), and offers more than promise. There are serious flaws in his work, however, the most blatant being a reliance on the conservative technique of the couplet, which a heavy inlay of sex and surprise does little to update. **"Ginger's Friday", "The Pocket Wars of Peanuts Joe"** and **"Allotments"** celebrate early sexual encounters. The wit is startling and assured, but Harrison imposes banal rhythms on his material, and the result is a relentless and, to my taste, rather thin jokiness, although this is partially redeemed by his fine dramatic sense. . . .

Also technically impressive are Harrison's Nigerian pieces, but the sexuality is overdone. Harrison, however, can create a convincing character, in this case an expat Loiner, the PWD Man, put across with much noisy enthusiasm in Kiplingesque metre. Apart from its interest as narrative, and its sheer readability, the only meaning here, as in much of Harrison's work, is a rudimentary Fuck and be Fucked, which in Harrison's distillation seems to be what the glamour of darkest Africa boils down to.

The two final poems, **"Newcastle is Peru"** and **"Ghosts: Some Words Before Breakfast"**, are much better. Harrison handles the notoriously difficult octosyllabic couplet well, and achieves more rhythmic subtlety than in the pentameters of the earlier poems.

World-wide in its topography, powerful in its effects, Harrison's poetry is a stunning addition to the scene. His contemporaries can already feel the competition breathing down their backs. (p. 70)

> *Douglas Dunn, "Snatching the Bays," in* Encounter,
> *Vol. XXXVI, No. 3, March, 1971, pp. 65-71.*

ALAN BROWNJOHN

The School of Eloquence is a work-in-progress on the theme of society, class and language, an area not neglected by dramatists and novelists during the last twenty years, yet only glancingly touched by the poets. Harrison mostly stands glaring ruefully over the great divide which a classical education and a literary career has opened up between him and his working-class family; a position in which he finds it so easy to be cruel, and touchy, very difficult to be tender, and at times quite possible to be patronising. . . . The class you leave behind doesn't automatically subside into pathos and ignorance. When he manages to drop the combative poses, he can produce a beautifully-modulated love poem like **"Durham"**; and write a sonnet called **"Book Ends"** which might easily command tears. (p. 64)

> *Alan Brownjohn, "Fascination of What's Difficult,"*
> *in* Encounter, *Vol. LII, No. 3, March, 1979, pp.*
> *61-5.*

ANDREW MOTION

The epigraph to *The School of Eloquence* admits that how [Harrison] became a poet is 'a mystery', and he spends a good deal of the book trying to explain its causes and effects. The 15 Meridithian sonnets which form the title sequence ["**The School of Eloquence**"] are his most determined attempt. Their stylish portraits of the artist as a young Leeds scholar show him torn between his family and his aspirations, his peers and his Latin proses, and his received idiom and an ideal articulacy. In each case, he opts for the chance of self-improvement, and the result is not to make him sound patronising, but guilty, rueful and unable to communicate with his past in its own terms. A coalminer is 'lost in this sonnet for the bourgeoisie', and the language of 'mi mam' is 'the tongue that once I used to know / but can't bone up on now'.

These tensions are no less evident in the form than the content of Harrison's poems. As his lines buckle, break up and collect themselves round rhyme-words, his diction veers from the lay to the learned. The effect is to create sustained disjuncture, rather than homogeneity, and most of the time it serves its purpose well. But there is a sense in which his expertise can be counterproductive. On a few occasions in "**The School of Eloquence**" his skilful conjuring tricks risk supplanting the very emotions they mean to produce: we are shown a beautifully polished top-hat and no rabbit. Fortunately such disappointments are rare, and the second part of his book more than compensates for them by including a few candidly straightforward pieces. In these, tenderness is never a prey to linguistic virtuosity, and doubts are persistently emphasised by the demands of technique. . . . (pp. 562-63)

Andrew Motion, "Self's the Man," in New Statesman, *Vol. 97, No. 2509, April 20, 1979, pp. 562-63.*

CHRISTOPHER HOPE

Tony Harrison called his first book of poems *The Loiners* and meant it though there were those who believed the title referred only to the citizens of Leeds—but it was the loins, too, that he considered, together with their fruits and failures, in his vibrant and invigorating fashion. [*The School of Eloquence*] displays again his prodigal talent. There is never any question of Harrison shirking risk; some of these poems build a career on it: can he match that impossible rhyme? Will the Greek bear just *that* gloss? Fancy finding just the right French to fit there! In such contests, with Harrison running in a winner just ahead of the bell, it's not always easy to judge the verse so dazzling is the prowess. . . . (p. 79)

And there is the burden of many of these poems. The prodigal returns wondering and worrying aloud in many languages how he must sound to the folks he left behind, trailing his t's and sundered s's in a parody of the northern eloquence he's lost, aware of the incongruity that crowns him like a cloth cap on the classics man and warning off the posh talking middle-classes who think they've got him. . . . Many of the poems are about the vexed question of pronunciation and class accents: '. . . The tongue that once I used to know / but can't bone up on now, and that's mi mam's' ("**Wordlists**"). However, the best poems in what is altogether an exciting collection, seem to happen away from home, in 'horny, horny Hollywood', or in the Hermitage where he contemplates the Amazons who dress the winter streets: 'Leningrad's vast pool of widowhood / who also guard the Rembrandts and rank Gents' / ("**Summer Garden**"). I think that Harrison's gift is his ability for doing

impersonations, as well as in recognizing them around him, in seeing how 'breasts become sombreros, groins goatees,' ("**Doodle bugs**"). And if his multi-lingual impersonations look more brilliant abroad (which is, after all, the place for prodigals) perhaps it is because he is free of the need to apologize or explain. (p. 80)

Christopher Hope, "Time and the Developers," in London Magazine, *n.s. Vol. 19, No. 3, June, 1979, pp. 74-80.*

JEFFREY WAINWRIGHT

The word *gob* has several meanings listed in the O.E.D. In Middle English it was a lump or mouthful which since the 16th century has become almost entirely "*dial.* or *vulgar*", "a clot of some slimy substance", and, still "*dial.* and *slang*", a word for the mouth and for talk, language. Certainly it was a word that my own respectable working-class upbringing and education rendered almost taboo as particularly "common". In Tony Harrison's *School of Eloquence,* however, the meaning and capacities of this word agglomerate to make it a focus for the class-ridden struggle for and with articulate language that is the subject of the title sequence ["**The School of Eloquence**"] and others of these poems. *Gob,* as Harrison's note to "**Working**" states, is also the word in coal-mining for the space where coal has been extracted, and that poem, commemorating Patience Kershaw, a pit-girl of the last century, ends with the serious pun,

> Wherever hardship held its tongue the job
> 's breaking the silence of the worked-out gob.
>
> (p. 57)

What Tony Harrison seeks to do in *The School of Eloquence* is to write poetry that will recover at least something of the words and the life of that "worked-out gob", and to do so in lines that will ravage the cultivation that has overlaid English poetry. . . . The sequence ["**The School of Eloquence**"] is also a personal and family history that evokes Harrison's painful initiation into accepted culture and learning as a member of that myth-laden group so beloved of the English Right, "bright children from poorer backgrounds". The stresses of this situation: that taunt of a schoolmaster as the boy begins "Ode to a Nightingale", "mi art aches"; the best front room, usually known only at Christmas, for funerals and for invalids, allowed him as a study, a card table for his Virgil; the forsaken pleasures—'*Ah, bloody can't ah've gorra Latin prose*'; all these are comically, sensitively and ironically brought into the poems. Also, the cultural disinheritance that came to him with the contradictory gift of his education opens to the wider spread of imperialism that has obliterated languages and cultures across the globe. Poetry itself, in which he has found his own voice, he sees in "T'Ark" as endangered, though

> A language near extinction best preserves
> the deepest grammar of our nothingness.

But of course is there not a profound contradiction in mounting this attack upon "owned language" in poetry, in *sonnets* moreover, one of the very forms its owners have appropriated as their own? . . . Perceiving this contradiction in *The School of Eloquence* will bring relief to some readers, and even . . . present an opportunity for cheap gibes. Harrison knows of course that there is no simple return to "his own class", and that the distinctiveness of his own voice is now composed also of that heavily imbibed education and the accompanying "conventional literary modes''. He is not easy in the situation, and its bitter irony is everywhere in the poems, as when he writes of all the

> tongues I've slaved to speak or read . . .
> Hausa, Yoruba, both R. C. Abraham's—
> but not the tongue that once I used to know
> but can't bone up on now, and that's mi mam's.
>   (**"Wordlists II"**)

The colloquialism ''bone up on'' is very consciously deployed, as is the deliberately strained phrase ''mi mam's'', whose plangency enacts the loss with its awkwardness and with the self-regarding ingenuity of its rhyme. The choice of strict form is evidently vital, for that itself proclaims Harrison's comprehension of the contradiction. It is naive to imagine that poetic convention, like cultural tradition at large, can be ignored and overturned at will. It has penetrated our consciousness too deeply for that, and rather than shirk the implications of this, Harrison takes on the tradition with the range and rhythms of its ''dulciloquy''. . . . A rioter in Bristol in 1831 was reported as exclaiming ''there would be no reform without books were burnt''. A culture in sullen, almost internecine turmoil seems to lie behind this, and is the historical ground of *The School of Eloquence*. These poems cannot solve the contradictions they embody, but they are a passionate, sad, and heroic struggle with them. They speak of our culture in a way that makes them some of the most important poems of the present day. (pp. 58-9)

> *Jeffrey Wainwright, "The Silence Round All Poetry," in* Poetry Review, *Vol. 69, No. 1, July, 1979, pp. 57-60.*

JOHN LUCAS

Continuous is so exciting a volume of poems that it's difficult to speak about it without making it seem even better than it is. For it does have some faults. In the first place the sixteen-line sonnet form, though Harrison usually manages it with astonishing authority and ease, becomes too much the expected thing, so that you wish he'd try something else. Then again, some of the poems exist to make a point and are therefore nearer to polemic than to poetry. Brilliant polemic, it's true, the kind that has you out of your chair and cheering him on:

> O gentlemen, a better way to plumb
> the depths of Britain's dangling a scholar,
> say, here at the booming shaft of Towanroath,
> now National Trust, a place where they got tin,
> those gentlemen who silenced the men's oath
> and killed the language that they swore it in.
>   (**"National Trust"**)

Their language isn't really killed, of course, and *Continuous* exists to prove as much. (You have to allow 'dangling' the ghost of a third syllable if the metre of the second line is to come out right, and that's of course how most people *do* say the word.) Yet Harrison knows that keeping the language alive requires him to handle it in a manner that can seem, and indeed often is, tendentious. 'Three cheers for mute ingloriousness! / Articulation is the tongue-tied's fighting', he says in his brilliant opening poem, **"On Not Being Milton"**; and in poem after poem he can make such ingloriousness appear as the mark of grace. But that is only because the working-class voices, chiefly those of his father and mother, which sputter through the volume with an angry, affectionate, desperate and touching inadequacy are given a final shape by the poet himself. And

as soon as he withdraws, or tries to limit his presence, he makes way for a clumsiness that works against all he hopes to achieve because it is condescending or plain careless. . . . (p. 18)

But these criticisms should not be allowed to obscure the fact that *Continuous* is a very fine achievement. More than any other English poet I have read in recent years, Harrison makes good Camus's claim that the function of art is 'to open the prisons and to give a voice to the sorrows and joys of all'. And if that seems to pitch the claim too high I can say only that the serious wit, the passionate knowledge and understanding of circumstances which the poems speak about and for, make the best of *Continuous* absolutely essential reading. It isn't so much that anyone who cares about poetry should read this book, as that anyone who reads this book will know what it is to care about poetry. (p. 19)

> *John Lucas, "Opening Prisons," in* New Statesman, *Vol. 103, No. 2650, January 1, 1982, pp. 18-19.*

PETER PORTER

I am kept from a proper appreciation of Tony Harrison's latest poems by my very different experience of childhood and education. *Continuous* is a volume with an *idée fixe:* a classically educated, working class Northerner summons up, through guilty recall, his dead parents and the world they brought him into, a world whose eloquence is based on suffocating closeness and inarticulacy. It is a very different eloquence, he believes, from that of poetry, with its upper-middle-class roots and allegiances. 'I'd like to be the poet my father reads!' Harrison writes.

We are not very far here from Richard Hoggart's *The Uses of Literacy,* and, just as that has always seemed to me a book of spurious insights, so Harrison's New poetry sounds to my ears to be full of hollow rhetoric and self-advertising guilt. Any middle-class Australian will have encountered even less understanding among his seniors when first experimenting with poetry, but he will not conclude that he is thereby separated from his family. High culture is neither made by the upper classes, nor belongs to them. It is the inheritance of all people who love truth and eloquence, and can be felt and imitated *sui generis.* This is as true of England as of any other country, and Harrison is fighting his enemies' battle for them by assuming that his schoolday Latin and his prize-winning verses have cut him off from his roots.

However, I suspect that his alienation is a strategy for getting his poetry written. He has pioneered a style for our times which matches the most corseted traditional forms with an acutely-heard vernacular speech. He is famous for introducing the apostrophe 's' into regular iambics, rather in the manner of the appoggiatura in music. Some critics have found in his poetry the perfect marriage of direct speech and formal precision. His earlier verse, especially *The Loiners,* goes some way to justify this claim, but since Harrison began to work on **"The School of Eloquence,"** of which *Continuous* is the latest instalment, his work has become more mannered and his dense lines more overbearing. Really he is looking for a backward-facing aesthetic which will not earn him the suspicion of being an English formalist, a type presumed to be middle-class and Oxbridge. . . . Neatness of structure is helping to produce glibness of response, a process assisted by the dominant mode of these sixteen-line sonnets, that of childhood and early manhood remembered. However, there are some moving poems on the death of his parents and the sardonic aspects of their obsequies.

"Timer", which won the 1980 National Poetry Competition, adapts a funny-postcard view of cremation with great poignancy. When he writes most directly, is least uptight, he produces his most sonorous and original poems. . . .

Peter Porter, *"The Latinist of Leeds," in* The Observer, *January 17, 1982, p. 31.*

ALAN ROSS

Nearly all the poems in *Continuous* read as a kind of post-mortem about Harrison's relationship with his mother and father, a doomed attempt across the grave to surmount the gap created by his education and 'way with words'. (p. 5)

Such a development most poets—whether 'working-class' or not—take as inevitable. Poetry is scarcely a serious career to many parents, of whatever background. For Harrison, however, the gulf between Yorkshire inarticulateness, on one side, emotion always reined in, and his own gift of the gab, leads to a kind of continuous verbal warfare conducted with the ultimate aim of establishing poetry as viable, common speech. Although death has made the communication one-sided, Harrison worries terrier-like at the intransigence of family patterns, determined to recapture and define a closeness that in life could never find expression.

No English poet has ever used dialect and the rhythms of working-class speech to such powerful effect as Harrison in these poems. In poem after poem details of childhood and adolescence are worked up to create portraits of his parents as vivid and four-square as those the Bradford-born Hockney painted of his. The muscularity and compression of the verse ought to be enough to convince anyone that poetry is a reasonable adult language. But one knows, and Harrison knows, that nothing would have broken through the parental disdain and contempt. His father, grousing and grieving, would have continued to grudge recognition by language.

Most of Harrison's main themes—in and out of the theatre—are to do with language; understanding and overcoming the impediments created by imperfect use of it, in both speech and writing, making words earn their keep. Harrison's unaffected use of his father's dialect takes nothing away from the generally sophisticated nature of these poems, but it raises certain problems. There was no use of dialect in Harrison's first book *The Loiners* (1970), a book of much wider range if less deeply felt, and it remains to be seen how much Harrison's present involvement in creating a family mythology conditions his future writing.

Continuous is a more domestic and restrained collection than *The Loiners,* a book in which Harrison's natural bleakness of outlook was more or less obscured by an intellectual exuberance deriving from his travels in Africa, Europe and the Americas. But in its similar firmness of stance and energy, irony and eloquence, *Continuous* makes a passionate companion to it. (pp. 5-6)

Alan Ross, in a review of "Continuous," in London Magazine, *n.s. Vol. 21, No. 12, March, 1982, pp. 5-6.*

BLAKE MORRISON

[*Continuous*] adds 33 new poems to the 17 that first appeared in **"The School of Eloquence"** sequence of 1978. At their simplest level, that of narrative (for the sequence does add up to a story of sorts), the poems describe the poet's childhood in Leeds during the 1940s and early 1950s; his endeavours as a scholarship boy; his mother's death and cremation; and his return visits, as a successful poet and play-translator, to see his lonely, grumpy and aging father, who in the end dies and is cremated too. The Leeds setting is every bit as accurately observed as Douglas Dunn's Terry Street: the 8 x 5 gardens, kept up or not kept up; the front doors used only by doctors, postmen and strangers and the backyards with their 'beaten hard square patch of sour soil' (a typically heavily stressed, heavily monosyllabic Harrison description); the cloth caps, coal fires, false teeth, ukeleles, wedding photos and Co-ops associated with this part of the North (but not the greyhounds, braces and tin baths a less informed observer would have gone for).

Continuous has a full complement of characters who in Harrison's hands avoid becoming 'characters'. . . . But the chief focus is on the family triangle—father, mother and only son—and the dislocation that ensues from the mother's death, a dislocation touchingly and even comically observed. . . . It is through the eyes of Harrison's father that we grasp, too, some of the changes that have overtaken the neighbourhood in the last ten years, not least the growing numbers of Pakistanis, whose presence he bemoans in frankly racialist language. . . .

If *Continuous* were only a part-family portrait, part-sociological record, it would add little to what *The Uses of Literacy* and any number of angry young novels from the North have made familiar. Its special edge comes from Harrison's interest in the question of what it means to acquire language in a community which has had none. The muteness of his uncles, 'one a stammerer, the other dumb', becomes a symbol of the suppression of working-class speech over the centuries. Harrison himself, believing with E. P. Thompson and other historians that 'the dumb go down in history and disappear' and that 'the tongueless man gets his land took', determinedly departs from that silent heritage. . . . He describes himself as a schoolboy in an intolerable wrestle with words and meanings, forcing down Latin and Greek, parroting dictionaries and lexicons, combing the 'thesaurus trove of trashes'. Or, resentful at being patronised by the guardians of high culture, who fob him off with the part of the drunken porter in *Macbeth* . . . , he chews up literature ('Litterchewer'), devouring it out of love but also in anger. His relation to language and culture is a paradoxical one. He aligns himself with what he calls the 'rhubarbarians': the Luddite barbarians (about whom Douglas Dunn has also written) who shout *'rhubarb rhubarb'* to drown out the linguistic civilities of their rulers. But he also, as these puns and coinages make clear, enjoys and feels liberated by the language his kin do not use.

Harrison is conscious that the acquisition of such language exerts its price: separation from his schoolfriends who go *'off tartin', off to t'flicks'* while he is left in his attic room working on translations of 'Cissy-bleeding-ro' (a cissy is what he feels, Cicero what he reads); separation from his family, who don't understand his poetry ('Sorry dad you won't get that quatrain') or who understand it to be 'mucky' (a library copy of his collection *The Loiners* has his mother weeping over his 'sordid lust'); and separation, ultimately, from his class, which he suspects may regard him as a panderer to 'the likes of them', the middle classes, whose property poetry is and for whom he has become a busker, flat cap in hand. Like some of Seamus Heaney's poetry, *Continuous* celebrates language while recognising that to acquire it is to become cut off from the tribe. . . .

He would like, really, to live in a special zone encompassing both the inarticulacy of ancestry ('the silence round all poetry', he calls it) and the articulacy of culture: 'Words and word-lessness. Between the two . . .'

These are contentious ideas about class and culture, and there are those who would accuse Harrison of melodrama when he posits an unavoidable opposition between the urban proletariat and high culture. Surely, they would argue, his picture of the scholarship boy as a heroic fighter against the odds is senti-mental and anachronistic. Can it be so very hard to be a work-ing-class writer and yet keep faith with one's class? And is high culture so heavily fortressed that it requires this kind of revolutionary clamour at the gates? . . . Is not Harrison in-venting difficulties, and does not his poetry suffer as result?

Part of the achievement of *Continuous* is to prove such diffi-culty on the pulses—in the very texture of the verse itself. It is a verse which coughs and splutters, all fits and starts. And though Harrison acknowledges this, describing how his poetry glugs 'like poured pop' and how it 'thickens with glottals to a lumpen mass', one's impression on a first reading is that he must have a cloth ear as well as a cloth cap. The clumping rhymes, the all-too-iambic pentameters, the awkward and re-petitive abbreviated 's's'—. . . the visually ugly breaking-down of the sonnets into units of one or two lines, the sheer confusion of lay-out and typography, as capitals, italics, Latin and Greek tags, brand-names, songs, advertising jingles, dictionary sym-bols and dialect rub shoulders on pages that have no pagina-tion—these must be some of the least fluent poems in the language. But they mean to be. The poetry that comes as naturally as leaves to a tree is, they imply, the poetry of the leisured classes, whereas these are poems that must work for their effects. To call Harrison's poetry 'laboured' is not to damn it but to describe it precisely: it is written with labour, and on behalf of labour, and out of the labouring class. Clank-ing and creaking like old machinery, yet formal in the extreme (*abab* 16-liners all the way through), it never lets us forget what a contrived and artificial activity poetry is.

> I strive to keep my lines direct and straight
> And try to make connections where I can,

he writes, and the stress falls on the words 'strive' and 'try', on the effort poetry costs. Yet *Continuous* repeatedly proves that effort to be worthwhile by discovering 'connections' which transcend the labour and become love. . . . (p. 10)

If Harrison's poems individually declare (and demonstrate) the value of poetry, the structure of *Continuous*—language poems in Part One, poems on the death of his parents in Part Two, reflections on art and extinction in Part Three—shows the poet's awareness of its limits. Being a poet cannot help him resolve his feelings about his mother's death (he returns to it obses-sively), nor allow him to pay tribute to her as movingly as his inarticulate father does. . . . At his mother's funeral Harrison decides

> If anyone should deliver an oration
> it should be me, her son, in poetry,

but all the years of Latin and verse count for nothing as he sits passively listening to a 'droning' vicar. In the light of these failures, Harrison's harping on about being a poet and inter-national figure, jetting between Leeds and the New York Met, seems less boastful than it otherwise might: it only underlines how little his literary success amounts to in matters of the heart.

Though it takes the risk of appearing monotonous, both because of the unwavering Meredithian form and because of its obses-sion with the same two topics, language and death, *Continuous* is one of the most rewarding books of poetry to appear in England in recent years. (pp. 10-11)

Blake Morrison, "Labouring," in London Review of Books, *Vol. 4, No. 6, April 1 to April 14, 1982, pp. 10-11.*

MICHAEL SCHMIDT

Milton and Keats are among the stars that Tony Harrison steers by. Why then does his *Selected Poems* . . . put me in mind of Kipling? It has to do with the pace of his poems, their lack of repose, the sudden clarification in images brilliantly rendered. It has to do with the emphatic rhyming, the bold awkwardness of technique, the use of dialects, the rich excess. Then there's the geographical and thematic range—evident not only in the exotica of working-class Leeds but in dedications such as "for Miroslav Holub, Havana, 1969" and "for Jane Fonda, Len-ingrad, 1978" (a sonnet about clitoridectomy). He's been around; that's part of what the poems are about. Then there's the button-holing manner, the narrative content, the insistent maleness of voice.

And the poems are steeped in politics. Harrison addresses not his political friends but agnostics and foes. He preaches to convert. He's praised for exploiting elements which "genteel practitioners" are shy of—bold statement, explicit sexual con-tent, a native dialect at once expressive and crude. When his work was not properly heeded, he had the excuse that no one seemed to be listening. When people started liking what they heard, he tended to play it again in different keys. There's an elegiac string on his Leeds lute that twangs too often. . . .

Harrison sets out to speak for those who haven't had "a voice" in the world of power and whose silence has meant repression. He speaks for them, not to them. Some critics claim he is easily "accessible". It's not a claim he would make. "Sorry, dad," he writes in one poem, "you won't get that quatrain (I'd like to be the poet my father reads!)" At public readings he spends three quarters of the time preparing his audience for what they are to hear.

What fascinates me is his use of many language registers and the tensions they create when brought together in traditional verse forms and subjected to his humanizing irony. And I love his recent free-wheeling poems, **"A Kumquat for John Keats"** and **"Skywriting"** for instance, with their intricate, easy verve. There, Harrison no longer has to prove himself—he *is* himself.

Michael Schmidt, "Speaking for the Voiceless," in The Sunday Times, *London, November 11, 1984, p. 42.*

CLAUDE RAWSON

The epigraph to a section of Tony Harrison's *Selected Poems* is called **"Heredity"** and asks where he got his talent from. The answer is *"I had two uncles, Joe and Harry— / one was a stammerer, the other dumb"*. The note is characteristic, both thrusting and coy. The poems sometimes embarrass by their self-cherishing, but the energies of a strong talent are seldom far away. The two uncles come to a vivid life in other poems, in proportion as they detach themselves from Harrison's fond self-mythologizing. . . .

[Harrison's] family occupies a high proportion of this book. They are not all "characters", like the two uncles, and a violent sadness usually attaches to them. A poem about his daughter's birth is a frenetic phantasmagoria of anxiety and elation, anticipating her later maiming in a road accident, an event which reappears with eruptive poignancy in several subsequent poems. Perhaps the best-known poems here are a series of sixteen-line "sonnets" on the death of his parents, of which the most affecting is **"Long Distance, II"**, about how his widowed father used to conduct an elaborate and surreptitious pretence that his wife was still alive, and how the poet himself becomes caught up in the same sad exercise. . . . There is in these poems a striking mixture of emotional vigour and patness. The formulations of grief come over in iambic pentameters which sometimes achieve a drumming neo-Empsonian starkness, and are at other times close to the kind of sub-Empsonian facility which used to be a distinguishing sign of weaker poems of the Movement. . . . Some of the attempts in these poems to blend the parents' Yorkshire speech with the stylish sweep of Harrison's own metrical fluencies seem affected or patronizing, or else overstrenuously willed or wilful. But at their best the poems in this idiom have a tender truthfulness, and Leeds, the place where he grew up, is a vividly evoked presence throughout the volume. . . .

A strong satirical note runs through the book. Sometimes it seems uncoordinated, flailing this way and that, as in some of the sexual/imperial rhapsodizing. By contrast, the poems about Audubon and about the American bald eagle from **"Art & Extinction"** have a wry power. The pastiche **"Oh, Moon of Mahagonny!"**, on the irony of "a big soirée" thrown by the Rockefellers "for the cast of *Mahagonny* by Brecht/Weill" is inventively funny, as is **"The Call of Nature"**, about tourists who visit the Lawrence shrine at Taos and its native "pueblo people":

> Their call of nature ends through separate doors
> branded in ranch pokerwork: BRAVES! SQUAWS! . . .

Claude Rawson, "Family Voices," *in* The Times Literary Supplement, *No. 4266, January 4, 1985, p. 10.*

DENIS DONOGHUE

Tony Harrison's *Selected Poems* includes 14 poems from *The Loiners* (1970), eight from *The School of Eloquence* (1978), 36 from *Continuous* (1981), all of *Palladas* (1975), and about twenty uncollected poems. . . . Most, but not all, of the poems are the kind that cats and dogs can read. Harrison hasn't lost any sleep over Eliot's assertion, in "The Metaphysical Poets" (1921), that 'the poet must become more and more comprehensive, more allusive, more indirect, in order to force, to dislocate if necessary, language into his meaning.' But 'the poet', in Eliot's sentence, has upper-class responsibilities which don't exert much of a claim upon Harrison's working-class sensibility. He prefers to write of local occasions: how things are going in Newcastle, what's new in Leeds, hard living in foreign parts, 'lovely Sodom's sin', a bout of tachycardia, sundry episodes in Brazil, Cuba, Beverly Hills, the Rosebowl at Pasadena, sex abroad. But the occasions that dominate his most telling poems are the old mortalities: in one poem, heartbreakingly, a dead child, in twenty poems or more a dead mother, a dying then dead father.

Many of Harrison's poems issue from images of the War in its first years. . . . When he alludes to other poems, they are mostly poems the War turned into momentously general truths. . . . But Harrison is even happier with the street-poetry of dialect words—yagach, faffing—and the shared pavements of the North.

His special tone arises, I think, from his sense of gallantry which makes an accepted claim upon him but which the conditions of his life haven't allowed him to sustain for long. This sense of unaffordable values appears in the poems from time to time as a grander style than any his normal themes would sustain. . . . There are also poems—**"On Not Being Milton"** and **"The Rhubarbarians"**—in which, enjoying a bit of rough stuff, he plays the Luddite. But mostly he doesn't take any greater authority than he needs to manage in an appalling situation. Indeed, his relation to the authority that a poet can resort to is quizzical, no more than a glance at big guns he knows he could bring forward. He ends **"Study"**, a poem about the best room in the house, reserved for deaths and Christmas, by alluding to two masters: 'My mind moves upon silence and *Aeneid* VI.' In Yeats's ''Long-Legged Fly'' mastery is possible—Caesar, Helen of Troy, Michelangelo—because the mind can accept its conditions by sequestering itself within them. . . . As for *Aeneid* VI, I assume that Harrison has in mind Aeneas's meeting at last with his father, who says: 'Have you come at last, and has your love conquered the difficult road?' . . .

Harrison is a learned poet, but the authority he calls upon for conviction and truth-telling comes, not from the poetic tradition, but from his family, mother, father, uncles, aunts and grandfathers, to whom *pietas* is a matter of remembering, reciting old woes, and holding on to a grandfather's knuckleduster so that, years later, it can be used as a paperweight, never far from the poet's hand. . . . (p. 18)

Denis Donoghue, "Venisti tandem," *in* London Review of Books, *Vol. 7, No. 2, February 7, 1985, pp. 18-19.*

DAVID McDUFF

Tony Harrison is a poet for whom the English North is an inherited, lived and living reality: it has been his nurturer and Muse since the outset of his career. . . . 'Working-class barbarian' is a clichéd expression—yet Harrison has, in a thoroughly original fashion, made it into his poetic persona, every bit as doggedly authentic as Auden's *Homo Abyssus Occidentalis* or MacNeice's Baudelairean, Hampstead Perseus. The equation of the concepts 'Northern' and 'working class' may not be an exact one, but it is sufficient for Harrison, who builds from it a cosmology that throws into glaring relief, in a way not hitherto attempted or achieved, those regions of the English psyche that are inhabited by the ghosts of the dispossessed, the inarticulate and the outlawed. Harrison's *Selected Poems* trace the development of that cosmology through a number of distinct yet subtly interrelated stages—from an early preoccupation with figures in an impoverished Leeds cityscape, through bouts of travel in the Third World to a darkly obsessive absorption in the realia of family life, and death, experienced directly, at gut-level and through a working-class perspective; and beyond this to an extended lyrical meditation on the nature of human existence and its relation to the void.

That it is an *English* psyche which constitutes the focus and centre of Harrison's poems seems beyond doubt. As in the case of Auden, the experience of foreign travel serves to make the poet 'reflect on [his] past and [his] culture from the outside.' Yet where the middle-class, Oxford-educated Auden sought to reach and surpass the limits of what seemed to him a parochial and world-blind culture by climbing to the 'vertiginous / Crow's nest of the earth' (MacNeice), Harrison—already at home in the North, working-class, Leeds-educated—seeks in the tropical wastes of Africa and the rainforests of the Amazon a barbarian antithesis and antidote to the culture that has given him birth. He approaches this experience as the civilized, even over-civilized descendant of a working-class cultural tradition (no less 'developed' than its middle-class countertype), and searches for metaphors to fit and plumb its stringently concealed abysses in the darkness that has been bequeathed by a colonial past. . . . Strangely, perhaps, for such an English poet, this is Rimbaud country, the ambience of the 'Fleuves impassibles'; it is also the terrain of an Aimé Cesaire, a 'Notebook of a Return to the Native Land', conceived less as a fixed geographical location than as an intensity of shadow, a *négritude* that in the very depth of its negation gives rise to the joy of light, the redeemed wholeness of a shared humanity. Nowhere in the *clapotement furieux des marées,* however, does Harrison abandon his craft to the vicissitudes of poetic prose or vers libre. Like Auden and, more especially, like MacNeice before him, he maintains a rigorous discipline of poetic steering: the forms he employs are classical and stanzaic, the meters elegantly precise, the rhymes judicious and assured. For his descent into the maelstrom of family affliction, love, death and grief chronicled in *The School of Eloquence,* he chooses the Miltonic sonnet. For his bitter, funny, witty and often cruelly painful jibes at the ineluctably *working-class* fate that has befallen him and those whom he loves, he selects the carefully-prepared techniques of the music-hall routine and the stand-up comic, punchlines and all. . . . By the end of [*Selected Poems*], we find Harrison's voice sounding gentler, his Englishness made all the more pronounced by his half-fascinated, half-repelled encounters with the American South. . . . Reading these most recent verse essays, which include the remarkable and virtuosic **"A Kumquat for John Keats,"** one begins to surmise that much of the posturing and bragging, the rhythmical battering and rhetorical browbeating, the coy Iron Curtain snook-cocking and Cuba-librism that mar some of the earlier work was nothing but a young man's conceit—what survives of the 'barbarian' persona in these later works is a deeply engaging and engaged voice, serious without being earnest, the voice of a scholar-poet who, while closely attached to England's Graeco-Roman heritage, sees through and beyond Judaeo-Christian England to the dark stretches of uncharted and unexplored territory that lie at the outer reaches of its spiritual domain. . . . I came away from Harrison's *Selected* with the feeling that despite certain weaknesses he is an uncommonly achieved poet, his voice more mature, more certain and more assured than that of practically any of his English contemporaries I can think of. In some ways the analogy is less with an Auden or a MacNeice than with some poet of a far earlier age—perhaps a Villon or a Ronsard (despite the poet's Englishness, one looks in vain for an English forefather—Milton's influence hardly goes beyond a formal level in Harrison's work), some poet whose struggle *is* his poetry,

and who goes constantly beyond his age, into the darkness of both past and future. (pp. 73-6)

David McDuff, in a review of "Selected Poems," in Stand Magazine, *Vol. 27, No. 1 (1985-86), pp. 73-6.*

CHRISTOPHER REID

Tony Harrison's treatment of the quatrain in his long poem *V.* might, at first glance, look as careless as Reed's, but to anyone forewarned by his previous work it will soon become clear that a conscious policy of disruption has been followed to bring about the frequent unevennesses of tone and texture that make an initial reading such a bumpy experience. Harrison appears to equate poetic and social form, and his rough versifying is a kind of bellicose bad behaviour, designed to emphasise his abhorrence of received opinion on the social matters that are his constant concern.

Thus in *V.,* as in the Meredithian sonnets that constitute his finest and most personal achievement so far, **"The School of Eloquence,"** time-honoured iambic pentameter and living Yorkshire voice are set against each other in an antithesis that generally resolves in favour of the latter, as one has only to hear the words spoken to recognise that the verses are sustained by an authentic and irreducible rhythm that will not be denied its claim to poetic status. Only at rare moments does a line appear to have been lazily filled out to make weight, or a measure needlessly botched in a spirit of literary vandalism.

But then Harrison is a wily operator, and even here he has pre-empted the complaints of his critics, for the central event of his new poem is a visionary encounter, in the Leeds cemetery where his parents are buried, with a graffito-daubing United supporter, a defacer of tombstones, who turns out to be none other than the personification of Harrison's own vandalistic impulses. One's judgment of the success of the poem will depend largely on whether one is persuaded by the poet's identification with this figure. . . .

Admirers of **"The School of Eloquence"** will no doubt be glad to enjoy again the punning word-play that is one of Harrison's most fruitful devices and that enables him to reveal such a wealth of V-significance in the single letter of his title: from the *versus* of antagonism to the optimistic 'V for Victory'. *Versus,* too, inevitably suggests verses, and with a single squirt from the skinhead's aerosol it can become a universally recognisable sexual emblem. Schism, defiance, the value of poetry and the healing power of love are all caught up thematically within this particular poem which, although it may lack the discipline of the 'sonnets', encouraging Harrison at times to over-indulge his penchant for bleeding-heart rhetoric, nonetheless confronts issues of real urgency and is capable of quickening the reader's responses more immediately than the performance of almost any other contemporary poet. (p. 21)

Christopher Reid, "Here Comes Amy," in London Review of Books, *Vol. 8, No. 7, April 17, 1986, pp. 20-2.*

Zbigniew Herbert

1924-

Polish poet, essayist, dramatist, and scriptwriter.

A leading figure in contemporary Polish literature, Herbert is acknowledged as a powerful poet whose work represents a search for strong moral and humanistic values. Having witnessed the brutal violence of World War II, totalitarian repression, and the failure of various ideologies to improve the human condition, Herbert stresses the need for poetry to confront the harsh realities of life. He frequently employs irony and experimental forms devoid of punctuation to free his verse from rhetoric and to directly address social, artistic, and metaphysical themes. While his verse is stark and unromantic, Herbert often relies on wit and fantasy to temper the bleakness of his subject matter. His work is infused with historic and mythic allusions as well as observations on the objects of ordinary life. Robert Hass has described Herbert as "an ironist and a minimalist who writes as if it were the task of the poet, in a world full of loud lies, to say what is irreducibly true in a level voice."

Herbert was born in an area of eastern Poland that was invaded by both the Soviet Union and Germany during the late 1930s and was annexed to the Soviet Union after World War II. As a teenager, Herbert fought in the Polish Resistance and began writing poetry during the war. Stalinist restrictions on literature after the war and Herbert's refusal, as A. Alvarez has written, "to relinquish his own truth and his own standards in the face of any dogma," prevented the publication of Herbert's work for fifteen years. This period of "writing for his drawer," as Herbert termed it, allowed him to forge a distinctive poetic voice that speaks for his generation and places their experiences within the context of historical and contemporary events.

Herbert's first three volumes of poetry, *Struna swiatla* (1956), *Hermes, pies i gwiazda* (1957), and *Studium przedmiotu* (1961), established him as a leading postwar Polish poet. These works introduce his characteristic use of classical literature, politics, history, moral issues, and everyday objects. Many of the poems appear in the two anthologies of Herbert's verse published in English, *Selected Poems* (1968; reissued 1986), translated by Czesław Miłosz and Peter Dale Scott, and *Selected Poems* (1977), translated by John and Bogdana Carpenter. Two of Herbert's best-known early pieces are "Apollo and Marysas" and "Study of the Object." The former poem, which focuses on the conflict between Apollo, the Greek god of art and beauty, and Marysas, a satyr flayed by Apollo, underscores Herbert's belief that art must reconcile beauty and the reality of human suffering. "Study of the Object," the title poem of *Studium przedmiotu,* is an attempt to define an object of idealized beauty by blending descriptions of ordinary objects with metaphysical speculations and mythic allusions. Such poems as "Why the Classics" and "Preliminary Investigation of an Angel" evidence Herbert's interest in history and political ideologies.

In the volume *Pan Cogito* (1974), Herbert follows the exploits of Mr. Cogito, a tragicomic character in search of moral certainties who meditates on history and his personal past and contemplates such topics as nature, hell, magic, and ethics. This character reappears in *Report from the Besieged City* (1986).

© Lütfi Özkök

Stanislaw Baranczak noted that Mr. Cogito has "become a model for the spiritual situation of a contemporary Pole: an individual who exists . . . and therefore, to reverse Descartes, has to think, to make a self-defending use of his or her conscience or its aesthetic equivalent, taste." The poems in *Report from the Besieged City,* which focus on life in Warsaw during a time of social turmoil and martial law, were written following Herbert's return to Poland in 1981 after having spent extended periods in France and West Germany. Through the use of historical allusions and observations on contemporary events, Herbert characterizes the problems in Poland as representative of the human condition.

Herbert has also published a highly regarded volume of essays, *Barbarzynca w ogrodzie* (1962; *The Barbarian in the Garden*). These pieces focus primarily on European art and architecture as viewed by the barbarian of the title, an individual who exists outside of the dominant Western tradition. In his essays, Herbert posits a view similar to that in his poetry, maintaining that art must unite pleasure and beauty with the hardships and realities of life.

(See also *CLC*, Vol. 9 and *Contemporary Authors*, Vols. 89-92).

THE TIMES LITERARY SUPPLEMENT

Hypocrisy, betrayal, violence: Poles do not need Albert Hall-style poetry readings to remind them of these. A brief allusion calls up quite enough sombre thoughts. What to do in the face of such thoughts, in the face of such facts: that is the insistent question. One of the reasons why Zbigniew Herbert is so highly regarded as a poet in Poland today is because he asks the question so doggedly, so intelligently, and so gently. . . .

In his teens [Herbert] fought in the Polish resistance; he was a student (of law, economics and philosophy) in the worst Stalinist years. . . . But few of his poems [in *Selected Poems*] simply recount the moral and physical horrors he must have witnessed. They are more directly concerned with virtue than with evil. Many of them are brief monologues-in-the-mind of men straining to see and feel with justice and generosity—or simply not to deceive themselves. One may regard these portraits as self-portraits of the poet without loss to him: there is a kind of modesty with which we have grown unfamiliar in presenting oneself as striving for virtue, and being glad to attain it in however small, uncertain a degree, or however belatedly. . . . Herbert is frank and rueful enough about the impediments to virtue; and irony—more at his own expense than others'—is a powerful instrument in his hands. But his irony never slips, as it can so easily, into immodest extremes of cynicism and self-disgust. Rather it is a kind of corrective in the name of truth which can round even on itself if necessary. . . .

In [his use of] inner monologues there is a direct miming of Herbert's efforts to render the complex justice due to different human situations. The strain to realize, the shock of realizing: this is the rhythm that the short lines embody. In other poems the reader's mind is more deliberately and rhetorically forced to consider, and reconsider. A final simile may press a further judgment on all that has preceded. . . .

But not all Herbert's work consists of examples, in his own words, of "the moralist's dry poem". There is also a haunting visionary element in his poetry, offered though it is with caution and often with grief for its fancifulness. **"Arion"** is a sketch of the fabulous singer who "restores world harmony". . . . Yet in spite of all his caution the poet grants a legitimate power to the vision, and makes that power come through at us, beautiful and disturbing. We find something similar in the poem of Herbert's that is probably best known in [Great Britain], **"Elegy of Fortinbras"**. Here Fortinbras takes farewell of the dead Hamlet, to return to his sewer project, his decree on prostitutes and beggars, and his "eternal watching"; yet even as he does so he has to say

> This night is born
> a star named Hamlet We shall never meet
> what I shall leave will not be worth a tragedy.

Gravely, and very movingly, Herbert locates the best examples of high human possibilities again and again in the dead and the non-human—fidelity in a wooden stool, dignity in a pebble. . . .

Herbert's rather dry, guarded diction, with its evocations under tight control, and his use of the line-break for many of his major effects, make him, fortunately, a poet less difficult to translate well than many other poets. These are very good translations, strong in their own right and close in force and feeling to the originals. The volume is introduced by Mr. A. Alvarez, who sums up very precisely and cogently that quality of Herbert's poetry—full of "fine classical yearning", yet

unshakably, practically, politically concerned with the obdurate world—that is representative of the best tradition of Polish literature; representative too, it might be added, of the best art and literature throughout eastern Europe at the present day.

"Armed with Irony," in The Times Literary Supplement, *No. 3454, May 9, 1968, p. 486.*

GEORGE GÖMÖRI

Perhaps the fact that Herbert left the town of his childhood before or during the war, never to return there, is significant: he is an expatriate and a wanderer. He must have felt like an expatriate in Cracow, Toruń and Warsaw, later on in Paris where he lived for a longer period, and in West Berlin where he is staying at present. The physical circumstances of his life are always provisional, his existence is precarious; only his quest for meaning, for a wider tradition and a spiritual home continues. All this is reflected in his poetry in an oblique way, as Herbert is not a man to express the collective feelings of *his* generation. This generation, as the word is normally understood, does not exist: comparatively few survived the holocaust of the Warsaw Uprising in 1944. . . . Who could tell what were the feelings of this truncated generation? At any rate, Herbert's allegiance bound him to the dead:

> the dead are gentle to us
> we carry them on our shoulders
> sleep under the same blanket.
>
> ("Our Fear")
> (p. 51)

In another poem published in his second book of poetry, *Hermes, Dog and Star,* Herbert is even more explicit. **"Biography"** describes a boy who "looked for a souvenir amongst the ruins / prayed with the names of the dead," a clear enough allusion to the Uprising, for years a forbidden theme in Poland. The poem continues with someone advising "the boy" to tear himself away from past memories, to look ahead, turn towards the future: "You have tried to outshout time / turning to the dead / try now to outshout time / turning to those yet unborn." This benevolent advice was certainly heeded by other poets, for instance by Różewicz in his politically most "committed" period, but not by Herbert who refused to fix his eyes on the imaginary paradise promised by the revolutionary chiliasm coming from the East. His later poems radiate the same spirit of courage and calm integrity that motivated the young people who had fallen on the barricades. Certain subjects though called for a different kind of courage, and in such cases Baczyński's bitter romanticism had to give way to the ironical realism of Zbigniew Herbert. (p. 52)

[**"Farewell to September"**] is about a national tragedy, the collapse of Poland in September 1939. There are many ways of speaking about such events: with pathos, with fury, or alternatively in sadness and sorrow. Herbert chooses the least expected stratagem and attacks his own pain (and the pain and frustration of every Pole) with irony which becomes, by extension, self-irony. The "anachronistic ballad," the *Warszawianka*, is sung over the megaphones in vain; uhlans will not win battles against tanks. The general can boast "we shall give the Germans not one button"—we know how much more the war cost Poland. The whole scene has the air of a comic opera until the last stanza, when suddenly the joke turns sour: those boys on the heath are dead. (pp. 52-3)

[Herbert is not] anxious to define his aims and allegiances in strict political terms. (In all truth one has to say that in the post-1956 context of Polish literature nobody pressed him to make declarations of loyalty.) At any rate, he is not a spokesman of either Them or Us, his detachment and implicit opposition do not make him a representative of definite political forces. . . . His untitled poem beginning with the words "We are standing at the border," written in 1956 to the fighting Hungarians, shows his deep concern for freedom and justice, while his **"Apollo and Marsyas"** is a reminder of the eternal reality of pain, is a human protest against divine cruelty. . . . [Herbert] condemns the violence of the stronger not on a historical but on a moral human level. (p. 56)

The best known poems of Zbigniew Herbert are dramatizations of what I would call "threshold-situations." The poet or rather his protagonist is about to take some kind of action which would commit him in one way or another. Whether it is hesitation between choices, as in **"The Return of the Proconsul"** where the poem ends on a not-too-enthusiastic decision taken by the protagonist ("I've decided to return to the emperor's court / yes I hope that things will work out somehow"), or cool contemplation of the *modus operandi* in taking over the reins of power in a rulerless country, as in the **"Elegy of Fortinbras"** (**"Tren Fortynbrasa"**), Herbert catches the moment that *precedes action*. One of his earlier poems bears the curious title **"Nike Who Hesitates"**—even the goddess of victory hesitates for a moment before letting a young man die unceremoniously for her. "Threshold-situations" favour meditation, personalized or projected from outside as the case may be, and meditations are not written for mass-audiences. In these poems Herbert fuses doubt and faith, hope and resignation into moments of inaction, and though his hero will have to act, his choice does not eliminate his doubts or the tragic element involved in the act of choosing. Scepticism is Herbert's self-defence against the crushing absolutes of history. (pp. 57-8)

History for Herbert is a complex process not reducible to schemes, a continuum which involves the rise and fall of civilizations, the blossoming and disintegration of cultures. Man and his culture fascinate Herbert who patiently follows the footprints of Man in the sands of eternity. Occasionally we have the impression that he is more interested in the cultural artefact itself than in the artist who produced it; but while he is detached as an art-critic, he is often involved in an interpretation of the past which is relevant for the present—I have in mind some essays, like the one on the Albigenses in the excellent collection *Barbarian in the Garden*. Nevertheless, Herbert betrays no prophetic inclinations. So many things happened throughout history and some of these things can happen again, though not in the way we imagine them. One should be prepared for the best (**"Report from Paradise"**) and the worst (**"Practical Recommendations in the Event of a Catastrophe"**), though neither is likely to happen. Herbert has no recipe for a perfect society and no confidence in ideologies which guarantee the Right Path leading to Paradise. On the other hand, he knows what to avoid. He is compassionate in a way which sometimes reminds us of the Stoics or the Humanists of the early Renaissance, and of Marcus Aurelius to whom Herbert addressed one of his early poems. Perhaps it is not an accident that his poetic practice to some extent follows the advice of the Emperor-Philosopher: "Make for thyself a definition or description of the thing which is presented to thee, so as to see distinctly what kind of thing it is in its substance, in its nudity, in its entirety, and tell thyself its proper name." This is exactly one of Herbert's main objectives in his last book of poetry appropriately named *Study*

of the Object (*Studium przedmiotu*). Things like a pebble or hair are described objectively, yet with a certain compassion. The title poem itself expresses highly speculative but not unimaginative praise of the pre-world of possibilities: "the most beautiful is the object / which does not exist." This sounds like a complete negation not only of historicism but of history, yet even this extreme withdrawal from the world of "realities" allows the poet an assertion of human creativity: "extract / from the shadow of the object / which does not exist . . . / a chair / beautiful and useless / like a cathedral in the wilderness" [**"Study of the Object"**]. . . . This rehabilitation of the cultural artefact against "the march of history" is a distinct feature of Herbert's more recent poetry. (pp. 59-60)

George Gömöri, *"Herbert and Yevtushenko: On Whose Side Is History?" in* MOSAIC: A Journal for the Comparative Study of Literature and Ideas, *Vol. 3, No. 1, (Fall, 1969), pp. 50-61.*

DEBRA NICHOLSON CZESTOCHOWSKI

"Study of the Object" is intrinsically Herbert's in its pervasive irony. And, typically, beneath that steel-plating of cynical intellection, paradox and tongue-in-cheek abstraction lies a softer core: the heart of the poem cries for affirmation of divinity, for revelation—a moment of clear insight to justify faith. But Herbert's words mock themselves, the plea is that of a skeptic.

From the outset, we are challenged by the poet to a metaphysical wordgame. Contrast and paradox give rise to multi-levels of meaning, which in turn shape the dilemma: concrete versus contemplative, a major preoccupation of Herbert and one that roots him firmly in the Polish literary tradition.

The very title of the poem is more than it seems. On one level it implies the close scrutiny of an entity that can be seen and touched. But after exposure to Herbert's ability to make the sparsest of language blossom kaleidoscopically, we are inclined to raise our interpretation of the title from the actual to the ineffable: "study of the object" implies a state of mental absorption, contemplation of the ultimate goal—pure consciousness, divine revelation, Nirvana.

> The most beautiful is the object
> which does not exist
>
> it does not serve to carry water
> or to preserve the ashes of a hero
>
> it was not cradled by Antigone
> nor was a rat drowned in it
>
> it has no hole
> and is entirely open
>
> seen
> from every side
> which means
> hardly anticipated
>
> the hairs
> of all its lines
> join
> in one stream of light
>
> neither
> blindness
> nor
> death
> can take away the object
> which does not exist

The first three words of the poem make clear that we are dealing with an absolute. Its exact nature, however, is ambiguous: the very notion of "object" implies existence; thus a mere couplet into the poem, we are confronted with an apparently irreconcilable paradox.

Lines three through six reinforce this paradox by emphasizing the nonutilitarian nature of this "object." It has no function, nor has it ever had one. It serves neither to sustain life, nor to retain the remnants of life. With mention of Antigone, the classical is evoked; the "object's" placement in that context is also denied. (pp. 131-32)

[The] poem emanates from a *nonimage*. The work is typically Herbert's in its stylistic economy and classical attention to detail, means that serve here not to define, but to defy the very geometric constructs applied by the poet. Western concepts of time, space and function are simply irrelevant to this "object." (p. 132)

                    2

        mark the place
        where stood the object
        which does not exist
        with a black square
        it will be
        a simple dirge
        for the beautiful absence . . .

Part 2 is an extension of the initial stanzas. Having failed to capture the "object" in terms with which we are comfortable, the poet removes the "object" and attempts to define its absence. (p. 133)

The strength of Part 3 resides in its dynamics. The "black square," once the site of our "object," expands—now a sail, then an island, sinking beneath a dazzle of salty white into oblivion. The blizzard erases these mutable black forms, and we are plummeted back to a "pre-world" of innocence and endless potential. . . .

Part 4 reflects a transition in the narrative voice: the poet addresses us directly. What seemed at the outset a fairly cerebral, distant problem becomes immediate and personal via the word "you". You and I may enter the "white paradise," but inevitably we will impose our logical constructs upon it, thus fulfilling, i.e., killing, its "possibilities." Here the poet's language functions superbly; the cry "vertical-horizontal" violates the "pre-world" and receives an appropriately angry response, as "perpendicular lightning strikes the naked horizon" in visual mimicry. (p. 134)

[In Part 5], Herbert extends his preoccupation with the visual to the image of the "canvas," which works as a metaphor for consciousness in his charge to the individual. Sham, chaos and unimaginative bulk—as suggested by "wadding," "slovenly," "gild" and "whale"—are forms pressing in from the outside and must be resisted. If we are compelled to "create" in our urge to complete the "pre-world," we are implored at least to retain the purity of our respective visions. Thus our paintings, the forms we impose on the "white paradise" of clean canvas, will be unique.

                    6

        extract
        from the shadow of the object
        which does not exist
        from polar space

        from the stern reveries of the inner eye
        a chair
        beautiful and useless
        like a cathedral in the wilderness

        place on the chair
        a crumpled tablecloth
        add to the idea of order
        the idea of adventure
        let it be a confession of faith
        before the vertical struggling with the horizontal

        let it be
        quieter than angels
        prouder than kings
        more substantial than a whale
        let it have the face of the last things

With the first stanza of Part 6, Herbert reverts to classical rigor and linguistic economy in a final proliferation of paradox. The cold precision of "extract" contrasts sharply with the compounded abstraction of "the shadow of the object which does not exist." "Polar" restricts "space"; "stern" inhibits "reverie"; and "chair"—that most functional of objects, created only to serve the human form—defies qualification as "beautiful and useless."

The poet's intent seems clarified by the words of stanza three, which ask us to "place on the chair a crumpled tablecloth." Thus we have summoned in our minds the vision of one functional object placed upon another. But, if chairs and tablecloths are defined by their functions, does not this juxtaposition, which renders these objects useless, rob them of their existence? This is daring imposed on our orderly minds; we have reached the highest abstraction. To maintain this vision, as *Ding an sich*, is our goal and equates a "confession of faith" precisely because it transcends the rational, on which we rely. We are asked, simply, to "let it be"—to refrain this time from imposing Euclidean constructs on the purity of the vision, the work of the "inner eye."

Then swiftly, almost as if in capitulation to his own irresistible urge, Herbert deals his ironic blow: four sharp, final lines that ridicule poet and reader alike.

        we ask reveal o chair
        the depths of the inner eye
        the iris of necessity
        the pupil of death

We are united with Herbert in worship of the chair. Thus the poet turns his cynicism back upon himself, desecrating his own lines by overextending his eye imagery in an absurd mockery of prayer. The formal rigidity of these last four lines bespeaks the death of divinity at the hands of theology, i.e., the "quadrangle." Our God is inanimate, His existence belied by reality; and we, the unknowing pagans, are fools.

The final stanza of **"Study of the Object"** confirms what has been implied throughout the poem: a disaffection with Western philosophy—with reliance upon its rational, Euclidean constructs to explain away phenomena; with the unbending, empty hierarchy of its "-ologies" and "-isms"; and with its inoperative checks and balances, the strongholds of Christian order: justice and mercy.

But in spite of its sharply cynical turn, the poem as a whole posits a quasi-affirmative view of experience. Disaffection with a philosophy of life need not imply distaste for living; Herbert does not yield to bitterness, but suggests a transition to a *Weltanschauung* derived from the East. Through simple focus on the concrete, a contemplative state may be realized. The goal is one moment of crystallized consciousness, during which the mundane assumes beauty and the purely functional exists in and of itself. Thus focusing on the objective from the very personal viewpoint of the "inner eye" offers relief, if momentary, from disappointing reality. Such temporary respite must suffice for salvation, as we learn to confront the true absolutes: "necessity" and "death." (pp. 136-37)

> *Debra Nicholson Czestochowski, "Herbert's 'Study of the Object': A Reading," in* The Polish Review, *Vol. XX, No. 4, 1975, pp. 131-37.*

BOGDANA CARPENTER and JOHN CARPENTER

The Polish poet Zbigniew Herbert is one of the most remarkable poets now writing in Europe. . . . Technically a member of the War Generation, Herbert has always resisted categorization: he has never been a spokesman for a group or school of any kind, and if he is a spokesman at all it is for individual conscience. . . . At times Herbert gives the impression of being entirely alone, answerable to no one except his own conscience. Usually his voice is deliberately subdued—it has been remarked that sometimes he seems to be "whispering" or talking to himself. Clearly he is an anti-rhetorical poet who has no need for any of the high literary styles or pompous attitudes of the past. Yet, if Herbert speaks for no current literary fashion or clique, he manages to pitch his voice in such a way that he is one of the most authentically public poets of our time. This is the paradox of Herbert which gives his poetry its particular stamp and which has been successfully imitated by no one else. It is important, therefore, to focus on Herbert the political and—above all—moral poet. To do this it is necessary to consider him in relation to his own generation, and then to define the unique relationship he has assumed toward the past, toward different traditions and the classics. To our knowledge, this has not been done before in a systematic manner; past studies tend to stress either Herbert the political poet, on the one hand, or, on the other hand, Herbert the classicist, and this has created an artificial dichotomy. Herbert's classicism has nothing in common with that of Jarosław Rymkiewicz, for example. Herbert is a poet who has expressed the theme of revolt, of *opór*, in one of its purest forms, and yet at the same time he has also read the Greek and Roman classics attentively and enlisted them in his revolt. It is a mistake to separate these, or to ignore how the classical aspect of Herbert's poetry greatly reinforces his rebellion. They are only seemingly contradictory, and in terms of Herbert's poetry they are entirely consistent.

Like other members of his generation—Tadeusz Różewicz, Miron Bialoszewski, and Tymoteusz Karpowicz—Herbert began to write poetry during World War II. (pp. 37-8)

The war was probably the most important experience in Herbert's life and left an indelible imprint on his poetry. As late as 1969, in the poem "**Prolog**" which introduced his fourth collection of poems, *Napis*, he wrote about those who took part in the war. . . . The war permanently changed his outlook; he was a young high school student when it broke out, and afterwards the place where he was born and brought up became part of a foreign country. The face of Poland was permanently changed, socially, politically, and physically. These experiences partly explain Herbert's insistence on a clear moral stance able to resist the fluctuations of history and ideology. Another

poet who lived through the war, Tadeusz Różewicz, has often been linked with Herbert, primarily because they are of the same War Generation and they are both moralists. But they can also be contrasted with one another: Różewicz's poetry after the war emphasized purely personal experience and denied all previous values, whereas Herbert drew entirely different conclusions. He has written: "Something makes me different from the 'War Generation.' It seems to me that I came away from the war without accepting the failure of the earlier morality. It is still attractive to me most of all because I painfully feel the lack of tablets of values in the contemporary world." . . . Herbert is a remarkably positive poet in the context of his generation, although rarely have positive values been won against greater opposition and with greater struggle. (pp. 38-9)

In America and Western Europe a positive attitude toward the culture of the past is sometimes associated with reaction. However, in Poland during the decade after World War II a paradoxical situation arose in which some of the writers who had most completely rejected pre-war Polish culture found they had little basis for rebelling against the repressions of the Stalinist present. On the other hand a poet like Herbert, who struggled to repossess (and revise) the culture of the past was able to express revolt in one of its most intense forms. For Herbert the past represents living experience rather than lifeless forms. (p. 39)

If Herbert is a political poet, he is political in the broad sense that he is a poet of revolt, of opposition. He is not a poet of parties or of platforms, he has never been a Nationalist, never a Communist or Marxist, never a Catholic. He is totally nondogmatic. On the one hand it is true that he constantly examines contemporary mechanisms of power, contemporary ideology, contemporary slogans. Poems such as "**Powrót prokonsula**," "**Sprawozdanie z raju**," "**Raj teologów**," "**Magiel**," and "**Damastes z przydomkiem Prokrustes mówi**"—and the list could go on at great length—are nothing if they are not political poems. Yet the word "political" should be applied to Herbert's poems with great care. If it is implied that they are political as opposed to lyrical or philosophical, this would not be true, and if "political" is defined as narrow contemporary relevance, a good case could be made for Herbert as an anti-political poet. The entire notion of ethics and politics was severely qualified in Poland by World War II, and all of "tradition" was put in a new light. The War Generation was not simply marked by the fact that they took part in the war or were profoundly influenced by it—this fact cannot be separated from the fact that after the war they took part in the reconstruction of the country. In Poland the War Generation is frequently called the generation of "Kolumbowie" ("Columbuses"). They were the ones who explored new social, political, and ethical territory for the first time. It is this fact which unites Herbert with Różewicz, and which prevents us from pushing the contrast between them too far. Both based their attitudes toward tradition on the physical, material destruction of the past which they had witnessed; both based these attitudes on the vantage point of what might be called the "rubbish heap" of the present. (pp. 39-40)

Herbert's attitude toward the past is not one of partisanship, that is, of attributing greater value to the past than to the present. Although he constantly returns to the themes of the past, it is never a static source of value. It is very difficult to call Herbert a classicist in the same sense in which the word can be applied to an academician or in the way it is applied to a Western European (or American) poet such as T. S. Eliot.

For Herbert, the past represents experience above all, common concerns, relevance, and life. Herbert never adheres to the past at the expense of the present, instead the past is the ally of the present. He is constantly saying both yes and no to the past, both yes and no to the present. His attitude toward the past is a constant balancing act and the final arbiter is his conscience.... As a moralist and political poet, Herbert assumes a position of extreme isolation. No group or party is automatically on his side, neither the present as opposed to the past, nor the past as opposed to the present. When he resists the repression or terror of the present, he might search for an ally in the past and stretch out his hand, so to speak, to that person in a gesture from one living person to another.... A Polish critic has noted that dialogue is fundamental to the structure of Herbert's poetry, and one of the most basic types of dialogue which Herbert carries on is with the past—the dead— whom he treats as if they were alive, made of flesh and blood.... Herbert's conception of the past always entails a highly imaginative act, and is of the greatest importance for his poetry. He insists on the life of the past, on its living, dynamic quality which is relevant to contemporary struggles not because it is dead but precisely because it is alive. The balancing act between past and present, the constant tension and dialogue between the two, do not restrict his poetry, far from it. By addressing his experience and his conscience directly, he confronts the world in all its breadth, both the past and the present. His experience is placed in a seamless historical continuum; his poetry becomes extremely broad and its range enormous. (pp. 41-2)

It is ironic that one of the most relentlessly political contemporary poets, who has little respect for authority and who uses a wide variety of avant-garde techniques in his verse, should admire the classics. Yet Herbert constantly returns to the classics and especially to their themes, not for their authority but rather to confront his experience with that of others. Herbert feels naturally, spontaneously at home with the Greek and Roman classics, and his interest in them seems to derive from his interest in the present and its very topicality; he has a need to see clearly, to let no assumptions pass unexamined. It is not, for example, the classicism of Goethe and his epigram, "Political verse—dirty verse." Herbert is a persistent critic of what might be called antiquarianism. The prose poem **"Klasyk"** is a critique of the antiquarian's lack of sympathetic imagination. (p. 43)

Herbert refuses to idealize the past, and he treats it with the same disabused irony with which he looks at the present. He demythologizes and deflates the past, and constantly tears down the barriers which separate it from the present. In a poem like **"W drodze do Delf"** Herbert clearly has the twentieth century in mind, its experience of the war and the Holocaust. In view of this, it could be said that Herbert's classicism is also anachronistic in that it has the frequent bias of the experience of World War II—Herbert's classicism is anti-idealistic, reflecting his experience, just as nineteenth-century classicism was idealistic, reflecting the experience of a different century. This is partly valid, yet Herbert's classicism is many-sided, and he treats myths from a variety of different points of view; generally the myth is a means for examining his own experience, and he does not consider it *per se*. (pp. 43-4)

It is a mistake to refer to Herbert's poems on classical themes as updating or revising them, because he conceives of them as fluid by their very nature. These myths do not represent Platonic forms for him, they do not contain immutable archetypes or permanence; Herbert's concept of myth is quite different from that of Jung. By treating them as experience, his focus is as much on the present as on the past. This experience is that of Poland, which was at the center of the destruction of World War II, the subsequent occupation and prison camps, propaganda, and terror. Consequently the myths are rarely treated with pious respect, although a deeper respect is usually present. In the prose poem **"Próba rozwiazania mitologii"** he treats the entire Greek pantheon as if it were a political organization which is being disbanded.... The poem is a light one. It is one of several which serve to remind the reader that Herbert does not put the Greek gods and classical myths on a pedestal, that they are neither remote nor separate from basic, everyday experience.

The classics, however, are also enlisted in Herbert's revolt against conditions in the present. This is one of the most serious and fundamental uses of the classics in Herbert's poetry: they are at the service of his revolt against repression and propaganda. Here Herbert's poetry often comes close to being topically political. (pp. 44-5)

In some of Herbert's poems he has used classical themes as vehicles for attacking the notion of transcendence, or even romantic idealism. This was the dominant meaning of the poem **"Historia Minotaura."** The Minotaur was actually a human, the slightly retarded son of Minos himself, who became a victim of pedagogical theory.... Probably Herbert has made his most scathing attacks on transcendence in poems which do not make use of classical themes, but use instead the figure of the angel.... the poem **"Raj teologów"** contains a biting critique of angels, theologians, and a paradise which is, in reality, totally empty. In the poem **"Przesłuchanie anioła"** an angel is interrogated, tortured, and the confession quickly follows; so much, Herbert seems to be saying, for romantic notions about the ability of the individual to resist physical force. Three more recent poems, **"Pan Cogito opowiada o kuszeniu Spinozy,"** **"Georg Heym—przygoda prawie metafizyczna,"** and **"Beethoven,"** carry the attack upon transcendence even further. Herbert seems increasingly convinced that the desire to improve or perfect mankind is one of the major causes for the repression or destruction of mankind. The desire to rise above the human condition becomes disrepect for life.... [From his post-World War II perspective, Herbert] associates the claims of romantic idealism with the ideological pretensions of Nazism, Stalinism, and totalitarian politics. In Herbert's poems the angel and religion usually shade into, and blend with, politics and political ideologies.

The corollary to Herbert's hostility to notions of transcendence and theory is his stress on practicality, on the importance of humble everyday details.... [In the] poem **"Pan Cogito opowiada o kuszeniu Spinozy,"** Spinoza expounds his philosophical ideas to God, then God turns against him and tells him ironically that, in effect, his ideas are nonsense. He should turn to the practical affairs which he has neglected. It is in this context that Herbert has written his many poems about humble everyday objects, about a stool, an armchair, a pebble. Herbert finds a source of value in these ordinary objects—used, dented, imperfect—rather than in the grandiose, the pretentious. Herbert continues to be fascinated by simple objects and to study them, finding unexpected new qualities and aspects of reality. He humanizes them, and at the sme time respects their fundamental opacity. Objects do not represent an escape from the human, it is not their inanimateness which interests him; on the contrary, he is intrigued by the community of interest between these objects and people. In Herbert's poetry there is no longer an abyss between people and inanimate objects; instead there is a new sense of identity with them based on the realization of human fallibility. Herbert is engaged in breaking down the barrier between the human and the inanimate, in extending the limits of the human. . . . [Everyday] objects have become one of the dominant themes of contemporary Polish poetry, and have given rise to the phrase "Poezja ubogiego konkretu"—"Poetry of humble concreteness.". . . [Eastern] European poets are often forced to create their freedom from virtually nothing, and they must use the humblest materials to wrest a small, livable, personally acceptable world from a hostile environment. Of all the contemporary Polish and eastern European poets, Herbert is the one who has probably been most successful in generalizing his revolt, who has tried to find its underlying principles. Here, the alliance he has made with the experience of the past and the classics is of fundamental importance. In the final analysis his position is one of extreme precariousness, and he is completely alone—with his conscience. (pp. 47-9)

Bogdana Carpenter and John Carpenter, "Zbigniew Herbert: The Poet as Conscience," in Slavic and East-European Journal, *Vol. 24, No. 1, Spring, 1980, pp. 37-51.*

JONATHAN AARON

One might say that history for [Zbigniew Herbert] is sometimes what religion is for the conventionally devout. In this, the poet Herbert most resembles is Cavafy. Typically, Herbert's subjects come from Greek mythology and classical history, as well as from specific moments in his own life during the war and its less than happy sequel. Herbert's poems, even in English, show he is a poet for whom past events and personalities provide the means to philosophical awareness, if not to consolation, in the face of boundless wrong. (p. 123)

But while his poetic voice . . . is generally even, sometimes low-key, there is a note which comes across in his work that is unique, sometimes hair-raising. His poems often bring one to recognitions that change one's sense of what can become known through poetry. In using history not as a source of mere analogy but as a mirror by means of which the past seems able to return and *possess* our particular present, Herbert proves himself over and over a poet of uncanny powers. . . . Herbert was first introduced to English and American readers by eighteen poems in Milosz's 1965 anthology [*Postwar Polish Poetry*]. It is no exaggeration to say that this selection composed the heart of that book. Reading it, one felt stung into a new, unfamiliar awareness; the poems, translated by Milosz, seemed even in English to be products of a sort of preternatural knowing. In 1968, Penguin's Modern European Poet's series published a *Selected Poems* consisting of seventy-nine poems translated by Milosz and Peter Dale Scott, with a short introduction by A. Alvarez. There was not a weak poem in the book. Stark and unadorned, powered by steely, unemphatic conviction, each touched with extraodinary concentration on the dilemmas of existence and suffering, on the search for perceivable moral essentials. The poem **"I Would Like to Describe"** (*Selected Poems,* 1968) explores what seems at first a simple aim:

> I would like to describe the simplest emotion
> joy or sadness
> but not as others do
> reaching for shafts of rain or sun

The speaker here is suspicious of language while being, of course, unable to convey his feelings and ideas without it. He would like to maintain logical distinctions such as the basic separation of "subject" from "object," but finds that such distinctions tend to blur in daily experience (". . . to say—I love / I run around like mad / picking up handfuls of birds"). The poem finally implies that a person is as much a part of the natural world as any other creature or element he may observe in it. But to be conscious of this fact is to feel apart. When we sleep "our feet abandon us / and taste the earth / with their tiny roots / which next morning / we tear out painfully." The sense of exile returns with wakefulness. Yet *with* this sense comes what amounts to a desire to be different, perhaps even to be separate from the very things it hurts one to be deprived of.

Herbert explores versions of this paradox throughout the poems translated in the Penguin volume, some of which must be among the most telling poems of our age. **"Three Subjects on the Study of Realism," "At the Gate of the Valley," "Apollo and Marsyas," "Elegy of Fortinbras," "Study of the Object," "Preliminary Investigation of an Angel,"** and **"Why the Classics"** are several of the stunning attainments to be found in this selection. Few readers, however, now have the chance to discover Herbert by means of the Penguin volume—it has been out of print for more than seven years and is all but impossible to find. . . . Unfortunately, this lack cannot be made up for by a different *Selected Poems* [1977] currently available, translated by John and Bogdana Carpenter. . . . Taken together, the out-of-print collection and the more recent one would constitute as rich and substantial a choice of Herbert's work as we might wish for. But because the Carpenters' selection emphasizes Herbert's recent work, we are at something of a loss without the early and middle work offered in the Milosz translations.

Part I of [*Selected Poems,* 1977] . . . is composed of work written through early 1969. However, as an attempt to represent almost twenty years of the poet's output, it is, perhaps unavoidably, a failure. It would seem an impossible task to convey the depth and complexity of his accomplishment in a mere thirty-three poems, two thirds of which are short takes in the ironic mode of which Herbert is a master but in which he sometimes sounds glib. (pp. 124-25)

The value of the Carpenters' effort is to be found in the second half of their selection, most of which comes from Herbert's 1974 book, *Mr. Cogito,* named for the dingy, aimless, silly, possibly tragic persona who wanders, deep in fruitless speculation, through many of the poems. His name an ironically truncated version of Descartes' motto, Cogito thinks—cogitates—from one poem to another in which he thinks about his father, meditates on suffering, reads the newspaper, considers the difference between the human voice and the voice of nature, reads old chronicles which enable him to experience the physical presence of persons long dead, tells about the temptation of Spinoza, thinks about hell, considers magic, seeks advice. But throughout all this he seems unable to complete the Cartesian equation; thought alone is not enough to supply him with moral certainty. . . .

It may be, however, that Cogito deliberately chooses not to assert "I am," because doing so would imply his giving in to a world he can only react to with bitterness. In fact, the Cogito sequence as a whole (in terms of what we have of it here, at least) suggests a crisis of perception on Herbert's part, possibly the increasing difficulty of keeping despair at bay through the morality of refusal. (p. 126)

Herbert's viewpoint in his snapshots of scenes from Cogito's life seems predominantly pessimistic. Classical motifs, restorative in his previous work, now assume grim forms as if to confirm the darkness of a present no longer worth rescuing. Instead of Marcus Aurelius or Thucydides (figures in earlier poems), we find the likes of Minos, Procrustes, Caligula. Procrustes speaks with particularly sinister effect in a monologue in which he offers a disingenuous reinterpretation of the crimes he committed with his famous bed ("experts on mythology are mistaken who call me a bandit / in reality I was a scholar and social reformer / my real passion was anthropometry"). He speaks with the aplomb of an established politician and concludes with a remark of chilling foresight: "I have a well-grounded hope that others will continue my labour / and bring the task so wonderfully begun to its end." This poem is a particularly intense instance of the political irony which is strong throughout the Cogito sequence. Indeed, one problem with the Cogito poems is that the rhetoric of irony tends to dictate too clearly how a poem is to turn out. But the recognitions of what might be called the governmental turn of mind accumulate in an atmosphere of oppression to which the final poem in the series, **"The Envoy of Mr. Cogito,"** comes like an explanation. Here Herbert rises above the limitations of irony, speaking both to and for his persona. . . . In this poem Herbert seems to turn on the lassitude, the bewilderment, and the carelessness he has shown in Cogito's world, allowing his undistinguished representative man the possibility of dignity by urging him to "be vigilant . . . / as long as blood turns in the breast your dark star." (p. 127)

> Jonathan Aaron, "Without Boundaries," in Parnassus: Poetry in Review, *Vol. 9, No. 1, Spring-Summer, 1981, p. 110-28.*

BOGDANA CARPENTER

One of the central themes in the writing of Zbigniew Herbert, which recurs in both his poetry and his prose, is that of the "barbarian." It is usually opposed to the concept of civilization, which for Herbert means primarily Western civilization. The opposition between the two is sharply drawn in the title of his collection of essays about Western art, **The Barbarian in the Garden** (1962), and at first glance the opposition seems clear. The barbarian is a savage, the inhabitant of a country at the periphery of the civilized world. For the ancient Greeks a barbarian was any person who did not speak their language, and for the Romans the term designated all the tribes living outside the empire. If in place of the Roman Empire we understand Western civilization and its cradle, the Mediterranean basin, then an inhabitant of Eastern Europe—of distant Poland, Lithuania, or the Ukraine—must certainly be counted among the barbarians.

As defined so far, the concept of the barbarian suggests a straightforward system of values based on a cultural hierarchy and implying inferiority on the one hand (the barbarian) and superiority on the other (civilization, the garden). However, a deeper reading of Herbert's work undermines this simplistic conclusion, revealing the ambiguity in his use of the term and the complexity of his attitude toward the West. This represents one of the most original and striking features of his writing. It challenges many of the commonly held attitudes about civilization—about what it is and what it is not—as well as the values we associate with it. (p. 388)

For the barbarian the West is a sweet and gentle garden, but it is also empty, distant, a foreign province where "trees have no roots houses no foundations the rain is glassy flowers smell of wax" (**"The Return of the Proconsul"** . . .). Herbert's barbarian is descended from primitive medieval warriors; but he is above all a man who knows suffering, and the garden has little place for this. Knowledge of suffering is a result both of certain temperamental characteristics that can lead "to a hurriedly dug out ditch" [**"Meditations on the Problem of the Nation"**], and of the accumulated lessons of history. It is precisely history, as well as the memory of those who have died in its course, that ties the poet-barbarian to the place of his birth, however tragic, violent or unspectacular it may be. . . . [The] experience of [World War II] has taught the barbarian that the truth of suffering and death is stronger than that of philosophy, art or beauty—and is more real. Confronted with the reality of war, "The omens of poetry are false / everything was different" (**"To Apollo"** . . .). As a result, the scale of values associated with the concepts of the barbarian and the garden is tipped; it is no longer a hierarchy. This is why looking at a painting is not simply a moment of esthetic contemplation for the barbarian, as it is for thousands of others. When Herbert is face to face with a great painting (e.g., Leonardo da Vinci's *Mona Lisa*) that has become a symbol of Western art, it is the moment of confrontation between the two worlds—and the two truths—of the barbarian and the inhabitants of the garden.

The concept of the garden is as complex as that of the barbarian and carries both positive and negative associations. On a superficial level it implies the geographical region around the Mediterranean and the "classical" tradition that took root there; the garden is opposed to the barbarian regions situated beyond this center. But the "garden" also stands for certain stereotyped attitudes toward this tradition, both uncritical acceptance and indiscriminate veneration, which transform the living garden into a lifeless museum. Opposing this process of "mummification," Herbert attempts to restore what was once the most essential part of the garden: its life. He does this by using his unique insights gained as a "barbarian." Thus the relationship between the garden and the barbarian is neither unilateral nor passive but involves an active exchange of perspectives and experiences. It is both a lesson for the barbarian and a test for the garden.

The poem entitled **"Mona Lisa"** . . . was written after Herbert's first trip to Western Europe in the late 1950s and is an excellent illustration of the complexity of his attitudes. Like a musical composition, the poem progresses by point and counterpoint: passages describing the painting alternate with passages about himself, flashbacks to his past (both recent and more remote) going back to the time of the war. Coming to see this "Jerusalem in a frame," the pilgrim from a faraway land not only has had to conquer physical and political obstacles ("seven mountain frontiers," "barbed wires of rivers"), but also has brought with him the heavy burden of the war. He is a survivor: "so I'm here / they were all going to come / I'm alone." This is why the encounter with the work of art occurs on two planes, esthetic and human. The spectator is a tourist ("I stand / in the thick nettles / of an excursion") and also a man with his own individual experiences. As a tourist and, what is more, an extremely erudite connoisseur of art, he is able to appreciate the expressive and painterly qualities of Leonardo's masterpiece. . . . (pp. 388-89)

So far the criteria of judgment are purely artistic, the painting a self-contained unity. . . . But Herbert's spectator never forgets, even for a moment, the place he has come from or the past he has lived through. Nor does he forget those who should be at his side but perished in the war.... The memories of his friends, the war and death lead to a second evaluation of the painting, this time from an entirely different perspective. Now the *Mona Lisa* is judged by a twentieth-century man who has lived through the Holocaust and totalitarianism, who is not a zealous "pilgrim" but a man burdened by experience. The eye is no longer admiring but judging and comparing, constantly measuring the distance between the two worlds—as well as the two experiences—of the past and the present. A duel takes place between the two, between suffering and beauty, between real life and art, and there is no victor, only a realization of the abyss that separates them....

What divides the spectator from the masterpiece, and the barbarian from the garden, is not only geographical, historical and cultural distance—one's "heritage"—but even more the nature of one's own experience. The abyss has been forged by "the sword," the second world war. (p. 389)

[The] idealization of the past is foreign to Herbert. On the other hand, he does not reject or depreciate art and tradition; instead the distance he perceives between himself and tradition makes him aware of the need to reevaluate it. He stresses the possibility of an interpretation of a work of art other than the purely esthetic one. Herbert's sensitivity to human experience allows him to see in the Mona Lisa a woman who was once alive but has now been turned into a lifeless object, "hewn off from the meat of life / abducted from home and history." Thus the comment in the last part of the poem that she is "a fat and not too nice signora" does not apply to the painting but rather is an attempt to see it in nonesthetic categories, to restore its purely human content.

Herbert's essays on Western art (most of which are included in *The Barbarian in the Garden*) as well as his poems about mythology are inspired by the same intention: to penetrate beyond the esthetic dimension, to find the living human elements which formed their original basis and matrix....

Although this collection of essays contains many passages of sensitive and learned analysis of works of art and architecture, Herbert's main goal—and one he admirably fulfills—is to conjure up, to reproduce the life they conceal. He is simultaneously a scholar of art, a historian and an anthropologist; above all he is a poet interested in concrete detail rather than erudite abstractions. His attitude toward art and the past is an active one: it demands not only passive contemplation and appreciation, but also an effort of re-creation.... Where scholarly evidence fails, the poet uses his intuition: "I cannot explain even to myself this union existing between the landscape of Greece and its art, its beliefs. Only a strong intuition tells me that the Greek temple, sculpture and myth grow organically out of the earth, sea and mountains." This is why the garden of art is full of action when seen with the poet's eyes, not a lifeless museum.... (p. 390)

Herbert's approach to tradition is not only active but also sharply critical. He refuses to ignore the dark side of the past simply because the extant legacy of the past, its art, has become for us a sacred canon of beauty. Therefore he mocks those for whom the past is a mere object of erudition.... His approach to art and tradition undercuts the opposition between the barbarian and the garden and puts both concepts into a new context. Much of his endeavor has been devoted to proving that the supposed "garden" of Western civilization has been in fact

a stage for quite barbarous exploits: killings and assassinations, bloody pursuits of animals, sacrifices and colonizations. It is precisely the barbarian, with his special experience of cruelty and his firsthand knowledge, who is able to re-create the life of past epochs (which is quite different from the dead art of museums) and to discover their barbarism....

Despite these conclusions Herbert's attitude toward the past is open and not closed; it is positive and constructive rather than negative or destructive. Instead of the isolation of the postwar period and the present, Herbert proposes a rapprochement with the rest of history. His is an attempt to reconcile and unite the two experiences, to create a dialogue rather than a monologue.... [Herbert's] experience of the war does not become an insuperable obstacle to participation in the common European heritage; instead it is the point of reference for a new examination of this heritage, and for the enrichment of European culture by the barbarian's unique experience.... Herbert neither turns his back on tradition nor uncritically accepts it; on the contrary, for him the past must rejoin the present, for only then is there a chance to salvage "the fragile human land." More than anything else, this is the redeeming value of poetry.

Herbert's attitude toward tradition carries important implications for his own writing and for his approach to it. (p. 391)

In a poem describing the execution of five men by a platoon of German soldiers, Herbert poses the inevitable question asked by ... many other contemporary writers and poets: "I did not learn this today / I knew it before yesterday / so why have I been writing / unimportant poems on flowers" (**"Five Men"** ...). The answer is not imposed from without by an arbitrary decision but has its justification, paradoxically, in the nature of that very experience. The night before their execution the five men talked about dreams, cards, vodka and girls—about life and not death. And so Herbert answers his question in the affirmative.... Herbert's answer suggests that the devastated world needs to regain its shattered faith more than to mourn or to despair, and that this might be the most important task of poetry. For Herbert the experience of war is a point of departure, not a closed circle.

Yet the war is never lost from sight. Even if "poetry" survives the apocalypse, it must always be able to sustain the confrontation with the reality of suffering. Apollo, symbol of the classical art of "gardens," appears several times in Herbert's poems, and Herbert's relation to the Greek god is clearly that of an adversary. Apollo symbolizes all that is sterile, abstract, perfect and therefore inhuman in art.... The opposition between Apollo and Marsyas in the famous poem **"Apollo and Marsyas"** becomes an open duel and at the same time a strong statement of Herbert's poetics. In the contest with Marsyas, Apollo is the loser, even though he has received the official victor's laurels. The howls of Marsyas, who has been flayed alive, are a poem of suffering, a new kind of art unknown to the god "with nerves of plastic." ...

As in **"Five Men,"** suffering does not annihilate poetry but becomes its new source. Herbert suggests the possibility of a different approach to poetry, and its power would be measured not by academic standards of perfection but by the effect it has on its listeners: Marsyas's suffering creates poetry that has the force to petrify a nightingale and turn a tree white. It is clear where the poet's sympathies lie. Marsyas's half-human, half-animal nature and his Phrygian origin make him a barbarian among the Greek gods. Even more important, Marsyas is acquainted with suffering, and his howls of pain are echoed by the barbarian cries of fear emanating from Herbert's contemporaries. It is this intimate knowledge of suffering that distinguishes the barbarian from those who live in the garden; it is his stigma but also his redeeming feature.

Both the experience of war and the reality in which he had to live made Herbert suspicious of any art based on harmony, order or beauty. (p. 392)

Herbert does not deny the validity of beauty, however. He does not advocate ugliness as an alternative esthetic ideal, as the "Turpist" poets did in the 1960s, nor does he castigate the artists who invented "a small round warm reality" because they thought "we would find happiness / in the tranquil heart of a landscape with a rainbow." He simply points out that his own experience cannot be contained within the poetics of "gardens" and "sunny white cities." . . . The only poetry that is compatible with his experience contains a moral imperative. This is for Herbert a third kind of realism. The link between realism and morality might appear surprising at first glance, but it is one of the strongest and most unusual features of his work. For Herbert, poetry must be subordinate to truth, and truth is faithful to reality—to life and to the past, to what has happened and what is happening. The poet is a witness, and his duty is to give testimony: "you were saved not in order to live / you have little time you must give testimony." This moral imperative is both heroic and demanding. It is ultimately positive; it avoids nihilism, martyrology and the masochistic scratching open of wounds. There is no glorification of suffering, only a sober determination not to avert the eyes. Above all there is the faithfulness of the barbarian to his experience and his allegiance to those who died for a cause. . . . For Herbert, loyalty entails still another emotion: compassion. In his way of looking, it is impossible to depict experience accurately, as it happened, without compassion.

From his extremely destructive experience Herbert manages to draw constructive conclusions, and he builds a bridge between realms that seem to be irreconcilable: the past and the present, suffering and poetry. As a "barbarian," Herbert is faithful to his experience of World War II and totalitarian terror, but in so doing he has also chosen a tradition of long lineage: of Gilgamesh, of Hector and Roland, "the defenders of the kingdom without limit and the city of ashes." The bridge that he has built gives both poetry and civilization another chance for survival. (pp. 392-93)

> Bogdana Carpenter, "The Barbarian and the Garden: Zbigniew Herbert's Reevaluations," in World Literature Today, Vol. 57, No. 3, Summer, 1983, pp. 388-93.

ROBERT HASS

[*Report From the Besieged City*] covers the period of the crisis in Poland and it is somewhat retrospective in tone. Herbert writes about the present, but he is also reflecting on what his art has been and has had to be in Eastern Europe. . . . [Herbert's] sense of history is deep. He is the kind of writer for whom nothing has happened only once. Traveling in Western Europe when martial law was declared in Poland, he might have chosen not to return. But he did return, and he wrote about it, or, rather, he wrote about a world in which, for ages, generals have been seizing power to restore what is called public order in what is called a time of national crisis in order to return the republic to what is called its true path. That is his report from the besieged city.

Herbert is an ironist and a minimalist who writes as if it were the task of the poet, in a world full of loud lies, to say what is irreducibly true in a level voice. His art has been compared to a calligrapher's—deft strokes, black on white, economy of motion; his chosen ground is a narrow and difficult human freedom, the freedom to think and see clearly, even if only in the privacy of one's own head. This explains the name of a character, Mr. Cogito, through whom some of Herbert's later poems are spoken. That somewhat comic and ironic persona stands for the fact that, in some circumstances, it is not our bodily freedom or the authenticity of our emotions that makes existence real, but our ability, however halting, to continue to think. One imagines that such a limitation of means in poetry would require a great purity of style. And that is the testimony of Polish readers. Czeslaw Milosz has said that the writing is "crystalline and austere." . . .

Plainness of speech is the rueful subject of several of these poems. In **"Mr. Cogito and the Imagination,"** for example, Herbert writes:

> Mr. Cogito never trusted
> tricks of the imagination
>
> the piano at the top of the Alps
> played false concerts to him . . .
>
> he adored tautologies
> explanations
> *idem per idem*
>
> that a bird is a bird
> slavery means slavery
> a knife is a knife
> death remains death . . .

This stance is based on the assumption that the ultimate power of poetry is witness. *Truth, Not Hope* might be carved above the entrance to Herbert's work. . . .

Though witness is the aim of Herbert's poetry, his poems on political themes are not reportorial. Here his method is much more that of a fabulist. In **"Babylon," "The Divine Claudius," "The Murderers of Kings,"** and in the title poem, **"Report From the Besieged City,"** he writes about events in the distant past or in some unspecified time to suggest the endlessly repetitive cruelty and injustice of human societies—and the perpetual struggle against them. **"Report From the Besieged City,"** widely read in Poland as a poem of the army's seizure of power, is the story, for Herbert, of any city:

> I am supposed to be exact but I don't know when the
>   invasion began
> two hundred years ago in December in September
>   perhaps yesterday at dawn
> everyone here suffers from a loss of the sense of time.

I am not sure that . . . brief quotations will convey the sense of a fierce, steady moral imagination which this volume conveys as a whole. Nor have I mentioned the special triumphs of the book like **"Mr. Cogito and the Soul"** in which that gentleman, feeling soulless, reflects like some eternally cuckolded husband out of Dostoevsky on the reasonableness and necessity of sharing his soul with others since there obviously aren't enough to go around, or **"Prayer of Mr. Cogito—Traveler,"** a poem which is moving partly because of the plainness of its gratitude. . . . The rarity of poems like this in Herbert's work give them a kind of grandeur; the vision of **Report From the Besieged City,** though its clarity seems heroic and though it glints with gallows humor, is not usually so tender. But neither is the history of Poland. Polish poets wrote a poetry of hope in the 1840s that moved all of Europe; they wrote a poetry of despair in the 1880s; and a poetry of hope in the 1920s, and a poetry of prophetic terror in the 1930s, and a poetry of resistance to that terror in the 1940s. They have been a kind of symbol, a weathervane of political emotion, for the rest of the world for the last two centuries. One can only not notice this cyclical pattern for so long, and Herbert notices. His resistance takes the form of refusing not to notice, and refusing to feel that the history of oppression, of force begetting force begetting force, because it is tedious and repetitive, is any less wrong. His own struggle, clear-eyed and stubborn, is to find a language which salvages from history the forms of personal and social integrity, so that he can write, as he does at the end of **"Report From the Besieged City"**: "The only thing we have not disgraced is our dreams."

> Robert Hass, *"The Austere Artistry of Zbigniew Herbert," in* Book World—The Washington Post, *July 21, 1985, p. 4.*

STANISLAW BARANCZAK

The title **Report from the Besieged City** could, in fact, stand above each and every poem of Zbigniew Herbert, who . . . is undoubtedly the most admired and respected poet now living in Poland. The image of a city under siege, one of the several symbols that constantly recur in his work, has a historic poignancy that makes it much more than just a figure of speech. In September 1939, as a 15-year-old, Herbert experienced the annexation of his hometown, the ancient city of Lwow, by the Soviet Union. After the Molotov-Ribbentrop pact turned sour, the city was seized by the Nazis, and then, at the end of the war, it was recaptured by the Soviets to retain it within the new borders of their empire. Young Herbert had to move to central Poland, but for him the state of siege continued. Now it was the entire country under the siege of "barbarians," the supporters of the new totalitarian order.

The final, unequivocal formulation of this crucial symbol came in the months of martial law, in the poem that lent its title to Herbert's latest collection. In retrospect, his entire work to date appears as a continuous "report from the besieged city." The poet identifies himself as a chronicler of the defense carried out against barbarians' ever-present threat. . . .

But, speaking of the symbolic rule of titles, it is very fortunate that almost simultaneously with **Report** another book by Herbert came out in English translation—his collection of essays titled **Barbarian in the Garden**. At first sight, there seems to be a contradiction here: the chronicler of the defense against the barbarians now portrays himself as one of them. It is, in fact, this deliberate contradiction that makes Herbert's poetic voice unique and meaningful. The fundamental paradox of his work is that his literary persona is both "the chronicler of the siege" and "the barbarian," someone who sticks, against all odds, to the traditional values and someone who has been forcibly disinherited of them. Like other defenders of the symbolic city, he doesn't want to be forced out. But sometimes he would welcome a little vacation abroad—with a reentry visa, to be sure. The trouble is, once he finally enters the quiet and manicured garden of the outer world, he is not able to identify himself with it. Combating the barbarians has had such an effect on him that he now seems to be a barbarian himself.

As everything in Herbert, this sense of incurable duality has its roots in a personal experience. **Barbarian in the Garden** appeared in Poland in 1962, after Herbert had made his very first trip to the West. Instead of "trip," one should rather say "pilgrimage." The poet had behind him several years of misery under Stalinism, when he was one of very few intransigent intellectuals who rejected the temptation to join the new order; as a consequence, he was reduced to poverty and isolation. (pp. 35-6)

Absent by his own choice from official literary life, he wrote "for his desk drawer." The breakthrough came in 1956 when, in the wake of political and cultural thaw, his first book of poems [*Struna swiatła*] was published, followed by the next two in 1957 [*Hermes, pies i gwiazda*] and 1961 [*Studium przedmiotu*]. The Western translations and literary awards that ensued provided Herbert with a chance to meet face-to-face with the world of culture he had known only from books and reproductions. Some of the effects of that confrontation are presented in his famous poem **"Mona Lisa"** . . . in which the Eastern European visitor finally, after many years of separation by "mountain frontiers" and "barbed wire of rivers," faces the legendary painting. His initial sense of triumph . . . soon evaporates. He realizes that another frontier, a psychological one, still sets apart his 20th-century Eastern European experience and the world of the Western cultural past. . . .

The notion of frontier or separation also accounts for the peculiar perspective of Herbert's essays. I don't mean by this that he has to relate his impressions of Italy and France to the not very well-traveled Polish reader of the early 1960s and thus is forced, for example, to explain in detail what a pizza is. More important, Herbert himself approaches the heritage of Western culture with a persistent sense of inner split: he looks at it with the eye of a legitimate heir and, at the same time, with the eye of someone who has been—illegally, but irrevocably—deprived of his heritage. After visiting the cave paintings at Lascaux, he confesses: "Never before had I felt a stronger or more reassuring conviction: I am a citizen of the earth, an inheritor not only of the Greeks and Romans but of almost the whole of infinity."

But such moments of uninhibited euphoria are rare. More typical are the instances when the perspectives of the "inheritor" and the "barbarian" merge: when, for example, Herbert tells the story of the destruction of the Templar order as if he were describing the atmosphere of the Moscow show trials in the 1930s. In such cases it is evident that he is concerned not merely with "the eternity of Piero della Francesca" and "how stone is laid upon stone in a Gothic cathedral," but also with the question of what all those triumphs of Mediterranean culture mean for a modern "barbarian" who, in his own part of the world, faces a methodical extermination of the basic values of civilization.

What is exceptional about Herbert is not the mere realization of that discrepancy but the fact that he is far from blaming culture and civilization for what has happened to them in our century. On the contrary, his respect for the common "heritage" of the Western cultural past never diminishes. He stubbornly reiterates that even though the "heritage" seems to be irreversibly lost the "disinherited" must claim their rights to it. This is, in fact, their only chance not to forget what is the difference between them and the true barbarians. Twenty years after the first Polish publication of *Barbarian in the Garden,* this particular motif has returned with striking force in Herbert's recent poetry, which, among other meanings, can be read as quite a direct commentary on the nature of totalitarianism and art's relation to it. I have in mind, in particular, the splendid poem **"The Power of Taste,"** which offers a surprisingly simple explanation of Herbert's own steadfastness during the years of Stalinism.... (p. 36)

[The poem is narrated] by a defender of the City who is back within its walls: after another prolonged stay in the West, Herbert returned to Poland in the beginning of 1981 eventually to experience both the harsh reality of martial law and the tremendous upsurge of his own popularity among Polish readers. Amazingly, Herbert's lyrical persona, Mr. Cogito—initially just a figure of a troubled modern intellectual—has recently become a model for the spiritual situation of a contemporary Pole: an individual who exists (in a given sociopolitical reality) and therefore, to reverse Descartes, has to think, to make a self-defending use of his or her conscience or its aesthetic equivalent, taste.

Is there any hope in this kind of defense? Not necessarily. Another of Herbert's features, without which his image as a poet would be distorted, is that he promises nothing. The conclusion of **"The Power of Taste"** is sober and bitter:

> Yes taste
> that commands us to get out to make a wry face draw
>   out a sneer
> even if for this the precious capital of the body the head
>   must fall

In other words, the defeat is more probable than the victory. If any notion of hope appears in Herbert's poetry, it is hope without guarantee. No philosophy, no religion, no ideology is going to assure us paradise on earth. The only thing we can count on is that, as one earlier poem put it, by not bowing to sheer force, by "maintaining an upright attitude," we will at least avoid "suffocation in sleep." Or, in the words of **"Report from the Besieged City"**:

> ... if the City falls but a single man escapes
> he will carry the City within himself on the roads of
>   exile
> he will be the City.

Whoever wishes to understand the spirit within the walls of the embattled fortress of today's Central European culture may well begin with memorizing these sentences. (pp. 36-7)

Stanislaw Baranczak, "The Power of Taste," in The New Republic, *Vol. 193, No. 11, September 9, 1985, pp. 35-7.*

MARK RUDMAN

I first read Zbigniew Herbert in Czeslaw Milosz's anthology of *Postwar Polish Poetry,* a book that has influenced a generation of American poets. At the time, I was struck by the purity of his diction and the strange blend of irony and negation in such poems as **"Elegy of Fortinbras," "Study of Objects"** and **"The Stone."** Milosz's description of Herbert as "a poet of historical irony" is apt because his work is critical in spirit....

"The Stone" exemplifies a poetry that attempts to salvage the remains of civilization. It is a poem that has become as integral to our way of looking at things as Wallace Stevens's "The Snow Man." ... What does this poem tell me about the state of things when it praises an object for having "a scent which does not remind one of anything," save that memory has only one route: to pain? **"The Stone"** could be mistaken for a minimalist gesture; but it isn't minimalist, it's metaphysical. The sparest poetry—especially when set beside the false eloquence of some American poetry—may ultimately be the richest. As Herbert says in **"Mr. Cogito and the Imagination"**:

> there is no place in it
> for the artificial fires of poetry
>
> he would like to remain faithful
> to uncertain clarity

It is a miracle in our overblown world to find something that is equal to itself. A stone is not subject to much self-inflation. Herbert practices a humanistic dehumanization of art. Reality stands independent of his/our designs on it....

Herbert's work has close philosophical links with that of Eastern European poets such as Paul Celan, Vasko Popa and János Pilinszky. These poets reduce their field of inquiry while at the same time enlarging their possibilities of vision. And so their minds turn to fable and other rigorous ways of saying that have moral rather than esthetic priorities. Take the title poem of the book, **"Report from the Besieged City."** Even if the "besieged city" is actually Warsaw, Herbert raises it to an archetype, as if that city's unremitting state of siege were an extreme and accurate image of the human condition.... (p. 287)

American poetry often remains a highly private affair, but these European poets speak for humanity, and without a trace of self-congratulation.... It is striking to find poets who have endured social and political oppression or witnessed the Holocaust and who have not tried to exploit these experiences. In his best poems Herbert makes us read beneath the literal level of information because he sets no scene. You will find no cinematic descriptions of men being leveled by machine guns or chased down dark alleys. No spectacles. Herbert trusts his art enough to let the bloody action occur offstage. Herbert affirms through negation. How effectively he negotiates the transition from IS NOT to IS should be clear from the opening lines in a haunting lyric from the Milosz anthology, **"Our Fear"**:

> our fear
> does not wear a night shirt ...
> does not extinguish a candle
>
> does not have a dead man's face either
>
> our fear
> is a scrap of paper
> found in a pocket
> 'warn Wojcik
> the place on Dluga Street is hot'

The poem embodies history. It has to, and it is through this sense of responsibility to history that the poem derives its tension, threading its way between the pitfalls of overcommitment and of aloofness. As a bridge between the void and the world, the poem insures that what is written is not swallowed up. Nowhere does Herbert better focus his consciousness of history as force than in these lines from **"The Murderers of Kings"**:

> not one of them managed to change the course of
>   history
> but the dark message has gone from generation to
>   generation
> so these small hands are worthy of reflection
> small hands in which the certainty of the blow is
>   trembling

I doubt if there is an American poet who has not puzzled over the question of what it means to write at peril to one's life and at the same time to write with the knowledge that you are being read, in the wrong way perhaps, but still being read. (pp. 287-88)

Herbert lets us know that he doesn't want to write only about the facts but that history has forced him into this circumstance. . . . It is no accident that *Report from the Besieged City* was first published by internees in the Rakowiecka Prison in Warsaw and that most of the copies were confiscated. (p. 288)

Mark Rudman, "A Calm and Clear Eye," in The Nation, *Vol. 241, No. 9, September 28, 1985, pp. 287-88.*

JOHN BAYLEY

"Classical" is the word most often used to describe Herbert's poetry, both in Poland and among readers who know his work in the West. The word is necessarily ambiguous. T. S. Eliot often appealed to the traditions of classicism, and implied, as did Ezra Pound in his way, that his own poetry endorsed them. But the interior of Eliot's poetry is deeply personal, full of romantic secrets and intimacies. These are notably lacking in Herbert. Not that Herbert is impersonal: he presents a Horatian simplicity and openness, a temperament like that of a traveller or classical scholar. His collection of essays on European cultural sites, *Barbarian in the Garden,* contains some of the best travel writing of our time, but is almost disappointing in the way it reveals nothing about the inner life or history of the man himself. One cannot imagine him writing a love poem, or investigating his emotion with the zestful precision of a Robert Graves. His poetry reveals sharply and by contrast how much modern poetry has come to depend on versions of self-pity, and on the way it feeds and builds up the individual interior of a poet's work.

This is not all gain where Herbert is concerned. His poetry can seem flat, formulaic and predictable. Even in the crisp and impeccable translations of Czeslaw Milosz and Peter Dale Scott [in *Selected Poems*] there is a certain sameness about the parallels along which each poem develops that may not show up in the variety and intimacy of its native tongue, where nuances of idiom and cadence would give it a specialness not available in English correspondence. As the translators point out, Herbert is not classical in the sense of using traditional metres or rhymes; his poetry is more like a spare form of conversation, obviously depending a good deal on word order and on the subtle use of cliché. Well-known poems like **"Apollo and Marsyas"** and **"Elegy of Fortinbras"**, are no doubt much funnier in the original. In English they depend rather too much on the points they make. In **"Apollo and Marsyas"** the god of restraint, proportion and clarity, having flayed the faun and cleaned his instrument, departs along "a gravel path hedged with box", leaving his skinless victim uttering one immense howl on a single note, perhaps a new kind of "concrete" poetry. The joke, at the expense both of classicism and of pop art, has a tenderness, but in English the message arrives without the full depth of its implication. No doubt the cruelty of art—even Herbert's own art—arises from the fact that in the very act of creation it necessarily separates itself from human suffering, which cries out from the force and nature of its whole body and blood, and is thus abhorrent to the "god with nerves of artificial fibre". . . .

It is indeed a striking thing that so many European poets who when young went through the full terror of the last war have written in consequence a poetry of extreme simplicity and precision, avoiding any overt expression of emotion, and setting the highest value on the old artifices of logic and reason. Vasko Popa in Serbia was one such, and Czeslaw Milosz is himself another. Man in extremity does not imitate the abyss and its moppings and mowings, but strives rather to detach himself from its absurdity. And it is a paradox that the sort of sounds made by Marsyas proceed, in our day and climate, not from anguish and loss of freedom and fatherland, but from the kinds of boredom and meaninglessness inherent in the affluent society. As Milosz implies, being a Pole connects one, in an intimacy which is almost comfortable, to the unchanging horrors of history. The idea that we live in a very special time that calls for a very special art would cause a Pole to smile. For him it is always the mixture as before, so that the attitudes and practices of classicism represent no arbitrary whim on the part of the poet, but rather the most natural response in art to the imperatives of survival. Herbert's poetry lives in the flow of history, and among the artefacts of European culture, as naturally as a pebble in the bed of a stream.

Herbert's great-grandfather was English, and the bizarre coincidence of his name with that of two English poets sharpens the fact of his wholly European rather than Polish status. . . . Herbert's mother was Armenian; his father, a professor of economics, a practising Catholic; his grandmother Orthodox. "And, all around, evidences of Hasidic culture . . . hence my syncretic religion." . . .

Paradoxically, this almost too nutritious background has probably been instrumental in producing the austerities of Herbert's verse. Instead of submerging itself in the past and in its milieu, with all the helplessness of which some modern poetry makes a virtue, Herbert's poetry detaches itself into a thinner air, almost that dimension of logic and mathematics in which recent Polish scholarship has specialized. Many of the poems in *Report from the Besieged City* employ a persona called Mr Cogito, a not altogether serious figure (sometimes he becomes "the suckling Cogito") who devotes himself none the less to some highly serious and abstract questions—on eschatology, autocracy, or death—varied by encounters with a monster who cannot be seen ("the proof of the existence of the monster / is its victims") or with Maria Rasputin, the historical daughter of that Siberian shaman who exercised his influence in imperial Petersburg.

Mr Cogito "would like to remain faithful / to uncertain clarity", and rejects "the artificial fires of poetry". . . . Of course, poetry is always rejecting its own devices, and acquiring new ones in the process. But Herbert is not just saying "My mistress' eyes are nothing like the sun"; his equivalents are precise and cryptographic. The poem **"September 17"** refers to the precise date in 1939 when the Russians invaded eastern Poland, ten days after the German army had struck in the west. But the date is only allowed its precision in and for itself: the poem is saying the opposite of *einmal ist keinmal*, for in Poland invasion is invasion, a simple and continuous fact, and as Pushkin put it tersely, more than a hundred years earlier and from the eastern side: "The history of Poland is and ought to be a disaster". . . . Herbert is not in the least afraid of the kind of platitude which goes with his simple and perpetual equivalents in history and logic.

My defenceless country will admit you invader
and give you a plot of land under a willow and peace
so those who come after us will learn again
the most difficult art the forgiveness of sins

At the end of the book the title poem, **"Report from the Besieged City"**, explores the same ground and reaches the same conclusion. . . . Nothing can be less exciting than the history of the siege, and once again the conclusion is what anyone might have expected.

> cemeteries grow larger the number of defenders is
> 　　smaller
> yet the defence continues it will continue to the end
> and if the city falls yet a single man escapes
> he will carry the City within himself on the roads of
> 　　exile
> he will be the City

Both in relation to Poland and to humanity at large the meaning is as obvious as a syllogism, but it carries its obviousness with the weight and delicacy which make Herbert so peculiar and so individual a poet. (p. 104)

> John Bayley, *"The Art of Austerity," in* The New York Times Book Review, *January 31, 1986, pp. 103-04.*

EVA HOFFMAN

[Herbert] has long been acknowledged as one of the commanding voices of his generation and a powerful influence on younger writers. One reason for his pre-eminence is undoubtedly his rare gift of speaking on public matters—a task imposed on Polish poets by their tradition and their country's situation—with no dissociation of sensibility or loss of personal voice. In *Report From the Besieged City* he brings to political and historical events the pressure and intensity of deeply felt experience. But then his experience has been inseparable from such dramas. . . .

Mr. Herbert's work was not published until the post-Stalinist thaw. By then he had forged a style that functions as a sort of antidote to the dangers of sentimentality or inflation—restrained, ironic, stripped of punctuation, averse to "tricks of the imagination" and passionate in its insistence on precision. . . .

But for all its terseness, Mr. Herbert's language manages to suggest an almost epic breadth. It is a largeness that comes from the austere objectivity he cultivates. . . . But it also comes from the scope of his historical perspective, his long, steady gaze. He not only uses historical allusions to mask references to events in Poland, but in his poetry the past becomes a unity in which events repeat and reflect one another. In some of the most acidly intelligent poems in this collection, notorious tyrants—Claudius, Procrustes—justify themselves, in highly familiar terms, in the name of practical achievements or noble ideals.

And in **"Report From the Besieged City,"** a poem written after the inauguration of martial law in 1981 in Poland, vast vistas of time and events are conflated until the city under invasion becomes not only Warsaw, or Poland, but a perpetually endangered realm of freedom and humane values. . . .

> the siege has lasted a long time the enemies must take
> 　　turns
> nothing unites them except the desire for our
> 　　extermination
> Goths the Tartars Swedes troops of the Emperor
> 　　regiments of the Transfiguration.

Against such cycles of violence, Mr. Herbert counterposes the modest virtues of accuracy and steadiness. Precision is such an important quality, a moral quality, in his poetry because it is a form of respect for the experience of those who are invaded or conquered, respect for voices that may be lost in the noise of history. In **"Mr. Cogito on the Need for Precision,"** Mr. Cogito, a skeptical *philosophe* who appears frequently in Herbert's poetry, expresses alarm at the difficulty of counting victims of natural and unnatural catastrophes. . . .

Mr. Cogito often implicitly mocks his own "naive" desire for logic and rationality. But the longing for truth is one of the deepest currents in Mr. Herbert's writing, and it ultimately goes beyond the concerns of politics to fuse with an almost Platonic dream of absolute intelligibility—a state in which things attain the clarity of being simply themselves, and in which "a forest was a forest the sea was the sea rock was rock." (p. 14)

> Eva Hoffman, *"Remembering Poland," in* The New York Times Book Review, *February 16, 1986, pp. 14-15.*

(Peter) Jeremy Hooker

1941-

English poet, critic, and editor.

In his poetry, Hooker evokes the countryside of his birthplace in southern England and his current residence in Wales to examine the relationship between the land and its history, legends, and people. Hooker, who often composes his verse in short trimeter lines, is praised for his ability to develop vivid images with emotional and technical restraint. Dick Davis described Hooker as "a poet always concerned to define the life he describes in terms of what is round about it and behind it, what encompasses it and what precedes it."

Hooker's first major collection, *Soliloquies of a Chalk Giant* (1974), includes a sequence of poems told from the perspective of the Cerne Abbas giant, an ancient monolithic figure with mythic and symbolic significance. *Landscape of the Daylight Moon* (1978) reprints many of Hooker's poems published in the pamphlet *The Elements* (1972) and also includes several new sequences relating to the English countryside. The poems in *Solent Shore* (1978) depict the coastal region of his native Hampshire, while those in *Englishman's Road* (1980) are set in Wales. The title poem of the latter volume focuses upon a nineteenth-century Englishman whose efforts to resettle in Wales are met with resistance from Welsh villagers. Hooker's reputation as a poet and critic was firmly established with *A View from the Source: Selected Poems* (1982) and *The Poetry of Place: Essays and Reviews, 1970-1981* (1982). Bill Ruddick noted that "Jeremy Hooker's poems show a search for understanding and for integration being carried on through elements of time, place and memory.... [The] succession of insights and discoveries that the search produces is individually and cumulatively bound to impress."

(See also *Contemporary Authors*, Vols. 77-80 and *Dictionary of Literary Biography*, Vol. 40.)

Photograph by Joe Hooker. Courtesy of Jeremy Hooker

PHILIP PACEY

[Jeremy Hooker's **The Elements** presents] an open-to-the-world sensibility that would rejoice in a surface polished to reflection, apogee of the polishing; for whom the uniqueness of place, the rhythm of earth, is enough, a benefaction to be held and handled in words, memory's symbolization that enables us to relish an experience even after its passing, pondering its intrinsic significance, mining it for its rich vein of metaphor (as in the beautiful love poem, **"There"**) rather than pressing on always to what's new; a sensibility willing to rest in the stillness of 'being', treasuring this, rather than an accumulation of mileage, at the end of the day. And this is the way to approach these poems, so with limited space I will say little more about them. But let this be clear: here is an exceptional writer, unwilling . . . to release a single line that is not achieved poetry. In my belief Jeremy Hooker is one of the most accomplished young poets writing, not merely in Wales, but in Britain, and in the relative poverty of his and my England his work—which

has advanced considerably since the publication of a group of poems in the Faber anthology *Poetry: Introduction One*, an advance most marked in the sustained longer poems, **"Landscape"** and especially **"Elegy for the Labouring Poor"**, in this first collection—deserves urgent and serious attention. The **"Elegy"** is perhaps the best of this pamphlet; as compared with the ironically turned statements, products of stunted vision, that too often pass for poems in the contemporary English scene, here is a rare imagination reaching deep into the past that's present, into the 'life that gave life' and that helped shape the landscape which would cradle life's continuing. Jeremy Hooker's importance consists, not so much in the critical care he brings to the exercise of his craft, more in the breadth of vision that is controlled but not stifled by that care, that is able to celebrate not what's new so much as what's known—known, that is, through that love that is the 'female element way of knowing'.... (pp. 89-90)

Philip Pacey, in a review of "The Elements," in Poetry Wales, *Vol. 8, No. 2, Autumn, 1972, pp. 88-90.*

RANDAL JENKINS

There are few superficial attractions in Jeremy Hooker's poems— little to satisfy a reader with an appetite for obvious excitements. There is almost no extravagance of incident, idea or language. The poems are not concerned with the pleasures and pains of private life, with fulfilments and conflicts within the self or in relationships (though there is one moving love poem). Nor is he primarily interested in public or political matters. *The Elements* contains a number of elegies on other writers and on his ancestors, and meditations on landscape. Running through the poems is a preoccupation with time and the elemental bases of existence. In them human life is set against a natural background whose essence is flux. . . . The meditative and melancholy tone is characteristic, as are the beautifully modulated, lyrical rhythms. Though the poet is present in his poems, it is as a shadowy observer whose own life can only be guessed at in the context of 'the living stream' that changes 'minute by minute'. It seems to me inevitable that these poems should remind us of W. B. Yeats for Jeremy Hooker too seems to be declaring that truth is not to be grasped in the fixities of knowledge but glimpsed in the movement of the stream.

"Landscape" describes scenes and incidents on a walk to trace a beck's source. It is concerned with what man has made of his natural environment. But its fundamental endeavour is to realise as completely, to hold in suspension as steadily as his poetic art can manage, the experience of the present moment—itself composed of multiple elements and time scales. In its first section, "Rock and Fern" fully grasping the momentary reality involves apprehending scales of time in which the man is made to feel 'invisible'. Thus the moment of 'rest under the last thorn' in which he catches his breath and 'The sun prints the shadow of a fern', which is then shaken by a breeze, causing the phenomenon in which the rock appears to flicker, is seen as conterminous with seasonal time scales in which plants are 'green', with geological time scales in which 'a beck slices the hill', the fern is fossilised, and with archeological time scales in which an arrowhead is 'The mottoed tablet to an aeon'. . . . The impressive success of the poem is in creating the unified consciousness in which all this is caught, and also in the sensuous richness of its realisation. . . . When in the third section he achieves a mood of abstraction in which he forgets 'The multiple unreckoned differences', he is reminded of other ties: 'In the heat my hands swell and flush / Tightening the ring on my finger'. He discovers that to identify the exact source is impossible. Thwarted, he stands beside 'A small clear pool with a hint of iron. / I breathe over it, earthbound and aching'. The consciousness that felt invisibly merged in the moment of the opening section has here become the man of flesh and blood, bound in by his physical limitations.

Far from wishing to escape from his roots, Jeremy Hooker is concerned in the grave and impressive "Elegy for the labouring poor" to 'grub in the past' for them; and not with the interest of an antiquarian, a philosopher or an elegist. . . . In this large, and properly poetic, ambition, he is successful to a marked degree.

Not all the poems in *The Elements* are as satisfying as the two major pieces; some of the shorter lyrics are slight and rather too abstract. But in this book we make contact with a considerable poetic intelligence. The best poems work in subtle and complex ways; they cannot be re-stated in prose without destroying them. Yet what is being said does not always emerge as plainly as it might. Perhaps it is because of this that I have the impression that these poems are likely to have a more restricted readership than they deserve. Jeremy Hooker may need to spell out rather more explicitly how his version of the past throws light upon how we live now. (pp. 226-28)

Randal Jenkins, in a review of "The Elements," in Anglo-Welsh Review, *Spring, 1973, pp. 226-28.*

PETER LEWIS

If Jeremy Hooker's ambitious sequence of poems, *Solent Shore,* is rather disappointing, it is because it fails to fulfil or even develop the considerable promise of an earlier sequence, *Soliloquies of a Chalk Giant.* The stylistic influence of Geoffrey Hill was marked in *Soliloquies* and is again evident in *Solent Shore;* and the structures of both sequences owe something to Hill's *Mercian Hymns.* But *Solent Shore* is an altogether looser sequence than the other two since it lacks a central persona (Offa in the *Hymns* and the Chalk Giant in the *Soliloquies*) to provide a focus for the multiplicity of experiences dealt with. To some extent it is the poet himself in *Solent Shore* who provides the organizing consciousness through which everything is filtered, but above all it is a part of England (again as in the *Hymns*) that defines the limits of the sequence.

Hooker was born and educated in the Southampton area (it is to him what Paterson was to William Carlos Williams), and as the title indicates, *Solent Shore* was inspired by the coastal region of Hampshire and the Isle of Wight. References to particular places and historical events occur frequently, and the long pivotal poem at the centre of the sequence, "The witnesses", which is sandwiched between shorter and more personal poems, is partly a collage of historical documents. At its best, as in "The water's edge" and "Solent winter", Hooker's writing is metaphorically vivid and subtle with typically Hillian *frissons,* but it can also be very mannered. In his attempt to achieve a highly concentrated form of expression, Hooker often uses very short lines of between three and six syllables, and thus puts a great deal of emphasis and even strain on every word and phrase. His desire to load every rift with ore is admirable, but when he overloads or does not succeed the effect can be portentous, cryptic and constipated. Perhaps the more relaxed and open-ended, yet verbally spare, approach of the untypical and tentative "Postscript" will point the way forward for this gifted young poet.

Peter Lewis, "Flake by Flake," in The Times Literary Supplement, *No. 3996, November 3, 1978, p. 1291.*

ANNE STEVENSON

Solent Shore should be read from the back forward. The strongest poems come at the end. "Gull on a Post", "Birth", "Monologue of a Shell", "Slack" have more to say than the impressionistic poems with which Hooker tentatively introduces us to his eye and voice. Like Grigson, Hooker is an exceedingly careful poet, but where Grigson evades the obvious through idiosyncratic syntax, Hooker relies on a loaded diction of description. . . . By telling us what he sees, Hooker suggests what he feels, sometimes implicitly, sometimes in an almost throwaway ending. (p. 386)

Anne Stevenson, "Being Happy," in The Listener, *Vol. 101, No. 2602, March 15, 1979, pp. 386, 388.*

ANNE STEVENSON

[In *Landscape of the Daylight Moon*] Hooker uses his eyes and brain to good purpose; the best of these poems connect image and idea with astonishing dexterity. . . .

Incisive, exact, sometimes haunting, Hooker's poems are wrought with care without being obviously worked over. Two longish sequences, some fine love poems and two landscapes of daylight moon and winter sun reveal important inscapes. Though never self-indulgent Hooker, like Seamus Heaney, is a poet with an acute sense of his own personal life.

Anne Stevenson, "All Their Little Ones," in The Times Literary Supplement, No. 4026, May 23, 1980, p. 586.

ANDREW MOTION

Jeremy Hooker relies for many of his poetic coups on close observation of the—predominantly rural—world around him. In his last book, *Solent Shore,* his perceptions were often crossed on one another to produce spare glancing narratives in which he enacted a search for harmony between himself and the landscape near Southampton. His new collection, *Englishman's Road,* continues the process—over the same ground in the first part, and then in Wales, where he has lived for the last 15 years. In certain respects the change of place seems to have had a deleterious effect on his talent. A sense of isolation from the Welsh language and from the country itself (Wales has, he says, 'A silence harder than the rock / To break and deeper than the snow') has prompted him to resort to pomposity as he presses his claim for integration:

> And I who desired
>   eyes washed clean
> as melting snow,
> radiant at the point of fall,
> know that every word obscures
> the one I want to know.

One way Hooker might find 'the' word is by bringing himself to act on an ambition shared by Peter Jay, who says, 'I would like words to be / clean as this life, / free as the water, / strong as the earth'. . . . The trouble is, Jay's sense of a subject is much less arresting than Hooker's—whose poems, for all their irritating aspects, sincerely grapple with a serious theme. (p. 23)

Andrew Motion, "Hating Directives," in New Statesman, Vol. 100, No. 2594, December 5, 1980, pp. 22-3.

JOHN PRESS

[*Englishman's Road*] is the fourth book of poems by a writer in his late thirties who has taught in Wales at University College, Aberystwyth, since 1965. His main theme is the interaction of place and history, or perhaps one should say prehistory and legend, since Mr Hooker responds more keenly to them than to events written in the history textbooks. "Englishman's Road", the title poem (though it is partly in prose), may seem an exception to that rule, since it deals with the attempt in the early nineteenth century of an Englishman, Augustus Brackenbury, to enclose common land near Aberystwyth. But even here the poet's main concern is with the rocks, the hills, the grass and the curlews. . . . Mr Hooker's vision is entirely self-consistent, owing nothing to fashion or to earlier writers, though he may have learned something from David Jones. This poetry of meditation may sometimes lack intensity and fail to awaken a response from readers who (perhaps wrongly) look for more variety and melody in a book of verse. But Mr Hooker has accomplished with devotion and skill what he set out to do.

John Press, in a review of "Englishman's Road," in British Book News, March, 1981, p. 180.

ANTHONY CONRAN

Hooker's warmth of feeling [in *Englishman's Road*], both about the culture and predicament of Wales and about his particular neighbours in the Welsh countryside, is richly conscious of Welsh attitudes, Welsh priorities.

Hooker is known chiefly as a poet with deep roots in Hampshire, as the titles of two of his books, *Soliloquies of a Chalk Giant* and *Solent Shore,* amply testify. Has he gone native, more Welsh than the Welsh, with these poems about Dewi Sant and Revivals, Pwyll the old god and boys called Gwion, Aled, Ifor and the rest? On the contrary, these poems insist on his exile status. He has lived for ten years in north Dyfed; it is both strange and familiar to him: "The mountain above has been rock to my drifting mind."

And yet, though it is his home, the "country with its language gives all things other names". He is the first poet, to my knowledge, to present a head-on racial conflict, English and Welsh, which is fair to both sides. ["**Englishman's Road**"], originally written for broadcasting, concerns one Augustus Brackenbury, gentleman, who in 1820 came from Lincolnshire and tried to found an estate on Mynydd Bach. After much bitterness and injury on both sides the local people burnt his house down and he fled to England. It is a theme with obvious relevance to contemporary Wales, with its burnings of second homes. Brackenbury has a vision of himself as a dispenser of civilization, and that, above all, is what the local people hate.

At the book's centre, as of Hooker's other volumes, is a vision of England. It is more sympathetically conveyed here than in the mythologizing of the Chalk Giant's soliloquies. At one point he asks why Brackenbury came to Mynydd Bach, and himself answers, Englishman for Englishman:

> Where there is land and sea
> . . . there is our image, and there
> our rootless tongue.
>
>   The stars
> reflect our fires; we are mirrored
> in histories we did not write.
>
>   And here,
> close to home, we have come
> sword against sword, tongue
> against tongue; and by our way
> the people leave, and we pass them, as if into our own.

The white man's burden is still with us: the guilt and yet the sense of destiny of the English has rarely been portrayed with such a troubled sadness, such a sensitivity to the dispossessed, such a feeling for men who work and marry and die. It seems right that Hooker prefaces these poems about himself in Wales with ten short ones about the Hampshire where he was so much at home. In many ways they seem the most complex in the book; yet the Welsh poems have a clean outline to them, like a silhouette, that these ten just miss.

Anthony Conran, "Anglo-Welsh Attitudes," in The Times Literary Supplement, No. 4066, March 6, 1981, p. 267.

JOHN SAUNDERS

In *Landscape of the Daylight Moon* Jeremy Hooker follows the 'idiotic rural poor' (Marx's phrase, from one of Hughes's poems) back into times which social historians like E. P. Thompson and Eric Hobsbawm have made more glamorous for us than any Merrie England. In **"Elegy for the Labouring Poor"** he turns to the past not for the picturesque, 'nor to savour lachrymae rerum', but to celebrate a people who left no monuments but the land they were driven from. . . . Hooker gives us strong, stark poetry, though at times a little self-consciously monumental in spite of his suspicion of the seductive power of images. **"A Note on a Poem by Thomas Hardy"** retells 'In the Time of "The Breaking of Nations"' from the point of view of the 'wight ' who goes whispering by, a girl on his arm, in Hardy's poem, leaving the 'aging man' who glances at them with an anthology piece but only some of the truth:

> But what became of you he could not tell,
> Nor whether, being universal, yet unwed,
> You had no sons to feed another war,
> Nor lay with her but with a shell instead.

Repeated returns to a landscape before there were figures occupy the second half of the collection, strange dream-like meditations on time and the elements over the country inland from Hooker's native Southampton. The past is source of brute creation, an unreflecting pool holding terrors and secrets which feed and threaten the mind. Measured against the 'sublime and oceanic vacancy' of the chalk downs, the mind's 'tender and precarious' seasons offer a little comfort. The past holds marriage and meetings, 'a soft response between two darknesses. . . . Our blood's branched source' (**"A Hambledon Sequence"**). The poem moves towards a kind of peace, the will relinquishing its overwrought patterns and oppositions:

> At times the hill is light as air,
> The life I tried to carry
> Scattered with the stones in grass
> Is borne with them
> Upon a current that I did not will.

> (pp. 72-3)

John Saunders, in a review of "Landscape of the Daylight Moon," in Stand Magazine, *Vol. 21, No. 4 (1981), pp. 72-3.*

DICK DAVIS

The contents of most modern poets' collections of verse are decided by little more than when the poems were written: a volume is brought out, over the next few years a sufficient number of poems on this and that come to be written and another volume is put together. Isn't this the normal way of working? But Jeremy Hooker's books are clearly not written in this way. He has to date published four books of poetry— one (*Soliloquies of a Chalk Giant*) in 1974, two (*Landscape of the Daylight Moon* and *Solent Shore*) in 1978, and one (*Englishman's Road*) in 1980; very few poems could be moved from one book to another without the reader sensing which poem did not fit its new home. In each book the poems belong to and illustrate a distinctive area of concern; they are meditations on a particular landscape and the forces that went to make it, and as such they are intimately bound up with the history and topography of a specific region. If a poem from *Englishman's Road* were to stray into *Soliloquies of a Chalk*

Giant it would be as conspicuously foreign as a conversation in Welsh in a Dorset pub.

This sense of poems growing from a particular context, and of themselves illustrating and finally contributing to that context, is itself part of the subject matter of the poems. Hooker's poetic strategy, and what the strategy focuses on, are aspects of the same concern—the definition of a context. He is a poet always concerned to define the life he describes in terms of what is round about it and behind it, what encompasses it and what precedes it. He will frequently draw attention to the ways in which what is immediately visible is but a part of the story, but a transient speck within the larger historical and geographical perspective. . . .

> You call me old
> But to the wind I am
> A novelty . . .

Hooker frequently juxtaposes the new, the temporary, with the abiding and constant in this way, nowhere more engagingly than at the end of the first poem of *Solent Shore*, **"New Year's Day at Lepe"** where a small boy sees the sea for the first time,

> and a small sunny boy running beside
> the great wet novelty shouting *wasser, wasser.*

but the charm of this should not blind us to the irony—it is, of course, the child who is the novelty, not the sea older than the hills that support the giant of Cerne Abbas. The contrast between what is fixed and what is constantly shifting runs through *Solent Shore,* as is indicated by the book's title—the shore being the area where the fixed land and shifting sea meet. . . . The small boy who runs beside the sea in **"New Year's Day at Lepe"** is but one of many lives in Hooker's poetry set in their vivid transience against the wider, more permanent context in which they have their being—but such lines frequently have a more complex point to make than the evocation of poignant mortality. The opening of the first section of the fine sequence **"For the Labouring Poor"** (from *Landscape of the Daylight Moon*) is set in motion by an image of Constable painting:

> Paint stiffens but the river swims forward;
> Clouds move on and the mill becomes ash,
> But the human features stay variable
> And the pliant earth defies stasis.

The only stillness here is that of art: in so far as the landscape is abiding it is a permanence made up of countless impermanences, of the lives that have lived and shaped it. The context is itself defined by the life it produces, it abides only in the sense that a swiftly rushing river abides. The paradox is beautifully caught by the phrase 'stays variable' (the ease and unobtrusive precision of which is typical of Hooker's exact and wholly unfussy technique). And if we return to the chalk giant for a moment we see how this emblem of a man cut into the hillside fits intimately into the vision that informs these poems— for the giant's context is chalk, a land made literally of other lives:

> The hill is a fine cloud
> Whitening the Cretaceous sea.
> Starfish, urchin, sponge.

The individual life—human or marine—contributes to an unimaginable geographical and historical vastness.

The momentary invoking of the myriad lives that make up the chalk hills is close in spirit to Hooker's constant questionings of the lives of the men who have lived before him in the landscapes he explores. He is not concerned with favourite sons or famous individuals but with those usually anonymous and unrecorded men like the labourer whose 'blunt boot-prints' are 'fugitive / As the cloud at his rear. . . .' (pp. 71-3)

Hooker's poetry is normally low-key in its emotional tone—he is more concerned to examine, record and understand than to excite. But his sense of the mutual need of a landscape and the individuals who live in it means that one theme is particularly emotive for him—dispossession, the enforced rupture of that intimacy which his poetry is always ready to explore and celebrate. Dispossession is the theme of the closing section of **"Elegy for the Labouring Poor"**, in which the peasant must leave behind him, for a life in the New World, the land which has nurtured his forbears. . . . It is also, more complexly and obliquely, the theme of the poem-for-radio **"Englishman's Road"**, the last section in the book of the same name. The poem evokes the memory of an Englishman, Augustus Brackenbury, who tried to settle, with the best of paternalistic intentions, in Wales and was driven out by the sullen hostility of his tenants. The rest of the book also celebrates Wales, but the landscape is one in which the poet, like Brackenbury, is clearly an outsider, and the celebration is not one of intimacy and understanding (as in *Solent Shore* or *Landscape of the Daylight Moon*) but of concern and respect, a recognition of otherness rather than of complicity. . . . (p. 74)

The poems of *Englishman's Road* are written by a deracinated sensibility, the sensibility of poet-as-rueful-outsider, which we have come to regard as specifically modern. But these poems share the distinctive tone of all Hooker's poetry, they are not an aberration in his development. Whether he writes of landscapes in which his consciousness is at home, or over the surface of which he moves as a watchful intruder, his attitude toward the landscape is remarkably consistent. An adverse critic once called D. H. Lawrence a chauvinist of all places: Hooker is a poet for whom the very notion of place, of a particular location with a particular history, provokes not anything so crude as chauvinism but rather a sense the Classical world would have recognised and applauded—of *pietas,* of a love compounded with reserve and awe before what is unique, abiding but always changing. His poetry is singularly lacking in hubris, in any grandiloquent claims for his or any other individual's importance. Typically, the poems occur at the meeting place of three factors—the past that has formed a place, the physical presence of the place, and the poet's consciousness. He is careful to allow his subjects to retain their identity and does not attempt to colonise them into emblems of his own sensibility. Indeed, the last of the three factors, his own consciousness, though it is of course responsible for the poetry, effaces itself as much as it well can in order to do justice to the subjects it addresses—in order to let them cleanly speak as it were for themselves. We learn almost nothing of Hooker the man from his poetry beyond the fact of the pietas I have suggested. And this seems right, for he clearly sees the individual's life as but a brief moment within the larger perspectives that hold his attention and towards which he directs ours. (p. 75)

The even tone of his verse is part and parcel of a vision that seeks to evoke and comprehend—his language is never meretricious and rarely thrilling, it refuses to draw attention to itself. But it is put together with the rare, precise skill that goes to making a dry stone wall: consider this, from *Englishman's Road:*

> there is a darkness on bright days

> and on the stillest a wind
> that will not let us settle,
> but blows the dust from loved
> things not possessed or known.

What seems to be a mere description of the weather deepens almost imperceptibly towards metaphor—the word 'settle' is a quiet pun, the Englishman indeed cannot in any sense 'settle' in Wales—and this pun leads us to question the 'wind' that is clearly more than merely atmospheric, and the 'darkness' becomes more than just the shadows of clouds. Yet at first reading the subtlety of the meaning that plays beneath the calm surface is barely visible. Jeremy Hooker's poetry is full of such moments of unforced deepening significance: in the sure skill of his technique, and in the rare, intense consistency with which he treats themes which are obviously far more to him than the occasion for literature, he seems to me to be one of the best of our poets. (p. 76)

Dick Davis, "Defining a Context: The Poetry of Jeremy Hooker," in Agenda, *Vols. 19 & 20, Nos. 4 & 1, Winter-Spring, 1982, pp. 71-6.*

ANNE STEVENSON

When a poet at mid-point in his career elects to give the world simultaneously a selection of his poems and a collection of his essays he is asking to be taken seriously. Serious indeed is the focused, intense thinking behind the essays and reviews Jeremy Hooker has collected into *The Poetry of Place;* no less serious are the carefully selected poems of *A View from the Source.* If there is one quality which distinguishes both these productions it is a predisposition (inherited, one suspects, from the author's Welsh mentor, Roland Mathias) to fix attention on an object, from literature or life, and hang on to it with dogged determination until its essential secrets are revealed. In both these books the discipline Hooker exercises with respect to his objects is a measure of his personal commitment to them. The result is a style of writing in which no self-mockery, no levity, no embarrassed asides of a witty or chatty nature are permitted to interfere with the gravity of the author's attitude to his undertakings.

If this seems an off-putting introduction to Jeremy Hooker's excellent work, then the assumptions underlying any notion of literature as a "criticism of life" must also be off-putting. . . .

The authors he chooses to understand and to praise (there are really no derogatory reviews here) are those like Edward Thomas and David Jones, for whom Wales represented a significant imaginative field. Hooker's concerns are with those delicate distinctions poets have to make between myth and history, reality and ideal, between a given "self" and those selves consciously or unconsciously realized through the imagination. . . . No one should attempt to read *The Poetry of Place,* then, with the naive expectation of finding here a fixed idea of beauty, loyalty or affinity. Instead this is a book which explores relationships between writers and localities, suggesting differences and similarities, but never relinquishing a certain self-consciousness which, in the end—for all his dogged objectivity—reflects the emerging identity of the author. . . .

Hooker's sympathies with Charles Olson's "projective" or "open" verse show how far removed he stands from the egocentric claustrophobia of much in the contemporary tradition—though he is careful to recognize the gifts a poet such as Sylvia Plath brought to her distorting expressionism. Hooker sees a ''limited individual consciousness'' even in the poems of T. S. Eliot, with his notion of the impersonality of the artist; so he turns, instead, to David Jones's introduction to *Anathemata* for a succinct enunciation of his (and David Jones's) principles: ''one is trying to make a shape out of the very things of which one is oneself made.'' In the same essay (an afterword to his poems) Hooker quotes from the Welsh of Waldo Williams: ''What is love of country? Keeping house / Amid a cloud of witnesses.''

The witnesses Hooker invokes in his essays are writers, natives and exiles, who have shared his sensitivity to ''belonging'', who have sought in their work to identify those ''sacred'' objects and memories out of which they were made and out of which in turn they made. The witnesses in Hooker's poems, however, are witnesses from his own history and childhood. The poems he wrote in Brynbeidog, Llangwyryfon, looking out over the Welsh uplands, take for their subjects the Chalk Giant of Cerne Abbas, the landscape of the Solent with its tarred gulls and flavour of sewage, the ships and kings and generations buried under the salt marshes near Southampton.

These poems, especially the later ones, are compelling and lyrical; while the language of the essays is so exact as to sound, occasionally, pedantic. Both poems and prose, however, speak authentically from a tension the poet can only resolve by defining or expressing his need for a *cydymdreiddiad*—a Welsh word untranslatable into English which means (in Ned Thomas's words) ''that subtle knot of interpenetration, which . . . grows in time (in people's consciousness) between a territory and its people and their language, creating a sense of belonging to a particular stretch of the earth's surface.'' . . .

The Poetry of Place seems an incomplete work, a book written in a middle period of a man's development to which he may look back as to a stone in the river on the way to a further bank. The same, I fear, must be said of the poems which, for all their purity and skill, record a stage in a poet's self-realization, a love of loveliness which the future may not permit him always, honestly, to enjoy.

> Anne Stevenson, ''The Spirit of 'Cydymdreiddiad','' in The Times Literary Supplement, *No. 4150, October 15, 1982, p. 1139.*

BILL RUDDICK

Jeremy Hooker explains in a prose foreword to . . . [*A View from the Source*] that most of his poems about southern England (his birthplace) have been writing at a distance, during a long residence in Wales. This fact arouses ambivalent feelings in him. The poems themselves achieve an exact, sharply-outlined interplay between childhood and the present, the historic past and actuality. . . . But is memory accurate? Do we not consolidate the past in a mould which is our own personality? And can we escape the fixed pattern that memory helps to impose? Revisiting a known scene would be no help. . . . With Hardy-like intensity the poet's mind returns to familiar places; but though visual surfaces can be recaptured (or remade?) with vivid clarity, an understanding of underlying significance eludes him. Yet, though baffled, he feels certain that past actions, past self and remembered places are still interactive. (pp. 40-1)

The quest for self understanding, needing to be achieved through a consideration of the self in relationship with time and place, leads Jeremy Hooker towards (in David Jones's words, which he quotes) 'trying to make a shape out of the very things of

which one is oneself made'. But the quest, while animated by a Hopkinsian sense of the glory of the specific, is also a Coleridgean one, for each element of self, time and the topos proves not only rich in potential but also in urgent need of imaginative exploration. 'Awareness of chalk and flint coincides with my earliest impressions' he confides, and therefore the sense of that landscape, its historic embodiment in art and the relationship between place and artistic expression needs to be explored in a remarkable sequence of poems, the **''Soliloquies of a chalk giant''.** The giant's egocentricity, his lack of concern for both the human and the divine, his primitive strength and oneness with his ancient environment are imagined with a Hughes-like power. But in the totality of Jeremy Hooker's poetry the sequence also earns its central place, for it manifests a recurrent preoccupation of his: his desire to set the individual poetic consciousness '*inside* a world which the poet shares with others, living and dead: a world in time and place, subject to all the influences that shape a specific human identity' while at the same time searching out the infinite complexity of the rhythms of living and inanimate nature. . . . Yet this Hopkinsian, Romantic vision, with its echoes of Wordsworthian reverence for natural things, can be checked, even frozen, by the human will; affected or even dominated by memory. . . . Jeremy Hooker's poems show a search for understanding and for integration being carried on through elements of time, place and memory. The elements of the search prevent a final answer, but the succession of insights and discoveries that the search produces is individually and cumulatively bound to impress. (pp. 41-2)

In Jeremy Hooker's poetry an imaginative but essentially alienated personality seeks for certainties which neither place nor memory can ever quite afford him. It is in the quest and its attendant revelations that the poetic consolations lie: there and in the discovery of the mind's own powers. (pp. 44-5)

> Bill Ruddick, '' 'These Shifting Constancies': Time, Place and Personality in Three New Collections of Verse,'' in Critical Quarterly, *Vol. 26, No. 3, Autumn, 1984, pp. 39-45.*

JOHN MATTHIAS

[Jeremy Hooker's Welsh poems in *A View from the Source*] come, indeed, to quite a lot, especially taken as a sequence or a cycle, all the poems from **''Under Mynydd Bach''** supporting or qualifying or completing each other. . . . In his essay **''Landscape of Fire,''** Hooker insists that Ronald Johnson, as an American and outsider in Britain, was able to see and record the old places and the local colors with a fresh eye and in a new way, free of the familiarity that breeds, if not contempt, then blindness or boredom or oblivion. Certainly the same is true of Hooker himself in Wales. The outsider, should he be both skilled and lucky, can sometimes see and name phenomena or ''rhythms'' which the native, and even the native poet writing in the native language, cannot see or name for being too caught up in them. This is the strength of the outsider's oblique perspective, and it is sometimes a compensation for the more obvious disadvantages of his situation which Hooker tends to brood on.

The poems in *A View from the Source* which were originally published in *Soliloquies for a Chalk Giant* and *Solent Shore* are offered with far fewer hesitations than the **''Under Mynydd Bach''** section, which originally appeared in *Englishman's Road*. In the poems about the chalk Giant of Cerne Abbas, and especially in the evocations of the tides and shingle spits and sunken wrecks and docks along Southampton's shoreline, Hooker has written his strongest work and achieved his homecoming as a poet. By a "sleight of imagination," he says, these poems were written as if from immediate experience and in immediate proximity to the things they remember and name, though the irony is that it was the distance from his native place and native *cydymdreiddiad*—for he wrote the poems in Wales—which sharpened his sense of both. In his Afterword, Hooker writes of his determination "to give primacy to [his] subject matter or materials" in these poems, and in *The Poetry of Place* he even says that he thinks of himself as working "not so much with words as with the materials which they name, with chalk and flint, or shingle and water and oil." Quoting and affirming David Jones's principle that "one is trying to make a shape out of the very things of which one is oneself made," he explains what he regards to be the "ground" of his poems, "a total environment, human and nonhuman, historical and personal, experienced through every form of relevant knowledge available to one, yet known as directly as the shock through one's whole body of treading on a stone, and through a language that was learnt there, in relation to the world it composes." If this begins to sound optimistic and affirmative, it is, and one wonders just how far these poems collectively serve to qualify Hooker's generally pessimistic picture of poetry of place after Wordsworth; a lot of this, in fact, sounds like Wendell Berry. One of Hooker's aims is clearly to "unspecialize" his poetry, though he has argued in his criticism, as we have seen, that "as the poet's grasp on a common human world has loosened" it is precisely through a preoccupation with place that he has "come to stress the specialness of other poets . . . and become a specialist talking to specialists."

The contradiction, if that is what it is, doesn't matter; what matters are the poems, and they are as vivid and alive as one could hope, as tangible and tactile as the chalk and flint and shingle they evoke, and written from an experience of the "ground" as deep as Crabbe's. Like Crabbe, Hooker sees the "gumboot-sucking ooze" at low tide, the weeds in the channel,

and—coming later than Crabbe—the oil and industrial pollution. Still, like his Welsh poems, the poems of the Solent shore constitute a poetry of celebration and praise—not of the grim present condition of the shoreline itself, but of life and work and love seen against the history and legend necessarily rooted there as deeply as a post in the harbor. And if praise can "turn the dust to light" in Wales, it doubtless can turn even oil slicks and blue-gray mud to light in Southampton. Emerging out of "water that is bottle green, with a salt crust / And an unmistakable flavour of sewage" as out of some antediluvian source of amphibious life, a characteristic poem notices "a tarred gull" floating past, "an orange box / And the helmet of a marine; a glove / With the hand still in it," as it struggles toward its (earned) vision. . . . I think Hooker would like his poems to be as essential as the necessities unladen in the harbor, "greased with use," as he has it in another poem. Imagining a seagull on a post, he wishes for the gifts both of post and gull: the post's gift to mark a channel and serve as a mooring, "standing ever / Still in one place," and the gull's gift to fly "inland or seaward; settle / At will—but voicing always in her cry / Essence of wind and wave, / Bringing to city, moorish / Pool and ploughland, / Reminders of storm and sea." Between the gull and the post, in the end, he sees no resolution, "only the necessity of flight / Beyond me, firm / Standing only then."

That is the note, in fact, on which the **"Solent Shore"** poems end, but I cannot leave Hooker's work without noticing briefly **"At Osborne House"**—his poem about the renovated manor house on the Isle of Wight where Victoria died—which connects so centrally with the poems on great houses by Jonson, Marvell, and Pope. . . . The poem should be read not only beside these celebrations of hospitality, wealth, and social or natural hierarchies, but also beside Robert Lowell's excellent "Doomsday Book" in *Day by Day*. Both Lowell's poem and Hooker's . . . bring a grand (and grandiose) tradition to an end. (pp. 197-99)

John Matthias, "Poetry of Place: From the Kentucky River to the Solent Shore," in The Southern Review, *Vol. 21, No. 1, January, 1985, pp. 183-203.*

L(afayette) Ron(ald) Hubbard

1911-1986

(Also wrote under pseudonyms of Frederick Engelhardt, Rene Lafayette, and Kurt von Rachen) American novelist, short story writer, nonfiction writer, and scriptwriter.

Hubbard is best known for his controversial work *Dianetics: The Modern Science of Mental Health* (1950), a volume of self-help philosophy upon which he based his Church of Scientology. However, he began his prolific career in the 1930s as an author associated with the "golden age" of science fiction. Encouraged by John W. Campbell, Jr., editor of *Astounding Science Fiction,* Hubbard contributed many stories to pulp magazines in diverse genres, using his given name for fantasy stories and the pseudonyms Rene Lafayette and Kurt von Rachen for his science fiction works. Many of these stories feature righteous heroes who develop superior mental powers as a means of overcoming their adversaries.

Several of Hubbard's early magazine serials were collected as novels beginning in the late 1940s. War-ravaged Europe is the setting of *Final Blackout* (1948), which Paul Walker described as "a bleak, harsh novel of a hopeless conflict and an idealistic lieutenant who fights it to its ironic end." A similar grim irony pervades *Death's Deputy* (1948), in which an immortal, forced to punish humans according to the whims of his race, seeks in vain his own death. The short novels *Typewriter in the Sky* (1951) and *Fear* (1951) are horrific fantasies which many critics consider to be classics of science fiction's golden age. *Fear,* which relates the existence of a man who alternates between psychosis and sanity, is considered among Hubbard's finest works. Hubbard's last book of this period, *Return to Tomorrow* (1954), is a "space opera" which anticipates future science fiction themes in its story about intergalactic traders for whom one month equals a century of earth time. Hubbard's stories written under the pseudonym of Rene Lafayette and collected in *Ole Doc Methuselah* (1970) relate the tales of a medical doctor who traverses time and space while opposing criminals and enemies of his profession.

With *Battlefield Earth: A Saga of the Year 3000* (1982), Hubbard returned to the heroic science fiction upon which he had initially built his reputation. This novel takes place one thousand years after humanity's near-extinction by an alien race called the Psychlos and centers on the accelerated mental powers by which the book's hero overcomes his oppressors. *Mission Earth* is Hubbard's "decalogy," a projected series of ten novels about an alien race which tries to save earth from human destruction in order to retain the planet for future exploitation. The first five volumes of the *Mission Earth* series, several of which have been published posthumously, include *The Invaders Plan* (1985), *Black Genesis: Fortress of Evil* (1986), *The Enemy Within* (1986), *An Alien Affair* (1986), and *Fortune and Fear* (1986). Although some critics welcomed Hubbard's return to science fiction, most considered his recent works less original and polished than his early serials.

(See also *Contemporary Authors,* Vols. 77-80, Vol. 118 [obituary].)

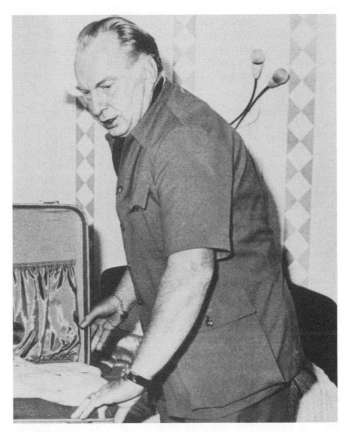

DAVID C. PASKOW

It's not often that one can believe a cover blurb, but Berkley is perfectly honest when it asserts [*Fear* and *The Ultimate Adventure*] to be "Two Classic Fantasy Novels." . . . *Fear* relates the nightmarish existence of James Lowry, an existence hovering between delusion and reality. Madness and murder intermingle to provide a roller-coaster, merry-go-round narrative which leaves the reader mentally exhausted by the climax. *Fear* is a fine psychological horror novel, comparable to Russell Greenan's *It Happened in Boston.*

The Ultimate Adventure is pure Arabian Nights fantasy with touches of horror (if one considers the appearance of a ghoul or two an element of horror) as Stephen Jebson fights for life and love in the City of Brass. At times the atmosphere is that of deCamp and Pratt's Harold Shea adventures, but Hubbard was first.

This double package of fantasy is a bargain in every way.

> David C. Paskow, in a review of "Fear" and "The Ultimate Adventure," in Luna Monthly, No. 23, April, 1971, p. 27.

PAUL WALKER

[*Death's Deputy* and *Final Blackout*] are both from the 1940 John Campbell *Unknown,* and are extraordinary. Whatever your opinion of Scientology or of its founder, I think you will find these two books quite different from anything you might have imagined. Both are unusual, advanced treatments of [fantasy and science fiction] themes, thoroughly readable, lucid, swift-paced, with detailed, effective characterizations and gut-oriented dramatic impact.

Death's Deputy . . . is the story of a tool of the gods, a reluctant immortal, who seeks death in vain while most all those he comes in contact with die violent deaths. It is somewhat dated in an odd sort of way and a bit overlong, but the characters and incidents come across very well. It seems just barely fantasy, with moments of quite vivid realism that rival Harlan Ellison at his best.

Final Blackout has an introduction by the author in which he comments on the controversy the book once aroused. It was written before America's entry into WWII and had some harsh things to say about the Soviet Union, but most of the events discussed are ancient history now and the story remains a bleak, harsh novel of a hopeless conflict and an idealistic lieutenant who fights it to its ironic end. It is longer and more effective than *Death's Deputy,* but again dated in that same inexplicable way.

Neither of these books are wastes, but I can't say they are especially worthwhile, either. Put it this way: as science fiction goes, these are two unusual works of some literary, some historical interest. As entertainment, they are of less interest.

> Paul Walker, in a review of "Death's Deputy" and "Final Blackout," in Luna Monthly, Nos. 35 & 36, April-May, 1972, p. 57.

P. SCHUYLER MILLER

Hubbard, before he found the pot of gold in Dianetics and Scientology, was a good writer of lively fiction. Seen from a modern perspective, most of [the stories in *Ole Doc Methuselah*] are really conventional action yarns dressed up in exotic trappings. "Doc Methuselah" is one Dr. Stephen Thomas Metheridge, graduate of Johns Hopkins in the Class of 1946. We meet him seven hundred years later as one of the Soldiers of Light, the six hundred space-roving members of the Universal Medical Society, and follow him through a couple of centuries. Accompanied by his extraterrestrial memory-bank, Hippocrates, he takes on a variety of con-men and nogoodniks in the name of medicine. Actually, the medical problems on which the seven stories are hung are largely cosmetic—an excuse for Doc Methuselah to wade in, a chip on his shoulder and the right in his hypodermic, with Hippocrates to back him up. The exception, and the best story in the book, is the one called **"Plague."**

I doubt that Hubbard has bothered to revise the stories to any extent . . . , but they read very well and date very little. Doc uses log tables instead of a computer, and when he does get one it is mechanical—not electronic—but the present fourth-generation micro-circuit computers were not predictable in 1947, even by John Campbell. The uninflated dollars of those long-gone days also seem faintly ridiculous when projected into the far future. (pp. 164-65)

> P. Schuyler Miller, in a review of "Ole Doc Methuselah," in Analog Science Fiction/Science Fact, Vol. XCI, No. 1, March, 1973, pp. 164-65.

[CHARLES N. BROWN]

[*Final Blackout,* a] future war novel of a devastated Europe, first appeared in *Astounding* in 1940 and became an instant classic. It still holds up pretty well but seems tame and romantic when compared to some more recent ones. Still an important book because it affected a lot of later books. . . .

When I first encountered [*Return to Tomorrow*] as ["To the Stars"] it really impressed me. Rereading it as an adult is embarrassing. Hubbard's knowledge of science is non-existent and he's managed to completely misinterpret the Lorentz-Fitzgerald equations. The gosh-wow pulp writing isn't too readable, either. If I was 13 again, I'd probably love it, but not now.

> [Charles N. Brown], in a review of "Final Blackout" and "Return to Tomorrow," in Locus, No. 182, December 17, 1975, p. 5.

LESTER DEL REY

[*Return to Tomorrow*] was Hubbard's last major story [at the close of the Golden Age of Science Fiction], and [he] was at the top of his form. It deals with men who trade between stars, traveling at nearly the speed of light; for them, time is greatly slowed so that a month for their ship may be a century for Earth. They can never return to friends they knew. And behind it all lies a strange mission. This is a grim novel that somehow manages to retain a feeling of hope and romance. The science is hardly accurate, but the writing makes up for that. (p. 172)

> Lester Del Rey, "The Big Boom," in his The World of Science Fiction, 1926-1976: The History of a Subculture, Garland Publishing, Inc., 1980, pp. 169-81.

FRANK KENDIG

L. Ron Hubbard is not your typical guru. First of all, he has periods with little to do, which probably can't be said of your average pope or ayatollah. Second, he is not burdened with humility. . . .

What Hubbard does share with other religious leaders is verbiage: *Battlefield Earth* runs 819 action-packed pages, piling up some 430,000 words. . . .

Watchers of scientology will be variously pleased or disappointed that *Battlefield Earth* contains not a . . . whisper of scientology's neural nonsense. What the book does contain is pure science fiction, reminiscent of a halcyon time in the pulps. The novel is set in the year 3000, a thousand years after the Earth was conquered by a race of cat-like people called Psychlos, who annihilated almost all of the human population. The hero, Jonnie Goodboy Tyler, aided by a band of surviving Scotsmen, drives the cat-people from the planet in a plot that, as Hubbard writes in his introduction, "contains practically every type of story there is—detective, spy, adventure, western, love, air war, you name it."

During the 1930s and '40s, before he got into the religion business, Hubbard was a professional writer, one of the most prolific during the so-called Golden Age of science fiction that also spawned such authors as A. E. van Vogt, Robert Heinlein, Edgar Rice Burroughs, Clifford Simak, and Isaac Asimov. *Battlefield Earth* is Hubbard's 101st published novel. It's a pretty good one, too, and that's the newest in a long list of reasons that he should never have switched professions.

Frank Kendig, "All Clear on Battlefield Earth," in Psychology Today, *Vol. 17, No. 1, January, 1983, p. 60.*

TOM EASTON

[Hubbard's most recent novel is] *Battlefield Earth: A Saga of the Year 3000,* and it's a real stinker.

Why do I bother to tell you, then? Well, I do have the feeling I haven't been mean enough lately. That's because few books deserve the full treatment of finger-pinched nose and loud noises of disgust. (pp. 160-61)

Hubbard barely tried, fell flat, and I invite you to share a chorus of "pee-yew." The problem may lie in Hubbard's egocentric (or even egomaniacal) conviction that as a messiah or god-on-Earth he can do no wrong. "Pure" SF is what *he* says it is. Certainly the book's long introduction supports this interpretation, for there Hubbard says such things as, "To handle [my] fantasy material, Campbell introduced another magazine, *Unknown.*" From what else I've read, I doubt that Hubbard was *Unknown*'s *raison d'être*. . . .

The story is a massive, save-the-universes (16—count 'em—16), wish-fulfillment fantasy wholly populated by the most one-dimensional of cardboard characters. The hero is Jonnie Goodboy Tyler. The alien villains are the Psychlos. (Others too have role-specific names.) Everyone looks his part—Tyler is noble and heroic, the Psychlos bestial, the cosmic bankers little grey men. No one plays more than a single note, over and over again. The characters are cartoons, and even so they are less believable than the ones in the funny papers. They are perfect examples of what novice writers should avoid.

The story is set a millennium hence, long after Earth has been depopulated by a world-wide gas attack. The Psychlos did it so they could gut the planet with mines. Only a few humans survive in isolated enclaves, descended to savagery. Tyler is one such savage, but he is driven by a noble curiosity and dissatisfaction with the status quo to leave his Colorado village and seek a wider life. Caught by a Psychlo with delusions of grandeur, he is educated with a telepathic machine, becomes civilized, contacts other humans, plots, and destroys the Psychlos lock, stock, and barrel, throughout the universes. He then manages to save the universes from the economic chaos that removing their Psychlo rulers has caused.

Sheeesh!

It's a story with scope, sweep, and grandeur. Human underdog conquers all, in the best *Astounding* tradition. Action galore, with gonads forgotten. Blood and thunder and mighty deeds. Gee, whiz! Is that what the Golden Age was all about? Gimme more! (p. 161)

For all the action, it plods and slogs, often lost in minutia. For all the sensawunda, it's as unlikely as a one-legged horse. And the thinking is sloppy, too.

Let me show you what I mean. [In one section], Hubbard writes of over-revving alien motors which, he has already told us, dont "rev" at all, ever; they're "continuous teleporters." Worse yet, the motors are presumably at rest with respect to the entire universe. When on, they move and hold position by continually adjusting their location coordinates. Momentum remains zero. Yet, when the motors are turned off, motor and vehicle just sit there. There is not conflict of momenta of the sort you

would see if you set a motionless brick in front of a speeding car or jet.

Maybe Hubbard just doesn't understand basic reality. [In another episode] he has his hero leap from a "plane" at hypersonic speed, unprotected—and he doesn't get smashed by the air.

More sweepingly, there's the Psychlos' excuse for raping Earth. They want metals, so they mine. But we know (don't we) that mining is easier and cheaper on small moons and asteroids, especially when you can't breathe a planet's air. And speaking of air, the Psychlos' "breathe-gas" detonates when exposed to radiation. So okay, they come from another universe, where the elements and chemistry are different from ours. But what about cosmic rays? Background radiation?

Most fundamentally of all, there's that "kill-gas" the Psychlos used to wipe out most of humanity. Hubbard reveals some hundreds of pages into the story that there's a simple defense against it: all you need to do is breathe through a filter of salt. In that case, the gas can be no poison for Earthly animals, whose body fluids are just chock full of sodium chloride. As soon as the gas entered the body, it would be neutralized.

Enough. *Battlefield Earth* is a crock. The only way you could possibly enjoy it is as a satire of the Golden Age, whose weaknesses it bloats to elephantiasis. Unfortunately, I doubt very much that Hubbard meant it that way. Judging by his introduction, he meant it quite seriously as the epitome of SF: what the stuff should be at its best. (pp. 161-62)

Tom Easton, in a review of "Battlefield Earth," in Analog Science Fiction/Science Fact, *Vol. CIII, No. 2, February, 1983, pp. 160-62.*

KATHLEEN ROMER

[Hubbard] has published again after thirty years' silence, this time falling far short of the talent and ingenuity displayed in such earlier works as *Fear* and *Typewriter in the Sky*. L. Ron Hubbard's newest "slug-fest," *Battlefield Earth,* is as trite and predictable as its unimaginative title suggests and exhibits the worst of the pulp tradition. So it is surprising to find that the "Introduction" contains an assertion by the author to the contrary: "[This work is] not in the old tradition. Writing forms and styles have changed, so I had to bring myself up to date and modernize the styles and patterns." . . . (p. 36)

Readers, consider: a protagonist and hero named Jonnie Goodboy Tyler (if you can stand it), blonde, American, pure (passionless), altruistic, selfless, who begins the story as an uneducated but adventurous boy-hunter, wide-eyed with curiosity about the rest of the human race . . . ; he ends up the reluctant hero of sixteen universes, staying alive through predicaments most authors would not dare ask their readers to believe, solving "Psychlo mathematics" when no other brain in the universe can, suddenly mastering the game of clever diplomacy when the fate of the human race finally hinges on a bank transaction. . . . and living to father a son (Timmie Brave Tyler) and retire humbly from the floodlights, having "done his work"—all in only a few years' time! Most authors would at least have the artistic sense to spread such a cosmic plot over generations.

Now consider: an antagonist, one alien Psychlo named Terl, who is motivated by greed and cruelty (aren't they all?), who is too easily duped and underestimates the cleverness and fortitude of our hero, and who manages to disappear from the story two-thirds of the way through, being replaced by a less interesting entire race (of Tolneps). The reader waits at least one hundred pages to learn Terl's fate—far too big a gap in the plot to maintain reader interest. In the novel's relentless effort to increase in scope with each successive chapter, characters are introduced late or dropped for long periods till the reader wonders that Hubbard bothers with any characters other than Jonnie Goodboy, who, in fact, very nearly engineers the entire unlikely plot single-handedly.

The cosmopolitan array of minor characters are forgettable except for the clichéd ethnic and national traits they exhibit: the Scots are clannish, argumentative, loyal; the Russians kiss avidly on both cheeks; the Chinese are heavy on tradition and ritual; the South Americans wear baggy pants and large, flat hats. You can fill in the rest.

One of the book's most serious flaws is the deplorably stereotyped female characters. They have occasional walk-on parts in which they cook, play nurses to the wounded, sit and wait for news of the action, or distract their men with trivial, "feminine" chatter. No reader need accommodate such a breech of literary ethics in a book with a 1982 copyright; therefore, Hubbard must be putting us on and getting a laugh himself.

Despite flat, stereotyped characters (there is even a "Captunk Moiphy"), obviously rigged plot coincidences, uninspired prose, and intruding passages of what surely are the author's profound views on banking, big government, and the evils of social suppression, this reviewer finds two redeeming traits—the book is far too expensive and long-winded to seriously tempt most discriminating buyers. (pp. 36-7)

> Kathleen Romer, in a review of "Battlefield Earth: A Saga of the Year 3000," in Science Fiction & Fantasy Book Review, No. 12, March, 1983, pp. 36-7.

THE ECONOMIST

Before turning his hand to religion, [Hubbard] wrote 101 science-fiction novels. By his own admission, he was one of the great writers of the golden age of space romance and was recruited to the trade by John W. Campbell Jr., the editor of Astounding Science Fiction. . . . He returns now with [*Battlefield Earth*] and invites comparisons with the best.

He lists the writers of his golden age on the dedication page— 84 in all, not including himself. . . . Does he belong in this company? Two of his dedicatees, A. E. van Vogt and Robert Heinlein, think he does. Regrettably, though, *Battlefield Earth* is an unsubtle saga, atrociously written, windy and out of control.

The hero, Jonnie Goodboy Tyler, begins his adventures as an illiterate hunter in the foothills of the Rocky Mountains. Spy drones patrol the skies, but none of his tribe knows their significance. It is the year 3000 and the earth has for a millennium been held by an alien race, the Psychlos, who are interested only in its mineral wealth. The gas they breathe explodes on contact with even traces of uranium and, for this reason, they keep clear of the mountains, where the last remaining 35,000 humans skulk in fear. . . .

Jonnie is captured by Terl, the chief Psychlo villain, who wishes to train humans to mine where Psychlos cannot go, but becomes so rapidly the master of their technology that he is able to wipe them out by page 596, leaving him with only a further 223 pages to deal with the several other interstellar predatory races who now take an interest in this bemused planet. Jonnie is assisted in his conquests by Chinese, by the remnants of the Red Army, by Tibetan lamas and most notably by Scottish highlanders, whom L. Ron Hubbard has drawn apparently from some old movie version of *Rob Roy*.

Some human villains also appear in the form of the Brigantes. These are inhabitants of the Congo, millennial descendants of mercenaries sent to topple the Zaire government, given to cannibalism and vile sexual practices and still awaiting rescue by the United Nations. This is one of the author's jokes, others being derived from his views on politics and economics. Science fiction, says he, ought to include such sciences as sociology and economics. There is even a ponderous joke about Keynes, of whom Mr Hubbard does not approve.

What is missing is the most elementary shred of characterisation. The good guys are all selfless and courageous and the bad guys uniformly sadistic. The plot clanks along like a giant, lumbering engine and Mr Hubbard is most at home (tiresomely so)—in laboured description of mechanical processes. Perhaps this secretive man was an engineer before he was an author. He writes like one. . . .

[*Battlefield Earth*] is unlikely to persuade the United States government to invest more heavily in space travel. The Psychlos, it seems, first came here in response to that probe NASA sent out, giving other creatures directions how to get here should they wish to pay earthlings a visit. That is Mr Hubbard's best joke. It comes, unfortunately, on page three.

> "Relic of the Golden Age," in The Economist, Vol. 291, No. 7336, April 7, 1984, p. 94.

GERALD JONAS

[Since his recent return to science fiction, Hubbard's] new books became best sellers, even though the plots were hackneyed in the extreme, the characters were thoroughly obnoxious (although not in any interesting way) and the sentences sounded as if they had been created on a non-English-speaking word processor. . . . [*The Invaders Plan*] is the first volume in a "decalogy" with the overall title **Mission Earth**. Decalogy is a neologism that we are told means "a group of ten volumes." In his introduction, Mr. Hubbard assures us that what follows is satire, a form of literature whose origins he carefully explains in what I take to be a satire on ponderous, self-serving pseudoscholarship. What actually follows is a paralyzingly slow-moving adventure enlivened by interludes of kinky sex, sendups of effeminate homosexuals and a disregard of conventional grammar so global as to suggest a satire on the possibility of communication through language.

> Gerald Jonas, in a review of "The Invaders Plan," in The New York Times Book Review, January 12, 1986, p. 22.

VICTOR W. MILAN

[Hubbard's] 1948 novel *Final Blackout* among other works is considered by many a classic of the [science fiction] genre. Recently, Hubbard returned to the field with *Battlefield Earth: A Saga of the Year 3000*, a lengthy epic of heroic Earthmen's resistance to alien invaders.

Alien invasion is once again on the agenda in *The Invaders Plan*, Volume I of a proposed *Mission Earth decalogy*. . . . This time we're treated to the viewpoint of the would-be invaders, very human humanoids of the intergalactic Voltar Confederacy. Earth's impending self-destruction through pollution and nuclear war threatens to throw off their age-old "Invasion Timetable," which causes great consternation until the head of the Gestapo-like Apparatus offers to mount a secret mission to save "Blito-P3"—Earth—from its inhabitants.

The narrative's first person, Apparatus functionary Soltan Gris, is assigned to guide combat engineer Jettero Heller, the real hero of the piece, through "Mission Earth." The problem is that his superior has ordered him to make sure the rescue scheme fails.

Though Heller starts out a prisoner, he escapes Gris' control the instant he's released from his cell to begin preparing for the mission, and Gris never catches up. But that's not surprising, since "Jet" Heller is a combination of Tom Brown, Albert Einstein, and the cartoon character He-Man, who throws a tournament to make a fellow officer look good to his sweetie, absorbs one-hour instruction tapes in 30 seconds, and twirls 100-pound exercise bags on one robust finger. Gris, on the other hand, is a boob, who hasn't even mastered elementary graft. . . .

Eventually we learn that the Apparatus boss plans to use Earthly heroin and speed to undermine the Confederacy's ruling aristocracy and enable him to become Emperor. Why he should want to derail salvation of the planet that supplies those drugs is as mysterious as why such a technologically advanced civilization can't synthesize them.

Parts of *The Invaders Plan* read as if poorly translated from the Japanese. "The blastgun barrel was into my stomach with violence!" goes one entire paragraph, characteristically substituting typographical stridence for the crisp prose and well-visualized action so conspicuously absent from the book.

Satiric intent cannot make up for weakness of prose, pace, characterization or lack of a credible plot—the more so since it's unclear what this book and the rest of the *decalogy* are intended to satirize. Bloated bureaucracy, perhaps—certainly an original target. The initials of Gris' employer, the Coordinated Information Apparatus, may provide a clue.

Satire can work as scalpel or as ax. Whoever its intended victims are, *The Invaders Plan* proves a fluffy feather pillow, wielded blindly.

> *Victor W. Milan, "The Invaders Plan," in* Los Angeles Time Book Review, *February 9, 1986, p. 6.*

JANRAE FRANK

Hubbard obviously had a strong personal antipathy to bureaucracy, particularly the military and espionage establishments with their callous manipulation of and disregard for people, things and events. . . . Hubbard has chosen to make fun of his target rather than dissect it. In *The Invaders Plan* . . . , Hubbard spins a satirical tale in which our world has been marked for potential exploitation by a more advanced, and equally ruthless, race. The jape: One of their advance scouts discovers that, between the threats of global pollution and nuclear warfare, we are in danger of destroying the earth before they can exploit it. . . .

Almost all of *The Invaders Plan* is a delicious read and, as one would expect of an experienced pro, Hubbard makes his points well; the major question is whether the book's flippant, light-hearted tone can sustain itself over some 5,000 pages. On the

other hand, Hubbard is no stranger to the form. Much of his best work of the '40s and '50s, *Fear, Slaves of Sleep, Typewriter in the Sky,* is written in exactly the same style and won reader polls at the time.

> *Janrae Frank, "Alien Economics," in* Book World—The Washington Post, *February 23, 1986, p. 10.*

TOM EASTON

If you want to embark on ten volumes of wheel-spinning, improbable action and soggy cardboard characters, if you want to be a literary masochist, then go right out and buy a copy of L. Ron Hubbard's latest sci-fi epic. It's *The Invaders Plan.* . . . and it's even worse than *Battlefield Earth.* It is so bad that I looked in vain for any sign that Hubbard intended it as a spoof of the field, but the signs all say he is serious. And it is so trite, so commercial, that it will surely be a best-seller, pushed by the kind of publicity campaign only a writer as rich as Hubbard, with a publishing house all his own, can afford to mount.

Hubbard gives us the expansionist Voltarian Empire, covering over a hundred worlds and moving slowly, according to a plan of conquest devised by the Empire's founders eons ago, to conquer the entire galaxy. Earth is scheduled for absorption centuries hence, but a routine patrol reveals that the Earthlings are ruining the real estate with pollution. The Apparatus, a government bureau staffed by thugs and run by Lombar Hisst, an egomaniac who makes Hitler look naive, wangles the assignment of teaching the Earthlings how to run a clean civilization, at least until the scheduled invasion date. However, Hisst has his own plans for Earth: it will be his base when he attempts a coup, it is already his source of corrupting drugs, and he insists that the salvage mission fail. Accordingly, he puts the mission in the hands of the inept Soltan Gris, ordering him to see that it fails.

However, Gris will be only the handler of salvage-expert Jettero Heller, a certified hero beloved of peers and public, a man who can inspire loyalty and clean living even in the thugs of the Apparatus (not in Hisst or Gris, but then no hero can be perfect) . . . *Plan* is thus largely the tale of Gris's frustrations as Heller prepares for the mission, which future volumes will take, step by step, to what seems a predictable defeat of evil and its minions.

If Hubbard's decalogy has any charm at all, it is in its focus on evil. Heller, ostensibly a villain but clearly the now and future hero, identifiable with Earth . . . , is very much in the background. He is a natural force with whom Gris must cope as best he can.

However, this small bit of charm is not enough. Avoid the book and its sequels like the plague. (pp. 174-75)

> *Tom Easton, in a review of "The Invaders Plan," in* Analog Science Fiction/Science Fact, *Vol. CVI, No. 4, April, 1986, pp. 174-75.*

RICHARD E. GEIS

There are those in the inner reaches of science fiction who think L. Ron Hubbard did not write *Battlefield Earth,* or the first two volumes of the 10-volume novel, *Mission Earth.* I'm almost positive he did write *Battlefield Earth,* but I have serious reservations about Volumes 1-2 of *Mission Earth,* [titled *The Invaders Plan* and *Black Genesis: Fortress of Evil*].

I couldn't get very far into **Battlefield Earth** before concluding it was too juvenile and pulpish for me. It was written skillfully, with talent, but it was written for the golden age of science fiction—13.

I can't recommend these **Misson Earth** volumes to the same readers for the same reasons. The opening Introduction is fine, clear, coherent, skilled, an education in understanding satire. The novel's cute stage-setting documents are jocular, tongue-in-cheek, suited to teenagers in style. They contain the elaborate pretense of having been written by an alien scoundrel as a confession to his lord and master Lord Turn, from prison in Government City, Planet Voltar of the Voltar Confederacy. . . .

But the fiction following the set-up material is awkward, clumsy, inept . . . simply bad, almost amateur in technique and skill. It leads me to think L. Ron Hubbard wrote the opening, and someone else completed the project.

(If ghost-written, couldn't a skilled writer be hired? But if Hubbard's brain were failing, the victim of subtle micro-strokes before the Big One. . . .)

Uncritical, read-anything kids will probably be able to consume **Mission Earth**. And parents shouldn't worry: all swear words have been bleeped out by the translating computer, 54 Charlee Nine.

I'm genuinely sorry I couldn't endure these, and more sorry still that L. Ron Hubbard wrote these and probably forced their publication. I doubt any other than his own publishing company would have accepted them and poured megabucks into their promotion.

Richard E. Geis, in a review of "Mission Earth," *in* Science Fiction Review, *Vol. 15, No. 2, Summer, 1986, p. 47.*

Tama Janowitz

1957-

American short story writer, novelist, and journalist.

Janowitz has drawn attention for her novel, *American Dad* (1981), and for her collection of short stories, *Slaves of New York* (1986). These works display her dispassionate approach to the bizarre experiences of unconventional characters. *American Dad* follows the growth to manhood of narrator Earl Przepasniak amid a tumultuous home life dominated by his hedonistic psychiatrist father and his eccentric mother, a poet. After his father is jailed for accidentally killing his mother, Earl leaves for college and then travels to Europe in search of debauchery. Janowitz was praised for her comic ingenuity and her fine ear for domestic dialogue. The Przepasniaks were modeled in part on Janowitz's own family, and reviewers found this portrayal to be the strongest aspect of *American Dad*.

Janowitz also drew on personal experience for the stories in *Slaves of New York*. She became a celebrity in New York following the book's publication and was the subject of several magazine and newspaper articles. Set in the bohemian milieu of Soho, the stories satirically depict the odd relationships of artists, nightclub patrons, jewelry designers, and other fringe characters of this society. Janowitz's sardonic, deadpan style and her choice of subject matter prompted critics to compare *Slaves of New York* to the works of Fran Lebowitz and Jay McInerney. Dinah Prince noted: "The protagonists [in *Slaves of New York*] . . . share with [Janowitz] a shyness and a sense of always being out of place. . . . Without ever taking themselves seriously, her characters are alternately befuddled and intimidated by the daily emotional and intellectual obstacle course that is Janowitz's New York."

(See also *Contemporary Authors*, Vol. 106.)

Photograph by Louis Psihoyos

KIRKUS REVIEWS

[*American Dad*] pops along with the energy of its youthfully pitiless stare. Earl Przepasniak is our narrator; with younger brother Bobo, he grows up in western Massachusetts with father Robert and mother Mavis—at least until divorce and unfortunate fates separate the couple. But Robert, the "American Dad," is anything but a Robert Young best-knowing father type. A psychiatrist at a private girls' school, he's every outlandish cultural aberration of the Sixties rolled into one: ecologist, mushroom-hunter, house-builder, philanderer, druggie, proto-hippie, eccentrically generous, totally self-absorbed. In other words, he's less someone a son can lean on than someone whose gunshot-behavior sends poor Earl scurrying around, dodging the ricochets . . . while mother Mavis, a late-blooming published poet who has suffered this man for years and years, is now doing her doughty best without him. . . . Janowitz has a smart-kid first-novelist's virtues: just about the right amount of premature jaundice, a long attention span (roughly half the scenes are *too* long), a good ear for nonsequiturs in domestic speech. But once out of the bosom of the wacko parents,

narrator Earl is cast off into an ill-prepared young adulthood that Janowitz just can't handle; a European rite-of-passage trip (mother dead, father in prison, what's a guy to do?) is dreary and toneless. So, when the live wires like dad Robert and mom Mavis are onstage, this book has a headlong, juicy appeal; when they're not, it's drably standard. (pp. 220-21)

A review of "American Dad," in Kirkus Reviews, Vol. XLIX, No. 4, February 15, 1981, pp. 220-21.

DAVID QUAMMEN

[The title character of *American Dad*] is Robert Abraham Przepasniak, a libidinous psychiatrist, three-time husband and father of two unpromising lads named Earl and Bobo. The real star of this family saga, however, is an American mom named Mavis Przepasniak, a late-blossoming poet who eats peanut butter with her fingers while she reads, who dreams of making money by producing an album of Telemann dubbed over with sounds from a public toilet and who fears she is fated to end her life selling miniature turtles at a Woolworth's. All the best comic moments in *American Dad* belong to Mavis. . . . Unfortunately Mavis disappears at the book's halfway point, when her ex-husband breaks down the barricaded door of her study and she is killed by a falling postage meter. Robert Przepasniak gets 10-to-15 years for involuntary manslaughter, but the chief loser is the novel itself.

Young Earl Przepasniak is the narrator and central character, and we are asked to accept him as a charmingly bizarre misfit whose unorthodox view of life—molded irrevocably by his overweening father and his nutty mother—is as affecting as those of Holden Caulfield or Alex Portnoy. But we are never so persuaded. Earl's perceptions, his poutish misadventures, his whining self-absorption are not sufficiently madcap or endearing to win us onto his side. Throughout his adolescence, his one year at Columbia, his lap-dog pursuit of several women, his Cook's tour of Europe, his own initiation into dadhood, he continues to seem precisely the pathetic, enervated schlemiel that he feels so wronged at being taken for. . . . Tama Janowitz has a fine comedic inventiveness, especially as applied in light dabs to character. But in *American Dad* that inventiveness is consistently undermined by the lack of grace—and, even more so, precision—in her language, the lack of subordination of emphasis among climaxes and interludes, the lack of narrative elision. The Przepasniak family might have been much more effectively portrayed in a tightly crafted short story. (p. 15)

> *David Quammen "Family Matters," in* The New York Times Book Review, *May 17, 1981, pp. 15, 24.*

GARRETT EPPS

Tama Janowitz is an extremely gifted writer, and her book [*American Dad*] is built around a memorable and original portrait of an authentic American type, the monster shrink.

Robert Abraham Przepasniak, MD, is a kind of psychiatric Great Santini, "Paul Bunyan, Abraham Lincoln, Hunter S. Thompson rolled into one, dark and strict, red and angry, a living legend." He jettisons his dreamy wife Mavis and their two children, Earl and Bobo, for a life of sexual freedom; but he is unwilling to let them out of his enormous shadow. When Mavis, a novice poet, shows faint signs of independence, Przepasniak flies into a rage, assaults her, and accidentally kills her in the melee. Then, on furlough from prison, he maims himself in a chain-saw accident.

There is not a false note in the presentation of this engaging villain. His intellectual but brutal appearance, his obsession with strength, his self-righteousness and manipulation, blend convincingly with a constant self-pity. . . . Janowitz has a sharp eye for the things of this world—the moldering contents of Przepasniak's refrigerator, the moldy old book Mavis collects, the flowers and trees on the family farm—and her sensuous writing enlivens the book. She also has a precocious satirical eye for literary humbug. Mavis's poems are "about Americans in the 1970s, strange, queer characters my mother imagined the United States was peopled with. There were men who fed flies to Venus Fly Traps, mailmen in the shape of fish who nibbled on letters they refused to deliver. Fat men, tumescent cake-eaters, babies with dandruff." But Dr. Przepasniak is offstage by page 137, and Earl takes over. Earl is a sorry fellow—a characterization he would not dispute. "I had turned out to be a drab, beaverish person with large nostrils, full of desires but lacking ambition," he explains. He rampages ignorantly around England and France, spouting dubious aphorisms ("Queer as bats, was all I could think about the French"). He also undergoes a half-hearted sexual initiation with Emma and Elmira, two London demimondaines who might easily live

next door to Johnny Rotten. This part of the book is thin gruel, though portentously presented:

> These are a young man's experiences in the world of sense and sensuousness that are, in their way, sacred and religious rituals of the highest order: a 'coming of age' by an American in England, food for thought for anthropologists in every land and climate, opening the publishing doors for many volumes of photographs, footnotes, explications, bibliographies and jobs for the masses of young would-be sociologists and paleontologists.

Earl may take all this seriously, but I couldn't. It wasn't exactly funny, either, and I began yearning for the stylish villainy of Poppa Przepasniak. Earl's adventures are mostly filler, marring what is otherwise one of the most impressive first novels I've read in a long time.

> *Garrett Epps, in a review of "American Dad," in* The New Republic, *Vol. 184, No. 23, June 6, 1981, p. 40.*

R. Z. SHEPPARD

The special effects [in *Slaves of New York*] are in the downtown style, a loose merger of traditional bourgeois bohemianism, '60s camp and the latest in celebrity mongering and real estate. In these advertisements for herself, Janowitz masquerades as a candidate for one of her own stories. Her characters include artists, gallery owners, designers and hangers-on, who seem to be stuck to the page with suction cups. Generally the humor ranges from adolescent to collegiate. Stash Stosz paints allegories using cartoon figures like Bullwinkle, Baba Looey, Chilly Willy and Mickey Mouse. Artist Marley Mantello takes the historical approach: a gouache entitled *Geoffrey Chaucer's First Date*. An occasional line has a graduate degree. Says Eleanor, an erstwhile jewelry maker: "If I ever get some kind of job security and/or marital security, I'm going to join the feminist movement."

Janowitz's intentions are satiric and sociological. Somebody orders Perrier and water; someone else proposes interior-decoration therapy for people with bad aesthetics. Sometimes it is hard to tell Janowitz from Lebowitz (Fran), who made a splash in 1978 with *Metropolitan Life*. Both writers rely heavily on a deadpan delivery. Lebowitz does more and better one-liners; the author of *Slaves* piles on more bizarre details with a heavy hand. Her stories can have arresting beginnings: "After I got my hair cut at High Style 2000 on Lexington Avenue, I was hit by a car"; "Fred had a problem: he liked to approach strange girls on the street and offer to take them shopping at Tiffany's." But Janowitz has no follow-through. Part of the problem is a lack of structure that presumably is meant to mirror the shapelessness of her characters' lives. Also her language is grating and imprecise. Lines such as "It's like drinking freeze-dried headache" and "Once again my vision is gathering detritus" suggest visceral connections that are not quite made.

Janowitz is energetic but too indiscriminate to be a good social observer or satirist. She is a flaneuse, a cultural pedestrian who wanders the streets of downtown Manhattan but does not exhibit any strong emotional or intellectual ties to her subject. As with MTV, style substitutes for values. (pp. 80-1)

R. Z. Sheppard, "Downtown," in Time, *Vol. 127, No. 26, June 30, 1986, pp. 80-1.*

JAY McINERNEY

Like Damon Runyon's Broadway, Tama Janowitz's Downtown is a stylized version of an actual tribal region of Manhattan. In Runyon's New York everyone is either a gangster or a moll. In *Slaves of New York* everyone is an artist—painter, performance artist, jewelry designer, makeup artist. Clearly there's at least one short-story writer lurking in the background, although this is more of a visual than a verbal culture, a fact that is reflected in the relative poverty of the local argot. The gangsters are more articulate. This particular locale has been much surveyed of late, on page and screen, but Ms. Janowitz carves out her own piece of the dance floor.

Slaves of New York anatomizes a class of Philistine Esthetes, careerist painters and hustling gallery owners whose knowledge of the tradition extends back as far as Hanna-Barbera and the early Warner Brothers cartoons, and whose role models are overnight millionaires. In this crowd, the name Raphael is more likely to conjure up a drug dealer than the painter. The concept of "important restaurants" is proposed.

The most consistently obnoxious of these Philithetes is Marley Mantello, a painter who narrates five of the tales. A self-proclaimed genius, Marley uses his grotesque self-confidence to make his peers miserable. Ms. Janowitz gives Marley more than enough rope to hang himself. "Ginger Booth, my dealer, handled only male artists and I was the most important. She had said this to me often, when I called her at three or four in the morning just to check." . . .

In **"The Slaves in New York"** we meet Eleanor, a 28-year-old jewelry designer *manquée* who lives with her graffiti artist boyfriend, Stash, and who subsequently reappears in five of the stories. A small-town girl who can never quite take her surroundings for granted, Eleanor is an ideal witness, a Dorothy in this land of Oz. She is still surprised by the world around her, still hick enough to consider a latex rubber evening dress something out of the ordinary, too naïve to realize that a fashion designer she dates after moving out on Stash is homosexual. In fact, she might be right out of a movie from the 1950's. "I was practically thirty years old, unmarried, and my marketability was going downhill fast."

Eleanor tries hard to be hip. A slave of fashion, like everyone else in the book, she's also a slave to the real-estate situation. She has moved in with Stash because—love and all that aside—she can't afford the rent on her own apartment. Then she finds that she can't afford to be herself, or be too honest with Stash, for fear he'll throw her out. It's his lease, after all. He's successful and she's not. . . .

The stories concerning Eleanor, as well as others in the collection, are photo-realistic in mode, mildly ironic in tone. Which is to say, they would not be out of place in *The New Yorker,* where in fact several have appeared. There is a second kind of story here—tales verging on fantasy and fable, with the artificial, playful texture of cartoons. They're fun, which is what they're supposed to be. These shorter pieces reflect a downtown esthetic, a campy postmodernism—the literary equivalent of the paintings of Kenny Scharf and Keith Haring. In **"You and the Boss,"** a young woman performs a lobotomy on Bruce Springsteen's wife and takes her place beside the Boss. (Bruce doesn't notice.) **"Modern Saint #271"** is a kind of middle-class slumming fantasy: a rich Jewish girl becomes a prostitute and dabbles in heroin. . . .

Frank O'Connor ended his most famous story, "Guests of the Nation," with a sentence he borrowed from Gogol, and which O'Connor suggested should be applicable to at least one character in any short story. A young rebel who has been forced to participate in an execution concludes, "And anything that ever happened me after I never felt the same about again." The closing words of one of Ms. Janowitz's stories in *Slaves of New York* strike me as equally emblematic of her own practice: a woman whose boyfriend has betrayed her has "settled into her old ways, neither joyful nor despairing."

Although the people in Tama Janowitz's stories frequently change partners and artistic media, though they expect to be discovered at any moment, they do not experience catharsis or epiphany. Most of these stories are static: actions and gestures succeed one another without much consequence. There is seldom much in the way of closure. Eleanor's maddening passivity is essentially reflected in the narrative stance.

Reading many of these tales, I couldn't suppress an image of the author wearing sunglasses, standing at a safe or, perhaps, sophisticated distance. One often feels she does not take her characters seriously enough, or far enough. As a writer, it *is* possible to be too hip. Some readers will wish that Ms. Janowitz pressed her characters harder, brought us closer to their secrets and their dreams, brought *them* closer to something— knowledge, passion, hope, despair. Others will be grateful for the shrewd observation, the skewed invention, which are the gifts of a singular talent.

Jay McInerney, "I'm Successful and You're Not," in The New York Times Book Review, *July 13, 1986, p. 7.*

CAROL ANSHAW

Tama Janowitz might want to start looking over her shoulder; she seems in imminent danger of being run over by her publicity machine. Relentlessly, it grinds her life into lore. Before you even get to her short story collection, *Slaves of New York,* you're knee-deep in Janowitziana. . . .

As a writer, Janowitz is much less egregious than she is as a celebrity. Like Mister Rogers, she tells us about her neighborhood—in this case, the downtown art scene. Most of her chronicles follow either Marley Mantello, a comically arrogant painter on the verge of making it big, or Eleanor, a listless earring designer in the long, inexorable process of being dumped by her artist boyfriend, Stash. They and their acquaintances are permanent transients in a dress-up and play-act milieu full of style without the slightest pretense of substance. And a certain number of readers will be attracted to Janowitz's stories (as they are to Jay McInerney's) for a peek inside her world, because they couldn't get an invitation or stay up late enough. They may be disappointed. Janowitz's pageant is elaborately costumed, but underneath the green hair and Day-Glo red mascara, the rubber dresses and accessory parrots, it's pretty much still Kerouac territory below her 14th Street. Boys get to be famous and outrageous. Girls get to be girlfriends—*if* they behave themselves, act like good little loftwives, and keep a fierce eye out for the Other Woman. They are resigned to loutish boyfriends, bad sublets, nowhere part-time jobs, and vaporous notions of self. Riding in a taxi, Eleanor says of herself: "I take out my little mirror from my pocketbook and check to make sure I'm still there, then I put on more eyeliner and lipstick.''

These are women so passive that drift is their aerobics. If they have hope, it's that something good might happen *to* them (as when Eleanor's desultory jewelry work is discovered and elevated to ''hot'' status). Their imagination stops short of making something happen themselves. The book is infused with a post-feminism that makes it look like the women's movement was just a wrong number. Art is negated in much the same way. Artists are shown as poseurs, self-aggrandizers, entrepreneurs. Most of their work is caricatured as the most conceptually bankrupt TV/movie referent pop. . . .

It's hard to know just how Janowitz feels about all this. She takes the comfy chair just above the action and chooses as protagonists the one-dimensional, foible-filled sorts who used to turn up as side characters. The Mr. Micawbers. While this makes for breezy, amusing stories, it keeps her from reaching in, pulling out the really interesting stuff—passion and fear and heartbreak. Typically, the worst traumas her characters experience are conversational *faux pas* and menu indecision. An exception is a story titled **"Snowball,"** about a gallery owner named Victor, who's on the entrance ramp to breakdown. Here, Janowitz harrowingly captures the moment when dawn loses its power to erase night terrors and becomes just a place for them to merge into daytime paranoia. Everything on the surface of her stories looks and feels and sounds righter than right, but in this one she gets under the high-gloss veneer with a central character she—and we—can care about. Maybe she'll do more of this, taking a cue from Truman Capote, who knew that, between parties, Holly Golightly had to get the ''mean reds.''

Carol Anshaw, ''Hype Springs Eternal,'' in The Village Voice, *Vol. XXXI, No. 31, August 5, 1986, p. 46.*

THOMAS DePIETRO

[*Slaves of New York* is a] collection as wild in its unevenness as it is deliberate in its weirdness. Janowitz thrives on the quotidian oddities found in the East Village and thereabouts. Her rock-and-roll sensibility is new-wave and, although her characters prefer groups like Teenage Jesus and The Circle Jerks, she herself comes off like a literary Cyndi Lauper, a connoisseur of kitsch capable of being assimilated into the mainstream.

Janowitz's masterful story, **"The Slaves in New York,"** introduces the haplessly hip couple who drift in and out of focus throughout the volume (**"Who's on First?,"** **"Physics,"** and **"Patterns"** are just a few of the stories in which they reappear). The ''apartment situation'' being what it is in Manhattan, Eleanor, a jewelry maker who's always slightly out of step with what's in—she's still making plastic James Bond-doll earrings—can't afford to leave the functional digs she shares with Stash, her graffiti artist boyfriend, best known for his painting, ''The Wisdom of Solomon,'' in which the cartoon characters Quick Draw MacGraw and Babalooey saw an Eskimo baby in half. When Eleanor, enslaved by both fashion and real estate, meets a South African who writes, in her words, ''political-type novels,'' Stash's slave-driver instinct asserts itself. Eleanor's innocent chats over coffee with Mikell, though infuriating to Stash, nevertheless suggest that something meaningful is going on in this story—an ironic commentary on Western forms of (self-) oppression perhaps. But none of the other post-modern parables collected by Janowitz, especially those told by her whacked-out narrator Eleanor, supply the kind of gloss needed here to sort out her intentions. In short, we're never certain whether these often disposable tales are a symptom or a parody of the junk culture Janowitz chronicles so well. Wicked send-ups of Yale feminist deconstructors (**"Engagements"**) and of Springsteen's proletarian posturing (**"You and the Boss"**) assure her status among those who blur the distinctions between high and low culture. The rest of us are desperately seeking guidance through her uncharted ironies.

Thomas DePietro, in a review of ''Slaves of New York,'' in The Hudson Review, *Vol. XXXIX, No. 3, Autumn, 1986, p. 489.*

Gabriel (David) Josipovici

1940-

French-born English critic, novelist, dramatist, short story writer, and editor.

Josipovici is an important contemporary literary theorist and a leading experimental fiction writer. Most critics agree that Josipovici most effectively posits his theories in *The World and the Book: A Study of Modern Fiction* (1971), a controversial work in which he urges readers to "remove the spectacles of habit" when reading unconventional fiction. Like antinovelist and theorist Alain Robbe-Grillet, Josipovici contests the value of the traditional realistic novel, believing that a work of fiction should concentrate on reconstructing rather than imitating the world. Josipovici adheres to this principle in his own fiction, utilizing fragmented dialogue, disjointed narrative, interior monologue, and other experimental techniques to challenge preconceived ideas about the nature of fiction and reality.

In *The World and the Book,* Josipovici extols the virtues of such authors as T. S. Eliot, Marcel Proust, and Vladimir Nabokov, comparing their unorthodox approaches to literature with the innovative techniques of François Rabelais and Miguel de Cervantes. David Lodge summarized Josipovici's outlook: "It is from literary realism (and all the fallacies about art and reality on which it is, in Josipovici's view, based) that modern fiction has freed us, restoring to us ... an understanding of the laws of existence, of the nature of human consciousness and human perception, of the inevitable gap between our desires and reality." While Josipovici's extreme anti-realist position was faulted by several critics, many agreed that *The World and the Book* presented a bold and imaginative approach to literature. Josipovici's other volumes of criticism, while not as highly regarded as *The World and the Book,* also display his insight. In *The Lessons of Modernism* (1977), Josipovici states that modern art, by definition, must be "anti-art," which demands that the audience concern itself with the process of creation rather than with the personality of the artist or the illusion produced by the artwork. In *Writing and the Body* (1982), Josipovici attempts to "examine the role which language, writing and books play in our lives, the lives we live with our bodies." *The Mirror of Criticism: Selected Reviews, 1977-1982* (1983) collects book reviews Josipovici contributed to various periodicals.

In his fiction, as in his critical works, Josipovici explores various ways of perceiving reality through unconventional approaches to fiction. Josipovici's reliance on dialogue to develop his themes has led critics to liken his works to the plays of Harold Pinter. His first novel, *The Inventory* (1968), concerns a young man who takes inventory of a dead man's belongings and becomes involved with acquaintances and relatives of the deceased. Josipovici creates a circuitous structure by juxtaposing recurring images and by repeating scenes and verbal patterns. *Words* (1971) examines a failing marriage and the inability of language to mend human relationships. *Migrations* (1977) focuses on a man in physical and spiritual anguish struggling to comprehend his condition. The novel's subtly varying repetition of events prompted critics to compare this work with the antinovels of Alain Robbe-Grillet.

Courtesy of Gabriel Josipovici

In *The Air We Breathe* (1981), a woman attempts to free herself from the stifling grip of her past. Considered one of Josipovici's most difficult novels, this work features a point of view that shifts between first-person consciousness and third-person narrative, as well as rapid temporal and spatial changes. In addition, unrelated conversations or events intrude upon the consciousness and memories of the characters. *Contre-Jour: A Triptych after Pierre Bonnard* (1986) consists of the interior monologues of painter Pierre Bonnard's wife and daughter and Bonnard's short note to a friend reporting his wife's death. Through the observations of the female protagonists, Josipovici explores the damaging effect of an artist's fanatical passion on those around him. In addition to his works of fiction and criticism, Josipovici has published several collections of short stories and has written a number of plays for radio and theater.

(See also *CLC,* Vol. 6; *Contemporary Authors,* Vols. 37-40, rev. ed.; and *Dictionary of Literary Biography,* Vol. 14.)

GILLIAN TINDALL

I wish I had more space to write about Gabriel Josipovici's first novel [*The Inventory*] which, though slight, suggests such an interesting view of reality and memory that one is eager for the next attempt. The 'inventory' of the title is being compiled in a squalid flat by a young man. To a girl who hangs around making coffee this mass of objects represents the sum of a father-and-son couple who lived here and whom she visited— or did she 'invent' them? We move from one time to another, from an actual conversation to a remembered one, or to one repeated with variations. Light relief is provided by the chatter of lost tourists, a ghastly housewife and her three brats. The shades of Pinter and Ionesco preside, but something original has been done here.

> *Gillian Tindall, "Bright Brute," in* New Statesman, *Vol. 76, No. 1960, October 4, 1968, p. 435.*

THE TIMES LITERARY SUPPLEMENT

Mr. Gabriel Josipovici's delicately structured first novel [*The Inventory*] is concerned with the way in which past events are transmuted by memory, by the need to dissemble, and by guilt; it is concerned, also, with emotional solitariness.

The book is at once complex (in its implications) and lucid (in its style) and any kind of plot summary is bound to do it less than justice. However, the basic situation is this: Joe Hyman is sent to make an inventory of the contents of a flat. Each day he is accompanied in this task by two women—Susan and Gill—who are relatives of the two men who once occupied the flat. Sam, the younger man, has died, but his influence in the story is considerable, for Susan, who lived with the two men for a time, claims to have provoked a crisis which led to Sam's suicide.

In Susan's anxious, faltering monologue, we are given the past—a memory made uncertain by her sense of guilt, by her evasions and by her inventions. The present consists of Gill— an inefficient mother at the mercy of her unruly and slightly sinister children—and of Joe's attempts to discover the truth about the relationship between Sam and Susan. Let into this pattern are fragments of the inventory Joe is compiling—the precise, ordered documentation of objects which form a palpable and immutable record of the past, in contrast to Susan's confused, partly falsified telling of it. The monologue is repetitious or, rather, it echoes itself; broken by dialogue or small events, it picks up and elaborates a previous memory or an ecdotal splinter, then hurries on. The structure, then, is fugue-like, and aptly so, for this term could also be applied (in the medical sense) to Susan's fragmented recollections. . . .

[There] is barely a superfluous line; nor, it should be stressed, is there any affected obscurity. The book is intriguing, certainly, and Mr. Josipovici's inventiveness, coupled with his skill in construction, makes *The Inventory* an impressive debut.

> *"Adding It Up," in* The Times Literary Supplement, *No. 3479, October 31, 1968, p. 1218.*

JOHN CAREY

Gabriel Josipovici's *Words* aims to reproduce the effect of desultory conversation, and succeeds. Composed entirely of smalltalk, frequently too small to struggle to the right-hand margin, it seems at first like a Pinter film-script which has somehow come adrift from its actors. The reader, one gathers, is intended to imagine vast emotional problems wallowing around under the dribble of dialogue. This makes it something of a do-it-yourself novel, though it does manage eventually to pose

one definite question. Will dull Louis elope with globe-trotting Jo who has dropped in on him and his wife en route to San Francisco? 'No' is the answer, of course, since any positive action would disrupt the tedium which the novelist has been scrupulously creating. Throughout Jo's little girl holds her tongue and glowers at the grownups. Wise child. (p. 625)

> *John Carey, "The Caressing of Fergus," in* The Listener, *Vol. 86, No. 2223, November 4, 1971, pp. 624-25.*

THE TIMES LITERARY SUPPLEMENT

Louis and Helen Rawlings, already cooped up in their not-long-purchased and half-renovated country house with Louis's brother, Peter and his wife Tina—we do not know how they all actually make a *living*—are visited briefly by Louis's old girl friend, Jo, en route for San Francisco, and her clinging, silent six-year-old. . . . Beyond this, most of Gabriel Josipovici's second novel [*Words*] is mystery; to be elucidated (which is the point of things) only through close reading of the constant dialogue in which the book is almost entirely couched. The situation emotionally is indeed obscure. . . .

Mr Josipovici's talent is real. His way with that mild, foolish inconsequential chatter which conceals lurking strengths of feeling, is beautifully witty and accurate. But the blurb invokes Harold Pinter, and his failure to put us in the clear about some essential features of his characters makes us wonder wheather he is relying too much on a received technique, setting things too firmly in that odd Pinter half-world where anything *could* be so but never actually *is*. The final outcome, and message, of *Words* is cleverly achieved, and altogether valid: time still operates while the chatter goes on, and time is the great decider. Jo and Louis fail to elope, even when they are planning it, the scheme is somehow talked out; things stay the same. The power of the book is certainly there in its tiny, chilling implications (offered with touches of alert and effective humour). But one begins to hope for evidence in future books that something more substantial and more clearly located in recognizable living will prove Mr Josipovici's abilities beyond doubt.

> *"Devious Dialogue," in* The Times Literary Supplement, *No. 3637, November 12, 1971, p. 1409.*

JONATHAN RABAN

[*The World and the Book* is] the most ambitious and complete apologia for the *nouveau roman* to have appeared in English. Josipovici is truculently anti-realist; he strides confidently through world literature, pointing out every self-conscious rhetorical gesture, every narrative sleight-of-hand, as evidence that the business of the book is to reconstruct, not dully mimic, the world. Langland, Chaucer, Dante, Rabelais, are formed into a scrum of heavy forwards to support the attack of his light-weight French wingers. It's an impressive, learned, often illuminating performance. His chapter on "The World as a Book" is a brilliantly documented mixture of medieval theology and astute criticism, centring on Hugh of St Victor's remark that the visible world was 'a book written by the finger of God'. Yet Josipovici's readings tend to reduce every work he discusses to a jumble of monkish pedantries and scholarly conceits. After the fire of an argument which takes in theology, the rise of science and its relation to realism, and the complicated crosscurrents of modern aesthetics, it is especially disappointing to reach chapters on Nabokov, Golding and Bellow which are merely predictable pieces of heavy-footed exegesis. He seems a prisoner of his own grim art; a critic who yearns for a world freed not just from the ordinary slow resistence of life, but from books as well—a world of pure structures where the reader-author can entertain a constant stream of unsullied fictions. (p. 864)

Jonathan Raban, *"Desperate Reveries," in* New Statesman, *Vol. 82, No. 2126, December 17, 1971, pp. 864-65.*

THE TIMES LITERARY SUPPLEMENT

Great literary criticism is the most evasive of achievements. Gabriel Josipovici seems blessed with all the gifts: a lucid style, vast imaginative energy, a huge storehouse of reading, a living concern for art, as well as a certain self-conscious humility at this whole buzz and fuzz in the face of aesthetic experience. . . .

Britain is not over endowed with critics of his range, who take in the classics, Dante, Chaucer, Rabelais as readily as Hawthorne or Bellow, Nabokov or Borges. Nevertheless there is something unsatisfactory about [*The World and the Book*], viewed as a thing in itself, a total world. The trouble, as so often, seems to be that the chance offers of academic life—to contribute to a symposium here, or a critical review there—have intervened. Though the argument is complete, its form is far from inevitable. This work too is controlled less by its structure within than from surface to surface as an organic experience as a critical *recherche*. . . . Himself a novelist, [Josipovici] has a deep intuitive grasp of the process of writing. Constantly alert to language itself as "process" rather than "meaning", his own critical practice seems to follow the endless path of Kafka's Sancho following Don Quixote, coming

> at last to the realization that this *activity* is itself the meaning for which he had been searching for so long. Then at last he understands that his perseverance has led him not to the discovery of a new world, but to the apprehension of the most alien yet nearest land of all: his own body.

Mr Josipovici, then, is that rare critical writer whose own responses suggest a series of self-explorations rather than an anatomy of criticism. No wonder, though he has learnt so much from Northrop Frye and Roland Barthes, he needs occasionally to take up cudgels with both. Yet he cannot divest himself wholly of the magisterial role. His brain is simply too active, perhaps. Take a passage, from [the concluding chapter "The World and the Book"], on Dante. That "Dante's universe is built on a series of analogies" is confronted with the contemporary paradox—"le démon de l'analogie", as Mallarmé called it:

> For to discover correspondences in the world around us does not lead to the sensation that we are inhabiting a meaningful universe; on the contrary, it leads to the feeling that what we had taken to be "the world" is only the projection of our private compulsions: *analogy* becomes a sign of *dementia,*

which is complex and arresting enough. Yet, like some Victorian decorator in his abhorrence of a white space, the imaginative trajectory or leap, he must rapidly list and analytically tick off a list of Dante's analogies:

between the physical and spiritual works; between secular and sacred history; between the history of the universe and that of each man; between the natural cycle and the Christian year; between the days of the week and the ages of man. . . .

Such processes are all-pervasive, leaving readers suitably dazzled no doubt. Because this is a bravura exercise. Yet on almost every page one may wonder whether the play of mind need release quite such a clutter; and, indeed, whether the analytic process, once begun, is not itself another slippery surface. Is it rigorous enough? Are there not, perhaps, further analogies than those listed? In the *Divina Commedia* are these really analogies, or correspondences, at all rather than variant *effects* from a single cause? Yet all this hardly matters if the argument can be sustained, as so often it can, even with a diminution of supporting detail.

For all his great gifts, then, Mr Josipovici has yet to decide whether he is writing as a brilliant academic or as a man of letters. . . . So the whole remains confused, now didactic, now persuasive, as if scholar and thinker, academic and novelist, were in constant competition; and if occasionally it rises to a more strident pitch, this is inevitable for the lone, sane voice, the lone, free voice in a wilderness of coterie jargon (French) and ossified common sense (British style).

Yet the barebone argument is not strikingly original. The translation of the medieval concept of the world as a book, via Mallarmé's "Grand Oeuvre" and Wittgenstein, Nabokov, Golding and Robbe-Grillet (among modern mentors) to the book as a world is not in itself an unusual journey of salvation. . . .

The contemporary North and South American scenes as well as certain Italian critics are noticeably absent. But, if nothing else, this is likely to be read as the most stimulating English textbook on the "anti-novel". Even on this pedestrian level it has few rivals and should help widen the context in which the works of a Borges, Beckett, Bellow are studied.

"The Contours of the Labyrinth," in The Times Literary Supplement, *No. 3652, February 25, 1972, p. 216.*

DAVID LODGE

Addressing an international Symposium on Literary Style in 1969, Roland Barthes concluded his lecture on "Style and its Image" with the following words:

> . . . if up until now we have looked at the text as a species of fruit with a kernel (an apricot, for example), the flesh being the form and the pit being the content, it would be better to see it as an onion, a construction of layers (or levels, or systems) whose body contains, finally, no heart, no kernel, no secret, no irreducible principle, nothing except the infinity of its own envelopes—which envelope nothing other than the unity of its own surfaces.

The editor of the Symposium's proceedings [Seymour Chatman] reports:

> Barthes' final reduction of content to form raised some questions. It was argued that it is one thing to say that even the smallest details of a

text have a structure, but quite another to say
that that is all there is, that there is nothing *but*
structure. Surely there must be such a thing as
the subject of a literary work. . . .

In this exchange we see exposed, with the clarity almost of
caricature, a disagreement about the relationship of art to reality
which divides not only French structuralists from Anglo-Saxon
empiricists, but also individual critics and schools of criticism
within these national and cultural groups; indeed, it would not
be an exaggeration to say that we have here a critical issue to
which all others, especially in the criticism of fiction, are
connected. As its title indicates, Gabriel Josipovici's *The World
and the Book: A Study of Modern Fiction,* is directly conerned
with this issue. For most of its length, the author appears to
be taking up a position very close to that of Barthes in the
quotations above, but towards the end it becomes evident that
(like, perhaps, Barthes' interlocutors) he is looking for a space
between the onion and apricot concepts of the work of art, in
which to operate dialectically. This conclusion is both understandable and commendable, but leaves one feeling a little
cheated by the militancy of the earlier argument: feeling, too,
that Mr. Josipovici hasn't earned the right to be quite so dismissive about Anglo-American criticism of the novel as he is.

Let me say at once, however, that *The World and the Book*
seems to me one of the best first books of criticism to have
appeared in England for a long time . . . and I warmly recommend it to anyone interested in literature of any period
between Dante and Robbe-Grillet. Not the least distinction of
The World and the Book is that it has that kind of scope and
fully vindicates the author's ambition in taking on so much.
Mr. Josipovici is intelligent, eloquent and formidably well-
read. He cares passionately about literature and can communicate his enthusiasm infectiously to the reader. At a time when
literary academia lies stifled and groaning under the weight of
its own loveless, unloved professional publications, Mr. Josipovici's stimulating and educative voice comes like a current
of cool and invigorating air. If his book is not, in the last
analysis, as powerful as it promises to be, it still leaves us
much to be grateful for.

The World and the Book has a somewhat misleading subtitle.
It is not so much a study of modern fiction as a prolegomena
to such a study. It offers both a theory and a history of literature:
a theory of literary value, and a polemical history which shows
how the theory is fulfilled in a certain kind of writing—'modern
fiction'. Thus the enterprise bears a close resemblance to that
carried out by T. S. Eliot on behalf of 'modern poetry' in the
early decades of this century. Like Eliot—like, indeed, many
grand theorists of a literary orientation—Josipovici is an exponent of the idea of a Second Fall. For Eliot, this Fall was a
politico-theological-literary complex occurring in the seventeenth century, in which Catholicism was dispossessed by Protestantism, Monarchism by Democracy, and a unified poetic
sensibility by a dissociated one. Modern poetry of the kind he
and Pound were writing aimed to put the dissociated sensibility
together again and to articulate—perhaps even redeem—the
wider cultural consequences of the Fall. That is a gross simplification, but not, I think, a gross distortion, of Eliot's position. For Josipovici, too, the Second Fall, though long in
preparation, occurred decisively round about the seventeenth
century, and the dire consequence for literature was not a dissociation of sensibility, but realism. It is from literary realism
(and all the fallacies about art and reality on which it is, in
Josipovici's view, based) that modern fiction has freed us,

restoring to us—not the unified and divinely meaningful universe of medieval Christianity, for that is lost forever, even to
Christians—but something equivalently valuable and liberating
for modern man: an understanding of the laws of existence, of
the nature of human consciousness and human perception, of
the inevitable gap between our desires and reality. It is for this
reason that he begins with a chapter on Proust and in his second
chapter goes back to Dante. For Proust is, in Josipovici's view,
the exemplary modern novelist, who makes the uncovering of
the 'laws of existence' the aim of his great novel [*A la recherche
du temps perdu*], and Dante the supreme voice of the medieval
Christian synthesis. . . . The *difference* between [*A la recherche
du temps perdu* and Dante's *Commedia*] is expressed by a shift
in the grammatical relationship between the two terms of Josipovici's title. The modern novel insists on the discontinuity
between the World *and* the Book, but to Dante the World could
be seen *as* a Book. This latter idea Josipovici derives from a
striking passage written by Hugh of St. Victor in the twelfth
century:

> For this whole visible world is a book written
> by the finger of God, that is, created by divine
> power; and individual creatures are as figures
> therein not devised by human will but instituted
> by divine authority to show forth the wisdom
> of the invisible things of God . . .

(pp. 171-73)

Drawing skilfully on [Erich] Auerbach and other, more spe-
cialised scholarship, Josipovici has written a very eloquent and
stirring chapter, entitled 'The World as a Book', celebrating
that 'medieval analogical synthesis' which, he suggests, began
to decay almost as soon as it had produced the *Commedia* and
the *Vita Nuova*. The decay is attributed to processes in both
religion and secular culture, which came to their maturity in
the Reformation and the renaissance. Dante's culture is, in
Josipovici's terms, the Paradise that writers and critics have
lost. 'It is only because the universe is itself seen as a book,
written by God, that the books of men can imitate it. Once the
universe ceases to be seen in this way then the criteria both
for understanding it and for understanding the 'real' meaning
of books and pictures seems to disappear'. It then becomes
essential for the literary artist to build into his fictions indications of the new, more problematical relationship between
the world and the book. Josipovici finds this happening as early
as Chaucer, those ironically presented narrative voices draw
attention to and question the reliability of his own artifice. . . .
This saving scepticism, this exposure of rhetoric in the very
act of exploiting it, is carried further in the work of Rabelais
and Sterne. But between these two writers occurred, finally
and decisively, Josipovici's Second Fall. This is dealt with in
a somewhat tendentious chapter entitled, 'Thoughts on the Rise
of the Novel'.

Ian Watt accounted for the rise of the novel, in his study of
that name, by showing how it responded, formally, to important developments in culture at large—individualism, puritanism, empiricism, etc. Josipovici, deploring these developments, uses them to account for the limitations of realistic
fiction. He maintains—convincingly, I think—that the Puritan
religious consciousness was inherently inferior, as a means of
generating allegory, to the medieval Catholic consciousness.
'The very ease with which meaning can be found (in *Pilgrim's
Progress*), the lack of any kind of tension such as we noticed
in Dante, gives us the feeling that there is something arbitrary
about this . . . it does not account for the opposition it sets up

between light and darkness, good and evil, and so on, it merely states it'. By a kind of sleight of hand, the relationship of the Puritan writer to experience is equated with the relationship of the reader to Defoe's realistic fictions: for 'the reader of any Defoe novel while he is immersed in it . . . there is nothing . . . to falsify what the imagination creates'. Proust is reintroduced as an edifying contrast: he describes the experience of being immersed, as reader, in the imagined worlds of novelists and he even provides us with such a world himself—but only to remind us of the inevitable falsifications of 'imagination', of the difference, for example, between the transparency of fictional characters and the opaqueness of real people. 'The act of perception or the act of consciousness is never a neutral one', says Josipovici, 'Proust and Homer and Virginia Woolf are all aware of this, but the traditional novel appears to ignore it. As a result it implicitly assumes that the world and the world as we are made conscious of it are one'. Represented by Defoe, and Defoe alone, the 'traditional novel' scarcely stands a chance in this contest. But such a reduction of realistic fiction is of course absurd and deeply misleading. *A la Recherche du Temps Perdu* is not, after all, the first novel which is 'a record of one disillusionment after another, the progressive discovery that nowhere does the world conform to my imagination of it'— such was also the theme of most of the great nineteenth-century novelists, from Jane Austen to George Eliot: indeed, it could be said to be *the* theme of the traditional novel, whence Proust himself undoubtedly derived it, rather than from Dante or Homer.

Josipovici uses the same manoeuvre when he turns to the language of realistic fiction, which in his view perpetuated certain fallacies about the relation between words and things that developed at the Renaissance. (The argument here depends fairly heavily on Walter Ong's work on Ramus, though Josipovici is anxious to dissociate himself from the Jesuit scholar's friend and ally, the most popular exponent of Second Fall theory in our time, Marshall McLuhan.) The idea that words might be disciplined into an exact one-to-one relationship with things, restoring a mythical state of primitive purity when, as Thomas Sprat put it, 'men delivered so many *things,* almost in an equal number of *words*', encouraged the false belief that words actually contained truths in a fixed and unalterable form, rather than belonging to a conventionalised communication system. Correspondingly it suppressed an overt recognition of the conventionality of art: 'From the start the writers of novels seem determined to pretend that their work is not made, that it simply exists'. Again, the sweeping assertion is attached to no specific novelist, other than Defoe. It might indeed be said of Defoe, and even of Richardson, but it plainly cannot be said of Fielding, to go no further. When Josipovici says, in this context, 'Talk of self-conscious narrators and the like is beside the point', he is saying in effect, 'I have made up my mind—don't confuse me with evidence'.

As the book proceeds, this impression is confirmed: Josipovici's defence of what he calls 'modern fiction', subtle and perceptive in its positive aspect, is damaged rather than reinforced by his prejudice against what he calls 'the traditional novel'—a prejudice which leads him not only to travesty the latter, but to deny its continuity with the former. Representative of the consequent distortions is this comment on Bellow's *Herzog*:

> Bellow, through his fiction, has been able to articulate the variety and richness of the world without being overwhelmed by it and without

on the other hand imposing upon it the rigid categorisations of the traditional novelist who only includes as much of the world as is necessary for his plot.

'Traditional novelist' here can only be a synonym for 'bad novelist', for as soon as one tests the description against one's experience of, say, Dickens or George Eliot, it collapses. It is almost a definition of the great nineteenth-century novelists that they articulated the multitudinousness of the world without being overwhelmed by it, and it is surely *non*-realist narrative forms, like allegory and romance, that are most likely to impose 'rigid categorisation' on experience, and to include only so much of the world as is necessary for their plots. In fact *Herzog* itself is a novel directly in the realistic tradition, and it is only the exigencies of Josipovici's thesis which compel him to argue that it is something else in order to express his admiration for it.

The other novelists to whom Josipovici devotes separate chapters—Hawthorne, Nabokov and Golding—fit the thesis better, in that they explicitly question the assumptions of realism. They also, of course, exploit the resources of realism, but this is something that Josipovici allows for, at least in the latter stages of his discourse:

> The modern novel is an anti-novel. Not because it sets itself up in direct opposition to the novel, but because it enlists the help of the novel to lull the reader into a false sense of security, and then, by pointing to its own premises, pitches him into reality.

This is certainly a kind of modern novel, and one particularly attractive to writers at the present time, but it is not the only viable mode for the novel, and the special value Josipovici attributes to it is, I believe, to be found in the other kinds of fiction, including his despised 'traditional novel'. That value is, in the last analysis, a moral or therapeutic one: it is the shock administered to 'our pride and narcissism' when the book 'reveals itself as a pure object', and thus compels us to recognise the gap between the world as it is and as we are made conscious of it. (pp. 173-76)

When Josipovici says that 'To imagine, like the traditional novelist, that one's work is an image of the real world, to imagine that one can communicate directly to the reader what it is that one uniquely feels, that is to fall into the real solipsism, which is, to paraphrase Kierkegaard on despair, not to know that one is in a state of solipsism', he expresses a genuine insecurity, in our culture, about knowledge and communication. This explains why so many modern novelists have built insecurity into the structure and texture of their writing, setting fiction and non-fiction, realism and fantasy, against each other within the same work; and why the techniques of the nineteenth-century realistic novelists will no longer serve in an unmodified form. (pp. 176-77)

I applaud Josipovici's defence of the anti-novel against prescriptive realists like John Bayley; I deplore his insistence that all good novels must be anti-novels in his own sense of the term. This attitude is not unconnected with my own practice of fiction. Since Gabriel Josipovici is the author of two published novels, it seems natural to look at them to see how far they exemplify the aesthetic expounded in the ***The World and the Book***.

The Inventory (1968) concerns a young lawyer who is cataloguing the effects of an old man who has just died, with the assistance (though that is scarcely the word) of two female relatives of the deceased—Gill Clem, the mother of three rambunctious children, and her cousin Susan. Susan, it appears, was emotionally involved with the old man's son, Sam, also dead in somewhat mysterious circumstances. Joe, the lawyer, falls in love with Susan. The narrative intertwines three time-sequences: the making of the inventory (distracted by casual conversation, coffee-drinking and the misbehaviour of the children); life with the old man and his son, as related by Susan in a rambling monologue; and Joe's dejected peregrinations around London after the inventory is finished, when he keeps phoning up Susan to make fruitless declarations of his love. There is a great deal of repetition. For instance, the characters frequently say the same things on different occasions. This is 'lifelike' to the extent that people *do* repeat themselves, but since the novel is highly condensed, the effect is artificial, drawing attention to the selectivity of the narrative. Furthermore, some scenes and exchanges of dialogue are repeated or 're-played', sometimes spliced with other scenes. There are also one or two farcical encounters in pubs and cafes which border on fantasy. In such ways the novel draws attention to its status as object. The atmosphere is weakly reminiscent of Beckett: a run-down physical environment, metaphysical vacancy, solipsism, a comically sad incapacity to cope with the contingency of experience, or to penetrate the minds of others. There is a gap between the empirical facts and the emotional facts which connected Susan with Sam and his father. Joe is cataloguing the former, Susan cannot communicate the latter, and is driven to making up stories to explain them. In short, there is no bridge between inventory and invention. The world is divested of poetry and rhetoric, which are invoked only to be mourned or parodied. (p. 182)

Words, published at the same time as *The World and the Book,* is even more self-denying in texture, consisting almost entirely of Pinteresque dialogue. Louis and his pregnant wife Helen are entertaining his brother Peter and the latter's wife Tina in their rambling house in the country near Southampton, when Jo, an old flame of Louis's, abruptly invites herself and her zombie-like infant daughter Gillian to stay, *en route* to America. This unexpected visitation, like a stone lobbed into a pond, sends ripples across the outwardly tranquil surface of the quartet's lives, setting up tensions between Louis and Helen, and placing a further strain on the already vulnerable marriage of Peter and Tina. The characters follow each other around the house and garden, feebly nagging, arguing, pleading, complaining and joking, in various permutations. Two questions preoccupy them: why has Jo come and what makes her daughter tick? Neither is satisfactorily answered. Lou and Jo toy verbally with the idea of running away, but inevitably it comes to nothing. It's a game, like most of the other conversations. Tennis and ping-pong, not surprisingly, are the main recreations of these characters.

The novel, then, is about failure in communication? Ah, but that is to fall into the apricot fallacy. *Words* is a novel about nothing but itself: hence the title. A novel should not mean but be. The words of the characters, flat and unpoetic in themselves, are arranged and counterpointed with subtle elegance. Framed, and often divided in the manner of a caesura, by a 'he said' or 'she said', they accumulate faint, tantalising rhythms, they fall into the pattern of stychomythia and enact other tropes of classical rhetoric: apoplanesis (evading the issue by digressing), aporia (true or feigned doubt or deliberation about an

issue), aposiopesis (stopping suddenly in mid-course, leaving a statement unfinished), epimone (frequent repetition of a phrase or question) and heterogenium (irrelevant answer to distract attention), to name but a few. . . . The unremitting banality of the experience rendered leaves our attention free to observe the formal patterns into which casual conversation falls. We peer myopically at the words, feeling, perhaps, that the patterns must conceal some depths of meaning; but no, there are no depths—none, anyway, that words could express—and we find in the polished surface of *these* words only the reflection of our own baffled eye. The little girl, Gillian, who retains the mystery of her motivation in the teeth of every adult attempt to break it down with cajolery, reproof, interrogation and badinage, is thus a symbol of the novel's aesthetic. Inasmuch as it defeats criticism by the total absence of pretensions, *Words* must be accounted a success; but it seems to me something of a Pyrrhic victory.

In *The World and the Book,* Josipovici says of the novel:

> it is the most natural literary form because in a sense it has no form . . . Provided it keeps within the very flexible limits of verisimilitude, it is entirely free to do what it pleases, to move in any direction it wants . . . for some writers, however, this freedom has been a souce not of pleasure but of irritation and anxiety. For if I can really say *anything* (provided I account for it in some vaguely plausible way) then what is the point of my saying anything? . . . And the reader of course is in a similar position, asking perhaps why he should continue with *this* particular book when the story it tells could just as well be told completely differently, or could even be replaced by another story altogether . . . modern art could be said to spring out of the artist's struggle to come to terms with these questions.

Here, as throughout his study, Josipovici seems to me to underestimate the extent to which the novel, at all periods, has observed its own laws, codes and conventions which keep it well to this side of formal anarchy. In particular, he greatly underestimates the importance of verisimilitude to the novelist *in the creative process.* The great realistic novelists did not feel it was enough to account for their fictions 'in some vaguely plausible way'—they expended enormous effort on making them totally convincing and consistent with the empirical facts of history. This commitment to history is thus a voluntary *restriction* on the writer's freedom which has the effect, precisely, of cutting out the question, 'Why this story rather than another?' It creates a bond of trust between writer and reader, for it is, however weak, the nearest equivalent our culture has to Irenaeus' 'rule of truth': as Josipovici admits, 'the premises upon which the novel is based . . . are the premises upon which most of us base our lives'. Which is not, of course, to deny that these premises may be questioned, subverted and transcended by other kinds of art: and Josipovici is right to point out how much modern fiction has done this, to the enrichment of literature. If his own novel, *Words,* does not seem very enriching, it may be because, instead of bursting through the conventions of realism, verisimilitude and plausibility, it contents itself with demonstrating how little can be said within them if you really try. By cutting down narrative to the bare minimum, by eliminating all the *description* (of people, weather, landscape, furnishings etc.) by which the novelist has traditionally conveyed attitudes and values under cover of providing factual information, by making the banal words of banal characters the only commentary upon their banal actions, Josipovici has written what is in many ways an ultra-realistic novel; but one in which one can scarcely say that realism is a voluntary restriction upon the writer's freedom, since there is little evidence that he wishes to exercise his freedom. The question *Words* raises is not whether there is point in saying anything, but whether the author has anything to say. In *The World and the Book* that is never in doubt, and one must hope that in future Mr. Josipovici will allow some of the creative energy of his criticism into his fiction. (pp. 183-85)

David Lodge, "Onions and Apricots; or, Was the Rise of the Novel a Fall from Grace? Serious Reflections on Gabriel Josipovici's 'The World and the Book'," in Critical Quarterly, Vol. 14, No. 2, Summer, 1972, pp. 171-85.

ROBERT W. UPHAUS

[*The World and the Book*] is full of learning and judgment. [Josipovici's] book is not merely ambitious in intent, for its intention, by and large, is more than matched by its execution. There is, as one would expect in a book of this length, a perceptible unevenness among its twelve chapters, but this is mainly apparent because some of the chapters, for this reader at least, are simply startling. At its best Josipovici's book is truly creative, for, like all good art, it transforms the reader's consciousness in such a way that we will never quite be able to return to our customary ways of reading literature. This is especially the case in chapters one through four and chapter seven which deal, respectively, with Proust, the world as a book, Chaucer, Rabelais, and Modernism and Romanticism. This is not to imply that these chapters, among others, do not cause some consternation. It is to say that in these chapters Josipovici successfully establishes himself as a committed "modern" by his own definition; that is, "What all the moderns have in common—perhaps the only thing they have in common—is an insistence on the fact that what previous generations had taken for *the world* was only *the world seen through the spectacles of habit.*" . . .

The key concept of the book, formed by the author's sense of literary history, may be explained by contrasting the two phrases "The World as a Book" and "The World and the Book." Dante stands as an example of the former concept, and Proust is an example of the latter. (p. 75)

Having established the above contrast as an analytic tool, Josipovici next examines two authors—Chaucer and Rabelais—for whom the world as a book is no longer a truth but a problem. If I understand Josipovici correctly, he wishes to establish the position that Chaucer and Rabelais, unlike Dante, no longer write out of a sense of "inspiration," which is to say they are not confident that their work is validated by a truth informing their work but larger than themselves. The presence of order and authority for them is now problematical; hence the works of Chaucer and Rabelais deal less with truth than with questions of interpretation. Indeed, it is Josipovici's view that with Rabelais and Chaucer "the whole question of critical attitude and mode of interpretation is the central *theme* of [their] work." . . . Art for Chaucer and Rabelais is not a book *of* Nature, but a book *about* Nature. What distinguishes Chaucer and Rabelais from Dante is a consciousness of convention. Josipovici thus observes about Chaucer's poetry, for example, that the reader is often led to contemplate the words of a poem rather than

participate in the poem's events; . . . similarly, he argues that in Rabelais "Language becomes a form of *action* rather than a mirror of a pre-established reality." (p. 76)

These first four chapters, then, both establish Josipovici's understanding of the uses of literary art from Dante to Rabelais and, just as importantly, they serve as a highly elaborate preface to his main interest: the nature of modern fiction. Chapter five, on the rise of the novel, thus acts as a bridge between the two halves of the book, with Shakespeare, for some reason, left conspicuously offstage. At any rate, to establish the radical nature of the modern novel Josipovici feels obliged to dispose of the 18th century novel, along with Ian Watt's influential study *The Rise of the Novel*. It is at this point that Josipovici distorts, or at least misunderstands, the kinds of novels written in the eighteenth century. He candidly admits that he distrusts most criticism of the novel written by "Anglo-Saxons," but this distrust leads him to argue, for example, that "From the start the writers of novels seem determined to pretend that their work is not *made*, but that it simply exists. . . . The effect is to divert attention from the fact that a novel, like a poem, is a made thing, a book, an object." . . . This statement is simply untrue, and the examples of *Tom Jones* and *Tristram Shandy* easily demonstrate why; for no two novels make the reader any more aware that what he thought was the world was, in fact, *"the world seen through the spectacles of habit."* Not only do these two novels represent this fact, but their respective narrators continually remind the reader of how much he is a creature of habit. If Josipovici has read *Tom Jones* and *Tristram Shandy*—and it's difficult to imagine he hasn't—then it appears he has uttered these statements mainly to highlight, and really exaggerate, the unique properties of the modern novel. I do believe that Proust and Robbe-Grillet are unique, but the really intriguing question, at this point, is, why does Josipovici engage in so blatant a distortion? I think the answer lies less in his general devotion to modernism than in his specific admiration for modern French criticism—Roland Barthes in particular.

Chapter eleven of this book is an examination of Barthes' criticism. Josipovici's ostensible intent is to mediate the quarrel between Barthes and his traditionalist opponents over what constitutes literary structure. But while this is an extremely useful chapter, its latent message is disturbing: the implication is that Anglo-Saxon criticism is so committed to the notion of tradition and the individual talent that it blunts what is truly modern, whereas recent French criticism, even in its excesses, is genuinely responsive to what is uniquely modern. This is why Josipovici rejects the eighteenth-century novel, along with Ian Watt. But this is also why chapters eight through ten, which deal with "the structuring activity of mind" in Nabokov, Bellow, and Golding, are disappointing and maddening. It's not that these chapters are uninteresting; it's simply that, because of his bias against Anglo-Saxon criticism, Josipovici has apparently failed to notice that what he says in these chapters has been said both before and, in some cases, better by Anglo-Saxons.

I do not, however, wish to end this review on a dissonant note. I remember once reading a review that began by saying that the primary question to ask of a new book is, "Did it need to be written?" I should answer . . . "Yes, in thunder!" about Josipovici's [*The World and the Book*]. (pp. 76-7)

Robert W. Uphaus, in a review of "The World and the Book: A Study of Modern Fiction," in Criticism, Vol. XVI, No. 1 (Winter, 1974), pp. 75-7.

DAVID LODGE

In the occasional essays collected under the title *The Lessons of Modernism,* Mr Josipovici has not added any substantially new ideas to those so richly provided in *The World and the Book,* and to that extent the more recent work is something of a disappointment. But there are some new applications of the ideas—to the Portuguese poet Fernando Pessao, to Walter Benjamin, to Stravinsky, Schoenberg, Britten, Maxwell Davies, Stockhausen—and some interesting adjustments of emphasis. Mr Josipovici's own concern with the practice of writing—he is, with Christine Brooke-Rose, a rare exponent of the *nouveau roman* in English—is more perceptible than before in his essays on writers (especially Kafka) who were obsessed by the imperative to write, and yet haunted by the gratuitousness of the activity, and the divorce it seems to entail from 'real life'. (p. 279)

Mr Josipovici views the human condition through the double lens of structuralism and a nostalgic post-Christian stoicism. Man is a mixture of culture and nature: a 'self' that is painfully constructed out of language and a biological body that is doomed to die. Post-Renaissance Europe, of which the realistic novel was the typical literary product, is characterised by Josipovici as 'a long nightmare . . . a mixture of lunatic pride and unbelievable naïveté', because it tried to pretend that the concept of the self was given by Nature, and to suppress the fact of death by such devices as the myth of progress and the creation of literary fictions that were lifelike, easily comprehended, uninterrupted, unselfconscious and reassuring. The value of modern art is that it restores the true picture, though without the promise of redemption and immortality that Christianity provided it is a somewhat bleak one.

Josipovici's critical stance has an undeniable appeal: he offers a justification of modern art that is not purely aesthetic or formalistic but is not crudely ideological either, dissociating himself with equal firmness from Leavisian and Marxist dogmatising, and from cultural doomwatching of the kind practised by George Steiner. He is also capable of beautifully phrased, brilliantly illuminating observations on particular texts. But I still feel, as I felt about *The World and the Book,* that his basic dichotomy between realistic post-Renaissance art and modern art is too simple and too exclusive. Criticism needs to discriminate between different kinds and phases of modernism (Josipovici implies that Robbe-Grillet's affinity with Eliot is as close as Proust's). More importantly, criticism should surely account for the continuing vitality of realistic modes of artistic presentation, and refine its methods of 'reading' them, rather than just wishing them away. It is symptomatic that Josipovici has in this volume a whole section of essays on modern music drama of the highbrow variety; but not one reference that I could remember to film, an artistic medium unique to the modern era, and one in which the possibilities of realism are still being explored to stunning effect. (p. 280)

David Lodge, "Make It New," in New Statesman, *Vol. 94, No. 2423, August 26, 1977, pp. 279-80.*

JOHN MELLORS

A man sits on a bed, reading *Migrations.* He twitches. He makes incomprehensible notes about identity, self-knowledge, alienation, double-glazing and rain. He vomits. Are you all right? she asks. No, he says, I keep thinking I have to review this book. If you're ill, you ought to see an editor, she tells him. He vomits. It's the resurrection, he explains. A Chinaman or a Western woman. Or Lazarus. Difficult to tell, with all those bandages. I'm a spider, he tells her. I'm a reviewer. Anything but a human being, she says. He vomits. . . .

Parody, of course, is the coward's way out for a reviewer. Also, a tribute: you can't parody a writer who has no individuality. What seems to me, though, to be wrong with *Migrations,* as with some of Josipovici's short stories, is a failure of technique. The means distort the ends. Vague, repetitive, ultimately tedious, the style slowly smothers the ideas, devitalising them. Or, to use the author's own metaphor, when Lazarus takes off his shroud, he does not exist: 'He's nothing at all.'

John Mellors, "Anon Events," in The Listener, *Vol. 98, No. 2528, September 29, 1977, p. 410.*

BLAKE MORRISON

A man walks up and down a bare, sunlit room, pausing occasionally at the double-glazed window. A man wanders in the vicinity of a railway station, dizzy and disoriented. A man picks his way through a well-furnished living-room, struggling to speak to the woman who watches him. A child in some kind of institution is being pressed to eat and talk. A man lies in bed with a woman, troubled by fantasies of spiders and suffocation. What is the relation between these unexplained and repeated episodes? Is this the story of one man, or of several? What is the timespan? Why are none of the characters named? Why does the text circle rather than move forward? What is the unspecified cause of the anxiety, nausea and bewilderment afflicting the main protagonist(s)?

At this point (anywhere in the first half of *Migrations*) impatient readers may decide not to have any further dealings with the text. But those who are familiar with Gabriel Josipovici's previous novels, and with the theories promulgated in his critical study *The World and the Book,* will accept that the frustrations experienced in reading *Migrations* are Mr Josipovici's means of making us share his protagonist's struggle to articulate a sense of life's purpose: we are made, by way of the difficult reading process, to identify with "the man's" search for meaning. Moreover, readers will find their experience of the novel mirrored by that of "the woman" in whom "the man" confides; though ostensibly a prostitute (or so her "vulgarly" sarcastic colloquialisms—"Go on!", "You're a talkative one", "Charming"—suggest), she takes on the role of the trustful reader to whom all will eventually be revealed: "Don't get upset . . . You'll explain to me. There's plenty of time. And then I'll understand." Mr Josipovici's novel is frequently self-referential in this way, focusing attention on the reading process, and on the rationalist expectations which underlie it. The reader of *Migrations* is made to "understand" not through narrative progression (though there is a small degree of this) but through repeated motifs, so that, for instance, the repeated phrase "No.I.No." comes to denote not just the protagonist's faltering efforts to speak, but his assertion of identity within the void.

Nevertheless, even patient readers will be disappointed by the latter part of the novel. The elusive and minimal procedures of *Migrations* increasingly submit to rational explanation, but as they do so something of the staleness and (for all the intended bleakness) sentimentality which underlie them is exposed. The central image through which "the man" eventually communicates his vision—that of Lazarus's linen being unwrapped to reveal of pile of dust—seems too derivative and too slight to be worthy of the considerable suspense which has been built up.... Both author and protagonist are subtle explicators of themselves, but their final anticipation of censure—"yes, it's been said before I'm not saying anything new"—is not persuasive enough to dispel dissatisfaction. Only one short passage—"if our eyes were good enough our lives long enough we would see everything always on the move, always migrating, islands separating from the mainland, mountains rising out of the sea, rocks crumbling into sand"—has the imaginative conviction to transcend the fairly undistinguished meanings which *Migrations* uncovers.

> Blake Morrison, *"Dusty Answer," in* The Times Literary Supplement, *No. 3965, March 24, 1978, p. 361.*

ALAN WILDE

[Gaps between perceptions and the things perceived], the burden or blessing of subjectivity, marks modernism as a whole, suggesting the source of its unresolvable paradoxes, its aesthetic evasions and tremendous blocked energies, its ubiquitous vision of discontinuity, in the world, in the self, and in the relation between them.

My special enthusiasm for *The Lessons of Modernism* can be explained, in part, by the fact that Josipovici not only sees but takes his reader directly to these gaps, abysses, and paradoxes—to the heart of the matter in its phenomenological particularity. He becomes fearlessly and trustfully coextensive with it, an insider. (p. 370)

I should say straightaway that Josipovici's notion of paradox is not entirely congruous with mine. Roughly speaking, the model I've proposed, though its roots are as subjective as his, is logical (in form) and antilogical (in effect): the modernists perceive, equivocally, A *and* not A—a configuration that paralyzes consciousness while ranging its perceptions of fragmentation into ordered and suspended symmetries of antithesis. Josipovici's model is temporally more dynamic, progressive, and, ultimately, hopeful; though it is not overtly religious, words like submission, conversion, and renunciation thread themselves through his discourse, feeding his paradoxes into determinable solutions of faith beyond reason. His central myth is the Fall, two Falls as it happens, the second having come about in that crisis of authority we call the Reformation. If the first produced a fallen language, a violation of silence and so, as Rousseau, Derrida, and now Josipovici would have it, a sense of guilt over the artifice and uselessness of our instrument of expression, the Reformation disperses the controlled investment of faith in traditional, objectifying structures: "We are in a world which springs out of the torment of having to live out an impossible paradox: the refusal to recognise any authority and the awareness of the suicidal nature of such a refusal." The shadow, here grown vastly historic, continues to fall between a fretful subjectivity and its world, between suicidal silence and conscious but, for Josipovici, not necessarily illusory effort: "By portraying the loss of innocence we may be led to a rediscovery of it, on the other side of despair." Sounding for a moment like early Sartre, Josipovici imagines an escape from irresolution that propels him not into the temptation of aesthetic heterocosms constructed by modernists like Woolf but through the quickening effect of paradox back to a reconstituted or at least a re-visioned world.

Innocence happily lost, and with it all the mimetic pretensions of realistic fiction, of pictorial perspective, and of language itself; the cult of the "I" and of certain knowledge through reason; "the long nightmare of post-Renaissance Europe, that mixture of lunatic pride and unbelievable naïvety"—we have heard these slogans before, in Heidegger, in the Frankfurt School, in Francastel, at Cerisy, and in *Tel Quel.* What is admirable about Josipovici is that these concepts, like the concept of paradox, instead of leading to the usual solipsistic or reflexive ironies, incite him to celebrate, as he discovers them in Kafka, Eliot, Picasso, Stravinsky, and others, "extreme moments, when we are taken up into the dance of the universe, when the reality we cannot bear very much of is forced upon us." (pp. 370-71)

Platonic "fury" and Christian agape, restyled into conscious mediation and working against the grain of traditional forms, are not for every taste; and though they are handled without the slightest solemnity by an exceedingly agile gymnast, to borrow Josipovici's own image of the artist, these undeconstructed winds of presence and inspiration do blow in and across the abyss of centuries. Modernism itself is made to extend seamlessly and commodiously from 1880 to the present, and the book neglects the case (which seems potentially strongest when focusing on art as game) for a distinctively postmodernist literature. Nevertheless, and despite some faults peculiar to books that are in fact collections of essays, this is a particularly exhilarating and engaging work, fused finally by its passionate unity of point and purpose. (p. 372)

> Alan Wilde, *"Modern/Modernist," in* Contemporary Literature, *Vol. 20, No. 3, Summer, 1979, pp. 369-76.*

PETER LEWIS

During a period when English literary conservatism has been strongly reasserting itself after the "aberrations" of the 1960s, and when few novelists have courted the label "experimental", Gabriel Josipovici has attracted attention as one of our more innovatory prose writers, deeply interested in foreign developments and prepared to try them out. The phrase "avant-garde" clings to him, though in England the label is more likely to be viewed as a noose than a halo.

His new novel, *The Echo Chamber,* is more immediately enjoyable and accessible than much of his previous fiction. Although the reader may find it difficult at first to distinguish between all the characters in the large country house in the Cotswolds where the action is set, *The Echo Chamber* is not only easy to read but positively racy. Josipovici achieves this pace by breaking his chapters into short sections and by writing most of the book in dialogue, so that it is really a chain of fairly short conversations. . . .

Josipovici's rigorous objectivity may owe something to the phenomenology underlying the *nouveau roman,* but it is not necessary to posit such an influence; one can just as easily relate his technique to an indigenous tradition of conversation fiction going back to Peacock. Indeed, the setting of a remote country house containing a number of eccentrics, and the frequently humorous way in which they present themselves, connect Josipovici's novel to a thoroughly English line of development. But given Josipovici's interest in radio, it is also feasible to see this novel as a kind of fictionalized play for voices: it is not only the very extensive use of dialogue that suggests this, but the sequence of short scenes, the straight cutting between them, and the grouping of characters in pairs or trios rather than in large gatherings.

Yet for all its resemblance to the comic-satiric mode of the English conversational novel complete with human oddities and caricatures, *The Echo Chamber* is not quite as it appears. It also has affinities with another kind of country-house novel, the mystery thriller, and during the second half the tension and suspense gradually build up as clues begin to fit together. The mystery is focused on the central character, Peter, who arrives at a house filled with a motley assortment of relations and family friends for a period of convalescence after an unexplained mental collapse. Of the circumstances precipitating his breakdown he has no memory. In the early stages of the novel all the inhabitants are introduced through their contacts with Peter and the emphasis is on these multiple interactions. Gradually, however, Josipovici foregrounds one strand, Peter's relationship with the sympathetic Yvonne or Vonnie, while the other figures provide a context for her attempt to help Peter recover his past. . . .

The more this "past" appears, however, the more like the present it seems to be and the more it prefigures the future. Are these echoes from the past reverberating in the chamber of the house really prognostications of what is to come? At the very end, when the "cause" of Peter's breakdown is finally revealed, both past and future are acted out in the present. It is as though Peter is trapped, rather like the characters in Beckett's *Play,* in an eternal cycle of breakdown and cure from which there is no escape. Here we are far from the country-house or conversation novel: *The Echo Chamber* proves to be a Borges-like *ficción* masquerading as something essentially English. . . .

The skill with which Josipovici fuses two very different fictional kinds is most impressive, as is the way in which he builds up suspense and subtly suggests that "time present and time past are both perhaps present in time future". Yet it is difficult to avoid feeling that the novel falls between two stools. Increasingly the conversation novel becomes secondary to the Peter-Vonnie relationship; and the "dreaming-forward" *ficción* is attenuated by being interwoven with various unconnected strands. Borges himself has adhered to short, compact forms since these suit his work admirably, and his most successful English-language followers, like the brilliant Australian Peter Carey, have done likewise. Gabriel Josipovici may have gone a long way to bridge a seemingly unbridgeable gap between tradition and experiment, but on this occasion it is possible to feel that he hasn't gone far enough.

> Peter Lewis, "Recovery Service," in The Times Literary Supplement, No. 4017, March 21, 1980, p. 312.

PETER LEWIS

Gabriel Josipovici's last novel, *The Echo Chamber,* succeeded in being ingenious and innovatory without being ostentatiously "experimental". In that mind-teasing book, he made considerable demands on the reader, but his sophisticated use of suspense ensured that the narrative was gripping from first to last. His new novel, *The Air We Breathe,* is both more difficult and more demanding, but it lacks the compelling impetus provided by the element of mysterious inevitability and the structural devices of its predecessor. As a result, the reader who is prepared to put in the effort and concentration Josipovici's fiction requires may well feel a sense of diminishing returns as he works through the novel, piecing together the fragments of the dislocated narrative.

In *The Air We Breathe,* technique comes perilously close to being an end in itself; the artistry of *The Echo Chamber* seems to have given way to artiness. There is an air of self-indulgent elaboration about the entire book, established by the long first paragraph, which opens and ends with "and" and contains no full-stop. Writers who fragment and intercut narrative can achieve great compression and intensity, communicating in a form of symbolic shorthand what would need far more space if related conventionally: Paul Bailey's *Trespasses* is a good example. In the case of *The Air We Breathe,* however, the opposite appears to be true. Told in a conventional way, the novel could easily have been much shorter than it is, since the content (to resurrect a forbidden term) is relatively insubstantial.

To provide a straightforward synopsis of this content—a woman, Gina, is in flight from her marriage to a Frenchman, Claude, whom she knew as a child during three summers spent in France, and so on—would be to give a totally false impression of the novel, since events both past and present are only gradually and often indirectly revealed; furthermore, much remains tentative, ambiguous, even unexplained. Josipovici's use of "he" and "she" rather than the names of the characters (although very occasionally some of them are named) adds to this air of uncertainty, as does his avoidance of locating the action in time: towards the end of the novel, the inclusion of a specific date, found on the back of a photograph, comes as a shock. What interests Josipovici is not what you say but the way you say it. . . .

The virtually unpunctuated stream of language brings Molly Bloom's monologue to mind, but Josipovici's indebtedness to Joyce is tempered by his individual adaptation of the technique, so that it fluctuates between a first-person representation of consciousness and a third-person narrative. Subjectivity and objectivity tend to overlap and merge.

Although the chronology and action are not linear, *The Air We Breathe* is conceived as a seamless whole: there are no divisions into chapters or sections. But if the book unfolds in one continuous sweep, more like a long story or novella than a novel, the narrative itself is extremely involuted and discontinuous. Time and place can change abruptly in mid-paragraph. Memories suddenly give way to unrelated conversations or events. Rapid transition and unexpected juxtaposition are essential to Josipovici's narrative method as he hints at certain key episodes and situations, then circles back to them, sometimes again and again, adding more information with each recurrence. As a result, what is initially obscure gradually becomes more intelligible. . . .

As we have come to expect from Josipovici's novels, *The Air We Breathe* is a technical *tour de force,* but the virtuosity is here supported by a flimsy infrastructure which could be recast in noveletttish terms. Josipovici's preoccupation with expanding the possibilities of the novel is leading him towards a formal and stylistic sophistication operating in a vacuum. Furthermore, *The Air We Breathe,* with its echoes of Joyce and Faulkner, illustrates how contemporary writing of the "advanced" and "experimental" sort often looks back more than it looks forward.

> Peter Lewis, "The Past's Suffocating Hold," in The Times Literary Supplement, No. 4102, November 13, 1981, p. 1330.

PETER KEMP

[Nicholas Mosley's *Serpent*] tackles intelligently the difficulty of communicating the complex. Gabriel Josipovici's book, *The*

Air We Breathe, huffs and puffs portentously in a travesty of such procedures. Suffering from a kind of verbal asthma, its nebulous heroine can't get things off her chest: 'again it came to her, that feeling . . . so that she gasped for air . . . the sense of having to say everything, everything, but also the impossibility of ever saying anything.' Groping through the novel's smog of unpunctuated prose, you gather she has, for some intensely enigmatic reason, married, and then left, an unusual man (one who 'has talked so little in his life that he is out of practice'). Congested with the unutterable profundity of it all, she now chokingly attempts to bring out the full significance. But it's hard to say whether she finally succeeds: the novel stays foggy to the end.

> *Peter Kemp, "Monied Monsters," in* The Listener, *Vol. 106, No. 2739, December 10, 1981, p. 728.*

KATHLEEN FULLBROOK

In order to be understood, Josipovici's experimental novel [*The Air We Breathe*] must be read with the intensity and attention usually reserved for poetry. As in the novels of Samuel Beckett and in the French *nouveau roman*, Josipovici's 'plot' emerges excruciatingly slowly from a welter of switching and overlapping time changes and from a kaleidoscope of images that grow in power as the novel proceeds. The central symbols of earth, water, fire, and, of course, the air of the title, dominate the book, but a Bergsonian union of time and the river as an encapsulation of the meaning of life is also crucial to the text.

The novel is a study of mind and meaning, and the mind which gives rise to the narrative is that of Gina. We follow her thoughts as she remembers her various attempts to make sense of life in general through a dissection of her own experience. This experience is dominated by a story told to Gina by her French mother-in-law. The story is that of the mother-in-law's father who spent most of his time in his latter years watching the Seine, in which he finally drowned. This tale seems to Gina, who has spent several childhood summers in the house of the dead old man, to contain a central meaning for her life. Her problem is to discover the meaning. This she attempts to do by marrying the old man's grandson and then, after leaving him, by attempting to tell the story to a series of men who refuse, in various ways, to help her get her story told. Gina's life becomes an odyssey of search for the listener who will understand her tale so that she may understand herself. . . . *The Air We Breathe,* then, is a novel which analyses language and silence and the nature of the gaps that occur in the attempt to think about and to communicate experience through words. It is a distinguished addition to the shelf of post-modernist fiction.

> *Kathleen Fullbrook, in a review of "The Air We Breathe," in* British Book News, *April, 1982, p. 259.*

DENIS DONOGHUE

Josipovici's aim [in *Writing and the Body*] was "to examine the role which language, writing and books play in our lives, the lives we live with our bodies". Put like that, it begs more questions than those it proposes. Who are "we"? What justifies the reference to role-playing? What are the "lives we live with our bodies": or rather, what is the force of that "with"? These questions are not released from beggary by Josipovici's assertion that writing and speaking "are at the crossroads of the mental and the physical, the orders of culture and of nature".

The figure is misleading. Writing and speaking are actions, a crossroads is the scene of a possible action. . . .

Given mind and body: or even given the words "mind" and "body", the inventive possibilities are considerable. If, on a count of heads, writers tend to be Idealists rather than Materialists, the reason is that words, whatever the character of the objects they denote, seem to be more mental or spiritual than material. This makes life hard for Marxists. Fredric Jameson has deplored "that instinctive idealism which characterizes the mind when it has to do with nothing but spiritual facts". Words are spiritual facts; which explains why some modern writers try to use them as if they weren't, making them opaque, as if the words were material things. Blake's *The Marriage of Heaven and Hell* complicates the issue, if once you take it seriously: or his marginal answer to Reynolds, which refuses the dualism: "Imagination is the Divine Body in Every Man".

Josipovici rarely invokes Blake, but he certainly has an interest in forcing literature and criticism out of the instinctive idealism to which Jameson refers. In *The Lessons of Modernism* (1977) he described a Brechtian theatre:

> Such a theatre rediscovers words, but as the expression of the total body rather than of consciousness. In an Ionesco or a Pinter play, for example, speech has a far more important function than in Ibsen or Shaw. For speech is used not to impart information or express views, but as a weapon or shield, as an extension of the arm or the chest, an instrument of survival or aggression.

This is a misreading of Shaw and Ibsen, whose characters speak, no less than those in the plays of Ionesco and Pinter, to defend themselves or attack others. But the important part of the passage is Josipovici's distinction between consciousness and "the total body". The distinction is vague in itself, but clear enough as indicating Josipovici's desire to render the separation of mind and body null in critical and rhetorical practice, even if it persists in strict theory. In *Writing and the Body,* as in *The Lessons of Modernism* and *The World and the Book* . . . he tries to enhance the body, as if by invoking "the total body", whatever that means, he could assign to the otherwise mundane body all the spiritual powers and attributes anybody could possibly want. Speaking of the silences that come between Othello's words, he says that "they are that out of which the words naturally spring and to which they return: they are his body, the totality of his being". In a somewhat grandiloquent reference to the novel, he says that it provides a universal language: "not in the words, not in the story, not in the book as an object, but in the book *as it is read:* a living body". . . .

The total body receives intense rhetorical stress in *Writing and the Body,* but not much explication. I have to contrast it, in that respect, with the patient argument and elucidation the question of mind and body has received from Jans Jonas in *The Phenomenon of Life,* especially in the chapter "Life, Death, and the Body in the Theory of Being", which is a more helpful meditation on the coincidence of inwardness and outwardness in the body. Jonas's purpose and Josipovici's are not, indeed, identical, but they have enough common ground to show that, on such a theme, recourse to rhetorical stress and italics is not good enough. . . .

The difficulty of *Writing and the Body* arises not only from the elusiveness of its theme but from a disproportion, in Josipovici's account of it, between illustrative matter and the object it is supposed to illustrate. Josipovici is like a novelist who is long on characterization but short on plot. Much of his discourse has only a tenuous bearing upon its official theme, and therefore has interest mainly intrinsic. The lecture on Shakespeare would be illuminating in any context, but is not especially appropriate to "the relations between writing and the body". There are passages on Sterne, Kafka, Borges, Eliot, Beckett, and Muriel Spark which read now like improvisations, however they sounded in University College London, two years ago; they float free from their context. Some of their details, however, are so perceptive that I could easily be persuaded to forget the context and any misgivings I have about it.

There is no evidence that Josipovici, like [Sterne's Tristan Shandy], has diverted himself from telling his "Life and Opinions": he ends every lecture on a ringing phrase. But it is hard to discover what, in the end, he wants the reader to do: are we required to change our lives? If the story has a moral, it is nearly as elusive as the official theme. I can find a semblance of one by putting together two brief passages which are separated by nearly a hundred pages. In the first, Josipovici says that Proust in the end remains faithful to his deepest insight, "that we are given back time by recognising that it is what inevitably passes". To avoid recognition of this, Josipovici says, is "to avoid recognition of one's own body: to accept the one is to be given back the other". I'm not sure how to reconcile this with a later sentence, that "writing reinforces our belief in our own immortality by helping us to avoid the acceptance of our bodies". But in any case, later still, Josipovici seems to commit himself to what he calls "trust", for which the image he gives is Kafka, in his final illness in Kierling, unable to speak but still scribbling notes to Dora Dymant, Robert Klopstock, and others. The notes are extraordinary; fragments, phrases, ellipses, Orphic now, whatever they seemed at the time. Josipovici's description of them is beautifully daring, the most touching thing in the book. He interprets Kafka's trust "in the ability of the hand to keep moving forward over the page" as "finally, trust, against all the evidence, in the beneficial aspect of time, in movement as opposed to stasis". Beautiful, indeed. But Kafka's hand isn't, except in a most enhanced sense of the word, a hand: it is, for the time being, his character, his will, the resilience of his moral being. It comes back, in our sense of it, to "the total body", and to whatever each reader is willing to allow that, under the persuasion of Josipovici's rhetoric, to amount to.

It may be contended that a reader of *Writing and the Body* will grant Josipovici's references to the total body, in any of its versions, whatever allowance the phrases need at the time. Doesn't the reader of "Ash-Wednesday" give Eliot the benefit of any doubt that clings to

                                       Redeem

The time. Redeem
The unread vision in the higher dream.

But "Ash-Wednesday", by the time we reach those lines, has suggested or enforced a context sufficiently stable, irrefutably there as the scene of certain images and rhythms. Josipovici's meditations have their own exaltation, but not enough, by way of an enabling or persuasive context, to make the reader complete for himself the meaning Josipovici has hardly begun to incite.

Denis Donoghue, "Materializing the Spiritual," in The Times Literary Supplement, *No. 4162, January 7, 1983, p. 6.*

DAVID MONTROSE

The Mirror of Criticism ought to be an exemplary collection. For one thing, Josipovici's personal vision of the reviewer's task—described in a rather long-winded introduction—is admirable for its espousal of a direct response to works, without the interposition of system or preconception. For another, as a sensitive reader and lucid writer, Josipovici is suitably armed to put theory into practice, especially as the subjects of these reviews are mostly ones in which he has long evinced particular interest: Dante, Chaucer, Kafka, Walter Benjamin, Nabokov, Beckett, Bellow . . . Inevitably, though, the knowledge Josipovici brings to them works against the openminded receptivity he considers ideal. This is mainly apparent in his criticism of criticism.

Josipovici is rightly distrustful of scholars pushing pet theses—a process which often involves twisting evidence to fit the argument—and is an unrelenting detector of their shortcomings. But, while a sceptical reviewer is certainly preferable to a gullible one, Josipovici occasionally gives the impression of being hard to convince because he has strong views of his own—which is scarcely surprising—that contrary opinions need to overturn. And there is no obvious instance here of that happening.

As a reviewer of fiction, too, Josipovici's views seem somewhat resistant to change, though this is probably less an indication of inflexibility than a worthy eschewal of literary faddishness. . . .

His only significant fault is an over-concentration on placing latest works in the wider context of the authors' oeuvres. A bottom-heavy excess of background often results. The same urge towards comprehensive statements informs Josipovici's non-fiction reviews, but there he usually has more space in which to operate and his wisdom is consequently saved from being spread too thin.

David Montrose, "Stubbornness," in New Statesman, *Vol. 106, No. 2737, September 2, 1983, p. 25.*

HAROLD E. LUSHER

Each chapter or lecture [in *Writing and the Body*] focuses mainly on the technique and contribution of a particular writer as that writer relates to the larger issue that Mr. Josipovici is examining. In the first lecture, for example ("The Body in the Library"), Sterne's *Tristram Shandy* is the centerpiece; in the second ("Everything and Nothing"), Shakespeare's *Othello* is the main object of scrutiny; the third ("Non Ego Sed Democritus Dixit"), is based on Thomas Mann's *Doktor Faustus* and also relies on Dante's *Divine Comedy;* and the final lecture ("A Bird Was in the Room") is a brilliant exposition of the otherwise often cryptic notes that Kafka committed to paper during his final illness at the sanatorium in Kierling. . . . [Josipovici] also cites ideas that crop up in the work of such widely disparate writers as Proust, Henry James, Borges, Virginia Woolf, T. S. Eliot, and Wallace Stevens. From music he draws on the examples of Mozart, Schönberg, and Stravinsky; from the visual arts, the work of Picasso; and from psychology, the speculations of Freud. What we have here, in short, is a rich and illuminating work, powerfully stimulating in its suggestions and in its cross-references among the arts. . . .

In spite of the perceptiveness of the mind at work in the book, however, in spite of the density of allusive material, the general reader comes to the end of this inquiry with curiously mixed feelings. On one hand, it is impossible not to admire the subtlety of mind and the range of erudition in these chapters. On the other hand, in the midst of so much to admire, the general reader is also surprised and not a little disconcerted to discover echoes of disappointment reverberating in his mind. Disappointment, of course, stands in direct proportion to the expectation aroused; and the title of the present work tempts one to believe either that the author has something essentially new to say about the interaction of the creative mind and the body it dwells in, or that known facts are seen in a wholly new perspective, bathed, as it were, in a new light. These expectations are regrettably not always as fully met as one might wish. At the beginning of his first lecture, the author defines his purpose for us: "... to examine the role which language, writing and books play in our lives, the lives we live with our bodies".... He mentions the paradox of the relationship we have with our bodies, how they are simultaneously familiar and yet forever mysterious to us, and claims a desire to explore such paradoxes. He is fully aware of the difficulty of the topic that he has chosen, and hopes to clarify the issue by speaking of *writing* and the body, rather than *literature* and the body, on the grounds that literature is an abstract idea, whereas *writing* concentrates on a living process. The thin line of argument that he proposes to lay down—and he concedes that he will be relying more on story and example rather than on rigorous abstract argument— he describes as "partly historical and partly what could be called phenomenological," and is content to hope that "it will emerge as these lectures proceed".... These are the channels in which the reader's expectations are led; and while one's curiosity is at least partly satisfied by the historical markers, the phenomenological are less distinct and to that extent less satisfying. If, when we have finished reading this book, we are persistent enough to ask ourselves what the links between writing and the body are, we are surprised to realize that they are still as tenuous and difficult to trace as they were, when we first asked the question. On our journey through these pages, however, we learn much that is valuable and of absorbing interest about the writers and the works examined, even if the answer to the basic question continues to escape us.

Part of the difficulty here is the essentially elusive nature of the topic itself. That writing affects, reflects, and sometimes governs the body is a widely acknowledged fact, but it is a point of information that we start out with rather than something that has to be established or illustrated. A greater part of the difficulty is that the focus of attention shifts, and the reader is actually invited to consider writing and the *mind,* particularly the emotions generated by the mind in response to a given set of circumstances, real or imagined. (p. 70)

The most rewarding parts of this book are the first and fourth lectures, which stay closest to the title and the author's declared intention. The title of the first lecture is based on a story by Borges, which Mr. Josipovici briefly recounts for us. The lecture's value lies in its historical perspective, in its reminders of the psychological origins of novel-writing (it stimulates a degree of curiosity which is fundamentally sexual), and of the close links between the novel and pornography, and in how Sterne implements a variety of techniques to arouse, defer, and finally satisfy the curiosity he has excited. The fourth lecture, "A Bird Was in the Room," is devoted mainly to the enigmatic work of Franz Kafka, whose attitude to life and literature was so pathologically hesitant, so utterly lacking in self-confidence, that he left a significant part of his work unfinished. Although Mr. Josipovici also discusses such central documents as The

Metamorphosis and the famous *Letter To My Father,* the chapter is chiefly concerned with the random notes and jottings that Kafka committed to paper during the final weeks of his life in a sanatorium. (According to Max Brod, he had developed tuberculosis of the larynx and was not supposed to speak at all.) In this lecture, the body moves into a particular prominence, not only because it is a source of intense and constant pain and is approaching its own extinction, but also because the imminence of death confers a special authority on whatever is said in one's last moments—or, in Kafka's case, on whatever is written down.

Quite apart from the degree of disappointment that the general reader may feel over the possibility of ever coming in terms with so impenetrable a topic, **Writing and the Body** is nevertheless a valiant and fascinating effort to widen our understanding and sharpen our awareness of how close the relationship is between the process and the organism. If that relationship is ultimately inexplicable, one must nevertheless give high marks to a writer who addresses the question anew with such courage and intelligence. (pp. 70-1)

> *Harold E. Lusher, in a review of "Writing and the Body," in* The International Fiction Review, *Vol. 11, No. 1, Winter, 1984, pp. 69-71.*

TOM PAULIN

[Josipovici's **The Mirror of Criticism**] demonstrates that he is an able reviewer. His analysis of C. H. Sisson's shoddy translation of Dante is wonderfully clever and learned, and his discussions of Chaucer are excellent. Unfortunately, Josipovici is unable to appreciate *Ulysses* and so has no understanding of what Joyce means by 'the classical temper.' This failure has damaging effects on Josipovici's whole critical manner and mode of address. For all his professed modernism he is really an old-fashioned affective critic who likes books which are 'moving,' 'profoundly moving,' even 'splendid.' A trim and nimble literary impresario, he tends to project his own face into the critical mirror. If he is sometimes lightweight and self-regarding, he is also a joyous and rather innocent enthusiast, a kind of singing wine-waiter with a pleasantly *dolce* patter.

> *Tom Paulin, "Slogging It Out," in* The Observer, *February 5, 1984, p. 53.*

MALCOLM BOWIE

[In **The Mirror of Criticism: Selected Reviews, 1977-1982,** Josipovici] talks his way rapidly through frontier-posts and checkpoints where other travellers might have had their cultural baggage searched for hours. Back and forth across the map of modern literature he goes (Joyce, Kafka, Nabokov, Grass, Robbe-Grillet, Beckett, Bellow, Malamud . . .) and back with equal self-assurance to the monuments of the European tradition (Dante, Chaucer, Rabelais, Cervantes . . .). Although the range both of his current sympathies and of his remembered literary pleasures is astonishing, there is little ostentation in his manner. What most excites him, and is most contagious for his reader, is the kindling by a new book of an unsuspected quality of response in himself. . . .

Criticism matters most, for Josipovici, precisely when an accustomed paradigm begins to come apart and when alternative opportunities for intellectual work and leisure become available. . . .

[Such] touchstone moments give Josipovici a clear sense of his own civic task: to transfigure the weeklies, fortnightlies and monthlies for which he writes, by purging them of their loose in-talk and by allowing his readers access to finer and more surprising perspectives of their own. Josipovici is telling us a good deal about his own practical notion of how this can be done when he writes of the contributors to J. P. Stern's *The World of Franz Kafka* that 'they all have a relaxed and sparkling quality rare in Kafka criticism, an exuberance and a willingness to abandon the central argument for the apparently peripheral insight which makes every paragraph exciting and thought-provoking.' At his best, Josipovici is indeed rather like this. What will make his book exhausting for its *in extenso* readers, as distinct from its dippers and skimmers, is that its relaxation and sparkle are as much those of the responsible seminar-leader as those of the hedonistic traveller in literary time and space. A patient, informative, improving voice is often to be heard— a voice much needed in the university classroom, no doubt, and well able to lend an air of fact-based authority to a short review: 'Graham Greene will be 72 this year, and he has been publishing novels for over fifty years. *The Man Within* came out in 1929, in the same decade as *The Waste Land, Ulysses* and *The Magic Mountain.*' But in a florilegium of such reviews, the reader may feel besieged by such facts as soon as they exceed a certain density and the factual mode itself may acquire, like Graham Greene frozen in his 72nd year, an oddly phantomatic air. To some extent, these are failings of the genre rather than of Josipovici's book, and there is much that is innovating and provocative enough to be worth retrieving from these pages. The reviews clearly were not written with an eye to their becoming a book and little has been done to disguise their occasional character. . . .

[*The Mirror of Criticism*] is the travel diary of a perceptive and generous-minded explorer, going where the reviewing road takes him and inventing his notions as the journey demands. (p. 22)

Malcolm Bowie, "The Shimmer of Transcendence," in London Review of Books, *Vol. 6, No. 12, July 5 to July 18, 1984, pp. 22-3.*

HERMIONE LEE

One of Josipovici's critical studies is called *The Lessons of Modernism,* and one too often feels that his fictions are meant as teaching illustrations, exemplary post-modernist texts. [*Conversations in Another Room*], though, seems less of a theoretical exercise. The 'conversations' between Sally, the niece who visits her difficult sick aunt Phoebe every Saturday, and between the aunt and her much-put-upon companion Mary, are marvellously acerbic and relentless, with a fine whiff of Ivy Compton-Burnett and Pinter. . . . Just off-stage from these female voices is an elusive male trio—Sally's silent friend who sits in the aunt's hallway taking notes, Phoebe's prodigal son who never writes (is he involved with Sally?) and Phoebe's vanished husband (and who is *he* involved with?). Just under the conversations are unspoken questions about guilt, power and inheritance. All this is powerfully suggested by the sharp comic voices. There is a falling-off into solemnity and pretension, however, as soon as the narrative starts to discuss the nature and purpose of narrative.

Hermione Lee, "Dabbling in the Occult," in The Observer, *August 8, 1984, p. 18.*

JOHN SUTHERLAND

Conversations in Another Room extends into fictional practice the investigation of literary obliquity conducted in Josipovici's recent critical work, *Writing and the Body.* (Particularly relevant is the fourth chapter, 'A bird was in the room'.) The novel's framing situation is the regular visit paid by a niece to her bedridden aunt. Their exchanges, reproduced with Sternean dashes rather than inverted commas, are largely banal, as are the other conversations which the old lady holds with her female companion. But a mystery, dealing with two broken marriages, emerges between the half-lines. Why did the old lady's husband desert her, after some unspecified misconduct in Italy? Why has her son gone to Saudi Arabia, leaving a broken marriage behind? One or other of her conversation partners may be responsible. There are brief excursions from the central dialogues: one to the old lady's husband, Robert, who hears a susurrus of women's voices in his flat in Positano. Beneath the old woman's bedroom, by a convex mirror (whose symbolism is tactfully indicated), a man takes notes. It is all poised, very deliberately, at the point where enigma borders sheer obscurity. Indeed, the whole thing may be the fictions of a failing mind: 'perhaps there was no husband, no son, no Rome, no Amalfi, no air-conditioned flat in the Gulf. Perhaps there are only two old ladies slowly dying together in a cramped flat in West London.'

My response to Josipovici's novel is mixed. It's easy to read, but hard to understand. There is a part of me that responds with: perhaps me no perhapses, Josipovici, tell me what's going on, for God's sake, or give the reader back his £7.95. Another part of me dutifully applauds the critic-novelist's intricate and tirelessly intelligent probing into the aesthetics of Modernist fiction. (p. 21)

John Sutherland, "The Great Exhibition," in London Review of Books, *Vol. 6, No. 16, September 6 to September 9, 1984, pp. 20-1.*

A. J. FITZGERALD

In a flat in West London (topography plays no great part, and certainly not its usual one, in Gabriel Josipovici's [*Conversations in Another Room*], but it is far from irrelevant: the place-names have their weight) sits Phoebe, advanced in years, more or less bedridden, conversing now with her young niece, who visits her at the same time every Saturday morning, now with her companion Mary, of indeterminate age but most probably somewhere between the other two. The conversations, or at least the voices of the women, are overheard (and, as it may be, transcribed, or invented) by the niece's friend Mike, who waits, scribbling in a notebook, biting his lower lip, tugging at his hair, in the hall. . . .

The comedy of their exchanges is fastidious and exact, having to do with an extremely accurate (though not mimetic) sense of timing, of the pauses, hesitations, evasions and sudden forward leaps, the artful, purposeful inconsequentiality of talk among intimates who have something to hide or something to discover, something important, that is, invested in their own words and the words of others. Skirting grim, familiar ironies, the talk is now easy, bantering, now strained, locked in struggle. . . .

All of this is economically and absorbingly done. The stylized surface propriety and consistency of the exchanges, their gravely comic rituals of interrogation, repetition and contradiction, have something in common with the dialogues Muriel Spark has been orchestrating in a series of dazzling short novels since the late 1960s; the undertones of fear, suspicion and genteel sadism recall, faintly, Harold Pinter. The conversations contain some of the sharpest and funniest writing Josipovici has done since his early novels *Words* and *The Inventory.* It will not be surprising, though, to readers of his fiction, his books of criticism or his unshowy, penetrating reviews that he is not content to leave it at that—at the satisfactions of form offered by his technique of withholding other satisfactions, at the shaping of speech patterns, and an implied anecdote of caricatural ordinariness, into a verbal sparring-match. With the intrusion, towards the end, of a first-person narrative voice ("And now at last I can speak") comes the—not entirely unexpected—turning back of dexterity on itself; anxious doubts take over, about the status of the ladies' slim and resonant sentences, about the conscious desires and hidden drives of their creator, about the ways of the self, at once intrusive and painfully self-conscious, in the ontological maze of fiction; finally and more hauntingly about loss, emptiness, failure, "the dust-heap of the imagination". These reflections are not without urgency, but there hovers too a whiff of over-conscious despair.

We grow accustomed to the unpredictability of the dialogues (notwithstanding the immense importance of routine and repetition in the household), to a sleight of tense and mood by which a given exchange can slip with no announcement of a forward or backward movement in time, into another, different "moment" in the ongoing conversation, giving each section the feel of something both specific and paradigmatic. When this is carried over into the artist's self-scrutiny, dissolving boundaries between the protagonists or between their inventions and his, blurring times and places, taking the anecdotal ground—shifting at the best of times—from under our feet . . . , the new paradigm, of fiction as a holding operation, as a succession of more or less improvisatory measures to keep off emptiness and dread, the gestures in this instance being spun out of silent, internal chatter, the murmuring of innumerable voices in the mind—all this comes a little too pat; the authorial throwing in and up of hands risks looking less like an inevitable end than a way out.

Josipovici, though, like his closest mentor among modernist writers, Robbe-Grillet, turns the knife again. The final short chapter comes back to the original anecdote, the unstoppable cycle, and an endlessly receding perspective which he cuts off, not with a flurry of self-doubt but a poised and beautiful tableau of terror and flight: the intent gaze, the moment of arrest and powerfully suggestive depiction releasing the trapped undercurrents of feeling and fascination that have given rise to the book.

> *A. J. Fitzgerald, "Voices Off," in* The Times Literary Supplement, *No. 4261, November 30, 1984, p. 1392.*

VALENTINE CUNNINGHAM

The scope of Gabriel Josipovici's [*Contre-Jour: A Triptych After Pierre Bonnard*] is minimal, but its translucence fosters an extraordinary purity of form and concept. In clear, obsessive, neurotic prose a mother and a daughter recall a painting husband and father. Known to their narratives only as 'he,' he could be Pierre Bonnard.

He sits always apart, silent except to reporters, cultivating the sideways glance, the edges of perception. His wife is always in the bath, unhappy, anointing her sore skin. Excluded from the work that sustains him, she's its constant object, his only model. She slashes the occasional canvas. Neglected by both of them, the daughter retreats to a high apartment.

The notation of all this anguish is cramped into a finicky, post-Laingian, sub-Jamesian prose. The general effect is of tasteful, well-read preciousness. Certainly the big bow-wow strain is not something Josipovici cares to go in for. The greater wattages of creativity are always going to blow his shy aesthetic circuits. But for all that he remains serious, even challenging, about the conditions of artistic production, especially the domestic tax art levies on all its worthwhile practitioners.

> *Valentine Cunningham, "Once More with Feeling," in* The Observer, *June 1, 1986, p. 22.*

GRAHAM HOUGH

[There] is something slightly anorexic about much current fiction, particularly perhaps about the *nouvelle,* a form which is apt to suffer from under-nourishment. On the analogy of the *nouveau roman* Gabriel Josipovici's *Contre-Jour* should be classed as a *nouvelle nouvelle,* for he still owes allegiance to that venerable tradition. Were the cats and the dog put down before or after the mother's death? We are told both. Why, when the central theme is the relation of mother and daughter, does the mother suddenly announce that she is barren and has had no child? Why is the letter from the father announcing his wife's death signed Charles when his real name was Pierre? Because this is a *nouvelle nouvelle* we are to be reminded by these hiccups in the narrative that we are reading fiction and there is no through road to fact. The disclaimer is all the more needed because *Contre-Jour* has a biographical foundation. It is well-known that the wife of the painter Pierre Bonnard had a passion for taking baths, only equalled by his passion for painting her in the nude. The result was a long series of paintings, of exquisite hazy luminosity, of Madame Bonnard either in the bath or entering it or emerging from it. Josipovici, with what biographical authority I do not know, bestows on them a daughter who feels herself totally excluded from her parents' life by their narrow and obsessive relationship. Soon she is indeed excluded by being sent away to school. The mother in her turn feels that she has been rejected by the daughter from the start. Meanwhile the father-husband-painter says pretty well nothing to either of them and gets on with his painting, to which everything else in the house is sacrificed. It is this bleak and comfortless situation on which *Contre-Jour* is based. It is called a triptych, but that must be to puzzle us, for the third member consists only of a half-page death announcement. Effectively the book is in two parts, the first the interior monologue of the daughter, the second that of the mother. They are in flat contradiction to each other. . . . It is at times suggested that the key to this stagnant imbroglio is the attitude of the father who refuses to engage himself in anything but his work. But he remains a shadowy figure, his one revealing remark showing him as entirely wrapped up in organising visual sensations: 'But it won't do to impose tension. It must spring from the subject. Otherwise you get expressionism, with every picture the same, the world transformed into the artist's anxieties.'

Curiously enough in a book about a painter, the visual quality is almost wholly absent from the writing. Josipovici gives a powerful rendering of anxiety and obsession, but of the untroubled dream of light and colour in which Bonnard seems to have passed most of his life we get no impression at all. One cannot doubt that this is deliberate, as everything else in this discourse seems to be, and the writing is far too skilful to strike an unintended note. But the impulse behind it remains obscure to me. Perhaps I have misread something, or missed some signpost. (p. 23)

Graham Hough, "Afro-Fictions," in London Review of Books, Vol. 8, No. 12, July 3, 1986, pp. 22-3.

ELAINE FEINSTEIN

There is a marvellous moment in Samuel Beckett's *Malone Dies* when the bedridden, curmudgeonly narrator, unable to cure himself of his habit of telling himself stories, finds that his fictions take on a human resonance, however absurd such a notion might be to him. At his best, Gabriel Josipovici has been similarly unfaithful to the ideology of French 1950s modernism. Altogether spikier than Nathalie Sarraute, funnier and livelier than Alain Robbe-Grillet, Josipovici is part of a longer European tradition. The attention he gives to the exact cadence of every conversational exchange readily betrays how sharply human need and pain concern him, even while he refuses to represent them in any traditional manner. The brilliant dialogue that opens *The Inventory* is a case in point; moreover, in that early novel the whole comic action that follows will hang on a lie of his central figure Joe: "There are just three subjects I prefer to avoid. The first is telephones. The second is my job. The third is human interest."

Contre-Jour is another case of an emotional response won from the reader by a piece of conjuring, though the lie on which this whole structure hangs is in some ways more perplexing. The relationship between Pierre Bonnard and his wife is presented as if through the eyes of a rejected daughter, a daughter for whom her mother has longed all her life, yet one who has been pushed outside the inturned daily rituals her parents have chosen. . . . Unsurprisingly, the daughter writes of their intimacy as a rejection of her own human needs, but this sadness, so eloquently voiced, is itself a trick; we are led gradually to the core of the wife's own reflections on her marriage, and eventually discover that no such daughter existed. The girl writes of herself "as a ghost" because she is no more than a figment of the mother's imagination. The reader cannot but ponder the epigraph from Bonnard: "There is a formula that perfectly fits painting: lots of little lies for the sake of one big truth."

The central preoccupation of the book is the relation between those who make art, and those who become victims of that obsession. Even when the painting is as great as that of Bonnard, there is some moral question about the artist's necessarily cruel attention to the surface of the model he observes, and the deep indifference he demonstrates simultaneously to the inner world, and even the words of the woman he is painting. . . .

Josipovici is questioning the primacy of art even as he celebrates it. The atmosphere of the house is one in which ordinary life is impossible. The terrible passivity of the wife is unprotesting, for all her long fight for breath (of which Josipovici has written elsewhere). Her stifled spirit imagines the shape of another relationship in which she could have breathed; the fiction of the daugher allows her to envisage herself as irreplaceably needed, to enjoy the fantasy of her husband's grief after her own death; and (perhaps most importantly) to believe that it is truly the absence of a child that has brought misfortune upon her. With a child the father "would not have turned in on himself, and taken it out on me". It seems likely that she is mistaken, for, in his own words, everything Bonnard sees becomes an inner mystery. . . .

It is strange, when one thinks of Bonnard's marvellous colours, how aside from the greenish water of the bathroom there is so little colour allowed to enter the novel; the garden of almond trees, mimosa and canvas deck-chairs is subsumed under the scratch of a pencil, a drawing. And though there is light in the book, it is most often the light of naked overhead bulbs, in which faces are grey. . . . Bonnard and his wife have been together for so long that it is possible she is not deluding herself that he could not live without her; certainly she can remember no other lover. There is a tragic absurdity in our increasing awareness that, for all the evident cruelty of their life together, she wants no other man. Josipovici allows her deepest knowledge of that emotional bond, the most hurt and shocking utterance of the novel, to emerge almost casually towards its close.

Elaine Feinstein, "Living with an Inner Mystery," in The Times Literary Supplement, No. 4347, July 25, 1986, p. 819.

RICHARD BATES

[*Contre-Jour*] is a novel about family relationships. The father, an artist . . . , is a peripheral figure only known to us through his pervasive influence on his wife and adult daughter. They can no longer relate to each other because of the way he played them off against each other to monopolize their affections. The women yearn for deeper contact, yet communication between them has taken the form of unwritten, unanswered letters and silent phone calls. . . .

Josipovici robs the novel of the melodrama with which a lesser writer would propel the reader through monotonous (not dull) familiar territory, a cross between the minimalism of Beckett and the alert consciousness of David Plante's fiction. Only the smallest, simplest, most intimate images furnish this novel and become more vivid than elaborate descriptions. . . . A blurring of the characters of the female protagonists occurs, as though they are both part of a split personality. The mother takes increasingly long baths. The daughter stares out of the window of her lonely flat—not the cure but the symptom of her affliction. This is the antithesis of an exciting book. 'Nothing happens and nothing happens and nothing happens and all of a sudden there is a whole life gone and you realize that all those nothings were in fact everything.' It is deeply moving to be robbed of one's illusions in such a subtle, perceptive and thorough manner.

Richard Bates, in a review of "Contre-Jour: A Triptych after Pierre Bonnard," in British Book News, August, 1986, p. 479.

Thomas (Michael) Keneally

1935-

Australian novelist, nonfiction writer, dramatist, author of children's books, and short story writer.

A prolific and eclectic writer, Keneally is best known for his novels based on historical personages and events. He offers a fresh perspective to his subject matter by focusing on individuals struggling with questions of conscience. "In Keneally's hands," Peter Ackroyd noted, "the historical novel is redeemed as the raw materials of the past are turned into a kind of fable." Keneally's subjects range from the history and people of his native Australia to the military campaigns of the Confederate Army during the American Civil War. He is consistently praised for his narrative voice, his careful characterization, and his sense of place.

As a young man, Keneally studied for the priesthood but left the seminary before being ordained. Two of his early novels are drawn from his experiences in the Catholic church: *The Place at Whitton* (1964), a gothic tale set in a seminary, and *Three Cheers for the Paraclete* (1968), which features a liberal Catholic priest. Keneally established his reputation as a historical novelist with *Bring Larks and Heroes* (1967). This novel, which depicts Australia's early years as an English penal colony, introduces some of Keneally's recurring topics, including conflicts between social classes and ethnic groups and the perception, even among its inhabitants, of Australia as an alien land. These issues are fully explored in one of Keneally's most important novels, *The Chant of Jimmie Blacksmith* (1972). This work is based on an actual incident in which a half-caste aborigine rebelled against the racism of the settlers and brutally murdered several white women before being killed by white Australians. Keneally explores other aspects of his country's social history in *The Cut-Rate Kingdom* (1984), which depicts Australia's unstable political structure and the moral character of its citizens during World War II. Manly Johnson wrote that "as a piece in the mosaic of [Keneally's fiction, *The Cut-Rate Kingdom*] contributes to our sense of his passionate involvement with moral issues."

Several of Keneally's novels examine war during various periods of world history. *Blood Red, Sister Rose* (1974) interweaves the brutalities of fifteenth-century warfare with the story of Joan of Arc. The novel was widely praised for Keneally's plausible and humane portrait of the peasant girl who become Saint Joan. In *Gossip from the Forest* (1975), Keneally recreates events leading to the Armistice of 1918 through the imagined thoughts of Matthias Erzberger, the German statesman whose role as negotiator was instrumental in bringing World War I to an end. Paul Fussell commented that "as fiction, [*Gossip from the Forest*] is absorbing, and as history it achieves the kind of significance earned only by sympathy acting on deep knowledge." *Season in Purgatory* (1977) recounts the story of David Pelham, a young English doctor who becomes involved with Yugoslavian partisans during World War II. The American Civil War is the subject of *Confederates* (1979). Critics noted Keneally's accurate rendering of the dialect and sensibility of his Southern characters in this book.

The Second World War is the setting for two of Keneally's later works, *Schindler's Ark* (1982) and *A Family Madness*

(1985). Keneally has said that he attempted to use "the texture and devices of a novel" in *Schindler's Ark* to tell the story of Oskar Schindler, a German industrialist who saved more than one thousand Jews from Nazi persecution. Keneally gathered most of his material from interviews with Holocaust survivors and others who knew Schindler personally. When *Schindler's Ark* won the Booker McConnell Prize, an award given only for works of fiction, Keneally's novelistic approach generated widespread debate. Most critics consider *Schindler's Ark* the novel that best exemplifies Keneally's skill at personalizing history. *A Family Madness* details the tragic legacy of Rudi Kabbel, a Belorussian emigré living in Sydney, Australia, whose parents had collaborated with the Nazis. A prosperous businessman, Kabbel isolates his children from society and instills in them his ill-fated patriotism toward his homeland and his vision of a forthcoming apocalypse. Interwoven with Kabbel's story is that of Terry Delaney, who falls in love with Kabbel's daughter, Danielle. The dominant theme of *A Family Madness*, that the past often reaches out to harm innocent people, is best reflected in Kabbel's warning to Delaney not to marry Danielle: "Sometimes, Mr. Delaney, history *does* make its claim on people. . . . [Danielle] belongs to forces you can't negotiate with."

Keneally's other works of fiction include *A Dutiful Daughter* (1971), a contemporary allegory about faith and redemption;

A Victim of the Aurora (1977), a combination historical novel and detective thriller which takes place during a polar expedition; and *Passenger* (1979), which examines such social issues as sex, parenthood, and abortion through the thoughts of an unborn fetus. Keneally has also written *Outback* (1983), a travel book about the land and people of Australia's outback territory.

(See also *CLC,* Vols. 5, 8, 10, 14, 19, 27; *Contemporary Authors,* Vols. 85-88; and *Contemporary Authors New Revision Series,* Vol. 10.)

MICHAEL HULSE

[The historical truth of *Schindler's Ark*] is beyond doubt: Keneally's work carries an acknowledgement of a list of survivors, now living scattered around the world, who provided the writer with personal testimony. So *Schindler's Ark* is a history. For this reason reviewers of the book, once they had retold the gist of the story, tended to focus on the question of whether it should have taken the Booker Prize, which after all is an award for fiction. (p. 45)

The inevitable debate set in even before publication, in Fiona Fullerton's brief commentary in *The Bookseller . . .* , which observed that *Schindler's Ark* 'is not, strictly speaking, fiction', placed the word 'novel' between inverted commas, and, anticipating the dissatisfaction which many reviewers were to feel with the realisation of the central character, concluded: 'since he chose the form of the novel to tell the story, he could have exploited it more fully to speculate on what really went on in the enigmatic heart and mind of Oskar Schindler.' (pp. 45-6)

[Throughout the reviews of Keneally's book], the most delicate question of definition has quite simply been evaded: is *Schindler's Ark* actually *fiction*? The Booker McConnell Prize is, after all, awarded for a work of fiction, and the resentment of 'one former judge' (unnamed), reported in *The Sunday Times . . .* , is quite understandable: 'A non-fiction novel is nonsense and an insult to fiction writers. I am very sad that a prize founded for fiction, the Cinderella of the publishing world, has been diverted off to one of the areas where everyone does very well anyway.' In the same report Keneally's informant Leopold Pfefferberg [who was saved by Schindler] is reported as saying, 'There is no fiction in it', and Keneally himself has repeatedly made almost identical statements.

The contention must presumably be between those who agree with tradition and the *OED* that fiction is invented and imaginary and those who would adopt the rather looser attitude of Paul Ableman in the *Literary Review . . .* :

> What essentially differentiates a novel from any other prose work is not the degree of literal truth but the power of creative imagination that informs it. Although Thomas Keneally's book is based on research and is, indeed, as carefully documented as a civil service report, literary art blazes in the language with which the work evokes and illuminates the terrible events with which it is concerned.

This strikes me as being irrelevant to the point of silliness. Literary art may well blaze in the language, but this still doesn't make *Schindler's Ark* fiction. Of course this history, though written in a far less overstated manner than *Confederates,* can certainly be read for its excitements. It matters that we know what becomes of the vile and murderous Amon Goeth, commandant of Cracow's Plaszów camp; that we know whether Helen Hirsch makes it on to the list of those allowed to move to Moravia; that we know whether those who accidentally end up in Auschwitz are got out again; that we see the final SS order, to liquidate surviving Jewish prisoners, thwarted; and so on. These things all bring with them a suspense that we expect in thrillers: Schindler and Amon Goeth playing cards for possession of Helen Hirsch is a grim scene. Such scenes—another is Rebecca and Josef's romance, with its perilously close escape—are played for all they're worth by Keneally, whose historical journalism seems here, as previously in *Gossip from the Forest* and *Confederates,* to need a certain amount of sensational leavening, at least in the author's eyes. Literary art, indeed: it is assuredly true that Keneally uses 'the texture and devices of a novel to tell a true story'. But what this actually means is no more than that a historical record of fact is subjected to a heightening treatment, is cast in the dramatic pacing and rhetoric of invented fictions. It doesn't need a pedant to point out that such pacing and rhetoric have never been absent either from the grand style of historical prose (Gibbon, Carlyle) or from the True Stories of the pulp market. At whatever extreme of integrity or intellectual propriety, factual records have a long history of being set in the 'texture and devices' of fiction: this does not make them fiction, does not make them novels. (pp. 47-8)

[Although most critics failed to confront the moral aspects of Schindler's story, this] issue is focussed by Keneally's use of the word 'virtue' in his 'Author's note' and by the inscription, a Talmudic verse, on the ring given to Schindler on the last day of the War by the Jews he has saved: 'He who saves a single life, saves the world entire.' . . . Schindler saved some thirteen hundred—but what, after all, of those millions of unsaved Jews who were not fortunate enough to have an Oskar Schindler? The large and ugly statistical context persistently obtrudes into our consciousness as we read. True, biblical rescues were hardly possible under the Nazis: Schindler was running life-and-death risks in any case, and handing out a personal fortune in bribes, and could hardly try to save a greater number without jeopardising what he *could* achieve. This is the realistic, pragmatic response, and probably the sanest: and most reviewers gave expression to it by expressing approval of, and agreement with, that Talmudic verse. If Schindler had saved even one single life alone, he would still be a Just Man.

Yet a dissentient voice was heard, in the only review to take serious issue with Schindler's claim to 'virtue', and here I think the moral discussion must begin. Marion Glastonbury's *New Statesman* review [see *CLC,* Vol. 27], vividly unlike any of the other assessments of the book, took exception to what she insisted was the hagiographical tendency of Keneally's work. . . . Ms Glastonbury went on to remind us—quite correctly—that Schindler was an immoral, loose-living character who in different circumstances would be seen quite simply as a racketeer and criminal, and concluded: 'The real Schindler owed his reputation for mercy and munificence to the company he kept. In the society of mass-murderers, the racketeer passes for a man of principle, distinguished only by the enormity of *their* crimes.' (pp. 49-50)

While some of Ms Glastonbury's account is manifestly overstated—it is quite untrue that *Schindler's Ark* is turned into panegyric, and indeed Schindler's dignity is repeatedly undermined—nonetheless it is salutary to have our approval of Schindler challenged, if only because it is strengthened in this way. Ms Glastonbury's side-swipe at 'the usual Catholic channels' may be a malicious glance at Keneally's early training for the priesthood (though he was not ordained), and the tone of her conclusion is surely too hysterically negative to deserve response; but the answer to her larger argument must necessarily return to the pragmatic terms of Keneally's work. What, after all, is a man in Schindler's position to *do*? He has a clear choice before him: either he callously exploits the expropriation of the Jews for his own enrichment, without giving a thought to the lives of the slave workers in his hands, or else, accepting the abnormal circumstances which create his wealth, he uses that wealth to buy and bully those workers back to life. It is the great paradox of Oskar Schindler's career that only the acceptance of the lesser evils could avert the greater: only because he was a man of vice could Schindler accomplish his pragmatic virtue. I have seen no commentary by a theologian on *Schindler's Ark,* and this strikes me as being the most reprehensible and disturbing omission in the reception of the book. But I would suggest that it needs no expert to draw conclusions from Keneally's evidence: that there is no good in this world unadulterated with evil, but also that, in a world as monstrous as that of the Nazis, we must expect to seek heroes or redeemers in men who at other times might be in our jails, and for good reasons. These are the ethics of an adult pragmatist, and I think constitute the most serious claim on our attention of Keneally's very fine work. The virtue of the virtueless, the pragmatic strength of the philosophic innocent, may be the only salvation in dark times. If this is a grim moral to draw from *Schindler's Ark,* it is still one that returns us to the truth of that Talmudic verse: 'He who saves a single life, saves the world entire.' (p. 51)

> Michael Hulse, *"Virtue and the Philosophic Innocent: The British Reception of 'Schindler's Ark',"* in Critical Quarterly, *Vol. 25, No. 4, Winter, 1983, pp. 43-52.*

MICHAEL HOLLINGTON

The title of Thomas Keneally's Booker Prize winning text [*Schindler's Ark*], with its overt Old Testament reference, may indicate that this book offers itself, as a consenting adult, to the kind of critical reading in which Christianity gets a large and sympathetic hearing. Keneally's Schindler, the Sudetan German who saved the lives of thousands of Jews in Poland between 1939 and 1945 is, like Noah, the 'one just man' of the dark and evil times of Nazi Germany—a type of Christ harrowing hell (Auschwitz, Gröss-Rosen, Plasów) to redeem the souls of the otherwise damned. Such a reading might construct him as a kind of Graham Greene hero, paradoxically bringing forth good out of the all-too-manifest corruption of his own flesh, so that in the end . . . it can be said of his urge to save Jews, 'that he desired them with some of the absolute passion that characterised the exposed and flaring heart of the Jesus that hung on Emilie's wall'.

Yet without dismissing such readings one notices a rather more secular paradox. For all its detailed, documentary striving after an accurate realist portrayal of wartime Poland—running to maps of Cracow, and plans of the concentration camp—*Schindler's Ark* is a peculiarly Australian book, owing more to the mythology of the bush than to that of central Europe. Although Australia figures overtly only once or twice in the text, the book seems to carry a subtext in which Australia functions as a discursive code to unlock the mysteries of the moral abyss of wartime Europe, explaining what it is that is lacking and why and how Schindler possesses it.

In a simple and general way, Keneally seems to imagine the issues at stake to be primarily personal and individual rather than social. He appears still to believe very much in the hero. There are other plausible 'just men' amongst the German inhabitants of the mad man's land of wartime Cracow. They have rather absurd names, like Bosko, Madritch, and Titsch, and no attempt is made to interest us in their stories, or their interaction, either with each other or with Schindler. And it is not for purely technical reasons (because Keneally wanted to write a particular kind of novel, perhaps) that only one can be allowed to fly over the cuckoo's nest; it is rather that a particular kind of individual space is imagined for this hero to operate in, space which is more strictly Australian than European. Keneally's Schindler is a hero on the run, a kind of Scarlet Pimpernel charging about central Europe on a train, fixing deals and saving souls. . . . Like the Australian bush hero he's essentially an outlaw who doesn't belong to the society of the respectable and orderly. . . . (pp. 42-3)

It is repeatedly emphasised that Oskar is a kind of child of nature, with a residue of unfallen innocence. This doesn't imply that he's a simpleton: a kind of peasant cunning in his nature is invoked by the application to him of the Good Soldier Schweik stereotype. It is very much suggested, however, that Schindler is profoundly anti-intellectual, opposed in particular, to theories of individual heroism emanating from Paris. . . . The anti-intellectualism is linked, both with a radical amorality, especially as far as sex is concerned—'To him sexual shame was a concept, something like existentialism, very worthy but hard to grasp'—and, just about simultaneously, with a fundamental morality of human kindness, stemming not from calculation but from spontaneous instinct: 'Oskar was a gambler, was a sentimentalist who loved the transparency, the simplicity of doing good.' Again, we are reminded of the babes and outlaws of the Australian bush. (p. 43)

A final point about Oskar Schindler's Australian parallels is that he's represented throughout as the 'most apolitical of Capitalists'. A pragmatic entrepreneur, his achievements reflect an anti-ideological work upon the givens that are to hand, rather than any abstract or theoretical form of protest against his world. In this respect he is pointedly contrasted with Wachmeister Bosko. This former theological student wafted by an afflatus of enthusiasm into the SS, later attempted to expiate his mistake by joining the Polish partisans, and 'had contempt for partial rescues . . . wanted to save everyone, and would soon try to, and would perish for it'. It is apparent that Bosko cannot be the hero of this narrative; there are kinds of *theoretical* innocence that it discriminates against just as vigorously as it favours 'intuitive naturalness'. This could be put another way by observing that Bosko, unlike Schindler, appears incapable of negotiating that distinctive antipodean contradiction whereby outlaws and rebels may at the same time be highly successful 'captains of industry', despite, or perhaps because of, their inherently anti-social behaviour.

What kind of truth claims are put forward by *Schindler's Ark*? Crudely put the question is, is it a novel or a true story? Keneally is suitably disingenuous on this point:

I have attempted to avoid all fiction . . . since fiction would debase the record, and to distinguish between the reality and the myths which are likely to attach themselves to a man of Oskar's stature.

The invitation, for any vaguely precise reader, is to see that whilst some kind of semi-plausible discrimination between reality and myth may be operative in the book, this in no sense implies that myth is disdained or eschewed. As the book will later tell us, 'the thing about a myth is not whether it is true or not, nor whether it *should* be true, but that it is somehow truer than truth itself'. (pp. 43-4)

The notion of the author with which Keneally is working in this book is by no means dissimilar to this conception of its hero. The homology is proffered in the prologue, which comments that 'it is a risky enterprise to have to write of virtue'— phrasing that clearly borrows its terms from Oskar's *salto mortale* to describe a purely aesthetic adventurousness. The book itself 'constructs' a fake concentration camp out of the testimony of those whose memories, working intensely upon the most nightmarishly vivid experiences of their lives, inevitably construct myths. It too attempts a 'redemption' of those 'just men' whom memory immortalises and weaves into heroes or gods, and a damnation of those whose crimes it once more exposes. And in doing this the author himself appears, like Schindler, to play the role of a minor god who is Janus and Bacchus.

If we remember Sartre's existentialist dictum . . . that the author must *not* play god with his own creation, an essential series of problems in *Schindler's Ark* are uncoverered. In a supposedly documentary work, what validates the highly emotional, moralistic ironies that dispense grace and damnation? How can we be sure that these moralisings aren't some form of gloss upon yet another attempt to cash in on the holocaust, Janus-facedly pointing up these unspeakable horrors once again in order to catch that fat film contract? (There are frequent reminders that Oskar looks like Curt Jurgens and has 'the outrageous Charles Boyer charm'.) And—to return to the Australian subtext once more—why should we believe that the values of 'natural spontaneous goodness', derived from the bush or anywhere else, can offer any antidote to, or even a means of understanding, what happened in Poland between 1939 and 1945?

I'm not proposing here to try to answer any of these questions: they are intended to serve, instead, as gestures towards the kind of terms in which critical debate about *Schindler's Ark might* be conducted. Yet—to make a tentative start on the specifically Australian question—there are probably quite a number of occasions in the text where the voting is likely to run fairly heavily in Keneally's favour, where indeed . . . those values associated with Schindler, the bush outlaw, seem firmly and convincingly 'realised'. I shall select two.

Mieczyslaw Pemper, a Schindler protégé in the Janus-faced position of secretary to the commandant of the real concentration camp, is accused late one night of plotting an escape. The commandant Goeth is invariably trigger-happy: what is Pemper, literally at gun-point, going to do? Both he and the text rise to the occasion quite brilliantly:

> looking around him for some sort of inspiration, he saw the seam of his trouser leg, which had come unsewn. How could I pass on the outside in this sort of clothing? he asked.

Here we have an example of 'work on the given' that justifies both Schindler's realism and the author's pragmatic handling of the writing's testimony.

The other example is more extended and central; it is indeed earmarked on a number of occasions as *the* paradigmatic correct instinctual response to an impossible situation. It's the day of the SS Aktion to clear the Cracow ghetto. Men, women and children are slaughtered indiscriminately, while Schindler watches like a film camera with a panoramic lens. One child stands out because she wears bright scarlet: the most conspicuous and vulnerable colour, one might have thought. As it is, the colour saves her, for there is no such thing as camouflage in this world. The SS men seem to use her as a kind of audience for their killings, paying no attention to her brightness, for they don't believe that any witness will eventually survive. The unlivable situation is mastered through a flamboyant gesture. This too is a 'realisation' of Schindler's mode of operation, a kind of gaudy, vulgar 'Australian' strategy of coping, in which instinctive flair counts far more than calculation. (pp. 44-5)

All of this is in part a way of establishing, *pace* the Oxonian lobby, that *Schindler's Ark* is indeed a worthy Booker Prize winner. . . . It's an ambitious book which cocks a snook at the metaphysical religiosity of Patrick White. Here we have Voss in the 80s, on the rebound from the Australian desert, back in his home patch, shorn of idealism. *Ach du lieber, rette mich nur!* is here rendered in a more prosaic and down-to-earth dialect.

But it's a pity that we still seem to have to be tossed into the great lap of God somewhere along the way. That flaming heart of Jesus on Emilie's wall, under certain lights in the book, looks a bit puce in colour, rather like a little something Dame Edna brought back from Cracow for the mantelpiece. 'Australia', read as the natural impulse of the heart, isn't ultimately an effective counterweight to 'Europe'. Whatever system it is that requires undermining underpins them both, and must be combatted, at least in part, with the weapons of intellect, intelligence and reason. Brecht's 'red statements' about Nazi Germany remain superior: his Schweiks are not heroes, but they do at least grasp that you get somewhere only when the office of 'just man' is abolished. (p. 46)

Michael Hollington, "The Ned Kelly of Cracow: Keneally's 'Schindler's Ark'," in Meanjin, *Vol. 42, No. 1, March, 1983, pp. 42-6.*

ALAN ROSS

[In *Outback,* Thomas Keneally uses the term "outback"] specifically to refer to the Northern Territory, that wedge-shaped state roughly bounded by the Gibson Desert to the west, the Simpson desert to the south and the Barkly Tableland to the east. Its main towns are Alice Springs near its southern boundary and Darwin, its disaster-ridden port on the Timor Sea.

Keneally appears to have had two main objectives in his book: first, to counteract any prevailing impression that nothing happens in the outback, and, second, to relate the lives of its present inhabitants to their nineteenth-century forebears, and most especially to the Aboriginals, who have lived in Australia for at least 40,000 years and for whom the Northern Territory is an area of historic significance. His method has been to build up a composite picture of outback life by means of character sketches and anecdotes, slices of history, geography, and mythology, descriptions of agriculture and police work, gold-mining and spy-satellite controls. About the only thing missing, until the last chapter, is the personality and presence of the author himself.

This is a pity, for what could have been a fascinating travel book is reduced by the lack of an individual narrative and personal involvement into something not greatly removed from a routine text-book. It may well be modesty on the author's part that has kept himself out of the picture, but the loss is a real one. . . . This is not to say that, in relation to his intentions, Keneally has not produced an interesting and informative book, merely that it is insufficiently recognizable as being by the author of *Gossip from the Forest, The Chant of Jimmie Blacksmith* and *Schindler's Ark.* More or less any competent journalist with a tape-recorder could have produced something similar.

At least, no one reading *Outback* and embarking on a comparable journey could fail to learn what they were in for. Keneally's genuine affection for the place and the people and his respect for their way of life and understanding of their problems makes him the most sympathetic of guides. . . . *Outback* is rich in incidental details, whether about camel trains or petrol-sniffing, cyclones or Dreaming trails, the Red Ochre men or two-up. Keneally skilfully suggests the space and isolation, the resourcefulness of the Territory's men and women, the vicissitudes of climate and economy that have contributed to their tough individual character.

The Aboriginals need all the attention and understanding they can get, and in this respect *Outback* can only do good. In the past the Aboriginals have had precious little to thank Australians for, and now, when their well-being is so crucially at stake, they need all the advocacy they can get in their war against the multi-nationals. Whether a "poofter" writer—anyone to do with the arts, Keneally reports, is usually so described—cuts much ice among the legislators in Canberra or the Foster's drinkers in Darwin is debatable, but the fact that Keneally spins a good yarn is on his side.

Alan Ross, *"Voice in the Wilderness," in* The Times Literary Supplement, *No. 4211, December 16, 1983, p. 1393.*

JOHN MELLORS

Thomas Keneally, perhaps mindful of the *Schindler's Ark* controversy, warns us that his new novel [*The Cut-Rate Kingdom*], about politicians and generals in wartime Australia, is fiction—and not even a *roman-à-clef.* He hopes that the book gives clues 'not to the privacies of any individual but to those that characterise the Australian soul'. Be that as it may, many readers will detect a MacArthur-ish colour in Keneally's portrait of the American General McLeod.

The narrator in *The Cut-Rate Kingdom* is a journalist, crippled at Gallipoli, who in 1942 has a 'grace-and-favour' apartment in Parliament House in Canberra. 'Paperboy' Tyson is a close friend of the Prime Minister, Johnny Mulhall, a staunch Labour man all his life but now suspected of allowing 'pragmatism' to erode principles. Is it also a sign of moral weakness in Mulhall that he has started a passionate liaison with the wife of the Australian General Masson? . . .

In a sense, the story is the working out of a myth. Mulhall is the king of 'a cut-rate kingdom' and has set up 'a fair model of the king-general-general's wife fable'. Looked at another way, the book has a simpler theme—that, in the words of one of Mulhall's critics, all politicians end up with 'souls like grocers'. And what about 'the Australian soul'? Do the citizens of *The Cut-Rate Kingdom* in 1942 share recognisable and distinctive character traits? They come across as prickly, mistrustful, regarding their American allies as 'gate-crashers'. They have inherited 'the tradition of convictism', and the older among them are full of 'Digger prejudices'. Keneally is adept at showing those characteristics in action, letting the Australian soul reveal itself in behaviour. *The Cut-Rate Kingdom* is a perceptive and provocative book. What it lacks, oddly enough, is 'soul'.

John Mellors, *"Australian Soul," in* The Listener, *Vol. 112, No. 2865, July 5, 1984, p. 27.*

MICHAEL WOOD

The year is 1942. Singapore has fallen, the Japanese have bombed the Australian mainland and are threatening to take Papua and New Guinea. Conscription, that old bugbear of Australian politics, hovers in the air, and minds are full of memories of a previous war in which Australian soldiers died at Gallipoli for a cause they could scarcely feel was theirs. Australia, in the view of Keneally's narrator [in *The Cut-Rate Kingdom*], is a marginal realm which has so suddenly been shifted to centre-stage that no one quite credits the text or the theatre. . . . There is more than one invader, though, in this "gangling, vacant continent". There are the English, departing lords of the past, more than half aware that Asia has been transformed, "tiffin . . . abrogated", and "gin and muffins . . . driven from that latitude"; and there are the Americans, masters of the timetable and public relations, on whose empire the sun is busy rising. The novel is not a *roman-à-clef,* Keneally says, his Australian public figures are not meant to "reflect the character and private life" of historical individuals. But he will forgive us, I imagine, if we see in his American commander, one Donald McLeod, subtly manipulating despatches, inflating statistics, surprising even his enemies by sudden bursts of simplicity, more than a faint shadow of General Douglas MacArthur.

Keneally is fond of straightforward characters who come across unwanted complexity, who seek to maintain the virtues of an older time in a newly muddled world, and this is the story woven into the historical fabric of *The Cut-Rate Kingdom*. John Mulhall, wartime prime minister of Australia, trying to save his country without betraying his socialist, anticonscription past, to keep the Japanese off his continent without plunging himself too deep in America's war, meets and has an affair with the wife of one of his generals. He is awkward and shy, has a dodgy heart condition and a wife in South Australia who won't come to Canberra and play first lady. The general's wife is beautiful, eccentric, slightly aggressive, and loyal in her way to the husband she doesn't love. . . . The affair finally founders on politics, on the mountain of compromises that go with power even in the most expensive kingdoms. . . .

The novel, published in Australia in 1980, two years before the appearance of *Schindler's Ark,* is sharply written . . . and its scenery is wryly observed, through the eyes and narrative voice of Paperboy Tyson, a crippled Gallipoli veteran, now a journalist and personal friend of Mulhall. . . . Tyson would like to be hardboiled but is really a softie, and his perspective gives the book its worried look. Is Tyson only a watcher, a man who has chosen the margins of life? Is Australia a watcher, a spectator whom history has somehow mistaken for an actor?

The questions can't be answered, merely tussled with, and in any case watchers get hurt along with the rest. Tyson is caught up in Mulhall's life, public and private, just as Mulhall and Australia are caught up in the Allies' needs. This is one of the suggestions of Tyson's (and by extension Keneally's) constant recourse to regal metaphors like the one in the novel's title. The Australians in the book are not royalists or nostalgics, and a previous prime minister is mocked for his clinging to old England. . . . Yet Tyson can't speak of Canberra without helpless scorn . . . and he can't resist the vocabulary of kingship. Mulhall is a "monarch", a "prince", his tenure of government is a "court"; he lopes up to make a speech "wearing a sort of Richard II grin, the rictus of a weak king".

Tyson is miming that feeling of secondariness which haunts all old colonies for longer than anyone would wish; that sense that the play originates elsewhere. "We're a race of bloody servants", a character says. "We're a race of . . . of bloody ostlers, that's what we are." And then later, more shrewdly, "Honest, it sometimes looks to me . . . that we couldn't do without someone to prove to us that we don't count." This thoughtful and kindly novel is about the cost of power, but it is also about the price of other people's troubles, which cannot sensibly either be espoused or denied. No man is an island, but it is at times possible not to know for whom the bell tolls.

Michael Wood, "Prince in a Wide Brown Land," in The Times Literary Supplement, No. 4247, August 24, 1984, p. 935.

PAUL STUEWE

Despite all the political, social, and sexual shenanigans of this novel set in wartime Australia, [*The Cut-Rate Kingdom* is] a surprisingly tame read. Keneally is a talented writer whose *Confederates* demonstrated a flair for historical fiction; *The Cut-Rate Kingdom,* however, doesn't offer a convincing period atmosphere to offset its aimless plot and uninteresting cast of characters. For those with a knowledge of things Australian, there may be resonances here that passed me by; but regardless of nationality, I can't imagine anyone getting excited about an essentially second-rate—although certainly not cut-rate—novel.

Paul Stuewe, in a review of "The Cut-Rate Kingdom," in Quill and Quire, Vol. 50, No. 10, October, 1984, p. 37.

MANLY JOHNSON

"A poor thing, but mine own": so might Thomas Keneally . . . think of *The Cut-Rate Kingdom,* as might others, because on a comparative basis it does not measure up to *Confederates* or *Schindler's List.* . . . But is it necessary for a novelist of Keneally's stature that it should? Granted that a writer is always in Olympic competition with his own achievements, still the requirements of each successive work make different demands on energy and imaginative power. One of the demands of the present novel is to say something about Australia and its precariously balanced political structure through incidents that occurred (or something like what occurred) during the early stages of the war in the Pacific. Another demand was to make some kind of revelation of the Australian character—not in itself so much as set over against the British and American and to some extent the Japanese. Here Keneally achieves a measure of success, variable only because the novel's 270 pages cannot encompass a persuasive, full-scale comparison.

The blurb reports that *The Cut-Rate Kingdom* is "a novel by the author of *Schindler's Ark*" (the British title of *Schindler's List*) which is corroborated by the writing, that economical use of language that gives to what might be otherwise incidental descriptions the vitality and power of art. . . . The difference between this novel and *Schindler's Ark* (also about the human spirit in time of war) is that Keneally provides in place of the Third Reich a "cut-rate kingdom" and nothing to compare with Oskar Schindler's bland subversion of the SS; neither is there a comparable magnitude in the number of lives destroyed.

Keneally's concern is not with quantity, however, but rather with quality—the quality of moral response to wavering principles and the ethical indeterminacy of governments and the military. This concern is made visible in the ever-present "Paperboy" Tyson, whose legs were shot off at Gallipoli in the previous war and who has returned to Australia to console the widow of his friend. Counterpointing Tyson's flawed heroism and compassion are the machinations of the familiar names Winston, Douglas, Franklin Delano, and Joseph, powers who loom in the background moving human pieces on a gigantic chessboard. *The Cut-Rate Kingdom* is not yet Keneally's great Australian novel, but as a piece in the mosaic of his other fiction . . . , it contributes to our sense of his passionate involvement with moral issues.

Manly Johnson, in a review of "The Cut-Rate Kingdom," in World Literature Today, Vol. 59, No. 4, Autumn, 1985, p. 656.

MICHAEL WOOD

It can't be news that the author of *Schindler's Ark* is interested in the secret passages of history and in decency entangled in horror, but I doubt whether anyone could have predicted where these interests would lead him next. In this powerful new novel [*A Family Madness*] a man is pushed from a train in Sydney because of events that occurred ten years earlier and half a world away. A family—father in his fifties, two grown sons, a grown daughter and a baby—commits joint suicide in 1984 because of "voices heard and insupportable fears" having their origins in the collapse of Nazi Germany. . . .

In a note [Keneally] mentions the historical case of a family of five who "willingly ended their lives" in a suburb of Sydney in 1984. There is, he says, a "broad similarity" between this event and the concluding horror of his story, but nothing more. He wants to know what roads could lead to such an ending, how people, as different characters in the book put it, can be marred or looted or grabbed by history. I don't think the ending has the grim necessity Keneally seems to want to suggest, and a slightly too artful reference to the Jonestown massacre . . . may mean that he is himself nervous about his implied argument. But the novel readily allows us to alter the proposition and say not that this history must lead here, to these deaths, but that even here, in this comfort-loaded and forward-looking Australia, history will get you one way or another.

The writing is too elegantly literary at times, and Keneally is perhaps too fond of metaphors of scent. His characters can smell the "musk of disappointment", the "acrid musk of lost faith". Some noses. And I winced a bit at the careful planting of a discussion of *The Tin Drum* just after we had heard about the invasion of Poland. Handy that the girl in the case should be taking a WEA literature course, handier still that they should be reading the right books.

But these are only mild excesses of craft. *A Family Madness* is an ambitious and successful book which makes connections we need to think about, and its deepest subject, the one that links all the odd and various strands of the story, is not history or violence or craziness but loyalty: the price of loyalty, and the blindnesses loyalty permits. Terry Delaney is [a] rugby player, solid Irish Catholic stock, married to the reliable, Italian-parented Gina, old worlds running through their union specially blessed by the Pope. He is a security guard during the week with a firm owned by Rudi Kabbel, a Belorussian who came to Australia at the end of the war. . . . In the course of the novel we read Rudi's history of his family, and Rudi's father's journals, which contain horrifying admissions about Belorussian complicity in the murder of Jews—the Nazis, the Belorussians thought, would reward their compliance one day by granting them independence. Loyalty to an idea, then, fosters disgrace and atrocity. But is disloyalty better? Rudi's mother passes information to the Russians in return for the sparing of her family, and is hanged in her husband's presence. It is from this haunting, unspeakable history that Terry, although he only intuits it, wants to rescue Danielle, Rudi's daughter. He loves her desperately, indifferent to all else, and she loves him in return; but she can't separate herself from her family. . . . When the end comes, when the family craziness kills the family, the same Danielle doesn't protest, doesn't defend herself or her tiny child, she only says mildly to her father, "Don't be cruel".

This is, I think, what Keneally would like to say to us. But can we hear him? Can we help ourselves? Terry's loyalty to Danielle and her baby is a cruel disloyalty to Gina; his brief return to Gina is a disloyalty to Danielle. What can he offer her in place of her father's magical certainty? And yet that certainty is horror and madness. Is this, to use Terry's phrase, why families go to hell in a group? Perhaps it is why families are both hell themselves and the only retreat from what feels like an alien hell outside.

Michael Wood, "Looted by History," in The Times Literary Supplement, *No. 4307, October 18, 1985, p. 1169.*

JOHN SUTHERLAND

Thomas Keneally likes to run his fiction close to historical fact. An appended note to *A Family Madness* indicates the novel's source: 'In a suburb of Sydney, Australia, in July 1984, a family of five willingly ended their lives. Their consent to their own destruction had its roots in events which occurred during World War Two, in voices heard and insupportable fears endured in that era.' Keneally's novel uses the genre's inventive licence to explore an event which the newspapers left as the week's inexplicable horror. The hero, Terry Delaney, is as straightforwardly Oz as Edna Everage. A security guard, he bumps up his earnings by playing Rugby League at the weekends. Terry is married to Gina, the daughter of an Italian couple from Palermo. When Terry loses his job, he drifts into working for a smaller security firm, oddly called 'Uncle', and run by a Belorussian patriarch, Rudi Kabbel, and his two sons. Delaney falls in love with Kabbel's daughter, Danielle, and she has a child by him.

A familiar novel of adultery could ensue from this mess. But Keneally's design is more ambitious. The narrative moves along three main tracks. There is Terry's match diary, recording his increasing ferocity (and success) on the playing field, as his involvement with the Kabbels deepens. Running alongside it

are Rudi Kabbel's reminiscences of his childhood in wartime Minsk and his father Stanislaw's journal from the same period. . . . Stanislaw is forced to witness his wife's execution, and young Rudi is imprisoned in a hole in the ground—a horror from which he never recovers. The surviving Kabbels emigrate to Australia. Essentially stateless, they fill the political emptiness of their lives with apocalyptic mysticism. Convinced that a purifying 'wave' is coming, they prepare for a new deluge. When it does not come, they calmly exterminate themselves. Terry witnesses this final solution but can only respond to it by a less deliberate act of violence of his own.

As in *Schindler's Ark,* Keneally has raked over World War Two for sub-plots to which the novelist can bring peculiar insight. In any balanced account of the war, the Belorussian theatre is pifflingly insignificant. . . . But fiction does not have to balance its sympathetic priorities. *A Family Madness* asserts that war robs humanity of more than life or territory. Imperial absorption, by denying survivors the comfort of national history and aspiration, leaves nothing but madness. . . .

Given the lavish success of *Schindler's Ark* it's understandable that Keneally should write another holocaust novel. But *A Family Madness* is, I think, better than its applauded predecessor. For one thing, its points strike nearer home. Keneally in this latest work projects a vision of the unfused fragmentariness of postwar Australia. An Irish hero has an Italian wife, but becomes involved with a Belorussian lover and her family. In this context, what is it to be 'Australian'? New nationality lies on these characters as lightly as wrapping paper. And Keneally's novel denies the cheerful a-historicism of the Australian dream, which requires that successful citizens simply forge their national and family pasts. . . . The memorial element is strong in Keneally's fiction. At its worst, it comes over as a 'lest we forget' preachiness. But here the nobility of the characters in the novel makes a genuine claim on the reader. (p. 24)

John Sutherland, "Carrying On with a Foreign Woman," in London Review of Books, *Vol. 7, No. 19, November 7, 1985, pp. 24-6.*

ROBERT TOWERS

Approximately half of the chapters of *A Family Madness* are set in the present and concern a young working-class Australian, Terry Delaney, who becomes involved with a family of Byelorussian origin, the Kabbels (originally Kabbelski), who immigrated to Sydney in the late 1940's. The other half deals with the terrible modern history of that family, a history reaching back to the early days of World War II. . . .

Mr. Keneally shuttles rapidly back and forth between his two stories, thematically counterpointing the relative "innocence" of the Australian present with the labyrinthine nightmare of the European past. In his fleshing-out of this hardly original but perfectly cogent theme, Mr. Keneally writes with customary briskness and ease, assembling the disparate elements of his story with an old pro's dexterity. The atmosphere of contemporary Sydney is nicely evoked: an American reader will feel immediately at home in that sprawl of suburban developments and shopping malls, of beaches and bars—and at home too, alas, with an ethos that tolerates murderous violence in sports and a casual acceptance of crime as simply one of the costs of doing business in a consumer-oriented society. Mr. Keneally is also effective in suggesting the kinds of anxiety and tension that underlie such an extroverted, breezy and frequently boozy way of life. The Byelorussian sections are, inevitably, of a very different order: they provide an often fascinating mini-course in the history of an area and an era with which most Westerners are scarcely acquainted.

The documentary interest of *A Family Madness* is therefore considerable. Its achievement as a work of literary fiction is much less secure. Mr. Keneally's characters—and this has been true of his earlier work as well—are curiously lacking in inwardness, in the suggestion of psychological depth. In the case of Delaney, his pal Stanton and Gina, this relative shallowness is perhaps not a crucial defect; Delaney is, after all, meant to be a fairly simple, ordinary fellow who gets into trouble. Even so, we have to take his wild passion for Danielle Kabbel entirely at the author's word; nothing that we have been shown in either character makes it fully credible, much less inevitable.

In Rudi Kabbel's case, however, the lack of an adequately realized psychological dimension is much more crippling to the novel's aspirations. Everthing is so externalized that the reader, while often interested, is never moved. The mystical, out-of-body states that Rudi experiences—once when he is nearly killed during the assassination of a local Nazi, again when he is buried alive in a latrine—are never made real for us, though they seem to be crucially related both to later quasi-epileptic seizures and to his mad obsession with security. This lack of inwardness also means that the various "voices" of the novel—not merely the dialogue but Stanislaw's journal, Rudi's family history and his sister'sletters—all sound explanatory, all sound, in fact, much the same. There are structural problems as well: the constant shifting back and forth between past and present is so rapid that scenes are seldom allowed to gain real momentum before being interrupted.

I finished *A Family Madness* glad that I had read it but feeling that Mr. Keneally's often admirable fluency and dispatch had, in the long run, let him down. While both the externalized approach to character and the stop-and-go narration might well have been effective, *mutatis mutandis*, in a more expressionist sort of novel, they can count only as flaws in a work so clearly realistic in its intentions. Mr. Keneally needed to have been much more patient, more exhaustive in his approach, more imaginatively and empathetically involved in his creation, for its fictional—as distinct from its documentary—ambitions to have been achieved.

*Robert Towers, "Breezy, Boozy and Byelorussian,"
in* The New York Times Book Review, *March 16, 1986, p. 9.*

TERRENCE RAFFERTY

Like all of Thomas Keneally's novels, *A Family Madness* is a history lesson in which the facts are less important than the voices, the old music we can't get out of our heads. This novel, set in Keneally's native Australia, tells the story of a young rugby player named Terry Delaney whose life is shattered by his encounter with the family of Rudi Kabbel, an émigré from Belorussia (also known as White Russia) haunted by his childhood memories of World War II. Keneally's typically objective third-person account of Terry's troubles also makes room for the wartime journals of Stanislaw Kabelski, Rudi's father, and for Rudi's own "History of the Kabbelski Family." These snatches of first-person testimony are, in a sense, the "explanation" for the Kabbels' bizarre behavior, evidence of a traumatic, definitive past that can't be shared with rugged Australian innocents. But for Keneally the past never explains itself

quite so simply, in the clear voice of an individual's memories. His Joan of Arc, in *Blood Red, Sister Rose* (1974), has a whole chorus of saints echoing in her adolescent body, driving her toward the glory of God and France; his murderous half-aborigine in *The Chant of Jimmie Blacksmith* (1972) has the music of tribal ceremonies in his blood, songs even his passionate desire for acceptance by white society can't quite silence; the unnamed sentient fetus who narrates *Passenger* (1979) is tuned in to more than his parents' voices—he hears their history and their ancestors' histories, the whispered messages in the DNA.

All those voices make his characters, more often than not, mad—and Rudi Kabbel is one of the maddest. . . . Kabbel's madness, like Joan of Arc's, is his belief that he's the incarnation of some greater principle (the small torch of Belorussian nationalism burns in him), and for him the survival of the Kabbels is therefore a transcendent value, the only thing in the world that really matters. In his Australian exile, Rudi's paranoia goes from bad to worse: from the acceptable form of the security service he runs from his home, to ever more frenzied preparations for an expected apocalypse (a great wave he believes will engulf the continent), and finally to a shocking self-destruction which is, for him, the only way of preserving his family intact from the forces that threaten them.

Rudi Kabbel is an example of something, all right—it's just not what he thinks it is. He isn't the savior of his people—either his nation or his family—and the notion that such heroism is needed in the free-form New World culture of Australia is clearly a comic (and tragic) delusion. . . . Against the background of a sprawling, half-developed abandoned colony like New South Wales, the Kabbel family survivalist army has a parodic, toy-soldier quality; Rudi's world was frozen, traumatically, in 1945, his responses fixed in the solipsistic intensity of an 11-year-old at play. His memoirs aren't an adequate account of World War II, even as a metaphor for the suffering of those years, and they aren't a reliable history of the Belorussian struggle, either. They're subjective and partial in a novelistic way: Kabbel has magnified his narrow, child's-eye view of experience into a complete system of belief, a faith that engulfs the world. Because Keneally surrounds Rudi's "history" with the drier, more practical narrative of the same period written by his father and with the contemporary realities of Delaney's story, we can see the full insanity of Rudi's writing.

What Kabbel is an example of, in fact, is a common madness, and a literary one: the writer's tendency to aggrandize his own consciousness, the assumption that an individual's trauma can be made to stand for all the horrors of history. Keneally's last book published in the United States, *Schindler's List* (1982), was a nonfiction narrative of Nazi-occupied Poland, patiently accumulated from the testimony of dozens of Holocaust survivors; he seems to have written *A Family Madness* as a demonstration of the dangers of that kind of consciousness, that kind of writing, as if to exorcise a madness in his own family. . . .

Keneally has given us a few sane people in his books, too, and they're invariably those who are skeptical of their ability to *represent*, who resist the burden of speaking for anyone else. Mathius Erzsberger of *Gossip from the Forest* (1975), the unlucky German cabinet minister designated by his defeated country to negotiate the terms of the November 1918 armistice, is one of them; so is Father James Maitland, the humane, beleaguered Irish priest of *Three Cheers for the Paraclete* (1968). These characters are, like the decent and confused Terry Delaney, caught in the middle of something, but Maitland's and Erzsberger's situations are almost too special, their responses too particular. The story of *A Family Madness* is deliberately—even self-consciously—more resonant: it is, along with *Passenger,* the novel that most fully embodies Keneally's complex historical sense. In *Passenger,* he makes us see the climactic birth of the fetus-narrator as the culmination of dozens of intricately interwoven forces—of destiny, design, and accident: when the baby arrives, he isn't the incarnation of anything special, but he seems nonetheless to be entering the world in a riot of significance. In the new novel, the forces are arrayed just as densely, and the consequences are tragic: poor Delaney loses his job, goes to work for Kabbel, falls in love with Kabbel's daughter Danielle (named for the dead mother), fathers her child, tries to pry her away from her crazy family, and finally witnesses the failure of all his good intentions. And although Delaney is never fully aware of the Kabbels' past, only its present-day effects, the narrative is structured as a demonstration of how the innocent are invaded by larger, more complex histories. At the novel's end, Terry is carrying the Kabbels' story as a part of himself, as if he'd inherited a disease. (p. 51)

The parallel narratives in *A Family Madness* turn out to be connected in a way that's both simpler and subtler than we'd imagined: the Belorussians, subsumed by the Soviet Union and (with their own participation) by Nazi Germany, extend history's chain of oppression in exile by engulfing a young Australian, making his troubled memory into their memorial. Terry Delaney has been singled out—he's White Russia's only colony. Keneally's point is that the Kabbels of the world can, when conditions are right, take possession of the Delaneys. The voices of particular and long-standing oppression make a more powerful claim on our imaginations than the shifting, everyday complaints of middle-class societies. Delaney's difficulty in finding a job, his setbacks on the rugby field, his mild boredom with his marriage seem trivial to him compared to the exotic Old World grief of the Kabbels. Keneally knows this as deeply as he knows anything, and it explains a lot about his writing: why he's attracted to the testimony of those the past has driven mad, and why, in recreating that testimony, he so frequently pulls back a little. He knows that a skillful novelist can, like Rudi Kabbel, be a persuasive madman, bending our ears, breaking down our resistance to his obsessions. And the words of priests, parents, teachers, and politicians—all those whose presence implies greater, more complete systems of knowledge—can likewise assume a terrible authority. In Keneally's version, these are the voices capable of colonizing those regions of the mind, crowding out doubts and rational apprehensions so we can act on these fragments of received knowledge: the ideas passed on to us have to turn into faith before they can become deeds, the stuff of history.

Keneally, who abandoned first the priesthood and then a teaching career before he became a novelist, may have turned to writing because it allows him at least the freedom of deciding how much, and what kind, of authority he's going to take on—he doesn't *have* to stand for something beyond himself. His

most distinctive quality as a novelist, especially as a 20th century novelist, is his reluctance to assume the voice of any one of his characters, to narrate from the point of view of a single consciousness. The form of Keneally's books is, in a sense, always the reflection of a moral attitude toward the material, and that approach has never been clearer than it is in *A Family Madness;* he wants to explore the ironies of history without turning himself, or his readers, into its victims.

Keneally's scrupulousness is a kind of modesty, a humility before the facts of history, though he never seems monotonously self-effacing, a passive recorder who wouldn't dare to merge his voice with the great voices of the past. Actually, the detachment of his method is anything but passive: he refuses to let the spirit of the past invade him, but seizes it instead by daring to interpret it. And in the body of his work—more than in any individual book—he even cuts a rather dashing figure. Tackling huge themes, he's averaged nearly a book a year since 1964: the promiscuity of his choices of periods and events to write about, and the sheer speed of it all, are the attributes of a reckless, heroic novelist, not a timid one. Keneally's books, as a result, are more distinct from each other than most contemporary novelists', which may make him seem elusive, a bit of a chameleon, and thus deprive his work of the attention it deserves. Not one of his characters really speaks for him, though the unborn narrator of *Passenger*—trapped in his mother's body, kicking with pure animal need, and trying to figure out what kind of world he's headed for—comes close. (As it turns out, he's headed for Australia.) And Keneally's treatment of Oskar Schindler—the German industrialist who was one of the ''just Gentiles'' of the Holocaust, rescuing over a thousand Polish Jews from death in the camps—is revealing, too. Schindler is no saint (he's a hearty businessman who eats and drinks too much and cheats on his wife), but his actions in an appalling time give him, for that moment, a radiant significance. He's someone who refuses to let the demented voices of his own country possess him; who lies a little and cajoles a bit in order to pull a few people free of a relentless wave, and he's the only real hero in Keneally's work.

In *A Family Madness,* there's no hero (just an ordinary, rather unformed young man waiting to be born into history), and no first-person testimony we can rely on (just the memoirs of another man who's waiting for an imaginary wave to submerge himself in). The voice of this novel is cumulative, like the chorus of witnesses we hear in the background of *Schindler's List,* growing from whispers to a low roar to a rich, pure chant. At the end of *A Family Madness,* Terry Delaney's mind is filled, resonant, with a phrase spoken innocently by Danielle, as if she didn't know it was a familiar refrain: ''Don't be cruel.'' Keneally speaks here, as he always does, through a complex, echoing structure, and what we hear, very clearly, are the impassioned, quietly subversive tones of a just man. (pp. 51-2)

Terrence Rafferty, ''Thomas Keneally Pleads Sanity,'' in The Village Voice, *Vol. XXXI, No. 18, May 6, 1986, pp. 51-2.*

Benedict Kiely

1919-

Irish novelist, short story writer, essayist, critic, journalist, and editor.

Kiely is regarded as a masterful storyteller in the tradition of the Gaelic *seanachie,* a teller of tales and history. Kiely's descriptive prose evokes the people, cities, villages, and rural landscape of Ireland, where all of his fiction is set. By combining humor, literary allusions, and humanitarian principles and employing such elements as symbol and myth, Kiely creates works that operate on several levels and examine how Irish social, cultural, and religious forces affect individuals. Thomas Flanagan noted: "Kiely is a man of wide literary culture, with a deep, unyielding tolerance for almost every range and variety of human experience." While many of Kiely's early works focus on such themes as provincialism, hypocrisy, and religious piety, his later books, notably *Proxopera* (1977) and *Nothing Happens in Carmincross* (1985), express his deepening outrage at the violence in Northern Ireland.

Two of Kiely's early novels, *In a Harbour Green* (1949) and *Call for a Miracle* (1950), ironically connect social and religious intolerance and pettiness with violence. *Honey Seems Bitter* (1952) is a psychological study of an introspective man whose attempts to understand himself are complicated by a murder mystery and a romantic triangle. *The Cards of the Gambler* (1953) is a supernatural allegory that updates a Gaelic folktale about a doctor who is granted three wishes by God. The story is infused with symbolic and mythic allusions relating to such diverse topics as Celtic lore, gambling, and pagan and Christian religion, and includes the doctor's dialogues with Death, God, and the Devil. *There Was an Ancient House* (1955) derives from Kiely's experiences at a Jesuit novitiate and offers a realistic and colorful account of this lifestyle while examining religious themes. In *The Captain with the Whiskers* (1960), a sadistic former sea captain tyrannizes his family. The captain's erudition serves as a means for discussing a wide range of topics, including evil and hypocrisy.

Dogs Enjoy the Morning (1968) secured Kiely's reputation as a major contemporary Irish novelist. This work humorously refutes pious Christian morality and features Kiely's use of a variety of literary devices to portray representative Irish characters and social attitudes. According to Daniel J. Casey, this novel "is Kiely's most humorous fiction . . . , but, at the same time, his most profound commentary on human strength and human fallibility." Casey added: "[*Dogs Enjoy the Morning*] establishes Kiely's claim as one of Ireland's important modern writers and ranks as one of the most outstanding contemporary novels in English."

Kiely has also written several well-respected works that focus on the political and religious divisions in Northern Ireland. His first novel, *Land without Stars* (1946), set during World War II, concerns two brothers who hold opposing political viewpoints; one brother is conservative and pacifistic, while the other is a revolutionary who bitterly opposes British influence on Northern Ireland. *Proxopera*, a novella which was republished in *The State of Ireland: A Novella and Seventeen Stories* (1980), relates the moral dilemma of a man coerced into plant-

Photograph by Mark Gerson

ing a bomb by terrorists who are holding his family hostage. In *Nothing Happens in Carmincross,* an Irish professor returns from a teaching post in the United States to attend his niece's wedding. His visit to his homeland, detailed with Kiely's characteristic humor and literary references, is marred by the persistent violence he witnesses.

Kiely's short story collections include *A Journey to the Seven Streams: Seventeen Stories* (1963), *A Ball of Malt and Madame Butterfly* (1973), *A Cow in the House* (1978), and *The State of Ireland.* Many of his stories present eccentric characters and offer further evidence of Kiely's humorous development of serious themes. Kiely has also written several works of nonfiction, including *Counties of Contention: A Study of the Origins and Implications of the Partition of Ireland* (1945), and two critical studies of Irish literature: *Poor Scholar: A Study of the Works and Days of William Carleton, 1794-1869* (1947) and *Modern Irish Fiction* (1950).

(See also *CLC*, Vol. 23; *Contemporary Authors*, Vols. 1-4, rev. ed.; *Contemporary Authors New Revision Series*, Vol. 2; and *Dictionary of Literary Biography*, Vol. 15.)

JANET EGLESON DUNLEAVY

In another city, in another country, to be labeled a journalist is often a liability for an aspiring young writer. . . . But in Ireland, where arts graduates of exceptional ability traditionally have begun their careers as staff members on Dublin newspapers, and even letters to the editor are written with style and imagination, such an offer was an opportunity. For Benedict Kiely, it meant becoming a colleague of such men as Brian O'Nolan (a.k.a. Flann O'Brien/Myles na gCopaleen), whose irreverent humor, subtle wit, and curious ability to combine the lyric and satiric were not unlike his own. It meant being turned loose to investigate the city that had produced such disparate talents as Sean O'Casey (whose ability to laugh at the edge of the grave Kiely shares) and James Joyce (from whom Kiely may have learned the technique of objectifying, through his older writer's eyes, the personal feelings and emotions of his younger, remembered self). . . . [In] 1946, Kiely's own reputation as a creative writer was publicly launched by the appearance of a novel, *Land without Stars,* and the publication of a short story, **"Blackbird in a Bramble Bough."** (pp. 159-60)

For Benedict Kiely, as for George Moore (a predecessor about whom he frequently writes with a certain ambivalence), it is the story that always holds him in thrall; in his fiction, as in Moore's, there is always the sound of a man's voice speaking. Yet his short stories have been called uneven by some critics. Daniel Casey, who prefers Kiely's novels, describes the narrative mode of the early stories as straightforward and conventional and at times finds his situations contrived, his characters stereotyped, his descriptions "unnecessarily elaborate" [see *CLC,* Vol. 23]. These are, of course, characteristics of oral narrative, the type of storytelling Kiely would have learned from listening carefully to the seanachie in Donegal; they are characteristics also of Carleton's *Traits and Stories of the Irish Peasantry,* to which Kiely has acknowledged a debt. Perceived as purposeful, they become not flaws but evidence of a stage in Kiely's development. A comparison of his two volumes of short fiction, *A Journey to the Seven Streams: Seventeen Stories* (1963) and *A Ball of Malt and Madame Butterfly: A Dozen Stories* (1973), confirms this judgment.

"Blackbird in the Bramble Bough," from the first volume . . . , is a tale of a young man's disillusion with a visiting poet. It begins with the young man looking at a clipping from an American newspaper, which contains a picture of a poet who had visited Ireland not many months before and a critic's description of his poetry as "like the song of a blackbird on a bramble bough." The rest is recollection: of the evening when the poet had come to lecture at the local convent school, of the young man's excitement when he, a young teacher, had been assigned to look after the distinguished visitor. The poet's stature had diminished in direct proportion to the time they had spent together; by the end of the evening, as the young man recalls—with amusement, chronicling the highlights for himself and the reader, but also with a certain sense of superiority—the poet had been completely demystified. Kiely's vivid descriptions and earthy humor leave the reader amused, too, but the story, a slight effort, provides neither insight nor heightened understanding. (pp. 160-61)

["**The Little Wrens and Roses**" is] also about a young man and a poet. The narrative I, Ben, is the young man; Cousin Ellen, the poet, is a "nonstop talker" who used to try his father's patience during her visits to the family. Ben mocks her to himself, to the amusement of the reader, by quoting lines from her sentimental verse and by reciting a parody of a typical Cousin Ellen monologue. But he also recalls that, to himself as well as to others, she was once something of a local celebrity, because her poems were published in the local newspaper. By the time he was eighteen he had realized that these poems were crude and banal. Still he had enjoyed Cousin Ellen's visits, for the show they provided: Cousin Ellen talking, talking, talking, apparently without need of breath; his father muttering that he was drowning, "drifting slowly, sinking slowly, brain and body numb, . . . but teetotally helpless." Ben remembers Cousin Ellen in the hospital, shortly before she died. In her usual fashion she had rattled on, a comic figure, threatening to make a poem out of every second observation. Later, he had walked to the station, talking of Cousin Ellen with the new servant girl from Mayo, a young woman with a sweet singing voice but an unfortunate birthmark on one cheek. To the young woman, as unsophisticated as once he had been, the published poet was an awesome figure. Tongue in cheek, he had declaimed one of Cousin Ellen's sentimental verses, but his mocking condescension had been lost on her: she had sung the words to a slow sweet tune that the narrator had "never heard before or since."

Far more sophisticated than **"Blackbird in the Bramble Bough,"** **"The Little Wrens and Roses"** is an example of Kiely's ability to play with narrative focus, first inviting the reader to regard Cousin Ellen as silly, self-centered, and vain; then asking the reader to admire her as a great character in the Irish meaning of that term; then making her an object of pity; and finally giving voice to her "poetic soul" in a tune that expresses the emotions Cousin Ellen could not convey. Another story from the same collection . . . reveals a different but equally skillful handling of narrative technique. **"A Great God's Angel Standing"** begins as a straightforward narrative, a fairly conventional tale of the friendship of a priest and a rake, with the narrative focused on the rake (he, of course, has the greater capacity to amuse the reader; he, like Milton's snake, gets all the good lines). Little by little a narrative presence enters the story, until "I" becomes a character deserving of the reader's attention. The jokes cease; the story develops an unexpected poignancy as the focus shifts to the priest; "I" has the last word. Whose story has been told? The reader—the humor still echoing in his mind, but with an unexpected pang in the heart—is left with the question.

For the most part critics have concentrated on Kiely's novels, noting his short fiction only in passing. . . . Exceptions are John Wilson Foster, who regards Kiely as "the equal of O'Faolain and within hailing distance of O'Connor"; Thomas Flanagan, who perceives in Kiely's Omagh resemblances to Faulkner's Yoknapatawpha [see *CLC,* Vol. 23]; and Mervyn Wall, who calls attention to the evidence in Kiely's short stories of his commitment to the traditions of Irish storytelling. Certainly, one significance of Kiely's short fiction is its debt to the techniques of the Irish storyteller. His contributions to the genre are notable also for the sheer poetry of their descriptive passages, especially those detailing the splendors of Ulster river valleys and countryside; for the skillful juxtaposition of humor and pathos, used by the author not just for effect, but to maintain subtle control of the narrative; and for a lustiness and earthiness that, according to Vivian Mercier, belong within a well-documented Irish comic tradition even older than that of the Irish folktale.

Like Mary Lavin, Benedict Kiely recently has begun to write fiction that is shorter than the conventional novel, longer than the conventional short story. *Proxopera* (1977), his first effort to employ the format of the novella or tale, also represents a departure in style and content. In its attack on terrorism it is more topical than Kiely's other work. Instead of subtle irony or witty satire, Kiely's usual verbal weapons, it depends on the evocative power of language more commonly found in Kiely's descriptive passages to achieve its effect. Whether it will remain a single work in the author's corpus or indicates a new direction for his shorter fiction remains to be seen. (pp. 161-62)

> Janet Egleson Dunleavy, "Mary Lavin, Elizabeth Bowen, and a New Generation: The Irish Short Story at Midcentury," in The Irish Short Story: A Critical History, edited by James F. Kilroy, Twayne Publishers, 1984, pp. 145-68.

JOHN GROSS

Carmincross, where nothing happens, is a small town in Ulster. Mervyn Kavanagh is a wandering son of Carmincross (Catholic as opposed to Protestant Carmincross) who has been teaching in America, at a women's college in "the semi-Deep South"— a well-cushioned exile in "a never-never land of dogwood and forsythia and chipmunks and young people." He has also acquired and then lost an American wife, who has left him and gone to live in New York, with a boyfriend in fitful attendance.

Now, at the outset of Benedict Kiely's new novel [*Nothing Happens in Carmincross*] Kavanagh is on his way home to attend the wedding of a favorite niece. When we meet him, he has just enplaned at Kennedy, with 10 brandy alexanders ("or brandies alexander") inside him, and some whimsical speculations on who exactly Alexander might have been buzzing round in his head. A genial sort, Mervyn, a man in his 50's, "big and fat and bald and Irish and cheerful." It isn't long before he "nibbles or nipples" at yet another brandy.

Leaving the plane at Shannon, he stops at a hotel owned by an old pal, and then sets off by car toward tranquil Carmincross in the company of Deborah, a former girlfriend with a sharp tongue but, on this particular occasion, an obliging disposition. Much of the novel is taken up with an account of the couple's leisurely, talkative journey north and of the fine selection of scenes and characters they encounter en route. Every so often their progress is punctuated by glimpses of Deborah's estranged husband, who is pursuing her, and by aggressive trans-Atlantic phone calls from Mervyn's wife, but such distractions aren't enough to cast a pall for long. And after all, they are on their way to a wedding feast.

One cloud, however, proves impossible to dispel. From the beginning of the novel, Mervyn has been haunted by dark thoughts of bombs, rubber bullets, political murder, political mutilation, terrorism and counterterrorism—not only in Ireland, but with the Irish example, naturally enough, uppermost in his mind. . . .

On his journey home, Mervyn samples some very different responses to the new Troubles—one man's gallant freedom fighter is another man's fanatical yahoo. And as the arguments bubble away, the sense of ominous possibilities grows stronger. When an outrage (cleverly prepared for in novelistic terms) finally takes place, when something does at last happen in Carmincross, it is no great surprise in itself, although the attendant circumstances are horrifyingly unpredictable.

Even readers who know of Mr. Kiely's comic gift from his previous novels may find it hard to see much scope for comedy in such material. Yet the first thing to say about *Nothing Happens in Carmincross* is that it is often brilliantly funny, and not just in its more boozy or boisterous episodes, that it brings a searing wit to the grim events it describes.

That wit is above all to be found at work in Mervyn's talk and still more in his thoughts, in the sudden leaps of his tumbling, fast-flowing stream of consciousness. He has a mind packed with familiar quotations, pop songs, learned allusions, running gags, all kinds of odd scraps and echoes—a mind where John Milton keeps company with Dolly Parton, where virtuoso mimicry and inspired wordplay come naturally.

He is also a master of abrasive irony, whose mock-rhetoric acquires a rhetorical, almost poetic force of its own. . . . A terrorist unit fails to phone through its warning to the local population in time, with dreadful results, because it overlooks the fact that another unit has put the telephone exchange out of action: "Should one patriotic perpetrator not remember what another patriotic perpetrator has recently perpetrated?" This is not just a merry tongue-twister, but an implied comment on both the action itself and the inadequacy of the flat or euphemistic words used to describe it in bulletins and communiques.

But then even a word like "wounded," as Mervyn remarks at one point, is "a mild word" when you think of what it can signify. The effect of his black humor, far from distancing us from horror, is to bring it home to us more vividly, to overcome the "mildness" of a settled response. The atrocities he conjures up are atrocities indeed. . . .

[There] can be no doubt that the principal thrust of the book is a revulsion against terrorism of both the homegrown and international varieties. It is an all too timely theme, and one to which this remarkable novel does justice in a masterly fashion.

> John Gross, in a review of "Nothing Happens in Carmincross," in The New York Times, October 18, 1985, p. C27.

RICHARD EDER

Nothing Happens in Carmincross is both novel and discourse, and extraordinary both ways. More than that, stupendously more, it is a way of thinking about Ireland. The Irish Situation comes down from the attic of our mind only when some particularly extravagant or bloody gesture catches our attention; and the news analysis that follows promptly sends it back into storage; not because the analysis is wrong, but because it is right in just the way such analyses have been right for the last couple of decades.

Mervyn Kavanagh flies from New York to attend the wedding of a niece in the little town of Carmincross, in the west of Ireland and just north of the border. He is big, bald, exuberant and middle-aged; a hard drinker, a womanizer when the opportunity offers, and of an inquiring mind.

From the moment the plane takes off, though, Mervyn's trip is touched by the elements of a quest. The passenger beside him is legless and Mervyn takes over the care of him from the stewardesses. His entry into Ireland, accordingly, is made pushing a cripple in a wheelchair.

Mervyn stops off to spend a day or two with a childhood friend who runs a hotel in the south. He picks up an old girlfriend,

Deborah, and takes her along with him on a leisurely drive up north. They eat, drink, sightsee, make love and visit acquaintances along the way. It is, or should be, a pleasure excursion to the most innocent of celebrations.

But it is invaded at every moment by The Situation. The radio reports bombings and kneecappings. Friends, ranging from cynics to enthusiasts, argue with each other and themselves. And Mervyn's consciousness becomes a great caldron in which Irish history, present-day politics, bits of old ballads, the brutal individual accounts on the radio, memories, jokes, and arguments swirl together.

It becomes a dream trip. At times, Mervyn, and Deborah—who is being followed by her strangely patient husband—become the Diarmuid and Grainne of legend, fleeing her warrior husband, Fionn. We think of Joyce's mingling of legendary Ireland with the small-minded Dubin of the 20th Century.

Kiely, one of the most important Irish writers of our time, intends us to think of Joyce. Also of Yeats, of Irish heroic poetry, love ballads, the war songs of each generation, the use of contemporary pop music to convey contemporary bloodshed, and the jokes, bulletins, slogans, epigrams, the precious and the cheap, the heroic, mock heroic and cynical. They all revolve, in wonderful and appalling fashion, in Mervyn's great bald head. . . .

The assemblage gives us all Ireland by the time Mervyn and Deborah reach Carmincross two-thirds the way through the book. Suddenly everything changes. Instead of the wedding there is a disaster. Its details and extent become apparent in disconnected bits and pieces, floating down like the debris of a bomb blast. It is difficult to grasp at first. The narration has gone into shock, and only gradually does the full awfulness become apparent.

Nothing I know has captured the Irish Situation so remarkably as *Nothing Happens in Carmincross*. It is Joyce's nightmare of history from which a nation is trying to awake. Contrary to Santayana, it is precisely through *remembering* history that the Irish seem condemned to repeat it. Through streets where girls go out in scarfs and curlers, where rock music comes through the cafe windows, where supermarkets sell frozen food and instant pie mix, medieval companies march along, impaling babies on their pikes.

Finally, Kiely suggests that the special case may not be so special. Other messages seep into Mervyn's clogged head. A woman stoned to death in Iran. Another woman burned in a racial incident in Boston. Nuclear submarines cruising under the Irish Sea.

Kiely does not press the point. Ireland is special, after all. Only he makes us ask: And what are we? Eight hundred dead in Ireland. How many in Dresden? How many dead of malnutrition in Africa? How many of speed, speeding or AIDS in the United States?

As I say, he is an artist and does not press it. It is the unique intimacy of the Irish tragedy and the unique brilliance of language around it that makes it so special and perhaps so inextricable. What would our disasters be like if we dared to use the language for them? Is the true birth of Yeats' terrible beauty not in the events of Easter, 1916, but, quite literally, in the poem itself?

> Richard Eder, in a review of "Nothing Happens in Carmincross," in Los Angeles Times Book Review, October 20, 1985, p. 3.

JOHN UPDIKE

[Benedict Kiely has produced] a novel tinged by the bitter wisdom of late middle age and raked by sore disenchantment; but his book, *Nothing Happens in Carmincross* . . . is lamentably diffuse, . . . muddied and meandering in its execution. . . . Mr. Kiely has always been a garrulous writer, most winningly so in such lilting short stories as **"A Journey to the Seven Streams,"** where the easy, talking prose tumbles along as brightly as a mountain brook. He has, Thomas Flanagan informed us in his introduction to Kiely's collection of stories *The State of Ireland* (1980) [see *CLC*, Vol. 23], a mind spectacularly stocked with quotations and songs; echoes drawn from this mental treasure have often deepened the run of his heroes' meditations and enriched our awareness of Ireland's complicated, incessantly verbalized history. But through his present hero, the historian and college teacher Mervyn Kavanaugh, Mr. Kiely has provided himself with too smooth a conduit to his own erudition and has drowned his tale in recollected words.

The tale is a slight one: in the summer of 1973, Professor Kavanaugh, who has been teaching at a girls' college in Virginia, returns to Ireland to attend his favorite niece's wedding; accompanied by an overweight and complaisant barmaid named Deborah, and pursued by phone calls from his estranged wife in New York City, he drives north from the vicinity of Shannon Airport to his home village of Carmincross, in Northern Ireland, where terrorist mischief mars the wedding. On this journey I clocked the literary allusions at two and a half per page, and braced myself every time the dialogue veered into the thudding rhymes of Celtic balladry. . . . [Deborah] calls him Merlin and her pursuing husband Mandrake, and Mervyn repeatedly indulges the fancy that the three of them parallel the legendary triangle of King Fionn, Queen Gráinne, and her lover Diarmuid. Another character, helpfully called Jeremiah, wields Biblical verses with a vengeance. "Quotations. Quotations," Mervyn's wife complains to him over the phone, and he himself reflects that "the mind of a reading man cursed with a plastic memory, who also goes to the movies, and watches television, is a jumble sale, a lumber-room." Irish history is discussed by the board foot, and a whole scrapbook of terrorist atrocities, Irish and other, is presented by way of conversation, rumination, and daily newspaper reading. Several long letters to the absent Mrs. Kavanaugh are indited in a style quite as leisurely and farraginous as the narrative method itself. Italics are never used to distinguish levels of reality, third person and first swing back and forth from sentence to sentence in Mervyn's stream of rumination, and Mr. Kiely's Joycean loyalty to the dash as the means of signifying speech (a typographical preference whose only conceivable utility is to brand the work at a glance as stubbornly, honorably avant-garde) further clouds the raddled flow. When the author does have an immediate, potentially affecting event to relate—and he has several, toward the end—he tends, Faulknerishly, to skim right past it and then reel it in by flashback. Though not quite incoherent, the novel appears to place coherence low on the list of aesthetic virtues. References to the Falklands War and the Ayatollah's Iran dot the 1973 scene, and an afterword blithely acknowledges such anachronisms with the question "Does it matter?"

Not that Mr. Kiely's fine native style is altogether suppressed. Individual sentences flash out smartly. . . . (pp. 147-48)

But the narrator's eye rather rarely focusses on external appearances. An extended wayward process of self-recrimination and consolation takes that eye inward and backward. The private aspect of Mervyn's journey, his sexual fling with Deborah, feels wishful and recalls Colonel Cantwell's amour with the Contessa in Hemingway's *Across the River and Into the Trees*. . . . The lady, indeed, is so purely the echo of Mervyn's desires and thoughts that when, late in their travels, she develops an individual decisiveness and a misfortune of her own the author and the hero both hurry, unchivalrously, to drop her.

The public aspect of *Nothing Happens in Carmincross* is of course the Ulster wars, the vicious pollution that Northern Ireland's competing terrorist factions have worked upon the beautiful land where Mervyn was reared, as a Catholic with Protestant neighbors. Carmincross is another version of Mr. Kiely's native town of Omagh, in County Tyrone. The bucolic scenes of his early fiction, to which war and violence travelled only as rumor and as legends spun by Ireland's adventuring sons, now are given over to the "Bombomb Yahoos" of both religious persuasions, whose explosives, homemade (a new cottage industry) of gelignite, fuel oil, and ammonium nitrate, are thrown into pub doors, dropped into letter boxes, and delivered by teen-age girls pushing prams. The gangs, whether I.R.A. (Irish Republic Army) or U.D.F. (Ulster Defence Force), extract "black rent"—protection money—from shops and businesses, pour appropriately colored paint (orange or green) over the heads of girls suspected of collaboration with the opposite side, and murder farmers in their fields and children in their beds. The centuries of Irish struggle against British rule have come, in Mervyn's view, to the triumph of "thuggery and blaggery" and the destruction of mutual trust, of every decent institution from the neighborhood pub to the public schools.

This is a sombre and mighty theme. And no living writer is better equipped than Benedict Kiely, out of the depth of his feeling and knowledge, to dramatize it. But Mervyn Kavanaugh offers a poor handle on the situation. . . . Our empathy with Mervyn feels obstructed; we want to like him better than he likes himself. Even as he visits the old sites and drives along the old ways his heart hangs back in America, with his unhappy, tenacious wife and "dogwood visions of slim girls like white fish in a blue pool." "They're a happy people," he jokes, of Americans. To the unhappiness of his own people he has returned as a tourist. Grieve though he does, Mervyn is merely visiting the distressed areas of Ireland; he does not have to live there, and the end of the novel sees him safely tucked back into the anesthesia of the New World. (pp. 148-49)

One would feel shyer in expressing reservations about this novel's treatment of a topic so momentous had not Mr. Kiely, in the story *Proxopera* (1979), already handled it consummately. In that long story, which concludes *The State of Ireland* and is dedicated "In Memory of the Innocent Dead," the hero, Granda Binchey, like Mervyn a teacher with a mind full of quotations, is, unlike him, a lifelong resident of his tormented village and has achieved all his ambitions there. Also unlike him, he is the protagonist of a dramatic action: with his son, daughter-in-law, and two grandchildren held hostage, the elder Binchey is forced to drive a car laden with a time bomb into the heart of town. This action, shown entirely through the old man's fluctuating observations and resolves, better conveys the agony of Northern Ireland than all the news items, horrific and deplorable though they are, that are strung on the crooked line of Mervyn's boozy peregrinations. At its most effective, *Nothing Happens in Carmincross* shocks us as a newspaper does: this happens out there. In *Proxopera,* it happens within us, as fiction makes things happen. Compared with the circumstan-

tial, suspenseful flight of the shorter work, the novel rushes ponderously about, feathered in quotations and wildly glowing, like an angel beating its wings but not quite getting off the ground. In this failure to rise we feel the heaviness of its theme. (p. 149)

John Updike, in a review of "Nothing Happens in Carmincross," in The New Yorker, *Vol. LXI, No. 35, October 21, 1985, pp. 146, 148-49.*

WILLIAM KENNEDY

Mr. Kiely's novel [*Nothing Happens in Carmincross*] is linked in subject matter to his book of short stories *The State of Ireland,* published here in 1980. Most particularly, it is linked to the novella in that collection, *Proxopera,* which is a small masterpiece about a bombing in a provincial town. But whereas *Proxopera* was constructed with great attention to plot and suspense, *Carmincross* is written as if plot and continuity were as inimical to the author as are the depredations of the British Army, and the murders by the Roman Catholic and Protestant fanatics of the North's political war.

He depicts Mervyn Kavanagh as a fat, bald, middle-aged storyteller incapable of not interrupting himself. . . . Add the fact that Kiely-Kavanagh is a man of great and curious erudition in literature, history, myth, song and barroom folklore, and what you end with is an incorrigible archivist, a manic associationalist.

Now he's with the legendary hero Fionn MacCumhaill, tracking Diarmuid and Grainne through mythic mountain heather, now with Helen of Troy and Olivia Newton-John, now with the MacDonnells of the Isles—foreign mercenaries with double-headed axes, hacking their way through medieval Ireland—now with Leila Khaled wreaking havoc for Palestine or with a half-dozen blacks setting a white girl on fire in Boston. At a oneness with all the violence of history, he finds vicious twists to the Irish-American ballads: "I'm dreaming of thee, dear little isle of the West, sweet spot by memory blest"—this after the bombs go off.

This style is the novelistic stream of consciousness writ large; the work of a man with a godlike view of history, and the didactic urge of an angry man for whom the tidiness of art (like *Proxopera*) is not enough. The man needs to sprawl cosmically, for how else can one tell the story of a heavenly garden decomposing into a backyard of hell? How else can the reader be made to see not only consequences but causes?

Mr. Kiely has succeeded so often as an artist that he needs no further consecration, but I sense that this work will be viewed as something of a tract, a political argument in which the politics are not only implicit but also imposed. The thin plot is Kavanagh's odyssey to the North from New York City, onto an airplane bound for Shannon, then to a nearby hotel where he is reunited with an old mistress and a childhood pal, and where he also meets people with whom he will eventually rendezvous at Carmincross. . . .

When the book is not an argument, it is a monologue, or a collage of actual, violent news stories, or a tissue of legendary or mythic tragedy, remembered in that plastic mind.

John Montague, one of Ireland's major poets and an old friend of Mr. Kiely's, has described him as one of the most beloved of Irish writers, who is "almost overcome by the variety of life." This book is testimony to the truth of that observation.

None of this demeans the book's achievements, especially for those Americans for whom the news of Ireland is always insufficiently reported, except when the roof is blown away. What is here, along with the bomb and the gun, is the madness behind them both. . . .

Benedict Kiely loves the North, but despite his great wit and exuberance of language, he must surely be one of the saddest men in Ireland because of what is going, and gone. No man not weighted with loss could summon the anger that is behind this book. He gives us the natural world, the evolutionary history and the society that is in shreds within them.

He also knows that Northern Ireland isn't the worst place in the world. Lebanon's violence is worse, Mexico's earthquakes produced more corpses. But one good man killed in his innocence, one family bombed away by inadvertence, one town smithereened by men who derive meaning only from death, deserve scrutiny and reverence. . . .

"So," writes Mr. Kiely, "are great deeds done or perpetrated in my homeland . . . in the name of God and of the dead generations," and in these lines fuses both his own sadness and the heroic, revolutionary rhetoric to whose cadences so much innocent blood is now blowing in the Irish wind.

> William Kennedy, "Heaven Is the Backyard of Hell," in The New York Times Book Review, *October 27, 1985, p. 7.*

DAN CASEY

Kiely's mastery of form owes an obvious debt to the yarn-spinner in the chimney corner. So many of his stories echo the tale-teller's voice—now discernible, now muted—or harken back nostalgically to a fading folk tradition captivatingly punctuated by songs and verse and historical anecdotes. The tales are crowded with unforgettable characters the likes of whom will never pass this way again. Even the landscapes—the ruins and crags and bracken—offer grand possibilities for reviving the wonder and magic of yore.

Though steeped in legend and lore, Kiely's stories are also deceptively sophisticated and thoroughly modern. A wise storyteller ever conscious of audience, he introduces current themes and psychological conflicts set against contemporary backdrops, so that the works are often layered, playing off past and present or extending the narrative symbolically and adding yet a third strand to the weave. In recent years Kiely has admitted to an obsession with the horror of the Northern "troubles," and that obsession has had a profound effect on his fiction. It has become more somber, more intense, less comic. *Proxopera* and the later stories attest to the grim spectre of sectarian violence and show an angrier side of the Irish storyteller. Though Kiely's rise to fame has been slow, he has, after thirty years, arrived and taken a place among the masters of the genre.

Since 1980, when *The State of Ireland* was published, the storyteller has further distinguished himself as a novelist. *Nothing Happens in Carmincross,* a controversial and curiously apolitical novel, surfaced in late 1985. Begun more than twelve years earlier as a chronicle of Northern Irish atrocities, a kind of stream-of-nightmare lament for the blood-strewn province, the project had several times to be shelved. The atrocities kept mounting and the lament finally gave way to depression. But periodically Kiely would return to the task and catalogue more neighborly Northern grotesqueries. The cataloguing added to the urgency of the mission. *Proxopera,* the spare, savage, sus-

penseful account of an abortive proxy-bombing, was likely culled from that chronicle in 1976.

Then, one day, an innocent young girl in Killeter, County Tyrone, a border village a few miles from Kiely's birthplace and a place where nothing ever happened, went out to post invitations to her wedding and was blown to smithereens by an incendiary. The obscenity of that mindless act moved the writer to finish the work.

This novel could not be a mere exercise in polemics, however. It demanded a sensitive and critical observer at a distance, so Kiely created Mervyn Kavanagh, an Irish-born academic teaching in America and invited him home to attend the wedding of a favorite niece in Carmincross. Kavanagh, fat, balding and in his mid-fifties, is a roaming encyclopedia of Irish history, literature, mythology, verse and song, and he is blessed with an unflagging *joie de vivre* and love of Ireland. No better man for a wedding or a wake.

On the flight from New York to Shannon, Kavanagh's fertile imagination, stirred by brandy and randomnalia, ranges over the whole of human experience. His exuberance is only slightly dampened by the legless, bladderless gentleman in the next seat, spokesman for all the innocent maimed. It is Kiely striking the theme and tone, saying, "Here is a mutilated man coming back to a mutilated country, mutilated in every way, because history has betrayed it."

Before trekking north to the nuptials in Carmincross, Kavanagh seeks out a few old friends—a hotel manager and school-chum with a generous nature; his assistant, a lusty former mistress; and a cynical civil servant, an associate from the past. Each will, of course, add dimension to the narrative. Deborah, Kavanagh's old flame, takes leave from her hotel job to traipse bog and vale with the inscrutable Mervyn, and the modern-day Diarmuid and Grainne hie off on adventures and bed-quests, keeping one step ahead of Deborah's husband, who is, in turn, Fionn and Mandrake and a pursuing shadow in a red car. The ensuing odyssey seems nearly frivolous in view of the work at hand, but it is not. There is, for example, the visit to a 1916 Republican hero that establishes contrasts in political philosophies and military tactics between old and new breeds of revolutionaries. There are the fresh reports of bombings and brutalities that dog them along the journey north and underscore the apparent hopelessness of the situation.

The novel occasionally rambles, but the digressions provide comic relief from the grand absurdity of a Pyrrhic war rumbling ominously in the wings. It sublimates tribal skirmishes but moves ineluctably toward a family gathering in Carmincross, a fateful scene where a favorite niece excuses herself from the best of company to step out and post her wedding invitations.

Kavanagh reflects on life after the bomb:

> On the sidewalk a lump of clothes with the blood running out of it. People flat on the sidewalk as if a steamroller had rolled over them. A priest tells of two legs sticking out of a pile of rubble, of shattered bodies, you could see the life going out of them. He anointed what he found there. In this car there was a body, decapitated, but no way of knowing whether it was a man or woman.

Gruesome details of a gruesome act. But why Carmincross? Why niece Stephanie? Why this hour of this day? Mervyn speculates with the reader: "To you there faraway in America, and far away from me and everything that I belong to or belongs to me, or that, for good or bad, made me that way I am, it may be difficult to explain how or why destruction came to Carmincross.'' But even he comes up short on the explanation. (pp. 2-4)

Nothing Happens in Carmincross has a nobility about it—it has grace and rhythm and style. Only a writer with Kiely's erudition and genius could have fathered ''Merlin the Magician'' and given voice to the indomitable spirit who stands steadfastly for life after the bomb. Kiely's tenth novel, and his best to date, is brilliantly conceived and brilliantly orchestrated. It's in a league with *Ulysses, At Swim-Two-Birds,* and other modern Irish masterpieces.

The 1980s have been especially kind to Benedict Kiely. He has, at long last, won international recognition for his fiction. But for forty years Kiely turned his considerable talents toward a wide range of subjects and wrote eloquently as historian, critic, essayist, and *savant.* (p. 4)

In spite of his obvious strengths as a novelist, Benedict Kiely reigns as successor to O'Connor and O'Faolain, doyen of Irish short fiction, and prince of Irish storytellers. He has over the years contributed some three-score stories to the most discriminating journals and won high marks for his virtuosity.

Though Kiely's stories, from the late-forties to the seventies and eighties, have had enormous appeal, they have also shown discernible aesthetic growth, a progression in narrative complexity. The early fiction offers relatively uncomplicated incidents, stories told in the first person or told omnisciently, but with a distinct sense of narrator. The later fiction is, by contrast, more subtle, more suggestive, darker and more complex. While, at times, they seem to lack narrative unity, the later stories move in loose psychological streams of consciousness that keep doubling back on one another, finally melding in a single cumulative effect. (p. 7)

[In ''Blackbird in a Bramble Bough''] the narrator examines a photo of a poet in a Philadelphia newspaper that is sent to a local publican. He reads the American critic's comment on the poetry; ''a note of freshness like the song of the blackbird on a bramble bough,'' it says. Then he recalls how he came to be at the lecture on Alice Meynell at the *aula maxima* in the convent school, and recollects the bald, obese poet of the clammy hand, Chestertonian cape, and book-and-bottle-laden grip. That night the young narrator's thoughts were far from the words of the caped wonder, the poetry of dear dead Alice, and the tea and sweetcakes offered by the withered nun from Waterford. He fantasized about soft white feminine loveliness lined row on row before him, exchanged knowing glances with a fair-haired lass, and imagined frothy pints and genial company in the town below.

The young man becomes the reluctant custodian of the distinguished visitor whom he comes quickly to despise. After transporting poet and valise to the hotel and standing more rounds than he should, the narrator succeeds in sending the drunken muse staggering through the rear gates of the convent garden in search of other after-hours' pleasure. The episode is hilarious and it is well enough told that the author selected it for *A Journey to the Seven Streams* seventeen years later.

Twelve years after he wrote of the poet, Kiely spins a wistful yarn that perfectly contrasts the imaginary and the real. ''The White Wild Bronco'' (1958) . . . uses a brilliant triptych effect to juxtapose an invalid's horizontal grey world of shops, warehouses, and railway yards with Edgar Rice Burroughs' lush African jungle of Tarzan and the Maoris and with Deadwood Dick's Dodge City of Wyatt Earp and Western villains. (pp. 7-8)

[Other pieces]—''The Heroes in the Dark House'' (1959), ''The Dogs in the Great Glen'' (1960), ''The Shortest Way Home'' (1962)—show similar authorial skill, managing two or three narrative strands while incorporating snatches of song and verse and history and memory and myth.

Twelve years after ''The White Wild Bronco'' and twenty-four after ''Blackbird in a Bramble Bough,'' Kiely offers his best short fiction in ''Down Then by Derry,'' a piece that merits close analysis. The narrator begins with an apparent digression: ''The first time Tom Cunningham saw Sadie Law's brother, Francie, that brother was airborne between the saddle of a racing bicycle and a stockade filled with female lunatics.'' He confesses, in the next breath, that neither Francie nor his sister is to be the chief character in ''Down Then by Derry''; nonetheless, he explains Francie's aerial predicament. In fact, Sadie Law and Tom Cunningham are two of a large supporting cast in the loose-knit narrative that shifts in slick Vonnegut-fashion between the ''now'' and the ''then.''

The middle-aged traveler returns, after an absence of thirty years, to his Northern hometown, dominated by a Catholic church with hopalong spires. He is accompanied by a clever, quizzical sixteen-year-old daughter and a no less curious fourteen-year-old son. The trio ascends and descends the High Street into the Market Street, reviving once-upon-a-time characters and events as they review the town. The haunting verses of an Omagh poem meanwhile play upon the father's consciousness:

> Thrice happy and blest were the days of my childhood,
> And happy the hours I wandered from school
> By green Mountjoy's forest our dear native wildwood
> And the green flowery banks of the serpentine Strule.

His octogenarian mother tells the children how their father was always fond of quoting poetry. The kitchen palaver continues, but he soon lapses into a reverie of Gothic spires overlooking the riverine beauty of the Strule, youthful caresses on hillsides, and that song that whispered the history of the place and the fate of the Gaelic woodsmen of Tyrone. The reverie spills into the momentary reality of a grave—his father's grave—but the relics of things past and the children's queries prompt memory again and again. Images of Sadie Law, Tom Cunningham, Angela Brown, an exiled woman in Wisconsin, the lady of Gleshrule are revived between the insistent verses of that poem. ''Down Then by Derry'' runs present, past, and distant past together, employing the cinematic effects of fading, blending, and continuous flashing back and forward to produce a unity of action. (p. 8)

The beauty of the story does not rely solely on Kiely's talent for manipulating three levels of life and three levels of history or in recreating the loveliness of the Strule. He also revives country customs—an aged mother spits slightly and politely into fire or handkerchief when the devil is mentioned and a feast sends young pagans climbing Slieve Drumond to pluck blayberries and insure local fertility. There are many humorous diversions as well. The author combines perfection of complex narrative technique with lovely poetic description and elicits a nostalgia heightened by comic relief.

Every phrase, indeed every word, contributes to the artistry of the piece. Here Kiely is the master of understatement, and when he tells his reader that Sadie Law was almost as famous as her brother, but not for track cycling, there is no mistake about the entendre. In the end Sadie Law, sixtyish and wearing the uniform of the hotel staff, comes from the kitchen to exchange memories and shake hands. She tells the traveler how Francie the cyclist has been confined to a chair since he broke his back in a racing accident years ago. Everything seems to have a place, after all.

Memory tries to alter truth but truth has a way of intruding itself. The puzzle of the past and the distant past begins to make sense, and the returnee confides to his children: "But once upon a time I laughed easily. It was easy to laugh here then." "**Down Then by Derry**" is in the complex mode of Kiely's later fiction.

After 1973 the short fiction—stories like "**The Night We Rode with Sarsfield**" (1973) and "**Bluebell Meadow**" (1975)—hints at the darker themes of a divided North. (pp. 8-9)

The more recent stories move in slower, sadder cadences. They move toward *Proxopera* and *Carmincross,* sounding a death knell over the recollections of a happier youth. It was, after all, easier to laugh there then.

In a survey of Benedict Kiely's short fiction, such as *The State of Ireland,* one immediately recognizes his mastery of genre, his narrative skills and sensitivity. What he has done is to combine the best in the traditional and the modern, and give *voice* to the "story," which has been too long without it.

If Benedict Kiely had never written a short story, he would be counted one of Ireland's most important contemporary novelists. To date he has published ten novels, at least half of which are in one way or another exceptional.

The earliest works—*Land without Stars, In a Harbour Green,* and *Call for a Miracle,* between 1946 and 1952—move through lush, green Ulster landscapes and against the starkness of Donegal seascapes toward the metropolitan sprawl of Dublin. They offer intriguing plots and credible characters and marvelous lyrical runs that lend wonderment to the scenes. *Land without Stars* develops the theme of divided loyalties in a divided North, introduced the year before in Kiely's *Counties of Contention.* *In a Harbour Green* portrays the narrowness of rural Irish life a la Brinsley MacNamara's *Valley of the Squinting Windows.* And, *Call for a Miracle,* a psychological study of four exiles adrift in Dublin who attempt to salvage something of their lives, is essentially a novelistic inquiry into metaphysical questions. There are obvious failings in these apprentice novels, but there is, too, in the progress from village to town to city, a discernible maturing of Kiely's narrative style.

Honey Seems Bitter and *There Was an Ancient House* advance that maturity. They are better novels because they move beyond intellectual bareness and existential preoccupations and flesh out characters like Donagh Hartigan and Jim MacKenna. *Honey Seems Bitter,* a psychological thriller and modern love story, involves the reader in a murder mystery, a romantic triangle, and the psychic introspections of a brooding Dostoevskian recluse. There is, for the first time in the long fiction, sufficient penetration to suggest genius. *There Was an Ancient House,* a novel of colors and contrasts set in an eighteenth-century house of religious studies, is anchored in Kiely's life as a Jesuit novice. It is well wrought, if sometimes esoteric.

The more enduring works are, with one notable exception, the later novels. The exception, *The Cards of the Gambler,* falls chronologically between *Honey Seems Bitter* and *There Was*

an Ancient House, and provides an engaging philosophical allegory framed by a Gaelic folktale. In it, Kiely keeps one foot in the tale and the other in the real world, and scripts a kind of "morality fiction" that conceptualizes God and Death and the Devil. He probes those elusive distinctions between "what is" and "what appears to be." It is, however, the unique structure of *The Cards of the Gambler* that particularly recommends it.

The seventh novel, *The Captain with the Whiskers,* places the writer squarely in the ranks of psychological novelists who matter. It is a brilliant warts-and-all portrait of Conway Chesney, a psychopathic martinet, his wife and five children and of the pervasive evil of Bingen House. The Captain brutalizes his family and eventually brings them to ruin. But *The Captain with the Whiskers* is also the study of Owen Rodgers, the young narrator, who, fascinated by Chesney and his diabolized ghost, maintains his distance and witnesses the disintegration of the Chesneys with a clinical interest. The book is compelling fiction, the first of Kiely's important novels.

Dogs Enjoy the Morning comes eight years after *The Captain with the Whiskers.* A complete departure from what has gone before, it is a rollicking romp through the oddball world of Cosmona, a serio-comic parody that falls short of savage satire but succeeds as an extravagant romance rich in myth and legend. In this mad, mad, mad, mad world, there is more reason for hilarity and more reason for hope.

The more recent novels—*Proxopera* and *Nothing Happens in Carmincross*—return to the theme of *Land without Stars,* but with a somber tone. There is no romance in the mayhem and destruction visited by the men of violence on the innocent and the young, and an angrier Kiely uses fiction as powerful invective. The strengths of *Proxopera* and *Nothing Happens in Carmincross* have been elsewhere noted. All that remains to say is that they are important works in the Kiely canon.

Novels published over forty years are apt to be uneven. In fact Kiely has provided a list of very respectable titles over that time, though four stand out as first-rate fiction: *The Cards of the Gambler, The Captain with the Whiskers, Dogs Enjoy the Morning,* and *Nothing Happens in Carmincross.* With the exception of the last, Kiely's best work in the novel has been seriously underrated by the critics. The attention given *Carmincross* may, however, spur rediscovery of those significant earlier works. (pp. 9-10)

Dan Casey, "Benedict Kiely: An Irish Storyteller," in The Hollins Critic, *Vol. XXIII, No. 1, February, 1986, pp. 1-12.*

DARCY O'BRIEN

Nothing Happens in Carmincross attempts to subdue by means of artistic sorcery sectarian demons of the North: this is Kiely's second such attempt. The first was *Proxopera* (1979), a novella about a proxy bombing, an austere work operatic in the power of its voice and in its schematic, flat characterizations. In *Carmincross* the characters, especially the narrator-protagonist, Mervyn Kavanagh, are more various, complex, and unpredictable. There is even a Mexican-American spitfire, something new in Irish fiction though not in life.

The voice of *Carmincross*—switching Joyce-fashion from third to first person and back—cajoles us in a kindly, contemplative, civilized way into comforting barbarism, cultural degeneration, the erosion of courtesy, delicacy and subtlety in our time. The voice ruminates and reverberates over great expanses of time and space, universalizing the parochial and the provincial in the accepted digressive Irish mode. Though dressed in the comfortable old clothes of the barroom raconteur, this is a serious narrator, his anger at the hard men and women of violence wrapped within yards of humorous anecdote, muted by a score of brandy alexanders or brandies alexander.

In the sonorous music of its prose and the range of its allusions, *Carmincross* bears little resemblance to most current fiction: its affinities lie more with *Ulysses* and *The Waste Land,* although the book is no imitation, rather its own unique self, reflective of its progenitors the way a son might show something in the gait of his going of his father or grandfather. These affinities are of both technique and of attitude and may be summed up by "These fragments I have shored against my ruins," as allusion after allusion, quotation after quotation from poem, song, myth accrete. Re-opening the book at random I find on one page allusions to Ninon, Helen of Troy, Cleopatra, Diane de Poitiers, Dolly Parton, Olivia Newton-John, Diarmuid and Grainne, prehistoric wolf-bones, Fionn, Mandrake, Burns, Ben Bulben, and Indian lovecalls. The technique is that ascribed to Joyce by Eliot: the continuous manipulating of mythic analogy. Yet the effect is closer to that of Eliot than of Joyce, because in *Carmincross* the presence of the past conveys always an acute sense of loss and of the inferiority of the present to the past.

Most often Kiely's juxtaposition of past and present, to the invariable advantage of the former, produces initially a humorous, even a ludicrous result, as when Simon and Garfunkel are contrasted with Bing Crosby. But on reflection the humor subsides into rueful regret, as Crosby's superior and genuinely melancholy tone obliterates the Simon and Garfunkel adoles-

cent whine. Similarly Kiely contrasts the new IRA with the old. Car bombers come off poorly beside General Tom Barry, who killed only soldiers and policemen, not babies and brides, and had a felicitous prose style.

Benedict Kiely's art, as Sean J. White has observed, is more that of the mosaic or the mobile than the narrative. *Carmincross* has less a plot than a central event, like Molly Bloom's adultery, around which characters and allusions swirl. That event is the explosion of a bomb in a letter box as a bride posts some last-minute wedding invitations. Although the bomb and the box are local phenomena, the explosion and the setting are as metaphorical as Joyce's Dublin or Eliot's London. Carmincross becomes the cultural background of modern life, where civilization loses again and again. . . .

Once in an unguarded moment Benedict Kiely, recumbent in a certain public house which he no longer frequents because it has become a gathering place for the hard men, announced that he had just observed in the form of a graffito the words he wished inscribed on his tombstone: "Growth, Self-Deception, and Loss." The course of a human life, any human life; the course of any civilization, from Aeschylus to Beckett. So too the course of the life of Mervyn Kavanagh and his native town of Carmincross where nothing happens except growth, the self-deception of harmony, and the loss imposed by a bomb.

Through his art, however, Kiely's sense of loss has become our gain, in this book melancholy and beautiful with the shards of a culture on the way out; a swan's song, like Lir's; a lament for the lost ones, like Anna Livia's last moananoanings.

Darcy O'Brien, "Our Gain from Kiely's Sense of Loss," in Irish Literary Supplement, *Vol. 5, No. 1, Spring, 1986, p. 33.*

Jamaica Kincaid

1949?-

West Indian-born American short story writer and novelist.

Kincaid's fiction centers on the intense emotional bonds between mothers and daughters and the ambivalent feelings that sometimes result from such relationships. Both her short story collection, *At the Bottom of the River* (1983), and her best-known work, *Annie John* (1985), are set in Kincaid's birthplace, the Caribbean island of Antigua, and are strongly autobiographical. Her prose, which combines West Indian dialects with European and American locutions, often imitates the forms and speech patterns of Caribbean folktales.

Kincaid's prose in *At the Bottom of the River* attains a poetic lyricism that evokes surrealistic qualities of ordinary objects and events. Many of the stories rely on repetition of phrases and images to reinforce her themes. In the story "Girl," for example, a mother repeatedly commands her daughter to "wash the white clothes on Monday and . . . wash the color clothes on Tuesday" and continually warns her not to walk "like the slut you are so bent on becoming." Several critics noted that Kincaid appears more interested in revealing character and consciousness in this collection than in presenting conventional narratives. As a result, some debated the effectiveness of her imagery and contended that Kincaid's stories are obscure.

Annie John was originally published as a series of short stories in *The New Yorker*. Some critics, however, regard this book as a novel because it focuses upon the life of the precocious title character, who struggles to assert her individuality and escape the influence of her domineering and possessive mother. As Annie John's mother gradually becomes unresponsive to her needs, a fierce love-hate relationship results between them. Annie's confusion is reflected in her surreal and often grotesque flights of imagination. Critics commended Kincaid for her ability to render Annie's distress and conflicting emotions. Jacqueline Austin commented: "Kincaid does write what she knows. What she knows is rare: pure passion, a past filled with curious events, a voice, humor, and above all a craft."

ANNE TYLER

"Wash the white clothes on Monday and put them on the stone heap; wash the color clothes on Tuesday and put them on the clothesline to dry. . . ." These are the words that begin this unusual little book [*At the Bottom of the River*]—a collection of ten stories, none of them longer than a few pages, most set in some unnamed spot in the Caribbean.

They're also the words that will give you the clearest idea of the book's general tone; for Jamaica Kincaid scrutinizes various particles of our world so closely and so solemnly that they begin to take on a nearly mystical importance. (p. 32)

Two themes dominate *At the Bottom of the River*. The first is the wonderful, terrible strength of a loving mother. "My mother can change everything," a narrator says, and she fantasizes

© Jerry Bauer

about spending the rest of her days with a woman who "every night, over and over, . . . will tell me something that begins, 'Before you were born.'"

The second theme is the mysteriousness of ordinary life. We skate across this mysteriousness every day, blindly. To make us see it, the author describes the most mundane events as if they were dreams. Her voice is the reflective, dazed murmur of a person just awakened from sleep. "Someone is making a basket, someone is making a girl a dress or a boy a shirt" lies cheek to jowl with the surrealistically matter-of-fact "Now I am a girl, but one day I will marry a woman. . . ."

"Either it was drizzling or there was a lot of dust in the air and the dust was damp," she tells us. "I stuck out my tongue and the drizzle or the damp dust tasted like government school ink." Is this a dream, or is it real life? Come to think of it, are the two all that different?

It should be plain by now that this book is more poetry than prose. It has the ring of poetry—actual refrains, at times, such as the repetition of "the slut you are so bent on becoming," that runs through the mother's warnings in **"Girl."** Or, in **"In the Night"**: "It's breathing, the little baby. It's breathing. It's bleating, the little baby. It's bleating." Moreover, the aim of the pieces is not to chronicle some specific event but to flood us with a mood or sensation. And that aim is realized, by and large.

But while these stories have all of poetry's virtues—care for language, joy in the sheer sound of words, and evocative power—they also have its failings. (Or at least, they're failings when present in short stories.) They are often almost insultingly obscure, and they fail to pull us forward with any semblance of plot. Not once in this collection do we wonder what happens next. Not once do we feel that the writer is leaning forward and taking our hands and telling us a story. Instead, she's spinning lovely, airy webs, with a sidelong glance in our direction every now and then to see if we're appreciative. For this reason, *At the Bottom of the River* in its final effect seems curiously cold and still.

This is not to say that readers should pass it up. At the very least, it's beautiful to listen to. And it introduces us to a writer who will soon, I firmly believe, put those magical tools of hers to work on something more solid. (pp. 32-3)

Anne Tyler, "Mothers and Mysteries," in The New Republic, *Vol. 189, No. 27, December 31, 1983, pp. 32-3.*

EDITH MILTON

Reading *At the Bottom of the River,* one feels drawn into an oddly futuristic sensibility, a literary equivalent of Rock video in which technical adroitness in manipulating an image and sensuous pleasure in what can be done with it rather preclude questions about why.

Perhaps I should confess at once that I have an unredeemed taste for the ironic and the logical in fiction, and that I found Miss Kincaid's penchant for apocalyptic imagery disturbing. Take this passage from **"My Mother,"** for instance: "My mother . . . grew plates of metal-colored scales on her back. . . . Her teeth now arranged themselves into rows that reached all the way back to her long white throat." I am not sure what this means or why it is happening, except that Jamaica Kincaid tells me it is. And I ask myself if her imagery may perhaps be too personal and too peculiar to translate into any sort of sensible communication. The answer to that question, of course, is equivocal, as it would be if it were asked, say, about William Blake. Sometimes eccentricity works, sometimes not. When it works for Jamaica Kincaid, she gives us sudden glimpses of a place seldom seen and makes us look at it in a way previously unthought of.

The ingredients of *At the Bottom of the River* are usually rather simple, even primitive. Many of the stories owe their structure to the folk tales of the Caribbean islands where most of them are set. They propose that things happen without any causal relationship, and they rely on repeated themes and phrases for coherence. Their language, which is often beautifully simple, also often adopts a gospel-like seriousness, reverberating with biblical echoes and echoes of biblical echoes. There is a strong sense of the pulpit. . . .

It might be just, perhaps, to give the book the latitude of its own vision and to read it as a series of prose poems rather than as stories. At its best, it achieves a haunting beauty—in **"In the Night,"** for instance, or **"What I Have Been Doing Lately"** (where the development of choral repetitions is used as a sort of anchor to hold down the increasingly surreal fantasy). But the most elegant and lucid piece of the collection is certainly **"Girl,"** in which the exhortations to "Wash the white clothes

on Monday," and not to walk "like the slut you are so bent on becoming," define in a few paragraphs the expectations, the limitations and the contents of an entire life.

If, for me, the book's difficult vision remained often obscure, for those who share its remarkable sensibility it will have all the force of illumination, and even prophetic power.

Edith Milton, "Making a Virtue of Diversity," in The New York Times Book Review, *January 15, 1984, p. 22.*

DAVID LEAVITT

Jamaica Kincaid's *At the Bottom of the River* is a brief, surreal, and thoroughly persuasive collection which defies paraphrase almost as much as it defies categorization. Though the 10 prose pieces in the volume contain the germs of traditional narratives, each moves forward according to a logic which is essentially private, and each is spoken with a West Indian rhythm and a metaphorical vocabulary created for itself and by itself. In the hands of a lesser writer, such self-contained fictions would be solipsistic, but Kincaid's particular skill lies in her ability to articulate the internal workings of a potent imagination without sacrificing the rich details of the external world on which that imagination thrives. . . .

The tangled love between child and mother, so clearly articulated in **"Girl,"** is the major preoccupation of Kincaid's work. Confronted by a mother who in later stories grows literally huge as a mountain, the child feels torn between a desire to declare her independence and a yearning to remain at the mother's breast, to be one with her. **"My Mother"** is a brilliant piece which in tone and content recalls ancient Hindu myths of origin; mother and daughter transform themselves into lizards by means of an oil prepared from lizard livers. They travel to a cave by the sea where the daughter attempts to defy her mother by building a house over a deep hole. She hopes the mother will fall into the hole and thereby into her power, but the mother once again proves her omnipotence by walking on air once she enters the house. Though the daughter rages for several millennia, in the end she returns to her posture of worship, and is rewarded by being allowed to join wholly with the mother. . . . In Kincaid's fiction, the relationship of a mother and daughter can recapitulate the genesis of mankind. Her imagination is unfettered by concerns about realism and consistency; she jumps with grace and ease from the mundane to the enormous, and, fascinated, we believe her.

In **"At Last,"** a dialogue between the voices of a mother and daughter, Kincaid interrupts the flow of her narrative to wonder whether the hen, in some future epoch, will be able to speak. "And what will it say?" she asks. "I was a hen? I had twelve chicks? One of my chicks, named Beryl, took a fall?" Kincaid describes lives not as they are lived, but as they are imagined: her stories offer brief glimpses into a mind which is ceaselessly transforming all it sees. Near the middle of **"At Last"** one of the voices asks, "Was it like a carcass? Did you feed on it? . . . Or was it like a skeleton? Did you live in it?" For Kincaid, the skeleton of a life—"I was a hen, I had twelve chicks"—is simply a chronology, a listing of events. Between these moments lie realms of experience; it's here, in the living and the feeding, that she builds her universe.

David Leavitt, in a review of "At the Bottom of the River," in The Village Voice, *Vol. XXIX, No. 3, January 17, 1984, p. 41.*

BARNEY BARDSLEY

This is not a story. There is no linear progression, no neat plot. *At the Bottom of the River* is instead a beautiful chaos of images, murky and tactile, which hint at the dreams and nightmares involved as a girl shakes off her childhood.

Jamaica Kincaid's first book is irritatingly difficult to read unless you let yourself go. The author has stepped boldly into dangerous territory—that of the subconscious—and demands that you go along with her, making no concessions as to ease of expression or understanding. Sometimes this works and sometimes it does not. But her unusual style is a welcome experiment in the world of novel writing. . . .

Jamaica Kincaid can seem pretentious. She repeats words and phrases in biblical monotone, and sometimes her vibrant inner landscapes are too elusive—or exclusive—for me to grasp. But then she comes back, to express something fundamental about the way we live.

Her description of a man who is lost in a 'world bereft of its very nature', unaware of his connection to 'the above' and 'the below', subtly explains an alienation many of us suffer in modern society. This is not a book for pedants or rationalists. It's not even a book to read straight through. But if you can bear to dig deep, Jamaica Kincaid's writing may unlock a piece of yourself you did not even know existed. Highly unfashionable, perhaps, but fascinating.

> *Barney Bardsley, in a review of "At the Bottom of the River," in* New Statesman, *Vol. 108, No. 2790, September 7, 1984, p. 33.*

PAULA BONNELL

Rarely has so much been done in so few pages. Jamaica Kincaid's second book [*Annie John*] is not much longer than her first, *At the Bottom of the River,* which had only 82 pages. But it would be fair to say that the excitement that has attended this remarkable new writer's work since it first began appearing in 1978 has made the publication of both these books, the first last year, eagerly awaited events.

Her work is recollections of childhood, full of the specifics of growing up in St. John's Antigua: breadfruit; Ma Jolie, the obeah woman; drought; the Anglican church bell; bathing in the sea with her mother "like sea mammals;" celebration of Queen Victoria's birthday; the pleats of school uniforms. But more importantly, it conveys the mysterious power and intensity of childhood attachments to mother, father and friends, and the adolescent beginnings of separation from them.

The tales themselves are gripping. Kincaid reawakens the child in the adult reader. The opening story in *Annie John* begins, "For a short while during the year I was ten, I thought only people I did not know died." This innocence is as fleeting as childhood itself. . . .

This power to bring home emotion so simply and directly animates the entire book, including an entirely believable account of a daughter's glimpse of her parents in bed ("**The Circling Hand**"), tales of the intoxications of girlish love ("**Gwen**" and "**The Red Girl**") and tomboy rebellions ("**Columbus in Chains**") in which our heroine is discovered having defaced a schoolbook, and "**Somewhere, Belgium**" in which the young Annie daydreams of living in Charlotte Bronte's Belgium, a place so remote that her mother could only write

to her there as: "Miss Annie Victoria John / Somewhere / Belgium."

The book culminates with a metamorphic sickness in which Annie lies ill of a mysterious affliction under the sound of a three-month-long rain coming down on the galvanized roof. "The sound the rain made as it landed on the roof pressed me down in my bed, bolted me down, and I couldn't even so much as lift my head if my life depended on it." This psychic illness and all the distortions with which it warps the narrator's world ("The words traveled through the air . . . but just as they reached my ears, they would fall to the floor, suddenly dead.") is given in beautifully awful detail, language that cherishes the peculiar pains of the self. And out of the sickbed arises a new being: the young woman who will leave the island of her childhood behind and set sail to seek her fortune. . . .

No one has yet fully explained why and how it is that art—including literature—is made. From Kincaid we might theorize that the artist is a self-willed being of extreme sensitivity who heals the wounds of experience by truthfully recreating the intense past. The memoirist, like the poet and the writer of fiction, is deeply concerned with expression of truths not conventionally acknowledged but instantly recognizable to anyone who has honestly examined his own grief and joy. . . .

On her first book, the publisher's dust jacket copy scrupulously avoided characterizing her work as fiction or nonfiction; on the second, her work is called a "fictional narrative." Should it matter whether we think of this as memoir or fiction? Perhaps not; memory and imagination are kindred faculties. *At the Bottom of the River* and *Annie John* are re-creations of the self in that emotional country where dreams and what might have happened are part of the truest story of one's life.

> *Paula Bonnell, "'Annie' Travels to Second Childhood," in* The Boston Herald, *March 31, 1985, p. 126.*

JACQUELINE AUSTIN

[*Annie John*] is one of those perfectly balanced wanderings through time which seem to spring direct from Nature. . . . In her collection of stories, *At the Bottom of the River,* and here, in *Annie John,* Kincaid does write what she knows. What she knows is rare: pure passion, a past filled with curious events, a voice, humor, and above all a craft.

Ten-year-old Annie John lives in a paradise: a back yard in Antigua overseen by a benevolent goddess—her mother. . . . Into this Eden come twin serpents: death and separation from the mother. At first they seem innocent. From the yard, Annie observes, with curiosity, "various small, sticklike figures, some dressed in black, some dressed in white, bobbing up and down in the distance": mourners at a child's funeral. Gradually, death comes closer. One day, an acquaintance dies, a deformed girl. "On hearing that she was dead, I wished I had tapped the hump to see if it was hollow." Annie surreptitiously views the corpse and then lies about it to her mother. This is the first in a series of evasions for which she is punished.

Until now, Annie and her mother were almost one. They wore dresses cut from the same cloth; they went shopping together; they even bathed together. "Sometimes it was just a plain bath. . . . Other times, it was a special bath in which the barks and flowers of many different trees, together with all sorts of oils, were boiled in the same large caldron . . . my mother would bathe different parts of my body; then she would do the same to herself.'' . . . Occasionally the pair would spend a gorgeous afternoon lingering over the objects in Annie's trunk—objects redolent of a shared past which seemed to promise to continue always.

But one day the mother cuts Annie a dress of fabric different from her own; this shock precipitates a slow decline in their relationship. They still keep the appearance of unity, but it's hypocritical: their smiles are false, and mask the most intimate kinds of treachery. The full break comes when Annie reaches puberty. She is now a stranger even to herself. Everything about her, from her nose to her habit of lying, is a mostly unpleasant surprise. This alienation worsens into disease, and ultimately into a total break with Antigua.

Derek Walcott has a poem, ''Love After Love,'' in which he prophesies to himself, and we listen in: ''The time will come / when, with elation, / you will greet yourself arriving / at your own door, in your own mirror, / and each will smile at the other's welcome . . .'' The poem closes with a command. ''Peel your own image from the mirror. / Sit. Feast on your life.'' Though Annie John replaces her mother with different objects of desire, first with the conventional schoolgirl Gwen and then with the wild Red Girl, she never does realize that both are reflections of herself, never experiences elation, except at her impending escape, and never feasts on her life—though Jamaica Kincaid does.

At the end of the book, Annie has just gone through a long illness. Having been treated by both doctors and obeah women, she rises from her sickbed several inches taller than her mother—that many inches farther from Eden. She decides to leave Antigua and become a nurse. As Annie embarks for England, the mother hugs her fiercely and declares, ''in a voice that raked across my skin, 'It doesn't matter what you do or where you go, I'll always be your mother and this will always be your home.''' Annie hides her revulsion and goes to lie down in her berth, where ''everything trembled as if it had a spring at its very center. I could hear the small waves lap-lapping around the ship. They made an unexpected sound, as if a vessel filled with liquid had been placed on its side and now was slowly emptying out.''

The past always threatens to contain the future; it's impossible for the future to break free while still embraced by the past. The daughter must tell her mother, ''No, I am not you; I am not what you made me,'' and this, whether truth or a lie, precipitates sexuality, originality, an honest relationship to personal truth. Annie is clearly an autobiographical figure, not perhaps in specific detail, but certainly in her internal development, her emotions, the tempering of her mind, the changes in her image from within the skin. How has Kincaid broken free? How has she acknowledged her past?

First novelists usually try to cope with their heritage: Kincaid has had to encompass two traditions. This has been the plaint, and the strength, of writers from the West Indies—both black, like George Lamming, and white, like Jean Rhys. In her two books, Kincaid makes an impressive start, fusing folk tale with novel, poetry with fiction, West Indian locutions and rhythms with ''European'' ones. She has proven herself to be a big, exotic fish in a small, brightly colored pond—the personal interior narrative. It will be interesting to see what happens once she throws herself into the ocean. (p. 6)

With *Annie John,* Kincaid has completed the themes begun in *River.* The two are companion volumes: an object lesson in showing how far a writer's technique can stretch. *River* seemed to be dictated straight from heart to hand, almost bypassing the mind. The voice in **''Girl,''** for example, quoted first mother, then daughter, in a rhythm so strong it seemed to be hypnosis, aimed at magically chanting out bits of the subconscious. Now *Annie John* fills in between the bits; it gives the passions of *River* a rationale. The surreality, imagination, internal and external detail are still there, but they now flow in a single narrative wave.

Kincaid's subject matter in these two books is so interesting that her style, sumptuous as it is, becomes transparent. She is a consummate balancer of feeling and craft. She takes no short or long cuts, breathes no windy pomposities: she contents herself with being direct. The reader feels that even if this writer had had the bad luck to be born elsewhere, she would have made it as wonderful as ''her'' Antigua.

Cynthia Ozick, Mary Gordon, and Susan Sontag have sighed over Kincaid's virtuosity with language, and they were right. Her language recalls Henri Rousseau's painting: seemingly natural, but in reality sophisticated and precise. So lush, composed, direct, odd, sharp, and brilliantly lit are Kincaid's word paintings that the reader's presuppositions are cut in two by her seemingly soft edges. Her wisdom, measured craft, and reticence will carry her on to more complicated and wider canvases, to larger geographies of the mind. (p. 7)

Jacqueline Austin, ''Up from Eden,'' in VLS, *No. 34, April, 1985, pp. 6-7.*

JOHN BEMROSE

Annie John confirms Kincaid's status as a subtle observer of girlhood. Like Kincaid herself, the heroine grows up in one of the most prosperous of the Caribbean islands, Antigua. Indeed, if ever a child has inherited heaven on earth, it is Annie John. Her carpenter father provides his family with an ample living, and 10-year-old Annie enjoys a mutually adoring relationship with her mother. But in spite of those advantages Annie becomes intensely unhappy. Kincaid's great triumph is that she imbues Annie's fall from grace with mysterious inevitability. *Annie John* reveals that evil grows everywhere, even in the middle of paradise.

The instrument of Kincaid's success is a prose style whose subtly varied cadences suggest the slow, dignified pace of life in colonial Antigua. She also knows her way around the human heart. Kincaid gradually shows that Annie's personality is too large for the society in which she lives. Being a good student and a virtuous girl is simply too easy and too boring. She abandons her friendship with her school mate Gwen for a rebellious ragamuffin she calls the Red Girl, because of her red hair. The two meet secretly to fondle each other with the clumsy urgency of adolescents. In the same story Annie takes up the ''boys only'' game of marbles, an activity that spells the end of her private Eden by bringing her into violent, hateful opposition to her mother.

Kincaid's vision grows darker throughout the stories, but it is never bleak. In the crucial, second-to-last tale, ''The Long Rain,'' Annie suffers a nervous breakdown from the strain of being a good girl in public and a rebel in secret. Miraculously, the sickness restores her to a new, healthy balance. The final story of *Annie John* describes her poignant departure from Antigua—the heaven that has become too small for her. With superb grace and insight Jamaica Kincaid has crafted her young heroine's life into a small but almost perfect book.

John Bemrose, "Growing Pains of Girlhood," in Maclean's Magazine, Vol. 98, No. 20, May 20, 1985, p. 61.

IKE ONWORDI

Jamaica Kincaid's highly personal world is that of an eccentric visionary. *At the Bottom of the River,* her first book, published in Britain last year, is a series of loosely connected prose pieces which together make up a picture of life as seen by a young West Indian girl during the period between her burgeoning adolescence and her eventual motherhood. The book's domain is the empire of things. It is unusual, to say the least, reading at first like a catalogue of proper nouns. . . . But it is through the cumulative effect of these fractured descriptions that her world begins to take shape. Kincaid writes with tactile sensibility; triumphantly self-effacing, she achieves objective effects through an intensely subjective style. . . .

This singular gift has been applied in her first novel, *Annie John.* Set on Antigua, it covers almost the same ground as *At The Bottom of the River.* It too is an account of a young girl's transition to womanhood and her discovery that she must leave her familial paradise for the uncertainties of the adult world. To this universal and well-explored theme Kincaid brings to bear a discipline that renders fleeting moments in the passage of a life with evocative clarity.

Annie John is a carpenter's daughter, a sensitive and precocious child whose morbid curiosity for the unlovelier side of life brings her, like the twice-born, to an early maturity. Her naive but none the less wise judgments concerning the nature of the universal and permanent amid transience are artfully expressed in the idiom of childhood. But the ambivalence of her love for her mother, her realization of the inevitability of suffering and death, are trials which she must successively overcome. In an ambience of confused affections Annie John learns that wisdom often lies in pursuing the broad path of honesty while fawning with a false heart.

The book is episodic in structure, and autobiographical—its development is that of Annie John herself. Her personal crises overflow into her perceptions and her triumphs lend the book new resonance.

Jamaica Kincaid uses language that is poetic without affectation. She has a deft eye for salient detail while avoiding heavy symbolism and diverting exotica. The result captures powerfully the essence of vulnerability.

Ike Onwordi, "Wising Up," in The Times Literary Supplement, *No. 4313, November 29, 1985, p. 1374.*

W(illiam) P(atrick) Kinsella

1935-

Canadian short story writer and novelist.

Kinsella has earned acclaim for his short story collections about modern-day Canadian Indians and for his novels and stories about baseball. His skill at blending fantasy with realism in a poetically whimsical style has prompted comparisons to Richard Brautigan. In his portraits of contemporary Indians struggling for survival in a white society, which most critics have found unromantic and uncondescending, Kinsella debunks stereotypes and distortions of the North American Indian. In the novels *Shoeless Joe* (1982) and *The Iowa Baseball Confederacy* (1986) and the short story collection *The Thrill of the Grass* (1984), the game of baseball "becomes the context and metaphor for imagination, commitment, and personal achievement," according to Steven G. Kellman. When Kinsella writes about baseball, he is less concerned with the onfield exploits of his characters than with the magical and rejuvenating force that the sport provides for its followers.

Kinsella uses Silas Ermineskin, a droll, self-conscious young Cree whose broken English is rich in metaphor and imagery, to narrate his Indian stories. The Indians in *Dance Me Outside* (1977) fight for honor and identity in the white-dominated world. Kinsella shows various ways in which Indians are conditioned to expect and resign themselves to victimization. The grimness of the subject matter is often lightened by the humorous dissimilarities of white and Indian lifestyles and world views. While Kinsella won praise for *Dance Me Outside*, *Born Indian* (1981) received a cooler reaction; critics found the stories in this collection to be excessively sentimental and faulted Kinsella for being blatantly unjust to whites and oversympathetic to Indians. *The Moccasin Telegraph* (1983) is widely regarded as the best of Kinsella's Ermineskin books. With what has been described as an original vision, Kinsella depicts an Indian community attempting to reconcile traditional customs with contemporary technological innovations and bureaucratic legislation. Without putting inordinate worth on ancient Indian culture or indulging in nostalgia, Kinsella extols those remnants and bits of native wisdom that have survived in modern North America.

In *Shoeless Joe*, Ray Kinsella, an Iowa farmer and baseball fanatic, builds a stadium on his cornfield in order to bring back to life the late baseball star Shoeless Joe Jackson. Ray then kidnaps baseball fan J. D. Salinger and gathers by supernatural methods sundry baseball figures, including his deceased father, so they can redeem their lives on his playing field. Through a childlike optimism, Ray succeeds in reviving the spirits of all he attracts to his ballpark. In the opinion of Randall Maggs, *Shoeless Joe* demonstrates that "the power of baseball to heal the human spirit arises out of its ability to evoke the 'lost past.'" *The Iowa Baseball Confederacy* again utilizes baseball—this time a game between the all-stars of the mythical Iowa Baseball Confederacy and the 1908 Chicago Cubs—as a sanctuary in which people can sustain their youthful ideals. Kinsella tampers with time and combines realism and fantasy to create a world in which a ballgame lasts forty days in a continual rain. In *The Thrill of the Grass*, Kinsella employs realism in half of the stories and fantasy in the other half. The

Photograph by White Rock Portrait Studio. Courtesy of W. P. Kinsella.

realistic pieces chronicle the monotonous, dreary lives of minor-league players waiting for their big break and their relationships with wives and girlfriends insensitive to their aspirations. In the fantasies, the game turns into "a microcosm of the human condition," according to Kieran Kealy. The book's central theme is the loss of youthful expectations and innocence and the disparities between dreams and reality. While most of the stories are ultimately pessimistic, they possess much absurd humor and include several memorable minor characters.

Kinsella is also the author of *The Alligator Report* (1985), which consists of what he calls "Brautigans"—fanciful, surreal vignettes involving unexplainable events that occur in a run-down city neighborhood inhabited by alienated people. In his introduction to this book, Kinsella acknowledges that no writer has had a greater influence on his style than Richard Brautigan; *The Alligator Report* thus serves as something of an homage. In a review of this collection, Harry Marten noted: "Kinsella defines a world in which magic and reality combine to make us laugh and think about perceptions we take for granted."

(See also *CLC*, Vol. 27; *Contemporary Authors*, Vols. 97-100; and *Contemporary Authors New Revision Series*, Vol. 21.)

JODI DAYNARD

These 15 stories [in *The Moccasin Telegraph*] by the West Canadian author W. P. Kinsella include possibly some of the most funny writing of recent times. Silas Ermineskin, 18, a born storyteller and Huck Finnian scamp, narrates tales about his Indian reservation in Alberta. There's his troublemaking buddy, Frank Fence-post, presenting himself as the chief of the Onagatihies (sometimes Onadatchies) to suburban hunters looking for a guide; Mad Etta, a 400-pound medicine woman whose office is a tree-trunk chair; the unanimously despised Chief Tom and his wicked girlfriend, Samantha Yellowknees; and other ne'er-do-wells whose lives we come to cherish. Bound together by a common history of official mistreatment, these people have a finely tuned instinct for silence, mutual help and deadpan trickery.... Not all the stories are funny, though, and some, like **"Strings," "Green Candles"** and **"Nests,"** seem to challenge the limits of human rage, jealousy and sanity. Unsentimentally poignant, full of the energy and drama of folk tales, these marvelous stories go far in dispelling many lingering myths and misconceptions about the North American Indians—none greater, perhaps, than the one that says they have no sense of humor.

> *Jodi Daynard, in a review of "The Moccasin Telegraph," in* The New York Times Book Review, *September 2, 1984, p. 14.*

LESLEY CHOYCE

W. P. Kinsella's *Shoeless Joe* performed one of the rarest acomplishments in my reading history: it successfully sucked me into one man's private modern vision of ecstasy, and that vision wrapped itself like soft calf leather around the sport of baseball. *The Thrill of the Grass* promised to do it all over again, this time with 11 short stories, each knitting a revised vision of the universe as potential but never fully realized no-hitter....

Kinsella is at his best when he lets the fantasy overtake the facts. In **"The Last Pennant Before Armageddon,"** for example, Chicago Cubs manager Al Tiller has been informed from on high that his team will finally win a pennant but that when it wins (according to some inexplicable holy design) it will signal the end of the world by nuclear war. For Tiller, it's a conflict of interests. For the reader, this unlikely plot works like pure magic.

TV baseball always bores me stiff, yet here's this West Coast Canadian writer, former Edmontonian, ex-life insurance salesman, and retired pizza parlour manager successfully selling me his personal euphoria over baseball. Even in the title story, I genuinely *care* about the absurd conspiracy to plant patches of real grass, tuft by tuft, back into a big-time ballpark, replacing the synthetic turf and thereby making a stand against the creeping artificiality in contemporary life.

Behind the ecstasy and the magic, however, lies an undercurrent of sadness whenever the real world takes a big enough chunk out of "the game." **"The Baseball Spur," "Barefoot and Pregnant in Des Moines,"** and **"Nursie"** exhibit the melancholy of professional (public) players trying to live out private lives with minimal success. **"Driving Toward the Moon,"** the only story actually set in Canada, does a masterful job of conveying the *angst* of a rookie leaguer willing to sacrifice the game for a woman he falls in love with. These are the sort of

trade-offs Kinsella worries about when he keeps his fiction down to earth.

Kinsella's baseball world is populated by few genuine winners, and he makes little use of any Howard Cosell play-by-play narrative. He admits in his introduction that stories about athletic heroics bore him. "Ultimately, a fiction writer can be anything except boring," he states, and since *The Thrill of the Grass* packs many surprises, it is freighted with no boredom. (p. 23)

> *Lesley Choyce, "Three Hits and a Miss," in* Books in Canada, *Vol. 13, No. 9, November, 1984, pp. 23-4.*

STANLEY CROUCH

In *The Moccasin Telegraph,* W. P. Kinsella uses modern literary techniques to render Alberta Indian life (it's apt that his title combines a traditional Indian image with Western technology). The 15 stories in this collection are inventively narrated by 18-year-old Silas Ermineskin, a writer who doggedly uses conversational patois that wreaks havoc on conventional agreements of subject and predicate. Like the rolling of a single cue ball from one corner of the triangular rack to the other, Ermineskin's tone reflects his attempted hipness, his self-conscious irony, and his purple attempts at the poetic. This voice demands a lot of authorial control, since a casual reader could easily think the gaffes are coming from Ermineskine's creator. What Kinsella allows us to witness is the failure of emotional bravado and the humbling of the narrator by the force and mystery of the lives around him.

For all its orchestration, Kinsella's style functions to get you some place, not just point at itself. He has learned from Twain, has definitely studied Hemingway, and he creates a vibrant Indian texture while taking on familiar modern themes. Kinsella brings his own variations to the crisis between old and new ways, the redefinition of individual and group identity in the face of technology, politics, bureaucracy, and the demons of pretension that dog every upwardly mobile step. He places no overwrought value on traditional Indian culture, but celebrates those poetic remains and insights capable of functioning beyond the self-pity that frequently results from nostalgia.

Kinsella's vision ranks injustice as but another aspect of the adverse—best handled with the stoic realism shown the dangers of the woods, if tragedy or disappointment is to be avoided. His characters pivot between Indian tradition and contemporary demands: the Indians who dominate these stories range from ne'er-do-wells to political opportunists; they can be stupid, cruel, clever, violent, jealous, compassionate, self-righteous, maudlin, brave, and so on. They're as aware of the mysterious convolutions of the human heart as of racism's double standards and the ruthless ways of the natural world.

The tension and the humor of these stories comes from the way they ricochet off familiar themes, especially from westerns. Things we're accustomed to seeing are significantly changed by the shift of social place and the nature of the age. The renegade Indian who gets drunk and goes on a rampage doesn't raid a farm, steal horses, and rape the settler women; he stumbles off the reserve full of homebrew and angel dust(!), barges into a 7-11 instead of a trading post, shoots a white clerk to death, leaves with $27, and meets his end holed up in a skating-rink shack. Indian raids have been reduced to shoplifting and car theft, hunting is turned into a show for a visiting member of the royal family (replete with a decrepit buffalo bought from a white man). But the mission Indian is no longer simply someone who, having been educated and Christianized by the whites, wanders among his people seeking relief from the spiritual migraine of an identity crisis. There are Indians who live in what is left of a traditional society and those who go into the world and return spiritually unscathed, armed to fight Indian battles with strategies learned in law schools. . . .

"The Mother's Dance" perfectly renders Kinsella's conception of contemporary Indian culture. It begins with the italicized description of a dance in which Indian men and women shuffle around a drummer in a circle.

> *. . . Each one of them dancers hold a baby, either their own or borrowed, anywhere from brand new to a year or so old. As they shuffle to the beat of the drum, the dancers hold them babies way up high, as if they was pushing them toward the sun. Some of the babies giggle, some of the babies cry, and some keep right on with their sleeping.*

By the end of the tale we learn that the dance is a present to Grace McGee, an Indian woman who has become well off through marriage to a white man. Though the Indians are usually saddened by such weddings, this woman proves that change of social place does not in itself mean a loss of soul or a denial of roots. Like a Cinderella figure, she has been taken away to live happily ever after by her fairy tale prince. "'I sat at home and had a houseful of kids,' she tells us. 'My husband makes all kinds of money so I don't have to work.'" At least to the poor Indians on the reserve, that seems like living happily ever after. But she also has a law degree she never used; McGee has arrived in a chauffeur-driven limousine on a rescue mission. As she pleads the case of some Indians about to be booted off the reserve by the government, Silas Ermineskin creates an image of her that is an Indian version of a pioneer woman, a heroine who has taken her values into a new situation and mastered it. . . .

Kinsella knows the true dynamics of cultural change. Any culture that's vital is given more sophistication by the introduction of foreign elements (save the kinds of corruptions that denigrate or erode through amorality and nihilism). The so-called white world—modern actually—is a frontier to the contemporary Indian or has been one for over 100 years. . . . When **"The Mother's Dance"** concludes with the same italicized description that began it, he's saying all has come full circle. Traditional Indian dance takes on a meaning beyond nostalgia because it recognizes a victory in the present. At the same time, the memory of tradition, usually expressed through style, shows its greatest importance was always the metaphor, which transcends time and place.

"Nests," an extraordinary variation on Kafka's "Metamorphosis," is also a turn-around of the familiar tale about a white man who witnesses the mysterious workings of some bush cult. Silas Ermineskin is hired by Gus Moon, a white man afraid to leave his house, who always feels cold and keeps the heat turned up as high as possible. His wife is dead and his daughter, like her mother before her, has become part of a conspiracy directed by a colony of wasps. Moon, the human trapped in his home, is reminiscent of Gregor Samsa, kept in his room because he is an insect who would be killed if he left. (p. 47)

In [**"The Moccasin Telegraph"**], Kinsella takes on opportunistic Indian political organizations. When Bert Lameman shoots up the 7-11 and dies at the hands of the mounties, AIM shows up. "These guys got shiny braids, hundred dollar black stetsons, and wear plastic Indian jewelry. AIM usually stand for American Indian Movement, but most people around here call them Assholes in Moccasins." Here is another story of exploiting a death for political interests, in this case getting more members in AIM, but it doesn't express a defeatist disavowal of political action.

Kinsella, consistently refusing to simplify things, says what true storytellers have always known: one can never predict human development or behavior, and what might look like one thing can often be something else. The Indian who is apparently most converted, who has chosen to have his family's last name legally changed from Two-brown-bears to Brown (an Ellis Island of the mind?), might be discovered practicing traditional religion late at night, using the body and feathers of an eagle illegally killed. Silas accidentally catches Lester Brown, whom the Cree call an "apple," for red outside, white inside, performing an ancestral ceremony. Brown's daughter, also thought an apple, learned things about historical Indian rituals at the University that even Mad Etta, the medicine lady, doesn't know. Daughter and father kept the information from the mother, who was totally committed to Catholicism. The point of **"Parts of the Eagle"** is that Western civilization, with its endless repositories of information and its Will to documentation, offers the individual in quest of internal satisfaction access to materials that can comfort, even if they exist outside convention. Since the book is a new thing to people from an oral culture, Kinsella is saying that those who want to know their past can use the library to buttress the living's limitations of memory. Documentation works in favor of any who would labor to shape either the individual features of their own faces or the collective conscience of their race. After all, when one chooses a religion, the point is accepting a poetic explanation compatible with one's spiritual needs. Kinsella knows this so well that he continually slips the noose of simplistic thinking. (pp. 47, 49)

Though some of Kinsella's stories don't stick and a few are almost parables, the talent that lifts up off these pages is special. Inside so many of those stories exist complex worlds and interwoven influences, amounting to what makes me consider ours the Age of Redefinition. The stage on which Kinsella's people struggle, die, and dream rose up in the faces of the Indians with a speed that must have been staggering. It is his refusal to sentimentally bemoan the loss of that far simpler world which makes him a modern writer fully aware that the tools of the times are here for all to use if they will only take on the job. Redefinition is a universal task, and the best of Kinsella's stories illustrate that fact with inspiring skill. (p. 49)

> *Stanley Crouch, "This Is The Modern World: W. P. Kinsella's New Frontiers," in* The Village Voice, *Vol. XXIX, No. 49, December 4, 1984, pp. 47, 49.*

KIERAN KEALY

Kinsella's *The Thrill of the Grass* includes two types of baseball stories. The first chronicles the tedious, dismal life of the eternal minor-leaguer, trapped in mediocrity awaiting his big chance, the day when he'll make the "Bigs." Ultimately the stories are not really about baseball, but about rural North America, small towns in Iowa and Alberta. The characters in these stories have a disturbing sameness, misunderstood men trying to sustain their dreams in a world of bitter, unfeeling wives and girl friends, women who don't really understand the game, who don't share the dream. It's a male world; women are seen as invaders. Even when the hero does make it to the "Bigs," the women don't understand. In **"Barefoot and Pregnant in Des Moines,"** for example, the hero, after desperately trying to preserve his relationship with his wife, acknowledges at the end, bitterly, that the story's title describes where women deserve to be. (pp. 168-69)

Fortunately, one need not judge Kinsella's collection on his "waiting for the Bigs" stories, for the second type of tale he tells is far more engaging: baseball fantasies, a category that includes **"The Last Pennant before Armageddon."** In one story Kinsella tries to decide whether to trade his life for that of a recently departed Thurman Munson; in another he joins the legendary 1951 Giants as a pinch-hitter and resident literary critic. Magically and wonderfully, the Giants become scholars, far more worried about how to interpret *The Great Gatsby* than about winning the pennant. Bernard Malamud, in fact, is a frequent dugout visitor. Yet another tale chronicles the lives of twins who began playing catch in their mother's womb. But perhaps the most delightful of the stories is the title tale. It takes place during the 1981 baseball strike, when a group of loyal baseball fans patiently re-sod a stadium recently doomed to artificial turf. Piece by piece, they bring in squares of sod and bring back the thrill of the grass. And here, baseball does truly become a microcosm of the human condition, and Kinsella and his gang of true believers find a magnificent way to fight back at all that is plastic and artificial and phoney in this ever-so-convenient age. (p. 169)

Kieran Kealy, "Armageddon," in Canadian Literature, *No. 105, Summer, 1985, pp. 168-69.*

PHILIP LANTHIER

[W. P. Kinsella] prefers to think of ball players as ordinary mortals "with the same financial and domestic problems as Joe Citizen," but whose lives are circumscribed by the brief time available for glory. He writes as a fan, not as an insider or functionary of the game; on the one hand he is an observer of each tug and twitch, scratch and shrug of the third-base coach, on the other a fabulist ready to perform entertaining outrages on baseball reality.

The real baseball fan, says the narrator in the title story of *The Thrill of the Grass,* is the man who stays for the last pitch no matter how bad the weather or certain the outcome. He stays because of the "beauty and mystery" of the game, taking quiet "joy from watching the first baseman adjust the angle of his glove as the pitcher goes into his windup." In *Shoeless Joe* Kinsella has his character speak rapturously of people watching the ideal, timeless game as if kneeling in front of a faith healer or dipping themselves in "magic waters where a saint once rose like a serpent and cast benedictions to the wind like peach petals." On this level, baseball is a cozy myth, a harkening back to a pastoral moment free of player strikes and monstrous salaries, a moment suffused with warmth and reconciliation under the happy skies of Kinsella's beloved Iowa.

Shoeless Joe overextended itself. Kinsella tried to stretch a single-base hit into a triple, but by the time he rounded second he was up to his knees in mythical goo. The first chapter did indeed have a kind of magic to it, transcending its sentimentality by virtue of Kinsella's originality and talent for creating atmosphere. In this latest collection of 11 stories [*The Thrill of the Grass*], that transcendant note is struck in the last story,

a lyric finale celebrating the clandestine replacement of artificial turf in a stadium with real grass, "little squares of soil, moist as chocolate cake with green icing." Baseball's real magic springs from deep in the soil itself, right up through cleat-shod feet. In the loose framework of the collection, this Eden-like story balances the opening, in which the end of the world through nuclear holocaust will depend on whether a manager orders his pitcher to throw a curve ball in the last of the ninth. In Kinsella's universe, paradise is retrievable and will prevail, mainly because of those fans who remember when the game was played on Real Grass, before the Fall into artifice and dopey club mascots.

Other stories in *The Thrill of the Grass* range hither and thither on the reality scale. Three are clearly fantastical: a teenage "W. P. Kinsella" joins the New York Giants as a pinch hitter and finds the players ready to talk Latin and argue about allegory in *The Great Gatsby;* another Kinsella-like figure is given a chance to reverse history by replacing a ballplayer in death; and in the Dominican Republic a woman gives birth to Julio and Esteban, the first in a catcher's crouch and with several broken knuckles, the second wearing cleats and with two splayed fingers on his pitcher's hand. This last story, **"The Battery,"** is a daft tall tale featuring a scruffy wizard, hot air balloons, baseball-crazy guerillas, and at the end, four blonde, pregnant ladies on the verge of giving birth to the ultimate infield line-up.

"I like to weave fact and fantasy. I like to alter history," says Kinsella in his introduction, echoing similar pronouncements by other practitioners of the New Fiction. Kinsella is the kind of wizard who knows there are no gods but summons them up anyway. Such candour is disarming. We enjoy the openhanded trickery and set ourselves to decode his thinly disguised messages, for example, some sacrificial Jesus business in **"The Night Manny Mota Tied the Record."** As long as Kinsella keeps his touch light and steers clear of sentimentality, as he does in **"The Battery"** and **"The Last Pennant Before Armageddon,"** the fantasies work; when he allows his lyricism to take over and his characters to speak like second-rate poets, the stories silt up with sugar.

Six stories deal with life on the periphery of baseball, most notably with the relationships between players and their women. Here Kinsella's male characters tend to be passive and evasive. They make odd half-moves which are very different from their moments of uninhibited physical grace on the field. In **"Barefoot and Pregnant in Des Moines"** a player who has finally made it big is defeated by his wife's silence and refusal to accompany him on the road as she has always done. He will not challenge her but resigns himself to living out an inevitable pattern of flight. In **"Nursie"** another player, setting out for spring training, refrains from hitting his very nasty wife; instead he buys flight insurance naming the girl he should have married beneficiary. Only if the plane crashes will the retaliatory blow be revealed. And in **"Driving Toward the Moon"** a good rookie-league pitcher sees his game deteriorate when he becomes infatuated with a sexy but married woman. "We're not going back, are we?" he says as they take off in his battered Plymouth, letting fate and good sex carry him away. This is one of the best realist stories in the book. Kinsella vividly evokes the loneliness of western minor league ballparks under uncertain skies, and makes the sexual chemistry between Rose and Johnny absolutely convincing. On the whole, Kinsella males are nice guys who love the wrong girls all too much; his women are either bad numbers or cheerful and supportive.

This is the other level of baseball, the ordinary human dimension with its has-beens, might-bes, edgy women, and fragile dreams. Its events are enacted far from the roar of ecstatic fans. The effect of these stories has little to do with any magical thrill imported from baseball; rather, we sense the game as a dramatic third character, sometimes near, sometimes distant, but insistently there.

Kinsella's mentors are the fantasist Ray Bradbury (*Fahrenheit 451*), who has bequeathed him the poetic simile; Richard Brautigan (*Trout Fishing in America*), who has given him a touch of surrealist absurdity (and more similes); and J. D. Salinger (*The Catcher in the Rye*), who has shown him how intensely and warmly characters can be made to relate to each other. Kinsella's stories work best where these influences are muted, as they are in **"Driving Toward the Moon."** When he tries to outdo Bradbury and Brautigan, as in **"The Thrill of the Grass,"** the mixture becomes undigestably rich.

I liked this book, probably because I like baseball and am happy to see a serious writer do something to advance the possibilities of the much neglected sports story. One does not have to be a fan to enjoy Kinsella, but it helps to have a more than passing acquaintance with baseball. These stories don't really let you into their world unless you're ready to surrender at least partly to the rituals of the game. But then isn't that true of any fiction worth the price of a seat along the first-base line? (pp. 29-30)

> *Philip Lanthier, "A Fan's Notes," in* The Canadian Forum, *Vol. LXV, No. 751, August-September, 1985, pp. 29-30.*

RANDALL MAGGS

In all of the stories [in *The Thrill of the Grass*] the central character is intimately involved with the game of baseball, either professionally or as religiously devoted "fan of the game." For Kinsella, baseball is obviously important for itself. It also provides him with a means of exploring the dreams and expectations of young men and the inevitable discrepancy between those dreams and expectations and what the world offers. "I am a failed shortstop," the middle-aged narrator confesses in the title-story, and in doing so broaches the theme central to the book. The collection includes both "realistic" stories and full-blown Kinsellian fantasies and the two types of stories are intricately related to one another. The former tend to deal with the limitations of life in a direct manner. The latter, with the obliqueness of an off-speed pitch, present other worlds where these limitations simply do not exist. They probably owe less to the current influence of Central and South American writers than to boys' dreams of heroes and heroic deeds. At one point in the title-story, the narrator finds himself stirred in recalling "the lush outfields of childhood." The title itself, *The Thrill of the Grass,* suggests emotion, beginnings, and innocence. It was taken from Kinsella's novel, *Shoeless Joe,* which attempts to redeem the reputation of the young White Sox outfielder, Shoeless Joe Jackson, whose brilliant career was destroyed by the World Series Scandal of 1919, for Kinsella, Shoeless Joe was much more the victim than offender. The source for the title to this collection seems appropriate; the stories all deal with baseball and the theme which is fundamental to the book as a whole is the destruction of the dreams and innocence of youth. In **"The Baseball Spur,"** Stan is a 36-year-old outfielder who is finally beginning to accept the fact that he is never going to make the major leagues. Reaching out tentatively toward the workaday world, he has gone to see his wife's brother, an employee at the rail yards:

> . . . last week I drove up to the stadium in Iowa City, I was running in the outfield, doing stretching exercises on the grass, stuff like that, when I happened to look up at the sky. There were little white puffs of cloud all across it, like a cat stepped in milk and then walked across the blue. I thought it was so beautiful I told Dmetro about it. He just stared at me. "I ain't looked at the sky in ten years," he said. I believed him.

Stan's dismay at what happens to men seems to reflect Kinsella's own. What appears to underlie this collection as a whole is an antagonistic attitude toward a world which causes men to forget to look upward. Characters are confronted with the inevitable fading of those vague but very powerful dreams of youth. Career hopes do not materialize. Love turns sour. The world, in general, seems to become a bleak, dishonest place. If Stan has to come to terms with his failure as a ball player in **"The Baseball Spur,"** the narrator has to deal with his not only in baseball but in love. . . . The collection does include stories in which gifted and hopeful players are seen working their way up through the minor leagues. In these stories, love too seems much more attractive. However, the characters involved are young, the relationships fresh, and the stories as a consequence seem to be placed in an ironic perspective by the collection as a whole.

The relationship between husband and wife, and the effect upon it of time, is very much at the center of this book. Annie, that impossibly wonderful dream-woman from *Shoeless Joe,* with her red hair, freckled face and cleavage, her radiant sensuality and her remarkable ability to deal with the everyday world turns up again as Dellie in **"The Firefighter."** Like Annie, Dellie is more than a match for the real world and is quite happy to free her husband to pursue his less mundane affairs: "you just keep hittin' the long ball and let me worry about the money." Talk about dream-worlds. In *The Thrill of the Grass,* though, Dellie is the lonely exception. For the most part, the women in the foreground in these stories are not presented very favourably. Nursie, in the story of that name, has a "mean whine"; she "really knows how to hate." In **"The Baseball Spur,"** Sunny (whose name is as ironic as Nursie's) cuts Jack cruelly in the midst of their lovemaking: " 'Can't you finish up,' Sunny said, not even in a whisper. 'I'm tired.' " In **"Barefoot and Pregnant,"** Dude Atcheson finds his world undermined by what he perceives as his wife's new "indifference" and "treachery." (pp. 106-07)

What I have suggested about the ideas in this book probably gives the impression that it is more sombre than it is. In fact it contains a great deal of humour. Even the more serious stories have their lighter moments. Thinking about his mother and her devotion to the Minnesota Twins, the narrator in **"Bud and Tom"** remarks wryly "My mother . . . knows more about Harmon Killebrew than she does about me." Kinsella has also a fine sense of the absurd. In **"How I Got My Nickname,"** Leo Durocher's Giants show off their Latin, and a running battle goes on in the dugout over whether or not *The Great Gatsby* should be read as an allegory. As in his earlier works, Kinsella reveals in these stories his gift for creating marvellous minor characters. One is tentative in referring to God as a minor character, but in **"The Last Pennant Before Armageddon,"** he does make a brief and amusing contribution. As long-suffering Cub fans plead with him for a National league pennant, he answers placatingly, ''I appreciate your interest . . . I want to assure you that I hold the Chicago Cubs in the highest esteem.'' (pp. 107-08)

Kinsella's success in creating character and setting, as in his humour, owes much to his sure hand with expression and dialogue. This can be seen in God's placating statement above. With colloquial speech Kinsella is especially deft. Seeing his lanky, far-from-brilliant son roar into the yard scattering chickens in every direction, Cal muses ''I be go to hell . . . It's Eddie with his new-to-him car.'' More than anything else, it is Cal's language which makes him hilarious and wholly convincing as a character. ''Ain't nothin' worse than a pussy-whipped man,'' he mumbles to Lefty, his son-in-law. ''Don't take no crap from 'em, boy. She's my own little girl, but I don't know where she gets off bein' so feisty.'' At the same time, Kinsella is subtle in his use of colloquial speech. As their voices are all quite distinct, his narrators easily differentiate themselves from one another. The way each speaks and the overall tone sought in the story which he narrates are never allowed to work against one another.

''First and foremost,'' Kinsella tells us in his short introduction to **The Thrill of the Grass,** ''I am a story-teller.'' In its range and richness, this collection makes that clear enough. The stories are all good and **''The Last Pennant Before Armageddon,'' ''The Firefighter''** and, perhaps, **''The Baseball Spur''** are excellent. If the book falters, it is in the few spots where the fantastical material may go a little flat. At times, there may be too much effort apparent and not enough magic. In these few flat spots, the writing seems to lose its element of surprise; it may even become predictable, and these are surely deadly failings in literature of this sort. But on the whole, the book is strong and the stories work well together. There is a lot of wonderful madness in it, most of it in response to a world that is both bland and harsh at the same time. There are also moving stories of characters defeated in that world and faced with having to come to terms with the loss of their dreams and with their lack of heroic dimensions. (p. 108)

> Randall Maggs, ''Failed Shortstops,'' in The Fid-
> dlehead, No. 145, Autumn, 1985, pp. 106-08.

HARRY MARTEN

''The humorous story,'' Mark Twain said, ''depends for its effect upon the *manner* of the telling; the comic story . . . upon the *matter*.'' The Canadian writer W. P. Kinsella has it both ways in the best of these whimsical tales and surreal sketches [collected in **The Alligator Report**], many of which he calls ''Brautigans'' in tribute to Richard Brautigan, whose influence is felt throughout. Working like a fast-talking confidence man, with self-conscious delight in his skill, he moves the reader back and forth across the line between fantasy and reality. Amid elaborately detailed, familiar portraits of slightly seedy city streets and houses, we encounter inexplicable events occurring in the unsuspecting bosom of the everyday. . . . But all is not playful performance in Mr. Kinsella's short tall tales. His quick glimpses of eccentric losers remind us that ''each of us lives with our own secrets, which may be as frayed as a favorite blanket or as vicious as a Tasmanian devil.'' And his fantasies frequently suggest the dangers of bureaucratic systems run amok, with networks of confused servants tunneling secretly under the foundations of all our activities. While some of the very brief sketches in **The Alligator Report** seem

curiously flat and over before they have begun, Mr. Kinsella continues, as he has done recently in his novel **Shoeless Joe** and his stories about Cree Indians in **The Moccasin Telegraph** to define a world in which magic and reality combine to make us laugh and think about the perceptions we take for granted.

> Harry Marten, in a review of ''The Alligator Re-
> port,'' in The New York Times Book Review, Jan-
> uary 5, 1986, p. 16.

JONATHAN WEBB

Perhaps [W. P. Kinsella] is most convincing when he takes his audience for granted. In **Shoeless Joe,** Kinsella's previous novel, the reader was never exactly asked to go along with the novelist's presumption. Sure, the author enticed a (real) reclusive author out of retirement, brought dead ball-players back to life, and played extraordinary phantom baseball games, but it was all for a good cause. It was to rectify old wrongs, to ease pain, and it was joyful throughout. How could a reader resist when compliance was at once so worthy and so much fun? And Kinsella wrote with conviction, as though his credibility was never in doubt.

The Iowa Baseball Confederacy contains bigger magic, larger and more spectacular effects, than anything attempted in **Shoeless Joe.** Kinsella is striving for grander meaning: the reconciliaton of immovable forces—love and darker emotions—on conflicting courses. And, while the effects are memorable and the story ingenious, the striving is too much in evidence, and so are the author's doubts.

The protagonist, Gideon Clarke, is haunted by the knowledge that there was once a baseball league in the hinterland of Iowa City. No one remembers it. There is no objective evidence that it existed. Neither newspaper accounts nor the testimony of a single witness have survived. But Gideon knows the IBC's history; the names of the players—even their statistics—are lodged in his brain. He also knows that the league played for the last time on July 4, 1908 in an exhibition staged between the IBC All-Stars and the major league-leading Chicago Cubs. The contest ended apocalyptically, but the course of the game and the actual cause of the league's demise are unknown to him.

To be obsessed with baseball is to be touched by grace in Kinsella's universe, and a state of grace gives access to magic. In **Shoeless Joe** such magic was sufficient in itself. Gideon, however, obtains additional assistance on his way to the game, first from a neighbour who (in defiance of the novel's own logic) turns out to remember the lost league after all, and then from a slightly creaky contrivance which Kinsella insists on in the early pages, the ''cracks in time''.

The game itself is densely, and rather magnificently, imagined. It is played over a period of 40 days, in steady rain, with supernatural interventions. For 2,614 innings there is stalemate: every run scored by one team is promptly matched by the other. Tens of thousands of spectators attend. The river rises and swells until the nearby town is flooded and swept away. President Theodore Roosevelt appears (he takes a turn at bat) and is followed by Leonardo da Vinci (who claims credit for the invention of baseball). There are other wonders and diversions.

To observe that the game goes on too long may seem churlish: its length is Kinsella's signal achievement. And yet the turning point, a mythical Indian's clutch hit, is anti-climactic. Too many marvels have gone on before.

Drifting Away, the mythical Indian, embodies the ambiguity that is at the centre of the novel. He reflects, in the variety of guises in which he appears and in his own revealed utterances, a lack of certitude that is wildly inappropriate given the pivotal role that he is called on to play.

He appears at first as an elusive presence, a giant striding silently by the side of the road. Later, we learn of his ancient grudge, his "power vision" (of a baseball game—*the* baseball game), and his encounter with the gods. He is, at this point, a formidable figure. But when he meets Gideon, he instantly loses stature. He strikes a curiously prosaic note, for instance, when he says, ". . . yes, I tamper with the reality of Johnson County, Iowa." And there is something discordant, again, when he admits to feeling lonely: "Do you know how long it has been . . . since I have spoken to anyone?"

Drifting Away's powers seem to wax and wane for no particular reason: they are simply variable. To the extent that he is uncontrolled, the novel is out of control. His uncertainty appears to be a reflection of the author's own.

Kinsella's seeming uncertainty has everything to do with his failure here to persuade the reader to go along with his magic. It is not in the imagining that *The Iowa Baseball Confederacy* is flawed, but in the convincing.

Jonathan Webb, "Seduction Just Part of the Game for Kinsella," in Quill and Quire, *Vol. 52, No. 4, April, 1986, p. 39.*

JODI DAYNARD

The problem with comedy is that it can be hellishly addictive. After relishing W. P. Kinsella's two riotous collections of Indian tales, I wanted to keep laughing. But the 26 stories in *The Alligator Report* differ strikingly from his other work. Gone is Silas Ermineskin, the 18-year-old Huck Finnian narrator of *The Moccasin Telegraph* and *Dance Me Outside.* Gone, too, are Ermineskin's picaresque pals, Indians determined to resist mistreatment by the whole world. Instead of the reservation, there's a decrepit rooming house in Vancouver, populated by faceless men who share only their isolation. Kinsella gives them identities, places them briefly—as he did the Indian community—on the map. Now, however, his focus has turned inward, to catch the strange, sad bonds formed out of loneliness. . . .

Kinsella's new stories replace humor with wit, regional dialect with high prose. Winos stumbling against building walls, the lone screech of a motorcycle tire, the sense of helplessness that comes with old age and indigence—from within and without, Kinsella's rooming house stands like a monument to urban indifference. . . . **"Gabon"**'s narrator peers in on life, . . . though what he finds is an isolation deeper than his own. Gabon, a former jockey, had passed him in the hallway for years with the salutation, "I pay my rent." One night, hearing stomping noises overhead, the narrator clambers onto the roof and stares into Gabon's window: "On a brilliant October night, in one of the loneliest places on earth, Gabon paraded around the winner's circle under the blazing sun of Hialeah, Pimlico, or Churchill Downs, accepting the accolades, remembering the clash of the starting gate, the yelp of the crowd as his horse lunged forward—sleek, powerful, pliant as butter between his thighs."

The echoes rising from the hooves of Gabon's pony—like those of D. H. Lawrence's "The Rocking Horse Winner"—are grotesque and sadly intimate. But Kinsella lends them a kind of grandeur that reveals how close the comic sensibility is to pathos. By comparison the short, surreal pieces that follow (dubbed "Brautigans" after the "delicate, visual, whimsical, facetious writing" of Richard Brautigan) are inchoate fragments. A huge rodent in **"The Gerbil That Ate Los Angeles"** gnaws his way across the continent, leaving (I imagine) steaming ruins where cities used to be. An "incorrigible little ankle-biter" in **"How I Missed the Million Dollar Round Table"** pours milk on his father's freckles and eats them while watching "Leave It to Beaver." In one of the early stories there's an octopus who works in the dead letter department of the post office, dreaming of lost crab. Rife with personified animals and humans whose quadruped perversions pin them securely to the lunatic fringe, these tales ring false, caricaturish, the jokes on which they pivot as awkward as those of a Borscht-belt comedian.

While paying homage to Brautigan's humor—with its myriad carnivorous animals and destructive, free-associative fantasies—Kinsella traduces his own. Brautigan's funniest passages have a luxuriant irony, very different from the tough-edged, wakeful sarcasm of Kinsella's underdogs. . . .

Stylistically Kinsella also differs from his mentor: he uses surrealism most effectively to highlight the delicate balance between solitude and alienation, not to achieve a comic effect. And animals serve more readily as symbols of human loneliness than vehicles of hyperbolic humor. Humans crouch beneath the false whimsicality of alligators, freckle-eaters, and octopi. "Tonight," the narrator of **"The Silver Porcupine"** recalls, as he awakens to his desolate surroundings after a long reverie,

> in this rooming house in Vancouver, a thousand miles and nearly as many years from the cold prairie and my past, I heard a silver porcupine tick across the front porch and snuffle at the door. And I could imagine yellow tines of streetlight shattering against his quills, bursting like fireworks in the rain.

These are the images that resonate—not comic ones, alas, but stirring, not woolly-wild, but urban gothic.

Jodi Daynard, "Strangers in the Night," in The Village Voice, *Vol. XXXI, No. 13, April 1, 1986, p. 56.*

ELIOT ASINOF

W. P. Kinsella loves fantasy. His characters do a lot of dreaming. His enjoyable first novel, *Shoeless Joe,* fantasized that baseball's great Joe Jackson was brought back to life and that J. D. Salinger was kidnapped to witness the glory of his return. In *The Iowa Baseball Confederacy,* Mr. Kinsella deals with the mystery of an amateur baseball league of the early 1900's of which there is absolutely no record, though the Chicago Cubs, the world champions of 1908, played an exhibition game against the league's all-stars. . . .

Mr. Kinsella teases us with an assortment of crooked pitches—dirty dinner dishes that wash themselves, houseplants that manage to survive on a wintry lawn. Eventually [Gideon Clarke] and his I've-got-to-make-the-big-leagues-obsessed friend, Stan, manage to penetrate that "crack in time," and zap! we are back in 1908 with the Cubs of Tinker to Evers to Chance and that exhibition game against the Iowa Baseball Confederacy, right there in Gideon's hometown.

Then the author really pulls out all the stops. During the course of a game that lasts more than 2,000 innings over 40 days in a torrential rain, a flood eventually washes away everything but the ball field itself. . . . The great umpire Bill Klem shows up to be the arbiter of the last thousand innings or so, as does Teddy Roosevelt to take a turn at bat (shades of E. L. Doctorow's *Ragtime*). Even Leonardo da Vinci floats through the clouds in a striped balloon and claims he invented baseball but a nation of boccie players ignored him (shades of Mel Brooks's "2,000-Year-Old Man"). . . .

Inevitably, you get the feeling you've read all this before, an irritation exacerbated by repetitious dialogue and incidents. Eccentricities are not amusing per se, and allegories are not necessarily profound.

> *Eliot Asinof, "Did Leonardo Invent the Home Run?"*
> *in* The New York Times Book Review, *April 20,*
> *1986, p. 15.*

STEVEN G. KELLMAN

"Baseball is the one single thing the white man has done right," says Drifting Away, a phantom Indian in [*The Iowa Baseball Confederacy*], a winsome fantasy in which one game lasts 2,614 innings and a fielder fades into the horizon while chasing a fly.

Kinsella's second novel is also his second baseball book. His first, *Shoeless Joe* (1982), was a metafictional whimsy about an Iowa farmer named Kinsella who constructs a diamond on his property. He conjures up the late Shoeless Joe Jackson, whose career was blighted by the 1919 World Series scandal, to play on a timeless team. He also recruits J. D. Salinger to join his visionary company in a game that is undiscernible to the unimaginative.

The Iowa Baseball Confederacy recycles many of the same elements. Like the finest baseball fictions—*The Natural, Bang the Drum Slowly, The Universal Baseball Association Inc., J. Henry Waugh, Prop.*—it is not exclusively, or even primarily, for the sports fan. The summer game becomes the context and metaphor for imagination, commitment, and personal achievement. This genial novel, in which Leonardo da Vinci materializes in a balloon gondola behind second base to announce he invented baseball in 1506, is itself a sport. Like baseball, the book inspires to infinity and eternity, in the hope that its fondest readers might share its narrator's wish: "*I want the game to go on forever.*"

He is Gideon Clarke, and he finds himself endowed with preternatural encyclopedic knowledge of an institution that has vanished from public memory: a baseball league that fielded a team seventy years ago in his hometown of Onamata, Iowa. Gid's father, who was killed by a line drive hit into the stands of Milwaukee County Stadium, was the only other person aware of the Iowa Baseball Confederacy. He even wrote a dissertation on it for the University of Iowa, but he was told by the history department to submit it to the English, as the book was brilliant fiction. Although Gid cannot find a trace of documentation to support his detailed claims about the Confederacy, he persists in his obsession, losing his wife and gaining the reputation of town eccentric.

It is the novel's amiable premise that there are cracks in time. And, one summer evening, accompanied by Stan Rogalski, a friend whose quest for a baseball career is as tenacious as Gid's is to authenticate the Confederacy, Gid walks into July 3, 1908.

It is the eve of an exhibition game between the Chicago Cubs and an all-star squad from the Iowa Baseball Confederacy.

At the end of nine innings, the score is tied at three runs each, but the players refuse to quit, continuing like maniacs in their inconclusive match. As if injected with pituitrin, the novel increasingly assumes the qualities of tall tale, as, despite rain and flood, the teams play on and on, day after day, in a game that would surely have earned a permanent niche in the record books were it not erased from collective consciousness immediately after its apocalyptic finale. Gid alone remembers. He also refuses to forget Sarah, the woman he loves and loses as 1908 floats away. *The Iowa Baseball Confederacy* is not above the facile humor of anachronism or the stock time-travel irony of an ingenue's assertion: "You can't live in the past." But when imagination challenges mutability, no one ought to leave the ballpark early. (pp. 409-10)

> *Steven G. Kellman, "Possessive Ghosts of Nostal-*
> *gia," in* Commonweal, *Vol. CXIII, No. 13, July 11,*
> *1986, pp. 409-10, 412.*

ELSPETH CAMERON

It's too bad Steven Spielberg didn't make a film of W. P. Kinsella's *Shoeless Joe* instead of Alice Walker's *The Color Purple*. Both books were among the highly praised novels of 1982, but it's Kinsella who shares Spielberg's devotion to naive optimism in a cynical world. With the audacity of a kid in a special-effects studio, Kinsella manipulates time and space until fact and fantasy merge in an absurd and mysterious mirage. His second novel, *The Iowa Baseball Confederacy,* is more of the same. Just as Spielberg's *Back to the Future* catapulted a 1980s teenager into the 1950s, Kinsella slips Gideon Clarke through a "crack in time" into 1908 so that he can prove that his father was right about the existence of a mythical baseball team. Both quests produce metaphysical musings, comical encounters, and the temptation to change history. (p. 45)

Like Spielberg, Kinsella draws us into a preposterous world by relying on our child-like longing to suspend disbelief. In less time than it takes to steal a base, he enchants us with such bizarre characters as Enola Gay, Gideon's sister, whose career as an urban guerrilla prevents her from claiming her share of the family inheritance—like her namesake, the plane that bombed Hiroshima, she blows things up. Even Theodore Roosevelt and Leonardo da Vinci horn in on the game, much as novelist J. D. Salinger makes an appearance in *Shoeless Joe.* Da Vinci arrives by balloon and says that he invented baseball before mankind was advanced enough to appreciate it. (pp. 45-6)

Baseball offers a ready-made world that Kinsella exploits for purposes quite different from the usual bottom-of-the-ninth, two-out cliffhangers, a genre he finds boring. Baseball has the qualities of myth: larger-than-life heroes, rituals, a symbolic language, a much-touted history, fervent followers. As a game of infinite possibilities, it has a dimension that might be called religious. Each play of every game can be seen as a contest between the individual and fate, the tangible re-enactment of man's destiny. . . .

[Kinsella] recreates vividly and persuasively the sensual pleasure and adolescent longings baseball can evoke. "I'd imagine," he has said, "that a tremendous proportion of the male population of America has had fantasies about playing major-league ball." Stan Rogalski, Gideon's best friend in *The Iowa Baseball Confederacy,* is a case in point. At thirty-three, the boyish Stan is still "strugglin' to make the Bigs." His constant refrain is, "I've still got a few hits left in me."

Stan might seem immature, a character right out of a beer commercial. But Kinsella lauds Stan's stubborn refusal to give up his dreams and knuckle under to a job that will never allow him time to look up and see how blue the sky is. Like Stan, Gideon—whose name recalls the Old Testament trumpeter who with his sword (or bat?) cut down the Midianites (Chicago Cubs?) to rescue Israel—gets to realize his personal fantasy. He comes up to bat against a major-league pitcher.

Almost all of Kinsella's fictions—he has published eight collections of short stories as well as the two baseball novels—centre on adolescent males. Like crusaders or knights errant, they seek some form of Holy Grail. . . .

Evil, according to Kinsella, lies in the institutions that run our lives: organized religion, banks, bureaucracies, military service, schools. In his books of Indian stories—*Dance Me Outside, Scars, Born Indian*, and *The Moccasin Telegraph*—Kinsella clearly delineates the destructive white culture. As Drifting Away succinctly puts it in *The Iowa Baseball Confederacy,* "The white man's world is full of squares . . . the white man always obsessed with bending the lines of nature, attacking the natural circles of nature, straightening the curving lines into grids, breaking circles, covering the land with prison bars."

Kinsella's bureaucrats lose sight of the vulnerability of the individual but possess the terrifying power to dispose of him. Human dignity is humiliated, and lives are brutally or casually taken. The conflict works on two levels: it's crucial for the individual to carry the innocent and tender vision of "good" forward into adulthood, just as it's essential that society evolve without sacrificing the ideals that inspired it in the first place.

Through the "constant" game of baseball, Kinsella presents us with an image of all that is wholesome, optimistic, and pure, and reminds us of the importance of keeping those ideals alive. The grouping of male adolescents into teams testifies to the impossibility of attempting such a goal alone. Baseball, with its playful nicknames (Three Finger Brown and Moonlight Graham), is a striking metaphor for male bonding.

Some reviewers have taken Kinsella to task for the inadequacies of his female characters, and his women do tend to be Raggedy-Anns: cute, red-haired, freckled little honeys who love their men and stand by them even when they are abandoned in favour of what must seem to them harebrained missions (a stereotype he attempts to modify with the dark, unreliable "travelling women" in *The Iowa Baseball Confederacy*). But such quibbling may be irrelevant. If women writers such as Alice Munro and Sylvia Plath can deliberately define the sensibility of women, why can't male writers explore the lives of boys and men?

Kinsella's fiction is infused with the recognition that the process of life—like the relentless course of a baseball game, or the subjugation of Indians by whites—is irreversible. His characters rebel against their powerlessness. What better way to rebel than to *claim* power by going back in time, bringing the dead back to life, and reliving events the way you wish they had happened?

The protagonist in *Shoeless Joe* gets to give his hero, Shoeless Joe Jackson, the chance to replay the fixed game that got him banned from baseball. In *The Iowa Baseball Confederacy,* Gideon gets the chance to vindicate both his father and Drifting Away, whose ancestral grievances against whites are legion. Gideon is tempted to abuse his new-found power. (p. 46)

"Can I control the urge to change history?" Gideon wonders. Can the adolescent, suddenly big enough to be called a man, control the urge to become like those who have oppressed him? Or will selfishness and power corrupt him?

Kinsella is almost never heavyhanded in addressing these issues. . . .

Kinsella's style, though occasionally overblown, is fresh, poetic, and delightful. His images have a down-home quality reminiscent of W. O. Mitchell. When Gideon's white-blond hair attracts the attention of the Iowa Baseball Confederacy, he feels "like a hamster in a cage, a whole kindergarten class about to pet me." A ball hit in the marathon game "sizzles along the earth like a stone skimming water." Watching the game is "like watching those delicate, long-legged insects skim over calm water."

Kinsella gently creates a fictional world so intimate and natural we feel we've been there before. (p. 47)

Elspeth Cameron, "Diamonds Are Forever," in Saturday Night, *Vol. 101, No. 8, August, 1986, pp. 45-7.*

Clarice Lispector

1925-1977

Ukrainian-born Brazilian novelist and short story writer.

Lispector is considered an important figure in Brazil's literary history for having helped introduce modernist experimental approaches to her country's fiction. Prior to the innovations of such writers as Mário de Andrade, João Guimarães Rosa, and Lispector, Brazilian fiction had been dominated by regional concerns rendered in the mode of realism. Lispector's contributions to the widening range of Brazilian literature included her focus on the subjective nature of reality, her intensely lyrical prose style rich in symbolism and metaphor, and her examination of the role of language in shaping and expressing identity. Lispector's work frequently centers on ontological concerns and the effect of society upon individual identity, which she often explored through the subjective viewpoints of her characters. She made extensive use of interior monologue and employed other elements which are commonly associated with such experimental fiction developments as modernism and *le nouveau roman,* or the antinovel. Alfred J. MacAdam called Lispector "the premier Latin American woman prose writer of this century."

Lispector was born during her family's emigration from the Ukraine to Brazil, where she was raised. She graduated from law school and published her first novel, *Perto do coração selvagem* (1942), while still in her teens. After writing two more novels, *O lustre* (1946) and *A cidade sitiada* (1948), and spending several years abroad, Lispector resettled in Brazil in the late 1950s. She first gained widespread acclaim for *Laços de família* (1960; *Family Ties*), a collection of short stories, and for her novel *A maçã no escuro* (1961; *The Apple in the Dark*). These are generally considered her most accomplished works.

Some critics believe that Lispector's short fiction is superior to her novels; Giovanni Pontiero noted that "her intensity makes her a natural short story writer." *Family Ties* is regarded as her most accessible book. The stories in this collection focus on female protagonists, ranging from adolescents to octogenarians, who experience epiphanic moments in which their sense of identity is challenged. Lispector won praise for the symbolic overtones and rich use of language displayed in these pieces. The stories in *A legiao estrangeira* (1964; *The Foreign Legion*) are set mostly in Rio de Janeiro and again concern females who must confront social and emotional problems. This book also collects journalistic pieces, or "chronicles," that Lispector contributed to various periodicals during her career.

The Apple in the Dark was praised primarily for Lispector's rich use of language and for her investigation of the relation between language and identity. This novel offers a symbolic, psychological portrait of an antihero who undertakes a quest for identity after he has apparently committed a crime. Much of the action takes place in the minds of the protagonist and two women with whom he becomes involved. Richard Franko Goldman stated that *The Apple in the Dark* "is about many things: the relation between speech and act, knowledge and being, perception and awareness, reality and imitation." Lispector's next novel, *A paixão segundo G. H.* (1964), centers on language and relates a woman's attempts to understand reality. Her failure to transcend her feelings of loneliness contribute further to her sense of alienation.

One of Lispector's later novels, *Água viva* (1973), while rooted in the consciousness of a character searching for meaning and identity, initiated Lispector's more intense, self-reflexive experiments in fiction. This feature also forms a major part of her last work, *A hora da estrela* (1978; *The Hour of the Star*), a novella concerning a young woman who moves from an isolated rural locale to Rio de Janeiro. The story is narrated by a man who relates her experiences and comments on how he will present them in fictional form. The adventures of the protagonist and the commentary of the narrator reflect Lispector's life and her ideas about art and language. This work exemplifies Lispector's interest in social issues, as she depicts the experiences of a poor female struggling to establish herself in a male-dominated society. Once again, Lispector was praised for her innovative use of language. In summarizing Lispector's contribution to Brazilian literature, Gregory Rabassa stated: "[Lispector marshals] the syntax in a new way that is closer perhaps to original thought patterns than the [Portuguese] language had ever managed to approach before."

(See also *Contemporary Authors,* Vol. 116 [obituary].)

E. R. MONEGAL

[The essay from which this excerpt is taken was originally published in Daedalus, *Fall, 1966.]*

[Since the mid-1950s] or so, a new group of Brazilian writers has been experimenting with a form that has been baptized *O Novo Romance Brasileiro.* The term *novo romance* acknowledges the influence of the *nouveau roman* and, to a degree, underlines the deep cultural ties that still exist between Brazil and France. (This is less true of the new group of Spanish-American novelists, who are strongly attracted to the Anglo-Saxon world as well.) But if some of the *novo romance* is only an adaptation of the *nouveau roman,* the best of it is really a new movement. Among the prominent novelists now writing in Brazil, Clarice Lispector is one of the most widely respected. She is not alone in the field: Maria Alice Barroso, Adonias Filho, Mario Palmeiro, and Nélida Piñón are also recognized as important or promising new novelists. But Clarice Lispector is the acknowledged master of the experimental fiction of the sixties.

She has already produced five novels: *Perto do Coraçâo Selvagem* (1944), *O Lustre* (1946), *A cidade sitiada* (1949), *A Maça no escuro* (1961), and *A Paixâo segundo G. H.* (1964). She has also published three volumes of short stories. Her first three novels passed almost unnoticed at the time they were published. Success came with her last two novels, which are undoubtedly her best. (pp. 13-14)

[*A Maça no escuro* and *A paixâo segundo G. H.*] reveal a turn of mind and an imagination deeply involved with a quest for reality, a determination to force appearances, and a burning desire to grasp the core of things. To a degree, [Lispector] can be compared to Virginia Woolf (as some of her critics have suggested) because of her rather obsessive philosophical attitude and obviously feminist bias. But it would be wrong to believe that Clarice Lispector is simply turning back the clock of fiction. In a sense, her novels are poetic novels, but they seek to go further than Virginia Woolf's experimental novels of the twenties and thirties. While the author of *To the Lighthouse* was influenced by writers like Frazer, Bergson, and Joyce, Lispector is influenced by the contemporary school of social and psychoanalytical anthropologists. In a very subtle way, her whole enterprise is linked with the one prematurely attempted by Mario de Andrade. As one of her critics pointed out recently, her novels are mythopoetic creations in which morose, and even exasperating, explorations of a given reality are reflected in very primitive types of consciousness. It has also been noted by the same critic that her two most recent novels retrace from the so-called primitive mind man's discovery of philosophical consciousness. According to José Américo Motta Pessanha, the mythical consciousness of man that Lispector explored in episodes of her previous novels and in her short stories is fully organized into a mythology in *A Maça no escuro.* The plight of this novel's main character becomes a symbol of the hero's return to the origins, to the roots, to the native land. In *A Paixâo segundo G. H.,* the problem of the origins of everything is presented in a more philosophical vein. Phenomenology and existentialism help Lispector to search beneath the surface of man's consciousness. Her task becomes increasingly more difficult and hard to follow. Quite recently, one of her most successful short stories, **"O Ovo e a Galinha"** (**"The Egg and the Hen"**), presents subliminal, almost quartet-like variations on an age-old question.

But even if one fears that Lispector's philosophical assumptions are sometimes a bit too lofty . . . , her skill in creating a totally fictitious world, her hypnotic power to extract from words, simple words, all their incantatory virtues, and the single-mindedness of her tragic vision tend to act on the reader as a charm. In *A Maça no escuro* . . . , the inner struggle of a man who believes he murdered his wife is the pretext for an unmitigated exploration of man's grasp of reality (both external and internal), of his power to cope with concrete objects, of his insertion into a foreign and always hostile environment— the world. At the beginning of the novel the man becomes lost in a desert, and in this emptiness even words are hard to find. In *A Paixâo segundo G. H.,* the main character, a woman, talks endlessly. She is trying to understand, trying very hard and obsessively to understand reality. Her effort to grasp the naked reality of the present moment and to recover her own soul reveals her *passion,* a word Lispector uses deliberately in a double sense, the Greek (to suffer) and the Christian. Paradoxically, the use of religious language in this novel indicates her profane turn of mind. (pp. 14-15)

Part of Lispector's works is lost to the common reader. What he generally finds is a brilliant and hard surface, a very morose tale, mysterious characters that suffer from some obscure disease of the mind. Captured by her prose, the reader discovers, in her novels, that everyday reality becomes hallucinatory. At the same time, hallucinations are presented as commonplace. Because of her mythological turn of mind, she is more a sorceress than a writer. Her novels show the incredible power of

words to act on the reader's imagination and sensitivity. On the whole, she has proved, going by a different route, what Guimaraes Rosa has also demonstrated: the importance of language in the novel.

All her work reveals an almost maniacal determination to use the right word, to exhaust the possibilities of each word, to build up a solid structure of words. Her last two novels are written like poems. They demand of their reader a concentration similar to that required by the best contemporary poetry. Once I asked Guimaraes Rosa what he thought of Clarice Lispector's work. He told me very candidly that every time he read one of her novels he learned many new words and rediscovered new uses for the ones he already knew. But, at the same time, he admitted that he was not very receptive to her incantatory style. He felt it was alien to him. His reaction is not unique and explains Lispector's limitations as a novelist. Critics often talk about some form of art that needs an acquired taste. Lispector's novels belong to this category, I think, while Guimaraes Rosa's have a more universal appeal. (pp. 15-16)

E. R. Monegal, "The Contemporary Brazilian Novel," in Fiction in Several Languages, *edited by Henri Peyre, Beacon Press, 1969, pp. 1-18.*

GREGORY RABASSA

The style in all of [Lispector's early] works is interior and hermetic. In most cases the action is seen from the point of view of the characters involved, and the description is also likely to be made through their eyes. This fact places her among the new vanguard of writers who have appeared in Brazil since the end of World War II and who have taken a further step along the path initiated by the so-called "Modernist" renovation of 1922. Because the Modernist movement was so broad as to defy exact definition, including, as it did, novelists and social scientists as well as poets like Mário de Andrade, who were most responsible for its inception, many of its effects were dissipated in the vastness of what would actually seem to be normal course of literary development in Brazil, whether a movement or not. The influence of social writers such as Gilberto Freyre led to a sort of regionalist bias in the novelist of the twenties and thirties, and even the most important of these, such as Graciliano Ramos, José Lins do Rêgo, and Jorge Amado, occupied themselves almost exclusively with their native Northeast.

The poets of the time were in many ways the real forerunners of the novelists of today. Their mythmaking tended to combine personal elements with national traits and realities. Beginning with Mário de Andrade's fantasy-novel *Macunaíma,* the story of "a hero without character," one can follow this combination through the work and styles of such poets as the protean Cassiano Ricardo—always in the vanguard—Jorge de Lima, and Manuel Bandeira down through Carlos Drummond de Andrade, in all of whom one finds introspection coupled with concrete circumstance. A second look at the novelists of the period, however, will reveal that beneath the surface of seeming regionalism there runs an extremely personal note. . . . (pp. x-xi)

The most obvious heir to this mixing of intents, one who has left the thirties far behind after having been spawned in its currents, is João Guimarães Rosa, with *Grande Sertão: Veredas* —Eng. tr., *The Devil to Pay in the Backlands*) and *Sagarana.* In the second book the very title gives away his intent as he appends the Tupi suffix -*rana,* meaning "in the manner of,'' to the Norse word *saga*. In Guimarães Rosa we have the frankest admission of re-creation and mythmaking plus a complex and often Joycean attempt to create new linguistic forms often derived from popular speech.

With the postwar years there is something of a reshuffling of elements, and the novel loses much of its regionalism, while some poetry returns to the native soil. João Cabral de Melo Neto of Recife writes about his native Pernambuco from abroad with nostalgic feeling reminiscent of the Brazilian romantic poets in exile, while in Rio de Janeiro the novelist Nélida Piñon makes biblical themes over into modern problems with an underlay that is Freudian and universal. . . . In all of these writers one finds this touch of the intimate, the universal, the existential, showing that many contemporary Brazilian writers are in tune with certain international currents such as the *nouveau roman* and that this has come about more naturally and less from outside influences than one might suspect. It is more a matter of the coincidences of modern society. This is where Clarice Lispector fits in, somewhere between a Guimarães Rosa and a Nélida Piñon.

The Apple in the Dark represents the high point in the development of Miss Lispector's work, the point toward which she was striving and to which her later novel is, in a sense, a footnote. Most of the elements that go to make up the current trend in Brazilian fiction can be seen in her work. The invention is not as obvious as in Guimarães Rosa because it is less a matter of neologisms and re-creation than of certain radical departures in the use of syntactical structure, the rhythm of the phrase being created in defiance of norms, making her style more difficult to translate at times than many of Rosa's inventions. Nor is the traditional vocabulary here anywhere as rich as in the works of Nélida Piñon. It is precisely in their styles of presentation that the three writers diverge: Guimarães Rosa using the primitive resources of the language for the creation of new words in which to encase his vast and until then amorphous sensations; Piñon extracting every bit of richness from the lexicon of a very rich language without falling into archaisms or other such absurdities; and Lispector marshaling the syntax in a new way that is closer perhaps to original thought patterns than the language had ever managed to approach before. These three elements are the stylistic basis of all good contemporary Brazilian literature.

Martim, the protagonist of *The Apple in the Dark,* is a perfect antihero, almost quixotic, except that Don Quixote knows only too well—and to his detriment—where he is going, while Martim is completely without direction, negative in the sense that his motion is directed by flight rather than pursuit. He is loath to act even when action means escape, thinking that his capture will be his salvation; whereas it is obvious that there is no real salvation either way: if he escapes the law, he will go on thinking that he is morally doomed; if he turns himself in, he will go on worrying about the very motivations that made him do so, and he will be equally unfulfilled.

It is a story with no sure future, no definitive accomplishments, with everything still doubtful at the end for all the characters concerned. It is the story of three people coming together, each with an aim or a fear or a combination of the two, and what at first seems to have been a tremendous accomplishment for each one: Martim's seeming re-creation of himself and his place in the whole universe, Ermelinda's outburst into love as a defense against her fear of death, and Vitória's softening into what she had felt she should have been—all are really futile in the end as they face their mean and shapeless reality. It is

in this sense that the book is quixotic. The words "hope" and "waiting" figure prominently. Don Quixote at least had the advantage of being mad, so that his view of what was around him was clear and definite to him. These people are conscious of their self-delusion, and this is what disturbs them and will be their lasting reality as they backslide out of their dreams and cogitations. (pp. xi-xiii)

The title is a kind of symbol of all that goes to make up the final theme of the book, and what message we are left with, hopeless as it may be, is summed up in it. The second time the notion is mentioned, it comes more clearly as part of the litany recited between Martim and the image of his father, his progenitor, toward the end of the book. We understand then why Miss Lispector has stressed the motif of darkness so much, perhaps why it is an apple, the popularly accepted fruit of the tree of knowledge. The apple can be felt and grasped and recognized in the dark, but there is always the danger and the fear that we may not have a good grip on it and may drop it. In this way the story ends on what could be a hopeless note. Adam and Eve knew what it was and bit into it, becoming human, with all of the tribulations entailed. Here there is the danger that we may drop it and go on being frustrated, even though its attainment means a new frustration. In this way the story seems to be telling us that there is consolation in holding on firmly to what we can recognize around us in the darkness of our ignorance, but it also makes us wonder whether we shall be any better off for it. (pp. xv-xvi)

> *Gregory Rabassa, in an introduction to* The Apple in the Dark *by Clarice Lispector, translated by Gregory Rabassa, Alfred A. Knopf, 1967, pp. ix-xvi.*

RICHARD FRANKO GOLDMAN

A fascinating and distinguished work, [*The Apple in the Dark*] more than explains the esteem in which Miss Lispector is held. Unlike much Brazilian fiction, its appeal derives not at all from its regionalism, for it is quite unconcerned with local color. It is fascinating simply because Miss Lispector is a superb writer, an artist of vivid imagination and sensitivity, with a glorious feeling for language and its uses. She employs words playfully, meaningfully, deceptively, and of course seriously, not necessarily as a poet does but as few novelists do. This makes translation more than normally difficult, and it should be said at once that Gregory Rabassa has succeeded remarkably well.

The book is about many things: the relation between speech and act, knowledge and being, perception and awareness, reality and imitation. Miss Lispector has considered the existentialists, and her ontology is essentially theirs. Superficially *The Apple in the Dark* is the story of a man who has committed a crime, which represents to him a genuine act. It tells of his flight and his attempt to reconstruct himself "from the exact beginning." On a remote farm the protagonist, Martim, becomes involved with two women in states of psychological isolation almost matching his own. At the end Martim is no longer sure even of the nature of his crime, let alone its meaning.

At least that is what appears upon the surface; but an outline of the "plot" is in this instance of little value; the action is in the minds and even more specifically in the words of the three principal characters. For Miss Lispector is telling us that the mind is made up in large part of the words it knows. A feeling of "horror" about his crime, Martim concludes, is "what the language expected of him," and he often "preferred what he had said to what he had really wanted to say.'' Each character is aware of ''how treacherous was the power of the slightest word over the broadest thought.''

Such conceits as these would be dangerous for anyone less skillful than Miss Lispector. Words are as elusive as the feelings and thoughts they attempt to represent, and this is true even for writers. Communication may be impossible among people, but the first-rate writer can work with elusiveness and allusiveness to create poetic meaning; and so Miss Lispector, while preoccupied with the difficulty and the danger of words, is able at the same time to demonstrate their power and beauty.

If her work is thoughtful and poetic, distinguished by touching insight and human sympathy, it is also full of irony and the wild humor that is a necessary part (cause or effect?) of verbal virtuosity. There are passages in *The Apple in the Dark* that bring to mind the blackest pages of Ivy Compton-Burnett, others that recall the saddest passages in Virginia Woolf's *The Waves*. It is feminine writing, but on this very highest level, and these comparisons are not meant to suggest that it is derivative. There are of course many influences: Kafka, Gertrude Stein, and perhaps even Lewis Carroll are in the background. But Miss Lispector is original and authentic, and her style is impressive.

The Apple in the Dark is heavily invested with symbolism, used vividly and effectively and, in general, discreetly. Occasionally Miss Lispector descends to the obvious, even to a hackneyed image or phrase; but one feels that this is done consciously, and more to reassure the reader than to shock him. She often relies on alarming juxtapositions, and the technique of the sudden let-down is handled with splendid effect. (pp. 33, 48)

The Apple in the Dark is susceptible to a variety of ''interpretations,'' and whatever one thinks it may be about, or whatever one may think it means, it remains a delight to read. (p. 48)

> Richard Franko Goldman, ''Deeds in the Mind,'' in Saturday Review, *Vol. L, No. 33, August 19, 1967, pp. 33, 48.*

JAMES NELSON GOODSELL

If Clarice Lispector were not already respected as one of Brazil's leading novelists, *The Apple in the Dark* would establish her reputation. Not that the book is a great novel. In many ways it suffers from stylistic lapses which detract from its theme.

Still Miss Lispector, like so many of her fellow modernists in Brazil, has broken ground in this new work which puts her name alongside those of João Guimarães Rosa and Graciliano Ramos. These are authors who are only now becoming known in English and whose pioneering efforts at radical departures from established storytelling and traditional syntactical structure suggest the richness of contemporary Brazilian literature.

Miss Lispector's hero—or antihero—is Martim whose story is one of flight, even though he does not know where he is going. He does not want to run, thinking that capture may be his salvation. Yet he does run because he fears his motivations in longing to be captured. Martim's story is thus a tortured one. Yet in many ways it is unimportant, as are the stories of the other two people who surface in the novel: Vitória and Ermelinda.

Like so much of modern Brazilian literature, the evoking of feeling through words and phrases with unusual and jarring twists to them is the important element. Martim only helps to carry the story along. The futility and frustration of human life is the feeling Miss Lispector wants to get across. Agree or disagree with this message, one cannot help but admire the ingenious use of words and the pictures they draw to characterize *The Apple in the Dark*. . . .

If this all seems complex and perhaps somewhat futile, this is exactly the feeling Miss Lispector is trying to evoke. For life in her view is just that: complex and somewhat futile. It may not be a particularly happy theme, but it partakes of the general themology of Brazilian literature of today, which despite the somewhat hopeless nature of the message is stylistically rich and vibrant.

It is with this in mind that works like *The Apple in the Dark* must be read. Even in translation, the way language is used suggests the color and breadth and depth of Brazil's modernist genre. The story may be mythical or abstract, the language is alive and real.

> James Nelson Goodsell, ''Brazilian Novelist's Complex Tale,'' in The Christian Science Monitor, *August 23, 1967, p. 9.*

C. D. B. BRYAN

Martim, the protagonist of *The Apple in the Dark,* is an antihero who believes he has murdered his wife. His escape is peculiarly negative in that he is neither running toward or away from anything—rather, he is running away from *being* anything. His crime has provided him with his freedom, ''with a single act he had made the enemies he had always wanted to have—other people, the others . . . in one fell swoop he was no longer a collaborator with other people, and in one fell swoop he had ceased to collaborate with himself.''

Martin's flight brings him to an isolated farm run by a dominating female, Victoria. Martim falls victim to her strong personality and the neuroses of her widowed cousin, Ermelinda. Martim's quest for his own place in the universe provokes Victoria and attracts Ermelinda, forcing a confrontation between the ''afraid to live'' Victoria, ''afraid to die'' Ermelinda, and ''afraid to be afraid'' Martim, as he characterizes himself and the others. The ultimate confrontation however, is that of each character with himself or herself.

The Apple in the Dark, like the majority of new novels coming from South America, is above all an interior novel, one in which the minds of the characters control and determine the action. Miss Lispector is an inspired and, at times, beautiful writer, but she lacks control; her overwriting flaws the novel, especially where she waxes lyrical about intellectual and emotional minutiae.

Martim's flight, complete with Edenic expulsion allusions, rivals Geoffrey Household's *Rogue Male* in intensity. Such passages are strong and believable; one feels the heat, the sand, the thirst, the sun, the solitude. But when Miss Lispector enters Martim's mind, she illustrates the literary fact of life that female authors can no more portray a man's search for identity than a male author can convey a woman's sensations during childbirth. (pp. 22-3)

The ''apple'' in the novel's title is symbolic not only of Eden and knowledge, but risk. An apple grasped in the dark may be recognized as an apple. Until seen in daylight, one is uncertain about its character, its color and maturity. Miss Lispector seems to suggest that it is better to be content with the knowledge one has of an apple (or one's self) in the dark, without any assurance that when light comes one is better off. For so capable a writer, one wishes she had had more to say. (p. 23)

C. D. B. Bryan, "Afraid to Be Afraid," in The New York Times Book Review, *September 3, 1967, pp. 22-3.*

EARL E. FITZ

Long and justly famous throughout Latin America for her sensitive, penetrating explorations of human consciousness, Clarice Lispector created a series of stylistically rigorous, hermetic, and often enigmatic novels and short stories that dealt, characteristically, with the working of the mind. Physical objects, such as those encountered in *O Lustre* (1946), or the presence of an external milieu, such as that depicted in *A Cidade Sitiada* (1948) or *A Maça no Escuro* (1961), function within her fictive universe in a way that reminds us of T. S. Eliot's understanding of the "objective correlative," that is, an object, situation, or action that, visibly and concretely, conveys the mood or state of mind that the author wishes to evoke in the reader. For Eliot, as for Lispector, the "objective correlative" is the vehicle by means of which emotion can be expressed in the objectivity of the art form, the only way the author can conjure up and express the proper emotional response in the reader without having to resort to a direct statement of that response. In this sense, a number of Clarice's characters, including the protagonist of *A Hora da Estrela,* show themselves to be rather like J. Alfred Prufrock or Rilke's Malte Laurids Brigge, hypersensitive beings in whose minds the outer world of objects and actions sets off a series of ostensibly uncontrolled flashes of silent, anxious speculation about the twin problems of identity and being. However, we should not forget, in view of the author's well-known ontological concerns, that Clarice Lispector never ignored the three dimensional world. To the contrary, she made use of it in a constant and unique way, one that would link together objects, our perceptions of them, and the impressions they make on our conscious and unconscious minds. This, as Lispector understood it, was at the heart of the process by which a human identity is formed, and it represents the all important bridge between much of what is "new" in *A Hora da Estrela* and that which we have grown accustomed to seeing in her earlier work. Her fascination with the always changing relationship between the inner and outer world also explains, in part, why we are reminded so strongly, at times, of the French "nouveau roman," especially as practiced by Robbe-Grillet and Nathalie Sarraute, the latter being especially close to Lispector in terms of her manner of characterization.

But Clarice's abiding interest in the objects of the external world and the effect they have upon our sentient minds also recalls for us the nature and function of phenomenology in Lispector's fictional world. Her distinctly phenomenological orientation towards life and literature involves a synthesis of object and one's awareness of it, a process in which a single human mind, usually that of her protagonist, becomes both the subject and the object of the act of cognition, of understanding. But while this kind of preoccupation has always been a vital element in her work, it must be noted that [*A Hora da Estrela*] . . . focuses on some overt social issues as well, specifically, on the chronic plight of a certain type of Brazilian northeasterner who undertakes a journey to the great cities of the south in search of a better life. But in this particular novel, and in typical Lispectorian fashion, we are led, additionally, into the mind of a realistically described young "nordestina," a woman who represents for us and for the author the continued presence of the "two Brazils," one rich and healthy, the other poor and sickly. In this double role, that of protagonist and symbol, Clarice's main character in this novel reminds us of the innumerable ways the harsh, tragic realities of the Northeast blight not only the land but the people as well. The image of the wasteland, geographically and psychologically, is thus constantly expressed, becoming, finally, the central or controlling image of the entire work. We can see, then, that, in a certain sense, *A Hora da Estrela* shows itself to be more of a shift of emphasis for Clarice Lispector, a different approach to get at an old concern, the tenuous relationship between language, existence, and consciousness, than it is any radically new tack or development. And yet . . . the openly ironic function of the narrator, and his dual relationship with the protagonist and the reader, adds a startlingly new element of narrative complexity to this work. Clarice elects here to deal directly with one of the most singular features of modern narrative: the unreliable, or fallible, narrator. In looking at how well she succeeded with her point of view experiments, we are able to get a better perspective on how she was growing, and maturing, as an artist, something which is crucial to our appreciation of this last work.

The style of *A Hora da Estrela* is less unabashedly lyrical than its immediate predecessor, *Agua Viva* (1973), but it does continue with Clarice's penchant for extracting every bit of connotative and denotative meaning out of apparently simple verbal icons. Lispector, a writer who, like Guimarães Rosa, always understood both the mystery of language and its pivotal importance for literature, especially the novel form, creates in this work a kind of allegorical regionalism, a mimetic tale of a certain place and time but one that turns in on itself. But in addition to this fascinating literary hybridism, Lispector links the structure of the entire novel to an ongoing discussion of what the creative act means to the artist, this being a theme first discussed at length by the author in *Agua Viva.*

A Hora da Estrela is, therefore, on one level the story of the writing, the creation, of a novel. As with Machado de Assis' *Dom Casmurro* (1900), or Graciliano Ramos' *São Bernardo* (1934), the development of the text itself becomes, to a large extent, what the narrative is about, its most compelling aspect. . . . [We] meet the person who tells the story in our novel, a man whose presence in the story is central to its structuring and, consequently, to its meaning. . . . [The] direct but self-effacing authorial commentary becomes a leitmotif of the novel, and its extensive implementation, along with its ironic function within the context of the story itself, marks an interesting stylistic development for Clarice Lispector. Indeed, for the first time, in any systematic fashion, Clarice has begun to deal with the delicate though critical relationship between narrator, author, and reader, or, to express it more precisely, between the real author, the implied author, the other characters, and the reader. . . . So the question of the narrator's reliability or unreliability is . . . one that is going to pervade the entire work, one that will affect the manner in which all the other elements in the story fit together. (pp. 195-98)

With the narrator's ruminations and interpolations omnipresent in the story, the point of view fluctuates constantly between first-person, either that of our struggling narrator or that of one of the characters most involved; second-person, which is generally reserved for the illuminating and often funny exchanges of dialogue between characters but which is also occasionally used by the narrator in direct discourse with the reader; and third-person, the omniscient, traditional mode of story-telling and one with which Clarice Lispector has been able to produce a very telling kind of psychological realism, one reminiscent, in its own inimitable way, of that of Machado de Assis. . . . The overall effect of this frequently fable-like tone, which is strongly reminiscent of Lispector's earlier work, is to draw the reader closer to the perspective of the narrator, a sensitive man who, like Clarice herself, was reared in the Northeast but who later on came to live in Rio de Janeiro. The narrator, as we have seen, seems to be talking with us directly as he ponders the how and why of fiction writing and, in a related issue, what it means to create something out of words. . . . So as the reader becomes privy to these types of concerns, which are simultaneously germane to the characters in the story and to the formulation of the story itself, he becomes an active and willing accomplice in the organic, but also ironic, process of the narrator's artistic functioning, its structuring. (p. 199)

Closely linked to this structural inventiveness are the three major themes dealt with in *A Hora da Estrela*. . . . [Operating] in close consort with the two more obvious themes in this novel, the ruinous and as yet unresolved human tragedy of Brazil's northeastern region, and the attempt of an essentially philosophical and lyrical writer to show a barren, blighted personality struggling, blindly and futilely, to develop into something more satisfying, there exists a subtle yet powerful third theme. This tertiary though no less vital impulse of *A Hora da Estrela* comes to grips with the implications inherent in being an artist, the ethical, humanistic, and philosophic meaning of creativity, what it really means to connect words with reality and then to give them form, to turn them into art, into literature. . . . (pp. 200-01)

The "death" of the narrator, supposedly the imaginative force behind the writing of the novel, also highlights an aspect of Clarice's fiction that has been a constant in her work, though often in an elusive, suggestive fashion. It is one, moreover, which places her, autogenerically, it would seem, in the mainstream of one of Western literature's most dominant themes— the isolation of the artist. In all of Clarice's fiction, but especially in her novels, art, or artistic sensibility, has been advanced, often symbolically, as the only possible antidote to the randomness and flux of existence. In Lispector's world, the artist, as seen in *Água Viva,* or an artistically receptive "common person," like Joana, of *Perto do Coração Selvagem* (1944), reacts to the baseness of quotidian reality by turning, often unconsciously, to the salvation and sense of worth found in the process of self-discovery and authentic self-expression. Typically, this process results in the attempted linkage of a person's private, personal sense of being and identity to what Clarice suggests are the eternal and timeless life forces at work in the universe, this being an impulse that is especially apparent in *A Paixão Segundo G. H.* (1964). Clarice's characters tend to rely on actual artistic creativity, as in *Água Viva,* the urge to create, as in *A Maçã no Escuro,* or on the liberating power of un-premeditated action, as in *A Paixão Segundo G. H.,* in an attempt to impose form, and consequently meaning, on their fragmented existences. In *A Hora da Estrela,* however, the narrator's own relation to life and death is inextricably bound up in the creation of his protagonist, Macabéa, and of "life" in literature. It is through art, Clarice is telling us, through imagination, selection, and ordering, that the artist—and the person who appreciates art—overcomes the formlessness and chaos of existence, succeeds in being constantly reborn, and achieves immortality. The cyclical, archetypal movement of

birth, death, and rebirth has become the means by which Lispector's characters, from Joana to Rodrigo S. M. Relato, gain in self-awareness and in a consciousness of where they fit into the general scheme of things.

So, in *A Hora da Estrela,* the death of Macabéa, an event paralleled by the narrator's statement that he, the protagonist's creator, "has just died with the girl," underscores the extent to which Clarice has, in the course of this book, artfully manipulated the viewpoint, the relationship between reader, character, and author. But in so doing, it also hearkens up important questions about the degree to which there are autobiographical elements in this story, about the degree to which Clarice chose to project herself into the action. There are numerous references which, given what we already know about Clarice's life, open the door to more speculation on this point. For example, Clarice, like Macabéa, knew what it meant to be a young girl obliged to move from her home in a small northeastern city and go to a huge southern metropolis. She knew, too, what it meant to be immediately bombarded with a plethora of utterly new sights, sounds, and ideas. She knew what it meant to find herself suddenly among strangers and to have to make up her life as she went along. (pp. 201-02)

[Although] the nature and function of the narrator is of considerable interest in *A Hora da Estrela,* there is another issue that needs to be studied in relation to it, an issue that speaks directly to the already alluded to autobiographical aspects of the novel. I refer to those sections of the work in which the narrator discusses his private feelings about life and its relation to literature, in which he indulges in some highly personalized digressions about his own troubled existence and the various ways it can, or cannot, be transformed into literature. . . . [A scene late in the novel seems] ineluctably to lead us to visualize Clarice herself, Clarice the isolated artist, confronting, at the very end of her life, the meaning of her own existence, her art, and her impending death. (pp. 203-04)

The attitudes and themes touched upon and alluded to here, almost as if in a literary summing up and farewell address, do not seem appropriate for Rodrigo S. M. Relato [the narrator]; they do, however, seem perfectly appropriate for Clarice Lispector, the artist who knew she was dying. It is as if Clarice slips, very unobtrusively, into Rodrigo's character and, with only a faintly discernible shift in tone to mark it, then proceeds to make her final accounting to us, as a writer and as a human being. The poignancy of this final realization and declaration of self, plus the concomitant explanation of what this story "is about," cannot be missed. Transmitted by a typically Lispectorian image involving sight, sound, a sense of anticipation, and the epiphany-like instant of cognition, the text, hauntingly ambiguous, carries us into the mind of the story's creator. . . . (p. 204)

In conclusion, we can say that, in *A Hora da Estrela,* Clarice Lispector continues to work with certain of the major themes that had held her interest, and ours, ever since her first published novel in 1944. But it also seems abundantly clear that there are present in this final, partially autobiographical work several elements that, if not wholly new, were certainly undeveloped previously. Among these, we should take special note of the author's controlled use of verbal and dramatic irony, her development of sardonic, even absurdist humor, her extended experiment with an intrusive narrator, and, most notable of all, the attention and stress she gives to the novel's sociologically related questions. Stylistically, however, and this does not surprise us since Clarice has always been a consummate stylist, she succeeds in blending all of these disparate elements, the old and the new, by means of a skillfully controlled perspective, one that allows her to merge her own comments about life, literature, and art with a narrative web that is based on the machinations of a fully self-conscious narrator, a man who, in many ways, is like Lispector herself. In addressing herself, then, through the text itself, to the unique experience that is the writing and reading of a novel, while, at the same time, plumbing the depths of an isolated human consciousness, Clarice Lispector has taken another important step toward legitimizing the place of Brazilian literature in the larger context of contemporary Western literature. Without being artistically perfect, *A Hora da Estrela* is a worthy addition to its author's lifetime of labor devoted to the creation of literature. In her penult effort as a novelist, Clarice Lispector succeeded in drawing together all of the themes that had preoccupied her throughout her illustrious career and in introducing some new ones as well. The organic, interconnected nature of her fiction and her concern over questions involving style and technique have never been more evident than they are here. (pp. 205-06)

So while it can be said that *A Hora da Estrela* does contain much that is vintage Clarice Lispector, we should not let this blind us to the new material that the author works with in this novel, particularly her attempt to merge social criticism with what remains basically stream-of-consciousness subject matter. But in all of this, it is Lispector's careful and coordinated shifting of perspective that establishes itself as the most outstanding feature of the entire work. Clearly aware of what she wanted to say, and of how she wanted it said, Clarice controls our response to *A Hora da Estrela* through her variations in point of view. Given the vigor and innovativeness of what we see here, one must wonder about the wonderful stories we could have expected from Clarice Lispector had she not died so prematurely. With her untimely passing, one of Latin America's most original and powerful voices has been stilled. Though her presence is already being sorely missed, her inspiration and example remain very much alive for us. While *A Hora da Estrela* may not be Lispector's best novel, its daring experimentalism tantalizes us with visions of what might have followed if she had been able to develop further. (p. 207)

> *Earl E. Fitz, "Point of View in Clarice Lispector's 'A Hora da Estrela'," in* Luso-Brazilian Review, *Vol. XIX, No. 2, Winter, 1982, pp. 195-208.*

MARTA PEIXOTO

Family Ties (Laços de Família, 1960), Lispector's most studied and anthologized collection of short stories . . . , offers a good starting point for investigating symbolic functions assigned to women in her fiction and for examining her models of female development. . . . *Family Ties* contains well-made stories, less idiosyncratic and difficult than most of her later work. In addition to the accessibility of these stories, it is perhaps its critical evaluation of family relationships and female life from youth to old age that has gained for this collection its readership.

In only three of the thirteen stories of *Family Ties* are the central characters male. The female protagonists, middle-class women in an urban setting, range in age from fifteen to eighty-nine. The stories in which they appear can be read as versions of a single developmental tale that provides patterns of female possibilities, vulnerability, and power in Lispector's world. The author assigns traditional female roles to her protagonists: ad-

olescents confronting the fantasy or reality of sex, mature women relating to men and children, and a great-grandmother presiding over her birthday party. Through the plots of the stories and the inner conflicts of the heroines, Lispector challenges conventional roles, showing that the allegiances to others those roles demand lead to a loss of selfhood. The protagonists' efforts toward recuperating the self emerge as dissatisfaction, rage, or even madness. The stories present the dark side of family ties, where bonds of affection become cages and prison bars.

All the stories in the collection turn on an epiphany, a moment of crucial self-awareness. In the midst of trivial events, or in response to a chance encounter, Lispector's characters suddenly become conscious of repressed desires or unsuspected dimensions of their psyches. These women experience the reverse of their accepted selves and social roles as mother, daughter, wife, as gentle pardoning, giving females. In their moments of changed awareness, they may realize not only their imprisonment but also their own function as jailers of women and men. Their epiphanies, mysterious and transgressive, bring to consciousness repressed material with potentially subversive power. The negative terms which often describe these moments—"crisis," "nausea," "hell," "murder," "anger," "crime,"—convey the guilt and fear that accompany the questioning of conventional roles. Internal monologues shaped by antithesis, paradox, and hyperbole display a wealth of opposing moral and emotional forces. After these characters' crises, when by recognizing their restrictions they glimpse the possibility of a free self, they more or less ambiguously pull back, returning to a confinement they can't or won't change. The intensity of their conflicts may be enlightening for the reader, but the protagonists return to their previous situations after questioning them for only a moment.

Of the three tales of adolescent initiation in *Family Ties,* two have women protagonists. It is instructive to compare the male and female patterns. In **"The Beginnings of a Fortune,"** a young boy suddenly fascinated with money grasps its connection with power and its usefulness in attracting girls. Yet he also sees the vulnerability to the greed of others that the possession of "a fortune" would entail. **"Preciousness"** and **"Mystery in São Cristovão"** have parallel plots on a symbolic level. Both hinge on the intrusion by several young men into a young woman's private domain. In **"Preciousness,"** the protagonist on her way to school undergoes a violent sexual initiation when two young men, strangers passing by, reach out and briefly touch her body. She accepts and turns to advantage this negative experience, darkly intuiting it as a lesson about her fragile individuality in a world of powerful men. Unlike the young boy, who realizes that acquiring his fortune requires purposeful activity, the young girl feels within herself "something precious." Something which "did not compromise itself, nor contaminate itself. Which was intense like a jewel. Herself." . . . But she is "precious" also in her new status as a coveted object, able to arouse men's lust. And this second kind of preciousness undercuts, compromises, contaminates her preciousness to herself. . . . As a lesson drawn from this incident, she keeps repeating to herself that she is all alone in the world. Sex and its concomitants, intrusion and violence, lead her to isolation instead of relationship. Yet she also learns the necessity of protecting herself. She confronts her parents with a request for new shoes: "Mine make a lot of noise, a woman can't walk on wooden heels, it attracts too much attention! No one gives me anything! No one gives me anything!." . . . She demands to be given things, possessions to compensate for the deeper dispossession, for her broken confidence in herself and in her relationship to others. And her assertiveness in demanding new shoes serves, paradoxically, her need for self-effacement, for camouflage, as a way of protecting herself.

"Mystery in São Cristovão" reworks in parable form a similar version of female sexual initiation. At the epiphanic moment, three young men on their way to a party, dressed up as Rooster, Bull, and Devil, trespass to steal hyacinths in "the forbidden ground of the garden" . . . at a young girl's house, as she looks on from her window. the moment when the four participants stare at each other seems to touch "deep recesses" . . . in all of them. The young men guiltily slip away leaving behind a "hyacinth—still alive but with its stalk broken" . . . ; the young girl screams, waking up her family. Like the protagonist of **"Preciousness,"** she too becomes passive and cannot explain anything beyond her scream. (pp. 288-91)

The male and female initiation tales offer, then, a number of contrasts: activity versus passivity; a young boy who seeks wealth and power versus young girls who are "precious" themselves, metaphorically identified with jewels and flowers; preoccupation with acquisition versus concern with self-protection; entrance into the world of economic and social exchange versus retreat in fear into oneself. Development, for the young girls, clearly will not proceed according to the male model.

It is in a context of attachment and affiliation with others that the women characters develop. After initiation into the vulnerability to which their female sexuality exposes them, they find protection and a measure of satisfaction in family ties. We see in other stories several of Lispector's women safely ensconced in a domestic life. The stories reflect the matrifocal organization of Brazilian society where the extended family still prevails, so much so that the word *família* usually refers not only to the small nuclear family but to a numerous network of relatives. The title story shows most clearly the ambivalent function of the family in the whole collection. In **"Family Ties,"** the power a woman wields within the family has a negative, constricting side: deprived of the chance to develop herself beyond the scope of the family, she attempts to control those close to her. (p. 291)

In **"Love,"** plant imagery conveys Anna's everyday awareness of herself in her thriving domesticity: "Like a farmer. She had planted the seeds she held in her hand, no others, but only those. And they were growing into trees.". . . Although "at a certain hour of the afternoon the trees she had planted laughed at her," . . . Anna feels steady in her chosen course. A casual encounter upsets her equilibrium. From a tram, she sees a blind man standing on the street, calmly chewing gum. His mechanical, indifferent acceptance of his fate perhaps mirrors for Anna her own blindness and restriction. The blind man is also a victim of the brutality of nature, which maims some of its creatures, a threat Anna usually forgets. When Anna continues her meditation in the botanical garden—a place that confines natural growth, making it follow a prearranged plan—a nausea analogous to Sartre's *nausée* overtakes her: "a vague feeling of revulsion which the approach of truth provoked." . . . The initial tranquility she perceives in this enclosed garden gives way to a disquieting vision of a secret activity taking place in the plants, as decay encroaches upon ripeness. . . . (p. 294)

"The Imitation of the Rose" contains a similar configuration of opposing forces: a familiar, domestic world threatened and undercut by the laws of another realm. For Laura, who has just returned from a mental hospital, images of light represent her powerful attraction to madness, suggesting that in madness she finds insights otherwise unavailable to her. Laura's dutiful relief at being "well" again, her drab descriptions of herself and her activities, contrast with her luminous, lively account of her mad self. Sleepiness, fatigue, obsession with method, cleanliness, and detail, a certain slowness of body and mind, boring to others as to herself—all signal that Laura is "well." An alert lack of fatigue, clarity of mind, a sense of independence, of possessing extraordinary powers, accompany her returning madness. In the encounter that sets off the struggle between sanity and madness, Laura admires the wild roses in her living room. The conflict between the impulse to send the roses to a friend and the desire to keep them for herself reflects Laura's life-long struggle between selflessness and selfhood. She can only satisfy herself and what she perceives as society's demands by an exaggerated rendition of the role of a giving, submissive woman. . . . The roses, in their beauty, exemplify a distinct, glorious selfhood that Laura denies herself: "something nice was either for giving or receiving, not only for possessing. And, above all, never for one to *be*. . . . A lovely thing lacked the gesture of giving." . . . Yet as soon as Laura decides to give away the roses, her madness begins to return. . . . (pp. 295-96)

In **"Happy Birthday,"** the protagonist belatedly rejects her family, implicitly questioning her own role as a prototypical matriarch. On her eighty-ninth birthday, when her power and the bonds of love have already been eroded, her family gathers to mimic the appearances of closeness. The narrative method—a mosaic of internal monologues interspersed with dialogues and the narrator's remote, at times ironic commentary—shows the resentment and hostility among members of the family and presents the protagonist from the outside as well as from the inside, what she is to others and what she is to herself. In a Kafkaesque progression reminiscent of "The Judgment," the old woman at first appears decrepit and later demonstrates a surprising, malevolent vigor. (p. 297)

The old woman rails against the loss of her power; in a sense she is a victim of old age. Her dominance stemmed from her personal capacity to play the most powerful role traditional Brazilian society allows women, that of mother in a mother-dominated extended family. Her ability to command attention is eerily revived when she cuts the cake, spits, and curses. These actions serve as a crude demonstration of the willfulness which in her prime she would have manifested in more subtle and socially sanctioned ways. Yet this old woman, like Lispector's other protagonists, is also ultimately a victim of her social role. Her power issued from a control of others that is neither healthy nor enduring. (p. 298)

After the old woman's outburst, the narrative method shifts back to external presentation. She relapses into an enigmatic passivity, clutching the ghost of her power. . . . Like so many of Lispector's female protagonists, she returns at the end to her initial situation. As they move from youth to old age, the protagonists of *Family Ties* also trace a circular path, beginning and ending in passivity—from the withdrawal of a frightened young girl to the abstraction of an old woman, her power over her family, repressive in itself, all spent.

Through the plots and internal monologues of her characters, Lispector questions, as we have seen, the conventional roles she assigns to her protagonists. A tendency similar to the subversion of stereotypes in characters and plot recurs on the level of language. Lispector destroys and recreates the meanings of certain ordinary words, redefining them through paradoxical formulations. In **"Love,"** the title word acquires multiple and contradictory meanings as the protagonist attempts to align her confused yearnings with the *eros* and *caritas* she had always believed gave direction to her life. In **"The Imitation of the Rose,"** madness takes on a positive value, signifying the expansion of Laura's independence and self-esteem—at the end of the story Laura is "serene and in full bloom" . . .—without of course losing its acceptation of illness, the delusion of power. (pp. 298-99)

Lispector's protagonists, as they shift from one set of specific circumstances to another, repeatedly find themselves in metaphoric prisons, formed by their eager compliance with confining social roles. Their potential development—the ability to integrate into their everyday selves the greater autonomy they desire in their moments of insight—again and again falters and stops short. For the youngest protagonists, the prison is their own fearful passivity in a society that accepts as normal intrusions by men such as the ones they experience. Anna's attachment to domestic routines blocks her from participating in a wider social and moral world, both frightening and exhilarating to her, the outlines of which she only obscurely intuits. For Laura, living according to others' expectations and suppressing her own desires leads to madness, an illusory escape into another prison. . . . [In] **"Happy Birthday"** and **"Family Ties,"** mother-love itself imprisons. These women start out and remain in spiritual isolation. Locked in desired yet limiting relationships to husbands and children, they find no allies in other women—mothers, friends, or daughters—who appear if at all as rivals and antagonists. Their only power lies in passing on an imprisoning motherly love to their children. (pp. 299-300)

Within the predominantly bleak view of female possibilities in *Family Ties,* there is a curious exception, represented by the grotesque, almost fantastic protagonist of **"The Smallest Woman in the World."** This story elaborates on a supposedly documentary anecdote: a bewildered explorer meets the smallest member of the smallest tribe of African pygmies—a tiny pregnant woman, measuring a foot and a half—and names her Little Flower. Readers of the Sunday newspaper react to her story and see her life-size picture. She herself does not experience an epiphany but instead causes moments of insight in other characters. Women of all ages seem fascinated by this hyperbolic representative of the fragility and powerlessness associated with their sex. One woman fights against an involuntary identification with Little Flower: "looking into the bathroom mirror, the mother smiled, intentionally refined and polite, placing between her own face of abstract lines and the primitive face of Little Flower, the insuperable distance of millennia." . . . While those considering Little Flower turn to her amazing smallness and supposed vulnerability with a greedy interest, wanting to possess the miracle and even use her as a pet, the small creature herself feels powerful and contented. Living constantly with the danger of being devoured by animals and members of other tribes, she experiences the triumph of having so far endured. . . . (pp. 301-02)

With the story of Little Flower, Lispector creates a comic parable of a native female power, sustained against all odds. The jungle inhabitant manages to retain the tranquil independence sought eagerly by city-bred women in their civilized world of enclosed spaces, prescribed behavior, and family ties. Lispector heaps on her protagonist multiple signs of powerlessness and oppression: membership in a black African tribe reminiscent of slavery and colonialism, the female sex, minute size, and the special dependence that pregnancy entails. She places her in opposition to a white male explorer (*explorador* in Portuguese means both "explorer" and "exploiter"). Yet the most vulnerable of women is not a victim. Unlike Laura, who cannot keep the roses, and unlike Lispector's other protagonists, who cannot hold on to and use their insights to change the forces that bind them, the smallest woman in the world, alone in her tree house, possesses herself—Lispector's wry symbol of a successful development, though not of the means to attain it. (pp. 302-03)

Marta Peixoto, "'Family Ties': Female Development in Clarice Lispector," in The Voyage In: Fictions of Female Development, *Elizabeth Abel, Marianne Hirsch, Elizabeth Langland, eds., University Press of New England, 1983, pp. 287-303.*

JOHN GLEDSON

It is a splendid coincidence (I assume that it is one) that these two volumes [*Family Ties* and *The Apple in the Dark*] by one of Brazil's most famous and individual modern writers should be given their first publication in Britain at the same time. . . . [Lispector] always formed part of a tradition in Brazilian fiction (represented also by one of her mentors, Lúcio Cardoso) of intense, almost exclusive interest in the subjective world. For this reason, her work may come as a shock to those familiar with other fictional Latin Americas.

The best entry into her often strange world is probably *Family Ties,* a volume of thirteen short stories. As Giovanni Pontiero says in his helpful afterword, her intensity makes her a natural short-story writer and the reading of [*The Apple in the Dark*] can be—was, quite certainly, intended to be—a challenge, at times as frustrating as it is enlightening. But no one who has read *Family Ties* could doubt the reality of her vision. Several of the stories are unforgettable, perhaps most obviously **"The Imitation of the Rose"**, a picture of a woman desperately and unsuccessfully trying to hold on to the few features in a blank world which might protect her from a relapse into the "nervous breakdown" from which she has just emerged; or again, **"Happy Birthday"**, a picture of a loveless family party presided over by a crippled, resentful grandmother. These stories, like **"Love"**, **"The Beginnings of a Fortune"** and [**"Family Ties"**], are set in the middle-class *milieu* of Rio, and to a degree are specific to that world—for instance, one of the problems faced by Laura in **"The Imitation of the Rose"** is how to deal with a maid to whom she herself feels inferior: the necessary mixture of authority and respect is something she is incapable of. Her trouble, and the trouble with many Lispector characters, is an overwhelming sensitivity. . . .

Most—indeed, with exceptions that are only apparently so, all—of the characters who are open to the world in this vulnerable sense are women, and indeed femininity is a theme in its own right in some stories, most explicitly in the grimly humorous parables **"The Chicken"** and **"The Smallest Woman in the World"**. Lispector's men are more difficult to understand. The best places to begin are again in *Family Ties,* **"The Dinner"** and most importantly, **"The Crime of the Mathematics Professor"** (would "teacher" be a better translation?). Mathematics, categorization, calculation: these are the implications of the title, and if they imply sexual stereotyping, the charge may be partly justified. But this is relatively unimportant beside the perverse complexity, the hypocrisy, or more exactly *mauvaise foi* which characterizes these men.

The difficulty of *The Apple in the Dark* is partly attributable to this—it is centered on a man, and such a man, the hero Martim. This means that a level of experience free from delusion, illusion, play-acting and false, specious argument is not often reached, and, when it is, the suspicion of further depths of falsehood always remains. . . .

In it we move out of the city of Rio to a recognizably Brazilian tropical countryside, but social distinctions have lost their weight in a world which is curiously lush and abstract at the same time. Martim, an engineer, is the mathematics teacher's successor. He too has committed a crime (the real or attempted murder of his wife), a fact which seems to arouse more interest than remorse in him; the book recounts his (failed) attempts to begin a new life, and his relationships with two women, Ermelinda and Vitória, who have their parallels in the stories too, representing extremes of abandonment and control. The stakes in this novel are high: it is an attempt to write a religious work (the apple of the title is *the* apple), while abandoning none of the specificity of human experience, whether physical, moral or emotional. One of the results is a very disconcerting use of language, which in its efforts to grasp complexity, occasionally drifts free from graspable meaning (the author was quite aware of this, as passages in the novel indicate.) The result is moving at times, at others quite puzzling. But anyone who has read *Family Ties* is likely to be tempted into this larger world.

> *John Gledson, "The Vulnerable World Inside," in*
> The Times Literary Supplement, *No. 4269, January 25, 1985, p. 86.*

MICHAEL WOOD

Martim, in *The Apple in the Dark,* has murdered his wife (well, he thinks he has, later he learns that his great crime is only an attempted crime) and in best existentialist fashion is busy reinventing himself on the basis of this radical bid for freedom. He flees to a sort of Brazilian waste land, meets the aging angry Vitoria, the dotty young widow Ermelinda, and thinks and thinks, revolving in his mind all the facets of his self-absorption. 'I understand by complicating,' a character says in one of Julio Cortazar's novels. Martim and Lispector just complicate: they run from understanding as if it were a disease or an intellectual gaffe. Indeed Lispector argues, with the brisk and wilful air of paradox which characterises much of her writing, that incomprehension itself is a form of understanding. Martim sees the countryside around him 'with a flash of incomprehension worthy of a genius'. Later he and Vitoria get each other's meaning without having any idea of what they are talking about, and Lispector celebrates the usefulness of 'words that are lost'. . . . The image of the apple in the dark has much the same implication. 'Understanding,' Martim thinks, 'is an attitude . . . as if . . . stretching out his hand in the dark and picking up an apple, he would recognise, with fingers that love had made so clumsy, that it was an apple. Martim no longer asked for the name of things.' This is wild talk for the author of a very long and very wordy novel.

However, Lispector can write in quite another way, and at her best she is not the Latin American cousin of anyone, even of other Latin Americans. Her recurring theme is the fragility of peace and order, and the swarming of temptations in unlikely places. She would have understood (and perhaps did) Brecht's phrase about the terrible temptation to goodness. The characters in *Family Ties,* a collection of 13 stories, are often afraid of

happiness, as if it were too blinding or too exhilarating a light. It is 'unbearable'. Life is not to be enjoyed, it is to be 'pacified'. A woman on her way home with her shopping sees a blind man at a tram stop and suddenly goes giddy with compassion, the whole pattern of her life is rattled by a ferocious and unmanageable love. She weathers the storm, though, and gets things back into place. 'Before getting into bed, as if she was snuffing out a candle, she blew out that day's tiny flame.'

The writing in this book is as sharp as that in *The Apple in the Dark* is foggy. Words are found and lost again instantly, scrupulously, so that we really do get a sense of whispered or intuited communication, are not quite sure we have heard what we have heard. The range is impressive too. A story like **"The Chicken"** is lightly comic. A fowl due to be killed decides to escape and is chased across the urban rooftops by the head of the family in his swimming trunks. 'The family was hastily summoned and in consternation saw their lunch outlined against a chimney.' The chicken is caught but lays an egg, thereby touching the family, who spare her. 'If you have this chicken killed,' Dad says roughly, warmly, 'I will never again eat a fowl as long as I live.' 'Nor me,' the little girl says. So the chicken survives, and is subtly anthropomorphised but not individualised. (pp. 20-1)

In **"The Imitation of the Rose"** the tone is sombre but still delicately managed. The story describes the return to health (and then alas to madness again) of a young woman who has had a nervous breakdown, and I don't think I have ever read anything more persuasive about the sheer difficulty of being normal, once your ordinary, relaxed claim to normality has been questioned. Everything you do will look weird, especially the things you do to show how humdrum you are. Laura is a tidy, modest woman, afraid of perfection in the way that Lispector's other characters are afraid of love or happiness. (p. 21)

> *Michael Wood, "Are Women Nicer than Men?" in*
> London Review of Books, *Vol. 7, No. 3, February 21, 1985, pp. 20-1.*

KATE CRUISE O'BRIEN

In both her book of short stories, *Family Ties,* and in her very lengthy novel, *The Apple in the Dark,* Clarice Lispector presents us with two kinds of real world. There is the mundane real world of rude mechanical happenings, of kitchens and women and repetitive tasks. And there is another realer, real world, a world 'so rich that it was rotting', 'a dark, fascinating world where monstrous water lilies floated'. In this realer, real world, luxurious parasites fasten themselves on trees, rats scurry in the undergrowth, insects swarm and decay is 'profound, perfumed'.

The humans involved in this dizzy natural carnival feel rather queasy or 'pregnant and abandoned' because of the fascinating repulsiveness of it all. Although it might be easier to choose mere existence in the mundane real world, where plants and insects know their place and dark fecund thoughts rarely obtrude, Ms Lispector's characters are a doughty bunch disposed to prefer doubt and decay, insects and rot to what the author disapprovingly describes as 'abstract' life, 'the opposite of natural rot'.

Martim, the hero of *The Apple in the Dark* was an 'abstract man' until he committed a 'true act'—a murderous attack on his wife. Martim then flees to the plain, where he communes with rats and birds. He lives on a farm where he identifies with plants, then cows, then mountains, until he ascends to the place whence he fell and is confronted by Man in the shape of two women. Martim's progress is slow, painful and almost unreadable. A respectful introduction to the book [by Gregory Rabassa (see excerpt above)], suggests that Ms Lispector marshals 'syntax in a new way that is closer perhaps to original thought patterns than the language had ever managed to approach before'—but even that submission cannot justify the turgid, dense and limping quality of Martim's endless monologues or the triumphant vapidity with which he contradicts himself. Ms Lispector writes with a kind of manic self-assurance, a blithe disregard for clarity, logic and her unfortunate reader.

> Kate Cruise O'Brien, *"Realer and Realer," in* The Listener, *Vol. 113, No. 2900, March 14, 1985, p. 27.*

ALFRED J. MacADAM

Brazil is scrutinized daily by economists and bankers, but Brazilian literature is subsumed into "Latin American writing," which usually means written in Spanish. But Brazil possesses the strongest literary tradition in Latin America; the Spanish Americans we read come from many lands, while Brazilian writers are isolated in one nation and the Portuguese language. There are women among the Latin American writers, of course, but precious few, and once again in recent years it is Spanish American women like Isabel Allende, Luisa Valenzuela and Rosario Ferré who have stolen the show. Clarice Lispector, the author of *The Hour of the Star,* is the premier Latin American woman prose writer of this century, but because she was a woman and a Brazilian, she has remained virtually unknown in the United States. . . .

Lispector produced several collections of short stories—*Family Ties,* reminiscent of Flannery O'Connor, is notable among them. She also wrote nine longer works of fiction, one of which, *The Apple in the Dark,* was published [in the United States] in 1967. She is studied by scholars, but she has never managed to catch the eye of the reading public. *The Hour of the Star* could change all that.

It is a novella (barely 79 pages), a form brief in length but dense as reading experience. Published in the year of Lispector's death, it meditates on the relationship between art and society and between the artist and the work of art. Like Michelangelo's *Slaves,* who only half emerge from their blocks of marble, Lispector's protagonist, Macabéa, only half emerges from the meditations of one Rodrigo S.M., her creator. Lispector assumes a masculine mask in telling the story of a poor young woman from the impoverished Brazilian northeast who migrates to Rio, works as a typist, fails at love and comes to a tragic end. She lives on hot dogs and Coca-Cola and longs to be a movie star. She will be, the narrator says, but only in an ironic sense and for a split second.

This is the bread and butter of Naturalist social criticism—the predetermined fall from indigence to nothingness that shapes so much protest writing, especially in Latin America. Lispector studies predestination: Macabéa, an orphan, ugly, poor and hopeless, has no chance for survival, because she is determined by heredity and environment; her narrator's artistic possibilities are also limited, because such a character offers virtually no room for development.

Why write about her? The narrator has philosophical and esthetic reasons for doing so. . . . He does not denounce society's inequities in order to change reality but because he thinks he can transform ordinary language and an ordinary person into art. Like Humpty Dumpty, he believes he controls words.

This is perhaps why Clarice Lispector chooses a masculine mask in *The Hour of the Star.* She needs this facade to project a story that reflects her own social concerns—poverty, the Brazilian military dictatorship of the 70's—while she simultaneously ridicules the masculine notion of dominating language. The writer who thinks *he* controls it is mistaken, because, like the repressed, language always returns to overpower the author. But the author must delude himself into thinking he can be the master. Lispector dramatizes the split between the person and the author: she knows that her writing is determined by language, just as Macabéa's life is determined by the Naturalist literary tradition. So she invents a self-possessed masculine narrator to destroy him through irony. The author, like her character, lives and dies through writing.

> Alfred J. MacAdam, *"Falling Down in Rio," in* The New York Times Book Review, *May 18, 1986, p. 27.*

JOHN GLEDSON

The Hour of the Star is [Lispector's] last book, published posthumously in 1977, the year she died (aged 56) of cancer in Rio. In the circumstances it would have been hard to call it anything but a masterpiece, "consecrated" writer as she was in Brazil. Yet, out of real necessity, because she thought of writing as a useless occupation unless it brought home something of the possible meanings and meaninglessness inherent in ordinary lives, she had to reject any form of consecration; here, in a novel of less than 100 pages, she again succeeds in upsetting expectations. She tells the story of Macabéa, a woman from the poor North-Eastern region of Brazil, who is, as far as Lispector can make her, a nonentity. Even her skin-colour is uncertain. She is poor, earning less than the statutory minimum salary, but she is a typist, who listens to "Radio Cultura", picking up useless pieces of information entirely devoid of context—"a man, who was also a mathematician, wrote *Alice in Wonderland*"—which she then "discusses" with her repellently *macho* and self-confident boyfriend, Olímpico, in conversations which go beyond banality to reveal unplumbed depths of intellectual and emotional deprivation. Not for nothing is "the most popular soft drink in the world" her favourite: yet even here, when we seem to be falling into stereotype, Lispector paradoxically admits that its attraction is real. As well as "sponsoring the recent earthquake in Guatemala", "this drink which contains coca is *today*. It allows people to be modern and to move with the times." This might seem to be said tongue in cheek: in fact, it is entirely likely that it is not. It is a measure of the book's success that it manages to make someone unlovable nevertheless such an uncomfortable presence. . . .

Poverty is a difficult subject for anyone, but it is only too comprehensible if for a Latin American it is even more so. Who could deny its crushing importance and visibility in the continent? Nevertheless, it is easy to feel that, like the Guatamalan earthquake, it has been "sponsored" for consumption at home and abroad. Desentimentalizing is part of Clarice's solution: Macabéa, I suspect, is the poor as no one would want them to be, whatever their political views. This is the measure, not only of an honourable (and anything but "magical") realism, but of the need for what at first reading is the most startling feature of the book; its very assertive and even unattractive male narrator, Rodrigo S. M. His maleness, as often with Clarice, is an index of coldness and calculation; here, it is something she needs to provide a barrier between her and her subject, yet is none the less more than that, for his intelligence and his battles with what he cannot help but narrate are part of the story's fascination.

The stories of *The Foreign Legion,* first published in 1964, are closer to the concerns of *Family Ties,* generally centred on the Rio middle class, and on emotional crises, especially those of adolescence. These are not books for children, however: rather, they remind us of the continuing presence within ourselves of the vulnerable, the awkward, the insensitive and callous beings that children often are—more openly than adults. At her best, which in her stories is frequent, Clarice combines intensity with precision.

John Gledson, "The Poor as No One Would Want Them to Be," in The Times Literary Supplement, *No. 4339, May 30, 1986, p. 587.*

Robert Ludlum

1927-

(Has also written under pseudonyms of Jonathan Ryder and Michael Shepherd) American novelist.

Ludlum is a prolific author of best-selling spy and thriller novels noted for their complicated plots and high-powered suspense. The diverse settings and time periods of Ludlum's novels are embellished by his protagonists, who are ordinary people either accidentally propelled or manipulated into participating in acts of espionage and political machination. While some critics find Ludlum's plots formulaic and his prose overwritten, others commend his ability to create plausible situations, evoke foreign milieus, and sustain reader interest.

The Scarlatti Inheritance (1971), *The Rhinemann Exchange* (1974), and *The Holcroft Covenant* (1978) are all set in the World War II era and depict the attempts of the Third Reich to gain world dominance. *The Scarlatti Inheritance,* which takes place during the early years of World War II, details the financial backing of the fledgling Nazi party by a group of Western business executives whose leader is an American expatriate and Nazi sympathizer. A corrupt military-industrialist faction is central to *The Rhinemann Exchange,* a tale of international double-dealing during the last year of World War II. *The Holcroft Covenant,* set in present-day Europe, revolves around the fruition of a scheme devised forty years earlier by German army leaders, who secretly bankrolled a large sum of money to be used by their descendants in reestablishing the Third Reich.

In several of his works, Ludlum unfolds speculative accounts of conspiracy in various facets of American society. In *The Osterman Weekend* (1972), the CIA enlists the aid of a television reporter to dissolve a conspiracy aimed at economic insurgency in which several of his close friends may be involved. *The Matlock Paper* (1973) centers on the criminal activities of a group of New England college professors and the reluctance of the school's dean to assist a government bureau in exposing the teachers. In *The Chancellor Manuscript* (1977), Ludlum alters history in his story of the assassination of J. Edgar Hoover by a group of government officials who seek control of his private files.

International terrorism is a prominent feature in many of Ludlum's novels. In *The Matarese Circle* (1979), several multinational corporations attempt to undermine governmental restrictions and regulations by using the services of a terrorist group. *The Bourne Identity* (1980) centers on a Vietnam veteran named David Webb, alias Jason Bourne, who is maneuvered by American intelligence officials into becoming a counterassassin in an effort to eliminate a notorious terrorist. In *The Aquitaine Progression* (1983), military leaders from several powerful nations conspire to destabilize and usurp their respective governments. *The Bourne Supremacy* (1986), a sequel to *The Bourne Identity,* revolves around a plot to destroy the People's Republic of China with the aid of a terrorist who masquerades as Jason Bourne.

Ludlum has also written three novels under pseudonyms: *Trevayne* (1973) and *The Cry of the Halidon* (1974) as Jonathan Ryder, and *The Road to Gandolfo* (1975) as Michael Shepherd.

© Jerry Bauer

The Osterman Weekend and *The Holcroft Covenant* have been adapted for film.

(See also *CLC*, Vol. 22; *Contemporary Authors,* Vols. 33-36, rev. ed.; and *Dictionary of Literary Biography Yearbook: 1982.*)

WILLIAM B. HILL, S.J.

The Osterman Weekend loses little time in pondering the imponderable and goes in heavily for mystery and suspense. If the ending is a bit weak, it is chiefly because it lets the rider down off a very high horse.

Not the least merit of this book is the creation of a marvelous web of surveillance and protection around the principal character, John Tanner, a big man in television. Tanner and his wife and two couples with whom they are friendly are expecting another couple from California, the Ostermans, coming in for a festive week end. Tanner is taken aside by a C.I.A. agent and told that the others are all involved in some sort of international conspiracy and it is up to Tanner to maintain secrecy, go on as though there were nothing extraordinary happening and help the C.I.A. to enmesh the conspirators. He tries; then his wife and children are almost suffocated, people are given ominous messages, the surveillance fails at crucial moments. It all adds up to a great deal of suspense and mystery. Occasionally the reader finds himself wondering why this or that is not done, and to that extent Mr. Ludlum fails to make his atmosphere all-pervading. Generally speaking, however, the tale is tautly told and the writing is vivid, the action gratifyingly rapid. The ending, the whole bent of the story, should have been thought out better; the excitement is allowed to dissipate instead of crashing to a finale. But there is plenty of said excitement through the course of the novel.

> *William B. Hill, S.J., in a review of "The Osterman Weekend," in* Best Sellers, *Vol. 32, No. 1, April, 1972, p. 5.*

NEWGATE CALLENDAR

Lockheed and I.T.T. and now Grumman—we know how corporations vis-à-vis the Government operate. Or we think we do, though obviously only the tip of the iceberg is showing. [Ludlum, writing under the pseudonym] Jonathan Ryder, in *Trevayne* . . . sets out to Tell All. A retired millionaire who made it big in aerospace contracts is recruited to head a commission in Washington investigating the military-industrial complex. He ends up taking on a super-corporation single-handed, fighting corruption (including actual murder) that extends to the highest levels. Finally, he discovers that if he cannot win one way there always are others.

Ryder touches something of great concern to millions of Americans, especially liberal Americans. There is no doubt that big business exerts an inordinate amount of pressure—more now, probably, than ever before, thanks to current White House hospitality. But how much pressure? Who is really running the country? Ryder has one theory, and he has written a taut book that spares nobody. It may be a black-and-white approach and the ending of *Trevayne* is a little hard to believe. But that does not affect the central thesis, or the horrid picture of capitalistic society presented in these pages.

> *Newgate Callendar, in a review of "Trevayne," in* The New York Times Book Review, *January 28, 1973, p. 20.*

KELLY J. FITZPATRICK

A good propagandist or a good liar will skillfully blend truths and half-truths, fabrications and happenstances, until the person for whom the blend is meant is unable to pinpoint the fabrications. Perhaps a good novelist does the same, earning for his work the term "plausible." Robert Ludlum has done it again [in *The Matlock Paper*]. . . .

The scene is a college campus in Connecticut. Here there is reality, deftly sketched in. The reality continues with the action. There is violence, but believable. There is suspense and terror. The plot revolves around Matlock (a youthful professor of English) and his interest in and, then, need to find when and where a meeting of crime chiefs is to be held. Representatives of the government have pushed Matlock into an untenable and dangerous situation. Ludlum, a powerful writer, sustains reader interest. The climax is effective and leaves the reader wondering. "Can it be so?" . . .

Ludlum discloses the forces of evil gradually—drugs, violence, extremism, militantism, an obsession with materials and fund-

ing. The clues are provided, but the action moves so swiftly that there is not time to consider them all. This is one author whose works of suspense should be eagerly awaited. *The Matlock Paper* is a good thriller and well written.

> *Kelly J. Fitzpatrick, in a review of "The Matlock Paper," in* Best Sellers, *Vol. 33, No. 2, April 15, 1973, p. 41.*

KAREN E. STEVENS

When Andrew Trevayne is appointed head of the Congressional subcommittee to investigate defense spending, he knows that he has a job that almost no one really wants completed, despite the loud protestations of support from the senators who confirm his appointment. . . . The deeper he goes into the affairs of Genesee Industries, the biggest of the defense subcontractors, the more clearly he realizes why no one dares expose Genesee, why ultimately even the President has to work with them; and, as the deadline for his report approaches, he discovers why they absolutely must be destroyed, regardless of the cost. A disgruntled Genesee employee gives him the information he needs, but Genesee has one more ace in the hole—the most colossal bribe ever offered, so cleverly set out that Trevayne doesn't even realize it is a bribe. [*Trevayne*] is an appalling, fascinating, frightening suspense novel, so realistic that one is tempted to check the Palo Alto phone book to see if there really is a Genesee Industries listed.

> *Karen E. Stevens, in a review of "Trevayne," in* School Library Journal, *an appendix to* Library Journal, *Vol. 19, No. 9, May, 1973, p. 100.*

NEWGATE CALLENDAR

[*The Matlock Paper* is a] book pegged to drug traffic in the colleges, organized crime, cancer in the college body politic, black militants, the United States Government's interest—and, behind it all, a Professor Moriarty type pulling the strings. Opposed to all this is a professor of English at an Ivy League college, trying to blow the conspiracy wide open. If action is what you want, action is what you get. The basic situation is unreal—indeed, it's unbelievable—but a good writer can make the reader suspend his disbelief, and Ludlum is a good writer.

> *Newgate Callendar, in a review of "The Matlock Paper," in* The New York Times Book Review, *May 6, 1973, p. 41.*

PUBLISHERS WEEKLY

There comes a point, fairly early on, in this novel of political intrigue [*The Cry of the Halidon*] when cleverness ceases to look like a virtue and becomes an irritant. If the writing were as rich or subtle as the plot is involved the reader might more happily stay the course, since there are features of the story, particularly its mise en scène, that are arresting; but the writing is in fact rather bare. A young American geologist is hired by a giant corporation based in England to conduct an industrial survey of a remote part of Jamaica. . . . But he finds himself in a hornet's nest of murderously conflicting interests—those of the corporation (in whose eyes he's expendable), of British Intelligence, and of factions of an underground movement of atavistic black Jamaicans. Ryder's picture of Caribbean racial tensions and murky politics is sinisterly effective, but the hectic violence of his action and the tropical density of his intrigue leave him little room for the development of character or the expression of thought.

> *A review of "The Cry of the Halidon," in* Publishers Weekly, *Vol. 205, No. 14, April 8, 1974, p. 76.*

NEWGATE CALLENDAR

Early last year, *Trevayne* by Jonathan Ryder attracted some interest. Now Ryder is back with *The Cry of the Halidon* . . . another long and ambitious book. But not really a very good one. Part of this is owing to Ryder's rather crude and obvious writing style. He is one of those rhetorical-question-posers: "What did it mean? What was it? Was it black?" He is not very good at suggesting real characters, and his hero is a cutout composite of any number of sources.

The Cry of the Halidon is about international finance. But there is a gimmick. The action takes place, mostly, in a Jamaican island, and Ryder introduces Shangri-la elements into the book. It's all very complicated (unnecessarily so) and stretched out much too long. It's also all unbelievable.

> *Newgate Callendar, in a review of "The Cry of the Halidon," in* The New York Times Book Review, *August 4, 1974, p. 26.*

PUBLISHERS WEEKLY

[In *The Road to Gandolfo,* Ludlum's novel written under the pseudonym Michael Shepherd, the] burlesque, comes crammed with zaniness and playful characters but, unhappily, neither asset produces comedy or the black humor indictment of the military mind the author intended. As détente becomes fashionable, Gen. MacKenzie Hawkins ("the Hawk") concludes that he had better get his kicks outside the service. So he launches a supposedly legit concern for "brokering the acquisition of religious artifacts." In reality his finances result from blackmailing the world's criminals while his organization exists for one purpose only: to kidnap the Pope. Naturally, such machinations require legal counsel, and this is where lawyer Sam Devereaux comes in. An anti-militarist nettled by the Hawk's less-than-candid job offers, he nevertheless plays along far enough to get intimately entwined with each of the General's ex-wives. But the coup itself comes a cropper in Italy and the madcap racing about strangely returns the plot to dead center, where it wilts.

> *A review of "The Road to Gandolfo," in* Publishers Weekly, *Vol. 207, No. 5, February 10, 1975, p. 52.*

HENRI C. VEIT

[*The Road to Gandolfo*] is a strange, lurching amalgam of thriller and fantasy. A gutsy, volatile, lunatic Army general is about to be sacrificed to the Chinese for mutilating a jade idol and a reluctant lawyer gets him out of the scrape. In no time the lawyer is conned into a harebrained scheme to kidnap the Pope with the help of the Mafia and other undersirables, and to substitute an unsuccessful tenor, a cousin of the Pope. Farcical, but heavy-handed, and not as funny as it should have been. (pp. 694-95)

> *Henri C. Veit, in a review of "The Road to Gandolfo," in* Library Journal, *Vol. 100, No. 7, April 1, 1975, pp. 694-95.*

RICHARD FREEDMAN

Paranoia buffs will have a field day with this latest thriller by Robert Ludlum. . . . For [in *The Chancellor Manuscript*] Ludlum's premise is that J. Edgar Hoover didn't die a natural death but was skillfully done in by a group of high-minded and high-placed intellectuals calling themselves "Inver Brass," who see a monstrous threat to the country in the Number One G-Man's unethical use of his scandal-ridden private files.

But the paranoia only starts there. After Hoover's death, it turns out that half the files are missing. The problem now is, who has lifted them, and for what nefarious purpose? The super eggheads of Inver Brass feed a heady potion of truth and lies to novelist Peter Chancellor, correctly assuming that he will somehow ferret out the truth for them in his never-ceasing quest for material to use in his factually based, deeply "authentic" novels.

Eventually, Chancellor comes up with more and grimier truth than anyone wants or can deal with. In the process, he dodges trucks and cars sent to wipe him out and becomes the target of more bullets than were fired in both world wars. He also uncovers more time bombs left ticking from the past than Lew Archer does in any three Ross Macdonald mysteries and comes to the dubious conclusion that no matter how idealistically motivated, assassination is never justified. . . .

But novelists, should avoid using novelist heroes. There's an overwhelming temptation to make them sexier, wealthier, more famous and, above all, tougher than their prototypes tend to be. Ludlum's virtually indestructible hero is also the purported author of *Reichstag!* and *Sarajevo!* (though he doesn't claim credit for *Oklahoma!*), and indeed, Chancellor's propensity for using exclamation points, those last infirmities of flabby prose styles, seems to be directly inherited from his creator. . . .

For all its breathlessness of style and repetition of effects, *The Chancellor Manuscript* nevertheless does exert a riveting appeal, as it seems to justify our worst nightmares of what really goes on in the so-called intelligence Community in Washington.

> *Richard Freedman, in a review of "The Chancellor Manuscript," in* The New York Times Book Review, *March 27, 1977, p. 8.*

BARBARA PHILLIPS

While there is nothing literary about *The Chancellor Manuscript,* the story idea is certainly inventive. J. Edgar Hoover does not die naturally in his sleep, but is assassinated. Why? To keep him from revealing the contents of his secret files which, according to this novel, contain enough damaging information to ruin the lives of every man, woman and child in the nation.

Five prominent personages who make up a secret group of self-appointed world savers are determined to get the files, ostensibly to save humanity. But they find half the files already stolen. Their hired killer, Varek, whose cover is the National Security Council, "programs" the hero, Peter Chancellor, a writer. Peter is to be the decoy who will lead the group to the mysterious somebody who got to the files first. Suspense, up to a point, is abundant.

There is no doubt that the book is entertaining. The characters are stock, the style melodramatic, the hero's durability preposterous. But the plotting is skillful, and the narrative races along with the speed of the expensive cars that Ludlum incorporates so lovingly into the plot. The novel also contains details about the secret workings of intelligence agencies that seem frighteningly accurate, as though Ludlum had his very own "Deep Throat." . . .

It is fashionable to maintain that internal conspiracies and international intrigues are the commonplace events which investigative reporters and fiction writers say they are, so no wonder we're all confused as to whether art or life is the real thing. Anything can happen and probably does in a world where daily headlines scream about Korean bribery of U.S. congressmen, CIA payments to King Hussein, or corporate bribery of high foreign officials. But if Mr. Ludlum's novel has any basis in fact, even the most respected among us had better review his past for indiscretions.

Barbara Phillips, "'Chancellor Manuscript': New Ludlum Thriller," in The Christian Science Monitor, *March 31, 1977, p. 31.*

EVAN HUNTER

Robert Ludlum knows how to write a great reader hook. In the first chapter of his new spy thriller [*The Parsifal Mosaic*], we are on a Costa Brava beach with an American undercover agent named Michael Havelock, who is witnessing the "termination" of his lover and partner in espionage, a woman now confirmed to be a double agent. A little while later, in Rome, he comes face to face with the presumably dead woman. What! How can this be? . . .

I believe it was Joseph Conrad who told us, "Never trust the teller, only trust the tale." It might seem lazy or unkind to allow Mr. Ludlum's fanciful tale to speak for itself, but what could be trusted more? The plot, then, as recapitulated in the novel: "So we have a mole called Ambiguity who cooperated with a fellow Russian we've labeled Parsifal, Matthias's partner in creating these insane agreements that could blow up the globe." Matthias, it should be noted, is the United States Secretary of State. In a spy thriller these days, it is no longer enough for someone to be a garden-variety mole working counterproductively within a nation's espionage system; Mr. Ludlum's mole is somewhere in the State Department itself. Similarly, the mere threat of a code being broken or vital secrets being leaked to the enemy is nothing when compared to the promise of nuclear extinction; a spy hero *must* get to the bottom of such scary hanky-panky or we will all be annihilated. But how can a hero *possibly* save us in these overheated, trigger-happy times? Simple. He must be Superman. Witness the invincibility of secret agent Michael Havelock:

On page 175, he is shot in the shoulder. On page 197, he is "tired and racked with pain." . . . On page 305, he is stabbed with a knife, "the razor-sharp edge slitting his flesh and marking his white shirt with a line of blood." On page 320, he is anesthetized with pure ethyl ether. On page 323, he is kicked in the throat by a booted brute. On page 331, he is kneed in the kidney, clawed on the neck, grabbed by the hair and kneed across the bridge of the nose. ("The darkness was splintered into fragments of white light.") On page 332, he is stabbed with a fork, and on page 333, when his latest assailant contritely says, "I've hurt you," he answers, "A minor cut and a few major scratches."

This pulp-hero reply may have been a deliberate attempt at humor, but the context and the evidence throughout seem to

indicate otherwise. Except for one richly comic scene in which a Russian spy details the impossible difficulties he's having with his intended defection, Mr. Ludlum's approach is as sober as his subject matter. But then, who would dare even *smile* when the end of the world may be 10 seconds away?

Evan Hunter, "Reincarnation and Annihilation," in The New York Times Book Review, *March 21, 1982, p. 11.*

ROBIN W. WINKS

The Ludlum phenomenon continues to defeat me. *The Parsifal Mosaic* . . . is the mix as served up nine times before, only fatter—630 pages. That's *Moby Dick*. No it isn't. One entire chapter is taken up with the hero making a fool of himself on an Italian wharf as racing footsteps are "Nearer . . . drawing nearer" and one hears "*Three Gunshots!*" (complete sentence and italics as in the original). What one is to make of a sailor who helps the reader follow his Italian by saying "What can you say to him *in riguàrdo a me* that he would *crédere*?" is utterly beyond my credere.

Robin W. Winks, in a review of "The Parsifal Mosaic," in The New Republic, *Vol. 187, Nos. 12 & 13, September 20 & September 27, 1982, p. 44.*

CHARLES P. WALLACE

The hero of *The Aquitaine Progression,* Robert Ludlum's latest novel, is fond of remarking that the only people who seem to prevail in tight spots are risk takers. Readers of this uneven novel might wish that the author had heeded his own advice.

In his latest outing, Ludlum's hero, Joel Converse, learns of a plot by generals in the United States, Germany, France, Israel and South Africa to spawn violent demonstrations. Once the violence bursts out of hand, the generals plan to step in and take over.

Converse, to Ludlum's credit, is not a product of the spy mills that have proliferated recently. He is an attorney with a New York law firm, specializing in international dealings.

The plot is laid out for Converse over coffee and croissants in Geneva by a childhood friend who has suddenly re-entered his life. By the end of the first chapter, the friend staggers into the room, clutches his bullet-riddled body and expires, but not before—you guessed it—whispering into Converse's ear "Aquitaine," the name of the secret plot.

Converse's job is to stop the plotters from reaching their goal. Early on, the men who hired Converse are killed off by the generals. Converse himself is accused of murder, meaning he becomes the quarry as well as the hunter.

If this sounds vaguely familiar, it is. Ludlum has given us some of the best thrillers in recent times; this time he has opted for a pretty dogeared story. . . .

Once his leviathan of a plot moves underway, Ludlum is more in his element. He is adept at re-creating European locales, and Converse travels through many of them, leaving a trail of dead villains as he tries to figure a way out of his predicament.

The problem with an Armageddon-but-for-me thriller is that it has been around since Ian Fleming created James Bond—long enough for just about every variation to have been tried. For every reader except the most gullible, the outcome is preordained.

Ludlum strives for verisimilitude in his plot, leavening the book with quotations from official-sounding dossiers and lines of untranslated German and Dutch. Yet Converse does not sound very lawyer-like until the denouement approaches and he wants to take everybody's deposition.

The result is a novel not quite believable and agonizingly slow-paced because of the large volume of dialogue.

After all, what is a thriller without the thrill?

> Charles P. Wallace, "The Military Minds and a World Obeys," in Los Angeles Times Book Review, March 11, 1984, p. 3.

CHRISTOPHER LEHMANN-HAUPT

It doesn't seem possible to spoil as overripe a plot as Robert Ludlum has committed in his latest fever nightmare, *The Aquitaine Progression*. Still, I won't say too much more than that it's about a plot by an international cabal of army generals to organize "a prolonged series of massive, orchestrated conflagrations designed to spin governments out of control and destabilize them." . . .

The ultimate objective? A multinational right-wing regime encompassing Western Europe, North America, Africa and the Middle East, to be called Aquitaine after the European realm of Julius Caesar's time. On the whole, a modest enough conspiracy by Robert Ludlum's standards.

But the question of interest is how does this Robert Ludlum compare with previous Robert Ludlums? Amazingly enough, the story starts off rather decorously, with dialogue that's almost believable and action that's nearly possible to visualize. For a while there, it seems Mr. Ludlum might be taming himself, maybe even writing a thriller plausible enough to be made into a movie or something.

But not to worry. Before long the action is careering out of control, the point of view is switching crazily all over the globe, and Joel Converse is surviving so many deathtraps that one begins to see him as the roadrunner in that Saturday morning cartoon show. Beep beep. Finally, and as always, one gets the feeling that the only motive behind it all is Mr. Ludlum's determination to tangle the yarn hopelessly and then untangle it again. Still, one does keep reading. Merely to be hunted all over Europe as a mad-dog killer, as Joel Converse ends up doing, or to know that any phone call you make will have no more consequence than someone's assassination—these activities seem such a relief compared with the threat of unpaid bills or inadequate snow tires.

> Christopher Lehmann-Haupt, in a review of "The Aquitaine Progression," in The New York Times, March 16, 1984, p. C23.

SAM CORNISH

Ludlum creates more than merely another Third Reich tale [in *The Aquitaine Progression*]. . . . Ludlum ambitiously creates a fabric of international intrigue in which both terrorist society and recent history—World War II, the Vietnam war, and the crisis in the Middle East—are interwoven. Converse is not the cool, self-contained hero of legendary spy fiction, but is a

hunted man with a nervous temperament which threatens to explode at every twist of the plot.

Other merits of *The Aquitaine Progression* include a procession of fascinating minor characters. The use of parallel plotting, wherein various characters retell incidents from the past—murders, escapes, and intrigues—is a structural device that neatly foreshadows the novel's conclusion. As usual, Ludlum's prodigious research is put to good use with his accounts of historical events and organizational detail. *The Aquitaine Progression* will be a popular novel. One hopes it will be read with the kind of care the author has invested in creating more than simply a facile entertainment.

> Sam Cornish, "Robert Ludlum's Newest Is More than a Mere Thriller," in The Christian Science Monitor, March 27, 1984, p. 22.

CHRISTOPHER LEHMANN-HAUPT

"Oh, my God!" one character in Robert Ludlum's 13th and latest doomsday thriller, *The Bourne Supremacy,* keeps gasping, staring with his mind's eye at the reader knows not what. It might as well be lost in the mists that in a typical Ludlum chapter opening "rose like layers of diaphanous scarves above" Hong Kong's "Victoria Harbor as the huge jet circled for the final approach into Kai-tak Airport."

Or have we missed something? One of the keys to what makes a Ludlum thriller so nerve-racking is the difficulty we have distinguishing between what we have been told and have not understood and what we don't understand because we haven't been told in the first place. So much is as obvious as an aboveground nuclear test: in the case of *The Bourne Supremacy* the decision by certain State Department honchos to reactivate the super-assassin Jason Bourne because someone in Hong Kong is murdering people in Bourne's name.

But why is this such a threat to world peace? So what if the People's Republic of China decides to break off talks with the British over the future disposition of Hong Kong? Is it our failure or the author's that we fail to feel sufficiently threatened by this? We begin to feel as paranoid as poor Jason Bourne, who, when asked to be Bourne again, has still not entirely recovered from his experiences in *The Bourne Identity,* although rest assured that even in his ragged state he makes Superman look like so much blue cheese. . . .

The Bourne Supremacy may be Mr. Ludlum's most overwrought, speciously motivated, spuriously complicated story to date. It's difficult to tell whether he's writing worse or it's just getting easier to spot his tricks. And yet—shameful to admit—one keeps reading. Is it the violence of the action? The adolescence of the fantasy? The maddening convolutions of the plot? Whatever, the effect is like dessert after certain rich meals. It's too much. One shouldn't. One doesn't really feel like it. "Oh, my god," one gasps, contemplating the enormity of it. And promptly devours the entire concoction.

> Christopher Lehmann-Haupt, in a review of "The Bourne Supremacy," in The New York Times, March 6, 1986, p. C25.

ARNOLD R. ISAACS

Those readers who have made commercial successes of Ludlum's previous novels will no doubt find [*The Bourne Supremacy*] equally to their taste. Its appeal lies, presumably, in the very absurdity of plot and characterization that will turn off those who don't care for the genre. In the last few pages of the book, Ludlum has one of his characters say, "These people do things the rest of us only dream about, or fantasize, or watch on a screen, disbelieving every moment because it's so outrageously implausible." It's a remark that may also help explain why this novel will undoubtedly join its predecessors up in the best-selling stratosphere.

If *The Bourne Supremacy* delivers exactly what Ludlum's fans want and expect, should it matter if a non-fan finds it bloated, witless and boring? Probably not. There's one point that should be made, though, and it has to do with Ludlum's portrayal of China and the Chinese. This is a book that depends on all the crudest stereotypes of the sinister Oriental. Whenever Chinese appear in these pages they are shown as diabolical, sadistic and depraved, practicing villainy as a sort of religious cult.

These have been staple images in Western popular fiction for a long time, of course, but they can still wound, and they grossly distort our view of a rich, ancient and complex civilization. To the extent that *The Bourne Supremacy* perpetuates that distortion, it is entertainment that is not quite harmless after all.

> Arnold R. Isaacs, "*Jason Bourne Returns,*" *in* Book World—The Washington Post, *March 9, 1986, p. 4.*

THOMAS R. EDWARDS

Near the end of *The Bourne Supremacy,* two mandarins of American intelligence wonder together at the feats of good field agents:

> "These people do things the rest of us only dream about, or fantasize, or watch on a screen, disbelieving every moment because it's so outrageously implausible."
>
> "We wouldn't have such dreams, or fantasize, or stay mesmerized by invention, if the fundamentals weren't in the human experience. They do what they do best just as we do what we do best."

It is in effect an apologia, or manifesto, for Robert Ludlum's outrageously implausible fiction. Though the notion that reading thrillers expresses a need to fantasize is all too familiar, it may be useful to ask who "the rest of us" are, and what we want from such writing, as compared with what we get.

First, we are people who buy books. . . . We are also males—though plenty of women read mysteries and even "tough" crime fiction, I know few who would give Ludlum the time of day, or who care much for even superior espionage novels like those of John le Carré. And of course we read such thrillers when we're not out working for our money, when in fact we're lying down—in bed, in the bathtub, on the beach—or sitting in commuter trains or airplanes.

But what is it that all we recumbent, reasonably well-to-do fellows *want* from what might as well be called a ludlum? First the thing needs to be defined. A *ludlum:* a long, turgidly written, and frantically overplotted novel, the literary equivalent of seriously wielding a plumber's helper. Its subject is conspiracy, the secret scheming of our collective enemies, foreign and domestic, and the equally secret and almost as menacing counterscheming of our supposed friends and protectors, the CIA or the NSC or the even more sinister "Consular Opera-

tions" branch of the State Department, which we may fervently hope is Ludlum's invention. To put it more grandly, the subject is the dreadful subsumption of private selfhood and its moral sense into a morally indeterminate public life. Ludlum's heroes are respectable, successful men—lawyers, scholars, businessmen, and the like—who are entrapped and used by hidden power; some of the manipulators are on our side, some not, and the hero's problem is to get them sorted out. But in an authorial move almost *de rigueur* in such fiction, the difference between good and bad is made maddeningly obscure, and the hero's fate is simply to survive and find some private happiness outside the labyrinths of power which may seem to enclose us all.

The Bourne Supremacy is a sequel to *The Bourne Identity,* and it would baffle a reader who didn't know the earlier book (an unlikely prospect). Both novels center on David Webb, who as Delta One led a ruthless guerrilla death squad in Vietnam. Webb was also known and feared as Jason Bourne, a name he took from a dead associate in this Medusa outfit, and in *The Bourne Identity* he is called Cain when American covert intelligence maneuvers him into collision with the terrorist Carlos, whom he foils and almost destroys.

When *The Bourne Supremacy* begins, Webb is a partial amnesiac, living quietly in Maine with his second wife, teaching Oriental studies at a small university and trying to erase the Delta-Bourne-Cain area of his psyche. But in Hong Kong someone calling himself Jason Bourne has begun a campaign of political assassinations that imperils the peace of just about the whole world, and Consular Operations conceives a plot to trick the real Bourne, David Webb, back into action against this imposter. Webb's wife is kidnapped, and Webb, knowing he's being recruited but not by whom, sets off for the Orient to rescue her.

I won't try to describe the layers of disinformation that Webb and the reader must peel away before the truth appears. That truth is that a potentate in Beijing, a "philosopher-prince" named Sheng Chou Yang whom I envision as a cross between Dr. Fu Man Chu and Ming the Merciless, is plotting to wreck the People's Republic and restore the Nationalists and the war lords. Sheng's chief instrument is the false Bourne, a wellborn but psychotic English ex-commando, whose murders are meant to create the illusion of gang warfare among the Triads of Hong Kong. Since the Red Chinese are as terrified of organized crime as we are, they will thus be provoked into occupying Hong Kong before the treaty expires in 1997, and this, Sheng knows, will start a general ruckus in which the Western allies and the Soviets will destroy the People's Republic, whereupon he and his Taiwanese cronies will take over.

When so abruptly undressed, Ludlum's plots seem scrawny, shivering things, but in the books, as in any striptease, the audience enjoys the process more than what they finally get. Any reader of ludlums knows that no sensible reference to geopolitical reality is intended. Nor are other sorts of realism needed, certainly not the sort that serious fiction invokes when it suggests that characters are not wholly the servants of the writer's efficient purposes. My interest woke, for example, when Webb, before leaving Maine to pursue his wife's abductors, pauses to set back the thermostat and cancel the newspaper, but Ludlum was too fast for me—knowing that motives must follow function, he quickly explains that Webb did this to mislead any hostile agents who might be observing him, by making it seem that he's gone away calmly and normally and can be expected back soon. The closest the book comes to suggesting irrelevant personal existence is when Webb, hiding out in a Chinese tourist hotel, hears an enraged matron from Short Hills shrieking, "The toilet doesn't work and you can *forget* the phone!"

Where then does our pleasure lie? Some of it lies simply in a second-hand, low-grade tourism. The book is packed with Chinese words and Oriental scenery and food; Ludlum loves it when someone can say something like "You have good joss." We can enviously assume that he's actually been to Hong Kong, and even more enviously that he deducted the cost as "research." For us ordinary men there is vicarious pleasure too in watching a mere college professor find it in him to survive and triumph over extreme physical and moral danger. It is bracing to look out from where our reasonable, stable, somewhat boring lives are led, upon a world full of "maniacs" (Ludlum's favorite word for enemies of any persuasion), a world where each new danger is met with cries of *"Incredible!"* *"Unbelievable!"* *"Insane!,"* which can be cries of delight as well as dread. (p. 12)

[There] is a strong if ambiguous appeal in the way Ludlum makes his heroes' motives personal ones. Those who manipulate Webb do so for the greater good even though it compromises their own moral values. But when Webb is forced back into the identity of Jason Bourne, the valueless killing machine he so deeply despises, his motive is immediate and selfish; someone has got his wife, and he wants her back. This is convenient for the author, since making Webb-Bourne the soldier of no cause but his own can offer no insult to the politics of any reader. But it also strikes a welcome note for a reader who is sick of politics altogether, worn numb by competing ideologies and slogans, wearied by demands that he care deeply about people and places that seem no concern of his.

Webb would have refused this mission if given a choice, because he doubts his capacities and because he resents being used even for "good" purposes. But his alter ego Bourne, the violent, selfish Hobbesian natural man we are born as and whom our socialized selves must bear ever after, can emerge and act with savage efficiency when Webb's civilized self is weakened by losing his wife. She, restored, tells Webb this as the book ends:

> "What do you do when there's a part of you that you hate?" said Webb.
>
> "Accept it," answered Marie. "We all have a dark side, David. We wish we could deny it, but we can't. It's there. Perhaps we can't exist without it. Yours is a legend called Jason Bourne, but that's all it is."
>
> "I loathe him."
>
> "He brought you back to me. That's all that matters."

Well, it's surely not all that matters, and for the reader the terms may be reversed; he may loathe not his dark side, the Old Adam within him, but the redeemed, acculturated self that goes to the office, makes deals, and tries to be liked, content to let the politicians, policemen, and spies do the dirty work. I imagine he sometimes wonders where his dark side went, and that he welcomes any news that it may still be around somewhere or other. (pp. 12-13)

Thomas R. Edwards, "Boom at the Top," in The New York Review of Books, *Vol. XXXIII, No. 8, May 8, 1986, pp. 12-15.*

Michael (Christopher) Malone

1942-

American novelist, nonfiction writer, critic, and journalist.

Malone's novels are usually picaresque in form and feature large casts of eccentric characters, numerous plot complications, and extravagant humor. Such influences as Miguel de Cervantes, Henry Fielding, and Charles Dickens are evident in Malone's expansive, adventure-filled works. Critics laud his colorful, diverse characters and his vivid evocation of place.

Malone's first two novels, *Painting the Roses Red* (1975) and *The Delectable Mountains* (1977), received sparse critical attention. *Painting the Roses Red,* Malone's only novel not written in the picaresque mode, takes the form of a journal kept by a confused graduate student who divides her love between her husband and another student. *The Delectable Mountains* concerns a young adult who becomes enlightened about life, love, and himself while working with a theatrical group in Colorado. *Dingley Falls* (1980) was Malone's first work to attract significant critical response. This novel depicts a small Connecticut town trying to maintain its "true American" spirit while combating a mysterious epidemic of heart problems. Ross C. Murfin called *Dingley Falls* "effective social satire as well as dark human comedy" due to Malone's literal and metaphorical interpretation of the townspeople's heart problems.

In *Uncivil Seasons* (1983), Malone "created two of the most memorable detectives ever to appear in mystery fiction," according to Evan Hunter. Much of the novel's entertainment evolves from the verbal interplay between Justin, the scion of the wealthy family that founded Hillston, North Carolina, and Cuddy, who feigns ignorance and is continually contrasting his rough upbringing with Justin's privileged childhood. In their quest for the solution to a mystery involving a rare coin, a design for a dormant textile loom system, and the murder of a senator's wife, the detectives encounter many bizarre characters. *Handling Sin* (1986) is another sprawling picaresque novel. In this work, Raleigh Hayes's stodgy, quotidian life as an insurance salesman is disrupted by a message from his moribund father. The father sends Raleigh on a scavenger hunt and instructs his son to meet him in New Orleans with the materials required by the dying man to atone for his past sins. While ostensibly a rollicking comedy, *Handling Sin* has at its center such serious themes as racism, the nature of evil, redemption, love, and death. Malone has also written two works of nonfiction, *Psychetypes* (1977) and *Heroes of Eros: Male Sexuality in the Movies* (1979).

(See also *Contemporary Authors,* Vols. 77-80 and *Contemporary Authors New Revision Series,* Vol. 14.)

KIRKUS REVIEWS

[*Painting the Roses Red* is a] first novel—just as nice and notional as it is frazzled and desperate—as told by Constance who is finishing up at Berkeley after five years and trying to wind up her indecision between Ty whom she loved best and

© Jerry Bauer

Gregory whom she'd married two years earlier. . . . [Constance is] very spacey and feeling "old" ("I'm getting old, I shall wear my Levis rolled") until she gets some help from a shrink called Dr. Waddle who is much more effective than he sounds. At the end you hope she's made it—learning to cede and compromise. . . . Right off the top of her head and her heart, this could easily sneak up on you from behind—it's fresh and raffishly appealing.

A review of "Painting the Roses Red," in Kirkus Reviews, *Vol. XLIII, No. 4, February 15, 1975, p. 196.*

PUBLISHERS WEEKLY

We've been here before. The Berkeley scene, getting in touch with yourself—it's all too familiar and so 60s it even seems curiously dated. [*Painting the Roses Red*] is the journal of Constance Mennagan, a graduate student from Southern California, married to Gregory (whom the reader never knows any better than Constance does), loving Ty whom she sees as somehow portentiously East Coast. . . . Innocence is what characterizes the novel and ultimately what goes wrong with it. Mennagan and her friends who sit around rapping at the Steppenwolf are likable enough but their problems are ordinary, the kind of problems that are interesting only to the people experiencing them. And what's off the mark here is Mennagan's sensibility; the author simply isn't wise enough yet to understand the turmoil in her head.

A review of ''Painting the Roses Red,'' in Publishers
Weekly, *Vol. 207, No. 9, March 3, 1975, p. 64.*

LARRY GRAY

The characters of [*The Delectable Mountains*] are a catalog of stereotypes: the alcoholic old artist; the whore with the heart of gold; the mean old, rich father who forecloses on the struggling young actors who are putting on *All My Sons* (allegory! insight!); the naïve homely understudy who takes over the lead and discovers herself as person and as artist (poignant! heartwarming!). By every right this novel should be corny, but it isn't. Despite these clichés and the author's disconcerting habit of writing in fragmentary and sometimes awkward sentences, the book succeeds.... This is not just a funny novel. It is a comedy in the best sense of the word.

Larry Gray, in a review of ''The Delectable Mountains,'' in Library Journal, *Vol. 102, No.1, January 1, 1977, p. 127.*

ALAN CHEUSE

You can hear it in the title of Michael Malone's third novel [*Dingley Falls*], the ever-so-slightly tinkly-sounding place-name that conjures up the hope, not unfounded, that this volume of almost heart-stopping length may be fun to read. Where the fun occurs is a small but ''well-off and white-bricked'' western Connecticut town that is celebrating its 300th anniversary in the year of the nation's Bicentennial. Dingley Falls is a place ''where the true America has been safely preserved, like an artifact in a time capsule,'' and thus a location in spirit as well as time and space. The comedy that arises in the telling of its long sad story is less black than it is red, white and blue.

But what the Dickens! The town is inhabited by more homey, colorful characters than all of Winesburg, Ohio, Raintree County and Batavia, N.Y., put together.... Each is convinced that life in Dingley Falls, U.S.A., is neither comic nor tragic but merely life.

At the novel's beginning, most of them have yet to see themselves in any plot beyond that of their own individual patches of consciousness. Waiting to unfold, however, are several designs grander than any that even the most astute citizens can imagine. On the comic side is a letter-writing campaign by an anonymous character assassin, which affects in small ways the daily life of just about everyone in town. In its more serious and virulent strain, destiny emerges as a top-secret government germ warfare project—''Operation Archangel''—which infects the region with a deadly and nearly undetectable form of bacterial endocarditis.

Although this news doesn't become apparent to the reader for about 50 pages (and never becomes fully known to the locals), we understand from the start that heart trouble, real and symbolic, is endemic in these parts. As the novel opens, Judith Haig, the attractive young postmistress whose husband ''Hawk'' is the local police chief, has just been diagnosed by old Dr. Scaper as a heart case, and not the first that day. (p. 14)

There are a number of other heart cases, both physical and metaphorical, wandering around the town....

With [several] interwined affairs running their courses against the backdrop of the government inflicted plague of heart disease, you might imagine that the novel would easily bubble up into soap or churn itself into melodrama. Indeed, the unruliness of its large cast, the episodic nature of its narrative, and the larger-than-life, almost Disney-like strokes of its style make this an extremely busy novel. But it is full of matters—large ones, such as love, conscience, politics and health, and small ones, such as gossip, sexual habits and the trivia of contemporary American culture—that will hold the attention of readers both serious and casual.

Ultimately, reading itself becomes an important aspect of the health of Dingley Falls. With rampant heart disease and violence, and other calamities surrounding them, most Dingleyans (there's that music again, half silly, half sad), rather than running for their lives, are reading for them instead. They read, Mr. Malone tells us, because ''unlike God and unlike the periscopes made by Dingley Optical Instruments [the town's one industry], they could not see around corners; because from any one perspective life is so much less full than fiction and so much more painful. Safe in fiction, they were testing their hearts.''

Patient fans of witty, intelligent, deeply felt and vividly narrated fiction will wish to do the same with this novel. (p. 29)

Alan Cheuse, ''All-American Town,'' in The New York Times Book Review, *May 11, 1980, pp. 14, 29.*

ROSS C. MURFIN

Dingley Falls, Michael Malone's novel about a fateful week in the life of a small self-congratulatory Connecticut town, deserves to remain a part of our literary landscape. Highly traditional in some ways, it nevertheless employs an unusually large range of tones and styles and gathers together an astonishing crowd of fifty-some characters who live in Dingley Falls and whose lives are being imperiled by seven others who do not.

On the first page of the novel, we are introduced to Judith Haig, who fears packs of dogs and her own mysteriously failing heart. On the second page we catch a glimpse of Winslow Abernathy, whose wife is about to discover love with a poet named Rage, and on the third we hear about Priss Ransom, who has painted the shutters of her Federalist home orange in a defiant act of ''defining herself.'' Still more characters appear until there is something ominous about the sheer numbers of people coming out of the wainscoting in the first bright, sunlit chapters of this novel.

When townspeople start dying, we know that the fall of Beanie Abernathy, who ''taste[s] the fruit'' of illicit sex until she is ''driven from the Garden'' by inclement weather, is not to blame. Nor is the anonymous local author of obscene messages. The source of darkness seems to have something to do with a sterile black spot in the nearby countryside that ''did not look like land cleared by fire . . . but like land annihilated forever.''

It hardly matters that, for a dozen or so chapters, Malone leaves the route to understanding his mystery as undeveloped as the Federal highway near Dingley Falls that was discontinued half a mile from where it was begun (and just short of the blackened wasteland). It doesn't matter because much that is revealed in the meantime seems even more pertinent. Encounters between checkout women and policemen's wives at the local A.&P.

speak with a discomforting kind of eloquence about the uncertain condition of life in Everytown.... (pp. 195-96)

Because of the manner in which the author eventually diagnoses the cause of the town's heart failure, his novel ends by being effective social satire as well as dark human comedy. *Dingley Falls,* which sometimes reads like the work of a New England Faulkner and at other times reminds us of *Catch-22* or even *V.,* ultimately owes more to Dickens than to any single American novelist. Malone's epigraph is taken from *Great Expectations,* but the vision of life he offers, however, has more in common with *Bleak House,* a novel that successfully combines satire and a ghost's walk, apocalyptic fire and scenes of life. (p. 196)

> Ross C. Murfin, "Ghostly Satire," in The Nation, *Vol. 231, No. 6, August 30-September 6, 1980, pp. 195-96.*

EVAN HUNTER

I am not at all sure Michael Malone will be pleased to hear he's created two of the most memorable police detectives ever to appear in mystery fiction. As the author of the highly acclaimed straight novel *Dingley Falls,* he may feel that rubbing elbows with murder is a form of slumming, a descent into the "cheap detective fiction" he mentions early in *Uncivil Seasons.* The literary title alone would seem to disclaim any familiarity with the mystery form, almost as though someone had convinced Mr. Malone that "transcending the genre" is all-important, when really the genre is not in desperate need of transcendence at all. Mr. Malone has written a rattling good mystery; he has also written an excellent novel. The two need not be incompatible.

The college town of Hillston, N.C., is a figment of Mr. Malone's vivid imagination, a beautifully rendered cross between what could easily be Durham or Chapel Hill were it not for the specifically stated distance from Raleigh. The Dollard family founded this town, and Justin Savile's mother is a Dollard. Justin, or Jay, as he is sometimes called, is a homicide lieutenant, not a proud calling for a scion of Dollard stock. His uncle is a State Senator whose wife has been brutally murdered as the novel begins. Justin and his partner, Cuddy Mangum, start their investigation....

[Cuddy] is the perfect foil to Justin's fading preppie cop. Learned but pretending to vast ignorance, he is forever and hilariously comparing his own mean upbringing to Justin's silver-spoon background, munching junk food, coddling his white poodle (named after Martha Mitchell) and doping out basketball scores in hope of one day winning a pool. He calls Justin's married lover Lunchbreak, referring to the hours during which they hastily meet and mate, and he is fond of run-on sentences that are witty, erudite and caustic. Together, they make a formidable pair—fresh and unforgettable....

Equally engaging are the colorful characters the detectives encounter in their search for the truth—the rambunctiously redneck Pope brothers and the women entangled in their brawling, larcenous lives; a rotund black fence who legitimately sells musical instruments and whose speech patterns are floridly Elizabethan; Sister Resurrection, the prophetess of doom who hangs around the halls of justice and with whom Justin enjoys a particularly touching rapport. These characters and many more share in the unraveling of a mystery involving a rare old coin, a design for an inertial textile loom system, an unrequited

love and above all the prestige of a rich and powerful family. But they serve as well to illuminate the characters who concern us most, Justin and Cuddy.

There are some flaws in the novel. Too many of the solutions are handed over on a silver platter, unearned. Unconvincingly, Justin falls madly in love with the least likable woman in the novel. And nowhere in the United States can anyone be charged with "*suspicion* of murder." But these are minor problems, and they are compensated for by the rich diversity of the cast, the compelling plot and the often poetically haunting beauty of Mr. Malone's prose—"Far away the wakes of menhaden and shrimp boats already ruffled, luring the white gulls down" or "everywhere on the trees along the branches swollen buds had burst to petals, unleafing snow and rose." That's impressive language for any kind of novel.

> Evan Hunter, "Detective from a Founding Family," in The New York Times Book Review, *November 13, 1983, p. 14.*

JEAN M. WHITE

[*Uncivil Seasons* bears Michael Malone's] imprint—the vividly drawn ambience of a small Southern milltown with an old-family structure that dominates local society and politics.

The narrator is Justin Savile, who rejected his family's plan for a career in politics to become a cop. At 34, he is carrying on a joyless affair with the wife of a textile mill executive and trying to shake the guilt he feels for having drunk himself into a sanitarium and possibly having caused the death of his father....

Malone brings a stylish gift for language to his first mystery. His small-town characters, notably Justin's cop partner with his witty patter, come alive. So does Justin's aristocratic mother, who rattles on like a flutter-headed society matron and then upbraids her son: "Justin, I had no idea you were so naive as to let me convince you I was."

> Jean M. White, in a review of "Uncivil Seasons," in Book World—The Washington Post, *November 20, 1983, p. 10.*

THOMAS D'EVELYN

Handling Sin is as raucous and jubilant as a bright spring morning....

From the title (which refers to a 14th-century English poem), to the hero and his side-kicks, to the Walker Percy-ish probing of Christianity, *Handling Sin* is ripe with allusion.

At the same time, we're gratefully carried along by the madcap adventures of the hero, who strikes me as a combination of Odysseus, Don Quixote, and Tom Jones. Pillar of his hometown Thermopylae, N.C., (talk about allusions!) Raleigh (named after Sir Walter) Hayes has avoided disappointment by asking of life only "modest and reasonable requests": "a wife he loved, unblemished children, good health, a house, an income to pay for it, leisure to care for it, the authority to serve the community, and their respect for having done so well."

What an improbable hero for romance! But just as Cervantes tested his bookish hero by a series of adventures, Malone has adapted the episodic romance to his modern middle-class hero. The result is both funny and touching.

Raleigh's father Early, who was long ago defrocked for trying to integrate his Episcopal church, disappears from a hospital in a Cadillac accompanied by a black girl in a white dress. He leaves behind a set of instructions for his insufferably upright son. Raleigh is ordered to bring certain things and certain people to New Orleans by Good Friday.

The trip does for Hayes what the Odyssey did for Odysseus: It makes a much-thinking man humble.

Gradually, Raleigh opens up to the color and form of the world. Accompanied by his fat neighbor Mingo (Sancho Panza?)

Sheffield, a man of faith who turns out to play a respectable jazz piano, Raleigh discovers something of himself in his half-brother Gates, in Gates's fellow-in-crime Simon "Weeper" Berg, and in a black saxophonist, Toutant Kingstree. Together, Mingo and Raleigh foil some nasty fun being had by a chapter of the KKK, deliver a baby girl in the trailer of an eighteen-wheeler, and battle a crime syndicate in Atlanta.

Through all this, Raleigh, who's a worrier, learns to laugh. The reader has been laughing all along. Malone's ear for voices and dialects, his comic timing, and his gaudy sense of the comic, are marvelous. Like the comedy of Charlie Chaplin, *Handling Sin* is relentlessly perceptive about the funny ways we have of being human.

There are quiet moments, too. On the road, Raleigh has time to think about the fact that his ruling virtue, indifference to the world and the concerns of other people (except when it involves insurance), is really a kind of vice. Malone suggests that it is a form of the deadly sin of acedia, or spiritual sloth. Hence the value of laughter. . . .

The heart of *Handling Sin* beats with the rapid languor of jazz. . . .

In his handling of his strong, vital black characters, Malone reminds me of Toni Morrison, author of *Sula* and other novels. It's they who prepare Raleigh for his final discovery of his own capacity for laughter and for "listening."

Unlike John Kennedy Toole's savagely funny *A Confederacy of Dunces*, *Handling Sin* lacks the bite of great satire. It is romantic and sentimental, but in the highest sense. As a treatise on sin, it rather celebrates the commandments of love enjoined by Jesus. As a book frequently preoccupied by the undertow of death, it rather celebrates the Resurrection. "It was the woman who had the guts to go in the tomb," Early had told Raleigh when he was young but already skeptical: "It was the woman that kept the faith. The best luck in life . . . is to keep a woman's love."

In the end, *Handling Sin* celebrates the love link Dante pointed to in the Commedia, *lo vincol d'amor che fa Natura* (the bond of love which Nature makes). . . . Laughter pervades *Handling Sin,* but it ends on a quietly paradoxical note and in silent contemplation of the strange happiness of being human and in love on Easter.

Thomas D'Evelyn, "Adventures of a Modern-Day Odysseus," in The Christian Science Monitor, *March 26, 1986, p. 21.*

RICHARD EDER

Among those acknowledged in Michael Malone's prefatory note to *Handling Sin* are 20th Century Fox, which may make a movie out of it, and Miguel de Cervantes, Henry Fielding

and Charles Dickens. He thanks the last three for their "friendship, nudges, winks and wise counsel."

All this nudging, winking and negotiating—the author's agent is also credited—seem to have produced creative wobble. Malone's attempt at a modern picaresque novel lurches in every conceivable direction on its way from North Carolina to New Orleans.

It is not hard to hypothesize the influence of the aforementioned writers, film company and agent in this tale of a small-town insurance man learning, through a series of adventures, to relax and get in touch with life. It is harder, but possible, to believe that Malone is a writer of some talent, wit and earnestness who has let his mentors shanghai him. . . .

Cervantes can be credited, I guess, for Raleigh's Sancho Panza, a greedy, clamorous but ultimately valiant naif, who comes along with him; and for a damsel in distress whom they succor. Dickens is more or less traceable from the notion of a mission imposed by an aged and long-gone relative, the reward for which will be an inheritance. Fielding may have suggested the tone, which the publishers describe as rollicking.

As for 20th Century Fox, there is the slapstick, the nurtured hilarity, the assortment of single-trait oddballs and a climactic scene involving a sword duel, a chase by pedal boat, golf cart and cable car, and an assault on an amusement park train. The only question is whether a film or a TV series is being aimed at.

Malone has a feel for Southern landscape and Southern tradition. He interlards Raleigh's adventures with long family accounts of the gaudy aviary that produced this sober penguin. Many of the characters are studiedly picturesque, as if Thermopylae were the Carolina franchise for Garrison Keillor's *Lake Wobegon*. But several of the family members are memorable. . . .

Raleigh's adventures are certainly varied and energetic. . . .

[But there] is a forced quality to all this, a spirit of "what can we think of next?" as if vast comic quotas had been set for the adventures and the characters, and the author were struggling to fill them. There are as many jokes as potholes on Raleigh's bumpy quest, and they have about the same effect.

The form of the book is picaresque, but the spirit is quite the opposite. There is none of the marvelous liberty that a Don Quixote or a Tom Jones gives us, the sense of free flight among the decaying pillars of the day. The wackiness of *Handling Sin* is not freedom but a decaying pillar of its own. It is the musty liturgy of the Situation and the Gag. The characters rarely embody their eccentricities; they mostly perform them.

Raleigh, the central figure, receives a lot of the author's care and affection. He is meant to teach a lesson, this conscientious but tied-down man who accepts uncertainty, danger and chaos in order to find his father. But the cards are stacked. All of the dozens of characters in the book preach the same message of liberation to him. And at the end, we get the feeling of pious imposition: of a lesson not taught, but simply recited.

Richard Eder, in a review of "Handling Sin," in Los Angeles Times Book Review, *April 6, 1986, p. 3.*

FRANCES TALIAFERRO

Handling Sin is a great big endearing picaresque novel. Its reluctant hero, a cautious middle-aged life insurance agent named

Raleigh Hayes, sets out on his quest from the little Piedmont town of Themopylae, North Carolina, accompanied by his bumbling fat friend Mingo Sheffield. Like their literary kinfolk Don Quixote, Sancho Panza and Tom Jones, Raleigh and Mingo leave many a complication behind them, but unlike their predecessors they drive off in a Pinto whose license plate reads "KISSY PU," and Raleigh is (to my knowledge) the first literary picaro ever to receive his marching orders from a tape cassette.

That tape was made by Raleigh's father, Earley Hayes, an antic septuagenarian who cheerfully disappeared from the hospital where he was supposed to be tending his heart condition. . . . As for the taped message he left behind, it sends Raleigh on a scavenger hunt all over the South as he searches for the people and objects specified by his wacky mentor.

For Earley—defrocked Episcopal minister, trumpet player, exuberant appreciator of life—has it in mind to shake Raleigh out of his prudent stodginess. The taped message ends: "I want you to enjoy yourself for once, Specs. I want you to think of this as a holy adventure, by God." In the course of a few hundred pages and dozens of escapades, even Raleigh begins to understand why his father used to call him a worry-wart and "uptight," just "shriveling with virtue." With affectionate relish, *Handling Sin* traces Raleigh's re-education, from dutiful prig to generous human being.

It's just about impossible to summarize the plot, which sprouts and ramifies like the Hayes family tree. The Hayeses have some of the random energy of *You Can't Take It With You* and the craggy quirks of a George Price cartoon, to wit Raleigh's formidable old aunt Vicky Anna, a retired missionary, who draws on a large supply of exotic anecdotes to put her home town in perspective. (p. 3)

In his prologue, Michael Malone acknowledges his debt to the "friendship, nudges, winks, and wise teachings" of Cervantes, Fielding and Dickens. What distinguishes all three masters is their energy—a yeasty and irrepressible bubbling-up of life. Like Dickens, especially, Malone cannot resist peopling his narrative with quirky souls who add nothing to the plot and everything to the texture of the novel. These "throwaway" characters, animated by the same appreciative spirit that produced the Aged Parent and Mrs. Jellyby, suggest a world of rapidly multiplying and largely benign eccentricity.

Handling Sin has none of the satiric edge of Malone's earlier novel *Dingley Falls*. Instead, *Handling Sin* is a larky tale that asks us to take its merry adventures at face value. We do, gladly. It's somewhat later, after the breakneck chases and the giggles have subsided, that we realize it's something wiser and deeper: the "holy adventure" Raleigh's father egged him on to. *Handling Sin* is pretty much the story of the Prodigal Son turned inside out, seen from the point of view of the stuffy, resentful "good" brother who stayed behind. It's a parable of love and reconciliation; It's also a celebration of plain old fun as one of God's great pedagogical devices. Funny, affable, and manageably sentimental, it's a delightful book. (p. 13)

Frances Taliaferro, "Rollicking across the South on a Scavenger Hunt," in Book World—The Washington Post, *April 13, 1986, pp. 3, 13.*

A. C. GREENE

[In] our absurd world there is a streak of insanity which, properly mined, yields the kind of humor that, while absurd, is nevertheless convincing. And funny. Sometimes it's simply because we give up, surrender to the ridiculous-made-common that now constitutes so much of our society's actions.

Michael Malone's *Handling Sin* operates from that base: that all of us today are a little cracked but some of us are more cracked than others. His characters are a collection of Everymans (and Everywomans, if there are such things). . . .

While comparisons will be made to *A Confederacy of Dunces* because of its Southern setting and its bizarre plot, the humor of *Handling Sin* is superior to that by now assumed classic. Mr. Malone's twists and turns and surprises are downright phenomenal, verging on genius. There are entire chapters in this book that are funny, sentence by sentence. And in about 90 percent of his plot twists, the humor works beautifully. Few strands are left to dangle wildly while the book moves on. But in a book of 544 pages and 1088 subplots (two per page, at least), there have to be saggy places and a few holes.

Mr. Malone overdoes the Jewish accent on one character and sounds not quite right on his teen-age girls. And a couple of his black characters are handled so gingerly as to render them flawlessly one-dimensional. (He also has a confusing habit of referring to his main characters alternately by first, then last, names.) The outrageous humor of the first 300 pages—capable of making a reader sick with belly laughter—isn't sustained throughout the remaining sections. In a sudden change of direction on the part of the plot and of several of the characters, a note of serious intent intrudes: we are suddenly, almost poetically, deluged with the beauty of Charleston by moonlight, the understanding love that can develop during 20 years of marriage unfolds before our wondering (why here?) eyes, characters push aside the prior rules of absurdity and begin to act predictably upright. And it is doubtful that any reader will be completely satisfied with the ending. It just doesn't fit. A goody-two-shoes ambiance takes over and a climax of near bathos almost drowns this previously irreverent, unafraid comedy.

But weighed on the scales of laughter, the work is a hilarious success. It is worth reading just to collect the full kernels of fine humor which are much thicker in this book than pecans in a Georgia fruitcake.

A. C. Greene, "Fruitcakes in the Carolinas," in The New York Times Book Review, *April 13, 1986, p. 11.*

TERRENCE RAFFERTY

Handling Sin, a comic road novel that begins in a small town in North Carolina and ends up in New Orleans in the week before Easter, is like *Easy Rider* with Bob Newhart as Captain America and John Candy as his sidekick. It's about the Old South and the New South, the Old Testament and the New Testament, race relations, jazz and marriage. The story is set in the present, but the author acknowledges his debt to Cervantes, Fielding and Dickens. Michael Malone's book is a rowdy, headlong picaresque which subjects its hero, the scrupulous Raleigh Hayes, to the indignities of marines, bikers, gangsters, sleazy businessmen, nervous adulterers, a Chinese restaurant owner who stuffs cookies with dire fortunes, and to the outrages of his own family of unreliable good ol' boys and hearty, aging party girls. But the novel's structure is tight as a fitted sheet: everything gathers perfectly at the end. There's almost no way of describing this huge, ambitious novel without making it sound fatally contradictory, a crazy hodgepodge. Yet all the contradictions are there for a reason: Malone has filled his book with as many disparate elements as he could invent, with the intent of bringing every one of them together for a final jam, a one-time-only chorus of reconciliation. When this novel reaches New Orleans, sinners and everyone in between come marching in, in precise formation.

This long parade of resolution, with its earthly and unearthly harmonies, is the only thing that's likely to worry anyone about *Handling Sin,* which is in most ways an obviously terrific performance: large-spirited, beautifully crafted and extremely funny. And this populist epic actually has *people* in it, dozens of them, vivid, eccentric creations who are as endearing and irritating as a houseful of relatives. Even the book's hero is a fully developed character (which isn't always the case in picaresques). Raleigh Hayes . . . spends the first 400 or so pages doing Bob Newhart-like slow burns and double takes at every outrageous bend on the road to New Orleans, but his straight-arrow's indignation isn't tedious. His exasperation has an explosive quality that's rather engaging and that suggests the livelier, more expansive spirit that's been buttoned into his solid-citizen disguise. Malone puts poor Raleigh through an awful lot in the course of this book, but does it with real sweetness and wit: the hero's rock-solid respectability is seen throughout as a kind of innocence, and his unsought adventures in the world outside Thermopylae, North Carolina, are like a kid's first experiences away from home, strange and unnerving and finally liberating. The best and most moving comedy in *Handling Sin* is the spectacle of this earnest middle-aged man growing up by letting himself have some fun. He's born-again to be wild.

The other major characters in *Handling Sin* are just as satisfying—deft mixtures of the representative and the weirdly individual—and they're all cleverly deployed to support Malone's immensely complicated structure. (p. 860)

The problem with *Handling Sin* is, perhaps, the most forgivable one a novel can have: even this maximum-capacity structure can't quite contain everything the author tries to fit into it. Throughout Malone's dazzling display of caricature and high-energy farce in his account of Raleigh's journey from Thermopylae to New Orleans, we've been picking up, like bugs on a windshield, hints of loftier purpose. The contrast between the anachronistic charm and civility of Charleston (where Raleigh stumbles into some wonderful *Tom Jones*-style bedroom chaos in an inn) and the gleaming businessman's paradise of modern Atlanta (where he finds himself involved in a duel and a frantic chase through an amusement park dominated by mammoth sculptures of Jefferson Davis, Stonewall Jackson and Robert E. Lee carved out of a mountain) seems to mean something, and so does the novel's increasing emphasis on music and race. It may occur to us somewhere along the way that Raleigh Hayes's roller-coaster tour of the South is also a lesson in moral geography, a blackboard sketch of the contours of that rich and contradictory region; that Malone, in the shadow

of his own great confederates, Cervantes, Fielding and Dickens, has undertaken the task of completing the unfinished business of Reconstruction in his imagination. He sees his native region as a paradise lost, and his fellow Southerners as a people whose virtues—grace, courage and a boundless appetite for living—have been spoiled by the original sin of racism. And the sin is to be redeemed, in this novel, by jazz: the common ground of blacks and whites, a traditional music that's bent on keeping itself new, refreshing itself every time a player picks up his instrument and blows his own experience through it.

So by the time Raleigh and his entourage get to New Orleans—that over-flowing jambalaya of music, Christianity, Old South beauty and the pleasures of the flesh—and form an ensemble with his father and the black woman named Billie, Malone's got a fair amount of symbolic luggage to unpack. He gets right to it. When his players assemble on the stage of a nightclub called The Cave, the first song they perform is a resonant standard: "Way down yonder in New Orleans / In the land of dreamy dreams / There's a garden of Eden . . ." In the scene that follows, as song follows song, family members reunite, whites and blacks pick up cues from one another and harmonize, and all the players surpass themselves in the making of a wild but elegant music—we should feel, at the end of this long and eventful trip, as if we'd died and gone to heaven. What we feel, regretfully, is that the novel's died, and remained on earth. Maybe it's unfair to be disappointed when Malone slides from high comedy to the resolution of his more serious themes, but after the exuberant riffs of the road portions of *Handling Sin,* we can't help feeling let down that he's returned to the melody at the end and is playing it straight: it sounds too familiar now. Malone's grand and lovely design has served him splendidly as a background for his improvisations, a tune drifting in and out among the exhilarating clusters of notes, deepening their tones. But in the end his attempt at synthesis doesn't quite come off, perhaps because he's finally too respectful of his elders, too committed both to reconstructing the traditional novel of Cervantes, Fielding and Dickens—which included, along with its rambunctious invention and variety, a good measure of didacticism—and to redeeming the debased religious heritage of the South by preaching a new, more forgiving kind of sermon, one that, for once, doesn't send anybody to hell. (pp. 860-61)

We're so self-contradictory that we can admire and agree with what Malone is saying and yet regret that he has to *say* it, that he won't let us reconstruct his vision for ourselves out of the brilliant characters and situations he's created. *Handling Sin* is never a bad trip, but a mysterious, rueful feeling—something like Captain America's cryptic "We blew it" in *Easy Rider*—hangs over us at the end. The author seems to have turned, helplessly, into a kind of father and the readers into children, and the generations remain—in their strange, probably inevitable way—apart, not quite reconciled. (pp. 861-62)

Terrence Rafferty, "*Glory-Bound Boys*," *in* The Nation, *Vol. 242, No. 24, June 21, 1986, pp. 860-62.*

Bobbie Ann Mason
1940-

American short story writer, novelist, and critic.

Mason has received considerable critical attention for her short story collection, *Shiloh and Other Stories* (1982), and her novel, *In Country* (1985). Set in rural western Kentucky, Mason's fiction depicts a rapidly changing South in which individuals who once lived and worked on farms and shared deep-rooted family traditions are now employed by national retail stores, live in subdivisions, and experience the modern world primarily through such commercial institutions as television, popular music, shopping malls, and fast-food restaurants. Unable to reconcile their present lives with the seemingly distant folk traditions of their past, Mason's characters have been viewed as grotesques who are experiencing, in Anne Tyler's words, "the sense of bewilderment and anxious hopefulness that people feel when suddenly confronted with change." Mason employs a plain, laconic prose style replete with brand names to illustrate the banality of mass culture and its effects on the society she portrays.

Mason's first book, *Shiloh and Other Stories,* contains several pieces which originally appeared in such national magazines as *The New Yorker* and *The Atlantic*. Set in and around the small town of Paducah, Kentucky, the stories document some of the social, economic, and moral changes that have accompanied the region's transition from farmland to commercial outpost and how these changes have affected the quality of life. *Shiloh and Other Stories* received overwhelmingly positive criticism, with reviewers commenting particularly on Mason's authentic regional dialogue and her vivid characterizations.

In her first novel, *In Country,* Mason continues to explore the themes and subjects she had established in her short stories. The novel concerns the experiences of Samantha, a seventeen-year-old Kentucky girl whose father was killed in the Vietnam War shortly before her birth and whose mother abandoned her as a child. Now living with her uncle, an emotionally and physically unstable Vietnam veteran, Samantha tries to come to terms with the war and the cultural context in which it occurred, but her attempts to uncover a heritage deeper than the commercialized culture around her are met with reticence and misunderstanding. Joel Conarroe called *In Country* "a timely variation on the traditionally male-centered *Bildungsroman*" in which Mason delineates a young woman's search "for a history that will validate her identity." While some critics faulted Mason for the predictability of her themes and for failing to develop her characters beyond flat sociological types, others praised her accurately rendered speech patterns and her ability to balance comedy, emotion, and poignancy.

(See also *CLC,* Vol. 28; *Contemporary Authors,* Vols. 53-56; and *Contemporary Authors New Revision Series,* Vol. 11.)

MICHIKO KAKUTANI

Published to much acclaim three years ago, Bobbie Ann Mason's *Shiloh and Other Stories* possessed the texture and density of a finely-crafted novel—though not interlinked, the stories worked together like episodes in a Robert Altman movie, fitting snugly, side by side, to give one an extended glimpse of a specific world. Miss Mason's setting was Kentucky —not the old Kentucky of small towns and gracious farms, but that proud territory of the new South speckled with shopping malls and subdivisions, fast-food franchises and drive-in movies, a shiny new place, vacuumed clean of history and tradition. Reeling from the swiftness of the transition, Miss Mason's characters all seemed to wander about in a fog, either spacing out in front of the television or passively drifting away from their families and friends, aware, however dimly, that they had misplaced something important along the way.

In her strong first novel, *In Country,* Miss Mason returns to this same geographical and spiritual milieu, and she returns, too, to her earlier themes: the dislocations wrought on ordinary, blue-collar lives by recent history—in this case, recent history in the form of the Vietnam War. In that respect, *In Country* may well remind readers of Jayne Anne Phillips's splendid novel *Machine Dreams,* for both books examine the intersection of that public event with private lives, and both specifically look at the repercussions it had on the psyches of young women who lost relatives to its horrors.

Miss Mason's narrative strategy and crackly voice, however, remain distinctly her own. Whereas Miss Phillips built up to the war, using it as a coda to her story of three generations—the disappearance of her heroine's brother in Vietnam became a kind of symbol of the family's dissolution—Miss Mason uses it as a starting point, moving backward from cold fact into a family's anomalous history. It is only by coming to terms with the war that killed her father that Miss Mason's heroine, Sam, can hope to discover her own relationship with him, and her own identity as a late child of the 60's. . . .

Like so many writers of her generation, Miss Mason chronicles these aimless lives in prose that tends to be as laconic and stripped down as her characters' emotional range. Where she parts company with such contemporaries as Ann Beattie and Mary Robison, however, is in her willingness to venture the occasional poetic image—"up in the sky," she writes at one point, "the daytime moon is a white fingernail hanging against the pale blue"—and in her desire to locate some sort of pattern or meaning in her people's spiritual malaise. Sometimes this can lead to rather strained configurations: Emmett's possible contamination with Agent Orange becomes a blunt, obvious metaphor for the insidious consequences of Vietnam; and Sam's attempt to imaginatively relive her father's experience in the jungle by camping out in the woods feels more like a novelist's contrived idea than a genuine gesture of passion.

Yet, all in all, the reader happily overlooks such miscalculations. It is Miss Mason's largeness of ambition and generosity of vision that invests *In Country* with the vitality of art; and her delineation of Sam's inner life remains so assured, so spontaneous, that we are swept along in the story, our trust sustained during such narrative lapses by our faith in the author's intimate knowledge of her heroine. Miss Mason has not only mastered the way teen-agers talk—their speech filled with allusions to television and rock-and-roll, nonsequiturs and sarcastic comebacks—but she has also understood and captured the ambivalence of youth: a young woman's craving for both knowledge and pristine innocence, her need to be both idealistic and cool. In doing so, Miss Mason has written a novel that, like a flashbulb, burns an afterimage in our minds.

> *Michiko Kakutani, in a review of "In Country," in* The New York Times, *September 4, 1985, p. C20.*

MARILYN GARDNER

Mason's spare prose, so perfectly suited to her unpretentious characters and setting, gives [*In Country*] a simplicity that is both deceptive and disarming. She displays an ear perfectly tuned to dialogue, an eye that catches every telling detail and quirky mannerism. Tiny, seemingly insignificant observations and revelations accumulate almost unnoticed until something trips them, turning them into literary grenades explosive with meaning.

Characters who in less-skilled hands could seem freakish become charming as Mason exposes their foibles with compassion, gentle humor—even love. One of the best portraits is Mamaw, Sam's paternal grandmother, a large, simple woman as baffled by credit cards as she is by "little tubs of non-dairy creamer" in a restaurant. The people are better than their out-of-joint times.

Ultimately, Mason seems to be saying that *nobody* comprehends war—any war, especially this war. In filtering a sad chapter in American history through the eyes and mind of a backwater teen-age girl, she offers insights that bring new perspective to years of confusing news reports and TV documentaries.

Not every reader will share Mason's sentiments about Vietnam. But only the most uncaring will be able to ignore the moral questions that lie at the heart of this little volume. . . .

> *Marilyn Gardner, "Bobbie Ann Mason's First Novel," in* The Christian Science Monitor, *September 6, 1985, p. B2.*

JONATHAN YARDLEY

On the strength of her previous book, ***Shiloh and Other Stories,*** Bobbie Ann Mason became a minor literary celebrity, a phenomenon for which she is not to be held responsible but which complicates one's reading of *In Country,* her first novel. . . .

The stories in ***Shiloh*** are amiable and appealing, but they are all pretty much alike and eventually they dissolve into a blur. They are more accomplished and interesting, though, than *In Country,* the good intentions of which are defeated by thematic predictability, unenticing characters and endless, pointless chatter. . . .

The young woman in Mason's novel is Samantha Hughes. She is called Sam and is 17 years old, soon to be 18. She lives in a Kentucky town called Hopewell with her 35-year-old uncle, Emmett, a Vietnam veteran who may or may not be a victim of Agent Orange. Her father, Dwayne, was killed in Vietnam shortly before her birth; now her mother, Irene, lives in Lexington with her prosperous new husband and infant daughter. Sam is about to head off for college, but before she does she feels a need to come to terms with Vietnam, a conflict of which she is an innocent victim.

This involves her in long if somewhat one-sided conversations with Emmett, who uncooperatively conforms to the cliché that veterans don't like to talk up their war experiences with the wimminfolks, and then with Tom, another veteran on whom she develops a strong crush. This leads her to attend a dance intended to draw local attention to what the vets did for their country, but even in patriotic Hopewell, not many people appear because not many people care—a theme that Mason bleeds for all it's worth and then some. . . .

[In] the novel's climax, [Sam] goes on a hegira to the Vietnam Veterans Memorial in Washington with Emmett and her paternal grandmother, who incredibly enough is called Mamaw.

All of this is meant to be painful and illuminating, but any power it might possess is eviscerated by its dreary familiarity. That many veterans of Vietnam have been put through hell is indisputable, and that the honor they have lately received is long overdue is equally so, but these points have been made many times before and nothing that Mason says adds anything to our understanding of them. Further, she has failed to transform these essentially political questions into the stuff of fiction; none of her characters comes to life, the novel's structure is awkward and its narrative herky-jerky, her prose wavers uncertainly between adult and teenaged voices. Her heart may be in the right place, but that isn't enough to bring *In Country* to life.

Jonathan Yardley, "Bobbie Ann Mason and the Shadow of Vietnam," in Book World—The Washington Post, *September 8, 1985, p. 3.*

JOEL CONARROE

A swatch of western Kentucky near the Illinois border constitutes Bobbie Ann Mason's private literary terrain. Encountered three years ago in *Shiloh and Other Stories* and now revisited in an impressive first novel [*In Country*], her landscape is populated by K Mart clerks, gas station attendants, young grandmothers who read Harlequin novels, and other "good country people," to borrow Flannery O'Connor's serviceable phrase. . . .

[*Shiloh and Other Stories*], by turns troubling and droll, resembles Joyce's *Dubliners* in communicating a pervasive sense of paralysis. Characters are unwilling (or unable) to break out of stultifying routines; some are reluctant even to leave the house. The men, typically, stay at home working with their hands, thus gratifying an unfocused creative urge. The divorce rate is high. . . .

Entrapment and mobility are also central to *In Country,* whose title is a veterans' phrase for Vietnam. Emmett Smith, 35, did a tour in the Army and now, 14 years later, suffers from skin rashes and severe head pains, probably caused by Agent Orange. The novel, at its most polemic, is an indictment of our Government's casual attitude toward those who survived an unpopular war but are having difficulty surviving civilian life. . . .

Emmett shares the house with his sister's daughter, Sam, a feisty teen-ager reminiscent of the tomboys in Carson McCullers and Harper Lee. Her father was killed in Vietnam before she was born and Emmett functions as a surrogate parent, though in fact the roles are usually reversed. In contrast to her immobilized uncle she is a distance runner, and in a quest for still more freedom she buys a used car from another of Hopewell's emotionally disabled veterans, with whom she has an unconsummated affair—the car, fittingly, has a faulty transmission. The novel's central material is framed by two brilliant sections describing a trip to the Vietnam Veterans Memorial in Washington. Sam and Emmett are joined by her grandmother, a comic figure who makes Sam think of "that Chevy Chase movie about a family on vacation, with an old woman tagging along." Those at home with books are more likely to be reminded of O'Connor's story, "A Good Man Is Hard to Find."

Sam, though, is no reader, and if the novel finally seems thinner, less resonant, than the tightly packed stories it is partly because her imagination has been nourished with such meager fare. . . .

It is a measure of Miss Mason's skill that despite her protagonist's minimal exposure to anything that is not banal she succeeds in communicating, persuasively, a movement toward adulthood and intellectual arousal. Working a timely variation on the traditionally male-centered *Bildungsroman*, she delineates Sam's quest for a father, which is to say for a history that will validate her identity in a way that Bruce Springsteen's lyrics cannot. By reading her father's battlefield diary and awakening to her uncle's deep grief, she gradually—and painfully—comes to recognize that there are things in the world more authentic than video games and "M*A*S*H." In the course of her moral education she passes through the phases traditionally associated with such rites of passage, progressing from separation to isolation (confronting a heart of darkness) and finally to integration.

If the rudimentary level of allusion revealed during this awakening is geared to Sam's inner life, so too is the novel's prose, which makes Hemingway sound almost Jamesian. . . .

[The] seemingly artless, brick-by-brick style is deceptive, however, and the novel, unlike the rock lyrics it quotes, is not intended for mass consumers with short attention spans—the very audience, ironically, best equipped to respond to its popular references. As in O'Connor, every detail, however trivial, is put in for a reason, and patterns of considerable sophistication—the several quest motifs, for example—eventually do emerge. *In Country* is written with disarming simplicity not because its author lacks linguistic resources but because she knows intimately the prosaic character of small-town life in her corner of the South.

She also knows exactly what she wants to say, whether about the difficult process of growing up, the daily routines of country people or the larger national dramas that unite all sorts of people. By the end of the meticulously constructed novel a literal journey has been completed, and in the dramatic final scene at the Veterans Memorial we watch Sam as she watches her uncle. Her figurative journey into understanding is in its early stages, and we can only speculate about how far from the bonds of Hopewell it might take her. As for her creator (who now lives in Pennsylvania), the book clearly reveals her own understanding of those mysteries that reside in the human heart. Her first novel, although it lacks the page-by-page abundance of her best stories, is an exceptional achievement, at once humane, comic and moving.

Joel Conarroe, "Winning Her Father's War," in The New York Times Book Review, *September 15, 1985, p. 7.*

THOMAS DE PIETRO

The just plain folk of Bobbie Ann Mason's fiction first lumbered forth in her widely praised collection, *Shiloh and Other Stories,* and there her poor rubes seem to dwell in an interminable present. Their mundane lives (circumscribed partly by Mason's numbing use of the present tense) remain buried under an accumulation of intentionally extraneous details ("Well, facts is facts") and inarticulate dialogue ("'I never was any good in English,' he says"). Mason's post-modern hicks typically work at Kroger's, shop at K-Mart, watch lots of TV, and occasionally dream of distant travel (to Florida or Arizona). Her prose signals REAL LIFE at every turn, and we're certainly meant to appreciate the passive heroism of those who endure it. But for a few nods to their Kentucky locales, these affectless tales could be by Raymond Carver, or Mary Robison, or Tobias Wolff, or Ann Beattie or . . . well, you get the idea. (If you don't, read any issue of the *New Yorker*.)

Shiloh offers some exceptions to be sure: **"Detroit Skyline, 1949"** and **"Nancy Culpepper"** among them. The latter, in particular, relies on an uncharacteristic point of view, that of a graduate-school-educated Kentuckian in exile, a woman no doubt much like Mason herself. (Like the author, she also lives in a small town outside Philadelphia.) In the story, what the protagonist Nancy (who's named after the kinswoman of the title) hopes to achieve by visiting her dying grandmother back west is what most of Mason's characters never attempt: to connect with the past, a time before fast food and Phil Donahue.

For her first novel, *In Country,* Mason exploits every literary notion and skill at her limited command. Though her narrative insists on its contemporaneity, and assumes a deliberately naive voice, it's organized like **"Nancy Culpepper"** as an effort in historical retrieval and recreation. The historian is a seventeen-year-old girl, Sam Hughes of Hopewell, Kentucky, who struggles to understand nothing less than the Vietnam War in all its grim detail. (pp. 620-21)

Like Nancy of **"Nancy Culpepper,"** Sam craves photographs, staring so much at likenesses of her father that "he was beginning to seem real." Much of the novel concerns Sam's dogged pursuit of such artifacts, and Mason includes a number of them in her text: mindless letters from Sam's father to his wife and parents, and the more revealing diary from his time in the jungle—an unexpected find which speaks directly to Sam's obsession.

Sipping Coke and reading her father's diary on a bench in the Paducah mall, Sam gags on his words ("dead gooks have a special stink") as it becomes clear he killed his share of Viet Cong without remorse. Before, the war had always been "like a horror movie. . . . Now everything seemed suddenly real. . . ." But not real enough. For as one of Emmett's buddies told Sam early on, until she's "humped the boonies" (i.e., survived "some godforsaken wilderness"), she'll never understand what it meant to go "in country." Her desperate attempt to recreate the Asian Jungle—the novel's first bit of real drama—finds her camping out in Cawood's Pond, "the last place in western Kentucky where a person could really face the wild." There, she fantasizes the sights and smells of Vietnam, with raccoons as V.C. and Granny Cakes as K-rations, but soon realizes something's wrong. No flares or rockets light the sky, no choppers or artillery pierce the quiet; this isn't war at all. (pp. 621-22)

When a frantic Emmett finds her the following day, he at last spills his guts, and tells her what "really happened." But she punctuates his long pent-up tale with the only reality she knows: "I saw something like that in a movie on TV."

Emmett's final maxim ("You can't learn from the past. The main thing you learn from history is that you can't learn from history.") forces us to realize another bloody truth. The bulk of this novel merely fleshes out another typically pointless Mason story. The narrative frame (the first twenty and last ten pages) simply recounts, in the present tense of course, what everything else in the book leads up to: a trip by Emmett, Sam, and Mamaw (her father's mother) to the Vietnam Veterans Memorial in D.C. The monument, with its ambiguous imagery, is the source of Sam's equally ambiguous epiphany. Walking past the rows of names (with a copy of *Born in the U.S.A.* under her arm) Sam confirms Emmett's earlier lesson. She thinks: "she will never really know what happened to all these men in war."

This diminished fiction, though loaded with surface details, fails to achieve even the modest effect of a story like **"Nancy Culpepper."** Instead, that earlier voice, insistent in its sophistication, intrudes on Sam's media-cluttered consciousness. . . . Though Mason begins with an admirable goal—to understand the aftershock of that horrible war abroad and those parlous times at home—she ends up trivializing both past and present. Snatches of rock lyrics and bits of TV dialogue provide Mason with an emotional shorthand; they're her cultural correlatives. But next to a pop masterpiece like *Born in the U.S.A.* or even "M*A*S*H," *In Country* seems bloated, condescending to its characters, pretentious in its feigned naïveté. Stripped

to its essence, it might make a decent young adult novel, or better yet, an after-school special on TV. (p. 622)

Thomas de Pietro, "In Quest of the Bloody Truth," in Commonweal, *Vol. CXII, No. 19, November 1, 1985, pp. 620-22.*

PATRICK PARRINDER

Bobbie Ann Mason's *In Country* portrays a strictly contemporary America in which the characters spend much of their time playing video games, watching TV reruns and listening to Bruce Springsteen. Nevertheless, this is a genuine rural novel, concerned with characters disinherited from, and trying to come back into connection with, the American land: both senses of 'land' are intended here. Mason is not a word-spinner or virtuoso stylist . . . , but she has an acute ear and eye and she writes in prose which is plain, stripped-down and adequate to its theme. . . .

Samantha Hughes, the central figure of *In Country,* ought to have grown up on a farm. Instead, her father enlisted in the Army and was blown to pieces in Vietnam in 1966. (Most of the names on the Vietnam Memorial in Washington are, we are told, 'country boy names'.) The novel is set in western Kentucky, culminating in a once-in-a-lifetime trip to Washington. Abandoned by her mother, and living with an uncle whose life is being wasted by post-Vietnam stress syndrome and possibly by Agent Orange, 17-year-old Sam Hughes develops a morbid desire to understand and, if possible, re-experience the late Sixties. She meets with a wall of reticence and inarticulacy as she tries to find out what Vietnam was like. Is it Vietnam or 'her own crazy family' which accounts for the weirdness of the people around her? Once she has found her father's letters home and the far more candid journal that was left behind among his personal effects, she thinks she has the key she was looking for. . . . *In Country* will doubtless be seen by some readers as uncomfortably moralistic. Sam Hughes was not an easy character to bring off wholly successfully: sometimes she seems too wide-eyed, and at other times her responses are too much those of her author. But this is a courageous and poignant first novel, a moral fable by a writer unafraid of sentiment—the climax comes with the characters' visit to the Vietnam Memorial—and capable also of expressing a precise and disciplined anger. Formally, *In Country* has strong affinities with some recent Second World War novels, notably David Hughes's *The Pork Butcher.* But it is also true to contemporary American life in the one sense that really matters, which is that of giving an unexpected and wholly persuasive meaning to that life. The party is over, and Bobbie Ann Mason, for one, has noticed. (p. 19)

Patrick Parrinder, "Last in the Funhouse," in London Review of Books, *Vol. 8, No. 7, April 17, 1986, pp. 18-19.*

ANNE BOSTON

Emmett, Dwayne, Earl, Dawn: the names [of the characters in *In Country*] twang like Country and Western guitar chords through this affecting, unpatronizing evocation of small-town Hopewell, where most of the folk take their style from the God-fearing or the sexy, and sophistication is a visit to the shopping mall in nearby Lexington. A few years ago England imported the label "dirty realism" along with Raymond Carver's pared-down stories; this year Bobbie Ann Mason's brand of rural nostalgia brings us "hick chic". Her preoccupation with authenticity dots the pages with the titles of television programmes, brand names of drinks and above all references to records. Major events past and present are dated by their rock-and-roll associations: Chuck Berry, the Beatles, Little Richard (the best legacy of that much overrated era) are the bridge between Sam and her parents' generation. As one of the vets says wistfully to her at the commemoration dance, "When you're in country, there's so little connection to the World, but those songs—that's as close as we came to a real connection."

Mason's deadpan, unornamented prose and faultless dialogue are well tuned to pick out the limitations of the place and people Sam is clinging to, even as she knows she is growing out of them: the "mating run" between McDonalds and the Burger King, where the boys cruise after the girls; Sam's best friend Dawn, pregnant and tied for good to Hopewell; her grandparents binding on about the tobacco crop; even the amiably weird Emmett, who can only "work on staying together, one day at a time."

The author is herself of the "Vietnam generation"; in her effort to exorcize those troubled years she perhaps over-emphasizes them in Sam's obsession. But the finale of Emmett and Sam's visit to the Washington war memorial with Sam's grandmother Mamaw redresses the balance. The picture of Mamaw, monstrously fat and leaning precariously from a borrowed painter's ladder to touch the inscription of Dwayne's name, is a finely balanced moment of comedy, pathos and understated emotion.

Anne Boston, "With the Vets in Hopewell," in The Times Literary Supplement, *No. 4333, April 18, 1986, p. 416.*

ALICE BLOOM

It's generally claimed that Bobbie Ann Mason is writing about the guts of the guts of the country, but to assume that *In Country* is therefore a nouveau pastoral dream of, when all's said and done, good hearts in simple people is like thinking Springsteen's "Born in the U.S.A." is a simple, warm-hearted, upbeat song and suitable for use at Super Bowl half-time festivities and as the basis for jingles urging us to vote America by buying Detroit-made cars. I mean let's look at what the words are really saying. I have no heart left for life in America at all, and no hope for any of her characters, or real-life people like them, when Mason is finished with them. They are grotesques, and their country is Franchise City. Maybe they are; maybe it is; Mason's prose does not work to go deeply into these lives but to distort their surface images as though they were being reflected off loose hubcaps. Diane Arbus, not Sherwood Anderson.

Which is legitimate of course; it's anyone's right, and maybe modern U.S.A. as it is lived by lots of people is thus most truthfully portrayed. What puzzles me, however, is why readers and reviewers continue to use words like "charming" and "deeply respectful" to describe a vision that is so terrifying, stripping, disheartening. It's not the story line of this novel, which is a conventional trajectory of hope. A just-on-the-verge-of-life, eighteen-year-old, small-Kentucky-town girl, Sam, is seeking the future by trying to know the past. For what substance and enlightenment she finds she may as well be seeking lost Atlantis, but all she wants is to understand an event less than twenty years old, and lived by many: the Vietnam War. (pp. 519-20)

But no one will talk about it, or else when they do they only kid around. They tell her to leave it alone, tell her to stop thinking so darned much, tell her she doesn't want to know. Sam is stubborn, keeps pushing and looking. We know she's searching for herself too, for grounding, for history, connection, roots, a father, a view of the world of her times, a view of what "adult" means before she tries it out. (p. 520)

Despite her pathetic hope and spirited ways, however, Sam is imprisoned, maybe for life, in the world that is Mason's America. The people around Sam are so anesthetized, paralyzed, brutalized, so sentimental or flippant or ignorant that they are no help because they don't know what she wants, or why, and they don't want it themselves. They want just to go along, let the past go. Mind their own business. And they have, though that is defined about as small as you could make it. Sam thinks there's a conspiracy of silence, that they're deliberately not telling her. But it's sadder than that: they have no language. And most of them, her own mother for instance, who's remarried and moved away, don't really remember all that much. You get the feeling they'd tell her if only they could remember. Along with all the t.v. shows, the videos, records, and movies that the characters constantly discuss, the re-make of *The Body Snatchers* is one everybody watches and talks animatedly about as though it were about people they actually know. The irony, of course, is that they do know them. Sam is like the major character of that scary movie, living out the last few minutes before he realizes everyone else is already pod people. We know that this realization is his future.

The source of deepest terror in this novel is not the plot or the characterization, but the style; and the recurrent, pervasive image of terror is brand-name junk. The nature of that junk, a piece of which appears in almost any sentence, is oxymoronic: this reiterated trash—Pontiac Thunderbird, Dairy Queen, Dodge Dart, Burger Boy, Exxon, K-Mart, Ford Cobra, Holiday Inn, Howard Johnson's, MTV, Billy Joel, the Kinks, re-runs of "M*A*S*H," *Reader's Digest*, plastic quarts of Coke and Pepsi and Mountain Dew, Doritos, chips 'n dip, Egg McMuffins, Ready-to-Heat Tacos, Gerber's "Blueberry Buckle," styrofoam cartons, Saran Wrap, Velcro, Acrylic, Tupperware, Formica—is terrifying because it's stuff that is cheap, flimsy, ugly, and utterly temporary, carrying no message, no texture, no touch, no history, no beauty, no way back or forward, no help for human life and, at the same time utterly permanent. Non-biodegradable nothingness laid as solidly across life and mind as the Interstates and Malls are laid across what used to be farm land.

When this is the junk that furnishes the words that the characters are given to think with, as though this ungodly man-made landscape of garbage were the only text available to our time, then what thoughts *can* people think? Sam is given youth, energy, and a kind nature, but Mason gives her no language to talk or think or feel with. When Sam describes a woman she really seems to like and admire, she thinks, "Anita smelled nice, like a store at the mall that had a perfume blower in the doorway," and she had a "hearty, warm laugh, like poppin'-fresh dough from the oven." I don't care how telling, mid-America, ain't it true, down-home and "significant" these analogies are supposed to be, or how cleverly observant on the part of the novelist; a person who sees, talks, connects, and thinks like this at age eighteen is not being equipped, by world or novelist, to look deeply into the nature of things.

At the conclusion of the novel, a ragged family group in a used VW with a broken transmission, a frail bug filmed from above, travels from Hopewell KY to the Vietnam memorial in Washington. Sam, Uncle Emmett, whose idea this trip is, and Sam's father's mother "Mamaw." (pp. 520-21)

They seem enormously uncertain of what they'll find or what they think or what they're doing, and because the narrative voice never tells us more than the characters know, as though in sticking so close to their side it has taken a sympathetic vow of poverty, we don't know what they're doing, either. The three characters seem like pilgrims who trudge uncertainly on without knowing what either journey or shrine ahead signifies: Defeat? Heroes? Hope? Healing? More P.R. hype? The black wall of the memorial is "massive, a black gash in a hillside, like a vein of coal exposed and then polished with polyurethane." It contains 58,000 names; Sam's mother has predicted that most of them will be "country boy" names, like "Bobby Gene and Freddie Ray and Jimmy Bob Calhoun." (I know this is stating a tragic, important fact, but I resent, again, the easy way it's done: is the reader to conclude by these diminutive brand-names for people that Robert and Frederick and James were all from Manhattan, enrolled at Harvard, and thus escaped being drafted? No; it's shorthand for saying "the draft was unfair," and so, most lamentably and shamefully, it was. Therefore it deserves being talked about in language suitable and exacting.)

They find Sam's father's name in the directory, and then on panel 9E of the black wall. First Emmett reaches up and touches the name, but Mamaw is too short. "I can't reach it," she says, "Oh, I wanted to touch it." (p. 522)

Sam's father, like thousands of others, was shipped home in a bag. A name we know on any gravestone is the worst poetry of all our lives. If you wanted to reach back to the reality of the dead and wanted through that touch to find your own reality, I don't know what you'd do with a name among 58,000 others on a black wall but reach out and rub it, and this scene is very sad. It is the wall here that is absurd, absurdly inadequate, and mute, and the words themselves that are "scratching on a rock. Writing." But there's something else here too, given the paucity of language in the whole novel, and the pathetic touching in this scene, that strongly suggests that Sam, Uncle Emmett, and Mamaw can't really read the words, with the eye, I mean. As though they have to touch; as though they suffered the awe of post-literate, future savages unearthing with dumb fingers a lost civilization's incomprehensible dictionary. (p. 523)

Alice Bloom, in a review of "In Country," in New England Review and Bread Loaf Quarterly, *Vol. VIII, No. 4, Summer, 1986, pp. 519-23.*

Henry (Valentine) Miller

1891-1980

American novelist, critic, short story writer, editor, and non-fiction writer.

Considered among the most controversial and influential of twentieth-century authors, Miller is best remembered for his first novel, *Tropic of Cancer* (1934). In this and other autobiographical works of fiction, Miller attacked what he perceived to be the repression of the individual in a civilization bedeviled by technology, Victorian mores, and politics. Miller's criticism of Western culture evidenced his affinities with such philosophers as Friedrich Nietzsche and Oswald Spengler. The explicit sexual content of Miller's work and his revolutionary use of scatological humor and obscene language underscored his rebellion and caused his works to be censored in many countries, including the United States and Britain, until the early 1960s.

Born in Brooklyn, Miller held a variety of jobs and had been married twice when he departed for Paris in 1930. There Miller's talent matured and he wrote the novels which earned him his greatest recognition. In *Tropic of Cancer*, Miller blends naturalism and surrealism in a spontaneous, anecdotal prose style which draws directly from American vernacular. Essentially a fictionalized rendering of Miller's first year in Paris, the book is both a chronicle of Miller's life in the city's impoverished sections and a life-affirming manifesto which revels in the unrepressed expression of bodily functions and sexuality. Miller's aim with this novel was to express his belief in the unconditional acceptance of all aspects of life, good and bad, as equally valid parts of existence. As Miller stated, "One reason why I have stressed so much the immoral, the wicked, the ugly, the cruel in my work is because I want others to know how valuable these are, how equally if not more important than the good things." Although many critics considered the book's bawdy humor, obscene language, and explicit sexual content to be gratuitous or sexist, others claimed that these elements served to exalt the human body in an era which celebrated technological advancement and to shock readers out of complacency.

In his other major works written in Paris, *Black Spring* (1936) and *Tropic of Capricorn* (1939), Miller continues his use of surreal and natural imagery to convey his outrage against Western culture. *Black Spring* contains segments originally intended for inclusion in *Tropic of Cancer* and *Tropic of Capricorn* along with surreal passages culled from Miller's personal "dream book." In other chapters, Miller reminisces about his youth in Brooklyn. Many of the events recounted in *Tropic of Capricorn* predate Miller's experiences in Paris, detailing his life in the United States, his various occupations, and the restrictive atmosphere he viewed as intrinsic to American life.

The novels of Miller's trilogy *The Rosy Crucifixion—Sexus* (1949), *Plexus* (1953), and *Nexus* (1960)—were written after he returned to live in the United States. Again based upon personal experience, *The Rosy Crucifixion* chronicles Miller's life in the United States during the 1920s. Focusing primarily on his first two marriages and his literary aspirations, the trilogy has met with less favor than Miller's previous novels because,

according to many critics, it fails to resolve the questions it raises regarding love and life. *Quiet Days in Clichy* (1956), a novel intended as a companion piece to *Tropic of Cancer,* is another Paris reminiscence, while *Book of Friends* (1978) concerns Miller's Brooklyn boyhood.

Miller also published many works in other genres. *The Colossus of Maroussi* (1941), a travelogue on Greece, is, according to Miller, "less a guidebook than an account of Greece as an experience." In *The Air-Conditioned Nightmare* (1948) and its sequel, *Remember to Remember* (1974), Miller recounts his impressions of consumer America during his travels across the United States. *Big Sur and the Oranges of Hieronymous Bosch* (1957) is a book detailing Miller's life in the 1950s on the California coast. Among Miller's critical works are *Time of the Assassins: A Study of Rimbaud* (1956) and *The World of Lawrence: A Passionate Appreciation* (1980). The latter, detailing the life and career of his literary compatriot, D. H. Lawrence, was begun prior to the publication of *Tropic of Cancer.* *Opus Pistorum* (1984) is a novel reputedly written by Miller in the early 1940s when he was in need of money. Most critics consider the work to be pure pornography, and some question whether Miller is the actual author of the book.

Since Miller's death, critics have reevaluated his influence and contribution to contemporary literature. That he laid the groundwork for such writers of the Beat movement as Jack Kerouac, Allen Ginsberg, and Lawrence Ferlinghetti by freeing language and subject matter from rigid censorship is generally acknowledged by literary authorities. While many of Miller's books contain passages of artistry, critics generally agree that *Tropic of Cancer* is his most sustained and successful work.

(See also *CLC*, Vols. 1, 2, 4, 9, 14; *Contemporary Authors*, Vols. 9-12, rev. ed., Vols. 97-100 [obituary]; *Dictionary of Literary Biography*, Vols. 4, 9; and *Dictionary of Literary Biography Yearbook: 1980*.)

KATE MILLETT

Certain writers are persistently misunderstood. Henry Miller is surely one of the major figures of American literature living today, yet academic pedantry still dismisses him as beneath scholarly attention. He is likely to be one of the most important influences on our contemporary writing, but official criticism perseveres in its scandalous and systematic neglect of his work. To exacerbate matters, Miller has come to represent the much acclaimed "sexual freedom" of the last few decades. One finds eloquent expression of this point of view in a glowing essay by Karl Shapiro [see *CLC*, Vol. 4]: "Miller's achievement is miraculous: he is screamingly funny without making fun of sex . . . accurate and poetic in the highest degree; there is not a smirk anywhere in his writings." Shapiro is confident that Miller can do more to expunge the "obscenities" of the national scene than a "full-scale social revolution." Lawrence Durrell exclaims over "how nice it is for once to dispense with the puritans and with pagans," since Miller's books, unlike those of his contemporaries, are "not due to puritanical shock." Shapiro assures us that Miller is "the first writer outside the Orient who has succeeded in writing as naturally about sex on a large scale as novelists ordinarily write about the dinner table or the battlefield." Significant analogies. Comparing the *Tropic of Cancer* with Joyce's *Ulysses*, Shapiro gives Miller the advantage, for while Joyce, warped by the constraints of his religious background, is prurient or "aphrodisiac," Miller is "no aphrodisiac at all, because religious or so-called moral tension does not exist for him." Shapiro is convinced that "Joyce actually prevents himself from experiencing the beauty of sex or lust, while Miller is freed at the outset to deal with the overpowering mysteries and glories of love and copulation."

However attractive our current popular image of Henry Miller the liberated man may appear, it is very far from being the truth. Actually, Miller is a compendium of American sexual neuroses, and his value lies not in freeing us from such afflictions, but in having had the honesty to express and dramatize them. There *is* a kind of culturally cathartic release in Miller's writing, but it is really a result of the fact that he first gave voice to the unutterable. This is no easy matter of four-letter words; they had been printed already in a variety of places. What Miller did articulate was the disgust, the contempt, the hostility, the violence, and the sense of filth with which our culture, or more specifically, its masculine sensibility, surrounds sexuality. And women too; for somehow it is women upon whom this onerous burden of sexuality falls. There is plenty of evidence that Miller himself is fleetingly conscious of these things, and his "naive, sexual heroics" would be far

better if, as one critic suggests, they had been carried all the way to "self-parody." But the major flaw in his oeuvre—too close an identification with the persona, "Henry Miller"—always operates insidiously against the likelihood of persuading us that Miller the man is any wiser than Miller the character.

And with *this* Miller; though one has every reason to doubt the strict veracity of those sexual exploits he so laboriously chronicles in the first person, though one has every reason to suspect that much of this "fucking" is sheer fantasy—there is never reason to question the sincerity of the emotion which infuses such accounts; their exploitative character; their air of juvenile egotism. Miller's genuine originality consists in revealing and recording a group of related sexual attitudes which, despite their enormous prevalence and power, had never (or never so explicitly) been given literary expression before. Of course, these attitudes are no more the whole truth than chivalry, or courtly, or romantic love were—but Miller's attitudes do constitute a kind of cultural data heretofore carefully concealed beneath our traditional sanctities. (pp. 294-96)

Miller regards himself as a disciple of Lawrence, a suggestion certain to have outraged the master had he lived to be so affronted. The liturgical pomp with which Lawrence surrounded sexuality bears no resemblance to Miller's determined profanity. The Lawrentian hero sets about his mission with notorious gravity and "makes love" by an elaborate political protocol. . . . But Miller and his confederates—for Miller is a gang—just "fuck" women and discard them, much as one might avail oneself of sanitary facilities—Kleenex or toilet paper, for example. Just "fucking," the Miller hero is merely a huckster and a con man, unimpeded by pretension, with no priestly role to uphold. Lawrence did much to kill off the traditional attitudes of romantic love. At first glance, Miller seems to have started up blissfully ignorant of their existence altogether. Actually, his cold-blooded procedure is intended as sacrilege to the tenderness of romantic love, a tenderness Lawrence was never willing to forgo. In his brusque way, Miller demonstrates the "love fraud" (a species of power play disguised as eroticism) to be a process no more complex than a mugging. The formula is rather simple: you meet her, cheat her into letting you have "a piece of ass," and then take off. Miller's hunt is a primitive find, fuck, and forget. (p. 296)

Lawrence had turned back the feminist claims to human recognition and a fuller social participation by distorting them into a vegetative passivity calling itself fulfillment. His success prepared the way for Miller's escalation to open contempt. Lawrence had still to deal with persons; Miller already feels free to speak of objects. Miller simply converts woman to "cunt"—thing, commodity, matter. There is no personality to recognize or encounter, so there is none to tame or break by the psychological subtleties of Lawrence's Freudian wisdom. (p. 297)

The Victorians, or some of them, revealed themselves in their slang expression for the orgasm—"to spend"—a term freighted with economic insecurity and limited resources, perhaps a reflection of capitalist thrift implying that if semen is money (or time or energy) it should be preciously hoarded. Miller is no such cheapskate, but in his mind, too, sex is linked in a curious way with money. . . . Before exile in Paris granted him reprieve, Miller felt himself the captive of circumstances in a philistine milieu where artistic or intellectual work was despised, and the only approved avenues of masculine achievement were confined to money or sex. Of course, Miller is a maverick and a rebel, but much as he hates the money mentality, it is so ingrained in him that he is capable only of replacing it with sex—a transference of acquisitive impulse. By converting the female to commodity, he too can enjoy the esteem of "success." If he can't make money, he can make women—if need be on borrowed cash, pulling the biggest coup of all by getting something for nothing. And while his better "adjusted" contemporaries swindle in commerce, Miller preserves his "masculinity" by swindling in cunt. By shining in a parallel system of pointless avarice whose real rewards are also tangential to actual needs and likewise surpassed by the greater gains run up for powerful egotism, his manly reputation is still assured with his friends. (p. 298)

The perfect Miller "fuck" is a biological event between organs, its hallmark—its utter impersonality. Of course perfect strangers are best, chance passengers on subways molested without the exchange of word or signal. Paradoxically, this attempt to so isolate sex only loads the act with the most negative connotations. Miller has gone beyond even the empty situations one frequently encounters in professional pornography, blue movies, etc., to freight his incidents with cruelty and contempt. While seeming to remove sexuality from any social or personal context into the gray abstraction of "organ grinding," he carefully includes just enough information on the victim to make her activity humiliating and degrading, and his own an assertion of sadistic will.

Miller boasts, perhaps one should say confesses, that the "best fuck" he "ever had" was with a creature nearly devoid of sense, the "simpleton" who lived upstairs.... Throughout the description one not only observes a vulgar opportunistic use of Lawrence's hocus pocus about blanking out in the mind in order to attain "blood consciousness," but one also intuits how both versions of the idea are haunted by a pathological fear of having to deal with another and complete human personality. Happily, Miller's "pecker" is sufficient to "mesmerize" his prey in the dark.... One is made very aware here that in the author's scheme the male is represented not only by his telepathic instrument, but by mind, whereas the perfect female is a floating metonymy, pure cunt, completely unsullied by human mentality. (p. 300)

Miller's ideal woman is a whore. Lawrence regarded prostitution as a profanation of the temple, but with Miller the commercialization of sexuality is not only a gratifying convenience for the male (since it is easier to pay than persuade) but the perfection of feminine existence, efficiently confining it to the function of absolute cunt. (p. 301)

Since "whores are whores," Miller is also capable of reviling them as "vultures," "buzzards," "rapacious devils," and "bitches"—his righteous scorn as trite as his sentimentality. He is anxious, however, to elevate their function to an "idea"—the Life Force. As with electrical conductors, to plug into them gives a fellow "that circuit which makes one feel the earth under his legs again." Prostitutes themselves speak of their work as "servicing," and Miller's gratified egotism would not only seek to surround the recharge with mystification, but convert the whore into a curious vessel of intermasculine communication—rhapsodizing: "All the men she's been with and now you . . . the whole damned current of life flowing through you, through her, through all the guys behind you and after you." What is striking here is not only the total abstraction Miller makes of sexuality (what could be less solid, less plastic than electricity?) but also the peculiar (yet hardly uncommon) thought of hunting other men's semen in the vagina of a whore, the random conduit of this brotherly vitality.

There is a men's-house atmosphere in Miller's work. His boyhood chums remain the friends of his youth, his maturity, even his old age. Johnny Paul and the street-gang heroes of the adolescence continue as the idols of adulthood, strange companions for Miller's literary gods: Spengler, Nietzsche, Dostoievski. The six volumes of autobiography, and even the essays, are one endless, frequently self-pitying threnody for the lost paradise of his youth.

As a result, the sexual attitudes of the "undisputed monarch" of the "Land of Fuck," as Miller chooses to call himself, are those of an arrested adolescence where sex is clandestine, difficult to come by, each experience constituting a victory of masculine diligence and wit over females either stupidly compliant or sagely unco-operative.... [The] reader is given the impression that sex is no good unless duly observed and applauded by an ubiquitous peer-group jury. And so Miller's prose has always the flavor of speech, the inflection of telling the boys.... His strenuous heterosexuality depends, to a considerable degree, on a homosexual sharing. Not without reason, his love story, *The Rosy Crucifixion,* is one long exegesis of the simple admission "I had lost the power to love." All the sentiment of his being, meanly withheld from "cunt," is lavished on the unattractive souls who make up the gang Miller never outgrew or deserted. What we observe in his work is a compulsive heterosexual activity in sharp distinction (but not opposed to) the kind of cultural homosexuality which has ruled that love, friendship, affection—all forms of companionship, emotional or intellectual—are restricted exclusively to males. (pp. 302-03)

Miller is very far from having escaped his Puritan origin: it is in the smut of his pals; in the frenzy of his partners; in the violence and contempt of his "fucking." We are never allowed to forget that this is forbidden and the sweeter for being so; that lust has greater excitements than love; that women degrade themselves by participation in sexuality, and that all but a few "pure" ones are no more than cunt and outrageous if they forget it. "The dirty bitches—they like it," he apprises us; clinical, fastidious, horrified and amused to record how one responded "squealing like a pig"; another "like a crazed animal"; one "gibbered"; another "crouched on all fours like a she-animal, quivering and whinnying." . . . (p. 306)

The very brutality with which he handles the language of sex; the iconographic four-letter words, soiled by centuries of prurience and shame, is an indication of Miller's certainty of how really filthy all this is. His defense against censorship is incontrovertible—"there was no other idiom possible" to express the "obscenity" he wished to convey. His diction is, quite as he claims, a "technical device" depending on the associations of dirt, violence, and scorn, in which a sexually distressed culture has steeped the words which also denominate the sexual organs and the sexual act. . . . Under this sacramental cloak a truly obscene ruthlessness toward other human beings is passed over unnoticed, or even defended. "Obscenity" is analogous to the "uses of the miraculous in the Masters," Miller announces pretentiously. He and the censor have linguistic and sexual attitudes in common: ritual use of the "obscene" is, of course, pointless, unless agreement exists that the sexual is, in fact, obscene. Furthermore, as Miller reminds us again and again, obscenity is a form of violence, a manner of conveying male hostility, both toward the female (who is sex) and toward sexuality itself (which is her fault). Yet, for all his disgust, indeed because of it, Miller must return over and over to the ordure; steel himself again and again by confronting what his own imagination (powerfully assisted by his cultural heritage and experience) has made horrible. The egotism called manhood requires such proof of courage. This is reality, Miller would persuade us: cunt stinks . . . and cunt is sex. (pp. 306-07)

The men's room has schooled Miller in the belief that sex is inescapably dirty. Meditating there upon some graffiti, "the walls crowded with sketches and epithets, all of them jocosely obscene," he speculates on "what an impression it would make on those swell dames . . . I wondered if they would carry their tails so high if they could see what was thought of an ass here." Since his mission is to inform "cunt" just how it's ridiculed and despised in the men's house, women perhaps owe Miller some gratitude for letting them know. (p. 309)

Miller's scheme of sexual polarity relegates the female to "cunt," an exclusively sexual being, crudely biological. Though he shares this lower nature, the male is also capable of culture and intellect. The sexes are two warring camps between whom understanding is impossible since one is human and animal (according to Miller's perception, intellectual and sexual)—the other, simply animal. Together, as mind and matter, male and female, they encompass the breadth of possible experience. The male, part angel, part animal, enjoys yet suffers too from his divided nature. His appetite for "cunt," recurrent and shameful as it is, is, nevertheless, his way of staying in touch with his animal origins. It keeps him "real." Miller staves off the threat of an actual sexual revolution—woman's transcendence of the mindless material capacity he would assign her—through the fiat of declaring her cunt and trafficking with her only in the utopian fantasies of his "fucks." That this is but whistling in the dark is demonstrated by his own defeating experience with Mara, and, even more persuasively by the paralyzing fear which drives him to pretend—so that he may deal with them at all—that women are things. (p. 312)

Miller has given voice to certain sentiments which masculine culture had long experienced but always rather carefully suppressed: the yearning to effect a complete depersonalization of woman into cunt, a game-sexuality of cheap exploitation, a childish fantasy of power untroubled by the reality of persons or the complexity of dealing with fellow human beings and, finally, a crude species of evacuation hardly better than anal in character.

While the release of such inhibited emotion, however poisonous, is beyond question advantageous, the very expression of such lavish contempt and disgust, as Miller has unleashed and made fashionable, can come to be an end in itself, eventually harmful, perhaps even malignant. To provide unlimited scope for masculine aggression, although it may finally bring the situation out into the open, will hardly solve the dilemma of our sexual politics. Miller does have something highly important to tell us; his virulent sexism is beyond question an honest contribution to social and psychological understanding which we can hardly afford to ignore. But to confuse this neurotic hostility, this frank abuse, with sanity, is pitiable. To confuse it with freedom were vicious, were it not so very sad. (p. 313)

> *Kate Millett, "Henry Miller," in her* Sexual Politics, *Doubleday & Company, Inc., 1970, pp. 294-313.*

NORMAN MAILER

[Henry Miller] exists in the same relation to legend that antimatter shows to matter. His life is antipathetic to the idea of legend itself. Where he is complex, he is too complex—we do not feel the resonance of slowly dissolving mystery but the madness of too many knots; where he is simple, he is not attractive—his air is harsh. If he had remained the protagonist by which he first presented himself in *Tropic of Cancer*—the man with iron in his phallus, acid in his mind, and some kind of incomparable relentless freedom in his heart, that paradox of tough misery and keen happiness, that connoisseur of the spectrum of odors between good sewers and bad sewers, that noble rat gnawing on existence and impossible to kill, then he could indeed have been a legend, a species of Parisian Bogart or American Belmondo. Everybody would have wanted to meet this poet-gangster, barbarian-genius. He would have been the American and heterosexual equivalent of Jean Genet.

In fact, he could never have been too near to the character he made of himself in *Tropic of Cancer.* One part never fits. It is obvious he must be more charming than he pretends—how else account for all the free dinners he is invited to, the people he lives on, the whores who love him? There has to be something splendid about him. He may even seem angelic to his friends or, perish the word, vulnerable. . . . (p. 2)

These few details are enough to suggest *Tropic of Cancer* is a fiction more than a fact. Which, of course, is not to take away a particle of its worth. Perhaps it becomes even more valuable. After all, we do not write to recapture an experience, we write to come as close to it as we can. Sometimes we are not very close, and yet, paradoxically, are nearer than if we were. Not nearer necessarily to the reality of what happened, but to the mysterious reality of what can happen on a page. Oil paints do not create clouds but the image of clouds; a page of manuscript can only evoke that special kind of reality which lives on the skin of the writing paper, a rainbow on a soap bubble. Miller is forever accused of caricature by people who knew his characters, and any good reader knows enough about personality to sense how much he must be leaving out of his people. Yet, what a cumulative reality they give us. His characters make up a Paris more real than its paving stones until a reluctant wonder bursts upon us—no French writer no matter how great, not Rabelais, nor Proust, not De Maupassant, Hugo, Huysmans, Zola, or even Balzac, not even Céline, has made Paris more vivid to us. Whenever before has a foreigner described a country better than its native writers? For in *Tropic of Cancer* Miller succeeded in performing one high literary act: he created a tone in prose which caught the tone of a period and a place. If that main character in *Tropic of Cancer* named Henry Miller never existed in life, it hardly matters—he is the voice of a spirit which existed at that time. The spirits of literature may be the nearest we come to historical truth.

For that matter, the great confessions of literature are apart from their authors. Augustine recollecting his sins is not the sinner but the pieties. Julien Sorel is not Stendhal, nor the Seducer a copy of Kierkegaard. *On the Road* is close to Jack Kerouac, yet he gives a happier Kerouac than the one who died too soon. Proust was not his own narrator, even as homosexuality is not like to heterosexuality but another land, and if we take *The Sun Also Rises* as the purest example of a book whose innovation in style became the precise air of a time and a place, then even there we come slowly to the realization that Hemingway at the time he wrote it was not the equal of Jake Barnes—he had created a consciousness wiser, drier, purer, more classic, more sophisticated, and more judicial than his own. He was still naïve in relation to his creation.

The difference between Hemingway and Miller is that Hemingway set out thereafter to grow into Jake Barnes and locked himself for better and worse, for enormous fame and eventual destruction, into that character who embodied the spirit of an age. Whereas Miller, eight years older than Hemingway but arriving at publication eight years later, and so 16 years older in 1934 than Hemingway was in 1926, chose to go in the opposite direction. He proceeded to move away from the first Henry Miller he had created. He was not a character but a soul—he would be various.

He was. Not just a *débrouillard,* but a poet; not just a splenetic vision but a prophet; no mere caricaturist, rather a Daumier of the written line; and finally not just master of one style but the prodigy of a dozen. Miller had only to keep writing *Tropic of Cancer* over and over, and refining his own personality to become less and less separate from his book, and he could have entered the American life of legend. There were obstacles in his way, of course, and the first was that he was not publishable in America—the growth of his legend would have taken longer. But he had something to offer which went beyond Hemingway. (pp. 2-4)

Miller is the other half of literature. He is without fear of his end, a literary athlete at ease in earth, air, or water. I am the river, he is always ready to say, I am the rapids and the placids, I'm the froth and the scum and twigs—what a roar as I go over the falls. Who gives a fart? Let others camp where they may. I am the river and there is nothing I can't join.

Whereas, Hemingway's world was doomed to collapse so soon as the forces of the century pushed life into a technological tunnel; mood to Hemingway being a royal grace, could not survive grinding gears, surrealist manners, . . . and electric machines which offered static, but Miller took off at the place where Hemingway ended. In *Tropic of Cancer,* he was saying— and it is the force of the book—I am obliged to live in that place where mood is in the meat grinder, so I know more about it. I know all of the spectrum which runs from good mood to bad mood, and can tell you that a stinking mood is better than no mood. Life has also been designed to run in the stink.

Miller bounces in the stink. We read *Tropic of Cancer,* that book of horrors, and feel happy. It is because there is honor in the horror, and metaphor in the hideous. How, we cannot even begin to say. Maybe it is that mood is vastly more various, self-regenerative, hearty, and sly than Hemingway ever guessed. Maybe mood is not a lavender lady, but a barmaid with full visions of heaven in the full corruption of her beer breath, and an old drunk's vomit is a clarion call to some mutants of the cosmos just now squeezing around the bend. It is as if without courage, or militancy, or the serious cultivation of strength, without stoicism or good taste or even a nose for the nicety of good guts under terrible pressure, Miller is still living closer to death than Hemingway, certainly he is closer if the sewer is nearer to our end than the wound.

History proved to be on Miller's side. Twentieth-century life was leaving the world of individual effort, liquor, and tragic wounds for the big-city garbage can of bruises, migraines, static, mood chemicals, amnesia, absurd relations, and cancer. Down in the sewers of existence where the cancer was being cooked, Miller was cavorting. Look, he was forever saying, you do not have to die of this crud. You can breathe it, eat it, suck it, fuck it, and still bounce up for the next day. There is something inestimable in us if we can stand the smell.

Considering where the world was going—right into the World-Wide Sewer of the Concentration Camps—Miller had a message which gave more life than Hemingway's. (pp. 5-6)

[Miller's] legend, however, was never to develop. With his fingers and his nose and his toenails, he had gotten into the excrements of cancerland—he had to do no more than stay there, a dry sardonic demon, tough as nails, bright as radium. But he had had a life after all before this, tragic, twisted, near to atrophied in some of its vital parts, he was closer to the crud himself than he ever allowed. So he had to write himself out of his own dungeons and did in all the work which would follow *Tropic of Cancer,* and some of the secrets of his unique, mysterious, and absolutely special personality are in his later work—a vital search. We would all know more if we could find him.

Miller is not a writer whose life lends itself to clear and separated aesthetic periods, for it is characteristic of him to write in two directions at once. Even *Tropic of Cancer,* which is able to give the best impression of a single-minded intent, still presents its contrast of styles.

Nonetheless, there is some pattern to his life. Miller has his obsessions, and they are intense enough for him to spend a good part of his aesthetic career working them out. If there is a gauge which separates the artist from everybody else who works at being one, it is that the artist has risen precisely from therapy to art. He is no longer fixed at relieving one or another obsessional pressure on the ego by the act of expressing himself. The artist's ultimate interest is to put something together which is independent of the ego; such work can make you feel that you are traveling through that fine and supple mood we may as well call the truth. *Death in Venice* or *Daisy Miller* has that quality, and *The Red Pony* by Steinbeck. *Breakfast at Tiffany's* by Truman Capote will offer it and Katherine Anne Porter's *Noon Wine.* There are a hundred or rather a thousand such pieces of literature and they are art. It is not to say that they are the greatest achievements of writing itself—nothing of Dostoevsky, for example, could fit such a category of art; indeed it may be said that all of Dostoevsky is therapy, except that he elevated the struggle from his ego to his soul, and so we can all partake of the therapy. Forever beyond art, happily, is genius.

On this herculean scale of measure, if considerably below Dostoevsky, can Miller be found. His life impinges on his work ceaselessly, indeed his relation to the problems of his own life is so unremitting yet so scatterbrained that it is as if life is the only true spouse Henry Miller ever had. A crazy spouse, of course, a confirmed nitwit in her lack of stability. He can never feel calm enough to live in the world of art. In this sense, everything Miller writes is therapy. No American author, not even Thomas Wolfe, emits so intense a message that the man will go mad if he stops writing, that his overcharged brain will simply burst. It is as if Miller was never able to afford the luxury of art—rather he had to drain the throttled heats of the ego each day. Yet his literary act takes on such intensity that we are compelled to awe as we read him. Awe can be a proper accompaniment to great art.

Never pausing to take a breath, it is as if Miller creates art as a species of spin-off from the more fundamental endeavor which is to maintain some kind of relation between his mind and the theater beyond his mind which pretended to call itself reality.

That he was successful is part of his greatness. Most souls who go in for literary self-expression to relieve their suffering end on a treadmill. As they relieve themselves so do they repel readers. Excrement is excrement even when its name is therapy. But Miller brought it off. His product transcended itself and became literary flesh. What he did was therapy in that he had to do it, but it rose above every limitation. Maybe it is because he kept one literary grace—he never justified himself (which is the predictable weakness of all therapy), rather he depended on a rigorous even delighted honesty in portraying his faults, in writing without shit, which is to say writing with the closest examination of each turd. Miller was a true American spirit. He knew that when you have a nation of transplants and weeds the best is always next to the worst, and right after shit comes Shinola. . . . So he dived into the sordid, and portrayed men and women as they had hardly been painted before. (pp. 7-9)

Miller captured something in the sexuality of men as it had never been seen before, precisely that it was man's sense of awe before woman, his dread of her position one step closer to eternity (for in that step were her powers) which made men detest women, revile them, humiliate them, defecate symbolically upon them, do everything to reduce them so that one might dare to enter them and take pleasure of them. . . . [According to Miller, men] look to destroy every quality in a woman which will give her the powers of a male, for she is in their eyes already armed with the power that she brought them forth, and that is a power beyond measure—the earliest etchings of memory go back to that woman between whose legs they were conceived, nurtured, and near strangled in the hours of birth. And if women were also born of woman, that could only compound the awe, for out of that process by which they had come in, so would something of the same come out of them; they were installed in the boxes-within-boxes of the universe, and man was only a box, all detached. So it is not unnatural that men, perhaps a majority of men, go through the years of their sex with women in some contract with lust which will enable them to be as fierce as their female when she is awash in the great ocean of the fuck. As it can appear to the man, great forces beyond his measure are calling to the woman then.

That was what Miller saw, and it is what he brought back to us: that there were mysteries in trying to explain the extraordinary fascination of an act we can abuse, debase, inundate, and drool upon, yet the act repeats an interest. It draws us toward obsession. It is the mirror of how we approach God through our imperfections, *Hot,* full of the shittiest lust. In all of his faceless characterless pullulating broads, . . . in all the indignities of position, the humiliation of situation, and the endless presentations of women as pure artifacts of farce, their asses all up in the air, still he screams his barbaric yawp of utter adoration for the power and the glory and the grandeur of the female in the universe, and it is his genius to show us that this power is ready to survive any context or any abuse. (pp. 17-19)

Norman Mailer, "Henry Miller: Genius and Lust, Narcissism," in American Review, *No. 24, April, 1976, pp. 1-40.*

D. C. KIERDORF

It is not surprising that Henry Miller, now in his 87th year, should write [*Book of Friends*], a volume about his earliest childhood acquaintances. Since *Tropic of Cancer* in 1934 he has been composing an extended autobiography in reverse; a life-long journey, as it were, back to his own beginnings. True, there have been digressions into the present, but the meat of his work, [*Tropic of Cancer, Tropic of Capricorn*], and *The Rosy Crucifixion,* are the story of his formation, his becoming a person and a writer, starting with his time in Paris and wandering, in this volume, back as far as his childhood in Brooklyn's 14th ward before the turn of the century.

Book of Friends does not have the urgency that makes *Tropic of Cancer* read like a juggernaut gone out of control. This latest book is a ramble, or rather the prolonged revery of an old man sitting on his front porch and reminiscing about his youth; taking time to reflect, to savour the smells and flavours, to consider certain points of particular or no interest, and to regale the listener with stories, funny stories, embarrassingly sentimental stories, pointless stories. This is a book for those already converted to Miller who wish to hear him spin a few yarns.

He claims that these memories of his childhood are more vivid, more 'real', than what he can recall of yesterday. It is as though he were on a time continuum that is running in the opposite direction of normal. If he is with us for another five years he will probably produce a volume of reminiscences of his life in his mother's womb.

It is surprising, considering how many volumes of autobiography he has filled, how unremarkable Miller's life has been. He is the son of a tailor who was neither wealthy nor poor, and his friends were the everyday creatures of the street, a street which Miller describes as, 'wide open like a corpse just dissected.' In these pages you may search and search and find nothing profound. Certainly you will not find any revelations into Miller's formation as a writer. That is unless you count the episode with his friend Jimmy.

Jimmy Pasta wanted to be president but his political ambitions were frustrated by his basic honesty. Nevertheless he did eventually end up working in the city administration and, finding Miller destitute on the street one day, gave him a job which provided breathing space at the right time. It was in Jimmy's office that Miller sat down one night and planned his literary career.

If that career has been like one long digression it is because essentially Miller has no point to make. By this I do not mean that he has nothing to say. His work is, he says, to 'imitate life', to chronicle the events and impressions which formed him as a person. By fixing himself firmly in the centre of his narrative and avoiding the devices of literature he has made limitless digression permissible. Nothing can be regarded as straying from the point because all experience is relevant.

He wishes to demolish the boundary between 'art' and life. The greatest artists have never written a word, never applied brush to canvas. Living is the highest art and if one allows oneself to be diverted into scribbling or daubing the basic quality of living will suffer for it. This urge to create works of art, finished dead items, will come between the artist and the immediate substance of life itself, and it is this substance, the essential ordinariness of life, which Miller celebrates. (pp. 102-03)

In his excellent essay, "Inside the Whale", Orwell remarks that the sensation for the reader of Miller is not one of understanding but of being understood. One experiences the minor ecstasy of *recognition*. Miller is writing about the average Joe and is more interested in the daily details of life than the great social and political issues of the day. He has recognized that most of our time, whether we are saint or devil, millionaire or mendicant, genius or fool, is spent on those simple acts which we must all perform to live. Eating, sleeping, fucking, breathing, excreting, waiting for things to happen. These things are the real substance of our lives and the common experience that binds us together. It is in his attention to these details, his acceptance of them, that he has made it seem extraordinary and has elevated the commonplace with a sense of wonder. (p. 103)

[Miller's] championing of life over 'art' has its unfortunate effects. Although he has a sure command of the language, he has produced a fair amount of dross. No artist, writer, painter, musician or whatever can ignore the demands of his medium with impunity. Miller is chronically careless when he writes and the results are occasionally painful. In *Book of Friends* there are sentimental, repetitive and sloppy passages which would have been better left out. In *Cancer* he announced that he wasn't interested in perfecting his thoughts, that he had no intention of rewriting anything. He could not have had much realistic hope that it would ever appear in print and he was alive with the joy of being able to write. That artless spontaneity, which occasionally leads Miller to compose passages of embarrassing amateurishness, also enables him to reflect the joyous radiance of life that only he, among living authors, can reproduce. (p. 104)

> D. C. Kierdorf, "Looking Back," in London Magazine, n.s. Vol. 18, No. 11, February, 1979, pp. 102-04.

LAWRENCE J. SHIFREEN

The one hundred books and pamphlets Miller wrote will certainly provide an important legacy when they are finally understood. For this major author is still considered a pornographer. While the writings are certainly obscene, one must understand that sex is a device that Miller used to satirize American self-righteousness; it was his express purpose to shock the reading public and, thereby, to make them aware of "reality."

Sex became the focus of Miller's work because he hoped that an accurate depiction of American society would help to undermine the country's long standing social, moral, and religious taboos. Once this aim was accomplished, Miller believed, people would gain an increased self-awareness and cultural understanding. To actively promote his position, Miller began writing a series of works—*Tropic of Cancer, Black Spring, Tropic of Capricorn,* and *The Rosy Crucifixion* trilogy.

Therefore, while Miller always claimed that he was apolitical, it is obvious that he was one of the most socially concerned writers of the century. It was his desire to educate people about themselves and about their world. In such essays as **"Glittering Pie," "Mademoiselle Claude," "Money and How It Gets That Way,"** and **"Let Us Be Content with Three Little Newborn Elephants,"** Miller studies various aspects of American society, focusing primarily on the individual-society split and on the subjects of personal freedom and social conformity within American society. In short, Miller is a moralist and a preacher. In fact, his preaching makes many of his essays appear dogmatic and all too literal. This criticism can certainly be levelled at such collections as *Sunday After the War, The Cosmological Eye, Stand Still Like the Hummingbird,* and *The Wisdom of the Heart.*

The best of Miller's works are the early novels. Written in the style of the "storyteller" (a word Miller himself used to describe the writings of such favorite authors as Sherwood Anderson and Isaac B. Singer) [*Tropic of Cancer, Tropic of Capricorn*], and *Black Spring* allow Miller to recapture two decades (the 1920's and the 1930's) in a way that none of his contemporaries was able.

Yet depicting reality undercut Miller's career, since the American public was not ready for the frank depictions of sex found in these works and wished to have "realism" rather than "reality." One readily sees why Singer and Saul Bellow have won Nobel Prizes for Literature while Miller, a man who did more to promote literary freedom throughout the world than any of his contemporaries, remains a literary outcast. For his efforts Miller was persecuted and his books banned throughout the United States and in such other countries as France, England, Germany, and Japan.

Depicting life too realistically shocked Miller's readers; rather than asking what Miller was trying to do in his writing, people dismissed the author. It is too bad that these men and women could not look past the works' sexual explicitness and realize that Miller provides an accurate account and is a historian attempting to recapture his times. These accounts of the 1920's and the 1930's are major contributions to American Literature according to Norman Mailer who suggests that *Tropic of Capricorn* provides one of the best accounts of New York in the Twenties and that *Tropic of Cancer* captures the flavor of Paris in the Thirties.

It is clear from Mailer's statement that Miller's fiction moves beyond the novel and combines fact (history) with fiction. For this reason I consider Miller the first writer of Twentieth Century *Faction*. Miller took the fictional techniques he had learned from reading and combined them with the story of his life and times. The result is a personal and societal history that affords both a study of the individual and of his society in the Twentieth Century.

It is extremely important to realize that the roots of Miller's writing are grounded in American Literature—not in Eastern or European traditions, as some readers argue. In fact, his works have the vision of his Transcendental predecessors—Emerson, Thoreau, and Whitman. They also incorporate the humor traditionally associated with the "Southwest Humorists" like Twain and use satire as a means of dismissing American propriety, much the same device that Benjamin Franklin employs in his *Autobiography*.

Yet, for all of these ties to the American literary tradition, Miller has been called a pornographer because he wrote about a world that none of his contemporaries dared to discuss. Depicting sex and society accurately and graphically allows Miller to explore such conflicts as those between sexual drives and morality and between basic human nature and society. His vision of his world offers a psychoanalytical perspective that demonstrates Miller's ties with Otto Rank. His study explores society's effect on the individual with a clarity and perception that is lacking in Gertrude Stein's language experiments, that is missing from Ernest Hemingway's masculine existentialism, and that cannot be found in F. Scott Fitzgerald's romanticism. Miller is truly the first American writer to depict sex in an open manner and to create a literary revolution in the 1960's.

To retaliate against societal abuse, Miller uses satire to criticize his country's moral standards. In fact, his aim becomes one of "cleansing" his country when he speaks of destroying American cultural taboos. . . . (pp. 2-5)

Hatred for America's lack of creativity led Miller to undermine his country's literature and, indeed, to attempt to destroy the novel as we presently know it. This assassination was first suggested in 1934 in *Tropic of Cancer* which was written as an "anti-novel" (a form that has been wrongly attributed to the 1960's and to such writers as John Barth, Thomas Pynchon, and Donald Barthelme). In fact, *Tropic* is the first American anti-novel, a vehicle used to prophesize a new type of historical novel. (p. 5)

The problem Miller saw in American writing was that it lacked the vitality of life, and he determined to capture life in his novels. (p. 6)

[Miller] was realistic in his appraisal of history and human nature. His desire to depict man as he had never been portrayed before shows Miller's attempt to explore the many facets of the human being. To better explore his subject, Miller created a first person narrator whose life, at times, paralleled Miller's own life in Paris and in Brooklyn, and who, at other times, was nothing more than a fictional creation. The persona was used as a device with which to recount Miller's past adventures; by using the persona as if he were a camera, Miller provided accounts of others, as well as himself. In this manner, the character was better able to depict a depraved culture. Therefore, it is no coincidence that *Tropic of Cancer* described Paris as a filthy city (much like T. S. Eliot's "Wasteland") and that this depiction contradicts Anais Nin's *Diary* which describes Miller's home as spotless. Thus the purpose of Miller's *faction* is to create a new reality which is more accurate in depicting society than is Nin's literal statement.

Miller achieved the distinction of creating a new genre that lacks the pretension of the novel and that looks to real events for its form, content, subject, and meaning. [*Tropic of Cancer, Tropic of Capricorn*], and *Black Spring* created a new American novel that is most certainly the basis for the "New Journalism" of the 1960's. It was Miller, not Truman Capote or Norman Mailer, who established the roots of this new genre and who certainly deserves the distinction of standing next to Herman Melville, William Faulkner, Henry James, and Gertrude Stein; for these are the American writers whose experiments helped to change the form and content of the American novel and who provided us with our literary legacy. Like them, Henry Miller was an author who refused to stand pat and copy his predecessors. Moreover, he refused to write *one* type of work and continued to experiment throughout his career. It is Miller's individualism and efforts that have helped to keep the American novel alive. For this, we owe a debt to Henry Miller. (pp. 6-7)

> *Lawrence J. Shifreen, "Henry Miller's Literary Legacy," in* Under the Sign of Pisces, *Vol. 11, No. 4, Fall, 1980, pp. 2-7.*

JAMES CAMPBELL

Rather than drop out of it, Miller chose to wallow in the brothels and gutters of a world whose atmosphere he believed to be polluted beyond recovery, to swallow it, lock, stock and barrel, and eventually turn the lot inside out. From the beginning of his writing career (*Tropic of Cancer* was written in 1932) he attempted to accomplish a metamorphosis in which the fluid of the gutter and the sewer become placentae nourishing new movement and new life. The outlaw and the sinner, not the

meek, would inherit because their 'sinfulness' is a mere definition of the act of opposing the automaton. Miller's defiance of progress meant going in the opposite direction to all norms, inverting every value of the 'civilized' world. He wrote in *Tropic of Capricorn* that he wanted to go 'exactly contrary to the normal line of development, pass into a super-infantile realm of being which will be absolutely crazy and chaotic, but not crazy and chaotic as the world about me'.

It was in the course of this inversion of society's mores and values that Miller discovered his major metaphor. His use of sex in books, plus his use of taboo words variously descriptive of sexual acts and parts and excretory functions, led to them being banned. (p. 34)

The sexual content was not included merely from a desire to shock—although that may have been part of it—but from a need to stand up against the sterility which was inherent in 'progress', which emanated from the 'smell of burning chemicals' and which also was inherent in the hypocritical puritanism of Western society's values. As a sexual liberator—and if anyone deserves the title, he does—Miller's value lies not in the pioneering of new varieties of sex (nothing in Miller is out of the ordinary, although his descriptions may make it seem so) but in simply owning up to the activity of his bodily functions and to the content of his mind. He was going to say, Look at me, I'm at one with this body which shits, farts, pisses, has erections and emissions, the same as it eats, talks, grows bald; my mind dwells on sex much of the time and I like to practice it as often as possible (though here, if Miller is to be believed, he *was* extraordinary). Miller's use of sex had a liberating purpose in that it sought to examine and to expose taboos, which is also where the subversive aspect of his writing came in. Although he was never overtly political, his anarchy and disregard of all norms and his refusal to acknowledge taboos had an implicit subversive intention.

A society's taboos are its secrets, and by keeping secrets it wishes to keep its members in ignorance, for they are not invited to share the secret which the taboo contains. Therefore, these taboos are inherently divisive and political since those who pretend knowledge of them are in a position to instruct those who do not regarding the taboo's content. By issuing a challenge to the taboo Miller was in effect demanding that this secret be revealed: a secret which was, is, not a secret but a lie: the lie of our society's pretended puritanism.

Therefore, it was necessary for Miller's books to be honest and if the honesty shocked, then so much the better. 'I am writing exactly what I want to write,' he said in a letter to Lawrence Durrell, 'and the way I want to do it . . . I am trying to reproduce in words a block of my life which to me has the utmost significance—every bit of it.' But there must be more to it than this since an anti-romantic tone such as pervades Miller's writing is surely deliberate and self-conscious: it is a strategy in his private guerilla war against hypocrisy and for the establishment of an ethos which subverts 'the smell of modern progress'. The consistency of tone demands the inclusion not only of warts but also syphilitic sores, of body odour and halitosis, of what at first glance appears to be a mild racism (niggers and 'smelly Jews'), xenophobia (he never liked the English) and of course a harsh male chauvinism. Opposition to the prevailing system and the lie of puritanism which clothes it, necessitated going contrary to 'the normal line of development' which in turn necessitated extinguishing any trace of the romantic in himself. The Song of Love, he writes in *Black Spring,* 'gives us the courage to kill millions of men at once just by pressing a button . . . gives us the energy to plunder the earth and lay everything bare'. Even with Mona—in real life Miller's second wife June, whose beloved spectre haunts the pages of *Tropic of Cancer* and is instrumental in determining its tone: a fact too seldom appreciated—he will not allow himself the luxury of the illusion of romance. . . . The anti-romantic attitude made Miller a predictable target for some exponents of the new puritanism, principally Kate Millett who delivered what she imagined to be an attack on him in her book, *Sexual Politics* [see excerpt above]. Miller treats women as things, she claims, and if not things then animals. Such is the perversion of a man who claimed to be undermining the myth of perversity. Millett criminally abuses the liberty of quoting Miller, as Norman Mailer showed in *The Prisoner of Sex*, and she does not discriminate between good and bad sex. Nevertheless, it would be pretentious to say that such a view of Miller's work as Kate Millett's is totally askew. It simply is not the whole story.

It is true that Miller's women do not have sex *lives*—they only have sexual qualities and these emanate almost totally from between the legs. With the usual endearing candour, Miller confessed to an interviewer: 'I love women. Is the fact that I also fuck them without asking their names the great sin? I never treated them as sex objects. Well, maybe I did at times . . .' But to dwell on this 'sin' is to overlook the importance of sex in his books, both as a means of subversion and as a metaphor of birth. The female sex organ is 'a symbol for the connection of all things'. It is the mouth of the stream, the delta, as he once described it: 'I love everything that flows', and the movement is away from all that is redolent of the real obscenity of hypocrisy and away from the smell of gasoline.

Millett is not the only writer to have misrepresented Miller. Gore Vidal wrote that Miller is unaware that 'not only is life mostly failure, but that in one's failure or pettiness or wrongness exists the living drama of the self'. Vidal, unusually, has missed a point of supreme importance about Miller's writings, which is that they begin from the station of failure and that their whole movement is towards a vantage point beyond death. In this respect, too, sex is primary since the purpose of sex is to augment life.

But the anti-romantic in Miller ensures that the actual creation of children not be among his goals (he is most casual about arranging abortions for his women, worried only about the cost), 'life' here pertaining to the already living. Although it is a flatulent book in places, *Tropic of Capricorn* is a great hymn to this 'life-rhythm'.

An interviewer once asked Miller what he thought perversion was. Miller hesitated, wanting but unable to provide an answer; eventually, he laughed it off and said he would have to think more about it. I believe he would have agreed that death is the perversion in his scheme, death among the living: 'Everyone who has not fully accepted life, who is not incrementing life, is helping to fill the world with death.' The ovarian trolley rolls away from death. The other perversion is voyeurism: to bring sex out into the streets by writing frankly about it—also, much of sex in Miller is witnessed by others, usually queueing up—is to negate voyeurism.

By the time Miller's books were legally available in Britain and America, other novels had been written, or were being written, in which sex was present for a purpose, rather than as a mere frill round the edge. To name only some of the more celebrated examples: *Another Country, The Naked Lunch, Last*

Exit To Brooklyn, Portnoy's Complaint; all American, and all employing sexuality as a means of overturning some of society's more fanciful ideas about itself. Burroughs in particular, although he is not the most readable of authors, has exploited this area fruitfully. His characters go berserk in the world of sex as a reaction to the forces of 'Control', copulation conveying—as in Miller—immunity from death. Philip Roth is perhaps more mundane than both Burroughs and Miller, but his opposition to the lie of puritanism is equally firm. He suggests that to the question 'Daddy, what did you do in the war?' the children 'could do worse than read *Portnoy's Complaint*'.

Despite the advances made by Miller and others towards complete freedom of expression, one can only wonder whether the dirty little secret really has been dispelled. Although there is a great deal more sex on display than there was when Miller was writing at his full power in the 'thirties, although it is talked about more freely, the secretive side of sex is still with us. Sex can still be seen to be partnership with filth, with hypocrisy, with the automobile. Although he helped to alter sensibility, Miller remained what he wrote about himself in *Tropic of Capricorn* in 1938, 'a monster who belongs to a reality which does not exist. Ah, but it does exist, it will exist, I am sure of it.' (pp. 35-8)

James Campbell, "Speaking Well of Whores and Henry Miller," in London Magazine, *n.s. Vol. 20, No. 7, October, 1980, pp. 33-8.*

ANATOLE BROYARD

In his foreword to the American edition of *Tropic of Cancer* [see *CLC*, Vol. 4], Karl Shapiro fatuously wrote that there is not a smirk, not a word of exaggeration or boasting anywhere in the book, when almost *everything* is smirk, exaggeration and boasting. It is one of the ironies of American literature that Miller was able to charm the public with his writing about sex because he was so palpably exaggerating, so innocent in his fantasies. His boasts were so pathetically ordinary, his smirk so un-self-conscious, that they immediately found their places as part of the American adolescent dream.

In the 60's, when *Tropic of Cancer* was made available here, Americans were enchanted by the idea of sex without anxiety because they hadn't yet realized how expressive, even enhancing, anxiety can be. The idea that sex could be liberated by mere proclamation, by a miracle cure of superficial promiscuity, was as simplistic as the 30's faith in Communism.

It is only in exposing the comedy of sex, the times when the partners are confused, intimidated or exhausted by the rhetoric and rituals surrounding the act, that Miller is original. In *Tropic of Cancer* he gives a brilliant description of Carl's half-imaginary affair with a rich woman, the "flower pot" letters composed of plagiarized passages that he sends her, his inhibition and delicacy as he becomes an American again in the face of her elegance and refinement.

Miller's straight sexual passages are among the worst part of his work, and they obscure what is best in it. What he liberated or made natural was not sex, but American fiction, which in the 30's and 40's was inhibited by self-consciousness and feelings of literary or social obligation. In the concrete incidents of *Tropic of Cancer,* Miller brought a largely unprecedented naturalness to narrative prose, an intimacy that we had heard only in Céline and in, say, Dostoyevsky's *Notes From Un-*

derground. Miller's autobiographical character anticipated Philip Roth's Portnoy by 35 years.

It wasn't Miller's sexual promiscuity that was remarkable, but his indiscriminate or promiscuous acceptance of life. He gave himself up to it with an abandon that was almost unknown before him in our literature. He was a wonderful *flâneur,* a kind of idle anthropologist, something for which most American writers had no talent or tradition. While his relations to women were self-serving, his real love was Paris. No one has ever described the beauty and the poverty of Paris better than he did. Like Joyce and Proust, he was one of the great poets of the city.

Next to Miller, the other American writers in Paris were mere tourists. Certainly Hemingway and Fitzgerald were. But Miller came as close to Paris as Céline himself. Though not as bitter as Céline, who was after all a slum doctor, Miller was not indifferent to the ugliness and brutality of Paris life among the poor. But he saw their poverty posed against the world's most beautiful city, while the poverty and sadness of American life were mocked by the sterile boast of the modern.

Miller expatriated our literature, taught us to see ourselves in what Kenneth Burke called "a perspective by incongruity," transplanted into foreign soil. Though Orwell prissily complained that Miller's characters were idlers, Van Norden, Carl and Fillmore in *Tropic of Cancer,* as well as Miller himself, were American picaresques, would-be heroes going the other way, like Wrong-Way Corrigan—not west, but back to Europe, as if their ancestors had forgotten something there that American writers had to go back and retrieve.

"A voice, a friendly American voice without humbug," Orwell said, but it was only half-true. There was in Miller's style a great deal of humbug: metaphors crawling like bedbugs, Joycean acrobatics, Célinesque snarls, Rabelaisian runs, Whitmanesque *longueurs* and worst of all the cracker-barrel philosophizing that suffocated the later novels.

It's as if Miller believed what was said about him and saw himself as a gargoyle atop Notre Dame, frightening away evil spirits. He began to bluster about life as he blustered about sex. He fell from a magnificent *flâneur* to a mere street-corner evangelist.

> *Anatole Broyard, "The Tropic of Miller," in* The New York Times Book Review, *May 9, 1982, p. 39.*

RALPH B. SIPPER

That *Opus Pistorum* existed is not in question. Jay Martin, in his definitive biography of Henry Miller, *Always Merry and Bright,* has determined that an indigent Miller tried to write pornography for money in 1940 but failed because his efforts were thought too "poetic." According to his biographer, Miller "farmed out" the job to a female acquaintance "with the suggestion that she simply take the cast of *Cancer* and the Paris scene and run amok with it." The six chapter headings in the published book bear the same crudely suggestive titles ("La Rue de Screw," "France in My Pants," etc.) that Martin cites in his biography. The documentation for these facts resides in unpublished Miller letters now institutionalized.

As things stand, Miller's authorship is neither proved nor disproved, though Martin has informed Grove Press that, in his opinion, Henry Miller did not write *Opus Pistorum.* I can only agree. The book is an uninspired disaster.

Miller could not have written so badly no matter how hard he tried. To believe that this literary ball of fire could have produced such a dull affair is to imagine Fred Astaire stepping all over his partner's toes, to visualize Lena Horne frazzled and dowdy, to conjure up a vision of Mozart composing punk rock.

Nowhere in a morass of unimaginative sexual incidents could I detect anything but the crudest parodying of Miller's writing style. Unfortunately, [due to the publisher's standards] I am unable to quote supportive examples from the text. . . .

The very things Henry Miller railed against during his life—inhumanity, oppression, mechanistic behavior—are here the sustaining structural elements. The sex is vindictive and desperate, devoid of the humor and high-spirited fervor of Miller's Paris books.

Conspicuously absent is any semblance of Miller's inimitable narrative style—the darting flights his free associations would take, the no-looking-back cliff dives into passionate waters that could propel a recondite philosophical aside for pages without in the least abating the reader's interest, the freshness of his first-person voice with its inspired meld of mysticism and Brooklyn colloquialisms, the thundering rhetoric that Norman Mailer found equal to Melville's. Those in search of vintage Miller will find themselves swigging Thunderbird locutions and Muscatel sentiments.

Henry Miller was one of this century's great writers. To saddle his reputation with such a pile of sludge when there is no conclusive evidence that he wrote it is a crying shame.

> *Ralph B. Sipper, "The Proper Attribution of Pornography: A Tropic of Commerce and Controversy," in* Los Angeles Times Book Review, *September 18, 1983, p. 2.*

PAUL E. HUTCHISON

Alf is not much of a hero. He wears the role of middle-aged-expatriot-American-living-in-Paris like a wet seersucker suit. His job is unimportant. His apartment is nondescript. His life is insignificant. He is, in fact, a cliché, a tired character out of a thousand plots who seems to have crawled into *Opus Pistorum* for a rest. But Henry Miller has plans for this worn-out hero, plans which surround him with a crowd of similar clichés and send them all out prowling Paris like a pack of dogs sniffing out sex. Poor Alf gets no rest, but what does it matter? He is not really human. He is, instead, an automaton, the imperfect creation of his master, and Miller uses him in this book with all the subtlety of a battery-powered vibrator. . . .

Grove Press fought successfully in the courts to lift the ban on *Tropic of Cancer* in 1961. It is therefore surprisingly regressive for them now to publish *Opus Pistorum,* a recently discovered pornographic novel written in 1941 when Miller needed money and willingly prostituted himself for a dollar a page. Surely they are not trying to prove the courts were right in banning Miller's works, but that is the impression one is left with after reading this book. For despite Grove Press's lame arguments to the contrary, *Opus Pistorum* is an avowed work of pornography (an affidavit appended to the text acknowledges this) and can only be judged on the relative merits of its chosen genre.

What is good pornography? Put aside your prejudices and consider the question. Good pornography is to writing what the dark side is to the moon. Good equals bad in this cosmology. Rape is good. Incest is good. Bestiality is good. In short, whatever filth can be pumped up from the cesspool of sexual perversion is good. On the other hand, characterization is bad. Plot is bad. Moral awareness is bad. Skillful writing is bad. Simple logic is bad. Judged against these criteria, then, ***Opus Pistorum*** is a work of good pornography. Judged by the wider standards of literature, ***Opus Pistorum*** is garbage. And don't even think about "redeeming social value."

Paul E. Hutchison, in a review of "Opus Pistorum," in Best Sellers, *Vol. 43, No. 8, November, 1983, p. 283.*

John (Clifford) Mortimer

1923-

English dramatist, novelist, scriptwriter, critic, translator, and journalist.

Mortimer, who began his literary career with such realistic novels as *Rumming Park* (1948) and *Like Men Betrayed* (1953), has gained his greatest renown as a playwright. His works make effective use of autobiographical experiences, particularly those relating to his career in the English legal system. As a lawyer, Mortimer has argued for the defense in several freedom-of-speech trials and helped to have government censorship powers over British theater abolished in 1968. As a writer, Mortimer is partial to comedy, believing that it is ''the only thing worth writing in this despairing age, provided the comedy is truly on the side of the lonely, the neglected, the unsuccessful.'' While containing fantasy and humor, much of his work has at its center such serious topics as human rights, the problems experienced by society's outcasts, corruption in the legal profession, and social and political attitudes.

Mortimer unites many of his interests in *The Dock Brief* (1957). In this play, an undistinguished lawyer is chosen to defend a man accused of murder. The lawyer, who has waited all his life for this opportunity, rehearses his defense with his client and fantasizes about the effect that his closing argument will have on the jury. However, once in the courtroom, the attorney is dumbstruck and loses the case. Nevertheless, his client is freed because, according to the judge, the lawyer's incompetence has caused an unfair trial. Such surprise endings are typical of much of Mortimer's work.

Although most of Mortimer's dramas are traditionally constructed, they treat many of the same issues dealt with by his more experimental contemporaries. For example, the failure of communication is a prominent theme in the one-act plays *The Dock Brief* and *What Shall We Tell Caroline?* (1958), among others. Critics often praise Mortimer's one-act plays for their eloquent dialogue and for his grasp of theatrical convention. However, many find his full-length plays less successful because their plots are either too ambitious or too slight for the longer format. Mortimer is praised perhaps most of all for his ability to incorporate humorous autobiographical anecdotes into his work. For example, the play *A Voyage round My Father* (1970) is a witty, sensitive portrait of his father, and *Clinging to the Wreckage* (1982) is an autobiographical account of his various occupations and acquaintances. Mortimer also gained critical acclaim for his script for the television series "Rumpole of the Bailey" and his adaptation for that medium of Evelyn Waugh's novel *Brideshead Revisited*.

In 1983, Mortimer retired from his position as a barrister and subsequently published two books, *In Character* (1984) and *Paradise Postponed* (1985). *In Character* collects interviews with various British celebrities that Mortimer conducted for the London *Sunday Times*. Critics lauded Mortimer for his skill as an interviewer, evidenced by his thoughtful questions and the sensitivity with which he treated his subjects. Aside from the *Rumpole* series, *Paradise Postponed* is Mortimer's first novel in almost thirty years. This social satire begins in 1985 with the death of Simeon Simcox, a wealthy socialist clergy-

© 1987 Thomas Victor

man who has surprised his wife and two sons by leaving his fortune to Leslie Titmuss, a young, opportunistic politician. Through flashbacks, the novel chronicles forty years of the Simcox and Titmuss families, ending with an answer to the questions about Simcox's will. To a large extent, however, the book is a social history of postwar England. Mortimer admitted that he intended to present a political premise: ''[*Paradise Postponed*] is about what we thought we would get after the Second World War—no unemployment, no class distinctions—but never got.'' Most critics agreed that *Paradise Postponed* is an accomplished work and praised Mortimer for his perceptive narrative ability and his exceptional comic talent.

(See also *CLC*, Vol. 28; *Contemporary Authors*, Vols. 13-16, rev. ed.; *Contemporary Authors New Revision Series*, Vol. 21; and *Dictionary of Literary Biography*, Vol. 13.)

FRANCIS WHEEN

Last week I heard John Mortimer being interviewed by Libby Purves on the wireless. I had always assumed that Mortimer's interviews with various notables, published in the *Sunday Times* over the past few years, were tape recorded. I was wrong.

Mortimer told the listeners that a pen and a notebook were his only companions. (p. 26)

Mortimer's fondness for the old technology is a necessary but not a sufficient explanation for this excellence as an interviewer, which shines through his collection of his *Sunday Times* articles [*In Character*]. What really distinguishes Mortimer from his rivals is his sensibility. It is now common practice for quality newspapers to describe almost any interview as a 'portrait' or 'profile'. In most cases, the title is undeserved. But Mortimer is an exception: he arrives at the interview armed with a humane morality of his own and a rare gift for avoiding the obvious.

Here, for example, is how he begins his interview with Tony Benn:

> 'I thought', I said to Tony Benn, 'that we might discuss Christianity. For instance, do you believe in God?'
>
> 'Christianity?' Benn started off with his usual enthusiasm. 'You know the bishops banned Tyndale's translation of the Bible. They didn't want the people to read Christ's social message.'
>
> 'Yes, but you were confirmed in Westminster Abbey. Do you . . .?'

Benn wriggles vigorously for several minutes in this fashion. Finally, at the seventh time of asking ('So you don't believe in God?') Benn gives a straight answer: 'Put it like that', he says, 'no.'

Although that extract may suggest otherwise, it would be wrong to think of Mortimer as a combative interviewer, bludgeoning his interviewees into a full confession. One cannot, for instance, imagine him dishing out the kind of treatment which David Frost gave to Savundra. Even when interviewing ne'er-do-wells, Mortimer is usually generosity itself. This makes his little outbursts of indignation all the more notable. For most of his interview with James 'Christian' Anderton, the chief constable of Manchester, Mortimer is content to let Anderton's thoughts on justice pass without comment. But when the chief constable dwells on the joys of caning, Mortimer can stand no more:

> He had the look of deep and complacent satisfaction which men assume when they speak of having been beaten in childhood.

Yet when one expects Mortimer to be severe, one is usually confounded. Lord Denning reveals that 'I must be one of the few people around who've ever sentenced anyone to death'. Not unnaturally, Mortimer asks how he felt about it. 'Didn't worry me in the least', Denning replies. Even the First World War, in which two of Denning's brothers were killed, doesn't seem to have given him any worries: Denning never questioned the war, because 'the King and Parliament had decided on it. That was all we needed.' Mortimer allows Denning to reveal this moral vacuum without adding any otiose editorial comments. (pp. 26-7)

My one regret about this book is that only three of the 27 interviewees are women. Does Mortimer find women uninteresting? Apparently not: there is a marvellous interview with Angela Carter, forthright and funny, and an astonishing piece about the novelist Catherine Cookson, who grew up in a workhouse. Mortimer says that Cookson 'is the only person out of the many I have interviewed who seems to have spent any time at all worrying about the condition of prisoners. But then she learnt her compassion in a hard school.' Britain is full of women who have been through a hard school; I wish Mortimer would seek out a few more of them.

That grumble apart, I have nothing but praise for this book. As Archbishop Runcie says, when Mortimer is taxing him on the subject of God, 'I still find a lot of trenchant truth in all sorts of people. Even people like you, of course.' Indeed. (p. 27)

Francis Wheen, ''Wire-less,'' in New Statesman, *Vol. 105, No. 2718, April 22, 1983, pp. 26-7.*

RICHARD INGRAMS

The combination of playwright and lawyer is one that serves John Mortimer very well in his new role [of interviewer]. As a playwright he is interested in all kinds of people and is able without the aid of a tape recorder to reproduce the way in which they speak; as a lawyer, he is expert in asking questions, at putting people at their ease and then coaxing them into admissions.

By and large the 27 subjects featured [in *In Character*] reflect Mortimer's own interests; the stage (Olivier, Gielgud); writing (Graham Greene, Dick Francis, Catherine Cookson); the Law (Denning and Anderton). But there are also quite a few politicians and one or two demagogues like Arthur Scargill and Ken Livingstone. A good mixed bag then with plenty of variety; even if it has some of the limitations you would expect of the *Sunday Times*. . . .

One ends up, however, being more interested in Mr Mortimer than most of the people he interviews. He calls himself an 'ageing radical' and obviously feels sympathetic towards the Benns and Livingstones of this world. He is a natural optimist who believes, sometimes a little too much so, in the basic goodness of his fellow men. What he likes about the novels of Dick Francis is their 'decency', a favourite word of George Orwell's, and not a quality that is highly valued nowadays. A surprising thing to those who still perhaps think of John Mortimer as a champion of the Permissive Society, the defender of *Oz* and *Gay News,* is his interest in religious matters. Almost every one of his subjects is asked about his religion. The most personal interviews and for that reason the most interesting are those in which Mortimer ceases to be the advocate of the *Sunday Times* and starts to ask questions because he personally is quite keen to know the answers. There is a distinct touch of the rich young man in the interrogation of Cardinal Hume—'Master, what must I do to inherit eternal life?'—even if the cardinal does not in the end provide any very helpful advice. The most revealing and successful interview, on both sides, is with Graham Greene, whom Mortimer meets very appropriately in a hotel bedroom in Leicester where they both drink whisky out of toothmugs—'Do you think a belief in God is a great advantage to a writer?' . . . 'Oh I think so. I've always thought it was having no belief that makes the characters of Virginia Woolf so paper thin.' How long, one wonders, will John Mortimer be able to maintain his belief in the absurdity of life?

Richard Ingrams, ''Ageing Radical,'' in The Spectator, *Vol. 250, No. 8077, April 30, 1983, p. 25.*

CRAIG BROWN

In the last few years, [John Mortimer has launched a career] . . . as a newspaper interviewer. *In Character* is a collection of these interviews. A public figure, however reassuring, is unlikely to be equipped with the necessary subservience (even if it is a malicious subservience) to interview another public figure. John Mortimer in this book is always stalwartly—one might almost say aggressively—John Mortimer, and he tends to be rather chummy with his subjects. Roy Jenkins is "as always, extremely pleasant"; John Gielgud tells him how much he enjoyed acting in Mortimer's play; Graham Greene asks him whether his eyes get tired writing plays (and gets a full answer). Mortimer seldom edits out his own questions, preferring to dress them neatly in quotation marks, even if the answers that follow fail to match up to their deadly importance. "Do you think we've got less concerned about each other, politically nastier? . . . What do you think about the Falklands affairs, for instance?" he asks Mick Jagger. "A most unnecessary war. And I hate the idea of people dying. English and Argentinian", comes the reply.

Together with detailing exactly what was eaten and drunk during each interview, Mortimer's distinctive journalistic quality is the asking of such crucial questions. He doesn't just ask Robert Runcie, Malcolm Muggeridge and Cardinal Hume whether their parents were religious, he asks computer whiz-kid Robb Wilmot and Mick Jagger as well. No, not really, they both reply. By and large, we learn more of the high drama of Mortimer's own spiritual despair than we do of his subjects. He asks Graham Greene whether he thinks a belief in God is a great advantage to a writer, adding, "I looked at him, and tried to keep the envy out of my voice".

This quirkiness does redeem some of the more boring interviews, and with his most forthcoming, and best, interviewees—in particular, Simenon and Gielgud—Mortimer is content to let his own personality be dwarfed, feeling no need to spring up between each sentence with some question for the prosecution. He can be very witty and astute in his descriptions of the external features of his subjects. Michael Foot has a voice which "varies strangely in volume, so that listening to him can become like hearing someone fiddling with the wireless"; Arthur Scargill looks like "an up and coming officer in the serious crimes squad"; police chief James Anderton "had the look of deep and complacent satisfaction which men assume when they speak of having been beaten in childhood". After he has added a restaurant guide and a thin pamphlet on agnosticism to his canon, Mr Mortimer might feel free to spend all his time as an interviewer in writing about those whom he interviews.

Craig Brown, "Quis and Ego," in The Times Literary Supplement, *No. 4183, June 3, 1983, p. 581.*

WILLIAM DOMNARSKI

[A] probing look into the mind of a defense attorney comes in *Rumpole's Return,* a short novel by John Mortimer, a distinguished English barrister. The novel follows two collections of short stories about Rumpole that were made into television dramas for public television. While the short stories and novel have been labeled as mysteries, they go far beyond that genre because Rumpole, the quick-witted, irreverent barrister, dominates. He wins some puzzling cases with some clever thinking, but the cases themselves remain less important than Rumpole, who is, as he should be, the star.

The Rumpole short stories have a distinct television flavor to them. Mortimer, in the manner of a one-hour television dramatist, adroitly pulls together two or more plot lines reflecting that week's theme. Substance, as a result, often lags behind form in such stories. Some plot developments are contrived, for example, and Mortimer, knowing that each story must have an easily grasped conflict, sometimes alters his characters to fit the needs of the moment.

Writing a novel instead of short stories geared for television adaptation allows Mortimer to present Rumpole as he wants us to see him. When the novel opens, Rumpole is basking in the Florida sun after reluctantly retiring from his chambers in London. His retirement, to his great relief, ends quickly when he returns to assist in a murder case featuring blood stains—Rumpole's speciality—as the key piece of evidence. How Rumpole wins the case, however, matters less than the way he handles life with and without the law. His gleeful exclamations that murder trials provide a bit of fun, as well as his irreverent humor, present only one side of Rumpole, distracting us from his other, serious side. Rumpole is, utlimately, a dedicated barrister, dedicated to both his clients and to the law itself.

Mortimer subtly uses Rumpole's wife, Hilda, to remind us of Rumpole's commitment to the law. On one level Rumpole's strained marriage to Hilda provides comic relief. He refers to her as She Who Must Be Obeyed, for example, and for good reason. She does more than just insist on having the last word—she always gets it. We might think that Rumpole would thrive when he returns to London and spends three weeks by himself before Hilda catches up to him, as he finally has a chance to eat what he wants and to keep a messy house, but amidst this happiness is a symbolic sagging practice. Rumpole, we begin to suspect, is not the same barrister when Hilda is absent because when examined closely she represents what American courts have termed the prosecutorial forces of organized society. Rumpole is a zealous advocate in court, where he can present a defense, because Hilda continually reminds him of what life would be like without the chance to defend oneself from authoritarian forces. Thus Rumpole's commitment to the law is reinforced daily. It is the motivating force in his life.

Mortimer uses Rumpole to tell us more about the law. The lines of poetry that Rumpole so often quotes, for example, reflect not so much his eccentricity as his sense of history, that sense that others before him have encountered the same problems, whatever they may be. Rumpole's sense of history as illustrated through literature can be applied to highlight the traditional obligations involved in upholding the law. The subplot about the attempt to force Rumpole out of chambers and back into retirement, in this regard, takes on additional meaning. Rumpole's eventual triumph over the young, ambitious, and hypocritical barristers urging his exit thus represents the triumph of Rumpole's—and by extension Mortimer's—commitment to the law, complete with its respect for history. (pp. 528-30)

William Domnarski, "Will the Defendant Please Rise," in The Virginia Quarterly Review, *Vol. 59, No. 3 (Summer, 1983), pp. 523-31.*

NICHOL FLEMING

Hats off to John Mortimer. He's gone and done it again! His new novel [*Paradise Postponed*] is a hugely enjoyable saga set in the four decades since the end of the war. The plot fairly canters along at a brisk pace and it is rare to find a page which is not enlivened by a sample of the author's genial wit—whether a sharp piece of observation or a humorous exchange between the characters, and anyone who is a fan of Rumpole on television will know this is an area where Mortimer excels. *Paradise Postponed* is a *roman à clef* of an unusual variety in that it is not the characters to whom one may require a crib to enjoy the story to the full—no one for instance turns out to be based on Cyril Connolly or Brian Howard. The key here belongs to the setting. We are in the Thames Valley. Hartscombe equals Henley, the author's home town. It all fits: the brewery, the regatta and the Leander Club—here named the Hellespont—where 'white haired ex-oarsmen, wearing . . . bright green socks and schoolboy caps . . . together with yellowing flannels and blazers which no longer button across their stomachs, sit on the lawn drinking Pimms and lamenting the decline in rowing.' . . . [Mortimer] scans the area with a perceptive eye that is both amused and affectionate.

The principal protagonists are the Rector of Rapstone Fanner, Simeon Simcox, his wife, Dorothy and their sons, Henry and Fred. The Rector is an enchanting Mortimer creation, a fervent socialist who sees not the slightest contradiction in being well-off thanks to his holding in the brewery and his somewhat muddled left-wing views on urban poverty, South Africa and the bomb. The man is an absolute poppet and therefore everyone is dumbfounded—not least his family—when on his death it transpires he has left his fortune to Leslie Titmuss, the odious local Conservative MP and minister in Mrs Thatcher's cabinet. Titmuss, in the words of his future mother-in-law (a prize bitch herself) is 'an oik'. As a youth he worms his way up through the Young Conservatives by that old ruse of making himself indispensable, then effects a shrewd marriage and so on up until the oik blossoms into the pompous, self-satisfied minister with a ready line in platitudes to match every occasion. . . . So why has dear sweet old Simeon Simcox left his fortune to this card-carrying stinker? It's a whydunit.

The mystery of the will—increasingly perplexing as the book progresses—is merely a plot which Mortimer spins in order to subject post-war England as represented by the area around Hartscombe, its inhabitants and their antics to his wry but not entirely unkind scrutiny. It is of course done with skill. Here we are back in the Fifties: we take our seats in

> a dimly lit jungle of rubber plants, among a lot of people wearing duffel-coats, scarves and beards, listening to the muted music of Cliff Richard and the Shadows, with the photographs of stars on the walls, Tommy Steele, Alma Cogan and Dickie Valentine, and [drinking] 'froffy' coffee out of see-through cups.

Rapture! Again, take the hotel in Hartscombe—before the war a raffish haven for illicit liaisons. Come the Eighties and it has been

> taken over by a motel chain, re-christened Ye Olde Swan's Nest and given piped music, colour TVs in every bedroom, Teasmades instead of discreet rustic chambermaids in black bombazine, an enlarged carpark and the Old Father Thames Carvery.

This is so engagingly written and the reader so keen to hasten on to the next gem that he does not pause to ponder if it is not also perhaps a shade over the top.

We observe in flashback the careers of the two Simcox brothers, first as children, then as pupils at their freezing public school—though not so cold as to deter the inmates from 'the usual thing'—and known in the school's jargon as 'jumping too low at leap frog'. Henry's first novel, *The Greasy Pole*, becomes a 'property' and carries him to Beverly Hills ('. . . a title like that must give serious offence to an ethnic minority,' remarks his producer.) His brother, Fred, . . . settles down to playing jazz and to becoming a doctor.

The brothers fall out over whether to contest their father's will, Fred being against on the grounds that they will have to prove their father to have been insane. Your reviewer aches to be able to claim to have twigged the motive behind the will but, in spite of the clues scattered by the author, has to admit to having flunked it.

> Nichol Fleming, "Rapture in Happy Valley," in The Spectator, *Vol. 255, No. 8202, September 21, 1985, p. 29.*

JONATHAN KEATES

There is so obviously too much of everything [in *Paradise Postponed*] that the tale of what happens when a clergyman's will sows discord in the family ducks discreetly from view amid the opulence of sociological detail, aided by a pace whose somnolent leisureliness would do credit to a Mudie's three-decker.

Few writers are better equipped than John Mortimer to catalogue the minutiae of postwar England, working-class Toryism, demos in Grosvenor Square, Gardeners' Question Time, Fairy Liquid, Mateus Rosé, Goose Green, you name it. A certain kind of indignant Orwellian *amor patriae* gives a fine acerbity to some of the laughter, and there is now and then a glimpse of that radiantly compassionate sense of the ridiculous which is Mortimer's strongest suit. But neither the comedy nor its actors ever quite manage to start from the page with sufficient life to engage us.

> Jonathan Keates, "Creaking Floorboards," in The Observer, *September 22, 1985, p. 27.*

D. J. ENRIGHT

One of the epigraphs to John Mortimer's new novel [*Paradise Postponed*] is Auden's lines about 'the dangerous flood of history, that never sleeps or dies'. The history in it, extending from the end of the war to the present, is less a flood than a small whirlpool with its tail in its mouth, the promised New Jerusalem having been sucked out of sight at an early stage.

Simeon Simcox is a socialist rector, the bane of his bishop and (some think) a bit of a saint. He keeps a small bust of Marx in his study and has campaigned for every good progressive cause you can imagine. So why does he leave his money to Leslie Titmuss, an unlikeable little working-class opportunist who, via the Young Conservatives, makes it all the way to Mrs Thatcher's Cabinet?

Although the attempt to contest the will, mounted by the rector's son Henry, doesn't come to court, the litigious and legal preliminaries may bring *Bleak House* to mind. But the novel's ending, as two of the nicer characters, chastened by experience, come together in a beech wood, is strongly reminiscent of *Great Expectations*. Mortimer's story is indeed one of great expectations largely unrealised: the earthly paradise fails to materialise, and the rector's money is found to be fool's gold. (p. 28)

The social history of the period is neatly docketed: Macmillan's 'never had it so good', Dr Stephen Ward, the Singing Nun, the property boom, the property slump, the three-day week, Goose Green and Greenham Common; and there is plenty of good uncomplicated fun as well as what, though the author leaves it unsignalled, we take as satire. In Rapstone Valley 'a solitary jogger is the only outward sign of urban pollution', and common criminals explain themselves in the language of social workers and psychiatrists. Mortimer's plotting is both ingenious in the extreme and watertight, all the loose ends tied up firmly in the long-awaited event, with a few sardonic twists thrown in.

The lefties are mocked as futile, quite explicitly, and quite explicitly the righties are obnoxious and self-seeking. At the same time, but not always convincingly, Mortimer manages to find an element of good in most of his characters. Henry Simcox is the notable exception; the author just can't stand him. Otherwise no one is hated very much, and—apart perhaps from England, or a Platonic idea of England—no one is loved very much. Whether devil or saint, each gets his or her due. That trying clergyman Simeon is posthumously revealed as shrewder and more human than he seemed. (pp. 28-9)

Though he has a more substantial story than is common in contemporary fiction, Mortimer doesn't have Dickens's density or depth of characterisation, and he doesn't really need Dickens's leisureliness and length. All the less so since he lacks Dickens's strength of feeling. His posture is that of a judge, a very decent one no doubt, dispassionately—most un-Rumpolishly—presenting the facts in the case but careful not to influence the jury. *Paradise Postponed* is, I suspect, just a little too judicial for its own good. (p. 29)

> D. J. Enright, "Green and Pleasant Land," in The Listener, *Vol. 114, No. 2929, October 3, 1985, pp. 28-9.*

PAT ROGERS

The historic span of *Paradise Postponed* is that of post-war England, as witnessed chiefly by the family of a fashionable left-wing cleric named Simeon Simcox. The story looks back from his death in 1985 and, neatly and undemandingly, intertwines events of the past forty-odd years. This family saga side works comparatively well, and John Mortimer could properly have been content with exploring his Thames Valley Forsytes in their several roles. But a demon whispered to the author that a chronicle of the nation was called for, and so we get periodic anatomies of Britain dropped into the book without much reference to anything else going on. As a result, the decent truth of Mortimer's observation is overlaid with unconvincing passages, asserting how representative these people all are. They *are*, but that is exactly the trouble, and something a more skilful artist might have suppressed.

As it is, the author's genuine talent for farce and comic anecdote is here laid aside in favour of humdrum versions of instant historiography: 'It was the end of the sad Seventies, a decade whose contributions to history, the Watergate scandal, President Carter, hot pants and the skateboard, vanished from the memory more quickly than a Chinese dinner.' The main characters are pre-packaged and fill their allotted space in the narrative with a depressingly perfect fit: the irritable elder son,

Henry Simcox, for example, who is described in the accompanying publicity hype as 'an angry young man turned crusty old Blimp' (the sad thing is that what we see of him in action doesn't add to this journalistic shorthand or make it seem an inapt idiom). At the centre of the book's intrigue is Leslie Titmuss, a working-class lad who ends up as a Tory cabinet minister. His background is evoked with wincing distaste. . . .

Potentially the most interesting areas of the book are those surrounding the younger son, Fred, and his lover Agnes. Fred is a doctor, a jazz fan with the awful traditional pieties of the days of New Orleans revivalism; Agnes an irresolute and impulsive girl who ends up marrying the wrong man (Henry, who is depicted as being wrong for anyone) and later catering for high-class dinner-parties in the region of Chelsea. Nobody ever travels north of Watford (except to study at Cambridge), though they zoom back and forward on the Los Angeles shuttle. Mortimer is guiltily aware of this, and makes characters with a conscience refer to their privileged location: but the fictional prospect of Britain remains irredeemably Home Counties in tone and perspective. Mortimer's narrative stance makes him oddly a part of the cultural history he purports to recount. (p. 18)

> Pat Rogers, "Street Wise," in London Review of Books, *Vol. 7, No. 17, October 3, 1985, pp. 18-19.*

ANDREW HISLOP

John Mortimer would, perhaps, not be the best of Prime Ministers but he would make a very nice God. A novel is a fair test of an author's suitability for ordering human affairs and *Paradise Postponed,* Mortimer's first for many years, is a delightful moral tale of post-war English society—told with much humour, cynical but affectionate, detached but with the insight of a game participant in the farce.

Mortimer plays God like the rare soul he is: an English liberal. He refuses in *Paradise Postponed* to exploit the omnipotence of the novelist. There is no intrusive narrator, certainly no stream of consciousness. Description is economical. The abundant dialogue is witty and poignant and many scenes end with a punchline. The structure of the plot with its flashbacks is of central importance. In short, this is the work of a very skilled comic dramatist. . . .

Mortimer has always had much fun with the comic embarrassment of even credulous Englishmen when confronted with a prospect of the divine. In his play *Fear of Heaven,* two Englishman think they have already reached the other side when they wake up in an Italian hospital on the ceiling of which is a Renaissance painting of Paradise and God's big toe. In another play, *Prince of Darkness,* two trendily doubting clerics are led to believe that a miraculous multiplication of loaves and fishes has taken place in a rectory fridge.

Paradise Postponed opens with the dying Rector of Rapstone Fanner embarrassed by a dream of "God on a cloud, a sort of electric light bulb behind his head. He was actually busying himself . . . judging people!" Simeon Simcox duly departs to meet his Maker, and his maker then begins his exploration of paradise postponed—postponed not for the lamented dead but for the lamentable living. . . .

Simeon is not lost to us, for he is allowed lengthy resurrections in flash-backs; but the narrative and symbolic crux of the novel is his legacy. He bequeaths his beer money not to his wife, the dreamy but verbally tart Dorothy, or to his sons—Henry, radical novelist turned New Right, old fogey film-writer, or Fred, part-time jazz drummer and unlucky lover turned village doctor—but to Leslie Titmuss, born into service but risen to become a wealthy Conservative Cabinet minister.

As in Mortimer's play *Edwin*—and indeed as in *Howards End*—sexual dalliance is linked symbolically to the future of society, but the solution of the relationship between Simeon and Leslie turns out to be more complex than one at first suspects. Leslie is not a figure to be pitied like Leonard Bast. His progress is due to a willingness not merely to get on his bike but to puncture the tyres of others. He is cynical, greedy, callous—particularly in his treatment of his wife Charlie, the daughter, officially at least, of a landed Tory MP. He is also a prig. You almost sympathize with the ghastly Hooray Henrys who throw him and his hired dinner jacket into the river after a Young Conservative dinner.

If Leslie is the future, no wonder Mortimer dwells so long on the past in the novel. . . .

[But] it soon becomes clear that in *Paradise Postponed* he is chronicling not the sudden rise of a real class of parvenus and the death of an actual way of life—parvenus, like the middle classes, have always risen—so much as a change in socially acceptable myths. The novel's setting—English village life—is itself a myth, one which easily accommodates Simeon's radicalism, for this never threatens the status quo of worlds either mythical or actual.

Leslie is less easy to accommodate. His 'crime'' is not his ambition—an English liberal cannot condemn a chap for just not wanting to be a servant. . . . But he makes a virtue of his unscrupulous methods. He boasts about them, while the old villagers' mythology allowed them to be hypocritically silent about their secret sins. He represents the new brutalism of the *mythology* of Thatcher's England, and it is not to Mortimer's liking.

Whether in reality the Titmusses are more brutal is another question; but the mythological shift is undeniable, even, it seems, in the attitude to God. Simeon is embarrassed by the prospect of the divine but Leslie prays for his selection as the Conservative candidate for Hartscombe and South Worsfield. Mortimer, soft touch that he is, answers his prayers. His thunderbolts are only dusted down to deliver Leslie a shock over the beer money.

> Andrew Hislop, *"Legacy to the Lamentable,"* in The Times Literary Supplement, *No. 4311, November 15, 1985, p. 1294.*

CHRISTOPHER LEHMANN-HAUPT

It would take an individual of considerable parts to resolve even half the complications of *Paradise Postponed*. John Mortimer brings more than the necessary talent and experience to the book. A barrister by training, the author of novels, stories, a memoir (*Clinging to the Wreckage*), film scripts and dramatic works for the stage, television and radio, and of course the creator of the popular Horace Rumpole *Rumpole of the Bailey* and so forth), he reveals on every page of his novel a sense of the absurd, a shrewd eye for human foibles, and an infallible sense of comic timing.

His vivid style is evident in the most casual phrases. The dying rector is "tall and thin, looks which gave him, in the course of his lifetime, the appearance of a rather bothered eagle."

His dialogue is charmingly eccentric: "Ha! Ha! Ha! Ha! Ha! Ha . . . le . . . lu . . . Hallelujah!'' Dorothy Simcox says apropos of nothing to a visiting solicitor whose passion for choral singing she happens to hold in contempt. "Taking forever just to sing one word! On and on and on until everyone dies of boredom. Why couldn't you just say 'Hallelujah' and get it over with, like a normal person?''

He juggles his plot adeptly back and forth in time, fast enough to be farcical yet slow enough to lend substance to his characters. Just at the point where many social satires of this sort begin to pall and grow static, he effortlessly shifts the plot's focus to the mystery of Mr. Simcox's will, thereby deepening the reader's involvement and sparing him the least moment of tedium.

Most engaging of all, the author never lapses into outright cruelty. No matter how angry he makes us feel at his characters—particularly the upstart Leslie Titmuss and the loud-mouthed older Simcox brother, Henry—he never cuts them up so badly that they cease to be human and ultimately sympathetic. Indeed, everything about *Paradise Postponed* is balanced. No matter how outlandish, the characters read true psychologically, and retain our affection. The most farcical developments are germane to the social satire. Even the solution to the mystery is all at once comic, morally satisfying and humane.

There is nothing esthetically radical about *Paradise Postponed*, nothing even adventuresome. If it captures contemporary England, it does so in traditional style. But it is so neatly put together that you can shake it and hammer it and never hear a rattle. It keeps its shape and it stays alive. And if it is true, as Simeon Simcox promised, that nothing was as simple as it looked, what did happen nonetheless retains a certain pastoral appeal. In that small sense, paradise was not postponed.

> Christopher Lehmann-Haupt, *in a review of "Paradise Postponed,"* in The New York Times, *March 24, 1986, p. C17.*

WENDY LESSER

Ever since Virginia Woolf and James Joyce dynamited the conventional English novel, those of us who love the old Victorian-Edwardian form have been looking for a modern-day equivalent. John Mortimer may well have provided one.

Yet *Paradise Postponed* is by no means a throwback to an earlier period of history (a feat of which Mr. Mortimer, who adapted *Brideshead Revisited* for televison, would undoubtedly have been capable). The novel is set firmly in late 20th-century Britain, amid episodes ranging from the imposition of postwar rationing to the 1974 coal miners' strike, from the Mandy Rice-Davies scandal in Parliament to the recent antimissile demonstrations on Greenham Common. But the book has an appealingly old-fashioned quality, inherent in the author's solicitous attitude toward plot, character and language. And even the novel's topicality is itself a kind of Victorianism, since by employing history in this way Mr. Mortimer reverts to a theme rarely found since the days of Dickens, Conrad and E. M. Forster: the idea that private experience only gains its full meaning in the context of public experience. In fashioning an appealing novel from this 19th-century idea, Mr. Mortimer evades both the pitfalls of historical pastiche (as practiced, for instance, by John Fowles and A. N. Wilson) and the limitations of much contemporary fiction. (p. 1)

What [Mortimer] has done in *Paradise Postponed* is to raise the mystery to the level of a serious novel while still retaining a kind of detached amusement that we rarely associate with the word "serious." . . .

The various occupations and preoccupations of the characters—enhanced by the degree to which Mr. Mortimer actively enters the mind of each—offer room for the novel to contemplate a range of subjects worthy of George Eliot. Through Dr. Salter's and Fred Simcox's medical duties, we are exposed to issues of mortality, public service and science versus faith. Simeon's ecclesiastical profession raises concerns about the existence of an afterlife, the connection between faith and good works, and the role of the church in politics. While Mr. Mortimer doesn't take sides as actively as, say, Dickens might have, the question of politics is clearly at the heart of the novel. Whereas the left-wing characters are at worst ineffectually silly, the right-wingers are vicious and consciously destructive. Thus part of the novel's tension stems from our distress at Simeon's money going to the Thatcherite Titmuss.

To allow us the fullest possible appreciation of the novel's intricate emotional twists, Mr. Mortimer runs his tale both forward and backward. That is, after beginning with Simeon's death and funeral in 1985, he rewinds to Fred and Henry in their boyhood in 1948, and then intercuts episodes from the present with past moments leading progressively closer to that present. Like Harold Pinter's similar technique in *Betrayal*, this enables us to know more than the characters without feeling superior to them: it becomes a question of *when* one knows rather than merely *what* one knows. In addition, the technique relies on public events as the necessary temporal signposts, making history essential rather than peripheral to the unfolding of the story. In an epigraph to the middle section, Mr. Mortimer quotes Kierkegaard to justify his method: "Life must be lived forwards, but it can only be understood backwards."

Kierkegaard notwithstanding, *Paradise Postponed* isn't at all pompous about the self-consciousness of its technique. In fact, the novels-within-the-novel written by the rather dislikeable Henry Simcox bear a satiric relation to Mr. Mortimer's own work. Thus one of Henry's most successful novels viciously mocks Hollywood from the viewpoint of an English screenwriter—just as segments of *Paradise Postponed* do. (These Hollywood sections are unfortunately the weakest part of Mr. Mortimer's novel: they come off merely as pale rehashes of Evelyn Waugh and Nathanael West.) . . .

Just as he revives the Victorian novel by updating both its subject matter and its techniques to suit the modern setting, Mr. Mortimer animates the old death-as-a-journey metaphor by making it literal. Moreover, the effect of this linguistic playfulness is both serious and moving.

Throughout *Paradise Postponed* Mr. Mortimer's wry authorial tone steers delicately between sentiment and satire. In his skillful hands, we seem to be viewing the world from a very great distance—far away enough to make even the tragedies slightly comic—while at the same time we are right inside the characters' heads. And Mr. Mortimer's prose is so easygoing, so companionable, that he appears to accomplish this act of literary ventriloquism without moving his lips. (p. 24)

> *Wendy Lesser, "The Rector's Will and Other Mysteries," in* The New York Times Book Review, *March 30, 1986, pp. 1, 24.*

Nicholas Mosley

1923-

English novelist, nonfiction writer, biographer, dramatist, and editor.

Considered one of the most original English novelists to have emerged after World War II, Mosley challenges literary norms through stylistic experimentation. Using disjointed narrative, spare dialogue, and complex associations, Mosley explores the nature of reality, the limitations of language, and the paradoxes of contemporary experience. Critics disagree in their assessment of Mosley's work: while some consider his fiction to be confusing and pedantic, others praise his novels as innovative and engrossing. According to Robert Scholes, "Mosley's writing is a bit 'difficult.' His perspectives are far from ordinary. But he deserves his share of whatever audience there is for genuinely creative fiction at the present time."

Mosley's first three novels, *Spaces of the Dark* (1951), *The Rainbearers* (1955), and *Corruption* (1957), are long, detailed, realistic stories that evidence few of the experimental qualities of his future work. These books introduce Mosley's characteristic examination of human behavior and his pessimistic view of life in England after World War II. While *Spaces of the Dark* and *The Rainbearers* unfold through traditional linear narratives, *Corruption* features shifts in time and narrative voice, elements which become more pronounced in Mosley's later fiction.

Mosley's fourth novel, *Meeting Place* (1962), indicates a distinct change in his style. Whereas in earlier works Mosley had relied on long, introspective sentences and paragraphs, *Meeting Place* employs a simpler sentence structure and an elliptical narrative style, leaving the reader to deduce much unstated information. The tone of *Meeting Place* also marks a departure from that of his previous novels, for this book ends on a positive note, in contrast to his largely cynical early work. *Accident* (1965) and *Assassins* (1966) further the innovations of *Meeting Place*, as Mosley again relates his story through fragmented narrative, examining various notions of reality and the inability of language to convey true meaning and expression. *Impossible Object* (1968) comprises eight seemingly self-contained stories about human relationships divided by brief, surrealistic pieces which complement the themes and ideas of the stories. The reader is left to make connections among the sections of the book and to discover, through multiple narrative viewpoints and interpretations of events, different levels of reality. *Natalie Natalia* (1971), which examines human relationships and the possibilities of language in a more conventional narrative structure, is regarded by some critics as Mosley's finest fictional achievement.

Catastrophe Practice (1979), Mosley's next work of fiction, marks another shift in style and is generally considered his most demanding creation. Composed of three "plays not for acting," three prefaces, a concluding essay, and a short novel, *Catastrophe Practice* displays Mosley's characteristic use of disjointed narrative and themes related to language in an unusual format which many reviewers found puzzling. Thomas Hinde summed up critical opinion of this book by stating: "Reading Mr. Mosley is . . . about as frustrating as reading a long coded

© Jerry Bauer

message to which you do not have the key." The protagonists of *Catastrophe Practice* are also the central characters of three later, more accessible novels: *Imago Bird* (1980), *Serpent* (1981), and *Judith* (1986). These books reinforce Mosley's ambition to better understand and interpret various levels of reality, and they emphasize his belief in the need for liberation from conventions which inhibit perceptions and responses.

In addition to his works of fiction, Mosley has produced several respected nonfiction books. These volumes include *African Switchback* (1958), a travelogue based on an automobile excursion he undertook with novelist Hugo Charteris in 1957; *The Assassination of Trotsky* (1972), about the life of Russian philosopher and political activist Leon Trotsky; *Julian Grenfell: His Life and the Time of His Death, 1888-1915* (1976), a study of the English poet who was killed during World War I and a sociopolitical analysis of the upper-class milieu of Great Britain during that era; and *Rules of the Game: Sir Oswald and Lady Cynthia Mosley, 1896-1933* (1982), a biography of Mosley's parents, members of British Parliament who endured a stormy marriage. Mosley has also written screenplays for the films *The Assassination of Trotsky* and *Impossible Object*.

(See also *Contemporary Authors*, Vols. 69-72 and *Dictionary of Literary Biography*, Vol. 14.)

THE TIMES, LONDON

Like most contemporary young authors, [Nicholas Mosley] is deeply preoccupied with the idea of romantic sensuality; like them, too, he is very good at describing it. *The Rainbearers* is essentially a simple story of a brief love-affair between a married man and a girl which, so the author contends, ultimately enriches the man by showing him for the first time what love can be at the expense, apparently, of the girl's soul. Another girl to whom the man is attracted is irrelevantly a Roman Catholic, and Mr. Mosley wisely refrains from pursuing this hare which is running much too fast for him yet. However, this is a promising book, and its faults, of rhetoric and oversubtle construction, are the faults of youth.

> *A review of "The Rainbearers," in* The Times, *London, October 6, 1955, p. 11.*

VIRGILIA PETERSON

Corruption is not a first novel, but the first by the young British writer, Nicholas Mosley, to be published [in the United States]. Its title, unenticing, is nevertheless apt, though the kind of corruption with which the author concerns himself is unexpected and, like the relationships he delves into, highly equivocal. For this is not a study of such obvious sources of corruption as money or power; rather, it is an attempt to show how the doubting and fearful self becomes, through its very doubts and fears, so corrupted in judgment that it can no longer distinguish between real and unreal either in its relations with the outside world or the world within.

"The hero in my book." Mr. Mosley has explained, "lives in a state of subjective fantasy." How his hero—Robert Croft—got into this state in the first place and what a morass of misunderstandings, not to speak of misdeeds, it led him into and how he finally came to see reality face to face makes the thread of narrative to which the reader must cling as he follows Mr. Mosley into this neurotic labyrinth. . . .

Stylistically, *Corruption* is unusual. A minimum of words (and these so fragmentary and ambiguous that they leave the reader floundering) is exchanged between Robert and the three women, two men and a child with whom he is involved; the action is largely abortive; and it is the lush, symbolic, and often breathtakingly odd imagery and description that give Mr. Mosley's novel not only its climate but its substance. Indeed, the equivocal psychological facts of his story are drowned in the baroque flourish of his embellishments.

> *Virgilia Peterson, "A Man Trapped in a Neurotic Labyrinth," in* New York Herald Tribune Book Review, *January 26, 1958, p. 5.*

RICHARD SULLIVAN

Surging talent all by itself does not necessarily make a good novel; but when unmistakably brilliant writing is combined with a degree of natural insight, the result, as in *Corruption,* is likely to be most impressive. . . .

[The novel] deals with a long, intermittent, desperate love affair. Eventually, like a grievous and irresoluble problem, this affair is not settled but perpetuated by mutual agreement to proceed no further. Not sweet reciprocal indulgence but reluctant yet deliberate separation is the end of this love in one sense and the confirmation of it in another.

The first-person narrator, Robert Croft—a young man still, at the end, in the post-war approximate present—tells his story in four major stages, with some nicely managed flickering about in time, and some stretches of truly lyrical, evocative prose. The novel begins with the name "Kate" and ends with the words quoted of Kate by her son to the narrator: ". . . she sends you all her love." Between beginning and end, beautifully and meaningfully, in climactic order, the four encounters of Robert Croft and Kate Lambourne, his slightly older and very distant cousin, are revealed.

These lovers meet first as children, in dimly forbidden childhood games; they meet again, sexually, when he is 16; after the war and another brief meeting he is named in her divorce suit; years later—in what is the actual time of this novel—they meet again, in Venice, to rediscover themselves in terms of all the intervening connivances and hatreds and deceptions. Finally they separate, presumably forever, though love has been clarified between them, as between the star-crossed. And love has at the end come to mean to them both not corruption but sacrifice.

But corruption is viewed steadily in this novel, as an involvement with self, as a proud and terrible loneliness pretending to be enlightened sensuality. There is, indeed, almost a religious note of compassion and understanding of the titled subject. This is, in essence, a romantic novel; but the romance is not treated in the currently popular naturalistic manner, nor in the traditionally romantic manner. This is romance written realistically, with admirable craft and surging talent. Here, too, is a high degree of the sort of graceful good sense that may occasionally be called natural wisdom.

> *Richard Sullivan, "Behind Love's Mask," in* The New York Times Book Review, *January 26, 1958, p. 5.*

CHARLES J. ROLO

[*Corruption* is a novel] in which a curious *mélange* of strains has produced a distinctly individual work: flawed, but splashed with brilliance. The first part traces, with Jamesian curvatures, the flowering of a Michael Arlenish heroine, Kate Lambourne, a wellborn and soon notorious beauty who appears to be mad and bad—"her specialty was scandal." She is the cousin of the narrator, who is desperately in love with her; and once in his adolescence, once some years later, she gives herself to him only to abandon him inexplicably.

In Part Two, the prose shifts into a rhythm which is startlingly Faulknerian (without Faulkner's obscurities), and the author suddenly displays a rich sense of comedy and a ferocious wit. He moves around London Bohemia, bringing into the story a wonderful character called Suzy: a doll at once infinitely demure and disreputable, who, each time she changes lover, is accompanied by a van loaded with her own enormous bed. This whole section is a tour de force—very funny, but serious and subtle in its perceptions.

Part Three carries the narrator to Venice with Suzy; and their involvement with Kate and her sinister Italian lover leads up to a dramatic denouement. Whatever the shifts of tone and style, the novel sustains a strong current of intensity. All in all, it is an attractive and out-of-the-ordinary book. (pp. 85-6)

> *Charles J. Rolo, in a review of "Corruption," in* The Atlantic Monthly, *Vol. 201, No. 2, February, 1958, pp. 85-6.*

THE TIMES, London

[Nicholas Mosley] has always been caviare to the general, so perhaps the plaintive and ludicrous note on the jacket of *Meeting Place* is understandable—"Few people will be able to read this without feeling that they have personal experience of such things as trying to bring rival gangs of teenagers together . . . being a pretty and successful woman journalist . . . attending a debate in the House of Lords . . . drifting around with television producers . . ." The "few" may rest assured that Mr. Mosley is, on the contrary, writing about one eccentric unhappy man, who some think a saint and others a frivolous upper-class do-gooder. Harry Gates, temporarily deserted by his wife, is tensely concerned with misfits—those who beg a few bob, the ex-mistress who is suicidal, the teenager on probation, his lonely schoolboy son, and most of all, God, who has turned his life upside-down. His worlds clash, because poetry and devout High Anglicanism are not easily reconciled with the raffish insider's commitments, and the clash makes for some disjointed sketchy moments in the novel and a patched-up end. But, as before, much must be forgiven a writer so original, witty, and immensely compassionate—like a kaleidoscope, it is worth holding Mr. Mosley still so that the pattern may settle.

> *A review of "Meeting Place," in* The Times, *London, October 5, 1962, p. 16.*

THE TIMES LITERARY SUPPLEMENT

Meeting Place centres on a rather older man, Harry Gates, separated from his wife, in revolt against the decadent life of his mainly rich relatives and friends, and seeking both escape and possibly salvation by working for a charitable organization which helps misfits and delinquents. At the same time it is a more ambitious novel, more intense—sometimes pretentiously so—and certainly much more difficult to understand.

Partly this is because for a long time the novel does not appear to have any particular sense of direction, and instead we get long passages of Harry's far from lucid intercommuning with his troubled soul, plus specimens of his poetry, intermixed with vignettes of his oddly assorted acquaintances and associates. . . . Partly it is because both the narrative and the dialogue are often extremely inconsequential. Life here exists in a spiritual vacuum; we get the boredom and the horror in full measure. There is no longer any glory left.

> *"Vile Bodies," in* The Times Literary Supplement, *No. 3168, November 16, 1962, p. 869.*

THE TIMES LITERARY SUPPLEMENT

Significantly shorter than Mr. Mosley's four previous novels, *Accident* is far more successful. It explores territory particularly risky to the English novelist: a highly sophisticated, adult world, in which all the grown-up characters are fully aware of the twisted and self-deceiving nature of their motives. As the narrator, a university don, writes, they "know all this now".

The situation explored is one that can best be described as an unholy, sordid and essentially commonplace mess; somehow it has been allowed to happen. The question to which *Accident* is an attempted answer is, Can anything of significance be salvaged from the kind of situation that has come into being in an entirely random manner, through a mixture of deliberate self-indulgence, lust and irresponsibility?

The plot concerns two older men, Stephen Jervis, the married don who is the narrator, and Charlie, the novelist who actually writes the book (although in the person of Stephen), and their relationships with two neurotic younger people, Anna and William, both of whom are Stephen's pupils. Both men make, in different ways, irresponsible use of Anna, and it is partly through their failure to act maturely that William, who loves her, dies in the car crash that opens the book. . . . [The] theme of *Accident,* an ambitious one, is the difference between aspirations and action. The solution it offers, in so far as it may be said to offer a solution at all, is presented in the form of a gloss on the text, "Resist ye not evil". But the element of religion is somewhat conspicuously absent—almost as if it had been cut away with scissors.

Technically, *Accident* is remarkable. Whereas in his former novels Mr. Mosley seemed sometimes to be indulging in obscurity for the sake of obscurity—a reflection of his dissatisfaction with the present capacity of the English novel to explore contemporary life—here he makes a fully coherent attempt to achieve a new form. The texture of the writing itself is deliberately simple; the complexity arises from the way in which the parts are put together—and from the fact, easily overlooked, that "the novelist", Charlie, is in fact supposed to be writing the book.

The very unconventionality of Mr. Mosley's methods will inevitably call to mind the French "anti-novel" and even the *nouvelle vague;* but these methods owe less to such manifestations than to his unusual and paradoxical combination of a highly sophisticated, determinedly "contemporary" and sympathetic awareness of atheistic despair, something that is much in the air nowadays, with an evidently well developed, even doctrinal, Christianity. A slightly manufactured, homiletic air pervades this fascinating and original novel, like a whiff of anaesthetic, chiefly because one feels, Mr. Mosley has tried to push what really preoccupies him into the background. It is more than likely that a writer of such seriousness and with such an impressive equipment to express it, will soon concern himself with the resolution of the paradox that obsesses him.

> *"Exploiting Anna," in* The Times Literary Supplement, *No. 3281, January 14, 1965, p. 21.*

ADRIAN MITCHELL

Mr Nicholas Mosley will never write a bad novel. He is very demanding. [*Accident,* his] story of two friends, a don and a novelist who become to a debatable degree responsible for a car crash in which a student dies, contains no waste paper. He often uses sentences like stepping-stones: the gaps between them may seem incredibly wide at first glance, but you can always get to the other side. His book is highly concentrated— a prose poem, if you like. It deals with the needs of man, especially his need for peace, and sometimes it sounds like a clear cry for help. I admit to a strong prejudice in favour of a writer who can be visionary without being vague, and I believe that tragi-comedy is the most effective approach to the world. *Accident* is seriously witty.

> Adrian Mitchell, *"Clear Cry," in* New Statesman, *Vol. LXIX, No. 1766, January 15, 1965, p. 82.*

TIME

[Iris Murdoch] has put readers on warning that novels by Oxford philosophy dons are apt to baffle as well as entertain. The same warning applies to *Accident,* by Nicholas Mosley . . . , which is about an Oxford philosophy don, and which raises the art of the intellectual tease to the level of mild torture. There is no doubt that in *Accident* a fictional design of subtlety and distinction has been attempted. But it is a literary jigsaw puzzle with perhaps some extra pieces belonging to another design slipped in.

The book seems perversely dedicated to confusion, like Oxford's linguistic philosophy which, from a puritan devotion to clarity, actually makes it very difficult to say anything about anything. Professor Stephen Jervis (and Novelist Mosley with him) struggles against this self-denying ordinance. After all, the intellectual show must go on. This is a novel. It is, the reader is told by one character, not about characters or society, but ''about knowing.''

Knowing what? Picking up clues or philosophic crumbs like a capriciously fed pigeon, the reader will learn that Stephen is married to a beautiful wife whom he loves, that he has two children, and that he does his job more or less well. He is also 40 years old, has problems of identity, and, more specifically, ''can't keep his hands off the girl students.'' It is not really his hands but his irresponsible voyeurism that is Stephen's trouble.

There is an automobile accident. William, an aristocratic undergraduate, is killed, and Anna, another student, is carried from the wreckage by Stephen—who is responsible in no ordinary legal or moral way, but is unhinged by guilt. Glimpses of his previous history indicate that he has enjoyed a sort of vicarious pleasure in the love affairs of his students and friends. He has had a doggish don's weekend in London with a former mistress, an affair that seems to have done no harm; yet, without apparent cause, his wife falls desperately ill in his absence. In one episode, a parody of war is enacted by rich undergraduates at a great country house; the aristocracy, we are told in a blurred Freudian attribution, is good only for causing death—their own and others. There is a fancy-dress party at another country house, once notorious as the scene of diabolic revels.

But these are all enigmas. Nor is the situation made clearer by the intimation that one of Stephen's contemporaries, a freelance careerist of the emotions called Charlie, is the hero's *Doppelgänger.* It is even suggested that the story is Charlie's, not Stephen's; thus, although written throughout in the first person, it should actually be in the second. If so, the moral of the story seems to be that a man cannot be trusted to write his own history, and that even his best friend will have trouble with his obituary. Is the don dead? And who donnit? (pp. 88, 90)

''All about Knowing,'' in Time, *Vol. 87, No. 16, April 22, 1966, pp. 88-90.*

ERIC RHODE

Most of the characters in *Assassins* are distanced; their names, when given, are disclosed reluctantly. Even the prose is tight-lipped. An unrelenting tone is sustained for the best part of the book, enough for the hardiest reader to quail at. The processes working behind it are most obvious at the climax—when a cameraman idly picks up a murder on the screens of a TV van in a way that recalls the shocking yet incoherent transmission of Lee Oswald's death. Nicholas Mosley captures a similar incoherence through his habits of visualising everything, as though writing with a Kodak, and of seldom hinting at anyone's motives (including his own); but the shock of actuality is soft-

ened out of all recognition. Visualisation and concealment are like his clipped and neat choice of words—ways of keeping the reader at arm's length.

The plot doesn't encourage us either. Its concerns are with politics and the present-day, yet it's bathed, incredibly, in an Imperialist glow. Mosley, it seems, isn't making a satirical point about backward-looking politicians: he shares their crankiness, their nostalgia, their refusal to observe. The secret meeting of Sir Simon Mann, a British Foreign Secretary, and Korin, elder statesman of some unnamed Iron Curtain country, is given the world-shattering importance that John Buchan once ascribed to the right interpretation of tide-levels. And Buchan's fascination with conspiracies re-emerges here in the shadow-boxing of mysterious forces, the rather aimless assassins of the title, while his anti-semitism is displaced, fashionably, onto an odious homosexual scapegoat. But then Mosley's view of England is unusual, to say the least: 'England was like poetry; bugles and cattle in a churchyard.' In such an ambience of country-house dottiness Sir Simon appears as no more than harmoniously odd: as silly as the don in a former novel, *Accident,* yet presented, without humour, as a great leader. His voice, we're persuaded, takes on 'a hypnotic lilt' as he praises Talleyrand for his pragmatism, or commends what he's glad to call the eternal verities: 'responsibility is complexity. The recognition of it. Evolution is revolution. This occurs when evil is assimilated. This is not appeasement. The battle now, on a world scale, is nemesis.' Meanwhile Sir Simon's daughter has been kidnapped by, and fallen in love with, a youth commissioned to murder Korin. . . .

The flatness of the writing forces us to take this story literally: we can't read it as an obscure allegory or as a hallucination. It's always controlled, defensive, polite—not grudgingly, but as though Mosley were too diffident to allow his conflicts to surface in public. The occasional violence, I believe, isn't the usual cheap attempt to jack up dead material: it's more a mark of undischarged feeling. Breeding, reserve, protects us from the 'darkness and confusion' within. The point is not to look too closely. And so in theory Mosley's manners and mannerisms suit his theme—which is, I take it, the assumption that the world consists of nothing but chaos beneath its show of appearances. As an apologist for Christian theology, Mosley probably views such a theme with unease: but one of the uses of the novel has always been to let writers test the worth of current ideas against the more precise demands of the imagination. In *Assassins,* though, the imagination never sets up a substantial challenge; appearances remain lifeless because the implied chaos is never directly felt. The theory is neither proved nor disproved.

Eric Rhode, ''Chaos Implied,'' in New Statesman, *Vol. 73, No. 1857, October 14, 1966, p. 553.*

THE TIMES LITERARY SUPPLEMENT

In this interesting but infuriating novel [*Assassins*] Mr. Mosley worries away at a question which might be put thus: is it possible to lead a public life and a private one concurrently and harmoniously or is it inevitable that either the one or the other must suffer impoverishment? He shows us a British Foreign Secretary and his country-house entourage engaged in crucial, detente-producing negotiations with Korin, Communist leader of some Eastern power. Korin has an appropriately ruthless past, and there are many—a student organization in particular—who oppose him.

A youth called Ferec attempts his assassination, but Mary, the lumpish, forlorn fourteen-year-old daughter of the Foreign Secretary, blunders into him while she is out pony-riding and unwittingly defeats his purpose. Ferec, not much older and not much less innocent than Mary, takes her off. The disappearance of the child creates problems and anxieties for the negotiators, held as they are in the unwavering searchlights of publicity. . . .

The novel is thoroughly imagined. It is crowded and detailed, yet Mr. Mosley is able to satisfy the reader that there is no routine padding. The child Mary, awkward, inarticulate, blown here and there by the strong winds of policy, yet demonstrating that there is a sense in which she is somehow stronger than they, makes Mr. Mosley's points for him, and is most movingly realized. The political crowd, burdened between them with the usual mixture of high purpose, low cynicism, careerist opportunism and sheer ineptitude, are also shrewdly observed.

Why, then, with so much to commend in it, should *Assassins* be infuriating? It is really a matter of style. Mr. Mosley refuses to have anything to do with the art of composition. He likes short, jerky sentences. He sticks them down one after another. He is like a literary grocer, dropping dried peas one by one into a paper bag until he has half a pound or so of paragraph. And then a fresh paper bag is reached for and the process renewed. It is all very daunting for the customer.

"The Wise Child," in The Times Literary Supplement, *No. 3374, October 27, 1966, p. 974.*

TIME

Q. Why is it that modern novels have to be different, that they can't just be stories of characters and action and society?

A. We know too much about characters and action and society. We can now write about people knowing.

This is a typically enigmatic bit of dialogue from Nicholas Mosley's recent thriller *Accident,* and it seems to apply even more to his new one, *Assassins,* which is half mystery, half "people knowing." During a top-level international conference, the motherless 14-year-old daughter of the British Foreign Secretary is kidnaped by a would-be political assassin. Her fate is in the hands of three of her elders: the chief government security officer, her father and his secretary, who is also his mistress. The latter is a disturbing woman—passive, manipulative, all things to the weaknesses of all men—seemingly a sister of the wife in Harold Pinter's *The Homecoming.* It is no accident that Pinter adapted Mosley's earlier novel for the movies. For both writers, ambiguity is truth itself. And for Mosley's characters, a mere problem of survival is too simple. The reader who follows the course of *Assassins* to its appropriately absurd end will be rewarded by a sophisticated plot, a cartographer's awareness of English landscape and a wealth of similes that are nearly as good as Mary McCarthy's. But characters, action, society? Hardly. (pp. D10, 100)

A review of "Assassins," in Time, *Vol. 89, No. 24, June 16, 1967, pp. D10, 100.*

THE TIMES LITERARY SUPPLEMENT

An affair between two lovers who are already married, well-to-do, well educated people who take family holidays in North Africa and Italy—this situation is not easy to make interesting. [In *Impossible Object*] Nicholas Mosley has tried to avoid banality by making his narrative hard to follow: it is like a cross-word puzzle, like a Royal Academy "problem picture". There are eight short stories about the central relationship, printed in an order which confuses the reader about the temporal sequence. In between these stories are printed surrealistic essays in italics, concerned with Nietzsche, bombs and "the population problem", the influence of sexuality and childhood on war and cruelty. . . . Mr. Mosley describes tortures in these essays, and concludes: "Once men found it easy to be hurt; now they have to advertise in shop windows." The "once" and "now" formula for his epigrams promises more than it offers. . . . The generalizations are huge, not well managed. They suggest ideas to the reader, but are too assertive for their content.

The reader is expected to relate these essays to the stories, several of which are good, conventional little tales. The effort demanded is considerable. Perhaps it is better to let the surreal images remain in the mind, unexplained, like last night's dreams, and read the straight stories in the ordinary way, hoping that the eerie parentheses will colour one's appreciation of the narrative. Thus one of the best stories, **"A Morning in the Life of Intelligent People"**, is coloured by the essays preceding and succeeding it. The story coldly tells of a married couple at bed and breakfast, each trying to put the other down with gestures and hints intended to prove the other selfish, unfeeling, frigid or otherwise guilty. The surrounding essays tell mysterious fables about the death of God, the glories and uselessness of warfare: the tendency is towards certain modern proverbs—"explore *inner* space", or even "it's all in the mind".

"Cross Words," in The Times Literary Supplement, *No. 3477, October 17, 1968, p. 1171.*

ROBERT SCHOLES

I note with shame that *Impossible Object* is Nicholas Mosley's seventh novel. With shame, because he is so good and this is the first of his books I have read. . . . And I wonder, has he always been this good, hidden among the unappreciative English? Or has he developed from book to book the mastery he exhibits in *Impossible Object?* All I know is that he now has under full control four of the novelist's priceless gifts. He knows how to exploit the metaphoric possibilities of language. He has a shrewd grasp of the dynamics of emotional and sexual relationships. He has a developed sense of the philosophical, which lends resonance to the situations and people he presents. And he knows how to handle the storyteller's fundamental tools: suspense and revelation.

Certainly no one is born with all these gifts. But I, for one, mean to look into Mr. Mosley's earlier work to find out just what was going on back there. At the moment, however, I must try to describe *Impossible Object*—no easy task. . . .

Mr. Mosley's book is an impossible object in that it is constructed of eight separate stories, all fairly straightforward and realistic in presentation, which cannot be brought into three-dimensional congruity. The same characters—or characters with many of the same attributes—reappear frequently, but it is hard to sort their lives into any single story. The central characters seem to be a woman with a daughter and a man with three sons, who love one another and labor furiously to keep their love and their lives from becoming ordinary. For the man in particular this is a major goal in life, almost an obsession. He knows that "love flourishes in time of war" and that life dwindles unless we "make impossibilities." Love itself, conceivable as an idea, is impossible as an object. It exists in two or four dimensions and cannot be brought into three; it cannot be realized and made permanent. And neither can life. The essence of life is that it is transitory yet repetitious. If we seek by an act of will to freeze certain recurring moments into the permanence of art, we engage in a heroic but doomed struggle. That is what Mr. Mosley's book is about.

In *Impossible Object* the struggle takes the form of various attempts by the man to keep his life and the lives of those connected with him at the most intense possible pitch. He is successful. He is also destructive of strangers, family, himself. He leaves a trail of dead and wounded behind him in his pursuit of "ecstasy." And we are not allowed the luxury of condemnation. After all, we are paying to observe all this. . . .

Interpolated among the eight stories, and standing as prologue and epilogue to the larger sequence, are nine little fables or parables on related themes. These are brilliant prose constructions, combining images and perspectives with a vigor and control reminiscent of the later work of Picasso. The scenes they present are grotesque and bizarre, but always rooted in life and returning to life. These little pieces frame the "real" action, but the word "frame" is too inactive to convey how they really operate. Mosley uses his perspectivist parables as a way of generating an emotionally charged field of ideas and attitudes which then cluster around the situations in the "real" stories, illuminating them with a fabulous phosphorescence.

> Robert Scholes, *"Life at the Highest Pitch," in* Saturday Review, *Vol. LII, No. 4, January 25, 1969, p. 31.*

SAUL MALOFF

The precision of Nicholas Mosley's highly figurative writing has the odd effect of creating, not an explicitness of statement, but an augmented elusiveness. Small gestures, looks, ways of talking and moving or maintaining silence are particularized, while the larger actions that enclose them move in widening circles from opacity to enigma.

Motives are hinted at, then denied, or left in suspension. Actions develop, then disperse. A sense of foreboding and mystery hovers over the most ordinary scene—a family game of hide-and-seek, for example, is charged with omens; a game of volleyball played on a beach portends catastrophe. Relationships are ambiguously "resolved" by means which seem only tenuously tied to their unnatural history. Mosley is the author, among other novels, of *Accident,* which provided the basis for Harold Pinter's recent screenplay. The conjunction is not just fortuitous.

As with Pinter, so with Mosley: style is everything—a way of seeing round corners and at sharply-tilted angles, a manner of perception and notation. At times, so thick is the atmosphere with literary contrivance, it is all but impossible to get past style to substance, as the two work not harmoniously toward a common purpose, but disjunctively.

When the manner fails to illuminate, or further to darken, Mosley's incipiently ominous scenes, it is merely fanciful—a kind of showy virtuosity that induces, at most, a grudging admiration in the reader exactly at those points in the sparse narrative where the writing is impenetrable; and Mosley is unrelentingly set on holding us there, transfixed by his maneuvers. Yet he can be a formidable writer, with a rare, unforced sense of the uncanny. He can bring off extraordinary

effects with an unexpected turn of phrase, a sudden veering that opens an obscure path in the brambles.

So, too, with subject and structure. The "impossible object" of [*Impossible Object*] may be said on a venture to be "contact," relationship, with oneself and with others. Or—to define the ground as closely as the book itself comes to definition—to "maintain ecstasy," the old romantic illusion, to "make impossibilities" in a society in which everything is possible. The dramatic occasion is an adulterous affair—complicated in the usual way, by families and children, but even more than that by the narrator's obsessions with mystification.

Beyond the most meager statement of premises, Mosley allows very little to happen by way of providing dramatic validation. The structure—a sequence of shifting episodes, some of them autonomous, bound by meditative interludes—while ingenious, finally deepens the felt absence of dramatic center. In consequence, Mosley gives us a series of tableaux; locale and point-of-view shift erratically, but without the effect of achieving the ostensible object, the intensifying illumination of the lovers and their destiny.

The narrative is without "plot" in the usual sense; without "line." The lovers meet, part, meet again. The scene shifts, or is statically transported, from a room to a pub to a beach. There are next to no "events" as such. The hermetic "drama" is one of perspective: taking an essentially stationary situation, Mosley registers the atmospherics surrounding it, and the barometric pressure within.

The narrator-lover is a writer (who is, alas, writing this book) and part of his credo is articulated. "We imagine we move," he reflects at one point, "according to cause and effect, whereas in reality we are particles with velocity and no location." No one seriously imagines any such thing any longer, at least in the simpler and consoling sense; this "principle of indeterminacy" is certainly one of the central ideas in modern literature. Unfortunately, without some notion of causation however complex or multiple—*necessarily* complex and multiple—*Impossible Object,* quite literally, begins dissolving before one's eyes.

And here, where it does, Mosley's remarkable gifts work best and most evocatively. Some episodes succeed brilliantly, especially where he really creates atmosphere out of particles, a sense of the eerie and unaccountable—or the emotional and psychic equivalent of war, as in one of the bed-ridden episodes, which, though it is an almost detachable set-piece, is the book's most fully realized dramatic encounter.

Like Pinter, Mosley is most effective—which is to say first-rate—when he is most menacing, deadly; when, laconically, he proposes, surprising our expectations, the tense union of affective opposites—the excitement of fear, the exhilaration of terror, persistent hints of the nameless and uncaused in human conduct.

> Saul Maloff, *"Volleyball Portends Catastrophe," in* The New York Times Book Review, *February 2, 1969, p. 35.*

ROBERT SCHOLES

Nicholas Mosley is a brilliant novelist who has received nothing like the recognition he deserves—either at home in England or in this country. His fifth novel, *Accident,* attracted some attention as a film, but the credit went largely to Harold Pinter for his excellent screenplay. Few people realized how faithfully Pinter had followed the original work. After his sixth novel, *Impossible Object,* was published, I had occasion to correspond with a young American writer living in England who shared my admiration for that book. He told me that Englishmen he spoke to about Mosley simply muttered, "Oh, yes, Oswald Mosley's son"—and refused to take his work seriously.

Being the son of Britain's leading Fascist must indeed have been a handicap for Mosley.... But surely... [we can] simply look at his work for the unique and powerful achievement it is. *Natalie Natalia,* his most ambitious novel, is a remarkable fusion of sex and politics seen through the eyes of a conservative Member of Parliament whose mental life is being drastically reoriented—not so much because he is losing his grip on the splitting fragments of the world as because he refuses to accept this world's false surface unity. One truth, one personality, one life—these are not enough. Thus Anthony Greville sees his mistress as two people: a ravenous angel, Natalie, and an angelic one, Natalia: "What Natalie said was often a code for what Natalia was meaning."

Both Anthony Greville and Natalia are married, though not to one another. For Greville this woman represents a necessary deranging of his orderly existence, which has become impossible....

Mosley's view of passion as both destructive and necessary to life is familiar to us from *Accident* and *Impossible Object.* His elaboration of that view has never been more eloquent than in his new novel. But the triumph of *Natalie Natalia* is that Mosley has found accommodation for a strikingly mordant view of geopolitics within his intense and personal perspective....

The bizarre appropriateness of [Mosley's] prose to the actualities of political life is dazzling. You have only to think of, say, C. P. Snow's *Corridors of Power* to appreciate the difference between Mosley's visionary insight and the unexamined reporting of received opinions. Snow *believes* in the dreams of politicians. Mosley exposes them. His disillusionment is cosmic—and it is persuasive....

Mosley's writing is a bit "difficult." His perspectives are far from ordinary. But he deserves his share of whatever audience there is for genuinely creative fiction at the present time. And he particularly merits that attention from academic audiences which is so important in preserving "unpopular" books until their readership establishes itself. One can only hope that Mosley's reputation will someday be commensurate with the quality of his fiction.

> *Robert Scholes, in a review of "Natalie Natalia,"*
> in Saturday Review, Vol. LIV, No. 45, November 6,
> *1971, p. 48.*

SAUL MALOFF

Nicholas Mosley's literary career is a melancholy reminder to anyone who supposes that these literary battles have long since been won that the more "difficult" a writer is the less his chances of crossing frontiers and oceans. Mosley's first six books went unnoticed in this country (in fact he didn't fare much better in his native England) and it took a famous movie (Losey's *Accident*) and a filmscript by a celebrated playwright (Pinter) to call attention to his novel of that title. Sufficient attention was paid the movie, though not the novel from which it was adapted, to alert Americans to his next novel, *Impossible Object,* an elusive, finely contrived and tautly-controlled—well,

narrative *object* more than it was a novel in any conventional sense, made memorable and (the exhausted word applies for a change) haunting by its persistent interplay of two voices, one nervelessly reporting the surface event, the other contrapuntally registering the subjective, unspoken response, both working together to create an effect of the hermetic self's radical isolation from the public person dutifully miming the required gestures tonelessly speaking the prompted lines. The novel's atmosphere was filled with an eerie silence, the public and private selves canceling each other out; the silence a measure of the desolate distance not only between innerness and facade but between the self and others. Thus crowded, the book's narrative space seemed uncannily empty: a still-life composed of inanimate human objects.

In [*Natalie Natalia*] Mosley yields nothing to the reader. Again the narrative elements are submerged, distorted, dreamlike as if apprehended by a consciousness for which the boundaries between the experiencing mind and external flux are continually shifting, adrift. The elements themselves are deliberately commonplace—an ordinary triangle with satellites: Anthony Greville, the narrator-dreamer-actor, Conservative M.P. and specialist in African affairs, his wife, their children and friends—all domesticated, suburban and solid middle-class; and Greville's mistress, Natalie Natalia, light and dark, the two versions of her name suggesting dual aspects of the "eternal woman." In the world beyond sensibility there is some sort of African revolution in progress, and Greville is in some way involved, but those events also are so veiled and oblique that they become like all other data material by which the world is ingested: private affair and public turbulence alike.

More than anything else—indeed to the exclusion of virtually everything else—Mosley is concerned to catch and somehow record the most tenuous states of consciousness; the bisecting lines where world and mind meet and dissolve; how the world seems when there is a "slight displacement of attention." Greville's consciousness is massively displaced by "explosive pressures in the personality that are universal and unavoidable." Oedipal and homosexual "pressures" are hinted at, but in Mosley's work hint never rises from its opaque depths to anything approaching explicit statement. In the absence of that, we must take as given a state of feeling, Mosley says at one point, resembling Dostoievsky's "just before he had a fit," where the fit itself is experienced as containing the "meaning of life" lived "at the edge of a dark wood." Greville lives at the edge of "perpetual anxiety" where "knowledge could not be formulated; only endured" and "the space between the inside and outside of me became a battle-ground." That "space," where one form of consciousness melts into another, is the ground Mosley as a novelist of extreme conditions has claimed for his own. (p. 283-84)

To sustain the sense of "perpetual anxiety" is a difficult achievement; and to evolve a style that seems its natural voice is Mosley's impressive gift. Yet along with the dazzlement in the end it becomes wearying, small-scale, thin—at times, because the obsessional range is so small, irritatingly repetitious and convoluted. Where *Accident* and *Impossible Object* succeeded in registering the implicit violence and menace of the ordinary acts, gestures, events in complex relationships, *Natalie Natalia* finally fails; and it does so both as novel and as a further working-out of Mosley's aesthetic of the novel. Transformations of consciousness, the slow turnings of sensibility from one mode of perception to another are Mosley's private province; but we ourselves, as receptors of and participants in the aesthetic act, are unable to plot their course largely for the reason that Mosley yields up so little of the world that is undergoing transmutation by and within the mind. The dark lady of the novel, if she can be said to exist as a character at all, is tritely mistress-y; by which I suppose I tritely mean hectic, feline, mercurial, given to hysterics, at once submissive and unpredictable. Yet these qualities are dramatically without substance; so, save as a disembodied mind, is Greville. In the earlier novels, each echo was resonant with portent and felt meaning; here they merely echo with sonic boom, interesting technical effects created by an imaginative engineer in a well-equipped studio. Before flesh can become mysterious it must have solidity and dimension; and before they can exist in the mind even women, like African revolutions, must live in the world. (p. 284)

> *Saul Maloff, in a review of "Natalie Natalia," in* Commonweal, *Vol. XCV, No. 12, December 17, 1971, pp. 283-84.*

JOHN NAUGHTON

[*Catastrophe Practice*] is a book whose author clearly aspires to something other than mere entertainment. Given that the British are inclined to regard abstract theorising on the human condition as a kind of disease, Mr Mosley had better resign himself to charges of pretentiousness—an intellectual vice which is tolerated in foreigners but abhorred in natives. . . . Before deporting Mr Mosley, however, let us see what he is on about.

The title of his book gets him off to a bad start. It was suggested, it seems, by a branch of mathematics called 'catastrophe theory' which has enjoyed a certain notoriety in recent years. Broadly speaking, this theory has been used to explain certain kinds of discontinuous phenomena . . . which conventional mathematics—based, as it is, on assumptions about the essential continuity of physical behaviour—cannot handle. The notoriety of the subject stems from the glibness and speed with which the theory was extended to 'explain' various kinds of human behaviour—where discontinuity appears to be the order of the day, if not the century.

Mr Mosley has sallied blithely into this minefield. If catastrophe *theory* exists, he seems to have asked, then why not have a bit of *practice* as well? And why not a book on the subject, as we're at it? The result is most unconventional—a network of three plays with prefaces, and a short novel—in which six characters 'try to find ways through some catastrophe that is not just in the world outside them but in their minds. They have felt that conventional ways of seeing things have become disastrous . . . yet it seems that they have only these to practise with to try to break through to something different.'

Or so, at any rate, says a blurb whose reputation for accuracy is not exactly enhanced by its garbled account of catastrophe theory. In actual fact, Mr Mosley's book does not seem to me to be much about catastrophes, nameless or otherwise, as about other grand themes with which literature is more properly concerned—themes like the ethics of ambiguity and the responsibilities of knowledge.

The clue to Mr Mosley . . . is to be found in his prefaces which, taken together, form a lucid essay on some contemporary problems of knowledge and freedom. In **"Skylight"**, the first of these, he discusses 'the gulf between the ways in which people are pleased to see others and the experiences they feel within themselves', and the attempts which have been made within

the theatre to bridge this gap. This leads, naturally enough, to a discussion of Brecht and an illuminating exegesis of some tantalising notes to the Berliner Ensemble written shortly before his death. . . .

This preface is followed by a 'play not for acting' involving the six characters immortalised in the blurb, set in some unspecified, vaguely sinister location, with dialogue consisting largely of non-sequiturs—rather as one imagines the small-talk at a convention of sports commentators. From this, it is clear that Mr Mosley is determined to obey Brecht's strictures against bourgeois realism. But then, perhaps it doesn't matter, given that the play's not for acting.

This pattern—preface followed by not-for-acting play—is repeated twice. The same 'actors' reappear in different roles, often saying much the same things in successive manifestations. It is clear that Mr Mosley is trying to convey the feeling that meaning has to be panned from verbiage much as gold is panned from silt. In all three plays the boundary between acting and 'behaviour' is consistently and deliberately blurred. The whole work is then topped off with a short novel, set in an unspecified university city in the throes of a violent—student?—revolt. The writing is suffused with ambiguity and suppressed violence, is thoroughly frightening and almost completely inexplicable.

For enlightenment, that classic bourgeois concept, one returns to Mr Mosley's prefaces, and especially to the second one, **"Landfall"**. This discusses the gap between *knowing* and *knowing that we know*, and our collective failure (lamented by Jacques Monod in particular) to face up to the ethical consequences of what is now known about genetic mechanisms. It is a delightful essay which links the philosophy of Sartre, Husserl, Monod, Popper and Gregory Bateson in one imaginative sweep. In it Mr Mosley gives the impression of a man who has thought rather more about the human predicament than is good for his own peace of mind. His book seethes with nearly-articulated wisdom, but fails to make explicit the links which clearly exist in his head; the result is a whole even more ambiguous than the sum of its parts.

> *John Naughton, "Changing Scenes," in* The Listener, *Vol. 101, No. 2617, June 28, 1979, p. 895.*

THOMAS HINDE

Catastrophe Practice, consists of three plays "not for acting" and one short novel. This much at least is clear, but despite three introductions and a postscript almost everything else is challengingly obscure. The short novel is called *Cipher* and prefaced with a definition: "Cipher, Cypher. . . . A manner of writing intelligible to those possessing the key . . . also . . . the key to such a system." Reading Mr Mosley is indeed about as frustrating as reading a long coded message to which you do not have the key.

The three plays are related to each other through their six actors. In the second and third the reader is reminded which parts they previously acted. In the novel they reappear with names from one or other of the plays. Mr Mosley is perhaps making a point about the mutability of human beings.

The problem is that he provides such a tenuous sense of character in the first place that subsequent transformations produce little except confusion. Deprived of most of the relationships to each other or to the surrounding world by which people are normally recognisable, they become mere names with voices.

The first play is set on the terrace of a mountain house, the second in a bar, the third underground, the stage showing various rooms in cross section. Sometimes the dividing floors collapse and the characters try to hold them up.

The novel seems to be set on a city campus. Bombs explode: indeed there is enough talk of barricades and liberation armies to suggest that a social catastrophe of some sort is occurring—though the title apparently refers to the biological term "catastrophe theory." This, one character helpfully explains means that "in physical sciences things change smoothly; in sciences to do with life changes happen in sudden jumps."

Mr Mosley would, I suspect, like to provoke a sudden jump in the way we look at ourselves, in particular at our myth-making inclinations. His introductions (complex and difficult, but lucidity itself compared to his fiction) convince me that he is attempting something of considerable interest. I only wish they provided a better key to what it is.

> Thomas Hinde, "Mosley's Mystery Plays," in The Sunday Times, London, July 1, 1979, p. 12.

VALENTINE CUNNINGHAM

Catastrophe Practice offers an impressively eager effort to corral and enact within its gatherum of plays, prefaces, a postscript and 'a novel', reflections on the (rather dubious) mathematical Catastrophe Theory; and thoughts on Brecht, Sartre, Monod, Husserl, Gregory Bateson, plus the theatres of cruelty and absurdity. Alas, Nicholas Mosley is no Stoppard: he just can't animate the ideas he's trying to dribble across the park. What's more, fictions within fictions, *tout simple,* look dog-eared now. Flann O'Brien got there ages ago. Even Conrad has chaps saying 'This is absurd'. Dialogue like 'Well, what is happening'; 'I don't know'; 'But someone must'; 'I don't see why'— and ciné-roman tricks like the reel within the real and shots of hands holding babies that might also be holding the pen—have rather made their little points already.

> Valentine Cunningham, "In the Wry," in New Statesman, Vol. 98, No. 2524, August 3, 1979, p. 171.

CRAIG BROWN

It must amuse Nicholas Mosley that reviewers so often become tongue-tied when writing about his books. They generally admit to a certain befuddlement before plunging in to talk of the evocation of the exuberance and pain of love, the trembling sense of detachment and so forth. In misunderstanding Mosley's work in this way, they are unconsciously demonstrating Mosley's principal and recurrent theme—the poverty of language as a means of understanding the world and the happiness within it.

Mosley's main characters are highly intelligent, self-conscious people whose constant struggle is to find a link between their interior lives and the world outside: they have an understanding of both, but can only connect them with the thin, frayed rope of words. *Imago Bird* treats this struggle with a greater intensity than ever before. . . .

Mosley never restricts himself to the narrowness of a solely literary discussion. Around the teenage boy, Bert, circle politicians and celebrities whose minds have been frozen by their need to build and inhabit plots—plots to explain themselves and other people, plots which cannot admit freedom of choice,

plots which cannot admit to being plots. Bert lives with his uncle and aunt at 10 Downing Street. Throughout the book, strange things are happening: a gun fires, a woman catches fire, a man is assassinated. With the searching energy of a teenager, Bert attempts to understand these things and, more, to understand himself understanding them. . . .

Mosley's prose jitters on the page, as if each word is conscious that it could be placed elsewhere in the sentence. Similarly, Bert communicates with himself in the characteristic, hesitant Mosley style, knowing that for each thought another is present and that for each direct speech there are many others—some entirely contrary—to take its place. . . .

Mosley has an uncanny ability to remember and scrutinzie the process of thought being transformed into external or internal speech and, like a scientist, he knows that the presence of observation alters the observed, so that Bert recounts people's actions and speech in a way that is necessarily stilted, as if the wind had changed and these ordinary people making faces had been petrified in all their oddness. The peculiarity of the roles people adopt when they see life as a plot is evoked further by the blank, childlike style of the narrator. Through his devotion to similes Bert continually suggests for himself worlds not chained by plots, worlds different, open and apart. . . .

Mosley's last work, *Catastrophe Practice,* was almost impossibly obscure. *Imago Bird* is the first of a planned series of interlocking novels, each relating to one of the six characters in the *Catastrophe Practice* plays. It is a much clearer, more self-assured work than its predecessor. . . . It looks as if each of the novels will add a new perspective on the riddle, in much the same way as each of the short stories in his book *Impossible Object* illuminated the whole. Mosley's concern with extending the dimensions of self-consciousness is taken to the brink near the end of this book, when the main character seems set to meet the man who wrote him. Mosley has started one of the very few genuinely experimental projects in modern English writing; while others cling to pessimism as if it is the artist's passport, he strives to communicate the real presence of optimism, its subtlety, its secrecy, its apparent incompatibility with the language.

> Craig Brown, "The Poverty of Language," in The Times Literary Supplement, No. 4042, September 19, 1980, p. 1012.

JOHN NAUGHTON

Nicholas Mosley's new book [*Imago Bird*] is the first of a planned series of novels about the future of the protagonists of *Catastrophe Practice*. Since the latter work was an ambitious (though, to my mind, ultimately unsuccessful) attempt to illuminate the discontinuities of human relationships using the perspective afforded by the branch of mathematics known as 'catastrophe theory', I must confess to approaching *Imago Bird* with some misgivings.

In the event, however, most of them turned out to be unfounded. The novel is on a much smaller scale than its predecessor, and is significantly more coherent as a result. The central character, Bert, is an 18-year-old with a stammer, an affliction for which a psychoanalyst has been prescribed by well-meaning relatives. As usual, however, the stammer is really a proxy for deeper difficulties. And besides, Bert is no ordinary teenager, but the nephew of the Prime Minister of the day, with whom he lives.

Living therefore at the hub of British politics, Bert's chief problem is that of sorting out reality from fantasy in this frenetic world. His friendships with Trotskyites and television personalities, and his perceptions of the shadowy intrigues concerning national security and the PM's domestic ménage are bounced off his analyst towards the reader. *Imago Bird* is a skilful, sardonic work with some contemporary references which resonate.

John Naughton, "Fascinating Faust," in The Listener, *Vol. 104, No. 2683, October 16, 1980, p. 513.*

PETER LEWIS

During the thirty years since Nicholas Mosley published his first book, his fiction has undergone two changes of direction, the second of which (marked by the publication of *Catastrophe Practice* in 1979) may turn out to be much less drastic than the first in the early 1960s. His novels of the 1950s are long, doom-laden books characterized by a fashionable pessimism, and by a stylistic and syntactical complexity owing much to James and Faulkner. Implicit in *Corruption* (1957), for example, is a belief that experience can be pinned down exactly by words—if enough are used, and in sufficiently tortuous configurations. Words operate as a completely closed system, and the world as depicted in these early novels is also closed: there is virtually no possibility of transformation or regeneration.

Then, after a five-year gap, Mosley transfigured himself as a novelist in a way that repudiated much of his previous work. In the 1960s, his novels (and sentences) became much shorter, his style simpler, and his narrative method more elliptical. In contrast to the exhaustive analysis of his previous novels, he now left many things unstated and unexplained. An unfashionable yet far from naive optimism replaced the modish gloom; a sense of potentiality replaced the closed system. Instead of the linguistic positivism underlying the earlier books, there is a radical questioning of the ways in which language can falsify experience and inhibit new possibilities. Mosley's novels of this second period, notably *Accident, Impossible Object,* and *Natalie Natalia,* are strikingly original but show no trace of meretricious experimentalism, and it is these books that won him a fairly wide readership.

After *Natalie, Natalia* in 1971 Mosley wrote no more novels for eight years; instead he worked on film scripts and wrote a study of Trotsky as well as his fine biography of Julian Grenfell. Then came *Catastrophe Practice,* which reduced even Mosley's admirers to stunned silence or bewildered incomprehension. At first sight, this highly intellectual, boldly experimental and apparently impenetrable novel seemed like another completely fresh start.

Mosley had never attempted anything as structurally complex before. At the heart of the book are many of the ideas he developed in his novels of the 1960s, but provided now with a scientific framework in the form of Catastrophe Theory, a startling mathematical development of the 1970s with far-reaching implications for the way we view the world. Partly to help the reader decipher this intricate book, Mosley promised a series of six related novels, one for each of the main characters of *Catastrophe Practice,* but he also intended these to stand on their own.

Whether readers of the well-received *Imago Bird* (1980), the first of the six, found that it illuminated *Catastrophe Practice*

or not, the book certainly succeeded on its own terms, and in many ways marked a return to Mosley's distinctive idiom of the 1960s. *Serpent,* the second of the six, also succeeds as a self-sufficient novel, and again looks back to the methods of Mosley's most familiar fiction rather than to those of *Catastrophe Practice;* though references to subatomic physics, quantum mechanics, and the principle of indeterminacy maintain the mathematical parallels of its predecessor. Nevertheless, the web of symbolism and the pattern of elusive correspondences in *Serpent* make it a more demanding book than *Imago Bird.*

The narrative itself is slight, most of it taking place on a plane during a flight. Jason, an extremely self-conscious screenwriter, is travelling to Israel with a small group of film people in connection with a script he has written about the Jewish revolt against the Romans in 66 AD, culminating in the siege of Masada in 73 AD when nearly a thousand Jews took their own lives rather than surrender. . . .

Sections of Jason's script are interspersed with the main narrative or otherwise incorporated into it, and some of the themes and situations of the script are echoed by events involving the modern characters. Also worked into the narrative of the flight are a few flashbacks concerning Jason and his equally self-conscious wife Lilia . . . and some episodes in Israel. One of these, featuring David Kahn, is actually set at Masada itself, thus connecting the siege in 73 AD with a contemporary "assault" on their rock by two men who die making a protest of some kind. The other, involving Kahn's wife, takes place at Lod Airport, and again involves an attack and violent death. Precisely what is going on in these episodes is unclear to the Kahns and is never fully explained. . . . In the final chapter, the narrative suddenly shifts away from both the flight and the script to describe the chance but symbolic meeting of Jason and Lilia and the Kahns on an Israeli beach, thus bringing together the two contemporary strands of the novel.

Running through the entire narrative are a number of leitmotifs: Plato's allegory of the cave and the sun; the Garden of Eden and the Serpent; Noah's Ark and the flight of the dove; the flight of the Holy Family into Egypt. Mosley organizes these mythic elements into an attempt to create his own myth of the human condition. In a book which stresses the paradoxical and contradictory nature of human experience, it is appropriate that most of the characters are both trapped inside an airliner and at the same time in flight. This contrast between imprisonment and freedom is one of a number of polarities at the heart of the novel: the individual and society; illusion and reality; orthodoxy and heterodoxy; the actor and his role; words and things.

As in a number of his books, Mosley explores the ways in which conventions, whether social, moral, or artistic, can be a form of imprisonment, inhibiting responses, closing the doors of perception instead of opening them. There is a strong Romantic, even Blakean, streak in Mosley, exemplified in a line from Jason's script: "The serpent was the angel who woke Adam and Eve from their sleep in the garden." *Serpent* is very much about the responsibility entailed by this awakening, and about how life can be made "a successfully going concern". Despite some of the difficulties of this novel the planned seven-decker of *Catastrophe Practice* and its siblings is turning out to be a less terrifying prospect than at first it seemed.

Peter Lewis, "The Flight from the Closed System," in The Times Literary Supplement, *No. 4098, October 16, 1981, p. 1192.*

PETER KEMP

'It's by connections we make things,' says the writer-hero of Nicholas Mosley's new book, *Serpent.* The novel itself supports this. It is linked with its predecessor, *Imago Bird:* some of the same characters appear; images recur; similar issues are examined. And both books stem from Mosley's earlier volume, *Catastrophe Practice:* dealing in detail with figures who featured briefly there, they put into operation literary theories Mosley outlined in it.

The first topic raised in *Catastrophe Practice* was the significance of myths: how, as 'expressions of ambiguities that a person feels but cannot readily comprehend', they relate to man's sense of 'himself as an individual and yet a member of a group'. This is something that had earlier attracted Mosley's interest. His absorbing biography of Julian Grenfell explored the part played by classical legend—instilled by the public schools—in cultivating ideals of self-sacrifice. . . .

Mosley's current venture, a linked sequence of six novels, aims 'to make myths about myths'—or to produce fictions in which legend and archetype are wittily paralleled, parodied, tilted at different angles to display what they contain of psychological or social truth. Part of his purpose is to depict the ambiguity and paradox of much human response—to the conflicting claims of mind, body, and emotions, or the differing demands of individual and community. Another part is to reproduce the never-neatly-patterned welter of experience. 'Human life,' he has said, 'is a matter of multifarious interlocking dramas, false starts, unfinished strands, might-have-beens, which jostle for the attention of the consciousness.' This could be a description of his current novel sequence.

Serpent, like *Imago Bird,* pushes into prominence a likeable intellectual. Jason is a writer whose mind effervesces takingly with theories, images, quick cross-connections. Eager as Saul Bellow to present the pleasurable procedures of thought, Mosley is like him, too, in his determination to establish that life is 'a successfully going concern'. Both *Serpent* and *Imago Bird* depict collisions between people of intellectual decency and those whose intelligence is used to pervert and sabotage. In each case, the former buoyantly survive—though evil is shown as far from negligible.

Serpent, as its title might imply, has at its heart a particularly repellent coil of slime: a tangle of film-grandees, dazed with power, drugs and sex, try to poison a happy marriage. Always excellent at monied monsters, Mosley portrays each twist and slither. Serpent legends drape the narrative. The events take place on a flight to Israel: Mosley fills his book with serious and jokey reminders of the Flight into Egypt—a contemporary Herod, family-destroyers, a menaced trio.

Also looming largely is Masada, the semi-sacred Jewish site with its connotations of heroic resistance. Jason has written a film-script intended to point up the ambiguities, as he sees it, of what happened there. Like so much of Mosley's recent fiction, the script aims at 'seeing things in two ways at once'. The extracts from it that we are shown are full of intellectual trampolining, jugglings with myth, tight-rope-walkings between farce and grimness, tonal somersaults. Though more liable than the rest of the novel to come to grief occasionally by toppling into the bathetic or grotesque, they still deserve attention and applause. Like everything else in *Serpent,* they derive from a willingness to take risks in emulating the dartingly, various nature of thought and response.

Peter Kemp, "Monied Monsters," in The Listener, *Vol. 106, No. 2739, December 10, 1981, p. 728.*

JAMES LASDUN

Since *Catastrophe Practice,* Nicholas Mosley has been engaged on a project that will win him admirers but not, I suspect, many readers. It consists of a series of experimental novels that explore the liberating possibilities of recording every shift in the mind's relation to itself, to the relation of that relation. . . . and so on ad infinitum, the point being that the more complete one's self-knowledge, the greater one's self-determination.

The setting for this exploration in *Serpent* moves between the first and tourist class compartments of an aeroplane, though from the first paragraph one is made aware of this more as symbol than as reality—'He thought—This is an image of the conscious and the unconscious?' In the first class compartment a writer called Jason is discussing his script about the Jews' mass suicide at Masada, with some surreal, and increasingly drunken, film men. Meanwhile, in the tourist compartment, Jason's wife is persuaded to perform a bizarre variation on fellatio in the lavatory. Flashbacks, sections of Jason's script (more Pirandello than Ben Hur), and a sub-plot involving an Israeli soldier stationed at present day Masada, and his airport security officer wife, interrupt the narrative and give to a story, that is at best oblique, a quality of arbitrariness that makes much of it impenetrable.

It is tempting to dismiss this enterprise as a vain effort to convince the reader that significant connections exist between events and symbols that seem, in truth, somewhat randomly dispersed. This would be a mistake; the nature of experimental writing is to take risks, and risks do not always pay off. When they do, the results, in this book, are isolated passages of highly original and disturbing writing. There is an encounter between the airport security officer and a girl who may or may not be carrying a bomb, in which Mosley's observations of the minutiae of consciousness in a state of fear, and his theme of survival versus self-sacrifice (as in the Masada Jews) gel together into a scene of enormous power.

Moments of such coherence are rare, but their existence at all suggests that this sequence, while never likely to be entertaining, may prove to be genuinely innovatory.

James Lasdun, "Obliquity and Whimsy," in The Spectator, *Vol. 248, No. 8008, January 9, 1982, p. 22.*

JOHN BANKS

Thinking about and articulating what Nicholas Mosley is doing is like trying to occupy a mental no-man's-land, an area of experience over which conceptual battles are fought but which is known to theory only by what it is not. If we first enlist the armies of theory—social, psychological, hermeneutic—in the study of his writings we will succeed only in pushing the ineffable back to known frontiers. . . . Instead I suggest that we begin by accepting his campaign as revisionary. We do know about the function and normative force of theory and methodology, that they order the ontology according to what they are able to denote and, interacting and layered in a cognitive network, constitute our conceptual scheme. Thus it would seem advisable to approach Mosley's writings by first trying to grasp the nature of his beliefs about the ineffable—both what it is that theory has not yet captured and, possibly, what there might be which is both knowable, part of public experience, and yet is by its nature beyond the frontier of theorizing. We might be guided by his figurative language, but this is not to allow at the beginning that we are concerned with mental territory and experience which is only penetrable with metaphor. . . . Still, his figurative language might helpfully be pressed into service on this meta-theoretic level: If our conduct is a strategy aimed at self-preservation, our language part of the weaponry used for defence or attack, then our words, like bullets, only rarely hit their targets bang-on; rather, they glance off objects, . . . ricocheting to an effect somewhere else. (p. 118)

It seems that almost all of Mosley's public writings contain passages which raise questions about language use. . . . Obviously his literary language is partly a function of his views of language in general; the problem of that mental no-man's-land is just that there seem to be important things which are occasionally being exhibited in the fiction but which have not been captured in his discursive writing. (pp. 118-19)

Although the main story of **Spaces of the Dark** (1951) has so much to do with postwar England, it does foreshadow many of the themes of the most recent work. One central implication is that the world is mad, mesmerized by empty words and causes. Truth is a matter of what is felt, what is shown in committed action. Here Paul, who understands little German, is leaning over a dying German soldier who is speaking unintelligibly.

> . . . but with such deliberation that I began to believe that I could understand him myself, believing with him and memorizing his statement although there was nothing to memorize; and I felt with him suddenly the precise importance of him holding me in the darkness and trying to convey something that perhaps could only be conveyed because it was unintelligible, believing something that he felt it necessary for me to believe in because it was otherwise incommunicable. . . .

Thus the speech achieves its point—a testament of faith, imparting it to Paul—precisely because it was unintelligible. . . .

A recurrent theme in the fiction is stated clearly in **Experience and Religion**: a central paradox of the human condition is that language is both the "stuff of life" and a confusion, seldom adequate to our higher purposes. These would at least include self-knowledge, self-expression, and moral action, but in each case language—for the most part literal, as it comes to us in discursive writing and speech—appears to work against us. It most effectively represents persons as consistent, indistinguishable from the public facade. Thus in the fiction there are all those examples of discontinuity between what is happening (public and private) and the language. This is part of another pervasive theme, that experience itself is paradoxical, good sometimes coming from evil, and the passion of love being mixed with doubt. Language aggravates this by continually presenting us with a formulation of the contrary; if we do not master this, making of it a dialectic at least, then we are its victims. (p. 119)

These effects of language are best combatted by our learning to manipulate them. Apparently Mosley shifted his attention to this sometime between **Corruption** (1957) and **Accident** (1965), though not exactly in **Meeting Place** (1962). There is some hope for Robert at the end of **Corruption:** evidently he is still

boggled by the potentials of language but he at least sees behind its illusions. In **Accident** Stephen-Charlie is almost too good at getting what he wants through language, having the skills to keep up the public face—and thus some freedom—but perhaps at first not the knowledge and feeling to direct him to right ends, the power of the tongue being a kind of seduction. But after **Accident,** all of the protagonists come to a more complete appreciation of their complexity. Having dissolved the conventional notion of character they are now like pure consciousness, "particles with velocity but no location," in **Impossible Object** exploring the usefulness of illusion, trying to generate contexts in which there will once again be meaning and passion. (pp. 119-20)

For my purposes here I would like to attend not to the uses of language within the stories—the protagonists' language—but rather to Mosley's literary language, for the central themes of these books have as much to do with what is not said in the text as with what is said. There is a remarkable phenomenon here, a kind of parallelism or interfusion of three things: what the protagonist is thinking and saying; what the reader is thinking and saying; and the theme. I think this is achieved to an almost magical intensity in some passages of **Impossible Object** and **Natalie Natalia.** The most common term for this sort of effect would be "immediacy," suggesting that the protagonist's consciousness comes to replace the reader's, or vice versa. . . . Mosley establishes a rhythm of shifts between the protagonist's public voice, his private voice, and his interlocutor's voice. Sentences tend to be short, impressionistic, to facilitate uptake and to eliminate the expectation of literalness. Descriptions are dropped in favour of the idiom of direct acquaintance, pronouns and lexicals. Then links between the protagonist's public voice and his interlocutor's public voice are stretched further and further, making the reader more avid for hints in the protagonist's private voice. Here, possibly the protagonist himself stumbles, expressing uncertainty, perhaps wonder, which gives the reader some hope and a feeling of camaraderie, or, at the very least, some liveliness of mind. But the protagonist's next utterance does continue the dialogue, not in a way that the reader could have foreseen, but in a way that he immediately grasps, for, after all, the protagonist and his motives are not unknown to him. This process continues, the thread of the dialogue stretched further and further, the reader having to participate more and more in order to make of the various voices some coherence. . . . (p. 120)

This is an area in which we have to try to bring to bear what is known about the expressing of thought—in modes direct and indirect, in contexts of varying degrees of epistemological complexity, and in layers of varying reflexivity. . . . At the same time it is important to add that in such an investigation we would not be looking only for the means by which the content of the protagonist's consciousness is given. It seems that Mosley intends to generate a sense of the *tension* in that consciousness, this being a means of demonstrating that there is an area in which we have some freedom. In short, the literary device is intimately connected with a complex psychological-epistemological view of thinking and interaction.

In the sixties thinkers like R. D. Laing and Erving Goffman gave up the last of the "coherent self" in exchange for something describable only as the function of certain linguistic and behavioral interactions. It seems that for Mosley this opened new horizons, both making it possible for people to distance themselves from the models and patterns which were destructive, and providing the means—a more sophisticated conception of the relationship between language and conduct—for creating something more hopeful. Interactions approaching this are exhibited in several parts of *Imago Bird*. . . . (pp. 120-21)

I have tried to intimate how Mosley's views of language might be revisionary. This is difficult because the shifts in the view of language, seemingly minor in themselves, radiate outward like waves, forcing almost everything else that there is—everything that is now in the ontology of theory—into some new equilibrium. . . . The thrust of much of Mosley's writing seems to be that the locus of truth is not in sentences and statements but in a different category altogether, approachable in language only along some odd tangent. This is not to make truth "relative" but to acknowledge that sentences or statements are not true in isolation from their context. . . . I think that when we allow that a person has understood a piece of language, or used a piece of language successfully, we are recognizing a relationship which is more complex than that between a person and a string of words, or a particular proposition, or, say, a speech-act. The piece of language, in and by its being understood, both constitutes and reflects the context of its appropriateness. . . . Such a view also entails that there is a sense in which events are created by being "framed" in language. The term is Goffman's, borrowed here because it suggests the extent to which language is implicated in our structuring of the world. . . . It is apparent that it is only through this process that our separate states, our separate understandings of what there is, become accessible and verifiable—in short, it is only through this that we acknowledge . . . a common world.

This path does lead back to Mosley's ficion. . . . [We] might at least learn the shape of no-man's-land—what is ineffable behind the eyes or, possibly, between us—by inferring from where our bullets have gone what they must have bounced off in order to get there! In speaking we listen for the echo which comes back true. Now there is even a visual model—the holographic image which is both there and here, reconstituted each time by our knowing the trajectories and ricochets of light rays. These are the processes of understanding which Mosley is inviting us to test—and, in the testing, to note—in the later fiction, particularly the *Plays for Not Acting*. Amidst the continual framing and reframing, and the hunting for what is recognizable, we might become infected with Mosley's style and sense the true power of the word, which is to create . . . worlds for one another. Conspiring with such freedom we may just be able to fashion something in our own best image. (pp. 122-23)

> John Banks, "Sleight-of-Language," in The Review
> of Contemporary Fiction, *Vol. 2, No. 2, Summer,*
> *1982, pp. 118-23.*

CRAIG BROWN

Having completed his extraordinary two-volume biography of his father Oswald, Nicholas Mosley has returned to his planned seven-volume series of novels. *Judith* is the fourth in the series. It reveals many of the same preoccupations that made the father-and-son biography so tense, so humane and ultimately so moving.

The father came to excuse evil as a possible force for good; as a politician and an orator, he became infatuated by the power of words and of acting: he believed that the ease with which

speech and image could be controlled was emblematic of the larger control the individual could gain over his own destiny and the destiny of others. Meanwhile, the son remained sceptical. In *Judith,* this scepticism has deepened towards mysticism. Question marks hold the narratives up like curtain-rings. By pulling away ideas of reality, Mosley seeks to view something grander and more far-reaching. One of the reasons that his novels are seen as "experimental" is that their eventual pursuit is out of kilter with others. Characterization—if characterization is the close delineation of the things that make people different—is virtually non-existent. Narrative, here, is self-conscious, jerky, repetitive, hard to follow, often just a demonstration of the protagonists' need for a narrative. "What falsifications result from the need for a story?" asks Judith, who is telling her tale in letters to three characters from Mosley's earlier *Catastrophe Practice*. With their repetitions, their questions, their obsession with symbols, their acknowledgment of a force beyond and inaccessible to words, Mosley's books often seem closer to psalms than to novels. "Of course the language is difficult. It has to circle itself: at the centre there is silence." Few novelists are so assured by their lack of assurance.

Judith is an ex-actress who is searching for a reality beyond her own reality by entering disparate contemporary worlds. . . . For all its spiritual concerns, the novel operates within solid contemporary worlds: from a *Private Eye* party . . . to an ashram in India, to the perimeters of an American airbase in Suffolk. It is the dislocation between the commonplace and what lies behind the commonplace—both in what is described and the words used to describe it—that makes the book so appealing. Mosley's usual technique of dialogue (I thought: / I said: / I thought I might say:) is used, and his confident and overt distillations of truth (rather more Victorian than experimental) are nicely saved from banality or sermonizing by the eccentricity of their means of expression. Even when pursuing his themes of free-will, the need to act, and the attraction of pessimism, Mosley can be both charming and funny. . . .

In Mosley's much earlier novel *Impossible Object,* a series of interlocking short stories in which the characters were now central, now peripheral, now observers, now observed, he began to play with Kleist's notion that human beings are never at ease because they are split between being doers and being observers of what they are doing. In this (so far unnamed) series, he is using the same pattern, though on a broader scale, to hint at something richer: the possibilities of salvation though this unease. "If, inside the theatre of memory, you have become yourself one of the figures that pop up at windows, what is it that you might see when you look out?" Switching perspective from one book to another, from one character to another, from a watchtower to a three-eyed sheep, from the Bible to a television flicker-switch, from the immediate to the eternal and back again, Nicholas Mosley is in the midst of constructing an answer as tricky and uneven, as holy, as powerful and as old-fashioned as prayer.

> Craig Brown, "The Psalmist's Voice," in The Times
> Literary Supplement, *No. 4350, August 15, 1986, p.*
> *894.*

VALENTINE CUNNINGHAM

It could not be claimed of Nicholas Mosley's *Judith* that it wears lightly its ambition to be an avant-garde experimental text. But this contemporary woman's epistolary report of sex with a satirical journalist and also with a high-life druggie, then of a retreat to an ashram, followed by a disruptive passage-at-arms at a women's peace camp, is nothing much out of the ordinary. And there seem few if any reasons why Judith should write her story so much in the interrogative mood, or worry about just who her audience is, or go in for bits of self-reflexive narratological smartness. In fact it's rather vexing to feel so frequently invited to grant this set of highfalutin' mannerisms an importance they keep failing to earn or justify.

> *Valentine Cunningham, "Skulls beneath the Skin,"*
> *in* The Observer, *September 7, 1986, p. 26.*

Joe Orton

1933-1967

(Born John Kingsley Orton) English dramatist, novelist, and scriptwriter.

An influential dramatist in England during the 1960s, Orton wrote anarchic comedies which have been subject to frequent revivals and critical exegeses. Evidencing his view of the ludicrous nature of life, Orton's plays are intended to shock audiences through the irreverent remarks and base actions of his characters. In *Loot* (1965), for example, a bankrobber hides the money he has stolen in his deceased mother's casket and moves his mother from the coffin to a cupboard. Subsequent appearances in drama of such overt forms of black humor are often called "Ortonesque." The characters in Orton's plays frequently affect genteel manners and language as they participate in ignoble acts, underscoring the disparity between their aspirations and the harsh realities of their lower-class existence. C. W. E. Bigsby noted: "[The] world that Orton describes is spiritually attenuated—a place in which a debilitated language reflects a parallel collapse of all other human values and civilizing qualities." Bigsby added: "It is a world that can accept violence and even murder. . . . It is a life in which the primary facts are sex and violence."

The son of working-class parents, Orton was raised in Leicester and attended the Royal Academy of Dramatic Arts. At the Academy, Orton met and began a prolonged homosexual relationship with Kenneth Halliwell, who introduced him to classical drama and encouraged Orton's literary aspirations. Orton and Halliwell collaborated on several novels that remain unpublished. After they were released from prison, having served sentences for defacing library books, Orton wrote the plays that would earn him recognition and notoriety. His burgeoning career abruptly ended, however, when Halliwell murdered Orton and then took his own life.

Several of Orton's early plays were influenced by the works of Harold Pinter. These dramas feature unusual individuals who create tension by disrupting the lives of other characters. Like Pinter, Orton relies on fractured dialogue to develop the mysterious and absurdist qualities of his plays. *The Ruffian on the Stair* (1964; revised, 1966) concerns the efforts of a despondent young man named Wilson to avenge the death of his older brother, with whom he was incestuously involved. Wilson tries to provoke his brother's killer into murdering him as well, thus incriminating the killer in both murders and saving Wilson, a Roman Catholic, from committing the sin of suicide. This play includes elements found in many of Orton's subsequent works, including incest, homosexuality, murder, and sexual ambiguity. The title character of *Entertaining Mr. Sloane* (1964) is a murderer who is blackmailed by the homosexual son and nymphomaniac daughter of his latest victim into dividing his sexual favors between the two. In typical Ortonesque fashion, the siblings' carnal opportunism outweighs all ethical considerations regarding their father's murder. In *Loot*, individuals from all levels of society are shown to be corrupt and avaricious. The one honest character in this play is presented as naive and foolish for trusting in the police and the medical profession, even though his wife is murdered by her nurse and a corrupt police officer arrests him on trumped-up charges. The

farcical elements of *Loot*, which include convoluted logic and exaggerated situations, foreshadow Orton's last play, *What the Butler Saw* (1969). Although Orton died before he could refine it, *What the Butler Saw* remains one of his most critically lauded and commercially successful pieces. Set in a psychiatric clinic, *What the Butler Saw* parodies the farces of French dramatist Georges Feydeau and features mistaken identities, transvestism, and incest.

Orton's one-act plays, *The Erpingham Camp* (1966), *The Good and Faithful Servant* (1967), and *Funeral Games* (1968), which were originally scripted for television, are regarded as less significant works. *The Erpingham Camp* is a retelling of Euripides's *Bacchae* set in a British holiday camp. *The Good and Faithful Servant,* a more somber effort, centers on the unfeeling usurpation of personal identity by authority figures. The protagonist, Buchanan, has worked in a large factory for more than fifty years and lost an arm there but retires virtually unnoticed by his employers. The play ends with Buchanan's son seeking a job at the same factory, thus repeating the cycle. *Funeral Games,* a satire on religion, is generally considered the least focused of Orton's plays.

Other works by Orton have been published since his death. *Head to Toe* (1971) is a fantasy novel recounting a man's journey across a giant's body. *Up against It: A Screenplay for the Beatles* (1979) was commissioned by The Beatles for their third film but was later rejected.

(See also *CLC*, Vols. 4, 13; *Contemporary Authors*, Vols. 85-88; and *Dictionary of Literary Biography*, Vol. 13.)

RAY GOSLING

On a body like a man's live many bodies. They have lives: consider the lice and the flea, the scabies and crabs, thousands of living things we can't see with our eyes. For them a right upper arm may be their whole world. Such is the cast of *Head to Toe*. Creatures living on the body of a man are in this novel made human: O'Scullion, Till, and Gombold. Gombold the hero makes a journey from his native forest of hair to toeland and back again.... There are kingdoms on the body, revolutionary republics, magazines and motorboats. Right buttock country is perpetually at war with the left. Journey into the bowels. Pitch your tent on the roof of the body's mouth. At the end of the novel the body dies.

Unlike Swift's Gulliver, Gombold is not the super-tourist/explorer. Gombold is ordinary, citizen X of the world, like Christian in *Pilgrim's Progress*. But *Head to Toe* is not a Christian book; neither easy to read, nor are its images for children. Joe Orton does not mask his commitments....

Sexual fantasy there is, a brothel scene: "Not just sex, it's poetry". But this is not a gay book, not Genet (nor nearly as good, for that matter). It is a kind of violent cricket: studs in the boot and green on the cream flannels. Another hemisphere, and another generation on from Burroughs. The style of *Monty Python;* but words last. Sometimes even like Dougal and *The Magic Roundabout*. Sometimes like Brigid Brophy, but not so sharp in language or contemporarily smart in fantasy nor as consistently amusing. (But, "I'm glad I'm a weed. I couldn't bear to be arranged".)

Joe Orton tested the words he used, the effect of adjectives. The images too, as where Gombold gets a job rolling stones up a hill, or making shrouds for another department to unpick. A wonderful zoo they go to where they are in cages, and the jailers are the keepers....

I think *Head to Toe* is an important novel of this time because it has caught where we are in a tale as short as a long poem. I like it better than the plays. Gombold/Joe Orton lived on the same body as us: crouching down, his ear all but brushing the earth, he overheard the conversation of half a bird, a cock, an aged lion, a melon and a daisy. I think he's the best and possibly the last of that genre "I'm glad I'm a weed, I couldn't bear to be arranged."

Ray Gosling, *"Creatures of the Body,"* in The Times, London, January 25, 1971, p. 7.

THE TIMES LITERARY SUPPLEMENT

[*Head to Toe*] is an account of a fantastic pilgrimage by a young man called Gombold in a magical territory. He has friends called Pill, Offjenkin, O'Scullion and Corporal Squall. He is innocent, childlike, something like Alice in Wonderland. Imprisoned with an old man called Doktor von Pregnant, he learns about "Saint Trimmer-Ac-whinous, Saint Ginn of the Crutch, Goitre, Dinty and Kneetchur", and such languages as "Finsh, Spoonish, Onlisch, Dallience and Greeman". (Had Orton been reading Joyce, or are the puns more like those of the Mock Turtle—about his education in Reeling and Writhing, and the classical languages, Laughing and Grief?) With the Doktor, Gombold digs a tunnel for escape, but the old man dies. Here we are deliberately reminded of Monte Cristo and his escape from the Château d'If.

The territory which Gombold is exploring is the body of a giant, "some hundreds of miles high". Gombold goes from the head to the big toe and back again. On the last page, we are told that the death of the giant (like the Death of God?) "could no longer be concealed: the Government had left the city; the countryside was considered unsafe". The countryside on this huge body includes the forests made by the giant's patches of hair; some parts of the surface are built-up areas and in one of them Gombold spends some time living as the kept man of the Chief of Police, a woman called Connie Hogg. The Government is all female, and Gombold gets involved in a male revolutionary group.

This section of the fantasy recalls Wyndham Lewis's *Childermass*, but Orton's treatment of sex, war and sexual indeterminacy has none of Lewis's jeering, authoritarian "masculinity". The bias is that of the English homosexual Left, with all its contradictions: pacifism and a fondness for soldiers; a tendency to identify with women but to fear their domination; an aesthete's passion for everything "exquisite" and "refined", and a delight in ribald vulgarity; an anger against cruelty, and a fascination with it; a primly reproving tone and a consciousness of sin. It is the spirit of Oscar Wilde and Denton Welch.

Another fantasist might be mentioned—Amos Tutuola, the Palm-Wine Drinkard, who found in the Bush of Ghosts a town of multi-coloured people at loggerheads with the "mono-coloured". Similarly, Gombold finds a town of multi-sexed people, happy folk who complete one male and one female phase every five years, on the average. In the next town are people who are "part dog-headed and part horse-bodied"....

There is some gentle mockery of the House of Windsor going on here, at much the same level as an earlier, fable-like passage about quarrelling animals—an aged lion, a capon that cries "Mon Dieu!", a shifty-eyed eagle trying to maintain an alliance, a Russian bear in the woods; to represent Rome, there is a she-wolf with a mitre, howling "Pax vobiscum!" Something of Orton's attitude to religion is represented by his account of the Jesus image—"I.N.R.I. encircled by a crown of thorns, the letters standing for I Now Represent Idiots." Another aspect may be recognized in Gombold's meeting with a holy woman who believes in the power of Love and longs for "the glory of the Infinite Morning when love and unbiased friendship is for everyone.... Until men can love men, and women do not fear to trust their own kind, we shall see no peace". There is a spirit of true religion struggling to express itself in this weird book. It is a rag-bag, a curiosity, but it helps to explain Orton's brief life and his handful of plays, those trim medleys of wit, horror and coolly expressed moral indignation. It is a surrealist account of his education in "Laughing and Grief".

"Reeling and Writhing, Laughing and Grief," in The Times Literary Supplement, *No. 3596, January 29, 1971, p. 112.*

MARY I. CASMUS

The two playwrights with whom Orton has been compared most frequently are Georges Feydeau and Oscar Wilde—the former because of similarities in farce method and the latter because of similarities in dialogue. Feydeau had an abundance of situational humor but only a moderate amount of humor in the dialogue itself. Wilde had abundant verbal humor but relied on a simpler plot, limited in physical action. Joe Orton tried to excel in both capacities simultaneously and to arrive at his own individual farce style. (p. 462)

In 1966, two years after the successful naturalism of *Entertaining Mr Sloane,* the first clear signs of a farce style emerged in *The Erpingham Camp.* The setting is a holiday area, and the hero, Erpingham, is the autocratic owner with dreams of expansion who turns over entertainment duties to an incompetent employee and dies as a result of the mob violence which soon erupts among the campers. The action is bedlam, made up of a series of brief scenes that are almost blackouts, featuring slapstick comedy, music and songs. Orton was trying for the frenetic speed and some of the traditional methods of farce, i.e., abrupt entrances and exits, deceptions and reversals, misconstructions, repetitions and monomania on the part of one or more characters. Orton's satire is established mainly in the dialogue. (pp. 462-63)

Within a few months of the initial production of *The Erpingham Camp* (1966), Orton presented his first full-length venture into farce. *Loot* opened in the fall of 1966 after censorship and revision, and won awards as the best play of the year. On the surface the play was blatant black comedy, reflecting Orton's preoccupation with the grisly and the morbid. . . .

Speed is implicit in the lightning reversals, the rapid character-shifting that Orton has written into the play. Situational humor demands this speed and so does much of the humor in the dialogue. Orton often sets up a scene in order to achieve a vaudevillian patter reminiscent of Marx Brothers inanity. He weaves a variety of types of humor into the tapestry of his lines. Sick jokes predominate, but there are also old gags, slick one-liners and refined witticisms. The continuous play on words includes even the lowly pun. . . . (p. 463)

Parody and social criticism are behind most of the humor in *Loot.* Throughout the play Orton takes every opportunity to parody the whodunnit, the police, the authority of the state and religion. . . .

Characterization in *Loot* is admittedly weak, but considerations of style, structure and situation are so dominant in traditional farce that it is debatable whether characterization can possibly be anything more than a subordinate element. Strictly natural character drawing cannot be pursued without cancelling out the factor of improbability which is so essential to the genre.

The brief re-emergence of Orton's interest in the creation of a convincing character may be seen in *The Good and Faithful Servant* (1967), his second television play and the last work produced before his death. Here is a compassionate portrayal of a man caught in a hopeless struggle with dehumanized company organization. Along the way we also get a frightening look at the invasion of privacy, the tyranny of the computer and the well-intentioned but unfeeling efforts of bureaucrats at regimenting the lives and even the thoughts of ordinary people who work conscientiously and aspire modestly. (p. 464)

The Good and Faithful Servant has none of the outrageous antics or frantic speed of the farce style that Orton was developing in this final period of his life. However, it does contain many funny lines in Orton's characteristic manner, i.e., the prim, absent-minded comment on a scandalous incident. . . .

Delightfully eccentric, Orton's verbal style was his most admired quality at the time of his death. Two plays were in rough draft but sufficiently worked out to warrant production. One was a television play, *Funeral Games* . . . and the other was a full-length stage play, *What the Butler Saw,* given its first London performance in March, 1969.

Funeral Games was a chaotic piece, the result of an attempt to combine fantasy and shock, and the two did not mix in this case. The action is set in a world so topsy-turvy that a religious leader, Pringle, is the object of adulation because he is believed to have murdered his wife. In the face of a reporter's challenge, he tries to prove his guilt by offering, as evidence of the crime, the severed hand of another corpse. It is difficult to tell whether Orton was more intent on playing games with the severed hand or castigating religious hypocrisy.

The title of Orton's last full-length play is itself a tease. There is no man-servant nor any voyeurism in *What the Butler Saw.* Orton borrowed the title of an old-fashioned peepshow (*and an old-fashioned play*) situated at the ends of wharfs in British sea resort areas. This unfinished final play divided audiences and critics down the middle. It drew clamorous protest in the provinces and mixed reviews in London. Those who praised it tended to be extravagant and those who objected tended to cavil. In 1975 the play was still generating controversy and will probably continue to do so for as long as Orton's influence is felt. *What the Butler Saw* does often violate its own logic; it is inconsistent in writing; its comic constructions are sometimes too flimsy; it sorely needs revision. Yet with all its shortcomings it is still a notable accomplishment in modern farce. (p. 465)

Feydeau literally grew up in farce; from his teens it took him many years to develop mastery in fashioning his inimitable imbroglios. Comparatively, Orton's *What the Butler Saw* was a giant leap in a short span of time as far as the rigorously complicated methods of farce are concerned.

It has been said that *Loot* was a farce which parodied the whodunnit, and that *What the Butler Saw* was a farce which parodied farce. The playwright systematically included the most familiar artifices of farce, principally mistaken identity, clothes swapping (not only for disguise but for transvestite change), concealments, deceptions, misconstructions, jack-in-the-box entrances and exits and running sight gags. To use so many contrivances in one play Orton had to devise an intricate plot. (pp. 465-66)

For all of Orton's nimble maneuvering through the maze of plot, situation was less important to him than language. That is why he was not the equal of Feydeau in structural soundness although he may have surpassed the French master in the sheer number and variety of situations he could pack into a single play. The razzle-dazzle deployment of farce contrivances may not have been intended so much to parody farce as to provide luxuriant opportunities for verbal play, and for impaling contemporary beliefs, manners and morals so unsparingly and implacably that it suggests a profound despair of society as it exists today. (p. 466)

Orton's bitterest and most scathing humor was directed in this last play against sexual modes and fashions, against the stereotyping which he only tentatively attacked in the early plays. When Prentice cites his marital state as proof that he is not homosexual, he is advised: ''Marriage excuses no one the freaks' roll-call.'' . . .

More than any previous play *What the Butler Saw* exhibited Orton's distinctive achievement, the forging of a unique, highly individual verbal style. Regardless of their social level, his characters all speak with high-toned airs. They are endowed with niceties of language and a vocabulary which in real life they would not be reasonably expected to possess. . . . Perhaps the most instructive example of the cynicism and callousness of Orton's comic idiom consists of Mrs. Prentice's suggestion, cooly and sweetly offered to Rance as he charges off to capture and certify her husband: "Try not to break his arms or legs. It makes the job of adjusting the strait-jacket doubly difficult."

Joe Orton broke no new ground in dramatic form, and the body of his work is slight. But he had begun to rediscover an old and honorable path too much in disuse. He found farce to be a genre more commodious for his vision of the world than any form of expression he could newly carve out. It was broad enough to contain both sides of his nature, the sunny as well as the dark and anarchic. And farce could be adorned, as Oscar Wilde had proven, with glittering language. (p. 467)

> Mary I. Casmus, "Farce and Verbal Style in the Plays of Joe Orton," in Journal of Popular Culture, Vol. XIII, No. 3, Winter, 1979, pp. 461-68.

BENEDICT NIGHTINGALE

To Orton, any form of authority, from the police to the Ministry of Health, was automatically suspect; all totems, all taboos, were to be challenged; and any show of virtue was certain to be sham. In the whole of his *oeuvre* I do not think there is one character with any capacity for altruism or affection. All are actuated by avarice, whether for power, applause, respectability, money, sex, or some concatenation of gain. And this is not a matter for rancour or even regret on Orton's part. On the contrary, he sees it as a plain truth, to be faced, accepted, and then cheerfully shrugged off somewhere between the counting-house and the knocking-shop. "The world", he once said, "is profoundly bad and irresistibly funny."

It would be absurdly puritanical to deny that the drama these attitudes produce isn't often, very often, entertaining, and even liberating. They produce the exuberance of *The Erpingham Camp*, a modern *Bacchae* in which Orton's Pentheus, the panjandrum of a seaside fun-prison, is punished for his tyrannous hubris by rampaging holidaymakers; and, of course, they produce the engaging scurrilities of *Loot*. Part of Orton's professed purpose in that play was to remind his audiences that a coffin was only a box and a corpse no longer a person; and he fulfils it with invention and dash, dwelling provocatively on details of teeth and eyes and those organs that have to be filleted out before embalming can take place. "My mum's guts were in there", says Hal, explaining why the money can't be stored in a convenient casket. "The damp would get into the notes." That is not just a "sick" joke. Rather, it is a deliberate challenge, a snook pointedly cocked at those who become reverential about death without asking what it is they are revering and why. (p. 57)

[Orton] wanted to remind the genteel that they, too, had bowels and genitalia, camouflage them though they might. His was an impish, teasing drama and, in some ways, an impish, teasing character. . . . His humour could be bumptious and naughty: it could also be contemptuous and malicious.

There is, of course, a place for drama that tweaks the upturned noses of the bourgeoisie, breaks open stink-bombs in their rough vicinity, and mischievously reminds the repressed of their carnality. It is a place that Orton fills with such flamboyance that it seems stingy to point out its limitations and pompous to accuse it of being "immature" or "irresponsible" or "not constructive." Such protests have the stamp of the stuffed shirt, successfully pricked. All the same, we are entitled to examine the conception of the good life that emerges from the plays and decide on the extent and degree to which we can share it. For what, to what, does Orton hope to liberate us? (p. 58)

Orton's plays celebrate the tripes, the glands and, of course, the genitals. They take delight in the overthrow of reason and the breakdown of order. Virtue in this gaudy, scabrous world is (on the whole) getting what one wants, and vice (on the whole) not getting it. "Pain", in so far as it means anything, is deprivation, and "anger" a justified reaction to those parental powers that presume to deprive others. This can, as I say, prove liberating, even exhilarating, in the theatre. There is also something about its greedy, sticky-fingered hedonism that can only be called infantile.

What will posterity make of these contradictions, or, to put the question more manageably, how has Orton's work weathered in the 11 years since his murder? In his iconoclasm, his mistrust of authority, his capacity for mischief and eagerness to shock, he seems very characteristic of the 1960s; and it comes as no surprise to learn that he was preparing a filmscript [entitled *Up against It*] for the culture-heroes of that callow, roistering decade, the Beatles, at the time he died. Yet he is a rather more original voice than this suggests, too individual to be tidied away into so vague a slot. And *Loot,* his best play, and *Entertaining Mr Sloane,* his next best, proved they still had power to amuse and sting when they were revived at the Royal Court three-odd years ago.

Ronald Bryden nicely calls Orton "the Oscar Wilde of Welfare State gentility", a phrase that helps sum up his more appealing qualities: his enjoyment of subversive aphorism, his considerable formal and technical skills, and perhaps also some of his satiric methods. He is constantly contrasting the outrageous with the mundane, the grotesque with the drab clichés and tatty furbishings of a plastic civilisation. (pp. 58-9)

Orton's satiric techniques did, however, change somewhat during his short career. In *Entertaining Mr Sloane,* the first and most naturalistic of his full-length plays, the net curtains are kept firmly drawn throughout. Kath and Ed, brother and sister, both have carnal designs on the lodger, Sloane, but they conceal them in euphemism, hiding their greed even from themselves. They have an extraordinary capacity for ignoring or explaining away anything that might contaminate their self-regard: so much so that Sloane can brutally murder their father, Kath and Ed can promptly blackmail him into agreeing to become their sexual slave for six months a year each, and Ed can end the play with a breezy "well, it's been a pleasant morning", without the least consciousness of behaving unusually. But in the later and more farcical *Loot* and *What the Butler Saw* the characters flaunt their proclivities unashamedly. They make conventions look foolish, not by hypocritically affecting an allegiance to them, but by openly, brazenly, ignoring them. "I'm an honest man", says Hal's father when the robbers try to buy his silence. "You'll have to mend your ways, then" is the instant riposte of the policeman on the case. "Your sleep won't be disturbed tonight, dear", someone promises Mrs Prentice, the nymphomaniac wife in *What the Butler Saw.* "Life is full of disappointments", she answers.

Orton spent his career looking for equivalents of Wilde's joke about the recently widowed duchess, ''her hair has turned quite gold from grief.'' Perhaps it is not too much to suggest, as [John Lahr, Orton's biographer] does, that he was searching for ''the perfect destructive sentence.'' Whether he ever found it is questionable; but he did evolve patterns of repartee that succinctly reflected his own brand of cynicism. The method is apparent in embryo at the end of his first play, **The Ruffian on the Stair:** one character kills another, incidentally smashing a goldfish bowl with a stray bullet, and the murderer's wife bursts into tears and wails, ''They're dead, poor things—and I reared them so carefully.'' It is, roughly, to cap an event or statement that would seem to expect a strongly emotional response, whether of outrage, horror or anything else, with one that wildly underreacts to that event or statement.

Thus Mrs Prentice reports that a pageboy has tried and failed to rape her. ''The service in these hotels is dreadful'' is the reply. Later she whimsically threatens to fly to Delhi and seduce its student population. ''You can't take lovers in Asia'', flings back her ''aghast'' husband, ''The air fare would be crippling.'' (pp. 59-60)

These examples all come from **What the Butler Saw,** which Mr Lahr is inclined to think the funniest, as well as the finest, of Orton's plays. Having seen it twice, and twice failed to laugh even remotely as much as the swaggering language and frenetic encounters seemed to demand, I find it difficult to agree. Part of the reason, I suspect, is that its increasingly elaborate subterfuges and disguises have no inevitability or even necessity. Why, for instance, should the wretched Prentice be at pains to conceal a minor indiscretion from a wife who herself tends to sexual athleticism? How can we laugh at someone's flouting of convention, or desperate attempts to regain respectability, when no one on stage is particularly conventional, respectable or shockable? Farce simply can't breathe in an atmosphere of amorality and permissiveness. And part of the reason is that the proceedings become increasingly unreal as the evening hurtles forward. Fantasy is not friendly to farce, either.

But it is its fantastic, indeed nightmarish, quality that gives **What the Butler Saw** special interest to a student of Orton. It is as if we were being treated to a tour of his free-associating subconscious. . . . By the hectic, frenzied denouement it is hard to distinguish who is sane and who is insane and, as much to the point, who is male and who is female. A drugged policeman meanders about in a leopard-skin dress; a girl reels across in the pageboy's uniform; the government inspector and Mrs Prentice draw revolvers and start shooting.

At this point the stage directions become surprisingly extreme. People are ''screaming with terror'', ''white with shock'', and ''anguished, fainting''; a wound ''streams with blood'', and blood ''pours'' down someone else's leg. Suddenly, unexpectedly and, for him, uniquely, Orton seems to be visualising a human abattoir, which even he finds less than hilarious. Before the final curtain the mood has changed again. Orton, who once declared that his work was ''a deliberate parody of bad theatre'', is reconciling everyone with everyone else in a burlesque imitation of *The Importance of Being Earnest.* Yet the violence that has preceded this is too graphic to be altogether forgotten. It is as if Orton, right at the end of his writing career, realised that the anarchy he was apt to celebrate could result in pain and that pain actually hurt.

It was a strangely ominous insight. Before he had revised **The Butler,** his skull had been smashed open by [his lover, Kenneth]

Halliwell, . . . and we shall never know to what extent, or even whether, that odd, flawed play betokened some deepening of his talent. As it is, we are left with a tantalising, maddening blend of the wit, the *agent provocateur* and the child hoodlum: enough to keep critical discussion and disagreement on the bubble for a long time. (pp. 60-1)

Benedict Nightingale, ''The Detached Anarchist: On Joe Orton,'' in Encounter, *Vol. LII, No. 3, March, 1979, pp. 55-61.*

DAVID ROPER

[**Up Against It** is a screenplay] originally intended for The Beatles via Oscar Lewenstein, but which was rejected without explanation by the boys and their manager, Brian Epstein. In fact, their decision was an obvious commercial compromise, in that the public could not be allowed to witness the nice lads from Liverpool engaging in revolution, assassination, transvestism and group sex.

But naturally, I overstate the case a little; what we really have is a weak idea around which Orton's anger is not focussed carefully enough, although textually the structure of the picaresque journey with its adventures and peripeteia is a standard, mythological device giving licence for anything to happen. The . . . boys leave their past to discover their uncertain, exiled future in a country where women govern, fight, police and are the heads of the Anglican church: if the dialogue remains flat, empty of ringing satire, it may be that Orton here forgot that fact can often be closer to farce than fiction. Fortune's wheel is spinning even faster than it did in Voltaire's *Candide,* and life is lived at the poles of extreme abundance or abject servility, with a fair amount of slapstick pandemonium from time to time, which is all intended to prove, in the words of the character Bernard Coates, that 'any well-regulated society must find room for anti-social activity'.

Orton himself flippantly remarked that it didn't matter if he repeated himself in the film (boys devoured by voluptuous women, as in **Mr Sloane;** middle-class with-its, as in **What the Butler Saw;** pastiches of romantic imagery) since the audiences wouldn't have seen the plays. And he used parts which were to appear after his death in the abandoned novel **Head to Toe.** If he had retained his first intention, of writing about four aspects of one man, four schizophrenic personae, there would have been more chance for the comic play of mistaken identity and role-switching.

There is also the typically acidic bitchiness against the status quo that can be found in any of his works: at a political rally Ramsey shouts, 'We all know why we're here! *(Crowd answers with a roar.)* We're here because there's nothing on the telly!' It's all part of Orton's comic revenge on society, as John Lahr points out, but **Up Against It** isn't a patch on the stage plays, and its only recommendation is that it brings the complete works nearer to completion, and allows for some interesting speculation on what the Beatles might have made of it, or rather, what it might have made of them. . . . (p. 101)

David Roper, in a review of ''Up against It,'' in Gambit, *Vol. 9, No. 35, 1980, pp. 100-01.*

MARTIN ESSLIN

Cocking a snook at the stuffed shirts, shocking the *bien-pensants* bourgeois, certainly was among [Joe Orton's] main aims in life. Behind it one can discern a violent desire to hurt their feelings, to revenge himself on society, to transgress its rules—even in cases when the stuffed shirts did not realize that the rules had been transgressed—merely for the elation of having got away with it. (p. 95)

This desire to shock at all costs, allied with a streak of extreme violence that runs through all of his work, springs from a *saeva indignatio* of great intensity; however, unlike that of Swift and most other satirists, Orton's rage is purely negative, it is unrelated to any positive creed, philosophy or programme of social reform. And it is this aspect of it, which, in my opinion, makes Orton's *oeuvre* so significant for an understanding of the social situation in Britain, and no doubt many other countries, in his lifetime and up to the present: for he articulates, in a form of astonishing elegance and eloquence, the same rage and helpless resentment which manifests itself in the wrecked trains of football supporters, the mangled and vandalized telephone kiosks and the obscene graffitti on lavatory walls. Orton, one might say, gives the inarticulate outcries of football hooligans the polished form of Wildean aphorisms. While thus Orton's writings have, quite apart from the sheer brilliance of his dialogue and plotting, considerable importance as manifestations of a whole society, the story of his life, which could well be the perfect specimen of the plot of one of Orton's plays, constitutes a cautionary tale of the first order, almost too apposite to be true, as though it had been invented by one of the moralizing philistines he so much detested. (p. 96)

That Orton had considerable talent as a playwright is beyond doubt; equally, the extravagant claims made for him by his biographer, John Lahr, who regards him as a major dramatist, seem to me to have to be taken with a grain of salt. Orton's earliest efforts were clearly derivative from Harold Pinter: the opening of the original (radio) version of *The Ruffian on the Stair* is an obvious imitation of the breakfast scenes in *The Room* and *The Birthday Party*. . . . (p. 97)

In the second (stage) version of *The Ruffian on the Stair* the Pinteresque breakfast dialogue has been omitted. A much more characteristically Ortonian note has been added. Now the play opens with:

Joyce: Have you got an appointment today?
Mike: Yes. I'm to be at Kings Cross station at
          eleven. I'm meeting a man in the toilet.
Joyce: You always go to such interesting places. . . .

The last of these lines, held over from the earlier version, thus gains a typically Ortonian flavour and becomes part of something like Orton's version of the Wildean paradoxical epigram. Altogether, a comparison between the radio and the stage version of the play . . . clearly shows the playwright's development. The plot line has been strengthened and the ending given a characteristically ironic twist. (p. 98)

The mature revised version of *The Ruffian on the Stair* . . . includes the very characteristically Ortonian *motif* of a 'good' ending brought about by the happy collusion of the guilty bourgeois and the police, also found in *Entertaining Mr Sloane* (at least in so far as all concerned agree to conceal Sloane's murder from the police), *Loot* and *What the Butler Saw*. . . .

In *Entertaining Mr Sloane* (1964) Orton's view of society as a conspiracy of the wealthy, designed to conceal crime and facilitate their lusts, had hardened. The suggestion that love could be the ruling passion motivating a play, which still informed *The Ruffian on the Stair*, has disappeared; it never

showed itself in any of Orton's further dramatic efforts. Yet, in this first full-length play of Orton's, the Pinter influence can still be discerned in the basic situation: an intruder who enters a household and disrupts it. Just as Aston offered to shelter Davies in *The Caretaker*, Kath has picked up Sloane 'in the library' and taken him to her home because 'he was having trouble. With his rent . . . His landlady was unscrupulous'. Sloane, a young man 'with very smooth skin', has murdered a photographer who had taken some pornographic nude pictures of him. Kemp, Kath's old father, happens to have been employed by that photographer and recognizes Sloane. Ed, Kath's wealthy businessman brother, is a homosexual who is attracted by Sloane. Sloane, who sleeps with Kath and has become Ed's chauffeur and prospective catamite, seems set for a successful exploitation of both. But when Kemp threatens to reveal Sloane's past crime to the police, Sloane kills him. This enables Ed and Kath to blackmail him into an arrangement which condemns him to remain bound to them indefinitely while they share his favours equally: six months with Kath, six months with Ed each year. Thus, as in *The Caretaker*, the play revolves around an intruder who, at first, seems to dominate two unequal and seemingly hostile members of the household, only to have the tables turned on him and to be dominated by an alliance of both insiders.

But, whereas in *The Caretaker* the situation is invested with genuine pathos, both in Aston's need for a companion and in Davies's for a home, so that there is a real feeling of human suffering and tragedy behind even the most grotesquely deprived and ludicrously incompetent characters, the atmosphere of *Entertaining Mr Sloane* is totally heartless. And while in *The Caretaker* the real action lies in a rich texture of subtext, in *Entertaining Mr Sloane* everything is on the surface. (p. 99)

While *Entertaining Mr Sloane* is still, outwardly, structured like a comedy, the mechanical nature of its characters and the explicitness of its language already clearly assign it to the realm of farce, even though it lacks the plot mechanisms of that genre (complications heaped upon complications or numerous doors opening with split-second precision). In *Loot* and *What the Butler Saw* Orton finally found the plot structure to match his vision of humanity and the style of his dialogue.

The television play *The Good and Faithful Servant* . . . still shows Orton groping towards his own style. Written for television mainly to make money, the play obviously represents an attempt to conform to the vogue for 'social' drama on the medium at that time. It is a simple tale about an old man who has served his firm faithfully as a doorkeeper for fifty years and is retired, having been presented with a toaster and electric clock as parting gifts. (p. 100)

On the face of it, this would be material for a touching little play, however hackneyed the theme. But again, in a story calling for at least some emotion and sympathy with the characters, Orton remains unwilling, or unable, to make his characters into more than mechanical functions of a schematic plot. Again there is no subtext, no suggestion that the people of the play have any life outside the actual lines they are speaking. We are left to believe that in the fifty years between his one amorous encounter (which lasted only one afternoon) and his retirement literally nothing happened to Buchanan. Nobody in the firm knows him; he cannot remember anything that occurred during that time. . . . The total passivity and acquiescence of those characters who are presented as victims of society thus not only deprives them of credibility as human beings but also renders them quite unsympathetic. The format of the play is that of realistic social drama with a touch of satire in the caricatured personnel officer, but the central characters are puppets who have strayed into this realistic world from the mechanical universe of farce.

In *Loot* (1965), at last, Orton had found his own voice and his own style. The plot is characteristically complex. Two delinquent young men, Hal and Dennis, have robbed a bank. Mrs McLeavy, Hal's mother, has died, and to escape detection by the police officer, Truscott, who is roaming through the house, Hal and Dennis remove the corpse from its coffin and hide the money there, stowing the corpse in the cupboard. Fay, the nurse who has been looking after Mrs McLeavy in her last illness (and has, in fact, murdered her in order to marry Mr McLeavy and add his fortune to the large sums she has amassed by murdering a long list of previous patients as well as men she had married after disposing of their wives) has had an affair with Dennis. After many macabre incidents involving the corpse, Dennis, Hal, the nurse and the policeman agree to share the loot from the bank robbery. The bereaved husband, old Mr McLeavy, the only character in the play not involved in a crime, is arrested and will have to be removed.... This, then is the farcical universe with a vengeance and at its blackest.... Here the onslaught on the values of the *bien-pensants* has become total: religion, death, the police, law and order, as well as all human emotion are under attack. What Orton is saying is that behind a façade of respectability there is literally *nothing*.... [*Loot*] is satire with a truly Swiftian acerbity and savage irony, even though there is no indication of a positive viewpoint from which society is being criticized. The tone is one of contempt and derision throughout, directed against all the characters equally. They all take it for granted that murder is an acceptable way of gaining one's ends—which, invariably, amount to no more than sensual gratification, sheer greed. And all this is expressed in language of studied and stylized elegance. There is no suggestion of a realist's concern for the vernacular, for class or regional differences. The lowliest characters express themselves in an eloquent standard English. This has led to Orton being compared to Restoration dramatists. And there certainly is something in this comparison with the traditional English high comedy of manners, except that Orton's best work might better be described as 'high comedy of ill-manners'. Yet the motivation for Orton's use of this style is different from that of the Restoration playwrights, who wanted to express the speech of elegant people in an elegant manner. Orton's aim was to achieve comic effects through the contrast between the coarseness of the subject matter and the refinement of its expression.... The television play *The Erpingham Camp* (1966) (later adapted for the stage as part of the double bill of *Crimes of Passion*) is a case in point. Orton spoke of it as his version, or recreation, of *The Bacchae* of Euripides, but, in fact, it is hardly more than a parody of that play.... The transposition of the plot into a British holiday camp—a favourite target of topical satire at the time—yields neither a contemporary reinterpretation of the theme of *The Bacchae* nor illuminating variations on its meaning: it merely lowers its social level and trivializes the plot. While Euripides deals with profound tensions in human nature, Orton is merely describing the inmates of a holiday camp getting out of hand through the incompetence of an entertainments manager who is too inexperienced or clumsy to control the evening's floor show. Thus the Dionysus of the play, Chief Redcoat Riley, is no God, no personification of primeval forces, while its Pentheus, Erpingham, is no more than a slightly authoritarian lay-figure, given to mouthing an occasional patriotic cliché. Even in terms of mere parody the parallels are extremely feebly drawn: the raging maenads amount

to hardly more than a pregnant lady, who claims that she has been insulted, and her feebly protesting husband. And Erpingham dies not under any assault by orgiastic, unchained revellers, but merely because the floorboards of his office give way so that he drops down among the dancers on the ballroom floor. The final scene of his burial, in a parody of a sanctimoniously conducted patriotic state funeral, has no organic justification and seems merely tacked on to make another hackneyed parodistic point. The suggestion that the holiday camp might be a symbol for contemporary Britain, with Erpingham as the embodiment of the establishment (the monarchy, the government), would, if it represented the author's intention, merely underline the shallowness of the concept. Orton himself had a high opinion of the play: but that simply confirms the absence in him of any serious thought about the society he was not so much attacking as 'cocking a snook at'. *The Erpingham Camp* is hardly more than an extended, and rather feeble, cabaret sketch.

Orton's last television play, written in 1966, but not broadcast till a year after his death, *Funeral Games*, reverts to the style of black farce that had been so successful in *Loot*. Again the satire is directed against sanctimoniousness and religious zeal; again there is a corpse at the centre of the action.... The language in which this preposterous tale ... is told is even more baroque than that of *Loot*; it exploits not only all opportunities to mix low subject matter with a biblically elevated phraseology, but, also—and above all—capitalizes on the opportunities for *double entendres*.... Indulgence in disgusting detail and baroque black humour are here driven to such extreme lengths that *Funeral Games* does achieve something like a superlative of inverted grandeur, and becomes a kind of Albert Memorial of mannerist preposterousness and execrable taste.

Orton's last play, completed shortly before he was murdered and generally regarded as his 'masterpiece', is *What the Butler Saw* (1969). It is a farce plotted in the style of Feydeau, and carries an epigraph from *The Revenger's Tragedy:* 'Surely we're all mad people, and they, whom we think are, are not'. (pp. 100-05)

[Orton] saw himself as having written a farce which, at the same time, was heavy with myth, the anthropology of *The Golden Bough* and allusions to classical drama.

It is certainly a dazzling performance. And yet, on reflection, does it amount to more than an impressive piece of juggling, of prestidigitation? Feydeau's characters, however mechanically they are moved about, still embody a satirist's insights into the realities of human nature. But even in this, undoubtedly Orton's most accomplished play, no insights are vouchsafed: the characters are simply not of this world, being pure constructs. That psychiatrists might be crazier than their patients is not an insight, not even an observation; it is simply an old, oft-repeated cliché. But there is not even a hint of genuine critique of psychiatry or psychoanalysis in the play. This aspect of it is no more than one of those semi-obscene seaside postcards blown up to giant size: the lecherous doctor who orders his patient to undress is a stock character of folk humour. So is the titillation derived from boys dressed up as girls, girls as boys, culminating, as it does here, in the demand 'Take your trousers down, I'll tell you which sex you belong to'....

This is not to say that Orton's work does not provide material for a psychoanalyst: his pre-occupation with incest, with sexual ambiguity, equally evident in *Head to Toe* and in the film script

Up Against It, with homosexuality and murder, might be a fit subject for investigation in greater depth (although at first sight the indications it provides seem fairly obvious) but that does not mean that the *oeuvre* as such provides insights as literature or art. (p. 106)

Behind Orton's attack on the existing state of humanity in the West there stands nothing but the rage of the socially and educationally under-privileged: having risen from the working classes of an ill-educated mass society that has lost all the religious and moral values of earlier centuries and has been debauched by the consumerism of a system manipulated by the mass media, Orton exemplifies the spiritual emptiness and—in spite of his obvious brilliance and intelligence—the thoughtlessness, the inability to reason and to analyse, of these deprived multitudes. This is neither the bitter laugh of which Beckett speaks, the laugh about that which is bad in the world; nor the hollow laugh about what is untrue; nor that mirthless laugh, the *risus purus,* about what is unhappy and tragic; but the mindless laugh which reflects the deprivation of the dispossessed and amounts to no more than an idiot's giggle at his own image in a mirror.

As such Joe Orton's *oeuvre* is both symptomatic and significant. (p. 107)

> Martin Esslin, *"Joe Orton: The Comedy of (Ill) Manners," in* Contemporary English Drama, *edited by C.W.E. Bigsby, Holmes & Meier Publishers, Inc., 1981, pp. 95-107.*

C. W. E. BIGSBY

Throughout his brief career [Orton] maintained a wry detachment not only from the social world but also from his own art. He was scrupulous in his attention to the details of craft, but undeceived by the mythologizing of art as an act of transcendence. For him it was a provocation, an act of revenge, a deliberate flouting of authority and flaunting of his own exhibitionist tendencies. It was designed to negate the conventional assurances of art and to corrode the link between that art and the assumptions of liberal humanism. Where, through its emphasis on the social and the psychological, liberal art offered a rational model of history and personal experience, he chose to stress the arbitrary, the irrational. Where it presented an image of a complexly motivated self in negotiation with a publicly verifiable reality, he presented a series of caricatures who exist in a self-evidently theatricalized world. Where it implied the possibility of social and moral order, the persistence of meaning, he dramatized an anarchic world, irrational, violent and self-consuming. (p. 23)

Like Pinter, Orton is concerned with underscoring the emotional and metaphysical void that he sees as lying beneath the surface of existence. Familiar settings are invested with a sense of menace. The surface realism is fractured by an external threat which exposes an internal insufficiency. *The Ruffian on the Stair* is set in 'a kitchen/living room with a bedroom alcove' and *Entertaining Mr Sloane* in 'a room' in a house situated in the middle of a rubbish dump. The cramped setting is an image of characters who are themselves effectively trapped in the narrow range of their own possibilities. But it is not a refuge that offers any protection. Once the familiar territory is breached, they are exposed, vulnerable, driven back on to resources they do not possess. Only vaguely conscious of a sense of pain and loss (in the former play) or not even aware of the existence of such emotions (in the latter), they happily embrace a vacuous

routine, compounding the absurdity of their situation by their blithe insensitivity.

Unlike Edward Albee's much misunderstood play, *The Zoo Story, The Ruffian on the Stair* is concerned with the efforts of one character to fool another into collaborating in his own suicide. . . . But where Albee's play is a direct plea for human communication, for the renewal of a love destroyed or sentimentalized by contemporary society, Orton's is a demonstration of the arbitrary power of primary instincts. Where Jerry's death, in Albee's play, is a sacrifice to demonstrate the need for human commitment, Wilson's is a pointless suicide which has no effect on those who survive it. In this world the word 'sacrifice' would have no meaning at all.

Orton's first play seemed in some sense counterfeit. The dominant influence of Pinter was so strong, indeed, that he felt obliged to delete some of the more obvious borrowings when he prepared it for the stage and to insist that 'The play mustn't be presented as an example of the now outdated "mystery" school—*vide* early Pinter'. . . . But there was some legitimacy in such a remark, for already he was inclined to resist the implications of metaphysics. Like Robbe-Grillet, he reacted against literary speliology—the assumption that art works by concealment, with the text merely hiding a subtext which is the real repository of meaning. Besides a predilection for mischievous innuendo, he was already committed to exposure as a method, inclined to realistic production values, more committed to the pace of farce than to what he regarded as the portentous mystifications of Pinter. 'The play', he insisted, 'must be directed without long significant pauses. Any pauses must be natural. Pace, pace, pace as well'. . . . Such mystery as exists derives less from the unexplained than from emotions that cannot be fully articulated—a problem not without its relevance to Orton. Indeed, if anything, the weakness of the play lies in a sentimentality not entirely neutralized by a mannered language. The loneliness that drives both male protagonists escapes the ironic treatment of their character and actions. Where later he would rigorously deny his characters any emotional dimension, making them no more than the embodiments of biological drives, here he compromises, opting for absurdist melodrama rather than absurdist farce.

Orton's early characters, like Pinter's, seem to inhabit a social and moral no man's land between the working class and the lower middle class to which they aspire; they are not quite at home in either. They reveal a severely limited emotional range which is reflected in a similarly restricted linguistic competence. Their pretensions to urbanity and their language, curiously inappropriate as it is to their situation, reflect a disruption between the apparent reality of their circumstances and their perception of that reality—a disruption that has implications beyond the social. The characters are mocked by the contrast between the studied, though seldom wholly correct, formality of their language and the substance of their lives. . . . [In *The Ruffian on the Stair*], we are clearly moving in a world in which reality cannot be adequately described or controlled by language—or, alternatively, in which language stands as a symbol of the kind of ordered and socially secure world which the individual would wish to occupy but cannot locate or inhabit. It is not just evidence of bourgeois pretensions, a bid for linguistic upward mobility. The secondhand expressions they use serve to underscore the degree to which they are the products of language rather than its master.

The clichés in which his characters perpetually speak imply a language drained of content. He derives his linguistic leverage from this juxtaposition of words to setting and character, both being voided of content. It is as though language were an almost dead battery he has stumbled on, able to generate only the minimum of power. It is a language marked by discontinuities, non sequiturs, incongruities. Conversations seem never to involve real exchanges. His characters are curiously autistic, incapable of communicating feeling or meaning with any conviction. (pp. 26-8)

[The] world that Orton describes is spiritually attenuated—a place in which a debilitated language reflects a parallel collapse of all other human values and civilizing qualities. It is a world that can accept violence and even murder as of no more significance than the accidental death of a pet goldfish. It is a life in which the primary facts are sex and violence. (pp. 28-9)

Like his first play, *Entertaining Mr Sloane* owes a great deal to Pinter. Sloane himself is close kin to Stanley in Pinter's *The Birthday Party*. Both are lodgers pursued by repulsive middle-aged landladies. Both move from being contemptuously dominant to being the pliant victims of others. Both plays end on an ironic note as the mindless pattern of existence reasserts itself and the disturbing revelations of insecurity and violence go disregarded. (p. 29)

[Sex] is central to [Orton's] work in a way that it is not, to the same degree, to Pinter's. For Orton, in his early works, it is at the heart of events, maiming, infantilizing, brutalizing. All other activity, with the exception of a sexually derived violence, is relegated to the wings. The grotesque power of the sexual drive is presented not only as an image of alienation but as, in some degree, its cause. The social world is merely cover for an aggression that projects tensions on to a public screen. (pp. 29-30)

In this world there is no structure, and the dominating sexual image is itself indicative of a fundamental dissonance. It is not only a world of grotesque mismatches, but one in which the incestuous relationship is the norm. It is hinted [in *Entertaining Mr Sloane*] that Sloane may be Kath's illegitimate child; in *The Ruffian on the Stair* Wilson has been having a homosexual relationship with his brother, a relationship described, by Orton, as a sexual perversion for which not even the Irish have a name. For Freud incest was an image of anarchy, and in all of Orton's work this anarchy dominates—either, in his early work, as a natural product of absurdity or, in his later work, as a redemptive volatility.

The world of *The Ruffian on the Stair* and *Entertaining Mr Sloane* is one of moral and linguistic incoherences. His characters are in control of neither their language nor their actions. Sexual impulses are the primary motor forces of their behaviour, but they each inhabit separate worlds. They are the objects of humour rather than its conscious generators. Thus the humour frequently derives from innuendoes lost on the characters, from an absurdly inappropriate register or vocabulary to which they themselves are insensitive. They are purely theatrical figures—a status to which the text itself confesses. . . . Much of the dialogue in the play consists of short sentences, quick-fire exchanges reminiscent of the music hall, which is plainly one of Orton's models. And as he chose to stress the theatricality of his characters, so he suppressed the sentimentality of his first play, opting for a world in which the density of character and the complexity of social reality are denied. The chief threat now becomes for him, as it did for Albee in *The American Dream* or Pynchon in *V.*, the pull of the inanimate, as his figures are slowly dismantled, invaded by the mechanical, from

Kath's false teeth . . . to Buchanan's artificial arm, in *The Good and Faithful Servant* . . . , and the corpse's glass eye in *Loot*. Indeed, Orton's plays are as littered with corpses as revenge tragedy, a genre whose fascination with death, moral anarchy and insanity attracted Orton to the extent that he used a passage from *The Revenger's Tragedy* as epigraph to his last play.

The violation of conventional modes and a refusal to accept the logic of narrative or character development are central strategies. Like Eliot and Pinter before him, Orton relies on the theatre's conventional function as a source of reassurance and entertainment for his subversive effects, making conscious use of the conventions he was intent on undermining. (pp. 30-2)

Orton's plays almost invariably conclude with a return to consonance which can be nothing but ironic. *Funeral Games* closes with the police getting their man (the wrong man, as it turns out), as the murderer remarks, 'Do not weep. Everything works out in accordance with the divine Will'; while *The Good and Faithful Servant* ends with the announcement of the protagonist's death to the accompaniment of 'On the Sunny Side of the Street'. The same reductive irony operates in the grotesquely inappropriate iconography and rhetoric that concludes *The Erpingham Camp,* in which, as the stage direction indicates, 'the body of Erpingham is left alone in the moonlight with the red balloons and dying flames in a blaze from the distant stained glass. A great choir is heard singing "The Holy City"'. . . . Orton seems intent on simultaneously satisfying and ridiculing the demands of a form that derives its effect from the re-establishment of rationality and structure after a simulated flirting with formlessness. While justice and morality seem to be victorious, in fact they have been profoundly subverted. (pp. 32-3)

Orton's characters are deliberately flattened, deprived of the supposed depth of realism: they are simple caricatures, reduced to the two-dimensionality of a painting. Jackson Pollock once observed that 'There was a reviewer a while back who wrote that my pictures didn't have any beginning middle or end. He didn't mean it as a compliment, but it was. It was a fine compliment'. By contrast, Orton chooses less to destroy such a structure from without, by abandoning it, than to undermine it from within, hollowing it out, draining it of its ideological force and its moral energy. In other words, parody was already an important element of his dramatic strategy; so was provocation. For, while Pinter's work may have perplexed and disturbed the West End audience, Orton's provoked it. (pp. 33-4)

[Parody] is an ambiguous weapon. Ostensibly it offers the audience a reassuring sense of superiority, a knowing complicity with the author. It flatters them with the assumption that they share a command of the models being subverted and are fully aware of the nature of those subversions. But Orton played a double game. Though his apparent models were the detective story, the melodrama and the light comedy, his other paradigms were buried deeper: classical drama, Restoration wit, Wildean paradox. Indeed, he relied on his audience's failing to recognize the parodic thrust and took pleasure in their discomfiture. The superiority of the writer over his characters mirrored a superiority of writer over audience in which he delighted. Relying on the ignorance of those he goaded, he needed the bourgeois audience to allow him the *frisson* that derives from delivering public insults with impunity. . . . His first plays, then, picture an antinomian world inhabited by spiritually debilitated characters, a world that is not so much a product of social forces as productive of them. In his subsequent work, however, he tended to become what Albee once described himself as being, a demonic social critic, as he focuses on the temporal agents of that determinism, the authoritarian figures who conspire to project metaphysical absurdity on to a social level. In his final plays he celebrates the splendidly anarchistic spirit that is liberated by absurdity, rather than delineating the ever-diminishing world of human action as Beckett had done. The sober madness of his earlier work gives way to the manic energy of the later. Sexuality is no longer seen as the painful source of human frustration and violence but as an absurdly trivial activity, the fit subject for a reductive humour.... Orton, in other words, presses the absurd towards farce—a movement that gathered pace after the most socially conscious of his absurdist plays, *The Good and Faithful Servant.*

While there is clearly a social dimension to plays that describe the world of diminished human possibilities, the deterioration of human relationships and the fragility of language, this is not his main concern in the early plays. For here he sees the metaphysical world as projecting a more fundamental dissonance than that which defines the individual's relationship to the social world. (pp. 35-6)

The 'meaning' of Orton's plays is clearly not recuperable primarily from an account of their plots or even a description of their characters. To a far greater extent than usual, the style of these plays, their wit and their internal processes are their meaning. Causalities are suppressed or mocked, the significance of action is dissipated, coherences dissolve, the presumed logic of moral process is disrupted and warped. *The Good and Faithful Servant,* therefore, is something of an exception in his work. It is a satire; and this implies something of a moral stance on Orton's part. The characters are what society has made them: they are infantilized, mechanized, quite literally demoralized by a system that values only its own processes. The protagonist, Buchanan, works for a company so large that he goes unrecognized and has a hard time finding his way through the labyrinth of its corridors. But the sense of anger here which generates Orton's satire is unique in a career more usually given to mocking the assumption that presentation conceals representation. (p. 37)

Orton's ironic view is directed not only at corporate capitalism but at the great unsocial present we each separately inhabit. Manipulated from birth, forced to adapt our sense of selfhood to the ready-made identities of the public world, we render absurdity doubly absurd, allowing habit and custom, utility and expediency, to become the only principles we can acknowledge, and nerveless passivity before an externally defined life to be the only philosophy to which we are prepared to grant any dignity. (p. 39)

Loot, completed in October 1964, was the first evidence of a shift in Orton's work away from the Pinter-influenced absurdism of the early plays to the absurdist world of anarchic farce. It was very clearly an act of public revenge for the humiliations society had inflicted upon him in an equally public way. He said in a letter to the actor-comedian Kenneth Williams, 'I'm writing a play to show all the inanities and stupidities I've undergone.' It was a play that very deliberately set out to flout all normal standards of good taste, an objective that did little to assure its stage success. It ridiculed the hypocrisy of polite society and exposed the cant of authority. The characters, with a single exception, are all totally corrupt, creating among themselves the only kind of society Orton seemed to believe possible: a society of the self-seeking.

But once again his most studied blows were reserved for the figures of authority, more especially for the police who, as a drug-taking homosexual, he regarded as a natural enemy, a necessary evil perhaps, but an image of all the restrictions into which he had run full-tilt over the years. The plot is, indeed, a neat reversal of the standard mystery play, a parody of that restoration of order which is inherent in the detective story and the well-made realistic play alike. (p. 41)

The only character with any sense of moral values, with any scruples that are not up for sale to the highest bidder, is McLeavy, and he is systematically insulted and abused. His touching faith in authority ... simply makes him a more convenient victim for the rapacious grotesques around him. When he insists that 'the police are for the protection of ordinary people', the police inspector can only reply in disbelief, 'I don't know where you pick up these slogans, sir. You must read them on the hoardings'.... (pp. 42-3)

[Orton describes a] world that has descended into unreality, so that Fay's concluding comment, 'We must keep up appearances'..., is not to be taken simply as a parody of middle-class hypocrisy. It is in fact a prescription for survival. In a world lacking in moral substance, the image may indeed be the only reality, a fictionalizing self the only protection against being trapped in the monolithic fiction of the state.

In this respect Orton's later plays are more thoroughgoingly subversive than the earlier ones, for farce becomes not merely a form of realism but a strategy to ensure survival. As he indicated in *Entertaining Mr Sloane* and *The Ruffian on the Stair,* the great risk is to be committed, to accept seriousness as a possible response to one's surroundings. His last works not merely present the fluid, confusing, amoral, neurotic, posturing world of contemporary existence; they celebrate it. It is in this sense that he regarded *Loot* as 'a plea against compartmentalization'. His characters are a series of 'performed selves' who evade the painful realities of existence by refusing to treat them with any seriousness, refusing to grant any connection between the roles they play and any other self which may be capable of suffering the ultimate traumas of birth and death.... Thus, too, in farce attention shifts from change deriving from the egregious circumstances of life and death to change deriving purely from the shifting perspectives and circumstances of social misunderstandings. (pp. 43-4)

[*The Erpingham Camp*] was very much in the new style that had emerged with *Loot.* Beneath the humour, which now deliberately smashes all pretence at realism, there is a mordant observer dispassionately remarking on the absurdity of all human passion and action. Mankind is seen as a scrabbling mass of grotesque creatures, uncomprehendingly enacting public roles in which they have been hopelessly miscast. *The Erpingham Camp* presents a Hieronymus Bosch world in which pain and degradation are the common currency, and the only structure is that imposed by the consistency of suffering or by the arbitrary act of the artist in choosing to locate the frenzied activity within a recognizable dramatic frame. It is a comedy of dislocation, an anarchic farce in which the sustaining myths of human rationality, dignity and integrity are seen as illusory. The view of human nature exposed here is much the same as that captured by the late Goya sketches: man as uncomprehending brute. Thus, despite the eponymous hero's proud assertion that 'we live in a rational world'..., the evidence of the play consistently contradicts him. For it consists of an elaborate act of decreation on the part of its characters as they enact the entropic process common to Orton's plays, as it is to the human organism itself. Faced with this ineluctable process, Erpingham can only exert an authority which is a substitute for will or fall back on what he calls the 'best in twentieth century civilization'. But, since this turns out to be 'Russ Conway on the gram and a browse through a James Bond' . . . , it proves a somewhat fragile resource. (pp. 44-5)

Yet, if Orton's contempt for authority is clear enough in a play that manages incidentally to ridicule the Queen, military pomp, nationalist fervour and the cant of politicians, he has no more confidence in the rebel. Indeed, *The Erpingham Camp* offers a mordant satire on the heroics of Establishment and revolutionary alike. It stands as a rejection of the whole world of politics and social action. (p. 47)

The move from *The Ruffian on the Stair* and *Entertaining Mr Sloane* to *Loot, The Erpingham Camp* and *What the Butler Saw* was a retreat from mystery, from implied depth, from density. In escaping Pinter's influence, Orton opted for a world in which his primary weapons became parody, sexual affront, visual and verbal humour and macabre juxtaposition. He learned from Pinter the need to treat the bizarre as simple realism and recognized the humour to be derived from a disproportion between social class and linguistic register; but, where Pinter aimed at a questioning of ontological status, Orton was concerned with a dislocation of the sensibility and turned his work into an act of aggression which did not stop at the boundaries of art.

In many respects Orton was more profoundly revolutionary than those playwrights who immediately preceded him, and who had been presented as bringing about radical changes in English theatre. Unlike them, he was as suspicious of dramatic form as he was of social imperatives. He set out to undermine both. . . . Orton was prepared to taunt his audience with the disturbing thought that only disorder can generate vitality and a compelling humour—that true liberation may lie in cutting loose from the moral world rather than trying to reconstruct it, in abandoning liberal notions of individual identity and social responsibility. Authority of any kind becomes a vicious and dehumanizing force. It serves only to frustrate an individual performance which is as much a reality as the fictions of society itself. The role playing to be found in the theatre is no longer contrasted with 'real life' but offered as an immediate strategy for those assailed by demands for social conformity. The authority of the camp owner, in *The Erpingham Camp,* is best opposed not by rational complaint and the assertion of legal rights but by a riot which, significantly, starts on a stage (the origin of Orton's own riotous subversion); the petulant demands of the Ministry-appointed psychiatrist, in *What the Butler Saw,* are frustrated not by a rigid adherence to norms of behaviour but by a disturbingly flexible approach to identity, with the characters repeatedly changing their roles as easily as they change their clothes.

Yet this is not simply a defence against the intrusive demands of society: it is, at base, a comment upon that society. For the artificial world of Orton's plays—a world in which character is provisional, violence imminent, language unreliable, reality uncertain—constitutes both a metaphysical observation and an image of contemporary life as he saw it. But, where society deliberately constructs a series of values which it then regards as absolute, Orton's protagonists behave as though the world were the antinomian place that Orton himself takes it to be. If they recognize the existence of social standards and sometimes pay them an ironic regard, their own energy is sustained not by observing the rules of the social contract but by playing their changing roles with vigour and commitment. Orton's plays

have the virtue of confessing to their artificiality, their fictiveness. (pp. 49-51)

The universal descent into unreality that has typified postmodernist literature surfaces in contemporary English drama as a fragmented world in which characters, purged of the rounded reality of liberal drama, move uncertainly or even obliviously through a strange landscape whose strangeness must simply be accepted. This is the world of Beckett's and Pinter's plays, as it is of Stoppard's *Rosencrantz and Guildenstern Are Dead*. It is also the world created by Joe Orton, who actually lived out the absurdity of his age, an age he could never take entirely seriously but which always threatened to devolve into violence and death—as, eventually, it did in reality for him.

The inhumanity of modern life is no longer countered by the assertion of liberal values but rather by a neutralizing madness or marginality. And the form embraced has frequently been that which defines itself by reference to marginality and inconsequence: farce, a new form of anarchic force derived from a wedding of the absurd and the old farce tradition. . . . The protagonists of this new farce-world are therefore themselves marginal, irrelevant to the slow unwinding of an entropic process, while the form itself is self-destructive, implying the existence of no Platonic idea in the mad logic of its own configurations. Indeed, entropy—a term drawn from thermodynamics and signifying the degree of disorder in a system, the progressive loss of energy in a machine—is as useful in an account of Orton's work as it is in a consideration of that of the American novelist Thomas Pynchon. For disorder characterizes both their worlds, as a progressive dismantling marks their characters (in Orton's case they are stripped or injured and even die). For both writers order is a phantom, the source of an irony that defines human experience.

If Orton was in some ways a representative of the post-modernist impulse, then it is worth recalling that post-modernism has two faces. On the one hand, it identifies the collapse of form, the loss of meaning, contingency, stasis, a marginality that is equally the product of social alienation and metaphysical abandonment; on the other, it celebrates that marginality, sees experience as a dimension of aesthetics, rejoices in the ludic and generates a manic energy. Orton, who began his career . . . as an exemplar of the former mode, ended as an embodiment of the latter. And in that he was very much an expression of his times. His stress on the sensual rather than the intellectual (though his wit plainly relied on intellectual processes), on an insurgency that derived from his own marginal position, his membership of a menaced subculture, was not merely widely shared but became itself something of an orthodoxy, more especially in America. (pp. 52-3)

Orton's work, and in particular the later plays, seems to reflect such convictions, to rest on the assumption that life is an elaborate performance, a fiction in which characters contain no more depth or reality than is demanded by the conventions of their role or permitted by the exigencies of social organization. In one sense this is to say no more than that Orton is indeed a *farceur,* for the world of farce is of course a world of partial beings, role players whose mask is constantly in danger of slipping, even if this is conveniently reinstated at the climax of the play. But here Orton differs. His social charades are made of sterner stuff. His characters cannot be so conveniently restored to their featureless norm as can the heroes of old farce; their wounds cannot be cauterized by a graceful arabesque of plot. They struggle to sustain illusions of purposeful existence with nothing more elaborate than a tissue of language.

If in farce action is substituted for feeling until human relations are little more than the extruded consequence of circumstance, in Orton's work the assault launched on individual character by the representatives of authority and normality is not without an edge of viciousness and a residual pathos. If this is farce, it is Pinter played as farce.

The only logic Orton could detect was the mad, circular logic of dementia; the only art he wished to generate, one that undermined models of social and artistic order. In the wildly absurd **Funeral Games** . . . he created a bewilderingly complex plot which turns on a neat reversal of conventional morality, the baroque arabesques of plot detail constituting an ironic comment on the narrative tradition in literature and, more significantly, presumptions of human rationality and spiritual integrity. (pp. 53-4)

It is scarcely any wonder that one of the play's characters should confess that he has 'learned to accept the irrational in everyday life'. . . . For this is a world in which 'the humble and meek are thirsting for blood' . . . , in which the church, whose ironic symbol is a bird of prey carrying an olive branch, is seen as merely a cover for violence. It is a world stood on its head, a place of mad logic, a frenzied correlative of a contemporary existence whose own style can perhaps best be described as neurotic. Like the complex interleaving conspiracies of Thomas Pynchon, which parody the compulsive human search for meaning and structure, it offers evidence of nothing but its own internal form. It is an impossible world, but one that is painfully close to our own in which religion has all too often proved simply another face of self-interest and violence, in which the existence of structured actions has been taken as evidence of cosmic meaning. Here the patterns are clearly self-destructive, wholly unrelated to any concept of reality or truth. . . . It is entirely appropriate that Orton's last play, **What the Butler Saw,** should be set in a mental hospital. . . . Like the *Marat/Sade* or *One Flew Over the Cuckoo's Nest,* it presents the institution as an image of contemporary society—a paradigm of a world in which authority seeks to define reality, impose rules, coerce the individual, and in which the individual can respond only with a corrosive anarchy, for, as one of the play's central characters remarks, 'You can't be a rationalist in an irrational world. It isn't rational'. . . . (pp. 55-6)

The play offers the by now familiar criticism of authority, with the Queen, Winston Churchill, the police and psychiatry being pilloried. But beyond its exuberant wit it does imply more substantial issues, the nature of the real, the desperate and ironic need to impose form on chaos, the inadequacy of the rational mind in a world not structured on rational principles. Unusual behaviour may indeed be the order of the day in a mental hospital, but the insanity with which Orton deals is not contained by the walls of an institution. It is a 'democratic lunacy'. Of course, farce has always sustained the notion that life is simply a game. The mistaken identities of French farce, the sexual taboos that are broken and the social etiquette that is momentarily abandoned are customary stages in a familiar and frivolous exercise. The indiscretions are themselves recognizable ploys in a game that will inevitably end with social roles happily reasserted, with broken relationships restored.

But where such endings occur in Orton's work they are painfully ironic. Where Feydeau has flirtation, Orton has rape; where Feydeau has sexual misadventure, Orton has incest. In Feydeau sensibilities are offended, in Orton physical injuries are sustained. Feydeau's characters are driven to cosmic despair and momentary desperation, Orton's are driven to madness and death. Where Feydeau depends on the existence of a structured society, with its recognized codes and values, Orton presents a world in which normative values no longer exist, in which anarchy is the only dependable reality.

Indeed, the byzantine complexities of the plot of **What the Butler Saw** can be seen as a deliberate attempt to parody the very structure of farce itself. (pp. 56-7)

The play is close in spirit and to a degree in detail to *The Importance of Being Earnest*. The confusion of identity and the critique of solemnity and pomposity are indeed familiar enough. Each individual perceives a different reality and makes this the basis for actions which, while logical enough given the nature of the initial premise, are irrational when viewed from any other perspective. And this is clearly proffered by Orton as an insight into human misunderstanding and the relativity of the physical and moral world. To some degree, of course, this would seem to be subverted by the privileged position granted to the audience, who believe themselves to be in possession of a perceivable truth, a reliable guide to the actual processes enacted in front of them. But this comfortable assurance, so necessary to the enjoyment of bourgeois farce, is destroyed at the end when they are made to see that what they took to be frivolous sexual games were in fact incestuous trysts in which a mother is raped by her son and a father attempts to strip and rape his daughter. The germ of moral anarchy is suddenly exposed at the centre of the conventional confection. And this is the essence of Orton's method.

Orton's consistent assault on authority, then, is both the gesture of a social rebel and an assertion of the contingent nature of the world we inhabit. His concern with the fragile boundaries of sexuality is not merely a defence of his own right to deviate from supposed norms but an assertion of everyone's right of dissent from all the principles and presumptions that form the basis of what we erroneously presume to be absolute standards of conduct and agreed codes of morality. His concern with the indefinable nature of reality, the fluid essence of identity and the relativity of truth constitutes a metaphysical as well as a social truth. It implies a conviction as to the antinomian nature of our universe; it is an assertion of the need to embrace uncertainty, the arbitrary, the neurotic, the kaleidoscopic fictions we create for ourselves. The authority he denounces is thus ultimately any kind of limiting or categorizing force, social or metaphysical, which is presumed to give shape and coherence to existence but which can do so only at the expense of the total freedom of action, that transgression of boundaries which is the only value he can identify. Dr Rance's claim that 'I am a representative of order, you of chaos' . . . is ultimately a validation of anarchy, of self-invention, and of the fictionalizing impulse. (pp. 57-8)

C. W. E. Bigsby, in his Joe Orton, *Methuen, 1982, 79 p.*

Frank Parkin

1940-

English novelist, nonfiction writer, and biographer.

Best known for his writings in the field of political science, Parkin elicited critical attention from the literary world for his first novel, *Krippendorf's Tribe* (1985). Set in a near-future England characterized by pension riots, uncollected garbage, and televised hangings, this book features black humor and farce in its story of James Krippendorf, an unemployed anthropologist who fabricates a study of a primitive South American tribe for publication in a scholarly journal. Krippendorf modeled this fictitious society after his three unruly children, who soon begin to resemble savages both in appearance and behavior. Parkin's comedic techniques, particularly his use of parody and his penchant for the grotesque, have been compared favorably to the works of English humorist Tom Sharpe. Although some critics faulted Parkin for an overabundance of jokes and an anticlimactic ending, others praised his inventiveness and his satirization of the academic community, familial relationships, and contemporary English society.

ANTHONY THWAITE

Anthropology is, I suppose, by definition more 'human' than philosophy, but in Frank Parkin's *Krippendorf's Tribe* it fares as badly. James Krippendorf is an anthropologist, no longer employed by a university, who now stays in Islington ineffectually looking after his three fearsome children while his wife does her TV-reporter stuff in foreign parts. His final research report for the Malinowski Institute, on the Shelmikedmu of the Amazon Basin, is long overdue. This is because he has never visited the Shelmikedmu, if they indeed exist. Instead, he has been sitting at home, inventing behaviour patterns for the tribe based closely on his observations of his dreadful family. . . .

Frank Parkin has a lot of bad-taste fun with the horrors of late 1980s England, in which bread riots, the jailing of the TUC, curfew enforcement and insurgency in the Home Counties are as commonplace as vandalised telephone booths and rubbish tips in the streets. Krippendorf's children are anarchic experimenters in sadism, incest, murder, and finally—with his surprised acquiescence—cannibalism. We leave them flying off to Brazil, leading a package-holiday expedition to the Shelmikedmu. Elements of Tom Sharpe and the Bradbury/Lodge team have been well mixed, though the black grin of shock-horror farce is a bit set.

> Anthony Thwaite, "Sex on the Brain," *in* The Observer, *March 3, 1985, p. 26.*

STAN GEBLER DAVIES

Since Tom Sharpe has taken to imitating himself, it is unnecessary that others should do likewise. Nevertheless, the school of Sharpe emerges as a blot on the literary landscape. It is rather a pity, really, but quite inevitable that once a writer has

© *Jerry Bauer*

devised a style so successful that his books sell in the millions, hundreds will ape him. . . .

There is an apparent simplicity to Sharpe's plots which must be beguiling to would-be imitators: it is that every last damn thing which could not conceivably happen, does happen. . . .

In order for the formula to work to comic effect, it is necessary that the victims should be utterly innocent, thereby demonstrating the awful malignancy of humankind and the nonchalance of God (*à la* Voltaire), or else thoroughly unpleasant, in which case one appreciates their comeuppance. Frank Parkin has got this formula only half-right [in *Krippendorf's Tribe*], for all of his characters are malignant and the most evil of them all, his hero Krippendorf, gets away with no more punishment than a passing dose of the clap.

The first half of [*Krippendorf's Tribe*] works very well. Krippendorf, an anthropologist so incompetent that he addresses the working classes in polysyllables in the belief that they will understand him, is engaged in the composition of a monograph on the subject of an Amazonian tribe whose acquaintance he has not been able to make because he has squandered his research grant on fripperies like a new Volvo. In the absence of his wife, a television reporter who roams the world recording revolutions and the executions attendant to them, he is required to look after his three children.

These are: a small boy who is interested only in the ingestion of food but cannot get it past his face; a larger boy who manufactures napalm and squirts it onto cats with his bicycle-pump; and their pubescent sister, a punk who beats the smaller boy for stealing the batteries from her vibrator.

Krippendorf, pressed for concrete results by the research foundation which has given him the squandered money, invents bogus behaviour for them, using as models his atrocious children and himself. When it takes off, it is very funny. . . .

The contemporary background is also excellently done. The author, who is Tutor and Fellow in Politics at Magdalen, has taken the collapse of the socialist-welfare-trade-union state a little beyond the point it had reached in 1979, before the happy intercession of Blessed Margaret, and imagined food riots, pension riots, trigger-happy police and televised hangings. I should imagine these passages, and those dealing with sex (well-observed, frightful; Krippendorf, on the job, notices that he is shedding dandruff onto the dark skin of the Filipino lady he is servicing), will greatly please vindictive and dirty-minded Tories, if there are any such creatures.

It is the second half of the book which goes wrong when it goes over the top. No longer are the imaginary Amazonians based on the children but the children are made increasingly to conform to a B-movie stereotype of jungle savagery, and at their father's direction take to incest and cannibalism. (Eating people is not necessarily funny.) This constitutes the happy ending.

Mr Parkin has an acute comic gift, and he will do very well for himself when he decides to do his own thing.

> *Stan Gebler Davies, "Look Sharpe," in* The Spectator, *Vol. 254, No. 8177, March 30, 1985, pp. 29-30.*

JIM CRACE

Frank Parkin has written what could pass . . . as a sequel to *Lord of the Flies* in the style of Tom Sharpe. His novel [*Krippendorf's Tribe*] is set in an England of curfews, pension riots, soup kitchens and uncollected garbage. The Lord, in this instance, is Jim-Jam Krippendorf, a house-husband in a "primitive Islington" where the most prized cultural totems are coach lamps, duvet covers and electric woks, and where (as evidence of national decay) the only whisky on the supermarket shelves is Korean. The Flies are the Shelmikedmu—the Krippendorf children, Shelly, Mickey and Edmund. They are studied by Jim-Jam, an anthropologist on domestic sabbatical, with affectionate and conniving indulgence, and then presented in a research thesis as a genuine South American tribe.

The structural anthropologists at the Malinowski Research Institute evidently find adolescent Islington so convincingly Amazonian that they award Krippendorf not only the Lévi-Strauss Memorial Prize (book tokens to the value of seventeen pounds) but also a £14,800 field study grant for air flights, interior travel, porterage and tropical clothing. *Exotica*, the journal of cheese-cake anthropology which vies with the *Gay Monetarist* and the *Home Counties Insurgent* for space on the magazine racks, commissions lucrative "illustrated" articles on the racier aspects of Shelmikedmu life—"Fantasies and Foreskins", "Amazonian Knockers" and "Savage Maidenhood". The Krippendorf children—and their Ethiopian babysitter—readily pose for photographs, naked in a jungle of potted plants and raffia mats from Habitat. They are quite happy to oblige their paterfamilias, too, with couvade and menarche ceremonies of his devising, or to experiment in hunting, body decoration, incest, murder and, finally, cannibalism. . . .

Regrettably, Parkin's treatment of what might have been a mordant social satire at the expense of Islington and academe is rarely funny or perceptive, despite its taboo-busting and its relentless chirpiness. *Krippendorf's Tribe* has the restlessness of a novel which has been inadequately planned and which is obliged to weave and wriggle with forced hilarity in order to compensate for the exhaustion of its ideas. The novel's thematic argument—that suburbia is no less savage than Amazonia—is made cumbersome by the constant and deadening levity of the narration. Parkin labours to pacify his audience with the regulation quota of jokes. But his visual japes—Krippendorf cutting Edmund's hair with the secateurs, for example, or mending Mickey's trousers with the staple gun—are thinly evoked and cannot be redeemed, as Parkin imagines they can, by arbitrarily summoning to their aid comic placenames, such as Worksop, Pontefract and Crouch End.

> *Jim Crace, "Looking at the Shelmikedmu," in* The Times Literary Supplement, *No. 4280, April 12, 1985, p. 406.*

PAUL KINCAID

The blurb compares [*Krippendorf's Tribe*] to *Lucky Jim* (1954), though it may be pitching it a bit high to suggest that it speaks for its generation in the same way. Nevertheless, *Krippendorf's Tribe* is a wickedly funny book that is both outrageous and perceptive about a society that has 'roughly identical moral beliefs and duvet covers.' Constantly in the background we are aware that our oft-bemoaned decline has taken one more step—the Black Death rages in Milton Keynes, there are pension riots in London. Against this we are told the story of unemployed anthropologist James Krippendorf. In his family the normal roles are reversed; his wife is a leading TV news reporter forever dashing off to the world's hot spots, he stays at home to manage the domestic duties and their unmanageable brood of children. Upstairs in his attic he writes learned anthropological articles about an obscure Amazonian tribe, the Shelmikedmu, where the roles are also reversed, the women being the hunters, the men cleaning the huts. . . . As the fantasy grows, capturing both the popular and academic imagination, Krippendorf finds his children gradually adopting the mannerisms and mores of the Shelmikedmu, and becoming less unruly as a result. *Krippendorf's Tribe* is a first novel, and clear evidence of a considerable comic talent in the making.

> *Paul Kincaid, in a review of "Krippendorf's Tribe," in* British Book News, *May, 1985, p. 300.*

RICHARD EDER

Eight or nine years ago, England had a prodigiously hot summer, marked by brilliant sunshine and whole weeks of blue skies. It started as a welcome novelty and ended up as something of a horror. Drought turned the emerald-green island into burnt-out amethyst. And it did more: It brought out an accumulating shabbiness and decay that had seemed less noticeable under the overcast.

In the different light, all the phrases about Britain's becoming part of the Third World took on a different light. A whiff of the tropics was no joke; they turned out to be Levi-Strauss' sad tropics.

I suspect that the memory of that summer is one of the things that underlies Frank Parkin's rattly but extremely funny satire. If Eliot's world ended not with a bang but a whimper, the England of *Krippendorf's Tribe* is going under, not with a whimper but something between a snarl and a smirk.

Set no more than three or four years into the future—and more disconcerting for being so recognizable—British life is an unpalatable blend of leftover egalitarianism, right-wing nastiness, decrepit consumerism and outbursts of violence.

In the most matter-of-fact way, we hear of bread riots, pension riots, mortgage riots. Hanging has been revived and put on televison. Union leaders face deportation. A school principal, wearing blue jeans and love beads, affably enumerates his more recent problems: stranglings in the boys' bathroom, an outbreak of religious mania in the fourth form and a leprosy scare.

Affability is the key; none of this matters much. The joke and the wink that symbolized a stalwart people during the Battle of Britain are now the symbol of a banal spinelessness. The normal is as discouraging as the extreme. The supermarkets carry Portuguese caviar, Korean whiskey and wine in six-packs next to the shelves of banana-fudge frosting. The universities are crowding out academic subjects in favor of practical ones. One of the crowded-out results is James Krippendorf....

Krippendorf is in full charge of his household of hellcat children. Having lost his university job, he is writing a paper on the Shelmikedmus, an Amazonian tribe, for which he has received a hefty research grant.

However, he has already spent the grant on a new car and a vacation. Furthermore, the Shelmikedmus are imaginary. They are, and it is the book's most ingenious conceit, a wacky image of his own surreal menage.

Among the Shelmikedmus, for example, domestic work is the principal source of self-esteem. Naturally, it is reserved for men. "In Shelmikedmu eyes," Krippendorf writes, "the only fully rounded personality, the only truly complete human being, is one who sweeps in the morning, scrubs in the afternoon and cooks in the evening." Women, he continues, are relegated to the despised task of hunting. Most accept the role, though there are occasional protests. Instances of spear-burning have been reported, he writes, "and now and then a young woman may be seen swishing her bow to and fro in pathetic imitation of a sweeping motion."

The children are a steady source of inspiration; sometimes in reverse. Treated with terminal contempt at home, Krippendorf writes that the Shelmikedmu children have their mouths bound so they won't speak. At night, they soothe their careworn father by rubbing him with alligator fat.

In a society that has lost its use for scholarly pursuits, no scholarly fraud goes unrewarded. *Exotica,* a soft-porn transfiguration of *The British Journal of Structural Anthropology,* offers Krippendorf handsome fees for doing a series of sensational articles on his tribe. Photographs are wanted as well, so Krippendorf colors his children with body paint and has them demonstrate circumcision rites with the household's potted plants as a tropical backdrop. When sexier material is required, he seduces and photographs the Filipino mother of one of his children's schoolmates.

Using an English family to derive a primitive Amazonian tribe is only part of Parkin's satire. As the book goes on, the children's primitivism turns tropical. By the end, they have killed and eaten their housekeeper—Krippendorf joins in, taking notes all the time—and have begun hunting the neighbors' pets for fresh meat.

Parkin is a political scientist and sociologist ... and *Krippendorf's Tribe* is his first novel. It has its weaknesses. A number of the incidents seem superfluous. The momentum is erratic after a strong beginning; the children's comical monstrosity gets more ciamorous but not more interesting as the book goes along, and the ending is more cop-out than climax. Finally, the author pops his jokes too often and too lavishly. Mickey's proposal to bury the housekeeper in the garden acquires whimsy but not humor when Krippendorf objects that he does not want his runner beans disturbed.

Still, Parkin has made his book something more than a comical contraption. His crooked anthropologist and the invented tribe swoop in at a flaring angle to the reality they satirize, and their passage more than makes up for a good deal of stumbling.

> *Richard Eder, in a review of "Krippendorf's Tribe,"* *in* Los Angeles Times Book Review, *February 9, 1986, p. 3.*

TIME

To the dictionary, civilization is social organization of a high order. To Frank Parkin, it is a coat of paint that washes off in a storm. In [*Krippendorf's Tribe*], the storm is the current decay of England, with its attendant riots and strikes. Unemployed Anthropologist James Krippendorf finds himself in charge of three children.... He has received a grant to do fieldwork in the Amazon jungle, but so far he has not set foot out of London, and the money is almost gone. Suddenly he is possessed by a brilliant notion: Why not take notes on his children, Shelley, Mickey and Edmund, and present them as observations about the rites and rituals of a distant tribe called the Shelmikedmu? ... His notes grow more detailed as his brood regresses, napalming the neighbor's cat, filing their teeth and, finally, living in a tree house in the backyard. Which has deteriorated more, the racially torn, economically battered society outside, or the wild-eyed members of the Krippendorf tribe?

Parkin ..., the author of four books on political science, including *Middle Class Radicalism,* knows whereof he piques. His is an ingenious performance, mad in every sense of the word. At the finale, Krippendorf is headed for the jungle, and funny as he is, good riddance to him. It is Parkin who deserves an encore.

> *A review of "Krippendorf's Tribe," in* Time, *Vol. 127, No. 7, February 17, 1986, p. 78.*

LORRIE MOORE

Krippendorf's Tribe [is] a short, bleak comedy that gives anthropology and Western manners a fair tromping. In Mr. Parkin's satirical world, Krippendorf's study is a resounding success. *Exotica,* the former *British Journal of Structural Anthropology,* publishes his work with more photographs than text and then phones Krippendorf for a sequel. It is a publication replete with glossy centerfolds and readers who "think Lévi-Strauss is a pair of jeans," but it is lucrative business. Krippendorf soon becomes the toast of a new, forward-thinking anthropological community and is called upon to give talks and lead expeditions. His children, too, take to the enterprise with enthusiasm, initially "in the manner of Hollywood Apaches" but subsequently with a solemn appreciation of ersatz tribal rites. They wear loincloths and sarongs. They experiment with animal sacrifice, sibling incest and, when the housekeeper dies and is stored in an improvised fashion in the freezer downstairs, inadvertent cannibalism. . . .

Easy to discount for its questionable taste, its old jokes, its prurience and prejudices (there is not a grown female character that the book doesn't seem to despise, although breast fascination abounds), *Krippendorf's Tribe* remains a novel of some accomplishment. And while it suffers from the first novelist's difficulty in gracefully moving characters through time and space, as well as from the weary comedy of empirical diction and field reports used in lieu of exposition and interior monologue, there are powerful descriptions of an ailing London that reveal Mr. Parkin's literary talent at its sharp-eyed, sharp-tongued best. These are succinctly depicted cityscapes, snapshots of the foundering British economy, and they mirror the protagonist's own fiscal and psychic chaos.

In these reflective passages, and in others that render in humorous detail English suburban life, the story itself really takes root. Mr. Parkin handles well Krippendorf's growing relationship with his children, one of tolerance evolving into tender engagement. "Name any sixty of the One Hundred and One Dalmations," Krippendorf says, to keep his brood occupied in the family car. But by the book's end, he has grown closer— saved his son's life, thrown his daughter a menarche party (to the strains of "Happy Menarche to You"), and insisted that they accompany him on an actual journey to South America. . . .

Mr. Parkin is an Oxford don who has published four books of political science. . . . In this, his first book of fiction, he has written a surprising kind of madcap *Mary Poppins*, a gender-reversed cautionary tale about the neglected house-spouse with the thwarted career. Those who emerge most engagingly and persuasively, however, are the Shelmikedmu themselves— Shelley, Mickey and Edmund—who, all Hobbesian energy, help demonstrate the horrible ease with which cultural assumptions fray, rather deconstructively, at the seams. They are tribe as diatribe. One wonders with interest what Mr. Parkin will write next.

Lorrie Moore, "Onward and Upward with the Shelmikedmu," in The New York Times Book Review, *March 2, 1986, p. 13.*

(Edward) Reynolds Price

1933-

American novelist, short story writer, essayist, poet, dramatist, and translator.

In his fiction, Price chronicles life in the American South during the twentieth century. His work is usually set in the backwoods areas of North Carolina where he grew up. Price's most highly regarded novels, including *A Long and Happy Life* (1962) and *Kate Vaiden* (1986), are character studies in which his protagonists come of age and contend with sexual desire and societal pressures. Although Price's liberal use of symbolism and irony lends a sinister tone to some of his works, his sympathy for his characters and his understanding of regional traditions combine to form affectionate portraits of growth and maturity in the rural South. Critics find in Price's work the influence of such Southern writers as William Faulkner, Eudora Welty, and Flannery O'Connor, and they consistently praise his realization of character, his sense of place, and his rich prose style.

Price's first novel, *A Long and Happy Life,* was widely acclaimed for his complex characterizations and lyrical writing. The novel follows Rosacoke Mustian's pursuit of Wesley Beavers and a conventional lifestyle while revealing the dangers of conforming to the standards of other people. Once she attains her goals, Rosacoke feels trapped until she begins to understand, through her portrayal of the Virgin Mary in a Christmas pageant, the exalted nature of marriage and motherhood. Rosacoke is also the protagonist of "A Chain of Love," included in *The Names and Faces of Heroes* (1963), Price's first collection of short stories. The Mustian family is the focus of Price's second novel, *A Generous Man* (1966), which details the sexual and emotional awakening of Milo Mustian, Rosacoke's older brother. Price's next book, *Love and Work* (1968), differs in subject matter from his earlier works. This novel examines a writer's need to balance his life between work and personal relationships. The protagonist is a teacher and novelist who forsakes emotional involvement to pursue his literary ambitions. When he discovers some of his parents' letters, which reveal to him the love and compromise inherent in their marriage, he comes to a better understanding of himself and his work and is able to look outside of himself for fulfillment.

In the foreword to his second collection of short stories, *Permanent Errors* (1970), Price writes that these pieces are "the attempt to isolate in a number of lives the central error of act, will, understanding which, once made, has been permanent, incurable, but whose diagnosis and palliation are the hopes of continuance." The tales take place in the present, but the characters are constantly aware of past actions that shape current events. Price's next novel, *The Surface of Earth* (1975), hinges on the same concept as the stories in *Permanent Errors. The Surface of Earth* follows four generations of the Kendal and Mayfield families and the ways in which parental mistakes affect children's lives. Price's protagonist in *The Source of Light* (1981), the sequel to *The Surface of Earth,* is an aspiring poet who represents reconciliation and survival for the two families. Reviewers generally praised Price's well-rounded characterizations, but most concluded that the novels are heavy-handed and ultimately unsuccessful. Price's recent work, *Kate Vaiden,* has generated uniformly positive critical response and

received the National Book Critics Circle Award for fiction. This book is narrated by the title character and chronicles nearly sixty years of her life, much of which is spent searching for her long-lost son. Robert Towers likened Kate to the heroine of Daniel Defoe's classic prose work, *Moll Flanders.* Critics generally agreed that Kate Vaiden is among the most memorable characters in contemporary fiction.

In addition to his novels and short stories, Price has published collections of essays and biblical translations, as well as *Early Dark* (1977), a play based on his novel *A Long and Happy Life. Things Themselves: Essays and Scenes* (1972) includes pieces on the status of contemporary Southern literature, Price's reaction to the critical reception of his own work, and criticism of the works of such authors as Eudora Welty, William Faulkner, Ernest Hemingway, and John Milton. Price has also published several volumes of poetry, including *Vital Provisions* (1983), his first large-press collection of verse. Reflecting the style and wit of Price's prose works, the poems in *Vital Provisions* were generally commended for their perception and clarity.

(See also *CLC,* Vols. 3, 6, 13; *Contemporary Authors,* Vols. 1-4, rev. ed.; *Contemporary Authors New Revision Series,* Vol. 1; and *Dictionary of Literary Biography,* Vol. 2.)

JOHN W. STEVENSON

The controlling theme of Reynolds Price's fiction is the revelation that comes through the quest for self-knowledge, not in any intellectual sense but in the discovery that meaning and identity are found in giving, and in giving is learned the fulfilment of love. Price constructs everything in his stories around the dramatic contrast between all those human and natural forces that defeat and wear down and those moments of devotion and commitment found only in love. And this love is not a towering, raging, selfdestroying passion, but the kind of love nurtured and made real in the relationships found in kinship, whether they be family or community. . . .

Price reveals this theme of love through an emphasis on setting and on character in which the fictional technique is all reminiscence. He reveals theme through character, and the subjects of his stories are studies in the obligations of love. The discovery of this obligation, achieved through a type of ritual act, becomes at the same time an insight into the nature of hospitality. It is never an intellectual discovery; the characters come to their knowledge through a simple act of selflessness, as if out of each one's private suffering and alienation from being gradually emerges the shared humanness of a common guilt, a guilt redeemed through an act of grace.

All of Price's published short stories are collected in a volume entitled *The Names and Faces of Heroes* (1963). (p. 300)

One discovers much of the underlying meaning in Price's short fiction in the . . . subtle drama of a character's developing moral awareness. Price reveals the significant action in what is going on in the character's consciousness: the discovery of his private obligation, his need to act out of a human responsibility to those who are if not in fact then in truth his kin. The commitment to action is the discovery that all action involves relationships. In many of the stories Price realizes this private discovery through the contrast between the young, for whom the knowledge of mortality is the awakening demands of love, and the middle-aged and elderly, for whom the knowledge is no longer an end but a beginning. The tension that dramatizes this contrast in all the stories is the nostalgia, the memory of an enfolding relationship that death cuts off. Because this loss involves a break up of the security and sense of community, the character perceives, if only briefly, the fragileness and the strength of the "chain of love." This is his passion, his discovery of the turning of time.

Another meaningful and important characteristic of Price's fiction lies in his setting. All of the stories are placed in the rural county of Warren, North Carolina—a setting which dramatizes through its simplicity and inherited moral values the source of kinship, the true place of hospitality. He contrasts the personal and inherited moral values of the rural setting with the nameless and impersonal urban morality, with those who live apart because of their fear of personal relationships. (pp. 301-02)

Price gives particular focus to [the] awareness of place as the source of knowing in his fiction in two stories about Negroes. Both of the stories are told by a first person narrator who as a young man has a strong family tie with two Negro servants. In the one, **"The Warrior Princess Ozimba,"** the action is in the present (rather than following Price's usual device of reminiscence), and the narrator takes on the family obligation started when his father was a boy of making an annual pilgrimage to the cabin of an aging and serene Negro woman. The occasion is her birthday. . . . And the gift, as it always had been from the very first, is a pair of blue tennis shoes. The crux of the

story hangs on the immense dignity and respect, on the unspoken wisdom of devotion that binds a relationship no one needed to define or explain. Each year, then, in the almost ludicrous yet childlike gift of blue tennis shoes there is renewed an unwritten covenant, a silent token of the obligation of love. For one brief moment the helpless, aged servant (blind, almost deaf, toothless) reveals to the heir of those whom she served all those years the nobility of service, that ultimate humility which gives her the exalted title, The Warrior Princess.

Like **"The Warrior Princess,"** **"Uncle Grant,"** the other story of a Negro servant, is a deeply moving study of the fidelity and childlike devotion of a man who becomes the means through which a family discovers the meaning of kinship, the tie that binds. Here again is the recognition, revealed suddenly in later years and far away from the original setting, of the strangely paradoxical knowledge of dependence found in the dependent, of strength in simplicity, of wisdom in innocence. In such characters as Uncle Grant and Aunt Zimby (The Warrior Princess), Price is not rendering an ideal of American primitivism; rather, like the old Negro woman in Eudora Welty's "A Worn Path" or Faulkner's Dilsey, these rural servants more nearly define the true pastoral character; their actions more specifically uphold the agrarian virtues and are in contrast to the stylized urban manners. It may well be that in modern American literature the only truly pastoral character is the Southern rural servant—presented not as a sentimentalized stereotype or as a subject for pity (hence, qualified for organized charity)—but as a way of measuring the order of myth (the past) against the fact of mortality (the present), of seeing pride in humility, hospitality in service.

The rural setting dramatizes the sense of nostalgia for a place once known and left behind, and these innocents recall this simpler world where a man knew who he was (knew without really knowing at the time) and accepted without calculation the obligations of love. It is, in fact, this technique of reminiscence that most effectively points up the contrast between the false and the real, the past and the present, the revelation of love and the knowledge of death that give dimension and force to Price's theme. None of Price's short stories presents this theme more sensitively than the one entitled **"The Names and Faces of Heroes."** He renders all of the action through the consciousness of a young boy as he searches his father's face for some one answer to the question he has set himself to discover. . . . [Although] he cannot know the complexity of his search, he is aware of the need to know somehow the nature of his father's identity. "I search it for a hero. For the first time. I have searched nearly every other face since last July, the final Sunday at camp when a minister told us, 'The short cut to being a man is finding your hero, somebody who is what you are not but need to be. What I mean is this. Examine yourself. When you find what your main lack is, seek that in some great man.'"

The story is a vision story, and it works because Price believes in the reality of the boy's final revelation and because the authority of the story comes from his never violating the limits of the boy's consciousness. The boy's painful dilemma is not resolved until he first strips away all the masks that disguise not only himself from his father but also his father from him. . . . What he discovers in the long reflection of his father's deeds and in his own need to earn his right as his father's son is the face of love, the source of his own being, and the name of his own identity. (pp. 303-05)

If Price finds his theme in the rural setting of northeastern North Carolina, he found also, I suspect, the place from which to explore in a less sweeping way the grandly epic theme of that other North Carolina writer Thomas Wolfe. Wolfe's restless energy and his cosmic agony for the lost home is refined and controlled in the nostalgia of Price's fiction. Perhaps it is the younger writer's knowledge of and belief in Wolfe's tremendous vision that gives him the stage to work out his own private need to define the quest for innocence and the obligations of love. Price selected, in fact, a sentence from Blake to introduce his collection of stories: "I met a plow on my first going out at my gate the first morning after my arrival, & the Plowboy said to the Plowman, 'Father, The Gate is Open.'" I cannot help thinking that the epigraph is Price's recognition of the seed of his literary source, the seed from which his fiction earns its right to sustain the vision Wolfe expressed in his large theme of "wandering forever and the earth again"—by which, Wolfe explained in a letter to Maxwell Perkins, "I mean simply the everlasting earth, a home, a place for the heart to come to, and earthly mortal love, the love of a woman, who, it seems to me, belongs to the earth and is a force opposed to that other great force that makes men wander, that makes them search, that makes them lonely." (p. 306)

> John W. Stevenson, "The Faces of Reynolds Price's Short Fiction," in Studies in Short Fiction, *Vol. III, No. 3, Spring, 1966, pp. 300-06.*

CLAYTON L. EICHELBERGER

Reynolds Price is one of the more promising young writers in the fictional mode on the American scene today. He has thus far published two novels, *A Long and Happy Life* (1962) and *A Generous Man* (1966), and a collection of short stories, *The Names and Faces of Heroes* (1964). All three books have received mixed reviews. Price has been criticized for being too Faulknerian, just another Southern writer imitating the master; he has been censured for stylistic incompetence; and he has been lightly dismissed as a young man who writes with facility but who has nothing memorable to contribute. His originality and "acute particularity" have been noted; his character portrayals have been praised as significant literary achievements; his future high rank among American writers, we have been encouraged to believe, is inevitable.

All of this could easily be interpreted as evidence of but one thing: the perennial divergence in the judgment of established reviewers. The fiction itself, however, cannot be put aside so casually; for something there is about the ambiguous and ironic patterns and endings of the Price novels and stories which is hauntingly provocative and which gives them a continuing life in the mind of the reader. One reason for this is the aching sense of discomfort they communicate. It is less intense, to be sure, than pain; but it is none the less real. Price repeatedly and willfully neglects to bring his characters to the degree of fulfillment which would permit the reader to wrap them up neatly, put them away in some properly labeled niche, and forget about them. One after the other they fall short of realizing their potential, and the ambivalent tension of disappointment communicated to the reader is left unresolved. As is often true in life, we would prefer to blind ourselves to the failure which surrounds them and of which we are uncomfortably aware, but we cannot. Price's offering is a bittersweet involvement with fictional characters that is carefully attuned to the frustration and sense of loss in our time. (pp. 410-11)

Love runs like a thread, not always a golden one, through the pages of Price's fiction. Its importance as theme cannot be denied. But the thing which gets hold of the reader in a most insidious and relentless way is the fact that the ordinary young people from the rural areas of North Carolina who are central to the narratives are ordinary primarily because they live and move on a level considerably below their capabilities. In *A Long and Happy Life,* Rosacoke Mustian is motivated by a sensitivity and an introspective realization of life that belie her years; and in *A Generous Man,* her brother Milo exhibits insight and knowledge rarely, if ever, found among fifteen-year-old country boys. Both demonstrate qualities which make them not ordinary but outstanding, which suggest their ability to rise above their mundane, provincial existence to a level of attainment unknown in their limited community. Both give indication of a blossoming individuality which will set them apart and so achieve identity for them. Both, having promised much, settle back into the morass of conformity. They win our affection only to disappoint us finally by their failure to become what they are capable of being; and we stand by like bound men, mute, helpless to reach out, to act, to save. Neither can we ignore. A banner in defeat flies over the work of Reynolds Price. (p. 411)

[Lack of fulfillment and] surrender to accepted patterns of behavior [are] the ironic substance of Price's first novel, *A Long and Happy Life.* For seven long years, ever since they were children, Rosacoke Mustian had loved Wesley Beavers; for seven long years she had waited in the pain and agony of her unrequited love for him to say that he loved her, thereby giving her the identity for which she yearned. For nearly seven years she listened to him talking of other girls and resisted his sexual advances, until, driven to the very limits of endurance, she plotted the moment at which she would give herself to him. Finding herself pregnant and feeling hate crowding love out of her heart, she is driven to make a decision: Will she, or will she not, accept Wesley's offer to marry her?

The conflict between what Rosacoke seeks to be and what she seems forced to be accurately predicts the dialectic ambiguity communicated at the end of the novel. From our first glimpse of her astride a motorcycle behind Wesley Beavers and clinging to him as if he is her only hope of being, her white blouse flying out behind like "a banner in defeat," to her final surrender to the patterns of traditional behavior, the dialectic tension is evident. . . . Through the painful years of waiting, Rosacoke rebels against the act which Milo, her older, sexually initiated brother, tauntingly tells her is necessary if she is to claim Wesley; but edged to the brink of desperation, she makes the penultimate sacrifice.

Even after her fall, she still has the chance to stand up against the world—her community, including Wesley Beavers—by confessing her moral failing; and in the strength and dignity of that confession she, like Hester Prynne, could have risen self-reliant and superior to provincial narrowness and conformity. . . . Decisions and possible decisions chase each other through her mind. She considers rejecting Wesley's dutifully proposed plan of elopement, thus establishing herself as a violated but inviolate being ready with strength and courage to shoulder all of the burdens of her individuality. Mentally she declares her freedom. (pp. 412-13)

But Rosacoke is not as free as she claims to be. Her courage is not equal to the challenge. . . . [She] imagines the community seeing through her disguise, penetrating to an instant awareness of her secret. She stands on the scaffold. Prophetically she experiences the inevitable ostracism which would result from the discovery of her moral violation. (p. 413)

Within herself Rosacoke Mustian had shouted her defiance to the world, but that shout dies away into unuttered humiliation. She answers Wesley's proposal with "yes"; and in that affirmative answer she makes final sacrifice of herself to the pressures of her provincial world and to the patterns of conformity. She can only look forward to living in rented rooms, eating Post Toasties and strong pork liver, pressing *his* shirts, and staring out of windows at concrete roads. The right ending, a young man and a young woman marrying to give their illegitimate offspring a proper name, leaves a bitter taste; for the right ending is purchased at the too dear cost of sacrificed fulfillment of individuality. The title, *A Long and Happy Life,* is wracked with irony, for the life that Rosacoke now faces falls far below the level of her potential. That life is her defeat.

A similar pattern of reversal and relapse into conformity and tradition constitutes the ending of *A Generous Man,* but in this case the ending is less poignantly moving and carries less impact for several reasons. One is that this novel, unlike *A Long and Happy Life,* suggests a mythic presentation. An aura of exaggeration and fantasy pervades it. A giant snake, a mad dog, and a half-wit boy chase each other in tangled pursuit through a briar-laced undergrowth; an unbelievably negligent posse is led by an unbelievable deputy unbelievably and ironically named Rooster; a spectre from the world of the dead appears in ghostly fashion to inflict a wound, the red badge of knowledge. In part this nightmare fantasy stands as a barrier to reader involvement; in part this lesser involvement can also be attributed to the method of external character presentation the author chooses to use instead of the probing, internal, Jamesian revelation of Rosacoke in the first novel.

The protagonist in *A Generous Man* is Milo Mustian, Rosacoke's elder brother.... Now fifteen, he is strong and lusty in youth, boastfully and narcissistically proud of his manly body, and somewhat awed by his suddenly discovered sexual prowess. In spite of vestigial adolescent acting out, he is an attractive and not unagreeable young fellow, primarily because he is bright and young and virile. But he tantalizes rather than convinces the reader.

The novel thematically centers on Milo's initiation into manhood through what might be described as a provincial puberty ritual in which Milo takes on the role of man by becoming a confidant of men and by accompanying them on a hunting mission. The behavior of the men toward Milo is motivated by both admiration and envy of his youth and capability. Milo, for the first time, is admitted into the ritual of man-talk. Even his essentially weak and unmasculine grandfather confides youthful sexual adventures. Such man-talk is unconsciously designed to point direction to the youth in his attempt to establish himself in the patterns of provincial masculine behavior which treats sexual prowess, or at least the sexual boast, not only as the mark of manhood but also the ultimate fulfillment of male being. A local reputation based on exaggerated sexual conquest is the means by which a young man can secure respect and acceptance; he proves his normality through adoption of the traditional patterns of the group. But the quick perceptiveness, the ready wit, the knowledge of life unexpectedly housed in the almost erotic body of this 15-year-old leads one to believe that Milo has an infinitely higher potential than that of the cuckold Rooster and the other country bumpkins, that he has the capability to stand tall as an individual outside the provincial group. And when he comes to experience love for Lois, the

snake tender, in a spiritual as well as a physical way, when he comes to the discovery that love is not simply giving generously of himself as he had naively thought and that it is not a matter of taking as practiced by the other men but a fusion of giving and taking in a shared experience, one is led to believe that he has come upon an avenue which will lead him into the largeness of soul and mind of which he is capable as an individual. (pp. 414-15)

Danger exists that while the process of maturation in itself seems to be an inevitable one and that while it suggests a physical blossoming forth into fulfillment of promise, it may also become negative in terms of spiritual and intellectual individuality if the independence and primal innocence of childhood is lost to the conformist patterns of adulthood and tradition. One hopes that Milo will overcome that threat. Persuaded of his capability and unusual promise, one naturally yearns to see him step free of provincial shackles, to rise on wings of non-conformity, and to soar superior to all he has known. For a while the reader is encouraged to view Lois as his means of escape, only to experience the shattering of that dream as the novel ends. Milo, who recognizes that he has a choice between living and working "like a mill from day to dark every day but Christmas doing what my Daddy did" and volunteering to change some things which need changing in the world, makes the least rewarding choice. He gives up his love for Lois, surrenders meekly to imminent marriage to Sissie (an unlovable, whining, demanding wench) and sinks back into the morass out of which he might have emerged. As in the case of Rosacoke, the fulfillment of his potential is doomed to perpetual diminution. The sudden turn from promise and hope to a passive acceptance of the traditional on this low level of existence can only be interpreted as defeat. Again conformity is the victor.

Each man, these novels suggest, has his chance to live up to his potential, but if, at the crucial moment, he loses his boldness and slips into the more comfortable precincts of conformity, he may waken to discover that he will not have a second chance, that it is too late to separate himself from the mass, to find fulfillment as an individual. (p. 416)

Buried beneath the mound of conformity lies sacrificed individuality, and the banner flies in defeat over the grave. An inherent part of the Price vision of life is the conflict between individuality and conformity, between self-reliance and tradition, between the challenge of establishing one's identity and the ease of turning one's back on promise and looking the other way. Here is no bright-eyed idealism. In this vision conformity is the victor, and the happiness spoken of in this state of conformity is an empty word, a pretense, a deceit wrought upon man by himself. (p. 417)

> *Clayton L. Eichelberger, "Reynolds Price: 'A Banner in Defeat'," in* Journal of Popular Culture, *Vol. I, No. 4, Spring, 1968, pp. 410-17.*

THEODORE SOLOTAROFF

Eight years ago Reynolds Price, then twenty-nine years old, published a first novel called *A Long and Happy Life,* which immediately established him as the legitimate heir of the great Southern writers of the past generations. The book is about a sweet, firm, country-wise girl named Rosacoke Mustian, who works for the phone company in a hamlet in the Piedmont region and waits for a boy named Wesley Beavers to stop running around and settle down.

Rosacoke's name is but the first of the indignities of her life that she bears with a natural and virtually unremitting grace, and Wesley's name is only the beginning of his intent, elusive, and horny nature. Otherwise, Price didn't have much to work with. But from these banalities, enclosed in a world where little happens except births, deaths, and Christmas, Price constructed a novel with what Mark Twain once called "the calm confidence of a Christian with four aces," one so full of feeling that it reverberates in every sentence. Here is the opening one:

> Just with his body and from inside like a snake, leaning that black motorcycle side to side, cutting in and out of the slow line of cars to get there first, staring due-north through goggles towards Mount Moriah and switching coon tails in everybody's face was Wesley Beavers, and laid against his back like sleep, spraddle-legged on the sheepskin seat behind him was Rosacoke Mustian who was maybe his girl and who had given up looking into the wind and trying to nod at every sad car in the line, and when he even speeded up and passed the truck (lent for the afternoon by Mr. Isaac Alston and driven by Sammy his man, hauling one pine box and one black boy dressed in all he could borrow, set up in a ladder-back chair with flowers banked round him and a foot on the box to steady it)— when he even passed that, Rosacoke said once into his back "Don't" and rested in humiliation, not thinking but with her hands on his hips for dear life and her white blouse blown out behind her like a banner in defeat.

Some beginning—of a book, of a career. Its sheer virtuosity is like that of a quarterback who on the first play of his first professional game throws a sixty-yard pass on the run, hitting the receiver exactly at the instant he breaks into the clear: a tremendous assertion of agility, power, timing, and accuracy. I won't try to give this sentence the English 31 treatment; I shall merely point out that detail by detail, image by image, Price has built up a complete synoptic view of the novel to come: its movement, figures, ground, issues, tonality, meaning. It is a sentence made up of charged essences—bits of imaginative uranium that radiate implications. It is also a sentence whose unfolding, suspenseful syntax marks the born storyteller. Finally, it is a sentence that could only have been written by someone in perfect touch with his material. The experience of connection with a society is behind every word, simile, cadence—a live experience caught at the point of overflow and then bodied forth as art.

I have paused too long over this one sentence, but no matter. I write of Price out of a sense of appreciation that I want you to share, and so I have to be specific. Also, the sentence marks a starting point in what has become a complex career. In his second novel, *A Generous Man,* Price returned to the Mustian family, this time focusing on Milo, Rosacoke's older brother, in his three days of passage into manhood and his one brimming moment of glory as the prince of his erotic desires and all they surveyed. Already moving on from *A Long and Happy Life* and from *The Names and Faces of Heroes* (a first collection of stories as sure in their realism as Chekhov's), Price turned Milo's story into something very different.

A Generous Man is a romance in form: the elegiac note of Milo's adventure rising and falling through melodrama, farce, and even literary burlesque. Partly the farce is there to convey

the leveling and coarsening that awaited Milo and would turn him into the bitter buffoon who appears six years later in Rosacoke's story. But it is also there as a kind of distance that Price was opening up between himself and the tradition of Southern pastoral in which he had begun so securely. Much of Rosacoke's world, though no less coarse, had been composed as a kind of vibrant emptiness of woods, fields, and lonely roads; Milo's was filled in by a community of misfits and clowns. It was as though Price had now brought together Faulkner and Erskine Caldwell: the theme of *The Bear* turned into a desultory, silly hunt for a carnival snake named Death; the motifs of rootedness—to place, family, folkways, etc.— undercut by a chronicle of displaced kin wandering into weird reunion attended even by a murderous family ghost. There is a lot of playfulness in Milo's story, but it is finally a bitterer one than Rosacoke's.

When the impotent sheriff, a kind of backwoods Montaigne, says to Milo, "Don't think it's morning when it's late afternoon," the burden of the novel which follows is that Milo's golden energy is not only his own valedictory but also that of a way of life, youth being the one glowing coal in these ashes. Among the losses, catalogued as well as foreseen, in *A Generous Man* is, I think, the loss of Price's early, full, harmonious relationship with the inhabitants of Mustian Corners, or whatever it's called, and possibly with the place itself.

In any case, his fiction since then has steered clear of it. His last novel, *Love and Work,* and this new collection of stories, *Permanent Errors,* are obviously intended to bring his writing level with his later experience and temperament. If he had grown up partly with people like the Mustians, he was also a boy from the Southern middle class who had gone to Duke and to Oxford University in England, and had returned to Duke as a teacher and writer-in-residence. Indeed, the last is mainly what these two recent books are about: a writer in residence in himself. They are also the work of a man who is further along in his life. The precocious brilliance and composure of his first novel no longer seem of much interest to Price; the artistry is still there but it is case-hardened, mainly by his own experience and the issues that relate to it. The sense of loss that still works through his themes like yeast in bread is now for a girl one has loved for years, or a mother, or a wife. Instead of the losses of life cresting, there are those of life already dwindling. (pp. 27-8)

Love and Work is a virtually complete portrait of a writer who has placed working before living, who expected his art to strengthen and redeem his life when the practice of it was chilling his already cool nature down to the freezing point. "The perfection of the life or of the work?" Yeats's choice isn't that simple, not if one lives with others, not if one is still attached to them by the chains (in both senses) of love. Thomas Eborn, a writer in his early thirties has kept his hostages to fortune down to two: his mother, who has an inoperable aneurysm, and his wife, who dutifully helps support both of them but is becoming skeptical.

While Eborn is writing an essay on the blessing of work. . . , his mother tries to reach him. But he has a deadline, can't be disturbed, and before he gets back to her the "time-bomb" in her forehead has gone off. His dreams tell him that he has been secretly willing it. A second death soon follows: a boy whom he has helped pull from a wrecked car.

Eborn feels himself to be the victim of some black destiny. When will it end, he asks. . . . But then his work begins to come through for him. Partly as reparation, he starts a novel about his dead parents' courtship, writing some thirty pages that have a genuine authority of detail and feeling (it most reminds me of Reynolds Price's early fiction). He coaxes a reaction from his wife; when it comes, it is devastating: "Easy lies," she says. Other revelations follow, the final one being a blinding vision of his parents' actual love for each other, which in his willed self-isolation he can now no more write about than share.

That's a superficial reading. In its deeper reaches, *Love and Work* is a novel about the unconscious and its circuits of love, fear, and punishment—what used to be called God. There is more than a hint of the spiritual in Price, rather like that in E. M. Forster or Rilke, which takes a psychological rather than a theological form: a powerful sense of dark unseen forces and influences that are only partly explained by the description of emotions and that require not just attention but supplication. This preoccupation comes increasingly into the foreground of *Permanent Errors,* a collection of stories and other pieces that, written over a period of seven years, lead up to and away from the issues of *Love and Work.*

In a brief, rather cryptic introduction Price tells us that the pieces are joined by a common intention: "the attempt to isolate in a number of lives the central error of act, will, understanding which, once made, has been permanent, incurable, but whose diagnosis and palliation are the hopes of continuance." Most of the errors in the book are committed by writers, who share Eborn's view that a writer needs solitude and detachment as a fish needs water (which happens to be true), but who use this need as a cover for vanity, timidity, selfishness, blindness, and other modes of withdrawal and assault.

There are two, possibly three, main examples. The first is Charles Tamplin, a young American writer living in England, who is involved in four pieces collectively titled **"Fool's Education."** Tamplin is something of an esthete and a prig who tends to view his experience from a self-protective literary attitude and to take his knowledge of life from the happiness and the scars of others. But he is not merely foolish: he has a quick, relevant understanding of what he sees, and though it comes too late to profit him in his life, it can, once recognized, accepted, and grieved over, perhaps help to strengthen him in his vocation. His situation is beautifully rendered in the first story, which deals with the last day of his longstanding affair with [Sara], a girl from home, a Rosacoke who has been to Vassar. To Tamplin, it is a day to get through, to kill gracefully and lightly, like the affair itself, and round it to a close. From their failure "to meet, to serve one another, to delight in the work" he will now gain his freedom to make art from it. (pp. 28-9, 46)

[Tamplin] is a young man in flight, one foot out the door of any entangling relationship, ready to pull the door of his privacy shut at any sign of invasion. He closes it on a desperate woman who wants to use his bed to steal a few moments of love, but he ends up worshiping the bitter mysteries of her love-scarred life. For there is a stern beneficence operating his fate that drives him out of his shell, turns his timidity to a certain kind of strength, leads him, some years later, to abandon his stiff-necked pride and ask forgiveness for not forgiving Sara's rightful distrust of him.

This difficult movement from grievance to grief surges powerfully through the last two stories in the book, which deal with an older writer, not unlike Tamplin, whose wife first

attempts and then commits suicide. **"Good and Bad Dreams"** is an extraordinary tracing of the borderland of the conscious and the unconscious that lies between a husband and a wife who have reached a terrible ultimate stage, in which her life hangs in the balance of their love/hate, but who can only communicate in their sleep.

"Walking Lessons," a long story, picks up the husband's legacy of rage after her death and takes him to an Indian reservation and to certain ordeals that his wife's act has reserved for him. The theme of an intolerable but seemingly unbreakable connection is doubled by the situation of the friend he visits there, a lapsed medical student who has a hopeless job as a VISTA worker and a more hopeless relationship with an Indian girl with multiple sclerosis. To Dora and the other Indians, the writer is a new affliction, the husband of a suicide, whose ghost, according to their lore, will follow him by night. To his friend, Blix, he is an unfeeling monster, "the killing kind." I won't try to trace the complex movement of this story or its mystical undertow, by which the writer is dragged to the admission of his responsibility, then to his atonement for it. I suspect that **"Walking Lessons"** brings to an end a long, grueling phase in Price's career, deeply though not congruently related to his own moral accounting, and bearing in its searching, potent artistry the healed scars of his own suffering. (p. 46)

Theodore Solotaroff, "The Reynolds Price Who Outgrew the Southern Pastoral," in Saturday Review, *Vol. LIII, No. 39, September 26, 1970, pp. 27-9, 46.*

MARSTON LaFRANCE

[*Love and Work*] may seem slight in poundage, but it is extremely well-done: soundly conceived, carefully constructed, well-written. If there is a cracked timber anywhere in the framework, it is probably the scene in which, by coincidence, the protagonist happens upon an automobile wreck; but whatever fissure exists Mr. Price has painted into a pleasant appearance with a prose style that has been noted by others. I do not happen to admire Mr. Price's overworking the dash, or the somewhat disjointed rhythm he favors, the result of dashes and semicolons laced into comparatively short sentences, but the author of such a novel as this has earned the right to indulge his own stylistic preferences.

Thomas Eborn, the protagonist—thirty-four, childless although seven years married, writer, English professor—is a psychological basket-case who would be tolerated in the worlds of Richardson, James, Proust, Hartley, Cozzens, but would be drop-kicked forthwith from the more knockabout preserves of Fielding, Melville, Crane, or Hemingway. . . . Some characters seem larger than life; Eborn, if only he could be pried out of the context of this novel, would seem smaller than life. An implicit measure of the author's ability lies in the fact that he is able to make this John Marcher of a protagonist not only vivid and alive, but also interesting, even sympathetic.

Eborn, an emotional remora ready to attach himself to anyone or anything capable of yielding him sustenance, occupies the center of the stage from first page to last. There is no attempt to move beyond him and his own problems—which certainly are sufficient—and thus there are no symbolic images that reverberate from any sounding-board other than his own shivering psyche. His function as a vehicle for truth develops from two great reservoirs of significance into which he channels his energies, and thus masks his own emptiness: love and work. Through the way in which he uses these two realities in a futile attempt to sustain his bankrupt personality, Thomas Eborn becomes a recognizable North American Tom Everyman, and the context that he brings to focus illustrates how even such noble pursuits as love and work can be turned to ashes. (pp. 345-46)

Work and love unite to reveal Eborn's monumental ego when he begins to create in fiction what he believes to be the unlived lives of his dead parents, to rescue them from having lived lives of insignificance. Given the examination of love and work through the personality of a conspicuous failure at both, the prose is freighted with a quiet irony that continues to unfold within one's mind long after one has read the book.

The only salvation for Eborn and his kind lies in an honest confrontation with the self. This encounter with truth implicitly occurs at the climax of the novel—the penultimate sentence—that aware readers will find at once obvious, ironic, and wonderfully ambiguous. Mr. Price's work, the opposite of Eborn's, is neither easy nor lies, and this novel is a worthy addition to his canon. (p. 346)

> *Marston LaFrance, in a review of "Love and Work,"*
> *in* Studies in Short Fiction, *Vol. VIII, No. 2, Spring,*
> *1971, pp. 345-46.*

STEPHEN G. NICHOLS, JR.

Sooner or later every successful author, bemused by the mystery of creativity, attempts to solve it. In *Things Themselves*, Reynolds Price, having established himself as one of the most important contemporary southern novelists with such works as *A Long and Happy Life* (1962), *A Generous Man* (1966), and *Love and Work* (1968), expresses firm, frequently controversial, ideas as to how literature happens, what it does, and how it should be approached.

As one might expect, Mr. Price ranks criticism well below creative activity. For him, thinking and talking about literature, art, and life are activities the writer busies himself with while waiting for inspiration to seize him. . . . Waiting resolves itself into reflecting upon the mystery of creation. The central question, Price finds, is not so much "What am I writing for?" as "Why am I waiting?" and "Why should anything be there at all?" For, once the writer knows the grounds of his faith in the ineffable, then form, matter, and theme will resolve themselves. The work will come. With Proust, Price seems willing to assert that art is a question, not of technique, but of vision—except that he refuses so Cartesian a word as "vision." Instead, he defiantly reiterates the word "mystery," and, to support his view of the artist as divine spokesman, he quotes Milton's *Elegia Sexta:*

> *Diis etenim sacer est vates, divumque sacerdos,*
> *Spirat et occultum pectus et ora Jovem.*
> (Indeed a poet is sacred to the gods, a priest to gods,
> And from his secret heart and mouth breathes Jove.)

An impossibly retrograde view of poetry and the poet's role? It might seem so at first blush, but, reading Price's smooth, incisive prose, one does not have the impression of listening to the lyrical effusions of a latter-day romantic.

The "things themselves" of the title are the author's response to the mechanistic view of art underlying the formalist school of criticism that dominated, until recently, the American scene. These essays ask us to take the viewpoint of the poet, rather than the critic. Price wants us to go beyond asking "How is a poem made?" to the more essential "*Why* was it made? Why is it this sort of a machine, not some other?" The question distinguishes the critic from the poet; for the poet, as Sartre long since showed, writes *for* someone, to cause something to happen.

In his first essay, **"Dodging Apples,"** Price argues that every work of art, regardless of size or length, has "kinetic intent"—it was created to change something in the world. To understand it, then, we need to know the nature of that intent: why it was created. Since the approach is nonevaluative, it may be used to urge a better understanding of works that have not received favorable attention. Thus, Price sensitively elucidates William Faulkner's *Pylon* not only as a commentary on a particular aspect of the American 1930s, but also as a personal act of exorcism, an attempt to lay the age-old fascination of the writer for the hero. Price's method serves him in good stead for another act of piety, in the best sense of the term: a long, reflective homage to Ernest Hemingway.

The essay devoted to Milton's *Samson Agonistes* is the most surprising in the work—surprising in the sense that adulatory essays of the classics written by contemporary authors are a rarity. Price's admiration for Milton, however, is central to his whole literary philosophy. It provides the literary and cultural rationale for a theocratically oriented world view that sees the future as a carrying-forward of the experiences of the past. This is the basis of Price's personal philosophy. . . .

The book closes with a glimpse into Price's literary future. The final piece describes alternative ways of treating the sacrifice of Isaac, suggested by a painting and three etchings by Rembrandt. Price's fleshing out of the bare bones of the legend, in a manner reminiscent of Kierkegaard's treatment of the same theme in *Fear and Trembling*, gives the reader the impression that a novel looms in the distance, perhaps another thundering, Miltonian proof of man's damnation, illustrative of Price's contention "that we in the South are the damnedest of all."

> *Stephen G. Nichols, Jr., in a review of "Things*
> *Themselves: Essays & Scenes," in* Saturday Review,
> *Vol. LV, No. 24, June 10, 1972, p. 62.*

MICHAEL WOOD

Reynolds Price, author of three novels and two collections of short stories, offers us his sixth book [*Things Themselves*] as something else: essays, reviews, notes, drafts, a set of instances of what a creative writer does while waiting for the muse. Of course, Price also hopes that these pieces will work for us in some way, will be "work themselves, looks at an exterior world, not just my waiting." They do and they are, but largely because the complacency of the whole project is redeemed by Price's perfect self-confidence and his unabashed joy in being a writer, and in talking about himself as one. It's refreshing to see a man so pleased with what he is doing and able to talk about it. Beyond that, the suggestion that novelists are just marking time when they are not writing fiction, that fiction is still crowned king of all the realms of prose, will appeal only to embattled creative writing instructors.

Still, Price is right to insist on the difference between his fiction and the work presented here, although the habits of his fiction create most of the flaws in this alert and intelligent book. The subdued poetry of his novels, for example, comes out here as a frequently strained raciness, a reaching for rich, jaunty language. The stripped simplicity that is a form of strength and tact in his fiction too often becomes merely dogged in his essays, a series of eloquent but brutal rejections of complexity. More generally, his self-esteem as a skilled narrative craftsman makes him something of a bully in discursive prose.

Literature is written to change our lives, Price asserts. Books are acts, objects, made things, things themselves. No word recurs more regularly in these pages than the word "usable." Initially, Price seems to mean it modestly, to be talking about the questions and answers and reasons that he can discuss sensibly and publicly, but respecting the rest, the private reasons, the essential but unusable portions of our motives and affections. . . .

One can respect his desire to work on the world, respect his analogies between writing and other crafts, sympathize with his horror of sterile criticism and the dead hand of academe, but such an insistence on the immediate effects of literature can in the end only hand us over to the philistines. . . . Too much of what is precious in our lives and in our books is useless in too many senses of the word. Literature is reflection, an activity of the consciousness, not of the hands and feet. It doesn't change our lives but, hopefully, the way we see our lives. Price himself knows this, I think, and makes it clear in his better moments. (p. 2)

Price writes well about his own work . . . , although the scenes from his screenplay based on his first novel *A Long and Happy Life* are curiously lifeless and hackneyed. Which would argue that Price's imagination is more purely literary, and less kinetic and visual, than he thinks it is, or that critics have said. The new work included here, the "notes before a novel" which take the form of meditations on four Rembrandts, four moments in the story of the narrowly averted sacrifice of Isaac by Abraham, seem strained to me, angling for significances they just can't reach; brilliant, but trivial.

The central pieces, then, are the essays on other writers: on Milton, an assured and sensitive reading of a difficult text; on Faulkner; on Eudora Welty; on Henry James; on Hemingway. Price is at his best when his own themes—loss, deprivation, isolation, ruin, the broken family—lead him into insights about others. He's at his worst when his own rather limited preoccupations swamp his subject. So he's at his best with Faulkner, seeing the importance of the disembodied scarecrow reporter in *Pylon*, with his offer of helpless love to the barnstormers; seeing the novel itself as needing us more than we need it. Or with Hemingway, where an uncovering of complicated and buried debts yields real perceptions, and where Price's pleasure in talking about himself really pays off, really leads us to Hemingway—to the poverty and the plea in all that lean and unclothed language.

But Price is then less successful with James and Eudora Welty because they leave no room for that tender but slightly condescending compassion, and because there are limits to what writers' criticism (as distinct from critics' criticism) can do for us. Writers, understandably, linger in the workshop, haunt what might have been, set up the books that got abandoned, and this can come to seem too persistent a flight from the words we've got on the pages we have. I finished *Things Themselves* with a sense of having been backstage slightly too long; but then Price himself by now is no doubt heading back for the boards and the footlights. (pp. 2, 24)

> *Michael Wood, in a review of "Things Themselves: Essays and Scenes," in* The New York Times Book Review, *June 18, 1972, pp. 2, 24.*

CHOICE

In his preface, Price warns that *Early dark* is not *A long and happy life* (1962) dramatized, but it is—and an excellent dramatization, too. Most of the characters from his first novel are here, as are many of the same events, though sometimes reshuffled. The novel had within it certain rites and rituals that seemed to be the natural property of drama. To these—the funeral of Mildred Sutton, the priapic strut at Mason's Lake, and the magnificent Christmas pageant—Price deftly reassigns a genre. The more objective demands of drama drain some of the lyrical richness of the earlier work, but the characters prove so durable that they please anew when they, in their own words and gestures, offer up their loves and burdens. Some minor characters . . . wear new dignities, and at least one major character, Wesley Beavers, displays depths only hinted at in the earlier work. Whether read or seen, *Early dark* will please long, for in it Price has accomplished what he aims for in most of his writing—"the tragic glee of the well-informed."

> *A review of "Early Dark," in* Choice, *Vol. 14, No. 9, November, 1977, p. 1216.*

RICHARD R. SCHRAMM

[In *Early Dark,* Reynolds Price's] first piece of writing for the stage, he returns to the story of *A Long and Happy Life* and successfully brings the vitality and humor of the novel through the difficult passage to stage drama. (p. 107)

[The title choices of *A Long and Happy Life* and *Early Dark*] are justified in both cases. The novel has its share of sorrow and death, but in the end we remember the Delight Baptist Church Christmas pageant and the image of Rosacoke kneeling behind the manger, holding little Frederick Gupton on her shoulder, Warren County's own madonna and child in a ritual of joy and renewal. The play does not end with the pageant, however, and instead of focusing on love, the drama's conclusion emphasizes separation and distance. We find also in the play a streak of bitterness and anger in Milo, Rosacoke's older brother. Milo's resentment, entirely absent from the novel, is directed against Isaac Alston, the patriarch of the county, for whom the play makes much more of the frustration and loneliness that characterized the relationship between Rosacoke's mother and her hapless, alcoholic father.

We see from those around Rosacoke that a long and happy life is a rare thing indeed, and now it seems that her simple dream is to be denied her as well, for that joyless vision of her future in Norfolk, merely a passing thought in the novel, is here not only articulated but also confirmed as her fate. The very love on which she had hoped to build her dream destroys it. In the retelling of the story the darkness settles around Rosacoke at the early age of twenty. Even with its abundant humor, the play is essentially tragic, the story of people who, as Price himself has pointed out in the preface, "could tell Sophocles or Beckett numerous complicated facts and possibilities." (p. 109)

> *Richard R. Schramm, in a review of "Early Dark," in* Southern Exposure, *Vol. VI, No. 1, 1978, pp. 107, 109.*

BENJAMIN DeMOTT

Hutchins Mayfield, hero of *The Source of Light,* is a 25-year-old Southern prep schoolteacher with literary ambitions who's ceased for the time being to wish he was in Dixie. At the start of the book he's discovered saying farewell to old family haunts and retainers in North Carolina and environs, just prior to leaving for a two-year stay at Merton College, Oxford. Much of the subsequent narrative focuses on Hutch's first experiences of Europe..., and upon various homosexual and heterosexual attachments he forms on foreign soil. The guilt induced in the hero by his flight is intensified by the death of his father (Hutch returns home to bury him), by his girlfriend's troubles (she aborts a child that may have been Hutch's), and by the not-so-veiled chiding of a number of loving elders who write him long letters ruminating about his clearing-out. But Hutchins Mayfield hangs tough: The book's closing scene shows him discussing Lewis Carroll in a pub with his Oxford tutor, and one concludes that, no matter what new pressures are exerted on him, he's likely to keep to his own schedules of self-development in the immediate future....

The Source of Light continues a family saga begun in *The Surface of Earth* (1975). And there's much to admire in its pages. Reynolds Price has an unplodding imagination; he's perfectly capable of diverging from conventional realism long enough to describe a visit by the ghost of Robinson Mayfield to his son Hutch's bedside—the purpose of the visit is to bestow a blessing—or a moment when Hutch himself, thousands of miles distant from his father, is so powerfully touched by a premonition of the man's passing that he's brought to his knees to pray there'll be no pain.

In addition to the family feeling and sense of the past that mark the novel, there's an intelligent awareness that one effect of integration will be to make blacks and whites strangers to each other. (The book is set in the mid-Fifties, on the eve of the civil-rights struggle.) I particularly liked the author's readiness to savor interruptions of the narrative business at hand.... And the structure of values throughout is admirable. *The Source of Light* is a 300-page narrative wherein absurdist savagery has no place and the idea of gentleness as a value isn't once mocked—which is to say, it's a rarity.

It's not, though, speaking bluntly, a compelling or exciting work of fiction. One failing is that the novelist merely assumes that the question whether his hero quits Europe or stays is momentous, but never demonstrates that it is. I was troubled too, by Price's difficulty in finding distinct voices for his characters. Nearly everybody in the book ... speaks a lingo best described as Southern-clever-wry, and in time the sameness of the speech becomes disconcerting.

Finally there's the Faulkner problem. Significant differences exist between Hutchins Mayfield and Faulkner's young masculine heroes—and between Faulkner's old people and Price's—and between Faulkner's literary allusions (the Bible and Keats) and Price's (the Bible and Shakespeare)—and between Faulkner's conviction of the uniqueness of the Compsons and Price's conviction of the uniqueness of the Mayfield clan. But while the differences exist, I'm afraid they're not as noticeable as the resemblances. The overall impression left is that of a fictional world rendered indistinct by the spreading shade of the great Faulkner tree; no action or person or style of utterance quite manages to achieve energetically independent being. Dignity and intelligence are always visible in *The Source of Light;* what's missing is the quality of freshness and surprise that makes novels novel.

Benjamin DeMott, "A Minor Faulkner," in Saturday Review, Vol. 8, No. 4, April, 1981, p. 72.

LARRY WOIWODE

Every novel is a separate existence that has to be taken on its own terms. This is as true for the novelist as the reader. No passing trends or contemporary fads should penetrate a novel's organic integrity (unless it's about such), and none do if the novelist remains true to the widening development of lives in the life under his hands; Reynolds Price is such a writer. For the rare modern novelist, such as Price, who is embarked upon an immense project, however, there can come a time when, out of empathy for his other half, the reader, he might say, "Some of this will have to go into another book." Price must have made such a decision in the midst of *The Surface of Earth,* as his new novel, *The Source of Light,* reflects.

The central character is Hutchins Mayfield, who appears as an adolescent in the final portion of *The Surface of Earth;* he's the last of the Kendal-Mayfield clan, and, over the approximate year of this new novel, is 25. He is the central character, yet most of the action revolves around his father, Rob. Hutch and Rob have the unique relationship of an only son and father, a relationship unfathomably deepened by the death of Hutch's mother at his birth.

The book opens with Hutch and Rob bathing in (ironically) curative mineral springs before both set off on their separate courses: Hutch, who has been teaching at a prep school in Virginia, toward Oxford, England, for further study and to pursue the career of his calling, writing; and Rob, who has just learned that he is dying of inoperable cancer, toward the end that awaits him, without telling Hutch, since it might prevent his leaving....

[Most] of the characters in *The Source of Light* come enveloped in an aura incomprehensible to anyone who has not read *The Surface of Earth.* They are rather too well-loved and doted upon, much as Salinger's Glass family became, in his later work, for reasons not every reader will find easy to discern. Nothing but the lovable, even when it concerns questionable characteristics, is communicated about Rob. His moving death, which Hutch returns to America for, is partly marred in its power because of this. And for other reasons. A shifting point of view that worked perfectly well for a cast of hundreds, in *The Surface of Earth,* here seems arbitrarily applied, when most of the book is centered around Hutch, and his relationship with Rob, and one of the most disturbing shifts comes near the end of Rob's dying, at a crucial point of the book, from which its title is drawn.

Echoes and recurring parallels, which in and of themselves might be bearable (even in greater abundance) in a book in which all of the essentials to the story were present and clear-cut, tend to take on the feel, in this one, of being imposed from the outside. If something is mentioned once, it will be followed by a parallel soon, and usually recapitulated in a dream. The book is filled with dreams. There is an endless play throughout on statues, dolls, children, and children with one or both parents missing; indeed, no child appears who isn't noticeably (momentously?) missing a parent or a parental relationship, as if to reflect Hutch's situation, or foreshadow his further state, after Rob's death.

Any of this, to any extreme, could be countenanced in a novel that, page by page, worked. For this reader *The Source of Light* ultimately doesn't, though it might for those who come to it from *The Surface of Earth;* indeed, devotees of that book might well like the present one. But this shouldn't be; a novel should rest on itself as that separate existence previously mentioned.

And just as extraneous fads should not enter into it, so one should not have to look elsewhere to fill in the spaces in it. *The Source of Light* arrives in wisps and fragments and stretches of brilliance, but without the interstitial substance that only *The Surface of Earth* can add.

To borrow from the imagery present in both books . . . an abundant amount of energy would be needed to warm and re-ignite the enormous *Surface of Earth* backward, and the present novel would have to be an even more burning, consuming source in itself to accomplish this, whether it were referring to Hutch as the bright point in the Kendal-Mayfield hopes, or all the way back to Christ. That this book doesn't bear this essential brightness is a disappointment to those who have come to respect and trust the bulk of Price's admittedly individual work, arriving as it usually does from the level of its own high standards.

Perhaps it is advisable for a novelist to put between two in-terrelated books a wholly other imaginative work that deals with radically different characters. For when a novelist has to say, "Some of this will have to go into another book," he sometimes also has to say, "But that will have to wait until I can see it clear." *The Source of Light,* as delicate as the dreams in it, like a mist above the surface of the earth, feels too tenuous and underlit for the world it must face, where readers and reviewers—not yet won over by Price's people, and entering a story already underway—approach with hearts and eyes of ice.

> *Larry Woiwode, "Pursuits of the Flesh, Adventures of the Spirit," in* Book World—The Washington Post, *April 26, 1981, p. 5.*

JOYCE CAROL OATES

[*The Source of Light*] is a portrait of the artist as son, as lover, as elegist; a romantic egoist who loves solitude, yet who reports on nearly every waking, and dreaming, hour of his life; a mourner who suspects that he must convert his private domestic suffering into something more substantial, into art, if he is to redeem it—and himself.

Hutchins Mayfield is a 25-year-old poet who thinks of himself as "an aging boy," who feels he must leave his North Carolina home, and his deep attachment to his father, in order to discover whether he is a genuine poet or a fraud. He goes to Oxford to read for a Bachelor of Letters degree, to write a thesis on "the love and nature of Andrew Marvell" and to work on his poetry in virtual solitude. (p. 3)

Hutchins Mayfield believes he has successfully cast off the hobbles that restrain him—his father Rob, who is devoted to him; his recollections of Mayfield-Kendal family history; his confused and painful thoughts about his mother, who died giving birth to him. But his father's unanticipated death calls him home and makes him realize that his subject will be his family, after all. In one of his final letters Hutch's father tells him, in essence, that he must be the means by which the various generations of their family are "made into a figure"—"a dia-gram"—"a writing in lines." "That's the hope, Son," his father writes, "that we make some figure. If we do you'd be the one to know (though it may take a while to know you know)."

This richly detailed and intensely romantic novel, which covers approximately a year in Hutchins Mayfield's life, is not a sequel but a continuation of Mr. Price's *The Surface of Earth.* . . .

Both novels are lyric, brooding, meditative, obsessive and pos-sess, at their most powerful moments, the histrionic clarity of a vast tapestry in which action is necessarily arrested and in-dividual figures exist only in their relationship to one another and the larger design.

Where *The Surface of Earth* had the structure of an old-fash-ioned family saga, *The Source of Light* is far narrower in scope, more centrally focused. If the "source" of light is Hutch's Mayfield-Kendal background, in all its melodramatic com-plexity, the "light" itself is Hutch—who, for good reason, is tormented by the possibility that he cannot be equal to it. Thus the mood of the novel is edgy, self-absorbed, questioning and uncertain. And, finally, it is elegiac, for Hutch, though capable of making his bold "high leap" to England, cannot escape obsessive thoughts of the deaths of his parents. (The depiction of Rob's death contains some of the most beautifully sustained passages in all of Reynolds Price's work.) Nor can he decide whether he loves a young woman well enough to marry her. Near the end of the novel, he learns, after the fact, that his girl has had an abortion to free herself of a baby that was probably, though not certainly, his.

As one might imagine, there are difficulties in assessing a writer in vigorous mid-career like Reynolds Price, and these diffi-culties are, in the present case, compounded by the fact that the novel under review is a continuation of an earlier work and gives every indication of leading to yet another Hutch Mayfield novel. It seems unfair to judge Hutchins Mayfield at this point and irrelevant to question whether he will ever be a poet, for that is not the concern of this novel. Mr. Price seems to be lightly satirizing Hutch, who believes that his self-obsessed letters home allow him to avoid "the rapt mirror-gazing that diaries invite"; then again, he indulges him at length, in long unedited letters that contain dreams recounted in full. One can see why Hutch's girl Ann becomes so impatient with him—he is romantically indulgent about himself and yet his manner with her is cautious and ironic, and he always seems to draw back from any forthright declaration of love. (Ann does not know, but perhaps can sense, that Hutch is attracted to other men—that, indeed, he has homosexual relations.)

Because he is so central to the novel, dominating virtually every page, it is disconcerting that Hutch remains so blurred to us and that Ann too lacks definition. We wonder whether she is as pallid as she appears or whether her passivity is part of her strategy to win Hutch for a husband? She takes pride, for instance, in confessing to a total lack of interest in a profes-sion or in what might be called the world. . . . (pp. 3, 30)

In this novel, as in Reynolds Price's previous work, the most appealing characters are garrulous storytellers, who are often peripheral to the central concern of a novel, but irresistible nonetheless, for it is through them that we experience the tex-ture of life in a given place and time. Since the publication in 1962 of his justly acclaimed first novel, *A Long and Happy Life,* Reynolds Price has been superb at capturing voices, and so it is not surprising that the older, talky women of *The Source of Light* (one of them Hutch's grandmother Eva, the mother of Rob) are marvelous, as are Hutch's male friends. . . . The women are warm, bemused, funny and wise, without neces-sarily being intelligent, and certainly without being self-con-scious; the male lovers are uncommonly intriguing, in ways poor Ann, locked into her claustrophobic "feminine" role, can never be. . . .

In all, *The Source of Light* is a somber, rather beautifully muted work, in which the melodrama of earlier generations has receded, leaving a hero who is, in his very uncertainty, absolutely convincing. It is a measure of Reynolds Price's integrity that he ends this novel on so restrained, and so unresolved, a note: Hutch back at Oxford, Ann at home, the Atlantic between them as well as the death of an unborn child, and a sense of great injury. Perhaps suffering will deepen Hutch, perhaps it will make him into the poet his father has required him to be. (p. 30)

> Joyce Carol Oates, "Portrait of the Artist as Son, Lover, Elegist," in The New York Times Book Review, April 26, 1981, pp. 3, 30.

J. O. TATE

The Source of Light, a continuation of *The Surface of Earth* (1975), covers a year (1955-56) in the life of Hutchins Mayfield, would-be poet. Mr. Price's strengths make themselves felt, as his readers have come to expect. Yet there is a crippling weakness at the center.

The second sentence of the novel gives its master image: a naked young man observes himself in a mirror. The narcissistic gestures of Hutchins Mayfield seem to compromise the narrator, who refers on page 12 to the hero's "pleasant and pleasing body." On page 14, Miss Fairfax Wilson, a "maiden lady," tells him, "Hutchins Mayfield, I consider you the finest young man now residing in the Old Dominion; and you know how stuck I am on Virginia." . . .

Later, in answer to the question, "How many books can there be you haven't read?" the apprentice poet replies, "Not many. . . . Now I'm writing my own." . . . Another admirer, impressed by Hutch's memory, gushes, "You're due to be Shakespeare." The author spurs the reader to believe in his protagonist's physical and mental wonderfulness, and his talent as a writer. But this reader, a jaded nag, must balk at the crude whip-hand.

As a portrait of an artist as a young man, the picture is High Romantic. But young Mayfield nowhere convinces us he is a poet. . . .

In spite of [his] failures and excesses, Price deserves every credit for the beauty of his supple prose, the velocity and ease of his motions, and the idiomatic reality of his characters. His Grainger and Min and Eva—particularly when they talk—have all the aura of human presence. Insight and humor—and an uncanny ear—have for Price always been available powers. I am struck by his convincing revival of the authority of the nineteenth century narrator: the dog Thal is rendered as a character with a consciousness, as Rob talks to her. Price dares further, and successfully, when he represents the spirit of Rob after death visiting his son's room. With god-like Tolstoyan simplicity, he specifies a moment of conception—a point that matters later on, concerning an abortion.

But the 25-year-old protagonist seems to cause the author to lose his touch: the best scenes are those in which the hero is absent. If he were an actual person, he would, I suppose, blight parties and ruin dinners in much the same way that he astigmatizes the vision of his creator.

Anyone who has read Mr. Price's symphonic essay on *Samson Agonistes* would anticipate from the phrase "the drowned-man act" in the first sentence of the book a series of allusions to "Lycidas" and Milton—and, by extension, to Mr. Price's fellow North Carolinian, Thomas Wolfe. And later there is a real drowned man, Miltonic geography, and other references. This

lends weight to the novel, if not meaning. But isn't another grand literary reference, the beautiful legend of Tristan and Iseult, put to ignoble use when one young man leaves "a dull table-knife" in the lonely bed of our hero? Now a symbol of flirtation rather than caution, this implement does not long separate them. Look homeward, Ganymede.

It is at the most crucial point—the failure to suspend our disbelief—that *The Source of Light* fails. Who would believe that this self-regarding beauty, Hutchins Mayfield, would have the *virtu* to "redeem back all [his] people pawned away"?

> J. O. Tate, "The Light That Failed," in National Review, Vol. XXXIII, No. 18, September 18, 1981, p. 1084.

DONALD NOBLE

The Source of Light is a much more intense, controlled, and focussed work [than *The Surface of Earth*]. Instead of following a large cast through forty-one years, this time Price tells the story of one year in the life of Hutchins Mayfield, sole son and heir and a young man quite believably going through the traumatic experiences which will, as they are endured and learned from, give his life its shape and direction. . . .

Hutch is not all that likeable. He is a vacillating, irritating character, and we wish he would get ahold of himself and commit himself to someone or something. He is redeemed somewhat, though, because we sense that he (and Price too, I think) feels the same way about himself. This is a novel of passage, and this young man needs to start his adult life, even if it turns out to be neither especially long or very happy. We leave the novel feeling that he will start.

This is not a book to rush through. Price's style, while sometimes lyrical and pleasing (Price is a writer of "prose-poems"), is paced and leisurely sometimes to the point of aggravation. The characters are so self-conscious and even narcissistic that they can all remember their many revelatory dreams and then relate them to one another, out loud and in their letters. Granted that the boy is bright and abroad and that folks do write letters still, Price forces these epistles to carry too much freight and thus gets out of creating the scenes that would show us, not merely tell us, what these people are like.

On balance, this is a successful and moving novel. Those who have not read *The Surface of Earth* need not fear; *The Source of Light* can stand alone. Those who have read and enjoyed the first have cause for cheer; the sequel is better.

> Donald Noble, in a review of "The Source of Light," in The Southern Humanities Review, Vol. XVI, No. 3, Summer, 1982, p. 276.

DAVID ROGERS

Reynolds Price has published eleven books, including five novels, two collections of short stories, a collection of essays, a play and translations from the Bible. From such an experienced writer we expect literacy and order, and that is what we get.

Vital Provisions is arranged in three parts: questions, mysteries and answers. A fair handful of the poems deal with matters central to Christianity . . . and these are powerfully imagined and convincing. Of the other poems in the book my favorite is **"The Dream of Lee."** The poet imagines he has been given the task of arranging for General Robert E. Lee to visit his university as a guest lecturer. Obviously Price, a teacher as well as a poet, is familiar with both the awkwardness and satisfaction of being a temporary guide for a great man. The situation is handled cleverly, and the poem is satisfying in its communication of a total experience.

Price's greatest difficulty in these poems is flatness. In **"Pictures of the Dead"** he remembers Frost, Auden and Lowell. These pieces are dull because the poet does little more than state the details of his meetings with these men. There is no overall or significant imagination of the events to give them meaning. When the wine of his reflection has been excessively watered with fact, the poems are more like catalogues of unassimilated observations than poems. On the whole, however, these pieces are rich and worth reading, particularly **"The Annual Heron,"** which is obviously something of a personal credo. The poem is personal, precise, literate and only a little less than great.

> *David Rogers, in a review of "Vital Provisions," in* World Literature Today, *Vol. 57, No. 3, Summer, 1983, p. 460.*

JAMES FINN COTTER

In his first book of poems, *Vital Provisions* . . . , novelist Reynolds Price combines narrative art with poetic perception. The opening poem, **"The Dream of a House,"** strikes the note of story and image which develop into the psychological and religious themes that fascinate this author. In his dream, a realtor guides the poet through the house of his dreams, its living room filled with his favorite paintings, books and recordings. He is told he will not live here alone, and he is led to a closed closet door. When it is opened, a crucified man hangs within, eyes shut and face level with his own. . . . The dreamer turns to his guide who answers: "Yours. Always." A terrible beauty stands revealed, the unconscious has spoken, and the reader stares into another world. **"The Dream of Lee"** that follows leads us into a further area of mythmaking. A college professor, Price is to pick up Robert E. Lee for two days at Duke University; but instead of the expected lecture, Lee wants to read from his poetry. Who ever heard of *The Poems of Lee*? Is there any such book? The dreamer worries. Lee reads a one-line poem dedicated to Price himself: "A country emptied by the fear of war," and he feels relieved, even transformed by the words. The poet, who here acts as guide, discovers that his private loneliness is national, his inner search is historic and his poetry is universal.

Price treats the religious theme explicitly in a series of poems on events in Christ's life, spoken by the participants themselves. . . . Like Salvador Dali's religious paintings, these poems present a weird surface reality that hints at depth without touching it. The best poem in the collection is the final one, **"The Annual Heron,"** a straightforward telling about a bird that for 10 winters visited a nearby pond. Here revelation breaks through in the phoenix figure of rebirth in "new grace" when the poet heeds the silent call of the heron to "Follow me." (pp. 93-4)

> *James Finn Cotter, "The Friendly Hand of Poetry," in* America, *Vol. 149, No. 5, August 20-27, 1983, pp. 92-4.*

CONSTANCE ROOKE

Although Price has never considered himself a regional novelist, he is undeniably and with sometimes visible pride a Southerner—whose work, moreover, shares a number of important characteristics with that of other Southern writers. Among these are a love of anecdote and colorful speech, a deep attachment to place, and a belief in the importance of the past and of family history. What Louis Rubin has defined as characteristic of the twentieth-century Southern writer is clearly true of Price: "His art has been crafted out of a deep sense of familiarity with the texture of community life, but also of a momentous distancing of himself from the community." That distance can be achieved in a meaningful way only when it has been preceded by familiarity; and what the South has given Price is that chance, the spectacle of human lives deeply entangled with one another, rooted in one place, enduring enough for the author's gaze.

An important fact of Southern life is its persistent rural flavor. For Price, that means the South can provide the artist with a sense of permanence. . . . The novel, Price remarks, has traditionally "turned on the poles of city and country"; and clearly his own work has employed each pole, as well as the tensions between them which are apparent now for any Southerner. Increasingly, Southerners must look back to discover that rural pole. The old way of life—God-and-family centered, rooted in the land—no longer flourishes; "but *surviving*," Price argues, "as opposed to *flourishing* has always been the supreme Southern specialty, black and white."

Most of the qualities we associate with Southern life and fiction are linked to the backward glance, a conviction that the past nourishes, guides, sometimes poisons our present lives. Religion, family history, and the oral tradition all operate in that way as the persistent backgrounding for contemporary life. "The past, as dream, condemnation, cause of the present," is for Price one grand design which imprints itself in several versions: Christian, Southern, and familial. The Christian doctrine of original sin, for example, has its counterpart in the tragic history of the South and in the family history that has determined so much of Price's fiction. The sin in each case seems to have been pride—which endures, despite guilt. Thus the South is also important for Price as a reflector of human history which is both larger than that (the story of man since Adam) and smaller (the story of Price himself). (pp. 8-9)

At the heart of Reynolds Price's fiction is a dialogue between love and solitude. Love is seen alternately as the ultimate reward and the largest threat in human life; solitude is both a blessing and a curse. . . . Thus his work contains both passionate testimonials to the importance of love and equally fervent, often shocking disavowals; it honors and blames people of both persuasions, the lovers and the solitaries—and it issues not from an aloof, Olympian perspective which sees and resolves all contradictions, but from a writer who has obvious personal stakes in the question that plagues and generates his work. Possibly because we expect any novelist to choose love, that side of the debate has generally been understood as victorious in Price's work. And it would be easy to find passages to support that conclusion—impassioned, unambiguous speeches; but there is strong evidence of a similar kind on the other side, proof that the dialogue must continue.

Price has described his theme as "an elaborate dialogue" between "free will and compulsion." He questions how far it is possible to escape the fate (the personality) that is laid on an individual by circumstance and particularly by family. As a Christian, he suggests that "one of the meanings of the metaphor of Original Sin" is "the accumulated genetic propensities-to-folly of man." Believing firmly in genetic and early environmental determinism, he also claims that man "both suffers from and is blessed by free will." Freedom might take the form of moving an individual toward love (if he were led in an opposite direction by nature or nurture) or away from it (if he had been guided otherwise). But most often in Price's work freedom is opposed to love; the loss of freedom is the price one pays for love, whether gladly or in bitterness. The loss of love is equally the price one pays for freedom. In that sense, he does believe in freedom as a human possibility, but he believes as well that we can exercise that freedom to make permanent errors. And the idea of a permanent error—nearly always, for Price, a violation of love—may suggest that we are not as free as we suppose, that our decisions finally are assessed by God in terms of an absolute code which we transgress at our peril.

If then, as seems to be the case for Price, one is consigned by family history to solitude and believes that God's code requires us to love one another, what hope remains? Have two kinds of law simply clashed, and is the violator of God's law damned by the circumstances of birth which God himself allowed? One kind of answer is to write books that describe for God and self and a few significant others the quandary in which such a person finds himself. In fairness to self, such books would acknowledge the claims of solitude and reveal the harm that love can do. The solitary author can also praise love, as Price does; he can exercise the faculties that God has given him, trusting that God will understand the solitude such work requires. he can remind all listeners as well that love is not restricted to the love between husband and wife, as Price has done through his emphasis upon odd couples of all sorts—masters and servants, parents and children, aunts and nephews, siblings, friends. He can point, finally, to another odd couple: the love between God and man, which is largely absent in the lives of Price's characters, but which is by implication their final consolation and his. (pp. 10-12)

[Price's] style is highly pronounced, unusual, and quite often difficult. The language generally is highly charged, the sentences are elaborate, the metaphors are often startling, and the precise description of all action (whether physical or emotional) often slows us down. . . . [His] goal is to force the reader, to shock him into recognition, to create a physical immediacy which gives the reader pause.

Price has claimed that he writes the most Anglo-Saxon prose currently being produced in America and has also defined his style (and that of the King James version of the Bible) as the "paradoxically baroque plain-style." The Anglo-Saxon qualities are what make it plain: an emphasis on concrete words rather than abstract, and a syntax which can be described as paratactic (that is, cumulative assault, an additive or horizontal syntax, rather than the Ciceronian style which depends much more on subordination). His prose in fact has a muscular, abrupt quality which we associate with Anglo-Saxon; it avoids what Price terms a "treacherous smoothness." Yet there is also undeniably a rhetorical quality, an elaboration which we tend to think of as baroque and which has misled some readers into thinking of Price's style as Faulknerian. While his sentences are often long, they tend to rely upon parentheses and noun phrases to accrete a total meaning, and they lack the quality of suspension found in more typically baroque syntax. Again, the goal is to keep us where we are, to wrench from each phrase of a sentence its immediate impact.

Perhaps the most striking feature of this style is its heavy reliance upon a core vocabulary. Most of Price's favored words are Anglo-Saxon rather than Latin in origin, nearly all are common and emotionally charged, and all are words that serve his central themes. Indeed, even a partial list of such words takes us into the heart of the author's vision: *protect, shield, threat, lethal, pain, loss, perfect, permanent, misery, pardon, plea, promise, blame, waste, warn, amends, ruin, error, wish, desperate, receipt, goal, gift, want, need, food, suck,* and *famine.* These words suggest the intensity of Price's concern with human interchange, both the damage it can wreak and the sustenance it may provide.

Those readers who accuse Price of overwriting claim by implication that he takes the complexity or the importance of his material too seriously. They would prefer that intense patches be relieved by something more casual and, in their view, more realistic. Their charge assumes either that his intensity is affected to make himself sound impressive or that if his intensity and complication are genuine they are still excessive. A strong argument, however, against the truth of the former assumption is that Price has demonstrated an absolute commitment to one thoroughly articulated vision. If he were concerned merely with a glossy surface, surely he would have applied that in a more random fashion to whatever matter would accept the glaze. Instead, what we find is a remarkably thorough correspondence between what the style signals and what Price believes about human life, as well as a remarkable concentration upon that set of beliefs. An evaluation of Price's style becomes, therefore, in large part a judgment upon his vision: if that is not excessive or distorted, then his style is not.

Other features of his style include a dense imagistic structure, a narrative voice which is often quite close to the speech of the characters, and considerable humor. Many of the same image patterns are used consistently throughout Price's fiction. Although such imagery (often verging on symbolism) is strikingly apparent, Price says he is "never conscious of symbols" when he is planning or writing a story, and he has a strong aversion to symbol-mongering on the part of critics. Again, what he would dislike is any suggestion of appliqué, of imposed decoration: the image patterns and symbols of his fiction grow naturally (and abundantly) from his diction and themes and from the physical world which Price creates. That same deep unity of fictional elements can be seen in the relationship of narrative voice and dialogue. Often, the narrative voice will echo folk rhythms (avoiding the subjunctive, for instance); at the same time, the dialogue is more literary, more studied and to the point than is strictly credible. Nearly everything the characters say contributes to the author's themes; and there is a strong similarity in tone, diction, and phrasing as we move from one character to another or from dialogue to the narrative voice. Roughly the same kind of humor (both extravagant and deflationary) appears in the dialogue and the narration. Humor functions in Price's fiction as it does in life—as a vital leavening, a delight, and a reminder of true proportions. (pp. 12-14)

Reynolds Price is a writer whose strengths may be perceived as weaknesses, according to the disposition of the reader. The intensity of his language and vision will either compel readers or disengage them; there is not much room for a middle ground, except perhaps for recognition of the author's formidable intelligence. This is not to say that we must share the author's Christian faith or his belief in the difficulty of contingency in order to appreciate his work. We may view marriage, for instance, or the relationship of parents and child very differently from Price and still admire or even love the fiction. We must, however, grant the integrity and genuine passion of Reynolds

Price if we are to penetrate the heart of his fiction and do him the justice of attention. He means every word he says; his manner leads to matter, not to the display of his linguistic facility. The surface of his work, however, has a stylized quality and a degree of polish that may tempt readers who are not in sympathy with his vision to suppose that Price's talents are restricted to the surface—that the author is hypnotized by the sound of his own voice.

In fact, there are few writers whose work suggests as strongly as Price's does the integrity of a single vision. The more deeply we penetrate into Price country the more insistent and thoroughly articulated does that vision appear. Nothing is accidental or extraneous or mere decoration. All of his elaborate imagery and the complex design of his fiction make final sense; each book repeats and expands the knowledge of the last. This intensity is ultimately a function of the author's concern with discovering the significance of his own life.

In *A Long and Happy Life* Price is apparently as remote from his own experience as he ever gets, and the success of that book (which many readers consider his best) complicates the picture of an artistic development that moves Price relentlessly always closer to the heart of his experience. That movement is unquestionably growth rather than a failure of the muse, and it is an exciting feature of his work for those readers who have followed it closely. *Love and Work* and *Permanent Errors,* which take the author into his personal heart of darkness, are extraordinarily powerful and courageous works of fiction. In *The Surface of Earth* we find magnified into epic proportions the essence of all Price has learned in his previous delvings of the self's core; it is a book executed in perfect confidence, a kind of demonstration of the author's life earnings. Continuing that demonstration, *The Source of Light* returns to a sophisticated and contemporary scene, extending and confirming some of the artistic choices made with *Love and Work* and *Permanent Errors.* But still we are faced with what seems an anomaly— the suspicion that Price's first book may be his most valuable

achievement. There is no accounting, finally, for the moment at which an author's finest work is cast up by his imagination. But if *A Long and Happy Life* is that book it should not lead us to the conclusion that Price's internal journey is a long mistake. Not all readers will feel inclined to follow him down those often-dark corridors of the self, but those who do will be amply compensated for their labor.

They will also be entertained, for Price knows how to tell a story. They will be amused, for he is often funny. And they will be instructed, for his vision is not so idiosyncratic that it cannot teach us much that is valuable for our own lives. (pp. 144-45)

Constance Rooke, in her Reynolds Price, *Twayne Publishers, 1983, 158 p.*

WILLIAM H. PRITCHARD

I felt . . . lack of form in Reynolds Price's first collection of poems [*Vital Provisions*], even though a publicity blurb quotes him as naming his "chief formal concern" to be "clarity." Mr. Price affects a direct speech in "language as common and conveyable as my own nature and the nature of the impulse will permit"; yet the poems which result seem flat, not quite turned into something memorable and too often bathed in the general aura of reverence which he also lays on thick in his novels. . . . More than one of these poems is titled "A Dream of" something or somebody; as a rule they tend to go on for a little longer than necessary, wander about in search of a situation, something around which the details could fall together. There is always the poet's assured tone, but the poems lack any distinction of rhythm, any formal pressure which might build them one way rather than another. So eventually they feel floating, arbitrary, a shade indistinct. (pp. 229-30)

William H. Pritchard, in a review of "Vital Provisions," in Poetry, *Vol. CXLIII, No. 4, January, 1984, pp. 229-30.*

Michel Rio

19??-

French novelist.

Rio garnered critical attention in the United States with his second novel, *Le perchoir du perroquet* (1983; *Parrot's Perch*). This highly philosophical work centers on Joachim, a Latin American priest who suffers a crisis of faith after being tortured by a despotic government for his political activities. Offered sanctuary in a French monastery but tormented by his memories of violence, Joachim renounces his values, including his belief in God and the redemptive worth of suffering. Much of the book consists of Joachim's philosophical and theological meditations, through which he attempts to understand the meaning of existence and attain spiritual peace. While faulted by several critics for failing to fully examine the reasons for undeserved suffering, Rio was praised for undertaking such an ambitious theme.

Rio's first novel, *Mélancolie nord* (1982), was described by Allen Thiher as a "philosophical adventure story" in the tradition of Ernest Hemingway's *The Old Man and the Sea*. In this work, a writer travels by sailboat from Paris to Norway to work on a book with a famous Scandinavian professor. Upon reaching Norway, he discovers that the professor has died. Thus, according to Thiher, "the trip has been made for its own sake, much like the narration of the trip, this novel, which now exists as its own goal, justified by an absurd choice to exist."

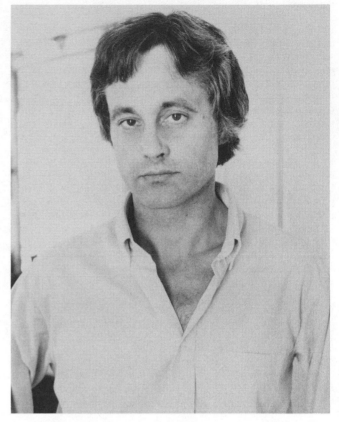

ALLEN THIHER

Michel Rio's first novel [*Mélancolie nord*] might be called a philosophical adventure story, one sharing a few traits with, say, *The Old Man and the Sea*. It begins in medias res with the narrator, alone in a small sailboat, having just survived a storm on the North Atlantic. The first-person narrator then tells how he got into this predicament: the storm had caught him in the middle of a rather extravagant trip that was to take him from Paris to Norway, where he was going to work on a book on the semiology of art with a famous Scandinavian professor. The rest of the work relates the narrator's ingenious struggle to survive in his sinking vessel. Against all odds he does survive, but upon arriving in Norway he discovers that the professor has died. The trip has been made for its own sake, much like the narration of the trip, this novel, which now exists as its own goal, justified only by an absurd choice to exist.

Reduced to this outline, the book may appear to offer a rather simplistic metaphor of the voyage and of fiction that links life and literature as gratuitous forms of excess, as irrational imponderables in a world that today is increasingly given over to the imperious forms of knowledge which seek to reduce life to fit rational schemes of explanation. This metaphor is not new, but it receives new life, thanks largely to the way Rio's style invigorates it. Much of the narration consists in a bravura description of the details of the narrator's struggle, of the hour-to-hour combat against the sea and the body's exhaustion and of the inventiveness that survival demands so that a lone man can convert the materials at hand into the instruments of a victory over an indifferent universe. One might see here a mixture of Stephen Crane and Lévi-Strauss, for the lone narrator is a heroic *bricoleur* who succeeds in defeating the elements.

The novel has a curious weakness in the portrayal of the narrator's rather fawning admiration of his Scandinavian intellectual hero as well as of the other major character, the isolated French writer who has loaned him the sailboat. Yet the narrator disarms this criticism by confessing his need for rather impossible father figures. Perhaps the presence of these fathers—a writer and a thinker—were necessary to give birth to this first novel. In any case, the Scandinavian thinker, a rather improbable mathematician, art historian and semiologist, leaves his protégé a final testament that provides a motivation for the novel's existence. He leaves him a letter that is a moving appraisal of the gratuitous power of literature in our modern era.

Allen Thiher, in a review of "Mélancolie nord," in World Literature Today, Vol. 57, No. 3, Summer, 1983, p. 422.

G. R. MERMIER

The narrator and hero of *Le perchoir du perroquet* is a South American priest in exile. Here he is talking to his brothers in a monastery somewhere in Brittany. He is angry and disillusioned and rejects all values, including God. He who had endured the most cruel tortures on the "parrot's perch" is now unable to cope with the haunting memories of the violence he experienced. In fact, memory and time have increased the absurdity of the act of torture to the point that death seems the only escape.

However, Joachim comes to realize that there is no escape from the acts or from his memory of them, but there is perhaps a chance to rediscover a form of serenity precisely in refusing compromises such as taking refuge in the imaginary or in some artificial paradise. By remaining true to his own authenticity, Joachim may attain peace. . . .

Le perchoir du perroquet is a dense and poignant story. Its power lies in its subtlety and in the harmony between mood and style which it establishes.

> *G. R. Mermier, in a review of "Le perchoir du per-*
> *roguet," in* World Literature Today, *Vol. 58, No. 4,*
> *Autumn, 1984, p. 570.*

PETER S. PRESCOTT

Billed as a novel, Michel Rio's *Parrot's Perch* . . . looks more like an argument set against a landscape. Joachim, an activist priest tortured in Latin America, finds refuge in a Breton monastery. . . . His own ordeal, which continues to haunt him in memory, prompts him to "hate suffering and humiliation," and thus to reject Christianity: by accepting the Crucifixion, "we have sanctified pain . . . This frightful idea, this madman's fantasy." Three tempters beset him: his torturer, who explains there is no right or wrong, only strength and weakness; the abbot of the monastery, a sophistical unbeliever who thinks religion a metaphor; a peasant woman of inarticulate, simplistic faith.

The French and the Russians have traditionally produced this kind of fiction, though they usually reinforce their arguments with character and action, both missing here. Rio instead describes in detail the monastery grounds. *Parrot's Perch,* named for the instrument with which Joachim was tortured, is an odd little book, but interesting. The problem of undeserved suffering has been with us since Job's day and never satisfactorily resolved—as it is not here.

> *Peter S. Prescott, in a review of "Parrot's Perch,"*
> *in* Newsweek, *Vol. CV, No. 23, June 10, 1985, p.*
> *81.*

LYDIA DAVIS

Michel Rio is a young Breton whose brief first novel [*Mélancolie nord*], a story of a struggle for survival against the elements in a foundering boat, was published in France three years ago to an enthusiastic reception. *Parrot's Perch* is another brief novel of almost incredible intensity, but here the struggle for survival is wholly in the mind of the main character. The power of this timely, unsettling story of a man's attempt to reconcile a devastating experience with his system of beliefs derives from the fact that in a short space Mr. Rio brings his protagonist into close personal combat with the great theological and philosophical problems—original sin, revelation, the redemption,

truth and lying, time and eternity, fiction and reality, acts and words, life and death, being and nothingness, to name just a few—and yet portrays the combat in such a way as to keep us anticipating the next word.

Brother Joachim is a Latin American priest who had been punished in his native country for his political activities by being subjected to the "parrot's perch," a form of torture in which "the victim is hung upside down naked by his feet" so that in time tremendous pressure is put on his forearms and "he becomes convinced that his fingers will explode." He tried to kill himself but was prevented by his torturers, and later was exiled to Brittany and took refuge in a monastery near the sea, where for a year he had "a peculiar status." He was not a monk; he lived in the hostel where those making religious retreats stayed, but he participated in the monks' activities.

Here, after an interval of "unconsciousness," he has suffered another kind of torture—the recurring memory of what he went through and the difficult recognition of what he believes to be mankind's innate cruelty, its taste for violence and its willingness to inflict pain. . . .

[In] the eyes of the monks, Joachim's experience has caused him to lose his faith, and the book opens with his "blasphemous declaration" to the assembled monks and other worshipers one Sunday. He rejects a religion and a God that have sanctified pain and suffering, and he lists the Christian martyrs and details their martyrdoms with a beautiful precision that proves another element in his disillusionment—that we are capable of taking esthetic and even sensual pleasure in suffering. For Joachim, this public declaration marks a figurative and literal point of no return.

After the service, he goes to his room, burns some of his papers and looks out his window at the landscape, a view he has studied so often that it has become a painting for him. He now urgently wants to "lose himself" in it, and leaving the abbey, he embarks on an allegorical journey that will take him, in less than 24 hours, from his indifference through states of mind that keep returning him to his initial despair and finally leave him with a feeling of vacancy. At the same time, he is walking through a variegated landscape toward the sea.

Part of the formal beauty of *Parrot's Perch*—and the reason for Mr. Rio's painstaking attention to Joachim's route and the exquisite detail of the landscape—comes from the fact that it is modeled very closely on the sort of late-medieval painting produced by Gerard David or Roger van der Weyden, in which time is collapsed so that the same biblical figure is shown at various points along a road that meanders up the panel through a sumptuously depicted landscape and off into the distance. And the experiences Joachim has along the way, like those of the figure on the painted wood, have a pointed symbolic significance in his larger story.

But whereas the saint or the Magus is on his way toward salvation, Joachim is going ever deeper into his pain and despair. Soon after leaving the abbey, for instance, he is overtaken by the abbot, who tries to reason with him and confesses his own lack of certainty in the church dogma; heading off in another direction, Joachim recalls the speech made to him by one of his torturers, a civilized young officer, after which all words appeared as lies to him, and his faith abruptly left him.

On the towpath by the canal, he meets the woman who keeps the lock, and the scene that follows is very close in spirit to

Pilgrim's Progress in its simplicity and directness of purpose, the characters being at once fully human and also the embodiments of attributes. The woman is, explicitly, "submission, convention, and ignorance" and Joachim is "passion, infinite experience . . . raw consciousness." On the path that winds through the fields toward the sea, he weeps, and then realizes that "these two explosions"—his tears and his earlier speech to the lock-keeper—have "broken him in two ways . . . He had cut himself off from words . . . from his own reasoning and . . . broken his extreme tension, ended the struggle his suffering body and sensibility had put up in order not to suffer." For throughout his walk he has been betrayed by his senses into registering feelings that no longer matter to his "dead soul."

He reaches the headland and watches night fall over the ocean. Then, standing at the point where the path loops away from the dangerously inviting edge of the wave-beaten cliffs, he looks across the valley at the abbey on its hill, and sees that it has, in turn, become a picture: "Cast in sharp chiaroscuro by the whiteness of the night, the monastery showed no lights; everyone, it seemed, was asleep." Joachim imagines himself back in his room looking out to the landscape where he now stands. "He had reduced or elevated nature to the state of artifice," and "now he had the odd impression that he was a part of the painting." But as the story nears its end, he knows there is no more refuge possible in the imaginary, in fiction, as no escape was possible in the "rigorous application of reason." At this point he lies down across the path and falls into a heavy, dreamless sleep.

The novel does not end with this state of oblivion, though it well could have—in fact, the only serious objection one might make to the book is that its end, while probably inevitable, is too predictable. For while the entire story is really a coda, an account of what happens after the end of the story, after everything has been decided, what is compelling about it is precisely that it does not answer the questions it raises.

Lydia Davis, "Joachim's Progress," in The New York Times Book Review, *June 30, 1985, p. 22.*

JOHN UPDIKE

[*Parrot's Perch*] begins with a sermon, a commentary on the Eucharist given in a French monastery near the Atlantic coast by a guest there, a young priest from Latin America, Joaquim Fillo. His remarks are announced as "about pain, about the cult of pain which is one of the bases of our religion." He begins with the Passion of Christ, an agony

> indissolubly linked . . . to the greatest good, which is the Redemption and the Life. The two blend indistinguishably in a fabric woven of blood and love, suffering and joy, the garden of tortures and the garden of delights, the victim and the executioner; and these produce a bread of man who is both his own victim and his own executioner.

He proceeds to a harrowing litany of the martyrs, with the specifics of their cruel deaths . . . and proceeds to the paradox of Christian cruelty in turn: "Whoever the torturer, whoever the tortured, suffering remains the route to Redemption. And for centuries the Holy Inquisition considered it a charitable duty to torture, burn, and destroy bodies in order to save souls." Father Fillo briefly describes his own acquaintance with torture,

after becoming a radical priest in his native land and then being "arrested and tortured by people who claimed to defend the values of Christianity." He ends by renouncing, before the assembled monastery congregation, Christianity:

> I reject that religion, a religion in which love has mixed with too much blood. I reject in it what is despicable, and so must also reject its sublimity. It reeks of human cunning, of the didactic imagination. For me God is other, or He doesn't exist . . . I want to make you feel the pointlessness of the pain and humiliation that gave rise to despair, to my despair—you who practice discipline and humility, in which you place your hope.

These are huge themes, and it is no very severe criticism of *Parrot's Perch* to say that the rest of the book isn't up to them. Mr. Rio, like Dostoyevski and Bernanos, Graham Greene and Shusako Endo, has posed a question—the problem of pain, of God's apparent silence—to which no novel can present a persuasive answer, though it may tend to confirm answers the reader has arrived at in the intimacy of religion and personal philosophy. There is no answer on earth, and the novel form is earthbound, properly and beautifully (as Henry James would say) confined to human perspectives. The body's answer to the problem of pain is brute endurance, mitigated by the numbness of shock and the eventual mercy of death. The average secular citizen's answer is stoicism, a narrow focus, and full use of the modern armory of anesthesia, ranging from alcohol to morphine. In *The Brothers Karamazov*, the troubled answer offered to Ivan's indignation over the death of children is the saintly life, as exemplified by his brother Alyosha. The Book of Job ends by appealing to the opaque, inimitable magnificence of Creation: the Creator will not be brought, philosophically, to heel. In *Parrot's Perch,* Father Fillo, having delivered his devastating homily, broodingly strolls in the countryside, has several impossibly stilted conversations with people he encounters, gazes at the sea, and succumbs to his own creator's portentousness.

The language proceeds from stately to awful: "He had cut himself off from his own reasoning, whose calamitous progress had contained the seed of its own negation, the possibility of a return or at least a detour in his rationalized trudging to the abyss." The priest's considerations begin to savor of too many graduate courses in ontology, and of Beckett's existential Gothic. . . . He is overtaken on his walk by the abbot, who cheerfully seems to believe rather less than Teilhard de Chardin, if a bit more than Jacques Monod. "I don't believe in original sin," says the abbot. "How can one believe in the guilt of amino acids and of protein, the origins of life and consciousness? . . . In denying the assumption of guilt, I logically deny its consequence, which is Redemption; and like you I admit the gratuitousness of suffering." Even burnt-out Father Fillo flares up, and asks what the abbot does believe in. "In the permanence, perfection, and universality of the Spirit" is the liberal answer. "And I believe in the morality of Christ, which is a morality of love." The young apostate is not coaxed back into the monastery, however; a little farther in his walk . . . he encounters a nameless woman operating the canal lock. "Her whole being emanated a kind of contained generosity, a spontaneous warmth held in check by a willed reserve." She had been in the congregation and heard his disavowal, yet greets him and invites him into her house. "Here were a man lost in a dark, inner space and a lonely woman—

uneducated, vivacious, and intuitive.'' Yet no dialogue, no exchange develops; she sits utterly mute while the disillusioned priest pours nihilism into her ears. As one of the book's better sentences puts it, ''her own, inarticulate hope had vanished in his void, and she saw now that she could expect nothing from this man save perplexity.''

Father Fillo walks on. His progress has become too baldly a pilgrim's, a self-absorbed pilgrim who doesn't need a novel's furniture around him. The little book has the weight, the seriousness, but not the movement and society of a novel. In the end, certain semiabstract scenic effects do for an epiphany. The Atlantic Ocean and evening are approached: ''The night, half day at the top, darkness at the base, seemed to have emerged from the ocean rather than from the sky.'' This black immensity of sea serves to emblemize the universe and prompts a page of cosmological meditation and such mind-twisters as ''He found himself in a hell he feared was eternal, which revolved around two poles: the relativity of nothingness and the absoluteness of the universe.'' His unrest now seems, like Hamlet's, centered on a faint doubt of oblivion: ''In an odd return to prayer, he asked only that the God Whom he found guilty of creating pain should also create oblivion.'' The scene before him has ''the palliative nightmare of reality, a peaceful mirror whose obverse was violence; and in it he saw himself.'' At last, in a final tortured twist of perception and of language, Joaquin Fillo sees himself as part of the landscape he often viewed from his window at the monastery, and this goads his thought and the hardworking translator to such words as ''topologic,'' ''metonymy,'' and ''alterity,'' and brings him peace. ''Flight became possible through the transmutation of place into image, of reality into illusion. He could escape into the fiction he had pulled from the truth of the setting, vanish beyond the field, beyond all the fields of the canvas framed by the sash of his window . . .''

Overwritten and underdramatized as it is, *Parrot's Perch* engages us, naïvely invites us into its strife. . . . The notion of the world as a testing stage has faded, and with it much that gave even the crudest adventure tale a certain dignity. Helplessness characterizes the typical modern hero; the most energetic and human acts that . . . Father Fillo [performs] are verbal acts of protest, registering . . . [his] astonishment that, as Flaubert said, the function of the sun is not to help the cabbages along. (pp. 87-90)

John Updike, ''A Pair of Parrots,'' in The New Yorker, *Vol. LXI, No. 22, July 22, 1985, pp. 86-90.*

MICHAEL WOOD

The protagonist of Michel Rio's *Parrot's Perch* has been close to silence for about a year. He is a Latin American priest who was tortured for resisting his government, and has been given refuge in a French monastery. The abbot asks him to give the commentary on the Eucharist one Sunday, and after some hesitation, in a voice whose very monotony speaks of trauma and despair, he preaches a remarkable sermon on pain; on 'the cult of pain which is one of the bases of our religion'. He lists the martyrs and their torments, their long, lovely names and their excruciations. Decapitated, racked, boiled, flayed, flogged, drowned, quartered, blinded, mutilated, crucified, fed to the beasts, broken on the wheel, they all died in Christ. 'Make up the cruellest tortures you can imagine,' the apostle Andrew is supposed to have said. 'The more constant I am in the torment I suffer in the name of my King, the more I shall please Him.'

'Such tribulations became and still are *exempla*,' the priest says,

> and we see in them not just a veneration for beings who refused to betray their ideas, but a veritable fascination with the redemptive power of pain. And if Redemption is a goal, it seems to me that suffering, which has coloured it in blood, is a goal as well, because the two cannot be dissociated. I dare not tell you what I make of Andrew's words, or of the words of those who find them fit subject for a sermon.

The sermon gets a little muddled after this, confuses the question of pain with the question of belief, and nothing in the book quite lives up to this austere and demanding beginning. The priest, Joachim, talks to the abbot, takes a walk in the Breton countryside, meets a peasant woman who moves him strangely, because she intuitively responds to his despair, and to 'the humility that lay at the very heart of his rebellion'. He stands on a crumbling cliff, watches the Atlantic breakers crashing in, and after trying to merge with the landscape, in a 'soothing coincidence of geography and mood', he finds peace, it seems, by walking off the cliff into a death which is the only possible erasure of intolerable memory. . . .

The novel is a bit thin-blooded, in spite of its fraught subject; highly literary and intellectual, as we might expect of a writer who confesses (on the dust-jacket) to 'a special affection for Conrad and Chomsky'. Too much signalling and symmetry in those names. There is a flimsiness even in this book's unmistakable elegance, a sense of difficult ideas being turned into philosophical dance-tunes. But if the ideas are entertained rather than suffered, they are not trivialised or thrown away, and it is good to see a writer using fiction as a place to think. Joachim's later meditations and his final peace are dubious, but his questions and his nightmares remain. Is it true that the courage of the saints is 'an inhuman response to an inhuman situation'? 'How are torturers born? Who are they? And doesn't their insanity lie solely in that conversion of the imaginary into action?' It is the officer in charge of torturing Joachim who reasonably (diabolically) says: 'I think no moral conviction justifies a scream of pain.' . . . [Rio is] trying to explore a mind severed from the world, or unable to find a home in it.

Michael Wood, ''Theory with a Wife,'' in London Review of Books, *Vol. 7, No. 17, October 3, 1985, p. 17.*

PHILIP SMELT

Michel Rio's *Parrot's Perch* has been hailed by critics in France as ''stunning'' and ''powerful''. Perhaps the novel has lost something in Leigh Haffrey's translation, but this sombre account of a priest's struggle with the religious implications of suffering seems somehow both slim and ponderous.

In exile at a secluded monastery in Brittany, Father Joachim is recovering from his torture at the hands of a Latin American dictatorship. *Parrot's Perch* records his emotional and intellectual reactions to the terrifying ordeal. . . . One morning Father Joachim shocks his gentle monastic hosts by delivering a sermon that criticizes the conventional Christian attitude towards pain and martyrdom. He tells the assembled brethren that his experience has shaken his belief in a merciful God and in the redemptive power of suffering, which he calls ''this frightful idea, this madman's fantasy'' that has ''terrorized legions of children''. The only other characters in the novel are the French Abbot, who is given a short speech in which he justifies the mystery of an all-knowing, all-powerful God; and a peasant woman who works as a lock-keeper on the canal, and says very little.

The further extravagant theorizing that Rio indulges in is confusing to the point of opacity. Like some religious Jean-Paul Sartre, Father Joachim launches into long meditations in which:

> He found himself in a hell he feared was eternal, which revolved around two poles: the relativity of nothingness and the absoluteness of the universe. He couldn't really imagine salvation, he strove simply to believe in it: it might lie in the relativization of the infinite and of eternity, and that imposition of limits might lead back on an enormously long detour, to nothingness.

Rio's own short detour, which when translated takes in such clumsy terms as ''cognizant'', ''exordium'' and ''alterity'', suggests a theology of non-liberation that leads nowhere.

> *Philip Smelt, ''Lost Cause,'' in* The Times Literary Supplement, *No. 4339, May 30, 1986, p. 597.*

Alain Robbe-Grillet

1922-

French novelist, essayist, scriptwriter, critic, and autobiographer.

Robbe-Grillet is among the foremost proponents and theoreticians of *le nouveau roman,* also referred to as the new novel or antinovel. In his volume of theoretical essays, *Pour un nouveau roman* (1963; *For a New Novel*), Robbe-Grillet questions the validity of traditional novelistic form and discounts the idea that realism necessarily offers the most accurate reflection of life. He strives for pure objectivity in his fiction, making camera-like use of point-of-view by spontaneously recording events without imposing subjective interpretation. Robbe-Grillet eschews standard chronology, character, and plot, favoring instead disjointed narratives, characters with vague or shifting identities, metafictional situations, and *chosisme,* the precisely detailed description of inanimate objects. *Chosisme* derives from such visual arts as painting and cinema and, according to Roland Barthes, refers to "the existential notion that human consciousness defines itself in relation to objects." Robbe-Grillet purposely leaves meanings ambiguous or contradictory to allow readers to exercise their individual perceptions, yet his fiction is not devoid of meaning, as objects elicit symbolic associations in the minds of readers. The major interest of Robbe-Grillet's work lies in the collaboration between author and reader, the process by which objective reality acquires subjective meaning. According to Robbe-Grillet, "literature is not a means of expression, but a search. And it does not even know for what it searches."

The discrepancy between objective and subjective reality is a central preoccupation in Robbe-Grillet's first novel, *Les gommes* (1953; *The Erasers*). In this book, a secret agent's investigation into the murder of a recluse leads the agent to confront and kill a man he supposes to be the murderer. The dead man is ultimately revealed, however, to be the recluse, who had feared for his life and had fabricated his death. According to Robbe-Grillet, such contradictory events are valid because an author's reality is the only admissible framework for a work of fiction. Like the secret agent, the author has made a nonexistent crime a reality and has "solved" both the crime and the murderer's identity. Easily defined identities such as hero, victim, and author are thus effectively obscured, or "erased." In Robbe-Grillet's next novel, *Le voyeur* (1955; *The Voyeur*), his hero exists on two separate planes of fantasy and reality and contemplates his attraction to sexual aberration, particularly sadism, in his search for identity. Similar protagonists recur in many of Robbe-Grillet's novels. *The Voyeur* is described from the viewpoint of a murderer; since author and reader share this viewpoint, both are guilty of voyeurism, and identities are again uncertain. *La jalousie* (1957; *Jealousy*) is considered a characteristic example of Robbe-Grillet's narrative technique. In this work, he juxtaposes objective description with the first-person fantasies and reflections of a man who suspects his wife of infidelity. As in *The Voyeur,* the reader is left to distinguish between internal and external reality.

Robbe-Grillet's next work, *Dans le labyrinthe* (1959; *In the Labyrinth*), is a novel within a novel. The internal work of fiction is created by an author whose room contains the objects

described in the narrative and who encourages readers to engage in pure investigation without expectations. This book recalls the myth of Theseus and the Minotaur in its story of a soldier who wanders a maze of alien streets attempting to deliver a package to a forgotten address. *Instantanés* (1961; *Snapshots*) is a collection of short exercises illustrating Robbe-Grillet's characteristic themes and techniques. *La maison de rendez-vous* (1965; *The House of Assignation*), like *In the Labyrinth,* is a novel within a novel, describing a "work in progress" in which the author appears to be reviewing a series of alternate scenes in his mind. In this book, one murder occurs under three different series of circumstances.

During the 1970s, Robbe-Grillet continued to explore metafictional possibilities in his work. In his preface to *Projet pour une révolution à New York* (1970; *Project for a Revolution in New York*), Robbe-Grillet predicts the emergence of a new form in which "the themes of the novel . . . become the basic elements engendering all the architecture of the story and even the adventures which unfurl in it." In this book, Robbe-Grillet uses colors and geometric figures as generative bases; for example, the color red symbolizes arson, rape, and murder in a surreal New York based on myths of popular culture. *Topologie d'une cité fantôme* (1975; *Topology of a Phantom City*) relates in colorful visual terms a hostile army's attack on an ancient city and the rape of a young girl. This and later works exemplify what Robbe-Grillet termed the "nouveau nouveau roman," which he stated was distinguished from the *nouveau roman* by "a proliferation of names and pronouns in a context of contradictory and conflicting situations, specifically designed to undermine all standards of realism." In *Souvenirs du triangle d'or* (1978; *Recollections of a Golden Triangle*), a story involving a sadistic cult that operates from within a labyrinthine opera house serves as a pretext for intertextual games in which Robbe-Grillet employs dead ends, reversals, circular reasoning, and other metafictional devices. The reader is invited to penetrate the heart of the text—the golden triangle of the title—and thus aid in the creative process.

Robbe-Grillet's first attempt at the *nouveau roman* was *Un régicide* (1978), a novel originally written in 1949. In this book, he varies objective narration with the first-person fantasies of a hero whose actual attempt to assassinate a king destroys his fantasy world. *Le rendez-vous* (1979; *Djinn*) is an experimental work which Robbe-Grillet produced with the intention of teaching French to Americans. Like his earlier works, this novel shifts between first- and third-person narrative; according to John O'Brien, "with each shift in person and tense, the 'facts' of the story are reshuffled and altered."

In addition to writing novels, Robbe-Grillet is also an acclaimed motion picture director and scriptwriter. Among his scripts and film productions are *L'anneé dernière à Marienbad, L'immortelle, Trans-Europ Express, L'Eden et après,* and *Glissements progressifs du plaisir.*

(See also *CLC*, Vols. 1, 2, 4, 6, 8, 10, 14 and *Contemporary Authors*, Vols. 9-12, rev. ed.)

WALTER A. STRAUSS

[*For a New Novel*] constitute[s] an indispensable companion volume to Robbe-Grillet's fiction and cinema-fiction; and, more broadly, an important apology for the *nouveau roman,* in a more immediate sense than Michel Butor's two volumes of *Répertoire,* which range more widely and more urbanely over the various provinces of literature. (p. 575)

[Robbe-Grillet is fascinated by] reflected visions, and his essays are attempts to justify the new novel as an enterprise in the subjective recording of viewed surfaces; he is also perhaps fascinated by the phenomenon of reflection itself, but tells us nothing about this problem in his essays. In this sense, he may be looked upon as a Valéry turned inside out: what is abstract in Valéry becomes relentlessly concrete in Robbe-Grillet: Monsieur Teste has become Monsieur le Voyeur, or better yet, Monsieur X. But one curious coincidence remains between these polarities of Valéry and Robbe-Grillet: they are both—along with every other major twentieth century artist—constructivists.

The reader should not begin by expecting too much from these essays; there is sufficient evidence in the essays themselves that Robbe-Grillet does not want them overrated. This volume is not The Art of the New Novel, nor its Theory; it is simply a very straightforward and honest discussion of what Robbe-Grillet's fiction is all about. There is more "theory" in Butor's *Répertoire; and* there is a more precise sense of the tradition and the problems of the contemporary novel in Nathalie Sarraute's *L' Ère du soupçon.* But there is a quality of common

sense and even of tentativeness here that is not quite found in Robbe-Grillet's more learned fellow-apologists. Nor will the reader find much "growth" in this present volume; there is a certain amount of progressive clarification in moving chronologically from the first important essay, **"A Future for the Novel"** (1956) to the most ambitious one, **"Nature, Humanism, Tragedy"** (1958) to the excellent **"Time and Description in Fiction Today"** (1963) and the succinct summarizing of **"From Realism to Reality"** (1955/63); but there is very little *approfondissement,* partly explicable by the fact that Robbe-Grillet appears to have a Pascalian kind of aversion to *profondeur.* The few shorter essays on other writers (Roussel, Svevo, Bousquet, Beckett, Pinget) are interesting primarily because of Robbe-Grillet's discovery of affinities with these writers; the Beckett essay, which surprisingly enough deals with Beckett's first two *stage* works, is quite perceptive.

It is unfortunate that we do not have more examples of Robbe-Grillet's personal and professional reactions to other writers; we ought to have lengthy essays at least on Flaubert and Kafka, even if those essays were merely in the form of *témoignages.* These two writers, in my opinion, are the major ingredients of Robbe-Grillet's craft: Flaubert, for insisting that his novels should be about "nothing" . . . and Kafka, for his uncanny sense of a precisely documented "reality" from which we are totally alienated. All the other "influences" on Robbe-Grillet—Balzac, Joyce, Faulkner, Proust, Beckett, the detective story, Graham Greene, and possibly Surrealist fiction—are important seasonings, but not basic ingredients. Robbe-Grillet's claim to *serious* attention lies in the fact that since his "Visions réfléchies," since *The Erasers,* he has consistently pursued a narrow and precarious path defined by himself in **"A Future for the Novel"** and achieved a strange kind of purification in his constructions and even in his expression (if this word is applicable to a writer who abhors all metaphorical literature as being falsely anthropomorphic and deceptively humanistic); his three finest achievements, ***Jealousy, In the Labyrinth*** and ***Last Year at Marienbad,*** bear this out.

The admirer of Robbe-Grillet's explorations (like Butor, he thinks of the novel as an instrument of "recherche") will, in all likelihood, *not* find the answer to the questions that interest him most: Robbe-Grillet is either not able or not ready to articulate the answers. In a sense, he has *presented* the problems to the best of his ability in his novels and *ciné-romans.* What we would really like to know is the source and the significance of Robbe-Grillet's fascination (and our own, too, as readers of his novels) with the obsessive emotional states of his characters and the hypnotic effect of those bizarre geometrical and at the same time labyrinthine topographies. This curious creative tension in Robbe-Grillet between the positivistic or phenomenological eye and the Jansenist mind—the observation of the world and the recoil from the world—this old-and-new Gnosticism, may have to be left for others to elucidate. (p. 576)

Walter A. Strauss, in a review of "For a New Novel,"
in The Modern Language Journal, Vol. L, No. 8,
December, 1966, pp. 575-76.

ROBERT KANTERS

Snapshot photography is a technique that attempts to retain the totality and diversity of the world in space while neglecting the diversity and the movement of the world in time, in consciousness and in history. And so the title [*Snapshots*] summarizes reasonably well the program or the intention of the New Novel according to Alain Robbe-Grillet.

To some extent, the six pieces that make up this small collection can also be considered as exemplary. They are short stories or prose poems, brief exercises in Robbe-Grillet's manual on style as well as content. So much so, in fact, that the first sentence of the first proof of these stories—''The coffeepot is on the table''—has since been derisively used as the title of a lampoon on Robbe-Grillet by a conservative and sometimes conformist critic, Pierre de Boisdeffre. . . .

The writing aims for the greatest possible clarity; it is pure objective observation, a simple list of particulars. The reader has no need to know too much about the characters in these brief evocations. The situation, and especially the material situation, must speak for itself and, without being interpreted through the consciousness of the author, impose on us a vision and if possible a sensation. The piece entitled **''Scene,''** dated 1955, the same year as *The Voyeur,* is like the vision of a performance at an imaginary theater, a performance that we become aware of, not one that we attend; all interpretation is reduced to the minimum reconcilable with minimum intelligibility.

The last piece, **''The Secret Room,''** is one of the most representative of Robbe-Grillet's approach and work. The very title brings us back to the somewhat mysterious enclosed site so important to the author of *La Maison de Rendez-Vous.* In addition, the dedication to the French artist Gustave Moreau—whose paintings, impregnated with a heavy and bizarre sensuality, had already aroused the interest of the surrealists—attracts us toward what Ludovic Javier, one of the best critics of the New Novel, has called ''the sadistic locale par excellence.''

A woman lies butchered, chained to a column, dead as the result of a wound in her breast, struck down by a man who is undoubtedly disappearing into the shadows. The foregoing could more easily be the description of a painting than the outline of a narrative. But these pages retain a heavy mystery. They do not relate a tragedy; they render it perceptible to us by means of this woman's body, by the odor of still-warm blood and perhaps that of sexual assault. The choice among objects of a privileged object—the woman's body—and the situation in which it is presented—chained, wounded—orients the objectivity of the story toward the world of dense sadomasochistic sexual obsessions whose presence imposed itself more and more in Robbe-Grillet's succeeding works.

In short, the reader will find in this very small volume something better than specimens. He will find pages that are not only very powerful and very characteristic of Robbe-Grillet's manner but that also offer important insights into the author's interior world. The dry technique of the book expands with an obsessional world, and the very brevity of these pieces permits the author to bypass the laborious scaffolding that sometimes slows up his novels and makes them cumbersome. . . .

While remaining faithful to his point of view about art and the world, [Robbe-Grillet] perhaps finds a more directly efficacious means of expression in dealing with the image by means of the image. Nevertheless, this small book shows how far a writer can go in dealing with the image by means of style, and Robbe-Grillet's style, deliberately elementary and flat, is no doubt one of those that lose the least in translation.

Robert Kanters, ''The School of the Look,'' in The New York Times Book Review, *January 12, 1969, p. 35.*

ANNA OTTEN

Alain Robbe-Grillet's first novel, *Un régicide,* which he finished in 1949, was turned down by a well-known French publisher. Absorbed in other writing, the author did not take time to revise the manuscript. Only now, after thirty years, has he decided to publish the original version.

Like Meursault and Roquentin, the novel's hero Boris is a stranger within his own society. Seeking his own identity, he moves between opposite poles: between stark realism and dream, between seemingly purposeless wandering and acute search, between passive contemplation and feverish activity. The narration too fluctuates like the waves on the seashore, where the hero, sometimes identical with the narrator, spends most of his time. Narrative fragments are arranged and rearranged, with commentary often added. Third-person comments may interrupt first-person narration; fictional modules vary greatly in length, and descriptions of place differ. From the sandy seashore, where beautiful women bask in the sun, the narration moves to fertile gardens rich with the scent of roses or to land totally barren. Observing through the author's eyes, we see steadily flowing images, as in a film. Robbe-Grillet borrows film techniques in his fiction, a method seen in his subsequent works. His very art is not to project patterns of a novel beforehand, but to be spontaneously guided by the text, by certain words and associations, and to form patterns as the work progresses.

One of the two most important fictional fragments of the novel is rooted in fairy tales of the young man and the sea sprite. It is Aimone, ''the daughter of sand and sea foam,'' who moves gracefully like seaweed on the waves. Indulging in verbal play, the narrator calls her ''Aimone . . . amie, amante, anémone'' and watches her as she glides into the waves to relax on the sandy floor. Another fictional module springs from the words on a tombstone: ''Ci-gît Red.'' Perhaps this refers to Red Eric the Viking, or to some other mysterious person. At any rate, a whistle is suddenly heard, and the words dance in the narrator's head to form the anagram ''Régicide,'' the word that generates the plot to murder the king. Thus the eroticism and violence, the humor and genius for rendering precise descriptions of dreams as well as of reality that mark all of his later works are already present in this first book.

A good introduction to Robbe-Grillet's whole work, *Un régicide* lends itself to a study not only of his fiction but also of his films. Less complicated and clearer than what was to come, it points the way deep inside the labyrinth of a man's mind, where his fantasies dwell.

The recent *Souvenirs du triangle d'or,* like all of Robbe-Grillet's works, arrays fictional fragments in ever-changing patterns. What is important is their relationship to each other within this book and their intertextual references to his other works, to other authors or to the daily press. Some fragments deal with murder, others with sex, torture, drugs or incest. As in *La maison de rendez-vous* and *Topologie d'une cité fantôme . . . ,* he also focuses on prostitution. But other references abound, some harking back to *Un régicide.* The author playfully composes these modules into one collage after another in repetition and variation. Each work of fiction appears to be created from these modules, and together they form a gigantic canvas where their interplay, their intertextuality, can be seen. There are dark colors and long corridors in what seem to be prisons, hospitals, houses of pleasure or city streets at night. But there are also bright beaches glistening in the sun and beautiful girls dressed in white set against backgrounds of red and blue. With a painter's eye, yet with geometric precision, Robbe-Grillet sketches his images.

From beginning to end, *Souvenirs du triangle d'or* deals with textual and sexual relationships. Fantasies are forever taking on new incarnations. . . . Fictional space is also seashore and city, but the city is no longer vague and undefinable. It is the old city that enemies partly destroyed in *Topologie d'une cité fantôme,* with its theatres, prisons and harems. In it a criminal is at work, with sexual and textual experiments. . . . Criminal experiences are revealed as "textual experiences"; intextuality is obviously connected to former books. The author is similarly fascinated with geometric shapes, in this book the triangle: triangular roofs, a triangular sign over the entrance of a mysterious house, the shape of women's pubic hair. The memory of the mythical golden fleece lingers on. (pp. 68-9)

Anna Otten, in a review of "Un régicide" and "Souvenirs du triangle d'or," in World Literature Today, *Vol. 54, No. 1, Winter, 1980, pp. 68-9.*

GABRIEL JOSIPOVICI

[*Djinn*] is Robbe-Grillet's funniest and lightest novel so far. He is taking on Calvino at his own game, but the overtones of menace and darkness are still present. The narrator enters a deserted hangar at the appointed time, makes out in the gloom a man standing waiting for him. . . . [He recites a] coded message he has been told to give. But the figure answers: "Ne prononcez pas Jean, mais *Djinn.* Je suis Américaine." So it's not a man but a woman: the conventions of spelling and thriller plots have misled him. However, a moment later he discovers that "she" is not a woman either but a tailor's dummy, animated only by the power of his imagination, and her husky voice issues not through her unmoving lips but from a sound system wired into the derelict building. He moves away in disgust only to be met by another dummy; identical to the first—only this one turns out to be a real American woman— or at least as real as anyone ever is in the pages of a book. For it may be that the narrator is imagining all this, the beautiful American girl, the whole bizarre world of Russian spies and an international ecological anti-machine movement into which he is drawn. We do in fact learn later that the narrator, Simon Lecoeur, is much given to fantasizing. But is he even called Simon Lecoeur? He gave his name as Boris, but this was the code, and though after his disappearance a French passport in the name of Boris Koershimen is found in his flat, the police think it's a fake. At the American school of the rue de Passy where he teaches he is inscribed as "Robin Körsimos, dit Simon Lecoeur", but his students call him Yann, spelt Ján.

The preface in which this information is given—shades of Nabokov and Borges here—only multiplies the hypotheses about his name and origins. It also directs our attention to the fact that the story of Simon and "Djinn" which follows was found on Simon's desk, ninety-nine neatly typed pages, divided into eight chapters of gradually increasing length and linguistic complexity. Eight weeks is the length of an American term, and so what we have here may not be either fiction or fantasy, but only a graded reader for students of French.

A comparison with Michel Butor may be helpful at this point. Butor, too, would have organized his material in a rigorous way so as to exhaust the possibilities inherent in it and in his initial decisions. But that would have been enough: symmetries and patterns are, for Butor, sufficiently satisfying in themselves. For Robbe-Grillet, however, they only represent what has got to be worked through if that which forever eludes definition is finally to be pinned down. Is not the educational character of the story merely one further lure? . . .

That, of course, has always been Robbe-Grillet's question, but in his recent novels the sense that narrative, as opposed to life, was free to do anything, quickly left the reader with the feeling that everything the narrative did was equally *un*interesting. But that is not at all the impression given by this novel. This is partly due to the irony and humour, which hint at a real desperation. Partly, too, it is due to the fact that when, as here, Robbe-Grillet does not make the erotic and the sadistic the central subjects of his work he taps unexpected resources in himself. That is partly why *Dans le labyrinthe* is the best of his early novels, the one in which the universal nature of essential themes is most fully realised. And here too, in the episodes with the two children—more than half the book—we are in the realm of myth, not science fiction or strip cartoon. . . . At one point Simon, for some reason he cannot even explain to himself, playing at being blind, eyes firmly shut, dark glasses on, a white stick in his hand, is led down endless alleyways by the little boy Jean (not Djinn). He could easily open his eyes, yet chooses not to. Why? "Je dois avoir un sacré complexe d'Oedipe", he thinks to himself, and it is of *Oedipus at Colonus,* not the banalizations of Freud, that the scene reminds us—not of Roy Lichtenstein but of the great Picasso etching of the little girl, a light in one hand, leading the blind minotaur by the other.

The artist is both innocent child and blind monster. He eliminates one or other at his peril. For too long—since *Dans le labyrinthe* in fact—Robbe-Grillet has tried to argue and to write as if art is merely a game. Of course it is not simply the imitation of reality; but it is also mystery, the confrontation of the unknown, unspoken. *Djinn* suggests a new humility in its author, a recognition of the fact that he may not hold all the cards. It is a pleasure to see a major artist finding himself once more.

Gabriel Josipovici, "Lessons in Storytelling," in The Times Literary Supplement, *No. 4076, May 15, 1981, p. 536.*

JOHN LEONARD

[*Djinn* is] the latest "antinovel" by Alain Robbe-Grillet, and his most ambiguous one since *The Voyeur* was published in France 27 years ago.

[The protagonist] Simon, answering a want-ad, appears at an abandoned workshop, where he meets Djinn, an American girl with a Boston accent. Djinn asks Simon to join her terrorist organization. Its purpose is not immediately specified.

Simon agrees. For someone who is supposed to "reason like a Frenchman positivist and Cartesian," he is astonishingly whimsical, almost Russian.

In the service of Djinn, Simon will meet Jean, a young boy who specializes in dying and resurrection, and who, because of a "dysfunction" of memory, dreams the future. He will meet Jean's even-younger sister, Marie, who attends a logic class on first-, second- and third-degree lying, "with two un-knowns," sometimes in harmony. He will be obliged to mas-querade as a blind man with a cane. . . .

I don't want to make the plot sound more complicated than it is. Mr. Robbe-Grillet has, anyway, always disdained plot, character, psychology and significance, anything that smacks of 19th-century "realism." Part of the fun of *Djinn*—and there is some—is in its send-up of the pop conventions of science fiction, espionage and occult novels. Little Marie tells us that, after graduating from "third-degree lying," she wants to study to become a heroine in novels. "It is a good job, and it allows one to live in the literary style. Don't you think that's prettier?"

What is complicated about *Djinn,* and let's not get into Islamic mythology to explain that title, are its reversals of plot and sex, its breaking down of narrative and identity into pins and needles to be rearranged in time and space. A former statistician and agronomist, Mr. Robbe-Grillet seems to be more interested in epistemology than he is in fiction. . . .

Simon keeps finding himself in the same blind alley until he is no longer Simon. He is, in fact, as blind as the alley, first in disguise, and then by an act of will. Returning to a strange restaurant, he is told, "Yesterday you could not see anything; that was the day we close." Are we blind, to past and future? Have we dreamed ourselves because of dysfunctional memory? Is this sad?

Djinn's organization is pledged to end the oppression of ma-chines on the human spirit and yet she speaks to her faithful through the mouths of mannequins, on tape machines. Is this a political comment, unusual for Mr. Robbe-Grillet, or are we being told that identity itself is a machine, a gearbox of dreams, memories, situations and gestures? That identity is an oppres-sion?

Simon at one point might be little Marie's father. At another he might be Djinn, or at least she might be the female half of his androgynous self. At the very beginning of their relation-ship, Simon tells Djinn, "The struggle of the sexes is the motor of history." Sex? Motor? History? Are they all machines?

Not having read any of Mr. Robbe-Grillet's recent criticism, I'm just guessing. And that criticism might not have helped. The antinovels of Robbe-Grillet, Nathalie Sarraute and Michel Butor seem to me to improve the more they depart from the critical theories of their authors, as if some sort of djinn were trying to escape from the laboratory and dream free.

And I shouldn't be guessing at all, according to French theory. The "analogical" method is beyond interpretation. It results in an object, like that "slice of tomato in an automat sandwich" mentioned by Roland Barthes in an essay on Mr. Robbe-Grillet, "without heredity, without associations and without refer-ences." Or, like the hamburgers, wash basins and soup cans of Pop art.

Djinn has its delightful moments and its gratifying perplexities. Italo Calvino and Stanislaw Lem would enjoy it. But I wonder if such an antinovel is any longer necessary. Writing years ago about himself, Mr. Robbe-Grillet announced that "the world is neither significant nor absurd—it *is*, quite simply." This statement now seems to me to be quite false, and perhaps even cowardly.

John Leonard, in a review of "Djinn," in The New York Times, *July 1, 1982, p. 18.*

JOHN O'BRIEN

Robbe-Grillet's *Djinn* is framed by the prologue and epilogue of a seemingly transparent narrator who finds a mysterious manuscript *The Rendez-vous* which he then reproduces. This Poe-like analyst limits himself in the prologue to providing the scanty and cryptic information available about the manuscript's author, Simon Lecoeur, and to vague speculations about its intent: "the ratio of probability of the reported event is almost always too low, in relation to the laws of traditional realism. Thus, it is not ruled out to see a mere guise in this pretense of a pedagogical intent. Behind that guise, something else must be concealed. But what?" The hand of this narrator is one possible answer to his question.

The first five chapters of *The Rendez-vous* record in first-per-son, present tense, Lecoeur's (or someone else's) response to a newspaper ad, which results in his taking an unspecified job with a clandestine organization that requires him to disguise himself as a blind man. He relates his bizarre experiences, culminating with a whack on the head when he lifts his opaque glasses to find himself in a room filled with others dressed identically, each apparently believing that he has been chosen for the same secret mission.

That whack leads to the last three chapters, multiple shifts in both person and tense, and to the structural game that Robbe-Grillet creates in this novel. A third-person narrator talks about Lecoeur in the past tense; then back to the first person, though not quite the same first person as before. Then other "I"'s enter. With each shift in person and tense, the "facts" of the story are reshuffled and altered. When the original narrator re-enters in the epilogue, he reshuffles the "facts" once more and incorporates them into his explanation of events, and thus the novel ever so gently slips back into retelling itself. Its variations and rearrangements are limitless, requiring no more than a change of tense, person, or fact to set in motion another possible arrangement.

Now, for any of this to work, Robbe-Grillet must know at exactly what point to place a wrinkle in the narrative, so that having made the story function on one plane, he can then cause that plane to intersect with another. As soon as the facts are known in one way, the introduction of a new fact, or the slight alteration of a previous one, will call into question all that has been understood up to that point. Robbe-Grillet invites the reader to inspect the devices of his composition, the devices which the naturalistic author keeps secret, the machinery qui-etly working its effects. Perhaps more than with the naturalistic writer, Robbe-Grillet cannot afford mistakes, because the very act of his invention is on display. He makes no mistakes. Like the magician, he explains his trick, only to perform another one that he doesn't explain.

John O'Brien, "Inventions and Conventions in the New Wave Novel," in Book World—The Washing-ton Post, *August 15, 1982, p. 10.*

JULIA FREY

To date, American reviewers seem completely mystified by *Djinn,* and I suspect Robbe-Grillet, that old *mystificateur*, of putting us on on purpose. What is irritating is that the trick is only on the Americans. In the French edition of the novel, you see, there is a paragraph in the prologue which (albeit obliquely) explains the truth. For unknown reasons, either Robbe-Grillet or his translators have cut this paragraph from the prologue in the American edition, denying the English-speaking reader access to essential clues to understanding the structure of the book. The secret is this: Robbe-Grillet, joining a recent move among contemporary French writers to try to earn some income from their writing, originally wrote this book not as a novel at all, but as a textbook to teach French to Americans. When published in 1979 as *Le Rendezvous* . . ., it had grammatical explanations and vocabulary inserted at the end of each chapter. For students using the book in a French course, the story is not mystifying at all. . . . There is a good-humored complicity between author and reader, because they both know the text is just a pretext. The subtext is learning French.

But what about the innocent American reader encountering this book in translation with no explanation and no teacher? How can we expect him for example to understand the density of meanings expressed by the title? For *Djinn* (Genie) reveals all the novelist's concerns. This is a now-you-see-it, now-you-don't novel about a disappearing American girl called Djinn/Jean (Genie = Jeanie). The title is a pun based on how a Frenchman would write the word Jean pronounced with the heroine's American accent. In French, of course, the name Jean (John) is masculine, as is the word Djinn. Robbe-Grillet further confuses genders by calling his hero by the nickname Jan (pronounced Yann), and by calling a little boy in the book Jean, explaining: "All little boys are called Jean. All little girls are called Marie. You would know that if you were from here". . . . But the hero is not sure if he's "from there" or not, and wonders what it all means. It should be mentioned that to any educated Frenchman, *Djinn,* immediately recalls *Les Djinns* by Victor Hugo, a poem/*exercice scolaire* in which each line is of increasing difficulty.

So the title plunges us into the book: a mystery where the heroine has strange powers, it is also a scholarly exercise by a serious writer trying to structure a fiction around the increasingly complex forms of French grammar. It is about the struggle to understand . . . be it a different language and culture, the power of obsession or the mystery of sexual ambiguity. The French or maybe Russian hero falls in love with an androgynous American girl his own age who looks strikingly like him. . . . Trying to follow her orders, at one point he finds himself as limited as if he were in a totally foreign world: blinded by dark glasses, unable to understand or to express himself, entirely at the mercy of his guide. Despite or perhaps because of his helplessness he becomes obsessed with solving the mysteries piling up around him, and we as readers come to share that obsession.

The theme of the unseeing voyeur is used by Robbe-Grillet to irritate that other voyeur, his reader, in an almost erotic way, continually frustrating his desire to see clearly, arousing him with titillating glimpses, leaving him at the end unsatisfied, still trying to see. . . . [The French edition's subtitle] is Djinn, *a Red Hole in the Broken Pavement*—an important statement of the author's point of view. He wants the voyeur to look into the conflictive, sensual imagery of the book: sex and death, seduction and violence, the shattering of time/place relationships, the interchangeability of all human experience. Frightened, daring, we peek through the broken boundaries of everyday reality into the threatening red hole. Exploring Robbe-Grillet's world of blindness, in comprehension, loss of will, and the frustration of desire is enlightening in its own way, even if it loses something in the translation.

> *Julia Frey, in a review of "Djinn," in* The American Book Review, *Vol. 5, No. 5, July-August, 1983, p. 10.*

ILONA LEKI

Robbe-Grillet rightly considers his long unpublished first novel *Un Régicide* (1978) more advanced than *Les Gommes* and perhaps even than *Le Voyeur* and *La Jalousie;* he finds it more disturbing, a more radical departure from traditional narrative form than the three subsequent novels even though he made no substantial revisions of the original 1949 text. Its oneiric and rather lyrical tone also sets it apart from the rest of his works. Furthermore, this early work makes obvious references to Robbe-Grillet's life. The opening sequences of the book describe a recurrent dream of Robbe-Grillet's and the entire island setting was inspired by his experiences and memories of living on the Breton coast. Perhaps the most surprising feature of this text . . . is the large number of elements in *Un Régicide* which were to resurface in Robbe-Grillet's later novels. (p. 145)

In an interview in 1959 Robbe-Grillet says somewhat tongue in cheek that his purpose in writing *Un Régicide* was to describe fog. Later in 1978, however, he says that *Un Régicide* is an attempt to describe a schizoid life lived on two planes at the same time. The fourteen chapters of the novel move along two levels, describing real events in the life of Boris, the young protagonist, and his fantasy life (his or that of an alter ego) on a desolate island perhaps off the Breton coast whose permanent, isolated population is only men. These two planes of existence occasionally make contact, but for the most part remain separate. The "real" life is written as third-person narrative from Boris's point of view; the life on the island is described in first-person narration. The novel opens with the description of a dream. The first-person narrator is walking along a beach at dusk and must cross a treacherous stretch of coast between rocks and pits into which the waves of the ocean rush, producing whirlpools which could drag the hapless narrator out into the sea. The fading daylight makes his chore all the more difficult, but he manages to reach a stretch of flat sand just in time. The narrative changes to third person with a description of Boris getting up on a Sunday morning in August. He is to meet his friend Laura, a political activist, at a café. As he waits for her, the narration slips, as if it were Boris's daydream, to the island again, which the first-person narrator describes as isolated, dreary, and with a suffocatingly unchanging climate. The brown and gray landscape is always shrouded in fog; no outsider ever visits the island.

The next day Boris goes to his job at a factory where he works calculating productivity, but again Boris seems to slip into a daydream in which the first-person narrator, walking along the familiar paths of his native island, spots a stranger. At the factory at lunch time and in the train on the way home from work Boris hears conversations about the political situation in the country where the Church party has just won a majority in the government. Conversation also centers around the reported murder of a foreign student whose body was found on a deserted construction site which Boris first says he did and then did not visit the day before. Abruptly he is described walking among the scaffolds and pathways of the construction area where he comes upon a tombstone inscribed "Here lies Red," the name of the murdered student. An anagrammatical recombination of the letters in the French phrase "Ci-git Red" produces the word "Régicide." . . . The next day Boris is eager to read anything he can find about the activities of the king. He decides that in order to become truly close to the king, to play a unique role in his life, he will assassinate him, and he is suddenly filled with a sense of well-being.

On the island the first-person narrator walks toward the lighthouse tower in which lives, perhaps, the stranger whom he had seen earlier. His dread of the tower dissipates as he climbs up to the top of its crenellated walls; he notices that the long-awaited spring is beginning. He soon becomes friendly with the solitary keeper of the lighthouse tower, Malus, who tells him of the coming of the sirens.

In town Boris learns that the king will be coming in September to visit the factory. On the way home from work he buys a poster of the king, hangs it on the wall of his room, and begins to devise a plan to assassinate him. He will wait for the king on the abandoned second floor of the factory; as the king rides the one-man, open elevator past this landing, Boris will stop the elevator and stab the king.

On the island the first-person narrator is anticipating the joy of the coming of the sirens when the island's perennial clouds will disappear and the puny, dull, barely noticeable flowers of the sunless island will be replaced by real flowers blooming in vivid colors. The narrator walks along the beach with his siren, Aimone, but Malus is anxious and warns the narrator not to return to the sirens the next day. To the sorrow of the narrator Malus stops appearing on the island and the weather again turns gray and damp.

On the day the king is to visit the factory, Boris awaits him on the second-floor landing; but time goes by so slowly that distracting images are superimposed on Boris's purpose, images of himself standing alone on the beach watching Aimone swim away into the ocean. Suddenly the elevator begins to move and the smiling king appears in front of Boris, who stabs him and, covered with blood, runs down the stairs and through the crowd. That night he sleeps deeply and long. The next day he tears up the king's picture, but then he hears the king's voice coming from the neighbor's radio; the picture reappears whole on the wall. Boris has his bloody knife to prove his assassination attempt but now the bloodstains look like simple rust, and he cleans the knife. (pp. 147-49)

[At] first glance what is perhaps most striking about *Un Régicide* comes as a result of its unusual publication history, a novel written in 1949 but not published until 1978, when the author's work is known worldwide. This most striking characteristic is the constancy of Robbe-Grillet's interest in certain scenes and other narrative fragments which would reappear throughout his works. The implication is not that Robbe-Grillet returned to this first work for inspiration but rather that certain narrative fragments, shapes, objects, and actions form a fairly permanent set in the author's mind and constitute for him cores of fascination or at least of potential sources which can be tapped for elaboration into the familiar, Robbe-Grilletian fictional networks. The most important names in *Un Régicide* reappear in later novels: Laura, Jean, Aimone (A . . . in *La Jalousie*), and Boris. Boris and the king finally merge into one figure in the subsequent works, fulfilling Boris's wish to have a unique relationship to the king and even eventually to take his place. Even in this early work Robbe-Grillet plays with the character's names. Aimone becomes Mona, *amie, amande, anémone, mon âme, mon amante*. Boris goes through transformations as well. As he awakens in his first scene and moves through different levels of consciousness, his name solidifies after going through homophonic variants: Maurice, Moritz, and then Boris. The name of the Solitary One, Malus, also bears a homophonic similarity to Boris, and the character of Malus plays a role in relation to the first-person narrator on the island which corresponds to the relationship Boris might wish to es-

tablish with the king. Like the king, Malus is a special person; he too lives separated from the rest of the people in a kind of castle, in the lighthouse with the top of its walls crenellated like a king's castle. (p. 151)

Themes which surface on nearly every page of *Un Régicide* provide further continuity. Communication, for example, is a problem: Boris cannot talk to Laura; the first-person narrator has difficulty expressing his thoughts to his companions; the sirens do not speak the same language as their lovers on the island. . . . In fact Boris waits to find out from the newspaper whether his attempted assassination of the king actually took place; he is then confused by the newspaper's contradictions not only of his own perceptions and memories of killing the king but also of Laura's statement that the king is dead. In addition to the theme of the impossibility of communication and the untrustworthiness of even the written word, the familiar and hopeless desire for order and causality in a world of confusion finds expression here. Boris's job at the factory is to calculate; he worries constantly about making errors in his calculations at work and in his assassination plot. His speculations and reconstitutions of scenes (past or future scenes) give this text a fabric foreshadowing the multiple scene variations that characterize later Robbe-Grillet texts. The same scene is played over and over or the same group of words is repeated as though the narrative were stuck. (p. 152)

Fear of chaos generates frequent references to traps, catastrophes, errors—the same dangers that threaten all of Robbe-Grillet's characters who try to make sense of events and to reconstruct a correct order from the debris of their physical and mental life. Boris's vain attempt to organize his possessions in his room is paralleled by the first-person narrator's attempt to find his way around his native island, where he has lived all his life and every path of which he knows by heart, but where he gets lost because the fog is so dense that he can perceive the world around him only in bits and pieces, never making out an object in its entirety. Similarly the major construction project which is a central issue in the platform of all the political parties in the country was begun with no ultimate goal in mind. . . . There is no overall plan, no whole, only bits and pieces. Nonetheless, in all the novels from *Un Régicide* to *Souvenirs du triangle d'or* Robbe-Grillet's characters make vain attempts to impose an order on events which refuse to cooperate. (p. 153)

The attempt to change the pattern of daily existence has failed for everyone, for although the king still lives for Boris, he has died for Laura, causing political problems in the country and forcing Laura to leave, like the sirens. Only the first-person narrator seems to have had a measure of success; he now lives in the old watchtower and looks over his island, which he no longer describes in the same negative terms he had used at the beginning. The final task for this first-person narrator is to eliminate Boris from the text as all the others have been suppressed. And in fact whereas Boris and the first-person narrator are quite separate at the beginning of the book, separated into a real life and a dream life, these two characters representing their respective levels of reality begin to merge until at the end Boris disappears altogether and his reality is assumed by the first-person narrator, who now lives in Boris's room, sleeps in Boris's bed. But he too is doomed. He is dying; he cannot continue to live after Boris is suppressed any more than the dream of a better life can survive the death of the king, the disappearance of Malus, and the departure of the sirens. The attempts to kill the father and possess the mother have both failed and once again, like Sisyphus, the narrator finds himself on a rocky coast at dusk. (pp. 154-55)

The publication of *Un Régicide* only in 1978 creates an interesting perspective on the characters in the novel. Names like Boris and Jean, which Robbe-Grillet chose because they connoted nothing in particular about the personalities of those who bore them, are suddenly charged in another way. They may remain undefined by their connections to the real world but they are defined or limited by the fictional world of Robbe-Grillet which has preceded them and in which their names figure. The king will have recurrent parts to play in the novels and he will become permanently associated with the name Boris. Boris and Jean, which is the king's name in *Un Régicide,* are the two once again merged characters in the film *L'Homme qui ment.* Laura too reappears regularly, sometimes much younger, as in *Projet pour une révolution à New York.* This is not to say that these names refer to characters who play roles in the novels and films but rather that the names themselves carry an intertextual weight, and the reader familiar with Robbe-Grillet is interested to see an early Laura, Boris, and Jean, before they were so carefully emptied of "personalities." Nevertheless, even though, for example, the introduction into the novel of Laura and the explanation of her political views follow the conventions of novel writing, as early as *Un Régicide* the characters have no past, no physical characteristics, no life outside the descriptions of them in the novel. From this point of view Robbe-Grillet's handling of his characters foreshadows his future, more conscious manipulations and already represents a departure from conventional novel form. (pp. 156-57)

Un Régicide is a fascinating work because it contains so many seeds of the themes and novelistic concerns which were to develop later throughout Robbe-Grillet's work. To the extent that the direction Robbe-Grillet's writing took was influenced by positive and negative critical reaction to it, *Un Régicide* has been a secret treasure for Robbe-Grillet from which he could pull these themes in order to explore them away from the watchful and influential, i.e., capable of making him change direction, eyes of his readers. Serving as an anchor and repository of Robbe-Grillet's literary interests, *Un Régicide* for nearly thirty years held the common roots of works like *Les Gommes, L'Année dernière à Marienbad,* and *Souvenirs du triangle d'or.* Where critics found contradictions in Robbe-Grillet's work, *Un Régicide* is proof of a profound continuity. That the book did not appear for so many years is not a sign of Robbe-Grillet's rejection of a work of his youth but rather a sign of its importance to Robbe-Grillet's conception of his mission in writing. Much of that mission is now literary history. Robbe-Grillet's career is established and deviations from what is perceived by the public to be his style can no longer be called contradictions but rather further developments. (pp. 158-59)

Ilona Leki, in her Alain Robbe-Grillet, *Twayne Publishers, 1983, 187 p.*

BETTINA L. KNAPP

Unlike the rigorously structured, precise, restrictive, detailed, and frequently pedantic novels of Robbe-Grillet—*Les gommes, Le voyeur, La jalousie*—*Le miroir qui revient* introduces readers to a new literary genre of his own manufacture. This freely felt, imagistic, and poetic autobiography differs from the conventional type à la Stendhal, with its causal, chronological, and systematized recording of events. Such an approach Robbe-Grillet considers false. *Le miroir qui revient* is a composite of mirror images, as the title suggests: interlocking visions, sequences of refrains which emerge and vanish prismatically. Consciously organized, it is not weighted down with a burdensome vocabulary; rather, words seem to float, to touch, to feel, despite the fact that Robbe-Grillet remains entrenched behind his objective and relatively feelingless façade. His story deals with the problematics of writing, displacements, alterations, referentials inherent in stylistic innovations and conformities.

Robbe-Grillet began writing *Le miroir qui revient* in 1976, but in a desultory manner, since his other novels were also published during this period. He does not believe in Truth, he states categorically, or in dogma. No sooner is a theory concretized than it is ossified. New ideas, fresh ways of envisaging literary art, cannot emerge in such restrictive terrain—only a reinforcement of established order. He still questions, probes, tries to understand the meaning of projection, both conscious and unconscious.

As a child, he tells us, he used to love gardens, not seas or oceans. . . . His parents were anarchists belonging to the extreme right. They sided with Pétain during the German Occupation, but most overtly during the Liberation and afterward, when they placed Pétain's picture in the most conspicuous area of their apartment. They were Anglophobes, believing that France and Germany should be united as they once had been under Charlemagne. They were anti-Semitic, and Robbe-Grillet's mother never believed in the reality of the concentration camps; as for the extermination of the Jews, that was all merely Zionist propaganda. . . .

For Robbe-Grillet, constant renewal and variety, as in *Last Year at Marienbad,* can transform the banal into the exciting, the well-worn into the fresh and provocative, blending new and old into new alchemical mixtures—as Robbe-Grillet has accomplished with such felicity in *Le miroir qui revient.*

Bettina L. Knapp, "Autobiography," in World Literature Today, *Vol. 59, No. 4, Autumn, 1985, p. 568.*

BEN STOLTZFUS

In the novel *Souvenirs du triangle d'or,* the prime generative theme is a golden triangle, an image composed of two ideograms: gold and triangle. From this shape and this color the author generates all the subsidiary themes and the mythology of the novel. . . . Whereas, in the past, Robbe-Grillet claimed to eschew all a priori symbolism, he now says that the triangle is a "divine symbolic form." Tongue in cheek and symbology aside (Robbe-Grillet seems to enjoy toying with his readers and his critics), the shape of an inverted triangle (∇) and the atomic number for gold (79) do allow him to generate numerical, geometric, mythological, and carnal forms. Accordingly, the atomic number for gold manifests itself as a "play" on two numbers: seven and nine. Both are incorporated into the nine rings of the archery target whose center is called "the gold" because it is so colored.

"La Cible" (The Target), is Robbe-Grillet's title for this particular section of *Souvenirs*—a passage that was first published as a preface to the Jasper Johns catalog for the 1978 exhibition at the Centre Pompidou in Paris. The target-text centers around and is generated by Jasper Johns's paintings of a broken target, a white target, green targets, targets with faces, and targets numbered in color and in black and gray. The number nine that Robbe-Grillet uses in his text comes from Johns's picture series entitled *Numbers*. The objects in Robbe-Grillet's nine circles are also objects chosen from Johns's art. "La Cible" begins with the number nine in the outer circle, and, in reverse order, moves toward one—the center of the target. Eight is a piece of rope, seven is a twisted coat hanger, six is a spoon, five is a handprint, four is an overturned chair, three is a half-eaten apple, two is a shoe, and one is a ruler. (pp. 32-3)

In the novel's many mirrors, objects such as the shoe [and] the triangle . . . , and colors such as blue, gold, and red reflect each other continuously. Nor is the shoe the only item generated by the inverted triangle: the green apple, the rose, the fur, the beggar-girl named Temple all issue from . . . within the triangle. One image slips into another as "contaminated" associations pass in and out of the cell of the author's playful imagination—an eye that sees reality but speaks it surreally: "the red-haired tuft of the sacred triangle" . . . is the shoe that is also referred to as a "sacred object," is also the *Golden Fleece* that is being performed at the Opera, is also Temple's "blond triangular fleece". . . . (p. 34)

Aurochs: Au is the Latin symbol for gold. The sound *aur* resembles the French word *or* (gold). The word *rochs* or *roc* (anticipating the novel's alchemy and search for the philosopher's stone) is also associated with the meteorite that appeared in *Un Régicide,* reappeared in *Topologie, La Belle Captive,* and now, once again, in *Souvenirs du triangle d'or*. It has a V imprint on it—an imprint that seemingly connotes "the ancient divinity of pleasure appearing doubly as Vanadis Victorious and Vanadis Vanquished". . . . The V of the inverted triangle (signifying and generating the concept *woman*) contains a circle and is contained within a circle: [The apple, the targets], and the egg are all circular objects, some such as the egg . . . verging on the elliptical. The bald Doctor Morgan (another round surface), who performs experiments on Angelica/Carolina/Christine, inserts an oval object, like a small hard-boiled egg without a shell, into her vagina in order to study her responses and the egg's programmed effects. . . . These round objects are all associated with the mysterious globe that makes its appearance in the narrator's prison cell and which seems to have its own autonomous existence. The globe, in turn, generates images of pleasure, syntagmas of a walking dream that slip in and out of the cell, through passageways, along the beach, or into the forest where young girls, like quarry, are pursued by hunters and dogs, to be captured and killed. *Le Triangle d'or* is, among other things, a secret society that allows such "games."

Le Triangle d'or is also the "Opera House" (notice the circle of the O) where the *Golden Fleece* is being performed, where a father (the author) masturbates his daughter (the text). *Le Triangle d'or* is also the temple of a religious society, symbolized by the girl whose name is Temple. The burning bush is a phoenix, the *femme-oiseau,* a mytical bird alluded to frequently. Thus, the sexual, mythical, visual, textual, geometric, and numerical connotations generated by the title ultimately converge on that one spot in the "golden center" of the circles and of the triangle. . . . (pp. 34-5)

The body of the text is consumed by fire. Its destruction is gratuitous, although like the phoenix, is eternally recuperated. The author, like an alchemist distilling gold, exploits the colors of the alchemical process: black, white, gray, red, green, and blue. In order to transmute base metals into gold, the metals are broken down into their separate component parts through the action of fire, purified, blended, and finally fixed at the appropriate stage. Fire is important, and the burning text is essential to the process—in this case, literary alchemy. Black, white, and red are the three main colors because black indicates dissolution and putrefaction, a sign that the experiment is going well. . . . The experiment must be proceeding well because the floor, ceiling, and walls of the narrator's prison cell—the generative cell—are white. The gray of the door signifies the passage from the black to white, and on the wall is the red imprint of the narrator's hand. Red, in alchemy, is the color of complete success. The fact that it is associated with the five fingers of the hand is even more significant since, in *Topology,* five was a generative number and the hand was the sign of authorial power and presence—the "signature." (pp. 35-6)

Many of the scenes in *Souvenirs* are borrowed from [one character's] books of childhood mythology, scenes that Robbe-Grillet uses as examples of the contemporary, ongoing, sadoerotic myth. . . . In alchemy care must be taken that the solution not return to black, for then the experimenter will have to begin all over again. Nevertheless, the text continues to evolve. . . . The green apple contains an electronic device that opens the "sanctuary's" black door. . . . The sanctuary is where Doctor Morgan's "sexual" and "textual experiments" take place. . . . The sanctuary is the secret room, the generative cell of fiction, the alchemist's laboratory where objects, e.g., base metals, like Rimbaud's "Voyelles," are transmuted into gold. Alchemy, as a metaphor for art, is not new, and the writer who transforms prosaic reality into poetry is performing functions that are not unlike the alchemist's. . . . (pp. 36-7)

The reader's role in this textual game is obviously to find the combination or the code that will open the black door to the text—to crack the electronic code of the green apple that will enable him to get inside where the experiments occur and insight begins. The sanctuary is the text, and Temple is a girl on whom the author leaves his red mark, whose body he sometimes paints with red paint so that breasts, thighs, and hands will leave red smears on a white wall, as they do, for example, in *L'Eden et après* and *Glissements progressifs du plaisir*. Since the hand's five fingers were also the generative themes of *Topologie, Souvenirs*'s intertextual nod is unmistakable. Unmistakable also is Robbe-Grillet's nod to Yves Klein's "body painting" on white walls.

The yellow color of the ruler, when mixed with the blue of the shoe, produces green, e.g., the apple. Mixing yellow (the ruler) with red (the hand) produces orange. Red (the hand) and blue (the shoe) produce violet, a play on the French verb *violer*. Since the purpose of the novel is to violate Temple, to penetrate the sanctuary, i.e., the golden triangle, the ambiguity of the words *violet-violer* is in line with the text's thematic thrust. The specular effects of words, colors, and things, . . . are contributing, generative aspects of the overall transmutation. If the shoe signifies Temple (i.e., *langue*) and the hand signifies narrator (i.e., *parole*), then the statement "strong hand on the delicate woman's shoe" equals the verb to violate. In its metonymic precision this equation leads to the following solution:

1. red and blue equal *violet*
2. hand on shoe makes *violate*
3. narrator violates Temple (the color violet is proof of that)
4. therefore *parole* violates *langue*
5. the author is free (since the narrator leaves the cell)
6. creation, i.e., free play, is art

    7. art transmutes objects into gold
    8. the author is therefore a magician
    9. the reader opens the door, i.e., penetrates
        the text

With the aid of the "philosopher's stone," the alchemists try to transmute gray lead into gold. Each color represents a stage in the process, indicating the likelihood of ultimate success. The green apple opens the bronze door that is lacquered in black, thereby providing access to the ordering process of the writer's imagination and the beach girls who have golden hair and golden skin. Pay dirt is inside the Temple, and gold is the name of the game. The golden triangle is thus both the generative theme and the answer to the puzzle of the text. The objects, colors, combinations, permutations, and slippages from one level to another, once decoded, trigger the secret mechanism, opening the door to the inside. Once inside the cell, the pearls, the light bulb, the globe, the circle, and the ovum perform their magic. Parthenogenesis occurs as the narrator and his twin Angelica give birth to fiction by means of the unfertilized egg that Doctor Morgan has slipped into her vagina. . . . (pp. 37-8)

This "globe," like the reader, is now "inside" generating its own imagery (*parole*) whose abrupt, seemingly implausible transitions between the inside of the cell and the world outside structure Robbe-Grillet's dialectical topology. There is one long, continuous co-mingling of the inside and the outside, of *parole* with *langue*, of the self with the other. The objective and the subjective meet at that mythic center in the golden triangle whose imagined memories generate the present fiction. Robbe-Grillet's stock-in-trade images are an emotional trap—crocodile bait—the girl trap he sets for the reader whose expectations are conventional and who is inevitably lured into recuperating the sexual signifiers in traditional ways. Accordingly, the nine key objects or stages of "Piège à fourrure," as they did in *Topologie*, form the combinations of the target's nine rings in whose center is the gold. The numbered objects of each ring appear and disappear as Robbe-Grillet continues to play with an imagery that is allegedly deprived of depth, but which, in fact, has all the symbology of traditional art. (pp. 38-9)

The reader can now generate order out of the initial disorder. Even after the code has been cracked, the linguistic and imagistic combinations within each New New Novel seem inexhaustible, every reading thus generating fresh, pleasurable, and blissful encounters. (p. 44)

        Ben Stoltzfus, in his Alain Robbe-Grillet: The Body of the Text, *Fairleigh Dickinson University Press, 1985, 187 p.*

WILLIAM W. STOWE

[*Recollections of a Golden Triangle*] could be read as Robbe-Grillet's tribute to the vibrant Latin American fiction that his own early works helped to inspire. It is set in a war-ravaged South American city whose still active opera house boasts a maze of corridors providing access to the boxes and the dressing rooms. The city jail has an analogous set of passageways, and the handleless door of a mysterious private club, the Temple of the Golden Triangle, swings open on another—or is it the same?—labyrinth. The plot centers on a sex cult, whose male members adore and violate their female victims, ritually crucify them and pack them in little cans labeled "salmon with spices." The narrative is sometimes delivered in the first person, sometimes in the third, the voice and the perspective are sometimes totally anonymous sometimes designated by an obscure "I". . . . All of this is in the most literal sense a pretext for one of Mr. Robbe-Grillet's most brilliant and hypnotic textual games, in which narrative transitions are motivated at least as often by association, metaphor or analogy as by more usual continuities of time and space. Mr. Robbe-Grillet's fictions are more abstract than the Latin American fantasies they in part inspired, and this work demands a degree of concentration some readers will be unwilling to grant. It is, however, a finely wrought example of a master's art, and will delight his old admirers.

        William W. Stowe, in a review of "Recollections of the Golden Triangle," in The New York Times Book Review, *September 28, 1986, p. 26.*

Evelyn Scott

1893-1963

(Born Elsie Dunn; also wrote under pseudonym of Ernest Souza) American novelist, autobiographer, poet, essayist, critic, and author of children's books.

Often overlooked in scholarly studies of American letters of the 1920s and 1930s, Scott was regarded by some as a considerable literary talent during that period. A feminist whose colorful and forceful opinions influenced much of her writing, Scott viewed women as victims of a social system that thwarted their intellectual abilities and prevented them from expressing their individuality. In her works, Scott attacked marriage, domesticity, and obsession with physical attributes—all of which, she contended, stunt the maturation of women and prohibit them from seeking meaningful lives. Scott's protagonists are usually strong-willed females who strive to overcome these obstacles and establish their rights, including the free expression of sexuality. In a larger sense, Scott believed that people cannot be truly independent until they no longer require societal approval for their actions.

Scott was born in Clarksville, Tennessee, and was raised in several small Southern towns and in New Orleans. Her social activism began at age thirteen, when she pursued a private education, defying the traditional Southern code of gentility which encouraged young women to obtain social skills aimed toward marriage. At fifteen Scott publicly advocated legalized prostitution as a means to control the spread of venereal disease, and at seventeen she became secretary of the Louisiana Women's Suffrage party, an organization devoted, in her words, "to champion the negro, the social outcast, and to insist . . . on the instant termination of industrial slavery." Although an outspoken opponent of what she considered the repressive and corrupt nature of American society, Scott did not belong to any national movements for social change. When she was twenty and a student at Tulane University, she eloped to Brazil with Frederick Creighton Wellman, a married professor who was more than twice her age. Their six years of poverty and illness in that country is the subject of *Escapade* (1923), the first of two autobiographical works. The second, *Background in Tennessee* (1937), examines the economic, cultural, and spiritual resurgence of the post-Civil War South within the context of Scott's own family and experiences.

Scott's novels are lengthy and ambitious. *The Narrow House* (1921), *Narcissus* (1922), and *The Golden Door* (1925) form a trilogy of domestic dramas revolving around three generations of a small-town family. *The Narrow House* introduces the elder members of the Farley family and examines the effects of their loveless marriage on their adult children, Alice and Laurence. *Narcissus* centers on the marriage of Laurence Farley to Julia, an educated woman whose outside pursuits alienate her husband, and *The Golden Door* focuses upon the inability of Laurence's daughter to resolve her own troubled marriage. Although these novels sparked critical interest, only *The Narrow House* received significant praise. Sinclair Lewis called the novel "an event," declaring that it "is one of those recognitions of life by which life itself becomes the greater."

Scott's next major achievement was a trilogy of historical novels chronicling four generations of two American families.

NYT Pictures

Migrations: An Arabesque in Histories (1927) concerns the California Gold Rush of 1849 and the resulting Western expansion; *The Wave* (1929) is a panoramic novel of the Civil War; and *A Calendar of Sin: American Melodramas* (1932) explores changing sexual roles amidst the vast industrial growth that occurred before World War I. *The Wave*, which became Scott's best-known and most respected novel, impressed many critics with its unusual structure. In this work, Scott does not rely on the conventional, sentimental depiction of the Civil War; instead, she articulates the tragedy of the conflict through more than one hundred characters from diverse social, racial, and economic backgrounds. The prominence Scott gained with *The Wave* prompted William Faulkner's publishers to request that she write a supportive essay to promote his novel *The Sound and the Fury*. Scott later expanded her essay into a book-length critical study, *On William Faulkner's "The Sound and the Fury"* (1929).

Three of Scott's later novels address the importance of intellectual and creative pursuits and urge the artist to retain idealism and integrity despite social pressures. *Eva Gay: A Romantic Novel* (1933), *Breathe upon These Slain* (1934), and *Bread and a Sword* (1937) range in theme from an affirmation of the potential for fulfillment through creative expression to a denial that people can remain true to their artistic principles in an unprincipled world. *Eva Gay* centers on an aspiring writer and her problems in balancing professional goals with the demands of her personal life; *Breathe upon These Slain* focuses upon a writer who is torn between producing literature of artistic merit or political fashion; and *Bread and a Sword* depicts an established author who compromises his art for financial reasons. The plots of these novels are frequently interrupted by lengthy commentaries on contemporary society, which Scott perceived as materialistic, oppressive, and violent. Critics generally regarded these novels as too heavily polemical and lacking the lively plots and characters of her earlier work.

In addition to her novels, Scott published two volumes of poetry, *Precipitations* (1920) and *The Winter Alone* (1930). Both collections consist of poems composed in free verse that were noted for their startling imagery. By the late 1930s, Scott's numerous physical and emotional problems had eroded her ability to write objectively. Her irrational behavior and erratic compositions estranged her from her friends, family, and potential publishers, and she published nothing after *The Shadow of the Hawk* (1941). Although Scott is regarded as something of a literary curiosity by many contemporary critics, she is respected for the technical skill of her early fiction and for her advocacy of freedom and fulfillment for women of her generation.

(See also *Contemporary Authors,* Vol. 104, Vol. 112 [obituary] and *Dictionary of Literary Biography,* Vols. 9, 48.)

LOLA RIDGE

I shall not forget the sensation—something like the suppressed excitement that you feel at the first inkling of some momentous event—with which I first read some of [Evelyn Scott's] poems. . . .

The union of strongly contrasting qualities that I then found in her work is emphasized in the present collection [*Precipitations*]. The clear searching vision, like an electric ray, that seems to focus—almost lovingly—upon decay and death, with a child's simplicity and eager response to every mood of earth. (p. 334)

Evelyn Scott's happiest (in the literal sense) reactions are to nature, though even then it is a nature already touched with decay. We are shown the stars like jaded dancing girls, their faces "Pale in the harshness of the sunlight"; and over many of the vivid pictures pours silvery wonder of a decadent moon. . . .

And when Mrs. Scott's vision turns upon humans, it becomes that of a ruthless eye which sees through rosy and gracious contours to the putrescence behind—an eye avid, searching, throwing a gold-harsh light on life. . . . (p. 335)

Most of these poems are short. The eye is a continually shifting ray that penetrates, impartially lights up whatever shape, be it swathed in bandages or merely coquetting behind veils; that hovers a moment and is gone, leaving the conception to be completed or explained in the mind of the recipient. Sometimes, as in "**Man Dying on a Cross,**" it uncovers a terrible beauty that throws out a flame like burning flesh—a flame that dies out swiftly, as with a great breath that blows in the eyes a live and silvery dust and leaves in the nostrils a smell, sweetish, faintly foul. Fortunately this vision does not see too much, nor does it stray from the spot that is the centre of the flung ray. Thus there is economy of detail, and we are not confused with a flickering and broken image. The method is at its best in the clean muscular beauty of "**Young Men**". . . . (pp. 335-36)

Occasionally, however, this concentration invites its penalty, and there is a lack of fluidity that is not so much stiffness as a halting movement that suggests the slight lameness of a beautiful body. Sometimes, too, an abrupt indifference to finish—perhaps something of that same refusal to chasten and refine which is manifest to life itself. Thus in three otherwise fine lines the words *drifts* and *melts,* following in succession, are left like grit under the teeth. (p. 336)

These poems show an astonishing and essentially modern awareness, an awareness that has nothing to do with "sophistication." . . . It is rather a consciousness that, while close to and keenly aware of instinct, has yet obtained its release; so that it watches, intent but calmly elect—impartial appraiser of its own pleasure and its own pain. This consciousness knows fear, the while it walks intrepidly forward to the pit and casts a stone at the coiled terrors within. But the fear walks unashamed and does not cloak itself in cynicism; or that chainarmor of the weak, a sneer. There is no sneer even in the devastating lines of "**Christians**" and "**Women**". . . . It seems to be that the experiencing mind, with an almost machine-like accuracy, records its inevitable emotion. The result is convincing. You do not question the data of this uncloistered spirit. You accept the authenticity of its emotional responses, even though they may not tally with your own.

And while it is difficult to say how this book—with its avoidance of the "typical" and absence of corroborated emotions, as well as its rejection of the anaemic doctrine of "escape"—may be received, it introduces a new and potent force into American literature. (pp. 336-37)

> *Lola Ridge, "Evelyn Scott," in* Poetry, *Vol. XVII, No. 6, March, 1921, pp. 334-37.*

SINCLAIR LEWIS

Salute to Evelyn Scott! She belongs, she understands, she is definitely an artist. Who she is, whether maid or matron, young or old, has not been told us, but she has in this new novel, *The Narrow House,* established her vision and her workmanship.

It is a tale of side streets, of side-street people and side-street pinching ugliness and amazing side-street beauty, in an American city which might equally be Seattle or Atlanta or Hartford. It is the story of a Family, a resolute hundred-per-cent Family which, without any special moral purposes about it, yet efficiently wrenches and breaks every soul in its "moral cellar." . . . The author has studied them with eyes which have not missed one wrinkle in the soft flesh beneath the chin, nor one gesture of the weary, lovely hands.

The Narrow House will not please devotees to the fiction in which all families are bodies of Florida water surrounding a dear little cripple whose smiles correct every ego urge in the neighborhood and make the man next door stop racing his Ford. But it will be hailed by people who liked May Sinclair's *Mary Olivier.* It fortifies the promise of *Poor White, Miss Lulu Bett* and *Moon-Calf* that American fiction has definitely and boisterously begun to rival the Young Britishers. There is nothing in Dorothy Richardson's snarled skein of emotions more real than the perceptions of Evelyn Scott. Real—that is the fundamental thing about her. . . .

To tell the scheme, the "plot" of the story, would be absurd. It is as plotless and as dramatic as the testimony of sensitive people in a divorce court; it is human agony and courage revealed by art. The astonishing thing about *The Narrow House* is that Evelyn Scott's hand is as well trained as her eye. An example: She is obsessed by sunsets, by the coming of night, when for a moment the manure-clotted street and the close-pressed houses assume the mystery of a wilderness; and that vivid-colored wonder she expresses competently....

Miss Scott—or Mrs. Scott—has that most uncommon and most valuable sort of observation: the power of realizing impersonally and accurately the things so close at hand that most of us never realize them at all. Out of the absurdly trivial incident of a woman carrying a breakfast tray up to a sick girl she makes an etching. Any one can see the Taj Mahal; almost any one can see a city sunset; but Evelyn Scott sees a plate of toast— and you jolly well see it with her!...

But it isn't really toast that Evelyn Scott is seeing; it is the tragic fact that to certain families toast is so important.... It would be an insult to speak with smug judiciousness of her "promise." She has done it! *The Narrow House* is an event; it is one of those recognitions of life by which life itself becomes the greater.

> Sinclair Lewis, in a review of "The Narrow House," in The New York Times Book Review, March 13, 1921, p. 18.

THE NATION

[The frame of Mrs. Evelyn Scott's first novel, *The Narrow House*], is small: a narrow house; her people few: Mr. and Mrs. Farley, Laurence their son, Alice their daughter, Winnie the son's wife. These five people have nothing of beauty and little of health in either body or mind. They are, especially in each other's vision, irritable and gross and ignoble and weak— bundles of ugly infirmities. But if you yield yourself quite passively to the enormous accuracy of the analysis, to what goes on so sharply and hauntingly in the brain and nerves of each of these creatures, you come to the conclusion that Mrs. Scott sees a way out for them all and that she is, as a matter of fact, more hopeful of human life and fate than the cheerful liar among novelists for the same reason that the diagnosis of a scrupulous physician is more hopeful than the promises of an oily quack. We do not know what happiness and comeliness the Farleys might not have made their own outside of that narrow house. But they are herded in it, doomed to fear and hate and love and rasp each other. They are united by consanguinity, duty, custom, opinion—by everything except healthy liking and voluntary choice; they are entangled by futile and febrile emotions; they live together in small, stuffy rooms and hear each other speak and sigh and mumble and masticate and yawn to the point of disgust and despair. Yet Mr. Farley stays, hiding cowardice under a mask of duty, and Laurence stays because he drifts and distrusts his impulses, and Alice because, in the present state of moral opinion, her life would be as sterile anywhere.... Guilt and horror belong here, in a word, to the narrow house, to an enforced litter as opposed to the freedom of voluntary companionship, to the will to obey a command that has neither sense nor sanction.

Except in a special and cerebral sense *The Narrow House* is not, indeed, a beautiful book. We hope, too, that Mrs. Scott will resist the temptation toward ultra-impressionism of style on the plain ground that coherent writing is just as expressive and far more permanent. But the book is beautifully brave and true and formidably searching. It would be not unimportant in any country; it is of the first importance to us. American literature is putting away childish things. The great style, the vision that is large as well as style, will come later. We are, at least, beginning to see with adult eyes. (pp. 596-97)

> "More American Chronicles," in The Nation, Vol. CXII, No. 2911, April 20, 1921, pp. 596-97.

THE NEW YORK TIMES BOOK REVIEW

There is an absence of the stereotyped in Evelyn Scott's undeniable talent which does much to compensate for its lapses and limitations, as revealed in her latest novel, *Narcissus*. Especially in her descriptions of the impressions of external things, as received by the individual, is this unhackneyed quality of viewpoint apparent. Every now and then one receives, through these pen pictures of hers, a faint thrill, a slight shock, as of stumbling against some unnoticed obstacle and so being brought to a sudden sharp awareness of it....

The author uses Blake's familiar lines, beginning, "Nought loves another as itself," to illustrate her book. Her men and women are alike prey to a restless, unhappy type of egoism, springing, in almost every instance, from one or another variety of inferiority complex. They long to express themselves, and, in expressing themselves, to establish their superiority and dominance over others. They are small of mind and spirit, deeply, essentially mean. And because they have no touch of nobiliity or of innate fineness, their seeking for dominancy is accompanied by a kind of petty malice, petty cruelty, which at times revolts even themselves. Mercilessly the author strips their souls bare, their poor, shivering, ungenerous little souls, calling attention to all their weaknesses and deformities. They never escape from her to reveal themselves, consciously or unconsciously, in speech or action. Always she is at hand to explain them. There is very little dialogue in the book; what little there is, receives an immense amount of explanation.

Two of the best and most carefully drawn characters in the book are those of the artist, Dudley Allen, and the self-deprecatory business man, Charles Hurst. As a child, Dudley had been physically weak and a coward, and this physical weakness, which he had almost forgotten, was the underlying factor influencing his life. "He needed to appear noble in his own eyes, and to assert his superiority with all those with whom he came in contact." Adverse criticism of his work he could not endure; he had a romantic conception of his destiny, and with it a terrible haunting fear of being ridiculous, and a craving to bring those in whom he was forced to admit the existence of something superior down to his own level. He wanted to believe in his own greatness, and could do so "only in the throes of emotion which exhausted him." Between his unwilling knowledge of himself and his desired conception of himself, he was tortured almost to the verge of insanity.

This inner struggle of Dudley's is the struggle of very nearly every character in the book.... The author speaks of the world as having become "too sophisticated to believe any longer in the sincerity of the noble gesture," and this disbelief permeates the book. Whatever is small and mean and weak, and therefore both "pathetic and absurd," is clearly seen and often vividly portrayed, but of generous emotion, of any sense of duty or honor or responsibility, there is none.

That ultimate, awful loneliness of the human soul of which every normally intelligent person is to at least some degree conscious, is an important influence in the book, especially at the last, when at the moment of reconciliation, "unacknowledged, each kept for himself a pain which the other could not heal. Each pitied the other's illusion, and was steadied by it into gentleness." And this loneliness is a part of the general hopelessness and pain and self-deception and futility. . . . One-sided in its viewpoint as the book is, within its very marked and obvious limitations it is well done, interesting and excellently written. To many it will no doubt seem profoundly and absolutely truthful, and they will admire it the more because its limitations are those of which they are themselves conscious as existing within their own personalities, while others of larger experience and broader outlook will find its dicta convincing only in part, perceiving that men and women, average men and women, are not such spiritual dwarfs as Evelyn Scott's interesting and in many ways penetrating study of their weaknesses and meannesses and petty cruelties would convict them of being.

A review of "Narcissus," in The New York Times Book Review, *July 2, 1922, p. 21.*

CARL VAN DOREN

Evelyn Scott, who called her first novel *The Narrow House* now calls her second one *Narcissus.* Her creative faculty has allowed itself to seem submerged by the troubled flood of life which it chooses to represent. It does not laugh, it is rarely ironical, or pitiful, it suggests no methods of escape. For the time being, at least, it is preoccupied with the inhabitants of the narrow house and with their careers. It accepts their own sense that the doors are locked and the windows tight and that there is nothing to do but run round and round in the sticky atmosphere. By thus accepting her neurotics Mrs. Scott intensifies her art: she brings her characters upon a cramped stage under a glaring light; she crowds them into a cage which they think a trap and there inspects their struggles. With the fewest reticences she gets them forth, making stroke after stroke of the subtlest penetration, shearing away disguises and subterfuges till she reaches the red quick. What she finds in all of them is essentially narcissism.

What further intensifies this biting art is that, narrowed to the narrow house and concentrated upon self-love, it anatomizes and subdivides self-love with minute analysis. The plight of practically all the characters in *Narcissus* has the complication that they are in love and are therefore habitually on edge as they might not be in calmer circumstances. But love does not liberate them. . . . Each of them, looking for love as Narcissus did in his pool, sees in lover or beloved something not entirely expected: sees, that is, another face and not a mere reflection of the looker's. Here lies the particular ground of their irritations. Whereas the lovers of the broad house reach eagerly out for qualities unlike their own, the Narcissus of the narrow house cannot endure unlikeness. And as there are no absolute likenesses in nature, they must be disappointed and must agonize.

One of the commonest devices in fiction is to show a narrow house with its inhabitants invaded and purged by a large breath from the broad house. Mrs. Scott denies herself this compromise. Her method, no less than her reading of life, compels her. She marshals her characters in a fugue of pain and exasperation. They have no career, in her novel, besides that of their passions; they do not appear at work or at play or in relaxed moments. When they try to speak lightly they speak stiffly. She never forgets the tense business in hand. That business, obviously, is not to make a general transcript of human existence, but to fit certain materials into a certain pattern in order to make a work of art. The pattern in this case does not quite equal the materials. Though the novel has form and proposition, its whole is partly hidden by the brilliance of its parts, which glitter with fiendish thrusts of observation delivered in a style of cruel curtness and vividness. The paths of the characters through the action seem tangled in a multitude of sensations. It is the tone which gives unity: the tone is passionate frustration sustained by art till the familiar sanities fade out of sight and the narrow house has shut out the sun, the wind, the soil, and the healing hands of time.

I see in the school of fiction best represented in England by D. H. Lawrence and in the United States by Evelyn Scott what I feel disposed to call a new exoticism. . . . The distinctive trait about the new exoticism is that its followers adventure among their romantic scenes with a precision which romancers ordinarily lack. The result is as striking as anything now being done by novelists. And praise of a high degree must be given Mrs. Scott, who, with less exuberance and splendor of language than Mr. Lawrence, has a better sense of art, a sharper intellect, a neater hand at satire, and a crisper wit. (pp. 803-04)

Carl Van Doren, "Broad and Narrow House," in The Literary Review [New York Post], *July 15, 1922, pp. 803-04.*

ELMER DAVIS

[*Escapade*] is an autobiographical document, and like most autobiographical documents more interesting to the writer than to the reader. Ten years or so ago, according to the story here presented, the author, then a young girl, eloped with a married man. His wife threatened him with the grotesque but occasionally very real penalties of the Mann act, so they fled to Brazil, where the man, an entomologist by profession, was compelled to make a living as bookkeeper for a sewing machine company.

The first half of the book is a record of life in the slums of Brazilian cities as it impressed a sensitive girl during pregnancy and long illness after childbirth; the latter part the story of the family in an unsuccessful ranching experiment in the interior, with poverty and its concomitant discomforts pressing more and more heavily upon them. One can understand how Evelyn Scott, after a fortunate break in the luck made return to the United States possible, began to write novels distinguished even in our time for their opaque gloom. Certainly she suffered in Brazil, suffered through sickness and poverty. But a great many people have suffered, and the story of their suffering is not always interesting to others.

The description of Brazilian low life is of some interest. Miss Scott has a good deal of descriptive skill. Unfortunately, every page is a personal record. . . . All this is no doubt of the highest significance to the author, but the cash customers may legitimately ask for something a trifle more interesting or significant to themselves.

Little is said about the personal relationship of the writer to John, her companion, but that little is always in praise of John, which he undoubtedly deserved. Only a great emotion or a sense of a Christian duty could have kept him on the job.

Elmer Davis, "An 'Escapade' in Brazil," in The New York Times Book Review, *August 5, 1923, p. 27.*

ROBERT MORSS LOVETT

Mrs. Scott's novels, *The Narrow House* and *Narcissus,* have served to mark her among the modernists as one who pursues farthest the evanescent, shifting, subjective experience which is so miraculously interwoven with the bodily existence which we lead among objects which we see and touch—objects which in turn acquire a curious symbolic connection with the inner life. She stands thus on the sheer verge of what we call reality, at the point where the perception of that reality through the senses and the fixing of it in words passes over into an altogether subtler process of suggestion and premonition, conveying the sense of something unprecise and unformulated of which the perceiving self is recognizably a part, and which thus partakes of the truth of our own existence. The effort to give utterance to this reality behind the real is implicit in Mrs. Scott's novels. Here in her autobiography [*Escapade*] it is explicit and measurable. In the former it was complicated by obligations of the novel form which Mrs. Scott had not mastered. In *Escapade* the effort is extraordinarily simplified and complete. The most poignant fact in Mrs. Scott's experience during the years of her narrative was her maternity. Perhaps her physical state before and after the birth of her child furnished her with more than a symbol of the book she so much desired. She has called *Escapade* boldly a creative autobiography. The book is at any rate a birth, a bringing into the world of consciousness and expression things which else remain hidden in the womb of the unconscious. . . .

The most obvious aspect of *Escapade* is the vividness with which the world of appearance and sensation is realized in the naturalistic manner. A girl of twenty, fleeing with her lover to Brazil, pursued by the "stench of public opinion," suffering pregnancy, childbirth, and an operation in an unspeakably foreign environment; seeing her lover give up his ambition, to become a bookkeeper, then an auditor, for a sewing machine company; the wretched little family, increased by the strangely incongruous figure of an aunt from the United States, thrown hither and thither in journeys by land and sea, from one provincial town to another, until in a last desperate gamble they buy a ranch in the mountains—and lose. The nightmare of all this is scarcely emphasized by the expressionist fantasia into which the experience merges. Throughout, the Brazilian scene is rendered with an acuteness of sensation to which the author's pathological state doubtless contributed. . . . (p. 363)

It will be seen that Mrs. Scott's effort is an ambitious one. Her autobiography makes the experience and reactions of Marie Bashkirtseff, Helena von Donninges, Marguerite Audoux and Mary McLane seem primitive and childish. Mrs. Scott has artistic resources far beyond these ladies, and she uses them lavishly. In her effort to evoke physical experience in terms which, in Henry James's phrase, will compete with life, and then pierce beyond that life into the mysteries about which it is woven as a spell, she must use words, not merely to give a single distinct and ever separable impression, but as notes with overtones; and rhythms not only in step with the pedestrian movement of life, but which soar into a region beyond. It is not to be denied, however, that in the conscientiousness of the artist Mrs. Scott loses something of the disinterestedness of the observer, that naiveté of the narrator. Of course it is unfair to ask her to be disinterested in the circumstances—who could

be? Yet for the sake of the reality which she so passionately seeks, a greater range of impartiality is demanded. There is danger that Mrs. Scott's view of the world will isolate itself from general experience and become a "case"—a pathological case at that. Again, in spite of all the intensely pathetic circumstances of the story, it fails to move us, as Mrs. Scott would desire, to the very bowels of compassion. On the contrary, like so much of expressionistic work, it leaves us indifferent. . . . Mrs. Scott is too constantly preoccupied with her art, naturalistic or psychic, and relief from this insistence is even more needed than from the intense brooding bitterness with which she sees her world. . . . She has not created but brought forth an impressive and a brilliant book. The question recurs—is it alive? (pp. 363-64)

Robert Morss Lovett, "Escapade," in The New Republic, *Vol. XXXV, No. 455, August 22, 1923, pp. 363-64.*

ISABEL PATERSON

How long is it since some Calvinistic critical beadle discovered and labeled "the literature of escape"? Surely not more than a decade or so; but in that time our younger writers have labored prodigiously to remove the reproach. The Dismal School of Fiction is not recognized and established as a sort of purgatorial antechamber to the delectable realm of letters. And with this latest addition even the most earnest literary flagellant should be entirely content. *The Golden Door* opens the other way, so to speak. If there is any escaping done in connection with it the refugee is more than likely to be headed toward real life. This deceptively gilded portal admits one into a region metaphorically resembling a sunless back basement kitchen, where the eye is chastened by a litter of unwashed dishes and discarded, dusty furniture from above-stairs, while the ear is exacerbated by the sound of a nagging quarrel between ill-suited neighbors over the back fence. Life may be just one darned thing after another, but this story is just the same darned thing all the time. . . .

May and Paul were married. Paul was a semi-Tolstoyan idealist, but he had dropped the celibate ideal which Tolstoy advocated. For that matter, Tolstoy only advocated it. Paul lived on a farm, went barefoot and couldn't stand being laughed at. As a matter of principle he objected to May giving the baby barley sugar in its milk. Scientific care of the infant he thought immoral, as if one didn't have faith. . . . He talked above love a good deal, but "he tried to love the baby and could not. It disturbed him. It was too oblivious to him." May went out to feed the pigs. . . .

Nina Gannett came to visit them. She was a bouncing, platitudinous, sentimental slob. Paul fell for her, all in a heap. . . . One wants to howl finally when the word "love" looms ahead. When Paul had done maundering about love he began pawing over "duty." It was his "duty" to get rid of May and take up with Nina. . . .

[May] consented to a divorce. There was a scandal, with headlines, in the papers. Nina scooted and May stopped the divorce and went back. They probably went on seesawing that way the rest of their lives, making maudlin scenes and talking hifalutin drivel. They have slatternly minds, slatternly souls.

As analysis of a certain type the book is good work; but good for what? . . . All these self-elected martyrs make one rather sorry for the lions.

Isabel Paterson, "Walk, Do Not Run, to Nearest Exit," in New York Herald Tribune Books, *May 17, 1925, p. 8.*

THE SATURDAY REVIEW OF LITERATURE

Evelyn Scott is a stylist of the highest order, vivid, terse, picturesque, with an exquisite sense of word values. With a phrase she can summon a mood. Her touch [in *The Golden Door*] is competent and sure as the Devil's, and not unlike it. She invests unpleasantness with an incredible richness.... Superlative praise is a dangerous thing, but this reviewer knows of no writer upon rain, animal passion, grief, hogs, mud, sweat, and futility, who can hold a stylistic candle to Evelyn Scott.

A review of "The Golden Door," in The Saturday Review of Literature, *Vol. 1, No. 44, May 30, 1925, p. 796.*

THE NEW YORK TIMES BOOK REVIEW

Migrations is at once an entrancing historical fiction of a new order and a considered statement of an attitude toward life. The novel deals with the time and the affairs and the preoccupations, the fashions of manner and speech and dress and thought of those who might have been the grandparents of almost anyone of the present generation. Yet the underlying sense of character operating from the mainsprings of conduct, which may be conditioned but not circumscribed by the complexion of an age, is a reminder that humanity changes astonishing little.

While the scene is laid in the imaginary town of Mimms, in antebellum Tennessee, the insecurity of the pioneer, revealed in terms of Mimms, must have been fairly typical of that period in the whole of the United States. At any rate, Mrs. Scott carries conviction of the authenticity of her vision. Reading of Mimms and the people who live there, the feeling of recently tamed land grows. An alarming vista of enlarging frontiers is spread. The reader views from outside the aging man, defeated in the new country of Tennessee, precisely as he would have been in the older country of Virginia, and watches, powerless to intervene, the operation of the same destiny upon the broken old man's son, bound for California. Mrs. Scott does not say it in so many words, but the inescapable recognition is none the less conveyed; spatial limitlessness must cease to foster delusions of grandiose capacity, and men must examine spiritual frontiers, also.

The new lands offer tempting mental mirages of uncleared, untried places, where a new start may be had. It is a truism, of course, that it is not an external circumstance, Mimms, Tennessee, so to speak, but a self, from which escape is desired. It is just that Mrs. Scott has seized upon varied aspects of the fundamental impulse to run away, in terms of a past remote enough to seem picturesque, that gives her seemingly romantic pictures their mordant, almost sardonic, irony. Mrs. Scott seems to be opening door after door to the oppressed imagination, and offering enough of a glimpse to persuade the seeker that living in this direction or that offers no more respite or enchantment of the self than the one this seeker may be determining to abandon. (p. 8)

Migrations is a splendidly crowded yet not a confused book. A large coordinated design molds the whole to its ends. The George family and the two McGuire girls, married by the two young men, are central figures, but the reader is equally concerned with [many of the secondary characters] . . . and, above all, with the vivid sketches of visual impression. *Migrations* is a revaluation of the past that is startling and provocative. Even those who disagree violently with its intimations will be impelled to search themselves for values of their own. It is a stimulating and beautiful use to make of history, transforming it into a keen weapon of criticism of the present. (pp. 8-9)

"Spiritual Frontiers," in The New York Times Book Review, *April 10, 1927, pp. 8-9.*

JOSEPH WOOD KRUTCH

Those who have read Mrs. Scott's previous novels do not need to be told of either her power to evoke an exotic scene or her capacity for the minute analysis of character. In her hands the present romantic, almost epic story becomes a series of intimate experiences, and where one would expect large sweeping gestures one gets instead intense, minutely developed scenes and brilliant bits of realistic character analysis which suggests anything but the romantic or the epic tradition. Considering her characters not as heroic figures but as essentially ordinary people who happen to have been born at a time when circumstance forced adventures upon them, she has written a historic novel [*Migrations*] as though it were a modern one, and as a result she has made of it something which is colorful without being, as most colorful things are, remote.

Yet for all the admiration which the fine texture of the book must arouse it cannot be denied that the author has neither fitted her material to the conventional form of the novel nor found a new and satisfactory one of her own; the further one proceeds in the reading of it the more scattered the interest becomes and the less possible it is for the author to draw the threads of her narrative into a single strand. Her story grows like a tree, branching out in every direction and becoming every instant more obviously incapable of being brought to any conclusion. New stories are continually begun before the previous ones have been even well started upon their way—fifteen pages near the end of the book are devoted to a detailed account of the ancestry and early experiences of a new character—and when one comes suddenly to the last page one seems merely to have finished the first volume of some gigantic work.

Migrations is, then, at once brilliant and disappointing. There is hardly a chapter, hardly a page even, that does not reveal talents amounting almost to genius, and yet the total effect is of something which failed to realize itself. In it is the material for half a dozen brilliant short stories and a score of vivid sketches, but there is no climax whatever and scarcely any cumulative effect, so that any one of the parts is more effective than the whole, and one is left with a never-to-be-satisfied interest in six or eight diverse people scattered over the whole face of America. Its theme is, to be sure, announced by the title. Its characters are wanderers diffusing themselves throughout the country and finally to be swallowed up by its vastness; but they are made too vivid to be thus vaguely disposed of. Mrs. Scott has made them individuals, she has caused us to feel for them an intimate concern, and one seems to have been deliberately cheated when they are left in mid-career with their fates not even foreshadowed and with decisive turnings yet to be taken. From a novelist who knows them so intimately, who has described in such details their minds and their actions, one has a right to expect some sort of completeness; it is merely irritating to have every conclusion withheld. (pp. 505-06)

Joseph Wood Krutch, "A Brilliant Beginning," in
The Nation, Vol. CXXIV, No. 3226, May 4, 1927,
pp. 505-06.

ISABEL PATERSON

If the facts were not in evidence, it would seem impossible that disgust could serve as the motive power for creative work. But there are Swift and Huysmans—and Evelyn Scott. Widely divergent in time and space, in theme and style, these three exhibit in common a concentrated, active, withering contempt for the human race, and indeed a revulsion from life itself, from the principle of energy which keeps the terrestrial globe spinning in space.... They hunger and thirst only for oblivion: Nirvana would be their true heaven. The vertiginous and uneasing flux of the material world occasions to these reluctant mortals a faint spiritual nausea. In the range of sensory impressions, it would seem that they are unhappily limited to perception of the painful and the discordant. Pleasure is an empty word in their vocabulary....

As a valid reason for refusing to accept the universe, Evelyn Scott depicts in *Ideals* five types of contemporary humanity who authenticate themselves by evoking the emotion of recognition.... Miss Scott defines her book as "farce and comedy." Well, of course, Gulliver is a nursery classic. But if that is what farce and comedy looks like to Miss Scott, she doesn't have much fun. These studies are as humorous as a surgical clinic. And, it must be conceded, almost as powerful and as thorough....

Consider "Queenie Abrams," described by her "gentleman friend" as "the finest little woman in the world." In retaliation, it must be put to her credit, she called him "Boy." Queenie was self-supporting, independent, and therefore prepared to be a "good pal" to a man. She "thanked God she had a sense of humor." She believed that you can always tell a lady by her gloves, shoes and hat. She was a nice girl, and a good woman, but broad-minded. When "Boy" overstepped the prescribed bounds for friendship, she told him he hadn't acted like a gentleman. Queenie is a behavioristic monster.... Her "responses" are "conditioned" to the last syllable, the least flutter of an eyelash; the product of New York, the subway, department stores, delicatessen and apartment house uniformity.

"Henry Ellis," the second specimen, is equally representative of the respectable middle-class commuter type of white-collar employee. Henry and his wife Gertrude both came of families which had had a little money for a generation and lost it. So they wished to keep alive in the minds of their children "the fine old traditions of American aristocracy." At the same time they avowed allegiance to a "democratic ideal." They spoke with placid conviction of "breeding" and "noblesse oblige."...

[Henry] loved and respected his wife, was proud of his son—who "made the great sacrifice" in the war—and of course he had no other wish for his daughter, Virgie, than that she should be happy. That is, until she married the "wop" chauffeur of the people next door. Then, as it is no longer customary and correct for a father to say, "I'd rather see you in your coffin than married to that man," Henry was at a loss. He couldn't admit that he hated Virgie for exposing his lack of resource in an emergency, and he did not hate her with anything resembling fervor. But the thought of what she had done made him rather sick. Just as, failing to find a stereotyped response to any

situation, any of Miss Scott's creations are usually rather sick. They fall back on that, one might say.

Herbert Young, the Young Intellectual, was reduced to the same squeamish perplexity when he tried to Realize the Absolute through an affair with a casual damsel. The casualness was deliberate; Herbert and his wife Jane were determinedly Free. Jane was aggressively Not Jealous. She declared she must be fundamentally Unmoral. She had two children, not wishing to "miss the experience." Herbert spoke of maternity as "the art function of woman." But in Maggie, the fourth-rate burlesque actress—a vulgar but refreshingly individualised little alley cat—Herbert hoped to achieve "the deep, dark secret of the Universal." He told Maggie she was "an instinctive artist vitiated by a commercial age." He adjured her further: "Art must remain aloof from moral issues, Maggie. All dynamic forms are expressions of the continuity of creation. My functioning is identically your functioning. We are an end, not a means." Maggie said yes; it was like the Colonel's lady and Judy O'Grady....

Enough. Too much, almost. Miss Scott is merciless. Herbert would applaud her stark sincerity; and Henry Ellis would say that nothing is sacred to her. Female virtue, the sanctity of the home, patriotism, religion, art, and even the "code of honor" of sport, she puts through an acid bath and lifts them out in rags and shreds....

It might be insulting to Miss Scott to call her satire salutary. It is improbable that she desires to benefit or improve her fellow creatures. More likely she wishes all men had but one neck, so she could wring it. And these Guy Fawkes effigies whom she takes it out on are uncannily realistic. One would not wish more power to her elbow; she doesn't need it. But a little selectiveness, and the sense of contrast, an appreciation of the fact that synthetic emotion and morality, like all imitations, presuppose something genuine, would advance her to the front rank of American satirists.

Isabel Paterson, "Five Patterns of Behaviorism,"
in New York Herald Tribune Books, *October 23,*
1927, p. 4.

THE NEW YORK TIMES BOOK REVIEW

[Evelyn Scott's] satire is less a protest than a denunciation, less a philosophic contention than a personal reaction. It is made with but little recognition of human frailty or human well meaning: from a superior level, Mrs. Scott sees people whole and rejects them whole. In any personal sense she would probably ignore her people as individuals; but they combine to make up the life about her and she has not the philosophic serenity to ignore the contemporary world. So she proceeds to belittle, to demolish the contemporary world, to hold up its inhabitants as so many specimens, to hold up their ideals as so many laughs for the enlightened. It is this contempt of hers which reduces such lives to the significance of a laugh and not a sense of amusement that leads her to call *Ideals* a book of "farce and comedy." Its people are a farce because they are without meaning; they are a comedy because they ought not to be taken seriously.

Yet for the purpose of dissection they are taken seriously enough. Their lives are dragged out into the open and seen beneath a spotlight of almost intolerable brightness. Their gestures, their ideals are shown up for what they are in contrast to what these people think they are. In her five novelettes Mrs. Scott manages to give us people we have seen in life and whom, through her agency, we shall not hereafter forget. (p. 6)

Mrs. Scott makes a clean job of [the] "ideals" which her characters take with such contemptible assurance. Accepting them so ready-made, so puncture-proof, her characters convert them into the stolid conventions which mold their lives. We are shown these lives with the utmost clearness and accuracy. There is nothing distorted, nothing exaggerated, about Queenie Abrams, or Henry Ellis, or Herbert Young. It is this photographic reality which makes them, in the end, so little interesting to the reader. One wishes that Mrs. Scott had made her people human beings we could meet a little more on our own grounds, people we could do something more than despise. As the book stands, realistic though it is, its "ideals" seem almost too patly and mechanically demolished. Mrs. Scott might have given her people the benefit of the doubt at times; she might have realized that character is fate and that to pity human character not at all is dangerous in a human being. Yet so just is her treatment throughout, so unquestionably deserving her indictment, that if one would be at all critical, one must praise her achievement rather than question her point of view. In its own way *Ideals* is masterfully done. Life seen truthfully from a point of view is always valuable; and the truth of the book becomes half-truth only when one has decided there might be something lacking in the point of view. (pp. 6-7)

> *"Satiric Portraits," in* The New York Times Book Review, *October 30, 1927, pp. 6-7.*

ALLAN NEVINS

For a few minutes [*The Wave*] puzzles the reader. It is obviously a piece of Civil War fiction; but the opening sketch of a Charleston lad who witnesses the bombardment of Fort Sumter from a rowboat is suddenly broken off for another brief sketch of a Baltimore clerk who participates in the attack on the Sixth Massachusetts, and this in turn is followed by a sharply-drawn picture of a Virginia family where the father is an ardent Confederate while the mother is a Yankee with brothers in the Union army. Then the reader catches the clue in Miss Scott's quotation at the beginning of the book from Philip Lake's *Physical Geography*.

> The water of the ocean is never still. It is blown into waves by the wind, it rises and falls with the tides. The waves travel in a definite direction, but a cork thrown into the water does not travel with waves.

The Civil War was like an immense wave which runs through millions of drops of water; it caught up, churned, exalted, crushed, and transformed millions of human beings, shook them into new positions and gave them new shapes, and passed on. Miss Scott traces the wave, in more than six hundred pages, from Fort Sumter to Lincoln's emancipation, registering its passage in typical impulses of agony and joy, bewilderment and comprehension, courage and fear, as given to perhaps two hundred Americans, North and South, soldier and civilian, black and white. Sketch follows sketch, episode follows episode; not one is related to another save as all are related to the overmastering wave called the Civil War. . . .

It must be said that an extraordinary talent has gone into Miss Scott's book. The kaleidoscopic succession of descriptions, incidents, stories, bits of drama—only with none of that continuity which the kaleidoscope possesses—required a remark-

ably agile and versatile imagination. It demanded something more. Miss Scott projects herself into the personalities of her wide array of characters with an intensity that is usually striking and sometimes amazing—though of course intensity is much easier in a brief episode than in a long narrative. . . .

Sometimes Miss Scott even achieves an excellent short story. . . . The episodes are naturally of uneven merit, and when she essays the very highest flights, she fails. She gives us inadequate sketches of Grant and Lee, and her study of Lincoln as he sat in the box at Ford's Theatre before the fatal pistol-shot lacks truth as lamentably as it lacks dignity and power. Though her style for the most part is quiet and simple, sometimes she overwrites. Yet most of the book is kept at a high level; it was well worth writing, and it is well worth reading.

Partly because of its novelty of form, it is one of the most interesting of all the efforts to deal with the Civil War in fiction. But many readers, while granting its power, will lay it down with the feeling that it embodies an artistic fallacy. A fluttering chaos of a hundred episodes and incidents, a rapid flickering of unrelated pictures on the screen, may achieve an arresting effect—but not the higher kind of effect. There is something fundamentally faulty in an art which arouses our interest in a character or scene for a brief moment, and then hurries to another and another. A great organic novel, where the characters are studied through a sustained action and where the interrelation of persons and events leads to a genuine development of individuality, demands an altogether larger and finer kind of talent; and it offers a truer, more penetrating medium for the study of a historical period. In such a book the whole can be far greater than the sum of its parts; here the whole is less than the sum of the parts, for the parts too often merely duplicate one another. They are all surface facets, and the inner truth of the matter—what the Civil War meant to its participants—is left largely unrevealed. Mary Johnston's *The Long Roll* and *Cease Firing* are not great novels; Stephen Crane's *The Red Badge of Courage* and Harold Frederic's *The Copperhead* are both brief studies, limited in scope. But they are better as art than this book, and when one searches for essentials, they give a deeper idea of the war. We do not know a character until we follow him through several scenes and events, not merely one, and till we see him in important relationships with other characters; we cannot understand the human impacts of a war until, abandoning mere panorama and episode, we study these impacts through characters thus fully realized.

> *Allan Nevins, "Cape-Smith's First Book," in* The Saturday Review of Literature, *Vol. V, No. 48, June 22, 1929, p. 1142.*

CLIFTON P. FADIMAN

For me, at least, the importance of Evelyn Scott's remarkable book [*The Wave*] lies in the fact that it is one of the few really formidable expressions in fiction of the anti-heroic viewpoint—or, if one may be permitted so lax a term, the modern viewpoint. It is not less sentimental than Barbusse or Remarque or Renn or Frey; but it seems to gain an added power and scope because it is so rigidly unautobiographical. Fine as is *All Quiet on the Western Front*, for example, one cannot help closing the book with the feeling that, after all, this is one man's war, fine-fibered and intelligent as that man may be. *The Wave* recounts no one man's war; it recounts the Civil War, whole and entire, by the one possible method: that of tracing its impact on several hundred individuals, from Abraham Lincoln down to a newsboy selling battle extras. . . .

By the time, these words appear so much just praise will have been lavished on Mrs. Scott's obviously torrential creative power that it hardly seems worthwhile to make further comment. She has set in motion a veritable army of characters, each provided with a complete background, as if each were originally conceived as the central figure of a novel. Indeed, Mrs. Scott's insight into and curiosity about her own creations are so vital and enthusiastic that it is only with great difficulty that she avoids what must have loomed up as her major difficulty: that of so subordinating the tragedies and comedies of her individuals as to give the reader a continuous sense of the great national drama in which they played their parts. That we do achieve this sense, despite the fact that there is little further connection between the hundred or more sections of the book other than that of vague chronological sequence, is an astounding technical triumph for the author.

Criticism has been directed, and will continue to be directed, against the "formlessness" of the book. It is hardly necessary to point out that this formlessness is designed, that it is in itself a way, a valid and exciting way, of viewing the national cataclysm which was the Civil War. It is, more than that, the only way in which a thoroughly modern temperament *could* survey the war completely because only thus can the utter madness and senseless horror of strife be completely communicated. The indictments of a Remarque or a Frey are powerful enough; but they are individual indictments; they have a quality of isolation; and, more pertinently, the indignant emotions they arouse are rather simple ones which tend to disappear after the book is read. But the emotions aroused by *The Wave* are not the simple ones of horror and indignation at all, but something far more profound. The most blighting as well as the simplest thing one can say against war is that it brings wretchedness to millions of people—and in different ways. It is the multifariousness, the incoherent and unrelated multifariousness of the tragedies, that is the most dreadful thing about war. And of these multifarious, senseless, individual tragedies no one, before the appearance of *The Wave,* has given us more than a schematic picture. There is a certain nameless horror that comes with the reader's realization that the meanest Negro and General Robert E. Lee are both made sick to their very souls by the same event. As one reads on and on, passing from one social level to another, . . . one begins to lose sight of the fact that this is a war between Confederates and Unionists, between two sharply demarcated economic and social ideologies. The "issues" of the war fade away, except in so far as they present themselves for our ironical survey; but the war as a tremendous *human* tragic event begins to engross us and finally to overwhelm us in its brutal variety and meaninglessness.

For myself, I find certain imperfections and disharmonies which are minor but perhaps worth pointing out. They are not the results of weakness but of an excess of strength. I could wish, for example, that Mrs. Scott's senses were not so keen and excitable, that she would refrain from packing every sentence with more visual and auditory metaphor than it will bear. Her style is so agonizingly alive that it occasionally becomes confusing. Similarly, she is so intent on avoiding a series of mere "snapshots" that (but very infrequently) she overloads her stories with biographical detail. . . . Finally, she may be charged once in a great while with selecting her stories too obviously in order to represent or typify some phase of the conflict. In

so far as we recognize these episodes as "representative," they lose in emotional quality what they gain in mere pertinency. . . .

There can be no doubt that *The Wave* is an outstanding achievement in recent American letters.

Clifton P. Fadiman, "A Great National Drama," in The Nation, *Vol. CXXIX, No. 3343, July 31, 1929, p. 119.*

EDA LOU WALTON

This book of poetry is difficult to criticize, for the reader is almost constantly of two opinions. *The Winter Alone* is the poetry of a novelist, one of the best of American novelists. There is no poverty of subject matter: the book is filled with individualistic observations upon life, with startling characters given in a sentence, with intricate emotional situations, with vivid backgrounds. The poet's outlook is at one and the same time mystic and intellectual. And yet, although the intention of many of the poems is lyric, there is a kind of looseness in rhythm and diffuseness in imagery which gives the reader the impression that many of these poems are notes for longer poems rather than the fused immediate statements of lyrics. And the lyric intention is only now and then focused clearly enough to arouse the called-for emotion on the part of the reader. In these verses there is the same subtlety and richness of imagination that makes Evelyn Scott a poet in her prose, for certainly much of her novel *The Wave* is highly poetic. Here is the same capacity for suffering, the same penetrative mind, and the same amazing gift for visualizing and using language. Here also is perhaps a little too much of human observation and not quite enough immediacy of emotional statement—the trick again of a novelist superseding the art of the poet. Mrs. Scott is too much inclined to walk into her scene and comment. . . . [Her] lines with their fine rhythm—and . . . [at times] the rhythm is identical with the emotion—lose just a bit through the author's rhetorical questions. [They] need not have been asked. The feeling of aloofness and grandeur could have been given directly.

Mrs. Scott has so much more to say than have most of our numerous poets, is so much more acutely sensitive to life, that we should not, perhaps, ask anything finer of her than that which she offers. And yet, the lack is there, a lack which some of the poems do not have—that of a convincing rhythm and a lightning-like fusion of several images into one consummate emotion.

But to quibble no more, *The Winter Alone* is a book of deeply and sincerely felt experiences. It exhibits no mere fluency of words, no mere playing with facile technique; the poems are of the stuff of life understood and the product of a mystic search never quieted. (pp. 100-01)

Eda Lou Walton, "The Poetry of a Novelist," in The Nation, *Vol. CXXXI, No. 3394, July 23, 1930, pp. 100-01.*

JOHN CHAMBERLAIN

A Calendar of Sin is what it purports to be—an explanation of American life in terms of a conception of sex that once provided Mr. Comstock with a considerable and very vocal following. The sin in Miss Scott's novel is the thinking that makes it so.

Granted her people, granted her perspective, she has sighted down the barrel of her gun with deadly enough aim. The beginnings of an industrial age are rapacious and drab anywhere whether in the England of James Mill's time or in the America of Matt Quay's and when these beginnings are complicated by the aftermath of a civil war they leave plenty of human wreckage as by-products. A good deal of Miss Scott's story unfolds in the town of Mimms, Tenn., and some of her best pages are those which evoke the days of the Ku Klux Klan.

It would require some of those fan-shape genealogical tables so popular in New England to straighten out the interlocked lives in *A Calendar of Sin*. There is no necessity, however, to spread out the tables here, for the stories of individuals are subordinated to the mass effect, which is that of presenting an America insensitive to joyousness. This subordination is the source of all that is dull in the novel. For example, the subtle corruption in marriage of Linda George, an appealing figure if there ever was one, is left to the imagination of the reader almost entirely. One sees her in the '70s, a lively, somewhat puckish figure, with fine instincts and a good brain, and one leaves her in old age, a being warped by a commonplace husband who has infected her with his banal views. One would give the whole "historical" gamut of virtues of *A Calendar of Sin* for a close study of Linda George—who marries one of those fabled Southern gentlemen who cannot forget, sir, that he might have had a very different heritage.

But Linda George must, inevitably, be swallowed up by the demands of the sort of novel that Miss Scott has undertaken. And the genre was worth the creation, for it brings us a new and fruitful concept of the historical novel. Ordinarily the novelist who works in this deceptive field will parade his erudition, his knowledge of acts of Congress, God, omission, commission and what-not. But the mass of historical detail that Miss Scott has at her fingertips . . . is used in *A Calendar of Sin* almost casually, and hence what happens in post-Civil War Mimms, Tenn.; in the Washington of President Grant's time; in Odessa, Ind., of the '70s; in St. Louis of the early 1900s, or in the haunts of the bad men of the West comes to us with a most grateful and easy contemporary air.

There are loose ends in *A Calendar of Sin*. One would like to know, for example, the precise functional value of giving us so much of the story of Memory Burgess in detail, or of telling us in elaboration of Wilbur George's death in New Mexico. These bits are inartistically tantalizing, for they are neither fully realized "melodramas" in themselves, nor are they necessary to the pattern that involves the Georges with the Dolans in a final tragedy that is a result of all the hates, both personal and sectional, that have gone before. One would like to have more completely divulged motivation for the careers of both John and James Dolan. We can sense what impelled them to acceptance of certain life-denying values, but we would feel more fully compensated were we let in on the absolute secret in detail. Because of these gnawing uncertainties in Miss Scott's scheme of things the novel cannot be called a final success. But neither can it be called a failure. Even if it is to serve chiefly as a beacon and a warning to other novelists. *A Calendar of Sin* was very much worth writing.

> John Chamberlain, "Three Generations in American Life," in The New York Times Book Review, October 18, 1931, p. 4.

CLIFTON FADIMAN

Now that Willa Cather has turned her back on anything likely to prove disturbing, Evelyn Scott emerges as perhaps our most important woman novelist. Her defects are many and exasperating: an idiom which oscillates between the strained and the banal; an inability to select and condense; a tendency to over-rapid composition. In short, she is not a first-rate artist. But she is something just as interesting—a *fearless* one. There is a convention, still flourishing in England and America, that the woman writer should deal with details rather than with wholes and prefer the touching to the tragic. To this convention Evelyn Scott is blind. As readers of that remarkable novel *The Wave* will agree, her eye turns naturally to whatever bulks large and serious in American life. The keynote of her work is courage, a sober willingness to follow wherever the intelligence may lead. For this reason alone *A Calendar of Sin*, unwieldy and diffuse as it is, enlarges the imagination far more powerfully than an idyll of evasion like *Shadows on the Rock*.

If not a great book, it has at any rate a great subject—the failure of American love, one of the basic tragedies underlying the national career. To get at the tangled roots of this tragedy the author goes back to the Reconstruction era and compresses into her narrative the broken lives of five generations. That perspective errs which views the collapse of marriage and the tumultuous uncertainty of our sexual conduct as peculiar to our own day. The causes of our erotic bankruptcy, like those of our industrial bankruptcy, lie deep in our history, though they are by no means so easy to disentangle. Similar in their contours, the records of these two failures exhibit the same features of horror, ugliness, bondage, and defeat. In one case the end-product is a paralyzing economic imperialism; in the other—Reno and tabloid murders. (p. 521)

What lies at the root of these tragedies? The lives of these men and women would seem to answer, a hysterical overvaluation of the emotion of sex. Particularly during the period which this book covers—that of our industrial expansion—the middle class discovered very few of the many normal outlets of emotional expression. Both the men and the women remained emotional juveniles. The males exhausted their energies in a mad economic battle; the females throttled theirs in an attempt at upholding the genteel cultural tradition which their husbands, excusably enough, had no time for. This general emotional starvation resulted in a deifying of the women as the conservers of the national idealism. This, in a way, was intended to compensate for the morally shabby life an industrial pioneer was forced to lead, as far as business was concerned. Also, in the course of a busy life, it became much easier to enshrine women than to understand them. It saved thought and therefore time. The first romantic experience, as a corollary, was overemphasized. It was received by most women and by many men as a sort of revelation of divinity—pleasanter if accompanied by carnal satisfaction, but not to be questioned if it were not. Calf love was taken with utter seriousness—most of the marriages in *A Calendar of Sin* are terribly premature unions—and marriages that should have been dissolved within a twelve month were religiously maintained by both parties, even though in so doing they suffered the agonies of the damned. Particularly in the South (most of Mrs. Scott's people are Southerners) where the puritan outlook was reinforced by the chivalric tradition, erotic disaster was inevitable. The morbid canalization of an emotion which is normally mobile and capable of growth and alteration resulted either in self-delusion, frequently to the point of mania, or in stoically accepted misery. And for those doomed ones whose bodies were too much for them, the only way out lay through the red door of violence. Therefore the subtitle of the book—*American Melodramas*. Murder, rape, self-mutilation, sadism, and suicide were the necessary products of any society which systematically distorted its erotic energies, confused them with spiritual nostalgias, or brutally sublimated them in the market place.

The final form which this mad sexual conflict assumed was the invisible matriarchate under which we now live. This had its first real development, as the pages of *A Calendar of Sin* show us, in the latter half of the nineteenth century during the era of feverish industrial expansion. The bourgeois, impotent to achieve a mature sexual adjustment to his woman, idealized her. Thus a seemingly significant relationship was established. The diffuse emotion it generated was useful in that it blinded him to the emptiness of his own emotional and economic life. As sophistication increased, this idealization became more difficult. But there still remained the necessity to relate the female somehow to the male career. Accordingly, a connection was made between the bourgeois's economic activity—his nearest approach to a real existence—and his perverted romantic idealism. The woman now became somebody not to adore but to *work for*. She developed into a sufficient reason for an otherwise meaningless technique of money-making. And in terms of this sufficient reason it is quite possible to interpret much of our apparently unique industrial energy and therefore of the history of the nation in general.

All these knotty and tragic problems achieve concrete meaning, if not complete clarity. . . . No one else has had the courage, or indeed the knowledge, even to attempt them in the form of fiction. It is an immense and important job and it is all the more regrettable, therefore, that the author has not tackled it supremely well. . . . Irrelevant episodes . . . would have been pitilessly cut away. Chunks of sociology and history would have been refined so that the background emerged unforcedly and unpedantically. And Mrs. Scott's English would have been purged of its unfortunate affectations and its frequent shoddiness.

With all its faults, however, *A Calendar of Sin* towers over most contemporary American fiction. There is no evasion in it, no prettifying, no substitution of style for intelligence. It must be read. (pp. 521-22)

> *Clifton Fadiman, "Eros in America," in* The Nation, *Vol. CXXXIII, No. 3462, November 11, 1931, pp. 521-22.*

JOHN CHAMBERLAIN

The American novel usually falls into one of the two broad categories. Either it is a "sociological" novel, such as Sinclair Lewis writes, or it is an "art" novel, such as Kay Boyle writes. The sociological novel came out of the period of the quest for social justice which died, temporarily, with the World War. . . . The "art" novel, which came to the fore in the middle '20s as Hemingway and others commenced writing about the individual soul of that lost generation which had said farewell to sociology, has had the best of the luck recently, even though a Lewis still commands his own great attention. But the luck is beginning to wane. Individual problems commence to seem silly when the group problem of food faces the nations.

What is Evelyn Scott's place in all this? With *Eva Gay* it begins to look as if she were the heir to the two traditions, mingling both the spirit of the sociological novel and the art novel. *Eva Gay* is a most ambitious book—more ambitious, even, than *A Calendar of Sin*. . . . In one sense *Eva Gay* is a continuation of *A Calendar of Sin*. It is an "international novel," paced to

parallel America's coming-of-age as a world power and creditor nation. Its characters, unlike those of *A Calendar of Sin,* experience Europe, the war and the aftermath. . . . One is always conscious, when reading *Eva Gay,* of the sociological pattern of an age, a nation, a world.

But Evelyn Scott differs from the usual sociological novelist. She does not write like a John Dos Passos; her nurses, her scientists, do not happen to be present at the Crillon when the Versailles treaty is being negotiated, or on the sidelines during a riot. There is no direct criticism of life in *Eva Gay,* no satire, no attitude toward events and philosophies that can be put into so many cold words. *Eva Gay* is a sociological novel with a difference.

The difference is one of concentration upon nerves. With the ordinary sociological novelist, the overt mental attitude of his people, as expressed in talk or social action, is important. Mrs. Scott seeks to cut below formulae; she doesn't care what the specific attitudes of her characters may be about the war debts, about liberalism, about women's suffrage, about the class struggle. Psychic shock, the trauma of two decades, is her province. In *Eva Gay,* with immitigable industry, and with a far better sense of style than was evident in *A Calendar of Sin,* she seeks to exhibit the impact on a nervous organization of events which would send a Sinclair Lewis or a Floyd Dell into minute description of environment, and into literal recording of talk.

The result [is] that Mrs. Scott has written another "difficult" novel. It depends, ultimately of course, on Freud, but she uses no clichés of psychoanalysis. . . . Evelyn Scott dispenses with the traditional means, and seeks solely to adumbrate successive states of mind as Eva passes from the emotional hungers of her 'teens to the psychic disintegration of "post-war." Similarly with Hans Haaska, as he breaks free from his sexual Puritanism, only to discover that he has been irrevocably conditioned by all he despises.

The novel closes on a note which must be disturbing to Mrs. Scott as artist. For, after the expansion of America into world prominence, after the war, after the peace, after the soul-searching of Eva Gay, of Hans, after the exploration of the individual's psychic reaction to currents of thought and feeling of three decades of "individualism" (which the novelist as artist must prize for his dramatic material, no matter what the world is coming to), Hans Haaska reflects upon the trend of events. He listens to arguments. "These new young men were hunger's Puritans." "For Marxians stuck very close to good biology, and the problem of nutrition was the problem with which every species was preoccupied." And, though Hans Haaska, a biologist himself, has seen life in the raw on the Antarctic continent and in Africa, it is cold comfort to fall back upon the stomach as the common denominator. Yet this is not all, even though it is nearly all. "Maybe, the general renouncing of personality was less an ordering of than a yielding to a circumstance." But Hans damned, nevertheless, "the young, inspired fanatics who would rub his nose in life which they so little understood." The individual snarls here at the close.

Eva Gay has a vast scope. One suspects that Mrs. Scott moves her characters about on the world chess board . . . merely to give the imagist poet that is in her an opportunity to write of whales, of "cat-agate spots, as though the dark grew eyes," of placid seas, of Swiss landscapes, of Kentucky Spring and Autumn. She does this superlatively well. Every now and again she breaks, probably unconsciously, into blank verse. . . .

This instinct for poetry probably violates the famous "other harmony" of prose, but it makes the book an adventure. It is an adventure that is at times maddening, specifically on those occasions when words fail Mrs. Scott in her attempt to body forth nebulous emotional states, but an adventure of any sort is certainly worth a little temporary exasperation.

John Chamberlain, "*Evelyn Scott's Cycloramic Novel*," *in* The New York Times Book Review, *April 9, 1933, p. 6.*

JONATHAN DANIELS

Far more than Ellen Glasgow or Elizabeth Madox Roberts, Miss Evelyn Scott is the articulate voice of the New South. Miss Glasgow and Miss Roberts, who might write in any place or time, write of the South in which they live. Yet Miss Scott, who easily encompasses an entire world in a novel, speaks the South's new voice and new mind. She builds miles of words as fast as the South of the twenties built miles of roads and to the same uncertain ends. Her books, like the rearing skyscrapers run up in every Southern city, are monuments of literary megalomania. With the rest of the South, too, Miss Scott has turned deliberately away from the romantic pattern of Thomas Nelson Page and turned quite as deliberately to new and equally romantic patterns in terms of the dark and already half-outmoded new psychology. . . .

No one can watch Miss Scott's huge books come out year after year and read them without being impressed with her tremendous literary vitality. While in none of her three chief figures in [*Eva Gay*] has she succeeded in creating a great character, she has with an amazing mass of detail built the incidents of three diverse and correctly drawn lives. Eva's story grows in the images of Miss Scott's own Southern past, but with equal certainty she has followed the Missouri childhood and wandering life of Hans, the son of a physician who was addicted to drugs, and a mother who clung bitterly to her small town ideal of goodness and religion. No less convincing are the details of Eva's unhappy childhood in New Zealand and London. In their three lives, Miss Scott carries her story with an amazing understanding of locale to Africa and the Antarctic, to New York and London, to Paris and the south of France. In all these scenes she builds minor characters who, in surface at least are as true as the lands she describes.

In *Eva Gay*, Miss Scott has written another big book but not a great one. There is much in it that is distinguished. Sometimes there is a poetic beauty in her prose. But underneath her prose, underneath so great a panorama of places and lives and conflicting ideals, there is somehow the lack of a philosophy strong enough for so much strong material. One feels that Miss Scott has made her sexual complexities and sexual fears in much the spirit that Mrs. Radcliffe devised her more frankly romantic horrors and mysteries. Both ladies are romantic, but Mrs. Radcliffe, despite the calumny that she went insane in the manner of her own well-wrought delusions, was a frankly romantic storyteller. A storyteller, and a good one, Miss Scott is, too, but her books give the unfortunate impression that she means to be something more. The truth is that Miss Scott merely frightens with the phallus as Mrs. Radcliffe did with ghosts. The fashion, not the method, has changed.

Jonathan Daniels, "*Old Wine in New Bottles*," in The Saturday Review of Literature, *Vol. IX, No. 39, April 15, 1933, p. 537.*

HORACE GREGORY

With each succeeding novel, it becomes more and more apparent that Mrs. Scott uncovers a number of uneasy problems for the critic and reviewer. Unlike her peers—and here I would include Mrs. Wharton and Willa Cather—she has arrived at no final destination; she eludes those categories that we are so fond of making for the novelist, those neat distinctions by which we separate the writing of a novel from other activities in literature. I would say that from the very start of her career Mrs. Scott has been interested in something far beyond the formal limitations of her medium, and one might add that her growth in mastery over that medium is almost incidental. She has, I think, proved her ability as an artist in all varieties of the form that she has chosen. . . . I believe that [**Breathe Upon These Slain**] is among the best of the dozen books that she has written, and listing a few facts about it will reveal, I think, its less obvious relationship to all the others.

In this . . . book there is a noticeable shift in environment; the scene is laid on the East coast of England and the central action of the novel is motivated by a series of events which took place forty years ago. The story is told by means of a special device: the narrator is living in a furnished house, and guided by family photographs hanging on the wall, reconstructs the history of the Courtneys who had made the house their home. It was one of those middle-class English families that wheeled slowly upward from moderate prosperity at the close of the last century to near wealth during the World War. (pp. 709-13)

The photographs disclose the entire company of Courtneys: Philip and Fedelia, father and mother of the household; Bertram the son, Tilly who died young, Ethel, Meg, and Cora, the daughters. See again Philip, the successful man of business, portly, middle-aged; wistful, inarticulate, inept at home; brutal, arrogant, and by no means scrupulous in business hours. Fedelia, his wife, carries her domestic, blind, harsh virtues before her as one might hold a banner. She rules the house as Philip rules his office and her drive toward power, clearly shown, is as destructive as every human reach toward earthly power becomes; blindly, she maims her children. The weaker variations of Philip and Fedelia are the children: the highly sensitized Tilly, a family sacrifice, to become a symbol of childhood death for Courtneys, then Ethel, nervous, ecstatic, trapped in marriage to a commissioned naval officer, then shallow Cora, then ugly Meg doomed to neurotic spinsterhood, and last, ineffectual Bertram who was to be the family hero, fulfilling his destiny by death on the battlefield of the Somme. Ethel in trapped rebellion and Bertram, closeted by an all too-conscious despair, are the central figures in the latter sections of the novel. Ethel's sons are citizens of the new world, the material out of which fascists and communists are made and their speeches are the means by which an epilogue is written.

So much for the particular range that Mrs. Scott has chosen for this latest novel, but on reading it one sees again the inner structure that was implied in *The Narrow House*. One may even go so far as to identify a similar cast of characters, but this detail is not important. It is the theme at the core of the two books that commands attention, a theme that reveals how human beings are trapped in their own toils. . . . The story is an old one, and how then does Mrs. Scott make it significant to us and to our times? In *The Narrow House* a rapid insight into human motives guided her way. It was a violent book, written with such conviction, that admitting certain flaws, its publication promised the arrival of an important novelist. Here, I would say, Mrs. Scott's prose instrument lacked the flexibility required for her more subtle observations, for what she has to say will admit no facile means of speech and to drive her point home, a number of specific instances must be placed before her readers. For the most part, she has selected her examples from American life and revealed them in the light of melodrama. I know that I am oversimplifying her statement when I say that her people are trapped and thwarted by the demands of sex, of money, of a transitory position in society. One must read the novels as one reads poetry, to get the full impact of Mrs. Scott's argument. In this last book she no longer turns to a melodramatic statement of her thesis and the result is that of subdued lyricism, an elegy, if you will, of a society that is now about to die. The danger that Mrs. Scott sees in the new order is that mistaken confidence that human beings have in the victories of material power, that very power which breeds ambition and then frustrates its final gratification. Her warning to the younger communists is that they too may fall into the narrow house that holds the bones of their grandfathers, the Victorians who celebrated the hollow conquest of iron and of steel.

As I said at the beginning of this review, Mrs. Scott voices no final solution of the problems she presents to her critics. She, like the old philosopher who sought an honest man by carrying a lantern, is seeking for some ultimate expression of reality. Her novels represent the road she has traveled during the past twelve years. As this moment only a few, I think, will realize the full importance of that journey. From the evidence of this book before me I doubt if Mrs. Scott will ever run to shelter; she will never relinquish, I think, her special power to observe the changing world. If I were looking for a parallel of this latest novel in modern literature I would be forced to reread Thomas Hardy and note again that courage to observe in human action the fatal end of earthly destiny.

Horace Gregory, "The Narrow House of Victorian England," in The Saturday Review of Literature, *Vol. X, No. 45, May 26, 1934, pp. 709, 713.*

LOUIS KRONENBERGER

I have seldom read a book whose appeal is so entirely to the mind. **Breathe Upon These Slain,** for all that it may have been written under emotional pressure, emerges dry and remote. The lives of [the] people are buried beneath words and ideas; when they are most vivid they are . . . reminiscent of the lives of people in other novels; and the device of a narrator who intrudes upon the story and reminds you, time and again, that the whole business of **Breathe Upon These Slain** is fabricated upon some faded photographs, proves the finishing touch to the unreality of it all.

There are further explanations of why it is all so unreal. Many of the separate episodes seem to fit badly into the scheme of the book. Many of the characters disappear from the story for such long stretches that when they re-enter it they are no more than names to the reader. Miss Scott has, besides, an unfortunate habit of introducing editorial comments on almost every page. But surely the most dismal and upsetting element of the book is its style—a style that whenever it is sharp is also cold, and that is very often the reverse of sharp. To the slow, verbose, colorless stretches of writing, more than to anything else, must be ascribed that lack of spirit and vitality which makes the book, whatever other virtues it may have, a novel dead at birth.

Louis Kronenberger, "Evelyn Scott Writes Now of England," in The New York Times Book Review, *May 27, 1934, p. 7.*

DOROTHY VAN DOREN

In a longish and sometimes clumsily written preface [to **Bread and a Sword**] Mrs. Scott offers the prolegomena for her problem of the artist today and how he shall make a living. Mrs. Scott of course knows that the problem is not peculiar to our own time. . . . But today, she avers, the machine has accelerated our tempo of living and flattened out our values; if an artist is not a commercial success, he is thrown to the dogs, or more specifically to the bread lines. If he has been so rash as to acquire a family, they, too, are not spared. When patronage is occasionally offered, it is either in the form of a grudging charity or it is capricious, vulgar, and irrelevant to the quality of the art that is being practiced. and the alternative, to get a job that will provide a living, is destructive to the art.

To illustrate this thesis, Mrs. Scott offers a novelist—husband of a woman who once thought of herself as a painter and poet, and father of two boys. He has written a couple of novels that have sold something like 15,000 copies each; but his royalty checks are diminishing steadily; he has taken the family to France, where living is cheaper and life is supposed to be simpler; he owes several thousand dollars; he is at work on another novel. And it doesn't work. . . . When they go back home, there is a stupid father-in-law beginning to suffer from the depression, with whom the family tries to live while the novelist, thoroughly cowed, is looking for a white-collar job. But there are no such jobs. The alternative, to take a farm laborer's job while the wife works in the farm kitchen, doesn't work either. Publishers refuse advances on problematical novels. And patronage, when it comes, is offered by a wealthy woman who discovers that her assistant gardener is really a literary lion in a small way, and who gets an erotic kick out of that fact.

It is a bitter story. Nobody describes family bickering brought on by poverty more relentlessly than Mrs. Scott does. Nobody delineates stupidity and vulgarity more devastatingly. Her hero is damned by a world that will not tolerate artists unless it is forced to—a situation which contains enough hard truth to give any artist pause. But she fails to make her case sufficiently convincing, first by lightening the gloom and providing the contrast which the reader must have in order to be able to endure her story at all. There is not a person in her book who is unquestionably sympathetic, or simply intelligent, or fundamentally good. . . . If this is really a world in which the only law is that of tooth and claw, in which every man looks only to his own advantage, in which bread is the only reality, then it is a world damned by its own shortcomings and not worth writing about. But Mrs. Scott's second failure is more serious even than this: she does not convince the reader that her artist is worth saving. . . .

All this is simply to say that Mrs. Scott is a novelist of power and much more than average intelligence, and that she has chosen a subject which is in itself powerful and worth attention. But having set herself a difficult and worthwhile task, she would have solved it better by attacking it perhaps—less directly. An oblique approach, which would have given her novelist a break or two—not necessarily by a happy ending—would have been more illuminating and more persuasive. It is permissible to harass and torment a reader, but he must be offered occasional balm, he must have time off to contemplate his scars. Otherwise the struggle has no meaning, and the end does not seem worth all the trouble.

Dorothy Van Doren, "Bread and the Artist," in The Nation, *Vol. 144, No. 17, April 24, 1937, p. 484.*

MARY ROSS

The bread of this title [**Bread and a Sword**] is bitter bread, the meager slice or contemptuously tossed crust that is likely to be the portion of an artist whose fidelity is to his perceptions rather than the market. The sword, I take it, is that double-edged power where with the artist has the delight of carving out some precise meaning clear and beautiful to himself, yet finds himself frustrated and isolated in the midst of his fellows. The force and intensity which so distinguish Evelyn Scott's work are here turned to the story of a writer, his wife, who once had wanted to paint, and their two children.

In a long preface Mrs. Scott has explained the basic philosophy out of which she writes the story of the struggles of an artist enmeshed in the modern economic order. It is fourteen years since this book was started. In this final form the story is laid in the period of the depression, but the questions it raises unfortunately would seldom be absent from the lives of people like Alec and Kate in the best of times. . . .

In the preface Mrs. Scott writes out her rebellion against the philosophies she finds implicit in current collectivist movements, fascism or communism. Her judgment is not against the ends of those who would socialize the economic system or against action to effect these ends, but against the slogans, the propagandas, that would give dialectics the oppressive sanctity of a cult. To her such a mood is as fatal to the artist as the standardization enforced by mechanization, advertising, or blind nationalism. . . . [She declares] "The artist's primary intention is never merely to convince mankind of the plausibilty of an opinion: it is to permit other men to share, through sense illusion, some unique, personally engendered envisagement of an actual."

So much for the frame of the book, the reason why the author believes the story of Alec significant. Evelyn Scott is too much of an artist herself to have used her characters as stalking horses. Once the preface is ended, the story is not in terms of general ideas but of explicit persons. The life of the Williamses in a little town in southern France, their return to New York and the charity of relatives, their desperate efforts to earn a living on a farm, Alec as a handyman, organist, reluctantly-exploited literary lion—all these are communicated with the beautiful integrity that characterizes Mrs. Scott's writing. A lesser writer would have used the story to point a moral. Here it is told as something important in itself, and it is because she believes such persons as these important that the author has reached the opinions she gives in the preface. Only an idealist, one who believes, with discrimination, in the importance of human beings, could attain the biting realism of this picture of frustration. . . . **Bread and a Sword** will anger those who are looking for an easy optimism. It will fail to satisfy those who have or want a stock answer for the sufferings and injustices of civilization which Mrs. Scott admits as readily as they. For those who are willing to consider the novel as such, or to read with open mind a preface with which they may not agree, this book, like its forerunners, presents a sincere and sensitive challenge, as distinguished in its quality of mind as in its artistry.

Mary Ross, "The Luxury of Integrity for an Artist," in New York Herald Tribune Books, *April 25, 1937, p. 5.*

LORINE PRUETTE

[In *Background in Tennessee*] Evelyn Scott has attempted a voyage of discovery backward in time, into her own background, from which she thought she escaped at the age of sixteen. Now, having swung through many countries and half a lifetime she comes back to try to learn what it is from she has never been able to escape. Depicting it in swift poignant little scenes, dissecting her Tennessee with her keen intelligence, her deftest phrases, considering it with her excited sensibilities, she tries to tell the truth and to make sense of it.

She does not make sense of it, but she makes it very believable. . . .

[The] pages are made vivid by vignettes of many of Evelyn Scott's relatives, so that we see the history of the country and the varying racial strains in this pleasant fashion. The story of her visits, as a little girl, into certain Negro shanties, is almost all we need to know. For the first time, so far as I can remember, the Negro man receives his due appreciation as one of the kindest, strongest influences in the development of the little white girls for whom he builds up the legend that they are little princesses. . . .

Here, too, is by implication the development of feminism in young Southern girls, of a special brand which never really made them feel at home with the more organized varieties of the North. "Wed, or unwedded, successful or confronted with defeat, they seldom lowered the banner they had agreed to carry, on which was inscribed, together with some genuinely noble sentiments: FIRST AND FOREMOST, SEX APPEAL!" It was against the implacable urge to please, to be pleasing to men, against the precocious sex consciousness, . . . against this premature concern with masculine opinion, that feminism grew here and there in the South. And against the realization that the women must carry so much of the burden of frontier living, or of Reconstruction days. . . . And against the task of being the professional belle, while yet recognizing the contribution made by "the cultivated, naive, yet eminently practical, cynicism of the Southern coquette."

And here the roots of compassion and of esthetic joy, which the South both develops and inevitably starves. "I became more and more aware of the precise qualities in happenings which make them beautiful to people with my type of response and limited understanding—responsiveness to what is transiently lovely, never dependable!"

On almost every page of **Background in Tennessee** are sentences so wise or so perceptive as to call for quotation; some of it shows that Evelyn Scott has escaped even less than she thinks, and this, doubtless, she would acknowledge. But this is intimate history, warm, personal, baffling and exciting, with almost all you need to know of Tennessee and much that you will want to know of Evelyn Scott.

Lorine Pruette, "In Intimate, Baffling and Exciting Tennessee," in New York Herald Tribune Books, *October 17, 1937, p. 4.*

ELEANOR CARROLL CHILTON

The material suggested by the title of this book [**Background in Tennessee**] is fascinating and important, but certainly difficult to handle, and perhaps it is unfair to have expected from Mrs. Scott any clear statement about the complicated relationship between her early environment and her contemporary self. . . . But the reader does ask of an author that he organize his material toward some thesis, however tentative and qualified, and *Background in Tennessee* gives the impression of being a long argument Mrs. Scott is having with herself before deciding whether or not she will be able to write a book about her background in Tennessee. The result is that what we read is lacking in both structural and essential form, and so breaks off without finishing and runs its course without making any point. It really sounds as if the author had simply noted down her memories of the first years of her life in Clarksville, taking them as they came, the free associations interrupted only when conscience reminded her to toss in some objective material. Tennessee, in other words, comes out a bad second.

Perhaps this is because Mrs. Scott really disapproves of her background. That, at least, is what one seems to glimpse behind the lines. On the showing of this book she is a rebel, and became one through realizing that behind the social order that had harbored her joyous childhood, lay injustice and pettiness. Injustice and pettiness, which abound everywhere, are of course notably conspicuous in a small town, but that does not reconcile Mrs. Scott, who hates provincialism. It is doubly a pity, therefore, that she did not in this book, line up side by side memories of the days when Clarksville was the accepted world and memories of the ensuing years of doubt, analysis, judgment, and escape. . . .

[The pattern of childhood acceptance and adolescent escape] has been told so often that to most of us it is no longer interesting unless the narrator has outgrown the rebellion—the driving power of which is egoism—and made at least a spiritual return and some peace with his origins. And there are decided implications throughout this book that the author still judges society from the point of view of an esthetic philosophy—a point of view which fairly precludes any warm interpretation of a small town anywhere on earth.

However, what one really complains about is not that *Background in Tennessee* fails to make this or that point, but that it fails to make any point. Some of the remembering is delightfully told. There is much material that is provocative, and some that is fresh. It is honest. But all this goes for nothing in the general shapelessness.

> Eleanor Carroll Chilton, "A Novelist Recollects," in The Saturday Review of Literature, *Vol. XVI, No. 26, October 23, 1937, p. 7.*

CLIFTON FADIMAN

It gives me little joy to acknowledge that Evelyn Scott's *The Shadow of the Hawk* baffles me. I have long admired her books, particularly *The Wave,* for my money the best Civil War novel ever written. But *The Shadow of the Hawk* is another thing again. I finished its 494 pages unable to determine exactly why it is so unsatisfying and much more unable to puzzle out why Miss Scott wrote it. Its content hardly seems to demand all the patience, invention, and intelligence lavished on it. The means are grotesquely more imposing than the end.

The Shadow of the Hawk studies, practically forever, the mind and character of young Angus Pettigrew and his mother as they live their lives under the blighting influence of a sordid and permanent disaster. . . .

Just what Miss Scott wishes to prove I cannot say. Mrs. Pettigrew is a weak and irritating woman at the outset of the story and at its close is a trifle weaker and more irritating. The boy is bewildered and resentful throughout. Their characters are studied with scrupulous care, but this hardly compensates for the fact that they are both dull. The minor personages, no less carefully conceived, are no more attractive. Indeed, Miss Scott would appear to be fascinated by gray, mean people. She doesn't like them, makes bitter fun of them, but simply can't let them alone.

I have a dismayed feeling that I am missing something in *The Shadow of the Hawk* palpable to more perceptive readers. Is this one of those imposing Dreiserian studies of the effect of society upon character? Is it a lower-middle-class satire, Dickens without humor? Does it purport to say trenchant things about justice and prison reform? All or any of these are possibilities. My respect for Miss Scott's talents leads me to believe the possibilities exist. They just don't seem to exist for me, that's all. (pp. 70, 73)

> Clifton Fadiman, "Disappointments," in The New Yorker, *Vol. XVII, No. 11, April 26, 1941, pp. 70, 73-4.*

N. L. ROTHMAN

It is best to read [*The Shadow of the Hawk*] in a purely receptive mood, from page to page, without trying to plumb Miss Scott's motives. For if you decide too soon just what she is doing, you will find almost at once that she has steered away from this to quite another course. And you will find, too, that whatever her plan, it is always exciting and original writing. . . . Angus Pettigrew is ushered into our presence as a seven year old boy in a court room, watching his father being given a life sentence for murder. He watches his father waste and die in jail, and he watches his mother degenerate and grow spiritually corrupt under pressure. . . . Inside this Miss Scott builds painstakingly out of the great miscellany of a boy's daily life, thoughts, words, dreams, and nightmares, as Angus recedes further and further from a hostile world.

Yet quite early in the story Miss Scott's attention passes from Angus to those about him. The focus of the novel expands, and the clinical study of Angus becomes lost in a widening series of light character studies. The whole atmosphere of the book has changed by now. The early study of Angus seems pointless, since even if he had not been marred by the first ten years of his life, he would have been anyhow by the second. The book, however, is a provocative work, always expressive of its writer's vigor and originality.

> N. L. Rothman, "The Story of Angus Pettigrew," in The Saturday Review of Literature, *Vol. XXIV, No. 8, June 14, 1941, p. 12.*

PEGGY BACH

Evelyn Scott's reputation as a major American writer of the twenties was based on two very different aesthetic achievements: *Escapade* (1923), an impressionistic memoir, and *The Wave* (1929), an experimental Civil War novel. But few critics and readers recognized that *Background in Tennessee,* published in 1937, was not only a unique blend of autobiography and history that deserved attention for its own accomplishments, but that it provided means for responding more fully to *Escapade* and *The Wave,* and indeed to Scott's other works, and more importantly to Scott as a southern intellectual woman who moved across the national and expatriate literary scene of the twenties and thirties as a distinctive individual. . . . Scott's life, in interest and notoriety, parallels her large body of work and both are explained in *Background in Tennessee* more effectively than in any of her other books. (p. 703)

Background in Tennessee will evoke interest in the writing of a serious artist, created from aspects of her own personality, revealing an independent southern woman who was an individualist and an intellectual. *Background in Tennessee* is an account of the position and growth of Tennessee in the South; with a strong autobiographical emphasis, it forces a realization of the power and intellectuality that produced Scott's books. . . . (p. 704)

Diverging from the usual chronological format used in the history of a region, . . . Scott, in *Background in Tennessee,* recreates an *atmosphere* for growing up southern and an awareness of the difficulty of being an intellectual southern woman. . . . [In this] book, Scott combines qualities of both [personal accounts and objective histories with lyrical undertones]. Scott's Tennessee is presented not only through her concrete knowledge of dates and events that formed Tennessee but through the scope and depth of the intellect and imagination that formed Evelyn Scott. She attempts to reconcile her existence with that of the South as she analyzes the slow growth of culture in the South, politics, religion, women, the Indian, the Negro, and the poor white. Scott weaves factual information about Tennessee with everyday happenings in the life of a charming child and a young woman searching for an identity that eventually led her outside the boundaries of the South in her life and writing.

The aspect of Scott's career that separates her from other southern women writers—Kate Chopin, Grace King, Mary Murfree, Ellen Glasgow, Elizabeth Madox Roberts, Caroline Gordon—is that while Scott is southern, she cannot be classified as a regionalist. The issues and character situations she treats in her novels are universal. Perhaps Scott's life and writing career more nearly parallel that of Katherine A. Porter. There is a comparison between Scott and Roberts in the way their works were perceived by the regions of their birth (Clarksville and Springfield, Kentucky). Neither was recognized for the range and value of her work. Philosophy was a major element in the fiction of both. Roberts in her fantasy work *My Heart and My Flesh* (1927) displays an imaginative power close to Scott's that produced the last enigmatic chapter of *Escapade*. (p. 705)

Like the Fugitives and the Agrarians, and others who created the Southern Literary Renaissance, Scott was deeply concerned with the slow growth of culture in the South and wrote three books about the problematic situation of the artist: *Eva Gay* (1933), *Breathe Upon These Slain* (1934), and *Bread and A Sword* (1937). The time span between the Revolution and the Civil War, Scott determined, was not long enough for a substantial cultural growth to occur. After the Civil War, pioneers looked for adventures in trade, new land, not always influenced by economic determinism, but by something in their characters that caused them to leave sometimes secure circumstances for something new and different, and though they always looked forward to good books, good music, they remained immature and never progressed beyond exploration. Once the adventures in trade and exploration of new land were over, establishment of schools should have taken place. Schools were established . . . where theology and some of the classics were taught to the gentry, but no cultural explosion took place. (pp. 708-09)

Brought up in the southern caste system, Scott ignored her teachers—"So much of what is done to you as child is done in the dark"—out of a fascination for the Negro, the Indian, and the poor white. She was particularly fascinated by the Negro, and her close association with nurses and servants is responsible for her affinity with Faulkner's intimate, intuitive portrayal of the Negro. (p. 709)

Scott's comprehension of the Negro as a silent partner in the South's history was jarred when Wade, who had a voice as magnificent as Paul Robeson's and who had been a porter at the *dee*pot in Russellville and worked for [Scott's family] on Saturday, announced that he had a birthday in May. The realization that Negroes had birthdays as whites do . . . shocked her. Scott's image of the Negro as always belonging in someone else's kitchen, always tending someone else's children, was challenged when she rode through "niggertown" and saw them at home in their own kitchens, taking care of their own children.

And she claims she began to "wear the albatross" when she and a cousin, sent in a wagon to summon a Negro servant, Aunt Polly, did not offer her a ride. "Negroes make themselves twice beloved because of a good-humored grace with which they accept being, in effect, sworn at. There is a genius born of social degradation which is as inspired as the genius for conquest and domination." Some of the eastern Tennessee mountaineers who despised the Negro slave claimed he lived softly. After the war, the Negro sometimes mourned the loss of the security of food and a roof. "How absurd of the northern idealist to suppose men were to be made free by mere proclamation." . . . Scott emphasized that Negroes were the only southerners with a time sense applied philosophically to their lives, the only ones who lived instinctually; they lent color and richness to life in the South. (p. 710)

Scott's statement that she could never identify with anyone who had not once been poor is born of her keen observation of the "poor white," not so fortunate as those who moved within the circle of Scott's family and friends. Her mother disclaimed the existence of poor people and the attitudes of many people were not unlike those of historian James R. Gilmore, who Scott says disposed of the poor whites in much the same manner as Hitler did the Jews. Court Days in "Strawberry Alley" when the country people came to town held a special appeal for Scott, and although she was confined, like all young ladies of her social position, to her yard on these days, she always tried to escape to watch the festivities. With her feminist attitudes showing, she notes the role of the women, walking behind the men, napping with the children on the open lawn of the Courthouse, waiting while their men got wildly drunk, and sometimes being in danger when a drunken husband careened crazily in the family wagon on the return home. (p. 711)

Evelyn Scott was an integral part of one of the most exciting and changing eras in literary history, the era of the lost generation. From 1919, when Scott lived in Greenwich Village and during later periods when she returned to New York from extended absences in . . . [many] foreign places, she published regularly in . . . [a variety of periodicals]. Scott moved among many of the major poets and writers of that period and the thirties: Sinclair Lewis, Hart Crane, Marianne Moore, Gertrude Stein, and Lola Ridge.

Lola Ridge, in a critique that appeared in *Poetry,* March 1921, says of *Precipitations,* Scott's first volume of poetry: "I shall not forget the sensation—something like the suppressed excitement that you feel at the first inkling of some momentous event—with which I first read some of these poems" [see excerpt above]. Ridge was instrumental in Scott's introduction to Kay Boyle and Scott's subsequent involvement with the expatriate group of artists in Paris that included along with many of those from New York, Robert McAlmon, Ford Madox Ford, Isadore Duncan, Djuna Barnes, and Harry Crosby. Boyle gave her first novel, then called *The Imponderables,* to Scott for criticism. In *Being Geniuses Together* (1920-1930), Boyle says she was so affected by the brilliance and the ruthlessness of Scott's criticism and her statement that a "veil hung between my work and the reader—tear the veil away," that she completely rewrote the book. Boyle described Scott "as desperately intellectual, with neither delicacy of bone nor subtlety of wit of Marianne Moore, neither saint-like head nor the burning presence of Lola Ridge nor Lola's shining aura of belief," and said Scott asked surrender of mind "insidiously, with a terrible, terrible hunger of everyone she met."

It seems that Scott, while being a major contributor to the literary climate of the 1920s, moving in and among other major artists, never was a continuous member of any group, perhaps because of her extreme individualism.

Her associations were not only with poets and writers but with intellectuals in every field. In the thirties, she contributed an article, **"A Note on the Esthetic Significance of Photography,"** to *America and Alfred Steiglitz, A Collective Portrait* (1934). Inclusion in this collection suggests that Scott was closely aligned with and respected by those who knew Steiglitz.... In his autobiography, William Carlos Williams names Evelyn Scott as a new talent among writers associated with the *Others.* Granville Hicks places her at Yaddo in 1931, along with Cowley, Louis Adamic, and Horace Gregory. Scott wrote **"Communist Mentalities"** for *America Now—An Inquiry Into Civilization in the United States* (1938), edited by Harold E. Stearn; among major American intellectuals in many fields, she represented the novelist.

The Agrarians recognized Scott as an important southern writer and she agreed with some of the views they expressed in *I'll Take My Stand* (1930).... Scott, however, was neither a fugitive, an agrarian, nor an escapist; she did try hard to be a pacifist. "In the sense of an intention to re-establish in the southerner a regional pride which may be his salvation," she said, "the I-take-any-stand agrarians are certainly on the right track." But Scott felt the agrarians' view of the South was a romantic one and that like many southerners whose very being was saturated with an either "before the war" or "after the war" time sense, they envisioned not only a South that had lost through the war, but a South that had never been. Scott realized that her own vision of the glamour of Tennessee was "generated by product of personal emotion."

The authorial personality is deliberately strong in all Scott's books; she wrote with a psychological intention, to convey philosophical contexts, wishing "to communicate what life is to me." She incorporated events and characters in her actual past fictionally into her books. Nannette in *Escapade* is Scott's mother.... In *A Calendar of Sin* (1932) the character Edwin George is patterned after Grandfather Thomas. *Migrations* (1927) is set in a fictional Clarksville, "Mimms." In *Eva Gay* she wrote about a childhood friend, Mary, whom she loved as no

one else—"certain feelings she engendered, which belonged to her, and to no other being, were forced so deep underground they cannot be brought to the surface again"—and this book contains information about C. Kay-Scott's earlier life in Africa. *The Wave,* of which Scott says, "the only hero of the book is war," depicts nearly one hundred episodes about people being caught up in the action of the Civil War.

Scott's autobiographical books, *Escapade* and *Background in Tennessee* are unique. *Escapade,* rich in imagist language, is written out of a strong emotional conception from a subjective point of view, and Scott, using the technique of interior monologue, and writing in a poetic prose style, shares with the reader an experience of senses. In *Backgrounds in Tennessee,* Scott filters her intellect and memory through a Socratic dialogue and produces a sweeping intuition and involvement with the complexities that gave impetus to the creative force of Evelyn Scott. Both autobiographies are atypical of the genre. *Escapade* progresses from arrival in Rio de Janeiro to return to New York, but immersed in feeling, one is unaware of time; there is no chronological order in *Background in Tennessee* as Scott mixes dates, events, and reminiscences. Neither book emphasizes the events. One has only to compare *Escapade* with C. Kay-Scott's autobiography, *Life Is Too Short* (1943), especially the section dealing with the same experience, to be fully aware of the aesthetic qualities, the conceptual approach, and the technical and stylistic composition of *Escapade.*

Scott's descriptive talent, likened to that of Virginia Woolf, is utilized in *Escapade* not to make the reader see, but to feel. The description in her history of Tennessee is more natural, more nearly in the oral tradition with its urgency and energy. Both *Escapade* and *Background in Tennessee* are subjective, highly personal, but the *degree* of subjectivity effects the most significant difference. *Escapade* sustains an inner-outer psychic relation, but the feelings expressed are self-generated, imagination produced. Outside influences in *Background in Tennessee* produce inner friction *in conflict with* outside reflections rather than *in contrast to* them as in *Escapade. Background in Tennessee,* says Scott, "is a sixteen year love affair with Tennessee, disturbed at intervals by a deep unhappiness, later disillusion." *Escapade* is a six year love affair, disturbed by poverty and extreme illness. Both are "reactions after a love passage."

Scott believed that her unorthodox behavior caused Tennessee to disown her, and she attempted for twenty years to retaliate and disown Tennessee. (pp. 713-16)

Despite the high critical acclaim she received, Scott was variously labeled a Freudian or a nihilist. She was accused of an "act of treachery toward the 'real' South" in her writing. But Robert Welker calls Evelyn Scott one of "Tennessee's own." ... And so she was, obsessed with and in possession of Tennessee.

But Evelyn Scott was more than a Tennessee writer, more than a southern writer. She was a demonstrably important writer, who may one day again be perceived as major. (pp. 716-17)

Peggy Bach, "Evelyn Scott: The Woman in the Foreground," in The Southern Review, *Vol. 18, No. 4, Autumn, 1982, pp. 703-17.*

Vikram Seth

1952-

Indian-born novelist, poet, and travel writer.

Seth elicited enthusiastic critical response for his verse novel, *The Golden Gate* (1986), which is modeled on Alexander Pushkin's *Eugene Onegin*. Like Pushkin's work, *The Golden Gate* consists of a series of sonnets through which the narrator relates and comments upon the adventures of several characters. Using iambic tetrameter for nearly six hundred stanzas, Seth examines the intertwined romantic lives of five young Californians in the early 1980s. Critics praised *The Golden Gate* as a work of technical virtuosity suffused with wit and accessible language that moves from elevated literary allusion to colloquial speech. Through his characters, Seth explores such topics as religious guilt, the nuclear arms race, the ethics of occupational choice, sexual politics, love, and death. Some critics claimed that the characters act as spokespersons for particular ideologies and could be construed as stereotypes. However, *The Golden Gate* is generally regarded as a bold achievement at a time when strict adherence to meter and rhyme goes largely unheeded. D. J. Enright commented: "*The Golden Gate* is a technical triumph, unparalleled (I would hazard) in English. We may not have scorned the sonnet, but we shall hardly have thought it capable of this sustained sequentiality, speed, elegance, wit and depth of insight."

In his first book, *From Heaven Lake: Travels through Sinkiang and Tibet* (1983), Seth chronicles the travails and observations of his journey from Nanjing University in China to his home in Calcutta, India, via Tibet. Seth spices the account with self-deprecating humor and ruminations on such topics as the consequences of the Chinese Cultural Revolution, the annihilation of Tibetan temples, and the treatment of foreigners by the Chinese. Critics lauded Seth's keen ability to convey the quirks and attitudes of Chinese culture. In his volume of poetry, *The Humble Administrator's Garden* (1984), Seth reflects on his experiences in India and at Oxford, Nanjing, and Stanford Universities. Claude Rawson noted that these poems are "observant of pathos, of ironies of behaviour, and of the unexpected small exuberances of life."

JONATHAN MIRSKY

[*From Heaven Lake*] is the perfect travel book. Its quality and promise are instantly plain in the picture inside the back jacket: it shows the author in the lotus position surrounded by marijuana plants. Vikram Seth does not bore you by saying that west China, through which he travelled by truck and on foot, through Tibet and into Nepal, is often covered with the Weed. He merely mentions that when the Gansu marijuana flowers the air is intoxicating.

An Indian, educated at Oxford, Stanford and Nanjing, Seth speaks and reads Chinese. He is a wonderful companion, therefore, as we follow his trip back to India in 1981, hitchhiking, walking, slogging through rivers and across the leech-ridden

Tibetan hills. He is grumpy, bored, beset by headaches and fascinated by the lorry drivers, officials, children and soldiers he meets along the way.

Most travel books feel wrong if one has made the same journey. Seth reminded me of the smell and bustle of the Gobi's one-camel towns, and of the pilgrims pressing through the aromatic and flickering temples in Lhasa. He can chill the blood, too. He describes Tibetan funeral practices, literally a form of butchery, but retains his objectivity enough to treat with disdain Chinese who watched the undertakers at work and laughed. . . .

Very few foreigners have spent the night in Chinese truck parks and country inns. Few have had even a meal with a Chinese family, unless it was carefully prearranged. Seth has, and he notices everything and tells us about it. . . . Seth is the sort of author who makes you glad he found out all the things that can be done with a yak—alive or dead.

> *Jonathan Mirsky, in a review of "From Heaven Lake: Travels through Sinkiang and Tibet," in* New Statesman, *Vol. 106, No. 2742, October 7, 1983, p. 25.*

ANDREW ROBINSON

[Seth's book *From Heaven Lake*], his first, illustrated with his own photographs, emerged from a desire to return to his family in Delhi, after seven years away, via Tibet, instead of flying back from Hong Kong in the usual way. He is a phlegmatic but sensitive traveller, delightfully alive to all that he sees and hears. Speaking quite good Chinese (and indeed travelling under his given Chinese name) gives him, and the reader, a tremendous advantage; in fact, without Chinese, we may be sure he would never have succeeded. Pitfalls *en route* are clearly tough: obsessive Chinese bureaucracy, numbing cold and searing heat, unpredictable hitch-hiking and appalling road conditions, loss of baggage and its miraculous retrieval, the 'language-rapists' who use him as a 'punchbag' for their English practice. The writing not only catches the immediacy of these hazards, especially in some well-chosen exchanges, it also never loses sight of the excitement of mixing with another culture. Seth has conveyed the odd tension of difficult, solitary travel with an overall schedule to keep, the juxtaposition of happy-go-lucky feelings and gnawing insecurity about what happens next; his complex sense of release on reaching Kathmandu and a broadly familiar culture at the end of the trip is almost palpable. (pp. 713-14)

Along with the lively descriptions of problems, people and landscape (informed by the author's academic knowledge of China) there are interesting reflections on the effects of the Cultural Revolution, the truly heart-breaking destruction of Tibetan temples, the curious continuing co-existence of Mao and the Dalai Lama as Tibetan deities, and the Chinese attitutde to foreigners: 'officialdom treats the foreigner as one would a valuable panda given to fits of mischief'. (p. 714)

> Andrew Robinson, in a review of "From Heaven Lake: Travels through Sinkiang and Tibet," in British Book News, November, 1983, pp. 713-14.

RICHARD COBB

The travel books that are the most enjoyable to read are about journeys that were extremely uncomfortable and occasionally perilous. There is any amount of discomfort and quite a few perils in Mr Seth's [*From Heaven Lake*], which is also wonderfully visual and with an acute sensitivity to speech, gesture and stance. It is beautifully written, always in a low key, and is enlivened by a gentle and kindly humour. The author is disarmingly modest and treats himself as a slightly comical figure.

> Richard Cobb, in a review of "From Heaven Lake," in The Spectator, Vol. 251, Nos. 8110 & 8111, December 17, 1983, p. 52.

NICHOLAS GARLAND

Vikram Seth, the 29-year-old author of *From Heaven Lake,* is adventurous, restless and inquisitive. When opportunity knocks he grabs at it, and when it doesn't he gives it a little push. During a vacation he decided on the spur of the moment to hitchhike home from his university in Eastern China through Tibet and Nepal to Delhi. The book is an account of that journey. He ponders on his taste for travelling and asks himself whether he ranges so far from his native Calcutta merely to accumulate material for future nostalgia. The question is not answered directly; Seth gives the impression that he wanders the world simply because it is there.

He shows that old-fashioned travel, felt by many to have been ruined by jet airlines and package tours, is still possible. If

you are as brave and resourceful as Seth, you too can get away from it all and explore.

He once plunged into an underground irrigation canal because the water looked so tempting and waded in pitch darkness up 50 metres of the icy stream. Half way along he began to get scared. His feet went numb with cold and it occurred to him there might be twists and even branches in the channel. '. . . It could still be a long way to the exit. Panic I tell myself is ridiculous—I can't be far from the mouth. . . . I talk myself forwards: a little further, a little further. . . .' There were many other times during his journey when panic would have been an entirely proper reaction to the difficulties and discomforts he encountered, but Seth is a very cool customer and triumphed over everything that climate, altitude, heat, insects and Chinese bureaucracy could put in his way. At last, without quite knowing he'd done it, he walked across the border into Nepal. . . .

One of the main pleasures of this book is seeing China through an Indian's eye. . . . [Seth] describes neatly a paradox: if you are born among the poorest of the poor you may be better off under the dictatorship of communist China, but as soon as your lot improves, free and democratic India, with all its problems, becomes infinitely preferable.

His reward for having endured considerable loneliness, illness and danger was the tremendous pleasure he took from the friendship and company of scores of strangers, many rare insights into life in modern China and the experience of having been close to the deserts and mountains and rivers of the mysterious lands he crossed. You cannot help but admire and envy him. Seth knows, however, that a travel book is bound to be a sort of self-portrait and he mars his account of this wonderful journey by an attempt to emphasise his poetic and dreamy side. He sometimes even breaks into bad poetry to express the intensity of his feelings, not realising that his material is so good it does not require more than honest telling. The sudden inclusion of some lines of verse on insomnia or a flight of fancy about the miraculous qualities of water is a distraction when the reader wants to know what happened next. It is perfectly clear that the author is as tough as old boots and extremely matter-of-fact. His image of himself as a gentle pilgrim leads him to sacrifice too much straightforward reporting. It is tantalising to the point of irritation to be taken, as it were, to a remote Chinese town and to learn so little about it.

However, one is grateful for what one does learn. For example, the terror of the Cultural Revolution is fading even if the pain is still felt, as China quite literally puts itself together again. Ancient buildings wrecked by teams of Red Guards are being repaired here and there, and the survivors of families brutally torn apart are reunited. Seth found that Chinese bureaucrats could be unexpectedly cooperative when they felt like it; it surprised me how many tourists he came across, including several individuals like himself going it alone. . . .

One forgives [Seth] a few horribly awkward phrases, such as his description of '. . . the last multi-coloured spasms of sunset', because, whatever his weaknesses as a writer, it comes through clearly that he is no mean traveller.

> Nicholas Garland, "Across the Himalayas," in The Spectator, Vol. 252, No. 8118, February 11, 1984, p. 24.

TOM D'EVELYN

Looking at *The Humble Administrator's Garden,* it's not clear that Seth has written poetry that will last forever. Can the quiet voice of this traveler be heard over the metaphysical feedback emanating from the poetry shelves these days? . . . [The poems **"Homeless"** and **"A Little Night Music"**] are "accessible," economical, plain. They approach universal experiences. **"Homeless"** appeals to the wayfarer in all of us.

The plainness of the diction, the cumulative force of the repeated syntax in the first stanza ("those who . . . who . . . who . . ."), the repeated infinitives in the second part ("To know," "to review," "to lie down," "to know"), and the sense of finality in the final two lines (repetition of the clause beginning with "that"): what could have been mere repetition and fatigue—analogues to the experience of the wandering—*adds up,* in this poem, to a sense of quiet, dignified pathos.

Quiet dignity is a quality exhibited by **"A Little Night Music"** as well. Where the rhymes of **"Homeless"** were spaced by unrhymed lines, in this poem rhyme is a crucial structural element. Notice which words are rhymed. Taken apart from their contexts, these rhymes would have to be called "easy" and yet in context they reinforce the meaning of the poem: a moment in time and space, repetitions within the uniqueness of that moment ("He . . . plays again"), an accidental meeting at night (the sound of the erhu more precious for the surrounding darkness), and the unity of mankind—in sum, the access of the universal causing unprompted tears.

These poems are typical of the verses in *The Humble Administrator's Garden.* Mr. Seth has chosen to represent in his poems feeling of the widest applicability. Given the exotic nature of his background, he could have gone in the other direction, toward the specialized feeling and idea, toward myth and cultural arcana, toward anthropology.

Instead of the pseudoscientific, Seth focuses on the mundane with unusual clarity. The clarity is not only in the image (that's not enough) but in the rhythm. He is one of the few young poets who has taken the trouble to learn, really learn, the disciplines of meter. (p. 21)

Furthermore, Seth is not afraid of the declarative statement, nor does he forget that the poem is its proper testing ground. When a poem entitled **"Unclaimed"** begins "To make love with a stranger is the best"—and to develop—and to subvert—the argument, testing its strength as it should, as other poems by Seth do, one is forced back onto the title and its real ironies: the experience is exhilarating. One lives through a little contemporary history, the history of a popular idea, in the process of reading the poem.

"Unclaimed" is ironical but not ambiguous. Ironies we've had enough of in recent poetry, but then there are precious few in *The Humble Administrator's Garden,* and this is cause enough to welcome its appearance and wish Mr. Seth a long life writing good verses. (p. 22)

> Tom D'Evelyn, "The New-Old Poems of Vikram Seth," in The Christian Science Monitor, *August 21, 1985, pp. 21-2.*

RAYMOND TONG

Although he was born and grew up in India, Seth's further studies have taken him to Oxford University, Stanford University and China, so that he has had considerable experience of four cultures from the inside. This experience is reflected in his first book of poems, *The Humble Administrator's Garden,*

in which he gently considers various aspects of these cultures, and gracefully observes the places and people encountered.

The poems are divided according to background into three sections: China, India and California (with occasional references to England). While a high level is generally maintained throughout, with little that is marginal, it would appear that the best poems are all contained in the oriental sections. Among the most attractive poems about China are **"The Accountant's House"**, recalling a visit to a Chinese family, and the title poem, in which Mr Wang, the Humble Administrator, proudly surveys his garden where among other wonders 'A plump gold carp nudges a lily pad / And shakes the raindrops off like mercury'. Such delight in exact observation is also evident in some of the Indian poems. . . . Equally enjoyable in this impressive first collection is the long poem, **"From the Babur-Nama"**, consisting of excerpts from the memoirs of the first Moghul emperor.

> Raymond Tong, in a review of "The Humble Administrator's Garden," in British Book News, *September, 1985, p. 559.*

CLAUDE RAWSON

There's no . . . folksiness in Vikram Seth's [*The Humble Adminsitrator's Garden*]:

> At home the grandmother has sat down to breakfast
> And complains that she is ignored, unloved.
> Her blood pressure is high, her spirits low.
> She is not allowed to eat gulabjamuns.
> The doctor has compiled an Index of Foods
> And today, to compound things, is a non-grain fast.
> Her dentures hurt. She looks at a stuffed tomato
> And considers how to darn her grandson's sweater.

The rich social notation and the ironic flatness recall Eliot's "Aunt Helen" or some of the social vignettes of *Lustra,* but Pound's idiom of sharp laconic observation is wholly assimilated into a fastidious probing language that becomes confidently Seth's own. It comes over without dialectal mannerisms or Poundian archaizing, despite its exotic settings, Indian, Californian and Chinese, the latter evoking or "imitating" Pound's Cathay: **"From a Traveller"** is a variation on "Exile's Letter" in a People's Republic setting. . . . The title poem and **"The Accountant's House"** are small masterpieces of delicate verbal and emotional discipline, observant pathos, of ironies of behaviour, of the unexpected small exuberances of life. And there are some beautiful stanzaic poems, with a sturdy Yvor Winters seriousness (he and Donald Davie seem to have been Seth's other formative influences) transfigured by a witty grace: **"A Little Night Music"** and the delightful **"Research in Jiangsu Province"**. (p. 138)

> Claude Rawson, "Knowing the Throne," in The Times Literary Supplement, *No. 4323, February 7, 1986, pp. 137-38.*

THOMAS M. DISCH

Like the bridge for which it is named, Vikram Seth's *The Golden Gate* is a thing of anomalous beauty: a long narrative poem set in present-day San Francisco, and that is odd enough, but what is odder, a rhyming poem in strict meter that is a "good read" after the manner of the better sort of fiction in the women's magazines. If Mary Gordon had written a contemporary romance that revolved around the "issues" of nuclear disarmament and sexual politics (viewed from an enlightened Catholic perspective) and had then boiled down her prose into 8,250 lines of verse, the result would be very like *The Golden Gate*.

The real surprise of this "novel-in-verse" is not that it has been done at all (for there has been a boomlet of narrative poetry lately) but that it has been done so well. (p. 7)

Seth writes poetry as it has not been written for nearly a century—that's to say, with the intention that his work should give pleasure to that ideal Common Reader for whom good novelists have always aspired to write. For most poetry professionals earning their living by the teaching of creative writing, Seth's ambitions, and his accomplishment, will be abhorrent if not simply incomprehensible. Does one write poetry to entertain? Are the affairs and courtships of five Bay Area yuppies—described as such on the very jacket of the book—a suitable subject for poetry? Are wit and grace and mere cleverness to be counted among the desiderata of poetry? Dullness forfend!

Yet if you have no vested interest in keeping poetry within the generic boundaries established by academic criticism and by the customary, sanctioned sloth of most poets (slim volumes take less work, after all, than thick), you will almost certainly find *The Golden Gate* an agreeable and judiciously balanced (not too heavy, not too light) tale that has been enhanced by the power of poetry to the narrative equivalent of haute cuisine.

This is not to say that there aren't stretches of the story that don't sag (but isn't that so of most novels, even very good ones?) or that the verse is unexceptionably fine. Some stanzas gush, some lines scan only under duress, and a couple of the larger scenes misfire. Seth's form accommodates most narrative needs naturally, but its artifice does become obtrusive when applied to long speeches and soliloquies. At one point a Berrigan-like priest delivers a 19 stanza-long peroration against the arms race, the effect of which was like hearing Jonathan Schell's *The Fate of the Earth* transformed into rhyming *bon mots*. Even the converted may become restive with such preaching.

Those few exceptions taken, I thoroughly enjoyed the book, following its quadrangular romance with the same degree of amused involvement or involved bemusement I would give to one of Woody Allen's sedater comedies of sexual intrigue. (pp. 7, 11)

The chief attraction of *The Golden Gate* is not its story as such, but its ever-recognizable and ever-fresh representation of upper middle-class life in the 1980s, a life that Seth celebrates with none of the dyspeptic acerbity of such prose chroniclers of the current scene as Ann Beattie or Frederick Barthelme. His characters are not invented to afford his readers the pleasure of knowing themselves to be more knowing. They are all of them quite nice people—good-looking, well-bred, prosperous, principled, affectionate—"yuppies" as the jacket copy has it, which is an easily broken code for "people like you and me." The effect of such characters, en masse, together with Seth's chroniclings of representative California pleasures is like seeing a great many Renoirs all at once. . . .

The rhyme-scheme of [*The Golden Gate*] is sonnetary, but the meter is four beats per line, not five. A four-beat line—the natural meter of ballads and doggerel—is much easier to sustain over the long stretch for both poet and reader. The model for this not quite-a-sonnet is Sir Charles Johnston's superb trans-

lation of Pushkin's *Eugene Onegin* (1977), and it is not alone the meter of that marvelous long poem that inspired Seth's emulation. The spirit of Pushkin's verse romance informs Seth's own tale at every turn, and Pushkin's intrusion of his own voice as commentator and master of ceremonies gives Seth a model for the proper balance between narrative momentum and poetic fun and games in his own poem.

Rarely has a poetic role-model been so sedulously imitated, and even more rarely has such imitation yielded so healthy an offspring. The least that can be said of both Pushkin's and Seth's novels-in-verse is that unlike so many would-be epics theirs are never monotonous. Both portray ordinary life without falling into banality, and one finishes both books with a sense that poetry rarely yields, a sense that life, however messy it may get from time to time, is really, pretty much, a bowl of cherries. (p. 11)

> *Thomas M. Disch, "Sunlight, Coffee and the Papers," in* Book World—The Washington Post, *March 23, 1986, pp. 7, 11.*

X. J. KENNEDY

[A] serious commotion in the air has preceded *The Golden Gate*. For all I know, it just might presage a literary storm. Already, Gore Vidal, a writer not given to gush, has dubbed the book "the great California novel." Another tough-minded critic, D. J. Enright, has chalked up for its author "a technical triumph unparalleled in English." In Massachusetts, one book dealer has been demanding $50 for a bootlegged set of the proofs. In Manhattan literary enclaves, I'm told, pirated photocopies of the book have been circulating more busily than cocaine with Perrier on the side. . . .

A novel about the manners and morals of Silicon Valley yuppies might well be expected to make at least a local stir, but why all this coast-to-coast hullabaloo? The answer is clear: It isn't merely Seth's revelations of yuppiedom. Awe strikes whoever casts a glance up this mountain of technical virtuosity. *The Golden Gate*—all of it, even its table of contents, its dedication to the author's friend and critic, UCLA poet and professor Timothy Steele, its autobiographical notes—is written in verse: 593 repeated stanzas, strictly measured and rhymed. (p. 1)

[Why] did he cast his novel in verse, anyway? Why has he used "The dusty bread molds of Onegin / In the brave bakery of Reagan"? He tells us why: for fun. He'd aspire to nothing higher than verse. Still, poetry keeps sneaking in—

> As in an airless room a curtain
> Parts to admit the evening breeze,
> So John's exhausted and uncertain
> Tension admits a transient ease. . . .

For all its metaphoric moments, though, *The Golden Gate* is a true novel, as author and publisher insist. Realistic, written in scenes, it conducts us on a psychological safari through five interesting souls. Upwardly mobile young professionals, they all live and work in San Francisco and the Silicon Valley. By night, Janet Hayakawa plays drums for the rock group Liquid Sheep; by day, she sculpts. Formerly, Jan slept with John Brown, a dour young bomb-builder who, feeling adrift now, admits, "The Dow-Jones of my heart's depressed." (That Jan can still stand to listen to this guy shows you the height of her generosity.)

When she does John a big favor, by advertising for a new lover for him, Jan looses an avalanche of fate. It sweeps on to involve Liz Dorati, a sensitive woman lawyer, and her brother Ed, an advertising man who writhes under the weight of a Catholic upbringing. Ed's sense of sin, more muscular than a pillar saint's, keeps wrestling with his gay nature. The wrestling match speeds up when he meets Phil Weiss, divorced single parent, a political idealist who has thrown over his high-tech job to crusade against the missiles he once made.

Seth, it soon appears, knows these people inside out. He understands the troubled conscience of the systems analyst who fears that his labors will speed the Big Bang. And Seth knows their habitat: singles bars and celebratory bashes, wine making feats and protest rallies. Besides, the novel abounds in vivid minor characters, some of them animals: Ed's pet iguana Schwarzenegger and, most memorable, Liz's formidable cat Charlemagne, lord of her hearth and bane of lover John.

What Robert Frost once affirmed was his big secret, Seth demonstrates anew. As Frost pointed out, the twists and turns of ordinary, idiomatic speech, when laid against a metrical line, give that line tremendous strength. In Seth's strict verse, today's small talk mingles with literary allusion—as when Jan tells John, "Choose a richer lens to see with. . . . Trade in that zoom for a wide angle. . . . You are the DJ of your fate." Even when such dialogue couldn't really come out of a human mouth, Seth persuades us that it just might do so anyway.

Deserving of applause though he is, Seth will probably get even more of it than he has coming. No doubt he will be proclaimed the reinventor of narrative verse in America, although in truth we've had a whole slew of long story-poems lately. At least, recent and notable efforts include those of James Merrill, Frederick Feirstein, Richard Moore, and Frederick Turner. Still, I don't know when a versifier has proved better versed in a verse-form than Seth. Such fluency probably hasn't been heard in English since Alexander Pope went around letting heroic couples effortlessly tumble from his lips.

Essential to an enjoyment of **The Golden Gate,** I'd suggest, is to read it slowly, silently pronouncing each line in the head's echo-chamber. Although this advice goes against the wisdom of every speed-reading course, the method may enable readers to savor more keenly the book's delectable art.

But isn't **The Golden Gate** stultifyingly artificial? To enclose a story in a strict verse form, I'll admit, is to place a conspicuous frame around it. Seth underscores this artifice with occasional asides that recall Lord Byron's in "Don Juan" ("Reader, enough of this apology . . ."). Some will be tempted to imagine Seth's novel translated into prose, without the stanzas. Even so denuded, it would still be well worth a read.

In that case, with the verse removed, a reader might complain that these people after all are ordinary; that the end of the affair between Janet Hayakawa and John the bomb-designer seems a bit melodramatic, like a climax in soap opera—or in a life. Seth gently preaches indirect sermons we have heard before; on honesty, on loyalty to friends, on the need for the human species to survive. I don't mind those sermons, myself, when the preacher is so eloquently wise.

Luckily, **The Golden Gate** could no more successfully be taken out of its Onegin stanza than a dolphin taken out of its tank could be kept alive. Like the frame that Edgar Degas casts around his ordinary drinkers of absinthe, Seth's verse-form calls our attention to people we know, or think we know. A

splendid tour de force, **The Golden Gate** finally hooks us into caring less about its author's skill than in caring how its sad and wistful comedy will turn out. For pages, we forget Seth's incredible dexterity. Mesmerized, we watch, as in a kaleidoscope, the shifting and resettling patterns of five lives. (pp. 1, 7)

X. J. Kennedy, in a review of "The Golden Gate: A Novel in Verse," in Los Angeles Times Book Review, *April 6, 1986, pp. 1, 7.*

JOHN GROSS

[**The Golden Gate**] is a thoroughly Californian novel, peopled by unmistakably Californian characters. But it is a Californian novel with a difference. Vikram Seth was moved to start work on it after reading Pushkin's *Eugene Onegin* in the translation by Charles Johnston, and like *Onegin* it is a novel in verse—fast-moving, rhyming verse, with the lines arranged in sonnet-like stanzas.

As such, it can hardly fail to be one of the curiosities of the season. Verse-novels of any kind are a rarity, and at first sight a verse-novel that takes in Fassbinder and Jane Fonda, bumper stickers and Gestalt groups, has the allure of the positively outlandish. But how much remains when the novelty has worn off?

A great deal. Mr. Seth is witty, dexterous and imaginative; he has fashioned a medium flexible enough to accommodate the most disparate material, from a game of Scrabble to an invocation to St. Francis, without losing momentum or sinking into doggerel (well, hardly ever). Love, death, cookies from Just Desserts—the varieties of experience are well represented in **The Golden Gate**. Equally important, the transitions between them are skillfully handled.

As in a traditional epic, a good deal of technical information is purveyed—about wine making, architecture, natural history. On the other hand it seems safe to say that some of the incidents in the poem have never been treated in verse before, and not very often in prose either—a discussion about the healthiest diet for a pet iguana (go slow on the calcium), an account of someone getting rid of somebody else at a party by doing the first uncouth thing he can think of (using the earpiece of his glasses to eat guacamole).

Incidental pleasures abound—a delightful conversation about the Tin-tin books, for example; some memorably evoked menus; a heartfelt diatribe against babies—"A pity that the blubbering blobs / Come unequipped with volume knobs." There is some effervescent wordplay (not too much, though). And the verse is often lightly allusive, with echoes of Andrew Marvell and Thomas Gray, a bare-faced borrowing from Hilaire Belloc's *Cautionary Tales,* a comic half-concealed reference to Sir Isaac Newton and his dog Diamond—this last in connection with Liz's cat Charlemagne, a creature that plays a sizable part in the story and deserves a place in any good feline anthology.

The inventiveness of the verse keeps the story going, and saves it from sentimentality. Recounted in prose, indeed, it might not be that much of a story. The characters come close to being stereotypes; stand back from them, and they start looking like the streamlined figures in advertisements. But rhythm and rhyme and imagery cast their spell, and Mr. Seth succeeds in making the idyllic moments and the sudden gusts of pathos much more credible than they would be if we encountered them in a conventional novel.

In the end—and it is the measure of his success—the story keeps the verse going as well. The verbal cameos and aerobatics, elegantly executed though most of them are, would not be enough in themselves to hold the reader's attention for 300 pages. But once we have been hooked by John and Liz and Janet and Ed and Phil (and Charlemagne), what would have been merely decorative or ingenious becomes infused with feeling.

It should be said, too, that Mr. Seth is wise enough not to overdo the fireworks. Perhaps the most noteworthy technical aspect of the poem is the naturalness of the dialogue, the lifelike, spontaneous-seeming manner in which the characters talk while simultaneously satisfying the demands of rhyme-scheme and meter.

Here and there *The Golden Gate* is too cute for its own good; occasionally inspiration falters, or we become aware of an emotional soft center. But for the most part the poem is a splendid achievement, equally convincing in its exhilaration and its sadness.

> *John Gross, in a review of "The Golden Gate," in*
> The New York Times, *April 14, 1986, p. 16.*

JOHN HOLLANDER

[This] brilliantly fashioned tale of life among a number of Bay Area yuppies [*The Golden Gate*] is never anything less than quaintly, and mostly unqualifiedly, marvelous. It is written entirely in (although, in a deeper sense, "through" and "with") the intricately patterned fourteen-line stanza of Pushkin's *Eugene Onegin*—down to the dedication, the table of contents, and the autobiographical note. The use of expertly controlled verse to give moral substance and extraordinary wit and plangency to a far from extraordinary tale is an astonishing achievement in its own right.

Seth's post-post-heroic protagonist, John (ex-Berkeley, now Silicon Valley), is launched into introspection—and, indeed, into interestingness—by an appropriate messenger:

> Successful in his field, though only
> Twenty-six, respected, lonely,
> One evening as he walked across
> Golden Gate Park, the ill-judged toss
> Of a red frisbee almost brained him.
> He thought, "If I died, who'd be sad?
> Who'd weep? Who'd gloat? Who would be glad? . . ."

Pushkin's poem starts with his hero complaining to himself of his lot while a post chaise carries him along a dusty road. Here, the subsequent events seem shaped by the character of the red, angelic plaything. John consults with his friend Janet Hayakawa, a sculptor and part-time musician (her group is called "Liquid Sheep") who puts a personals ad in the *Bay Guardian* on his behalf. It is answered unsatisfactorily at first. . . . But finally it yields a letter, leading into the plot and the rest of the novel's characters. These include Elizabeth Dorati, a lawyer from a family of Sonoma County winegrowers; her brother Ed; John's friend Phil Weiss; a host of background figures and family members; and many cats.

The events themselves—meetings, parties, partings, concerts, recognitions, peripeties, deaths—provide the occasions for Seth's verse. And his narrative strategies and control of tonal range proceed to do their remarkable work, giving to his personages and places a depth that they would seem to belie. (Readers may find him visiting the world he has created, on page 78, in the person of one "Kim Tarvesh.") Indeed, the book's major character may be the narration, and its true post-heroic hero its verse. The way in which that verse tells stories is central to the novel's substance.

Pushkin's octosyllabic stanza (well handled, in English, in the elegant translations—pace Nabokov—of Oliver Elton and Charles Johnston) is a complex instrument. Its rhymes group the lines so as to allow many shifts and turns of syntax and arrangements of rhetorical moves: deferring punch lines or bringing them up quickly, framing descriptive set pieces or stringing together rags of talk, allowing rhymed couplets to sum up, or to undercut, a quatrain that has preceded them. The stanza deploys the three possible ways of building quatrains with two rhymes, and leads the reader through these modes. A somewhat crude self-descriptive example might go like this:

> The stanza of Pushkin's *Onegin*
> Unrolls in strict *abab*'s
> Of quatrains (rhyme can be a plague in
> Lines that are quite as short as these);
> Then a mere couplet seems to break
> The quatrains' flow—only to make
> Adjacent couplets we should call
> A form of quatrain after all.
> Then comes the final way to play
> (In the form we remember from
> Tennyson's *In Memoriam*)
> A quatrain on rhymes *b* and *a*,
> Until at Closure's stern commands, a
> Couplet will terminate the stanza.

But in practice, the reader is made aware not of the structure of this intricate framework, but of what is being woven onto it, so that the aphoristic or meditative asides, or the several remarkable occasions on which the character and behavior of cats are pointedly discussed, move effortlessly along, showing none of the skeletons of contrivance. And yet whenever, as a local device, the stanza's operations are momentarily pushed into the foreground, it is in the great old way. A rhyme's brightly calling attention to itself will point out some significant incongruity that may have general import for the story. Thus at one point the author himself asks, "How can I (careless of time) use / The dusty bread molds of Onegin / In the brave bakery of Reagan?" and the moral and aesthetic fall across the two rhyming words defines the book's kind of softly rueful comic space. Seth uses his stanza's frame to catalog the tokens of this bakery's world with a mildly Popean irony:

> John looks about him with enjoyment.
> What a man needs, he thinks, is health;
> Well-paid, congenial employment;
> A house; a modicum of wealth;
> Some sunlight; coffee and the papers;
> Artichoke hearts adorned with capers;
> A Burberry trench coat; a Peugeot;
> And in the evening, some Rameau
> Or Couperin; a home-cooked dinner;
> A Stilton, and a little port;
> And so to a duvet. In short,
> In life's brief game to be a winner
> A man must have . . . oh yes, above
> All else, of course, someone to love.

Or he can cut away at his line groupings with the rhythms of carefully staged conversation. . . . The author can build, through a splendidly paced series of 20 stanzas, a homiletic oration of a mildly activist priest at an antinuclear demonstration. Or he can shape a descriptive set piece right up to where it bumps against a gentle reminder of the nature of its own sentiment. . . . The narrative distancing that gives an edge to Seth's accounts of his young people oscillates from far to close: his authorial hand can point its finger and, some lines later, caress. It is not only that this writer's ear for rhymed verse is perfect; so is his ear for colloquial discourse, for the inadvertent ironies of commercial product-naming, for the tonalities of callow and sincere self-expression. And so is his almost John O'Hara-like eye and ear for the cultural fact and the revealing detail. But in this case, the elements of such detail are almost magically formed so that their sociological rightness and their rhymed and rhythmic role seem to echo each other.

Throughout this admirable book the sheer delight in technique is a figure for a kind of ultimate intellectual joy taken in attention and discourse itself. So many moments in this book make the reader want to grab someone and read lines aloud to him or her. (I remember in my youth doing this with Thurber, Perelman, Parker.) The narrative's control of pace, of nuance, of discovery, of implication makes the reader trust the worthiness of the objects of its attention. And yet this book was written for readers skeptical by nature of these objects, these slightly more than Neil Simonish people, this range of incident. Its triumph is to set up that irony and overcome the dangers it exhibits.

There are very few masters of rhymed verse writing in America (Wilbur, Hecht, Merrill, Daryl Hine), and very few prototypes (the later parts of *Don Juan,* Clough's *Amours de Voyage,* parts of Hine's *In and Out,* parts of—yes—*Evangeline*) for its sustained rewards to the informed attention. *The Golden Gate* is a charmingly unique sort of minor masterpiece, a tour de force of the transcendence of the mere tour de force. As Wilde's Algernon said of his own bon mot, when asked was it clever, this book is "perfectly phrased, and quite as true as any observation in civilized life should be." (pp. 32-4)

> *John Hollander, "Yuppie Time, In Rhyme," in* The New Republic, *Vol. 194, No. 16, April 21, 1986, pp. 32-4.*

PATRICK PARRINDER

Why not a novel in verse? It's all a question of expectations, and in *The Golden Gate* the Indian-born poet Vikram Seth singlehandedly overturns most readers' expectations about what can, and cannot, pass as a novel. Whatever the frame of mind in which you begin it, by the end it has come to seem the most natural—and the most accessible, and easily assessable—thing in the world. One takes the poetic dexterity for granted, and begins to see its faults as a novel. Perhaps neither reaction is wholly fair to the author, but it is he who has taken a gamble and broken the rules.

The Golden Gate is in no sense a pastiche of *Eugene Onegin,* though both books are concerned with the romantic entanglements of gilded youths. Seth's characters are not Russian transplants, but Californians seen in their native habitat. We begin and end with John, an upwardly-mobile computer scientist whose work is connected (just how is never made clear) with nuclear weapons manufacture. At the age of 26, John belatedly realises that he is a workaholic with no private life. Jan, an ex-girlfriend, diagnoses his trouble and secretly inserts a heart-search ad for another lonely workaholic: 'Young handsome

yuppie seeks . . .'. The replies from female yuppies (real and pretended) come pouring in, and John meets the significantly-named Liz Dorati.

John's background is half-English, but we are invited to make little of that, or of any of the presumed contents of his mind. Some lip service is paid to nanoseconds and megabytes, and in his spare time, we are told, he 'likes to read / Eclectically from Mann to Bede'. If so, he reads merely from boredom, since it has no measurable effects upon his life. There could hardly be a more striking contrast with Pushkin's characters. Onegin and his Tatyana may not have been great readers, but they were steeped in a well-defined cultural and literary tradition stretching from Richardson to Rousseau and Byron. They tended to re-enact the romantic roles that their contemporaries had become so excited about. In *The Golden Gate* the choice is between a hereditary and pastoral mode of life (Liz Dorati's parents are wine-growers), the culture of protest and rock music, and the 'yuppie' state of mental and imaginative barrenness.

Luckily, John has some non-yuppie friends. Alternative life-styles, civil disobedience, the problems of single parenting, and the Catholic Church's teaching on homosexuality all play their part in the story, which at times threatens to become a forum for discussing contemporary ideas, and at other times a relaxed soap-opera in verse. There is a scene or two on the Golden Gate Bridge, but by the end the Dorati family's vineyard and the nearby 'clapboard church with the white steeple' have come to loom much larger than anyone could have expected. Thanksgiving at the Doratis' may fall short of Christmas at Dingley Dell in some respects, but it is here in a harvest festival atmosphere that John's real claims on Liz's affections (the two have been lovers, of course, ever since she answered his ad) are conclusively weighed in the balance. It is his best friend and rival, an anti-nuclear protestor called Phil, who is chosen. The golden gate in this novel leads not so much to the Pacific Ocean as to a durable marriage. . . .

Morally, *The Golden Gate* is surprisingly simplistic, and apart from the idea that both sexes can now sow their wild oats, its message for the 1980s would have sounded old hat in 1880. The cost of writing a verse novel, it would seem, is to turn a blind eye to virtually all that Hardy, Joyce, Lawrence and their successors have done in prose. The result is a strange blend of racy, colloquial literary enterprise and static neo-Victorian values.

> *Patrick Parrinder, "Games-Playing," in* London Review of Books, *Vol. 8, No. 14, August 7, 1986, p. 8.*

CAROL IANNONE

To have written the "perfect book for the 1980's" may sound like a dubious achievement, but in the case of Vikram Seth's first novel, *The Golden Gate,* a publisher's blurb may for once approach accuracy. The thirty-four-year-old author, a Stanford Ph.D. candidate in economics, has spun an up-to-date tale of San Francisco "Yuppiedom"—and he has done it, what is more, in verse, broadly modeling his book after the subject (young love) and the tone (mild bemusement) of Pushkin's *Eugene Onegin,* and adopting that classic Russian poem's intricate form as well. . . .

And he makes it work. As a formal device, Seth's versification is engaging, clever, and responsive to the subject matter. One is pleased, and even (although that may not have been the intention) reassured, to find that computers and nuclear arms can be treated without embarrassment in narrative verse. The vocabulary is rich and varied, ranging as needed from the lofty, erudite, and archaic to the trendy and quotidian. The verse can be lyrically fresh or dramatically intense. Line groupings and sentence structure are handled flexibly and, when necessary to punctuate an idea or shape a point, ingeniously. If occasionally a rhyme seems forced, a word choice awkward, a meter strained, overall the language proves remarkably elastic and capable. (p. 54)

Unfortunately, there is a problem with this elegant literary divertissement, and that is its content. The ideas and themes of *The Golden Gate* derive wholly from the arsenal of contemporary liberal orthodoxies, now apparently so deeply entrenched in the literary imagination as to have achieved defining moral status. Of course, there is nothing wrong with a writer's appealing to current ideas and beliefs, or to his incorporating them as elements in telling his story and shaping his vision— but in *The Golden Gate,* the ideology *is* the vision.

The story begins when one John Brown, a successful twenty-six-year-old product of Berkeley and Silicon Valley, is nearly "brained" by a frisbee while walking through Golden Gate Park, and is thus with amusing improbability made to feel the loneliness of his emotion-dry, work-centered single life. His ex-girlfriend, Janet Hayakawa, a Japanese-American sculptress and part-time drummer in a rock band named Liquid Sheep, sympathetically takes out a personal ad in his name. Through this thoroughly contemporary contrivance, John meets and falls in love with Liz Dorati, a Stanford Law graduate. As they blissfully set up housekeeping, Liz's brother Ed, and John's best friend Phil, a young divorced father who has quit *his* Silicon Valley job to become a peace activist, also begin an affair. But Ed, deeply in thrall to traditional Christianity, raises religious objections to their love and Phil sadly gives him up. In a sudden twist, partly precipitated by the news that her mother is dying of cancer, Liz realizes that her own relationship with the still emotionally rigid John cannot work and decides to marry the more easygoing Phil, not out of "love" but out of "like," which both now believe is the more reliable emotion.

For his part, John is horrified and disgusted to learn of Phil's homosexual indulgence, and is further hurt and angered by Phil's and Liz's marriage. After a bitter spree of one-night stands and singles bars, he starts up again, promisingly if tentatively, with Janet, only to lose her in an automobile accident. While Phil and Liz care for their expanding family, which includes Phil's son, a child who survived the auto accident that killed Janet, and their own newborn baby boy, John is left aching and alone. But the book closes on a note of bittersweet possibility: now that he has learned of life's fragility, John may at last be ready to accept whatever love or friendship comes his way, on whatever terms.

More than one critic has conceded that, the feat of versification apart, the plot of *The Golden Gate* is slender, the characterizations sketchy and flat. It might be closer to the truth to say that, in the hands of a lesser artist than Pushkin, versification of this sort actually seems to encourage flatness and superficiality of a kind that would be intolerable in prose. But whatever the reason, *The Golden Gate* sports a slick emotional veneer such as one associates less with serious fiction than with a Hollywood film like *The Big Chill,* with a few Snoopy greeting-card sentiments about love and friendship thrown in for good measure.

But its problems go deeper than this. Seth does not so much create characters, round or flat, as grade them on a scale of prefabricated moral possibilities. As one critic remarked, apparently in admiration, "the novel's ultimate morality is severe. Crucially, it's the bisexual and idealistic Phil . . . who quit his job at Datatronics to join the peace movement, who ends up favored by fortune while priggish homophobic John emerges with his initial desolation intact." Characters are defined in terms of where they stand on the issues, with life's sweetest secrets yielding to those on the correct side of the correct causes.

Take, for example, that *summa* of causes, peace. As an activist, Phil is obviously the most advanced on the moral scale. Next comes Liz, who grows increasingly enlightened through contact with Phil; at a peace rally, she makes an impromptu speech in defense of "all the other fauna / that have developed here on / the earth." Ed, who belives in working for peace in the individual heart—"to curb our own complicity / In violence and in exploitation"—is judged to be simply ineffective; as Phil puts it, "By the time your catholicon / Acts on our guts, we'll all be gone." Finally there is John, who despises the antinuke movement.

John believes the U.S. is superior to the Soviet Union, and he worries that the peace movement will "*give* them the rope to hang us with." He remarks to Phil: "Spout here: you'll come to little harm. / Spout there: the KGB will sell you / A ticket to a dexterous shrink / Who'll drug you dumb to help you think." But Phil has a response to this: "But their state wouldn't look so bad / To someone sunk in unemployment / —Of which we've plenty—or disease. / Bankrupted by his medical fees, / I doubt that he'd get much enjoyment / From all his fabled freedoms." And besides, Phil asks, "How can you think of we or they / When we're both in the soup?" The two go back and forth, with Phil predictably gaining the upper hand each time.

Seth lays out the case for "peace" in other ways as well. He mockingly describes the presumed attitude of the scientists who make the bombs: "When something's technically attractive / You follow the conception through, / That's all. What if you leave a slew / of living dead, of radioactive / 'Collateral damage' in its wake? / It's just a job, for heavens sake." And he devotes a large section of his book to a loving evocation of a peace demonstration (no mildly bemused tone here) including a ten-page speech by an activist priest who follows a Christianity clearly more to Seth's liking than Ed's. In this speech the whole argument against nuclear defense is piously set forth, and we are reminded how our country always seems to need an enemy to hate—"Even before we'd reached Berlin / Moscow was our new sump of sin." (pp. 54-5)

Perhaps even cruder than these judgments is the book's system of racial and ethnic characterizations. John, for example, is the only child of an apparently loveless Wasp home. His father, his only surviving parent, is English, and "Retired in his native Kent, Rarely responds to letters sent / (If rarely) by his transatlantic / offspring." The presumed emotional aloofness of the Anglo-Saxon appears, indeed, to be a cardinal sin of the West in the eyes of the Indian-born Seth. Phil's former in-laws do not care for "Claire Cabot marrying Philip Weiss— / For all their Wasp stings of advice." As a "good atheist Jew," Phil serves in Seth's universe as a desirable foil to a poker-spined

Anglo society. . . . But on the book's terms it is the Oriental Janet Hayakawa who is the most firmly fixed in a sense of nurturant family solidarity, selfless, giving, unconditionally loving, creative (one of her sculptures is entitled ''Mother Hen'').

As a woman, Liz is by definition emotionally more elastic than John, while John, a typical young male of our time, is of course a problem to begin with. In his emotional reserve, his tendency to possessive jealousy, his disdain for peace activism, and his repudiation of homosexuality, we are clearly meant to discern the root problems of patriarchy. At times *The Golden Gate* almost seems patterned after an episode of *All in the Family,* with John, a younger, educated, sophisticated Archie Bunker being tutored in simple truths by representatives of various human groups in possession of the warmer and more natural impulses of life.

Perhaps nowhere is Seth's trusting subscription to current orthodoxies more glaring than in his casually sophisticated portrayal of homosexuality. It is taken for granted in this book that the only permissible attitude toward homosexuality is one of complete and favorable acceptance; indeed, in Seth's eyes, whatever moral complications may surround homosexual practice are ascribable not to that practice itself but to cultural and religious prejudices against it. Ed's objections, religious in nature, are rendered in caricature. . . . (p. 55)

But to say that Seth's attitude toward homosexuality is one of casual sophistication is not to say that he regards it as without moral content. On the contrary, for him it possesses decisive moral weight—it is life-enhancing and spiritually expansive. The ability to accept homosexuality in oneself or in others becomes one of those measures of a character's entitlement to emotional rewards. Moreover, in Phil, who effortlessly and unreflectingly travels from a homosexual affair into heterosexual domesticity, Seth goes beyond respect for the separate integrity of the homosexual experience to a vision of breezy bisexual integration as an ascendant moral norm. In this vision above all *The Golden Gate* decisively earns its credentials as a ''book for the 1980's.''

Henry James, in an acute insight into Pushkin's complex attitude toward Eugene in *Eugene Onegin,* wrote that the poet both saw through his hero and admired him. This is emphatically not true of Seth's attitudes toward his characters. Whom he admires (Phil, for example) he does not see through; whom he sees through (John, chiefly) he cannot really admire. In any work of art, and especially in one with aspirations as high as those of *The Golden Gate,* this is a fatal failing. One may therefore assume that most of the critics who praised this book were entranced with its view of life as well as its technical virtuosity, while others may have been willing to overlook its view of life precisely because of its technical virtuosity. But as Vikram Seth has himself asserted, ''it is a truism that in a work of art one can't easily separate form and content.'' One not only can't; one shouldn't. (p. 56)

Carol Iannone, ''Yuppies in Rhyme,'' in Commentary, *Vol. 82, No. 3, September, 1986, pp. 54-6.*

Jon Silkin

1930-

English poet, editor, critic, dramatist, and translator.

In his poetry, Silkin often utilizes imagist techniques while exploring moral and social themes. Among his major topics are human relationships, political issues, and the Holocaust of Nazi Germany. Although frequently focusing upon brutality, cruelty, and suffering, Silkin's verse evidences his belief in love as a unifying force that makes existence meaningful. Silkin's poetic style has evolved from his early use of assonant rhythms influenced by the Old Testament to experiments with form and syntax. Edward Larrissy noted that Silkin's poetry ''is convincingly pressed into the service of a stringent, thoughtful and indignant compassion for the suffering and exploited: it enacts an austere pity.''

The title of Silkin's first volume of poetry, *The Peaceable Kingdom* (1954), is derived from an emblematic painting by Edward Hicks. The visionary lyricism of many of the verses prompted critical comparison to the work of William Blake. Like Blake, Silkin metaphorically emphasizes the dualistic nature of life, seeking to effect, in his words, ''harmony composed from tension.'' This volume contains the poem ''Death of a Son,'' one of the most popular and successful of Silkin's early works, which describes his feelings toward his brain-damaged son, ''who died in a mental hospital age one.'' The poem contrasts the physical misery of Silkin's son with his own mental anguish and repudiates abstract phrases that attempt to ennoble what Silkin perceives as the meaningless suffering of humankind. In his next collection, *The Two Freedoms* (1958), Silkin again examines moral and humanitarian concerns but employs longer lines and more complex syntax. Silkin abandoned this approach in favor of the shorter lines and didactic style of *The Re-Ordering of the Stones* (1961) and *Nature with Man* (1965). In the former volume, Silkin indicts the hypocrisy of a society unwilling to put its morality into practice. The poem ''Respectabilities,'' for example, chastises posturing liberals who scrutinize problems instead of acting upon them. *Nature with Man* features the highly regarded ''Flower Poems,'' a sequence in which Silkin describes flowers in anthropomorphic terms to metaphorically explore their connections with humanity.

Silkin's visit to Israel and his travels to the United States to participate in the Iowa Writer's Workshop inform his next collection, *Amana Grass* (1971). *The Principle of Water* (1974) includes ''The Killhope Wheel,'' a sequence in which Silkin defines an area of Northern England in terms of its natural and sociopolitical elements. Ostensibly about an abandoned lead mine in the Pennine Mountains, this sequence commemorates those miners who were killed in 1860 during a bitter strike. In the title sequence of *The Little Time-Keeper* (1976), Silkin contrasts belief in the existence of God with the notion that the universe may be subject to entropy. In other poems in this volume, he illustrates the fragility of love in the contemporary world. He continues his examination of these themes in *The Psalms with Their Spoils* (1980). Silkin's most respected works appear in *Selected Poems* (1980).

Silkin has furthered his reputation through his association with *Stand,* a literary magazine he founded and edits with poet Ken

Smith. He has also published two works on the poetry of World War I: *Out of Battle: The Poetry of the Great War* (1972), a critical analysis of verse of that era, and *Gurney* (1985), a verse play based on the life of English poet and composer Ivor Gurney, who was injured during the war and never fully recovered.

(See also *CLC,* Vols. 2, 6; *Contemporary Authors,* Vols. 5-8, rev. ed.; and *Dictionary of Literary Biography,* Vol. 27.)

JOHN CIARDI

[A] book that held me fascinated in dismay to the very end is *The Two Freedoms*. . . . This, [Silkin's] first book published in America, is my year's discovery of the unintelligible. Silkin is a poet of great skill. His rhythms, his individual phrases, and his ability to conjure a dance of half-lit suggestions is fascinating. It still adds up to a real experience in unintelligibility. (The point to be made by the way is that the unintelligible is not nearly as common as some believe.)

I don't think Silkin is deliberately unintelligible. Rather, he seems so wholly preoccupied in the development of a poetic mannerism that he consistently falls into unintelligibility, and even preciosity. Neither mannerism nor difficulty in the reading is a final charge against a poet, if he can make it work. The good poet can lure us into the dark forest and we can wander there happily lost, if the shadows are full of enough song, and if the song comes from real birds, whether we see them or not. Poem after poem of Silkin's, however, goes by with no objects in it. Even his poem to the victims of a Nazi concentration camp opens on a self-satisfied discussion of a (to me at least) wholly unintelligible symbol:

> Love, when you ask me forgiveness
> I see not you but hairless wrists involved
> With love's embrace, he a friend the sufferer clasps;
> Who is in shackles, whose wrists soar, who is a bird
> Wrenched into focal agony. This charged symbol,
> Stripped by brutality of fictive detail,
> Stark to the pain it symbolizes. . . .

And so on. It's hardly my idea of a "charged symbol." If that is the best a poet can do with human suffering, I prefer newspaper coverage. The champions of clarity in poetry may take Silkin as their whipping boy for unintelligibility, and welcome to him, but let no man claim that he is typical of what is happening in poetry these days.

> *John Ciardi, in a review of "The Two Freedoms,"*
> *in* Saturday Review, *Vol. XLI, No. 39, September*
> *27, 1958, p. 18.*

HARVEY SHAPIRO

[Silkin] is disturbing to his fellow poets. He comes forward crying "Human Agony," addressing God in his verses. . . . [In *The Two Freedoms*] Silkin stands out like Blake in a roomful of Rotarians.

Unconventional (in terms of the conventions of the moment) in theme and manner, he writes a poetry of social protest that, like Langland's or Blake's, has a religious base. Against the modern scene ("The brass fiction of the industrial King") and its citizens ("meanness scrubbed into the face"), he levels "Great Language, / With his huge crown and religious body." . . .

Turning from this world, "whose image is / Reflected by a brass screw," he writes about birds and insects, and they become unmawkish symbols of innocence as he works upon them with the same primitive intensity that permits him to change the events of his own life (the death of a son, for example) into something resembling religious myth. He is a moving poet of death. His openness and his concern with love and pity enable him to take one of those untouchable subjects, the victims of the concentration camps, and raise it into verse: "Pain / Nor agony nor heart can put a heart again / Into that stone the dead are."

It would be misleading to say that all the poems in *The Two Freedoms* are successful. In some, the language, though striking, fails to carry the animating experience. But Silkin is only 28. In the best of his verse it is impossible not to see a powerful new talent.

> *Harvey Shapiro, "Figures in the Patterns," in* The
> New York Times Book Review, *November 30, 1958,*
> *p. 42.*

BARBARA GIBBS

[In *The Two Freedoms*], Mr. Silkin's subjects are generally metaphysical, paradoxical, involving the intellect and the emotions about equally. A poem is made when a certain number of formal gyrations or permutations of the subject have been performed, like figures of a dance. It is often necessary to signal the ending by a commonplace, like the long chord of music that tells the dancers to stop. In other words, the poem could have gone on, but the poet thought it was time to stop (for whatever reason). Thus there is unity, as between poem and subject, but not identity. On the question of seriousness of commitment, I do not feel that Mr. Silkin withholds himself, he commits himself wholly, if in a somewhat cool manner. And as to his language: it is rhetorically heightened, and perhaps derivative of certain past models, only mildly heightened in vocabulary, tasteful as to sound, and . . . without slack. Thus, Mr. Silkin's model of a poem . . . would have a subject, would not have a merely decorative relation to that subject, would take its subject seriously, and in language be well-wrought, close-fitting and addressed to the ear. (p. 191)

Mr. Silkin's poetry is carefully well-made, married to tradition, civilized, yet within these purlieus new, as each voice that takes up a theme is a new voice. *The Two Freedoms* is a good book to read, because everything in it is good. There are few lapses, the themes are serious and intelligent, the textures interesting—complex and lucid at once—each poem in its way well-made, not a copy. Perhaps I miss idiosyncrasy, would be glad if there were more. (p. 194)

> *Barbara Gibbs, in a review of "The Two Freedoms,"*
> *in* Poetry, *Vol. XCIV, No. 3, June, 1959, pp. 191-194.*

DONALD DAVIE

Names of things can beautifully check and vary the flow of verse; names of ideas seem by comparison very smooth stones indeed. 'Love', 'sex', 'affection', 'creature', 'unit', 'love', 'end', 'love', 'image', 'universe', 'man's love'—in the first 14 lines of a poem by Jon Silkin, these are the nouns; and their abstractness is typical of a cerebral poet whose mind [in *The Re-Ordering of the Stones*] moves naturally among ideas rather than perceptions. His solution to the musical problem this sets him is interesting and ingenious: by using short unrhymed lines, he weakens the rhythmical impetus to a desultory trickle, in which even the smoothest pebble can make a little eddy. Unfortunately he has other ways of making snags and snarls—by manipulating what he calls 'syntax, that Interlockage of human action', and this produces sentences like

> Disaffection means letting go what man
> Had in the way that soul, a fabric
> Of experience, is disentwined
> Be he Man as thorn, Man as candle.

Or there is the indeed stupendous 'interlockage' when

> Those who raped Tibetan girls castrating men
> To prevent a fruitful Tibet
> Are accused of genocide.

Despite these hilarious miscalculations, and monotony and obscurity, and a humourless portentousness on almost every page, Silkin is an interesting writer. He is working at a higher level of abstraction than anyone else, even Thom Gunn. And when he succeeds (as I reckon in this book he does just once—with a piece called **"Depths"**), the result is a poem unlike anyone else's, and achieved against all the odds. By the same token, his failures are sometimes worth more than other people's successes. But I had better admit that in saying this I am struggling against a strong antipathy to his tone of voice, and to very many of his social and political and moral attitudes. (pp. 794-95)

Donald Davie, "Snags," in New Statesman, *Vol. 62, No. 1602, November 24, 1961, pp. 794-95.*

ROBIN SKELTON

Jon Silkin has always been an uncompromising poet, following his own line and avoiding the merely fashionable. [*The Re-Ordering of the Stones*] marks an important stage in his development. He has created a form of balanced, disciplined, unrhymed verse that has all the force of rhetoric with none of its specious glitter. The poems are controlled by a firm syntax, that can move easily from formal to vernacular gestures, and by a taut sparse vocabulary which only rarely astonishes with an epithet, but often surprises with its concrete strength. The poems are dignified, and honest. They explore suffering, pain, exile, love, with the passionate precision of a surgeon. They are not, however, cold or unmoving. Nor are they speciously profound, as work of this kind so often appears to be. The discoveries are valuable. . . .

From the majority of these poems I get the impression that Mr. Silkin has begun to tackle all the problems which most concern him in an effort to remake his values, and reshape his universe. His problems are only occasionally different from every man's problems, of course, but I would emphasise the sense I have of a particular poet probing deeply personal questions because it is the total personality of this book, as a man (one might say) which most impresses me. I have not, in the past, rated Mr. Silkin's work as more than promising and interesting, having enjoyed and been deeply moved by much of it, but never convinced completely by any one book. Always I felt that something was missing (though not as much as from the work of many more fashionably accepted writers). Now, however, I take my hat off to him. This is a book to convince anybody of his significance. Occasionally the abstractions get a little too rarified; sometimes the syntax falters and loses its grip; once or twice there is a suspicion that a statement is intellectually specious, and a shade evasive. These are, however, minor smirches on an admirable and rewarding book. I am eager to see what happens next; it is likely to be very exciting.

Robin Skelton, in a review of "The Re-Ordering of the Stones," in Critical Quarterly, *Vol. 4, No. 1, Spring, 1962, p. 92.*

MARVIN BELL

Of the thirty-four poems in *Nature with Man*—his fourth collection—Jon Silkin apparently wishes us to pay particular attention to fifteen on flowers—having published and broadcast groups of them previously, and now surrounding them with pieces closely related in content and a relevant three-page essay.

According to ["**Nature with Man**"], ". . . The whole / Of nature is turning slowly / Into an eye that searches / For its most developed / And treacherous creature, man." Mr. Silkin's attempt to define the real situation of "nature with man," both in the flower poems and in their fellows, is heavy with aphorism ("The whole of nature / Is a preying upon"; "What

can't be stopped must be nourished"; "It is not natural to / Grow by separation."), anthropomorphism (peonies are "confident"; daisies, "candid" and "glad"; violets, "courageous"), and insistence ("Take care of Nature . . . ."; [God] is our carnivore / And we, His feeling plants. / And that's the complex part."). The poems labor to deliver their messages.

(I take the presence of the essay as an indication of the book's technical and perceptual mediocrity. Here, the poet tells his theories, intentions and methods in the flower poems, and a bit of his political philosophy. Having read the poems first, I was not convinced by the essay. Returning to the poems, I felt the essay had said everything, and more interestingly.)

Jon Silkin has already written well, and importantly. . . . These flower poems, on which he has placed such emphasis, seem to me neither artful nor educational—not half-successful. Of the (better) poems which lead up to them, I like two particularly: "**Defence**" and "**Community.**" (pp. 411-12)

Marvin Bell, in a review of "Nature with Man," in Poetry, *Vol. CVII, No. 6, March, 1966, pp. 411-12.*

THE TIMES LITERARY SUPPLEMENT

Jon Silkin's pursuit of both the craft and the cause of poetry has been austere and unremitting, a fifteen-year dedication winning much less credit and recognition than it deserves. To those who look for easy and comfortable writing his talent has never appealed: it has too much rigorousness and edgy intensity. As far as the cause goes, the toil of personally sustaining a little literary magazine—as Mr. Silkin has sustained *Stand*—is usually accounted more "heroic" than important. . . . [*Poems, New and Selected*] is therefore particularly welcome, offering an opportunity to assess the quality and extent of his achievement.

The Peaceable Kingdom, the title of Mr. Silkin's first volume, was taken from the name of a celebrated American primitive painting. The painter's animals mounted into his ark with placid innocence and ceremony; the poems in the Silkin book enacted simple tenderness, compassion for the hunted fox, the wounded bird and even a dead fly, with the same naive power. This standpoint and these themes were too naked and ingenuous-seeming for the 1950s. But Mr. Silkin was more than the raw and earnest primitive. These poems (see "**A Space in the Air**") were also groping towards a definition of the obscurer components of deep personal emotion, and searching for a style.

The dual quest continued actively in the next two books, where a good many poems were gravid, slow-moving meditations affirming involvement and tenderness against violence and guilt. The very title of *The Re-ordering of the Stones* somehow suggested both Mr. Silkin's reverence for the poet's vocation and its essential difficulty for him. . . .

In [*Poems New and Selected*], the group of "**Flower Poems**" from *Nature With Man* is reprinted complete. This is Mr. Silkin's finest work to date. The nearest precedent for this minute scrutiny of flowers in distinctly anthropomorphic imagery is Ted Hughes's "Snowdrop"; but the final achievement here derives from Mr. Silkin's own manner. . . . These flowers grip the reader unnervingly through the medium of this gritty patience and precision: the sequence finally justifies Mr. Silkin's uncompromising struggle to find his own voice. *Poems New and Selected* should help to establish the solid reputation he deserves.

"The Craft and the Cause," in The Times Literary Supplement, No. 3365, August 25, 1966, p. 765.

JOHN FULLER

In the 'fifties there was much talk of poetry's desperate need to involve itself with real life, real people and real feelings. A felt connection with the individual and his sufferings, some understanding of social forces: these were offered panaceas to an etiolated verse. No poet has campaigned with a more isolating persistence for these qualities than Jon Silkin.... Silkin's editorial prescription for poetry [in Stand] dangerously paralleled his own developing creative sensibility ('The trouble with much of the verse written nowadays is that it rarely subscribes to the passion which makes it poetry') and led him to print much that was falteringly or grindingly nerve-baring or quasi-devotional. Again, in a review of Philip Larkin's The Less Deceived ... Silkin proposed 'passion' as a missing ingredient. 'Current fashion has it that the book, or most of it, is very good poetry. But current fashion is wrong.... If only Mr Larkin would let go and become passionate.' Silkin himself was soon to be drawn to the ill-fated Mavericks. (pp. 100-01)

[It now seems] that Larkin had indeed involved poetry with life, in a detailed and worryingly introspective structure that was all the more poignant for being formal. The heart-throbs were carefully avoided, but this was a poetry aware of suffering: surely Silkin's 'passion' could recognize Larkin as a fellow-subscriber? Or did Silkin perhaps more narrowly mean a self-surrender to the extremes of painful experience as a means to understanding others? When, years later, he chastised Larkin for being 'too knowingly present' in "Church Going", he surely pointed as much to his own reliance on the instinctive as he did to Larkin's self-consciousness. There seems a basic difference here between the idea of the poem as a self-evident process of discovery, and of its being an account rather than a representation of the discovery. If one compares "Church Going" with, say, Silkin's celebrated "Death of a Son" [in Poems New and Selected] one sees what Silkin has in mind, but one also I think sees that though Silkin rightly refuses to indulge in his pangs, he has not tackled them in his mind either, and this seems to show up in his reliance on incantatory syntax and bare, vaguely Old Testament imagery to connote a groping sense of spiritual realities.... Larkin's patiently discursive effort in "Church Going" is of quite another order: the feelings are understood at each stage. To call this being 'knowingly present' is one thing, but surely it implies (and is evidenced by, in reading) a corresponding absence in Silkin's poem. One likes the poem and finds it moving, but it does present the kind of stunned feelings that one would expect and takes one no deeper: one senses that the poet is making up, in the ceremonious language, for some unfaced emotional circumstances.

In just this way, Silkin rarely has been interested in fact or analysis. One may find a poem about the massacre of the Jews at York in 1190; or a half-acid, half-clumsy attack upon three half-recognizable critics; or references to Civil Defence inanities, the National Assistance Board or Chinese atrocities in Tibet: but Silkin is very far from the conventional poetry of 'commitment' that such topics might suggest. These things appeal to him only as paradigms of the individual's failure to respond to love or to the social environment. Literature to him is a barometer of moral health, not a platform. His career up to now is, in a certain sense, rather Wordsworthian: the political concern gets edged out by the mystical one.

Indeed, some of Silkin's judgments are short of the charity he prescribes. The scorn heaped upon conventional liberal attitudes in a number of poems ("Respectabilities", "For a Child pronounced Mentally Defective", "Sacred") derives from an assumed conviction that these attitudes imply reservation, that they reveal no instinctive response to human needs.... There is something unflatteringly Holbrookian in this sort of attack on supposed immaturity in relationships. If liberals ask permission before making love to each other, it can indeed be made to seem absurd: but as a symbol it looks more like a good way of negating rape and tyranny than a crabbed denial of the universal brotherhood. Silkin is, in the most creditable sense, a revolutionary idealist. Where Godwin and Shelley fulminated against King and Priest, Silkin lodges his hatred in the liberal. Passion is again the panacea, but does this passion have time for compassion for those without passion?... This is not to say that these accusatory poems of Silkin's are not effective: he writes with an honesty and urgency which demands, and receives, sympathetic attention. But his effects are often blurred by an unconsidered gesture, a small piety or sentiment. An example might be taken from another well-known, and perhaps unusually rhetorical poem, "Furnished Lives". Here the secret wish of the poor London children for 'a dinner-service, austere, yet gay: like snow! When swans are on it' is a charming yet convincing image. Its development in the poem to relate to the God they are praying to, and who does not visit them, is so less finely perceived than this that to me it becomes involved and presumptuous.... Unevenness of this sort implies a lack of just that cerebration that Silkin found to be an impediment in Larkin.

What I have so far suggested is only a bulky, but not over-riding, qualification to be made of Silkin's work. On the whole, it is plain that his talent has not been sufficiently recognized. Much of his recent poetry has been tighter, more jagged, more emblematic and more aphoristic than before. By encouraging these qualities he has left behind the faltering musicality, the Biblicisms and occasional fantasy of his earlier work. The poem about the seal girl in The Peaceable Kingdom, for instance, seems now a very faded mode.... (pp. 101-03)

[Compare his early poems to] the recent flower poems (terse, accurate, eccentric, yet wholly absorbed in the human situation) and one sees how far Silkin has matured as a writer. It was perhaps necessary for him to pass through the phase of earnest moralizing represented by The Re-ordering of the Stones in order to achieve the power and relaxation that one senses behind this later work:

> They look like plates; more closely
> Like the first tryings, the machines, of nature
> Riveted into her, successful

("Dandelions")

This is assured writing, and pleasureable. Its idiosyncrasies seem fully required by the nature of the insight and comment aroused by the new range of subject-matter. The Silkin ceremoniousness is still there, but there is much that is observed and conversational: the result takes one close to Marianne Moore. Not as witty, but quiet and necessary and humane. (p. 103)

[Poems New and Selected] is intended to serve only as an introduction to Silkin's work. There are only four new poems: another flower poem, and three others which could be said to be narratives, oblique, but intriguing. The first, and longest, particularly catches the attention, with its neo-imagist melange of the meditations of a pioneer with descriptions of a waterfall and local vegetation, and the pioneer's identification with all living things, as 'an ingredient' among them. . . . This cinematic range of images, realized with great determination in Silkin's peculiarly Latinate diction, seems at once mysteriously vague and finely adjusted: the effect is of an organic involvement in the world described, both natural and authoritative. (pp. 103-04)

[*Poems New and Selected*] is very thin on both new and familiar work. Anyone who possesses *Nature with Man* and some good anthologies has little need of it. The claims of the blurb that we can now compare the flower poems with the bestiary of *The Peaceable Kingdom* are made nonsensical by the paucity of the choice from that volume (only three poems about animals); and both author and publisher conspire to hide from us the existence of a fifth volume of poems, *The Portrait*. . . . I mention this not to betray juvenilia to the inquisition of bibliography, but to put on record a collection of fourteen poems in an earlier style of some interest to readers of Silkin. In a fullish collection there would be several poems to be retrieved from it, one would have thought.

Thus [*Poems New and Selected*] serves as a breathing space for a poet who is flexibly and confidently moving towards new and better things. One hopes it will enable him to see in perspective where his best talents lie. . . . At any rate the Apollonian/Dionysiac absurdities of the 'fifties already look severely dated. (p. 104)

> *John Fuller, in a review of "Poems New and Selected," in* London Magazine, *n.s. Vol. 6, No. 7, October, 1966, pp. 100-04.*

RALPH J. MILLS, JR.

[*Poems, New and Selected*] by Jon Silkin, one of the most impressive and productive of the young British poets, is long overdue. . . .

Jon Silkin's work is quiet, rich in detail, and may be said to constitute both a poetry of observation or description and a poetry of meditation. Certainly the most obvious characteristic in the present selection is an accurate and loving eye for the particulars of creation reminiscent of Roethke or Francis Ponge. Such concentrated attention is especially noticeable in the very recent flower poems. . . . (p. 114)

There is a passionate yet objective, exact vision moving through these poems which reveals the long familiarity, the intense scrutiny, and the personal reflectiveness behind them. Occasionally we catch a brief glimpse of human analogies, but that practice is more in evidence elsewhere in the book. In such poems as **"Caring for Animals," "The Wholeness," "A Space in the Air," "Death of a Bird,"** and **"The Two Freedoms,"** Silkin explores with compassion and understanding the bonds between birds, animals, nature, and man. Something should likewise be said about the poet's deeply moving elegy for his son; his poem on "London's poor", **"Furnished Lives"**; and the haunting indictment of **"The Coldness."** (pp. 114-15)

> *Ralph J. Mills, Jr., in a review of "Poems, New and Selected," in* Poetry, *Vol. CIX, No. 2, November, 1966, pp. 114-15.*

HELEN VENDLER

[In *Poems, New and Selected*], Silkin writes often about single objects—stones, flowers—but his flowers seem like stones,

and might as well be, for the grinding abstraction he uses on them endows them with an iron life. . . . To see clearly, for Silkin, means recently to see flintily, and with a froth of deliberately repellent and clenched language he measures, like a snail, or an inchworm, "the differing planes of surface . . . / Which employ the sunk depths." This is a great improvement over his early style (pseudo-Hopkins, pseudo-Thomas) and the hoarded pain which is his subject might turn later to freer expression. Besides the static flower poems, he has done a striking narrative, taken in part, he has said, from the pardoner's tale, but in fact it is more like a horrifying reworking of Wordsworth's encounter poems. Silkin's equivalent of the old Leech-Gatherer at first seems neutral, but at the end, his tenacious resentment of life issues in an appalling gesture. . . . This grim tension, drab violence, is Silkin's best new version of himself. (pp. 543-44)

> *Helen Vendler, "Recent American Poetry," in* The Massachusetts Review, *Vol. VIII, No. 3, Summer, 1967, pp. 541-60.*

ROBERT L. STILWELL

To observe that Jon Silkin has consistently proved himself one of the more interesting and accomplished of the "younger" British poets is, in my opinion, not exactly to heap him with accolades. Yet Mr. Silkin's achievements transcend this rather limited judgment, at least to some extent: at his infrequent best, in perhaps a dozen of his poems across the past dozen years or so, he has struck me as potentially among the more interesting and accomplished poets, of whatever age, currently writing in English. It is true that large areas of poetic possibility, areas that count profoundly, appear to lie well beyond his attainment. It is true, furthermore, that to like him you have to like a particular order of verse: a hard, tight, economical verse in which (usually) words are employed as grudgingly as Webern employed notes: a verse in which (usually) the tiny lines rest on the page with a snowflake's ease and lightness. You also have to like love poems: love that discovers its occasions in flowers and birds and animals, in the death of a one-year-old son in a mental hospital or the "small brown death" of a fly. On such terms, however—on his own carefully chalked-out terms—Mr. Silkin can occasionally be very good indeed, a poet gratifyingly free of fuss and clutter and posturing. Scarcely any of his poems [in *Poems New and Selected*] are faultlessly sustained from beginning to end. He is prone to irritating disruptions of syntax, and of punctuation, that I for one find absolutely pointless (except in his widely admired flower poems, where such disruptions assume a notational form and thereby register something of the breathless, quirky wonderment with which the flower is being examined). Also, his tone sometimes becomes jaggedly uncertain. **"Caring for Animals"** is an indisputably moving poem, a sort of scholium on Blake's "Auguries of Innocence"; but watch how its two opening lines—

> I ask sometimes why these small animals
> With bitter eyes, why we should care for them.

—get shot down by the sentimental triteness (not to mention that ugly tautology) of its third and fourth lines:

> I question the sky, the serene blue water,
> But it cannot say. It gives no answer.

On the other hand, one can forgive much from a poet capable of saying something like this (in **"The Wholeness"**):

> The branches
> Stir above the healed lovers.
> The huge halves
> Of this life are one for once.

After exploring Mr. Silkin's *Poems New and Selected* . . . , I must confess a keen disappointment with the cross-section that he has picked from his earlier writing; for it seems to me that he has passed over some of his better poems (particularly several from his first book, *The Peaceable Kingdom*) but given room to a number of others (**"The Coldness"**, **"To My Friends"**, **"The Centre"**, **"Respectabilities"**, **"Three Critics"**, **"Defence"**, **"A Kind of Nature"**, and **"Depths"**) that I fervently wish he might somehow unspeak. Still, he has included **"A Death to Us"**, **"The Return"**, **"Furnished Lives"**, **"The Two Freedoms"**, **"Death of a Bird"**, **"The Wholeness"**, **"A Space in the Air"**, **"The Child"**, **"Death of a Son"**, and **"Nature with Man"**, work that should be sufficient to establish a narrow but secure reputation for any poet. He has also chosen twelve of those poems in which he celebrates—through really *looking at*—such small flowers as violets, dandelions, bluebells, and lilies of the valley. And if one adds that his four "New Poems" draw close to being as pared and sharpened as anything that he has ever done, it becomes evident that anyone who has responded to Mr. Silkin in the past will enjoy this little collection, despite all its omissions and (in my opinion) regrettable inclusions. (pp. 533-34)

> Robert L. Stilwell, "The Multiplying of Entities: D. H. Lawrence and Five Other Poets," in The Sewanee Review, *Vol. LXXVI, No. 3, Summer, 1968, pp. 520-35.*

DOUGLAS DUNN

Jon Silkin's writing grows thicker and thicker. His expressions [in *The Little Time-Keeper*] have come to rely on an extraordinary diction. They wear signs of the dictionary; or, if not that, then of too painstaking an effort to employ full powers of language—by that, I mean the painstaking is as conspicuous as the resources to which it is directed. Too often, his richer idiom expels anything so simple as direct poetic utterance. There is an appearance of the "thought-out," rather than of imagination and mind responding to phenomena or occasions. These lines from **"Entropy at Hartburn"** are a fair example—

> The huge energies untwine, and stars
> slither away on the braids. The wagging stems
> of sex slather to inane fruitfulness.

Here, sound of words evokes as much as their meaning. As in his previous collection, *The Principle of Water,* Silkin has taken his interest in enacting word-sounds a step further. But by now the result, I feel, is too heavy; the unfortunate result is portentousness as much as music. Some lines, I fear, have to be taken on faith, extraordinary perceptions like these, for instance—

> Prophecy is an ear coiling on entropy

> Huge elisions pass
> through the eye-rimmed sea

> . . . the dense shade, in the spaces, runs
> to hydrogen

laconic as its dull copulars.

You cannot *see* what is said in these lines. They sound strong, and are, arguably, both scientific and sensuous. Yet they seem to have lost touch with the world. They seem too deliberate.

Composing on the same principle, Silkin can write [unproblematic] lines. . . . Or he can write as directly as in these lines which end an **"Untitled Poem"**—

> We will not last, love, as we are. Love,
> I would have us stay, ever, like this.
> My conscience, my fear, and our sex, stir.

These lines are singular and authoritative in a way which the other lines I have quoted are merely singular. In removing himself from the laconic or ironic modes of writing most contemporary poets have come to consider debilitating, Silkin may have gone too far in the opposite direction and into a willed poetic manner. It has been brewing in his work for some time. His ability to impact one word on another in the creation of a sensuous idiom is not up for sacrifice. But it ought to be possible to retain it within a more direct form of writing. I note that, like Hughes, Silkin's music is all annotated below the stave. Both sound grand. I almost said "grandiose" which, being mischievous, is what I mean. Grandiose tones bother me. That, I think, is part of Silkin's weakness in this book. He has not lost touch with realities—a long poem about Australia in *The Little Time-Keeper* proves this effectively—but he may be in danger of losing touch altogether with their language. (pp. 82-3)

> Douglas Dunn, "The World and His Wife," in Encounter, *Vol. XLVII, No. 5, November, 1976, pp. 78-83.*

BEN HOWARD

The dominant impression made by *The Little Time-Keeper* is that of a mature style in the service of private obsessions. In general the style is that of Silkin's work since *The Re-Ordering of the Stones* (1961). Its structure is jagged, angular, and irregularly stanzaic, and its texture is thickly compacted, employing assonance ("Is it our sullen-hung selves numb us?") and consonance ("the dulled rose of texts, desert mica") in equal measure. Its diction is colloquial and concrete, heightened by a high concentration of transitive verbs ("the heart / glebes sharp, hard water"). Its rhythm is pointedly spondaic ("the bench will have its forked play / of their clasped forms"), its tone laconic and solemnly insistent. Its imagery spans a range from the celestial to the natural to the domestic, circulating around a few central motifs, such as milk and water, darkness and light. Its syntax is alternately gnarled and notational, combining the truncated phrase with the most convoluted construction ("Of no use if beauty affirm the techniques / work anneals; and, what droops away / is beauty as consolation—in the flame / work is of cash drudged for"). When it finds an appropriate subject, it can render a statement with considerable force. . . . (pp. 298-99)

[**"Entropy at Hartburn"**] explores Silkin's own characteristic themes, placing the wagging stems of sex in close proximity to steaming beasts, slithering stars, and the poet's religious anxiety. That cluster of images and themes, discernible in Silkin's earlier work, appears recurrently in the new collection. Here it converges upon a specific place, Hartburn in Northumberland, and forms a basis for a meditation on what Silkin (in a prose note) calls his "fear of eternity". The poem is the first in the sequence entitled **"The Little Time-Keeper,"** in which Silkin mingles an exploration of Northumbrian history with dark broodings upon his own finite existence. It is one of two long sequences in this collection, the other being **"Honey and Tobacco,"** which is set in Australia and contrasts Aboriginal views of that country with those of its white settlers. At one point Silkin speaks of writing a poem "from which breathe / the silences"—a phrase which might sum up the strengths and limitations of his larger canvases. On the whole their successes lie less in clarification than in the creation of atmospheres and the evocation of buried mysteries. The most memorable poems are in fact the short concentrated studies of personal relationships. Their tone is both intimate and precise. . . . (pp. 299-300)

Ben Howard, "British Wells," in Poetry, Vol. CXXXI, No. 5, February, 1978, pp. 292-305.

JEFFREY WAINWRIGHT

Jon Silkin has always been a tendentious poet, and it is this, and the clarity and openness with which he takes his stance, that has tended to embarrass his critics. He will insist on *saying* things. This is clear enough in his first book *The Peaceable Kingdom*, first published in 1954. The volume is no collection of mere observations: a place here, a 'character' there, an unstrenuous meditation or two, inevitable landscapes, but a determined, integrated set of poems built into their theme. The book's sentinels, **"Prologue"** and the matching refracted **"Epilogue"**, announce the collection's organisation, and throughout several vivid emblems, the fox, and the fragile insect among animals, the colours red and black, recur, along with the central figure of the child—his presence and his absence. Merle Brown writes correctly of the volume's 'seamless wholeness'.

The book's theme is proclaimed by its title, *The Peaceable Kingdom*, after Edward Hicks's visionary paintings evoking in American settings the prophecy of Isaiah. The words of Isaiah XI verses 6, 7, 8, 'The wolf also shall dwell with the lamb . . .' stand as epigraph recalling the beautiful notion that the world might yet become peaceful, that it has within it the capacity for that, it is *able* to be so. Such tendentiousness at the outset of a poetic career, and in the midst of the ever more sunken pragmatic 'realism' of the fifties. The very idea of such a hope, never mind expectation, is so readily seen as naïve.

Silkin's kingdom is drawn in strong lines of oppressed innocence and a corruption and deathliness that is also self-devouring and pitiful,

> All the animals in my poems go into the ark
> The human beings walk in the great dark
> The bad dark and the good dark. They walk
> Shivering under the small lamp light
> And the road has two ways to go and the humans none.
>
> ("Prologue")

It is not only the reference which makes these and other lines of Silkin's sound Biblical. Without any regular stress pattern, and with their simple repetitions, they have the pace and rhythm of the Biblical verse which Silkin has often acknowledged as a vital formative influence. The lines also have the broad, clear openness and uncluttered presentation of the essential that is shared both by the Biblical statement and narrative and by a 'naïve' painter like Hicks. Both are characteristically unconcerned with naturalism. Just as the scene is visionary, so that painter is not representing the lion or the lamb, the ox or the child, as life-like, or bothering much with the illusion of perspective. The Biblical narrative, as Erich Auerbach suggests, sets no scenes and renders only as much definition of time and place as the action strictly requires. This ignoring of context in favour of what is central to the action, or more often in Silkin's poems the experience, can be seen again and again. . . . To say that a painting is two-dimensional is commonly to disparage it, indeed it is often used as sufficient definition of the 'naïve' or 'primitive'. But the simple use of the horizontal and vertical can often be liberating and enable the clearest and most open of statements. Something of this quality is in *The Peaceable Kingdom*. . . . But the objection will be made that just as the method is simplified, non-naturalistic, so is the vision, that it is not 'realistic' about the world. **"Death of a Son"** could hardly prove such a charge, and a poem like **"A Death to Us"** sees in the 'tiny fly' a peculiar complexity to manifest innocence in which, too certain of itself, its proper invasion of another's space becomes aggressive,

> And I think now as I barely perceive him
> That his purpose became in dying, a demand
>
> For a murderer of his casual body.

This is the kind of moral complexity that Silkin has persistently explored in his later work, and for all the simplicity of its presentation here and elsewhere it can hardly be seen as simple-minded. The bold outlines of Silkin's enterprise always contain this kind of awareness, just as his 'kingdom' is inhabited by close personal experience. Nevertheless I want to insist upon the scale of the vision of *The Peaceable Kingdom*. What that implies and enacts is that the world need not be seen as a shapeless chaos of details occasionally endearing but mainly engendering despair or cynicism, but as a history where recognisable forces contend. The contention includes the political persecutions of the poor and the Jew, though through the recurring emblematic but real animals in the book this becomes part of the world's predatoriness. The forces then might be seen as no less familiar than the red and black, life and death, good and evil, though I do not think that they are therefore dissolved into anodyne generality. **"Caring for Animals"** is certainly a rhetorical poem but its questions and its statement are persuasive and vital because of the perspective the rhetorical mode imposes:

> I ask sometimes why these small animals
> With bitter eyes, why we should care for them.

Why? Why care for the son who is only 'something like a person'? Such questions and their answers might be taken as read, and the charge of naïveté presents itself again. But what **"Caring for Animals"** truly implies with its deliberate gaucheness is that the question is taken as read and that the true answer is that we do not and even that we need not. Can we then be impatient of the poem's measured advice? . . . The force of the advice lies of course not only in the sentiment, a matter of the heart being in the right place, but in the measure, the perfect pacing of the lines. The stylisation of the poem too, its conscious rhetoric, deflects the portentousness that would come of trying for such an affirmation colloquially. The poem has an intelligent beauty. (pp. 3-7)

Jeffrey Wainwright, "The Peaceable Kingdom," in Poetry Review, Vol. 69, No. 4, June, 1980, pp. 3-7.

PAUL MILLS

'To think hurts.' This sentence from **"Jerusalem"**, the fourth poem in Jon Silkin's [*The Psalms with their Spoils*], makes sense. It is clear that Silkin is telling a truth, and is doing so uncomplacently, but from an impression of the whole book one could say, or must say: 'To read this, hurts.' It does not initially hurt the heart but the head. Somewhere there is the world towards which these poems move: complex, full of events, baffling, sensuous. But instead of trying to approach a little of it and make contact through the tentative medium of verse with its outsideness, this book tries to cram, enfold, rather than to render coherent. The world has to be classified, has to be somehow digested into each sentence. The sentence soon breaks down. Too much of what might have become meaning falls away, and the reader is left with simple questions he would rather not ask. One is: What does this poem say? Another: How can I learn to enjoy this text and benefit from the presentation of life it gives? Where, in other words, is its sanity? One expects to be offered different answers by different texts but coming to a new one there must always be a residue of expectations. It is not that this book forces one to ask questions about what poetry is, but that if it fulfils any expectations at all they are ones we have not set out with, and those we have set out with we shall need to eject. To do so requires either courage or the wrong sort of meekness. I am not yet clear which. (p. 25)

Jagged and odd as the poems in this book may seem they nevertheless have a music. It is one which was delivered more smoothly in Silkin's earlier collections. It sinks further underground as his writing develops, but it can still be heard even here. It is a music of postponed repetition or restrained echo. Emphatic in Hebrew poetry of the psalms, in Silkin it weaves obscurely. . . . [In] *The Psalms with their Spoils* the physical world and its disjointed, awkward condition is brought up hard against what would be otherwise merely pure and unsoiled. In **"The Cathedral Chair"** the poet discovers the relic of the poem's title in a workmen's skip of rubble. 'Of a skip: of a monument.' The word 'skip' (Icelandic) is the ancestor of our modern English word 'ship' just as 'navis'—a ship, is of our word 'nave'—part of a church. So etymologically-speaking the chair may not be as out of place as it seems. A simple poetry could have been made out of these connections but Silkin's interest in the conjunction of meaning between Cathedral and skip develops through a choice of words which are rubble-like, selected from mixed contexts, words torn up from their roots. What seems at first a poem misshapen by too much verbal exhibition and Thesaurus-reading may in the end be faithfully serving its point. Connections are disrupted, refused wilfully. Not until the last poem in the book can we be completely clear though that the disruptions of music and simplicity are deliberate. . . . [In] **"Wildness makes a form"** this problem is argued out:

> Spring's tinct is urinous on the heart-shaped leaves
> marsh-water's flexions cringe. With reed and bird
> is mutuality, hospitable
> to each one's sounds—music is sound threaded
> on each one's listening, amongst wildness,
> this sluggish jamming of impatient forms,
> this enclaving of form
> in authentic dishevellment.

Is the dishevellment authentically observed or merely willed? It may be an attribute of the poem's subjects, of reality, or it may be invented. The opening line of this passage (which is the opening line of the poem) is on the point of forgetting (or perhaps even beyond that point) that what it must as language approve is fact. Why is the urinousness of that particular spring's

tinct on those heart-shaped leaves a fact of any importance or resonance? Is it a fact at all, or merely an intrusion to serve 'authentic dishevellment'—with the accompanying dishevellment—of language? All through the book unfactual lines persist: 'The pigeon's feathery / limb grins at the cobble face. / Mild-trained as a falcon, raspberry quartz / rings the palm's acquiring limb.' No context can elevate these statements to anything other than nonsense. If they fail as fact, how can they ever hope to succeed as meaning?

In spite of this, although it may well be that some of the poems are redeemable from their oddness and that many are not, when they are the freakishness can seem unexpectedly apt and there is a personality in the book as a whole which emerges, something furious and tense and, in the end, conciliated and innocent. (pp. 27-9)

Paul Mills, ''A Purposeful Dishevellment,'' in Poetry Review, *Vol. 69, No. 4, June, 1980, pp. 25-30.*

JAMES CAMPBELL

Jon Silkin's poetry is ''difficult''. This difficulty does not lie chiefly in what he has to say, however, but in how he says it, which makes his poetry hard to read, and even harder to understand. He makes no concessions to the reader, seeming at times to have no need or awareness of him—or so Silkin's lack of general comprehensibility would indicate—and *The Psalms with their Spoils* contains many poems in which all but the brave will lose their way and be forced to backtrack what seems like a mile or so in order to find it, so dense and lush is the jungle of Silkin's diction and syntax.

Most of the familiar preoccupations of Silkin's past work are represented in his new book: Jewishness, man's relationship with nature and animals, the uses of love. The epigraph, from Psalm 147, ''Praise is comely'', echoes throughout the book in lines such as ''Mend, I'd say; the spirit, mend, mend'' and suggests, along with the title, that Silkin intends his work to be devotional. He is indeed devoted to bridging the divide between body and soul which is the premise of many of these poems.

Silkin has often been accused of perpetrating wilful obfuscation in his poems. In his defence it should quickly be said that his imagination is inhabiting a realm in which all movement is of birth, death, pain, guilt, love. It may be that, if the poet is to be true to his ''word'', extreme states of being demand extreme modes of manifestation. We do not go to Silkin for acute social perception, or for exquisite descriptions of love, or for wit, (nor, incidentally, can I see that we should regard him as a ''committed'' poet, as at least one critic has suggested); his problem is the problem of being and his exploration of it requires that grammar and syntax be adapted to suit the demands of his vision. His language is primarily imagistic: the temporal movement of the poem is crammed so tightly with image and metaphor that it almost ceases to be temporal at all and becomes architectural. . . . The last thing this poetry means to be is mere drama or description; instead it seeks to enact its own content, to become the thing itself phenomenologically. In the best of the book's longer poems, **"Wildness makes a form"**, Silkin writes that the ''Gaudy practitioner'' enacts ''coordinates of our growth with that wild growth''.

But if Silkin's grammatical and syntactical liberties are to be justified in terms of his seeking a grammar which will measure his vision, then we want to be sure that the vision itself is exacting, that he has something worthwhile to *say*. Since most of his poems eschew "statement", depending instead on accretions of imagery which counterpoint and eventually congeal the narrative, what Silkin has "to say" cannot be defined or paraphrased. Yet when he does drop his syntactical guard, the poems can be disarmingly simplistic for one whose linguistic skill demands so much attention. . . . (Beside that it should be said that some of the best poems in *The Psalms with their Spoils* are those in which Silkin leaves his nerve exposed.) Occasionally, too, his lush diction slides into self-parody. . . . To touch briefly on that favourite grouse of Silkin's critics, his syntax, the instances of virtual impenetrability are legion: "It's if / not all we are, yet what a great prince throws / of deep confusion into certainty''; ''Of the fly's eye, blinded majesty / the loss indented by a fed pin''. I am not suggesting that these constructions have no meaning, only that their meaning is exceedingly difficult to reach and that even if one does succeed in cracking the shell, it is still in question whether the nut was worth the bother. Silkin's dense sensuality is too often claustrophobic, while his "Holy holy" gestures towards illumination are mostly heavy-footed. And while his insistence on finding a suitable language for his experience is to be respected and, in places, strongly admired, the main objection to his practice must be that by rejecting the grammar of shared experience he is squeezing the heart—human, if not poetic—out of his poetry.

James Campbell, "To Asyntactical Extremes," in The Times Literary Supplement, *No. 4032, July 4, 1980, p. 762.*

PETER BLAND

I'm not as familiar with Silkin's previous work as, probably, I should be, but I find his poems [in *The Psalms with Their Spoils*] hard going. A very personal style (I'm all for that) seems forged out of contraries. The lessons of 'open field' writing result in a tightening rather than a widening of experience. The real 'field' in these poems is not so much the visual world outside him as the state of the poet's own emotions. His lines, though often lean-looking, belie the cramming and jarring of syntax within. In addition to these problems of form and language the poems often exist as a sort of dialogue between the universe and the self, so that the reader feels doubly excluded. I found it helpful to copy out some of the shorter poems in longhand. This seemed to hold me into the poems and helped me feel out the physical shape of Silkin's thinking. I also found a dictionary useful as he's inclined to suddenly tighten up a poem around a rather unusual word (sepalled . . . integument . . . dihedral . . . ululations) or unusual combination of words. I'm not being entirely negative about this. It's part of a poet's job to chivvy up the language and Silkin is one of the few around who's obviously got his heart set on doing just this. If the poems, for the most part, don't have a set 'subject' as such, then they *are* trying to be their own experience. In this he's learned something from the mainstream modernism of the Americans (Pound, Williams, Wallace Stevens) with far more openness than most English poets have. Modernism, apart from some uses of condensed speech, seems largely to have been ignored by 'established' poets in this country. All this said I still have the nagging feeling that Silkin could be more sympathetic to his readers without sacrificing his own essence. (pp. 109-10)

[At times Silkin moves] from the particular to the universal with admirable energy and insight. . . . At other times the con-

stant changing of imagery and metaphor within any one poem is very off putting and, for me, not always vindicated by the 'wholeness' of feeling that struggles to keep the poems together. . . . Silkin's overall context always strains to give us the physical equivalents of feeling. But by the end of the book I felt as though I'd read one long poem in which a lot of the parts were somehow interchangeable. On a powerful elemental level something underneath the poems keeps smouldering through. A compassion for the natural world has its equivalents in a strong physical feeling for language. Silkin mauls his words as though they were clay. If I often feel excluded from his concerns it's largely because of the poet's own self-absorption in what he's doing. I admire Silkin's determination to take risks. But how can one use 'the blinded mind' . . . 'the mind's awry' . . . 'baulked energy' . . . 'pity's flight' . . . 'excess of rage' . . . and 'seething heart' all in one 13-line lyric, and hope to get away with it? It's a measure of Silkin's emotional strength that he *almost* does. (pp. 110-11)

Peter Bland, "Exile and Late Vuillard," in London Magazine, *n.s. Vol. 20, Nos. 5 & 6, August & September, 1980, pp. 109-12.*

NICK MALONE

Jon Silkin uses language more directly than any major contemporary English poet; attitude and experience are expressed without any attempt to hide behind the language transmitting them, and without any concessions to 'taste', either in the verse form or the feeling that forged it. A healthy sign of the present poetry readership is that this directness has already achieved a wide popularity for some of the poems [in *Selected Poems*]. . . . (p. 331)

But Silkin's most important achievement lies ironically in the reasons for which he is frequently considered 'difficult' and 'obscure'—a genuinely radical vision whose statement is normally quite plain. At one level, one of the difficulties in approaching Silkin's poetry is simply the insistence on *what* is being said, expressed as it is with an immediacy, unfamiliar to much modern poetry; there is no gentle immersion in sound in which the reader can bathe before tackling complex thematic issues; (in contrast to the way in which many readers can initially enjoy Eliot's *Four Quartets* for instance). This is not to say that Silkin's poetry is without great vibrancy; but its intonations are rhythmical rather than metrical with delayed cadences that perhaps have their roots in Hebrew. . . . (pp. 331-32)

But what gives this language its forged acerbity is the dramatic shift in standpoint that the poems demand of the reader—a move from the position of comfortable, detached observer to a direct identification with the object, where ideas and experience are in this sense 'lived in'. . . .

It seems to me that it is this shift from the hidden gentility of modernism, (and by 'gentility' I mean here the protected elitism implicit in its frequent detachment and impersonality), that is the triumph of these poems, and it is the political demands of this shift that most frequently results in their misapprehension. For the book is fiercely political, not just in its overt pieces like **"Killhope Wheel"** and **"Breaking Us",** but in its entire perspective of the world and its value judgements on how we should relate to it. (p. 332)

Nick Malone, "The Politics of Compassion," in Contemporary Review, *Vol. 237, No. 1379, December, 1980, pp. 331-32.*

EDWARD LARRISSY

Looking back through Jon Silkin's earlier work [contained in *Selected Poems*], I was struck by the absence of that quality of "concreteness", of faithful observation, so often mentioned in praise of various poets. Not unfavourably struck, mind you. "The kingdom of God cometh not by observation", as Joyce remarked. Since this quality is absent from a fair amount of good poetry, we may assume that poets can get along without it. And Silkin does.

Some of the early poems, especially from *The Re-ordering of the Stones* (1961), remind one of another poet who offended against Life and Leavis: W. H. Auden.... Silkin's style, though, unlike Auden's, is convincingly pressed into the service of a stringent, thoughtful and indignant compassion for the suffering and exploited: it enacts an austere pity.

The suffering may be close to the poet, and deeply felt, as in the famous "Death of a Son"; but Silkin's response generally implies a wider political attitude....

Not that Silkin does not occasionally fall foul of the dangers both of his style and of his stance. Sometimes he offers no recompense for his sparseness, or the elliptical and intellectual style results in a dense, knotted obscurity which yields to no strategy. The recurrent imagery of small animals and birds (vulnerable) and stones (invulnerable) can seem perfunctory and mechanical.

At other times we are subject to a rude assault on our complacency, which, though motivated by an indignant humanity, does not turn into a poem: "The beggar's bowl is formed from hands.... / You, into this gnarled hand put / Bread, and drop meat; raw / Boned and moist, but donate no pity." The poem is in part a taunt offered to a supposed liberal attitude: a theoretically compassionate but in fact unfeeling detachment, a sense of fairness based on social privilege. In "Respectabilities" we learn that "Many liberals don't just / Make love, they first ask each other ... / Nothing hasty, nothing unconsidered / Catches the liberal by / The hairs of lust." Many radicals allow qualities such as fairness and tolerance no autonomy, and even speak of them as if they went with limp wrists. Self-righteousness is the peril peculiar to moral earnestness. In early Silkin it may be connected to an over-simple rejection of "the inner heart" when faced with the begging bowl raised by half the world.

The poems in *Nature with Man* (1965), especially the "Flower Poems", represent a change and an advance. Here our old friend "close observation" is happily married to Silkin's gift for terse, memorable phrasing.... One is made to feel that the attention to these humble flowers is analogous to a considerate attention to humanity in general; the poems succeed in evoking a moral sense through lively description. They are impressive, unusual, and show that Silkin has learnt something from William Carlos Williams: a nice lesson, since both Williams and his imitators sometimes give the impression that they are not interested in poetic language. Silkin, however, retains a sense of excitement in his quirky phrasing and inventive diction.

Silkin has gone on developing: from being a poet who had done some fine things he has become a fine poet. A further change comes in *Amana Grass* (1971), where among a number of poems of place are some about Israel. He now explores the link between the personal (for instance his Jewishness) and the political in a more serious way. The poems are sometimes reminiscent of Neruda, not only in their sense of the connexion

between people and places, but also in their expansive rhythm, capacious lines, and exalted, sombre meditativeness. This style can be seen to advantage in "Six Cemetery Poems" (the cemeteries are American) and in one of the Israeli poems, "Divisions": these divisions are religious and "tribal". The setting of the poem is where the border divides Israel and Lebanon.... The poem conveys the arbitrary feel of the border, but soon comes to focus on two dead men, one circumcized the other not. There is a strangely clinical description of the two penises. The poem ends by stating that "None attends them. The sabbath intervenes like a blade."

The verse of *The Principle of Water* (1974) represents a stylistic continuation, but something of a disappointment. "Killhope Wheel" is a long poem about a disused lead mine in the Pennines. It successfully evokes the reality of an extinct community. But there is a sense of effort about this self-consciously committed piece of social history.... The interminable poem "The People" is a terribly portentous, more or less obscure family romance. There are good patches, but the private references do not take on a logic of their own, do not transcend their privacy as they do in, say, Plath.

But for the poems of *The Little Time-keeper* (1976) reprinted here, nothing but praise is due: they move in a realm where the public and private worlds are one, where thought and sensuous experience flow into each other. Their language is rich, striking, authoritative, with a powerful compactness. All these things could be said of Geoffrey Hill's work, and Silkin is indeed sometimes reminiscent of him. This is no mean praise; and anyone surprised by it should turn to the last pages of this varied and interesting selection and look at such poems as "Two Images of Continuing Trouble", or "At Nightfall".

Edward Larrissy, "Holding in Affection," in The Times Literary Supplement, *No. 4059, January 16, 1981, p. 65.*

MARY KINZIE

[As evidenced in Silkin's *Selected Poems,* the] oppression of the physical enters into his work at every point, whether in his themes or because, whatever his theme, he gives the impression of having been trapped in the wrong body, the wrong voice. In a ghastly way, he writes like Caliban: "flesh deciduates in passion"; "The wagging stems / of sex slather to inane fruitfulness"; "Blackmen, abiding their wilderness, / scorch the defoliated, wriggling grub"; "the bee / Grapples the reluctant nectar / Coy, suppurating, and unresigned." He is an expressionist, turning his mind to the inner workings of speechless things, but marring the effort with odd points of dogma....

> Despair is texture; without it
> We should not know how to face
> The thing with such certainty
> Of loss.
>
> ("Depths")

What does it matter what "texture" can be imparted to despair? Isn't it more vital to find its cause, its cure, or at least to distinguish the false from the true kind? Silkin plays so loose with the Great Ciphers (Despair, Pain, Passion, Agony, Suffering) that his work has neither the plainness of experience nor the subtlety of thought.... All his poetic gestures are designed to convince the reader that gnarled logic, mixed metaphor, and rapid feints of syntax are commanded from him because the feeling is so deep. Like Dylan Thomas, Hart Crane, and Galway Kinnell, Jon Silkin is a cosmic sentimentalist, a writer who wants the world to be understood as essentially biological and emotional as it makes its direct private appeal to him. . . .

Even when Silkin writes about the two subjects of most significance to him, the death of his infant son and the holocaust (which he frequently intertwines, as in the long poem **"The People"**), it is plain that experience is occasion for writing about it. Moreover, experience is to be written about in terms that send us, not back to our lives, but to the side-apse of the chapel in which the poet enshrines his own professionally pained sensibility. The parading of strong response and the sheer congestion of Silkin's verbal associations make excessive demands on the faithful.

> *Mary Kinzie, in a review of "Selected Poems," in* The American Poetry Review, *Vol. 10, No. 6, November-December, 1981, p. 40.*

NEIL PHILIP

Jon Silkin's play *Gurney* is an ambitious piece, using the life of the poet and composer Ivor Gurney as a loose framework for a verse enactment of themes of artistic talent versus artistic genius, the sanity of madness, and the will to destruction. Silkin, himself a notable poet and an expert on Gurney's period, is well equipped for such a task. Nevertheless, the play, at least on the page, does not seem to me very successful. The language is often rather flat, with little of Gurney's anguished precision, and the scenes of violence seem melodramatic and untrue to the essence of the experience they attempt to express. Gurney may, for instance, like Wilfred Owen, have been accused of cowardice or malingering, but the scene here of him being tortured in hospital with cigarette butts does not adequately convey the dynamics of such accusations. One of the problems of reading this play—as opposed to seeing it on stage, where it might sweep one past such reservations—is that it is never clear quite how closely to identify Silkin's 'Joseph Gurney' with his model. . . . [Some characters] are given their real names; others are lightly disguised; others seem to be composites, in one case (Benjamin Critchley) crudely distorting an important area of Gurney's life.

In *Gurney* Jon Silkin has concentrated with passion and intelligence on a period of history and an aspect of creativity that have long occupied him. The result will interest anyone who cares for Silkin's work or for Gurney's. It does not seem to me, however, either to free itself properly from its source material—the story of Gurney's 'hour of agony'—or to do justice to the desperate pathos of Gurney's prayers for 'Death, Release, or Imprisonment. An end to pain.'

> *Neil Philip, in a review of "Gurney: A Play," in* British Book News, *September, 1985, p. 561.*

James (Stewart Alexander) Simmons

1933-

Irish poet, songwriter, editor, critic, dramatist, and biographer.

A prominent member of Northern Ireland's respected Ulster Poets who gained recognition during the late 1960s, Simmons is noted for the personal nature of his verse and his entertaining use of colloquial language, lyrical form, and rhyme. He typically addresses such themes as marriage, divorce, love, art, and the political unrest and violence in his homeland. Although Simmons's poems often stem from disillusionment and pain, they characteristically feature a lively wit and a celebratory approach to life. Critics have noted that Simmons's experience as a songwriter has influenced his use of rhyme and meter and helped him to achieve clarity in his poetry. Simmons is also the founder and former editor of *The Honest Ulsterman*, a literary magazine that serves as a forum for Irish writers.

After gaining attention for several poems published in respected British magazines, Simmons wrote *Ballad of a Marriage* (1966), a pamphlet of personal verse centering on marriage. In his first full-length volume, *Late But in Earnest* (1967), Simmons continues his examination of familial, romantic, and marital relationships and begins to develop his personal view of world events. In his next collection, *In the Wilderness* (1969), Simmons examines a variety of topics and includes a sequence of poems based on *King Lear,* using Shakespeare's work to parallel aspects of his own life, including his marital difficulties and loneliness, and to underscore the need to acknowledge simple joys even in the face of life's tragedies. Many of the poems in *Energy to Burn* (1971) reflect the breakup of Simmons's marriage and his disenchantment with love in bluntly honest lines tempered with self-irony. In *The Long Hot Summer Still to Come* (1973), Simmons expands his thematic scope to encompass public concerns, including the political problems in Northern Ireland. Perhaps the harshest of his works, this book was praised by several critics for the vitality of Simmons's straightforward approach.

West Strand Visions (1974), which contains both songs and poems, perhaps best displays the positive influence of songwriting on Simmons's poetry. Terry Eagleton explained: "There is an obvious kinship between the dry satirical wit of [Simmons's] best poems and the disciplined blend of graphic detail and moral aphorism which writing songs and ballads enforces." In the songs of this volume, Simmons satirizes the historical failures of Ireland, while in verse he focuses on Irish myths. Almost all of the poems in *Judy Garland and the Cold War* (1976) are about other poets, including T. S. Eliot, John Donne, and W. B. Yeats. In the long poem "No Land Is Waste," which had been previously published as a pamphlet, Simmons attempts to refute the bleak view of life Eliot presented in *The Waste Land.* Poems from Simmons's first six volumes are collected in *The Selected James Simmons* (1978). In his review of this work, Gavin Ewart commented: "Humane, entertaining, honest, Simmons is certainly one of the very best English language poets we have."

Constantly Singing (1980) reveals Simmons's celebratory spirit, even though many of the poems in this volume are concerned with divorce and political turmoil. Simmons also includes such

Courtesy of James Simmons

new elements as evocative imagery of the Irish countryside and a thematic interest in middle age. Criticism of his next volume, *From the Irish* (1985), focused on the tension between Simmons's desire to be a popular and accessible poet and his frequent use of sophisticated literary allusions. While some reviewers asserted that this conflict sometimes resulted in trite verse and contrived rhymes, others praised the naturalness of Simmons's language and his perceptive observations.

(See also *Contemporary Authors,* Vol. 105 and *Dictionary of Literary Biography,* Vol. 40.)

ELIZABETH JENNINGS

James Simmons is, in *Ballad of a Marriage,* an adamantly personal poet. He writes of those things which most poets neglect, he is not afraid of his own body or its functions. In a poem called **"Connections,"** he writes very immediately and sharply of love:

That small, gay spurt of semen made, became
　　Brain, limbs and organs, nerves for joy and pain. . . .

Yet there is no desire to shock, only to link the reader with the poet's own experience. Not all the poems in this pamphlet come off, however. Some fail because they are unashamedly poetic, others because they thrust too much personal experience at the reader without supplying that necessary reticence and distancing important to all art. For the truth is that we are most engaged when least is overtly demanded of us. But Mr Simmons has some valuable things to tell us. (p. 324)

> *Elizabeth Jennings, "War and Peace," in* The Spectator, *Vol. 217, No. 7211, September 9, 1966, pp. 323-24.*

THE TIMES LITERARY SUPPLEMENT

James Simmons *is* entertaining, or mildly so, but the ironical style which Graham Greene praises in the blurb [for *Late but in Earnest*] turns out hardly to warrant the invocation of the late Norman Cameron: Mr. Simmons is in fact much more like, say, Philip Hobsbaum, though with less glumness and a greater would-be winsomeness.

> *"Taking a Strong Line," in* The Times Literary Supplement, *No. 3423, October 5, 1967, p. 937.*

JOHN HORDER

[*Late but in Earnest*] is abundant in life and vitality and is grounded in a basic humanity. The blurb makes a simple statement which proves to be true, 'Mr Simmons allows us to know him.' The poet's essential humanity is felt very firmly behind each word. The poems are simple, flowing statements on what it is like to be alive.

Mr Simmons, who has accepted the defects and flaws in himself, is able as a result to love others, defects, flaws and all. There are many very fine poems here, in particular **"Husband to Wife"** and **"This Seems True."** They will all be read with relish and delight, not least for their gusto. (p. 502)

> *John Horder, "Physical Responses," in* The Spectator, *Vol. 219, No. 7270, October 27, 1967, pp. 502-03.*

IAN HAMILTON

In The Wilderness, [James Simmons's] second book of verse, aims to impress us as both honest and a little dotty. It is an entertaining volume, glib and witty in the Kingsley Amis manner. When Simmons sets aside his smiling mask and attempts some small thrust of moral wisdom, he invariably falters into the banal, and there is a tendency throughout to let whole poems pivot on inadequate punchlines. At his best, though, a gifted and engaging writer.

> *Ian Hamilton, "Tremblings of Promise," in* The Observer, *April 13, 1969, p. 28.*

THE TIMES LITERARY SUPPLEMENT

Except for a sequence of lyrics which try to expatiate on *King Lear* and understandably fail to push frontiers forward, James Simmons's new book of poems *In the Wilderness* contains nothing which does not show the benefits of his very smooth, song-trained line, his fine worry or his good wit. **"The Theft Partial"** shows these qualities together: a principled disagreement with those dummy epigrams of Robert Frost which a

receptive culture has further debased to cracker-mottoes, it's a real punch-up of a poem. . . . Mr. Simmons is a redskin. Outside of civilization in much more than a Ginger-Mannish sort of way, he seems to inhabit, as well as hold, reservations. Unforced, not noticeably concocted, a genuinely trend-dodging and socially unfunctional personality comes across in every poem. Individual poems are rarely perfect but they add up, and likeability, a literary quality that can never be managed but can only happen, happens.

> A night with drama students. The party lasted till four
> And I woke next morning among bodies on a floor.

This happened while King George VI was dying, and the poem expiates a chance remark on the subject which the students took literally. Written in ambling couplets loosely handcuffed at the ends with obvious rhymes, it is nevertheless a clean job formally with the poet's style of life (that evening, if at no other time) presented guilelessly as a good, like the King's.

> The King was one of those who lived to please us
> Like Santa Claus and Dr. Johnson and Jesus

This line of his work, reigned in well short of cuteness, is one of his two best things. It shows well again in **"Remember thy Creator"**:

> In penultimate inspiration God
> Lifted a likely lump of sod
> And, pummelling at it half the night,
> Made Adam, to his great delight.
> Seeing his work a few weeks later,
> He pursed his lips: "I could do better."
> Into fresh clay his thumbs pressed,
> Left out the penis, made the breast
> Breasts, etcetera: "This is fun;
> It's the best thing I've done."

The comic organization which ensures that the last quoted line will bounce, instead of just lying there, is probably what Graham Greene had in mind when he suggested (in a statement now much in evidence on this book's wrapper) that Simmons could be mentioned in the same breath as Norman Cameron. That's probably putting it a bit high, but certainly effects like this have to be diligently worked for.

His other best thing is a strain of terror, on show in **"Rough Sketch"**: once more, and perhaps too reminiscently of the Dai poems of Kingsley Amis, the white-collar libertine slavers after the knickers flashing before him in the fog. . . . **"In the Desert War"** and **"Death of a Poet in Battle-dress"** are likewise terror-stricken. One gets the sense, here from a fragment and there from a balancing of sections, that Mr. Simmons might push through to a stronger poetry yet: but to do so he will have to put aside his too-forgiving guitar and tighten up. As it is his poems seductively invite an examination they can't long sustain. The music's all round instead of inside.

> *"Smooth Songs and Irish Echoes," in* The Times Literary Supplement, *No. 3504, April 24, 1969, p. 437.*

THE TIMES LITERARY SUPPLEMENT

James Simmons and Basil Payne are both Irish poets, and it is not fanciful to see here something of the sources of their poetic strength. The Irish context seems to offer in both cases a wry sense of the grim seediness of things enlivened by a quick, humorous self-awareness and (in Mr Simmons's case especially) a trick of quietly devastating irony. That irony seems a habit of sensibility which draws its nourishment from the wider social environment of which both poets are continuously aware: a disillusioned sense of a spent cultural tradition (symbolized for both in Yeats) which nevertheless still survives vestigially in a mode of perceptive wit which checks disillusion from sliding into cynicism. The neat, pointed impersonal regularity of Mr Simmons's metrical forms [in *Energy to Burn*] seems itself a kind of irony enacted at the expense of his drably confessional subject-matter: a precise poetic ordering is played off, in a sardonic, poker-faced way, against the depressed anecdotes of wife-swapping and marital strife which constitute its themes. . . .

> *"Floating in Spiritual Space," in* The Times Literary Supplement, *No. 3619, July 9, 1971, p. 798.*

JOHN SAUNDERS

[Simmons] knows that poetry can be fun. Much of [*Energy to Burn*], which includes poems from the earlier *No Ties* and *Memorials of a Tour in Yorkshire,* is frankly ephemeral, yet I have enjoyed it. . . . There are two parts, the first involving the life and loves of the artist, the second occasional verse on a variety of subjects. Most of the memorable things come from the first, although **"Censorship"** is amusing and effective. His theme is marriage and the woe that is in marriage. He uses rhyme very cunningly, the slight suggestion of formality offset by the colloquialisms and the metre regular but not settling to a fixed rhythm. Sometimes he approaches an almost Byronic lilt, and he can cover quite a range of effect as in this, one of the **"Marital Sonnets"**:

> In age's Leamington our joys last longer,
> the libraries are good, the tea rooms neat,
> good arguments aren't broken off by anger,
> new appetites are fed, we are replete.
> Let's call this love, that alters when it finds
> alteration, the marriage of two minds.

The attitudes to himself and the situation are more complex than the initial pose would suggest ('Our youth was gay but rough, / Much drink and copulation.'). Perhaps the underlying warm, undestructive self-irony is Irish. . . .

> *John Saunders, in a review of "Energy to Burn," in* Stand Magazine, *Vol. 12, No. 4 (1971), p. 65.*

THE TIMES LITERARY SUPPLEMENT

James Simmons is the liveliest of the Belfast poets, with the valuable quality of enjoyability. His poems are almost never dull and are usually entertaining. The technique is sometimes a little rough, but the straightforwardness, the honesty, and the intense appreciation of the fact of being alive, compensate for this. In a way, the roughness is part of the charm.

The main documents in the case are *Energy to Burn* . . . , *No Land Is Waste Dr Eliot* . . . and the present book [*The Long Summer Still to Come*]. With his wit and directness, Mr Simmons seems more at home in the world—even the troubled world of Belfast—than most poets. . . . His attitude to the troubles is oblique. **"Ulster Today"** contains the lines "If the next bomb / kills *me* it will still be irrelevant" and "the farcical and painful history of Ireland / is with us, unchanged".

Although the forms he uses are never complicated, not all the poems are ideologically simple—for example, **"The Bridge**

Players"**,** in which two psychiatrists, married, and a husband with a neurotic wife make up the four. On the other hand, a very simple poem like **"Drowning Puppies"** is also effective. Mr Simmons has always been good on marriage, and **"The Complaisant Husband"** is one of the best poems in this book. **"Wish Fulfilment"** is aimed at Betjeman, not exactly a parody but more a gloss on his uneasy attitude to sex. The short epigrammatic pieces aren't, in general, as satisfying as the longer poems, of which **"Uncle Jack"** and **"Before Hanging"** are fine examples.

> *"Rough Edges," in* The Times Literary Supplement, *No. 3715, May 18, 1973, p. 548.*

HAYDEN MURPHY

[*The Long Summer Still to Come*] has been one of the most invigorating books I have been given to review for some time. . . .

Simmons with affection and humour, discipline and energy (an earlier book was called *Energy to Burn*) and with an unfailing ear for our absurdities has compiled an answer to the 'bitter rage' that we too often accept as the only true sign of dedication. His poems on the page sing through his ability to juxtapose the absurd with the intense. His awareness of the pornography of loneliness and his exposé of the futility of hatred provide me with a book that I can return to and remember.

He irritates, he over-simplifies, he breaks all the codes of conduct, he is conservative and may for all I know be a dedicated Unionist, but for once all this seems irrelevant. In a poem, graphic and noisy, called **"The University Toilet"** he writes—'the partitions are frail' and in the total honesty of his work, and even into political context this poet can break down all induced partitions. The cynical eye that rhymes U.I.A. with 'those who pay' (**"The Field of Roses"**) is also the tender eye that writes:

> If God treats the human race like my father
> Treats customers we needn't worry.

It is good for us to have to face the reality of our similarities. We are lucky that Simmons still will play the wise fool to our sententious Lear. (p. 113)

> *Hayden Murphy, "Human: Irish & Ulster," in* The Dublin Magazine, *Vol. 10, No. 2, Summer, 1973, pp. 112-13.*

DOUGLAS DUNN

Contingency makes prose. That is both James Simmons's method and sentiment:

> Can a sheltered writer of poetry,
> sheltered by class and a teaching post
> at the University from the people
> he wants to serve, expect to have written
> songs for a new society? What nonsense!

Nonsense, yes; but why did the writer allow himself to be "sheltered"? And if he knows he's sheltered, why not leave the teaching post?

When Simmons gets tuned up, his lines have the plangency of
"**Bagpipe Music**":

> So, won't you now step off the carousel?
> There's no alternative to intercourse.
> However scary or exasperating,
> Hating the buggers only makes them worse.

While these lines have the virtue of truth, one reads the rest
of [*The Long Summer Still to Come*] longing for an imaginative
insight, something to prove that he has more than opinions and
a bad temper with which to project them as plain words inel-
egantly suspended over the unmetrical rise and fall of a doggerel formality. Simmons works from that dull and controversial quality, common sense. No doubt these lines will be
applauded as accurate recognition of "facts." To me they are
offensive:

> When speakers dissipate their breath
> demanding basic inalienable rights
> I know we are in for a boring night
> and morning paper headlines of death.

Why? The answer is that there are more than Simmons who
feel that the whole business of demanding rights is contemptible
and "boring."

Simmons's intention is to be *effective* rather than poetic; he is
after poems that *hurt,* and he doesn't care what he has to do
to get them. In his previous book, *Energy to Burn,* his subject
was conjugality—the presbyterian word suits him—either clandestine or official, a territory which [Michael] Longley calls
"the great indoors." *The Long Summer Still to Come* has the
same bite; but although harsh facts of domestic and married
life are here as before, he distributes vitriol over a more public
and political range. A state of mind formed by private experience is now directed at public events. One result of this is
that he promotes his own counter-ideology of feelings about
how life ought to be lived. Like Frank Sinatra, Simmons's
message is "*My* way!" And his advice is suspect: his subur-
banly bedroomised vision has its merits, but most of the time
it's nothing more than provincial agony in which virtually everything is found "boring" or, as he says of Camus's mind,
"bent." Nothing ever seems to live up to his hypothetical
standard of normality. His writing denies imagination its rights,
and language its sensuousness. His meaning is that the domestic
must triumph above all else.

Although Simmons's poems are perversely on the side of life
and personal happiness, his stance makes it necessary for him
to be not only disrespectful to those he dislikes, but to anything
larger than he is. Irish history is "farcical and painful" in his
opinion. All history is painful, at least intermittently; but to
associate farce with suffering is to degrade what might have
been justified, and elevate what was vicious. (pp. 73-4)

> *Douglas Dunn, "The Speckled Hill, the Plover's*
> *Shore: Northern Irish Poetry Today," in* Encounter,
> *Vol. XLI, No. 6, December, 1973, pp. 70-6.*

TERRY EAGLETON

James Simmons's songwriting has always been productive for
his poetry: there is an obvious kinship between the dry satirical
wit of his best poems and the disciplined blend of graphic detail
and moral aphorism which writing songs and ballads enforces.
In previous Simmons collections this has resulted in the paradox of an essentially subversive wit finding expression in
trimly metrical stanzas, turning poetic form itself into a kind
of structural irony. *West Strand Visions,* however, divides ge-
nerically in two: first some poems, then a sheaf of songs and
recitations culled from the performances of the Resistance Cabaret group of writers and musicians which Mr. Simmons has
formed in Belfast.

The songs, concerned as they mainly are with Northern Ireland
violence, successfully mix the acerbic, grotesque and pun-
gently realistic; in one darkly sardonic piece a couple of Belfast
Zoo monkeys come across the corpses of the last two men left
alive in the world and glumly confront the tedious prospect of
having to start the whole business over again. That vein of wry
disillusion runs through the poems too, but there it is held in
tension with a dream of fabular possibilities, played off against
the memory of a mythical past more heroic than the slackened,
devastated present . . . A personal disillusion . . . ; but also,
one senses, part of a deeper deadlock between heroic aspiration
and historical failure which is Irish society:

> The Man with the hat falls on the floor.
> Their fields are full of stones
> when they want bread and a job so much more
> than TVs and cinemas and telephones
> but they're laughing now, every man a star.
> Possessed by three unities they will never escape—
> ignorance, poverty, hate—they definitely are
> stylish, passionate and in great shape.

Direct references to Ireland of this kind are fairly rare in the
poems, and maybe, given that facilely Olympian "never", all
to the good; but it is interesting to see how the historical conflicts starkly exposed in the alternately tight-lipped and knockabout ballads are transformed in the poems into sharply probing
debates between vision and reality.

> *Terry Eagleton, "Diminished Hopes," in* The Times
> Literary Supplement, *No. 3808, February 28, 1975,*
> *p. 214.*

ALAN BROWNJOHN

James Simmons has always been the maverick of the Ulster
poets, rough, clumsy and talkative where his colleagues are
often technically fastidious and reticent. Half of *West Strand
Visions* consists of "**The Resistance Cabaret**", ballads and
poems sung and recited by the poet with other singers, writers
and musicians: untidy, angry and sorrowful stuff, worlds away
from those mandatory nods towards social content given by
folk-singers in English bars. He can write touchingly about the
anxieties of being a poet, which most poets can't (and how
often they try!). . . . (p. 557)

> *Alan Brownjohn, "Opening Lines," in* New States-
> man, *Vol. 89, No. 2301, April 25, 1975, pp. 557-58.*

D. M. THOMAS

Almost all the poems [in *Judy Garland and the Cold War*] are
about other poets, dead and alive, English and Irish. [Simmons]
is stern about the stern ones (the religious Donne, and Eliot,
whom he calls by his second name, Stearns), and genial about
the genial ones. The style is cool, colloquial, vigorous. It makes
for a lively book; but, when he strikes out at much finer poets
than himself the blows rebound embarrassingly. . . .

[While] Mr Simmons's response to *The Waste Land* contains
skilful portraits of seedy likeable people from his earlier years

in London, this long poem, **"No Land is Waste"**, is damaged by its aggressive air of "correcting" Eliot's vision.

Elsewhere, Mr Simmons's frequent passages of parody are not quite witty enough. There are good poems about a few unnamed poets, and also about Judy Garland and Fanny Hill, where something real is being said, skilfully and wittily, about the human condition. The rare breaks from the mirrorfuls of poets work best: for example, the droll humour of **"Buchanan's Fancy"**, where body-searches in Belfast are seen as sought-after sexual titillation. Here, an echo of Donne works well as a climax, so to speak: "Do you license / their roving hands? I do."

D. M. Thomas, "Corrected Vision," in The Times Literary Supplement, *No. 3921, May 6, 1977, p. 548.*

EDNA LONGLEY

In the poetry of James Simmons art and life never look like becoming polite strangers. Their intimacy declares itself through the effortlessly natural tones of the poet's voice—at once source and focus of the pervasive vitality. Whether lyrical or plain-spoken, confiding or confessional, pointing a moral or telling a tale, the poems have an air of very immediately addressing the reader out of the immediacy of experience. Simmons's theory, too, favours direct methods that connect on a live fuse the poet, his subject matter and his audience. In the sequence **"No Land is Waste"** he argues, in a suitably demotic idiom, for a democracy of the imagination as opposed to the remote, aristocratic stance of T. S. Eliot:

> The pompous swine . . .
> that man's not hollow, he's a mate of mine.

Simmons's other and inseparable career as songwriter and singer both explains and sustains such an aesthetic. **"Didn't He Ramble"**, a tribute to jazz, affirms the origins of the artist's words and music in the tribe and its unpurified dialect:

> the word of life, if such a thing existed,
> was there on record among the rubbish listed
> in the catalogues of Brunswick and H.M.V.,
> healing the split in sensibility.
> Tough reasonableness and lyric grace
> together, in poor man's dialect.
> Something that no one taught us to expect.
> Profundity without the po-face
> of court and bourgeois modes. This I could use
> to live and die with. Jazz. Blues.

Although Simmons's range encompasses many 'classical' effects, his commitment to 'the word of life', as a touchstone for style and content, makes him one in spirit with these jazzmen. If we grant the term its full weight, he is a 'folksinger' in his poetry as he is a poet in his songs.

Simmons's 'word of life', however, does not confine itself to the good news. In **"Me and the World"** he personifies the world as an unpredictable lover, often 'estranged by flaws of mine or withdrawn / for her own reasons'; while in **"A Muse"** inspiration itself assumes the same fickle guise: 'Her / charm is in being chancy'. The special immediacy of Simmons's poetry also derives from its authenticity as the fluctuating response of a representatively 'flawed' individual to a 'chancy' universe. And the rough course of true—or untrue—love is central to the plot of the continuing drama thus established. . . . [A] stanza, from **"The Silent Marriage"**, epitomises and holds

in a rare poise the conflicts in Simmons's perception of love, and perhaps of life: ecstatic moments, all-too-probable decline or betrayal, the incompatibility of passion and permanence, a slightly over-optimistic faith in the resolving power of honesty. Similar perspectives condition his larger exploration of the tensions between romance and domesticity, freedom and responsibility, youth and age. Simmons has taken some highly unflattering 'photographs' of marriage, which attempt to fix the reality beneath the 'Arcadian' mask. . . . But time, in traditional manner, is seen as the ultimate betrayer of idylls and ideals. . . . (pp. 1-2)

This needling consciousness of how time and ties can devour the free spirit instals the Ulysses myth as a subterranean point of reference in Simmons's poetry. It eventually surfaces in **"On Circe's Island"**, but many other poems conjure up the liberating sea, voyages of discovery, the thrill of an exotic landfall. . . . [Simmons, like] Ulysses, tends to come round full circle, to the full complexities. . . . The complexities, including death—that inescapable destination and commitment—are most completely felt in his **"King Lear"** sequence, which also incorporates Simmons's most completely developed mythological framework. He sets up camp on the edge of 'the wilderness' and of Shakespeare, and, partly by mocking the pretension of both these actions, holds up perhaps his largest and clearest mirror to the mortal predicament. . . . (p. 3)

Simmons's flirtations with Shakespearean drama draw attention to the variety of his own *dramatis personae*. He generally plays the lead himself, of course, or rather his voice, modulating to express different moods and attitudes, from 'passion, grief and fear' to tenderness, humour and satire. **"Written, Directed by and Starring . . ."**, a fine example of Simmons's ironic mask, can be read as a gloss on such self-dramatisation, and on the way in which his 'scripts' have kept pace with the changing stage of his world:

> The hero never hogs the screen because
> his wife, his children, friends, events intrude.
> When he's not on the story doesn't pause—
> not if he dies. I don't see why it should.

Wife, children, friends and lovers are only some of the characters that crowd the screen. Many others take their bow in this densely-populated poetry: shell-shocked **"Uncle Jack"**, a chain-smoking professor, an **"Old Gardener"**, the bizarre celluloid figures of **"Summer Lightning"**, 'business girls', 'The head commissionaire at the Odeon, Marble / Arch', writers and the characters *they* have created, idolised entertainers. . . . The imagery, like the way his people straddle the boundaries of fact and fiction, indicates once again Simmons's own 'integrated' view of art and life. His theatre includes some memorable final acts in which the power of the completed performance mitigates pity and terror. . . . (pp. 4-5)

But there is a didactic as well as a dramatic element in Simmons's poetry. One part of his imagination desires to change the world, not simply to stage it as it is. When he founded the literary magazine, *The Honest Ulsterman*, in 1968, he called it 'a monthly handbook for a revolution'. With varying degrees of self-mockery, he adopts the persona of a 'teacher', a 'reformer', in several poems. . . (p. 5)

In its visionary aspect, his poetry is that of a Blakean Utopian who, somewhere beyond irony and qualification, believes with

Judy Garland in 'the promised rainbows', in the millennium he outlines in **"For Thomas Moore"**:

> when youth finds its singers
> and old men find peace
> and beauty finds servants
> and genius, release . . .

Songwriters, singers and musicians are often given a prophetic role that reflects Simmons's wish to see his own 'songs' used 'to live and die with'. The original jazz revolution points the way towards a society free of oppression and repression, founded on and cherishing the unaggressive values of art, true to the spiritual implications of 'the word of life':

> Here was the risen people, their feet
> dancing, not out to murder the elite . . .

Yet another deftly turned couplet emphasises the shapely clarity of Simmons's style, a clarity which is integral to the democracy of his approach. Songs and ballads of course aim at instant penetration of the mind and emotions, and it is likely that the discipline of these modes has toned up the muscle of Simmons's other verse, helping him to achieve surprisingly often his ideal of 'Tough reasonableness and lyric grace / together'. The Elizabethan simplicity of phrasing in **"The Silent Marriage"** and **"The Blessed Mary Fogarty"**, the streamlined economy of such different narratives as **"Summer Lightning"** on the one hand, **"The Ballad of Gerry Kelly: Newsagent"** and **"Claudy"** on the other, have their echoes and equivalents throughout his work. In some ways the basis—or at least the base—of Simmons's poetry is statement, the medium of 'Tough reasonableness'. Despite an abundance of precise detail and vivid impressions, sensual impact generally plays second mate to the moralist or seer at the helm. Their idiomatic and dramatic energy rescue Simmons's statements from the pitfalls of abstraction, but his eagerness to place, as well as evoke, experience makes the epigrammatic couplet, the sonnet, the neat quatrain, forms to which he homes a trifle automatically. . . . The mimetic quality of . . . **"Birthday Poem"**, however, proves Simmons's ability to break free of the rhythmic straitjacket (and fixed viewpoint) which his addiction to firmly rhymed iambic assertion does at times become. . . . Myth supplies a further dimension still: in addition to the *Odyssey* and *King Lear* many subsidiary legends, folk tales, works of literature, as well as the poet's own inventiveness, open out, heighten and universalise a vision that occasionally risks becoming too particular or personal.

"Stephano Remembers" seems to me Simmons's most profound interpretation of an archetype; perhaps because dramatic and mythic qualities fuse at a whiter heat than usual, the imagery achieves a bolder 'sweep':

> on a huge hogshead of claret I swept ashore
> like an evangelist aboard his god . . .

But the fundamental source of the poem's excellence must be its extra distillation of the warmth and compassion which are the controlling emotions of Simmons's best work. They not only blossom forth in his love poems and his poems about children, but also determine a celebratory bias ('celebrate' is a favourite word). . . . It may be harder for Ulster poets these days to 'join in celebrating' or come up with affirmations of life. Certainly **"Claudy"** and **"The Ballad of Gerry Kelly"** magnificently meet the new demands that have been made on Simmons's compassion. . . . The last two lines of **"Lullaby**

for Rachael" sum up the spirit of the whole achievement which is saluted by the publication of [*The Selected James Simmons*]:

> I've made, while trying to tell no lies,
> a noise to go with love.

> (pp. 6-9)

Edna Longley, in an introduction to The Selected James Simmons, *by James Simmons, edited by Edna Longley, Blackstaff Press, 1978, pp. 1-9.*

GAVIN EWART

Edna Longley, in her introduction [to *The Selected James Simmons* (see excerpt above)], writes "In the poetry of James Simmons art and life never look like becoming polite strangers". This is surely the heart of the matter, and the main virtue of what might be called the Ulster School—Michael Longley, Michael Foley, Frank Ormsby and, at a distance, Derek Mahon (Andrew Waterman is more of an expatriate outsider) and others of equal, or nearly equal, talent. The verse is usually simple, iambic quatrains being standard, and traditional. There is nothing that anyone could call experimental or avant-garde about it. Fantasy is rare and ordinary everyday life, described or commented on, is its subject. Any issue of *The Honest Ulsterman* will prove this point.

Simmons is even more a part of this simplistic tradition than the others, because he writes his own songs and sings them, to the guitar. Mrs Longley claims that he is a folk singer in his poetry, as he is a poet in his songs. This is true—but there are snags. The trouble is that songs can be made to sound good, even when they have inexact rhymes and very simple forms; poems (which are frequently stared at on the page by dons and people like me) can't afford so much roughness. They can afford some, if they're good enough—imaginatively and poetically. The rhymes of **"Our Hunting Fathers"**, for example, are very approximate; but, like butterflies in a collection, page poems are pinned down. The song, in its flight, moves so quickly that the mind accepts things that would trouble it in written-down verse.

"Claudy" is a marvellous ballad, in the same class as "Danny Deever"; and it works both ways. Yet the folk singer can be glib, too. "If our luck should run out / and love withers and dies, love, / don't try out of kindness / to save me with lies, love". Here "withers and dies" is a songwriter's dead metaphor, and "save me"—what does that mean? The songlike techniques have their triumphs of humour: "But the girls who read Vogue / and are bored by Ted Hughes / are easy to look at / but hard to amuse." It is careless, all the same, to use "but" twice.

There is, though, an "academic" side to Simmons's talent. . . . The sequence that takes issue with Eliot (perhaps rather unfairly, as Simmons himself suggests), and contains the line "that man's not hollow, he's a mate of mine", is dealing in commodities known to English Departments. So is the whole **"King Lear"** sequence and (naturally) **"Shall I Compare Thee to a Summer's Day?"** and **"Death Be Not Proud"**. The formal, rhymed poem **"Lot's Wife"** could easily have been written by Roy Fuller or Yvor Winters. Equally neat is **"A Man Whistling"**—not included here. Yet, if anything, Mrs Longley has played down the roaring qualities. *Late But In Earnest,* his first book, so praised by Graham Greene ("Surely this is the most readable volume of ironic poetry since Norman Cameron died?"), contained **"If The Cap Fits"** (birth control) and *In* *the Wilderness* had **"Songs of the Old Sod"** (reflections on the Catholic faith), **"The Use of History"** (the troubles beginning, 1969), **"Seasonal Greeting"** (a Tom Moore-like song of unbelief). . . . I would rather have had these in, and the **"Lear"** poems out.

But this is devil's advocacy; though even Shakespeare does, actually, abide our question—particularly when he strays too far into fustian or boring lists of noblemen, like football teams, in the Histories (and "O saucy Worcester!" was a fair parody, in *Beyond The Fringe*). This selection is a good one, and the list of good poems here is a long one. . . .

The poems become more interesting technically in the later volumes. . . . Humane, entertaining, honest, Simmons is certainly one of the very best English language poets we have, and anybody with an eye or an ear for poetry will enjoy this selection.

> Gavin Ewart, *"Singing and Roaring," in* The Times Literary Supplement, *No. 3982, July 28, 1978, p. 846.*

GREVEL LINDOP

Simmons has always been ready to report on immediate personal experience, but more than any of the earlier volumes *Constantly Singing* seems a set of dispatches from a personal battlefield: emotion recollected sometimes in tranquillity, but just as often in perplexity or anger.

The new book follows quite soon after *The Selected James Simmons*. . . . He is a prolific writer, and during this period his output has also included several plays as well as musical settings of his own and other poets' work which he has sung in concert and recorded on a series of albums. Through all this work the strengths and weaknesses have been fairly constant, closely related to each other and to the fact that he sees himself first of all as a performer, an active communicator rather than a creator of timeless artefacts. The central virtue of his work has been its plain-spoken clarity, a refusal to evade issues or clutter feeling with rhetorical ornament. Coupled with precise observation, this can be a technique of revelatory honesty, as in the fine early poem, characteristically entitled **"Experience"**, about being forced into a pointless fight by a belligerent drunk. . . . And it works well in the memorable ballads he has composed in response to the "troubles" of the past eleven years which, as a native resident of Northern Ireland, he has had to watch at close quarters—**"The Ballad of Gerry Kelly: Newsagent"**, for example, which recounts with desperate sanity a senseless sectarian murder. . . .

But clearly these styles impose their own limitations, and there are depths and subtleties which such a purely demotic manner, in this age at least, probably cannot reach. How far Simmons is aware of the problem is unclear, but his entertaining onslaught on Eliot, **"No Land is Waste"**, does not inspire a great deal of confidence, referring to Eliot as a "pompous swine" and even inviting him to refresh his vision by "com[ing] round to meet the boys tonight, / to see the hollow men get full and fight", as if Simmons had forgotten his own **"Experience"** and what the much-sentimentalized bar-room punch-up is really like at close quarters. It is easy enough to dismiss Eliot's vision as "the spiritual DTs", but the tendency to go for the easy laugh and the quick stock-response, a dangerous temptation for the song-writer and "performing" poet, can betray him into conventional falsehoods which are at least as far away

from reality. When, in a poem from the 1976 collection, *Judy Garland and the Cold War,* Simmons admits "I wish my lovely lucid songs / had the conviction Elton John's / get from just knowing they're wanted", one senses all the problems of wanting to be wanted, of depending on an audience that may need to be wooed in ways that will cost the poet, eventually, all that he has.

By their truth to experience, the best poems in *Constantly Singing* avoid these dangers, registering with detached precision the cheerless pretences of an unhappy marriage . . . or the freshness and disorientation of divorce. . . . The poet, however, is still "the star", and persistent irony never quite succeeds in neutralizing a note of self-congratulation. **"Meditations in Time of Divorce"**, the opening poem sequence of the book, is often starkly moving—. . . but a tendency to autohagiography keeps breaking in:

> Behold the change-shaper,
> now Ulster's leading
> lighter of a fire
> with screwed up newspaper,
> a dish-washer of genius . . .

Despite the calculated absurdity, and the self-judgment a few lines later—"Platitudinous old pseud"—one feels that at some level Simmons means it, as he does when later in the same sequence he describes himself as "in good faith embracing / necessity, constantly singing, not / putting a sour face on it", in rather too obvious contrast to the wife, who is busy "seizing the house-beautiful, the car, / the kids, lacking other resource". This might be dislikeable, but it is not, probably because, like the whole book, **"Meditations in Time of Divorce"** carries a strong impression of honesty. At times the poems admit pomposity, but they are not pompous. **"After Eden"**, perhaps the best poem in the book, shows the poet making a furtive visit to the former marital home—"after midnight, woozy with drink, / on a quick foray for old tapes"— and presents with equal clarity and innocence the sensation of punching his wife on the nose—"When he hits her, precious tapes unreel / and roll on the pavement. Again they are sharing / intimate touch—her nose, his knuckles, sore". . . .

This openness to the untidy immediacy of experience gives Simmons's work some similarities to that of the jauntier wing of the American "confessional" tendency: the Berryman of *Love and Fame,* for example. There is also a certain debt to the poetic mode associated with the "Movement". . . .

And at some moments Simmons seems to be deliberately evoking some of the more famous exercises in risk-taking by poets of that generation. **"Interior Decorating"** strives to outdo the memorable opening line of Larkin's "Sad Steps": Larkin wrote "Groping back to bed after a piss . . .", so Simmons begins, grandiloquently, "One night I strode from you to ease my bowels". Donald Davie's sombre and often-quoted "A man who ought to know me / wrote in a review / my emotional life was meagre" seems to be emulated in the last lines of **"At the Post Office"**: "The critic, Mrs Longley, was to write / years after, / 'He must have had very large / illusions.' By God she was right."

Occasionally plainness of speech can lapse into dullness, the language slithering into a mixture of dead metaphors, as when, at the end of **"Five American Sonnets"**, "my host breezed in / just as our dying fall was wearing thin", and the love poems lapse sometimes into soft-porn cliché: "our glowing bellies, heaving / in ecstasy" and so on. At other times, as if to hint that he is aware of broader perspectives, Simmons can be over-allusive, and *Constantly Singing* is studded with phrases from the Masters—Shakespeare, Donne, Crashaw, Wordsworth, Browning, Whitman and, of course, Yeats—most of which add very little, while some are absurdly inappropriate, as when, in **"Ballad of a Marriage"**, a husband enquires

> "This sweet mysterious country
> explored by my right hand.
> Am I the first, my wife, that's burst
> into this silent land?"

—the Coleridge echo seeming merely a distracting, embarrassed mannerism. Yet, typically, **"Ballad of a Marriage"** recovers almost immediately. The husband's response to the answer he feared is precisely and painfully delineated:

> I'd slept with girls myself, but I
> was trembling, I was hating
> these men, and her, and yet I found
> her stories titillating:
> first fascination, then disgust;
> first pain and then a surge of lust.

And self-judgment is delivered unflinchingly: "Freedom and truth, by which I swear, / in fact were more than I could bear."

The personal, autobiographical tone of *Constantly Singing* also governs its one poem about the political situation in Ulster, **"Coleraine: 1977"**, which describes the psychological impact of a bombing—not a murderous outrage but rather an event that seems, in its context, an almost trivial affair of noise and broken glass. Simmons's account, excellent merely as documentary description, is muted and self-critical, sensing the inadequacy of his own responses and the shallowness of the liberal aestheticism which seems the only present alternative to barbarism. The poet and his friends are "middle-class magi with no star / in the heavens or on our chests", who "all have a certain flair / for enjoying each other / in a mildly bohemian fashion". When the explosion is heard, other postures appear: first the stilted indignation, then the furtive, prurient curiosity: "quick, cautious, we sidle into the night air / like the rest of Coleraine . . .". The poem's most powerful statement is a confession of helplessness:

> You might define decadence
> by our ambivalence, unable to see or hear
> exactly what's going on, only
> the old words and music, our eyes
> curiously impaired.
> Shops, churches, uniforms look
> as they used to, but don't fill
> the role. The rare policeman
> with wit and integrity
> is a poignant figure, like the clergyman
> who embodies faith, or the rigorous teacher.

One can scarcely avoid comparing this bleak scepticism, this hesitancy of thought and rhythm, with the forceful, almost visceral reactions of Heaney: his instinctive revulsion, for example, at the sight of British armoured cars and his grimly sympathetic understanding of atavistic tribal conflict. To admit that Heaney's treatment of political themes has so far been more powerful than Simmons's may be to say only that Simmons has undertaken the harder task. The lyric tradition accommodates itself rather easily to the terrible beauty of commitment; the beauties of scepticism and detachment demand

an ability to use tradition against itself, to criticize the stock response. . . .

Constantly Singing carries, throughout, the warmth of lived experience. At some points Simmons seems not to be writing at full pressure; and there are indications that both his view of poetry and an undue sense of his own importance may be placing limitations on his work. But he has produced another lively, challenging book, at its best scathingly direct and memorably terse, presenting (as he has written in a poem about jazz) "Tough reasonableness and lyric grace / together, in poor man's dialect".

Grevel Lindop, "The Beauties of Detachment," in The Times Literary Supplement, *No. 4060, January 23, 1981, p. 91.*

ALAN HOLLINGHURST

An elevated or transfigured commonness is part of [Simmons's] achievement, and the reasons for it lie partly in his experience as a songwriter and singer. He knows about the openness of sound, the clarity of idea, the directness of syntax demanded by words for music, but unlike those of most poets his songs when printed do not look like gauche and simplistic botches of a different kind of poem. He has discovered a voice of effortless fluency, natural and virile in diction and wide in range, a tough but transparent medium in which the performer's voice is preserved in limpid perpetuity after the performance has ended. . . . [He] has the ballad in various forms and with its conventions more or less unruffled as a major vehicle. And his brief for fiction is more generous, more simple: "Anything processed by memory is fiction!"—a dictum which makes no special case but reminds us of the fictional autonomy of life when transmuted into poetry.

Simmons's new collection [*Constantly Singing*] contains a number of songs—poems at least in ballad form but with a literary rather than popular discipline: entirely lucid and accessible, they contain no banalities. . . . Some people may feel that Simmons is too prolific, fear his mastery has become parnassian or his subject too easy; but everything in this book refutes it. . . . (pp. 82-3)

Alan Hollinghurst, "Telling Tales," in Encounter, *Vol. LVI, Nos. 2-3, February-March, 1981, pp. 80-5.*

RODNEY PYBUS

'Anything processed by memory is fiction!' James Simmons warns us, quoting Wright Morris, as an epigraph to his latest collection [*Constantly Singing*]; and well he might, though it does not diminish a flicker of guilt in the reader confronted by the saga of the poet's public 'private' life. What we still get, though, is the unmistakable sound of someone telling the truth about his emotions and things as they are. The sexual explicitness, the celebrations of harmony and discord in or out of the domestic-marital framework (usually dressed in traditional forms that are dropped less frequently than lovers' underwear), have always been some of Simmons' characteristics. They figure again, but here with poems of divorce and only-half-regretful middle-age: his poetry is still a full-frontal quarrel with all that Ulster (and British) Protestantism holds most dear. In Simmons respectability, fidelity, sobriety and the work ethic become signs of the inauthentic. At its best his work has 'grace under pressure, / style and sense of form under duress' (**"The Happy Worrier"**, *Energy to Burn*), and the remarkable wholeness of his several collections to date is pointed up by the reprinting here of one of his earliest poems, **"Ballad of a Marriage"** (minus the original's last two relatively optimistic stanzas), and it seems not at all out of place in style or quality. While it might be argued that this implies no 'development', he has always had a variety of forms and tones to work, and here there is a deepening insight into the possibilities of human sympathy and compassion, and the effects of their absence.

It's too easy to write him off as a sharp-eyed, witty and musically-gifted balladeer: he is very much in earnest, and for all the cavalier brio of poems like **"My Friend the Instrument"** (no, it's about his guitar) and **"Five American Sonnets"**, what's relatively new is the tone of 'Failing is all right, / a sort of roughage to the appetite' (**"The Honeymoon"**). In **"After Eden"**, one of the best poems about divorce and separation, the man 'on a quick foray for old tapes' meets his ex-wife and they come to blows. The last stanza movingly images the continuing grip of their marital past:

> His last glimpse is of her standing
> in faded chiffon nightwear, humble, beautiful,
> like a dark harvest etching, The Last Gleaner,
> a woman, lit by a street lamp, winding
> tangles of gleaming tape on a plastic spool.

Even in Simmons' cocksure or bitter poems there is usually a genuineness, and a democratic generosity, towards human beings and their feelings, that incline one to forgive him. . . . (p. 75)

When Simmons does engage with the public world of Ulster, he refuses to take sectarian sides: in no predictable way, at least. In **"Coleraine: 1977"** after a bomb attack an angry, nervous plain-clothes policeman points his gun at some students. . . . But the policeman, 'abandoned by craven citizens' (and the poet does not try to exculpate himself or his friends, the 'middle-class magi', who crept into the street to watch), 'is our only law-hero, / facing chaos alone, strong in a way . . .' Not the response one might expect: it is in fact the inadequacy of 'normal' responses in this situation that Simmons captures well here in unusually (for him) flat verse which moves with a tone, both weary and wary, to a conclusion where no-one's feelings are assuaged:

> . . . we work and wait
> where desperation and hate
> thrive and move the desperate

in which the poem's only rhymes hammer out the repetition and exhaustion of the experience. In other poems (**"The Imperial Theme"**, **"Younghusband"**) he intimates suggestive connections between the politics of imperialism and sexual relationships, history and lust, the aggressions and conciliations and couplings of dominant and dominated. Indeed, the poems of divorce and separation in *Constantly Singing* cannot help but carry resonances from the public world which is their implicit context. Simmons' libertarian stance and persona seem to me no easier poetic response to the conflicts of modern Ireland than that of contemporaries who have tackled them more often and more explicitly. (pp. 75-6)

> *Rodney Pybus, "Matters of Ireland: Recent Irish Poetry," in* Stand Magazine, *Vol. 22, No. 3 (1981), pp. 72-8.*

S. J. WISEMAN

James Simmons's new collection [*From the Irish*] is divided into four sections. The first of these . . . gives the volume its title. Of this section Simmons writes 'my love for what I know of Gaelic literature was in tandem with my impulse to use it for my own ends'. Thus "The Hag of Beare" becomes one of the more interesting poems in the collection, **"The Old Woman of Portrush"**; "The Lament for Art O'Leary" becomes **"Lament for a Dead Policeman"** on the grounds that 'a humble policeman's widow could feel grief as strong'. This poem introduces one of the pervasive problems of Simmons's work. He seeks, in subject-matter and simplistic versification to be a popular poet (he is in fact a singer). He writes: 'I would certainly rather have written "The Ballad of Joe Hill" than *Paradise Lost*.' However, he is an intensely literary poet. He also handles the Ulster working class with the charm of a bulldozer in a greenhouse. It is deeply embarassing to realize that the characters Simmons creates speak platitudes about the 'troubles' not because they are caricatures but because this is the way this writer imagines working-class people think.

Some of the poems from the second section, **"Domestic and Personal"**, are less disturbing: **"The Father to His Children"**, **"New Every Morning"**, **"The Professor's Morning Ride"**, **"Playing With Fire"** are all illuminations, sad or happy, of personal themes—life in the country, his failed marriage, and so on.

The third section contains some early uncollected poems. **"The Archaeologist"** . . . is a sad poem of a return, and it is much more metrically exciting than most of the other poems in the collection. The final section, **"Songs and Recitations"**, is a section of Simmons's work that he usually sings. . . .

> *S. J. Wiseman, in a review of "From the Irish," in* British Book News, *July, 1985, p. 434.*

PETER PORTER

James Simmons has been a consistent adder to the gaiety of nations. He writes better when the rhythms and cadences of songs and ballads are worked into poems of contemporary life than when he essays the folk forms themselves. *From the Irish* is an attractive up-dating of poems from the great Hibernian heritage, the Gaelic as well as the English, plus domestic and urban poems centred on Simmons's life in Portrush and Coleraine. His adaptations work very well, most notably the long **"Lament for a Dead Policeman"** which humanises a piece from *The Penguin Book of Irish Verse* and manages to say truthful and unpopular things about attitudes on both sides of the killings in Derry.

To be pro-booze-and-sex, 'on the side of life' and the rest of it, and not seem strained, is Simmons's achievement. I suspect that many years from now his handling of the vernacular will seem one of the lasting styles of a very confused literary period. Consider the naturalness of the language in this final stanza from his lament for an old house in Portrush:

> Great herring gulls still strut the roof,
> eyes bright and hurling down
> what sounds like lyrical abuse
> that echoes round the town.
> There's style and courage in those cries,
> ferocious love and hate,
> indifference to vicissitude
> I cannot emulate.

> *Peter Porter, "Cassettes of Atrocity," in* The Observer, *September 1, 1985, p. 19.*

DENIS DONOGHUE

Much of James Simmons's *From the Irish* is accomplished doggerel: it seems to ask to be set to music for The Dubliners or The Wolfe Tones and sung in a pub in Howth. His persona is that of the honest Ulsterman, 'The Poet's Breastplate' something to be beaten in public. There is nothing wrong with his themes—the IRA, a dead policeman, Joyce, Sligo, Derek Mahon, divorce, the woe that is in marriage, 'our ruined century', *Othello,* and one of the hotels in Newry. But most of them are approached by way of nothing more exacting than irritation. . . . They are also designed, apparently, for a wretchedly undemanding audience:

> the loftiest climber
> only reveals his arse
>   more clearly.
>   Poets today
> are likely to bungle
>   the tragic modes.
> What they know is farce.

But farce, too, has its criteria: a disability in the tragic modes isn't a qualification for the rough stuff. (p. 22)

Denis Donoghue, ''Ten Poets,'' in London Review of Books, *Vol. 7, No. 19, November 7, 1985, pp. 20-2.*

Clark Ashton Smith

1893-1961

American short story writer, poet, and essayist.

Smith is known primarily as a fantasist who used baroque language to create lushly detailed supernatural settings and events. He is often linked with H. P. Lovecraft and Robert E. Howard; these three writers shared correspondence and an interest in the supernatural, and they are regarded as having been the most prominent contributors to *Weird Tales* magazine during the 1920s and 1930s. Smith, who resided in California throughout his life, first secured recognition there as a poet. In the late 1920s he turned to short fiction, composing more than one hundred stories by the mid-1930s. Smith's literary output abruptly diminished after 1936. Although never again a prolific author, he continued to write poetry and prose while increasingly representing his fantasies through such visual media as painting, drawing, and sculpture.

Smith's first three volumes of poetry—*The Star-Treader and Other Poems* (1912), *Ebony and Crystal: Poems in Verse and Prose* (1922), and *Sandalwood* (1925)—drew attention in the San Francisco area, where he was regarded as a promising young poet. Using conventional poetic forms and formal diction, Smith richly evokes natural landscapes and exotic and mystical images. In his most famous poem, ''The Hashish-Eater; or, The Apocalypse of Evil,'' Smith creates a dreamlike atmosphere and presents a series of desolate images. Smith's best poetry was collected and reissued in *Selected Poems* (1971).

Contemporary interest in Smith generally focuses on his fiction. His stories are usually set in remote, imaginary worlds where magic thrives and where characters encounter supernatural forms of beauty, evil, and horror. Smith creates this Gothic atmosphere through ornate language replete with rich and painstaking descriptions of otherworldly environments. Within these decadent and decaying settings, Smith's protagonists typically attempt to recapture past glory. A pervasive sense of death, loss, and impending doom characterizes the atmosphere of his fiction. Smith's work contains elements of science fiction and the macabre, as his characters frequently move between different dimensions of time and space. For example, in one of his most widely anthologized pieces, ''The City of the Singing Flame,'' the protagonist passes back and forth between parallel realities, one of which contains a perpetually burning flame that mysteriously lures people to self-immolation. Six collections of Smith's stories have been published: *The Double Shadow and Other Fantasies* (1933), *Out of Space and Time* (1942), *Lost Worlds* (1944), *Genius Loci and Other Tales* (1948), *The Abominations of Yondo* (1960), and *Other Dimensions* (1970).

Much of Smith's fiction was reissued during the 1970s in four books, each of which contains stories set in a particular imaginary locale. These regions are reflected in the book titles: *Zothique* (1970), the last surviving continent in Earth's distant future, where science has been replaced by necromancy; *Hyperborea* (1971), an arctic setting in Earth's remote past; *Xiccarph* (1972), a planet society similar to several Martian settings in science fiction literature; and *Poseidonis* (1973), set in the mythic undersea realm of Atlantis. *Planets and Dimensions: Collected Essays of Clark Ashton Smith* (1973), which

contains many of Smith's nonfiction pieces on fantasy literature, helps explain his approach to fiction. Smith believed that fantasists should not apply realistic techniques to their works to make them more accessible but should create fully-realized fantastic settings and events that excite the imagination.

HOWARD PHILLIPS LOVECRAFT

Of younger [American horror-tale writers], none strikes the note of cosmic horror so well as the California poet, artist and fictionist Clark Ashton Smith, whose bizarre writing, drawings, paintings and stories are the delight of a sensitive few. Mr. Smith has for his background a universe of remote and paralysing fright—jungles of poisonous and iridescent blossoms on the moons of Saturn, evil and grotesque temples in Atlantis, Lemuria, and forgotten elder worlds, and dank morasses of spotted death-fungi in spectral countries beyond earth's rim. His longest and most ambitious poem, **''The Hashish-Eater,''** is in pentameter blank verse; and opens up chaotic and incredible vistas of kaleidoscopic nightmare in the spaces between the stars. In sheer daemonic strangeness and fertility of conception, Mr. Smith is perhaps unexcelled by any other writer dead or living. Who else has seen such gorgeous, luxuriant, and feverishly distorted visions of infinite spheres and multiple dimensions and lived to tell the tale? His short stories deal powerfully with other galaxies, worlds, and dimensions, as well as with strange regions and aeons on the earth. He tells of primal Hyperborea and its black amorphous god Tsathoggua; of the lost continent Zothique, and of the fabulous, vampirecurst land of Averoigne in mediaeval France. Some of Mr. Smith's best work can be found in the brochure entitled *The Double Shadow and Other Fantasies* (1933). (pp. 74-5)

> *Howard Phillips Lovecraft, "The Weird Tradition in America," in his* Supernatural Horror in Literature, *Ben Abramson Publishers, 1945, pp. 60-75.*

LIN CARTER

When we speak of the golden age of *Weird Tales,* we refer largely to the decade 1928-39, when this greatest American magazine of the bizarre and the fantastic reached a peak it was never again able to attain, although the magazine lasted until the issue of September, 1954.

During that decade, the magazine was chiefly dominated by three writers of fantasy whose talents were immense and whose popularity and influence were to grow even more significant in afteryears. These three writers were, of course, H. P. Lovecraft (1890-1937), Robert E. Howard (1906-36), and Clark Ashton Smith (1893-1961). Of these three gifted men (who were all good friends and correspondents although I do not believe they ever actually met), it is Clark Ashton Smith alone who has yet to achieve the wide recognition his artistry so rightly deserves.

It is to be hoped that [*Zothique*] will help make his mordant and imaginative talents known to the many thousands of fantasy enthusiasts who have not thus far discovered him. (pp. ix-x)

Much like Lovecraft, Smith lived as a recluse for the greater part of his life in a sort of self-imposed exile from his century. In his early twenties he was very much a part of the bohemian literary and artistic life in the San Francisco area, a circle which had included such people as Jack London, Ambrose Bierce, Bret Harte and Joaquin Miller. Smith gained entree to these circles as the protégé of the poet George Sterling. . . . (p. x)

Smith turned from poetry to the writing of short stories in about 1925. . . . However, Smith did not settle down to work on the short story form with any great degree of industry until the beginning of the Depression. He began to hit his stride in about 1929; between then and August 1936, he produced more than one hundred short stories and novelettes. At that point, although still only in his early forties, he for some unknown reason virtually stopped writing. The remaining twenty-five years of his life . . . produced only a negligible output. No one has yet come forward with a convincing explanation of this curious and very unfortunate decline. (pp. x-xi)

The short stories of Clark Ashton Smith are very much his own, and nothing quite like them has been written in America, at least since Poe. The real progenitors of his prose style are William Beckford's nightmarish and erotic novel of the "Oriental Gothic," *Vathek,* and two novels by Gustave Flaubert: the luxurious Carthaginian romance, *Salammbô,* and the phantasmagoric extravaganza, *Tentation de Saint Antoine.* Smith's jeweled and darkly evocative prose is closer to the style of these three novels than to that of Lovecraft or any of the more recent writers of the macabre. But the influences he most fre

quently admitted to were those of Robert W. Chambers, Ambrose Bierce and Edgar Allan Poe.

Smith's short fiction—he once attempted a novel but abandoned it after about 10,000 words—falls into several groups. There are cycles of tales laid against mythic and imaginary backgrounds such as Hyperborea and Atlantis, cycles set in the imaginary medieval lands of Malneant and Averoigne, and a few stories laid on the planet Xiccarph. But in my own opinion, the most exotic of his tales take for their locale the Continent of Zothique (rhymes with "seek"). . . .

Smith's conception of Zothique is that of Earth's last continent in the very distant future when the sun has grown dim, the world has grown old, and the remorseless seas have overwhelmed all other Earth continents. The Sciences have been forgotten through the long ages; the shadowy arts of sorcery and magic have been reborn. The result is a dark world of older mystery, where luxurious and decadent kings and wandering heroes quest and adventure across dim landscapes, pitting their strength and wisdom against powerful wizards and alien gods, under a dying sun. . . .

Smith's concept of a final continent where magic is reborn to rule man's sunset as it did his dawn has proved of considerable influence on the writers who came after him. Several books have used much the same idea, among them, A. E. Van Vogt's *The Book of Ptath* (1947); while Jack Vance used an identical theme for *The Dying Earth* (1950), and its sequel, *The Eyes of the Overworld* (1966). I also used the same idea in a novel called *The Giant of World's End* (1969). (pp. xi-xiii)

This present collection of all the Zothique stories will introduce you to one of the giants of modern fantasy, a puzzling, brilliant and enigmatic man of many gifts. (p. xiii)

> *Lin Carter, "When the World Grows Old," in* Zothique *by Clark Ashton Smith, edited by Lin Carter, Ballantine Books, 1970, pp. ix-xiii.*

BENJAMIN DeCASSERES

When I received from Clark Ashton Smith his *Ebony and Crystal* in 1923, I had not read far before I was conscious that I was in the presence of one of the rare company of the Brotherhood of the Unearthly Imagination.

He is brother-prince to Poe, Baudelaire, Shelley, Rimbaud, Laforgue, Leconte de Lisle, Keats, Chopin, Blake and El Greco. . . .

He is, in a manner, a far greater anomaly in America—hardbitten, realistic America—than was Edgar Allan Poe. Poe lived in a time when America was still somewhat romantic, when the iron collar of industrialism and the ball-and-chain of machinery had not been fastened upon us, before the stench of "proletarian" literature had yet arisen from the privies of mental and spiritual sterility.

Ashton Smith hovers over the corpse of matter like a beautiful, ironic Chimera over a Sphinx that is silent because it has nothing but imbecility in its eyes and an eternal vacuity in its brain—the Sphinx of "modernity".

You will find nothing of today or yesterday or tomorrow in the four volumes of Ashton Smith's poetry [represented in *Selected Poems*]. Nothing but beauty, immortal, speechless beauty, and the record of the dust of worlds and the decomposed illusions of man.

He is a sheer Nihilist, a devaluer of all values in the alembic of an "Olympian ecstasy" and "the darkness that is God". (p. 3)

Humor? Yes—vast and terrible. The humor of the mocker, but a mocker whose head is crowned with thorns and from whose eyes flow tears of ice.

"The Hashish-Eater," one of his longest poems, is a glut of beauty that leaves me breathless in one continuous reading. Here are magnificent words piled on words until the keyboard of sounds seems exhausted; vast visions that open, as always in the poetry of Ashton Smith, on perilous nightmares in super-terrestrial fairylands accursed—until we come upon those final lines of a black apocalypse:

> A huge white eyeless Face
> That fills the void and fills the universe,
> And bloats against the limbs of the world
> With lips of flame that open. . . .

Like Baudelaire, Poe and Blake, he has seen profoundly into another world. In that world he is immortal, one of the Rishis that sit behind the suns and write the epitaph of all living things in the waveless sands of eternity. (p. 4)

> Benjamin DeCasseres, "Clark Ashton Smith: Emperor of Shadows," in Selected Poems *by Clark Ashton Smith, Arkham House, 1971, pp. 3-4.*

GAHAN WILSON

It's said that Clark Ashton Smith may have met Ambrose Bierce in the Bohemian San Francisco of the early nineteen hundreds. Of course Smith would have been very young, and Bierce getting on to be remarkably sour, neither of them really at their best, but the confrontation would have been intriguing all the same. Few authors held less hope for our species than these two, or considered it less important in the general scheme of things.

The vast difference between them was that Bierce's understanding of man's sublime futility infuriated him and made him bitter, whereas Smith's clear vision of it braced and cheered him and spurred him on to endless, lively speculations on the awesome possibilities of impartial disaster. It isn't surprising to learn that he veered toward Buddhism in his later years, since one of the basic paradoxes of that orientation is that we should take heart, as all is hopeless. (p. 73)

Smith began selling fiction to the pulps in the late twenties, appearing in publications with such magnificent names as: *Stirring Science Fiction, Thrilling Wonder Stories, Amazing Detective Stories,* and . . . *La Paree Stories.* . . .

Smith's stories stood out rather starkly against the all-pervading, well-nigh unbelievable innocence which was the hallmark of most pulp writing. Now and then he did wander into the Golly-gee-whiz-will-you-look-at-this-planet! school, but mostly his tales were sly and subtle jibes at mankind's aspirations, chilling little fables of a startling bleakness. They were beautifully constructed, full of lovely images and absolutely sumptuous English, but they were deadly. Reading them was a tiny bit like being skillfully murdered with a Cellini stiletto, or dining well at the Borgias.

The message patiently taught the reader of Smith's bejeweled little bear traps was that man's evil and stupidity is beyond plumbing; but that for all of it, and for all of his good what's

more, he is doomed to be snuffed out by forces only vaguely aware of him, if aware at all. You can see how this might have been a little rough on a reader of, say, *Wonder Stories Quarterly,* particularly when he'd just finished something assuring him that all would be well with us once we'd managed to perfect the interstellar space ship. (p. 74)

This sixth . . . [collection of Smith's stories, *Other Dimensions*], is in the nature of a final wrapping-up and so contains some material that is decidedly not Smith at his best, but there is plenty of lovely work in it, and certainly no serious collector of his writings would consider passing it by. . . . *Zothique* is an anthology of stories that share as a common background one of Smith's most ghoulish fantasy worlds—an Earth where the sea has swallowed up all but one continent, where the sun is slowly fizzling out, and man has regressed to ignorant, ugly magic. Necromancers thrive, dark and inescapable curses abound, and extinction chews at the edges. [Lin Carter, the editor], has arranged these fascinatingly morbid fantasies in a perfectly satisfactory kind of chronological order so the thing may be read as a novel, if you like. Myself I would suggest you nibble rather more cautiously at these dainties, taking them one or two at a time. A reading of *Zothique* at a sitting might do something serious to the cellular structure of your brain. (p. 75)

> Gahan Wilson, "The Darker Corner," in The Magazine of Fantasy and Science Fiction, *Vol. 41, No. 1, July, 1971, pp. 73-6.*

LIN CARTER

Few writers really get a chance to do something entirely new and original in the genre they have chosen for their own. Clark Ashton Smith was one of the lucky ones.

The phenomenon of Clark Ashton Smith is a curious one, and much of it cannot be explained and may never be fully understood. He won his first reputation as a poet, but about September 1929 he suddenly began producing short stories of a type seldom seen in American letters. Macabre tales, written in a lapidary prose, jeweled and studded with exotic words, ornamented with obscure mythological allusions—stories piquant and even witty, written with a mordant humor.

The majority of his tales, and there are approximately one hundred and twelve known to have been completed, are set against backgrounds of ancient times; either in fabulous prehistoric civilizations like Atlantis and Hyperborea, semilegendary Eastern lands, or in a mythical province of medieval France. But much of his superior work in the genre of macabre fantasy borders upon what any purist would call science fiction—such as his story cycle laid in the far future supercontinent of Zothique toward the end of terrene history.

[*Xiccarph*] illustrates the second phase of his work, and more nearly approximates genuine science fiction than even the Zothique tales do. But Smith's prime market was not the science fiction pulp magazines, although he did in fact sell stories to them, but Farnsworth Wright's great *Weird Tales,* for which Smith wrote in its golden age. And since *Weird Tales* quite logically had a right to prefer tales that were weird, Smith conformed.

In so doing he invented a minuscule sub-genre all his own.

To see precisely what I mean, turn to the story called **"The Vaults of Yoh-Vombis,"** which is included in [*Xiccarph*]. The tale, you will see, is set on the planet Aihai, or Mars, and it takes place in the near future. These facts alone qualify it as belonging quite firmly to the province of science fiction. But now read the tale and savor the prose style: this rich, bejeweled, exotic kind of writing is the sort we most often think of as being natural to the heroic fantasy tale of magic kingdoms and fabulous eras of the mysterious past. Finally, read the story straight through and notice the actual plot. As you will find, it is precisely the sort of thing we call weird or horror fiction.

In composing a horror story set in the future or another world and told in the luxuriant, "gorgeous" prose traditional to heroic fantasy, Smith did something quite new and different and exciting, something all his own.

It must have been rather difficult to write this kind of story, for few writers have followed Smith into this new area of fantasy fiction. In fact about the only one I can think of who did it at least as well as Clark Ashton Smith was C. L. Moore, who in her celebrated "Northwest Smith" cycle of tales worked the identical vein of ore.

I must admit that I find this kind of fantasy delicious fare. And it seems to me that in creating this minor sub-genre, Smith rose above his own limitations as a prose writer and suggested for the first time his real importance as a fantasy writer. For— these extraplanetary weird fantasies set aside—the remainder of his prose work, while certainly delightful to read, lacks originality to some extent. That is, his tales of Hyperborea or Poseidonis, the "last isle of foundering Atlantis," are not really very different from the sort of thing Robert E. Howard wrote in his tales of Conan of Cimmeria or Kull of High Atlantis. And several of Smith's Averoigne tales, and certain out-of-series stories, simply draw upon the Cthulhu Mythos yarns H. P. Lovecraft was writing at the time. But with such tales as **"The Vaults of Yoh-Vombis,"** or **"Vulthoom,"** or **"The Doom of Antarion,"** or many of the other stories in this latest of our three Klarkash-Tonian collections, Smith was doing something that had not really been done before him to any great extent, and it is this that sets him apart from his colleagues. (pp. 3-5)

> *Lin Carter, "Other Stars and Skies," in* Xiccarph *by Clark Ashton Smith, edited by Lin Carter, Ballantine Books, 1972, pp. 3-8.*

CHARLES K. WOLFE

Clark Ashton Smith was one of our foremost practitioners of fantasy, but he was also a writer very much aware of exactly what he was doing and why he was doing it. Unlike some of his contemporaries, who all too often saw themselves as entertainers rather than artists, Smith from the very first of his writing career saw himself as a serious artist, and saw his work as realization of a cogent and well-formed aesthetic theory. . . .

During his lifetime Smith wrote well over thirty non-fictional essays of varying lengths. Unlike his friend, H. P. Lovecraft, Smith seldom wrote essays on topics of "general interest," such as cats or geographical locales; nearly every one of Smith's essays deals directly with literature or literary influences. Included among these essays are assessments of George Sterling, Lovecraft, M. R. James, Ambrose Bierce, Poe, Hodgson, and Donald Wandrei. But the most interesting essays are those in which Smith talks about his own art. Significantly, he never talks much about his poetry in these public essays (though he did frequently in his private letters); his attention is directed almost exclusively to his stories. A possible reason for this is that his short stories were much more public than his poetry; they were being exposed to all manner of reader in the pages of mass circulation magazines like *Wonder Stories* and *Amazing Stories*. With such a wide and occasionally hostile audience, Smith was more inclined to explain his intentions and defend his art.

Since over half of Smith's stories were written and published in the mid and early 1930s, it is not surprising that most of his important critical statements also date from that time. Especially interesting are a series of public debates Smith engaged in through the letter columns of *Wonder Stories, Amazing Stories, Strange Tales,* and *The Fantasy Fan* in 1932-33. Smith came under attack from those who were insisting upon more "realism" in science fiction; psychological realism was in vogue in mainstream literature in the 1930s (with Anderson, Dreiser, and Hemingway setting the pace) and various writers and fans of speculative fiction insisted that the only way by which speculative fiction would ever be accepted as "serious" literature would be for it to adopt more "realistic" modes. Smith perceived that realism was only one tradition, and that romanticism was an equally valid tradition. He rejected the definition that literature was a study of human reactions and character development; he called such a definition "narrow and limited."

Smith saw the folly of people who equated "realism" with quality in literature; only in the last decade has literature begun to recover from the tyranny of the realism criterion, the assumption that the only function of literature is to tell it "how it is." Smith fought his lonely battle during the height of the realistic movement, in the 1930s; only today is the literary mainstream beginning to appreciate the fact that some writers are not *trying* to be "realistic," and that reading them requires a different set of standards. . . . (p. 20)

Of course, no one can deny that Smith's prose style is romantic by any definition of the word; the texture, color, sentence structure, and, especially, the vocabulary is in the best tradition of the self-conscious story-teller, always reminding us that we are in the hands of an artist, and what we are reading is indeed art, and reminding us of the difference between the world of the art and the everyday world. The recent textual work of Lin Carter and others is showing us just how rich Smith's prose style was; it was richer even than we had imagined, for the editors of the time apparently were quite ruthless in editing his stories. One could, indeed, make a good argument for style being the most important aspect of Smith's art, and that his style is frequently an end in itself. But for the sake of argument let us artificially divide style from content, and look at some of the structural patterns in Smith's stories: how are they romantic?

If any basic structural pattern emerges from Smith's various stories, it is one of the journey by the hero into some other world, some sort of magic world; it may be via a space voyage, via dimension, via the past, or a mystic experience. But frequently Smith's heroes must make this journey; they must cross the threshold into some sort of *alternative reality*. (This term seems better than the term "fantasy world," since "fantasy world" implies an unfair distinction; it implies that the "real" world—the common, recognizable world—is more basic or more important than the other world; Smith would have insisted that both worlds were equally important, were equally "real.") Stories of this sort are multifold; the titles of two Smith collections, **Lost Worlds** and **Other Dimensions,** testify to the pervasiveness of this theme in his work. Perhaps the most centrally significant of these threshold stories is **"The City of the Singing Flame,"** which suggests multiple alternative realities.

In many stories Smith goes out of his way to stress the significance of this threshold; he does this by creating in his readers a feeling of incredible *remoteness* from these alternate realities. A reader is hardly impressed by a threshold to a world very much like his own; thus a successful fantasy, like *Alice in Wonderland,* will strive to make the alternative reality as different as possible from the "control," everyday reality. Smith was fond of manipulating his readers by attempting, through various devices, to "distance" the events of his story from the reader's world. For example, **"The End of the Story"** is presented through the manuscript of a law student found sometime after 1789; the real plot of the story thus is distanced from us, first, by the fact that it is second-hand, coming in a manuscript, and second, by the fact that the manuscript is removed from us by history. In **"The Testament of Athammaus,"** we have the obviously ancient narrative of a chief headsman in Commorion, who then tells the story of *his* youth of how Commorion fell; again, we have two stages of distancing. The story of Commorion has already become a misty legend to the narrator; and yet the narrator is already remote to us because he is from Hyperborea; the actual story of Commorion is thus infinitely more remote to us. But Smith did not need to rely on the past in creating a sense of remoteness; he just as easily used space travel and the future. For instance, **"The Dweller in the Gulf"** contains no less than four "distancing" elements: 1) the Martian setting; 2) the time setting (obviously the future); 3) the antiquity of the cavern into which the party wanders and the antiquity of the Martian surface; and 4) the bizarre descent into the sub-world of Mars. In short, we have an alternative reality within an alternative reality, . . . like a series of Chinese boxes, one within the other. Of course, these distancing devices have been used since the time of Irving and Hawthorne to try to lend an aura of antiquity to relatively recent and commonplace events; but Smith's imagination allowed him to develop this art of distance to striking perfection. And when it works, his readers are made acutely aware of the alien quality of Smith's other worlds. This is perhaps what Smith meant when he said the function of imaginative literature was to lead the imagination outward. (pp. 20-1)

But what happens to characters who encounter these remote alternative realities? And what is the nature of these realities: are they hostile, beneficent, or what? These complicated questions need longer answers than we can provide here, but one or two points are obvious. We might first note that Smith's basic plot—the hero crossing the threshold into an alternative reality—is closely related to the classic hero myth as traced throughout the ages from primitive myth to folk legend to literature. Joseph Campbell, in *The Hero with a Thousand Faces,* has defined this basic structural pattern, or monomyth, as follows: "A hero ventures forth from the world of common day into a region of *supernatural wonder* (italics mine): fabulous forces are there encountered and a decisive victory is won: the hero comes back from this mysterious adventure with the power to bestow boons on his fellow man." Now the first part of this structure fits the stories of Smith well; the hero does go, frequently, from a recognizable world into a world of wonder: the past, a remote planet, another dimension, or even occasionally a dream. But here the pattern breaks down, for in many of Smith's stories, the heroes do not return from their alternative realities. Some of them strive to return, but fail; witness stories like **"The Dweller in the Gulf," "The Weird of Avoosl Wuthoqquan," "The Weaver in the Vault,"**

"The Second Interment," or **"Master of the Asteroid."** Others, like Giles Angarth in **"City of the Singing Flame,"** make it back but are shattered by the experience. A few, like the law student in **"End of the Story,"** prefer to stay in the alternative reality; the speaker in the poem **"Amithaine"** says, "who has seen the towers of Amithaine / Shall sleep, and dream of them again," and, in the end, chooses to remain in the romantic dream world, the "fallen kingdoms of romance."

Now exactly how romantic is this pattern? On one level, readers of extremely popular writers like Burroughs expect and receive their heroes' return from the alternative reality to the "natural" world; here Smith is writing a different sort of fiction, to be sure. But on a literary level, even with a more abstract definition of romance, it would seem Smith is writing something different. One of the keystones of romanticism as a philosophy is the ability of man to triumph over his environment; Smith's characters seem defeated by their environments, even though the environments *are* alternative environments created by Smith. In one respect, there's not much difference between Stephen Crane's Maggie being crushed by social and economic forces—a hostile environment—and Smith's heroes being destroyed by the Dweller in the Gulf; in both cases, attempts of the heroes to assert themselves and to escape are futile. (The editors of *Wonder Stories,* incidentally, found the ending of **"Dweller"** so bitter that they changed it.) . . . Nor is this pessimism simply apparent in Smith's fiction: he often seems quite naturalistic in certain aspects of his critical statements. In a letter he published in *Amazing Stories,* October, 1932, Smith protested the view that saw man as the center of the universe; the real thrill of properly done fantastic fiction, he said, "comes from the description of the *ultrahuman* events, forces and scenes, which properly dwarf the terrene actors to comparative insignificance." Fantasy should emphasize the non-human or extrahuman; "isn't it only the damnable, preposterous and pernicious egomania of the race," that insists on realistic fiction? In **"The Tale of Macrocosmic Horror,"** . . . Smith said that in the "tale of highest imaginative horror," "the real actors are the terrible arcanic forces, the esoteric cosmic malignities. . . ." Thus most of Smith's characters are hopeless pawns in the face of some alternative reality; they seldom assert themselves, and all too often pay the ultimate price for crossing the threshold.

In this one respect, then, we can hardly call Smith a romantic. This side of Smith certainly has affinities with someone like Ambrose Bierce . . . , or Kurt Vonnegut, whose notion of human civilization in *Sirens of Titan* would surely have appealed to Smith. The point is, that, like most serious writers, Clark Ashton Smith was too complex to be pigeon-holed into a single term. He was uniquely himself, and, for me at least, his appeal lies in this uniqueness. But he should show us that "fantasy" and "romance" are not necessarily synonymous terms, that Smith knew this, articulated it, and illustrated it in his fiction. (pp. 21-2)

Charles K. Wolfe, "CAS: A Note on the Aesthetics of Fantasy," in Nyctalops, No. 7, August, 1972, pp. 20-2.

CHARLES K. WOLFE

[*Planets and Dimensions: Collected Essays of Clark Ashton Smith*] brings together most of the important non-fiction prose of Clark Ashton Smith. . . .

The guiding principle behind the selection of [the] essays was quite simple: each piece included was designed as some sort of public statement, or was presented as a public statement with Smith's approval. This means that [*Planets and Dimensions*] includes not only the formal, eloquent essays and book reviews that Smith wrote for the various fan magazines, but also a series of long published letters, actually self-contained essays, that Smith sent to various commercial magazines, such as *Wonder Stories* and *Amazing Stories*. At times these letters were part of a longer debate being conducted in the letters columns. . . . (p. ix)

Unlike his close friend and correspondent H. P. Lovecraft, Clark Ashton Smith did not write many essays on topics of general interest; he did not seem to be very interested in the art of the essay as such. Most of his writings in this volume stem from quite specific occasions, and reflect ideas Smith felt most passionately about. The essays range in time from 1927 . . . to 1953. . . . The essays thus reflect Smith's entire life, though the most interesting of them date from the 1930s, which, not coincidentally, was Smith's greatest period of productivity of short fiction. The subject matter includes homages to literary influences. Some literary influences, like George Sterling and H. P. Lovecraft, Smith knew as personal friends; indeed, the two essays on Sterling are two of the longest pieces included, and the three different tributes to Lovecraft attest to the effect Lovecraft's death in 1937 had on Smith. Other literary influences are simply writers whom Smith read and studied; these include the British scholar and writer of ghost stories, M. R. James; Ambrose Bierce, and Edgar Allan Poe ("**Atmosphere in Weird Fiction**"); William Hope Hodgson; and Donald Wandrei. The subject matter also includes personal statements about Smith's life and career, and several cogent comments about some of his more important individual tales. One subject rather conspicuous by its absence is a discussion of poetry itself; Smith thought of himself primarily as a poet, and turned to short-story writing only as an expediency. Yet, aside from his tribute to Sterling's poetry, and his review of a book of poems by Marianne Moore, there is little here about Smith's first love. Perhaps he felt his verse was sufficient testimony for itself.

By far the most frequent topic in these essays is Smith's own theories about weird fiction and speculative fiction in general. In the early 1930s Smith, in a sudden creative spurt, composed over half his corpus of short stories, and published a good many of them in magazines at that time; it is not unusual, therefore, to see him also turning with interest to critical justification for his work during that time. These critical statements are of interest to any student of imaginative literature, in that they provide one of the most cogent and well-informed aesthetics evolved and articulated by any major writer of speculative fiction. Smith was a poet and well-versed in literature; as such, he was more able than many of his peers to fit his craft into a larger perspective. For instance, Smith was able to see that the demands for "realism" in his genre were contradictory to the basic spirit of fantasy; he stubbornly asserted the validity of the romantic tradition at a time when this tradition was much in disfavor with the mainstream of literary thought. If "realism" was part of "high culture," then Smith wanted no part of "high culture." Also Smith repeatedly insisted upon the all-important distinction between realism as a literary school and simple writing proficiency; much of the criticism of science fiction and fantasy, he suggests, would be eliminated if the writers and editors would simply write better, not write in a different mode.

We know today that history has vindicated Smith's stubborn refusal to acknowledge realism as the ultimate development of literature; for today the cycle has come full circle again, and the romantic tradition, represented by the increasing popularity of fantasy and science fiction, as well as a strong fabulist and neo-romantic tradition in mainstream writers, dominates the literary scene again. Smith's defense in itself is important, but he offers a coherent and extremely valid system of aesthetics *within* this tradition. For the best exemplification of this system, we have Smith's collected body of stories; for Smith's own account of what he was trying to do, we have these present essays. Seldom do we find any serious discrepancy between intention and accomplishment.

To some this collection may appear to be a rather ragged assortment of bits and pieces, of marginalia and uneven documents. However, the collection comprises one of the few articulate critical testimonies we possess from a major writer of science fiction and fantasy of the 1930s and 1940s. Few at that time took science fiction or fantasy seriously enough to interview its creators or even treat them as serious artists, and Smith's explanations of his craft survive only through letter pages of magazines and the graces of the fan magazine movement (and no student of imaginative literature can fail to feel grateful for what the fanzines did do with such limited resources. But even if we possessed lengthy autobiographies of every major science fiction writer of the time, Smith's essays would still be of interest today; his growing popularity with new generations of readers, and the increasing recognition he is receiving around the world as a master of fantasy, justifies the issuance of this collection. (pp. x-xii)

> Charles K. Wolfe, in an introduction to Planets and Dimensions: Collected Essays of Clark Ashton Smith *by Clark Ashton Smith, edited by Charles K. Wolfe, The Mirage Press, 1973, pp. ix-xii.*

HARLAN ELLISON

It is seldom a writer is able to cast back through memory to locate the specific stories that influenced him in his work. Who can remember that this particular image was fostered by Conrad or that specific syntax was employed by Céline? But in one isolated instance of my own professional career, my impetus remains as bright and compelling as it was the day I removed it from a library shelf in a high school in Cleveland, Ohio and passed—incredibly!—out of that building through a portal to the City where the Singing Flame lived. . . . And I found it in an August Derleth anthology, *The Other Side of the Moon*. It was March of 1949, and the book had been in the library only a few days. I took it down because of the title. Yes, by God, what *was* on the other side. Not only of the Moon, but of time, of thought, of my own nature. . . . I began to read at once. An hour later I left the library. I had stolen the book. I own it to this day. It would have been impossible for me to leave behind the weird story of Giles Angarth and Ebbonly and the "**City of the Singing Flame.**"

Almost immediately, I began writing fantasy and science fiction. Within a year or two I was deeply enmeshed in the writing in the field—no single example of which *ever* brought on the shock of stimulation caused by that first reading of Smith. . . . It is often impossible to say where a man's inspirations come from, but in the lineal descent of my own writings, I have no hesitation in saying had it not been for Clark Ashton Smith and the wonders he revealed to me, at that precise moment of my youth in which I was most malleable, most desperate for direction, I might well have gone in any one of the thousand other directions taken by my contemporaries, and wound up infinitely poorer in spirit, intellect, prestige and satisfaction than I am today. As I owe a great debt to science fiction as a whole, to fandom as a particular, and to the other writers who encouraged me in my work . . . I owe the greatest of debts to Clark Ashton Smith, for he truly opened up the universe for me.

Harlan Ellison, in a letter to Donald Sidney-Fryer in Emperor of Dreams: A Clark Ashton Smith Bibliography, *edited by Donald Sidney-Fryer, Donald M. Grant, Publisher, 1978, p. 153.*

SAM MOSKOWITZ

Whether Clark Ashton Smith will ever come to be regarded as a minor writer in the honor roll of American literature we cannot know, but that he made some very tangible contributions to fantasy fiction, particularly science fiction, we can be sure. His science fiction had the same objective as H. P. Lovecraft's; it was intended to evoke horror. In this objective he was completely successful, far more so than Lovecraft. **"The Vaults of Yoh Vombis"** and **"Dweller in the Martian Depths"** all but exceed the tolerance factor for physical horror of the average reader. As a parallel to horror it was required that he create a mood in his science fiction and this quality transcends all others in his best work: **"Master of the Asteroid,"** where the trapped spaceman watches the fragile cycle of life on a tiny asteroid; **"Visitors from Mlok,"** the consequences suffered by an earthman who has permitted his senses to be altered to conform with the requirements of an alien world: **"City of the Singing Flame,"** of a siren force that drew diverse intelligences from many worlds and dimensions to probable extinction; **"Flight Into Super-Time,"** which displays remarkable humor and satire as well as the incredible ability to maintain fever-pitch interest while writing in a style not too dissimilar to some of his prose poems. . . .

Clark Ashton Smith understood the world around him, sex and life's rules far better than H. P. Lovecraft despite his even more intense hermit-like existence. A brief tale like **"The Mother of Toads"** is a masterpiece *only* because Smith's understanding of the world's workings gives it allegorical depth.

There is greatness in a few lines and certain passages in Smith's poetry, but he sacrificed his shining promise in verse on the altar of an unabridged dictionary.

Sam Moskowitz, in a letter to Donald Sidney-Fryer in Emperor of Dreams: A Clark Ashton Smith Bibliography, *edited by Donald Sidney-Fryer, Donald M. Grant, Publisher, 1978, p. 162.*

STEVE BEHRENDS

The writings of Clark Ashton Smith display a continuity of idea and image that can only be described as remarkable. Fantastic settings and happenings from his early poems crop up twenty years later as the bases for short stories; prose-poems written in Smith's mid-twenties were fleshed into the elaborate fictions of his forties; he would write of Medusa in 1911, in his verse masterpiece **"Medusa,"** and in 1957, four years before his death, in the ironic tale **"The Symposium of the Gorgon"**. Evidence for the interconnectedness of Smith's literary

output is discernible in nearly every poem and story. The endurance of his imaginative vision should give us all pause.

Equally impressive is the tenacity with which Smith clung to certain emotional themes throughout his work; and of these themes, he returned most frequently to "loss."

Perhaps a quarter of Smith's fantastic stories (twenty-five or thirty out of some 110) deal in a basic fashion with the subject of loss, and we shall concern ourselves with the most prominent of these; but nearly every Smith tale and many of his poems make some reference to loss, or use an image of loss metaphorically to set an emotional tone. . . .

The structure of the essay has been inspired by **"The Song of the Necromancer"**, a poem in Smith's jotting notebook, *The Black Book,* that seems to encapsulate nearly all the major aspects of his relationship to loss. The poem strikes me as a piece of some importance for an understanding of Smith's stories:

> I would recall a forfeit woe,
> A buried bliss; my heart is fain
> Ever to seek and find again
> The lips whereon my lips have lain
> In rose-red twilights long ago.
>
> Lost are the lands of my desire,
> Long fled, the hours of my delight,
> The darkling splendor, fallen might:
> In aeons past, the bournless night
> Was rolled upon my rubied pyre.
>
> In far oblivion blows the desert
> Which was the lovely world I knew.
> Quenched are the suns of gold and blue. . . .
> Into the nadir darkness thrust,
> My world has gone as meteors go. . . .

Coming from a man whose tales abound with mages and wizards, and who had a poetic image of himself as a solitary sorcerer . . . , the poem's title is a very suggestive one. In fact, **"The Song of the Necromancer"** is Smith's own "song". (The final version of the poem appeared in the February 1937 issue of *Weird Tales;* Smith later included it in the "Incantations" section of his *Selected Poems.*)

Like any writer who ever had to scramble to provide motivation for some character, Smith used loss as a plot-element in several of his tales, including **"The Ghoul"**, in which a man's despair over the death of his wife drives him to bargain with a demon; **"The Flower-Women"**, wherein Maal Dweb's yearning for his action-filled youth leads him to challenge the denizens of an untamed world; and **"Thirteen Phantasms"**, whose main character witnesses some bizarre hallucinations of his lost beloved. But for Smith there was an importance to loss that went far beyond plot: his real interest was not in what loss could make his characters *do*, but in how it could make them *feel*.

Smith created scores of situations in which individuals lose the things closest to their hearts, and live on only to regret their loss and to contrast their fallen state with the glory they once knew. He gave his characters the capacity to realize the extent of their loss, and to express the pain they felt; and he used their scrutiny—their comparisons of "now" and "then", of "what once had been" and "what is no more"—to spotlight the emotions he wished to convey to his readers.

These emotions, attendant to "falls from grace", were very special to Smith, and he worked all their shadings and manifestations into his literary output: regret, nostalgia, homesickness, alienation, grief, ennui, loss of innocence, age, death, decay. Certain verbs and adjectives literally ring in our ears after a session with his stories or poems, so often do we encounter them: "sunken", "faded", "fallen", "lost", "irretrievable", "longing", "yearning", "seeking".

This intense fascination with loss has been misdiagnosed or oversimplified from time to time as a preoccupation with death . . . ; and while it may be true, as L. Sprague de Camp once said, that "no one since Poe has so loved a well-rotted corpse", it was not death that obsessed Clark Ashton Smith so much as yearning and loss. We should hear Smith's own voice in the words of his character John Milwarp from **"The Chain of Aforgomon"**, who is presented, importantly, as a writer of imaginative Oriental fiction: "In the background of my mind there has lurked a sentiment of formless, melancholy desire, for some nameless beauty long perished out of time."

As a writer, the actual techniques Smith had for bringing loss into the lives of his characters were of only secondary importance: the emotions involved were of more interest to Smith than any mechanisms he had for generating them. His concern was not really with the object lost, whatever or whoever it was, but with the feelings associated with losing it, and living without it. (The Necromancer of **"The Song of the Necromancer"**, for instance, laments the absence of his sweetheart, but he also craves the return of his splendrous and powerful past.)

For purposes of organization, though, one can sort Smith's stories according to the kind of loss suffered, and the following two sections discuss stories that feature the most readily discernible forms of loss: of love, and of the past. But this division will also make it possible to touch upon the different reasons that drove Clark Ashton Smith to portray these two kinds of loss in his fiction.

As might be expected of a poet, Smith was greatly attracted to the strength of the emotion of love, and the fervor with which we cling to it and to our lovers. (pp. 3-5)

The textbook example of such a "loss of love" story is **"The Venus of Azombeii"**. The central character of this tale, Julius Marsden, has felt throughout his life "the ineffable nostalgia of the far-off and the unknown" . . . , which compels him to make a journey to dark and mysterious Africa. In a wilderness region he meets a beautiful black woman, Wanaos, whom he comes to love. Marsden experiences a time of wild happiness. . . .

As Smith would have it, though, their life together is soon shattered through the treachery of a rival suitor to Wanaos. Both lovers are poisoned with a slow-killing brew, by which, please note, Smith gives them plenty of time to realize the sadness of their fate and the fullness of their loss. "Dead was all our former joy and happiness. . . . Love, it was true, was still ours, but love that already seemed to have entered the hideous gloom and nothingness of the grave. . . .

Identical in its emotions but with a slight twist to its development is the extended prose-poem **"Told in the Desert"**. A young traveller loses his way while crossing a desert expanse. He eventually stumbles upon a cool and fertile oasis where dwells a beautiful girl, Neria. We are told that the young man's sojourn with Neria, like that of Marsden and Wanaos in **"Azombeii"**, was "a life remote from all the fevers of the world, and pure from every soilure; it was infinitely sweet and secure."

Unlike Marsden in **"Azombeii"**, however, the hero of **"Desert"** abandons his idyllic love-nest, his "irretrievable Aidann", instead of having it taken away from him. But Smith does not end the story there. The man comes to yearn for his "bygone year . . . of happiness"; and seeking in later years the splendor of the oasis, he is doomed to wander in vain, and all his days thereafter are filled with "only the fading visions of memory, the tortures and despairs and illusions of the quested miles, the waste whereon there falls no lightest shadow of any leaf, and the wells whose taste is fire and madness. . . ."

The next two stories to be discussed, **"The Chain of Aforgomon"** and **"The Last Incantation"**, have necromancers as their main characters rather than adventurous young men, and display some other common features to which we will return later.

In **"Aforgomon"** the sorcerer Calaspa invokes the powers of an evil god to win back a flown hour with his dead beloved, Belthoris. The past is temporarily regained through this necromancy, and in typical fashion Smith presents their resurrected love in the grandest of terms. "We dwelt alone in a universe of light, in a blossomed heaven. Exalted by love in the high harmony of those moments, we seemed to touch eternity." We are left to contrast this with Calaspa's mood after the hour has passed: "Sorrow and desolation choked my heart as ashes fill some urn consecrated to the dead; and all the hues and perfumes of the garden about me were redolent only of the bitterness of death."

"The Last Incantation" contains some of Smith's finest descriptions of the emotions of loss, and the story also serves as a bridge between the "loss of love" and "loss of the past" tales.

At the height of his powers as the mightiest sorcerer of Poseidonis, Malgyris the Mage sees only the empty, unchallenging years ahead of him, and the barren moments of the present, and takes but a cold and hollow joy from his exalted position. . . . Amid this desolation, Malgyris is sustained only by a gentle memory from his innocent youth which "like an alien star . . . still burned with unfailing luster—the memory of the girl Nylissa whom he had loved in days ere the lust of unpermitted knowledge and necromantic dominion had ever entered his soul."

Like the male protagonists of the other stories discussed, Malgyris aches for his lost love. Unlike the others, however, his mind also dwells upon the passing of his former, untarnished self, the "fervent and guileless heart" of his youth, and the glorious, sun-filled days of his past. This sentiment leads us to a group of stories featuring Smith's second method for bringing loss and regret into the lives of his characters. (pp. 6-7)

Smith set his most famous cycle of stories, the tales of Zothique, in a "fallen" world where the past infinitely outweighs the future. "On Zothique, the last continent, the sun no longer shone with the whiteness of its prime, but was dim and tarnished as if with a vapor of blood." There are constant reminders of age and decay, of a glory withered away by Time: vast deserts of tombs and buried cities, frequent references to the greater potency of the potions and spells of elder wizards, etc.

On the level of the individual, Smith dishes out the same bitter meal. His fiction is filled with characters haunted by memories of a more desirable past, and from whom Time has stolen something precious. Depending on the person in question— again, Smith's focus is on loss itself, not the object lost—they desire the power and glory they once knew, the simplicity and vigor of the years of youth, a lost innocence, some splendrous state of being, or the vanished beauty and grandeur of incomparable cultures and beloved worlds. (pp. 7-8)

As a simple example of this yearning for the past, consider the following paragraph from **"The Testament of Athammaus"**, a story which details the desertion of the Hyperborean capital Commoriom as seen through the eyes of the one-time public executioner:

> Forgive an aged man if he seem to dwell, as is the habit of the old, among the youthful recollections that have gathered to themselves the kingly purple of removed horizons and the strange glory that illumes irretrievable things. Lo! I am made young again when I recall Commoriom, when in this grey city of the sunken years I behold in retrospect her walls that looked mountainously down upon the jungle . . .

Note that the years after Commoriom are "sunken", and its glory is "irretrievable". Also note that Athammaus is alone in his suffering: "And though others forget, or happy deem her no more than a vain and dubitable tale, I shall never cease to lament Commoriom." While others were healed, Smith chose to center his tale on a man whose feelings of regret have remained strong and vivid.

In **"Xeethra"**, perhaps his most famous tale of Zothique, Smith presents multifold loss alongside monstrous irony. A young goatherd, Xeethra, eats an enchanted fruit and is henceforth tormented by the memories of a past life wherein he was Prince Amero, ruler of the fair kingdom of Calyz. The bewildered and newly awakened king is repelled by the rude and simple life of Xeethra; he longs for a dimly recalled life of opulence. He journeys in search of Calyz, but discovers that the land has become a parched desert. Xeethra/Amero is "whelmed by utter loss and despair" at the sight of his ruined and crumbled homeland.

At this point in the story an emissary from Thasaidon, the Satan of the future, appears and offers him a strange deal. At the price of his soul, the life Amero once knew will be returned to him—but it will remain *only so long as he wishes it to*. Not really understanding this clause, the young man accepts the bond; and suddenly the past lives again for him, and he is the king of a bountiful land. But in time he succumbs to ennui, and finds himself wishing for the simple life of a goatherd. In an instant he is back once more in the leper-peopled desert of Calyz. "His heart was a black chill of desolation, and he seemed to himself as one who had known . . . the loss of high splendor; and who stood now amid the extremity of age and decay. . . . Anguish choked the heart of Xeethra as if with the ashes of burnt-out pyres and the shards of heaped ruin . . . In the end, there was only dust and dearth; and he, the doubly accursed, must remember and repent for evermore all that he had forfeited," both the powerful life of a monarch, and the carefree and uncluttered life of a shepherd. He can never return to either life.

An even grander scale of personal loss and suffering is displayed in the prose-poem **"Sadastor"**. On a distant planet, "dim and grey beneath a waning sun . . . a token of doom to fairer and younger worlds", the demon Charnadis discovers the mermaid Lyspial wallowing in a small briny pool that had once been a far-flung ocean. She has witnessed the slow desiccation of the sea and the destruction of the glorious world of her past; she is tortured with the knowledge of her present state, and of all she has lost. (pp. 8-9)

A fallen world is presented in another prose-poem, **"From the Crypts of Memory"**. The setting is a shadowy world orbiting "a star whose course [was] decadent from the high, irremeable heavens of the past." The people of this world are unspeakably ancient and have fallen far from their golden past. Only in memories can they haltingly recapture "an epoch whose marvelous worlds have crumbled, and whose mighty suns are less than shadow." But such memories add to the burden of age and sorrow, and by contrast their lives are made to seem even more pale and ghostly: "Vaguely we lived, and loved as in dreams—the dim and mystic dreams that hover upon the verge of fathomless sleep. We felt for our women . . . the same desire that the dead may feel."

It is worth mentioning that for Smith not even death is an end to yearning and despair. On the contrary, although "a living death" was used in **"From the Crypts of Memory"** as a metaphor for a great suffering, a literal "life in death" is employed in **"The Empire of the Necromancers"** as a tool for generating feelings of loss. Here the loss suffered is the loss of life. Ultimate and striking contrasts are produced between the living past and the dead present. The race of people drawn forth from death, who serve as slaves to a pair of necromancers, find themselves living a sort of half-life. . . . We hear of their longings through the resurrected Prince of the people, who "knew that he had come back to a faded sun, to a hollow and spectral world. Like something lost and irretrievable, beyond prodigious gulfs, he recalled the pomp of his reign . . . and the golden pride and exultation that had been his in youth. . . . Darkly he began to grieve for his fallen state."

And on the other end of the scale, Smith wrote a handful of stories in which individuals lose not life, but a glory beyond life, some "unnatural" state or condition, like "the suns of gold and blue" of **"The Song of the Necromancer"**. In every case the "unnatural state of being" is an ecstatic and desired one, and this follows directly from Smith's own interests. He wanted his characters to *long* for the splendor they had experienced, beside which everyday life is wan and inadequate. And given such "glorious" experiences, they would naturally make the contrasts and comparisons of "then" and "now" that Smith liked to use, and feel the kind of regret and empty despair that so fascinated him.

The visions that are presented to these hapless characters are often so completely strange and wondrous that they can only be seen or understood in part. They are too far beyond the mundane sphere of human experience, like the image of incarnate Beauty glimpsed in Smith's poem **"A Dream of Beauty"**: "Her face the light of fallen planets wore, / But as I gazed, in doubt and wonderment, / Mine eyes were dazzled, and I saw no more." This itself is a technique Smith used to intensify and magnify the effect of the passing of the "unnatural" state and the resumption of commonplace reality, as it points out how high the pinnacle of the past had been.

Stories of this type include **"The City of the Singing Flame"**, **"The End of the Story,"** **"The Light from Beyond"**, and **"The White Sybil"**. There is no need to describe the distinct wonders found in each of these tales. We need only note the similarity of their characters' attitudes as they "come off the high" of their unique experiences. . . . For the heroes of these stories the past shall always be more resplendent and desirable than either the present or the future, a time always to be longed for. And for some it is a thing they must try to regain, whatever the cost. (pp. 9-11)

This article ends as **"The Song of the Necromancer"** begins. In a general sense, this poem has been our guidebook to Smith's relationship to loss, and we should note that it starts off with a declaration of intent: the unhappy sorcerer (we learn of his unhappiness in the subsequent stanzas) would seek to resummon his lost past, and to draw back his dead love from the tomb. The same is true of several of the characters we find in Smith's short stories.

Why Smith should have them strive to recapture what they've lost is obvious—such striving serves to underscore their unhappiness, and the depths of their dissatisfaction.

That all these attempts either fail or end in self-destruction reflects Smith's generally pessimistic outlook. "You can never go home again," he says. Or if you do make it back, it is a very mixed blessing.

In a story like **"Told in the Desert"** what is sought after is literally unattainable, for though he may search the desert for the rest of his life, that young man will never again find the fertile oasis in which he lived so happily with Neria.

And what Malgyris seeks in **"The Last Incantation"** is just as unattainable, though more figuratively so. Believing that he would be content to have his lost Nylissa beside him again, he summons her spectre from the grave. Once she has materialized, however, he begins to find fault with her manner and appearance. Dissatisfied and unsettled, he dismisses the phantom, at which point his familiar explains the true nature of his yearning and its predestined failure: "No necromantic spell could recall for you your own lost youth or the fervent and guileless heart that loved Nylissa, or the ardent eyes that beheld her then."

This same lesson is learned in Smith's unfinished tale **"Mnemoka"**. Space-Alley Jon, a drifter of the space-lanes, purchases an illicit Martian drug called "mnemoka" which brings back memories with all the strength of real experiences. Jon intends to relive his first sexual experience, back in his innocent adolescence. . . . But after downing the drug, he is haunted instead by visions of a brutal murder he had recently committed. His life has become too soiled to allow retrieval of the moment he longed for. The boy who had lain with Sophia no longer existed.

Calaspa's quest in **"The Chain of Aforgomon"** is also unsatisfying, and is self-destructive as well. His conjured hour with Belthoris vanishes back into the past just as a temporary spat develops between the two lovers. Ending on such a sour note, he proclaims that "vain, like all other hours, was the resummoned hour; doubly irredeemable was my loss." And even more tragic is the price Calaspa must pay for casting the time-distorting spell. . . . The local priesthood torture and kill him, after laying their own spell upon him, that his soul should travel from body to body into the future, until in some other incarnation he shall die again for his crime.

Indeed, even when the acknowledged price is their own destruction, Smith's men go forward unhaltingly to retrieve what they have lost, so great is their despair. The narrator of **"The City of the Singing Flame"** ends the tale by saying that he will return to the City and immolate himself in the Flame, that he might merge with the unearthly beauty and music that he had sampled and lost; and the hero of **"The End of the Story"** makes the same resolution, to return to the couch of a deadly lamia, from which he had been taken by force, rather than live out his years without her. . . . (pp. 11-12)

But whether they seek to regain their loss or choose to suffer through a life of torment and regret, the characters in the stories we've discussed are all made to feel "the loss of high splendor", to live through "sunken years", and to long for the return of "a buried bliss"; and as each is the puppet-creation of Clark Ashton Smith, their songs of woe should be seen as those of the Necromancer himself. (p. 12)

Steve Behrends, "The Song of the Necromancer: 'Loss' in Clark Ashton Smith's Fiction," in Studies in Weird Fiction, *Vol. 1, No. 1, August 1, 1986, pp. 3-12.*

John (Hoyer) Updike
1932-

American novelist, critic, short story writer, poet, essayist, and dramatist.

A major contemporary American author, Updike is particularly noted for the subtle complexity of his fiction, verse, and criticism. His values derive from myth and Christianity and are evidenced in his work by his emphasis upon morality. Updike's major subject since the mid-1960s has been the domestic life of the American middle class and its attendant rituals: marriage, sex, and divorce. Against the mundane setting of American suburbia and in concurrence with his interpretation of the ideas of philosopher Sören Kierkegaard and theologian Karl Barth, Updike presents average people—usually men—searching for aesthetic or religious meaning in the secular awareness of their own mortality. Updike stated that his books center upon "insolvable dilemmas," and the dialectical tension in his work is often the result of the struggles of his characters to determine what is morally right in a constantly changing world.

In 1954, Updike graduated *summa cum laude* from Harvard University. He soon began contributing stories, poems, and criticism to *The New Yorker* and served as a reporter for the magazine's "Talk of the Town" column from 1955 to 1957. Although Updike left *The New Yorker* to pursue his literary career, he has regularly published fiction, verse, and criticism in the magazine; much of this work has been collected in numerous volumes. Updike's first major work, *The Carpentered Hen and Other Tame Creatures* (1958), contains poems that whimsically attack such topics as modern values, sports, and journalism. Critics particularly praised "Ex-Basketball Player," discerning in Updike a talent for the exacting rhyme and meter associated with light verse. Reviewers warmly praised Updike's second volume of poetry, *Telephone Poles and Other Poems* (1969), in which he blends wry wit with esoteric reflections. The title poem of *Midpoint and Other Poems* (1969) is considered Updike's most experimental work of verse. In this piece, he makes use of photographs and typography to reflect upon his life up to age thirty-five. Updike called "Midpoint" both "a joke on the antique genre of the long poem" and "an earnest meditation on the mysteries of the ego." *Tossing and Turning* (1978) secured Updike's reputation as a master of light verse. This volume examines such topics as suburbia, middle age, and the illusory nature of success. *Facing Nature* (1985) also elicited praise. The alternately humorous and serious reflections in this collection prompted comparison to the verse of W. H. Auden.

Updike's early short fiction, collected in *The Same Door* (1959), earned him a reputation as a leading practitioner of the short story form. Most of Updike's early stories are set in the fictional town of Olinger, which he modeled after his hometown of Shillington, Pennsylvania. Small-town concerns are the subject of Updike's second short story collection, *Pigeon Feathers* (1962), which addresses adolescent anxieties regarding love, marriage, and children. Further tales of small-town life are collected in *Olinger Stories* (1964). In the mid-1960s, the fictional Boston suburb of Tarbox largely replaced Olinger as Updike's setting, reflecting his actual move from New York City to Ipswich, Massachusetts. The stories set in Tarbox fea-

© Jerry Bauer

ture sophisticated, urbanized individuals whose marital problems and quests for identity mirror the social anxieties of their times. Tarbox is the setting of *Bech: A Book* (1970), in which Updike introduces his alter ego, Henry Bech. A Jewish bachelor and writer who fears the commitments of marriage and success, Bech aims in these stories to "confess sterility"—to demonstrate how authors betray their integrity for monetary or fashionable reasons. In *Bech Is Back* (1982), another collection of short stories, Bech concludes thirteen years of insecurity and writer's block by getting married and by writing an offensive, best-selling novel. Despite his success, however, his old fears return and his marriage ends in divorce. In *Too Far to Go: The Maples Stories* (1979), a husband and wife separate in mutual friendship. The moral of these stories, according to Updike, "is that all blessings are mixed." *Problems and Other Stories* (1979) also centers on domestic conflicts. Updike received an O. Henry Award in 1966 for his story "The Bulgarian Poetess."

Updike's first novel, *The Poorhouse Fair* (1959), established his reputation as a major novelist. Set in Olinger, the book centers on the intense rivalries between elderly members of a poorhouse, who are permitted to stage an annual fair by a bureaucracy insensitive to their greater needs. Interpreted as an attack on behavioristic psychology and the welfare state,

The Poorhouse Fair elicited a diverse critical response. D. J. Enright proclaimed it "a perfect little cameo of old age." Updike's second novel, *Rabbit, Run* (1960), is among his best-known and most widely analyzed works. This book explores the prolonged adolescence of an inarticulate working-class father and husband who misses the excitement of his high school years. Fearing responsibility, middle age, and an unhappy marriage, Harry "Rabbit" Angstrom seeks escape in an extra-marital affair before realizing that "there can be achievement even in defeat." Updike wrote two sequels to *Rabbit, Run,* each reflecting a new decade in Rabbit's life. *Rabbit Redux* (1971) mirrors the unrest of the late 1960s, this time centering on the threat posed to Rabbit's marriage when he brings home a young drug addict and a black revolutionary. Critical reaction to the book was largely negative, but reviewers were nearly unanimous in their praise of *Rabbit Is Rich* (1982), for which Updike received the National Book Critics Circle Award, the American Book Award, and the Pulitzer Prize. A quiet tone of acceptance permeates this work, in which Rabbit, middle-aged and basically content with his marriage, must resolve his feelings regarding his daughter's death and his own mortality.

Updike won the National Book Award for his third novel, *The Centaur* (1963). In this allegorical work, a rebellious son and his father are modeled after the mythological figures of Prometheus and Chiron. Like Prometheus, the legendary hero for whom the centaur Chiron sacrificed his immortality, the son learns to appreciate the value of his father's life only after the man has died. *Of the Farm* (1965) according to Updike, is "about moral readjustment" and "the consequences of a divorce." In this book, Updike focuses on a man who returns to his widowed mother's farmhouse with his new bride and stepson and soon realizes that his mother and his wife are equally demanding. Peter Buitenhuis called the novel "very clearly and very completely, a small masterpiece."

Beginning with *Couples* (1968), Tarbox replaces Olinger as the setting of Updike's novels. In this controversial work, Updike examines the sexual and spiritual quests of ten suburban couples. Religion and sexuality are again the focus of *A Month of Sundays* (1975), in which an adulterous preacher is unable to feel guilt even after he is cast out by his congregation. In *Marry Me: A Romance* (1976), two adulterers are caught in the ambiguous dilemma of wanting to marry but not wishing to hurt their respective families. *The Coup* (1979), a novel inspired by Updike's 1973 lectureship in Africa, represents a radical departure in his subject matter. Narrated by the black dictator of an emerging African nation, the book ridicules the idea of revolution as a vehicle for change as well as the attempts by superpowers to make third-world countries serve their economic interests.

Updike's recent novels have elicited mixed reviews. *The Witches of Eastwick* (1984) centers on three divorced women who acquire the powers of witches, casting evil spells and pursuing unhappily married men in their suburban community until the arrival of a demonic stranger throws them into competition. Greg Johnson summed up diverse critical interpretations of this work: "An allegory, a fable, a romance, a meditation on the nature of evil—*The Witches of Eastwick* is all of these, while remaining a high-spirited sexual comedy and a caricaturist's view of women's liberation." *Roger's Version* (1986) centers on a divinity school professor's dualistic feelings regarding a student's proposal to prove the existence of God by computer. This novel, which blends theology, eroticism, and science, is narrated by the ambiguous Roger, who claims to be the tale's villain. As its title indicates, Roger's version of the story is only one among many.

Updike's criticism, originally published in *The New Yorker,* appears with articles, anecdotes, and other pieces in three acclaimed collections: *Assorted Prose* (1965), *Picked-Up Pieces* (1975), and the National Book Critics Circle Award-winning volume, *Hugging the Shore: Essays and Criticism* (1983). Updike has also written a biographical drama, *Buchanan Dying* (1979), about James Buchanan, the fifteenth President of the United States. Several of Updike's novels and short stories have been adapted for film and television.

Critics rarely agree on the artistic value of Updike's works. Such literary figures as Norman Mailer and John W. Aldridge regard his style as superficial, masking a lack of statement or substance. Most critics, however, concede Updike's breadth of knowledge and mastery of presentation, and many consider him among America's most distinguished and erudite authors. John Cheever deemed Updike "the most brilliant and versatile writer of his generation."

(See also *CLC,* Vols. 1, 2, 3, 5, 7, 9, 13, 15, 23, 34; *Contemporary Authors,* Vols. 1-4, rev. ed.; *Contemporary Authors New Revision Series,* Vol. 4; *Dictionary of Literary Biography,* Vols. 2, 5; *Dictionary of Literary Biography Yearbook: 1980, 1982;* and *Dictionary of Literary Biography Documentary Series,* Vol. 3.)

LAWRENCE GRAVER

With playful modesty Updike offers **Picked-Up Pieces** as consignments from an artist's workshop—miscellaneous prose made to order during the past ten years; but it looks more like a splendidly cluttered Italian museum where profane and sacred treasures, monuments and miniatures, make dizzying claims on our attention. Brilliant, sustained essays on Kierkegaard, Borges and Nabokov mix with travel sketches, accounts of golf, body cells, Indians, cemeteries, Satanism, and the ambiguous gratifications of the writing life. A garland celebrating our luck (and our children's) at having E. B. White's *The Trumpet of the Swan* is soon followed by thoughts on oral sex and buggery in the American novel. . . .

Even the footnotes sparkle. Having said in 1968 that he must be one of the few Americans with a bachelor-of-arts degree never to have met either Robert Lowell or Norman Mailer, Updike now feels compelled to revise the record with an asterisk:

> True in 1968 but no longer. Lowell who seemed to be leaning above me like a raked mast, later described me to a mutual friend as "elusive and shy." I think I was afraid he would fall on me from his height of eminence. Mailer, as much shorter than I had expected as Lowell was taller, danced about me on a darkened street corner . . . , became not elfin but an entire circle of elves in himself, taunting me with my supposed handsomeness, with being the handsomest guy he had ever seen. I took it to be Maileresque hyperbole, absurd yet nevertheless with something profound in it—perhaps my se-

cret wish to *be* handsome, which only he, and that by dim streetlight, at a drunken hour, has ever perceived.

Who else but Updike could offer in a footnote his talent in microcosm? Lowell as "raked mast"—the image is worth a thousand pictures of that looming, exposed, tormented poet; and metaphors as fresh animate much of *Picked-Up Pieces.* The sentence that follows has that irresistible blend of vulnerability and pluck, self-effacement and self-regard that is often the quality of an Updike confession. With the appearance of Mailer, we get a bizarre, suggestive vignette: the prize-ring and the fairy tale, banter and illumination, plus a stubborn respect for mundane circumstance, the verifiable fact.

As one reads along in *Picked-Up Pieces* such dazzle becomes customary light, and a more confident feeling for the form of an Updike literary essay emerges. The initial impulse is usually celebratory: the reviewer wishes to share his enthusiasm for a book he admires. More often than not, the author is foreign, in some way exotic, in craft and vision unlike himself. . . .

Updike seems obsessed with finding out what the best people elsewhere are doing, partly from a desire to talk shop, partly from a need to peer through other masks, but also from an almost mystical passion for human connectedness in a clefted, precarious time. Bonds, ties, relationships, transactions, alliances—the urge to make them and the difficulty; how they are formed and dissolve; the joys they offer and the penalties they exact—this has been one of Updike's persistent subjects in fiction and in journalism. . . .

Updike's search for coexistence offers a clue to one of the most satisfying features of his best essays and reviews: the simultaneous expression of diverse, many-layered experience. Sometimes he does it through his remarkable gift for figurative speech. Describing the limits of Nabokov's *Glory,* he isolates one of those "landlordly prefaces that slam shut the doors of unsightly closets, inveigh against the Freudian in the hall, and roughly nudge the prospective tenant toward the one window with a view." On a larger scale the effect works as a structural and thematic principle, as can be seen in the final tribute to Borges.

It begins quietly with facts about publication and translation history (in the clear, low-keyed style that can serve as cement for an Updike mosaic). A moment later comes personal reminiscence:

> I myself had read only "The Garden of the Forking Paths," . . . [and] I was prompted to read Borges seriously by a remark made—internationally enough—in Rumania . . . by a young critic in a tone he had previously reserved for Kafka.

Funny yet unobtrusive, the juxtaposition does its work; our critic is equally relaxed with detective stories and the heady talk of a literary conference. The allusion to Kafka slides almost unnoticed into an analogy and a question. Will the appearance of Borges prove as important as the publication of Kafka in the 1930's? Unlikely; but might not his work "in its gravely considered oddity" provide a clue "to the way out of the dead-end narcissism and downright trashiness of present American fiction?" Three paragraphs into the essay and we have a compacted structure with four main elements: literary history, personal reminiscence, a promise of textual analysis, and generalized cultural commentary. From this point on, Updike's own

delight in Borges's work, his skill at conveying its originality and felt life, its place in history, and its meaning for the present are elegantly woven together.

In the foreword to *Picked-Up Pieces,* Updike laments that his flirtation with journalism has too often kept him away from fiction, his one true love. . . . Without wishing to hex his novels and stories, one might hope that for the sake of criticism he keeps his frustrating, fruitful balance.

Lawrence Graver, "Even the Footnotes Sparkle," in The New York Times Book Review, *November 30, 1975, p. 39.*

ANATOLE BROYARD

John Updike is such a conscious craftsman, such a deliberate conjurer with words, rhythms, forms and ideas, that one would expect him to be more disdainful, less generous, toward the cruder gropings of most of his contemporaries. However, *Picked-Up Pieces* contradicts this impression. In fact, in his major essays, those on Jorge Luis Borges, Kierkegaard and Nabokov, he strikes me, at least, as being too kind.

As I see it, the relationship between Updike and Nabokov might be described as "there but for the grace of God go I." The implacable archness, the gratuitous word games, the lepidopterous frivolity, the sense of the author's ego breathing down your neck, in Mr. Nabokov's fiction are potential faults that John Updike has increasingly repressed or brought under control in his own work. It must be nostalgia for his avoided vices that impels Mr. Updike to call the author of *Ada* and *Pale Fire* "the best-equipped writer in the English-speaking world." His reading of *Ada* is so ingeniously convoluted as to be almost indistinguishable from parody. . . .

In treating Borges, Mr. Updike is only slightly less indulgent. While he concedes that "discouragingly large areas of truth seem excluded from his vision," he forgives Mr. Borges by remarking that "his driest paragraph is somehow compelling." That uncharacteristic "somehow" is a confession of Mr. Updike's inability to justify Borges's bibliomaniac sereneness, those pages that make you feel you are locked in a library during an earthquake, in danger of being buried under the weight of books.

I like *Picked-Up Pieces* better when Mr. Updike observes that "modern fiction does seem, more than its antecedents, the work of eccentrics. The writer now makes his marks on paper blanker than it has ever been." . . . One agrees gladly when he remarks that "even intelligence does not commend a fictional character to us. No, in the strange egalitarian world of the novel, a man must earn our interest by virtue of his—how shall I say?—*authentic sentiments.*"

I found Mr. Updike's piece on Kierkegaard disappointing. It evokes neither the literary brilliance nor the fatiguing obscurity and verbosity that compete in Kierkegaard's pages and concentrates instead, to an almost perverse degree, on his narrowest approaches to religion, as if his chief interest to us today was as a maverick theologian. . . .

In an essay on the novels of Knut Hamsun, Mr. Updike is like someone who discovers, dusty and neglected in an attic, a small hoard of valuable country primitive antiques. The review of John Cheever's *Bullet Park* seems to betray, in its peculiar praise, an unconfessed ambivalence. "The tender, twinkling prose'' is one of those compliments that seem to imply a reluctance overcome. . . .

The daily reviewer, who has to eat the plat du jour and gulp it down at that, may feel a pang of envy on reading the luxurious lucubrations of *Picked-Up Pieces*. After this, he ought to be grateful, for John Updike is an unassailable refutation of the old saw that those who can do, while those who cannot, criticize.

Anatole Broyard, ''On a Spree With Updike,'' in The New York Times, *December 2, 1975, p. 37.*

MARTIN AMIS

As a literary journalist, John Updike has that single inestimable virtue: having read him once, you admit to yourself, almost with a sigh, that you will have to read everything he writes. At a time when the reviewer's role has devolved to that of a canary in a pre-war coalmine, Updike reminds you [in *Picked-Up Pieces*] that the review can, in its junior way, be something of a work of art, or at least a worthy vehicle for the play of ideas, feeling and wit. His stance is one of ultimate serviceability: the alert and ironic layman unanxiously detached from the world of literary commerce. . . . And the hectic pungency of his prose is answered by the intense, if erratic, strength of his responses. Updike's reviewing is high-powered enough to win the name of literary criticism—which is to say, it constantly raises the question (a question more interesting than it at first sounds), 'What is literature?' The fact that he never finds a good reply to it is just one of the reasons why he needs to be judged by the highest standards, his own standards.

A rather workaday grumble to be made about *Picked-Up Pieces* is that many of its pieces ought never to have been picked up—at least not without emendation. Complaints about the price of particular novels or a book's margin-sizes may look well enough in the columns of the *New Yorker* but appear footling between hard covers. Several books-received notices on humdrum theologians should have been exorcised, and it is hard not to be startled by a 60-word citation to Thornton Wilder (which carries a 50-word footnote humourlessly justifying its inclusion). Include away: here, plainly, Updike is more interested in his personal filing-system than in his normal courteousness towards the reader. (p. 368)

The heart of *Picked-Up Pieces,* however, is its fiction reviews, where Updike can always revert to first principles and so remain unimplicated by the frequent banality of his material. Updike goes at fiction with a firm idea of what he takes a novel to be, but he is incomparably good at conveying the *weight* of an author's prose, the lineaments of the talent behind it. Even when he is scorning what seems admirable or praising what seems mischievous, there is never any clouding of the issues involved. Yet the readings are intractably polemical; and although Updike's methods are close to irreproachable, one can only react polemically to his findings.

For some reason, most of the novels Updike has chosen to review are translations. I thought at first that Updike must have some gluttonous craving for local colour. . . . Surely, one reads even the foreign classics in translation as a guilty duty, to get some blotched silhouette, as one might look at snapshots of inaccessible paintings. But Updike regards the language barrier as a rut which any frog could straddle. . . . Updike can keep a straight face while noting the linguistic tang of translated 'Arab and Bantu exclamations'; and he is perfectly capable of

talking about the *style* of a novel translated from the French translation of the Polish—which is like analysing the brushstrokes in a Brownie. It is an insensitivity that points to a radical imbalance in Updike's view of how novels work, and it loiters in everything he says about fiction.

Even Nabokov's fiction—and the seven essays on Nabokov are perhaps the most valuable thing in the book. The swank of Updike's prose provides the ideal window for the teeming haughtiness of Nabokov's: from his excesses . . . to, very nearly, his essence: 'Nabokov's is really an amorous style . . . it yearns to clasp diaphanous exactitude into its hairy arms.' Here, you feel sure, is a critic unimprovably equipped for and attuned to his author. But here too, suddenly, Updike's linguistic blindfold . . . is whipped off to reveal tightly shut eyes. 'Is art a game? Nabokov stakes his career on it'; he makes 'airtight boxes . . . detached from even the language of their composition'. If you substituted 'embodied in' for 'detached from even' you might get within hailing distance of Nabokov's art, but by now Updike is in full retreat. Nabokov, *horrible scriptu,* spurns 'psychology and sociology', confronting us 'with a fiction that purposely undervalues its own humanistic content'.

Uh-oh, one thinks. Updike is a Catholic, of the small-town Dionysian sort, and this does his writing no harm; yet he is also a Humanist, of the numinous Apollonian sort, and this does seem to account for that vein of folksy uplift which underlies his novels as well as his criticism. . . . Thus, Erica Jong's appallingly written and irreducibly autobiographical *Fear of Flying* is a 'lovable, delicious novel', because, well, in Updike's view Erica Jong has a lovable and delicious lifestyle. Would Updike defend this on the grounds that a writer's life can 'matter more than his works'? Or because, as Updike says five pages later, books can 'exist less as literature than as life'?

Life. 'Life.' Some people seem very keen on stressing their approval of this commodity, almost as if the rest of us had no time for the stuff. Updike, who likes fiction to believe in 'improvement' and 'a better world', crucially asserts that 'by a novel we understand an imitation of reality rather than a spurning of it', and grades them accordingly. . . . If Updike granted art the same reverent autonomy he grants life, some 'improvement' would indeed take place: he would become a better critic. Meanwhile, get to grips with his funny, clever, butter-fingered book. (pp. 368-69)

Martin Amis, ''Life Class,'' in New Statesman, *Vol. 91, No. 2348, March 19, 1976, pp. 368-69.*

VICTOR HOWES

John Updike's poems, like his novels, are timely, urbane, wise, and rated PG (parental guidance recommended). They are, in [*Tossing and Turning*], the poems of ''an aging modern man / estranged, alone, and medium gray,'' a man who attended the Harvard of the 1950s in company with a generation steeped ''in Doctor Spock, TV, and denim chic.''

Now, a father whose children have fled from home ''to grow voices and fangs,'' the poet finds himself insomniac, ''Tossing and Turning'' on his undulant waterbed, a bed that utters ''Gurgle gleep'' and ''sings / of broken dreams and hidden springs.''

The hidden springs of Updike's poems are his memories: memories of a sheltered boyhood in Pennsylvania where ''My parents' house had been a hothouse world / of complicating inward-feeding jokes''; memories of a sudden cold exposure to a wintry ''world of snowmen named Descartes, and Marx and

Milton''; memories of a youthful romance, a marriage, parenthood, Caribbean vacations, writing novels. . . .

Though Updike's poems take no daring leaps toward either despair or affirmation, vault no logical or rhetorical fences, they are good, literate vehicles of thought and feeling. Exposing no intimate private world, they image instead our shared contiguous environment, a place of golfers, bicyclists, putters-on of storm windows, watchers of moon-landings on TV. . . .

At his best, Updike suggests no comfortable vision of modern urban man. Here we are, he seems to say, afloat on a salt, estranging sea, tugging at-our oar, rattling the handcuff that binds us to it, but afraid to rock the boat, and counting our mixed blessings with a stiff upper lip.

> *Victor Howes, ''Updike Verses Tally Some Mixed Blessings,'' in* The Christian Science Monitor, *June 29, 1977, p. 19.*

MATTHEW HODGART

[In one poem in *Tossing and Turning*], Updike visits Hartford, Connecticut, which is said to have the highest per capita income in the United States, and looks at the opulent houses of Mark Twain and Wallace Stevens; he reflects that no authors today possess such residences, ''And I, I live (as if you care) in chambers / That number two—in one I sleep, alone / Most nights, and in the other drudge . . .''. Well, I do care, in a way, enough to ask if this famous novelist . . . is really as poor as all that. Should we do something about it? The only suggestion I have to make is that the causes of this poverty, if it is real, are private education for several children plus amateur photography. **''Commencement, Pingree School''** tells how the poet goes to see ''his lovely daughter graduate''. As each of the girl graduands ''accepts her scroll of rhetoric / Up pops a Daddy with a Nikon. Click.'' A Nikon is a very classy camera, and even film is dear on top of school fees.

Updike, who once illustrated an autobiographical poem [**''Midpoint''**] with real black-and-white snapshots, is at his best in family reminiscences. **''Leaving Church Early''** is a restatement of his novel about his family in Pennsylvania in the 1940s (*Of the Farm*) but no less poignant for that. His recent experiences are more melancholy than those of this childhood (true of nearly all the poets). The particularly sad poems are the ones that ought to be happy: being driven, very fast, from Milan to Como by a beautiful Italian lady; sailing in a large yacht; flying over the Atlantic (agony). His family connections extend backwards and forwards, interestingly but on the whole unhappily. The one subject he is happy about is, one supposes, sex; but the long poem with the unprintable title is more ingenious than euphoric.

Updike remains a master, perhaps the master in our time, of light verse. Whether he is a poet or not will not be decided until twenty years after his death. . . . This cannot matter to him, since he must remain in the company of Chesterbelloc and Auden, a good man and better *faber*. He is even a literate writer, if one defines literacy as the willingness to read through the *Scientific American* every month without necessarily understanding every word. . . . In the strange world of poetry (still largely unknown) Updike may be a weak force but he nevertheless has in him something of the stars.

> *Matthew Hodgart, ''Family Snapshots,'' in* The Times Literary Supplement, *No. 3993, October 13, 1978, p. 1158.*

CHRISTOPHER LEHMANN-HAUPT

[Henry Bech's writing style in *Bech Is Back*] doesn't sound at all like the Henry Bech we have come to know from John Updike's earlier sketches [in] *Bech: a Book*. . . . Or rather, it doesn't sound like Mr. Updike writing about Bech. It echoes more of Mr. Updike's most writerly, exquisite self. . . .

What accounts for the contrast between [the styles of the two books] . . .? The shortsighted view would be to blame it on sheer inconsistency, of which there happens to be a moderate amount in *Bech Is Back*.

After all, some of the seven episodes are little more than clever but offhand scribbles—**''Three Illuminations in the Life of an American Author,''** in which Bech encounters some of the pitfalls of being a famous, if fallow, writer in our endlessly trendy society; and **''Bech Third-Worlds It,''** in which Bech collides with various cultures. . . .

Only in the long climactic piece, **''Bech Wed''**—in which Bech settles with his Protestant bride in Ossining, N.Y., and cranks out a million-dollar best seller—are we given anything substantially complex to chew upon. And even here, so violent is the contrast between Bech's intricate interior musings and a nearly silly parody of the contemporary publishing scene that we wonder for a moment if Mr. Updike hasn't lost control.

One can blame the varying styles of *Bech is Back* on inconsistency, but it would probably be a mistake to do so. Mr. Updike . . . usually has a reason for everything he does. Anyway, it's as easy to work out a defense of what he's up to as it is to blame. The key, I think, to the relative exquisiteness of Bech's writing style—or, more precisely, the style that describes Bech's writing—is that the passages in which it appears in **''Bech Wed''** are the first in which we've really glimpsed Bech's interior. Up until this point, he's been something of a vacuum, someone more acted upon than acting. Indeed, this has been the source of his comedy.

Now suddenly, as Bech's block breaks, we glimpse an intricately sensitive, almost romantic Bech, and just as suddenly the terms of the comedy are reversed. Having completed his book against his own better judgment, and having in the process betrayed the complexity of his imagination he must now come up against a publishing industry so vapid and trendy that a reader would wince if he weren't so busy smiling.

That Bech writes like Updike when he finally gets going—that is, like Updike when he *isn't* writing about Bech—also reveals the simple truth that despite their contrasting exteriors, Bech and Updike have been one and the same all along. What's more, this likeness makes it possible to float a few theories on why Mr. Updike's esthetic ego happens to be Jewish: the artist as wanderer (Bech is so often depicted on tour); the artist as an individual lacking nationality (Bech happens to disapprove of Israel).

But I am leaning somewhat heavily on a book whose pleasure lies in its levity. Let us therefore simply rejoice that Bech is back. And if this volume happens to be the *Rabbit Redux* of an eventual Bech trilogy, then let us now begin to look forward to the publication of *Bech's Bucks*.

> *Christopher Lehmann-Haupt, in a review of ''Bech Is Back,'' in* The New York Times, *October 14, 1982, p. 20.*

EDWARD HOAGLAND

Since 1970 Henry Bech has been one of John Updike's several alter egos. In *Bech: A Book,* Bech was the author of three novels and a miscellany and was beginning to find that leading the literary life was easier than writing. He was also a bachelor afraid to commit himself to marriage, and the fact that in this respect he was the opposite of Updike may have made him all the dearer to his creator. But in *Bech Is Back* his dry period has stretched to 13 years, and though the descriptions of poor Bech's collisions with rare book collectors, Third World cultural attachés and sexual hostesses in the Commonwealth countries may be funnier than ever, they are sadder. He is running out of stalling tactics. At last he relinquishes his timidities, marries his mistress, finishes a long-awaited, best-selling book called *Think Big* and exchanges his shyness for disillusion, thereby becoming a formidable literary figure.... And in accomplishing this ambiguously welcome transition, he is like Updike, which—though Updike evinces no undue interest in the books Bech writes—should keep him available for the future. (p. 1)

It wasn't till Updike had started publishing distinguished criticism that he was taken seriously in all [literary] quarters.... [Many writers and critics] tended to regard the likes of Updike with indifference, condescension or even antipathy. It was especially explorations of the Jewish experience in America they were "hailing."

Boldly and good-humoredly Updike set out to explore that experience himself in [*Bech: A Book*]. He may have begun it as a bit of a Nabokovian joke. Anyway, I don't believe his timing was a coincidence, having published an essay called **"On Not Being a Jew"** ... in 1968, which was probably the same year that he sat down to think Bech up.... But this was also a midpoint of Updike's life—his most recent book had been *Midpoint and Other Poems*—and he was investigating middle age, the nature of a writer's life and other matters pertinent to him, by way of Bech. He has kept on juggling Bech's fate and fortunes, along with those of Rabbit Angstrom, the Maples and a successor couple and many inhabitants of Brewer, Olinger and Massachusetts towns.

Bech, like Updike, is quite Bellovian. He ruminates with Saul Bellow's sort of moderation and similar, intensely crafted, eye-stopping observations stemming from and leading toward good will.... Bech is humbler than Bellow and less productive but no less prudently ironical—a tired fellow, much anthologized, and on the lecture circuit to Mennonite and Indian colleges to support himself. He realizes that as his artistic activity has diminished he has grown to look more and more like an artist. He has reached the point, after signing 28,500 "tip-in sheets of high-rag-content paper" for a fancy edition of an early novel, that "he could not even write his own name."

Then, marrying a methodical gentile woman, he finally gets around his difficulty and submits this best seller to his old publishing house.... [The] conversations Bech has with [his editors] are hilarious. Bech had left Riverside Drive and 99th Street and gone up to Ossining for his transformation, though he often feels "like a strolling minstrel" among the *goyim.* Jewishness, thinks Bech, "became a kind of marvel—a threadbare fable still being spun, an energy and irony vengefully animating the ruins of Christendom, a flavor and guile and humor and inspired heedlessness." ... But after Bech's book is successful Bech's marriage breaks up. We see him at a television producer's white-on-white costume party lined up for the night with a mud wrestler.

Bech Is Back is not a novel but a group of pleasantly linked stories, a minor Updike performance. Nevertheless, its pigeons have "a Chaplin-tramp style of walking." ... Bech is not overly "Jewish." He takes to Scotland more than Israel, while his Scottish-American wife prefers Israel to Scotland. He is Jewish in about the way that James Buchanan—Updike's choice to write about among the Presidents, in a play called *Buchanan Dying*—was a President. But more than Buchanan, he's also Updike, a vehicle for future ventings by the author of the travails of authorship. (p. 32)

Edward Hoagland, "A Novelist's Novelist," *in* The New York Times Book Review, *October 17, 1982, pp. 1, 30, 32.*

ISA KAPP

Eager to cover much more territory than there was scope for in his fine, small early novels, *The Poorhouse Fair* and *Of the Farm,* [Updike] has been making his books thicker, his sentences longer, Rabbit richer. *Bech: A Book,* the most unexpected and clever of the volumes that followed, fulfilled the rather nervy ambition of this Congregationalist to speak in the cadences and mannerisms of a Jewish writer....

[In *Bech Is Back*], Updike has definitely gone too far, swooping [Bech] (courtesy of the State Department) through a whirlwind "cultural exchange" tour of seven Third-World countries, then grounding him in the peevish marital complaints of the familiar Updike hero. No wonder he has grown so waspish that we cannot distinguish him from the WASP husband of *Marry Me.* Whether at home with his new wife [Bea] and her three children, ... [or writing] a big new novel that sounds dishearteningly like the author's *Couples* with a Lesbian postscript, ... the Jewish element in Bech is exceedingly hard to locate.

But the notion that Bech is either literally or phantasmagorically Jewish finally reaches the level of the preposterous in the story (more accurately, spotty travel diary) titled **"The Holy Land."** Here Bech is impelled to observe (justly) that "His artist's eye, always, was drawn to the irrelevant: the overlay of commercialism upon this ancient way fascinated him." ...

Jewish life and the Israeli population go virtually unnoticed in this voyage to Jerusalem. Bech does attend a dinner with some Israeli writers, but the conversation is sparse and sympathies veer mainly to the Arabs who, "Bech perceived, are the blacks of Israel." ... Ever the artist, Bech notices that the female novelist is overweight but flirtatious, and he ponders the lag between the fading of an attractive woman's conception of herself and the fading of the reality. These are the responses of a Jewish writer during his first visit to Jerusalem? Only if he is created with or by a *goyisher kopf.*

Lest anyone suspect that a racial angle lurks in this lopsided travelogue, I can testify that in the Scottish setting of **"Macbech"** the behavior of the Bech and Bea combo is equally incongruous. (p. 5)

[Updike] has regretted in interviews that he knows so little about the ordinary working world. Though he convincingly portrays the linotype setter in *Rabbit Redux* and has done thorough enough research to create an authentic African dictator in *The Coup,* the truth is that compared to a large-minded novelist like Dickens or even a smaller-minded one like the maligned James Gould Cozzens, Updike and his characters give the impression of living in a stale domestic backwater that no amount of verbal athleticism can refresh.

In the most substantial portion of [*Bech Is Back*], "Beck Wed," muddled marriage is once again Updike's beat. The urban author is out of place in his wife's suburban house where "squirrels or was it bats danced over his head," and he keeps his one window closed against the distracting variety of bird calls. . . . Eventually Bea retreats into a furious obsession with her teen-age daughter's loss of virginity, blaming Bech's erotic novel for her fall, and Bech, demoralized, goes the way of Updikeans, committing adultery with his sister-in-law.

Updike undoubtedly has a genius for conveying chronic tensions between male and female, for painting a rueful portrait of marriage brushed simultaneously with flecks of an old Tolstoyan sympathy for one's mate and splotches of anxious modern bellicosity. His friends could do worse, however, than advise him to quit forever the (for him) lugubrious preoccupation with sex and marriage.

Much too capricious to be more than a wet blanket over romance, Updike allows the unpredictably genial and witty side of himself (by far the better half) to take over when he sizes up other forms of susceptibility and adulteration. An amusing major theme of *Bech Is Back* is the cornucopia of temptations dangled before the contempoary novelist to lure him from his typewriter. He can now, by lecturing, trips abroad, conferences, seminars, and multimedia interviews, contrive to keep respectably busy without ever putting a word on paper. (pp. 5-6)

It is intriguing to realize how very intelligent John Updike is, yet how much that intelligence is a matter purely of atmosphere and language—very different indeed from the analytical intelligence of the Jewish novelists who have so magnetized him. Not really an intellectual, he can be caught out in such unfinished thoughts and loose remarks as the one about Arabs being the blacks of Israel. . . . This difference of intelligence makes it easy for Updike to envision the words a Jewish writer might *say* (like "Craziness, down through history, has performed impressively.") or how he might feel in his senses (the urban Bech squirming in country greenery). But when it comes to the Jewish writer's emotional imagination and his true metier, the drama of the soul, Updike is in a foreign country.

Still, Updike's territory, words, also count. They identify us, betray us, and in *Bech Is Back,* more often than not, entertain us. The most hilarious episode of the book is the telephone introduction of Bech to the editor-in-chief of his old publishing house. . . .

None of this satire requires deep thought or feeling, and there is in fact some question whether the business and publicity of writing are legitimate subjects for novels; maybe television has so accustomed the novelist to seeing his own image while he talks that he now believes anything, including sales reports, are fair game for fiction. On the other hand, it is fun for the reader to find Updike out in the big lively world of impersonal rather than personal corruption. (p. 6)

Isa Kapp, "Updike in a Foreign Country," in The New Leader, Vol. LXV, No. 23, December 13, 1982, pp. 5-7.

JONATHAN YARDLEY

[In *The Witches of Eastwick*], John Updike is at his most calculatedly puckish and thus least attractive. By turn, and often simultaneously, *The Witches of Eastwick* is arch, fey, self-indulgent, showy, precious, windy, goatish. It will enjoy a great success, because Updike's inexplicably inflated reputation assures a large audience for all his books, especially his novels. But it is at best a silly book and at worst a disagreeable one; it is most difficult to imagine that many among Updike's loyal readers will take much pleasure from it.

There can be no doubt, though, that we are meant to be charmed. Updike presents himself to us in *The Witches of Eastwick*—just as he did in *A Month of Sundays* and *Marry Me* and many of his short stories—as a pied piper, luring an enchanted audience into his tunnel of love. There we are treated to what he clearly regards as a panoply of delights, most of them having to do with the flesh, and less frequently the minds, of women. The occasional appearance of an austere New England steeple reminds us that there is serious business being attended to, as do the frequent references to various emissaries of God; but in *The Witches of Eastwick* Updike is at play in the fields of the Lord, indulging himself in a bit of a frolic, a lark, a gambol.

But *The Witches of Eastwick* is none of the above. Like so much else Updike has written it is less a work of art than of artifice. That it is the artifice of a talented and intelligent writer must not be gainsaid, but it remains that what we have here is mere cleverness and contrivance. The play in which Updike would have us join is false and self-conscious; the atmosphere is not joyful but brittle.

The witches are three women who live in the small Rhode Island settlement of Eastwick, a place that "had for decades been semi-depressed and semi-fashionable." They are Alexandra Spofford, Jane Smart and Sukie Rougemont; the first two are in their late thirties, the last is six years younger. All of them have children, whom to all intents and purposes we never meet—an omission that is most uncharacteristic of Updike, who if nothing else usually writes about children with real feeling and understanding—and all of them have been liberated from their husbands. . . .

They seem quite ordinary women of the privileged, cultured middle class, but as Updike presents them, they are intended to be quite extraordinary. Separated from their men, they have acquired the power of witches—the power to see into the minds of others, to alter the lives of others, to translate their darkest thoughts and wishes into reality. . . .

They are as happy as can be: convening their meetings, doing their little witchy tricks, having their various affairs with local gentlemen seeking a dash of excitement in their monotonous married lives. But the peculiar tranquility of their existence is disturbed by the arrival in Eastwick of the mysterious Darryl Van Horne, "a bearish dark man with greasy curly hair half-hiding his ears." . . . That all three women are strongly attracted to this creature is likely to be, for most readers, sufficient mystery in itself; but Updike, who is working lazily in *The Witches of Eastwick,* seems to feel under no obligation to do more than present Van Horne as a given and leave it at that.

Whatever the case, the women quickly draw themselves into Van Horne's orbit. . . . [Readers] of Updike's previous novel, the loathsome *Rabbit Is Rich,* will be relieved to know that in *The Witches of Eastwick* the pokings and lickings to which his characters are inclined are described with somewhat less detail than he has of late been accustomed. These encounters lead, predictably, to yearnings and jealousies that do no one very much good, especially when a younger woman named Jennifer arrives on the scene and attracts—or at least seems to attract—Van Horne's singleminded attention.

So the witches turn on Jennifer. They have been imbued by their creator with the power to transform wish into action, and this they do—with consequences most grievous for their poor victim. . . . [The witches] have the power to do real evil when the rest of us can only imagine it; thus the novel is a contemplation, though a most tedious one, of what society would be like were it rid of the constraints that civilized people place upon their animal instincts—and what a jolly nice thing it is that in the real world we don't have witches.

The moral is not worth the labor of reaching it. *The Witches of Eastwick* is a tired, half-hearted novel by a writer who seems to believe that, with critics and readers adoring his every simper, he can get away with anything that comes out of his typewriter. The genuine charm and intelligence of his early books—*Of the Farm, The Poorhouse Fair,* the Maples stories [in *Too Far to Go*], even the bloated *Couples*—has degenerated into something that looks a great deal like complacency and arrogance. The prose has gotten self-conscious and exhibitionistic; the preachments against the degenerate state of contemporary society are repetitive and predictable; the obsession with the bodies of women and the curiously condescending depiction of the workings of their minds betray more than a suggestion of misogyny; the preoccupation with the minutiae of upper-middle-class life is narcissistic. That Updike's later work is considered among the literary adornments of the age is a telling comment on the age itself and on those who are setting its "standards."

> Jonathan Yardley, "The Sorcery of John Updike," in Book World—The Washington Post, *May 13, 1984,* p. 3.

MARGARET ATWOOD

The Witches of Eastwick is John Updike's first novel since the much-celebrated *Rabbit Is Rich,* and a strange and marvelous organism it proves to be. Like his third novel, *The Centaur,* it is a departure from baroque realism. This time, too, Mr. Updike transposes mythology into the minor keys of small-town America, but this time he pulls it off, possibly because, like Shakespeare and Robert Louis Stevenson before him, he finds wickedness and mischief more engrossing as subjects than goodness and wisdom.

Mr. Updike's titles are often quite literal, and *The Witches of Eastwick* is just what it says. It's indeed about witches, real ones, who can fly through the air, levitate, hex people and make love charms that work, and they live in a town called Eastwick. It's Eastwick rather than Westwick, since, as we all know, it's the east wind that blows no good. Eastwick purports to be in Rhode Island because, as the book itself points out, Rhode Island was the place of exile for Anne Hutchinson, the Puritan foremother who was kicked out of the Massachusetts Bay colony by the forefathers for female insubordination, a quality these witches have in surplus. (p. 1)

How did these middle-class, small-town, otherwise ordinary women get their witchy powers? Simple. They became husbandless. All three are divorcées and embodiments of what American small-town society tends to think about divorcées. Whether you leave your husband or are left "doesn't make any difference," which will be news to many abandoned women stuck with full child support. Divorced then, and, with the images of their former husbands shrunk and dried and stored away in their minds and kitchens and cellars, they are free to be themselves, an activity Mr. Updike regards with some mis-

givings, as he regards most catchwords and psychofads. (pp. 1, 40)

[The witches are at first] merely restless and bored; they amuse themselves with spiteful gossip, playing mischievous tricks and seducing unhappily married men, which Eastwick supplies in strength; for if the witches are bad, the wives are worse, and the men are eviscerated. "Marriage," one of the husbands thinks, "is like two people locked up with one lesson to read, over and over, until the words become madness."

But enter the Devil, the world's best remedy for women's boredom, in the form of the dark, not very handsome but definitely mysterious stranger Darryl Van Horne, who collects pop art and has an obvious name. Now mischief turns to *maleficio,* real evil occurs and people die, because Van Horne's horn becomes a bone of contention—nothing like not enough men to go around to get the witches' cauldrons bubbling. And when Van Horne is snatched into marriage by a newcomer witchlet, the eye of newt comes out in earnest.

This may sound like an unpromising framework for a serious novelist. Has Mr. Updike entered second childhood and reverted to Rosemary's babyland? I don't think so. For one thing, *The Witches of Eastwick* is too well done. Like Van Horne, Mr. Updike has always wondered what it would be like to be a woman, and his witches give him a lot of scope for this fantasy. Lexa in particular, who is the oldest, the plumpest, the kindest and the closest to Nature, is a fitting vehicle for some of his most breathtaking similes. In line of descent, he is perhaps closer than any other living American writer to the Puritan view of Nature as a lexicon written by God, but in hieroglyphs, so that unending translation is needed. Mr. Updike's prose, here more than ever, is a welter of suggestive metaphors and cross-references, which constantly point toward a meaning constantly evasive.

His version of witchcraft is closely tied to both carnality and mortality. Magic is hope in the face of inevitable decay. The houses and the furniture molder, and so do the people. The portrait of Felicia Gabriel, victim wife and degenerate afterimage of the one-time "peppy" American cheerleading sweetheart, is gruesomely convincing. Bodies are described in loving detail, down to the last tuft, wart, wrinkle and bit of food stuck in the teeth. No one is better than Mr. Updike at conveying the sadness of the sexual, the melancholy of motel affairs—"amiable human awkwardness," Lexa calls it. This is a book that redefines magic realism.

There's room too for bravura writing. The widdershins dance, portrayed as a tennis game in which the ball turns into a bat, followed by the sabbat as a hot-tub-and-pot session, is particularly fetching. Students of traditional Devil-lore will have as much fun with these transpositions as Mr. Updike had. Van Horne, for instance, is part Mephistopheles, offering Faustian pacts and lusting for souls, part alchemist-chemist, and part Miltonic Satan, hollow at the core; but he's also a shambling klutz whose favorite comic book is—what else?—Captain Marvel.

Much of *The Witches of Eastwick* is satire, some of it literary playfulness and some plain bitchery. It could be that any attempt to analyze further would be like taking an elephant gun to a puff-pastry: An Updike should not mean but be. But again, I don't think so. What a culture has to say about witchcraft, whether in jest or in earnest, has a lot to do with its views of sexuality and power, and especially with the apportioning of powers between the sexes. The witches were burned not because they were pitied but because they were feared.

Cotton Mather and Nathaniel Hawthorne aside, the great American witchcraft classic is *The Wizard of Oz,* and Mr. Updike's book reads like a rewrite. In the original, a good little girl and her familiar, accompanied by three amputated males, one sans brain, one sans heart and one sans guts, go seeing a wizard who turns out to be a charlatan. The witches in "Oz" really have superhuman powers, but the male figures do not. Mr. Updike's Land of Oz is the real America, but the men in it need a lot more than self-confidence; there's no Glinda the Good, and the Dorothy-like ingenue is a "wimp" who gets her comeuppance. It's the three witches of Eastwick who go back, in the end, to the equivalent of Kansas—marriage, flat and gray maybe, but at least known.

The Witches of Eastwick could be and probably will be interpreted as just another episode in the long-running American serial called "Blaming Mom." The Woman-as-Nature-as-magic-as-powerful-as-bad-Mom package has gone the rounds before, sometimes accompanied by the smell of burning. If prattle of witchcraft is heard in the land, can the hunt be far behind? Mr. Updike provides no blameless way of being female. Hackles will rise, the word "backlash" will be spoken; but anyone speaking it should look at the men in this book, who, while proclaiming their individual emptiness, are collectively, offstage, blowing up Vietnam. That's *male* magic. Men, say the witches, more than once, are full of rage because they can't make babies, and even male babies have at their center "that aggressive vacuum." Shazam indeed! . . .

The Witches of Eastwick is an excursion rather than a destination. Like its characters, it indulges in metamorphoses, reading at one moment like Kierkegaard, at the next like Swift's *Modest Proposal,* and at the next like Archie comics, with some John Keats thrown in. This quirkiness is part of its charm, for, despite everything, charming it is. As for the witches themselves, there's a strong suggestion that they are products of Eastwick's—read America's—own fantasy life. If so, it's as well to know about it. That's the serious reason for reading this book.

The other reasons have to do with the skill and inventiveness of the writing, the accuracy of the detail, the sheer energy of the witches and, above all, the practicality of the charms. The ones for getting suitable husbands are particularly useful. You want a rich one, for a change? First you sprinkle a tuxedo with your perfume and your precious bodily fluids and then. . . . (p. 40)

> Margaret Atwood, *"Wondering What It's Like to Be a Woman,"* in The New York Times Book Review, *May 13, 1984, pp. 1, 40.*

GREG JOHNSON

[*The Witches of Eastwick*] comes as a surprise—so clever, lighthearted and puckish a work that it seems naturally immune to criticism. Light-hearted, but not lightweight: Updike's stylistic pyrotechnics have never been more in evidence, and his sexual frankness is accompanied by his typically wry, wistful skepticism toward human couplings of all kinds. Updike has been criticized for dealing superficially with women in his fiction, merely spinning out mythologized fantasies of the male imagination, and in his new novel he seems to answer this charge, creating not one but three women who live alone, support

themselves, and raise children single-handedly; what's more, they are all artists. But he also makes them, alas, unhappy and gossipy women who are obsessively focused on a man, who are poor mothers and not very good artists. And he makes them into witches.

The best way to approach this novel is the way Updike seems to have written it—with tongue planted firmly in cheek. In method and tone it bears a family resemblance to his 1976 novel *Marry Me,* which was subtitled "A Romance," rather than to the more somber and realistic mode of the recent, much-awarded *Rabbit Is Rich* (1981). For all its playfulness, however, *The Witches of Eastwick* has its own patches of shade, presenting a world where human magic is no match for the dark and whimsical forces governing natural creatures. For, despite their supernatural powers, the three witches . . . fall victim to every malaise that plagues ordinary mortals and in particular to those which are traditionally "credited" to women: jealousy, spite, and the desire for revenge.

It's certainly true that the witches aren't "nice." . . . Even Alexandra, the most sympathetic of the three, isn't above an "irritated psychic effort" that causes an old lady's necklace to come unstrung, and the old lady herself to take a bad fall when she trips on the scattered pearls. But the women have reason to be nervous, for they have all begun vying for the attentions of a newcomer to Eastwick: the arrogant, hirsute, reputedly wealthy Daryll Van Horne, who becomes a Satanic force that sets the witches' (and the novel's) powers into motion.

Alexandra, who sculpts squat and rather unprepossessing female figures she calls "bubbies," is particularly vulnerable to all the foibles of divorced women in middle age. She is slightly overweight, she feels out of step with the times, and she is simultaneously the most needful of the intrepid Van Horne's approval and the most perceptive about her true motives. . . . [Her disappointment over Van Horne's indifference]—combined with that of her two sisters in power—precipitates the climactic events of the story. The mordant comedy of the novel's first half gives way to a darksome romance, reminiscent of Hawthorne, in its final sections. Updike's conclusion is rather pat, but meaningfully so; the novel suggests the power of blackness in the lives of all concerned, then quickly retreats back into the daylight world.

An allegory, a fable, a romance, a meditation on the nature of evil—*The Witches of Eastwick* is all these, while remaining a high-spirited sexual comedy and a caricaturist's view of women's liberation. There are some marvelous set-pieces: Alexandra, wanting the beach to herself, conjures up a magnificent thunderstorm that has scores of teenagers running for cover (and for the storm, Updike conjures up five pages of his most glittering descriptive prose). . . . The three witches, who get together once a week for a friendly coven, have rip-roaring and uninhibited conversations that only a male novelist both perceptive and admiring of women could manage. (pp. 342-43)

[Set] in the 1960s, [*The Witches of Eastwick*] foretells the darker side of the sexual and feminist revolutions to follow, while retaining its broadly human sympathies. In his rich allusiveness and his more somber passages Updike has provided ample fodder for the critical acolytes who await each new book by one of our finest novelists, and our premier prose stylist; but he has also provided, for everyone else, one of his most elegant and provocative entertainments. (p. 344)

Greg Johnson, "Weird Sisters," in Southwest Review, Vol. 69, No. 3, Summer, 1984, pp. 342-44.

ALICE BLOOM

Do not be misled by the high-toned maroon dust jacket [of *The Witches of Eastwick*], with its tasteful, elevating Dürer etching: this novel is intended to be a cute, playful romp. In actuality, however, it is a book of such hysterical meanness it seems that only the victim of a prolonged evil spell could have endured the writing of it. From coy and turgid beginning to flat end, it is malicious cliché tarted up as sniggering, smart humor. Was it written with an eye on a female audience? Because real men don't smirk? Real women don't either. Lest someone bristle up like a Halloween cartoon suspecting only anti-feminist fun and vileness here, it might be some relief to know that everyone in the novel of whatever sex is equally empty, vulgar, uninteresting, forlorn, and nasty.

Witches, small town uproar, orgies in hot tubs, a fat cat of a Devil, tricks and endless treats, what could be dull about all this? I'm tempted, imitating the tongue-in-cheekness of the reigning humor of the book, to reply: God only knows; but I won't. It's dull because it's unrelentingly vicious. It's dull because only one voice, that of the narrator, has anything even remotely interesting to say. That voice, vaguely identified twice as "one of us in Eastwick," is the only presence that thinks, feels, notices, knows something about near anything, and gets to strut its verbal stuff. On top of that, this voice continually drags attention—for a long lyrical peroration on beach pebbles, or clouds, or trees in autumn, or Bach's cello intricacies, or the history of Rhode Island—*away* from the characters, so that you have a sense of the character trying to escape into his own being but held by the neck and drowned like a tree-toad in a boiling brew, and you realize, in case you'd forgotten, that the real MoJo in novels is words, after all, and the narrative voice is given the best and by far the most of those.

Third it's dull because, honest, nothing happens but the usual tedium, pissy small talk, hypocrisy, gossip, sleeping around, heaps of self-justification, and the shallow hell on earth that has come, by now, to constitute Updike's New England village life. (p. 624)

[What Updike's witches] do is turn ex-husbands into madras plaid placemats and tennis balls into raw eggs; kill squirrels and puppies and, when they really get into it, friends, lovers and neighbors and with a glance and some obviously researched hocus-pocus. Aside from casting spells, blabbing on the phone, and enjoying hot-tub orgies at the Devil's mansion, mainly what the witches do is sleep around with stray husbands they feel sorry for. It is mischievously suggested throughout that the witches are instruments of a larger force, nature maybe, that works through them to keep some necessary duality alive. . . .

What's further hinted at is that all the victims of the coven roundly deserved being ground to dust or tripped on the ice or riddled with cancer: that woman was just too uppity, this husband a wimp and a jackass, that lover a sad, sick drunk with whiskey breath, a partial plate, and a big-mouthed wife who deserved to belch thumbtacks, dirty straw, parrot feathers, and finally to be bludgeoned with a poker. Besides this, life is dull, dull, dull in Eastwick where the citizens plod through their "civic and Christian duties." As if that weren't enough, there's the bad times: widespread moral disintegration and all that, crappy values, "window-trashing LSD-imbibing youth," . . .

and other such sour, heartless, facile observations made in the interest of establishing the feckless mood of the times, in this case with about as honest and useful results as you'd get taking someone's pulse by checking the labels in their clothes. Collectibles as Zeitgeist.

The dialogue is as meagre and utilitarian as the stuff we overhear at the checkout counter: is that a new skirt? *God,* I'm tired of canning tomatoes. (p. 625)

Most of it on the phone, too. The witches can cause storm, withering, chaos, murder, no matter—there's no looking into that on their parts, they don't know or care why they can do it, just a bemused acceptance and an ooooh, aren't we devils humor. No wondering, nothing learned, no psychology of magic, and I *think* there's supposed to be an extended joke in this along the lines of see, they're just your average, etc., just like you basically, same little nagging doubts and worries. Put forth as funny because so typical, these women are dull, ignorant, horny, sloppy, petty, bored single parents trying to make both ends wearily meet who just happen to be able to do, as a kind of accidental side-line, dark, dirty, and ultimately dismal deeds. (p. 626)

Alice Bloom, in a review of "The Witches of East-wick," in The Hudson Review, *Vol. XXXVII, No. 4, Winter, 1984-85, pp. 621-30.*

GAVIN EWART

Good novelists who also write good poetry are very rare. . . . Among the Victorians, we remember Emily Brontë, Thackeray and Meredith. Dickens interpolated "The Ivy Green" into *The Pickwick Papers,* along with Mrs. Leo Hunter's famous "Ode to an Expiring Frog" and the anonymous "Lines to a Brass Pot." In fact, Victorian novelists had a tendency toward parody and light verse—very noticeable in Thackeray ("Little Billee" and "Sorrows of Werther").

It is to this tradition that John Updike belongs, though what he writes is light verse rather than directly humorous verse like Thackeray's. In *Facing Nature* there is actually a section headed "Light Verse," containing 112 short poems, but even the serious section has its share of lightness, for example, unrhymed sonnets with lines like "Our bottoms betray us and beg for the light." This euphemism for the sexual and excretory organs has been used by no other serious poet except Auden, and Mr. Updike and Auden have a lot in common. Urbane, controlled, contemplative and original, Mr. Updike writes about dying and madness and loss of love with coolness and great technical aplomb. The sex, with the above exception, is straight and avoids the English nannyish locutions of the late Auden. The words are often unusual ("like a purse being cinched") and Latinate ("The palms are isolate"), the lines compact with meaning ("Burdensome summer has come").

Mr. Updike is a mandarin writer, not much given to colloquialism, full of culture (the painters Goya, Rouault, Turner, Francis Bacon and Hopper all appear), with a liking for travel (mainly Spain) and with a Wordsworthian side, consisting of a very modified form of the "egotistical sublime." Lines like "If people don't entertain you, / Nature will" are one aspect of this, and keen observation is another. . . . The Auden-style generalization is also there—sleep is "the flight the chemical mind / must take or be crazed." This is from **"Sleeping With You,"** a beautiful poem in the domestic category.

Many of the poems in the main body of the book could be labeled light verse. **"Head of a Girl, at the Met"** is traditional light verse, for example, but the theme is the shortness of human life. **"Crab Crack,"** with its everyday subject matter—catching and eating crabs—is light in its touch but [evokes serious reflections]. . . .

Mr. Updike has the ability to make the ordinary seem strange, as all "metaphysical" poets have always done: "and the barber himself asleep in two chairs, / snoring with the tranquillity of a mustached machine." He can also make good use of fairly ordinary material. . . . There are seven very original **"Odes to Natural Processes"**—rot, evaporation, growth, fragmentation, entropy, crystallization and healing. These in particular seem late Audenesque. . . . [One poem, **"Ode to Rot,"**] also has a touch of Erasmus Darwin, who expounded a certain botanical system in a long poem.

The poems actually billed as "light" are a little disappointing. They seem too minimal in subject and not interesting enough in shape or form—or wit, the most important factor.

Gavin Ewart, *"Making It Strange,"* in The New York Times Book Review, *April 28, 1985, p. 18.*

JOEL CONARROE

[As] if to prove just how many strings are in his bow, [Updike] has produced one of the year's more appealing books of poetry [*Facing Nature*]. Since this is his fifth such collection his gift hardly comes as a surprise, but the consistently high quality of these verses provides cause for celebration.

It has been said that a limousine is not an acquired taste—one gets used to it right away. Updike's poetry is like that. *Facing Nature,* in fact, will likely engage anyone who picks it up, both those who usually avoid poetry as well as the happy few who are addicted. Why? It is accessible, witty, wise, and, like a limousine, stylish and comfortable. Moreover, it has the rare capacity to evoke laughter one moment and tears the next. (I am not sentimental, but **"Another Dog's Death"** does me in.)

As in his novels, Updike demonstrates a rage for order, precision and plenitude. Apparently existing in smiling harmony with all that is, he persuades us that since life spins miracles we should die rejoicing. Moved by patterns and cycles, he exhibits a childlike wonder at nature's mysterious beauty—"And shadows on water!" he exclaims, astonished, echoing the delight of Hopkins's "Look, look at the stars!" He also echoes Stevens' belief that death is the mother of beauty, that our transience lends intensity to our apprehension of the physical universe. . . .

The most winning segment of this book, interestingly enough, is not the selection of light verse, a genre in which Updike has few peers, but a sequence called **"Seven Odes to Natural Processes."** These lyrics document not only his obsession with the mysteries of physical phenomena but also his dependence on the revelations produced by knowledge. He is a scrupulous scholar of natural change.

[That Updike is] reckless, productive and cheerful (like nature itself) helps account for the delights of this companionable book. (p. 8)

Joel Conarroe, *"Updike, Clampitt and Merrill: Poets in Their Prime,"* in Book World—The Washington Post, *July 28, 1985, pp. 1, 8.*

CHRISTOPHER REID

John Updike is such a lavishly gifted novelist, and so lavish in the employment of his gifts, that his occasional ventures into the field of poetry have in the past tended to be rather disappointing. The miraculous exuberance of his prose, seemingly so inexhaustible in its gathering of perceptions and engendering of conceits, might have led one to hope that his verse would display something of the same unstoppable vitality: yet his earlier volumes showed him to be, at best, a competent dabbler in the art. . . . In this light, *Facing nature* comes as an encouraging surprise. It is bulkier than any of Updike's previous collections and the poems attempt more, and achieve more, than anything he has hitherto tried in this line.

Two kinds of poem stand out above the rest: the first a loosely assembled set relating the observation of nature and landscape to autobiographical matters; and the second a group of **"Seven Odes to Seven Natural Processes"**. These odes, characteristically learned and witty, address topics—rot, evaporation, entropy and so on—that other contemporary poets may be thought to have neglected, perhaps because of the modern inhibition that prevents them from seeming to address any topic too blatantly. It must be confessed that some of my own doubts about the success of these poems arise precisely from such qualms. It is certainly astute of Updike to have hit upon the ode as the form most suited to his habitual headlong manner, and these specimens contain more than their share of startling exposition and metaphorical panache. At the same time, I cannot help wondering if they are not organised a little too much like essays, each part of the argument presented in its logical order so as to add up, not so much to a poem, as to a point.

An air of Augustan sententiousness, amounting in some passages to a cheery complacency about the workings of nature that Dr Pangloss himself would have applauded, increases one's dissatisfaction. As an example of what is both pleasing and regrettable in these poems, the first few lines of the **"Ode to Healing"** will serve. 'A scab,' Updike writes,

> is a beautiful thing—a coin
> the body has minted with an invisible motto:
> In God We Trust.

The conceit is delightful, its glib moral application rather less so. Yet Updike appears to believe that the instances mustered in his poem will ultimately support such a contention, and he concludes with the sermon-like flourish,

> Faith is health's requisite:
> we have this fact in lieu
> of better proof of *le bon Dieu,*

which is not redeemed from patness even by the suspicion that the final terrible rhyme is meant as a comical let-out.

The poems that deal with the writer's personal history in terms of what he has observed about his native landscape—**"Accumulation," "Plow Cemetery"** and **"Planting trees"** being among the finest—are what one comes to value most in *Facing nature*. Here the view generously accommodates ample tracts of space, time and emotional development. . . . Mythic gestures are accomplished with seemingly casual grace, and the drama that unfolds in each separate poem, that of the poet's gradual rapprochement with his own past and heritage, engages one quietly but with utter conviction. Updike's handling of metre is never more rigid than in the easygoing pentameters of **"Plow Cemetery"**, but it does not need to be, and one is seldom jarred by a false quantity or misjudged line-break. (p. 20)

Christopher Reid, "Here Comes Amy," in London Review of Books, *Vol. 8, No. 7, April 17, 1986, pp. 20-2.*

JOHN CALVIN BATCHELOR

John Updike's wonderfully tricky and nakedly sharp-minded 12th novel, *Roger's Version*, throws down that most threatening of Christian challenges: Can you love the loathsome? And there are sleights-of-hand here that make this twice-told New England tale of adultery even more taunting. The reader must determine the needful culprit among a pirate's crew of characters. For it is not the narrator Roger's 19-year-old niece Verna one must love despite her vulgarity, her unwed motherhood, her sadism with her mulatto infant Paula. And it is not Roger's rebellious 38-year-old wife Esther one must love regardless of her porn-queen seduction of a young computer student. Nor is it even the seduced computer wizard Dale one must love, forbearing his wacky vanity to seek God inside a terminal monitor, scrambling cosmological constants like someone scheming to predict this week's lottery pay-off.

No, the impossible assignment here is that the reader must learn to love and even to forgive Roger Lambert himself, 52-year-old divinity school professor and as hard-hearted and fork-tongued a hypocrite as was ever found in an Updike morality tale. And there is a most worrisome catch. Roger is not only the villain—he admits it—he is not only his wife's pimp and his niece's corrupter and the fool student's tormentor, he also just might be the horned one. Updike was only kidding around with demonology in *The Witches of Eastwick.* Faithless, shameless Roger sounds like the Devil himself.

The story opens in the fall of 1984 at an unnamed city indistinguishable from Cambridge/Boston. Roger Lambert, specialist in Christian heretics, is called upon by the grad student Dale, who is as goofily pious as he is eager.... What Dale wants is Roger's help with his pet mystical project to deduce God out of a number-crunching machine. (p. 1)

[The situation leads to] an overwhelming dialogue about physics, chemistry, biology and astronomy;... [there are] several fact-crammed expositions in the book, any of which may weary the impatient reader's mind and body.

Updike has too much craft to surrender his genius to natural philosophy, however, and it is one of the pleasures of the novel to watch the author both outmaneuver avalanches of theories by other folk..., and also outfox chatty, raunchy Roger.

As the hanky-panky unfolds, Roger tries to take control of the story: he projects himself into the minds of the lovers Esther and Dale; he appeals to the reader as his confessor; he toys with sex, math, theology, racism, and the supposed male territory of sadism.... Roger does everything but listen to himself, because if he did he might realize that he was incarcerated inside a slippery reworking of Hawthorne's *The Scarlet Letter.*

[In Hawthorne's novel], Roger Chillingworth abandoned his young wife Hester (rhymes with Esther) Prynne to the New World. Love-starved Hester melted into the arms of the God-fearing if faint-hearted Rev. Arthur Dimmesdale. Boston's good folk condemned Hester to that famous embroidery while Chillingworth sought revenge with what Hawthorne called "the black arts." After soulful travail, Hester outlasted Puritanism, Dimmesdale escaped cowardice, Chillingworth sputtered out, and the beatific child Pearl ascended to miraculous happiness.

These are modern times though, and Updike turns his version upside down and re-imagines the drama before what would be the birth of Pearl.... Updike's Roger Lambert is a perfectly 20th-century beast—boastfully wicked in all directions. He abandoned his first wife because she was infertile and quit the pulpit not out of honest doubt but because it was inconvenient once he had acquired the hot-blooded Esther in a scandalous episode. He took up teaching God-talk not because he believes in a Savior, but because he enjoys mocking seminarians with the arcane heresies of such as Pelagius and Tertullian and whipping his colleagues with Barthian cruelties. (pp. 1-2)

Roger is so rotten that just a few words of dialogue from one of his victims airs out the book like an open window. The reader must fight the urge to garrote Roger or just to stuff his cloven feet in his mouth. The odd, tiny successes of Verna, Esther, and Dale become triumphs when they are scored against Roger. And there is genuine suspense in the struggle when Verna, manipulated by Roger into an abortion she does not want, falls toward child abuse. One reads faster for fear that Updike will permit Roger to engineer a catastrophe like the baby drowning in *Rabbit, Run*—a scene so unforgettably scary that it might be the Big Bang of Updike's global career.

Roger is finally beaten back by the nifty goodness in lustful humanity; yet there is no comfort. Updike has written admiringly of Hawthorne elsewhere as a skeptical believer in Christian spirituality, as a disabused Puritan who nonetheless held "that the soul can be distorted, stained, lost" by wrong conduct. One argues then that, though Updike clearly enjoyed fashioning this positivistic tribute to Hawthorne, Roger's gloomy fate is not meant as entertainment to be put aside like cold coffee.... *Roger's Version* does not choose to be affirming or touching.... The warning is that the Devil in Roger is potent, classy and most persuasive, and that this should hurt to admit; but it does not, so woe is us. (p. 2)

John Calvin Batchelor, "The Hacker and the Heretic," in Book World—The Washington Post, August 31, 1986, pp. 1-2.

DAVID LODGE

There are at least five distinct discursive strands interwoven in the texture of John Updike's *Roger's Version.* Four of them will be familiar to readers of his previous novels, but the fifth is, I believe, a new development, or acquisition, and a remarkably interesting one.

To start with the familiar: there is the discourse of theology. The central character and narrator, pipe-smoking, 52-year-old Roger Lambert is a professor of divinity, a former Methodist minister who adopted an academic career after the scandalous breakup of his first marriage and his union with Esther, 14 years his junior.... He is a somewhat dilettantish disciple of Karl Barth, the austere Swiss theologian who fiercely insisted on the utter separateness of the divine and the human, and the utter dependence of the latter on the former. Roger admits to insulating this "hot Barthian nugget" in "layers of worldly cynicism and situation ethics." Mr. Updike is well able to evoke the ethos of an academic theology department, and to have sly fun with its professional rivalries, pretensions and jargon (this one has specialists in "Ethics and Moral Logistics" and "holocaustics"). He has manifested an interest in religion and theology in previous books. If there was ever such a species as the Protestant novelist, comparable to that much discussed animal, the Catholic novelist, Mr. Updike may be its last surviving example.

There is the discourse of eroticism, or pornography—the distinction is not always easy to draw, and Mr. Updike has taken a leading part in the tendency of contemporary art to blur it, incorporating previously taboo matter and diction into serious fiction.... [Roger's descriptions of sex] certainly have the sharp focus, the closeup detail, the glossy sheen and vivid color of pornographic photography—with the added perversity, or poignancy, that they are mostly imagined rather than reported, mental projections of his conviction that he is being cuckolded by a young graduate student, Dale Kohler.

There is the discourse of domesticity—the faithful rendering of small quotidian activities such as cooking a meal, fixing a drink.... From his earliest *New Yorker* stories, Mr. Updike has shown himself to be a master of domestic realism, enhancing our awareness of the way we live. (pp. 1, 15)

Closely related to this discourse of domestic behavior is a discourse of physical description—of streets, houses, furniture, trees, clouds and the whole mesh of culture and nature that makes a suburb or a city: "the irrepressible combinations of the real," in Roger's words. Again, Mr. Updike has always been famous for his ability to defamiliarize the commonplace with a nifty trope, sometimes jeopardizing the authenticity of his characters by attributing to them metaphors and similes that a professional poet might envy. Roger, however, is cultivated and clever enough to carry [these] off....

There are several extended—perhaps overextended—topographical passages in the novel that trace Roger's movement from the relatively affluent and commodious residential streets around the university to a run-down housing project where Verna, the daughter of his half sister, lives precariously on welfare with her baby, Paula, whose black father has absconded. Made aware of Verna's plight through Dale, and motivated by family loyalty, social guilt and—increasingly—lust for the sexy Verna, Roger makes several trips to the housing project, and his negotiation of its decaying environs reflects his uneasy consciousness of social and economic divisions in American society....

The fifth, and unfamiliar, discourse in *Roger's Version* is that of science—mathematics, physics, biology and, above all, computing. Dale Kohler is a graduate in computer studies and a fundamentalist Christian. At the beginning of the story he visits Roger not just to tell him about Verna but to ask his assistance in obtaining a grant from the theology department. He is convinced that the more science discovers about the mathematical equations underlying the universe, the more unavoidable becomes the conclusion that they are not the result of chance. "God is showing through," he assures Roger, though the scientific establishment is desperately trying to conceal the fact....

[Dale's] ambition is to prove this assertion by calculations and model manipulations on the university's giant computer. The project is as repugnant to Roger as its tall, gawky, virile proponent. It offends his Barthian theological principles, but it also threatens his cynicism and "situation ethics." "Your God sounds like a nice safe unfindable God," Dale shrewdly observes. Much is at stake.

The pair debate the issue in a series of set pieces that cover cosmology, evolution and the relation of body to mind. These are fascinating and important issues—topical too, given the

rising tide of Christian fundamentalism in America today—and it is heartening to see a literary novelist taking them on board. A note on the copyright page gives some indication of the research that all this entailed, and one can only salute Mr. Updike's energy, boldness and sheer brainpower in undertaking it. He is not content to give us a mere impressionistic whiff of physics, math and biology. He makes Dale Kohler speak with the passion and particularity of the true enthusiast....

[The] scientifically illiterate reader (like myself) may find that much of [this discourse] goes over his head, at least on first reading. The book seems initially to be shaping up as a rather static novel of ideas, but as it proceeds the different discourses within it begin to interact excitingly. There is, for instance, a remarkable chapter in which Roger's wrestling with Tertullian's arguments for the resurrection of the body elides into a startlingly explicit account of Esther and Dale making love, which in turn gives way to a debate between the two men about the body-mind problem. Each strand illuminates the others.

Admittedly the plot (never Mr. Updike's strong point) ticks on rather slowly. The cracks in the Lambert marriage begin to show. Verna gets carelessly pregnant again, and Roger shoulders both the financial and the moral responsibility of arranging an abortion....

Since all the discourses in the novel are uttered or mediated by Roger, as narrator, the question of his reliability becomes crucial. The title of the novel suggests that there might be other, very different versions of the story, and a number of clues seem planted in the text warning us not to trust him. Early on he begins to put himself in Dale's place, and see the world through his eyes with what he himself calls "an odd and sinister empathy." His detailed narratives of Esther's infidelity appear to be based on pure suspicion, and could well be the voyeuristic fantasies, at once compensatory and self-punishing, of middle-aged impotence. As the novel moves toward its narrative climax ..., [it] seems poised for a reversal that will reveal Roger's suspicions as delusory. But at the very end they are casually confirmed by Verna....

The absence of an expected reversal is itself a reversal. This twist is effective in narrative terms, but does not entirely solve the problem of authority in the novel. Where did all the detail of Roger's erotic imaginings come from? How does he know what Dale's room looks like, down to the Korean crucifix, of ambiguous substance, that hangs above the bed? How is Roger, in a tour de force chapter, able to give a minutely circumstantial account of the Cube, the building that houses the university's computer services, where Dale works all night in a supreme effort to conjure the hand or face of God on his computer terminal, when he (Roger) states at the outset of his narrative that, "I have never entered it, nor do I hope to"? First-person narrators are allowed, by poetic license, to borrow some of the author's eloquence, but not his omniscience.

One is tempted to seek a clue in Roger's comment on the inconsistencies and circularities of early Christian documents: "First-century people just didn't have the same sense of factuality that we do, or of writing either. Writing was sympathetic magic ... writing something down was to an extent making it so."

So, of course, is writing fiction. If Mr. Updike were a novelist given to metafictional tricks, we might suspect him of holding up a mirror to the reader's credulity, by making his character claim the same freedom to invent that we grant the novelist. But everything we know about Mr. Updike suggests that he shares the modern sense of factuality and believes that fiction should create the illusion of it. Otherwise, why take all that trouble to get the scientific discourse right?

There is, then, an unresolved enigma or contradiction at the heart of *Roger's Version,* blurring the exact nature and degree of the narrator's "bad faith." For all its richness and virtuosity, the novel makes its effect by a somewhat arbitrary suppression of the discourse of objective report. Nevertheless, one finishes it with gratitude—for it is challenging and educative—and with renewed respect for one of the most intelligent and resourceful of contemporary novelists. (p. 15)

> *David Lodge, "Chasing After God and Sex," in* The New York Times Book Review, *August 31, 1986, pp, 1, 15.*

RHODA KOENIG

Faith and science, God and sex are the matter of *Roger's Version,* a sour, rather constricted novel about the striving and swiving of two mismatched couples. While Roger engages in a protracted game of teasing and groping with his sluttish niece, his wife is being rogered by the god-struck hacker [Dale]. Esther Lambert, at 38, is bored with her marriage, and her friskiness comes out in sardonic, stagy gestures. "*Voilà.*" she says to Roger, bowing, as she produces her dinner. "*Le* meat-*loof*." After Dale and Verna come to the Lamberts for Thanksgiving, Esther appropriates Dale for a last, desperate plunge before the horrible dark of 40 descends. They copulate anally, orally, normally, amid a welter of anatomic and spiritual detail. . . .

Dale is convinced that, if you feed enough physical, mathematical, and biological data into the computer, God will manifest Himself. . . .

[Roger] is repelled by Dale's search for certainty, his desire to make God part of the vulgar, comprehensible, banal human world so that there would be no need for any leap of faith. . . . Dale finally loses his faith at a cocktail party, when another professor hits him with such damning arguments as "Inside the Planck length and the Planck duration you have this space-time foam where the quantum fluctuations from matter to non-matter really have very little meaning, mathematically speaking." There is much more, some of it even less compelling.

The complex, clotted computer and science talk sadly counterpoints the simplistic nature of the characters. Esther is merely a figure representing Marital Discontent, and Roger a windbag. Though Roger disdains the certainty of God, he is aware of the inexorability of death, and so he, like his wife, holds it off for a while with a young lover—the teenage Verna. But Dale and Verna—parsimoniously—are not given any advantage but youth. He is a gauche, earnest young sprout, she a foulmouthed lazy brat who knocks her baby around. The young people service the bodily needs and anxieties of the middle-aged, then vanish like a daydream when the phone rings.

Though this chilly novel does not offer the satisfactions of plot or character or philosophy, there is still Updike's brilliance of description. Like a busy little dog, Updike sniffs at everything (including dog turds), evoking the sights and smells of a forlorn housing project, an antiseptic glamour restaurant, a prosperous New England autumn. There is a playful running metaphor about a fish (and we know what that stands for), one that always proves elusive. . . . As the men talk, "our eyes, our souls, seemed to be sliding back and forth like ghostly eels." As always, with John Updike, God is in the details.

> *Rhoda Koenig, "Soul on Ice," in* New York Magazine, *Vol. 19, No. 35, September 8, 1986, p. 76.*

MARTIN AMIS

[In *Roger's Version*], Dale Kohler [is] a spotty, pallid, wised-up eternal student, who wants a grant that will enable him to prove the existence of God by computer. . . . Roger is repelled and intrigued by Dale—and by almost everyone and everything else (this is a novel of weighty dualities). In Dale, perhaps, he sees a version of his younger self, though one hopelessly degraded by modern 'head-culture,' by the era of big brains and microscopic sensibilities.

At any rate Roger adopts Dale and helps him get the grant for his doomed and blasphemous project. . . . Meanwhile, via feats of empathy which teeter on psychosis or fictional innovation (what one might call the Wandering or the Floating Narrator), Roger starts to 'live through' Dale, to see through his eyes, to yearn through his loins. This is a particularly absorbing hobby; for Roger, because Dale is now dividing his time between his quest for the evident God and a rather more successful quest for Esther, Roger's neglected little wife.

All according to Roger, of course. This is merely Roger's version, the gospel truth according to Roger. It is never quite clear, for instance, whether Dale is really having an affair with Esther, or whether Rog is indulging in marathon erotic fantasy as he pictures their epic couplings and unglueings, their squattings and squirtings. Here too we encounter one of Updike's few faults or excesses, his undifferentiated love of detail. Faced with a character's genitals, we don't get the phrase or sentence we think we could make do with: we get a paragraph of peeled-eyeball close-up. On the other hand, maybe the obsessiveness can be granted structural status for *Roger's Version:* it is Roger's obsession, and provides an overlong but necessary glimpse of his duplicitous, sublimating, sleepwalking soul.

Even by the standards of late-middle Updike, Roger is a grossly paradoxical figure, exalted and demonic, heartless and sentimental, magnanimous and mean. . . . He is caught between heaven and hell—or between heaven and earth, which will do these days. Equally keen on pornography and theology, he is alike addicted to the 'rat scrabble' of Dale's God-seeking computer and to the helpless *nostalgie* that leads him back to the smells and secretions of Verna's two-room walk-up. She calls him 'evil'—and he is flattered. He revels in his own heresy. . . .

This is a tremendously expert novel. Updike, by now, is the 'complete' player, an all-court wrong-footing wizard who has lost none of his speed. As with Roger, the book's cargo of disgust (disgust for the corporeal, disgust for the contemporary) is perfectly offset by the radiance of the humour, the perceptions, the epiphanies. Dale Kohler seeks the designer universe. I direct him to the fiction of John Updike. It is a very dinky place. Too dinky, perhaps. I sense genius, but not the heavy impact of greatness, not yet.

> *Martin Amis, "Designer Universe," in* The Observer, *October 12, 1986, p. 29.*

Vernon (Phillips) Watkins

1906-1967

Welsh poet, translator, editor, and nonfiction writer.

Watkins has been linked with the "New Apocalypse" poets, a neo-Romantic movement of the 1940s that also included Dylan Thomas and George Barker among its proponents. These poets explored metaphysical themes through the use of descriptive and symbolic natural imagery, often verging on surrealism, and they rejected the expression of social and political concerns in their verse. While many of Watkins's poems display the influence of the later visionary writings of W. B. Yeats, critics also note similarities between the work of Watkins and Henry Vaughan, a seventeenth-century Welsh metaphysical poet. Like Vaughan, Watkins vividly evokes the Welsh landscape, and his verse is infused with allusions to both Christianity and Welsh myth. Watkins's strict avoidance of temporal references reflects his attempt to liberate art from time and to express the concept of eternity.

The title poem of Watkins's first volume, *Ballad of the Mari Lwyd and Other Poems* (1941), is one of his best-known and most critically appreciated pieces. In this poem, Watkins depicts the ancient Welsh New Year's Eve custom—in which the bearers of the *Mari Lwyd,* a decorated horse's skull, challenge the occupants of a house to a rhyming contest in the hope of gaining entry—as a symbolic confrontation between the living and the dead. *The Lamp and the Veil* (1945) consists of three extended pieces. One of these, "Yeats in Dublin," recounts Watkins's visit to Yeats's home in Ireland and documents his conversations with the poet.

The Lady with the Unicorn (1948) firmly established Watkins's reputation as a gifted lyric poet and introduced the first poem of his ongoing "Music of Colours" sequence. The poems of this visionary series contrast the mutability of nature with the idea of eternal perfection and affirm Watkins's Christian faith. *The Death Bell: Poems and Ballads* (1954) and *Cypress and Acacia* (1959) contain portions of a poetic sequence that focuses on Taliesin, a sixth-century Welsh poet. According to a legend of the *Mabinogion,* an ancient text, Taliesin boasted that time was powerless over him. Watkins uses this claim to underscore his belief in eternity and the mystical capabilities of poets. *Affinities* (1962) and *Fidelities* (1968) contain poems about poets whom Watkins admired for their artistic vision, including William Wordsworth, John Keats, Marianne Moore, and Dylan Thomas. *Affinities* prompted Stephan Stepanchev to comment: "[Watkins] has many admirable qualities: a supple rhetoric, an opulent imagery of natural scenes—of seascapes, fields at harvest time, waterfalls, valleys—and a vision that successfully unifies the contraries of the world."

Several anthologies representing Watkins's career have been published. *Selected Poems* (1948), *Selected Poems, 1930-1960* (1967), *I That Was Born in Wales* (1976), and *Unity of the Stream* (1978) reprint many of his previously published pieces, while *Uncollected Poems* (1969) and *Ballad of the Outer Dark and Other Poems* (1979) consist mainly of posthumously collected and unrevised poems. The title poem of *Ballad of the Outer Dark* is a continuation of the themes and motifs begun in "Ballad of the Mari Lwyd." *Selected Verse Translations*

© Rollie McKenna

(1977) contains Watkins's renderings of such poets as Heinrich Heine, Rainer Maria Rilke, and Friedrich Hölderlin.

Although Watkins is not generally regarded as a major figure of twentieth-century poetry, critical appraisal of his work has been widely favorable. Louis L. Martz proclaimed Watkins "one of the finest religious poets of our century," and Dylan Thomas thought Watkins "the most profound and greatly accomplished Welshman writing poems in English."

(See also *Contemporary Authors,* Vols. 9-10, Vols. 25-28, rev. ed. [obituary]; *Contemporary Authors Permanent Series,* Vol. 1; and *Dictionary of Literary Biography,* Vol. 20.)

THE TIMES LITERARY SUPPLEMENT

The long ballad which gives its title to Mr. Watkins's [*Ballad of the Mari Lwyd*] is based on an ancient custom still prevalent in many parts of Wales according to which a band of singers carry a grey horse's head modelled in wood and hung with ribbons from house to house on the last night of the year and challenge those within to a rhyming contest. When the inmates failed to supply a rhyme the challengers had the right of entry and were entertained with food and drink. Like most ancient customs this one was full of hidden meaning. What Mr. Watkins finds in it is best stated in his own words. "I have attempted," he writes, "to bring together those who are separated. The last breath of the year is their threshold, the moment of supreme forgiveness, confusion and understanding, the profane and sacred moment impossible to realize while the clock-hands divide the Living from the Dead." Such a mystery in which the bounds are broken down that keep death and life, night and day, the outcast and the redeemed, apart, is hard to express powerfully without slipping into melodrama. . . .

[*Ballad of the Mari Lwyd* shows] the originality of Mr. Watkins's imagination, and his rhythm is as potent as his imagery. He translates the actual, whether it be the stark life of a Welsh collier or a tree in a **"Thames forest,"** into an essentially poetic reality. And he is equally passionate when he sings the **"griefs of the sea"** or of the shooting of Werfel in Paris or in **"A Lover's Woods,"** of the supreme ecstasy of love. But his verse, too, has at times the defects of passion, when it is impatient of the daylight world of sensibility and obscures the actual in heavy and complicated folds of myth.

> *"Beyond Time's Realm: The Changing Myths of History," in* The Times Literary Supplement, *No. 2073, October 25, 1941, p. 534.*

RICHARD EBERHART

The poetry of Vernon Watkins [in *Selected Poems*] is opposed to almost all of the major poetry of the last forty years. To read it is almost to think you are living in the early part of the nineteenth century. This verse is divorced from what is considered modernism and is written, with its differences, in a Shelleyean tradition. Watkins can sustain a long, philosophical lyric, using ancient, simple and universal terms for twenty-four pages, which happens in the last pages of the book. Of moderns, he is not opposed to the lyricism of late-early and early-middle Yeats.

The poems are selected from Watkins' two books published in England, *Ballad of the Mari Lwyd* and *The Lamp and the Veil*. If there is such a thing as Welsh imagination, he has it.

The book begins somewhat unpromisingly, but rises to powerful instances of verbal and conceptual splendor. . . .

The splendor and magnificent imagery of Watkins are showered in the last two long poems, **"Sea-Music for my Sister Travelling"** and **"The Broken Sea."** The counters are old, worn, but the effect is new, sensitive.

> *Richard Eberhart, in a review of "Selected Poems," in* The New York Times Book Review, *August 8, 1948, p. 12.*

GERARD PREVIN MEYER

Vernon Watkins is a Welshman, of the folk that produced the metaphysicals: Donne, Herbert, Vaughan and Traherne, Wilfred Owen and Dylan Thomas, Henry Treece and Alun Lewis, leaders of the New Apocalypse; to say nothing of the Mabinogion, the Eisteddfod, and the poetic prose of Caradoc Evans.

In *Selected Poems* the Welsh poet presents the intangible and spiritual (his belief in which stems from absorption in Bible reading as well as from the dark Celtic heritage) through the medium of the concrete. . . .

Watkins will repay reading aloud, for he has the Welsh music in his lines; he is a master of repetition, of phrase as well as sound, particularly. He calls for rereading because his imagery tends to follow a psychological rather than a logical pattern (though not always). In this connection he is more symbolist, even surrealist (under control, the added note of the Apocalyptics), than metaphysical, although suggestions of Donne are not absent.

He commands terror ("You taught us first how loudly a pin falls"), word-magic ("Gaping, we groped with unawakened hands"), and is a myth-maker of no mean stature. Old myths, too, are recalled to life, in a manner that not so long ago was deemed obsolete by new poets. In such vein is the longest poem in this book, **"The Ballad of the Mari Lwyd,"** which has a fine eeriness coming out of Welsh legendry.

> *Gerard Previn Meyer, "Individualists, Yankee and Welsh," in* The Saturday Review of Literature, *Vol. XXXI, No. 41, October 9, 1948, p. 32.*

ROLFE HUMPHRIES

Vernon Watkins is a young Welsh poet, and that is part of the trouble with his *Selected Poems*. There is apt to be in the young Celt, especially when he is a little over-conscious of himself as such (the real Ur-Welsh, I believe it has been claimed, were not Celtic at all, but never mind), more than a trace of an *überspannt* quality that is hardly distinguishable from the Teutonic. The Welsh, however, usually, have more interested ears; and that this is so Mr. Watkins gives evidence in his use of the spondee in his poem **"Thames Forest,"** written in sapphics, or in the slant rhymes of **"Yeats's Tower."** In general, the shorter lyrics in this book are the more interesting; Mr. Watkins takes after William Butler Yeats a good deal, and no better practice could be recommended, but he has not yet quite learned how to bring off effects of original terseness. The trouble with the long poems is that they contain too many words: **"The Ballad of the Mari Lwyd,"** for instance, creates an atmosphere successfully; there is much to be said, in this kind of poem, for the use of a refrain, but when the lines "Midnight. Midnight. Midnight. Midnight. / Hark at the hands of the clock" are used nearly forty times in seventeen pages, one begins to wonder whether the repetition is always incremental. From verbiage to verbalizing is a dangerously short cry, and adjectives and adverbs can sometimes do a poem to death. (p. 471)

> *Rolfe Humphries, "Young Welsh Poet, Maybe," in* The Nation, *Vol. 167, No. 17, October 23, 1948, pp. 471-72.*

THE TIMES LITERARY SUPPLEMENT

The world of Mr. Watkins's poetry is a dazzling one, transfigured by an awareness of supernatural light. There is hardly a poem in [*The Lady with the Unicorn*] of which the key images do not come from a sort of mystical colour sense. . . .

Fading and shining, vividness and obscurity, simplicity and mystery, these are the marks of this poetry which, like Vaughan's, conveys through sensuous images the meaning of a spiritual experience that has, in fact, for the poet transformed the sensuous world.

A reader who looks in poetry for a commentary on common experience will, therefore, be disappointed with this volume. A devout Christian, Mr. Watkins is not concerned to argue the grounds of his faith, but to express a certain clear, pure joy that arises from it. He does express this joy, sometimes, as in the title-poem, with the innocent precision the Pre-Raphaelites aimed at.... There are many contemporary poets more subtle, more intricate, more dense (Mr. Watkins's one technical weakness is a certain tendency to diffuseness), more uneasily aware of the complications of our time. There are many who strike a more varied note. There are, however, few contemporary poets of whom it may be said that the most striking characteristic of their work is its images of joy and light, its beauty. That may be said of Mr. Watkins.

> *"A Christian Poet," in* The Times Literary Supplement, *No. 2444, December 4, 1948, p. 683.*

THE TIMES, LONDON

Mr. Watkins is a Welshman, and in his earlier volumes, **The Ballad of the Mari Lwyd** and **The Lamp and the Veil,** he cultivated a richness of utterance which ran parallel to Dylan Thomas. He has now pared his exuberance to a much greater economy of phrase [in **The Death Bell**], and at the same time adopted a stricter metrical framework, both in the ballads which comprise one part of his book and in the lyric poems, which make up the rest. His poetry is thus more accessible than formerly. It exemplifies a very general tendency to break away from the gnomic or the ambiguous modes which were fashionable before [World War II], in search of a fresh simplicity, and there is no reason why even those who are chary of modern poetry should miss the pleasures which are scattered through these pages.

> *"Two Successful Poets in Search of Simplicity," in* The Times, *London, May 8, 1954, p. 9.*

THE TIMES LITERARY SUPPLEMENT

The central experience of [**The Death Bell**] is a sustained wonder at the glories of the created world, told in twin and merging moods of rhapsodic acceptance and grave meditation. The themes that Mr. Watkins chooses to dwell on are relatively few; but they are the great ones, and it is a measure of the intensity of his gift that, in trying to give them fresh expression, he seems to be straining at times at the very limits of the communicable. At times, indeed, the sound alone must carry the major burden of the sense. But then, in Valéry's definition, this is the true realm of poetry: "la poésie, cette hésitation prolongée entre le son et les sens."

Mr. Watkins's poems are written out of an avowedly religious inspiration, but they are in no sense mere illustrations to particular dogma. They grow, rather, out of a sense of an ultimate cosmic harmony, so that, not infrequently, one is reminded of that other Welshman, Henry Vaughan.... Several of these poems are, in fact, rooted in pagan themes. And if these seem, at a first reading, the most hermetic, the explanation may be sought in a note appended to the title-poem: "The pathos of pre-Christian love lies in its incompleteness, the prophetic nature of pre-Christian death in its reticence." They are the fruit of what one might call a retrospective compassion, in which the poet seeks to relate the two worlds that hinge about the offer of redemption. There is an unbearable sadness in the dereliction of the pagan dead: but with it goes a sense of continuity as well, a profound feeling for tradition which recognizes that, while man cannot escape the necessity of his earthly role, he can at least, by his patient art, assure himself

of a lesser immortality. This is the implication of poems like **"A Book from Venice"** and **"Art and the Ravens."** ...

The ballads are less intent in mood but not less careful in craftsmanship; ballads of dead men rolled in ocean pools, of moonlight poured in a barrel, of the destruction of Sodom.

It should be clear from the foregoing that these are poems which yield their full riches only after repeated readings.

> *"Great Themes," in* The Times Literary Supplement, *No. 2728, May 14, 1954, p. 311.*

LOUIS L. MARTZ

Though **The Death Bell** is the fourth volume of poetry by Vernon Watkins (he is 48), he is still not widely known in [the United States]. Yet here is one of the finest religious poets of our century: religious in a frank, disarming way.... Watkins, a countryman and friend of Dylan Thomas, strives to convey that sense of a "unity of being" which Thomas also reveals in his better poems; but Watkins' sense of unity is given more dogmatically, more explicitly, in Christian terms. No doubt "intuition" discerns this unity—but with Watkins, at least, it is intuition trained by what he calls "right argument": he gives "That dignity of line / From doctrine pounded fine."

His poems plunge into the heart of the natural object, the sea, the pool, the shell, the blossom, the rock, the bird, and through bardic showers of imagery (**"Taliesin in Gower"**) build up a sense of some "primaeval music" moving through it all.... Thus in the most impressive poem of this volume the Niobe of Dante's "Purgatorio" is transformed to a sea-whipped rock in Wales, and all the images of nature fuse to form a symbol of maternal grief, enduring and undefeated.... Aside from Hopkins and Eliot we have not seen religious poetry like this since the seventeenth century; and indeed the poetical ancestor of this poetry is Henry Vaughan, whose meditiative vison also found these flashings in the landscape of Wales.

> *Louis L. Martz, "New Poetry: In the Pastoral Mode," in* The Yale Review, *Vol. XLIV, No. 2, December, 1954, pp. 301-09.*

THE TIMES LITERARY SUPPLEMENT

[**Cypress and Acacia**] is Mr. Watkins's first volume of verse for five years, but it represents a steady development of gifts his admirers already knew about rather than a radically new departure. There are, however, certain new tendencies. There is more argument and reflection, perhaps, than there used to be, and less reliance on a vivid, uncommented presentation of natural beauty to carry its own transcendental message. There seem more poems bringing in people, particularly dead people: a dead friend of Mr. Watkins's whose likeness comes back to him precisely only in dreams, or, in the poem from which the title of the book comes, the dead English Romantic poets in the Protestant Cemetery at Rome. Some lines on Shelley in that poem, a fine one, are typical of Mr. Watkins's fairly new reflective vein:

> Shelley, who from the first began
> His concept of a sinless man,
> Inspired by passion's desperate stream
> Translating substance into dream,

Yet who transfigured him to thought,
Making of life what it is not,
Ignored that resurrection must
Come of true substance, and of dust. . . .

But there is still plenty of dazzling evocation, in long lines which Mr. Watkins handles with a peculiar confidence and a peculiarly individual tone. . . .

Mr. Watkins is very consciously a Romantic, in a decade in which younger poets have, on the whole, turned against Romanticism; and he is very unself-consciously a Christian in a decade in which many younger poets are indifferent or hostile to Christianity and in which Christian poets like Mr. Auden or Mr. Betjeman feel their creed under attack and present its attitudes often with an oblique sophistication. Irony and wit are not among Mr. Watkins's poetic weapons. Like Hopkins, he sees and feels God in nature. . . .

[One] poem describes in detail an actual meeting with a dead friend in a dream. The friend seems happy, in the dream. Mr. Watkins feels reassured in his surmise that his friend is among the saved, but is immediately reproached by the dream-ghost:

"What right had you to know, what right
To arrogate so great a gift?"
I woke, and memory with the light
Brought back a weight I could not lift.

Earlier in the same poem Mr. Watkins says interestingly,

This that moved me most
Was first a vision, then a dream,

and readers may wonder whether this dream, so precisely evoked, is the same sort of dream as Shelley is reproved for translating substance into. In fact, Mr. Watkins's vision, especially in certain poems in short lines, a little too reminiscent in cadence of Yeats, seems sometimes vaguer than his dreams. But he is a poet who has created his own immediately recognizable world; and who, in an age in love with ambiguity and hedging, can declare with obvious dignity, "Truth is simple."

"Vision and Dream," in The Times Literary Supplement, *No. 3015, December 11, 1959, p. 727.*

LOUISE BOGAN

Three recent books of poetry break through the season's rather unexciting level of general competence to give the reader unexpected pleasure and surprise. Vernon Watkins' *Cypress and Acacia* . . . is one of these. Born in 1906, a Welshman educated at Cambridge and an early friend of Dylan Thomas, Watkins never succumbed to the influence of his younger compatriot either in manner or in point of view. His poetry, disciplined from the beginning . . . , is completely free of ambiguity, irony, and skepticism. He continually expresses his belief in the virtue of simplicity, and he shows a reverence toward nature and a sympathy for the various bafflements of mankind with an emphasis that might easily lapse into blandness and piety but that never does. He is quite willing to deal with the past and allows only one machine (a tractor in a field) to show up in his description of the present. This separation from the harsh modern scene has given some critics the opportunity to call him neo-Romantic. Watkins has certainly kept hold of the Romantic poet's right to reflect, meditate, and have intimations of one kind or another, and there are moments when his poetry seems distinctly nineteenth-century. Under the surface, however, a modern sensibility is at work. His experience is so genuinely

felt, so exactly observed, and so freshly expressed that any initial sense of the old-fashioned and the *déjà vu* soon disappears. This is delightful poetry, whose subject and technique show a complex temperament and a craftsman's hand. (p. 154)

Louise Bogan, in a review of "Cypress and Acacia," in The New Yorker, *Vol. XXXVI, No. 6, March 26, 1960, p. 154.*

ROBERT HILLYER

The high admiration that Dylan Thomas expressed for Vernon Watkins' genius will not influence an objective reviewer, but the conclusion is still unqualified praise. If the names of great poets in lyric mood occur to us in reading *Cypress and Acacia,* it is not from any derivative elements in Mr. Watkins' work but because of his equal claim on our attention. He is an artist to whom long discipline in rhyme and meter has given the assured and musical expression that we so often look for in vain among other contemporaries.

His phrasing seems as easy as it is effective. Among the many forms he uses are the four-stress couplet, the five-stress couplet, the sonnet, blank verse, an adaptation of the Sapphic stanza and many ingenious stanza-forms of his own, including the sixteen-line strophes of the **"Ode at the Spring Equinox,"** which sustain the beauty and meaning of the seasonal apocalypse. Throughout the book, images that are fresh, and yet seem inevitable, embody large themes, some of them philosophical or religious, which indicate a poet of contemplative mind and profound emotions. The Arthurian **"Camelot"** reminds us that Mr. Watkins is a Welshman and entitled to his heritage of song and magnificence.

Robert Hillyer, "Mixed Quintet of Harmonists," in The New York Times Book Review, *March 27, 1960, p. 10.*

THOM GUNN

Vernon Watkins's first book, **Ballad of the Mari Lwyd and Other Poems,** is now, it appears, being distributed in [the United States] for the first time. The poems in it combine a considerable musical power with violent imagery of the type that was popular at the time they were written. One poem begins

The keen shy flame holding this poem's ash,
Texture and syllable,
Bears on its point the precious crucible
Transforming utterance to a breath more rash.

Silence is there within the flying bowl
Bright as a waving poppy.
Still from the ignorant pattern falls the copy.
That pivot has all time in its control.

It would be difficult to explain in rational terms exactly what Mr. Watkins is saying here, but the ideas apppear to derive from the French symbolists, perhaps through Yeats. There is a suggestion of meaning barely but deliberately eluded in both the manner and the content of these lines. In them as in most of the poems in the book there is—if it is not a contradiction in terms to say this—a rich but imperfectly realized imagery, imagery that is introduced more for its quality than for its meaning.

Twenty years later, in *Cypress and Acacia,* the same sort of thing is going on, though with far greater accomplishment. The rhetoric has been freed of its more violent elements, and there is frequently a beautiful control over meter (Mr. Watkins' sapphics, for example, are probably the best by any living poet after Ruth Pitter). He seems to be aiming, even more deliberately than before, at a kind of "pure poetry". The gesture, the stance, the sound are all-important. The meaning, since it cannot be entirely suppressed, is still present, but present in a rather unsatisfactory manner. There are, for instance, as in the earlier book, heavy hints of a type of Yeatsian mysticism, supported at times by embarassinging imitations of Yeats's style like "I praise the eagle and the dove". The mysticism is, for me at any rate, almost entirely impenetrable. At the other extreme we find meaning as cliché. (pp. 264-65)

Mr. Watkins's trust in the clichés of symbolist mysticism and of the newspapers can at times, however, become something more modest—a trust in the known, resulting in passages of impressive simplicity. (p. 265)

> *Thom Gunn, "Certain Traditions," in* Poetry, *Vol. XCVII, No. 4, January, 1961, pp. 260-70.*

THE TIMES LITERARY SUPPLEMENT

Irish poetic language tends towards rhetoric, Scottish towards a fine but sometimes bleak bareness, Welsh sometimes (not always, for Mr. R. S. Thomas is a striking exception) towards the musically mysterious, and towards a fullness of celebration. . . .

What has seemed peculiarly Welsh in Mr. Watkins's work in [volumes previous to *Affinities*] has . . . been a visionary sense of landscape, of the landscape of the sea and coast of the Gower peninsula where he has his home; a sense, in particular, of light and colour in the sky and sea, and of these things as symbols, or intimations, of infinity. The stress of this new volume is more on the theme of the poet, his task and his glory, and there are some fine poems of commemoration and compliment to poets and other artists living and dead. Through the whole volume there runs a delight in praising the good and great which is certainly amiable, and certainly also Welsh.

> *"Irish, Scots and Welsh," in* The Times Literary Supplement, *No. 3179, February 1, 1963, p. 78.*

ROBIN SKELTON

Vernon Watkins, [in *Affinities*], is clearly Proud of Poetry. He laments the death of Keats and pays tributes to Wordsworth, Heine, Holderlin, and Dylan Thomas. The fundamental laziness of Mr. Watkins's verse is shown over and over again. For example,

> The barren mountains were his theme,
> Nature the force that made him strong.
> This day died one who, like a stone,
> Altered the course of English song.

This, the opening verse of a poem on Wordsworth, is typical of Mr. Watkins's pedestrian moments. Other moments there are, of course, but not too many. It is a sad business, for Mr. Watkins clearly is an earnest and good man who is completely possessed by his poetic vocation. His language, however, is dead, his rhythms are mechanical, and his cadences, though carefully made, only superficially attractive.

> *Robin Skelton, in a review of "Affinities," in* Critical Quarterly, *Vol. 5, No. 2, Summer, 1963, p. 190.*

STEPHEN STEPANCHEV

As a poet, Vernon Watkins has been overshadowed by his friend and fellow Welshman, Dylan Thomas (whose *Letters to Vernon Watkins* appeared posthumously in 1957), but he is a remarkable poet who demonstrates in [*Affinities*], his fifth book of poems, that he has many admirable qualities: a supple rhetoric, an opulent imagery of natural scenes—of seascapes, fields at harvest time, waterfalls, valleys—and a vision that successfully unifies the contraries of the world. This vision is essentially religious and rests, ultimately, on a belief in salvation through the intercession of Christ.

One finds contraries and paradoxes everywhere in Mr. Watkins' poems. . . .

Among the most stirring poems in the present collection are **"Waterfalls," "The Crane," "Expectation of Life," "Bishopston Stream,"** and **"Music of Colours—Dragonfoil and the Furnace of Colours."** Least interesting are the poems about the making of poems and poetic tributes to such literary figures as Wordsworth, Eliot, Browning, Heine, and Hölderlin. These make up a fairly large portion of the book. The chilling self-consciousness of this poetry suggests that, perhaps, poets should look for subject matter in the lives of carpenters, farmers, and physicians.

Technically, Mr. Watkins is a traditional poet in the best sense of the term: the poetic tradition is renewed through him. He shows how the rhythmic pulse of the accentual-syllabic system that has dominated English poetry since Chaucer's day can animate contemporary poetry. It is this rhythmic pulse that enables him to sing, setting him apart from many recent poets who merely talk.

> *Stephen Stepanchev, "Out of the Shadow," in* Books, *August 11, 1963, p. 6.*

KATHLEEN RAINE

[Watkins] chose tradition (vital memory) as against education, and inspiration as against the new positivist spirit of the age; he remained true, as Yeats said poets must, to "certain heroic and religious truths, passed on from age to age, modified by individual genius, but never abandoned." One may say that he was lucky to be able to make the choice at all; Yeats, coming to the same realisation, had to re-graft himself within the tradition of Ireland; Edwin Muir brought from his "distant isle" (Orkney) only memories; and other poets know themselves exiled beyond all possibility of return to ancestral roots. . . . [By] their reiteration of faith in the imagination the English poets, from Spenser to Milton, from Blake and Coleridge to Keats and Shelley, from Yeats to Edwin Muir and Vernon Watkins, have preserved in English culture a knowledge obscured by her philosophers (Locke, Blake's enemy, was the type of all later positivists who believe man to possess no knowledge except through the senses) and indeed by her religion, which has taken the bias of a temperamental pragmatism. Without knowledge of this mind and access to its fountains no true poetry can be written, but only an imitation which, while it may appear indistinguishable to those deaf to the "other" voice, cannot for a moment deceive those attuned to it. Thus it is that in discussions of verse with such people one so often has the sense of talking about two different things. To those who rule out life an acorn is a poor kind of pebble: the difference is not of degree but of kind.

No doubt Vernon Watkins is well acquainted with Coleridge's thought and with Blake's, and probably with the Platonic philosophers who were their teachers as they were Yeats's. He is also well acquainted with the parallel history of German poetry; he himself has published a volume of fine translations of Heine, and a sequence of poems to Hölderlin. . . . But one may guess that it was not by way of learning of this kind that the initiatory knowledge of the poet came to him first; but rather, as he implies by way of the vital memory of the Welsh bardic tradition. This tradition transmits, as surely as Plato or Coleridge or Blake, the doctrine of the "other" mind of poetic inspiration.

This "other" mind of inspiration (Coleridge's and Milton's higher reason, Blake's "Jesus the Imagination," Yeats's *anima mundi,* as such so wonderfully described also by Edwin Muir in his *Autobiography,* Jung's collective unconscious, Plato's world of ideas and perhaps the Christian Logos itself) is beautifully expressed in the Welsh mythological story of the poet-child Taliesin, a theme to which Vernon Watkins often returns. Taliesin dies and reincarnates, unageing and indestructible: his knowledge is as old as the world. Robert Graves and Charles Williams have given versions of the famous "Lay of Taliesin" and Vernon Watkins descants on the theme. . . . This spirit of the divine wisdom is also in the Taliesin legend identified with the prophetic tradition both Christian and pre-Christian. The same wisdom that was present when the mountains were laid was present at the Crucifixion, and inspires all prophetic (that is to say poetic) utterance. . . . (pp. 174-76)

Through his participation in a still living tradition Vernon Watkins commands great advantages over poets whose sources are solely literary. Inseparable from the poetic doctrine of Taliesin is the mythical story itself and the symbols associated with it; and in using these the poet is assured of being understood by those to whom his poems are most immediately addressed. A second advantage is that the dress of his mythology is identical with the natural world of present Wales. All Taliesin's stars and birds and rivers, and also the Hebrew and Christian themes of the "Lay," remain contemporary. The Welsh poet has even the advantage over the Irish poets who, led by Yeats, attempted to revive ancient Irish mythology, for Taliesin's symbols are cosmic and timeless in themselves and can be understood without previous knowledge. I say this with reservation, however, since there is doubtless an esoteric meaning within the Bardic tradition which is perhaps not to be understood apart from the Druid learning perpetuated presumably in the Taliesin poems. Yet it is certainly true that, while loaded with the riches of the past, these symbols are no less appropriate to the present.

How very much within this tradition Vernon Watkins was and was to remain may not have been apparent to readers who saw in his early **"Ballad of the Mari Lwyd"** a tour-de-force (which it is) evoked by a picturesque custom which the poet remembers from childhood. On the last night of the old year a horse's skull decked with ribbons was carried from house to house by "a party of singers, wits and impromptu poets who, on the pretext of blessing, boasting of the sanctity of what they carried, tried to gain entrance to a house, for the sake of obtaining food and drink. The method they used was to challenge those within to a rhyming contest." Thus our poet's first experience of the art of verse was in a context at once popular and sacred. The horse (which in other Celtic countries also is associated with the dead) is the symbolic vehicle of all those powers outside the world of the living who in every tradition seek to gain admittance. Perhaps (as Y. Evans Wentz argues in his

Fairy Faith in Celtic Countries) reincarnation was part of the teaching of the Druids and therefore part of the Bardic tradition which has lingered into the modern world as folklore. Be this as it may, for Vernon Watkins the dead and the unborn are near akin; the state of life is continually besieged by inextinguishable life which desires admittance. Yeats in his later years said that the only two themes to hold the interest of an intelligent man are, finally, the mysteries of sex and the dead; and the cosmic mystery is, seen now from the side of birth, now of death, the central theme of Vernon Watkins's poetry, expressed on many levels and in many moods. (pp. 177-78)

The wits and impromptu poets who carried the Mari from house to house boasted of "the sanctity of what they carried." The *Mari* is a sacred cult object associated with the dead who themselves are the memory of the world immortal in the "other" mind. Must we not perhaps define the sacred as whatever comes from that world, speaks from it, is born from it or returns to it? Since the bard is the oracle of that mind, that world, his office was traditionally held to be sacred, and is so still insofar as his inspiration comes from that fountain. It is no doubt precisely this different (though traditional) conception of the role of the poet which sets Vernon Watkins apart in the profane modern world. He is a true initiate; he does not carry a horse's skull, but he carries the symbol.

The evocation of the "other" mind by incantatory rhythms is as old as mankind; and whatever the reason may be (to consider such a question would be beyond the scope of this article) the gift of lyrical and incantatory speech seems at all times to accompany "inspired" utterance and to be the natural gift of those who know how to tap the springs. Plato in the *Ion* describes this characteristic of inspired speech of the poets, who in their sober minds are incapable of rhapsodic utterance. Vernon Watkins has this gift to a marked degree. His **"Ballad of the Mari Lwyd"** is a poem which seems rather given than made, the utterance rather of the race than of an individual poet. It is by the compulsion of their incantation that the dead strive to break down the defences of the living. . . . This poem seems an initiation which the poet has received from the ancestors, which has continued to fertilise all his future work.

David Jones in an essay, "The Myth of Arthur," has described the characteristic evanescence, melting and mingling of contours and planes of reality which characterise the Celtic genius. "A half aquatic world . . . it introduces a feeling of transparency and interpenetration of one element with another, of transposition and metamorphosis." Both Dylan Thomas and Vernon Watkins share this delicate, intricate and dazzling web of intermingled elements as they weave the texture of a world less concrete than that of the English, more like the glittering veil of *maya* as conceived by the Indian metaphysics, a system made up not of solid substances but of appearances. Yeats and the Irish poets turned to India for a metaphysics to match their own Celtic inheritance of subtle myth and a cosmic sense of the whole implied in every separate part—the past and future in the present, the dead in the living and rebirth in decay—rarely found in England. Vernon Watkins lets fall the names of Plotinus, Blake, and Yeats; he gives always the impression that he writes from a great reserve of knowledge, kept strictly under control. Initiate he is: and in this he perhaps differs from Dylan Thomas, for whom indeed the word "holy," which he so often used, had a personal meaning whose emotion colours all he wrote. But if Dylan Thomas surpassed his friend in dazzling richness and the fullness of the flow of life in his work, Vernon Watkins has the greater metaphysical sense.

It would be wrong to suppose that, a friend and contemporary, Vernon Watkins is the same kind of poet as Dylan Thomas, only not quite so good; neither judgment would be true, although there are, of course, resemblances. . . . [*The Lady with the Unicorn* (1948) is] the collection in which the resemblances to Dylan Thomas seem most frequent. They have in common that prodigality of dazzling images declaimed in what Blake called "the voice of a true orator," a voice perhaps made possible for both by the emotional climate of Wales, in which such voices do not go unheard, as in England they are likely to do.

But all along Vernon Watkins adheres to his symbols with a more conscious dedication to their sacred and traditional content. All life is foaled by the sacred *Mari*

> And whoever watches a foal sees two images,
> Delicate, circling, born, the spirit with blind eyes
>   leaping
> And the left spirit, vanished, yet here, the vessel of
>   ages
> Clay-cold, blue, laid low by her great wide belly the
>   hill. . . .

In the fine poem **"Niobe"** the bereaved mother turned to stone is herself a landscape, a threshold between life and death; she is the dark face of the cosmic mystery, arrested, in mourning, under its aspect of tragedy. . . . (pp. 178-82)

At a time when it is so widely assumed that no more is needed in poetry than the description of something perceived by the senses or some emotion felt by the poet, or a complexity of images and feelings (at which point Dylan Thomas frequently was content to remain), it is necessary to point out that a characteristic of Watkins's poetry is the presence of some organising idea which can only be apprehended poetically, some true cosmic or metaphysical apprehension of what Coleridge calls "the eternal in and through the temporal." Inevitably, either everything in nature has this dimension or nothing has; no poet can be sometimes merely descriptive of physical or emotional sensations, and sometimes writing "symbolically," since those poets for whom there is an eternal dimension must be aware of it at all times. The symbol one may call the measure of wisdom, since its reach is in depth, in virtue of the analogy by which every plane of reality expresses and reflects every other; and Vernon Watkins's soundings are deep. How easily, for example, can we imagine the kind of conversation piece many poets could have written instead of **"The Lace Maker"**! Such poems seem endlessly popular nowadays. To the present writer (who shares Vernon Watkins's vision in depth) merely descriptive poems, however well made (as we are often assured, though in what sense those of us who look for imaginative ideas as the necessary structure without which there can be no poem at all find it hard to imagine) are mere blanks on the page. But, as does Blake, whose women are all weavers of the texture of the world, or Edwin Muir, whose Penelope wove human lives upon the loom of history, Vernon Watkins employs the images of lacemaking for the purposes of a symbolic statement; this is but normal traditional practice and only at an abnormal time has it become necessary to point to so obvious a usage. The lacemaker's hand is weaving, like light, the "minute particulars" of the veil of the visible, quietly accomplishing the eternal triumph of light over darkness. . . . Beauty and nobility are at all times the distinguishing mark of traditional poetry: necessarily so, since such poetry is concerned with the "sacred" themes of the cosmos and not with mortality. Irony and vulgarity, so often associated with modern realism (and mistakenly regarded as more "truthful" than beauty and nobility), are incompatible with the vision of the "other" mind; they are never to be found in any poem of Vernon Watkins's, nor for that matter in the work of Dylan Thomas.

Another characteristic gift of the "other" mind, lyrical form, is perhaps Vernon Watkins's most outstanding mark as a poet. But if the gift is innate it has certainly been perfected through learning. To a naturally gifted poet knowledge is attracted like iron fittings to a preëxisting magnetic field. Thus we find Vernon Watkins using with ease Sapphics and Alcaics, besides many free or strict English lyric and ballad forms: he is none the less a craftsman for his access to the fountain. His favourite borrowed form seems to be the Sapphic metre, which in his hands never sounds like an exercise. He does not use, so far as I know, Welsh metrical forms or those assonances borrowed from the Welsh by Hopkins: but in all his verse one finds something David Jones points to as characteristic of "the Celtic thing," "an elusive hardness, a bent towards the intricate and the abstract"—characteristic also, though differently, of Dylan Thomas.

Yeats's influence is often present, riding the feminine Welsh *Mari* like the high horse of Ireland, sometimes with effect. . . . At other times Yeats's influence is unfortunate, and makes apparent the difference between the gossamer-light weaving and interweaving which is Watkins's Welsh native bent, and the proud stateliness of Yeats. . . . It is not in the direction of Yeats that Vernon Watkins's natural development seems to lie. Rather it is to some modern return to a poetry like that of the English metaphysicals, especially Herbert and Vaughan, whose roots also were Welsh. It seems that Mr. Watkins has been for a long time moving from pagan rite to Christian sacrament; his lyricism tends more and more to diverge from the abundant rhapsodic image-laden poetry of his own youth and that of Dylan Thomas; his themes, as they become more austere in feeling and image at the same time become more complex and more reflective. Like Vaughan and Herbert "one place" suffices to give him themes whose complexity is all in depth. Yeats was in this sense a more worldly poet. So, curiously enough, was Edwin Muir, whose visionary poems embraced the European history of his time in a way not Auden himself, most extroverted of poets, has done. Every poet has his limitation, but this is not necessarily a weakness; it merely defines his field. Certainly Vernon Watkins's field is, in a worldly sense, a narrow one; but I do not find his poetry so any more than that of those earlier metaphysical poets who by choice withdrew from the world to seek for wisdom in depth rather than knowledge in extent.

"The Death Bell" is the title poem of his last volume but one (1954) and is a return to the theme of the **"Mari Lwyd,"** the two worlds of the dead and the living. This poem could never have the popularity of the earlier incantatory magic; it is a more austere, restrained, profound and, though less immediately impressive, a more finely written poem. It is also, so it seems to me, a better poem than Dylan Thomas's "Do not go Gentle into that Good-night" because subtler and more sober in its searchings, as it is in its expression, of the themes of death and immortality. Dylan Thomas assumes annihilation, and for those who share his view of death his emotional response to the situation of his father's blindness and impending death must seem as sufficient in its content as it is natural in its intensity. Vernon Watkins's theme (also occasioned by the death of his father) is not so much death as the mystery of immortality. The image of the bell, swinging between the two extremes of dust and spirit, hope and despair, is used with that exhaustive searching of every possible implicit symbolic analogy which characterises the metaphysical poets of the seventeenth century. "The bell itself is more than an instrument. It is involved with all for whom it has tolled, and its resonance has the power to beckon everyone whom its sound has touched. Before it rises, it must sink to its full weight at the end of the rope, and lie there, as a dead body must, under a single thread, expecting resurrection. The harmony within the bell, and within the dead body, is musically controlled, and depends upon the mercy and judgment of the heavenly scales for its pace. These scales are discernible everywhere in nature, but they may be discerned only by intuition, not by the reason." Let us admit it, Mr. Watkins's theme is not only unfashionable at this time: it is difficult and profound, embodying a knowledge not to be bought at the cheap rate which this age demands. Thought and language alike suggest Herbert or Vaughan (far more than Donne from whom the theme of the death bell—"It tolls for thee"— is taken). . . . The complexity of the ideas [interwoven in **"The Death Bell"**], within the terms of a symbolism of ponderosity, musical resonance, font, rope and bell, is in form, even in vocabulary, as timeless as its themes, perhaps because the vocabulary of our subtler thought changes more slowly than the words of common usage. We are reminded of the perfect manners of Herbert and Vaughan, who in writing upon the most intimate themes never intrude their own mortality or attempt to evoke ours.

The elusive figure of Taliesin indeed unites pre-Christian with Christian themes; and in **"Taliesin and the Spring of Vision"** the prophetic Bardic spirit itself seeks baptism; the cosmic spirit is reluctant to leave the freedom of timeless nature for human history, yet makes the choice. . . . (pp. 183-87)

"Taliesin took refuge under the unfledged rock" from time and history; but realisation comes to him that the time-bound human condition taught Shakespeare and Dante and Blake; the cosmic voices seek to hold the poet to a world of perfection that for that very reason falls short of human perfection. . . . Vernon Watkins's Christianity is thus a seed or acorn into which the essence of the pagan cosmic sense, which filled with blossom and bough, with sea foam and rock and wings his earlier poetry, has been distilled; the tree of life has been diminished to a grain which in its simplicity holds the potential complexity of the tree both as memory and as promise. The "sanctity" of the old mare's skull is deepened into the exploration of themes which will set in even farther apart from contemporary profane English culture. It may be that his deliberate baptism of the bardic spirit is reflected in his attempt in his last volume, *Affinities,* to write on human rather than natural themes, odes to poets dead and living, friends or strangers. **"Revisited Waters"** was written for the Quartercentenary of Repton School—an unpromising subject, though Gray immortalised the Eton playing fields. Surprisingly, this occasional poem is a very fine one. I would expect Vernon Watkins in the nature of things to follow in the future religious themes to their source, "out of nature." If he becomes more explicitly a religious poet, he is likely to be less appreciated than ever but his choice was made long ago, and its price known. (p. 188)

Kathleen Raine, "Vernon Watkins: Poet of Tradition," in The Texas Quarterly, *Vol. VII, No. 2, Summer, 1964, pp. 173-89.*

ELIZABETH JENNINGS

Vernon Watkins has always been a rather lonely figure in English poetry. He has never been associated with any move-

ment or involved in any coteries. . . . It is good, then, to have these *Selected Poems 1930-1960* and to be given a chance to assess his contribution to English literature.

Just as Mr. Watkins does not fit into any school of poets, neither can he be easily classified by subject-matter or method. He is a poet who deals with the largest themes—birth, death, love, renewal—yet he is not a nature poet in the strict sense of the word. He does not, as Wordsworth did, identify himself with natural forms. Rather, he celebrates them. This is very evident in the beautiful poem, **"Music of Colours—White Blossom"**:

> White blossom, white, white shell; the Nazarene
> Walking in the ear; white touched by souls
> Who know the music by which white is seen,
> Blinding white, from strings and aureoles,
> Until that is not white, seen at the two poles,
> Nor white the Scythian hills, nor Marlowe's queen.

This is poetry of praise, neither intellectual nor philosophical. It is, too, a poetry of sensuousness, though the imagination is always alert and will not allow the senses to run riot. Perhaps one can convey some idea of Watkins's unique quality if one compares him with two other Welsh poets—Dylan Thomas and R. S. Thomas. The first is a poet of pure celebration and of limited subject-matter; he lacks the play of mind which is always present in Watkins's work. As for R. S. Thomas, most of his work deals with a dark religion and a hardy set of parishioners. At times (though not very often), Watkins reminds me of W. S. Graham. Mostly, he remains entirely his lonely self. . . .

Watkins's Christianity is an essential part of his poetry; he writes in praise of nature for the sake of God. Yet his religion lacks that dark side which we find so often in the poems of R. S. Thomas. On the contrary, it is something which brings gladness and rejoicing to his verse.

In some ways, Watkins reminds me of Edwin Muir. Like Muir, he pursues his own course, his individual way. Like Muir, too, there is an intense seriousness about his work, a feeling that to be a poet is a very special vocation, closely allied to religion. Vernon Watkins's poems, selected from thirty years' work, make a deep impression.

Elizabeth Jennings, "Very Special Vocation," in The Spectator, *Vol. 218, No. 7235, February 24, 1967, p. 230.*

ISABEL HARRISS BARR

In the forefront of contemporary British poets, Vernon Watkins is unequivocally a Romantic and holds his position with dignity. Never succumbing to the wiles of ambiguity, he has created his particular, recognizable world; he writes with a distinct reverence for words, which sets him apart. The poems [in *Selected Poems*] are for the most part long and the majority of them are rhymned. Place names, such as Carmarthen, Goleufryn, Swansea, Cwmdonkin, all add to the leavening music of Mr. Watkins' work. . . . Of special interest are the poem, **"Ophelia"**, with its nunnery of sorrows, drowned in oblivion, the eddies rippling through cresses, wollow-trunk and reed-root; **"Good Friday"** with its profound final lines;—**"Griefs of the Sea"**,—and the closing poem, **"Great Nights Returning"** with these ending-lines: "Death cannot steal the light which love has kindled / Nor the years change it." Never as gay, lavish or ecstatic as Dylan Thomas, his close friend, Vernon Watkins writes with precision, yet with ease.

Isabel Harriss Barr, "Leavening Music," in Spirit, Vol. XXXIV, No. 5, November, 1967, p. 159.

KATHLEEN RAINE

A year or two ago I published on Vernon Watkins' poetry an essay [see excerpt above] full of admiring respect but which somehow missed the essence which upon the occasion of that reading I felt so strongly: 'an unworldly, or inhuman quality', so his wife, Gwen Watkins, wrote to me in a letter. I replied surely not *in*human but perhaps trans-human; and she, 'I think the impersonal or "trans-human" quality in his work—and in a way in his attitude to personal relationships—was due to the fact that he saw people as immortal souls, not as personalities; and presumably the soul, though *beyond* personality, has put off things such as sex and age which it needed in time'. . . . Perhaps in this rejection of the personality lies the explanation of a fact which has often surprised me, the failure of quite a number of 'literary' people to realise what an incomparable poet he was. There is in all his work that quality at once remote and compelling which belongs to that part of consciousness, outside sex and age and the temporal personality, to which music (because so entirely outside and beyond such accidents) supremely addresses itself.

Vernon Watkins is perhaps 'a poet's poet': the best of his work, with the possible exception of his ballads, is undiluted pure poetry; like white light or distilled water his invisibility to the common kind and degree of attention is an attribute of this purity. The common reader very often prefers verse which has none of this quality at all but comes within the range of ordinary attention. Vernon Watkins' work addresses the spirit, and the temporal mind scarcely at all; which is perhaps nearer the truth than calling him a poet's poet, for in this sense there are readers who are poets and writers who are not.

Indeed, I have read his poems at times without the miraculous shift of focus and found their intricate shifting patterns of words and images impossible to follow; there is nothing in their woven veil for logic to hold on to, no more than in the sound of a waterfall. But then the attention is caught up and, committing ourselves to the swift yet gentle current, we flow with the verse; and perceive that the order of the poetry is not below that of reason but above it; nor formlessness but an interplay of forms so subtle and so finely interwoven that only the poet can hear what the poet speaks. Reading his work I no longer seek to apply the relatively crude instruments of *Practical Criticism* or *Seven Types of Ambiguity*, but await the miracle. Once attuned, the 'minute particular' come into focus; for in addressing the spirit no poet could be less abstract, less theoretical, less 'religious': we are shown the visible, sensible world in all its precision of form, but in a different focus, so that at first we do not recognise in a transfigured landscape familiar headlands and hills.

I belong to a generation for whom iconoclastic avant-gardism was the norm, the accepted convention; it holds no surprises. All my epiphanies have come from the astonishment of discovering, in Eliot, in David Jones, in Yeats, in Vernon Watkins, even in Joyce, the roots of tradition unsevered. Vernon Watkins' choice to live his life on the Gower peninsula was in itself an affirmation of traditional loyalty. 'The history of Welsh poetry has been dominated by the sense of tradition', H. I. Bell wrote in *The Development of Welsh Poetry*, 'a persistent loyalty to the past'. Vernon Watkins, though writing in English, had this loyalty in its most extreme degree, a cosmic loyalty extending to the pre-human rock and water and light of Gower; a quality which comes round full circle and lifts his sense of the past out of time altogether and back into the ever-present; a quality his poetry has in common with the *Lay of Taliessin* which must be, for any Welsh poet, his classical ground rather than the Greco-Roman or Renaissance poetic tradition.

The bards and *fili* of Wales and Ireland served a long apprenticeship in learned schools where they were taught not only complex rules of versifying, but also the proper themes of poetry. . . . It must even now be impossible—and in this way they are greatly to be envied—for any Welsh poet, whether writing in English or in Welsh, to be altogether outside this bardic inheritance from the Hyperborean Abaris to whom Pythagoras said he had nothing to teach, for he already possessed full knowledge of the Mysteries.

Robert Graves in his finest work, *The White Goddess*, writes of 'the Theme' of true poetry. It is not generally held, at the present time, that there is any one particular theme more than another proper to poetry. Shelley called poetry the language of the imagination, which, though true, many sense, seems to make the choice a personal one. Here again the Welsh inheritance gives a more objective and a more instructed meaning to the Theme. Graves quotes

> the Welsh poet Alun Lewis who wrote, just before his death in Burma, in March 1944, of 'the *single* poetic theme of Life and Death . . . the question of what survives of the beloved'. Granted that there are many themes for the journalist of verse, yet for the poet, as Alun Lewis understood the word, there is no choice. The elements of the single, infinitely variable theme are to be found in certain ancient poetic myths which though manipulated to conform with each epoch of religious change—I use the word 'myth' in the strict sense of 'verbal iconograph' without the derogatory sense of 'absurd fiction' that it has acquired—yet remain constant in general outline. Perfect faithfulness to the theme affects the reader of the poem with a strange feeling between delight and horror, of which the purely physical effect is that the hair literally stands on end.

Poetry to the uninitiated, Graves concludes, must seem 'a preposterous group of mares' nests'; the metaphor is deliberately chosen, for the Night Mare—Vernon Watkins' *mari*—is 'one of the cruellest aspects of the White Goddess', the Muse.

Robert Graves's own cult of the Muse is perhaps idolatrous: directed, that is to say, towards the externals of the symbol; which nevertheless has upon his imagination, even while he strenuously denies its metaphysical context, an irresistible power. Vernon Watkins experienced the *mari* numinously; and his ballad does, more than any modern poem known to me, make the hair stand on end. *The Ballad of the Mari Lwyd* embodies and transmits an ancient knowledge whose roots are in a forgotten past, which the poet has inherited rather than adopted. Unexplained, inexplicable, the truth of poem and poet to 'the Theme' is something more radical than a belief or a poetic enthusiasm. Neither is the Theme historically determined or bounded by any one period more than another within the centuries through which it has been transmitted; with a living tradition archaelogical purism is incompatible. The pre-Christian Taliessin has taken into its continuity the Christian revelation; and Vernon Watkins, within the continuity of Taliessin, expresses a vision unambiguously Christological. Throughout all the intricacies of its weaving every moment of time and atom of space (to take an image from Blake, one of Watkins's poetic masters) within his cosmos is oriented within that Revelation. In mood, often even (as in *The Death Bell*) in his 'metaphysical' imagery, Vernon Watkins calls to mind Vaughan or Herbert or Traherne; but the scope of his vision belongs peculiarly to his own time, with the cosmology of Teilhard de Chardin and the poetry of St John Perse.

Dr Bell, whom I have already quoted, says that 'Welsh poetry as a whole suffers from a lack of the architectonic faculty'. The Theme does not in its nature lend itself to the kind of forms to which Greco-Roman rationalism have accustomed us; it is elusive and pervasive rather than definable. The vision of such writers as David Jones, Dylan Thomas and Vernon Watkins lends itself to other forms, and to look for the architectonic is to miss the peculiar and fluid beauty of their kind. 'It is on the line, the couplet, the stanza, the units of which the poem is composed, that the poets of Wales usually lavish their attention.' Not Yeats himself could spin those gossamer lines, strung with their words like perfect spheres of dew, that characterise Vernon Watkins' finest lyrics; yet that gossamer is held by forces strong and coterminous with the universe. All his best poems seem—as Robert Graves suggests as a characteristic of poets dedicated to the Theme—like parts of a single poem; his elegies flow into an affirmation of rebirth, his poems for a birth or a christening are rooted in the world of the dead within the rocks, and out of the graves flowers grow for some epithalamion, or foals are born to the shadowy *mari*. He sought always, as in his Ballad of the *Mari,* a unity of vision which should include life, death and rebirth; but in his work the theme is not doctrine, but experienced in a manner wholly poetic. He communicates this Pythagorean life-in-death, death-in-life, terrible in the darkness of the *Mari Lwyd,* joyous in the birth of foal or child, bird, bud and blossom into the light, but always numinous, as it must have been experienced in the archaic rites of the Goddess. His poetry whether of death or of rebirth is without nostalgia, like a field of flowers whose roots are always in the graves; an ever-present paradise beyond pathos and beyond tragedy.

Vernon Watkins' respect for tradition was not confined to his bardic inheritance; he was a learned poet, well-read in French and German literature. He lacked nothing the finest English culture (that Public School education which in another generation will have ceased to exist) could impart to an heir of the Bards. Doubtless he was influenced, like all his generation, by the critical writings of T. S. Eliot. Yeats, certainly, was nearer to Vernon Watkins in his understanding that tradition is not anything and everything that has historically occurred, but a few heroic and religious themes, passed on from age to age; yet Eliot's more historical view of tradition he would certainly not have rejected; the poet may inherit the Theme, but he is free to choose his themes; history and tradition are not identical, yet each has its own importance. Vernon Watkins was well read throughout the whole range of European literature; Dante, Blake, Browning, Yeats are names that stray often into his poems; he translated Heine, but admired and read French poetry no less than German; his skill in the use of Sapphics and Alcaics came from his appreciation of Greek lyric poetry, which he read generally (though he knew some Greek)

in translation. He spoke of some avant-grade versifier who had reproached him for his excessive interest in writers of the past: '*They*' won't help you', this knowing one pointed out; on the contrary, Watkins replied, it was precisely to those that he owed everything. (pp. 49-52)

Much could be said of Vernon Watkins' verse, of his skill in the use of many forms both English and Classical. Perfectionism of verse has been the heritage of Welsh-born poets down to Vernon Watkins' generation, perhaps the last inheritors. English poets, whose ears are attuned to blank verse, sonnet and couplet may envy poets of the Celtic tradition the intricate rhymes and assonances of the *cynghanedd*. We can already see in retrospect that the innovations of modern poetry have not been those much-publicised rejections of traditional forms— the 'free' verse of Pound and Eliot, French prose-poetry or the succeeding chaos—but the skilful, careful and gifted prosody of poets within the Celtic tradition of Wales and Ireland, and perhaps of the 'makars' of Scotland. Hopkins, an Englishman, studied Welsh verse. In this use of verse Vernon Watkins comes perhaps nearest to his early friend Dylan Thomas, with whom he shared the years of learning the poet's craft. Yet it is not in those poems in which he most resembles Dylan Thomas that Vernon Watkins is at his best—rather the reverse—and the same is true of the influence upon him of Yeats, whom he already had taken as a model while his Cambridge contemporaries were concerned only with Pound and the Imagist theories of T. E. Hulme. His note is his own; yet at the same time a voice more of the race than that of Dylan Thomas.

Like Dylan Thomas he was a perfectionist, never allowing any poem short of attainable perfection to appear in print; he has left unpublished more poems than he ever passed for publication. Like David Jones it was his habit to keep poems and to work over them at long intervals or over a long period, until he was satisfied that they were right. He was cut off in the prime of a talent slowly and continuously developed. (p. 53)

> *Kathleen Raine, ''Intuition's Lightning: The Poetry of Vernon Watkins,'' in* Poetry Review, *Vol. LIX, No. 1, Spring, 1968, pp. 47-54.*

ALAN BROWNJOHN

Friendship with Dylan Thomas, and certain affinities of theme with the younger poet, helped to link the late Vernon Watkins decisively with the Forties neo-Romantics. When the Forties mode lost favour, his reputation lost ground with the rest. He was Welsh, he tended to get excited and rhapsodic about nature, and he admired some of the mystics and sages adopted by the New Apocalypse—what more was needed to place him? And his uncompromising pursuit of poetry as a sacred and honourable vocation didn't exactly impress Fifties poets busy being sceptical, robust and ironic. As a result, one looks almost in vain for any fair and considered assessment of Watkins's verse in critical writings published since 1955. Yet his was, by any standards, a major talent; and the publication of *Fidelities,* his last and perhaps his best book, should help to correct a persistent underestimation.

For Watkins, poetry was a continual celebration of the forces of nature, a deeply honest aspiration to truth through sea, wind, sky and stone. Despite the ambitiousness of his themes, the power in his poetry is of a quiet kind. The splendour of his effects is hardly ever sudden: the very deliberate diction does lack a final grandeur or resolving excitement, his shots at sturdy Yeatsian sonorities didn't work, and he too often wrote lengthily in strict forms which encouraged a sort of high-flown, orderly vagueness. But his best work has a grave purity and measured impressiveness that stands firmly based on exact and brilliant observation.

In *Fidelities,* a longish collection, he returns to some old heroes—Taliesin, Heine—and meditates widely on history, art and the nature of man's life. But it is in a quite small group of short poems—**"The Guest"**, **"The Razor Shell"**, **"The Crinoid"**, **"Means of Protection"**—where the diffuseness drops away, and the thinking is beautifully controlled and precise, that he achieves a splendid late perfection of his style. (pp. 843-44)

> *Alan Brownjohn, "Craft and Art," in* New States-
> man, *Vol. 76, No. 1970, December 13, 1968, pp.*
> *843-44.*

THE TIMES LITERARY SUPPLEMENT

[*Fidelities*] could be divided into poems whose cadences were imposed by a ready-made metre, and poems in which Vernon Watkins relied on his extraordinarily fine ear for modulations and improvisations of his own. The ready-made metres, in turn, were apt to impose an excessively formal diction, forced rhymes and awkward syntactic inversions. The same obstinate traditionalism often prevented this poet from drawing on his immediate visual experience, as he did in **"Fisherman"**, **"Fingernail Sunrise"** and **"The Snow Curlew"**, poems that stand out in this collection because they fuse the real with the imagined. In other poems experience and vision fall apart, either because the immediate occasion remains private, as in **"Poem for Conrad"**, or because its symbolic extension is elaborated to the point of abstraction or obscurity.

Vernon Watkins's art, like his creed, aspired to timelessness, and this sets him apart from the mainstream of modern poetry in its post-Romantic-Symbolist phase. Many of his most characteristic perceptions were of a kind that defies verbalization, as he recognized once more in **"Means of Protection"**:

> As plovers trail their wings
> To hide a nest from men's concern,
> Right lovers turn
> Talk that nears treasured things.
> The best of judgment says
> No case is won by what speech proves,
> Least of all love's.
> We live by silences.

The paradox of language demanded an explanation of the inexplicable, as in the very lines quoted here, an expression of the inexpressible, an articulation and enactment of those silences. No task could be more difficult. Vernon Watkins was equal to it in poems—like **"Cornfields"**, **"Movement of Autumn"** and **"Triad"** in this volume—that come closest to Symbolist practice in its liberation of music and vision from the control of prosaic argument. Yet Vernon Watkins's affinities and fidelities were apt to forbid this freedom; they were too generous and too eclectic, and included too much that pulled him in the opposite direction. The tributes in *Fidelities* to Marianne Moore and Heine, poets whom Vernon Watkins admired for being utterly different from himself, show how his various allegiances tempted him into formal exercises close to imitation or parody. The poetic pantheon that meant so much to him in later years, eliciting so many poems of homage and celebration, was at once too isolated and too capacious.

Yet the same isolation is inseparable from the strength and purity of Vernon Watkins's best poems—poems essentially anachronistic in their aspiration to timelessness and their rejection of temporal material which more worldly poets have been able to use. Those best poems are not worldly, but most of them are earthly enough to outlast many changes in the world.

> *"Too Timeless," in* The Times Literary Supplement,
> *No. 3486, December 19, 1968, p. 1434.*

DOUGLAS DUNN

There are positive virtues in the poetry of Vernon Watkins, its seriousness, sometimes its acceptable profundity, and it is good to have a visionary-romantic poet to suggest the universal significance of everyday things. But there is something unsatisfying about his work, as there must always be in poetry where the writer's beliefs make it difficult for us to respond to the work in the same way as he responded to what the poems are about. Watkins's ideas about life and about literature are simply and totally at odds with most of the trends in the modern world. . . . His poetry [as exemplified in the volume *Fidelities*] seeks permanent qualities. The ideas of permanence, of fixed laws in art and nature (see, **"Sonnet"** and **"The Compost Heap"**), of the existence of sacred things (of which poetry is one) and a Christian God (**"The Sibyl"**), are behind everything he wrote, as well as his close observation of the Welsh landscape and his Wordsworthian belief that nature can teach. Some of these underlying notions are likely to deter us, to say the least. Watkins's achievement, however, is to have been able, to some extent, to get away with the tense, heightened language and the not particularly elegant 'strict numbers' that his beliefs resulted in. There is in his poetry something of the 'order' and harmony that he complains is missing in the modern world. In a very good poem in this book, **"Resting Places"**, phrases that in other poets might be frowned at, and that in writers under forty would be jeered, don't really jar at all—for example 'The moment's magnitude', 'Time's holy scaffolding'. Our response to his poetry should be able to assimilate a diction that in newer poets would be reprehensible.

Watkins's poetry as a whole is a process of remembering a time when song and the synthesizing visionary experience were not only acceptable in literature but were a part of the perfect life. We may call this activity 'post-romantic', but we cannot deny that it is often moving, beautiful, and above all, in a literary if not a social context, useful. (pp. 101-02)

> *Douglas Dunn, "Old Faithfuls," in* London Maga-
> zine, *n.s. Vol. 9, No. 7, October, 1969, pp. 101-03.*

LESLIE NORRIS

Diffidently at first, and then with growing assurance and understanding, Watkins began to explore and interpret the eternal world of his vision. There were hints in *Ballad of the Mari Lwyd,* mainly in the use of symbols. The sycamore tree, for example, in the weak little poem **"Autumn Song"** or more positively in **"Sycamore"**, is seen to be a symbol of the defeat of time, an example of something near timelessness. Not only is it a particularly long-lived tree, but it achieves a kind of immortality through the high fertility of its keys, and its wood is used to make musical instruments and carvings, works of art—again a means of immortality, and one which Yeats, Watkins's master, had explored in the "Byzantium" poems and in "Lapis Lazuli". The sycamore also has a further importance since it was into the branches of a sycamore tree that Zachaeus climbed in order to see Christ pass, and there he received his vision of the eternal world which changed his whole life. Zachaeus, 'that short-statured man', is obviously a person with whom Watkins can identify, and the sycamore tree is linked with this identification.

This relationship is more closely examined in **"Zachaeus in the Leaves"** (from *The Lady with the Unicorn*), a poem in which Watkins attempts to recreate the experience of the chief of the publicans and to relate the interdependence of Christianity and myth. But it should not be forgotten that there are many other significant symbols, particularly those which employ the Platonic image of water, either as stream or fountain, perpetually flowing and perpetually renewed. These, too, suggest to us an eternal world.

What Watkins came to believe, then, was something like this. Firstly, that time does not exist. This he took as a simple and Christian truth. He did not have to invent the gyres of Yeats or any other complexities; rather it was a simple and unblemished faith like that of Vaughan or Blake. There existed, he felt, a perfect world of which this world was only a flawed copy. This he first suggested in **"Prime Colours"** (*Ballad of the Mari Lwyd*) and went on to elaborate in his **"Music of Colours"** poems, perhaps most importantly in **"Music of Colours, White Blossom"**, from *The Lady with the Unicorn*. This collection has always seemed to me the first of the mature Watkins. Not only is the title-poem his most explicit statement of the power of art over time, but also that human love, which inspired the making of the tapestries he describes and celebrates, is akin to divine love, sacred in its own right and a powerful force in the destruction of the idea of time. The book opens with the marvellous introductory poem, **"Music of Colours, White Blossom"**, first of a series with related titles, and one essential to the understanding of Watkins's thought. In this he makes plain his idea that for any revelation—any true revelation—of the eternal world, Christ's intervention, presence even, is necessary.... The true colours of the eternal world are visible only in the perfect white of Christ. (pp. 90-1)

From the natural world ["**Music of Colours, White Blossom**"] moves into a stanza in praise of the glorious examples of whiteness to be found in myth. The curious juxtaposition of Christian and pagan imagery, reminiscent of Renaissance poetry in this at least, is really perfectly logical. (Watkins was intensely interested in myth as a kind of genuine but faulty recognition of truth, a kind of pre-Christian, half-knowledgeable religion. It is partly this which makes the poetry of Hölderlin, combining as it does Christian and Greek belief, so attractive to him.) Having been made aware of perfect whiteness, Watkins is all the more able to recognize and appreciate the less perfect.... True inspiration, argues Watkins, is that knowledge of the perfect and timeless world which Christ allows, briefly and occasionally, to the true artist. It is the task of the artist to see that eternity clear when the vision is offered to him, in a flash of 'blinding white', and to recreate it as humbly and as perfectly as possible for his fellow-men through the practice of his art. (pp. 92-3)

Watkins's position at this time must have troubled him deeply. For so modest a man to discuss the nature of inspiration directly and personally would have been unthinkable, yet it is obvious from poems in *The Death Bell* and *Cypress and Acacia* that these are the concerns that obsessed him. His solution was beautifully simple and successful. He assumed a mask, a persona which allowed him to speak in the first person; not as Vernon Watkins the twentieth-century bank clerk, but as Taliesin the sixth-century poet.

Why Taliesin should so have attracted Watkins is fairly obvious, for Taliesin in his *Hanes Taliesin* claims to be quite out of the sway of time.... It was this prophetic power of poetry in which all time, past, present and future, remained as one that so attracted Watkins. He identified himself with the old poet, he laid claim to him. His first such poem was **"Taliesin in Gower"**, in which Watkins walks, as Taliesin, over his own Gower cliffs:

> Late I return, O violent, colossal, reverberant,
>   eavesdropping sea.
> My country is here. I am foal and violet. Hawthorn
>   breaks from my hands . . .

(It is worth pointing out here that foal, violet and hawthorn are all symbols of regenerative life in Watkins's work, all stand for the defeat of time and can be met in many poems.)

But the important Taliesin poem is **"Taliesin and the Spring of Vision"**; important for my argument that is. For Taliesin in the Mabinogion story had, as a child, drunk the three magic drops of inspiration that splashed onto his finger from the Cauldron of Knowledge, and all time was revealed to him. Now Watkins can look at the nature of inspiration, can make all his great claims, not on his own behalf but on behalf of all true poets, through the mouth of Taliesin. He can examine his own position and the modifications he may wish to make in his idea of the nature of inspiration, time, religion. For Taliesin is the witness at once of present, future and past; in his presence, we learn, 'time's glass breaks'. (pp. 93-4)

"Taliesin and the Spring of Vision" is included in *Cypress and Acacia*, a volume in which Watkins, as I have suggested, has been concerned to examine the nature of inspiration and, if I am right, to state publicly his assumption of the poet's heroic responsibility, that of seeing and interpreting Eternity. To complete his task he must have read very widely the work of other poets and considered the work of artists in other media. My belief is that, in *Cypress and Acacia*, Watkins marshalled all the support he could. My first hint of this—outside the identification with Taliesin—is to be found in the charming poem, **"The Mare"**. Stephen Spender's poem, more famous, perhaps, thirty years ago than it is today, has these lines:

> Eye, gazelle, delicate wanderer,
> Drinker of the horizon's fluid line . . .
>   ("Not palaces, an era's crown . . .")

This image is picked up, surely deliberately, by Watkins in the opening lines of **"The Mare"**:

> The mare lies down in the grass where the nest of the
>   skylark is hidden
> Her eyes drink the delicate horizon moving behind the
>   song . . .

It is as if Watkins is reminding us of the examples of truth he finds in other poets: for this is only one of a number of passages in which he recalls the work of other men, sometimes, as here, in the borrowing of a simple image, sometimes by writing a whole poem in a manner that irresistibly recalls another poet. It is as if, having made his enormous claims for the importance, the necessity, of the poet's task, he is claiming support of his peers, he is 'numbering them in the song'. He has already called on Taliesin, Shakespeare, Blake, Dante, Spender, but they are only the first in a long line of poets named or remembered in this extraordinary volume; sometimes, as in **"The Mare"**, by specific use of unmistakable lines or images, sometimes, as in **"The Return"**, by the use of forms and titles which recall those used by other poets; and sometimes, as in **"A Wreath for Alun Lewis"** and **"In the Protestant Cemetery, Rome"**, by writing his elegies for the young poets whose moments of truth were curtailed by death. (pp. 97-8)

All this is an achievement of a most rare kind. For despite these deliberate references to the work of other poets, Watkins retained his markedly individual voice. His exploration into the nature of poetry remained a personal journey, his assumption of poetic responsibility, despite the examples he displays to us, is clearly his own realisation. Even his interest in old Welsh poetry, of which his **"Taliesin"** poems are evidence, is used to further his purpose. Some of the rhymes in **"Angel and Man"**, for example, may remind us of the rhyming of stressed and unstressed syllables we find in the *cywydd*. This is not an easy form to sustain in English, but Watkins attempts it in rhymes such as 'field/fulfilled' and 'lived/deceived'. . . . Accepting, then, that Watkins, in *Cypress and Acacia*, was proving the necessity of true art, explaining to us the purpose of the true poet, we can find additional significance in the three elegies for young poets which are included in the collection; **"In the Protestant Cemetery, Rome"**, in which Watkins, recalling his first visit to the graves of Keats, Shelley and Trelawney in that spot 'where cypress and acacia stand', tells us that it was a time of deep personal trouble, a moment 'when I still / Knew no remedy for time's ill'; **"A wreath for Alun Lewis"**, his lament for one who is 'needed now, for you knew men's strength and failing, / Their death by storm who could manage intricate chords . . . '; and **"The Exacting Ghost"**, a splendid elegy for, as I take it, Dylan Thomas. This last is a fine poem, moving with a simple solemnity that I find very impressive. Nowhere strained or unsteady, its calm surface reveals a profound and unrelieved sadness over the death of his friend, and it achieves a direct, uncomplicated statement which is almost new in Watkins's verse, although it is to appear more and more frequently in subsequent poems. . . . (pp. 101-03)

An interested reader can trace for himself the importance of poems like **"Poet and Goldsmith"**, **"A Man with a Field"**, and others, to my general theme, and consider whether these poems may not be best thought of as one single work almost, so closely related are they to Watkins's great obsessions.

And his giant purpose is continued, modified and expanded in *Affinities,* the collection published in 1962 when Watkins was fifty-six years old. 'In this book Vernon Watkins is ploughing old ground', said the poet wryly, when his publisher asked him for a blurb for the book. It has a certain truth: many of the poems are written on themes he has examined before, and some rely for a full understanding on a knowledge of these earlier poems. His statement implies, too, that it is a collection of considered work, that the excitement of discovery may well be missing. And it is true that the exploration of the nature of poetry and inspiration which resulted in the Taliesin poems among others is here only as a statement of belief. There is an extension of his interest to true interpreters in other arts; Michaelangelo and Nijinsky are celebrated. There is an important dialogue conducted between the poet and his muse in **"Demands of the Poet"** and **"Demands of the Muse"**, in which Watkins states the essential labour ('I set my heart against all lesser toil') and continuous struggle of the true poet ('It is by conflict that he knows me And serves me in my way and not

another'). As in *Cypress and Acacia,* true poets are invoked and honoured, among them Thomas (**"A True Picture Restored"**), Lawrence (**"Zennor Cottages"**), Wordsworth, Eliot, Keats, Charles Williams, Heine, Browning and Hölderlin. There are, in addition, two **"Taliesin"** poems which keep the great theme before us.

The Browning poem, **"Browning in Venice"**, is a particularly interesting example of Watkins's uncommon skill. . . . We have seen that Watkins possessed so marked a sense of style that he could, very successfully, use a manner clearly reminiscent of the poet he was discussing without ever losing his own voice, and in this poem he invents a stanza form so markedly Browningesque that I searched the *Collected Poems* for the model; but Browning has used no form exactly like the one Watkins has 'forged'—a necessary pun—for him. The ten-line stanza, using lines of varying but strictly-controlled lengths and a complex rhyme scheme, often give us an eerie echo of Browning's voice. . . . Again, as in the Keats sonnet in this same collection (**"The Death of Keats"**), Watkins is at pains to claim, not the individual achievement of any one poet, but the primary affinity of true poetry:

> The achievement does not matter, nor the fame;

and in this his purpose is not unlike that he examined and displayed in *Cypress and Acacia.* But the heart of this more recent collection is his absorption with the poetry of Hölderlin, and **"The Childhood of Hölderlin"** occupies the central section of the book. This long poem, written in nine parts is prefaced by Watkins's own translation of Hölderlin's "To the Fates" (An Die Parzen). Watkins had admired Michael Hamburger's translation of this famous poem, and its importance to his own preoccupations at this time is obvious. It is a statement absolutely in accord with his own belief that the poet's gift was a 'god-like right', and that having once composed his 'full-ripened songs' he has lived 'as gods live'. It is not the sort of completely romantic statement that Watkins could make in his own person or claim directly for himself, but he has been in effect making such a claim on behalf of all the artists he has been celebrating. Now, in the first person, even if momentarily speaking as Hölderlin, he can make his eloquent boast of the heightened, indeed 'god-like' perceptions of the poet, make open the peculiar satisfactions they bring and the risks that are attendant. . . . It is the sort of high gesture not really open to a contemporary poet, but essentially it is what Watkins had been wanting to say for some time.

For a full understanding of the long **"The Childhood of Hölderlin"**, some knowledge of the German poet's life and work is necessary; without them the poem is certainly the reflection of Watkins's excited recognition of his own central beliefs vividly anticipated by the older poet, but it could also be an obscure work. It is probably enough here to say that Hölderlin shared Watkins's interest in the interrelationship of pagan and Christian belief, that his attempts to integrate Greek myth and Christianity must have been most helpful and encouraging to Watkins, and that his opinion of the high and necessary nature of the poet's task was identical with that of Watkins.

Beginning, then, with his first true poems, Watkins's work had been a long revelation of eternity as he was allowed to see it; he had searched for the example, the support and assurance of other true artists, finding his greatest help in the work of the old Welsh poet Taliesin and that of the modern German poet Hölderlin. His own world, compounded now of what he saw about him with his ordinary eyes and what he knew of the eternal world, was ready for exploration. In the beautiful poem **"Waterfalls"**, the first in *Affinities*, we see Watkins treat, almost for the first time, the natural world about him with the intensity he had reserved for the immortal world. In **"Poem for Conrad"** there is a beautifully exact and humorous observation at work to create an extension of his sensibility that I, for one, had not thought possible. In **"The Guest"**, a miraculous poem from *Fidelities*, he makes our mortal world eternal, and proves his claim for art's defeat of time through lines which are so perfect that they seem without art. . . . He had achieved the synthesis of the mortal and eternal worlds, alas almost too late.

For he was a very rare type of poet indeed, one who spent most of his life to make with infinite labour the groundwork of an enormous edifice, his ambitious plans embracing the deepest mysteries of life and art. He was wholly serious and dedicated; his concerns were those of absolute great poetry. Whatever his stature, and we are too near to him in time to discuss this, his work is certainly unique in our generation. (pp. 104-08)

Leslie Norris, "Seeing Eternity: Vernon Watkins and the Poet's Task," in Triskel Two: Essays on Welsh and Anglo-Welsh Literature, *edited by Sam Adams and Gwilym Rees Hughes, Christopher Davies, 1973, pp. 88-110.*

JEREMY HOOKER

I That Was Born In Wales contains thirty poems arranged thematically under the four headings "Wales", "Poetry and the Poet", "Dylan Thomas", "Life and Death", and provides brief introductions to each group consisting of information about the poet and his poetry and extracts from his prose statements about his art. Naturally, this method of presentation simplifies; which is precisely what many of us need to aid our understanding of Vernon Watkins, and in serving this end the method can only help to reveal the unity of the poetry. It is a pity, though, that no poem from the **"Music of Colours"** sequence was chosen. This omission may be justified on the ground that the best of these are "well-known anthology pieces," but for my taste the selection is too limited to carry under the heading "Poetry and the Poet" so many rather similar poems—namely **"Rewards of the Fountain"**, **"Demands of the Muse"**, **"Demands of the Poet"**, **"Muse, Poet and Fountain"**—that are schematic and somewhat rhetorical in their affirmations when compared to this sequence or to **"Taliesin and the Spring of Vision"** (also included under this heading) and other poems whose lyricism depends on the cadence of long lines or lines of varying length, on patterns of sound, and startling transitions from metaphor to metaphor. This is not, of course, to argue with the "metaphysical truth" with which Vernon Watkins said he was "entirely concerned", but rather to express admiration of poems that embody or explore that truth in metaphors and symbols discovered in loved places, creatures, parables or myths, and coolness towards poems that use traditional metaphors and symbols without either renewing or naturalizing them. In his study of Vernon Watkins . . . Roland Mathias is right, obviously, when he says that Watkins was "much less interested than David Jones in the collection of 'particulars' to validate the ultimate order he postulates". Nevertheless, his Taliesin is a poet of Gower, and his poems set in Bishopston Valley have a freshness of diction, metaphor and image which conveys metaphysical truth more livingly than his waters and fountains which are without local habitation and name. . . . I

believe his great poems to be those which either subtly ("**Foal**") or explicitly ("**Taliesin and the Spring of Vision**") baptize traditional symbols in his native Welsh element. **"Foal"**, alas, is not in this selection although the much-anthologized **"Peace in the Welsh Hills"** is. The latter I think overrated, a mixture of some of Watkins's strengths and some of his weaknesses, and would compare the freshness of the third stanza to the more literary (Yeatsian) introduction and presentation of the fountain in the last two stanzas. What I find least congenial in the poetry as a whole occurs in this poem, where a confident poetic manner and deployment of traditional symbols suggest both excellence and profundity, but act almost as substitutes for meanings or assurance *earned* by the poem, though the poet in his life has earned them. Any criticism, however, either of the selection or the poet, must pale beside the fact of this book's existence. That it seems likely to be all that will represent Watkins, outside the anthologies, for the foreseeable future is at once a bitter comment on present fashion and cause for pride in publishing in Wales. (pp. 121-22)

Jeremy Hooker, in a review of "I That Was Born in Wales," in Anglo-Welsh Review, *Spring, 1977, pp. 121-25.*

DAVID WRIGHT

Vernon Watkins is an undervalued poet. I was about to adorn the adjective with some modification like 'inexplicably' or 'strangely', but reflected that his comparative neglect, given the kind of poet he was and the kind of age we live in, is neither inexplicable nor strange. On further reflection, I should strike out 'and the kind of age we live in' because so far as poets of uncompromising spiritual honour like Watkins are concerned, the times in which they happen to live make no difference. Such poets do not offer their own day sufficient flattery, even the mild flattery of attention—as Tennyson did and Philip Larkin does—to win much contemporary acclaim. Two examples are William Blake and William Barnes. I don't claim for Watkins either Blake's stature or Barnes's microcosmic provinciality; but apart from sharing their integrity and unworldliness, he had affinities with each.

Unlike Blake, Watkins was a deliberately visionary poet. That is, where Blake is spontaneous, Watkins *consciously* set out to look for, and celebrate, the ideal or eternal form behind the transient shape—sometimes unluckily. Watkins would have acknowledged that matter of luck—in **"Yeats in Dublin"**, his remarkable tour-de-force verse report of a conversation with the older poet, he records Yeats as saying: 'For the poem is always / A piece of luck'. This is a craftsman's as much as an artist's observation. Both Yeats and Watkins were craftsmen; they did not 'write poetry', they made verses. After all, verses is what a poem is made of. Yeats's point was that good poets, like good generals, are lucky; the implication is that, like generals, they have to be prepared for luck. Watkins's great piece of luck, for which when it came he was well prepared, was *The Ballad of the Mari Lwyd,* that dialogue and dialectic of the dead and living, the eternal and ephemeral, the spiritual and corporeal, the transcendental and material, art and philistinism, God and Mammon: the real subject and focus of all Watkins's poetry. In the ancient Welsh custom of carrying a horse's skull from house to house on the last day of the year, its bearers challenging the inmates of each house to a rhyming contest— the forfeit being the right of entry for the challengers, and feasting them with food and drink—Watkins found the ideal objective correlative for what he had to say. Though Watkins's use of language is less innovatory, for my generation the impact of *The Ballad of the Mari Lwyd* in 1941 was almost as electric as that of Auden's *Paid on Both Sides* had been a decade earlier. Its combination of a plain diction and hammerbeat rhythm is immensely effective in building suspense. . . . (pp. 7-8)

It was probably inevitable that Watkins should eventually write a sequel to the **"Mari Lwyd".** That poem ends with the singers, who represent the dead (and all transcendental values) failing to get into the house of the living. The sequel, **"The Ballad of the Outer Dark",** takes up at this point. . . . The sequel to the **"Mari Lwyd"** ends with a transmutation, a reversal of roles. The returning dead take possession, while the inmates of the house find themselves bearing the horse's skull, the Mari Lwyd, through the outer dark. It is a resolution that serves both poems; the two can be read as one.

Watkins wrote **"The Ballad of the Outer Dark"** more than twenty years after the publication of the **"Mari Lwyd",** and it was broadcast on the BBC in the year he died. It is astonishing that he did not include it in his last book of poems; but Watkins was a rigorous editor of his own work, and would focus each of his collections on a certain theme, or themes. Poems, however good, that did not fit he left out. Some of these rejected poems were among the best he wrote. (pp. 8-9)

What strikes one, apart from the workmanship, is the variety of forms and metres that Watkins was able to handle with success, yet preserve, in every case, his own unmistakable voice. Here I am reminded of William Barnes, another writer of apparently simple poems which in fact obey strict and complex metrical patterns. Take, for example, such metrically intricate poems as Watkins's **"Matrix of Morning"** or **"Secrecy".** And one of Watkins's late poems, **"The Dry Prophet"**— it is about R. S. Thomas—has a new and harder music. . . . But Watkins does not depend on dexterous handling of intricate metres. Plainness is the test of a poet. (pp. 9-10)

I have already remarked that Watkins's use of language was not innovatory. This was a virtue, even a strength. 'Write for the dead, if you will not disappoint the living' was one of his maxims. His poetry is 'modern' and 'contemporary' even though his manner belongs—as Martin Seymour-Smith has pointed out—to the seventeenth rather than the nineteenth or twentieth century. Thus Watkins remains 'contemporary' while the work of some of his trendier coevals is already acquiring a period air.

With Patrick Kavanagh, another late developer, Watkins was one of the two poets of real quality to appear in the 'forties. (p. 10)

David Wright, "Introduction," in Poetry Wales, *Vol. 12, No. 4, Spring, 1977, pp. 7-10.*

JOHN ACKERMAN

Two years ago I had the pleasure and excitement of devoting six months to the study and interpretation of Vernon Watkins's poetry. It was an exacting experience, and I often recalled the almost similar intellectual and emotional wrestling with Dylan Thomas's poetry twenty years previously. I emerged from my poem-by-poem absorption in Vernon Watkins's writing with one dominant conviction: in his metaphysical exploration of the relationship between time and eternity, his paradoxical vision of the interpretation of life and death—usually explored through the natural world, Vernon Watkins is a major poet. At the same time it seemed to me that the profundity of his

vision and the splendour of its expression was somewhat unfocused by his fecundity of composition. Reading the poetry chronologically I felt that the achievement of the finest poems (e.g. the **"Music of Colonis"** sequence, **"Taliesin in Gower"**, **"Peace In The Welsh Hills"**, **"The Heron"**, **"The Curlew"**, **"Taliesin and the Spring of Vision"**, **"The Replica"**, **"The Mare"**, **"Great Nights Returning"**, **"The Snow Curlew"**— these are randomly recalled, and could be easily added to) seemed dimmed by the unevenness of the volumes in which they occurred. Unlike his friend Dylan Thomas's poems which have a primary energy and vitality of language even when almost impenetrably obscure Vernon Watkins's weaker poems are diffuse, as Dylan Thomas observed of this sometimes 'literary' fecundity: 'I can see the sensitive picking of words, but none of the strong, inevitable pulling that makes a poem an event, a happening, an action perhaps, not a still-life or an experience put down, placed, regulated' (*Letters to Vernon Watkins*). Unlike Dylan, and also R. S. Thomas, Watkins lacked the Midas touch, and where the words do not turn to spare or profligate gold they cloud the visionary gleam.

I have mentioned my own recent involvement with Vernon Watkins's poetry because it then seemed to me that a judicious selection of his verse, drawn from the eight volumes already published, would make his finest poetry more accessible to the reader; for my guess was—and is—that Vernon Watkins's poetry is not as widely read as it merits—both inside, and beyond Wales.

I was therefore delighted to receive recently this selection of poems, felicitously titled *I That Was Born In Wales*. . . . It certainly goes much of the way in meeting the need I personally felt, and is to be warmly welcomed. Most of the poems here have that quality Dylan again so rightly commended in the same letter: 'I want my sentimental blood . . . the blood of leaves, wells, weirs, fonts, shells, echoes, olives, bells, oracles, sorrows.'

The poems are helpfully arranged according to their themes, and in this respect, as the "Foreword" suggests, they throw light one on another. Generally, I found the chosen themes provided illuminating arrangement of the poetry; and of course one appreciates the reluctance to include the more anthologised verses, however appropriate. In the opening section "Wales", the poem **"Rhossili"** is not included; though I think there might usefully have been more of the poetry of place since it is usually more accessible and among the poet's best work. Next, "Poetry and the Poet"—a preoccupation paralleled in Dylan Thomas, is a section revealingly and luminously prefaced by some of Watkins's views on poetry. The third section, "Dylan Thomas", includes some of Vernon's poems on the friend whose 'death in November 1953 was a grief from which Vernon never recovered,' we learn. I was fascinated to see **"The Snow Curlew"**, undoubtedly one of his finest poems, included in this section, not having sensed the connection. The last section is called (perhaps rather too vaguely) "Life and Death" and contains 'poems he wrote in the last years of his life which seem to anticipate death.' I would have liked another, possibly a final, selection of those strikingly visionary verses, the poems of epiphany—Watkins's 'seeing eternity'—to borrow Leslie Norris's phrase, the poet's glimpse of 'the white light', his discovery of which seems to me to be of the order of Eliot's similar search for 'the moment outside of time' in *Four Quartets*. I think of such poems as the **"Music of Colonis"** sequence, **"Taliesin in Gower"**, **"Great Nights Returning"**. Perhaps, too, a short selection of poems on "Natural Life"—birds, beasts etc.—would illuminate important facets of his work; for though Watkins was not simply a nature poet as he himself asserts in this volume (what major poet is?), his poetic redemption of the sparrow's—as well as man's—fall was, like Dylan's, integral to his religious vision. (pp. 118-20)

I That Was Born In Wales contains quotations from Watkins's own notes on poetry, usually delivered during poetry readings or lectures. There are rare and invaluable insights on poetry in general as well as the poet's own; for they are not the exterior commentaries of the critic, but the distilled, heuristic experience of the artist. The appetite whetted by these short notes, one eagerly looks forward to the promised publication of the 'selected prose pieces'. (p. 120)

As well as Vernon Watkins's own comments *I That Was Born In Wales* has a valuable "Foreword" and informative editorial notes preceding each section of poems, and also at the end of the collection. (p. 121)

> *John Ackerman, in a review of "I That Was Born in Wales," in* Poetry Wales, *Vol. 12, No. 4, Spring, 1977, pp. 118-21.*

D. M. THOMAS

It seems a peculiarly apt and happy circumstance that poems by Vernon Watkins should still be pouring off the press, ten years after his death. He was a poet who constantly disputed the borderland between life and death, and his most-celebrated poem, **"The Ballad of the Mari Lwyd"**, relates an attempt by the dead, at midnight on New Year's Eve, to enter the house of the living and share their feast. . . . [Watkins reworked this theme in] **"The Ballad of the Outer Dark"**. There is a gap of twenty years between the two poems; the later ballad—it is really a compressed verse drama—was broadcast in the year he died.

The return to an earlier success should have been disastrous, but it succeeds brilliantly. There is the same hammering, full-blooded rhythm, the same dignified but simple and natural vocabulary and word-order. . . . It is not a sequel to the **"Mari Lwyd"**, still less a revision; it is analogous, rather, to a variation on a theme in music. The folk-custom on which the poems are based—the New Year practice, in Wales, of bearing a horse's skull from house to house and engaging in a rhyming contest in order to gain right of entry and hospitality—is so perfectly and concretely a symbol for Watkins's obsession with the antinomies of life and death, body and spirit, "dying the other's life, living the other's death"—that there seems no reason why he could not have written as many variations as Bach did for Goldberg. He was in the grip of his daimon. Too often in Watkins, an ornate superstructure disguises a vacuum; the poems are so well-wrought that the life is lost or never found, like a child's skeleton in the foundations of a bridge. Yeats may have had an intuition of this when he emphasized to his awestruck visitor in 1938 . . . that nonchalance and luck are essential qualities in a poem. "The young poets toil too much." Vernon Watkins toiled too often to make a poem that wasn't there. But the horse's skull of the **"Mari Lwyd"** custom *was* there, and kept grinning at him. It was his necessary poem. . . . [W. B. Yeats's] disastrous influence on Watkins is all too apparent. *The Influences,* a Yeatsian masque begun in 1935 and finished, as a script for radio, in 1947, is almost wholly pastiche. Here indeed was too much toil, on a work that had no chance of coming to life. Allegorical figures, an Old Man ("blear-eyed wisdom") and a Girl ("O body swayed to music"), never find any plain, dramatic reason why they are talking to each other. The Girl introduces herself with a lyric, to music, which starts, "Plato is dead these ages / And Aristotle's learned school. . . .". Not surprisingly she fails to quicken one's pulse.

I That Was Born In Wales is a slim, pleasant selection. As the editors intend, it will be a useful book for introducing new readers to Watkins. The poems are thematically grouped, and although the chosen themes look naively uneasy at first sight—Wales, Poetry and the Poet, Dylan Thomas, Life and Death—in practice they work quite well. The sections, and the individual poems, throw light upon each other, and there are brief, helpful notes. The introduction points out that it is not intended to be a representative selection; it does not, for example, include any of his ballads; but the poems have been taken from among those the editors consider his best. Their judgment is good, and their book duplicates very little of the work included in the . . . *Selected Poems* of 1967.

More valuable, because more surprising, is [*Vernon Watkins: Selected Verse Translations*]. . . . Watkins, a modern languages scholar, made nearly 200 translations of European poems. Apart from his versions of Heine, they have not, until now, been gathered together. It is a rich harvest. He admirably reconciles the two impossible, contradictory aims of the translator: to serve the foreign poet faithfully and modestly, and at the same time . . . "to create an English equivalent which reads like an original poem".

His practice lives up to his theory. The versions unmistakably remain poems by Ronsard, or Rimbaud, yet with the freshness of originals in English. In fact, they often seem more original than many of his own poems. The *joie de vivre* of the French Renaissance poets, and the harsh, electric style of the Symbolists, release his own style from abstraction and artifice. The problems of reconciling metre with meaning created more lively rhythms than he usually allowed himself in his own verse, and the vocabulary takes on more of the "nonchalance" that Yeats advocated.

> *D. M. Thomas, "The Odour of Death," in* The Times Literary Supplement, *No. 3944, October 28, 1977, p. 1272.*

BEN HOWARD

[For Vernon Watkins] the "past" is not *materia* or "raw stuff" but a fount of inspiration. "What is fresh must also be ancient", Vernon Watkins insisted. "What I owe I owe to the Past." And yet the central theme of the [*I That Was Born in Wales*]—a posthumous selection thematically arranged—is not the importance of the past but the transcendence of the temporal order: the redemption of time in the lyric moment. The editors make no claim that their selection, which excludes among other things Watkins's ballads, is representative of the poet's work. Their intention is rather to provide a selection of poems "which not only form a unity in themselves, but . . . throw light on one another." They have divided the poems into four categories—"Wales, Poetry and the Poet, Dylan Thomas," and "Life and Death"—whose rubrics might suggest thematic diversity, but in fact the themes are remarkably convergent. Even the eulogies of Dylan Thomas tie in closely, since Thomas (who was Watkins's closest friend) was for Watkins the archetype of the lyric poet. And for Watkins it was the lyric poet—symbolized as the curlew, the heron, the fountain where "Ages are linked by water in the sunlight"—who made "all transience seem an illusion / Through inward acts, acts corresponding to music''. In lyric intensity Watkins found the inner peace for which he yearned, the song of ''Harmonious joy with stillness at the core''.

Not everyone will be enchanted by the old-fashioned lyricism of Watkins's own poems. ''I cannot see'', writes the poet in an accompanying statement, ''how any poet whose roots are deep can be influenced by a living contemporary''—a telling comment from a poet whose work seldom reflects twentieth-century idioms, pressures, and dislocations. The fact is that Watkins was rather heavily influenced, if not by contemporaries than by the English lyric tradition; and when he declares that his ''strength is from the sepulchre / Where time is overthrown'', one thinks less of an Anglo-Saxon burial mound than of Westminster Abbey. Echoes abound, notably those of Shakespeare (''Has the brook ears?'') and the late Yeats (''But he has fixed his golden eyes / On water's crooked tablet, / On light's reflected word''). When the English tradition makes its appearance in less specific ways, it is in the form of Victorian and Romantic conventions—inversions, ''poetic'' diction—which are often fatally distracting. To paraphrase Oscar Wilde, one would have to have a heart of stone not to be made tired by such lines as ''Here, where the earth is green, where heaven is true / Opening the windows, touched with earliest dawn . . .''

Nevertheless, one can understand T. S. Eliot's admiration for Watkins's verse. Watkins believed that poetry is ''more closely related to music than to prose'', and his lilting cadences are sometimes compelling. . . . And amid so much that is softly mellifluous, one also finds complex syntax, muscularity, and strict compression. A gentle romantic, possessed of infinite patience and what Heidegger has called ''openness to the mystery'', Watkins also projects integrity, tenacity, and, in his best moments, a tough-minded resolution. . . . (pp. 294-95)

> *Ben Howard, ''British Wells,'' in* Poetry, *Vol. CXXXI, No. 5, February, 1978, pp. 292-305.*

KATHLEEN RAINE

Vernon Watkins was a fine scholar in both ancient and modern languages; but it was from inherited tradition he took his deepest themes. The first poem by him that I remember is **''The Ballad of the Mari Lwyd''**, in which the restless, life-hungry dead seek through their *mari* to barter their wisdom for human food. In 1941 this wonderful poem may have seemed a spellbinding adaptation of a folk-lore theme asking for a 'suspension of disbelief'. Now we can see that it was—though nearer than any other of his poems to the popular idiom of those bearers of the beribboned skull—a first indication of what was to be Vernon Watkins's exploration of that 'deep but dazzling darkness' which surrounds and sustains daily consciousness. The dead are not imaginary, they are imagination itself. Paradoxically (or so it might seem to the naïve realist) this holy unholy mystery is the warp upon which Vernon Watkins weaves his woof of evanescent joy. Light and shadow, leaf and wing, flowing water and mossy stone, bird and butterfly weave and unweave their pattern, which is a perpetual celebration:

> All I love, all I have,
> Green one, from the grave you give.

All is flowing, and the poet who has learned the dreaded secret of the unity of life and death does not seek to stay the flux. I find in Vernon Watkins's nature-poetry the same evanescent delicate sense at once of form and of transience in which David

Jones's water-colours celebrate the Welsh Persephone, Blodeuwydd, *Flora Dea*, who is also queen of the underworld.

''The Ballad of the Outer Dark'' is **''The Ballad of the Mari Lwyd''** re-conceived and re-written to say all the mature poet had learned from the age-old Welsh traditional custom. Vernon Watkins is seldom personal in his writing, and would doubtless have held the Bardic view that those poets write best who 'confine themselves gladly to some inherited subject-matter known to a whole people'. In such a case does the poet choose the theme, or the theme the poet? Our separate selves belong to the day; the mind of the night interpenetrates, and of the inspirers we know only that they are 'other'. The voice of the poet is least of all his own.

Wales gave Vernon Watkins myth and landscape; but he is also one of the last poets to write the English language of the educated and the cultured. He makes no concessions to a demotic revolution. He belongs to past and to future, transmitting words he inherited without diminution of meaning and value. He is perhaps a national, but not a popular poet; certainly a great poet. Some great poetry—I think of Vaughan and of Herbert, Welshmen also—is never popular yet remains because there will always be those attuned to its music and its meaning.

Technically Vernon Watkins was a master of the craft of verse, untouched by the fashion for 'words taken over from science or the newspapers'—to quote Yeats again. As one among other techniques of verse-writing he admired Lawrence's and Lorca's use of 'free verse' but seldom himself used it. Generous and open to the work of other poets, he followed undeflected his own genius. It seems that rhythm, whether of music, dance or verse, is the natural expression of the soul, but not of the daily reasoning mind. At one time poets not drawing upon the deeper source would produce mechanical imitations of those natural patternings to produce 'the puppet on ambition's wire', as Watkins (unsparing towards the false) wrote. (pp. 11-12)

But it remains true that the lyric gift is the signature of inspiration. Yeats found few good lyrics among the poets of the 'thirties; but, like Dylan Thomas, Vernon Watkins was a 'singer born'. His gift seems spontaneous, yet he had perfected it by the study and practice of the Greek lyric metres (which he uses more beautifully than any modern poet) and also of the English verse-forms. The Welsh patterning of both vowel and consonant in rhyme and assonance is found to perfection in (for example) **''Secrecy''**; yet never does the poet's labour obtrude itself, all seems as effortless and spontaneous as Menuhin's playing of viola or violin. (p. 13)

> *Kathleen Raine, in an introduction to* The Ballad of the Outer Dark and Other Poems *by Vernon Watkins, edited by Ruth Pryor, Enitharmon Press, 1979, pp. 9-13.*

LAWRENCE SAIL

Unity of the Stream, a new and well produced selection of Vernon Watkins's poems, spanning more than thirty years' work, contains fifty-one poems, most of them taken from *The Lady with the Unicorn* and *Cypress and Acacia*. . . . Watkins's voice is always distinctive—measured, prayerful, intent on weighing the transient against the eternal. This is very much the work of a man who was in the world, yet not of it: and if he is sometimes mannered, especially in the earlier work, and if his own faith seems too bland for the times in which he lived, nonetheless these poems are superbly and lovingly crafted, enacting the defeat of death which was one of the poet's obsessive themes. It is good, too, to be reminded of how finely Vernon Watkins wrote about the sea—'Ocean, kindler of us, mover and mother,' as he put it in one poem.

*Lawrence Sail, in a review of "Unity of the Stream,"
in* Stand Magazine, *Vol. 21, No. 1, (1979-80), p.
79.*

JEREMY HOOKER

There should be a Collected Vernon Watkins, but in my view the first need is for a good Selection which will be kept in print. **Unity of the Stream,** despite having two striking misprints in one poem and half a page of the Notes devoted to a poem which is inexplicably absent from the book itself, is the best to have appeared so far. Its chief virtues are that it includes among its fifty-one poems three outstanding sequences whose individual poems its brings together in one book for the first time: the Taliesin poems, the **"Music of Colours"** poems, and the Platonic replica poems, and omits, for the most part, examples of Watkins's weaker poems: the formal exercises in which he gave the theory but not the practice of vision or the poet's role, his sub-Yeats poems and those most touched by New Apocalypse excesses. The choice of poems has been made by the poet's widow, Gwen Watkins, and one of his best critics, Roland Mathias. **The Ballad of the Outer Dark and Other Poems** is a new selection of unpublished and uncollected poems, also chosen by Gwen Watkins, from the large number left by her husband at his death. Although there are several poems in it which I doubt whether the poet himself would have included in a book, it is still a valuable addition to the work already collected, and its long title poem, which develops the theme first treated in **Ballad of the Mari Lwyd,** is among Watkins's finest achievements. This is magnificently dramatic both as a poem for voices and as a metaphysical dialogue between the Living and the Dead.

"A Dry Prophet", Watkins's poem inspired by the character of R. S. Thomas and included in **The Ballad of the Outer Dark and Other Poems,** may be taken, in part, as his tribute to his poetic antithesis:

> Say of this man
> He was sure in his affection
> For the things he loved,
> But did not commit his tongue to praise.
> Excess of words galled

His instinct. Rather he called
Reticence a truer servant,
More likely to lead to grace.

Vernon Watkins, on the contrary, did 'commit his tongue to praise', at his best in poems combining verbal richness with density of significance, but in weaker poems with 'excess of words' that did not gall his instinct. On the other hand he too was 'sure in his affection / For the things he loved', and his poems are far more reticent about his spiritual autobiography than are R. S. Thomas's about his. They are, however, the reverse of reticent in their affirmations. He was, in fact, a praise-poet who adopted the bardic role, writing either as the Poet or as invisible maker of his poems, but rarely as his existential self, and using words rich in colour and sound, and symbolic and mythic implication. His dynamic rhythms, variety of carefully crafted forms, and mastery of cadence and echo in the long, sustained lyric further distance him from the 'dry prophet'.

The present relative unpopularity of Watkins's poetry is probably due to its opulence and difficulty, which may suggest a verbal spendthrift and mystifier instead of a true visionary. His poems can be very difficult, not only because he uses a traditional symbolism, pagan, Christian and Platonic which it is usual to describe as a lost language in the twentieth century, but because he uses it with a strong individual twist, and, in some of his earlier poems, confusedly, in struggling with contraries by which he only later progressed. Yet his symbolic language of light and darkness, trees and creatures, music, spring, river and sea can be felt to convey more than the natural magic of his Gower even when it is not fully understood. He can write with genuine rhapsodic power. . . . and a dramatic, epigrammatic, rhetorical authority that occasionally equals Blake's. . . . Natural magic with all its Arnoldian connotations seems to me the right term to use of Watkins's evocations of Gower, but by association with romantic ideas of the 'Celtic' it also suggests the isolation of this visionary poet within his actual common world. As a metaphysical poet concerned above all with community between the living and the dead, Vernon Watkins exemplifies the tragic paradox of the great poet with no community among the living except that defined by family and friends. If in spirit he belonged to Europe and to Wales, most of his spiritual contemporaries were among the dead. This, it seems, is a condition of the great modern metaphysical poet, and it is an aspect of his greatness that he makes us see it. To which it must be added that his book is open; 'the kingdom of love' it articulates can be shared. (pp. 67-9)

Jeremy Hooker, "Natural Magic," in Poetry Review, *Vol. 69, No. 4, June, 1980, pp. 67-9.*

Philip (Gordon) Wylie

1902-1971

(Also wrote under pseudonym of Leatrice Homesley) American novelist, short story writer, nonfiction writer, essayist, and scriptwriter.

A prolific writer and an outspoken voice in American literature for more than forty years, Wylie established his controversial reputation with novels of ideas and polemical nonfiction works. The collection of essays *Generation of Vipers* (1942), Wylie's best-selling indictment of American society and culture, outlines issues which he also examined in his fiction and which led to considerable critical debate: a distrust of religious, scientific, and academic authority, an adherence to the psychological theories of Sigmund Freud and Karl Jung, and Wylie's belief that humans are motivated by their own self-interests, avariciousness, and stupidity. Wylie handled these topics in a variety of literary styles, ranging from early novels of manners and science fiction to later philosophic and apocalyptic books.

Many of Wylie's early novels derive from personal experience. The son of a minister, Wylie rejected the rigid morality of Christianity and endorsed the "new morality" that favored a more relaxed attitude to sexuality. Wylie dramatized this dilemma as the generational conflict between a strict Presbyterian minister and his free-spirited daughter in his first novel, *Heavy Laden* (1928). *Babes and Sucklings* (1929), drawn partially from Wylie's troubled relationship with his first wife, questions the validity of the institution of marriage in the twentieth century. *Finnley Wren* (1934), considered by many critics to be Wylie's finest novel, features a protagonist who is married to an adulterous woman and who is charged in a paternity suit—circumstances based on actual incidents in Wylie's life. *Finnley Wren* experiments with narrative and displays Wylie's command of satire and social commentary.

Finnley Wren was followed by a series of novels intended by Wylie to reveal the shortcomings of the "new morality." These novels, as well as foreshadowing the topics discussed in *Generation of Vipers,* assert the necessity of moderating sexual freedom. *As They Reveled* (1936) involves the unsophisticated responses of jealousy, divorce, and separation that occur when a single woman disrupts the patterns of casual infidelity among four "modern" couples. *Too Much of Everything* (1936) chronicles the plight of family members who reexamine their values after losing their fortune in the 1929 stock market crash. *An April Afternoon* (1938) challenges the openmindedness of a family whose mother abandons them to live with her lover.

Many of Wylie's works are informed by his controversial studies of American society, culture, psychology, and morals. In *Generation of Vipers,* a vicious, often humorously exaggerated attack on revered American institutions, Wylie isolates flaws in the American system of beliefs that encourages capital gain in favor of self-knowledge. Many of the ideas and concepts expressed in *Generation of Vipers* are based on Wylie's interpretations of the works of Freud and Jung. The book achieved considerable notoriety for its vehement attacks on American womanhood, for which Wylie applied the term "mom." "Momism" refers to the social pandering of women, whose reproductive role renders them helpless and bitter. Like many

of the female characters in his novels, "moms" manipulate their husbands by withholding sex for material gain and granting sex as material reward. Men, on the other hand, compound this difficulty by their unquestioning worship of the female. *An Essay on Morals* (1947) is a more detailed examination of the assertions of Jung and Freud and concerns the sublimation of human instincts, primarily sexual urges. According to Wylie, sexual demystification could forestall the disintegration of the nation, the family, and the individual. Many readers found these essays difficult to comprehend, and critics accused Wylie of misinterpreting Jung, although Jung himself expressed admiration for the work. In *The Magic Animal* (1968), Wylie turns from psychology to the natural sciences, insisting that the sole basis for all moral judgment is whether humans may continue to populate and nurture the planet. These concerns are the focus of Wylie's prophetic novels of nuclear apocalypse and ecological disaster.

Many of the theories Wylie propounded in *Generation of Vipers* are also expressed in the novel *Night unto Night* (1944). The protagonists of this work, who serve as spokespersons for many of Wylie's beliefs, are forced to confront real and metaphysical aspects of mortality. *Opus 21* (1941), echoing the theories promulgated in *An Essay on Morals,* details a weekend in the life of the novel's protagonist, a writer well-versed in Jungian theory named Philip Wylie. While awaiting the biopsy results of a growth removed from his throat, Wylie encounters, assists, and converses with a variety of characters. Like *Night unto Night,* the characters are given ample opportunity to expound upon crucial elements of Wylie's personal philosophy. Both novels feature extended passages independent of the main narratives, a device Wylie first employed in *Finnley Wren* and which he used extensively in his speculative fiction.

Several of Wylie's early novels rely upon science fiction motifs and reflect his understanding of scientific concepts and his reading of the novels of Edgar Rice Burroughs and H. G. Wells. *Gladiator* (1931), considered by many critics to be the original inspiration for the character of Superman, concerns an ordinary man coping with his extraordinary physical strength. *The Murderer Invisible* (1931), borrowing its premise from Wells's *The Invisible Man,* explores the darker side of human nature, as a scientist uses his power of invisibility to tyrannize the world. *When Worlds Collide* (1932), a collaboration with Edwin Balmer, employs Wylie's characteristic scientific veracity and highly charged narrative style. A sequel, *After Worlds Collide* (1934), another collaboration with Balmer, was less highly regarded.

Later in his career, Wylie turned to science fiction to examine contemporary issues. To offset the label of misogynist applied to him after *Generation of Vipers,* Wylie wrote *The Disappearance* (1951), a novel in which he divides the world into two separate realities—one without women, the other without men—to demonstrate the interdependence of the sexes. The need for men to rely on their intuitive capacities and the negative effects of male dominance upon women are two of the novel's main themes. Wylie's novels about nuclear holocaust, *Tomorrow!* (1954), *The Answer* (1956), and *Triumph* (1963), are characterized by gruesome depictions of atomic battles. The environmental concerns raised in *The Magic Animal* are also expressed in Wylie's last two novels, *Los Angeles, A.D. 2017* (1971) and *The End of the Dream* (1972).

(See also *Contemporary Authors,* Vols. 21-22, Vols. 33-36, rev. ed. [obituary]; *Contemporary Authors Permanent Series,* Vol. 2; and *Dictionary of Literary Biography,* Vol. 9.)

THE NEW YORK TIMES BOOK REVIEW

[*Heavy Laden*] is a spectacular first novel. Bursting with vitality it sputters and thunders by turns, telling the story of a vigorous minister of the gospel and his headstrong daughter through the medium of a style which is such a welter of impressionism, bombast, excellent writing and sensationalism at all costs as can hardly be contained between book covers.

Hugh MacGreggor is the dominate. A forceful, red-headed man, he first makes himself the dominant figure in an Ohio town, goes through two marriages and one war, and then proceeds to become the dominant figure in ''Glendale, the wealthiest suburb in America''—hypothecated in citerieur New Jersey. Then his daughter Ann goes native among the post-modern-generationists, and her run eclipses his wane. . . . (p. 6)

Now, that looks like a harmless little fable, but wait till you see the lurid colors Mr. Wylie dresses it in. He goes about the writing of prose in a manner reminiscent of the vaudeville man who plays an entire orchestra single-handed. The result is entertaining, in all but those passages in which he takes himself too seriously, or pretends that there is something radically new

about some of his methods. Then one must remind him of his masters and predecessors. For instance, he stops the story now and then to give the reader a direct lecture in the first person. Well, Henry Fielding was doing that when the novel was young; it's still a good trick, but hardly new. Then, after heroic effort, he digs up one or two of the proscribed words and phrases which might be considered rather daring things to mention— if *Tristram Shandy* had not been written so many years ago. But it's all done with such a fine gusto that one wants to cheer rather than chasten this self-conscious sowing of literary wild oats. . . .

A great deal is touched upon, but little is gone into thoroughly. The best part, perhaps, from the reader's point of view, is the first half of the book and the casual humor. The war scenes are chiefly notable for their echoes of other writers. The exhaustive analysis of the modern clergyman is simply a magazine article. The views on sex have a little news value by way of distinction. All the talk bearing on the current younger generation's earth-shaking views on life and how to live it sound strayed out of a college novel. These remarks do not, however, alter the fundamental fact that Mr. Wylie apparently had the time of his life writing the book and that no reader will find it dull. (p. 14)

"An Ohio Clergyman," in The New York Times Book Review, *April 1, 1928, pp. 6, 14.*

ROBERT MacDOUGALL

Of every hundred readers who come across **Heavy Laden,** ninety will cry, ''Obscene! Disgusting! Suppress it!''; the other ten will understand Mr. Wylie and bless his wisdom. For this first novel by Mr. Wylie . . . is an uncompromising statement of the case for the Younger Generation, that rowdy band of disquieting independents. It is not impossible that **Heavy Laden** may interpret, explain, show cause, and even perhaps persuade; it is the novel of all that have recently appeared that should be the manifesto of this Younger Generation, its answer to its critics. Yet I am sure that Mr. Wylie and his writing will be condemned by those who should be tolerant and sympathetic; I am sure that the novel will be widely misunderstood. And the fault will be not entirely the readers', for Mr. Wylie is bitter and he is brutal—seldom urbane or respectable.

But perhaps I am in danger of treating **Heavy Laden** too solemnly. Let me say, therefore, that in demonstrable essence it is a lusty story after (and in some particulars, beyond) the most strenuous modern models. Although in no real way similar to *Elmer Gantry,* it slaughters a man of God, and many of its moments are Lewis-ian in their mocking photography. Furthermore, there are definite resemblances to the Ben Hecht of *Erik Dorn* and *Gargoyles.* But after all, Mr. Wylie smashes his way through an excellent narrative in a manner that is fundamentally his own. (p. 945)

Throughout his novel, Mr. Wylie gives us chapter after chapter of excellent narrative: we know no more thoroughly admirable treatment of the War than his account of Hugh McGreggor's days in France with the Y.M.C.A.; Ann's few sad months in college and her drunken brawls in New York are written with high sincerity and truth; and, very differently, the description of the flood in the Middle Western town shows mastery of a more conventional sort of writing. **Heavy Laden** is a memorable novel, therefore, entirely aside from its sensationalism or its propaganda.

Heavy Laden probably never can be put in free circulation by public libraries; it will disgust all those who have a definite notion of what is decent in a novel and what should not be mentioned. As likely as not it will do more harm than good— simply because it will be so often misunderstood. But to those who do see what Mr. Wylie is driving at, who by experience and by temperament can sympathize with him, the novel will be a notable success. No one can deny its occasional brilliance; no one can be lukewarm in his attitude. (pp. 945-46)

> Robert MacDougall, *"A Lusty Story,"* in The Saturday Review of Literature, *Vol. IV, No. 46, June 9, 1928, pp. 945-46.*

THE NEW YORK TIMES BOOK REVIEW

Mr. Wylie's first novel [*Heavy Laden*], which appeared with a good deal of accompanying condemnation from the conservatives last year, was essentially a bombastic piece of work, intended to startle. Strong, even narrative was broken into by such tirades on the part of the author as indicated first, an animosity that amounted to contempt for the reader, and second, the desire to attract by a display of that animosity.

In *Babes and Sucklings* a good deal of the bombast has simmered down to more orderly turbulence. As far as the subject matter of his tirades is concerned, Mr. Wylie has learned no better manners in the last year, but he has at least reconciled his animosities to a consistent literary style. Where the author himself stepped out of a page to shake his fist at the reader in the first book, in this one the characters manage to say for him what Mr. Wylie has to say. To be sure there sometimes seems little reason for their saying it, but at least this method is the less distressing.

In back of the fireworks, *Babes and Sucklings* tells, as did *Heavy Laden,* a good story. This too is the story of young moderns. In *Heavy Laden* we had the conflict between the older generation and the younger; between the old morality and the new. In *Babes and Sucklings* the conflict is purely individual, and in that way the book is not as big a one as its predecessor, for it lacks that touch of the universal that made the other strike home to all of its readers. . . .

Naturally, with people who think more than they say, and contemplate more than they accomplish, conversations and actions cannot bring out the full flavor of their characters; so the author is forced to choose between presenting them as their friends see and talk about them and as he sees them. Here he does a little of both, but a good deal more of the latter, with the result that there are long passages of nothing but character analysis. It is consistent analysis, sympathetic and revealing, but it smacks too much of a case history chart to be fully artistic.

The result, however, which may justify the means, is a thorough acquaintance with the people who inhabit the book. Though their pasts are obscure, their futures are left pretty certain in the minds of the readers, and their presents are at all times vivid.

> *"Complex People," in* The New York Times Book Review, *April 14, 1929, p. 6.*

THE SATURDAY REVIEW OF LITERATURE

The author of *Heavy Laden* lives up to the title of his first novel in [*Babes and Sucklings*], one of those Manhattan cocktail things, compacted of synthetic sin and orange-juice. He actually succeeds in making vice as boring as virtue, and combines all the familiar features of the rising-young-writer story with all the dreary preachments of Sigmund Freud and Lucy Stone.

The tale deals with a rather unspecified young man named Thornton and a blonde divorcée from California named Cynthia who live "beautifully" in free love and eventually become reconciled to each other in spite of it. Around these, against a background of advertising offices, writing, studios and gin-parties, writhe a frieze of bankers, writers, artists, "sugar daddies," and "teasers" all of them afreud of life, and all of them unutterably dreary.

On second thought it is not quite fair to *Babes and Sucklings* to dismiss it as only a dull book. One has the feeling that the author felt under tremendous urgency to get it all off his chest, at the cost of jerky construction, banal plot, and prolonged preachments. He has aimed to show that people can fall in love, even when they are not married, so long as they Face Life Honestly. Perhaps in his next book he may make concessions to the fact that life is a little bigger than the people who live it and that living it, rather than facing it, honestly or otherwise, is a human drama.

> *A review of "Babes and Sucklings," in* The Saturday Review of Literature, *Vol. V, No. 39, April 20, 1929, p. 935.*

THE SATURDAY REVIEW OF LITERATURE

[*Gladiator*] is the third novel by Mr. Wylie to be published. The earlier two, *Heavy Laden* and *Babes and Sucklings,* showed a vivid, undisciplined talent, a talent that suggested the possibility of high excellence in the future. But *Gladiator* shows neither development nor growth; it is the novel of a writer who, though obviously gifted, lacks literary common sense. That is, Mr. Wylie does not know what is practicable and what is impracticable in the writing of a novel.

The whole trouble is this: *Gladiator* is written around too good an idea. It does not, as a piece of sustained narrative, attain the slightest effectiveness; indeed, it is almost an affliction to the reader looking for entertainment. And the reason for this failure to tell a good story is that Mr. Wylie starts merrily out on the development of an idea that by its very brilliance can never be properly finished; his premises admit of no logical conclusion. *Gladiator* is satisfactorily startling in its first third, but after that Mr. Wylie no longer controls his narrative; it runs away with him—downhill. The protagonist of *Gladiator,* by means of a fantastic pre-natal treatment, is far stronger and more nearly invulnerable than the average human being. He can lift tons, jump scores of feet, run at an extraordinary speed. As we might anticipate, his great prowess brings him only unhappiness; he asks merely, "What can I do to justify my power? How can I be useful?" His life is a series of disasters, spiritual and physical.

It is probable that no author . . . could resolve such a dilemma satisfactorily. Really, it is far from a discredit to Mr. Wylie that the novel turned sour on his hands. He was to blame, however, in his injudicious attempt to make a novel of the "strong man" notion in the first place. He ought to have seen that the idea was too good to be usable.

A review of "Gladiator," in The Saturday Review of Literature, Vol. VI, No. 39, April 19, 1930, p. 971.

THE NEW YORK TIMES BOOK REVIEW

Though its main idea is rather preposterous, this romantic tale [*The Savage Gentleman*] soon captures one's interest and steadily tightens its grip as the well-wrought and ingenious action progresses to a close. The father of the hero is a distraught multi-millionaire who, in 1898, deserted by his faithless wife, embarks in his steam yacht with only his infant son, a Scots engineer and a Negro servant upon a voyage which ends when he deliberately drives the ship aground upon an uncharted island in the Indian Ocean. Marooned there, the three men and the child, completely cut off from all communication with the rest of the world, spend the ensuing thirty years, while Henry, the son, meticulously reared and educated by his misanthropic father, grows to stalwart, if somewhat naïve, maturity. After his father's death, leaving Henry the missing heir to an immense fortune consisting of a chain of American newspapers, the young man and his two aging companions are salvaged and transported to New York. Henry at first finds the complexities of civilization, and especially of womankind, a dire problem for his keen but unsophisticated intelligence, in the solving of which, we are glad to report, he performs no miracles. How he battles his way to mastery of a singularly difficult and sinister situation provides the climax of a story which develops far more sensibly than the somewhat steep earlier stages portend.

"Castaway's Return," in The New York Times Book Review, November 20, 1932, p. 19.

WILLIAM ROSE BENÉT

Despite his publishers' annoying jacket blurb, which positively yells at you what they wish you to think about the book, and immediately stiffens your backbone against it, I found myself launched upon young Philip Wylie's latest opus [*Finnley Wren*] with the feeling that "here might be something." But how could they confuse him with Sterne and Rabelais? . . .

[Mr. Wylie] can write. There is no doubt about that. After he gets through his sophomore year in letters, he may quite possibly do a novel "as is" a novel. All the nonsense-pornography of this volume and all the Thorne Smithing—the kind of thing provincial New Yorkers think is sophistication, the kind of thing the ex-speakeasy boobs fall for in wide swaths—all that kind of thing is shown to be the trash it is beside the simple account of Finnley's first affair at the beginning of the book, and the positively remarkable account of the forest fire at Rangadam. . . . Those episodes are really worth reading.

Rabelais, my Aunt Ermintrude's anti-macassar! Rabelais would roar himself hoarse at the information that all this fiddle-faddle about copulation and all this wish-fulfilment writing had anything to do with his abbey or his ilk. Finnley Wren is disillusioned, cynical—all the sawdust has come out of all his rag dolls. In his big moment, consequently, "he yelled at the top of his mighty voice and threw himself at my feet and began to kick and bite the earth and to beat it with his fists." This is just after he has told with horrible unction of his wife's having been burned to death. Oh, that's Rabelais for you. Gosh, how like that is to Laurence Sterne!

Physical love is a perfectly clean thing. Does the point still need laboring? Apparently. Promiscuity won't work. The proof is all about one in a big city like New York. But these matters crowd into the foreground of a book that might have got somewhere, and it is all in some weird way blamed on the Gargantuan creator of Pantagruel.

Undoubtedly I have been somewhat unfair to Mr. Wylie, which is because I recognize how well he can write when he wants to. As to what he regards as his clever writing, his "notions" and "literary misdemeanors," his monkeyshines and quiddities, they are all very well for awhile. But that's all. Just because you have one gigantic word (like "so" in quotes) printed alone on a page, you are not Laurence Sterne. Really, you're not.

As for Mr. Wylie's criticism of modern civilization, most of it is entirely valid. He is doing his own thinking. I hope he writes a perfectly swell, completely integrated book for his next one. This isn't it. But I believe he can do it.

William Rose Benét, "Brilliant in Spots," in The Saturday Review of Literature, Vol. X, No. 39, April 14, 1934, p. 631.

THE NEW YORK TIMES BOOK REVIEW

"A book in the spirit of Sterne and Rabelais," say the publishers, and indeed [*Finnley Wren*] is a Tristram Shandy and an Abbaye de Thélème easily identifiable despite sea changes, modern dress and airy allusions to the latest scientific theories—a Tristram become an executive in a New York advertising agency, a Thélème in Connecticut.

Yet with equal truth they might have declared that it was in the spirit of Aldous Huxley, Gertrude Stein, Christopher Morley, Lewellyn Powys and several other contemporaries, for the narrative manner constantly changes—one is ever pursuing new scent, familiar like the last but of a different fox. The title page gives a foretaste of the stylistic range: *Finnley Wren: His Notions and Opinions together with a Haphazard History of His Career and Amours in these Moody Years, as well as sundry Rhymes, Fables, Diatribes and Literary Misdemeanors. A Novel in a New Manner.*

Scorning the fiction convention of a depersonalized author-narrator, this author tells how he, Philip Wylie, first met Finnley Wren in a speakeasy one Friday afternoon, and how the barroom chance acquaintance (evidently under some strong emotional compulsion) commenced to tell the story of his life. . . .

Viewed in the large, the tale is one of Rabelaisian humor, though it contains, too, episodes that are tragic, gruesome and sometimes revolting. Not a book for tender-minded readers, but Hemingway addicts will find it flavored to their taste.

"More Mad Moderns," in The New York Times Book Review, April 15, 1934, p. 7.

T. S. MATTHEWS

Finnley Wren fulfills none of the grandiose claims made for it. It is as much in the spirit of Sterne and Rabelais (what a combination!) as this review is in the spirit of Carlyle and Cervantes. It obviously was not written purely for amusement; its "new manner" strongly resembles an old notebook. As for its "humanity, whim, brilliance, roaring humor, volcanic horror," etc., they are all chimerical—semaphored with sophomoric violence, but with the signals mixed. The hero, Finnley Wren, is a New York advertising man who passes in these pages for an original, a desperate liver and a bold thinker, a fine flower of intelligent and lusty manhood. The whole thing is undergraduate and—in Dashiell Hammett language—screwy, but there are enough bedroom-and-bar scenes to keep the reader going.

Mr. Wylie has for some years knocked violently at the door of Literature, but it has not opened to him. That is certainly no crime. But when he allows a publisher's legerdemain (which does sometimes fool part of the audience) to give the illusion that he is another Aladdin, then he is compounding a felony. To give him his due, Mr. Wylie is himself under no illusions about what kind of book he has written. The last words on the blurb—which give a fillip of cynical honesty to the whole farrago—are his: "But since I felt so certain that all writing nowadays is myopic twaddle, I had no hesitation in writing some twaddle of my own." If Mr. Wylie really feels that way about modern fiction, what the devil is he doing in that galley?

> T. S. Matthews, "Rackety Jackets," in The New Republic, Vol. LXXIX, No. 1016, May 23, 1934, pp. 51-2.

VINCENT McHUGH

Rewriting The Country Wife, Mr. Wylie's new novel [As They Reveled] takes his eight youngish married people and a girl to Wycherley, Conn., fifty miles out of New York on the Sound, and there sets out to crossbreed them with the experimental intentness of Thomas Hunt Morgan poring over his drosophila flies. "Sweet love," says Mr. Wylie. "Modern, civilized, biochemical, endocrinological, adept, expert, unemotional, functional, promiscuous, unbigoted and unenlightened love."

The last adjective, at least, is not ironic. These mild amateur Dillingers of the emotions, worldly as they supposed themselves to be, had never comprehended that first precept which enjoins that if light loves, like killings, must be multiple, they ought at least to be widely scattered. The Wycherleyans played in each other's backyards. They began to take in each other's wives, like washing, and everyone complained about the laundry. The result was a very complicated and embittered hi-de-ho, with divorces flowing like water.

Out of it, and the series of compound cohabitations which led up to it, Mr. Wylie has arranged a skittery and fertile comedy, full of the chop-logic of ironic situation, moody and gay by turns, with a respectable depth to its conclusion. . . .

Mr. Wylie's first book, **Heavy-Laden**, was plainly a job of talent, charged with certain durable qualities inherent in its theme: Calvinism and the revolt from Calvinism. His subsequent novels, with the exception of **Gladiator**, moved more and more in the direction of a circus-tinsel virtuosity which threatened to make him a kind of Tiffany Thayer for sophisticates. This tendency—a whirl of scene-changes, tricky phrasing, shock-writing, determined ribaldry, a knife-juggler's byplay with manners and ideas—was apparent even in the best passages of **Finnley Wren**. But it was clear, too, that this legerdemain was not merely or entirely Hechtian. The evidences of genuine feeling and talent remained.

In **As They Reveled**, the more ambiguous effects of **Finnley Wren** have been omitted or brought under the dominant tone of satiric comedy. It is in many respects a better novel. The first half or so sets out to be not much more than superior

popular writing, but it gains in gravity and depth. The end passages have a good deal of vehemence, humor, pathos and essential truth to the subject. They retain interest and enlarge it, despite a certain amount of stringing out after the climactic party. Of Mr. Wylie's characters, shrewdly but partially vivified, one has the sense that a deeper knowledge of their beginnings would be more revealing than any estimate of their fluctuant present.

> Vincent McHugh, "Summer Love in Connecticut," in New York Herald Tribune Books, March 8, 1936, p. 8.

THE NEW YORK TIMES BOOK REVIEW

"The vagaries of love are greater than the vagaries of any other human occupation," says Philip Wylie. And this is the reason that romances of all varieties, light and heavy, continue to sell well and offer endless entertainment. Philip Wylie has elected to write about the vagaries of love on the Connecticut shore of the Sound [in As They Reveled]. He has produced a smartly sophisticated, entertaining story, not lacking in humor and sound sense. It hasn't the sparkle or the body or the rich variety of his **Finnley Wren**. But it is a book that readers who enjoyed **Finnley Wren** will find satisfactory in its own right.

The characters are the sort of people one associates with a smart suburban community. The men are in advertising, selling, Wall Street. The women go in for sports, bridge, clothes, and one of them has ideas about social uplift. There are four young married couples who pride themselves on holding very modern views. This modernity is expressed almost exclusively in the business of flirting and philandering with each other's wives and husbands and in drinking to what used to be known as excess. (p. 19)

The problem of temporarily trading partners is more nerve-racking than the usual modern game, because this shore colony is geographically limited. The four couples live in four comfortable houses on four plots which formerly made up one large estate. They share a common swimming pool and are inevitably thrown together a great deal—too much, in fact. The arrival of a pretty Southern visitor, a predatory and unscrupulous belle, upsets the balance of the group, sets all their nerves on edge. For the visiting Claudette is an out-and-out terror. All the easily accepted precepts of letting love wander where it listeth receive a rude shock when Claudette puts them into practice. Cool and sophisticated tolerance flies out the window when the Southern belle comes in the door.

Mr. Wylie's story brightly weighs the relative merits of married love and extramarital amours. Occasionally he throws in a brief and sagacious sermon. Mostly he sticks to the carryings-on of one Connecticut Summer. Of his nine not very pleasant people, one man and one girl are outstandingly likeable. They manage to survive the nightmarish Summer but—surprise!—not in each other's arms. And not one of the four couples renews the lease on its Connecticut house.

The Wylie style is, as usual, bright, light and smart. The Wylie humor is equally apt at wisecracking and at popping up in unexpected places. The book is good entertainment, more realistic than satirical in its suburban picture. (pp. 19, 22)

> B. S., "Suburban Worldlings," in The New York Times Book Review, March 8, 1936, pp. 19, 22.

FLORENCE HAXTON BRITTEN

Philip Wylie has written—perhaps a little belatedly, in view of the novel's extremely superficial qualities—a story set in the months immediately following the October, 1929, Wall Street crash. In *Too Much of Everything* Mr. Wylie gathers fictionally, but in considerable realistic detail, for one brash, underbred, nouveau riche family, the Bentlans, the kind of material which R. C. Angell has recently compiled in his research into a wider social scene, *The Family Encounters the Depression*.

The Bentlans are, in October, 1929, breathlessly engaged in the various pursuits appropriate to their several ages: father, absorbed in money-making: mother in social-climbing: Daphne, eldest daughter of these two, in sleeping about pretty recklessly with boys in her own set. Her engagement has not been announced, nor is likely to be. Jim, a brother about her own age, is busily engaged in parallel pursuits suitable to his sex. . . .

Then along came the depression, a blessing in disguise for all the foundering Bentlans. Each of them Mr. Wylie now takes and remakes in terms of a new and self-respecting life. Daphne goes to work behind the remnant counter of a cheap department store, attempts suicide when her depression-shot boy friend forsakes her for a rich, older woman, and comes to herself at last through the revaluation that tragedy and the nice young surgeon provide her. Jim goes to sea and gets beaten by the first mate and a storm into manhood. And so on, et cetera, through the rest of the adults and adolescents of the Bentlan menage. Until happy days are here again—happier days by far than they could ever had known had it not been for the shock of poverty and a changed way of life.

Too Much of Everything is written with a combination of daring and naive seriousness that is most disconcerting. Every fifty pages or so Mr. Wylie builds up some new situation calculated to startle attention. In fact the whole undertaking reminds me of nothing so much as a small boy firing off a whole boxful of Cather wheels one after another in broad daylight on July 3.

Mr. Wylie, novelist, is to me a puzzling phenomenon. He has an observant eye and a rather unusual amount of literary energy and skill. His difficulty, in such opuses as *Too Much of Everything,* seems to be a vast unwillingness to let his obviously capable brain discover what his facile typewriter is doing.

> *Florence Haxton Britten, in a review of "Too Much of Everything," in* New York Herald Tribune Books, *August 23, 1936, p. 10.*

BEATRICE SHERMAN

The reformation of a parvenu family, due to the wholesome effects of losing their money in the depression, is the Pollyanna theme of [*Too Much of Everything*]. . . . In spite of its happy moral lesson, the book's atmosphere is gloomy. The emphasis is all on the problems, frustrations and tribulations of the individual Bentlans. It is only when each finally decides to turn over his own new leaf that sunshine breaks through the clouds.

The Bentlans in 1929 are an ill-assorted, cornery family who make no effort to understand one another. Rich and unhappy, they batten on the dollars that Bentlan piles up for them in Wall Street. . . .

The October crash knocks the props from under this wabbling family. With keen discernment and shrewd understanding, Mr.

Wylie sketches the family reactions, from Bentlan down to Junior. . . .

The story, engagingly written, is entertaining but not very original. It has its humorous and its tragic moments, leaning rather heavily to the sensational for its dramatic effects. The Bentlans' troubles and turmoil are more convincing than the Bentlans' reform, which smacks slightly of good resolutions due to a bad hangover.

> *Beatrice Sherman, "Fiction in Lighter Vein," in* The New York Times Book Review, *August 23, 1936, p. 18.*

HARRISON SMITH

For a long time Philip Wylie has disapproved, violently and caustically, of this generation of Western civilization and especially of American habits and thoughts and pretenses. Since his first philosophical novel, *Finnley Wren,* ten years ago, and that bitter tirade, *Generation of Vipers,* his wrath has not lessened; it has become only more convincing and more eloquent. But his new work, *Night Unto Night,* is far more than a sermon and a philosophical quest into the meaning of life and death; it is a novel in which his characters live and move, and in which there is action and suspense and inner conflict. That his novel was planned to illustrate his idea that we are an irresponsible and childish nation hiding from reality, that the men and women in it talk more effervescently and at greater length than the people in any other book I can remember, does not alter the fact that it is constantly stimulating and entertaining. He has conceived of a dramatic situation and of the protagonists to give it life. There isn't much more a novelist can do, except to conform to the rules of the game, which Mr. Wylie throws out of the window.

In his preface . . . the author starts, one would think, with two strikes against his book. "Here is a novel about death," he writes in his first sentence and adds, as if he had suddenly remembered that it really was a novel he had started, "that is, about the living and their thoughts about death." He goes on to say that in our increasingly materialistic world we attempt to overshadow and forget our approaching doom (death) by the absorption of our senses with everything that can serve to stave off introspection, "for a moment, an hour, a lifetime. . . ." If that were true of all of us he would find precious few readers. As a matter of fact, he will find a great many, and they will not all be readers who are vitally concerned with Mr. Wylie's ideas about death or with the follies of American civilization today. They will be concerned and moved by the story of Ann Gracey whose young husband dies at sea, not far from her gloomy home on a lonely beach south of Miami, and who returns to haunt her. And they will be stirred by the dilemma of John Galen, a professor and a biochemist who flees from Chicago to Florida to find solitude and the time to think of the appalling discovery he has made about himself, that he is an epileptic who may be cured or who may die in a year or two, a slobbering maniac.

Ann certainly heard young Bill Gracey's voice and is forced to believe that though his body has disintegrated in the sea he has somehow returned to tell her that "it is here," though what it is she does not know until later. So she has to think about death in an unconventional manner, as a present and living fact. Her younger sister, Gail, beautiful and so consciously streamlined that her constant drinking and lovemaking leave her apparently untouched, has secretly to ponder the same engima, because she does not know whether or not she was responsible for the death of her husband and baby by monoxide poisoning some years before. All of them are facing what Mr. Wylie calls "terrifying uncertainties."

But the men, rather than the women, are the sounding boards of Mr. Wylie's theories; John, who has rented and has gone to live in Ann's haunted house; a psychiatrist who flies to Miami to be with his friend after his first ghastly epileptic seizure, and a stalwart and successful commercial artist whose pet aversion is science and the scientist, and who must be one of the most prodigious non-stop talkers in American literature. Shawn Mullcup is fat, bald, has two children and a lovely wife. . . . He is a gargantuan creature, bursting with vitality, kindliness, and vituperation, and the author handles him with a master hand, for, however fantastic he may seem at first glance, he is certainly alive and three-dimensional. He adds the necessary lighter touch to a novel that Mr. Wylie designed to be deadly serious. . . .

[The essential purpose of the novel], I gather, is the author's desire to convince the reader that he is on his way to hell, along with the rest of the American people. Not the hell of the revivalist preacher, but the hell of the generations of suffering that we must undergo as a people because we have become slack, because we refuse to think, or to take life and our own sins seriously, because we have become the servants of the machines we have created, and so, until we awaken, we must live through a long series of future wars and catastrophies. He has the zeal of a missionary with not one, but twenty, sermons to preach. (p. 9)

[Is *Night Unto Night*] a successful novel from the standpoint of a critic of literature? I doubt it, but I do not believe for a moment that Mr. Wylie expected, or wanted it to be so. But he has, I believe, achieved his purpose. He has created a group of characters whom the reader will not forget in a hurry, and has placed them in the midst of a situation as daring as the thought behind it. He has been able to exercise his remarkable talents and his brilliant gift for writing volcanic prose, and he will not leave many of his readers untouched. If some of them refuse to take life more seriously, or to consider death as anything but a depressing subject to take to bed at night with them, they will at least have had a startling experience and will have been subjected to dynamic ideas, whether they like them or not, that may never have entered their heads before. Some day when Mr. Wylie has stopped railing at humanity for so many of its errors and sins of omission and commission, all in one volume, he may sit down and write a novel that will knock everyone out of their seats. (p. 20)

> Harrison Smith, "'Such Stuff as Dreams Are Made On'," in The Saturday Review of Literature, Vol. XXVII, No. 39, September 23, 1944, pp. 9-10, 20.

THOMAS SUGRUE

Some eighteen months ago Philip Wylie, hitherto listed in the geography of American literature as a pleasant, fertile plain, erupted like Mexico's Paricutin, showering lava and hot ashes on the consciousness of his readers. The crater was called *Generation of Vipers,* and the dust from its explosive birth still reddens the sun for those who entered its atmosphere. Now a vent, fictional in form, has appeared in its side, and a second molten flow has begun. It is less spectacular than the initial outburst, but just as hot and even more purposeful, since the primary job of a volcano is metamorphosis, with destruction

second and pyrotechnics a poor third. A mind caught in the path of *Night Unto Night,* then, will receive the same pelting and scalding it suffered from *Generation of Vipers,* but it will also be given the benefit of hope, and the sight, seen mistily through steam and fire, of a new world coming to birth.

"Night unto night sheweth knowledge," says the psalmist, and knowledge is the preoccupation of the new Wylie characters—knowledge of death, and wonder about its meanings, its implications, its conditions of form, its mental patterns. They are not mystics, not medievalists, not Hindus, but Americans—scientists, artists, business men, pretty girls. They operate within the framework of slick fiction; they inhabit Miami and Miami Beach. They drink and dance and swim and eat as does most of middle-class America. They worry about the war (it is 1942); they worry about America's future; they fret about morals, Fascism, materalism, post-war economics, politics.

But something else bothers them, haunts them, claws at their spirit. Out of their studies of bio-chemistry, psychology, metaphysics, esthetics, nuclear physics, love, sex, longing, there has come a certainty, a realization, a knowledge: life, the seeming reality, is a barrier against actual existence, a certain shutting off the truth with five very small peepholes and a rudimentary machine for computing what can be ascertained through these sense apertures. Death holds the promise, not of extinction, but of an astronomically expanded awareness and a transcendent art. Faced by this result from his own empirical experiments, the scientist feels he must do something; led to this thesis by his reason, the psychiatrist knows he must act; likewise the painter, the widow, the tart. . . .

They drift together, John, Ann, Gail, Shawn, in the hot summer of southern Florida. It is an apt setting—the naked eye can see nature at her work of evolution in the mangrove swamps and in the warm, swarming sea. In the old Gracey house on the dunes and in Shawn's studio, amid the voices of ghosts, the roaring of a hurricane, the spiraling growth of human love; speaking now in the jargon of psychiatry, now in the symbology of higher mathematics, now in the satirical pomposity of Menckenian scorn, the characters work at their problem. It is exciting, interesting, sometimes amusing, to observe how they are able to see, from the frontiers of modern science, precisely what mystics from time immemorial have sighted from the minarets of meditation. Except for a difference in vocabulary and symbols, some of the conversations might have taken place between St. John of the Cross and Teresa of Avila. One paragraph, purported to be from a book by a man named Gaunt (Gaunt is Wylie in didactic form) is a condensation in scientific prose of the fifth chapter of St. Matthew.

What is the result of all this? In his preface the author says, "This is a . . . religious book—even when it attacks organized religion." That is true: religion is the heart of the story. The characters, John and Shawn in particular, reach the conclusion that, however rudimentary may be science's present understanding of life and death, enough has been proved to make sure that the fundamental principles of mystical exercise and religious dogma rationally belong to man's way of being. They recognize that morality, labor, knowledge and prayer (with them a kind of brooding or yearning) are proper instruments for man in the attempt to liberate his consciousness from its present level and expand it toward total reality.

All this is not new, either in fiction or in life, but Mr. Wylie has put the notion in a way which makes it fresh, provocative, and understandable to the average reader. By putting the story in a pattern of conventional romantic fiction he has brought a new audience to the subject and brought the subject to a level where it is intelligible to the audience. All but psychology buffs will stumble over some of the mumbo-jumbo terms, but the general idea is hard to miss, and it is one that will be hard to forget—that out of the test tubes of laboratories and the consulting rooms of healers of neuroses has come, miraculously, the Sermon on the Mount.

> *Thomas Sugrue, "Rediscovering First Principles,"*
> *in* New York Herald Tribune Weekly Book Review,
> *September 24, 1944, p. 4.*

RICHARD MATCH

I don't know whether G.P.U. agents ever poisoned Philip Wylie's drinking water, or whether an itinerant chemistry professor got Mr. Wylie's sister Georgianna with child, or even whether he ever spent an awful week end in New York waiting for the biopsy report on a cancerous-looking growth in his throat. Chances are none of those things ever befell the "real" Philip Wylie, the author of *Generation of Vipers, An Essay on Morals,* and other books, who has no sister named Georgianna. But all of them, and many more too outrageous for any one but Mr. Wylie to mention, very definitely did happen to a fictional character named Philip Wylie, who is the hero and central figure of Author Wylie's new novel, *Opus 21....*

[In *Opus 21*] prostitution is a socially desirable, a thoroughly commendable endeavor (besides being a lot of fun), while homosexual love is recognized and applauded for what Kinsey says it is: a normal sex activity of human beings and other animals. ("I have published such data in my books, years before Kinsey," Wylie adds.) In *Opus 21* Mr. Wylie continues to kick over cherished mental bric-a-brac with an abandon born of long and deadly practice. Who will be surprised when, along with the junk, he topples a couple of pieces by which most of us—even those who would go much of the way with Wylie's house cleaning—still set quite a store? I refer to Reason and Faith, which Wylie would supplant with Instinct.

Somewhere in *Opus 21* Philip Wylie says, "I've come to understand a good deal by searching for blunder, by hunting for the sense of what brighter guys have learned." If *Generation of Vipers* was his merciless catalogue of blunders searched out, of soul-sicknesses diagnosed, this new book may be regarded as the "constructive" sequel: the Cure—one character calls it "Dr. Wylie's elixir for the self-righteous." And as he freely admits, his prescription is borrowed from a "brighter guy." Wylie's acknowledged master is Jung, the psychologist who rescued instinct from the Freudians.

"To Freud," Wylie explains, "the id"—i.e., instinct—"was pretty much what sin is to a preacher. A disgraceful bunch of bestial lusts and impulses." To Wylie, by way of Jung, instinct is "all good," and it is only by honestly recognizing and encouraging the instinctual, the animal, nature of man that we can safely steer between the Scylla and the Charybdis of this tormented century: the two Reports, Kinsey and Smythe. As a corollary, of course, we must recognize that "the sexual behavior of people is mammalian in every respect." Faith and reason must be sent packing, because both try to "elevate" man above the joyous animal he wants to be.

This business of repressing instinct is an old, old error. It's been going on, Mr. Wylie grants, since the Stone Age, a matter of perhaps forty thousand years now.... But when it comes to demolishing folly, Philip Wylie is no respecter of age. In a series of remorselessly quotable, if rather unilateral, "dialogues"... he trots out all his resources of vocabulary, erudition, wit, ribaldry, charm, contumely, tirade, invective, sophistry, word play, personal philosophy, and hygienic common sense, and takes arms, Wylie-nilly, against a sea of ignorance. It is a brilliant forensic exercise, but whatever "action" there is in this story must fit itself between lengthy conversations. Read consecutively, they may be conducive to mental indigestion.

There are all sorts of possible reactions to pure Wylie, depending largely on the reader's own premises and ranging outward in complexity from the simplest of all: an apoplectic stroke. This book will elicit the whole outlandish gamut. It may not be a good "novel" in any sense in which the term has previously been used: it is superlative Wylie.

> *Richard Match, "Dr. Philip Wylie's Elixir," in* New
> York Herald Tribune Weekly Book Review, *May 22,*
> *1949, p. 6.*

DIANA TRILLING

Because Philip Wylie describes his new volume, *Opus 21* ... as a novel, it has come to this department for comment. Actually, however, there would seem to be little fiction about it. The author speaks in the first person and in his own name and describes a few days in his recent life—a trip to New York to consult his physician about a possible throat cancer, an involved encounter with a girl he picks up in a bar, a trying experience with a young nephew who has got himself engaged to a prostitute. Upon this slight narrative skeleton he hangs discussions of politics, art, science, love, psychiatry, sexual morality, and so on which are, of course, the reason he wrote the book. Not having read any of Mr. Wylie's previous work, I do not know if this is his usual method, but I admit myself drawn to the unorthodox form he has contrived for himself.

I also admit a rather disarmed affection for the author of *Opus 21.* When one deals with so personal a performance—in the course of his book Mr. Wylie tells us not only what he thinks on all the topics of our times but also what he likes to eat and drink, what he enjoys and what he fears, how he feels about his wife and daughter, how much money he earns and how much insurance he has accumulated—it is impossible not to be personal oneself. Mr. Wylie has an abundant curiosity and energy; but he is not a very disciplined person. His egocentricity is embarrassing, his lapses of taste too numerous to specify. But he is so aware of his own excesses that for the reviewer to call attention to them is to labor the obvious, to punish for mistakes already confessed. I feel the impulse to protect Mr. Wylie as one wants to protect a small boy who simply cannot help misbehaving.

On the other hand, Mr. Wylie is assuming the role of an educator in morality. He boasts a large public influence, and he may indeed be reaching a wide and susceptible audience with his opinions. He must therefore be held to some intellectual and moral account, especially for his sexual ideas, which are the ones that will be most interesting to the general reader. Mr. Wylie speaks in his own person, but he also claims the authority of Freud and Jung. Still alive, Jung can of course refuse his spokesman if he chooses. It is the reviewer's responsibility to make the disclaimer for Freud: enough nonsense is already ascribed to Freud without some of Mr. Wylie's strange notions being laid at his door too.

I refer particularly to Mr. Wylie's mad prescription for the sexual health of the young woman he picks up in a bar. The girl is reading Kinsey: she has recently discovered her husband in a homosexual partnership and is trying to find enlightenment on this woeful marital problem. Mr. Wylie talks to the girl at great length, learns that she has herself been frigid in her marriage, and promptly diagnoses her trouble: it is her own sexual repressiveness that sent her husband to a male companion and that accounts for her dismay at his present behavior. But Mr. Wylie not only diagnoses, he cures: he introduces the girl to a prostitute, with whom he encourages her in a Lesbian relationship. The girl experiences her first sexual fulfilment; she becomes transformed. Accepting her own bi-sexuality, she is now able to accept her husband's bi-sexuality as well. She returns home with the author's happy assurances that all her matrimonial difficulties have been solved; she and her husband will now achieve a fine sexual union.

This reconstruction of a marriage is only about half of the "plot" of Mr. Wylie's novel, but obviously it will be the whole lesson the casual reader will draw from the book. It is not only foolish talk, and a complete perversion of Freudian practice, but very dangerous stuff to bandy about. . . .

And it is a great shame that it is particularly in the sexual sphere that Mr. Wylie goes so wrong, because he has a basic perception about the sexual source of our ills which one must be glad to help him propagandize. Mr. Wylie understands what few better-disciplined moralists are willing to acknowledge— the extent to which a faulty attitude toward man's biological nature creates the horrors of modern society. . . . But surely the general public will need more discrimination than it is yet equipped with to be able to take Mr. Wylie's sexual premise without the faulty construction he builds upon it. Either the one will be thrown out with the other or the one accepted as an inevitable development of the other—and it is hard to say which outcome is the less desirable.

Diana Trilling, in a review of "Opus 21," in The Nation, *Vol. 168, No. 24, June 11, 1949, p. 668.*

JOHN J. MALONEY

Philip Wylie, as just about every one must know by now, is one of God's angrier men. In a series of novels and essays he has zealously hacked away at some of our most cherished superstitions leaving behind him a broad trail of shattered idols. As an idol smasher Mr. Wylie is no slouch—perhaps the best we have had since Mencken—although he is inclined to use the scatter-shot technique rather than the single telling bullet accurately aimed.

Having tried just about every method short of the rubber hose in his endeavor to make a benighted populace see the light, Mr. Wylie, in [*The Disappearance*], has resorted to popular fantasy. William Percival Gaunt, one of America's outstanding philosophers, is in his study preparing a lecture. He looks out of the window and sees his wife, Paula, watering a gardenia bush in the garden. When he glances up again, she is gone. Paula Gaunt looks up from the garden and sees her husband at work in his study. As she watches he disappears. Man has disappeared from woman's world and woman has vanished from man's. Thus does the author begin what is, at the very least, a formidable technical exercise. Purely as craftsman, Mr. Wylie is equal to every occasion. Back and forth he leaps nimbly from male to distaff showing us in a series of contrapuntal chapters, first Gaunt's womanless world, then Paula's

world without men. In both cases the effects of the fantastic occurrence are pretty harrowing, since Mr. Wylie has exploited just about every possibility that could arise from his rather spectacular idea. We are treated to a long series of holocausts, including an atomic war with Russia, a famine, a cholera epidemic, and a great many others only slightly less dire, before the happy denouement is finally reached.

It is all, on the surface level at least, the sort of highly exciting stuff of which good popular fiction is made. Consequently, in view of the rigors of this highly specialized mètier, it is a much tamer Wylie that we encounter in his role of society's gad fly. To be sure he takes time out now and then to belabor his particular *bêtes noires* (sex taboos, organized religion, objective science) but these interlardings are fewer and farther between and they have lost much of their old zing. As a matter of fact, if it were not for an occasional half-hearted jeremiad and a twenty-page essay embodying Mr. Wylie's central hypothesis, *The Disappearance* would be merely a good and exciting fantasy, a kind of *Mr. Adam* in dead earnest.

Obviously, as old Wylie adepts will have surmised by now, he intends much more than this. Man and woman, he says, were meant to be one, and yet they have become separate. This schism occurred when man, in order to feed his insatiable ego, made himself superior to woman, and, by so doing, split himself in two. Woman became a slave and sex became secret and shameful. Modern woman is in a worse plight than even her chattel ancestors. Given all the outward symbols of freedom, she is still hemmed in by the same old fears, phobias and taboos. Hence there is no pattern to her life, she is spiritually dead. What Mr. Wylie does in his novel, of course, is to make this separation an actual physical fact, and then, after four long years of chaos and disintegration, he brings man and woman back together again, chastened and presumably wiser.

Now whether or not you agree with this thesis, you must, I think, admit that it is provocative. The trouble is that Mr. Wylie has cheapened it, not only by his usual leather-lunged, chest thumping assertions that he, and he alone, is right, but by wrapping it up in a rather gaudy swatch of entertainment. Taken purely as a piece of fantasy-fiction, *The Disappearance* would hold its own quite well with the best in the field. Taken as a novel of ideas, it falls considerably short of the mark. . . .

In a way I find it quite painful to have to report unfavorably on a Wylie book, since I have, more often than not, found myself in sympathy with what he was trying to say, although I have never been able to concede that his ideas were as shocking and profound as he seemed to think they were. Mr. Wylie is a fair-to-middling thinker, and, when he wants to be, a topflight entertainer. If I am to have him as a thinker, I prefer to take him straight in slambang essays like *A Generation of Vipers*. If I am to have him as entertainer, I will gladly settle for Des and Crunch. When he attempts to mix them both into a frothy brew like *The Disappearance,* then it is not my drink.

John J. Maloney, "Sex-Segregated Worlds: A Swatch of Gaudy Fantasy," in New York Herald Tribune Book Review, *January 14, 1951, p. 4.*

HARRISON SMITH

Philip Wylie has been scolding and entertaining the public ever since his *Generation of Vipers* began to sell all over America eight years and six novels ago. Whether you look at Mr. Wylie as a novelist, a prophet, or a propagandist of his own ideas on science, love, education, psychoanalysis, women, and almost everything else that he thinks is wrong with America, he has succeeded through various startling books in bringing his theories before a wider and more popular audience than any present-day philosopher or educator can command. His *Opus 21* of last year was in many ways an outrageous and yet a highly amusing performance, in which the writer cast too obvious a shadow over his sexually maladjusted characters. His latest, *The Disappearance,* is the most successful of his attempts to drag his readers by the thousands into his theatre to watch a pyrotechnical show and then to give them the now familiar Wylie treatment.

He has proved long ago that he can turn to fantasy of the science-fiction variety with the greatest of ease, a middle-aged man on his own flying trapeze, now swinging up into the sky, now suddenly plummeting to earth. *The Disappearance* is quite certainly the most brilliant of his improvisations. In the hands of almost any other writer his plot would be monstrous, clumsy, and even ludicrous. The reader is asked to believe that at four o'clock in the afternoon of the second Tuesday in February all the women, girls, and babies in the world disappear from the sight of all the males, and that at the same split second of time no male human beings of any shape or form can be discovered by any female on earth. . . .

This conception would be hard to swallow even by the most hardened of fantasy fans if Mr. Wylie was not so ingeniously or diabolically persuasive. His persuasiveness is obviously the result of his ability to create characters, as could the late H. G. Wells, in whom the reader can almost believe. (p. 10)

This awesome device enables Mr. Wylie to dramatize with obvious gusto what would happen to human beings and to civilization in these two separate worlds—one in which there were no females and the other totally bereft of males. The reader is thus presented with two parallel novels, both of them an outragcous attack on his common sense. It is difficult to decide in which one Mr. Wylie finds the most pleasure . . . since the author's voice can clearly be heard in all of his philosopher's lengthy comments on the idiocy with which the human race has conducted its practical, metaphysical, and amorous affairs through the ages. Mobs of men slaughter each other, an atomic war with Russia breaks out, homosexuality is rampant, and there are fires and explosions wherever women have disappeared from the kitchen stove. Nevertheless, some kind of order and flow of gas, electricity, and goods is maintained because men are the lords of the machine.

[The] women have an even rougher time. They have the ability to organize eventually, to establish shaky and somewhat silly governing bodies, but they cannot dig coal, replace oil and gasoline, run complicated machines, or find enough food. And of course like their tortured husbands they cannot find a satisfactory substitute for normal sex.

Long before the book is over the reader wonders how in the name of reason Mr. Wylie is going to end this four-year debauch in two sexless worlds. Dr. Gaunt's theories about the nature of this disturbance on our planet are many and long though rarely tiresome. . . . His essay on the philosophy of sex, which gets the world nowhere since it cannot restore a single female to her mate, is worth reading because it presents the basic ideas about which Mr. Wylie has been shouting for so long. There is a great deal of common sense and truth in it, and surely no other novelist would dare to ask his reader to plunge into a twenty-four page argument of this nature. . . .

Fortunately, Mr. Wylie resolves their difficulties and unites his males and females again, freed at last from the superstitions, taboos, and insane ideas that have forced God to take a hand in ameliorating human suffering and perversity.

But just how this is accomplished the reader should be left to discover. At any rate *The Disappearance* is a book that will stimulate, shock, and perhaps illuminate some of the darker corners of human behavior and thought—unless the reader is already convinced that Mr. Wylie has never known what he has been talking about for the last ten years. (p. 11)

Harrison Smith, "Four P.M.—No Sex," in The Saturday Review of Literature, *Vol. XXXIV, No. 3, January 20, 1951, pp. 10-11.*

AL HINE

In his seriously directed works of fiction or semi-fiction Philip Wylie has often combined the righteous wrath of an evangelical puritan with the antics of a side-show barker, the glib sonority of an advanced amateur in analytical psychology with the glamour trimmings of a gossip columnist. In *Tomorrow,* a tract in the form of a novel, he sticks closer to the narrative framework of an action and suspense story on the theme of atomic (and hydrogen) Armageddon. There are tart paragraphs of the familiar Wylie in which he impales, deftly and deservedly, such phenomena of our age as bad advertising, radio comics and their cretin audiences, and so on; but the story is the thing.

The story is of two American cities living side by side and of their reaction to the threat of atomic attack and finally of their reaction to actual atomic attack. Wylie has a sometimes surprising gift for uncovering the ordinary confusions of decent people especially when, as in the case of Civil Defense, their confusions are worse confounded by apathy and more confusion among the men they look to for leadership. It would be a different reader who would not be caught up, perhaps in spite of himself, in the politics and chicanery of River City and Green Prairie, in the swift movement and brutal detail of the last half of the book. For Wylie makes his atomic disaster terrifyingly real and true and close and possible without ever sounding the unconvincingly shrill and nervous note of the perennially jittery alarmist.

It is amazing that the book *is* so real, a tribute certainly to the intensity and feeling with which it is written, for it is, as noted, not a novel in any literary sense, but sheer tract with all the flaws of a tract. As in those old remembered tomes about coffee, tobacco, or booze, the characters are one-dimensional, and all that is evil happens to the flouters of the author's code, while the virtuous folk flourish (in atomic terms only comparatively) like the green bay tree. Young and old alike of the families who scorn Civil Defense are blasted (as young and old alike suffered the curse of caffeine, tobacco, or whiskey), and all the good folk who serve CD survive pretty well unmaimed to build a brave new world. But these are critical afterthoughts perhaps a trifle unfair to a book which kept me up far into the night. Its very faults of haste and evangelism lend it some of its strength, and its message of sane, non-chauvinistic preparedness is one which cannot be ignored. (pp. 15-16)

Al Hine, "Hiroshima, Connecticut," in The Saturday Review, *New York, Vol. XXXVII, No. 3, January 16, 1954, pp. 15-16.*

VAL PETERSON

Because of his past writings, Philip Wylie has long occupied a unique place as tireless goader of civic consciences in positions high and low. In that frame of reference, his shocking new book [*Tomorrow!*] must be ranked among his best. The story of an atomic attack on two neighboring American cities, it is penned not only in vitriol but in blood—a writing fluid more commonly used by the science fiction and murder mystery purveyors than by ranking novelists.

Mr. Wylie's many deaths, while outnumbering even those of the indefatigable Mickey Spillane, are not in the least mysterious. And his science, unhappily, is far from being fiction. It is, instead, an authentic reflection of what President Eisenhower called, in his speech before the General Assembly of the United Nations, the "new language" of atomic warfare. (p. 4)

Either of Mr. Wylie's two cities might be your city today— Green Prairie, where the Civil Defense has always been a model of its kind (and the measures taken after the holocaust, from geiger-men to fire-fighters, are truly inspiring); River City, where an it-can't-happen-here psychology has its own ghastly aftermaths. The uncomfortable sense of familiarity attaches itself throughout to both characters and settings and contributes in large part to the book's stunning impact on the American reader. And that's as it should be, since *Tomorrow!* seeks first of all to arouse the literate and thoughtful citizens of these United States to the age of peril in which we live.

Mr. Wylie foresees failure in our attempts to reach honorable and peaceful atomic agreement with the men of the Kremlin. I hope he is wrong about that. With much of the rest of his novel I must agree, however reluctantly. (pp. 4-5)

> Val Peterson, "They Said It Would Never Happen . . . ," *in* The New York Times Book Review, *January 17, 1954, pp. 4-5.*

EDMUND FULLER

It has pleased the fancy of Philip Wylie in *The Answer* . . . to describe the explosion of an American H-bomb (dropped from a plane, as in the current series of tests) which results in the death of an angel. The celestial being flutters down to a crash landing on an atoll, before the eyes of an astonished missionary's son, and expires. Word of this occurrence spreads with nearly the speed of light, confounds the high command, and precipitates a Cabinet crisis. To paraphrase an old wartime saying, there are no atheists left on the atolls. Pretty much the same thing happens to the Russians when they set off H-bombs in Siberia. It wouldn't be fair to give you the message the angel is delivering, but I must confess that as far as I was concerned I found it an appalling anti-climax.

Wylie is going soft. He has recanted on Momism recently and now it's angels yet. It's brutal to carp about the structure of a fable, but this one is painfully weak within its premises, sweetness and light notwithstanding. The greatest question is just why Mr. Wylie's angels should be rushing so urgently, at just such times and just such places, to deliver a message which is to be found already delivered in the Gospels, minus the gimmicks and the saccharine, and which although tragically ignored most certainly has been neither lost nor forgotten. (pp. 50-1)

> Edmund Fuller, in "Message from Above," *in* The Saturday Review, *New York, Vol. XXXIX, No. 24, June 16, 1956, pp. 50-1.*

NEW YORK HERALD TRIBUNE BOOK REVIEW

[*The Answer*] in essence is a parable or fable. On an island in the Pacific, American military specialists and observers dropped an H-bomb to test its power and efficiency. In Siberia, at the same time, the Russians were conducting a similar experiment. In each instance the project was successful but in each case there was a casualty which could not be explained in terms of realism or science. One must read *The Answer* to savor its message which is rooted in denunciation of human destruction by warfare. . . . An able storyteller, Mr. Wylie makes his plea for peace in incident and language geared to today's life—and death.

> "Atomic Fable," *in* New York Herald Tribune Book Review, *August 5, 1956, p. 7.*

WILLIAM B. HILL, S.J.

[*Triumph*] is a scare-book, calculated to make people think about the consequences of a thermonuclear war and, presumably, to make them do something to prevent it. The book is well done, graphic, crisp, readable, exciting. Its value is, however, chiefly that of a thriller; it comes complete with a melodramatic rescue of the few Americans who survive. Perhaps no more horrifying description of our country's destruction has yet been concocted by any prophetic novelist; yet the Robinson Crusoe security of the survivors does much to soften the horror of what goes on outside the shelter. By a perusal of this book, some people might be frightened into an attitude of submission to Russian threats but it is questionable how many will be won over to constructive action for peace.

The hero of *Triumph* is Ben Bernman, a physicist. He is visiting the palatial home of Vance Farr—sometime in the 1970's, apparently—when the warnings sound and he is rushed into a most elaborate shelter buried deep in a hill of limestone, each adit carefully protected by a series of doors. The fourteen people who finally reach the shelter are a mixed lot, including Mr. and Mrs. Farr, their daughter, Farr's mistress, a Chinese and a Negro girl—both very beautiful—and a Japanese employee who helped construct the place. The supplies are ample: oxygen fed through an ingenious system, electricity, water, powerful radios for sending and receiving, television equipment, food, games, even a hobby shop. . . .

Mr. Wylie has gone out of his way to frighten people. He wants us to believe that the Soviet Union might be willing to sacrifice itself, China, and our northern hemisphere in order to insure Russian Communist control of what would be left— a wild surmise that slips by in the rapid movement of the novel. He says that there will be no survivors except those who are in secret spots on the ocean or in deep shelters such as that built by Vance Farr, shelters that would cost about ten million dollars per person saved. If Mr. Wylie succeeds in making anyone more anxious to work for peace, good for him; but he may defeat his own purpose. Life in the shelter is so cozy as to be attractive, and the destruction outside is so horrible that it is incredible. . . . Whatever its initial intent, this is primarily a book for those who like a good yarn and are not afraid of some violent shudders. It should be added that though Philip Wylie has been criticized in the past for coarseness he has gone out of his way to preserve decency of dialogue and incident in this novel; I suggest its restriction to adults only because of the nature of the sexual relationships involved, not because of the way they are described.

> *William B. Hill, S.J., in a review of "Triumph," in* Best Sellers, *Vol. 22, No. 22, February 15, 1963, p. 429.*

ROBERT DONALD SPECTOR

On the huge stockpile of literature about "The Bomb," Philip Wylie has tossed a small firecracker. His new novel [*Triumph*], not his first contribution to this genre, sputters and fusses, but fails to explode. Whatever is stirring about the virtual annihilation of Wylie's generations of vipers and mother-worshipers comes less from what he has written than our own fear of his awesome subject.

To be sure, he has managed an incredible amount of technical detail in his story of fourteen American survivors of an atomic holocaust, but he has done it at the expense of credibility and readability. . . .

Wylie's conveniently chosen characters—an atomic physicist, male and female mathematicians, and even a gigolo whose talents as a miner develop when needed—have time to concentrate on their personal romances, to straighten out their confused lives, and to demonstrate the truisms of Wylie's interminable sermons. When he is not too busy with his scientific explanations, Wylie preaches the laudable doctrine of the brotherhood of man, for which purpose he has included Chinese, Japanese, Negro, and white; Jew, Christian, and agnostic, a veritable League of Nations, as his characters remind us.

And yet for all of its weaknesses, *Triumph* has moments of real terror. Despite its clumsy prose, there is the reality of the extinction of the entire Northern hemispheres. . . .

[*Triumph*] seems no more realistic than most of Wylie's novels, but truth and fantasy may prove after all to be one in today's world.

> *Robert Donald Spector, "Everything Explodes Here Except the Story," in* Books, *April 21, 1963, p. 5.*

ARNO KARLEN

Philip Wylie is narrator and protagonist of his latest book [*They Both Were Naked*]. Except for his wife, a disclaimer warns, the other characters are invented. The result is a curious arraying of autobiography, fiction and essay, often a glaring contrast, telling about the real Wylie's fictional adventures among the big guns of science and business, their immense establishments, occasional virtue, frequent corruption and deranged private lives. Throughout, he exhibits his old virtues: satiric wit; steamroller indignation; a sharp eye for the disguises of emotional and intellectual fraud. He delivers deeply-felt asides on anything, you name it—scientific specialization, childhood sexuality, conservation, the right-wing mentality, democracy, love, alcohol, retirement, genius.

And as always, his faults are striking. The book is much too long, from the landing of planes and ordering of meals to descriptions of people and their feelings. Of hybrid genre, it lacks the elegant economy of first-rate reporting and the fire of fictional imagination. The verbosity and jarring diction are compounded of many things: journalese and phrase-making;

unlovely neologisms; muscular verbs and adjectives; italic reinforcements and proofs by repetition. Rhetorical questions lead to one-line paragraphs running down the page like a Beethoven coda, but ending on a shrug. ("That was it? Or was it? It might be!") The dialogue is often the ersatz language of ersatz people, such as you hear from hearty ministers and scoutmasters. Or perhaps it is just Wylie, the writing voice of the Midwest decades ago.

Wylie attacks his usual enemies—cities, churches, business, amoral science, cultural lag, castrating women. But it is an older, mellower Wylie, his tendentious harangue softened to stern, avuncular monologue. He becomes chatty, Tells All with long self-examination on his writing and financial problems, with domestic gossip and family jokes. This intimate garrulity creates a confessional tone, which is heightened by continual, shuffling demurral. It is as though his angry lectures have finally begun to embarass him, and he keeps assuring you that he, too, is guilty of all he damns. He does it with convincing humility, but to a point that begins to embarass the reader, too.

Wylie's voice has always been that of the village atheist seeking a secular faith, trying to shock, inform and change his neighbors. He is less a novelist or thinker than an educator, an impassioned pamphleteer—in fact, like many village atheists, a nondenominational preacher. His angers are strong and honest, and usually aimed at worthy targets. He has sound instincts and an intelligent heart. How can you help liking, even admiring, a man like that? Or help, once you've left the village, growing impatient and finally bored with him?

> *Arno Karlen, "Novelist Onstage," in* The New York Times Book Review, *December 12, 1965, p. 39.*

TRUMAN FREDERICK KEEFER

In April, 1934, appeared *Finnley Wren,* Wylie's most original and possibly greatest novel. In one sense, it is the natural successor of *Heavy Laden* and *Babes and Sucklings,* both of which had earned him a reputation as a chronicler of the lives of the young people of his generation, the first one to experience the full impact of what it meant to be liberated from the Victorian ideas about God, marriage, and social behavior in general. Both books, though causing a small furor when they appeared, seem as mild as Sinclair Lewis' *Main Street* does today—and in fact have been quietly forgotten.

But *Finnley Wren* lives on, a furious, magnificent act of creation that is no mere document of rebellious sons or young free lovers in the 1920s and early 1930s, not just a clever satire of the absurdities of the day: it is a man's outraged outcry against those things that outlast all topicality: man's ineradicable stupidity, cruelty, and selfishness; his inescapable burden of suffering, pain, loneliness, and death; and, most of all, the lack of any meaning or explanation of his tragic fate. But, though this novel is a savage and unforgiving indictment that spares nothing and no one, it is also paradoxically an affirmation of all that is infinitely precious: courage, love, honesty, self-knowledge, beauty (whether in nature or in a human heart), and the love of life that will not permit the truly alive to "go gentle into that good night." And, not incidentally, *Finnley Wren* is a dazzling and audacious display of stylistic virtuosity and of technical ingenuity, a work which both parodies the "modern" novel and employs its methods to achieve its own ends. (p. 66)

The baroque title (in eight different kinds and sizes of type, both red and black) is a fairly complete account of the story he produced: *Finnley Wren: His Notions and Opinions together with a Haphazard History of His Career and Amours in these Moody Years, as well as Sundry Rhymes, Fables, Diatribes and Literary Misdemeanors. A novel in a new manner.* Set in New York City and a country house in Connecticut, it is a first-person account by a fictional novelist named Philip Wylie of his forty-eight hour acquaintance with the title character. During this period, Wylie spends most of his time listening to Finnley telling the story of his life and enlarging on his opinions—or to other characters who give him their views of the remarkable Finnley. (pp. 68-9)

The various techniques and literary devices used by Wylie in the novel range from the functional to the merely ornamental. Point of view is the most important; basically, he uses three. The framework story is a first-person narrative, with "Wylie" as narrator. Finnley's monologues are reported by Wylie; but, since Wren sometimes talks for pages without interruption by "Wylie," the effect is of a second first-person narrative within the first-person account. The novel also has sections of third-person narrative told from the point of view of the omniscient author.

Another of Wylie's techniques is his insertion and extended quotation of various pieces of written material, most of them from Finnley's hand. These compositions reveal the hero's character as well as provide a change of pace for the reader— and all of them are delightful in themselves. In fact, Wylie may have included them more for their own sake than to characterize Wren. He would again use this kind of insertion in a number of later novels, including *Night Unto Night, The Disappearance,* and *Opus 21.*

The style of *Finnley Wren* is an awesome *tour de force,* the most extravagant display of vocabulary Wylie was ever to make. Illustrations of Finnley's varied diction are almost too easy to find. The nonstandard English includes "the brashest slang" and many of the well-known profane and obscene terms; "son of a bitch" was the most shocking one to the audience of 1934. Wren also draws upon scientific and technological terms. His formal vocabulary, a reflection of his extensive reading and awareness of beauty in language, is made up of many of the unusual "big" words with which Wylie had been ornamenting his novels for years. Here, however, they are appropriate because they are entirely consistent with the extravagant nature of the speaker. Wren is also fond of intermingling words from his different vocabularies to produce astonishing and bizarre juxtapositions.

The main aim of the novel was to give the reader a complete exposure to the personality of the title figure. To do that, Wylie drew upon the methods he had perfected in earlier books: Finnley himself tells us what he is; other characters comment on him; some of the characters in the flashbacks state their views; there are reports of the world's view of him; and "Wylie," too, draws his conclusions. We also have the opportunity of seeing Finnley's actions in various key events in his life, and he reports, apparently quite honestly, on his thoughts at these times. But vastly more important is the constant barrage on our ears of his opinions. The overall effect is the creation of an extraordinarily believable character—perhaps Wylie's best. There is no one like him in fiction, and perhaps no one in real life, except Wylie himself, who supplied Finnley with many of his own qualities and opinions. Yet every reader who has ever responded to this novel has recognized in Wren much of himself. Thus, this unique being is also, paradoxically, a perennially universal one.

We would hardly expect a "one-man show" like this novel to have well-developed or even memorable supporting characters. Nevertheless, there are four remarkable ones in *Finnley Wren:* Dr. Gordon Wren, Helen Holbein, Hope Jones, and Ricardo Jones—Hope's father. Hope and Ricardo are drawn with love and affection, but the other portraits, inspired by Wylie's raw hatred of their prototypes, are among the most despicable beings in literature. Doctor Wren is characterized by every method except his thoughts, but the savage use of his physical appearance to discredit him borders on genius. His hypocrisy is summed up by his clothes: he wears a well-cut suit over frayed underwear, a girdle, and a "moldered jockstrap." The true nature of his spiritual condition is suggested by a Swiftian catalogue of his bodily defects; and, when we are given a list of the eleven classes of germs that live on various parts of his anatomy, our feelings of revulsion toward him are insurmountable. (pp. 70-1)

Finnley Wren owes much of its notoriety to the fact that in it Wylie was able, for the first time, to speak his mind without restraint on everything that irritated him. At one point, Finnley says, "Everything's wrong—wrong—wrong. Hideously wrong. It has always been wrong. It will take thousands and thousands of years to make it right. It will take forever. And yet—it could be set right—if it weren't for the plethora of greedy fools. Nitwits. Nincompoops. How I hate people!" The indictment seems too sweeping to fit into one book, but only when we try to list the objects of satire in *Finnley Wren* do we realize fully how many targets Wylie has hit. Not only Finnley but also Estelle, a nameless sad man who appears in tears five times, and "Wylie" himself contribute to the diatribes. On one occasion, Wren reads aloud an eight-page article someone sent him—and that piece is an attack also. Of course, some subjects receive greater attention than others—these are exposed in their shortcomings by being dramatized in episodes— while others are dismissed with a mere epithet.

The following is a mere sampling of the pungent opinions that grace the novel. The principle of giving everyone a vote—both the foolish and the wise—has caused the failure of representative government. The actions of Christians expose their complete lack of any religion whatsoever, especially when tenets of their faith are criticized. So-called sex offenders are punished extravagantly for actions that are so widespread as to be correctly called normal. Newspapers are printed to make money by appealing to the lusts of a lascivious, thrill-seeking people. American businessmen dedicate their lives to inventing gadgets and then creating an artificial desire or "need" for them.

The educational system is dedicated to presenting facts without correlation or explanation, to instilling a thousand lies instead of the hard truths, to avoiding the discoveries and implications of science, and to making sex and the body a subject of shame. The chief result of the feminist movement has been to convince women that they must abandon their function as mothers and turn themselves into men in order to find freedom and happiness; men have encouraged women's latent selfishness by giving them every material comfort they want. The *New Yorker* set—like any similar group of intellectuals—has no real claim to superiority: they're "run-of-the-mill human beings." Finnley's most compelling polemic is addressed to the stupidity of the great American masses: "The melting pot has turned out to be a cesspool." He therefore proposes the passage of the "Ass-reduction Act," under which seventy-five percent of the population would be legally executed as not fit to live, not to mention reproduce.

If Wylie's views of his fellow Americans, especially of their self-righteousness, were even partially valid, then *Finnley Wren* was certain to offend a greater proportion of the population than had any other book written on this continent. In fact, during the Cold War of the 1950s, the novel, along with *Generation of Vipers,* was excluded from United States Information Agency libraries in foreign countries as too anti-American.

But whether or not we feel that Wylie is right, it is still possible to enjoy the diatribes. In the first place, the attacks are so cleverly phrased, so uninhibited in expression and vehemence, so imaginative, so Shakespearean in their uses of the resources of the language, that they compel admiration. At times, we become aware, too, that Wylie is consciously enjoying his deployment of the language, and this knowledge somehow is cathartic: his ridicule and vituperation are the actions of a strong and confident man, not a victim; and we therefore find ourselves believing, against our wills, that his words are capable of changing the world. (pp. 71-3)

The reader cannot efface from his mind [the impression] . . . that the life of every human being is in constant peril of unthinkable horrors. Wylie put into *Finnley Wren* his most unbearable scenes. They are understated and—to use Wylie's description of Finnley's own style—couched in "words so passionately compressed that they emerge small, hard and individually alive." After a forest fire sweeps a Canadian town, Finnley attempts to aid the horribly burned survivors. One woman has a face "that looked like an ill-butchered ham cooked too long, and in that red and gummy gobbet she opened a hole from which she emitted a long, agonized shriek." Another still-living being found another, more horrendous fate: "the wolves had been eating him."

The torments of the mind are not omitted. After Finnley quietly tells how his wife died in his arms, he "suddenly yelled at the top of his mighty voice and threw himself at my feet and began to kick and bite the earth and to beat it with his fists." No reader of this novel will feel safe ever afterward, for Wylie has made him share his own private nightmare: death and horror are the unavoidable and primary fact of life. . . . None of this suffering has meaning or even a pattern. Yet, because it is so universal, it provides a kind of makeshift justice: the guilty who escape punishment do so only for a time; ultimately, they will suffer enough in the ordinary course of human experience to satisfy all the longings for vengeance in the hearts of their victims. Thus, in the closing pages of the novel, Wylie with grim pleasure shows the fate of those who sinned against Finnley. Dr. Wren is aging alone; Libby is a sodden alcoholic; Helen finds her hold loosening on her current victim; his first girl friend, her beauty gone, nurses her fourth child and flounders in hideous domesticity.

Astonishingly—and perhaps necessarily in a story so full of anguish—*Finnley Wren* is one of Wylie's funniest books. Most of the humor comes from his satiric comments on whatever he dislikes. The style itself produces comedy through its self-conscious exaggerations. And, as always in Wylie, there is also plenty of slapstick, as when Finnley pursues an intruding photographer down the street and repeatedly "kicked him so hard that he was lifted clear off the ground," and when an amiable drunk "fell face forward, narrowly missing one of the Whittington cats." Such moments make both life and *Finnley Wren* bearable. (pp. 73-4)

Truman Frederick Keefer, in his Philip Wylie, *Twayne Publishers, 1977, 168 p.*

CLIFFORD P. BENDAU

No less than Superman himself, the creator of the original Superman, Philip Wylie, burst forth from the unassuming facade of mild-mannered writer to become the "superwriter" of the Forties and Fifties. Representing truth, justice, and the American way, he was the voice of America and the vociferous critic of Americana. From his earliest novels through his polemical essays to his final work, he vehemently disapproved of his generation's decline in manners and morals. Out of his fiction and nonfiction alike came a portentous warning: awaken to the follies of the modern age or prepare to meet destruction and chaos in the future. (p. 3)

Wylie became one of the most ambitious and outspoken writers of the twentieth century. Although he was not a product of the university, he felt comfortable with its most sophisticated concepts, considering his self-acquired knowledge equivalent to several doctorates. His irreverence for academic propriety was legend, as was his prolificacy. He was a generalist who scoffed at those specialists who were unable to follow a problem from start to finish, and he took great pleasure in flouting scholarly "rules."

He was primarily concerned with truth. He believed mankind to be suffering from chronic self-deception. He saw humanity taking refuge in falsehood whenever life became too difficult. By inveighing wrathfully against self-imposed blindness, he made himself the gadfly to the mid-twentieth-century Americans. With books that attempted to "throw light on the curtain we Americans draw across our minds," his mission was to reveal "the gulf between our pretensions and what we really do."

No single area could have contained Philip Wylie's bursting energy. He jumped into controversy. He studied human nature, searching for and formulating new theories about man's tendency to self-destruction. It was a lifetime endeavor. His half-century of writing was a search for order. Using the intellectual evangelism he inherited from his father, he mercilessly exposed the sin of self-deception. With missionary zeal, Wylie sought to convert those who believed in disordered superstition into science-minded believers.

Science was his first love: it met the need for honest investigation. Wylie's universe was orderly and rational; it could be investigated by the scientific method. Although science meant different things at different times to him, rational thinking characterized his writing. His early books would employ the hard physical sciences. His fiction, especially his science fiction, would prove that a writer could be scientifically accurate *and* interesting. Using a contemporary understanding of physics, chemistry, biology, and mathematics, Wylie projected future technologies, always balancing scientific realism with inventiveness. This is most evident in his early speculative fantasies.

The soft sciences marked Wylie's middle years. Psychology (not the behavioristic variety of Watson or Dewey, but the depth-psychology of Freud and Jung) became the hub of his writing. Wylie reasoned that man was an animal with animal instincts. To deny this because of egoistic-religious reasons was the cause of modern man's apparent insanity. Drawing first on Freud and then on Jung, Wylie argued that instinct was of prime importance in man. Man could not deny the existence of instinct without producing dire consequences. These ideas are clearly presented in Wylie's nonfiction such as *Generation of Vipers* and *An Essay on Morals* and in novels such as *Opus 21* and *The Disappearance*.

In his final years, science included the biological sciences and the conclusions of naturalists. The natural sciences, dealing with man's evolutionary nature, reaffirmed Wylie's belief in man's animal instincts. He would take issue with those who denied man's animal nature, drawing on men like Konrad Lorenz and Robert Ardrey, and then arguing through analogy. This phase of Wylie's thought is definitively written in *The Magic Animal* (1968) and the posthumously published novel, *The End of the Dream* (1971).

Although his career is neatly delineated into different scientific orientations, the various objects of Wylie's hostility give the best clue to his major concerns: man's destruction of man, dogmatic thinking, the destruction of the environment, and the relationship between the sexes. (pp. 5-6)

Philip Wylie was one of the most prophetic, persuasive, and currently relevant thinkers of the mid-twentieth century. Although revered by some and reviled by others, few can deny the validity of his concerns, the forthrightness of his conclusions, or the impact of his style. The complete honesty with which he confronted his times gave us an early glimpse of a world we are presently struggling with. America was never the same after *Generation of Vipers*, perhaps because Americans were finally exposed to themselves for what they were—human. (pp. 7-8)

> *Clifford P. Bendau, in his* Still Worlds Collide: Philip Wylie, and the End of the American Dream, *The Borgo Press, 1980, 63 p.*

Appendix

The following is a listing of all sources used in Volume 43 of *Contemporary Literary Criticism*. Included in this list are all copyright and reprint rights and acknowledgments for those essays for which permission was obtained. Every effort has been made to trace copyright, but if omissions have been made, please let us know.

THE EXCERPTS IN CLC, VOLUME 43, WERE REPRINTED FROM THE FOLLOWING PERIODICALS:

Agenda, v. 6, Autumn-Winter, 1968; v. 19 & 20, Winter-Spring, 1982. Both reprinted by permission of the publisher.

America, v. 147, August 7-August 14, 1982 for a review of "Forsaking All Others" by Joseph Browne; v. 149, August 20-27, 1983 for "The Friendly Hand of Poetry" by James Finn Cotter. © 1982, 1983. All rights reserved. Both reprinted with permission of the respective authors.

The American Book Review, v. 3, March-April, 1981; v. 5, January-February, 1983; v. 5, July-August, 1983. © 1981, 1983 by *The American Book Review.* All reprinted by permission of the publisher.

The American Poetry Review, v. 10, November-December, 1981 for a review of "Selected Poems" by Mary Kinzie. Copyright © 1981 by World Poetry, Inc. Reprinted by permission of the author.

The American Political Science Review, v. 72, June, 1978. Copyright, 1978, by The American Political Science Association. Reprinted by permission.

American Review, n. 24, April, 1976 for "Henry Miller: Genius and Lust, Narcissism" by Norman Mailer. Copyright © 1976 by Bantam Books, Inc. All rights reserved. Reprinted by permission of the author and the author's agents, Scott Meredith Literary Agency, Inc., 845 Third Avenue, New York, NY 10022.

Analog Science Fiction/Science Fact, v. XCI, March, 1973. Copyright © 1973 by the Condé Nast Publications, Inc./ v. CIII, February, 1983 for a review of "Battlefield Earth" by Tom Easton; v. CVI, April, 1986 for a review of "The Invaders Plan" by Tom Easton. © 1983, 1986 by Davis Publications, Inc. Both reprinted by permission of the author.

Anglo-Welsh Review, Spring, 1973 for a review of "The Elements" by Randal Jenkins; Spring, 1977 for a review of "I That Was Born in Wales" by Jeremy Hooker. Both reprinted by permission of the respective authors.

Ariel, v. 13, October, 1982, for "The Song of the Caged Bird: Contemporary African Prison Poetry" by Chikwenye Okonjo Ogunyemi; v. 17, January, 1986 for "The Troubador: The Poet's Persona in the Poetry of Dennis Brutus" by Tanure Ojaide. Copyright © 1982, 1986 The Board of Governors, The University of Calgary. Both reprinted by permission of the publisher and the respective authors.

Arizona Quarterly, v. 19, Spring, 1963 for "Summoned by Nostalgia: John Betjeman's Poetry" by R. E. Wiehe. Copyright © 1963 by *Arizona Quarterly.* Reprinted by permission of the publisher and the author.

THE EXCERPTS IN CLC, VOLUME 43, WERE REPRINTED FROM THE FOLLOWING BOOKS:

Bendau, Clifford P. From *Still Worlds Collide: Philip Wylie, and the End of the American Dream*. The Borgo Press, 1980. Copyright © 1980 by Clifford P. Bendau. All rights reserved. Reprinted by permission of the publisher.

Bigsby, C. W. E. From *Joe Orton*. Methuen, 1982. © 1982 C. W. E. Bigsby. All rights reserved. Reprinted by permission of Methuen & Co. Ltd.

Bogan, Louise. From *A Poet's Alphabet: Reflections on the Literary Art and Vocation*. Edited by Robert Phelps and Ruth Limmer. McGraw-Hill Book Company, 1970. Copyright © 1970 by Ruth Limmer as Trustee. All rights reserved. Reprinted by permission of Ruth Limmer, literary executor, Estate of Louise Bogan.

Brée, Germaine and Margaret Guiton. From *An Age of Fiction: The French Novel from Gide to Camus*. Rutgers University Press, 1957. © 1957 by Rutgers, The State University. Renewed 1985 by Germaine Brée and Margaret Otis Guiton. Reprinted by permission of Rutgers University Press.

Callan, Edward. From *Auden: A Carnival of Intellect*. Oxford University Press, 1983. Copyright © 1983 by Edward Callan. Reprinted by permission of Oxford University Press, Inc.

Carter, Lin. From "When the World Grows Old," in *Zothique*. By Clark Ashton Smith, edited by Lin Carter. Ballantine Books, 1970. Introduction copyright © 1970 by Lin Carter. All rights reserved. Reprinted by permission of Lin Carter.

Carter, Lin. From "Other Stars and Skies," in *Xiccarph*. By Clark Ashton Smith, edited by Lin Carter. Ballantine Books, 1972. Copyright © 1972 by Lin Carter. Reprinted by permission of Lin Carter.

Christensen, Paul. From *Charles Olson: Call Him Ishmael*. University of Texas Press, 1979. Copyright © 1975, 1979 by Paul Christensen. All rights reserved. Reprinted by permission of the publisher and the author.

Dawe, Gerald. From "The Permanent City: The Younger Irish Poets," in *The Irish Writer and the City*. Edited by Maurice Harmon. Barnes & Noble, 1983. Copyright © 1984 by Gerald Dawe. Reprinted by permission of Barnes & Noble Books, a Division of Littlefield, Adams & Co., Inc.

DeCasseres, Benjamin. From "Clark Ashton Smith: Emperor of Shadows," in *Selected Poems*. By Clark Ashton Smith. Arkham House, 1971. Copyright 1971, by Mrs. Clark Ashton Smith. Reprinted by permission of Arkham House Publishers, Inc.

Del Rey, Lester. From *The World of Science Fiction, 1926-1976: The History of a Subculture*. Garland Publishing, Inc., 1980. Copyright © 1980 by Garland Publishing, Inc. All rights reserved. Reprinted by permission of the author.

Dunleavy, Janet Egleson. From "Mary Lavin, Elizabeth Bowen, and a New Generation: The Irish Short Story at Midcentury," in *The Irish Short Story: A Critical History*. Edited by James F. Kilroy. Twayne, 1984. Copyright 1984 by Twayne Publishers. All rights reserved. Reprinted with the permission of Twayne Publishers, a division of G. K. Hall & Co., Boston.

Ellison, Harlan. From a letter in *Emperor of Dreams: A Clark Ashton Smith Bibliography*. Edited by Donald Sidney-Fryer. Donald M. Grant, Publisher, 1978. Copyright © 1978 by Donald Sidney-Fryer. Reprinted by permission of Donald Sidney-Fryer.

Esslin, Martin. From "Joe Orton: The Comedy of (Ill) Manners," in *Contemporary English Drama*. Edited by C. W. E. Bigsby. Holmes & Meier, 1981. © Edward Arnold (Publishers) Ltd. 1981. All rights reserved. Reprinted by permission of Holmes & Meier Publishers, Inc., IUB Building, 30 Irving Place, New York, NY 10003.

Fergusson, Francis. From "Excursus: Poetry in the Theatre and Poetry of the Theatre, Cocteau's 'Infernal Machine'," in *Literary Criticism—Idea and Act: The English Institute, Selected Essays, 1939-1972*. Edited by W. K. Wimsatt. University of California Press, 1974. Copyright © 1974 by The Regents of the University of California. Reprinted by permission of the publisher.

Grimm, Reinhold. From an introduction to *Critical Essays*. By Hans Magnus Enzensberger, edited by Reinhold Grimm and Bruce Armstrong. The Continuum Publishing Company, 1982. Introduction © 1982 by Reinhold Grimm. All rights reserved. Reprinted by permission.

Guicharnaud, Jacques with June Beckelman. From *Modern French Theatre from Giraudoux to Beckett*. Yale University Press, 1961. © 1961 by Yale University Press, Inc. All rights reserved. Reprinted by permission of the publisher.

Keefer, Truman Frederick. From *Philip Wylie*. Twayne, 1977. Copyright 1977 by Twayne Publishers. All rights reserved. Reprinted with the permission of Twayne Publishers, a division of G. K. Hall & Co., Boston.

Kettle, Arnold. From "W. H. Auden: Poetry and Politics in the Thirties," in *Culture and Crisis in Britain in the Thirties*. Edited by Jon Clark and others. Lawrence and Wishart, 1979. Copyright © Lawrence and Wishart, 1979. Reprinted by permission of the publisher.

Literary Criticism Series
Cumulative Author Index

This index lists all author entries in the Gale Literary Criticism Series and includes cross-references to other Gale sources. For the convenience of the reader, references to the *Yearbook* in the *Contemporary Literary Criticism* series include the page number (in parentheses) after the volume number. References in the index are identified as follows:

AITN: *Authors in the News*, Volumes 1-2
CAAS: *Contemporary Authors Autobiography Series*, Volumes 1-4
CA: *Contemporary Authors* (original series), Volumes 1-118
CABS: *Contemporary Authors Bibliographical Series*, Volumes 1-2
CANR: *Contemporary Authors New Revision Series*, Volumes 1-18
CAP: *Contemporary Authors Permanent Series*, Volumes 1-2
CA-R: *Contemporary Authors* (revised editions), Volumes 1-44
CDALB: *Concise Dictionary of American Literary Biography*
CLC: *Contemporary Literary Criticism*, Volumes 1-43
CLR: *Children's Literature Review*, Volumes 1-12
DLB: *Dictionary of Literary Biography*, Volumes 1-53
DLB-DS: *Dictionary of Literary Biography Documentary Series*, Volumes 1-4
DLB-Y: *Dictionary of Literary Biography Yearbook*, Volumes 1980-1985
LC: *Literature Criticism from 1400 to 1800*, Volumes 1-5
NCLC: *Nineteenth-Century Literature Criticism*, Volumes 1-15
SAAS: *Something about the Author Autobiography Series*, Volumes 1-2
SATA: *Something about the Author*, Volumes 1-44
TCLC: *Twentieth-Century Literary Criticism*, Volumes 1-24
YABC: *Yesterday's Authors of Books for Children*, Volumes 1-2

Author Index

Author Index

Author Index

Author Index

Author Index

Author Index

Author Index

Author Index

Author Index

Author Index

Author Index

Author Index

Author Index

Author Index

Author Index

CLC Cumulative Nationality Index

Nationality Index

Nationality Index

Nationality Index

CLC Cumulative Title Index

Title Index

Title Index

Title Index

Title Index

Title Index

Title Index

Title Index

Title Index

Title Index

Title Index

Title Index

Title Index

Title Index

Title Index

Title Index

Title Index

Title Index

Title Index

Title Index

Title Index

Title Index

Title Index

Title Index

Title Index

Title Index

Title Index

Title Index

Title Index

Title Index

Title Index

Title Index

Title Index

Title Index

Title Index

Title Index

Title Index

Title Index

Title Index

Title Index

Title Index

Title Index

Title Index

Title Index

Title Index

Title Index

Title Index

Title Index

Title Index

Title Index

Title Index